DATE DUE

Demco No. 62-0549

METROPOLITAN COLLEGE
OF NEW YORK LIBRARY
75 Varick Street 12th Fl.
New York, NY 10013

The UN Human Rights Treaty System in the 21st Century

Edited by
Anne F. Bayefsky
York University, Toronto, Canada

KLUWER LAW INTERNATIONAL
THE HAGUE / LONDON / BOSTON

Published by:
Kluwer Law International
P.O. Box 85889, 2508 CN The Hague, The Netherlands
sales@kli.wkap.nl
http://www.kluwerlaw.com

Sold and Distributed in North, Central and South America by:
Kluwer Law International
657 Massachusetts Avenue, Cambridge MA 02139, USA

Sold and Distributed in all other countries by:
Kluwer Law International
Distribution Centre, P.O. Box 322, 3300 AH Dordrecht, The Netherlands

Library of Congress Cataloging-in-Publication Data is available

Printed on acid-free paper.

ISBN 90-411-1415-7
© 2000 Kluwer Law International

Kluwer Law International incorporates the publishing programmes
of Graham & Trotman Ltd, Kluwer Law and Taxation Publishers
and Martinus Nijhoff Publishers

This publication is protected by international copyright law.
All rights reserved. No part of this publication may be reproduced, stored in a retrieval
system, or transmitted in any form or by any means, electronic, mechanical,
photocopying, recording or otherwise, without the prior permission of the publisher.

Printed and bound in Great Britain by MPG Books, Bodmin, Cornwall.

For Aba and Evelyn Bayefsky

Table of Contents

Preface xiii
Contributors xv
Introduction xvii
   Anne F. Bayefsky

I. An Analysis and Evaluation of the System of State Reporting   1

  1. An Analysis and Evaluation of the System of State Reporting   3
     Jane Connors
  2. State Reporting and the Convention on the Elimination of All Forms of Discrimination Against Women   23
     Carmel Shalev
  3. Reporting and the Committee on the Rights of the Child   35
     Judith Karp
  4. State Reporting and the Role of Non-Governmental Organizations   45
     Laura Theytaz-Bergman
  5. State Reporting: an NGO Perspective   57
     Rachel Brett

II. Fact-finding as Part of Effective Implementation   63

  6. Human Rights Fact-Finding   65
     Joan Fitzpatrick
  7. The Role of a Human Rights Field Presence   97
     Ian Martin
  8. Fact-Finding in the Inter-American System   105
     Douglass W. Cassel, Jr.
  9. Fact-finding as Part of Effective Implementation: the Strasbourg Experience   115
     Andrew Drzemczewski

III. An Effective Individual Complaint Mechanism in an International Human Rights Context   137

  10. An Effective Complaints Procedure in the Context of International Human Rights Law   139
     Andrew Byrnes
  11. Commentary on Complaint Processes by Human Rights Committee and Torture Committee Members   163
    (a) The Human Rights Committee   163
      David Kretzmer

		(b) The Committee Against Torture *Peter Burns*	166
	12.	Reflections on the Effectiveness of the European System for the Protection of Human Rights *Michael O'Boyle*	169
IV.	**Defining the Role of Non-governmental Organizations**		**181**
	13.	Defining the Role of Non-Governmental Organizations with Regard to the UN Human Rights Treaty Bodies *Andrew Clapham*	183
	14.	Women's Human Rights NGOs and the Treaty Bodies: Some Case Studies in Using the Treaty Bodies to Protect the Human Rights of Women *Alice M. Miller*	195
	15.	The NGO Role: Implementation, Expanding Protection and Monitoring the Monitors *Stefanie Grant*	209
	16.	Defining the Role of Non-Governmental Organizations: Splendid Isolation or Better Use of NGO Expertise? *Mark Thomson*	219
	17.	The Committee on Economic, Social and Cultural Rights and Non-Governmental Organizations *Virginia Dandan*	227
V.	**Follow-up of Treaty Body Conclusions**		**231**
	18.	Follow-Up Mechanisms Before UN Human Rights Treaty Bodies and the UN Mechanisms Beyond *Markus G. Schmidt*	233
	19.	The UN High Commissioner for Human Rights: A Link Between Decisions of Expert Monitoring Bodies and Enforcement by Political Bodies *Manfred Nowak*	251
	20.	The Effects of Final Decisions of the Supervisory Organs Under the European Convention on Human Rights *Leo F. Zwaak*	255
	21.	Follow-Up in the ILO Context *Jane Hodges*	273
	22.	Follow-Up of Treaty Body Conclusions by the Treaty Bodies and the UN Mechanisms Beyond *Bert G. Ramcharan*	277
VI.	**The Future of the Human Rights Treaty System: Forging Recommendations**		**285**
	23.	The Future of the Human Rights Treaty System: Forging Recommendations *Elizabeth Evatt*	287

	24. A Court and Two Consolidated Treaty Bodies *Thomas Buergenthal*	299
VII.	**The Role of National Courts: A Canadian Example**	303
	25. Enforcing International Human Rights Law: The Treaty System in the 21st Century *Rt. Hon. Antonio Lamer*	305
VIII.	**Conference: Discussion and Recommendations**	313
	26. Discussion	315
	27. Conclusions and Recommendations	331

Appendices

Appendix 1:	**The Text of the Treaties**	343
	(a) International Convention on the Elimination of All Forms of Racial Discrimination	345
	(b) International Covenant on Civil and Political Rights	356
	(c) Optional Protocol to the International Covenant on Civil and Political Rights	372
	(d) Second Optional Protocol to the International Covenant on Civil and Political Rights	375
	(e) International Covenant on Economic, Social and Cultural Rights	378
	(f) Convention on the Elimination of All Forms of Discrimination against Women	387
	(g) Optional Protocol to the Convention on the Elimination of Discrimination against Women	398
	(h) Convention against Torture and Other Cruel, Inhuman or Degrading Treatment or Punishment	403
	(i) Convention on the Rights of the Child	414
	(j) Optional Protocols to the Convention on the Rights of the Child on the Involvement of Children in Armed Conflict and on the Sale of Children, Child Prostitution and Child Pornography	431
	(k) Effective implementation of international instruments on human rights, including reporting obligations under international instruments on human rights, A/RES/47/111	444
	(l) Conference on States Parties to the Convention on the Rights of the Child, A/RES/50/155	448
Appendix 2:	**Status of Ratifications**	449
	(a) Status of Ratifications of the Principal International Human Rights Treaties	451

Appendix 3:	**Status of Individual Communications**	459
	(a) Statistical survey of individual complaints dealt with by the Human Rights Committee under the Optional Protocol to the International Covenant on Civil and Political Rights	461
	(b) Statistical survey of individual complaints dealt with by the Committee against Torture	465
	(c) Statistical survey of individual complaints dealt with by the Racial Discrimination Committee	467
Appendix 4:	**Draft Amendments to the Treaties**	469
	(a) Draft Optional Protocol to the International Covenant on Economic, Social and Cultural Rights	471
	(b) Report of the Working Group on the Draft Optional Protocol Proposed to the Convention Against Torture and Other Cruel, Inhuman or Degrading Treatment or Punishment on its eighth session	490
Appendix 5:	**Report of the Independent Expert on Enhancing the Long-Term Effectiveness of the United Nations Human Rights Treaty System**	513
	(a) Interim report on study on enhancing the long-term effectiveness of the UN human rights treaty regime (1993)	515
	(b) Final report on enhancing the long-term effectiveness of the UN human rights treaty system (1997)	593
	(c) Effective Functioning Report of the Secretary General, Corrigendum, Addendum (1998)	629
	(d) Effective Functioning Report of the Secretary General (2000)	663
Appendix 6:	**International Law Association Report on the Treaty System**	679
	(a) International Law Association, Committee on International Human Rights Law and Practice, Report on the UN Human Rights Treaties: Facing the Implementation Crisis	681
Appendix 7:	**Meetings of Chairpersons of the Treaty Bodies**	701
	(a) Report of the first meeting of chairpersons (1984)	703
	(b) Report of the second meeting of persons chairing the human rights treaty bodies (1988)	716

	(c)	Report of the third meeting of persons chairing the human rights treaty bodies (1990)	738
	(d)	Report of the fourth meeting of persons chairing the human rights treaty bodies (1992)	754
	(e)	Report of the fifth meeting of persons chairing the human rights treaty bodies (1994)	774
	(f)	Report of the sixth meeting of persons chairing the human rights treaty bodies (1995)	787
	(g)	Report of the seventh meeting of persons chairing the human rights treaty bodies (1996)	797
	(h)	Report of the eighth meeting of chairpersons of the treaty bodies (1997)	810
	(i)	Report of the ninth meeting of chairpersons of the treaty bodies (1998)	827
	(j)	Report of the tenth meeting of the chairpersons of the treaty bodies (1998)	839
	(k)	Report of the eleventh meeting of chairpersons of the treaty bodies (1999)	853

Appendix 8: **Resolutions of the Commission on Human Rights relating to the Human Rights Treaties (2000)** — 871

- (a) Effective implementation of international human rights instruments — 873
- (b) Status of International Covenants on Human Rights — 877
- (c) Question of the realization in all countries of the economic, social and cultural rights contained in the Universal Declaration of Human Rights and in the International Covenant on Economic, Social and Cultural Rights, and study of special problems which the developing countries face in their efforts to achieve these human rights — 881
- (d) Torture and other cruel, inhuman or degrading treatment or punishment — 888
- (e) Draft optional protocol to the Convention against Torture and Other Cruel, Inhuman or Degrading Treatment or Punishment — 896
- (f) Rights of the child — 898
- (g) Racism, racial discrimination, xenophobia and related intolerance — 914

Appendix 9: **Resolutions of the General Assembly relating to the Human Rights Treaties** — 923

1998
- (a) Effective implementation of international instruments on human rights — 925

	(b)	International Convention on the Elimination of All Forms of Racial Discrimination	931
1999			
	(a)	International Covenants on Human Rights	935
	(b)	Torture and other cruel, inhuman or degrading treatment or punishment	939
	(c)	Convention on the Elimination of All Forms of Discrimination against Women	943
	(d)	The girl child	946
	(e)	The rights of the child	950
	(f)	Measures to combat contemporary forms of racism, racial discrimination, xenophobia and related intolerance	959

Appendix 10: Regional Human Rights Instruments — 963

	(a)	Convention for the Protection of Human Rights and Fundamental Freedoms	965
	(b)	European Social Charter – Revised	978
	(c)	European Convention for the Prevention of Torture and Inhuman or Degrading Treatment or Punishment	1002
	(d)	Protocol No. 1 to the European Convention for the Prevention of Torture and Inhuman or Degrading Treatment or Punishment	1009
	(e)	Protocol No. 2 to the European Convention for the Prevention of Torture and Inhuman or Degrading Treatment or Punishment	1011
	(f)	American Declaration of the Rights and Duties of Man	1013
	(g)	American Convention on Human Rights	1019
	(h)	The African Charter on Human and Peoples' Rights and the Rules of Procedure	1033
	(i)	Protocol to the African Charter on the Establishment of the African Court on Human and Peoples' Rights	1069

Index — 1075

Preface

The papers comprising this volume were presented at a Conference held at York University, Toronto, Canada on 22–24 June 1997. The Conference was entitled: "Enforcing International Human Rights Law: The Treaty System in the Twenty-First Century". In the production of the final version, the editor updated the chapters to 1 January 2000.

The conference was convened in order to address the problems of implementation faced by the human rights treaty system. The aim was to consider steps to improve the enforcement of international human rights law and to develop a vision for the advancement of the treaty regime, a goal consistent with the broader imperative and context of U.N. reform.

Participants included a wide variety of international human rights actors: members of each of the six treaty bodies, representatives of three U.N. specialized agencies, U.N. officials from the Office of the High Commissioner for Human Rights, the Division for the Advancement of Women, and the Division for Political Affairs, individuals from eight major non-governmental organizations, representatives of states parties, representatives from the Council of Europe and the Organization of American States, representatives of U.N. special procedures mechanisms in the field of human rights and U.N. human rights field missions, and leading international human rights academics.

At the conclusion of the Conference, as Rapporteur, I summarized the ideas for constructive change, both short-term and long-term, which emerged from the papers and the discussion at the Conference itself. The dialogue over the three days is summarized in Chapter 26. The range of conclusions and recommendations which emerged from the Conference are set out in Chapter 27. The appendices which have been added provide the reader with a compilation of central documents for the study of the human rights treaty system and the project of reform.

The financial support of the Canadian Department of Foreign Affairs and International Trade, the John Holmes Fund, the Department of Justice, and Heritage Canada, is gratefully acknowledged. Research support from the John D. and Catherine T. MacArthur Foundation and the Social Sciences and Humanities Research Council of Canada has also been appreciated.

Special thanks to those individuals which assisted in the editing of this collection: Gillian Collins, Anne Molgat, and Angie DiTuri. I also wish to thank M.B. Fenton, then Associate Vice-President (Research & Faculties), and the students at York University, including those who helped both during the conference and in the subsequent research for this publication: Marika Giles, Dzovag Kevork, Rachel Li Wai Suen, Gail McCabe, Stella Militano, Heather Northcott, Purushothman Panchalingam, Maria Vamvalis, and Goli Yohannes.

Anne F. Bayefsky
York University, Toronto, Canada, 2000

Contributors

Anne F. Bayefsky
Professor, York University, Canada.

Rachel Brett
Associate Representative, Quaker United Nations Office, Geneva; Fellow of the Human Rights Centre, University of Essex.

Thomas Buergenthal
Judge, International Court of Justice (formerly, Member, Human Rights Committee; President, Inter-American Court of Human Rights).

Andrew Byrnes
Professor, Faculty of Law, University of Hong Kong.

Peter Burns
Chair, Committee Against Torture.

Douglass W. Cassel, Jr.
Executive Director, International Human Rights Law Institute, DePaul University, College of Law; Legal advisor to the United Nations Commission on the Truth for El Salvador.

Andrew Clapham
Associate Professor of Public International Law, Graduate Institute of International Studies, Geneva (formerly Representative of Amnesty International at the United Nations in New York).

Jane Connors
Chief, Women's Rights Unit, United Nations Division for the Advancement of Women.

Virginia Dandan
Chair, Committee on Economic, Social and Cultural Rights.

Andrew Drzemczewski
Head of Secretary General's Monitoring Unit, Council of Europe, Strasbourg, France.

Elizabeth Evatt
Vice-Chairperson, Human Rights Committee (formerly, Chair, Committee on the Elimination of Discrimination Against Women).

Joan Fitzpatrick
Jeffrey and Susan Brotman Professor of Law, School of Law, University of Washington.

Stefanie Grant
Chief, Research and the Right to Development Branch, Office of the High Commissioner for Human Rights (formerly Lawyers Committee for Human Rights, New York).

Jane Hodges
Standards Branch, International Labour Organization.

Judith Karp
Member, Committee on the Rights of the Child.

David Kretzmer
Member and Special Rapporteur on New Communications, Human Rights Committee.

Antonio Lamer
Chief Justice, Supreme Court of Canada (1990–2000).

Ian Martin
Human Rights Centre, University of Essex, (former director for Human Rights/ Deputy Executive Director, UN/OAS International Civilian Mission in Haiti (MICIVIH), and Chief, UN Human Rights Field Operation in Rwanda (HRFOR)).

Alice M. Miller
Director, Women's Rights Advocacy Program, International Human Rights Law Group.

Manfred Nowak
Judge, Human Rights Chamber for Bosnia-Herzegovina; Member, Working Group on Enforced or Involuntary Disappearances; Director, Ludwig Boltzmann Institute of Human Rights.

Michael O'Boyle
Section Registrar, European Court of Human Rights (former Head of Division of the Registry of the European Court).

Bert G. Ramcharan
United Nations Deputy High Commissioner for Human Rights (formerly United Nations Director, Africa 1 Division, Department of Political Affairs).

Carmel Shalev
Member, Committee on the Elimination of Discrimination Against Women.

Markus G. Schmidt
Office of the High Commissioner for Human Rights, Geneva.

Laura Theytaz-Bergman
Liaison Officer, NGO Group for the Convention on the Rights of the Child.

Mark Thomson
Deputy Director, International Service for Human Rights, Geneva.

Leo F. Zwaak
Lecturer, International Protection of Human Rights, Utrecht University; Researcher, Netherlands Institute of Human Rights (SIM).

Introduction

Anne F. Bayefsky

The United Nations system, created fifty years ago, was erected upon the ashes of the Second World War. Embedded in its foundation was the promise to better protect human rights and a recognition of the sanctity of individual human dignity. At the same time, the international legal system continued to regard states as the primary players in its evolving network of rules and obligations. Binding international legal obligations which would require states to protect individual human rights challenged traditional theory.

The United Nations Charter itself did not resolve the original tension between state sovereignty on the one hand, and international interest in the well-being of individuals within the state on the other.[1] During the Cold War, that tension was exhibited in a number of ways. One bloc championed peace and security and described international scrutiny of human rights situations as interference in domestic jurisdiction. Other states maintained that peace and security were dependent upon the protection of human rights.

In this antagonistic environment, the United Nations drafted the core human rights legal standards, the six major human rights treaties, and created their concomitant implementation machinery, the six human rights treaty bodies: the International Convention on the Elimination of All Forms of Racial Discrimination (1965), the International Covenant on Civil and Political Rights (1966), the International Covenant on Economic, Social and Cultural Rights (1966), the Convention on the Elimination of All Forms of Discrimination Against Women (1979), the Convention Against Torture (1984), and the Convention on the Rights of the Child (1989). The human rights treaty system was conceived as of central importance to the international protection of human rights because legal standards could offer benefits which political fora could not: the potential to generate remedies and greater accessibility to human rights victims.

With the end of the Cold War, many anticipated a new era of vigorous international protection of human rights. The conflict in theory would be

---

[1] The United Nations Charter, 1 UNTS xvi (in force 24 October 1945), says both that its purposes include promoting and encouraging respect for human rights (Article 1(3)), and that the United Nations should act in accordance with the principle of non-intervention in matters within the domestic jurisdiction of states (Article 2(7)).

replaced with a common agenda to improve the welfare of individuals everywhere. Indeed, few states would now take issue with the principles that protection of human rights is not merely a matter of domestic jurisdiction, and that human rights limit the scope of state sovereignty. The opposition of economic, social and cultural rights to civil and political rights, has been replaced by agreement on their indivisibility.[2] Ratification of human rights treaties is high, three-quarters or more of the world's states having ratified five of the six treaties, fifty percent the sixth. Every United Nations member state is part of the system, through the ratification of at least one of the treaties. Theory is apparently shared. Universal standards are codified and to a large extent legally binding.

The consensus, however, is misleading. When the treaties were drafted, it was easier to arrive at pious statements of intention than effective mechanisms to ensure those commitments were actually implemented. The current mechanisms for implementing human rights treaties, devised when the power of the argument about domestic jurisdiction was at its peak, exhibit significant weaknesses which are exploited by many of today's participants. There is, therefore, a schism between the standards and their implementation, between rules and reality, which must be directly confronted if the benefits are to be imparted to the actual victims of human rights abuse.

The major implementation shortfalls of the UN human rights treaty system, (which are discussed in detail in the Chapters herein), include the following:

- State reports, due to each treaty body, are overdue to an enormous extent. A large number of overdue reports are initial reports. States having the largest number of overdue reports are frequently those with extremely poor human rights records.
- If all the overdue reports were actually to be submitted, expunging the backlog would take years. Even with respect to reports which have been submitted, the meeting time now available to the treaty bodies means that delays in considering those reports for some treaty bodies run into years.
- The treaty bodies spend only a few hours considering a single report, on average every four years. The time spent in an actual dialogue or exchange with a state party when treaty bodies consider reports is often severely circumscribed.
- The proceedings of the treaty bodies in general are often poorly attended, particularly by national non-governmental organizations (NGOs) and national and international media.
- The availability to the treaty bodies of reliable, independent information on human rights conditions in states parties is a significant problem: the treaty bodies generally do not engage in fact-finding, state party reports are less than candid, NGO material can be highly selective or focussed, and the U.N. secretariat is ill-equipped to produce in-depth country studies.
- In the case of two of the six treaties the individual complaint procedure is not available. In the case of three treaties which include a right of petition, access is limited by the rate of ratification of this optional mechanism. (The fourth petition system for the Women's Discrimination Convention is not yet in force.) Even in the case of the mostly widely ratified individual petition

---

[2] Vienna Declaration and Programme of Action, A/CONF.157/23 (12 July 1993) at 5, para. 5.

mechanism, the Optional Protocol to the Covenant on Civil and Political Rights, there have been relatively few cases over the years in comparison with the potential complainant population in ratifiying states.
- The follow-up of treaty body conclusions is often minimal and reduced to promises of answers in a next state report years away.
- Access to the process is circumscribed both because actual attendance of the treaty body meetings is difficult, and because a comprehensible (in sufficient languages), timely, written account of the proceedings in the form of the questions asked, the answers provided and the record of the dialogue, is difficult, if not impossible, to obtain.
- Concluding observations, which follow the consideration of a state report by a treaty body, often lack sufficient specificity in their critique of domestic laws and practices to serve as useful domestic tools for governments and NGOs alike.
- There is a significant level of non-compliance with the Human Rights Committee's views on individual communications under the Covenant on Civil and Political Rights.
- Although the General Assembly, and other U.N. bodies such as the U.N. Commission on Human Rights and the Commission on the Status of Women, have responsibility to follow-up treaty body conclusions, they generally do not do so.

The Final Report of the Independent Expert on the effective functioning of the treaty bodies, produced for the 1997 session of the U.N. Human Rights Commission, concludes: "... the principle of holding States accountable for non-compliance with their treaty obligations by means of an objective and constructive dialogue, on the basis of comprehensive information and inputs from all interested parties, has been vindicated in practice ..."[3] While the principle is certainly laudable, the reality is unfortunately different. In practice the information available is not comprehensive, input is not obtained from all interested parties, the dialogue for these reasons as well as constraints upon time, accessibility and follow-up is often not constructive, and with those states which need it most, frequently never takes place.

Where then should future implementation efforts be placed? The contributions to this volume seek to respond to this question. At the outset, however, it is important to reiterate some first principles. The treaty system today contains a significant number of states which do not share democratic commitments or aspirations. But when non-governmental organizations are fearful of participating, or inhibited from sharing information with the treaty bodies, when individuals are prevented from criticizing their governments and complaining of violations of human rights, when a nation's media is not permitted to monitor and reveal proceedings critical of its government, the treaty system will fail. Successful implementation machinery requires sufficient familiarity with country situations (which may entail capacity for investigation or fact-finding), and fully functional rights and procedures of individual petition. Yet extensive resistance to reforms directed at these ends can be expected from states unwilling to further empower either international monitors or their own citizens.

---

[3] Philip Alston, *Final Report on Enhancing the Long-Term Effectiveness of the United Nations Human Rights Treaty System*, E/CN.4/1997/74 (7 March 1997) at para. 9.

Consequently, two fundamental questions must be borne in mind throughout this inquiry. Firstly, what is the best method for securing reform aimed at empowering and protecting individuals everywhere? Through democratic preconditions for participation within the treaty system, or through alternative venues for interchange outside the treaty system? Secondly, who is the system for? Is it aimed at assisting democracies or aspiring democracies, to adjust and calibrate their laws and practices? Or is it aimed at the unrepentant social deviant, and intended to expose the depravity and provide a tool for critics everywhere? Reforms necessary to improve the usefulness of the system to democracies or aspiring democracies, will discourage non-democracies from joining or participating. Low levels of resources and feeble institutional methodologies which expand state participation, undercut effective implementation. In the final analysis, the price to be paid by failing to advocate far-reaching reforms may be too high for the sake of adding the voice of the treaty bodies to the volume of public criticism directed at extreme delinquents.

I. An Analysis and Evaluation of the System of State Reporting

CHAPTER 1

An Analysis and Evaluation of the System of State Reporting

Jane Connors*

(1) Introduction

At the Vienna World Conference on Human Rights, participating governments set the year 1995 as the target date for universal ratification of the Convention on the Rights of the Child (CRC)[1], 2000 for the ratification of the Convention on the Elimination of All Forms of Discrimination against Women (CEDAW)[2], and urged the universal ratification of all other human rights treaties.[3] Universal ratification of the six core human rights treaties is becoming a real possibility. The number of states parties to human rights treaties has expanded significantly over the 1990's, with the CRC almost universally accepted and CEDAW running second, with one hundred and sixty-five states parties.[4]

Since the human rights treaties have been increasingly accepted, commentators and activists have shifted their efforts away from encouraging states to become parties to treaties[5] and toward ensuring that obligations undertaken by existing states parties are respected. Methods of international implementation of human rights obligations have consequently come under increasing scrutiny.

Though some of this scrutiny has been directed at the individual communications procedures established under some of the human rights treaties,[6] these procedures

---

*The views expressed in this paper are in the author's individual capacity and do not necessarily reflect the views of the United Nations.
[1] Convention on the Rights of the Child, 1577 UNTS 3 (in force 2 September 1990).
[2] Convention on the Elimination of All Forms of Discrimination Against Women, 1249 UNTS 13 (in force 3 September 1981).
[3] Vienna Declaration and Programme of Action, A/CONF.157/23 (1993) Part 1, at paras. 21, 39 and 27.
[4] As at 31 December 1999. However, the International Convention on the Protection of the Rights of All Migrant Workers and Members of their Families, G.A. Res. 45/158, adopted on 18 December 1990, is not yet in force, and as of 1 January 2000 there were only 12 ratifications.
[5] While the number of states parties to human rights treaties has increased significantly since 1993, there is unevenness across the six treaties, with over 22% of states not party to either of the Covenants and almost 40% not party to CAT. Some commentators point out that increased ratification has led to a treaty body crisis (see *infra*, Anne Bayefsky, Appendix 6, *International Law Association, Committee on International Human Rights Law and Practice, Report on the UN Human Rights Treaties: Facing the Implementation Crisis*, at 681). Others emphasize the promotion of universal ratification as essential in order to strengthen and consolidate the universalist foundations of the United Nations human rights regime, and put forward strategies to achieve universal ratification:

have emerged relatively free from significant criticism. As a result, recent efforts successfully ensured the addition of such a procedure to CEDAW and efforts continue with respect to the International Covenant on Economic, Social and Cultural Rights.[7] In contrast, periodic reporting, the most widespread and established method of implementation at the international level of human rights standards,[8] has received extensive, and frequently scathing, criticism.[9]

In essence, those who have subjected the system of state reporting established under the six international human rights treaties to any level of analysis reach conclusions which range along a continuum. At one end of this continuum is the view that the entire system is an empty diplomatic ritual and should be disbanded, while at the other is the view that, while not flawless, the system is a valuable tool in ensuring the implementation of agreed human rights obligations and operates as best it can given its various constraints.

Along this continuum, the view that prevails is best expressed in the premises of the Final Report of the Independent Expert on enhancing the long-term effectiveness of the United Nations human rights treaty system, submitted to the 1997 session of the Commission on Human Rights:

> ... the basic assumptions of the treaty supervisory system are sound and remain entirely valid. ... [It] has the potential to be an important and effective means by which to promote respect for human rights. The potential contribution that it can make has not in any way been superseded by other approaches or mechanisms that have been created ... considerable achievements have been recorded by all of the treaty bodies in recent years, although there has been significant unevenness in that regard ... progress, both in improving the quality and effectiveness of monitoring and in reforming the

---

see Philip Alston, *Final Report on Enhancing the Long-Term Effectiveness of the United Nations Human Rights Treaty System*, E/CN.4/1997/74 (27 March 1997) at paras. 14–36.

[6] Rein Mullerson, "The Efficiency of the Individual Complaint Procedures: The Experience of CCPR, CERD, CAT and ECHR", in *Monitoring Human Rights in Europe: Comparing International Procedures and Mechanisms*, Arie Bloed et. al. (eds.), Nijhoff (1993) 25; Bernhard Graefrath, "Reporting and Complaints Systems in Universal Human Rights Treaties", in *Human Rights in a Changing East/West Perspective*, Allan Rosas and Jan Helgesen (eds.), Pinter (1990) 290.

[7] International Covenant on Economic, Social and Cultural Rights, 993 UNTS 3 (in force 3 January 1976).

[8] Periodic reporting as a means of implementation of human rights standards has a long history: art. 22, League of Nations, 225 CTS 195 (in force 10 January 1920); arts. 19 and 22 of the Constitution of the International Labour Organization, 1 UKTS 47(1948) (in force 10 January 1920); arts. 73e, 87a and 88 of the United Nations Charter, 1 UNTS xvi (in force 24 October 1945); art. VIII of the Constitution of UNESCO, 4 UNTS 275 (in force 4 November 1946); ECOSOC established a system of periodic reporting on development and progress in human rights in 1956; ECOSOC Res. 624B (XXII), adopted 1 August 1956. This system was terminated by the General Assembly in 1980: G.A. Res. 35/209, adopted on 17 December 1980.

[9] Anne Bayefsky, "Making the Human Rights Treaties Work" in *Human Rights: An Agenda for the Next Century*, Louis Henkin and JL Hargrove (eds.), American Society of International Law (1994) 222; see *infra*, Anne Bayefsky, Appendix 6, *International Law Association, Committee on International Human Rights Law and Practice, Report on the UN Human Rights Treaties: Facing the Implementation Crisis*; Andrew Clapham, "UN human rights reporting procedures: An NGO perspective", in *The Future of UN Human Rights Treaty Monitoring*, Philip Alston and James Crawford (eds.), Cambridge University Press, 2000 at 175.; Scott Leckie, "The Committee on Economic, Social and Cultural Rights: Catalyst for change in a system needing reform", in *The Future of UN Human Rights Treaty Monitoring*, Philip Alston and James Crawford (eds.), Cambridge University Press, 2000 at 129.

procedures and institutions, is inevitably a gradual process and there are no "miracle cures" to be found.[10]

But even those most sympathetically disposed to reporting conclude that: "the present system is unsustainable and ... significant reforms will be required if the overall regime is to achieve its objectives".[11]

The reporting system has the potential, if properly used, to be an important means of ensuring the implementation of human rights standards at the domestic level, and this potential has been realized on numerous occasions. At the same time, it is a system with clear limitations, particularly in the context of politically unstable states and urgent situations. It is also a system which requires attention at various levels to preclude it becoming an empty ritual and thereby a process which serves to bring the UN's central legal framework for the protection of human rights into disrepute.

The perspective of the paper is based, to a large extent, on reporting in the context of CEDAW. It is also based on the author's personal experience in drafting a state party's report required under that Convention and as a part of the Secretariat to CEDAW.

(2) The reporting system described

The system of reporting established under the six operative international human rights treaties consists of a voluntary system of self-monitoring by way of reporting supervised by six independent and expert international committees.

Each treaty provides that states parties will report periodically, generally every two to five years,[12] on the measures they have adopted to give effect to the rights enumerated in the respective treaty, the progress made in the enjoyment of those rights and any factors and difficulties affecting the fulfilment of the treaty's objectives. The report is then considered by an international committee

---

[10] Philip Alston, *supra* note 5 at para.9. This report was submitted by Philip Alston as the independent expert appointed by the Secretary-General pursuant to G.A. Res. 47/111 adopted 16 December 1992. Mr. Alston submitted two earlier reports, an initial report, *Long Term Approaches to Enhancing the Effective Operation of Existing and Prospective Bodies Established under United Nations Human Rights Instruments*, A/44/668 (8 November 1989); and an interim report to the World Conference on Human Rights, *Interim Report on Updated Study of Mr. Philip Alston*, A/CONF.157/PC/62/Add.11/Rev.1 (22 April 1993).

[11] Philip Alston, *supra* note 5 at paras. 9 and 10.

[12] Convention on the Elimination of All Forms of Discrimination (CERD), 660 UNTS 195 (in force 4 January1969), art. 9: the report is due within one year after the entry into force of the Convention for the state concerned and thereafter every two years and whenever the Committee so requests; International Covenant on Civil and Political Rights (CCPR), 999 UNTS 171 (in force 23 March 1976), art. 40: within one year of the entry into force of the Covenant and thereafter when the Committee so requests; Covenant on Economic, Social and Cultural Rights, art. 17: within one year of the entry into force of the present Covenant; CEDAW, art. 18: within one year of the entry into force for the state concerned and thereafter every four years and when the Committee so requests; Convention on the Prevention of Torture and Other Cruel, Inhuman or Degrading Treatment or Punishment (CAT), 1465 UNTS 85 (in force 26 June 1987), art. 19: within one year after entry into force of the Convention and thereafter every four years or when the Committee so requests; CRC, art. 44: within two years of the entry into force of the Convention for the state party concerned and thereafter every five years.

of independent experts in the presence of representatives of the state party[13] in a public process of question and answer, or what is described as "constructive dialogue." The constructive dialogue is non-contentious and non-adversarial and, although the treaty body is sometimes openly critical of states parties and identifies areas of non-compliance with the treaty, there is usually no open accusation of human rights violation. After the consideration of the report, the relevant treaty body writes concluding observations or comments[14] on the report and the constructive dialogue. The observations outline the extent to which the reporting state actually meets the required standards of protection elaborated in the treaty, and the measures required at the national level to improve compliance with the obligations in the treaty and to bring the state into line with international standards. Depending on the particular treaty body, there may be some follow-up mechanism which aims to ensure that recommendations emerging during constructive dialogue or included in concluding comments are acted upon by the state.[15]

The central purpose of this system is to promote compliance by states with the obligations which they have undertaken by consensually becoming party to the various human rights instruments. In its first General Comment, written in 1989, the Economic, Social and Cultural Rights Committee identified seven further objectives of the reporting process. They are:

(1) to facilitate a comprehensive review by a state of its national legislation, administrative rules, procedures and practices in implementing the treaty;
(2) to ensure the ongoing monitoring by a state of the actual situation with respect to each of the rights on a regular basis, and to ensure that the state is aware of the extent to which the various rights are or are not being enjoyed by all individuals within its territory or under its jurisdiction;
(3) to facilitate public scrutiny of relevant government policies to encourage the involvement of various sectors of society in the formulation, implementation and review of relevant policies;
(4) to provide a basis on which a state, together with the Committee, can effectively examine the extent to which progress has been made towards the realization of the obligations in the treaty;
(5) to identify factors and difficulties inhibiting implementation of the treaty; and
(6) to enable the Committee and states parties to facilitate the exchange of information among states and in so doing encourage a better understanding of the common problems faced by states in the implementation of the treaty

---

[13] The treaties themselves do not foresee the participation of the representatives of states in the consideration of reports by the various treaty bodies. The practice of inviting the state party's representatives to respond to questions by Committee members when the report of the state is being considered was introduced by CERD in 1972 and has been adopted by every other treaty body.
[14] The first treaty body to adopt concluding observations reflecting the views of the Committee as a whole was the Economic, Social and Cultural Rights Committee in 1990. It was followed by the Human Rights Committee in 1992, CERD in 1993 and CEDAW in 1994. The Child Committee has adopted concluding observations from the outset (third session, January 1993).
[15] For example, the Economic, Social and Cultural Rights Committee may stipulate that information be provided within a stated time limit, usually six months, or in urgent cases, three months: *Committee on Economic, Social and Cultural Rights: Report on the Tenth and Eleventh Sessions*, E/1995/22 (1995) at para. 38. The Secretariat of the Child Committee provides it with documentation tracking the implementation of measures recommended in concluding comments. CEDAW has now begun to review some states parties with regard to which it formulated concluding comments at earlier sessions.

and a fuller appreciation of the type of remedies that might be taken to promote effective realization of human rights.[16]

Even the harshest critics of the human rights reporting system can point to its successes in meeting at least some of the objectives delineated by the Economic, Social and Cultural Rights Committee.

In Chapter 13, Andrew Clapham questions whether, given the expansion of opportunities for human rights work within other parts of the United Nations system, non-governmental organizations (NGOs) are best advised to direct their energies and limited resources towards the treaty bodies and the treaty reporting system.[17] At the same time, he details several clear successes of the system, at least from the perspective of international NGOs, and Amnesty International in particular.[18] Andrew Byrnes has concluded that the reporting system under the various human rights treaties has played a helpful role, particularly in the case of Hong Kong. He argues the reporting system has raised awareness of applicable human rights standards in the community as a whole and amongst law and policy makers, who have become alert to the need to take these into account in the formulation and review of laws and policies.[19] Although suggesting that a procedure which would allow issues to be examined individually should now be considered where the CRC is concerned, Ursula Kilkenny documents the successful use of reporting by a consortium of NGOs in regard to the United Kingdom's first report to the Child Committee.[20] Michael O'Flaherty presents a similar analysis in relation to the consideration of Ireland's first report required under the International Covenant on Civil and Political Rights by the Human Rights Committee.[21] The United Nations Development Fund for Women (UNIFEM) has taken joint initiatives with International Women's Rights Action Watch (IWRAW) – Asia/Pacific, which have facilitated the presence of representatives of NGOs from those countries reporting to the recent sessions of CEDAW. They have found these efforts have contributed significantly to the capacity of those NGOs to engage in domestic human rights advocacy.

These and other more anecdotal examples point to the capacity of the reporting system to provide a forum for public examination of state activity and a focus for human rights education for a broad range of individuals. They make it clear that the system can assist varied groups to integrate the language of international human rights into arguments for legal and policy change at the domestic level. These examples also indicate that the system provides civil society with opportunities to engage in dialogue with governments and the international community.

---

[16] Economic, Social and Cultural Rights Committee, *General Comment 1*, in *Committee on Economic, Social and Cultural Rights: Report on the Third Session*, E/1989/22 (1989) at Annex III, paras. 2–9; see also *UNITAR Manual*, first edition (1989) at 14–16.
[17] See *infra* Andrew Clapham, Chapter 13.
[18] *Ibid.*, at 186–7.
[19] Andrew Byrnes, "Uses and Abuses of the Treaty Reporting Procedure: Hong Kong Between Two Systems", in *The Future of UN Human Rights Treaty Monitoring*, Philip Alston and James Crawford (eds.), Cambridge University Press, 2000, 287.
[20] Ursula Kilkenny, "The United Nations Committee on the Rights of the Child – An Evaluation in the Light of Recent UK Experience", 8 *Child and Family Law Quarterly*, (1996) at 105.
[21] Michael O'Flaherty, "The Reporting Obligation under Article 40 of the International Covenant on Civil and Political Rights: Lessons to be Learned from Consideration by the Human Rights Committee of Ireland's First Report", 16 *Human Rights Quarterly* (1994) at 515.

Whether the reporting system fulfills its central purpose of promoting state compliance with agreed treaty obligations is a more difficult question to address and one that would require sustained analysis of the response of governments to the recommendations of treaty bodies in their review of reports. Some commentators have traced the adoption of domestic legal reforms directly to the efforts of treaty bodies,[22] but, as Andrew Byrnes has pointed out, identifying the origin of change in law and practice is complex, particularly where such change is gradual or long-term.

In the final analysis, however, those who are intimately involved in the work of the treaty bodies are insufficiently impartial and thus unable to judge, on the basis of cost and benefit, whether the reporting system meets its goals. Our instinct is that it does, but that its success depends, as less partial observers point out, on many factors.[23] Some of those factors are open to influence and change, and are addressed below.

The most crucial dependency of the system, and least open to manipulation, however, is the commitment of individual states parties to their treaty obligations. In the absence of genuine commitment, the success of the process, which is essentially dependent upon shame to encourage compliance, is likely to be limited. However, even in these cases the reporting system is a tool for human rights education and a focus for inspiration at the national level.

(3) Dependencies

There are two central factors, which predicate the success or failure of the reporting system. They are the compliance of the state with the reporting obligation, and the expertise and independence of the treaty bodies. Related factors are also of critical importance. These include the interest of NGOs in the system and their ability to be part of it, the involvement of the media in the process, and the financial and human resources within the UN Secretariat available to treaty bodies to assist them in their task.

(a) State compliance

The compliance of a state party with its reporting obligation has various dimensions. The most fundamental of these is its willingness to draft and submit reports as required by the various treaties in accordance with the periodicity that they establish.

More states parties to human rights treaties fail to comply than comply with this most fundamental of obligations. The 1999 annual report of the Human

---

[22] José Inglès, *Study on the Implementation of Article 4 of the International Convention on the Elimination of All Forms of Racial Discrimination*, A/CONF.119/10 (1982).
[23] See *infra*, Anne Bayefsky, Appendix 6, *International Law Association, Committee on International Human Rights Law and Practice, Report on the UN Human Rights Treaties: Facing the Implementation Crisis*, at 683.

Rights Committee expressed serious concern that nearly two thirds of all states parties were in arrears with their reports, a factor which the Committee felt impeded its ability to monitor the implementation of the Covenant.[24] More reports required under CEDAW are seriously overdue than are on schedule; of those overdue, fifty-three are from states parties who have yet to submit their initial reports.[25]

Responses to the delinquency of states parties in this regard have included appeals to the General Assembly to intervene,[26] repeated letters of reminder, meetings between treaty body members and permanent representatives of offending states, the release of documents listing overdue reports, and the publication of lists of recalcitrant states at treaty body press conferences. Other responses have included the agreement of CEDAW to allow states parties, in exceptional circumstances, to combine up to two reports[27] and concession by the Human Rights Committee, in very exceptional circumstances, to invite a state party whose report is overdue "because of material difficulties" to send a delegation to discuss those difficulties or to submit a provisional report dealing with only certain aspects of the Covenant.[28]

Since 1991, as a measure to ensure a minimum level of review of all states parties and to encourage constructive dialogue with defaulting states, CERD has reviewed implementation of the Convention in those states parties whose periodic reports are five or more years overdue, on the basis of their previous reports.[29] A more robust approach has been taken by the Economic, Social and Cultural Rights Committee, which examines states parties, even in the absence of initial reports, on the basis of all available information, an approach that the Child Committee has indicated it will emulate in cases of persistent non-reporting states parties.[30]

Recalcitrance in the submission of reports is only one aspect of state party failure to comply with reporting obligations. Alston has noted that:

> The process of satisfying a state's international reporting obligations should be seen as an occasion for achieving a variety of objectives. Ideally, it will be considered to be part of a continuing process designed to promote and enhance respect for human rights rather than an isolated event absorbing precious bureaucratic resources, solely to satisfy the requirements of an international treaty. In others words, the process should be treated as an opportunity, rather a chore or formality. It is an opportunity for domestic stock-taking and for the adoption of measures to remedy any shortcomings

---

[24] *Report of the Human Rights Committee*, A/54/40 (1999) at paras. 48–49.
[25] *Report of the Committee on the Elimination of Discrimination Against Women*, A/54/38/Rev.1 (1999) at Annex V. See also *Report of the Committee against Torture*, A/54/44 (1999) at paras. 25–26.
[26] CERD, General Recommendation VI, in *Report of the Committee on the Elimination of Racial Discrimination*, A/37/18 (1982) at 121.
[27] CEDAW Decision 16/III, adopted at the sixteenth session, in *Report of the Committee on the Elimination of Discrimination Against Women*, A/52/38/Rev.1 (1997) at 1. Note that CEDAW has allowed states parties to combine up to three reports. For example, one of the reports considered by it at its sixteenth session where this decision was taken was a combined first, second and third report.
[28] *Report of the Human Rights Committee*, A/50/40 (1995) at para. 32.
[29] *Report of the Committee on the Elimination of Racial Discrimination*, A/51/18 (1996) at paras. 601–607. See also paras. 579–582.
[30] CRC, *Overview of the Reporting Procedures*, CRC/C/33 (24 October 1994) at para. 32.

which have been identified. And it is an opportunity to proclaim to the international community that the government concerned is serious about its international commitments.[31]

Perusal of a sample of submitted reports suggests that in many cases the process of preparing the report has indeed been viewed as an isolated event and a formality. Preparation of reports is entirely a matter for the state concerned, although each treaty body has formulated guidelines relating to the content of reports. Some reports fail to follow the established guidelines.[32] Others are so inadequate that treaty bodies, notwithstanding their constructive and non-confrontational attitude, have openly criticized reports[33] and, on occasion, encouraged their withdrawal.[34] Many reports are self-serving and non-critical, descriptive of the formal legal and policy framework, rather than reflective of *de facto* implementation of treaty obligations in states parties and the difficulties confronting such implementation. Only a minority of reports suggest that states parties have taken the views of civil society into account in their preparation[35] or that the state is working to integrate the reporting process into domestic policy-making and seeking to align domestic and international objectives through that process. It is well-known that very few countries publicize the fact that reports are being prepared. Nationals frequently have difficulty gaining access to the reports of their countries except through the United Nations, which makes all submitted reports available on request and is in the process of entering all states parties' reports onto its websites.[36] It is unusual for states parties to make it widely known that their reports are being considered. Despite the fact that one treaty specifically mandates wide dissemination of information about the process at the domestic level,[37] and that treaty bodies usually request translation into local languages and extensive distribution of their concluding observations at the national level, available evidence suggests that the results of the process are rarely transmitted by states beyond government ministries.[38]

In many cases, presentation of the report by the state party to the relevant

---

[31] Philip Alston, "The Purposes of Reporting", in *Manual on Human Rights Reporting*, United Nations (1997) at 20.
[32] Some sympathy may be felt for states parties who are currently preparing their periodic reports required under the CRC, the general guidelines for which run to 49 closely typed pages: *General Guidelines Regarding the Form and Contents of Periodic Reports to be Submitted by States Parties Under Article 44, Paragraph 1 (b) of the Convention*, CRC/C/58 (20 November 1996).
[33] See the Human Rights Committee, *Summary Record of the 1325th Meeting, 7 July 1994*, CCPR/C/SR.1325 (13 July 1994) at para. 34 with regard to the report of Togo.
[34] See CAT, *Summary Record of 230th Meeting, 15 November 1995*, CAT/C/SR.230 (20 November 1995) at para. 5 with regard to the report of Belize.
[35] Of reports submitted to CEDAW, those submitted by Nordic States most suggest that the reporting process is integrated domestically. Notably, the third report of Denmark included a response to the government report by NGOs, submitted as part of Denmark's report (CEDAW/C/Den/3 (7 May 1993)).
[36] Both the Office of the High Commissioner for Human Rights (www.unhchr.ch) and the Division for the Advancement of Women (www.un.org/dpcsd.daw) have websites which operate collaboratively and seek to incorporate all material concerning the treaty bodies for which they are responsible.
[37] CRC, art. 44.
[38] The representative of the Kingdom of Morocco undertook to ensure wide dissemination of the concluding comments of CEDAW in Morocco at the conclusion of consideration of the report of Morocco by CEDAW at its sixteenth session. Moroccan NGOs unsuccessfully sought to gain access to these comments in Morocco.

treaty body appears to be an extension of the notion of report preparation as an isolated event. States parties are usually informed at least one year in advance that they have been scheduled by the relevant committee to present their reports. Some states parties request deferral of consideration to a later date so that they can prepare supplementary material to be considered with the report and acquit themselves adequately. Others do not respond at all to the information that they have been scheduled to present their reports and join the growing list of states parties whose reports have been submitted, but who are still awaiting consideration because they have failed to appear to present their report before the committee.[39]

Those states parties which accept a committee's nomination to present their reports often manifest their attitude to the reporting obligation by the level and size of the delegation assigned to present the report and by the degree to which the delegation is familiar with the treaty obligations, their implementation in the country, any factors that might hamper implementation, and the content of the state party's report. In the case of the CEDAW, which meets in New York, large and high-level delegations are now routine and are usually very well-prepared for Committee scrutiny. It is increasingly unusual, where CEDAW is concerned, for the report to be presented by the Permanent Representative of the state party to the United Nations, a trend possibly connected with the increased interest in gender issues since the Fourth World Conference on Women in 1995.

Nonetheless, even in those cases of full state party compliance with treaty obligations – a well-prepared, publicized and timely report, reflective of the *de jure* and *de facto* implementation of those obligations, presented by a well-informed and cooperative delegation – the presentation of states parties' reports is perceived by some commentators as a mere formality. For example, Clapham notes:

> The first impression of most outsiders attending a meeting of one of the human rights treaty bodies is that the human rights inquiry one might have expected has been replaced by a strange diplomatic ritual. Government representatives explain all the things that the government has been doing to fulfill the requirements of the treaty, and the expert members of the treaty body then pose gently worded questions which imply that certain issues are being ducked. Often the officials sent to answer the questions are unable to respond to the questions but are particularly able at talking around the subject in a lengthy and uninformative response.[40]

To some extent this perception is as a result of a misunderstanding of the nature of the process, sometimes fuelled by media reports that the process is adversarial.[41] It also results from the limitations of treaty bodies themselves.

---

[39] In the case of CEDAW, for example, the Dominican Republic was scheduled for consideration for two sessions, but did not agree to present until February 1998. It is as well to remember that although the presence of the state party during the consideration of reports is now required by virtue of the Rules of Procedure of each of the treaty bodies, such presence is not foreseen in the treaties themselves.
[40] Andrew Clapham, "UN Human Rights Reporting Procedures: An NGO Perspective", in *The Future of UN Human Rights Treaty Monitoring*, Philip Alston and James Crawford (eds.), Cambridge University Press, 2000, 175 at 176.
[41] The reports of the *Daily Mail*, *The Independent*, *The Times*, *The Guardian* and the *Daily Telegraph* on 28 January 1995 with regard to the consideration of the UK's report by the Child Committee are suggestive of a judicial process.

(b) The expertise and independence of treaty bodies

Each of the six treaty bodies is comprised of nationals of the states parties to the relevant treaty elected at the regular meeting of states parties. Experts are to be of high moral character and recognized competence and expertise. In their election, attention is paid to equitable geographical representation, and representation with respect to such issues as the different forms of civilization and principal legal systems.[42] Each expert serves in his or her personal, rather than representative, capacity.[43] In the case of CEDAW, the Human Rights Committee and the Child Committee, each expert receives a modest honorarium. When attending committee sessions, treaty body experts receive the daily allowance of a United Nations' Assistant Secretary-General.

Although the membership of treaty bodies is predicated primarily on expertise and recognized competence, it is also dictated by diplomatic considerations and is often dependent on successful lobbying by states parties and bloc voting across the six committees. A significant proportion of treaty body members are functioning diplomats, including active ambassadors, and members of their governments, sometimes cabinet ministers. While not doubting the expertise of these individuals, it is clear that it might well be difficult for experts so close to their governments to act independently and in their personal capacities on all occasions during the process of monitoring states parties' reports. Allied to this obstacle to impartiality is the issue of the participation of members in aspects of the consideration of their national reports. The eighth meeting of persons chairing the human rights bodies recommended that members of the treaty bodies refrain from participating in any aspect of the consideration of the reports of the states of which they are nationals.[44] This issue, as well as the concern that the often very close connection of members with their national governments, have serious implications for the substantive impartiality upon which reporting depends. Neither issue has yet to be addressed seriously by all the committees, or by the states parties to the various treaties.

While genuine independence of committee members is a necessary precondition to effective monitoring of reports, so too is the capacity for expert analysis. Increased acceptance of human rights treaties by states has meant that committee members are now unlikely to be expert in regard to all of the legal and factual situations they are called upon to scrutinize, and they are thus unlikely to be able to examine each report with the same level of proficiency.

The growing numbers of reports requiring consideration also demands increased commitment from treaty body members. Many are required to meet in formal session for up to twelve weeks per year[45] and to be able to undertake intersessional work. Many experts have demanding full-time positions and are unable to devote

---

[42] A number of the treaties stress the importance of legal expertise, while CAT provides that in electing experts, states parties shall bear in mind the usefulness of nominating persons who are also members of the Human Rights Committee and who are willing to serve on CAT: art. 17(2).
[43] CCPR, arts. 28–35; CERD, art. 8; CEDAW, art. 17; CAT, art. 17; CRC, art. 43.
[44] *Report of the Eighth Meeting of Persons Chairing the Human Rights Treaty Bodies, 15–19 September 1997*, A/52/507 (21 October 1997) at para. 67.
[45] The Child Committee meets for three annual sessions of three weeks and three further weeks are required for its pre-sessional working group; CEDAW meets for two annual sessions of three weeks and members are also required to meet in two one-week pre-sessional working groups comprised of four experts.

themselves to significant intersessional activity.[46] Committee sessions are therefore very intense. In order to fulfill their monitoring role as well as possible, most members, who are subject to other pressures at the time of sessions, must attempt to familiarize themselves in a few short weeks and usually with the help of NGO material, with the relevant issues in states parties. The period available for the consideration of individual reports is limited.[47] Although the practices of committees differ to a certain extent, the constructive dialogue of most remains formalistic, unstructured, and sometimes undisciplined, with duplication of questions addressed by experts to representatives during the examination of periodic reports and repeated remarks of praise for reporting states.[48] Consideration takes place over unbroken periods of three hours, and during this time committee members have limited opportunity for consultation with each other, with the Secretariat or with NGOs. At the conclusion of the constructive dialogue, experts have a very short time frame in which to formulate their concluding observations.

A number of strategies have been introduced by the treaty bodies to ensure that report consideration is as thorough as possible, given the constraints outlined above. These include the formulation of detailed but thematic reporting guidelines reflective of the expertise of treaty body members[49] and the nomination of individual country rapporteurs charged with the responsibility of studying a particular report in detail in the light of all information available. Based on this study, the country rapporteur is asked to introduce the report and point to pertinent areas for review, or to take the lead in constructive dialogue.[50] Another strategy has been the introduction of a pre-sessional working group to prepare lists of questions or issues for submission to reporting states in advance. The Child Committee,[51] the Economic, Social and Cultural Rights

---

[46] Although all members are asked to do so, only a minority of CEDAW members, for example, contribute questions in advance to the pre-sessional working group of the Committee which prepares the list of questions submitted to states parties presenting periodic reports.

[47] CEDAW devotes up to three three-hour meetings to initial reports and up to two meetings to periodic reports.

[48] Roberta Jacobson writes with regard to CEDAW:
> Each member seems to feel compelled to repeat congratulatory remarks and to reiterate questions already posed by a colleague. An even worse tendency is to associate one's self with the question of another, often at greater length than the initial question... Members also occasionally feel compelled to demonstrate that they have read the report by quoting whole sections before finally arriving at their question.

Roberta Jacobson, "The Committee on the Elimination of Discrimination against Women" in *The United Nations and Human Rights: A Critical Appraisal*, Philip Alston (ed.), Clarendon (1992) 444 at 461.

[49] See, for example, the Child Committee guidelines for initial and periodic reports: *General Guidelines Regarding the Form and Contents of Periodic Reports to be Submitted by States Parties under Article 44, Paragraph 1 (b) of the Convention*, CRC/C/58 (20 November 1996).

[50] CEDAW's practice is for the country rapporteur to introduce the state party's report in a ten minute closed session. Thereafter, each Committee member is at liberty to pose questions, normally on an article-by-article basis. The country rapporteurs nominated by CAT and CERD are charged with the responsibility of leading the dialogue with the state party.

[51] In its *Overview of the Reporting Procedures, supra* note 31, the Child Committee pointed out:
> ... the principal purpose of the working group is to identify in advance the most important issues to be discussed with representatives of states. The intent is to give advance notice to the states parties of the principal issues which might arise in the examination of their reports... the possibility for government representatives to prepare answers in advance to some of the principal questions is likely to make discussion more constructive (at para. 8).

Committee,[52] the Human Rights Committee,[53] and CEDAW[54] schedule the pre-sessional at the end of the previous session, an approach which gives states parties an opportunity to prepare comprehensive responses, thereby making constructive dialogue more fruitful,[55] and ensures that these responses become part of the formal process. The Child Committee, the Economic, Social and Cultural Rights Committee, and CEDAW also require written responses from states parties to the lists of issues. The scheduling of pre-sessional consideration of reports some months in advance, moreover, provides a further opportunity for the reporting process to become an integral part of state implementation of the treaty.

The concluding observations or comments of the committee are the most immediate and tangible results of the reporting process, and have the capacity to offer individual states parties and civil society clear direction for implementation of the treaty concerned. The quality of concluding observations is dependent on the quality of the constructive dialogue and the ability of the treaty body, in a limited amount of time, to isolate strengths and weaknesses in implementation in individual states parties. Study of concluding observations reveals that they are uneven, considered from both the standpoint of individual treaty bodies and across treaty bodies.[56] Indeed, as Alston has observed "... there is still considerable room for improvement of the quality of concluding observations, especially in terms of their clarity, degree of detail, level of accuracy and specificity."[57]

There is some variation between treaty bodies in the method of preparation of concluding observations, but the general pattern is that following the consideration of the state party's report, the relevant body meets in private to discuss elements to be reflected in the observations. The draft is then prepared by the country rapporteur with the assistance of the Secretariat and later considered and adopted by the committee as a whole in a closed session or sessions.[58] Formulation of concluding observations is governed by strict time constraints, which intensify as the session progresses. Their content is dictated by the information available to the members at the session, and is sometimes limited to that

---

[52] The pre-sessional working group of the Economic, Social and Cultural Rights Committee comprises five members and its purpose is to:
   identify in advance the questions which might most usefully be discussed with representatives of the reporting states. The aim is to improve the efficiency of the system and to facilitate the task of states' representatives by providing advance notice of many of the principal issues which will arise in examination of the reports.
Committee on Economic, Social and Cultural Rights: Report on the Tenth and Eleventh Sessions, E/1995/22 (1995) at 13.

[53] *Supra*, note 25 at para. 39.

[54] CEDAW began scheduling the pre-sessional meeting at the session prior to the consideration of a state's report at its 20th session. *Report of the Committee on the Elimination of Discrimination Against Women*, A/54/38/Rev.1 (1999) at para. 15. At an earlier stage, for example, the pre-sessional working group of the sixteenth session of CEDAW dispatched up to one hundred and twenty questions to states reporting at that session. Despite the number of questions, however, there were some suggestions that the Committee had failed to identify the fundamental trends in the countries concerned.

[55] *Supra*, note 30 at para. 8.

[56] Eric Tistounet, "The Problem of Overlapping Among Different Treaty Bodies", in *The Future of UN Human Rights Treaty Monitoring*, Philip Alston and James Crawford (eds.), Cambridge University Press, 2000, 383 at 389–394.

[57] *Supra*, note 5 at para. 109.

[58] See, for example, *Committee on Economic, Social and Cultural Rights: Report on the Tenth and Eleventh Sessions*, E/1995/22 (1995) at paras. 32–33; the same pattern was adopted by CEDAW at its sixteenth session.

reflected in the state report and the state's responses during the constructive dialogue. Quality could be enhanced by greater involvement of the Secretariat in their drafting, or perhaps by the participation of NGOs. Concluding observations might also be prepared in advance by the country rapporteur and circulated to other members for comment and finalized at the session. Concluding observations might also be prepared over more than one session. This would not only improve quality, but also emphasize the seriousness of the reporting process for states parties and keep the situation in states under active review.[59]

(c) *The role of non-governmental organizations*

All who have commented on the reporting mechanism point to its dependence on a state party that is willing to participate openly in critical self-analysis, an expert and independent committee, and well-coordinated and efficient NGO involvement. Most who analyze the system conclude that its most critical dependency is on NGO participation during report preparation at the national level, during the consideration by the committee and thereafter. NGOs are crucial players in ensuring that preparation is a dynamic process, that consideration is a moment of critical monitoring, and that the results of that monitoring are an important part of civil society's interface with government.

The importance of NGO participation in the work of the treaty bodies has been underlined repeatedly by the meeting of the persons chairing United Nations human rights treaty bodies[60] who have pointed to the vital role of NGOs in supplying the treaty bodies with documentation and other information on human rights developments. At their seventh meeting in 1996, the Chairpersons encouraged NGOs to continue to take an active role in "critically examining the role of the treaty bodies" so that more effective performance by treaty bodies as a whole, as well as by individual experts could be achieved.[61]

Current practices of individual treaty bodies with regard to NGO participation differ, with CAT[62] and CERD retaining only informal links with NGOs, and CEDAW, the Human Rights Committee, the Economic, Social and Cultural Rights Committee and the Child Committee encouraging informal country-specific briefings from NGOs, as well as allowing NGOs to participate in the closed pre-sessional working group.[63] Perhaps as a result of the significant involvement of NGOs in the drafting of the CRC and article 45 of that

---

[59] In the past, CEDAW has finalized concluding comments at the session following the session where the state party's report was presented. This was more as a result of time pressure than it was a reasoned decision.
[60] *Report of the Sixth Meeting of Persons Chairing the Human Rights Treaty Bodies, 18–22 September 1995*, A/50/505 (4 October 1995) at para. 23; and *Report of the Seventh Meeting of Persons Chairing the Human Rights Treaty Bodies, 16–20 September 1996*, A/51/482 (11 October 1996) at paras. 35–38.
[61] *Ibid.*, at para. 35.
[62] It is to be noted that Rule 62 of CAT's Rules of Procedure states that the Committee may invite, *inter alia*, NGOs in consultative status with ECOSOC to submit information, documentation and written statements relevant to the Committee's activities under the Convention. Notwithstanding this, NGOs, even those in consultative status, have not been accorded any official role in the process of report consideration.
[63] In 1998, for the first time CEDAW's pre-sessional working group "had invited representatives of national and international non-governmental organizations, on an experimental basis, to provide it with information with respect to the states parties under review" and recommended that "this practice also be adopted as a normal practice of the pre-session working groups." The Committee agreed

Convention (which empowers the Child Committee to invite the specialized agencies, the United Nations Childrens' Fund (UNICEF) and other competent bodies to provide expert advice on the implementation of the Convention in areas falling within their respective mandates), the Child Committee has developed the closest relationship with NGOs of all the treaty bodies. So close is the interface between this Committee and NGOs that NGOs are formally part of the system of reporting under this Convention. Material from NGOs is included in the country files available to the Committee and in the country analysis, prepared by the Secretariat, of those states parties which are to be reviewed.[64] In addition, individual NGOs are invited by the Committee to attend its pre-sessional working group and present country-specific information.[65]

Despite professed enthusiasm for greater NGO participation in treaty body work, the relationship between treaty bodies and NGOs is ambivalent. While all treaty body members appear to welcome informal contact with NGOs and certainly rely on their information in the monitoring process, their views towards more formal NGO participation are mixed. Some experts take clear national positions in this regard and express fears that the approach to NGO participation in the human rights treaty bodies might be out of step with the approach to participation of NGOs in other UN contexts. At the same time, although there is a hard core of NGOs which follow the work of the treaty bodies, NGO interest in this work remains limited and varies in degree from committee to committee.[66] These NGOs sometimes question the value of devoting their scarce resources to the treaty bodies, criticize them, both constructively and less constructively, and sometimes expect them to tailor their working methods to NGO needs.[67]

The success of the reporting system is predicated upon the capacity of treaty body members to engage in meaningful discussion with states parties in relation to implementation of human rights obligations. Such discussion is only possible if members are able to draw upon information independent from that presented by the state party. While it may be possible for members to access independent

---

with this recommendation. *Report of the Committee on the Elimination of Discrimination Against Women*, A/53/38/Rev.1 (1998) at paras. 19–20 and 433. Decision 18/I, *Report of the Committee on the Elimination of Discrimination Against Women*, A/53/38/Rev.1 (1998) at 3. In 1999 the Committee "urged its Secretariat to take all possible steps to make the entities of the United Nations and non-governmental organizations aware of its changed pattern of work so as to encourage these bodies to provide inputs in the future." *Report of the Committee on the Elimination of Discrimination Against Women*, A/54/38/Rev.1 (1999) at paras. 19 and 47. Decision 20/I, *Report of the Committee on the Elimination of Discrimination Against Women*, A/54/38/Rev.1 (1999) at 7.
[64] CRC, *supra* note 30 at para. 9.
[65] *Ibid.*, at para. 11.
[66] The Child Committee has perhaps the best following of NGOs, by virtue of the efforts of the NGO Group for the Convention on the Rights of the Child. The Human Rights Committee is followed by the mainstream international human rights NGOs, such as Amnesty International and the Lawyers Committee for Human Rights. Informal consortia of NGOs have been organized through Anti-Racism Information Service (ARIS), in regard to the CERD, and the International Women's Rights Action Watch (IWRAW), in regard to CEDAW.
[67] Gerison Lansdown, "The Reporting Process under the Convention on the Rights of the Child", in *The Future of UN Human Rights Treaty Monitoring*, Philip Alston and James Crawford (eds.), Cambridge University Press, 2000, 113. Lansdown complains that although the pre-sessional working group is critical to the effectiveness of the reporting process, the practice of timing the pre-sessional meeting at the end of the previous session should be reviewed because Committee members may be tired or absent and NGOs disappointed.

information themselves or for the Secretariat to assist in this regard, there is no question that NGOs, especially national NGOs, are better placed to provide it. Where most states are concerned, moreover, it will be NGOs, rather than the state itself, which will publicize reporting and disseminate results of the review process.

As their role is crucial, it is incumbent upon all treaty bodies to treat NGOs as equal partners in the process, rather than as poor relations on sufferance. At the same time, efforts must be made by NGOs to coordinate their work and collaborate with one another to exploit fully the potential of the reporting system.

Just as NGOs are critical to the success of the reporting system, so too are the media. All of the activities of the treaty bodies, and particularly the reporting system, are disadvantaged by a lack of public knowledge or understanding of their actual and potential significance for the promotion and protection of human rights. To some extent this is a result of the comparatively lackluster efforts of the United Nations Department of Public Information with respect to the treaty bodies, but it is also as a result of limited media interest, in particular with regard to the reporting process. It often surprises those who work with the treaty bodies that their activities are not inherently newsworthy and that newspaper, television and radio coverage of these activities is not routine. The primary responsibility for raising media interest in the reporting system rests with the UN Secretariat and, particularly, the UN Department of Public Information. More imaginative approaches to raising the interest of the media in the treaty system must be devised. The opportunities offered by new technology should be exploited fully and steps taken to ensure that the reporting system is accessible at all levels.

(d) Human and financial resources available to support the reporting system

Although the treaty bodies are autonomous independent entities, each is serviced by the UN Secretariat. All committees, with the exception of CEDAW, whose Secretariat is the Division for the Advancement of Women, are supported both technically and substantively by the Geneva Office of the High Commissioner for Human Rights. It is well known that the human resources and financial resources available within the Secretariat to support each of the treaty bodies are limited. Despite calls by the World Conference on Human Rights[68] and routine resolutions of the General Assembly,[69] it seems unlikely that the existing levels of funding and staffing will increase or even remain at their current levels. These constraints can be addressed to a certain extent by greater use of modern information technology, as well as by the employment of interns, externs and research fellows. Concrete and long-term strategies to confront existing limitations are required, however, so that the respective Secretariats of the treaty bodies will be able to meet their growing needs in relation to reporting. Strategies might include concerted efforts to seek extra-budgetary funds and the establishment of a trust fund specifically earmarked for the support of the treaty bodies. Independent foundations might also be persuaded to support the reporting system.

---

[68] *Supra*, note 3 at paras. 9–12.
[69] G.A. Res. 50/170, adopted on 22 December 1995; G.A. Res. 51/87, adopted on 12 December 1996; G.A. Res. 52/118, adopted on 12 December 1997; G.A. Res. 53/138, adopted on 9 December 1998.

In November 1996, the Office of the High Commissioner for Human Rights unveiled the Plan of Action to strengthen implementation of the Child Committee. The Plan envisaged an integrated approach to the implementation of the Convention. A substantive support team of four UN professional officers with research, coordination, follow-up and advisory functions would be recruited to serve the Committee. Additional support was to be made available at the national level to assist in report preparation and in the implementation of the Committee's recommendations. The Plan, was implemented for an initial period of three years to July 2000.[70] A Plan of Action was also adopted for the Economic, Social and Cultural Rights Committee.[71] In addition, a Global Plan of Action concerning CAT, the Human Rights Committee, and CERD was discussed at the Eleventh Meeting of Chairpersons.[72] In the fall of 1999 and early 2000 the High Commissioner for Human Rights launched an Annual Appeal which included a comprehensive two-year programme to improve the servicing of all five treaty bodies.[73]

Approaches such as the Plan of Action are crucial to strengthening the resources available to the reporting system. In addition, the wider UN system must become alert to the value of the reporting system in the promotion of human rights generally and their mandates in particular. The support of United Nations Children's Fund (UNICEF) has been critical to the early success of the Child Committee, affecting the rate of ratification and the capacity of the Committee to monitor its Convention as effectively as possible. The support of UNIFEM has ensured that CEDAW and the work of CEDAW have become part of the agenda of the grass roots women's movements that UNIFEM promotes. Other entities within the UN system, such as the United Nations Population Fund (UNFPA), the United Nations Development Program (UNDP) and the Bretton Woods institutions (International Monetary Fund (IMF), World Bank), could be encouraged to further incorporate human rights into their work and to take account of, and to support, the reporting system and the efforts of the treaty bodies.

(4) Limitations

While the thrust of the reporting system established under the human rights treaties is a cyclical mechanism of report preparation and review, a number of the treaty bodies have sought to develop means to address human rights situa-

---

[70] According to the Plan at the cost of $US 1.39 million per annum. *Plan of Action to Strengthen the Implementation of the Convention on the Rights of the Child*, CRC/SP/26 (21 January 1999) at para. 4.
[71] Programme of Action to Strengthen the Implementation of the International Covenant on Economic, Social and Cultural Rights, *Report of the Committee on Economic, Social and Cultural Rights*, E/1997/22 (1997) at Annex VII. As at 9 April 1999 enough funds had been received to recruit one specialist. *Follow-up to the Recommendations of the Tenth Meeting of Chairpersons*, HRI/MC/1999/3 (15 April 1999) at para. 21. According to the Plan, the cost is US $547,372 per annum.
[72] *Draft Proposal for a Plan of Action*, HRI/MC/1999/Misc. 3 (1 June 1999). See *Report of the Eleventh Meeting of Persons Chairing the Human Rights Treaty Bodies*, (4 June 1999), A/54/805 at para. 46.
[73] *Annual Appeal 2000: Overview of Activities and Financial Requirements*, Office of the High Commissioner for Human Rights, (January 2000) at 93. The Annual Appeal 2000 seeks $1.9 million for Support to the Treaty Bodies at 95.

tions requiring immediate attention.[74] In 1993, CERD commenced "early warning" and "urgent" procedures whereby it examines the situation in states parties identified by members as causing particular concern because of actual and potential circumstances.[75] The procedures, which by the end of 1999 had been invoked with regard to seventeen states parties, result in consideration of the situation in public or private session.[76] Representatives of the relevant state party may be invited, as may UN non-conventional human rights mechanisms, such as country rapporteurs.[77] Results of CERD's procedures in this regard have included formal decisions, declarations expressing the views of the Committee, bringing the situation to the attention of the Office of the High Commissioner for Human Rights, the Secretary-General, the General Assembly or the Security Council, requests for an immediate report from the state party, and undertakings by the Committee, (with the consent of the relevant governments) of good offices or technical cooperation missions. The Human Rights Committee has periodically also requested exceptional reports.[78] CEDAW has introduced the practice of calling for "exceptional reports" in situations where it considers implementation of treaty obligations to be compromised.[79] The Economic, Social and Cultural Rights Committee has, on occasion, nominated its Chairperson to follow-up feared imminent violations of the Covenant,[80] and although the Child Committee has yet to develop a practice of reacting to urgent situations, it has indicated that it might do so in the future.[81]

The notion of treaty bodies as a mechanism of early warning and as effective tools to encourage the implementation of human rights in urgent situations is attractive, but some have suggested that the efforts of treaty bodies in this regard serve to highlight the clear limitations of the system as a whole. Consideration of situations must be deferred until the relevant Committee is in session, and it is questionable whether there is much value in requesting exceptional reports from states parties which are in crisis or where the identification of authoritative government is difficult. There are other mechanisms within the U.N. system, including the non-conventional mechanisms, which are directed to early warning and urgent situations and it might well be appropriate, particularly in the light

---

[74] These initiatives appear to have been inspired by the *Report of the Secretary-General on the Work of the Organization*, A/47/1 (1 September 1992) at para. 101; and *Report of the Fourth Meeting of Persons Chairing the Human Rights Treaty Bodies, 12–16 October 1992*, A/47/628 (10 November 1992) at para. 44.
[75] *Supra*, note 29 at paras. 609–613.
[76] *Report of the Committee on the Elimination of Racial Discrimination*, A/54/18 (1999) at para. 20.
[77] For example, in the case of the former Yugoslavia, CERD met with the special rapporteur concerning the situation of human rights in the former Yugoslavia: CERD, *Summary Record of the 1071st meeting, 27 February 1995*, CERD/C/SR.1071 (6 March 1995).
[78] Work of the Human Rights Committee under article 40 of the CCPR: see *Report of the Human Rights Committee*, A/48/40 (1993) Part 1, Annex X at 219; and Rule of Procedure 66, para 2, in *Rules of Procedure of the Human Rights Committee*, CCPR/C/3/Rev.5 (11 August 1997).
[79] Decision 21/I, *Report of the Committee on the Elimination of Discrimination Against Women*, A/54/38/Rev.1 (1999) at 45.
[80] Economic, Social and Cultural Rights Committee, Twelfth Session, *Summary Record of the 4th Meeting, 2 May 1995*, E/CN.12/1995/SR.4 (5 May 1995); and *Summary Record of the 5th Meeting, 3 May 1995*, E/CN.12/1995/SR.5 (8 May 1995).
[81] Rule 66 of *Provisional Rules of Procedure*, CRC/C/4 (14 November 1991). No request for an exceptional report has been made.

of existing pressures, if treaty bodies were to discontinue their efforts in this regard.[82]

Related to the question of the value of the treaty bodies' early warning and urgent action procedures is that of missions by treaty body experts. In the past, the Child Committee has engaged in regional and sub-regional missions facilitated by UNICEF. On occasion, members of other committees have also taken part in country missions. These missions certainly allow committee members to gain greater insight into the conditions in states parties and this inevitably enhances their report review. There is also some evidence to suggest that missions by committee members enhance the implementation of human rights treaties in individual countries.[83] At the same time, it is possible to question whether treaty body members are best equipped to undertake the direct role envisaged in a mission, or whether this should be left to non-conventional mechanisms or United Nations technical and advisory services instead.

(5) Conclusion

In his report to the Commission on Human Rights, Alston predicts a future of almost universal ratification of the six core human rights treaties, with states expected to produce six reports for the consideration of the six treaty bodies and to answer additional ad-hoc requests from the committees, as well as to respond to complaints in regard to four or more communications procedures.[84] The growing burden on states will mean a growing burden on treaty bodies, with increased meeting time and increased sessional and intersessional commitment from experts being essential. In addition, the pressure on an already stretched Secretariat, in substantive and technical terms, will be overwhelming while human and financial resources will remain inadequate. In the face of an almost continual reporting process in individual states, national and international NGOs will divert their efforts to promote human rights elsewhere within the United Nations framework, while media interest will be minimal.[85]

To some extent, this future is already upon us. States are currently subject to a heavy reporting burden which, as has been noted, many address by failing to report. All of the treaty bodies are under intense pressure. The resulting additional meeting time remains insufficient given the backlog of reports awaiting consideration.[86] Human and financial resources available within the UN Secretariat are inadequate to service the system appropriately, and strict limitations on conference servicing, affecting provision of documentation, translation and interpretation, are being introduced.

As a result, treaty bodies and their Secretariats are seeking creative solutions to avert what Anne Bayefsky has called an "implementation crisis ... of dangerous

---

[82] *Supra*, note 5 at paras. 78 and 79.

[83] A parliamentary inquiry into the plight of children disadvantaged by discriminatory nationality laws in Egypt is said to have been inspired by the joint meeting of the Child Committee and CEDAW in Egypt in late 1996, where Egypt's reservations to both CRC and CEDAW were a topic of discussion.

[84] *Supra*, note 5.

[85] *Supra*, note 5 at paras. 82–84.

[86] *Supra*, note 5 at paras. 48–50.

proportions."[87] These solutions include simplified reports, the elimination of comprehensive periodic reports in their present form, and the introduction of thematic reports or reports tailored to the particular state party concerned.[88] Other ideas being discussed include reports, which could be considered by more than one treaty body, or the consideration of reports by individual committees with the assistance of experts from other committees. In this context, the detailed analytical study called for by the General Assembly of the human rights treaties to identify duplication of reporting required under these instruments[89] may set the scene for collaboration and cooperation between and across treaty bodies and their Secretariats. In addition, the replication of the Roundtable of Human Rights Treaty Bodies held in late 1996[90] would facilitate further dialogue amongst treaty body members towards integrated and creative solutions.

Until now, however, the approach to enhancing the system of reporting has been reactive and remedial. Radical solutions have been eschewed, although the twin notions of the permanent super-treaty (consolidated) body and the global report remain definite subtexts in discussions of the current system.

Observers have suggested that the merger of the existing treaty bodies into a single, permanent and comprehensive body would serve to reduce the burden on states parties, improve the effectiveness of existing procedures, and allow the development of uniform standards. But such an initiative would, inevitably, have significant financial implications[91] and might result in a less expansive interpretation of human rights obligations by omitting particular perspectives, such as gender or economic, social and cultural rights. For those of us whose daily work is bound up with the reporting system, and who believe it is a valuable mechanism for human rights implementation, however, the time has come for a radical approach. Significant efforts are required to sustain the system in its current imperfect form and still greater efforts will be needed to ensure that the potential of the process is exploited to the fullest. One can only hope that in the context of UN reform, the reporting system – perhaps the best available means of overseeing the implementation of human rights obligations – is not forgotten.

---

[87] See *infra*, Anne Bayefsky, Appendix 6, *International Law Association, Committee on International Human Rights Law and Practice, Report on the UN Human Rights Treaties: Facing the Implementation Crisis*, at 689.
[88] *Supra*, note 5 at paras. 92 and 93.
[89] G.A. Res. 51/87, adopted on 12 December 1996, at para. 5; G.A. Res. 52/118, adopted on 12 December 1997 at para. 10; G.A. Res. 53/138, adopted on 9 December 1998 at para. 14.
[90] *Report of the Roundtable of Human Rights Treaty Bodies on "Human Rights Approaches to Women's Health, with a Focus on Reproductive and Sexual Health Rights"*, unpublished, Glen Cove (1996).
[91] Markus Schmidt, "Servicing and Financing Human Rights Supervision", in *The Future of UN Human Rights Treaty Monitoring*, Philip Alston and James Crawford (eds.), Cambridge University Press, 2000, 481.

CHAPTER 2

State Reporting and the Convention on the Elimination of All Forms of Discrimination Against Women

Carmel Shalev

(1) The reporting obligation and guidelines

Under article 18 of the Convention on the Elimination of All Forms of Discrimination Against Women (CEDAW),[1] states parties agree to submit a report on the legislative, administrative or other measures which they have adopted to give effect to the provisions of the Convention and on the progress made in that regard. Reports are submitted to the Secretary-General of the United Nations "for consideration by the Committee [on the Elimination of Discrimination Against Women]." Initial reports are due within one year after the entry into force for the state concerned, and subsequent periodic reports are to be submitted every four years. States parties also further agree to submit, on an exceptional basis, reports "whenever the Committee so requests."

The guidelines issued by CEDAW for the preparation of reports by states parties[2] relate to the initial and subsequent periodic reports. Initial reports are to provide specific information on the constitutional, legislative and administrative provisions in force, as well as the developments that have taken place and the programmes and institutions that have been established since the entry into force of the Convention. The guidelines note the distinction between the *de facto* and the *de jure* positions. They recommend that the reports provide information, including sex-disaggregated statistical data, which indicates how the legal instruments are reflected in the actual economic, political and social realities of the country. States parties are requested to reveal obstacles to the participation of women on an equal basis with men in the political, social, economic and cultural life of their countries.

Subsequent periodic reports should include information on measures adopted to implement CEDAW since the previous report, actual progress made to promote and ensure the elimination of discrimination against women, and any significant changes in the status and equality of women since the previous report.

---

[1] Convention on the Elimination of All Forms of Discrimination Against Women, 1249 UNTS 13 (in force 3 September 1981).
[2] *Guidelines for Preparation of Reports by States Parties*, CEDAW/C/7/Rev.3 (26 July 1996).

In addition, they should include information on matters that were not covered in the previous report, as well as on matters raised by the Committee, that could not be dealt with when the previous report was considered.

The guidelines for reporting were amended at the Committee's fifteenth session in 1996, following the Beijing Platform for Action adopted at the Fourth World Conference on Women in September 1995. States parties were invited to take into account the twelve critical areas of concern in the Platform for Action insofar as is pertinent to the mandate of the Committee in monitoring effectively women's ability to enjoy the rights guaranteed by the Convention.[3]

(2) Preparation of reports

The government body responsible for preparing the report will vary from state to state. In some countries, the national machinery for women's affairs may be responsible. In others, such machinery does not exist or is ill-equipped to fulfil the reporting requirements. The responsibility may be assigned to the ministry in charge of legal affairs, in conjunction with the foreign ministry. Preparation of a report requires technical knowledge of the treaty body system and expertise in human rights reporting, which may be lacking. Reporting requirements may not be altogether clear. Indeed, the Committee's guidelines have been criticized for being too general and failing to specify the kind of detailed information required under each of the articles of the Convention. Reporting manuals issued by the Office of the High Commissioner for Human Rights, and by the non-governmental Commonwealth Secretariat and the International Women's Rights Action Watch (IWRAW), might not be at hand. In addition, given the broad scope of the Convention – which covers the fundamental human rights of women in all aspects of their daily lives and in all areas of public and private life – the preparation necessitates co-ordination between many governmental departments, as well as non-governmental organizations (NGOs), which have relevant information and expertise in women's affairs. Government bureaucrats are unlikely to appreciate the importance of human rights reporting and might resent having to spend time compiling information at the bequest of some other government unit.

(3) Committee meeting time

The reporting obligation is the major implementation mechanism created by the Convention, and two major shortcomings of the system are the same as those faced by other treaty bodies:[4] on the one hand, the failure of states parties to

---

[3] Para. 323 of the *Beijing Platform for Action* A/CONF.177/20 (17 October 1995):
States parties to the Convention on the Elimination of All Forms of Discrimination Against Women are invited, when reporting under article 18 of the Convention, to include information on measures taken to implement the Platform for Action in order to facilitate the Committee on the Elimination of Discrimination Against Women in monitoring effectively women's ability to enjoy the rights guaranteed by the Convention.

[4] See Anne Bayefsky, "Making the Human Rights Treaty Bodies Work", in *Human Rights: An Agenda for the Next Century*, Louis Henkin and JL Hargrove (eds.), American Society of International Law (1994) 229 at 234–5.

submit reports in accordance with the time frame set by the Convention, and, on the other hand, a significant number of reports submitted but not considered by the Committee due to backlogs. As of 1 August 1999, there were over 160 states parties to CEDAW, and there were 53 initial reports, 53-second reports, 40 third periodic reports, and 56 fourth periodic reports overdue. On the other hand, there were 9 initial reports, 11-second periodic reports, 14 third periodic reports, and 6 fourth periodic reports awaiting consideration by the Committee.[5]

The backlog is due primarily to a structural flaw in the system, namely, the inadequacy of the meeting time. Article 20 of CEDAW provides that the Committee shall normally meet for a period of not more than two weeks annually. As a response to the Committee's concern that it was becoming overwhelmed by its workload, the General Assembly granted the Committee a total of three weeks annual exceptional meeting time, preceded by a pre-sessional working group. This too was insufficient. The report of the fifth meeting of the chairpersons of the human rights treaty bodies, held in September 1994, noted with serious concern that the Committee was seriously constrained by the lack of sufficient meeting time. It described as "wholly unacceptable" and "deplorable" the situation that owing to the resulting large backlog, state party reports may not be examined until three years after their submission.[6]

At its fourteenth session, in 1995, CEDAW issued General Recommendation No. 22, out of concern for the workload of the Committee. The workload had increased as a result of the growing number of ratifications, the backlog of reports pending consideration, and the long lapse of time between the submission of reports of states parties and their consideration. The Committee noted that it is the only human rights treaty body whose meeting time is limited by its Convention, and that it has the shortest meeting time of all the human rights treaty bodies. The Committee recommended, therefore, that states parties amend the Convention so as to allow the Committee to meet annually for such duration as is necessary for the effective performance of its functions.

The states parties subsequently took up the recommendation, and the amendment is now pending acceptance by a two-thirds majority of states parties in order for it to enter into force. Meanwhile, for an interim period, the General Assembly decided at its 51st session in 1996 to approve the Committee's request for additional meeting time and to allow the Committee to hold two sessions annually, each of three weeks' duration, preceded by a pre-sessional working group.[7]

(4) Committee practice

The Committee's practice in considering reports is different for initial than for subsequent periodic reports. The rationale for the different procedures is that when a state party presents its initial report to the Committee, it is important

---

[5] *Report of the Committee on the Elimination of Discrimination Against Women*, A/54/38/Rev.1 (1999) at Annex V.
[6] *Report of the Fifth Meeting of Persons Chairing the Human Rights Treaty Bodies, 19–23 September 1994*, A/49/537 (19 October 1994).
[7] G.A. Res. A/51/68, adopted on 12 December 1996.

to establish a constructive dialogue first.[8] Interestingly enough, the Committee's practice is not reflected in the rules of procedure that it adopted in 1982.[9] The Committee is in the process of revising these rules. The changes proposed would, among other things, formulate the existing practice that provides governments with the possibility of submitting additional information, up to a certain deadline, so as to resolve the difficulty of reports becoming outdated between their submission and the time they come up for actual consideration. The proposed revision would also formally allow states parties with more than one overdue report to submit a combined report, pursuant to the Committee's decision at its tenth session (February 1991).[10]

(5) Initial and subsequent periodic reports

As mentioned, the form for consideration of initial reports is different than that for subsequent reports. For initial reports there is a formal introduction by the representative of the state, followed by questions of the Committee members article by article. The representative is then allowed a few days to prepare a reply in consultation with her government. The procedure extends over at least two meetings of the Committee.

Compared to this, the procedure introduced in 1990 for periodic reports was that a pre-sessional working group would convene one week before the Committee's session to prepare a coordinated list of questions on the report under consideration, based on suggestions by Committee members as well as on a comparison of the current report with the reports previously submitted. The list of questions was then sent to the representative of the state, so that she

---

[8] *Report on the Elimination of All Forms of Discrimination Against Women*, A/52/40/Rev. 1 (1997) at paras. 25–28. The purpose of a constructive dialogue between the Committee and the reporting state party is to establish that consideration of reports by the Committee is a joint enterprise designed to advance the goals of the Convention, rather than an adversarial process. The state party provides information, and the independent expert members point out shortcomings and suggest ideas for further implementation of the Convention, through a series of questions and answers. States are able to discuss progress and obstacles, and to benefit from the Committees expertise in evaluating the fulfilment of their obligations under the Convention: *Report by the Committee on the Elimination of Discrimination Against Women*, Fourth World Conference on Women, Beijing, A/CONF.177/7 (1995) at paras. 31, 43. The notion of a constructive dialogue is found in the work of other human rights treaty bodies. It embodies a distinction between an inquisitorial investigation of allegations of specific human rights violations, and a cooperative procedure of reviewing the overall progress made in the implementation of a convention. See *infra* Andrew Byrnes, Chapter 10 at 149.

[9] Chapter X of the Rules of Procedure relates to reports from states parties under article 18 of the Convention. Rule 46, concerning the form of reports, provides merely that the Committee may formulate suggestions and general recommendations as to the form, content and dates of the periodic reports. Rule 49, concerning attendance by states parties, provides that representatives of states parties shall be present at meetings of the Committee when the state's report is being examined, and shall participate in discussions and answer questions concerning the said report.

While the Rules of Procedure are not very enlightening on the practice of the Committee in considering reports and on the form of its constructive dialogue with the state party under review, the guidelines for the preparation of reports are more informative. See *supra* note 1 and *infra* note 11.

[10] *Report of the Secretariat on Ways and Means of Improving the Work of the Committee*, CEDAW/C/1995/6 (26 October 1994) at para. 7 and Annex I. See also *Report of the Committee on the Elimination of Discrimination Against Women*, A/46/38 (1991) at para. 370. *Revised Draft Rules of Procedure of the Committee on the Elimination of Discrimination Against Women*, CEDAW/C/2000/I/WGI/WP.1 (January 2000, Twenty-second session).

could prepare her answers ahead of time. Normally one meeting would suffice for this.

At its sixteenth session (January 1997), however, the Committee found it necessary to revise this procedure after having become overwhelmed by the amount of information it elicited. The pre-sessional working group had prepared diligently many detailed questions on the periodic reports and, in some cases, the answers were provided conscientiously in writing at comparable length. The state party representatives then proceeded to read through them laboriously for the record, as well as for the benefit of simultaneous interpretation. Aside from the tedious nature of this proceeding, it was also counter-productive to the goal of a constructive dialogue, since it was time-consuming in the extreme, and left little room for the Committee members to engage with the state representatives in a focused way.

The Committee recommended in consequence that the pre-sessional working group be convened henceforth at the end of the session prior to that at which the state party would be presenting its periodic report. The pre-sessional working group would formulate a short list of questions concentrating on major areas of concern, which would be submitted to the state party to be answered in writing in advance of the session. On this basis CEDAW could then enter into a constructive dialogue with the representatives. The Committee also decided that the reporting guidelines should be amended to indicate that the state party would address the Committee for up to one hour before opening the floor to the expert members for constructive dialogue, and that one and a half meetings would be available for consideration of a periodic report.[11]

(6) Reports on an exceptional basis

At its twelfth session (January 1993), CEDAW decided that it may request a state party to submit a report on an exceptional basis, within the obligation of states parties under article 18(1)(b) to report "further whenever the Committee so requests." The Committee decided to restrict its own discretion to exceptional situations of alleged grave violations of the rights of women in the country concerned.

So far, the Committee has received four reports on an exceptional basis: from Federal Republic of Yugoslavia (Serbia and Montenegro), Croatia, Rwanda, and Democratic Republic of the Congo (formerly Zaire). The first three reports were actively requested by the Committee in response to situations of alleged massive violations of human rights in areas of armed conflict. This was consistent with the recommendation made at the fourth meeting of the chairpersons of the human rights treaty bodies, and reiterated at their fifth meeting,[12] that treaty bodies take all appropriate measures[13] in response to such human rights violations. Indeed, the Chairpersons would welcome initiatives to develop procedures

---

[11] "Action taken by the Committee on the Report of Working Group I" in *Report of the Committee on the Elimination of Discrimination Against Women: Sixteenth and Seventeenth Sessions*, A/52/38/Rev.1 (1997) at paras. 369–371.

[12] *Supra*, note 6 at para. 27.

[13] "[I]ncluding the possibility of bringing those violations to the attention of the High Commissioner for Human Rights as well as the Secretary-General and the competent organs and bodies of the United Nations, including the Security Council": *ibid.*

aimed at the *prevention* of human rights violations, including early warning alerts to prevent escalation of conflicts and immediate responses to limit the scale of ongoing violations in areas identified as problematic. Yet it is not clear that the reporting process is at all useful as a preventive measure.

Obviously, one of the major tools of human rights work at all levels and throughout the world has been the collection of information and the documentation of violations. This appears to be most effective as an *ex post factum* instrument. It is of the utmost importance to tell the stories and expose the atrocities that human beings perpetrate against each other. Certainly there is enormous value in identifying and naming the gender-specific forms of violations of *women's* human rights, which have often been overlooked in the annals of history. But the effective use of the reporting process to collect and disseminate information as a preventive and early warning measure is no simple matter.

The case of Democratic Republic of the Congo is instructive. Zaire (as it then was) had been scheduled to present its initial report under CEDAW at the Committee's sixteenth session in January 1997. It did not, however, respond to repeated communiqués from the Secretariat that attempted to establish whether the government was ready to send a delegation to UN headquarters in New York to present its report before the Committee. Given the lack of response, the assumption was that Zaire would not be reporting, and arrangements were made for another country to present its report instead. Nonetheless, when the Committee convened, a delegation from Zaire arrived in New York expecting to present the state party's initial report. After some deliberation the Committee agreed to allot limited time for Zaire to make an oral report on an exceptional basis, in view of its understanding that the unstable political situation in the country had been responsible for the difficulty in communication and out of appreciation for the efforts made by the government of Zaire to send its representatives.

The Committee expected the delegation to report on the extraordinary circumstances of the crisis that the country was experiencing in the wake of the conflicts in the neighboring countries of Rwanda and Burundi, and in particular on the situation of women among the displaced refugee communities. It was also clear to the Committee and the Secretariat that the oral report would not be considered to satisfy the periodic reporting obligation of the state party according to CEDAW's ordinary procedures, and that the regular report would be rescheduled for consideration by the Committee at a future date. But when the representatives of Zaire took the floor, they proceeded to present a standard, albeit brief, overview of women's general situation in the country. In response to questions posed by Committee members, the representatives reluctantly acknowledged, in a perfunctory manner, the state of rebellion in eastern areas of the country, noting the internal displacement of several hundred thousand people and a significant number of refugees from Rwanda and Burundi. They emphasized that many parts of the country were not affected by the civil war in the east, but also expressed the sentiment that the international community was not truly concerned with the human rights situation in Zaire.

The main feature of this exchange, which lasted approximately one hour, was general embarrassment. The representatives of Zaire were clearly not at liberty to discuss openly the real issues of human rights violations in their country. The Secretariat was frustrated with its failure to explain effectively to the delegation the purpose of the exceptional oral presentation. And Committee members were confused as to their role in such politically sensitive circumstances, being unable to elicit any substantial information from the state party delegation in a situation that would explode within a short while and be catapulted into newspaper headlines all over the world.

The concluding comments of CEDAW on the report of Zaire[14] were formulated in the style of diplomatic understatement that is typical of constructive dialogue. The Committee reiterated that the oral report had been heard on an exceptional basis as a matter of courtesy to the delegation, and as an expression of concern for the situation of Zairean women "in those areas where conflict occurred and refugee populations were high." It regretted that the state party's presentation had not sufficiently reflected the close link between discrimination against women and gender-based violence, on the one hand, and the violations of fundamental human rights and freedoms of women in the current situation, on the other. The Committee was of the view that "effective and immediate measures need[ed] to be taken to protect the physical and moral integrity of refugee and displaced women and of all women victims of armed conflicts." And finally, it encouraged Zaire to provide information in subsequent reports on the consequences of armed conflict within the country for both Zairean women and refugee women from neighboring countries.

(7) Concluding comments

At its thirteenth session in 1994, CEDAW decided to dispense with a lengthy written account of the presentations and comments during the constructive dialogue without substantial conclusions, and introduced the practice, similar to that of other human rights treaty bodies, of preparing concluding comments in respect of each state party's report. The concluding comments constitute the Committee's collective appraisal of the report, and have been described as "the communication of the Committee with the country concerned."[15] Their objective is to highlight the most important points raised during the constructive dialogue, and to identify, on the one hand, particular areas of progress and, on the other hand, issues of special concern which the Committee wished the state party to address in its next periodic report.[16]

A pronounced goal of the concluding comments is to make CEDAW's work more accessible to government policy makers, civil servants and NGOs. The comments are included in the official report of the Committee, and are on average three or four pages long.[17] It has been suggested that they should be disseminated immediately after their adoption not only to the governments of the reporting states parties, but also to national NGOs and UN agencies.[18]

---

[14] *Report of the Committee on the Elimination of Discrimination Against Women: Sixteenth and Seventeenth Sessions*, A/52/38/Rev.1 (1997) at paras. 344–351.
[15] *Report of Working Group I*, CEDAW/C/1997/WG.I/WP.2 (1997) at para. 2.
[16] *Supra*, note 10 at para. 8.
[17] *Report of the Secretariat on Ways and Means of Improving the Work of the Committee*, CEDAW/C/1997/5 (6 December 1996) at paras. 12–14.
[18] *Report of the Roundtable of Human Rights Treaty Bodies on "Human Rights Approaches to Women's Health, with a focus on Reproductive and Sexual Health Rights"*, unpublished, Glen Cove (1996) recommendation 1.8.

Likewise, it has been suggested that CEDAW ought to be more forceful in its conclusions, in that it should clearly identify incompatibilities with the Convention and violations of specific articles, and suggest specific measures to be taken in remedy.[19]

At the Committee's sixteenth session (January 1997), Working Group I (a sub-committee of the Committee meeting during the session) developed a standard format for the concluding comments, following a pattern elaborated at its fifteenth session (January 1996).[20] After a brief summary of the presentation of the state party, the introduction should assess the nature and quality of the report in terms of adherence to the reporting guidelines, incorporation of gender-disaggregated statistical data, and the governmental level of the delegation. The second section, entitled "Factors and Difficulties Affecting Implementation of the Convention," should include general comments on overarching legislative, social, traditional, cultural and behavioral factors, including the impact of structural adjustment and transition on the women of the state party under review, and including the issue of state party reservations to the Convention. The following section on positive aspects should be presented in the order of the articles of CEDAW, while the principal subjects of concern should be addressed in the order of the importance of the issues. The final section should provide concrete recommendations and suggestions from the Committee to solve the problems identified in the rest of the comment, and should also include reference to commitments made by the state party at the Fourth World Conference on Women. Concluding comments should close with a recommendation relating to the dissemination of the Convention, the reports and the concluding comments themselves.

At CEDAW's sixteenth session (January 1997), it decided further that there would be a closed meeting of Committee members, after the constructive dialogue with each state party, in order to discuss the main issues that should be reflected in its concluding comments. Two experts,[21] designated as country rapporteurs, draft the comment accordingly, to reflect the actual views expressed by the other experts at the meeting during which the report was presented. The draft is then taken up for discussion and, finally, adoption by the Committee as a whole. These meetings are closed to allow for the unconstrained exchange of views between the expert members of the Committee.

(8) Processing the information

It is clear that the effectiveness of a monitoring system based on state party reports is enhanced where the monitoring body receives additional information from external independent sources. In the most serious cases of human rights violations, the reporting government is unlikely to be wholly forthcoming on the matter. However candid the state party may be, it will tend to present its

---

[19] *Recommendations of the Colloquium of the International Women's Rights Action Watch and the Committee on the Elimination of Discrimination Against Women*, New York (14 January 1996).
[20] *Supra*, note 15 at paras. 3–6.
[21] One expert is designated as the main country rapporteur, and another as back-up rapporteur: *supra* note 15 at para. 2.

report in the most favourable manner. Matters that are of serious concern to human rights activists within the country may go unmentioned, or may be camouflaged by innocuous language. Given the broad scope of the Convention, even in the best of circumstances, where relevant information is actually presented in a comprehensive report, its significance may be lost among the wealth of facts, figures and legal analyses.

The independent expertise of the Committee members is a primary resource for deciphering the mass of data included in the states parties' reports. Aside from the personal knowledge and understanding they bring from their diverse backgrounds, Committee members develop an innate skill in separating the wheat from the chaff. However, this skill alone is insufficient, especially when one takes into account that the Committee may consider up to ten reports in addition to other items on its agenda in the course of one session of fifteen working days, and that many of the reports are extremely lengthy, sometimes reaching over 200 pages.

External sources of additional information serve, therefore, at least two purposes: to provide a wider perspective on the actual human rights situation in the reporting country, and to assist the expert members of the Committee in focusing on matters of central concern.

Indeed, the Committee has, in recent years, expanded its access to independent sources of information. The Secretariat of the Committee has for several years routinely prepared a somewhat obscure compendium of statistical information on the countries under consideration.[22] A most valuable source of information for many years has been the informal contribution of IWRAW, which publishes brief reports on the countries reporting at any given session, based on shadow reports solicited from local NGOs and independent research. In some cases national NGOs have taken the initiative to provide local materials directly to the Committee members, and their ability to shed light on the *de facto* implementation of the Convention is unquestionable.[23] At its sixteenth session (January 1997) the Committee recommended that the Secretariat should facilitate an informal meeting with NGOs at the beginning of its sessions, which would include country-specific information.[24] In 1998 the Committee further decided that NGOs would be invited to provide it with information with respect to states parties under review at the pre-sessional working group.[25]

---

[22] At the Committee's sixteenth session in January 1997, Working Group I of CEDAW reached the conclusion that "the diagrammatic comparisons of the states parties' reports provided by the secretariat in the analysis reports were not necessary": *supra* note 15 at para. 11.

[23] IWRAW was established specifically to monitor the work of the Committee at the non-governmental forum of the World Conference to Review and Appraise the Achievements of the United Nations Decade for Women, held at Nairobi in 1985. For further discussion of the Committee's relations with NGOs, see *Report of the Secretariat on Ways and Means of Improving the Work of the Committee*, CEDAW/C/1997/5 (6 December 1996) at paras. 30, 43–48, and *Report of Working Group I*, CEDAW/C/1997/WG.1/WP.2 (1997) at para. 7; *Report of the Committee on the Elimination of Discrimination Against Women*, A/53/38/Rev.1 (1998) at paras. 19–20 and 433; Decision 18/I, *Report of the Committee on the Elimination of Discrimination Against Women*, A/53/38/Rev.1 (1998) at 3; *Report of the Committee on the Elimination of Discrimination Against Women*, A/54/38/Rev.1 (1999) at paras. 19 and 47; Decision 20/I, *Report of the Committee on the Elimination of Discrimination Against Women*, A/54/38/Rev.1 (1999) at 7.

[24] *Supra*, note 11 at para. 362.

[25] See also *Report of the Committee on the Elimination of Discrimination Against Women*, A/54/38/Rev.1 (1999) at paras. 19 and 47.

In addition, other human rights treaty bodies also serve as sources of information. Since its fifteenth session in 1996, the Secretariat has made available to the Committee the concluding observations of the other human rights treaty bodies on the reports of the state party under consideration.[26] The Committee has also asked the Secretariat to ensure that its own concluding comments are transmitted immediately to other treaty bodies.[27]

The Committee has discussed the information it receives from specialized agencies and other bodies of the United Nations under article 22 of the Convention.[28] Several of these bodies regularly submit reports to CEDAW, and their representatives may make oral presentations at its meetings. The Committee has also designated individual expert members to act in liaison with focal points at these bodies. The Committee suggested at its sixteenth session (January 1997) that the input of specialized agencies into its work should be more structured, and that information submitted under article 22 of CEDAW should be country-specific and should include country or regional studies about the state party, new statistics collected by the agencies, and a description of the country-level programmes of the agencies in the state party under review.[29]

A roundtable of the human rights treaty bodies, held in December 1996 on the issue of women's reproductive and sexual health rights, made some interesting recommendations in this respect. The roundtable was a collaboration of the Division for the Advancement of Women, the United Nations Population Fund and the United Nations High Commissioner for Human Rights. Its aim was to bring the issue of women's reproductive and sexual rights into the mainstream of the human rights agenda in the wake of the International Conference on Population and Development held in Cairo in 1994 and the Fourth World Conference on Women held in Beijing in 1995. It was the first occasion at which members from all the treaty monitoring bodies met to discuss a thematic issue. The recommendations that ensued from the substantive discussion put a strong emphasis on developing working methods that would encourage cooperation between the treaty bodies and UN agencies and NGOs. It included one recommendation that treaty bodies should notify the agencies of their meetings and provide them with state party reports scheduled for consideration, so as to allow the agencies to analyze the reports and provide country-specific information which would be relevant to their consideration by the treaty bodies.[30]

---

[26] This practice was adopted upon the suggestion of the Colloquium convened by IWRAW with members of the Committee in January 1996: *supra* note 20 at para. 24.

[27] *Supra*, note 11 at para. 363.

[28] Several specialized agencies had requested guidance in relation to the information that they could contribute to the work of the Committee: *Report of the Secretariat on Ways and Means of Improving the Work of the Committee*, CEDAW/C/1997/5 (6 December 1996) at paras. 9–11, and *Report of Working Group I*, CEDAW/C/1997/WG.1/WP.2 (1997) at para. 9; see also: *Ways and Means of Expediting the Work of the Committee, Report of the Secretariat*, CEDAW/C/1998/I/4 (24 December 1997) at paras. 4–5; *Report of the Committee on the Elimination of Discrimination Against Women*, A/53/38/Rev.1 (1998), Decision 18/II at 3, and 37, paras. 431–433.

[29] *Supra*, note 11 at para. 365. The Committee also asked the Secretariat to ensure that its concluding comments should be submitted to the heads of specialized agencies as soon as possible after their conclusion.

[30] *Supra*, note 18, recommendations 1.6 and 2.7.

(9) The rationale of reporting

The rationale for the periodic reporting obligation is that it provides an occasion for comprehensive review of the situation of women in a particular country. In this respect, the actual presentation of the report to the Committee is for just one moment the focus of a process that is an essentially domestic dynamic of self-scrutiny and public debate. Under the pressure of deadlines for submitting reports, the state party takes a close look at its own laws and practices. The initial reporting requirement may result in the first detailed, official examination of the situation of women in that country. Some governments avail themselves of NGO expertise and knowledge, give them the opportunity to contribute to preparation of the report, or include them in a public discussion of the report. The constructive dialogue with CEDAW may shed light on core issues and produce suggestions for remedial actions from the diverse experience of individual expert members. The concluding comments of the Committee might form the basis for the domestic elaboration of targeted policies to advance the goals of the Convention, eliminating discrimination against women and furthering their equality.

Yet the reporting system also plays the role of external monitoring. Naturally, as time goes by, the number of initial reports will decrease and the Committee will spend more and more time considering second and subsequent periodic reports of the states parties. In doing so it must assess significant developments during the four-year period of the report and attempt to ascertain the degree to which the Committee's comments and suggestions at previous reviews have been internalized and implemented. This requires a comparative analysis of the initial and subsequent reports so as to identify issues that have not been addressed or that remain unanswered from the Committee's previous examination of the state party, and to highlight issues of concern.[31]

(10) Conclusion

CEDAW has devoted much attention to matters that would enhance the effectiveness of its functioning. One of the major difficulties that has arisen in this regard is an overload of information as regards the ongoing monitoring of the implementation of the Convention. While CEDAW has been creative in addressing its own working methods and producing what appear to be appropriate technical responses to pointed problems of the reporting system, the underlying question remains to be addressed: now that we have all this information, what do we do with it? On the other hand, as the exceptional report of Zaire demonstrates, the existing reporting system suffers from a lack of information in relation to its potential to serve as a preventive or early warning mechanism. Clearly then, issues of information processing and management are central to

---

[31] The Committee has indeed asked the Secretariat to provide an analysis of whether the recommendations it made in its concluding comments have been addressed in subsequent reports of the state party concerned: *supra* note 11 at para. 368.

the future development of the reporting system as a monitor of the situation of human rights in the vast majority of the world's states which have ratified the Convention.

CHAPTER 3

Reporting and the Committee on the Rights of the Child

Judith Karp*

(1) Introduction

The evaluation of the process of state reporting must focus on the effectiveness of reporting as a tool for international monitoring of compliance with obligations under human rights treaties. But it must also address its impact on, and contribution towards, the actual implementation of these treaties at the national level. These two parameters may initially seem one and the same, or at least concurrent. They are indeed indivisible and intertwined, yet they are also distinct in their nature. Evaluation of the reporting process depends therefore on a conceptual frame of reference for the notions of "reporting", "monitoring" and "implementation".

This commentary depicts a conceptual framework for reporting, based on a holistic vision of implementation, as reflected in the *modus operandi* of the Child Committee. I shall draw an outline of the Committee's dynamic perception that considers the process of reporting to the Committee to be an integral part of the actual implementation of the Convention on the Rights of the Child (CRC).[1]

---

*The views expressed in this commentary are the author's and do not necessarily reflect the outlook of the other members of the Committee.

[1] Convention on the Rights of the Child, 1577 UNTS 3 (in force 2 September1990). The duty to submit reports offers an opportunity and a forum for those in government who are truly concerned about children's rights and their promotion. Almost all the states' reports include a certain degree of self-criticism, which is the first step towards finding solutions. The writing of reports provides an opportunity to assess the conditions and status of children, and to plan measures for reform. In the eyes of the Committee, the reporting process and the duty of states parties to indicate in their reports any factors and difficulties affecting the fulfillment of obligations under the Convention and to provide the Committee with a comprehensive description of the implementation of the Convention in the country concerned (art. 44(2)), offers an opportunity for states parties to monitor their policies on a regular basis and to focus on areas where further action is required.

According to the *General Guidelines Regarding the Form and Content of Initial Reports to be Submitted by States Parties under Article 44, Paragraph 1(a) of the Convention*, CRC/C/5 (30 October 1991) at para. 3:

The Committee believes that the process of preparing a report for submission to the Committee, offers an important occasion for conducting a comprehensive review of the various measures undertaken to harmonize national law and policy with the Convention and to monitor progress made in the enjoyment of rights set forth under the Convention.

(This is repeated in *General Guidelines Regarding the Form and Content of Periodic Reports to be*

According to this view, the Committee plays an active role in the implementation process through its monitoring functions at the international level.

(2) Reading the process of reporting in a holistic way

The CRC is a holistic document.[2] Its nature calls for a holistic approach to implementation, which implies a comprehensive approach to children's rights and an all-embracing strategy for the development and adoption of legislation, policies and plans of action. It also implies an integration of efforts and a maximization of resources of all kinds – human, material, organizational, technological, and informational. It calls for cooperation, coordination and integration of all measures taken, of all actors and at all levels. It also calls for the cooperation and partnership of public authorities with national and international non-governmental organizations (NGOs), UN specialized agencies and other relevant internal UN or international bodies. Above all, holistic implementation means the mobilization of all parts of civil society to participate in a comprehensive and dynamic development process of social action and change, directed towards empowerment of the weaker elements of society through access to knowledge, provision of information, and the entitlement to rights.

The Committee also understands the process of reporting and monitoring in a holistic manner. According to article 43 of the CRC, the Committee was established "for the purpose of examining the progress made by states parties in achieving the realization of the obligation undertaken under the Convention." It follows, therefore, that the role of the Committee is that of a monitoring body. The Committee also regards itself as the international conscience for children's rights and as the representative of all children throughout the world. It regards its ultimate rationale as the task of improving the conditions and status of every child worldwide. In a working paper considered during the third session (January 1993) of the Committee, it was suggested that as a treaty body, the Committee was expected not only to assess the states parties' compliance with the Convention, but also to assist governments in fulfilling their obligations. It was also suggested that the Committee should allocate adequate time to activities related to the promotion of the rights of the child.[3]

Submitted by States Parties under Article 44, Paragraph 1(a) of the Convention, CRC/C/58 (20 November 1996) at para. 3.) Thus, the reporting system contributes to highlighting "children's rights" problems especially in those countries where such problems might have otherwise been hidden or neglected. This is also an opportunity to formalize a state's need for technical assistance and advice, and to take advantage of the Committee's procedures for providing such assistance. Similarly, the obligation of states parties under art. 44(6) to make the reports widely available to the public in their own countries is identified as an innovative follow-up system. In these ways, the system of reporting has direct implications on the national level. In addition, the obligations under the educational provisions of the Convention (art. 42 and 44 (6)) that refer to education in the context of implementation methods may have a substantial impact in the long run.

[2] The holistic nature of the Convention lies not only in its universality (as of 31 December 1999, 191 countries have ratified or acceded to the CRC) which accords it an holistic territorial dimension, but also an holistic approach to rights. It encompasses in a comprehensive way, rights from all fields: civil and political, economic, social and cultural. It also reflects the "indivisibility and interdependency of rights" approach, and the holistic approach that is needed in all issues of children's rights.

[3] Marilia Sardenberg, "Committee on the Rights of the Child: Basic Processes", in 6 *Transitional Law & Contemporary Problems* (1996) 263 at 271.

Accordingly, the role of the Committee in the process of reporting does not appear to end with the task of formal international monitoring. The Committee views itself as a partner in the enhancement of actual implementation through advocacy, education and awareness-raising, dialogue with government as well as with civil society, and cooperation and coordination with national and international NGOs, UN specialized agencies and other similar organizations.

The Child Committee interprets its role in the process of reporting as including involvement in the capacity-building of a state party, especially through grassroots mechanisms at the national level. In other words, reporting is seen as an opportunity for the Committee to participate in the process of turning the implementation of the CRC into a human-development endeavor in which human-rights norms are reflected, developed and enhanced.

(3) Reporting and the culture of rights

The Committee envisages and uses reporting as a tool to transform public discourse at the national level into a discourse on the norms of children's rights. Reporting is considered as a means to develop human rights language as the basic language of implementation-discourse, and to promote a better understanding of the content and meaning of the commitments undertaken by states parties under the Convention.

Reporting and monitoring – though to a certain extent a frustrating exercise – may prove to be an invaluable catalyst for bringing countries within reach of a common human rights language and thinking, which would ultimately be reflected in legislation, policies and actions. Reporting may prove to be an effective means to develop a universal culture of rights, one in which the actual meaning of rights and their implications for specific individuals and groups are commonly understood and internalized by governments and civil society alike. The importance of developing such a culture of rights cannot be minimized. One clear lesson that may be learned from the experience of reporting and monitoring is that we have yet to grasp the practical implications of human rights on governments and on individuals. This is true not only with respect to children's rights[4] – a relatively innovative concept – but also with respect to human rights in general. It is therefore important that these practical implications be conveyed to public authorities, as well as to human rights promoters, including national and international NGOs, UN specialized agencies and other concerned bodies. Those who work with, and for, children and the public at large must also be made aware of the Convention, its requirements and the reporting process. Reporting may thus serve as a meaningful facilitator, an opportunity to involve governments and civil society in a dialogue on rights at the national and international level and as a catalyst for growth.

This desired outcome may be achieved through the mechanisms of reporting: dialogue with the delegation of a state party that is constructive and instructive

---

[4] The need to teach the implications of rights under the CRC is much stronger, not only because of the innovative approach of the Convention, but also because of the comprehensive scope of the rights set out under it.

in nature, the diverse expertise of the Committee members,[5] and the concluding observations adopted by the Committee. The reporting process encompasses some additional devices to reach this goal. In the discussion that follows, some of these expanded elements of reporting will be highlighted, namely: detailed guidelines for reporting, thematic discussion days, the initiation of studies and field visits, interaction with NGOs, and the linkage with technical assistance and advisory bodies.

(4) Detailed guidelines for reporting

The common language and the culture of rights, as described above, may be promoted through detailed and elaborate sets of guidelines for reporting, such as those developed and adopted by the Child Committee.[6] The General Guidelines – especially those regarding the periodic reports – give a comprehensive review of the practical meaning of children's rights, as well as concrete illustrations of the situations in which they apply and the circumstances in which they may be endangered or violated. They may serve, therefore, as a practical tool for implementation and education.

The drafting of the guidelines was intended to promote, through the process of reporting, a new approach based on the understanding that the implementation of each right should take into account the realization of all of the other rights.

These guidelines reflect the "cluster approach," according to which closely related articles of the CRC are grouped under specific headings and according to certain themes, rather than dealt with on an article by article basis. It is the Committee's view that the thematic approach will better stress the interrelationship between the Convention's articles, in addition to promoting a holistic view of rights under the Convention. This approach is also reflected in the formulation of the General Principles of the Convention.[7] They group under one heading

---

[5] Under art. 43 of the Convention, the Committee consists of ten experts. They are all experts on different children's issues. The current Committee consists of four lawyers (two judges, an international law professor and one Deputy Attorney General), two psychologists, one pediatrician, a professor in education and two diplomats. The members are from diverse regions (Barbados, Brazil, Burkina Faso, Indonesia, Israel, Italy, Lebanon, Russian Federation, South Africa, and Sweden). It is composed of seven women and three men. The composition of the Committee promises diversity of approaches – legal as well as social, psychological, health-oriented and educational.
[6] During its first session in October 1991, the Committee devised and adopted the *General Guidelines Regarding the Form and Content of Initial Reports to be Submitted by States Parties under Article 44, Paragraph 1(a) of the Convention*, CRC/C/5 (30 October 1991). In its thirteenth session in November 1996, the Committee adopted the *General Guidelines Regarding the Form and Content of Periodic Reports to be Submitted by States Parties under Article 44 Paragraph 1(b) of the Convention*, CRC/C/58 (20 November 1996). This second document of 49 pages is a much more elaborate and updated version of the first set of guidelines. Due to its comprehensiveness, it is expected by the Committee to serve also as a practical guideline for the initial reports for those states parties who have not yet submitted their report. These two sets of guidelines supplement the *Compilation of Guidelines on the Form and Content of Reports to be Submitted by States Parties to the International Human Rights Treaties, HRI/GEN/2 (14 April 2000)* which relate to the general part of states parties' reports (the core document). In the General Guidelines, the articles of the Convention are grouped under eight thematic sections: general measures of implementation; definition of the child; general principles; civil rights and freedoms; family environment and alternative care; basic health and welfare; education, leisure and cultural activities and special protection measures.
[7] Non-discrimination (art. 2); the right to life, survival and development (art. 6); the best interests of the child (art. 3) and the right to express views and be heard (art.12).

matters to be dealt with together in the state party's report as well as in the dialogue between the Committee and the government.

In the long run, detailed reporting guidelines may serve as the only comprehensive practical human rights language that can guide a state party towards the actual meaning of proper implementation.[8] Such guidelines may help to produce appropriate reports, save time in the process of drafting the list of issues and in the process of the dialogue[9] and serve as indicators for the concluding observations. Equally important, the guidelines serve as indicators for national monitoring bodies, for national and international NGOs, and for the public at large. These indicators help to evaluate the progress achieved and the difficulties encountered in the implementation of the Convention. Education and the raising of awareness by means of detailed guidelines are therefore seen by the Committee as part of the process of reporting and monitoring.

The Committee also systematically stresses[10] the need to develop quantitative and qualitative indicators and to collect desegregated data for assessing the implementation of all rights under the Convention, and about all children, especially those belonging to the most disadvantaged groups. The development of indicators to measure not only achievements in social development – particularly in education and health – but also to measure violations of the human rights of a child (including his or her economic, social and cultural rights), is essential to the evolution of a common discourse on human rights and the creation of a human rights culture.[11]

(5) Thematic discussion days

Under rule 75 of the Rules of Procedure, the Committee may decide upon a general discussion theme concerning one specific article of the CRC or a related subject, as a means to enhancing a deeper understanding of the contents and implications of the Convention. The practice of the Committee is to hold one "special discussion day" a year.[12] The topics for the thematic days are chosen by the Committee based on their importance for promoting and protecting children's rights and their potential contribution to improving implementation. The thematic days usually reflect a number of the Committee's major concerns regarding state reports. They are held within the framework and spirit of partner-

---

[8] This is true notwithstanding the proposal to simplify the guidelines for reporting as one possible solution to the "reporting crisis," and despite the sympathy felt by Jane Connors for the states parties currently preparing their periodic reports under the CRC: see *supra* Jane Connors, Chapter 1 at note 32.

[9] This is on condition, of course, that written answers arrive in time to enable the Committee members to read them before the commencement of the dialogue with the delegation.

[10] This is done in the guidelines, the dialogue and concluding observations and recommendations.

[11] The development of indicators is also important for raising awareness and understanding of the comprehensive scope of the Convention. It plays a vital role in promoting a systematic monitoring of the status of children, and in evaluating the progress achieved and difficulties encountered in the realization of children's rights as a new language of commitments. The real value of indicators can be assessed only by a consideration of the periodic reports.

[12] Discussion days have been held on children in armed conflicts, economic exploitation of the child, the role of the family in the promotion of the rights of the child, the girl child, the question of the administration of juvenile justice, on the child and the media, children with disabilities, and children living in a world with HIV/AIDS.

ship with UN specialized agencies, international and national NGOs, and other competent bodies and experts on children's rights.[13] The resulting recommendations are sent to each of them. The importance of these thematic days lies in their educational, advocacy and awareness-raising value, and in the contribution they make towards developing a common language and culture of rights. They highlight the activities of the Child Committee and its understanding and interpretation of the Convention. The days are also a valuable forum for a dialogue between the Committee, specialized agencies, international and national NGOs, and experts working with and for children.

(6) Initiating of studies

The Committee may also initiate studies of specific issues relevant to rights under the Convention. According to article 45(c) of the CRC, the Committee may recommend that the General Assembly request the Secretary-General to undertake on its behalf, studies on specific issues relating to the rights of the child. This is a unique and powerful feature of the Child Committee. Under rule 76(2) of the Rules of Procedure, the Committee may also invite the submission of studies from other bodies on topics of relevance. The thematic discussion days may also generate – and have generated in the past – a request for a more thorough examination of a particular issue in the form of a special study.[14]

(7) Field visits

Until 1997 the Committee made informal field visits to different regions of the world.[15] These were another example of combining the process of reporting with other activities which together, led to enhanced implementation. The aim of these visits was to examine directly the situation of children, to listen to them and hear their views, and to exchange views freely with government officials, NGOs, public organizations and private institutions. The visits were also aimed at sensitizing the media to children's issues.

In the Committee's view, such meetings provided a greater awareness of its work and of the Convention outside the United Nations, as well as a more comprehensive understanding of the actual situation of children in various regions of the world. The Committee also believed the informal visits enhanced international cooperation and joint efforts between different UN bodies, specialized agencies and other competent bodies active in the field of children's rights

---

[13] Sometimes representatives of governments are also present.
[14] For example, after the discussion day on children in armed conflict (1993), the Committee recommended to the General Assembly that the Secretary-General be requested to undertake a study on the means to protect children in armed conflicts, in the hope that an optional protocol to the CRC would be drafted whereby the minimum age for participating in hostilities would be raised to 18 years. The study was undertaken and completed (*Study on the Impact of Armed Conflict on Children*, A/51/306 (26 August 1996). Similarly, after the discussion day on the child and the media, a working group was established to implement the resulting recommendation. *Committee on the Rights of the Child: Report of the Fifteenth Session*, CRC/C/66 (1997) at para. 327.
[15] These informal regional meetings were facilitated by UNICEF. They have been held in Latin America and the Caribbean, Asia, and Africa.

at the national level.[16] The informal visits helped not only to make the Child Committee visible on the national level, but they also enabled the Committee to make itself and the Convention known to individuals in the field and to national NGOs who work with and for children. These visits also contributed towards improving the system of reporting and the role of the Committee in that process. At the moment, however, these informal visits are currently not funded.

At the same time, members of the Committee serve as resource persons in seminars, workshops, conferences, and other meetings throughout the world concerning children's rights issues, the Convention and the reporting process. UNICEF, either through headquarters or regional or national offices, currently fund approximately a dozen such trips by Committee members a year. These activities contribute to making the CRC and the Committee more visible outside the international arena and to promoting better implementation of the Convention.[17]

(8) Partnership with NGOs and Others

The crowning function of the Committee within the framework of reporting and monitoring is its role as facilitator of cooperation, coordination and the dissemination of information among non-governmental actors.[18] The spirit of partnership, and the formal and informal cooperation which has developed between the Committee, UN specialized agencies and intergovernmental organizations,[19] and other international and national NGOs working for the cause of human development and protection of children's rights,[20] has led to a widening of networking circles between such organizations at all levels. This spirit of partnership has also initiated a process of concerted efforts by NGOs to place the rights of the child on the political agenda as a priority, both in international and national fora.

During the Committee's first session, it was recognized[21] that the CRC provided a particularly valuable framework to guide activities and programs affecting children for specialized agencies, the United Nations Children's Fund

---

[16] *Committee on the Rights of the Child: Report on the Second Session*, CRC/C/10 (1992) at 14.
[17] The Committee played an active role in the World Conference on Human Rights in Vienna, 1993, and in the preparations for that conference. It also took part in the World Conference on the Commercial Sexual Exploitation of Children, held in Stockholm in August 1996, and in its preparations, and played a similar role in the World Conference on Housing (Habitat) and other international conferences. Members also participate in seminars on reporting organized by regional NGOs and by UNICEF, as well as in meetings of other UN committees or specialized agencies on subjects concerning the Convention.
[18] Art. 45 of the Convention serves as the normative base for such interaction. NGOs fall under the reference to "other competent bodies as it may consider appropriate" in art. 45(a) and (b). These provisions enable the Committee to invite NGOs and other competent bodies to provide expert advice on the implementation of the Convention in areas falling within the scope of their respective mandates. They also provide for the Committee to transmit to the NGOs and other competent bodies requests from states parties for technical advice and assistance. It is the Committee itself, and not the Secretary-General, that sends state requests for assistance to the appropriate body.
[19] Note the Committee's relationship with UNICEF, the United Nations Educational, Scientific and Cultural Organization (UNESCO), the World Health Organization (WHO), the International Labour Organization (ILO) and the United Nations High Commissioner for Refugees (UNHCR).
[20] The NGO Group for the CRC is included.
[21] *Committee on the Rights of the Child: Report on the First Session*, A/47/41 (1991) at 11.

(UNICEF), other UN organs and competent bodies. In addition, it was noted that the "Convention served as a useful basis for meaningful cooperation and dialogue among all the bodies concerned." The Committee also emphasized the need for "effective coordination in the provision of relevant information from inter-governmental and non-governmental sources."[22]

Accordingly, the Committee periodically exchanges views with these bodies in order to foster international cooperation and interaction between the different agencies who work on programs for technical assistance, advocacy and training,[23] and to make the CRC a focal point in the planning and implementation of such programs. This exchange of views is designed to evaluate progress and consider further ways for strengthening dialogue and interaction between the different partners involved in the implementation of the Convention. In its ninth session the Committee decided to hold these meetings once a year to allow for continuing evaluation of the progress achieved and any difficulties encountered.[24]

The Child Committee is unique in its cooperation – in policy and practice – with non-governmental bodies. It is also unique and privileged in having the assistance of the NGO Group for the CRC and a capable liaison officer. This is a mutually beneficial partnership. It enables the Committee to broaden its sources of information and knowledge beyond the information provided by the states parties. It also allows the Committee to play an indirect role in the encouragement and establishment of a grassroots infrastructure to assist in the implementation and monitoring of the CRC. The presence of all partners in the pre-sessional meetings of the Committee clearly promotes a mutual exchange of information, expertise and experience, and fosters the development of new ideas essential for the effective monitoring process at both the international and national levels. It is also critical for the enhancement of cooperation and the integration of programs amongst all actors at the national, regional and international levels, as well as for the maximization of efforts and resources[25] and the building of a spirit of solidarity.

The pre-sessional meetings and other formal and informal meetings of the Committee with non-governmental partners may also serve as a valuable tool for the empowerment of NGOs, especially those at the local level. For them, knowledge, education and accessibility to the Committee are the key elements.[26]

This partnership is recognition of the new status of NGOs as essential players

---

[22] See CRC, art. 45: "[i]n order to foster the effective implementation of the Convention and to encourage international co-operation in the field covered by the Convention. ..."

[23] *Supra*, note 17 at 16.

[24] *Committee on the Rights of the Child: Report on the Ninth Session*, CRC/C/43 (1995) at 37.

[25] This includes a variety of actors such as, the International Monetary Fund which has begun to attend sessions (for exmple, the seventeenth session (January 1998) and twentieth session (March 1999)).

[26] Other instruments of empowerment that may support NGOs in their role of monitoring and sharing in the implementation of the Convention are: the joint exchange of information, views and experience; the guidelines for NGOs adopted by the NGO Group for the CRC and based on the Committee's reporting guidelines; the "shadow reports" written by the NGOs to the Committee; the obligation of states parties under art. 44(6) of the Convention to make the reports widely available to the public; the Committee's concluding recommendations to governments to cooperate with NGOs in the preparation of the country's report; and the Committees' recommendations to governments to work towards an effective partnership between government and civil society. The Committee looks into the scope of cooperation of the various states parties with NGOs and includes, when necessary, specific recommendations in this regard.

in the international and national arena of human rights. Indeed, the Child Committee believes that the reporting process "... should be one that encourages and facilitates popular participation and public scrutiny of government policies" for the purposes of promoting a positive and fruitful partnership between government and civil society as a whole.[27] The NGOs, in turn, use the reporting process to raise awareness about the Convention and its implications, and to make concerted efforts for better monitoring and implementation of the Convention.[28]

(9) Linkage with "technical assistance-and-advice" bodies

The Committee views its role as one of assisting and enabling states parties to comply with the Convention. It follows that if a state party is having difficulties meeting the standards of the CRC, the Committee will help to coordinate technical assistance from the Office of the High Commissioner for Human Rights, other UN agencies or international NGOs.

Direct linkage and partnership with the Office of the High Commissioner for Human Rights, the UN Crime Prevention and Criminal Justice Division, UN agencies and organizations, and international NGOs help to provide a network which enables technical advice and assistance to be provided when needed and in accordance with the Committee's recommendations.[29] In this context, the concluding observations of the Committee are gradually becoming a major reference tool for international and national programs at the national level. Technical assistance may consist of fellowships, seminars and expert services to create internal infrastructures, to aid in law reform, or to assist in the preparation of the state's report.[30] The Committee has also noted the importance of ensuring closer coordination between the work of the Committee and those working in the area of advisory services and technical assistance. It requests that the relevant information concerning countries whose reports are to be examined gathered by the latter be systematically shared, thus allowing for better evaluation of existing activities at the national level and consideration of possible areas for future cooperation.[31]

---

[27] *General Guidelines Regarding the Form and Content of Initial Reports to be Submitted by States Parties under Article 44, Paragraph 1(a) of the Convention*, CRC/C/5 (30 October 1991).
[28] The creation and development of national coalitions of NGOs working with children, with the support of the NGO Group for the CRC, and the working subgroups of the NGO Group, on specific topics of universal interest, are important examples. They are a significant source of information for the Committee as well as for concerned UN bodies and interested NGOs. They contribute to the development of policies and strategies, and make information, decisions and recommendations of the Committee and other concerned UN bodies available to other NGOs and individuals in the community.
[29] According to art. 45(b), the state party may make a request or indicate a need for technical advice or assistance from the Committee. The latter shall then transmit this request along with its own observations and suggestions to the specialized agencies, UNICEF and other competent bodies that it considers appropriate.
[30] The follow-up process on the Committee's recommendations concerning technical assistance warrants improvement. A *Draft Program of Action in the Field of Juvenile Justice* was developed by a group of experts in Vienna (23–25 February 1993), which includes a proposal to establish a Coordinating Panel on technical advice and assistance in the field of the juvenile justice.
[31] *Committee on the Rights of the Child: Report of the Ninth Session*, CRC/C/43 (1995) at para. 213.

(10) Conclusion

In conclusion, reporting should not be evaluated solely as a mechanism of international monitoring. It should also be assessed on a holistic basis, as a process that is part of the implementation process at the national level. It should be judged mainly for its impact on promoting human rights as a living and spoken language, to be used in the everyday life of governments, NGOs and individuals alike.

CHAPTER 4

State Reporting and the Role of Non-Governmental Organizations

Laura Theytaz-Bergman*

(1) Introduction

The six major international human rights treaty bodies[1] form a comprehensive system of internationally recognized human rights. The treaties are monitored through a system of reporting by states parties to monitoring bodies in the form of committees of independent experts. States parties are required to submit reports to the treaty bodies on the progress that has been made in fulfilling their obligations under the treaties. States parties are requested to follow guidelines for reporting that have been established by the treaty bodies and to submit comprehensive initial and more focused periodic reports for scrutiny by these bodies. The theory behind reporting is that the process of preparing reports should serve as an exercise of internal analysis, which might prompt improvements in national law and practices. In addition, the scrutiny of these reports by independent experts should expose non-compliance with treaty obligations and such exposure and publicity should encourage change.

Although the system itself has been severely criticized, the majority of states parties do submit reports to the treaty bodies and participate in a more or less constructive dialogue with committee members. The treaty bodies adopt concluding observations, most of which now reflect the factors and difficulties impeding the implementation of the Convention, the principle subjects of concern, and concrete suggestions and recommendations for future action. Is this enough to ensure the effectiveness of the system? Although the concluding observations represent the monitoring body's considered views of the treaty's meaning, and

---

*This paper is based largely on the author's experience with the Committee on the Rights of the Child.
[1] The International Convention on the Elimination of All Forms of Racial Discrimination, 660 UNTS 195 (in force 4 January 1969), the International Covenant on Civil and Political Rights, 999 UNTS 171 (in force 23 March 1976), the International Covenant on Economic, Social and Cultural Rights, 993 UNTS 3 (in force 3 January 1976), The Convention on the Elimination of All Forms of Discrimination against Women, 1249 UNTS 13 (in force 3 September 1981), the Convention Against Torture and Other Cruel, Inhuman or Degrading Treatment or Punishment, 1465 UNTS 85 (in force 26 June 1987) (CAT) and the Convention on the Rights of the Child, 1577 UNTS 3 (in force 2 September 1990).

the steps necessary to effect that interpretation, there are no sanctions for non-compliance. The treaty bodies do expect, however, to see their concerns addressed in future reports. These are not submitted on a yearly basis and it is therefore impossible for the treaty bodies to monitor continuously the human rights situation in a country. The committees can merely emphasize the importance of a national discussion about human rights, point out problems and suggest possible remedies. Who then is truly responsible for monitoring the implementation of the human rights treaties? The treaty bodies must rely on domestic monitors in the form of non-governmental organizations (NGOs), particularly those working at the national level, as one of the mechanisms to ensure that the treaties are being implemented in each state party. But where do NGOs fit into this system?

(2) The role of NGOs in the reporting process

A role for NGOs in the system of state reporting has slowly emerged. For most of their existence, the treaty bodies rejected a formal role for NGOs in the system of state reporting. Information submitted by NGOs (usually by international NGOs) was made available to committee members, but was tolerated and used to varying degrees. Some even argued that the treaty bodies should only consider information that came from governmental sources.[2] In recent years, however, this argument has been rejected in practice as the treaty bodies have come to depend more and more on information submitted by NGOs in order to obtain a serious assessment of the progress and difficulties encountered. This is basically due to the fact that the reports submitted by states parties tend to present only the legislative framework and infrequently consider the implementation process. It is difficult for the treaty bodies to obtain a complete and accurate picture of the human rights situation in the concerned state. The consideration of NGO information is therefore an essential element in the monitoring process.

At present, however, the system of reporting to the treaty bodies remains a best-kept secret. Although governments are aware of their reporting obligations, one or more bureaucrats (usually in the Ministry of Foreign Affairs) often prepare the report at the national level with little or no consultation with other government offices or NGOs directly involved in the implementation of the relevant treaty. The report is usually submitted to the relevant treaty body with little or no mention in the country itself that this has occurred. Civil society is usually not informed that the report has been scheduled for consideration by a treaty body, that the report has been examined, and that, conclusions have been adopted. In this system, the national level is left out of the picture and the impact at the national level is virtually non-existent.

(3) A formal role for NGOs: Convention on the Rights of the Child

Only the Convention on the Rights of the Child (CRC) formally recognizes the

---

[2] See Philip Alston, *Interim Report on Updated Study of Mr. Philip Alston*, A/CONF.157/PC/62/Add.11/Rev.1 (22 April 1993) at para. 218.

role of NGOs in the reporting process. Under article 45(a)of the CRC,[3] "the Committee on the Rights of the Child may invite ... other competent bodies" to provide expert advice on the implementation of the Convention. The Committee recognized early on that the expression "other competent bodies" included NGOs.[4] In order to formalize the fundamental role of NGOs, the Committee has encouraged them to "submit reports, documentation or other information" in order to provide it with a comprehensive picture of how the Convention is being implemented in a particular country. The Committee welcomes written material from international, regional, national and local NGOs and seeks specific, reliable and objective information that deals with all of the different areas covered by the Convention in order to monitor effectively its implementation in a country.[5]

The Committee has also established a procedure by which NGOs who submit written information in advance may be invited to participate in the Committee's pre-sessional working group meeting. The pre-sessional working group identifies the main questions to be discussed with states parties who will appear before the Committee during the next session. The pre-sessional working group meets in private. This means that no governmental representatives, media or outside observers may attend, although representatives from relevant intergovernmental organizations[6] (IGOs) are also invited to participate in the discussion. NGOs are only invited to attend the meeting related to the country on which they are able to provide expert advice. These meetings last approximately three hours for each country being considered. NGOs are encouraged to provide the Committee with a constructive, critical analysis of the government report and to help set priorities and identify key issues for discussion with the government.

The Child Committee is further helped in its outreach to NGOs by the Liaison Officer of the NGO Group for the CRC. The role of the Liaison Officer is to ensure that the Child Committee receives information from NGOs for all countries on its agenda. The Liaison Officer tries to identify NGOs working at the national level that may have information on the situation of children in a country. National NGOs are informed that the report of the government has been submitted for consideration to the Committee and, if necessary, they are

---

[3] Art. 45(a) of the CRC states:
The specialized agencies, the United Nations Children's Fund and other United Nations organs shall be entitled to be represented at the consideration of the implementation of such provisions of the present Convention as fall within the scope of their mandate. The Committee may invite the specialized agencies, the United Nations Children's Fund and other competent bodies as it may consider appropriate to provide expert advice on the implementation of the Convention in areas falling within the scope of their respective mandates. The Committee may invite the specialized agencies, the United Nations Children's Fund and other United Nations organs to submit reports on the implementation of the Convention in areas falling within the scope of their activities.

[4] See CRC rules 34, 70, and 74 of the *Provisional Rules of Procedure*, CRC/C/4 (14 November 1991). In addition, at the 1988 meeting of the working group of the Commission on Human Rights to consider the question of a Convention on the Rights of the Child, there was a request that "the record state clearly that the words 'other competent bodies' were to be interpreted in their widest sense to include intergovernmental and non-governmental bodies. It was agreed...": *The United Nations Convention on the Rights of the Child: A Guide to the Travaux Préparatoires*, Sharon Detrick (ed.), Dordrecht (1992) 582 at para. 185.

[5] *Committee on the Rights of the Child: Report of the Eighth Session*, CRC/C/38 (1995) at para. 261.

[6] Examples are: UNICEF, the International Labour Organization (ILO), The United Nations High Commissioner for Refugees (UNHCR), and the World Health Organization (WHO).

provided with a copy of the state party report.[7] They are also informed of the Committee's timetable for consideration of the report as well as the time limit established for the submission of written information. The NGO Group for the CRC has also prepared a guide for NGOs reporting to the Child Committee[8] which carefully explains the reporting procedures as well as provides recommendations about the preparation of written submissions. NGOs are informed by the Liaison Officer as soon as possible of the submission of the state party report in order to allow them ample time to prepare comprehensive information on the implementation of the Convention. Due to the enormous backlog that exists at present, most NGOs have between six and nine months in which to prepare written information for the attention of the Committee.

The NGO reports are written by the national NGOs themselves and the NGO Group for the CRC merely provides support for this process. The Liaison Unit of the NGO Group for the CRC helps to ensure that national NGOs are invited to participate in the pre-sessional working group meetings, provides assistance in making travel arrangements and may even be able to provide financial support to national NGOs for travel and accommodation costs. The Liaison Officer has a close working relationship with the UN Secretariat of the Committee and helps to relieve some of the workload of the Secretary by eliminating much of the direct contact between the UN Secretariat and members of NGOs, particularly on routine matters.

The relationship between the Child Committee and the NGOs has become a strong, mutually dependent one, which functions with a high degree of trust. The Committee has come to count on the NGO Group for the CRC to ensure that it is receiving reliable information from national NGOs. This relationship has been officially recognized by the Committee[9] and has helped the NGO Group for the CRC to raise funds in order to secure the services that the Committee requires.

(4) A limited role for NGOs: experience of the other treaty bodies

Although the CRC is the only treaty to grant a formal role to NGOs, the other treaty bodies have moved toward a closer form of cooperation with NGOs. Most of the treaty bodies generally invite NGOs that closely follow its activities to submit information concerning states parties whose reports have been scheduled for consideration. In general, these invitations are issued only to international NGOs approximately two months before the consideration of the report.

The Economic, Social and Cultural Rights Committee formalized its cooperation with NGOs in May 1993, and NGOs are now encouraged to provide

---

[7] Although art. 44(6) of the CRC states that "States Parties shall make their reports widely available to the public in their own countries", it is still difficult for NGOs to receive copies of the government report in most countries. The Child Committee has therefore made it clear that state party reports will be made available to NGOs: *supra* note 5 at para. 264.
[8] *A Guide for Non-Governmental Organizations Reporting to the Committee on the Rights of the Child*, NGO Group for the Convention on the Rights of the Child (1998). www.crin.org/crc/guidelns.htm.
[9] *Supra*, note 5 at para. 265:
   The Committee welcomed once again the meaningful establishment... of the NGO Group for the Convention on the Rights of the Child. It further welcomed the crucial role played in that framework by the Coordinator [note: title has since been changed to Liaison Officer] of the Group.

written information to the Committee.[10] In addition, the Committee grants a half-day meeting during its plenary session for NGOs to address the Committee, and also invites NGOs to participate in its pre-sessional working group. The Committee has recommended that a coordinating body of NGOs be established, much like the NGO Group for the CRC, which could assist the Committee in the implementation of the International Covenant on Economic, Social and Cultural Rights.[11]

Although the Human Rights Committee does not have formal relations with NGOs, it does receive a considerable amount of unsolicited information, particularly from a core group of international NGOs. Members of the Human Rights Committee also attend informal briefings organized by NGOs during sessions. As more and more NGOs were requesting briefings with Committee members, in October 1996 the Committee instituted a procedure by which it invites selected NGOs to attend meetings of its pre-sessional working group in order to brief Committee members.

The Committee on the Elimination of Discrimination Against Women (CEDAW) profits from the services of the International Women's Rights Action Watch (IWRAW), which provides country-specific information to the Committee. CEDAW also invites NGOs to attend an informal meeting in which they are asked to offer country-specific information on states parties to be reviewed during the session. The other two treaty bodies (Committee on the Elimination of Racial Discrimination (CERD), and the Committee against Torture (CAT), have weaker links to NGOs. CAT invites NGOs to submit written information. Its Rules of Procedure allow NGOs in consultative status with the Economic, Social Council (ECOSOC) to submit information, documentation and written statements concerning states parties whose reports are scheduled for consideration.[12] In addition, article 20 of Convention Against Torture and Other Inhuman or Degrading Treatment or Punishment allows the Committee to undertake investigations based on the examination of "reliable information" without limiting the sources of the information.[13] CERD does not have a procedure whereby it may formally request or receive information from NGOs. Nevertheless, CERD receives support from NGOs which endeavor to ensure that they are receiving information from NGO sources. The Anti-Racism Information Service (ARIS) collects and distributes NGO information to interested Committee members. At the moment these two treaty bodies do not have a regularized procedure by which they may meet with representatives of NGOs.

Through such a mechanism, the comprehensive national approach followed by the Committee... would certainly enhance the system of promotion and protection of children's rights.

[10] *NGO Participation in Activities of the Committee on Economic, Social and Cultural Rights*, E/C.12/1993/WP.14 (12 May 1993).

[11] *Follow-up Action on the Conclusions and Recommendations of the Sixth Meeting of Persons Chairing the Human Rights Treaty Bodies: Report of the Secretary-General*, HRI/MC/1996/2 (15 August 1996) at para. 66.

[12] See CAT rule 62(1) of the *Rules of Procedure*, CAT/C/3/Rev.2 (31 January 1997).

[13] Art. 20 (1) and (2) of CAT states:

20(1) If the Committee receives reliable information which appears to it to contain well-founded indications that torture is being systematically practised in the territory of a State Party, the Committee shall invite that State Party to cooperate in the examination of the information and to this end to submit observations with regard to the information concerned.

(2) Taking into account any observations which may have been submitted by the State Party concerned, as well as any other relevant information available to it, the Committee may, if it

As seen from the above information, although the other five treaty bodies have made progress in incorporating NGOs into the process of state party reporting, none of the treaty bodies comes close to the level of cooperation that has been fostered by the Child Committee.

(5) Potential NGO contributions to the reporting process

NGO participation in the reporting process may help to reduce or at least mitigate some of the weaknesses of the treaty body system. Although the main responsibility for reporting lies with the state party, the experience of the Child Committee has shown that national NGOs can have an impact on this process. National NGOs can and should lobby their governments to comply with reporting obligations by direct approaches to ministries, the lobbying of parliamentarians, media discussion and other forms of campaigning. In the case of the CRC, this process has been greatly helped by the United Nations Children's Fund (UNICEF)[14] and the Office of the High Commissioner for Human Rights that have organized training sessions on reporting to which national NGOs are sometimes invited. In a number of countries, UNICEF has facilitated the preparation of the state party report by identifying and, in some cases, providing human and material resources.[15] Although little can be done to overcome a lack of political will, lobbying and providing technical assistance can help to reduce some the obstacles to compliance with reporting obligations.

At present, measures for examining compliance with various treaties in the absence of state party reports are unsatisfactory. The dependence of CERD on information submitted by the state party to other UN organs, and its refusal to use NGO information in this process,[16] is unacceptable. The majority of information submitted by states parties is legalistic and contains little acknowledgment of the problems of implementing international human rights obligations. Although the Economic, Social and Cultural Rights Committee takes into account NGO information, the lack of information from national NGOs has led to undue influence by certain international NGOs who regularly contribute information to the Committee on only one of the many themes covered by the Convention. Examination of the human rights situation in the absence of a state party report must take into account information submitted by national NGOs in order for a true analysis of the human rights situation in a country to be conducted.

The use of the treaty bodies in cases of urgent action has also proved to be a failure as the treaty bodies are constrained by their reporting cycle and lack of flexible procedures. For example, the so-called "urgent action procedure" of the Child Committee has served only the purpose of frustrating NGOs who expect that the Committee will react immediately to the information that has been submitted, only to be met with silence and no reaction from the Committee as

---

decides that this is warranted, designate one or more of its members to make a confidential inquiry and to report to the Committee urgently.

[14] *The Reporting Process to the Committee on the Rights of the Child, A UNICEF Resource Guide,* UNICEF (February 1997) at 10–12.

[15] *Ibid.,* at 2.

[16] *Report of the Committee on the Elimination of Racial Discrimination,* A/51/18 (1996).

to whether the information has been considered or acted upon. The better-established urgent action procedures of CERD and the Human Rights Committee have also not been very successful in addressing urgent situations. There are other mechanisms within the UN system, which are better suited for these types of actions and it would probably be a better use of resources if the treaty bodies left these issues to others.

On the other hand, the treaty bodies are often the only juridical forums in which the human rights situation in a particular country is discussed. The high number of ratifications of some of the treaty bodies has created an opportunity for NGOs to raise issues of concern in countries which have ratified few international instruments. This creates an increased responsibility on the treaty bodies to raise issues effectively with the state party in the spirit of constructive dialogue and possibly to elicit some acknowledgment of the problem and the necessity for improvement.[17]

The process of report preparation is also an area where national NGOs should be more involved. Clear signals from the treaty bodies as to the appropriate role for NGOs in the elaboration of the state party report can help to ensure that civil society is involved in the report's preparation. In its guidelines for periodic reports, the Child Committee recommends that the preparation of reports be an opportunity to review law and policy, and that this process should "encourage and facilitate popular participation and public scrutiny of government policies."[18] In addition, the guidelines ask a series of questions about the extent to which NGOs participated in the preparation of the report and in the implementation of the Convention.[19] This line of thinking is pursued on a regular basis by the Child Committee which systematically asks about NGO cooperation with the state party in its List of Issues (a list of questions given to the state party in advance of the dialogue) and during the actual dialogue. These clear signals combined with the now well-known fact that national NGOs are systematically preparing "alternative reports" have led to a marked increase in the number of governments requesting NGO input in the preparation of the state party report. This collaboration takes many forms, including sending letters to NGOs with requests for information on the implementation of the Convention, holding meetings with NGOs in order to solicit their views or to discuss copies of a draft report, or creating joint government-NGO drafting committees. NGOs need to be cautious of maintaining their independence, while at the same time collaborating with the government in the preparation of the state party report. Nevertheless, the participation of NGOs from the start of the reporting process may help to ensure that the report is submitted on time and that it is a serious, well-prepared document.

(6) A model in need of improvement

Once the report has been submitted to the treaty bodies, the role of NGOs in the reporting process becomes even more important. The Child Committee has

---

[17] The Child Committee has examined, for example, the reports of Myanmar and Bangladesh which have ratified few international instruments.
[18] *General Guidelines Regarding the Form and Contents of Periodic Reports to be Submitted by States Parties under Article 44, Paragraph 1(b) of the Convention the Rights of the Child*, CRC/C/58 (20 November 1996) at para. 3.
[19] *Ibid.*, at para. 22–23.

considerably involved the NGOs in the reporting and monitoring process. This relationship has proved beneficial to both the NGO community and to the Committee itself. Why is this successful and could it be used as a model for other treaty bodies?

There are advantages that the CRC has over other treaty bodies that cannot be duplicated. First, the Convention itself gives NGOs a role in monitoring the implementation of the Convention and second, as the newest treaty body, it does not have the same Cold War history as most of the other treaty bodies. On the other hand, the other treaty bodies have gradually moved towards more cooperation with NGOs and have begun formalizing their relationships with NGOs in their rules of procedure. In particular, the Economic, Social and Cultural Rights Committee has established procedures quite similar to those of the Child Committee.

The Child Committee also has the advantage of being supported by the NGO Group for the CRC which aims to promote full implementation of the Convention and facilitates the flow of information between the NGO community and the Committee. In a time where the level of servicing of the treaty bodies is limited and the workload of the treaty bodies increasing, it is doubly important that NGO cooperation with the treaty bodies relieve pressure on the Secretariat and not add to its work. For example, a request of the Economic, Social and Cultural Rights Committee to send copies of reports pending consideration to a range of national NGOs in each state party[20] put an undue burden on the Secretariat.

The primary concern for all the treaty bodies is how to ensure that the information that has been received from NGOs is reliable and objective. In order to deal effectively with this complex problem, the NGO Group for the CRC has promoted the creation and development of national coalitions of NGOs working with children. A national coalition that is broadly based and representative allows NGOs working with children to cooperate and coordinate their work in certain areas. National coalitions should be composed of a wide range of organizations, both human rights and development, which reflect the full range of issues raised by the Convention as well as the interdependency of economic, social, cultural, civil and political rights. In addition, members should represent the diverse jurisdictional and geographic as well as ethnic and cultural differences that may exist in a country. It is equally important that the views of children and young people are taken into consideration, although this principle has been difficult for most national coalitions to implement in practice. This allows for more effective monitoring of the implementation of the Convention at the national level due to the specialist knowledge of coalition members and the variety of points of view that may be represented, and may thereby present a more comprehensive picture of the situation in a country.

NGO reports prepared by coalitions rather than individual NGOs are much more difficult to disregard or discredit and therefore tend to lend greater legitimacy to breaches of rights being identified. Governments can easily claim that information submitted by one NGO should not be taken seriously because that particular NGO is politically motivated, linked to the opposition, not reliable,

---

[20] *Report of the Secretariat on Ways and Means of Improving the Work of the Committee*, CEDAW/C/1997/5 (6 December 1996) at para. 38.

or is basing its criticism on fantasy rather than fact. It is much more difficult for a government to discredit a report prepared by a group of NGOs. In addition, a single comprehensive report allows Committee members who are under intense time pressure to familiarize themselves with the relevant issues[21] to study only one NGO document from, for example, twenty organizations rather than twenty reports from twenty organizations. This practice differs greatly from that of the other treaty bodies who rely mostly on the information of a "hard core"[22] of international NGOs. Although the Child Committee welcomes information from international NGOs, the NGO Group for the CRC (presently composed of 41 international NGOs) has preferred to request that its national sections, offices and partners collaborate at the national level in order to prepare comprehensive reports for the Committee.

Although this system has succeeded in bringing in the points of view of national NGOs, as a model several concerns remain. The main problem is that even by working with a group of national NGOs, it is still difficult for the NGO Group for the CRC to know whether or not this group is representative of civil society. In some countries, there is more than one "national coalition" and in others NGOs complain that they have been excluded from the "national coalition" or that their views have not been taken into account. In addition, the NGO Group for the CRC has come to rely on certain members of the Group to initiate the formation of coalitions at the national level, which has led to criticism of bias against those who "control" the national coalitions. Even when coalitions exist and function well, the Child Committee often receives additional reports from national NGOs who bypass the coalition in order to ensure that their organization or their views are recognized by the Committee.

The structure and quality of the reports varies greatly, despite the fact that the NGO Group for the CRC has prepared recommended guidelines for submission of NGO reports. In addition, the NGO Group for the CRC does not have the capacity to translate NGO documents and the United Nations will not do so. Therefore, NGO documents submitted in any language other than English[23] are not taken into full consideration by the Committee. In order to combat these weaknesses, the NGO Group for the CRC has prepared additional guidelines on the content (not simply structure) of NGO reports. The guidelines recommend that international NGOs working at the national level translate NGO documents into English.[24]

Participation at the Child Committee's pre-sessional working group is perhaps the most exciting aspect of NGO cooperation with the Committee. The Committee may invite NGOs who have submitted information in writing to participate in the pre-sessional working group. Although the UN specialized agencies are also invited to the meeting and generally attend, only UNICEF is represented on a regular basis by members of its field offices,[25] and therefore

---

[21] *Supra*, Jane Connors, Chapter 1 at 13.
[22] *Ibid.*, at 16.
[23] "As English is the working language of nine out of ten experts on the present Committee, documents submitted in French and Spanish should, whenever possible, be translated into English." *Supra*, note 8 at Section II, Practical Information.
[24] *Ibid.*
[25] UNICEF's field office participation is a recent practice. UNICEF's resource guide on the reporting process to the Child Committee, *supra* note 14 at 13, recommends that UNICEF field offices make "every effort" to participate in the pre-sessional working group.

NGOs are often the only source of information from the national level. The Committee devotes a full three hours to each country and NGOs are considered on equal par with all other participants. In fact, NGOs are often the focal point for the discussion as they assist the Committee by identifying key issues of concern, indicating central questions which need to be raised with the government, providing information on the practical implementation of legislation, highlighting gaps in the government report and in general providing information which might not otherwise be available to the Committee.[26] The NGO Group for the CRC has raised funds to cover travel costs for one person from each developing country, which almost guarantees regular NGO representation.

Once again, however, this system is in need of refinement. At present, funding to attend the pre-sessional working group is limited to one NGO representative per country. It would be beneficial to the Child Committee to have more than one NGO representative present, as the issues covered by the Convention are too vast to be addressed by one person. In addition, funding is not available for developed countries, which sometimes prevents representatives from these countries who have prepared reports from attending the meeting.

Although in principle all ten Child Committee members may participate in the Working Group, attendance is unreliable and often quite thin. This is disconcerting, as the Committee has emphasized the importance of this process on numerous occasions. Committee members who are present have not read the written information that has been submitted in advance and are frequently unprepared for the discussion. This often leads Committee members to ask inappropriate questions and prevents them from taking full advantage of NGO participation in the preparation of their meeting with the state party. The NGO community has suggested that perhaps the timing of the pre-sessional Working Group needs to be modified in order to allow Committee members to better focus on preparing for the upcoming session. The experience of other treaty bodies may be relevant in this regard. In the past, the Human Rights Committee and CEDAW held the pre-sessional working group during the week prior to the session; this, however, did not allow enough time for the state party to prepare responses to the Committee's List of Issues and both Committees now schedule the pre-session at the end of the previous session.[27] On the other hand, Committee members often have trouble remembering the issues that were discussed during the long gap of three to four months between the pre-sessional working group and the discussion with the government, and the information may be out-of-date at the time of the discussion.

Another solution to this problem might be for the Child Committee to assign Committee members to attend the pre-sessional working group on a rotating basis as is done in some of the other treaty bodies. This could help to ensure that at least a few Committee members feel responsible for the outcome of the pre-sessional working group and may encourage them to become more fully engaged in the discussion. Although Jane Connors suggests that NGOs should not expect the treaty bodies to "tailor their working methods to their needs,"[28]

---

[26] Gerison Lansdown, "The Reporting Process under the Convention on the Rights of the Child", in *The Future of UN Human Rights Treaty Monitoring*, Philip Alston and James Crawford (eds.), Cambridge University Press, 2000, 113.
[27] *Supra*, Jane Connors, Chapter 1 at 14.
[28] *Ibid.*, at 16.

the present system leads NGOs to believe that the Child Committee is not interested in the information that they have been invited to present. This is completely contrary to all the other signals being sent out by the Committee. If the treaty bodies want increased commitment from NGOs, then in return NGOs must feel as though their contributions are playing a valuable role in this process, otherwise NGO interest in the work of the treaty bodies will remain minimal or even decrease.

The true test of the usefulness of NGO information to the reporting process is the extent to which the treaty bodies use the information during their discussion with the states parties and in the production of the concluding observations. A study conducted by the NGO Group for the CRC on the NGO impact on the conclusions of the Committee showed that it was "undeniable that the NGO alternative reports have greatly influenced the conclusions of the Committee on the Rights of the Child."[29] Contributing to the reporting process has engaged the NGO community in the promotion and monitoring of children's rights and has helped to create a better understanding of the usefulness of the Convention in the day to day work of national NGOs.

(7) Future perspectives

Although state non-compliance with reporting obligations is a serious weakness of the system, the present backlog of reports to almost all the treaty bodies makes prolonged discussion of this situation almost amusing. What would the treaty bodies do if all state party reports were submitted on time? At present, the backlog of initial and periodic reports to the Child Committee is two and one-half years long, with reports received in 1999 being scheduled as far ahead as the January 2002 session. Other treaty bodies are faced with similar backlogs. Not only are state party reports out-of-date, but NGOs who are charged with monitoring the implementation of the Convention are unsure of deadlines and are likely to produce information that is out-of-date. In addition, the momentum of the reporting process is lost. Radical solutions are necessary to deal with these problems and the consolidation of the reporting process[30] either by reducing the number of treaty bodies or through a single "global" report appears to be the only viable long-term option. Although each treaty body is intent on protecting its "turf," the overlaps in the system are obvious and create a burden on both the states parties and those contributing to the monitoring of the implementation of the human rights treaty bodies.

In the short term, better information sharing among treaty bodies could enhance the reporting system. For example, NGO reports submitted to the Child

---

[29] Stephanie Hill, *NGO Impact on the Conclusions of the Committee on the Rights of the Child*, NGO Group for the Convention on the Rights of the Child, unpublished (July 1995).
[30] See Philip Alston's reports on enhancing the long-term effectiveness of the United Nations human rights treaty bodies: the initial report, *Long Term Approaches to Enhancing the Effective Operation of Existing and Prospective Bodies Established under United Nations Human Rights Instruments*, A/44/668 (8 November 1989); an interim report, *Interim Report on Updated Study of Mr. Philip Alston*, A/CONF.157/PC/62/Add.11/Rev.1 (22 April 1993); and the final report, *Final Report on Enhancing the Long-Term Effectiveness of the United Nations Human Rights Treaty System*, E/CN.4/1997/74 (27 March 1997).

Committee often include information that is relevant to other treaty bodies. The treaty body database[31] has helped to ensure the sharing of "official" UN information (state party reports, summary records, concluding observations). Nevertheless, there is only a weak system within the United Nations, and none within the NGO community, for ensuring that NGO information that already exists is transmitted to other treaty bodies who may have the same state party under consideration. What a shame that such information exists and is not utilized to its full extent.

Realistically, the treaty bodies alone cannot solve the problems in any country. Instead, they can play the role of a catalyst by helping to prioritize problems, offering suggestions for improvement at the national level, and perhaps by generating public debate. Although the treaty bodies can pressure governments for change, the solutions themselves must come from the national level. The treaty bodies must therefore rely on domestic monitors in order to ensure that the human rights treaties are being implemented. The development of sound national monitoring is essential, therefore, in order to provide the strongest basis for effective international monitoring. Although the primary responsibility for implementation of the human rights treaties rests with the government, NGOs have a significant role to play in monitoring the extent to which compliance is being achieved. In order to fulfill this role, NGOs must become partners in the monitoring process from the very beginning. The Child Committee has on numerous occasions emphasized the importance of the role of NGOs in enhancing the promotion and protection of the rights of the child. The other treaty bodies would be well advised to follow its example in order to ensure that the human rights of all are promoted and protected to the fullest extent possible.

---

[31] The web site for the treaty body database is http://www.unhchr.ch/tbs/doc.nsf.

CHAPTER 5

State Reporting: an NGO Perspective

Rachel Brett

(1) Introduction

The system of state reporting under the international human rights treaties has advantages and disadvantages. Government representatives are quietly but persistently questioned *in public* about their countries' human rights records. Governments drafting the treaties probably had little idea of the consequences to them of establishing this apparently innocuous reporting procedure. But much that was then new and challenging has become routine.

In the early days, the involvement of non-governmental organizations (NGOs) was in itself a contentious issue. In principle this is no longer the case, and the crucial role of NGOs as providers of information to supplement or challenge information provided by governments is now well-recognized. There is also increasing recognition of the important role of national or local NGOs in the country concerned during the preparation stage of the country's report. This may be in relation to the actual preparation of the report. It may also be through the creation of a public debate about human rights issues, by entering into discussions with the government about matters of concern. Further, unless NGOs follow-up on the treaty body's consideration of the report, the tendency of governments to view the committee's consideration as the end of the process is likely to prevail until the next report has to be prepared.

(2) The reporting system

The treaty body reporting system is the only forum in which virtually every country in the world comes under scrutiny at one time or another. This is very important from the perspective of NGOs, both national and international. For the former, this may be their one opportunity for a thorough international review of the human rights situation in their country. It may also provide a focus for a thorough debate within the country on these matters. International NGOs must be selective and use their limited resources to try to address the most pressing needs. Frequently, there is a tendency for countries which do not have the worst human rights records, or which are "off limits" in political human rights bodies, to escape international attention. The reporting system, however, affects a much wider range of states. Furthermore, the importance of being able to raise issues of law, policy and even proposed legislation, without having to ground it in "violations" or "individual cases", presents NGOs with the opportunity to take preventive action in relation to human rights, as well as to address actual violations of the relevant treaty. The fact that this scrutiny operates on a timetable also means that it is possible to avoid the danger of continually postponing human rights in that particular country from the top of the agenda.

In addition, the dynamic of the consideration of state reports by the treaty bodies is quite different from other UN human rights bodies. Rather than the NGOs confronting or accusing "offending" governments, the NGOs work *with* the members of the treaty bodies primarily for the promotion and protection of human rights in the reporting country. This is assisted by the fact that the governments have all voluntarily accepted the obligation of reporting by choosing to become parties to the treaties.

(3) Issues

Some of the problems with the reporting procedure are practical, and at least in principle easily soluble, such as the difficulty in obtaining copies of the state reports. Others are inherent in the system: the slowness of the process, the long lead time between the preparation of the report and its consideration by the relevant committee, the rather formal and "diplomatic" nature of the consideration, the expense of attending meetings in Geneva or New York. Still others could be changed, but would require shifts in attitudes in order to be effective. Consider for example the isolation of women's rights from the mainstream human rights work at the UN because of its different geographical location and different Secretariat. This leads NGOs, including my own, to treat women's rights as a separate issue and not as part of our main international human rights work. This practice is conceptually unsound and leads to possible marginalization, and lack of cross-fertilization with other human rights bodies.

The simplest problem to solve should be that of NGO access to documentation. NGOs can, of course, provide information even without seeing the state report. One of the particular values of NGO contributions, however, especially those of national NGOs, is that they provide a commentary or alternative to the state report. Therefore, NGOs not only need to know when the report is to be considered, but also need access to the report itself. Ideally, the report should be widely available within the country, but since this is not always the case, it must also be readily available from the UN. The ability to access state reports on the internet reduces some of the difficulties of getting these documents. The Office of the UN High Commissioner for Human Rights has its own home page on the Internet, and those with access should be able to obtain information about the meetings of the treaty bodies, which countries will be considered, and the reports. Not all NGOs have access to the internet, however, so another method should also be available, such as through the UN Information Centre in the country concerned. A further possibility would be to both equip the Information Centres with access to the Office of the High Commissioner for Human Rights' home page and to provide a room and a terminal for the use of

NGOs, so that those who do not have their own equipment are not excluded from this valuable source of information.

Not all states are parties to all treaties, and therefore although virtually every state's record will be considered by one or more treaty bodies, not all aspects will be considered. The near universal ratification of the Convention on the Rights of the Child[1] means that – at least in theory, every state will be considered by at least one treaty body. However, the fact that some states are only considered by the Child Committee raises questions about the effectiveness of that Committee, and of the NGO information submitted to it, in relation to human rights in general rather than only to child-specific rights. These questions have come up when such general human rights concerns as summary executions and freedom of assembly have been raised by the Child Committee because some of the victims were children. The Child Committee should take into account whether states are parties to other human rights treaties, and the need to be particularly vigilant to ensure that fundamental rights are not overlooked in favour of child-specific ones. General human rights NGOs should also submit information to the Child Committee for countries not covered by other treaties. Overall, there is little coordination between treaty bodies, and the fact that a state is or is not a party to another treaty may not be taken into account when the report is being considered.

The reporting interval means that a state's record is generally reviewed only every 4 or 5 years. At a minimum, a follow-up mechanism is required in order to monitor whether the treaty body's recommendations are being implemented and whether the human rights situation is deteriorating. If the human rights situation is deteriorating, there should be means to institute immediate action. Such action could include calling for a special report, asking government representatives to appear before the treaty body to discuss the situation without asking for a written report, or referring the situation to the Office of the High Commissioner for Human Rights.

There appears to be no coordination of the reporting cycle between the different treaty bodies. As a result, a state may present several reports to different treaty bodies in one year and then none for several years. Although states do not always or even usually present their reports on time, and there are different numbers of states parties, and the different treaty bodies meet at different times, it would be preferable if states which are parties to several treaties reported to only one treaty body per year. This would ensure that the burden on the state would be more evenly distributed, and that an aspect of the human rights situation would be under scrutiny by the treaty bodies and NGOs annually or regularly. However, if reporting is too frequent on the government side it may become a formality and a chore, and on the NGO side there may also be reporting-fatigue, unless the issues are of sufficient continuing concern and the reporting procedure seen as sufficiently valuable for it to remain an NGO priority.

Not all treaty bodies give adequate warning of when countries will be considered. This makes it difficult for NGOs to prepare and submit information in a timely manner, and also to plan for attendance. All treaty bodies should follow the example of the Child Committee and produce a schedule for reports a year

---

[1] Convention on the Rights of the Child, 1577 UNTS 3 (in force 2 September 1990).

in advance, including two "reserve" reports for each session should additions to the session become necessary. In this way, NGOs can plan the preparation of counter-reports and other information, and likely times for attendance at meetings.

The fact that the report is being prepared should also be made known to national NGOs. Ideally, the requirement to prepare a report should be seen not as a bureaucratic chore but as an opportunity for domestic debate about the state of human rights in the country and the changes required. Conceptually, this is akin to the "domestic remedies" rule that requires an individual complainant to exhaust domestic remedies before taking his or her case to the international level; it would be helpful if governments could be persuaded to perceive it in this light. Issues could thus be raised and some problems resolved even before the report is prepared. There are many different models for NGO involvement in the preparation of the report. However, it is essential to remember that the report is a report by the government, and that NGO involvement should neither reduce governmental responsibility for the preparation of the report and for its substance, nor preclude or inhibit the NGOs from submitting alternative information or views to the treaty body.

Discussion between NGOs and committee members prior to the consideration of a state report is valuable for NGOs. It enables representatives of NGOs to be identified by the committee members, to highlight particular points of concern, including adding more recent information than that submitted, to draw up specific questions for the committee if it so desires, and to understand the needs of the committee and the issues the committee is likely to consider. The fact that such discussions are possible, whether formally or informally, should be more widely known to NGOs in order to enable NGOs to request and prepare for them. Without having a sense of how written material should be prepared, for whom it is intended, and how the committee's wish it to be presented or how much they already know, it is difficult to do it well. Furthermore, if it is not clear that the material is being used and no explanation when it is not used is provided, NGOs can quickly become discouraged from trying to use the treaty body system. This highlights the benefits of informal, personal contacts. At the same time, meeting with NGO representatives may enable committee members to form a better judgment on how seriously to take material from an unknown NGO. Practical information about making submissions could usefully be featured on the Office of the High Commissioner for Human Rights' home page, including information on such matters as: the date by which material should be submitted, to whom it should be sent, the language and form committee members prefer.

Only governments report to the treaty bodies. Thus when there is no government (as in Somalia), or no legitimate government (as in Haiti before President Aristide was reinstated), the reporting mechanism ceases to function. This may be an insoluble dilemma for treaty bodies, but it suggests the need for alternative procedures to be instituted automatically in such circumstances. A member of a treaty body might be nominated to monitor the situation and report to the Office of the High Commissioner for Human Rights.

Even when there is a government, it may not in fact be in control of the whole territory. Although this does not alter the legal obligation in relation to human rights violations and reporting under the treaty, the practical effect will be the same. There may be a need in such circumstances to provide a link to some other form of human rights monitoring such as country or thematic rapporteurs of the Commission on Human Rights.

In addition to country-specific discussions, it could be useful to set aside time at which NGOs could raise issues of concern for discussion with the committee, at least once a year if not at each session of each treaty body. Although the Child Committee and the Economic, Social and Cultural Rights Committee have valuable thematic discussions with NGOs, these are on one specific theme decided by the committee in question. At present there is no official channel for an NGO to raise with a committee the question of the committee's interpretation of a particular right or an area which does not appear to be adequately covered in the committee's considerations in general.

Such discussions could also be an opportunity to consider changes, or developments, in the committee's procedures. NGOs could be encouraged to make written statements as well as oral contributions. However, the sessions should be sufficiently informal to allow for real discussion.

Finally, there is also a need for NGOs to have ready and timely access to the concluding observations of the treaty bodies on the reports. Such access would allow NGOs to try to ensure that the concluding observations are indeed taken into account and acted upon by the government. The posting of these on the Office of the High Commissioner for Human Rights home page is a significant step forward in this regard. In addition, however, they could be sent directly to those NGOs that submitted information at the same time as they are sent to the government in question. If both governments and NGOs knew that this was happening, it might in itself be an incentive to act upon the observations. They would be still more useful if they were issued rapidly in the UN language in which the report was submitted. It would also be helpful if the member of the treaty body designated as country rapporteur prior to the treaty body's consideration of the report were to continue that function afterwards in relation to the follow-up of concluding observations. This role could include receiving information from NGOs on the government's response to the committee's comments and following up this action or inaction with the government. Not only would this assist in ensuring that serious consideration is given to the concluding observations by the government, but it could also form a valuable basis for the start of the next round of reporting by the government.

(4) Longer term approaches

As a longer-term strategy, perhaps a state party to more than one treaty, particularly those who are parties to several of the treaties, could submit a single report to be considered jointly and/or consecutively by the respective treaty bodies. Such a process would be made easier if there were an overlapping membership of the treaty bodies, which could in any case be a pragmatic way of moving towards the "super-committee" discussed by Philip Alston in his interim expert report to the UN on reform of the treaty body system.[2] The

---

[2] Philip Alston, *Interim Report on Updated Study of Mr. Philip Alston*, A/CONF.157/PC/Add.11/Rev.1 (22 April 1993).

advantages to the state would be that it would only have to submit one report every five years, and have one delegation to meet with the various treaty bodies during a single concentrated period. The advantages to the NGOs would be that they would know of the schedule well in advance, and that all issues would be under consideration at the same time. There could also be considerably more media interest, since the consideration would be concentrated at one time. It might also be possible to hold the meetings in the reporting country. This approach could also be advantageous for the treaty bodies. If a state had not submitted a report to one body but had to another, that report could be the basis for a more general, serious consideration. The information from non-UN or other sources could be sent at one time. The treaty bodies could learn from one another and benefit from the questions and responses prepared by, and for, each treaty body. They could perhaps divide the issues between them.

The major disadvantage of this process happening only every five years could be counteracted if a proper follow-up mechanism were provided for each country consisting of one member of each relevant treaty body. NGOs could relate to this person or group of persons, who would continue the "dialogue" with the government in relation to concluding observations. If the situation seemed to be deteriorating, it could be referred to treaty bodies for further action before the end of the five-year period, or be referred to the High Commissioner for Human Rights or other appropriate body.

The next periodic report would then be based on the concluding observations in relation to the previous consideration, together with questions and issues brought forward by the follow-up group. This would not preclude other issues being raised.

(5) NGOs should ...

Finally, there is a tendency by governments, independent experts and UN staff to tell NGOs what they should do. They fail to recognize the distinct and significant features of NGOs. They are independent actors. Most are relatively small, with limited human and financial resources. Any human rights NGO that is good at its job will always have more to do than it can do well, or even at all, with the resources at its disposal. It will set priorities. If the reporting system as a whole, or the performance of a specific committee, does not produce an adequate return on the NGO's investment in it, that NGO will *and should* redirect its activities elsewhere. Any committee, which feels that it does not receive adequate attention from NGOs, should look to its own performance and procedures. Although many NGOs do not know enough about the treaty body system and its possibilities, and could do much to enhance their own effectiveness, repeated statements beginning with "NGOs should ... " are no substitute for human rights procedures which produce results in themselves or which provide NGOs with additional tools in their own struggle for the promotion and protection of human rights.

II. Fact-finding as Part of Effective Implementation

CHAPTER 6

Human Rights Fact-Finding

Joan Fitzpatrick

(1) Introduction

The international human rights regime, having elaborated standards defining fundamental human dignity and freedom with ever-increasing specificity, faces a crisis of implementation. Varied participants in the regime – treaty and political bodies of inter-governmental organizations, national authorities, non-governmental organizations (NGOs), scholars, the international media – agree that disclosure of human rights violations is crucial to compliance. A range of implementation mechanisms, including individual petitions, country and thematic rapporteurs, special reports on country situations, state reporting, inter-state complaints, deployment of human rights monitors, NGO reports and litigation at the national level, have important fact-finding dimensions. Human rights fact-finders are proliferating at a prodigious rate, producing a plethora of information. A system constructed on the optimistic premise that exposure of human rights abuse will shame perpetrators into compliance is weakened by the vulnerability of its fact-finding apparatus to accusations of bias and incoherence.

Describing an occurrence as a human rights violation is pejorative, and not a factual categorization. As a result, human rights bodies strive to provide fair opportunities for rebuttal to alleged perpetrators and accused states. But because human rights fact-finding takes so many forms, no singular set of procedural and evidentiary guidelines presently exists or could easily be crafted.[1] Although

---

[1] Human rights fact-finding can be approached from many angles. Two collections of essays provide a good general introduction to the subject: Bert G. Ramcharan (ed.), *International Law and Fact-Finding in the Field of Human Rights*, Nijhoff (1982); Richard B. Lillich (ed.), *Fact-Finding Before International Tribunals: Eleventh Sokol Colloquium*, Transnational (1990). Two casebooks on international human rights contain thoughtful chapters exploring the practical and ethical difficulties of human rights fact-finding: Richard B. Lillich and Hurst Hannum, *International Human Rights: Problems of Law, Policy and Practice 3rd ed.*, Little, Brown (1995); Frank Newman and David Weissbrodt, *International Human Rights: Law, Policy and Process 2nd ed.*, Anderson Pub. (1996). On the particular topic of fact-finding by non-governmental organizations, very useful analyses are offered by Diane Orentlicher, "Bearing Witness: The Art and Science of Human Rights Fact-Finding", 3 *Harvard Human Rights Law Journal* (1990) 83; and David Weissbrodt and James McCarthy, "Fact-Finding by International Non-Governmental Human Rights Organizations", 22 *Virginia Journal of International Law*, (1981) 1. Interesting methodological data is provided in Hans Thoolen and Berth Verstappen, *Human Rights Missions: A Study of the Fact-Finding Practice of Non-Governmental Organizations*, Nijhoff (1986).

this chapter addresses its recommendations primarily to the United Nations human rights treaty system, it canvasses a wide range of fact-finding mechanisms for useful lessons. The following issues will be addressed: (1) differences between fact-finding focused on a particular incident versus documentation of patterns of human rights violations; (2) the endemic problem of bias, real or imputed; and (3) interrelationships among human rights fact-finders, resource limitations and the optimal means to enhance fact-finding through collaboration.

(2) Incident facts and situation facts

Human rights fact-finding is not a singular, definable process. It occurs in many different settings, involving a variety of actors seeking diverse goals. Fact-finding may be the core of one process, while being a collateral, even coincidental, product of another activity.

Fact-finding focused on a specific incident, however, tends to be distinct from fact-finding that describes a general human rights situation or that documents a pattern of violations. Generally, procedural formality and precise evidentiary standards are more vital to processes focused on specific incidents.

Where a state is suspected of a pattern of human rights abuse, the fact-finder must bring a more interpretive, and less purely descriptive, intelligence to the assessment of the available facts. Because of the subjectivity and the greater informality of evidentiary standards, to assure reliability and credibility the fact-finder must avoid methods that are needlessly careless or biased.

The classic commission of inquiry, limited to gathering data and testimony and leaving normative evaluation to the parties or to another body, has only a vestigial existence in the human rights treaty field,[2] although such commissions play a significant role within the enforcement regime of the International Labour Organisation (ILO).[3] Human rights fact-finding by treaty and political bodies, whether focused on incidents or situations, combines in a single evaluator the

---

[2] Art. 41(h) (ii) of the International Covenant on Civil and Political Rights (CCPR), 999 UNTS 171 (in force 23 March 1976), for example, provides that the Human Rights Committee in an inter-state case is restricted to reporting "a brief statement of the facts" in cases that cannot be settled amicably. Subsequently, pursuant to art. 42, an *ad hoc* Conciliation Commission may be appointed, consisting of five persons acceptable to the disputing states, to state its findings on questions of fact and "the possibilities of an amicable solution...". No inter-state complaints have ever been filed under the CCPR, so this two-stage process has never been tested.

[3] See Thomas M. Franck and H. Scott Fairley, "Procedural Due Process in Human Rights Fact-Finding by International Agencies", 74 *American Journal of International Law* (1980) 308 (praising meticulous methodology and impartiality of ILO investigatory bodies). For example, in response to complaints of forced labour by workers' delegates, the ILO established a Commission of Inquiry on Burma/Myanmar, which issued a report in July 1998: *Report of the Commission on Inquiry Appointed under Article 26 of the Constitution of the International Labour Organization to Examine the Observance by Myanmar of the Forced Labour Convention, 1930 (No. 29)*, Geneva (2 July 1998). In hearings held in Geneva and during a visit to the region (India, Bangladesh and Thailand), the Commission heard the testimony of NGOs and eye witnesses. While in the region, the Commission asked NGOs to provide a pool of potential interviewees selected at random from as many Burmese regions and ethnic groups as possible. The Commission also invited IGOs, governments in the region, governments having economic relations with Burma/Myanmar and companies mentioned in the complaint to submit information. The Commission made findings of fact and recommendations of necessary steps to remedy problems. These findings were made without the benefit of an on-site visit, as the Government of Burma/Myanmar denied access to ILO representatives: *ibid*.

tasks of gathering the relevant information, describing the events and drawing a conclusion as to whether a violation has occurred.

(a) Fact-finding concerning specific incidents

Punishment of perpetrators and compensation of particular victims remain marginal aspects of human rights implementation, despite increasing resort to individual complaint mechanisms under human rights treaties, the establishment of *ad hoc* international criminal tribunals for the former Yugoslavia and Rwanda and more frequent tort and criminal actions for human rights victims in national courts. The greater number of human rights fact-finding mechanisms paint a general picture of the human rights situation or document patterns of violations. Proving the facts of a specific incident in detail and under tightly controlled evidentiary rules is unimportant if no particular consequences will ensue from a fact-finder's reliance upon the information. Where significant consequences attach to the outcome of an inquiry into a specific incident, however, human rights fact-finders pay greater attention to their investigatory and evidentiary methodology.

(i) Judicial methods

Where fact-finding is geared toward a single occurrence, such as an act of official torture of an identified individual at a specific place and time, it is more likely that judicial or quasi-judicial methodology will be employed. A variety of bodies engage in this type of human rights fact-finding, ranging from treaty bodies with an almost exclusively quasi-judicial function (for example, the European Court of Human Rights), to treaty bodies with mixed functions (for example, the Human Rights Committee or the Committee on the Elimination of Racial Discrimination (CERD), to the *ad hoc* criminal tribunals authorized by the UN Security Council, to national authorities of either a judicial or an administrative character (for example, courts conducting tort litigation against human rights violators or asylum adjudicators).

Little consensus exists on the appropriate methodology for human rights fact-finding, though various proposals for standards or rules of procedure have been floated over the years.[4] Even among bodies employing quasi-judicial fact-finding to assess individual claims, no single approach dominates. Each treaty body is authorized to establish its own rules of procedure, which vary in their precision concerning investigatory and evidentiary matters. Factors explaining variance in judicial fact-finding methodology include the availability of evidence gathered by other reliable sources, the potential consequences of an adverse finding, the degree of cooperation from governmental sources in the state that is the alleged site of the human rights abuse, and material resources available to the fact-

---

[4] In 1974, the United Nations Commission on Human Rights forwarded to the Economic and Social Council a set of *Draft Model Rules of Procedure Suggested by the Secretary-General of the UN for Ad Hoc Bodies of the United Nations Entrusted with Studies of Particular Situations Alleged to Reveal a Consistent Pattern of Violations of Human Rights*, E/CN.4/1021/Rev.1 (1974), reprinted in Bert G. Ramcharan, *supra* note 1 at 239. In 1980, the International Law Association adopted the *Belgrade Minimal Rules of Procedure for International Human Rights Fact-Finding Missions*, reprinted in Bert G. Ramcharan, *supra* note 1 at 250.

finder. The most extensive experience in judicial implementation of international human rights norms can probably be found within the Council of Europe system established to implement the European Convention for the Protection of Human Rights and Fundamental Freedoms.[5] Prior to the restructuring of the European Court of Human Rights pursuant to Protocol 11,[6] in first-hand factual investigation or the taking of testimony, the European Commission on Human Rights possessed the authority under Article 28(1)(a) of the European Convention to "undertake ... if need be ... an investigation" of individual applications under Article 25, and in some instances took testimony in Strasbourg or on-site, at either the admissibility or merits stage.[7] This investigatory task has now devolved to chambers of the new Court or to surrogates selected by a chamber.[8]

Especially in light of this broad investigatory authority, the rules of evidence and burden of proof standards applied by the Council of Europe human rights bodies have been fairly rudimentary.[9] The sketchy nature of these evidentiary

---

[5] Convention for the Protection of Human Rights and Fundamental Freedoms, ETS 5 (in force 3 September 1953).

[6] Protocol No. 11, ETS 155 (1998) (in force 1 November 1998).

[7] David J. Harris, Michael O'Boyle, and Chris Warbrick, *The Law of the European Convention on Human Rights*, Butterworths (1995) at 595–599 (describing on-site visit at admissibility stage in *Ensslin, Baader and Raspe v. Federal Republic of Germany*, 14 DR 64 (8 July 1978); taking of testimony in Strasbourg, including expert medical testimony concerning torture in *Cruz Varas v. Sweden*, Series A, Volume 201 (20 March 1991); and visit to Maze prison in Northern Ireland to confirm whether prisoner consented to application filed on his behalf in *Marcella and Robert Sands v. United Kingdom*, Decision No. 9338/81, unreported (1981)). Under Art. 38 (old Art. 28) of the revised European Convention, the Court now possesses the power to "undertake an investigation, for the effective conduct of which the States concerned shall furnish all necessary facilities."

[8] Rule 42 of the *Rules of Court* adopted on 4 November 1998 provides, in part:

1. The Chamber may, at the request of a party or a third party, or of its own motion, obtain any evidence which it considers capable of providing clarification of the facts of the case. The Chamber may, inter alia, request the parties to produce documentary evidence and decide to hear as a witness or expert or in any other capacity any person whose evidence or statements seem likely to assist it in the carrying out of its tasks.

2. The Chamber may, at any time during the proceedings, depute one or more of its members or of the other judges of the Court to conduct an inquiry, carry out an investigation on the spot or take evidence in some other manner. It may appoint independent external experts to assist such a delegation.

3. The Chamber may ask any person or institution of its choice to obtain information, express an opinion or make a report on any specific point.

4. The parties shall assist the Chamber, or its delegation, in implementing any measures for taking evidence.

[9] *Supra*, David J. Harris et al., note 7 at 598, observe:

[A]part from a duty to cooperate with the Commission, the applicant does not bear the burden of proving his allegations since at [the merits] stage it falls to the Commission under Article 28 of the Convention to establish the facts. In this process the proceedings are governed by the principle of free admission and assessment of evidence. The Commission has no fixed rules of evidence concerning illegally obtained evidence, privileged documents or perjury...

Neither the Convention nor the Rules of Procedure prescribe a particular standard of proof. However, the Commission has consistently held that facts constituting a violation of the Convention must satisfy a reasonable doubt standard... (citations omitted).

The Court will not regard itself as bound by the Commission's findings of fact if exceptional circumstances indicate that the facts found by the Commission were not proved beyond a reasonable doubt: *Aydin v. Turkey*, Series A, Volume 1997-VI (25 September 1997) at para. 70. Proof beyond a reasonable doubt "may follow from the coexistence of sufficiently strong, clear and concordant inferences..."; *Mentes v. Turkey*, Series A, Volume 1997-VIII (28 November 1997) at para. 66, 37 *International Legal Materials* (1998) 858.

Where the respondent state refuses to cooperate in the Commission's investigation, for example

standards may possibly be explained by the fact that most applications have been the subject of elaborate adjudication at the domestic level. Only rarely has the requirement of exhaustion of domestic remedies been waived on the grounds of futility or lack of availability. The European Court has functioned largely as an appeal or review body, deriving the facts from the record of the domestic case and performing a primarily legal-interpretive function.

The European Court is aware that its judgments in individual cases bear considerable weight with states parties and that on occasion the life of the applicant may be at stake. Under the prior bifurcated system, the Court stressed that, while it would engage in first-hand fact-finding only in exceptional circumstances, it was never bound by the Commission's findings of fact and it was free to make its own assessment and to take note of developments occurring after the Commission's review.[10] The Court may review the factual record with special care where violations of absolute rights related to fundamental democratic values are at issue.[11] In such cases, the European Court has tended to question more deeply the factual basis for the respondent government's assertion that the applicant's Convention rights are not at risk.

The deference extended to domestic fact-finders by the European bodies in more ordinary cases can, however, be problematic. The facts concerning the individual applicant are often uncontested and clearly documented in the record of the domestic proceedings. In such cases, the real controversy relates to the weightiness of the state's justification for restricting the applicant's rights. These situations range from classically political cases concerning the arrest of an anti-militarist demonstrator,[12] to the denial of parents' wishes in naming a child.[13] The background social and political situation, which must be proven in order to justify the limitation of rights under the European Convention, is often the subject of no independent factual inquiry. Such factors are generally assessed under a forgiving "margin of appreciation," deferential not only as to the facts, as described by the state, but also as to the proper balance to be struck between individual and social interests.[14] As the Council of Europe bodies encounter

---

by refusing to permit entry of a Commission delegation to its territory in order to conduct an investigation, the Commission does not automatically presume the truth of the applicant's allegations: *supra* David J. Harris *et al.*, note 7 at 598. The Commission seeks to "satisfy itself that the information before it is sufficient to express a well-founded opinion"; *ibid.* (quoting Commission Report in the *Greek* case).

[10] *Chahal v. United Kingdom*, Series A, Volume 1996-V (15 November 1996) at paras. 95–97, 23 *European Human Rights Reporter* (1997) 415.

[11] *Ibid.*, at para. 96.

[12] *Chorherr v. Austria*, Series A, Volume 266B (25 August 1993), 17 *European Human Rights Reporter* (1994) 358 (finding applicant's arrest for holding placard and distributing leaflets at a military parade in Vienna to be justified to prevent a breach of the peace, despite the authorities' interference with his freedom of expression under Art. 10).

[13] *Guillot v. France*, Series A, Volume 1996-V (24 October 1996) (involving refusal of French authorities to permit parents to confer forename "Fleur de Marie" on their infant daughter; no violation of Art. 8 found).

[14] In the *Chahal* case, *supra* note 10, however, the Court asserted a degree of international judicial control in cases of national security involving confidential material. The Court cited as a potential model the Canadian procedure for *in camera* consideration of secret evidence. Under that approach, the litigant is given a summary of the damning information and is provided with an attorney and the right to present exculpatory evidence. In addition, another security-cleared counsel is appointed to review the secret evidence on behalf of the litigant, though that counsel may not disclose any details to the client and must attempt on his or her own to contest the accuracy of the information

applications from victims in states with less reliable judicial systems, fact-finding methodology will take on increasing importance. It is not surprising that the need for European Commission delegates to take testimony on-site increased after Turkey's acceptance of the Article 25 individual application process. Taking on-site testimony in an adversarial setting has been no simple matter, with Commission delegates forced to make difficult judgments concerning the credibility of witnesses and the sorting out of conflicting evidence.[15] As states of Central and Eastern Europe ratify the European Convention managing the caseload will require a greater investment of fact-finding effort.[16]

As Protocol 11 is implemented, chambers of the European Court may regularly be called upon to take testimony on site in order to create a factual record sufficient to permit an informed decision. The European Court will cease to resemble the classic appeals body of the past, and may grapple in greater detail with technical questions concerning admissibility of evidence, burdens of proof and confrontation of adverse witnesses.

Among human rights bodies that combine quasi-judicial competence with the monitoring of general human rights situations, the most extensive practice and most elaborate development of methodology in individual cases is that of the Human Rights Committee and the Inter-American Commission on Human Rights. Neither has found it possible to rely to the same degree as the Council of Europe bodies upon factual records created by reliable domestic tribunals. In a significant number of cases, exhaustion of domestic remedies is waived on grounds of unavailability or futility. Though more heavily burdened as a result with fact-finding in individual cases, neither the Human Rights Committee nor the Inter-American Commission has developed highly elaborate investigatory or evidentiary mechanisms. They have been impeded by governmental non-cooperation and by a lack of material resources for field investigation and verification of testimony through highly structured trial procedures.

The Human Rights Committee has faced difficult challenges under the First

---

to assist the court in a just disposition of the matter. The Court has since reiterated its insistence that the judiciary must be given access to supposed sensitive national security information in order to assure that important individual rights, such as the prohibition on invidious discrimination, are not unjustifiably violated. See *Tinnelly and Sons Ltd. v. United Kingdom* and *McElduff and Others v. United Kingdom*, Series A, Volume 1998-IV (10 July 1998).

The Commission and Court have sometimes differed on the extent to which general social conditions indicate the proper disposition of a particular applicant's case. In *H.L.R. v. France*, Series A, Volume 1997-III (29 April 1997) for example, the Commission accepted the applicant's claim that conditions in Colombia indicated that he faced a serious risk of torture or cruel treatment if he were deported. The Court disagreed with this assessment and denied relief under Art. 3 on the grounds that the applicant had failed to establish a sufficient degree of personalized risk: paras. 31, 37–44.

[15] In *Mentes v. Turkey*, supra note 9 at paras. 67–69, the Court seriously considered Turkey's objections to the validity of the Commission's factual findings but accepted those findings. The Court noted that full cross-examination had been provided at the adversarial hearings in Turkey, that the Commission addressed the inconsistencies and contradictions in the evidence and that Turkey had failed to cooperate in providing documents and access to a key witness.

[16] For example, in *Assenov and Others v. Bulgaria*, Series A, Volume VIII (28 October 1998) at para. 100, the Court held that it, like the Commission, "finds it impossible to establish on the basis of the evidence before it whether or not the applicant's injuries were caused by the police...". However, the Court found a violation of Art. 3 based on Bulgaria's failure to undertake a thorough and effective investigation into the applicant's complaint of serious ill-treatment: *ibid.* at para. 106.

Optional Protocol[17], which permits individual communications concerning violations of the International Covenant on Civil and Political Rights (CCPR)[18]. It depends almost entirely on the parties to the dispute for pertinent evidence, provided in written form. The quality of evidence submitted by the individual applicant varies with the quality of his or her representation and access to vital sources of information. In no case is the applicant able to maximize the impact of favorable evidence with credible personal testimony in the presence of the adjudicator, nor may either party probe the veracity of the other's evidence by in-person cross-examination of opposing witnesses. Cases concerning detained or disappeared applicants pose special difficulties, especially where the government is uncooperative or disingenuous.[19]

Where, however, a communication concerns a person convicted of a common crime and the record of the domestic proceeding is available, the Human Rights Committee may be quite deferential to the state, given its weak tools for uncovering the truth in a complicated or contested case.[20] The Inter-American Commission has similarly signalled its reluctance to serve as an appellate body of the "fourth instance".[21]

Being unable to engage in independent fact-gathering, yet reluctant to act decisively upon the uncontested allegations of an obviously self-interested (and possibly politically motivated) petitioner, the Human Rights Committee provides respondent states with prolonged opportunities to contest the petitioner's allegations. The Human Rights Committee's reaction to government unrespon-

---

[17] First Optional Protocol to the International Covenant on Civil and Political Rights, 999 UNTS 171 (in force 23 March 1976).
[18] International Covenant on Civil and Political Rights, 999 UNTS 171 (in force 23 March 1976).
[19] The *Laureano* case, for example, involved a disappeared girl in Peru. The Human Rights Committee rejected the Peruvian Government's suggestion that the victim might have been abducted by the Shining Path, in light of credible evidence that she had been seized by Peruvian security forces and that the authorities had failed to undertake a serious investigation. The Human Rights Committee noted that Peru had over an extended period simply reiterated that the disappearance was being investigated; in such circumstances "due weight must be given to the author's allegations, to the effect that they have been substantiated"; *Laureano v. Peru* (540/1993), A/51/40 Vol. II (25 March 1996) 116 at para. 8.2, 4 *International Human Rights Reports* (1997) 54.
[20] In one 1996 case, for example, the Human Rights Committee found no violation of art. 10 relating to the detained author's claim that he was denied reading materials and visits, noting that authorities keep no records of such matters; a similar finding was made regarding the author's claim that his rights under art. 14 were violated because of inadequate access to counsel to prepare for his trial on criminal charges, the Human Rights Committee noting that "the facts before it" did not permit the finding of a breach of the CCPR: *Kulomin v. Hungary* (521/1992), A/51/40 Vol. II (22 March 1996) 73 at paras. 11.4 and 11.5. The Human Rights Committee cautioned, *ibid.* at para. 11.8:
> The Committee takes this opportunity to reiterate that it is not for the Committee, but for the courts of the states parties concerned, to evaluate facts and evidence in a criminal case, and that the Committee cannot assess a person's guilt or innocence. This is so, unless it is manifest from the information before the Committee that the Courts' decisions were arbitrary or amounted to a denial of justice. In the present case, nothing in the written submissions before the Committee permits such a conclusion.

In its 1996 Report to the General Assembly, the Human Rights Committee noted that it "is not an instance of final recourse intended to review or reverse decisions of domestic courts and that it cannot be used as a forum for pursuing a complaint on the basis of domestic law"; *Report of the Human Rights Committee*, A/51/40 (1996) at para. 390.
[21] *Marzioni v. Argentina*, Report No. 36/96 (15 October 1996), in *1996 Annual Report of the Inter-American Commission on Human Rights*, OEA/Ser.L/V/II.95 Doc.7 (1997) Chapter III.

siveness is limited to a somewhat unsystematic resort to evidentiary presumptions.[22]

An interesting development is the designation of a Human Rights Committee member to follow up on views on individual communications,[23] including on-site visits to pressure state authorities to provide the remedies recommended by the Human Rights Committee.[24] On-site visits at the earlier evidence-gathering stage do not yet appear to be feasible or contemplated.

Unlike the Human Rights Committee, which may consider individual communications only as to states that have ratified both the CCPR and its First Optional Protocol, the Inter-American Commission possesses a broad authority to decide individual cases concerning all Organization of American States (OAS) member states, including those that have not ratified the American Convention on Human Rights. While individual cases have generally been a secondary focus of the Inter-American Commission's work, it has adopted noteworthy fact-finding innovations, including a presumption of veracity for allegations that have met either with no government response, or with denial unsupported by serious investigation.[25] This presumption is intended to stir governments from complacency and to prompt concrete responses that will advance the Inter-American Commission's truth-finding function. The Inter-American Commission has occasionally undertaken on-site visits to gather evidence prior to deciding individual cases, although it has eschewed formal judicial taking of testimony in these instances.[26]

---

[22] Where the government has not made a serious response to the allegations and the other evidence in the record appears credible, the Human Rights Committee may apply a mild presumption of credibility to the author's allegations: *supra* note 19.

[23] The designated member requests follow-up information in all cases where a violation of the CCPR has been found. As of 12 July 1999 information had been received as to 152 cases, compared to 84 cases where no information was received. The Human Rights Committee categorized approximately thirty percent of the follow-up replies as satisfactory in terms of the state's willingness to implement the Committee's views or as indicating an effective remedy for the violation: *Report of the Human Rights Committee*, A/54/40 (1999) at para. 458. From 1996 to 1999, the Human Rights Committee regretfully noted that the Office of the High Commissioner for Human Rights had not budgeted funds for follow-up missions: *Report of the Human Rights Committee*, A/51/40 (1996) at para. 466; A/52/40 (1997) at para. 557; A/53/40 (1998) at para. 510; A/54/40 (1999) at para. 474.

[24] The Human Rights Committee delegated a member to make an on-site visit to Jamaica in 1995 to follow up on implementation of its views in several cases involving prisoners on death row: *Report of the Human Rights Committee*, A/50/40 (1995) at paras. 557–562. The Human Rights Committee explored the possibility of a follow up visit to Trinidad in 1996, but could not secure the necessary financial resources from the Secretariat: *Report of the Human Rights Committee*, A/51/40 (1996) at paras. 453, 466. In the context of death penalty scrutiny, in 1998 Jamaica withdrew from the Optional Protocol. Trinidad and Tobago withdrew but ratified again with reservations concerning the death penalty. Guyana also withdrew but ratified again with reservations concerning the death penalty. Bert Wilkinson, "Another Government Withdraws from UN Body", Inter Press Service (18 November 1998), available in *LEXIS*, News Library, Curnws File. The Human Rights Committee has issued a general comment on renunciations of this type: *General Comment No. 26*, CCPR/C/21/Rev.1/Add.8/Rev.1 (1997).

[25] Pursuant to art. 42 of the Inter-American Commission's regulations, if a respondent state does not provide pertinent information within the time specified by the Inter-American Commission, "the facts reported in the petition... shall be presumed to be true... as long as other evidence does not lead to a different conclusion"; *Handbook of Existing Rules Pertaining to Human Rights in the Inter-American System*, OEA/Ser.L/V/II.65 Doc. 6 (1985).

[26] Art. 44 of the Inter-American Commission's regulations provides authority for such on-site visits. On-site visits can occur simply to verify the facts in an individual case; alternatively, the Inter-American Commission may gather information relevant to a pending individual case while conduct-

The vigorous approach of the Inter-American Commission and the increased responsiveness of OAS political organs to human rights crises in the Americas produced a backlash from certain OAS states during the mid 1990s. The initiative was led by states experiencing severe human rights violations (for example, Peru) and supported by states with an exaggerated concern for state sovereignty or a reluctance to accept rigorous external scrutiny (for example, Mexico).[27] With particular relevance to fact-finding, the proposal called upon the Inter-American Commission to apply more stringent admissibility and evidentiary rules, increasing barriers to redress without necessarily correcting any verifiable pattern of serious error by OAS human rights organs.[28]

Such pressures for reform of the OAS human rights system[29] pose a dilemma for human rights advocates. Insiders recognize the flaws in the existing system for human rights fact-finding. Moreover, they are likely to possess a strong attachment to rule of law principles and an interest in shoring up the credibility of the Inter-American Commission's conclusions. But exaggerated formalization of human rights fact-finding can undermine processes that have been consciously devised to compensate for government unresponsiveness, official monopoly on relevant evidence and the vulnerability of victims and witnesses.

The finding of a human rights violation against an identified individual, announced by an expert treaty body, is never entirely without consequences. At the least, pressure for redress or cessation ratchets up incrementally. However, where respondent states frequently choose to ignore factual conclusions and prescribed remedies, as is the case with many individual petitions to the Human Rights Committee and the Inter-American Commission, informality in evidentiary and procedural rules tends to predominate.

As the stakes attached to a finding of violation increase, greater formality tends to be incorporated into the fact-finding procedure. The European Court and the Inter-American Court of Human Rights possess the authority to order substantial damages against culpable states. The Inter-American Court, facing its first contested and factually difficult individual cases and anticipating that its pronouncements would carry some weight, produced sophisticated analyses of

---

ing an on-site visit in preparation of a special report on the country situation. For examples see *1990–1991 Annual Report of the Inter-American Commission on Human Rights*, OEA/Ser.L/V/II.79 Doc.12 Rev.1 (1991) at 193–223; *1994 Annual Report of the Inter-American Commission on Human Rights*, OEA/Ser.L/V/II.88 Doc.9 (1995) at 71–112; *1996 Annual Report of the Inter-American Commission on Human Rights*, OEA/Ser.L/V/II.95 Doc.7 (1997) at 23–26; *1997 Annual Report of the Inter-American Commission on Human Rights*, OEA/Ser.L/V/II/98 Doc.7 (1998) at 28–31.

[27] See Richard J. Wilson, "The Inter-American Human Rights System: Principal Activities in 1996", *ACLU International Civil Liberties Report* (March 1997) 30.

[28] *Ibid.*, at 30.

[29] The OAS Secretary-General issued a report outlining possible reforms in 1996: *Toward a New Vision of the Inter-American Human Rights System*, OEA/Ser.G/CP/Doc.2828/96 (1996). Several other reports have been issued addressing reform proposals: *Seminar on the Inter-American System for the Promotion and Protection of Human Rights: Conclusions of the Inter-American Commission on Human Rights and Minutes of the Statements made by the Participants*, OEA/Ser.L/V/II.95 Doc.28 (1995); *Report of the Permanent Council on Evaluation and Improvement of the Workings of the Inter-American System for the Promotion and Protection of Human Rights*, AG/Doc.3481/97 (1997). See also: remarks by the Chairman of the Inter-American Commission on Human Rights, Robert K. Goldman, at the Opening of the One Hundred and Sixth Regular Session, Washington, D.C., 22 February 2000, http://www.oas.org/cidh/discursos/2.22.00english.htm.

burden of proof questions that serve as a model for handling individual petitions.[30] It is noteworthy that the Inter-American Court was required to grapple with these issues in disappearance cases, a violation deliberately contrived to obscure the truth.[31]

The two *ad hoc* criminal tribunals established by the UN Security Council in recent years have adopted elaborate rules of evidence in order to insure that criminal penalties will not be imposed without reliable evidence of the defendant's guilt presented in a formal, adversarial process.[32] Particularly striking is the fact that existing human rights bodies provided little useful methodological and evidentiary guidance to the tribunals.[33] The unique human rights context of these prosecutions has required special adaptation of ordinary judicial evidentiary principles, especially with respect to witness protection.[34] While these evidentiary adaptations have been controversial,[35] it is interesting to note that the 1974 model rules of procedure proposed by the UN Commission on Human Rights for *ad hoc* fact-finding bodies and the International Law Association (ILA) Belgrade Rules both envision the possibility of witness anonymity.[36] Evidentiary issues have been given careful attention in some of the significant judgments of the *ad hoc* tribunals.[37]

---

[30] *Velásquez-Rodriguez Case* (July 29, 1988), in *1988 Annual Report of the Inter-American Court of Human Rights*, OEA/Ser.L/V/III.19 Doc.13 (1988) at 35. The Court laid out a framework for addressing the difficult evidentiary and burden of proof issues posed in contentious disappearance cases: *ibid.* at paras. 127, 130, 135:

> The Court must determine what the standards of proof should be in the instant case. Neither the Convention, the Statute of the Court nor its Rules of Procedure speak to this matter. Nevertheless, international jurisprudence has recognized the power of courts to weigh evidence freely, although it has always avoided a rigid rule regarding the amount of proof necessary to support the judgment...
>
> The practice of international and domestic courts shows that direct evidence, whether testimonial or documentary, is not the only type of evidence that may be legitimately considered in reaching a decision. Circumstantial evidence, indicia, and presumptions may be considered, so long as they lead to conclusions consistent with the facts.
>
> ...
>
> In contrast to domestic criminal law, in proceedings to determine human rights violations the state cannot rely on the defense that the complainant has failed to present evidence when it cannot be obtained without the state's cooperation.

[31] *Ibid.*, at para. 131.

[32] See for example, *International Tribunal for the Prosecution of Persons Responsible for Serious Violations of International Humanitarian Law Committed in the Territory of the Former Yugoslavia Since 1991, Rules of Procedure and Evidence*, 33 International Legal Materials (1994) 484.

[33] Kim Carter, "Proof Beyond a Reasonable Doubt?: Collecting Evidence for the International Criminal Tribunal for the Former Yugoslavia", 1993 *Canadian Yearbook of International Law* 235.

[34] Christine M. Chinkin, "Due Process and Witness Anonymity", 91 *American Journal of International Law* (1997) 75.

[35] Monroe Leigh, "The Yugoslav Tribunal: Use of Unnamed Witnesses Against Accused", 90 *American Journal of International Law* (1996) 235.

[36] *Supra*, note 4.

[37] For example, in the *Akeyesu* case, ICTR-96-4-T (2 September 1998), the International Tribunal for Rwanda held, *inter alia*, that it was not bound by the civil law principle of *unus testis, nullus testis* and thus did not require corroboration of every allegation of crime (at paras. 243–253) and that hearsay evidence was not categorically inadmissible (at para. 255).

Where victims request closed sessions, the International Tribunal for the Former Yugoslavia requires objective evidence of danger to justify closure to the public and media. *Prosecutor v. Delacic et al., Decisions on the Motion by the Prosecution for Protective Measures for the Prosecution Witnesses Pseudonymed "B" through to "M", IT-96-21-I (28 April 1997)*, available on the Internet at www.un.org/icty.

The most prominent accused, such as Radovan Karadzic and Ratko Mladic, have so far avoided trial. The "super-indictment" device of rule 61 provides a truncated opportunity for the prosecutor to present to the Tribunal factual evidence against these individuals, without imposing punishment beyond the risk of international arrest.

National tribunals also engage in human rights fact-finding, especially in the realm of asylum adjudication and tort or criminal actions against human rights violators. This chapter will briefly note some of the significant fact-finding challenges encountered in these settings.

States parties to the 1951 Convention relating to the Status of Refugees and its 1967 Protocol[38] enjoy a wide discretion in structuring their refugee status determination systems. The United Nations High Commissioner for Refugees (UNHCR) produced a Handbook to provide guidance on significant substantive and procedural matters.[39] Administrative bodies susceptible to foreign policy concerns unfortunately play a significant role in asylum adjudication in many states. Review by an independent judiciary is sometimes available, but the factual record is generally created at the administrative level. Asylum adjudicators may derive much of their information concerning human rights conditions in the applicant's state of origin from data provided by foreign policy officials, whose objectivity is open to question.[40] While foreign ministries, especially those of the developed democracies, have unparalleled access to information concerning human rights conditions in other states, they may have strong policy reasons to avoid candor or even to disseminate disinformation about those conditions.[41]

Human rights fact-finding in the asylum realm is unusual in that it is primarily predictive, rather than retrospective. The key issue in most asylum cases is whether the applicant has a well-founded fear of becoming the victim of persecution if he or she is repatriated. The temptation to engage in wishful thinking, for example to assume that the applicant has a safe internal flight alternative, is sometimes indulged. Determination of refugee status may occur in settings so informal and hurried that error is inevitable. Seeking to deter perceived abuse of asylum, many Western states have initiated summary review of asylum claims at the border, without providing applicants a realistic opportunity to obtain representation or to compile supporting factual information. While the burden of proof is sometimes lowered to compensate for this procedural informality and truncation,[42] the risk of factual error is grave.

---

[38] Convention Relating to the Status of Refugees, 189 UNTS 137 (in force 22 April 1954); and Protocol Relating to the Status of Refugees, 606 UNTS 267 (in force 4 October 1967).
[39] *Handbook on Procedures and Criteria for Determining Refugee Status*, UNHCR (1979).
[40] For example, while the creation in 1990 of a corps of asylum officers in the United States improved objectivity and professionalism in the asylum system, both asylum officers and immigration judges continue to place heavy reliance upon information on human rights conditions in the state of origin provided by the United States Department of State. See, for example, *Marcu v. I.N.S.*, 147 *Federal Reporter, 3rd series*, 1078 at 1082 (9th Cir. 1998). The personal testimony of the applicant and information supplied by experts and non-governmental organizations is also considered: *Code of Federal Regulations, Title 8: Aliens and Nationality*, 8 C.F.R.(1998) Reg. 208.12.
[41] See, for example, *Gailius v. I.N.S.*, 147 *Federal Reporter, 3rd series*, 34 at 46 (1st Cir. 1998) (noting tendency of Department of State to soft-pedal human rights conditions in friendly states).
[42] Under 1996 legislation in the United States, for example, an arriving alien who lacks proper documents for admission must demonstrate a "credible fear" of persecution to an interviewing asylum officer in order to avoid summary removal: *Code of Federal Regulations, Title 8: Aliens and Nationality*, 8 U.S. Code (1996) Reg. 1225(b). If credible fear is demonstrated to the asylum officer

The litigation of human rights cases in national courts has developed rapidly in recent years, primarily through United States tort suits.[43] While many of these lawsuits have resulted in default judgments, premised on an offer of proof rather than formal presentation of admissible evidence subject to challenge by the defendant, several have gone to trial, testing the human rights fact-finding capabilities of domestic courts. Judges conducting these trials apply ordinary, well-established rules of evidence. Nevertheless, the challenge of proving human rights violations in the setting of a domestic court unfamiliar with the human rights situation in question should not be underestimated:

> [A human rights tort suit] raises the same issues as any case – any case, that is, where the events took place in a foreign country; the plaintiff was the victim of traumatic human rights abuses and often is a refugee, far from home, who may not speak English; witnesses have scattered and may be afraid to testify; documentary evidence is scarce; and the defendant was a government official at the time he committed the abuse, with sufficient authority to commit such human rights abuses with impunity.[44]

In these human rights cases it is indispensable to present expert testimony by credible persons with extensive factual knowledge of human rights conditions in the state where the violations occurred.[45] Without a factual context in which to situate the stories of the victims, the typical domestic judge or jury is unable accurately to assess difficult issues such as attribution of command responsibility. Domestic courts thus benefit from the fact-finding prowess of human rights IGOs and NGOs through the testimony of such expert witnesses. However, the programmatic or ideological orientation of the experts provides counsel for the defendants ample opportunity to challenge the reliability of their evidence. In class actions, such as the extensive litigation against former Philippine President Ferdinand Marcos, testimony concerning representative victims was admitted to establish the extent of damages suffered by the entire class,[46] an indispensable efficiency but one raising concerns about strict accuracy of individualized proof.

Because foreign sovereign immunity is a serious barrier to litigation, few of the successful cases have been brought against states rather than individual perpetrators. However, Argentina's agreement to settle the *Siderman* case[47] suggests that, where a foreign state is not immune to civil jurisdiction in a foreign court for human rights torts, it may have a powerful incentive to avoid trial and judgment. Such states may be prepared to provide sizeable compensation to

---

or a reviewing immigration judge, a full hearing on the asylum claim is granted, with judicial review. If not (and also in those cases where border officials improperly refuse to provide credible fear screening), the asylum seeker is removed without detailed investigation of the facts of his or her claim.
[43] See Benedetto Conforti and Francesco Francioni (eds.), *Enforcing International Human Rights in Domestic Courts*, Martinus Nijoff (1997); Joan Fitzpatrick, "The Role of Domestic Courts in Enforcing International Human Rights Law", in *Guide to International Human Rights Practice 3rd ed.*, Hurst Hannum (ed.), Transnational (1999).
[44] Beth Stephens and Michael Ratner, *International Human Rights Litigation in U.S. Courts*, Transnational (1996) at 197 (citation omitted).
[45] *Ibid.*, at 202–204, 208–209 (noting testimony in one class action by former U.S. officials with knowledge of human rights conditions in the Philippines under President Ferdinand Marcos and by experts employed by reputable NGOs).
[46] *Supra*, note 44 at 208–209.
[47] *Siderman de Blake v. Republic of Argentina*, 965 Federal Reporter, 2nd series, 699 (9th Cir. 1992).

II. Fact-finding as Part of Effective Implementation 77

victims in order to avoid having the factual details of their depredations subjected to the glare of media scrutiny in as authoritative a setting as a domestic court of law.

(ii) Non-judicial mechanisms

That a human rights fact-finder focuses on individual victims does not necessarily imply that quasi-judicial fact-finding methods are optimal. The Working Group on Enforced or Involuntary Disappearances, authorized by the United Nations Commission on Human Rights, can be seen as relentlessly factual in its approach to individual disappearances, although it eschews judicial-type procedures. The Working Group considers a case resolved once it has determined whether the disappearance victim is dead, or alive in a particular location. The Working Group does not strive to establish responsibility for the victim's disappearance; it seeks to convey the most detailed factual information obtainable to the victim's family. At the same time, the Working Group's reports supply noteworthy statistical information on patterns of reported disappearances and its program of on-site visits yields recommendations for systemic reforms to reduce violations.

The Working Group also monitors compliance with the recommendations of the Declaration on the Protection of All Persons from Enforced Disappearance.[48] This mandate involves issuing general comments clarifying the Declaration's terms and adoption of observations on the situation in particular countries experiencing a significant number of disappearances. With respect to a proposed convention on disappearances, the Working Group has recommended that either an existing treaty body or the Working Group itself take on the function of reviewing implementation by states parties.[49] The Working Group would continue to function as a thematic mechanism with respect to non-parties.

The Working Group on Arbitrary Detention adopts a methodology more akin to that of treaty bodies with competence over individual communications, such as the Human Rights Committee. The Working Group conducts an exchange of written communications between representatives of a claimed victim and the respondent state, and reports whether a violation of norms protecting personal liberty has occurred. At the 1997 session of the Commission on Human Rights, the Working Group's mandate was altered to diminish its factual and evaluative conclusions from "decisions" to "views,"[50] to restrict its capacity to judge the behavior of non-party states by the standards of the CCPR, and to limit its role in assessing the legality of the detention of persons whose situation has been examined by domestic judicial authorities. This experience suggests

---

[48] Declaration on the Protection of All Persons from Enforced Disappearance, adopted by G.A. Res. 47/133 on 18 December 1992.

[49] *Report of the Working Group on Enforced or Involuntary Disappearances*, E/CN.4/1998/43 (12 January 1998) at para. 19. Draft International Convention on the Protection of All Persons from Forced Disappearance, E/CN.4/Sub.2/1998/19, annex (19 August 1998). See also Commission on Human Rights Res. 1999/38, adopted on 26 April 1999; Sub-Commission Res. 1999/24, adopted on 26 August 1999.

[50] See UN Commission on Human Rights Res. 1997/50 adopted on 15 April 1997, in *Commission on Human Rights: Report on the Fifty-Third Session*, E/CN.4/1997/150 (1997) at 164. The Working Group responded in May 1997 by altering its conclusions on individual cases from "decisions" to "opinions"; *Report of the Working Group on Arbitrary Detention*, E/CN.4/1998/44 (19 December 1997).

that where a thematic mechanism adds a strong evaluative approach to fact-finding in individual cases, an adverse reaction among some states may be anticipated, premised in part upon the relatively weak legal authority of the body.

One of the great innovations of the UN thematic mechanisms, the "urgent action," focuses on individual incidents, though primarily for preventive rather than fact-finding purposes. For cases that qualify as urgent actions, rapporteurs and working group chairs promptly send messages to state authorities requesting immediate clarification concerning reports of recent violations.[51] Other, more belated reports are processed less promptly and may languish in a backlog before state authorities are asked for a response. Where early contact is made with authorities concerning an individual case, the victim's situation is more likely to be illuminated.[52] Thus, even though the contact is intended to prevent violations rather than to document them, rapidly establishing the facts significantly improves accuracy.

As intergovernmental organizations (IGOs) place greater stress on preventive human rights monitoring, however, detailed fact-finding concerning individual victims may sometimes take a lower profile. For example, CERD, which has devoted relatively little effort to resolution of individual communications under article 14, has undertaken on-site visits in the context of its efforts to defuse crisis situations involving racial and ethnic strife.[53] While these visits no doubt provide useful background information to CERD to assist it in monitoring the general situation in a crisis state, they are not intended to produce detailed documentation on the circumstances of specific victims.

Redressing the plight of individual victims, including accurate determination of responsibility for particular violations, may also assume secondary importance in the deployment of human rights monitors.[54] The human rights monitoring mission to El Salvador (ONUSAL), while in many respects a success, was often unable to determine the truth about incidents reported to it. Eventually, ONUSAL chose to emphasize institution building at the national level over

---

[51] The Working Group on Enforced or Involuntary Disappearances, for example, subjects a reported disappearance to its urgent action procedure if the disappearance allegedly occurred within three months preceding the Group's receipt of the report, or if relatives or others seeking to aid a disappearance victim are subjected to intimidation, persecution or reprisal: *Report of the Working Group on Enforced or Involuntary Disappearances*, E/CN.4/1996/38 (15 January 1996) at para. 4; E/CN.4/2000/64 (21 December 1999) at para. 4.

[52] The Working Group on Enforced or Involuntary Disappearances, for example, was able to clarify 39 of the 163 cases treated under its urgent action mechanism in 1995: *ibid.* at para. 32. In the report of the Working Group to the 2000 Commission on Human Rights (Fifty-sixth session), the Working Group notes that it sent urgent action appeals in respect of 125 cases; it transmitted a total of 300 new cases of enforced or involuntary disappearance; and during the same period, it clarified 70 cases. *Report of the Working Group on Enforced or Involuntary Disappearances*, E/CN.4/2000/64 (21 December 1999) at paras. 4, 14, 16.

[53] *Report of the Committee on the Elimination of Racial Discrimination*, A/51/18 (1996) at paras. 24–36 (noting 1993 "good offices" mission to Serbia and Montenegro). A CERD member undertook a mission to Croatia under the auspices of the advisory services program of the UN: Michael Banton, *International Action Against Racial Discrimination*, Oxford (1996) at 162.

[54] An excellent survey of the mandates, methodologies and accomplishments of human rights monitoring missions is contained in Alice Henkin (ed.), *Honoring Human Rights: From Peace to Justice*, The Aspen Institute (1998). The contributors to this volume analyze problems of recruitment, training, coordination, resources and mandate confusion, drawing upon extensive first-hand experience.

investigative work on specific complaints.[55] This was true even though ONUSAL's human rights monitors had the unusual advantage of close collaboration with civil police experts sent by the UN to train the Salvadoran police.

Learning to adapt police investigatory techniques effectively is an important challenge for human rights bodies seeking to investigate violent human rights abuses that are analogous to serious crimes. The UN is developing an increasingly sophisticated understanding of forensic techniques and has created a data bank on forensic experts who might assist the fact-finding process.[56]

(b) Human rights situations and patterns

Placing an individual human face on violations can be an effective strategy for mobilizing pressure against entrenched patterns of abuse, as NGOs such as Amnesty International have long shown. Mechanisms for individual complaints offer the added benefit of direct and concrete redress to victims, in addition to exposing the truth about their experiences. Nevertheless, fact-finding by IGOs and NGOs primarily addresses situations and patterns rather than individual cases. Some UN treaty bodies lack competence to consider individual complaints, though active proposals are pending to extend such authority to the Economic, Social and Cultural Rights Committee.[57] States parties are generally reluctant to accept implementation mechanisms invocable by individuals. As a result, the work of the UN human rights treaty bodies, as well as most other human rights IGOs and NGOs, concentrates upon assessing the general human rights situation or exposing patterns of violations. Effective performance of this task is extremely difficult, and many human rights bodies are severely hampered by limited resources and inefficient coordination.

(i) Judicial methods

Judicial fact-finding methods have been employed in inter-state complaints decided by the European Commission and the European Court, addressing patterns of violations of the European Convention, typically in the context of a state of emergency. Extensive testimony has been taken from large numbers of witnesses in these proceedings; for example, over one hundred witnesses were heard in *Ireland v. United Kingdom*.[58] An on-site investigation may be crucial in establishing facts relating to identified victims, such as incidents of torture. For

---

[55] Reed Brody, "The United Nations and Human Rights in El Salvador's 'Negotiated Revolution'", 8 *Harvard Human Rights Journal* (1995) 153.

[56] *Manual on the Effective Prevention and Investigation of Extra-Legal, Arbitrary and Summary Executions*, United Nations (1991); *Human Rights and Forensic Science: Report of the Secretary-General*, E/CN.4/1998/32 (5 January 1998).

[57] See for example, the Draft Optional Protocol to the International Covenant on Economic, Social and Cultural Rights, E/CN.4/1997/105 (18 December1997).

[58] *Ireland v. The United Kingdom*, Series A, Volume 25 (18 January 1978). A delegation of the Commission at the merits stage heard thirteen witnesses proposed by the applicant Government. The respondent Government insisted upon extraordinary security measures to protect its witnesses; eventually the Commission agreed to take testimony at an airfield in Stavanger, Norway, guarded by Norwegian security forces. Some of the respondent's witnesses were permitted to conceal their identities and to testify behind screens. A total of 118 witnesses were heard by Commission delegates: Arthur H. Robertson and John G. Merrills, *Human Rights in Europe 3rd ed.*, Manchester University Press (1993) at 279.

example, after hearing several dozen witnesses in Strasbourg, the European Commission in the *Greek Case*[59] sent a delegation to Greece to hear the testimony of thirty-four witnesses on the question of patterns of torture, securing the services of forensic experts from Switzerland to examine certain claimed torture victims. The Commission delegates also visited several prisons and police stations, though they were not granted entry to all requested locations. Most strikingly, the Commission delegation took testimony on-site from twenty-nine witnesses, including prominent former politicians and current military leaders, concerning the politically charged question whether a state of emergency, as defined in Article 15 of the European Convention, existed at the time the military government seized power.[60]

The Inter-American Court, while not yet seized of an inter-state case of this type, has actively taken evidence in contentious individual cases,[61] which make up an increasing portion of its docket. The Inter-American Court has found it necessary on several occasions to order provisional measures to secure the safety of persons whose lives had been threatened because they testified or were scheduled to testify before the Court, pursuant to article 63(2) of the American Convention and article 25 of the Inter-American Court's rules.[62]

The International Court of Justice (ICJ) has never played a prominent role in international human rights fact-finding. However, the ICJ has reached the merits stage of the pending case between Bosnia-Herzegovina and Serbia and Montenegro, the first to be brought under the Genocide Convention.[63] The ICJ will presumably employ its traditional fact-finding methodology in deciding whether the Serbian Government bears international legal responsibility for ethnic cleansing during the war in Bosnia-Herzegovina.[64] In light of the ICJ's recent experience in conducting an on-site fact-finding visit,[65] it is possible that similar evidence-gathering techniques might be employed in complex human rights cases.

---

[59] *The Greek Case*, ECHR Yearbook 12 (5 November 1969) 1.
[60] *Supra*, note 58 at 278–79.
[61] The Inter-American Court's rule 44(1) gives it broad authority to hear witnesses:
The Court may, at any stage of the proceedings:
    1. Obtain, on its own motion, any evidence it considers helpful. In particular, it may hear as a witness, expert witness, or in any other capacity, any person whose evidence, statement or opinion it deems to be relevant.
Under rule 44(4), the Court may delegate one or more of its members "to conduct an inquiry, undertake an *in situ* investigation or obtain evidence in some other manner"; *Rules of Procedure of the Inter-American Court of Human Rights*, approved by the Court at its XXVI Regular Session (9–20 September 1996).
[62] Scott Davidson, *The Inter-American Human Rights System*, Dartmouth (1997) at 139–141.
[63] Convention on the Prevention and Punishment of the Crime of Genocide, 78 UNTS 277 (in force 12 January 1951).
[64] See Stephen M. Schwebel, "Three Cases of Fact-Finding by the International Court of Justice", in *Fact-Finding Before International Tribunals: Eleventh Sokol Colloquium*, Richard Lillich (ed.), Transnational (1990) 1–17; and Thomas M. Franck, "Fact-Finding in the I.C.J.", *Ibid.*, at 21–32 (suggesting that the ICJ, when hearing politically charged cases arising out of armed conflict, will find it necessary to engage in more active fact-finding, including on-site visits).
[65] *Gabčíkovo-Nagymaros Project (Hungary/Slovakia)*, International Court of Justice Reports 1997 (25 September 1997), 37 *International Legal Materials* (1998) 162. The visit was undertaken pursuant to art. 66 of the *Rules of Court*, based upon a joint proposal of the parties. The visit occurred between the first and second rounds of oral hearings. Delegates of states assisting in the visit were instructed to limit their responses to technical explanations and to avoid argument on legal issues: Peter Tomka

(ii) Non-judicial fact-finding

The heart and soul of human rights fact-finding is the disclosure of patterns of human rights violations. This is the core function of human rights NGOs, and it is also undertaken by many IGOs and the international media. The evaluative nature of such fact-finding exposes its participants to charges of bias, especially in circumstances where verification of factual data is difficult. This section focuses selectively on the experiences of country and thematic rapporteurs of the UN Human Rights Commission, the Inter-American Commission, human rights monitoring missions, and the Committee Against Torture (CAT). This background will then inform the evaluation of the report-review functions of the UN treaty bodies in Section 3, which theoretically strive to present a general picture of state compliance with treaty obligations.

The proliferation of fact-finding mechanisms under the authority of the UN Human Rights Commission can be traced to concern in the 1970s over notorious situations of gross and persistent human rights violations. While the *ad hoc* conciliation commissions envisioned by Economic and Social Council (ECOSOC) Resolution 1503 have at best a ghostly existence, public fact-finding mechanisms have grown to amazing dimensions. Being the subject of a human rights fact-finding mechanism of the UN Human Rights Commission at first was a form of implicit condemnation restricted to pariah states. The methodology employed by the groups monitoring practices in those states was designed with non-cooperation by the target in mind; objectivity was not their hallmark. However, they experimented with fact-finding techniques in some instructive ways, for example by holding public sessions in neighboring states to receive testimony and by establishing on-going information exchanges with informed NGOs.

The Special Rapporteur on Torture visited Chile in August 1995, and set an important precedent by making on-site visits a central element of his fact-gathering endeavors.[66] This approach has been adopted by subsequent country rapporteurs as well as by special representatives of the Secretary-General who, while undertaking a "good offices" function, produce similar fact-finding reports. The thematic rapporteurs and working groups established by the UN Human Rights Commission also undertake on-site visits, in addition to responding to communications concerning individual victims and conducting theoretical analyses of their focal norms. UN treaty bodies, in contrast, rely only rarely on on-site visits in the discharge of their reviewing function over state reports. Outside the UN human rights system, on-site visits have figured prominently in Inter-American Commission special reports on the situation of human rights in selected OAS states. The Organization for Security and Cooperation in Europe (OSCE) is an enthusiastic participant in on-site methodology and has deployed a number of human rights monitoring missions,[67] such as in Kosovo. Such missions have preventive as well as verification objectives.

---

and Samuel S. Wordsworth, "Current Development: The First Site Visit of the International Court of Justice in Fulfillment of Its Judicial Function", 92 *American Journal of International Law* (1988) 133.

[66] *Report of the Special Rapporteur, Mr. Nigel Rodley: Visit by the Special Rapporteur to Chile*, E/CN.4/1996/35/Add.2 (4 December 1996).

[67] See, for example, Michael O'Flaherty, "International Human Rights Operations in Bosnia and Herzegovina", in Henkin, *supra* note 54 at 71, 73, 76–77, 81–82 (describing dual human rights and election monitoring functions performed by OSCE in Bosnia).

The problematic aspects of on-site visits thus merit scrutiny in an evaluation of human rights fact-finding. There is a fairly well-established protocol for IGO on-site visits, but the accepted methodology is more diplomatic than evidentiary. The terms of the visits must be negotiated with governmental authorities, giving rise to the risk that information will be filtered. Visits cannot be incognito, creating danger for witnesses who approach the fact-finding delegation during the course of the visit, as illustrated by the extraordinary events in East Timor in March 1997 when security forces injured dozens of persons seeking contact with the Secretary General's envoy.[68] Assurances of non-reprisal following the visit cannot be effectively guaranteed by IGOs. Visits are brief and thus highly selective. Data gathering tends to be informal, and mechanisms for cross-checking the accuracy of statements are not elaborated. Confusion of role may result where the rapporteur or envoy attempts to combine fact-finding with diplomatic overtures.

The best-known initiatives to set standards for human rights fact-finding, for example draft rules of procedure referred by the UN Human Rights Commission to the ECOSOC in 1974 and the International Law Association's 1980 Belgrade Principles,[69] have taken on-site visits by *ad hoc* IGO delegates as a focus. Yet these standards do not address in detail such questions as selection of interviewees, cross-checking the accuracy of statements, role and identity of interpreters, and similar practical concerns affecting credibility. These standards envision the appearance of witnesses in the relatively formal setting of a hearing, at which representatives of the state may also be present to challenge the veracity of the testimony. In reality, the on-site investigatory techniques of UN *ad hoc* bodies tend toward much greater informality.

One alternative to the flying visit of a fact-finding body is a sustained field presence by human rights monitors. Growing recognition of the human rights dimension of international peace and security has resulted in the establishment of a number of human rights monitoring missions in the past decade.[70] While a comprehensive analysis of the work of these bodies is not possible here, certain aspects of their fact-finding deserve mention.

The Office of the High Commissioner for Human Rights, symbol of the organization's shift in focus to preventive, early warning mechanisms, has been given administrative responsibility for missions or offices in states experiencing acute human rights crises, such as Rwanda and Colombia. Several monitoring missions were initiated as a component of an internationally brokered ending to an armed conflict, for example United Nations Transitional Authority in Cambodia (UNTAC)[71] and La Mission d'observation des Nations Unies en El Salvador (ONUSAL).

The deployment of numerous human rights monitors throughout a state experiencing severe human rights violations seems an ideal means to overcome

---

[68] "East Timorese Shows Torture Video at UN Rights Meet", Agence France Presse (April 9, 1997); "Timorese Killed Under UN Envoy's Nose, Says Horta", Reuters N. Am. Wire (April 9, 1997), both available in *LEXIS*, News Library, Curnws File.
[69] *Supra*, note 4.
[70] See *supra* note 54, Henkin, for a systematic comparison of significant human rights monitoring missions.
[71] See Brad Adams, "UN Human Rights Work in Cambodia: Efforts to Preserve the Jewel in the Peacekeeping Crown", in Henkin *supra* note 54 at 189.

the barriers to accurate fact-finding that have long plagued the treaty bodies, IGO *ad hoc* mechanisms, and NGOs. Monitors have access to detailed information from numerous sources and an opportunity to become deeply familiar with the political situation, enabling improved assessment of the accuracy of complaints. However, the human rights monitoring missions to date have not been ideal exercises in objective, timely, comprehensive, public fact-finding.

The UN-OAS mission to Haiti and the Human Rights Field Operation in Rwanda (HRFOR) provide insight into potential drawbacks. It is difficult to staff a mission quickly with substantial numbers of persons who possess the necessary background knowledge, language ability, objectivity and field operational skills to produce credible evidence of a human rights situation in crisis. The mission may be confused as to whether its focus is moderating ongoing human rights violations or investigating and documenting massive violations of the immediate past.

For example, HRFOR attempted to collaborate in the gathering of evidence for the trials of genocide perpetrators by the International Tribunal, at the same time that it sought to monitor human rights conditions under the post-genocide regime of the Rwandan Patriotic Front (RPF).[72] Amnesty International questioned whether HRFOR staff possessed the technical capability to gather admissible evidence for the criminal prosecutions, and noted that, since information relating to pending prosecutions required a high degree of confidentiality, an unfortunate impression was created in Rwanda that HRFOR's concerns related exclusively to the RPF's own human rights problems rather than to the 1994 genocide.[73] Ian Martin notes that the failure at the outset to clarify a productive working relationship between HRFOR and the investigative staff of the International Tribunal resulted in delay, inefficiency and loss of the opportunity for HRFOR to issue a general report on the genocide.[74]

Where the presence of human rights monitors has been negotiated as part of a volatile political process, it is subject to manipulation by state authorities and those with significant influence in IGO political bodies. The UN-OAS mission to Haiti was undermined by doubt expressed by United States officials concerning the veracity of its documentation of grave human rights violations contributing to the irregular flow of Haitian asylum-seekers. At several points the mission was required to evacuate as the *de facto* Haitian authorities perceived an erosion of high-level political support for its work.[75]

The UN treaty bodies have made only rudimentary use of the on-site visit as a fact-finding tool and lack the capacity to initiate on-going monitoring missions even in states severely out of compliance with treaty norms. The treaty body with the greatest potential for a field presence, if an indirect one, is the Child Committee. The Child Committee has crafted a close working relationship with the United Nations Children's Fund (UNICEF) under article 45 of the

---

[72] *Supra*, note 1, Newman and Weissbrodt at 311–319; Ian Martin, "After Genocide: The UN Human Rights Field Operation in Rwanda", in Henkin, *supra* note 54 at 97, 106–108.
[73] *Supra*, note 1, Newman and Weissbrodt, at 316–319 (quoting AI Index: AFR 02/24/95 (1995)).
[74] *Supra*, note 72, Martin at 107.
[75] Ian Martin, "Haiti: Mangled Multilateralism", 95 *Foreign Policy* (1994) 72; William G. O'Neill, "Human Rights Monitoring vs. Political Expediency: the Experience of the OAS/U.N. Mission in Haiti", 8 *Harvard Human Rights Journal* (1995) 101.

Convention on the Rights of the Child (CRC),[76] including a regular flow of detailed empirical information on the condition of children in states scheduled for review. Up until 1997, the relationship with UNICEF also permitted the Child Committee to convene "informal meetings" in a variety of African and Asian states, during which Child Committee members stressed the importance of state reporting, made contact with local governmental and non-governmental experts on children and discussed with them pertinent thematic issues, such as child labor.[77] These were not on-site fact-finding missions in the ordinary sense, but members of the Committee did induce states to provide more pertinent data, and occasionally took the opportunity to monitor the implementation of its recommendations from previous reviews of state reports.[78] Since that time UNICEF has suspended the funding of such informal field visits by Child Committee members, but continues to fund travel of individual members to attend conferences and meetings on an ad-hoc basis. Other treaty bodies have expressed an interest in drawing more intensively upon specialized agencies of the UN in order to gain access to similar valuable factual information.

An interesting model for evaluation of a pattern or situation of human rights violations in a particular state party is presented by CAT's capacity to undertake a confidential inquiry into allegations of systematic practices of torture under article 20 of the Convention Against Torture and other Cruel, Inhuman, and Degrading Treatment or Punishment (CAT).[79] CAT published a summary of the results of such inquiries, into practices involving Turkey[80] and Egypt.[81] CAT must rely upon data supplied by NGOs, the Special Rapporteur on Torture and Other Cruel, Inhuman or Degrading Treatment or Punishment and by witnesses contacted by its delegates during the on-site visit.

In its summary report on Turkey, CAT frankly confronted the state's challenge to the sufficiency of the proof available to it.[82] CAT was hampered by Egypt's

---

[76] Convention on the Rights of the Child, 1577 UNTS 3 (in force 2 September 1990).
[77] *Report of the Committee on the Rights of the Child*, A/51/41 (1996) at paras. 1036–1047.
[78] In November 1996, for example, the Child Committee used its visits to Morocco and Egypt for such follow-up purposes: *Report of the Committee on the Rights of the Child*, A/53/41 (1998) at paras. 1341–1352.
[79] Convention Against Torture and other Cruel, Inhuman, and Degrading Treatment or Punishment, 1465 UNTS 85 (in force 26 June 1987).
[80] *Report of the Committee Against Torture*, A/48/44/Add.1 (1993).
[81] *Report of the Committee Against Torture*, A/51/44 (1996).
[82] As CAT noted in the summary report on Turkey, *supra* note 80 at paras. 36–38:

The Committee wishes to state that it has received numerous allegations of torture in Turkey originating mainly from five international non-governmental organizations and five Turkish non-governmental organizations engaged in action to promote respect for human rights. The report which the Committee members making the inquiry addressed to it also contains detailed information on dozens of testimonies which they gathered within and outside places of detention during their mission to Turkey from 6 to 18 June 1992. In addition, the Committee has received precise information on the examinations of presumed torture victims by the medical expert who lent his assistance during the inquiry, and on the talks which the Committee members had with the Turkish authorities about the torture allegations received.

The Government of Turkey has informed the Committee that it rejects all the allegations of torture submitted by non-governmental organizations, since those organizations are, in its view, deeply politicized or have never given credible proof of their impartiality. As to the testimony gathered during the mission to Turkey, the Government stated that it was derived essentially from persons presumed to be terrorists who, in line with their strategy, had every reason to claim that they had been tortured.

The Committee considers that, even though only a small number of torture cases can be proved

refusal to cooperate in an on-site visit, but chose to proceed based on other information:

> In the absence of a visit to Egypt, the Committee ... could neither support the Government's position nor call into question the allegations of torture, and it had to draw its conclusions on the basis of the information available to it.[83]

CAT emphasized that this information came from different sources, appeared to be well-founded and indicated the systematic practice of torture by Egyptian security forces.[84]

The concern for identifying gross and persistent human rights violations has sometimes been misused to disguise geopolitical assessments as factual determinations. As Diane Orentlicher has convincingly demonstrated,[85] the "certification" mechanisms adopted by the United States Congress have not been successful experiments in objective human rights fact-finding. These mechanisms delegate to the President the responsibility to verify that certain factual conditions exist (for example, a reduction in the rate of serious human rights violations), as a prelude to a Congressional decision respecting financial assistance, arms sales or other elements in the bilateral relationship with the foreign state subject to the certification. In the case of human rights certifications during the 1980s, the Executive Branch disseminated palpably misleading depictions of human rights conditions in states such as El Salvador, drawing NGOs into a destructive cycle of charges and countercharges of bias. Rather than take the hard political judgment to impair trade and other relations for the sake of human rights objectives, the United States Congress prefers to impose on the President the obligation to make periodic "factual" findings[86] that would supposedly trigger disruption of diplomatic relations. Not surprisingly, factual accuracy is one of the main victims of this politically charged process.

Some IGOs are setting themselves the task to determine trade policy on the basis of factual certifications concerning human rights conditions in particular states. In a noteworthy decision, the European Union withdrew modest trade preferences from Burma/Myanmar on the basis of uncontested factual allegations, supported by extensive documentary evidence compiled by labor unions,

---

with absolute certainty, the copious testimony gathered is so consistent in its description of torture techniques and the places and circumstances in which torture is perpetrated that the existence of systematic torture in Turkey cannot be denied.

[83] *Supra*, note 81 at para. 39.

[84] A draft optional protocol envisions that CAT would also conduct a regular program of on-site visits to places of detention, in order to strengthen protections against risks of torture and cruel treatment: *Report of the Working Group on the Draft Optional Protocol to the Convention Against Torture*, E/CN.4/1998/42 (2 December 1997); *Report of the Working Group on the Draft Optional Protocol to the Convention Against Torture*, E/CN.4/1999/59 (26 March 1999), E/CN.4/1999/59/Add.1 (26 April 1999); *Report of the Working Group on the Draft Optional Protocol to the Convention Against Torture*, E/CN.4/2000/58 (2 December 1999).

[85] Diane F. Orentlicher, "Bearing Witness: The Art and Science of Human Rights Fact-Finding", 3 *Human Rights Law Journal* (1990) 83.

[86] An example is the International Religious Freedom Act adopted by the U.S. Congress in 1998, Public Law 105–292, which establishes a Commission on International Religious Freedom and obliges the Secretary of State to issue an annual report on patterns of violations of religious freedom in specific countries. Congress refrained from imposing automatic diplomatic and trade sanctions under this statute after considerable debate.

that the Burmese regime is engaged in a systematic practice of forced labor in violation of fundamental human rights norms.[87] The European Union process is interesting in that it is open to NGO petitioning and is determined by an inter-governmental body, rather than being delegated to political authorities in a single state.

Finally, a review of human rights fact-finding cannot ignore the phenomenon of truth commissions established by transitional regimes. Factual information is their stock in trade. Their exposure of the truth is generally intended to serve multiple objectives – to prevent recurrence of violations, to acknowledge in a formal manner the suffering of victims and survivors, or to achieve reconciliation among hostile social groups. No consensus exists on the ideal model, or even on the basic question whether the emergence of truth commissions has measurably advanced human rights protection.[88]

Some truth commissions focus on documenting the fates of victims (for example, the Argentinean report Nunca Mas). Where a conscious decision is taken not to "name names" of perpetrators, as in Chile, a victim focus naturally results. In some cases, however, such as "lustration" in Eastern Europe and the truth commissions established under UN auspices in El Salvador, identifying and purging violators are a central concern. Where the establishment of a truth commission has been secured at the cost of an amnesty for perpetrators, creating a thorough historical record may be impossible as no incentive exists for cooperation by those in possession of the vital information. The Truth and Reconciliation Commission in South Africa has, with some notable success as in the Stephen Biko case, overcome the information barrier by conditioning amnesty on full confession. However, the controversy surrounding the South African Commission also brings into acute focus the question whether factual disclosure should take precedence over punishment[89] or material assistance to victims.

(3) Bias

Facts in the human rights context are socially constructed. Their determination cannot occur, as in the sciences, in an objective manner designed to exclude the possibility of data manipulation and to facilitate the replication of research results by other investigators. Human rights facts must be interpreted through a filter of values and perspectives. So long as these values and perspectives are known and understood by the fact-finder, the information sources and the consumers of the data, the fact-finding process can make a positive contribution toward implementation of human rights guarantees.

IGO and NGO fact-finders should not be expected to approach their fact-

---

[87] "EU/Burma: Council Suspends Industrial and Agricultural GSP Benefits", *European Report* (March 26, 1997) available in *LEXIS, News Library, Curnws* File.

[88] See generally, Naomi Roht-Arriaza, *Impunity and Human Rights in International Law and Practice*, Oxford (1995).

[89] As the case of the murderers of anti-apartheid leader Chris Hani illustrates, even human rights violators whose factual guilt has been established to the demanding standards of the domestic criminal justice system may seek amnesty (and early release from prison) pursuant to the Commission's regulations. Suzanne Daley, "Apartheid Inquiry Takes Up the Killing of Mandela Associate", *New York Times* (12 August 1997) at A7. The full report of the Truth and Reconciliation Commission is available at http://www.truth.org.za.

finding endeavors with a completely neutral, value-free attitude. They should have a "human rights bias" – that is, an institutional and personal dedication to the goal of eradicating violations of internationally recognized human rights. They should be expected to place a high priority on revealing the truth about human rights practices, even where competing values may be at stake. This is not to suggest that confidential fact-finding has no place in the regime, but it should result in the suppression of the truth only for the most weighty reasons.

Sufficient inter-subject agreement exists among participants in the human rights regime for human rights fact-finding to be regarded as a genuinely empirical exercise. For example, certain types of egregious physical harm inflicted on detained persons will generally be recognized as internationally illegal acts of torture. The types of evidence that may credibly establish an allegation of torture are also broadly agreed (for example, testimony by the victim and eyewitnesses, forensic medical evidence, psychological evaluations for trauma, impeaching evidence that the victim's injuries were incurred accidentally, and so on).

Despite this shared understanding of the types of facts that are relevant in assessing events from a human rights perspective, perceptions of the reality of particular situations are likely to be wildly divergent. Governments are predictably defensive, denying the accuracy of allegations of human rights abuse and typically casting aspersions on the motivations and knowledge base of those making the accusations.[90] Egypt's response to CAT's article 20 inquiry was an argument that even examining reports of systematic torture would give aid and comfort to fundamentalist groups whose aims and methods are deeply adverse to human rights values.[91] NGOs without direct, extensive access to the country in question and under time pressure to perform an early warning function may report nonverifiable "allegations" rather than strictly provable "facts."[92] NGOs and media at the local level have invaluable access to factual information, while being especially vulnerable to accusations of politically motivated distortion or invention. Many IGOs are forced by resource constraints to rely upon government, NGO or press data which they cannot validate through rigorous, adverse, open evidentiary testing. Those same resource constraints may impede IGOs from developing sufficient expertise to be informed and appropriately skeptical consumers of factual information from either governmental or non-state sources.

With respect to some rights, divergent perceptions of reality may hamper the treaty bodies' fact-finding function. States may not perceive that certain practices (for example, homelessness and hunger resulting from economic policies, rigid gender roles in marriage, corporal punishment of children), which may be deeply imbedded in the political or cultural traditions of the society, are problematic under human rights treaties. Treaty bodies monitoring compliance with economic and social rights and with non-discrimination norms must communicate the

---

[90] In one absurd instance, in the face of several broadcast videotapes depicting unprovoked acts of violence by Brazilian police against ordinary civilians, the state security chief in Rio de Janeiro dismissed a coincidentally published study of Brazilian police brutality by Human Rights Watch/Americas, labeling the study's author a "space alien." Diana Jean Schemo, "Video in Brazil Captures Police Brutality; 6 Arrested", *New York Times* (9 April 1997) at A5.
[91] *Supra*, note 81.
[92] Hurst Hannum, "Fact-Finding by Non-Governmental Human Rights Organizations", *supra* note 1, in Lillich at 293.

human rights dimension of such policies and practices before a genuine fact-finding process can commence. Fortunately, some egregious practices are disclosed through review of relatively objective demographic and statistical data or of facially invalid national legislation. However, certain problems (such as violence in the family) may be concealed by a lack of empirical data, uncollected due to the state's failure to recognize the practice as a social problem or as a matter relevant to its compliance with human rights treaties.

(a) State reporting

The primary implementation mechanism in UN human rights treaties is state reporting. The drawbacks of this system are not ordinarily approached as a problem of fact-finding bias. However, many of the deficiencies of the state reporting system can be traced to the fact that the primary source of information has a strong incentive to dissemble, indeed a virtual conflict of interest. Governments are essentially asked to investigate their own human rights practices and to file a self-critical public report. Candid, detailed reports indicating significant and specific failures in compliance are, not surprisingly, almost non-existent. The report review system is posited on a utopian vision of constructive dialogue between knowledgeable and candid state representatives and treaty body members who can, through careful questioning informed only by a general expertise on human rights norms, assist the state to achieve compliance with the treaty.

It is now generally acknowledged that this model for report reviewing is unrealistic. The alternatives are to jettison state reporting as a human rights fact-finding procedure or to supplement state reports with alternative data that can be effectively incorporated into the treaty bodies' reviews. In recent years, the treaty bodies have vigorously pursued the second option, though with imperfect success. While members of treaty bodies have for some time benefitted from informal contacts with NGO sources, a rapid evolution in the formalization of input both from NGOs and specialized agencies is occurring. Moreover, initiatives for information-sharing among treaty bodies and extra-conventional mechanisms are multiplying.

Section (4) of this chapter will explore proposals to rationalize and integrate the data-gathering functions of UN human rights bodies, with a particular focus on the prospects for enhancing the fact-finding functions of the treaty bodies. This section will examine the particular problem of compensating for inherent bias in the most readily available sources of information.

Because of the pejorative aspects of admitting to human rights violations and lingering attachment to strict definitions of state sovereignty, some states take extreme self-defensive postures in the reporting process. CERD, for example, was required to educate its states parties that their own problems of racial and ethnic divisions were the focus of its legitimate concerns, even though some of these same states parties perceived the Convention primarily as a vehicle for critiquing the racial and social policies of other states.[93]

For many years, and despite explicit guidelines for state reporting promulgated

---

[93] *Supra*, note 53, Banton, at 102–121.

by the treaty bodies, state reports have typically emphasized the state's constitutional and legal framework, providing little or no factual data indicating whether citizens actually enjoy the rights guaranteed by the treaty. State authorities charged with the preparation of reports often fail to gather pertinent factual data, either to save expense or out of political calculation that few consequences will result from the submission of a dry, abstract, cursory report. Data disaggregated on the basis of gender or other important markers may not be provided. State representatives who attend sessions of treaty bodies are frequently unprepared to answer questions of a factual nature.

Worst of all, many states simply fail, often over a number of years, to submit any reports at all. Some of the treaty bodies have reacted to this default by scheduling reviews of states whose reports are seriously overdue. In the absence of any alternate data, however, such reviews can be a relatively unproductive exercise, at least from a fact-finding perspective.[94] CERD in 1996 decided to conduct such reviews on the basis of any prior reports submitted by the state, any information supplied by the state to any other UN body and any information on that state "prepared by organs of the United Nations."[95] The Economic, Social and Cultural Rights Committee has enjoyed some success in extracting overdue reports from states scheduled for such reviews. The prospect of a review without a report poses a real dilemma for states, given the committee's access to what is described by one observer as "detailed research work" and "a wide range of sources of information," and its willingness to reach "detailed, accurate and comprehensive" concluding observations following such a report-less review.[96]

The UN treaty bodies have moved to streamline the state reporting system, taking steps that, in part, increase its value as a fact-finding tool, but in other respects unfortunately diminish it. The end of the Cold War defused ideological tensions on the treaty bodies, creating greater possibilities for consensus on questions of state compliance. The treaty bodies took the opportunity to adopt concluding observations at the end of the review of each state report, expressing concern with specific aspects of compliance by the state in question. These observations are fact-finding exercises in a real sense, though their depth and explicitness varies among the treaty bodies. They have been widely disseminated, in an effort to increase the publicity for the report review process, to attract greater involvement by informed NGOs and, consequently, to place greater pressure on states to redress their failures.

For reasons of efficiency, some of the treaty bodies have also moved in the direction of specialization, by appointing country rapporteurs charged with the responsibility of familiarizing themselves with problems of treaty compliance in a state scheduled for review and the preparation of questions for the treaty body to pose. While this innovation in some instances will increase the intensity of

---

[94] For example, CERD's March 1996 review of Gambia, which had not submitted a report since 1977 and failed to send a representative to the session, draws no factual conclusions on the human rights situation in Gambia and simply exhorts the government to submit its overdue reports and to seek advisory services and technical assistance: *Report of the Committee on the Elimination of Racial Discrimination*, A/51/18 (1996) at paras. 257–258.
[95] *Ibid.*, at para. 22.
[96] Mr. Philip Alston, *Final Report on Enhancing the Long-Term Effectiveness of the United Nations Human Rights Treaty Bodies*, E/CN.4/1997/74 (27 March 1997) at para. 47.

the committee's scrutiny, the country rapporteur's own biases, insensitivity or limited sources of information to certain types of violations, may skew the process and impede fact-finding.

At the same time, the treaty bodies have deleted valuable factual information from their annual reports to the General Assembly. This information consisted of a condensed version of the dialogue between committee members and state representatives, exchanges that often contained interesting factual information pertaining to particular events and human rights conditions. These dialogues are still reported in the summary records of the committees' meetings, but these summary records are less easily available than the annual reports and are no longer being produced as systematically and accessibly as in the past.

Bias in sources of information is one problem in the state reporting system; bias among members of the treaty bodies poses an additional danger to the system. Persons who are employed by their governments, sometimes in the diplomatic service, are frequently appointed to treaty bodies as "independent experts." Moreover, it is possible that members of treaty bodies might participate in reviewing reports filed by their governments or in individual cases against those governments. While this is the norm in international adjudication, and the European Commission and Court have managed to maintain credibility despite the fact that their members have a tendency to support the views of their home governments, this apparent conflict of interest is more troubling where information supplied by the state plays such a prominent role in the treaty bodies' deliberations. Thus, the initiative of CERD to examine the question of participation by members in the review of their own states' reports is noteworthy, especially given CERD's experience with dissenting views appended to the Committee's concluding observations concerning India and China.[97] The Committee on the Elimination of Discrimination Against Women (CEDAW), for example, excludes its members from participating in the review of their own states' reports.[98] While members naturally bring a greater depth of factual knowledge to the review of their own state's report, they also inevitably bring the appearance, and sometimes the reality, of bias.

(b) Bias-reduction techniques

Both IGOs and NGOs must grapple with their own biases and limited perspectives. The feasible steps to reinforce credibility without the infusion of dramatically increased resources are largely self-evident. *Ad hoc* bodies should avoid appointing fact-finders who have prejudged the human rights situation or who lack receptivity to contrary data; the same is true of NGOs composing human rights missions and treaty bodies devolving focused fact-finding tasks upon their members. Candor concerning sources of information is vital to insure that biases are exposed and the factual information weighed accordingly, so long as disclosure of informants does not threaten their physical security. Opportunities for states to contest allegations of human rights violations should be provided, subject to the same proviso.

---

[97] *Supra*, note 94 at para. 21.
[98] *Report of the Committee on the Elimination of Discrimination Against Women*, A/53/38/Rev.1 (1998), Decision 18/III.

Truly rigorous human rights fact-finding is at this point beyond the scope of resources available to human rights IGOs. It would require an on-going field presence or access to a constant stream of detailed factual data, organized, easily accessible and subject to strict verification for accuracy. It would require changing the composition of the bodies to insure rigorous objectivity and high levels of empirical as well as legal expertise. Until this vision becomes feasible, interim steps to increase the efficiency of the existing regime may advance the fact-finding endeavor to a modest extent.

(4) Greater efficiency and reliability through collaboration

Human rights fact-finding will never be consolidated into a single, unified whole following uniform protocols for data gathering. Nevertheless, it is regrettable that with such modest resources devoted to human rights fact-finding, reasonable steps toward collaboration are not taken, where these would promote efficiency and amplify the impact of available information. The time is ripe for substantial alteration of the fact-finding techniques of the UN treaty bodies.

(a) UN steps toward information-sharing

In recognition of the proliferation of its treaty-based and political human rights fact-finding bodies, the UN has begun to promote collaboration among its IGO elements and integration of NGOs into the fact-finding process. While still in their infancy, these steps are promising and should be embraced with enthusiasm. More ambitious proposals have been made to establish centralized country databases or to consolidate the treaty bodies into a single organ.

An important collaborative step was taken when the chairs of the six UN treaty bodies instituted a series of annual meetings to explore common procedural difficulties and prospects for information sharing. These meetings were followed by similar gatherings of rapporteurs and working group chairs appointed by the UN political bodies. The interchange between the political and treaty-based fact-finding components of the UN has also been advanced by attendance of the chairs of the treaty bodies at the similar group session of rapporteurs, and also to have meetings of the chairs of the treaty bodies concurrent with the meeting of all rapporteurs.

The meetings of treaty body chairs address, among other things, non-procedural issues. For example, one session was devoted to the need to incorporate a gender perspective into the work of all the committees. In December 1996, a separate meeting was conducted on the topic of reproductive health rights, attended by two members of each treaty body, and representatives of UN units, specialized agencies and NGOs, as well as independent experts. Such thematic sessions improve the fact-finding capabilities of the treaty bodies, not by supplying them with empirical data of immediate relevance to their next round of report reviews or to their disposition of pending individual cases, but by sensitizing them to issues which they might not otherwise explore. The sessions tend to focus on clarification of substantive norms, against a background of general data on state practice. Similar thematic sessions have been held by single treaty bodies, such as the Child Committee and the Economic, Social and Cultural

Rights Committee, to deepen the understanding of committee members concerning specific human rights.

Where the focus of a treaty body is relatively specialized, its close collaboration with a special rapporteur in the same field is obviously desirable. CAT, for example, relies upon information provided by the Special Rapporteur on Torture. However, CEDAW has expressed concern that resource limits and inadequate planning have impeded its collaboration with the Special Rapporteur on Violence Against Women.[99] The Chair of CERD voiced chagrin that a Special Rapporteur on Contemporary Forms of Racism, Racial Discrimination, Xenophobia and Related Intolerance was appointed by the UN Commission without any consultation on how that person would interact with CERD.[100] Treaty bodies such as the Human Rights Committee have a much more difficult task to develop close links with the numerous country and thematic rapporteurs and working groups producing information on matters relating to compliance with the CCPR. While the published reports of these non-treaty mechanisms are of obvious value to the Human Rights Committee, direct interaction is likely to be episodic at best.

The inability of the treaty bodies to launch on-site fact-finding missions can contribute to an appearance of remoteness or irrelevance. Because treaty body members have only a limited amount of time to devote to their committee work and because resources for conducting on-site visits as a matter of course are unlikely to materialize, the best means to bring the UN treaty bodies into the arena of on-site visits is through joint participation in fact-finding missions conducted by UN *ad hoc* mechanisms. This participation could be organized according to the schedule of report reviews or through an assessment of particularly pressing needs for first-hand verification of contested factual matters, either regarding the broad human rights situation or the specifics of an especially significant incident.

While the UN human rights conventions have long empowered the treaty bodies to receive information from the specialized agencies, links have often been minimal or non-existent. Following the lead of the Child Committee, which has established significant connections with UNICEF and other agencies pursuant to article 45 of the CRC, other treaty bodies are seeking to establish much closer relationships with specialized agencies. This impulse stems in part from a desire to enrich the committees' access to objective factual data on states scheduled for review. CEDAW has appointed individual members to serve as focal points for various specialized agencies, and is exploring means to enhance these links by framing particularized requests for information.[101] The Human Rights Committee and the Economic, Social and Cultural Rights Committee have taken initiatives to invite representatives of specialized agencies to attend pre-sessional meetings in order to brief them on relevant human rights conditions in states scheduled for review.[102]

The UN treaty bodies, seeking to improve the rate of submission of state

---

[99] *Report of the Committee on the Elimination of Discrimination Against Women*, A/51/38 (1996) at paras. 27, 336; *Ways and Means of Improving the Work of the Committee*, CEDAW/C/1997/5 (6 December 1996) at para. 22.
[100] *Supra*, note 53, Banton at 41–42.
[101] *Ways and Means of Improving the Work of the Committee*, CEDAW/C/1997/5 (6 December 1996) at para. 9.
[102] *Ibid.*, at para. 10.

reports, have called on states to submit "core" reports, containing basic background information to be made available to all the UN treaty bodies with review authority over the reporting state. The move toward "core" reports may be a harbinger of greater change in the UN human rights system, such as the creation of centralized country files or even the consolidation of the six treaty bodies into a single committee with specialized chambers.[103]

(b) *Closer collaboration with NGOs*

The treaty bodies have long since overcome their concerns that review of state reports must be informed solely by information supplied by the state. After years of informal contact, primarily with the major international NGOs, the treaty bodies are increasing the transparency of their interaction with NGOs. The chairs of the treaty bodies have requested the Office of the High Commissioner for Human Rights to develop a database of national and local NGOs to be alerted to the scheduled review of state reports.[104] How the various committees react to NGOs who accept this implicit invitation varies, however. CAT and CERD continue to pursue a relatively informal interaction with interested NGOs, soliciting information in advance of reviews of state reports and permitting members to make direct contact with NGO representatives outside the formal meetings of the Committee.[105] The Human Rights Committee advanced from informal contacts by members with NGOs, to informal briefings organized by NGOs to coincide with its sessions, to invitations to NGOs to attend pre-sessional working groups of the committee in order to provide data relevant to the issues pending for state reviews.[106] The Economic, Social and Cultural Rights Committee grants permission for NGO oral presentations at the opening session of its meetings. Further, the Economic, Social and Cultural Rights Committee requests the Secretariat to disseminate state reports to relevant NGOs in advance of the review session, in order to prompt their critical or supplementary response.[107] The Child Committee invites interested NGOs to contribute data to country files maintained by the Secretariat and benefits from the coordinating efforts of the NGO Group for the Convention on the Rights of the Child, which seeks to establish coalitions of children's rights groups at the national level and provides limited funding to permit attendance of national NGOs at pre-sessional working groups of the Child Committee.[108] CEDAW also benefits from information provided on state compliance by a coordinating NGO dedicated to improving its effectiveness, the International Women's Rights Action Watch (IWRAW), and also permits NGOs to interact orally with the Committee members on country-specific situations.[109]

As NGOs with knowledge of and interest in the treaty bodies' work proliferate, however, the committees risk being drowned in a flood of (often last-minute)

---

[103] Discussed briefly *infra*, section 4(c).
[104] *Supra*, note 101 at para. 29.
[105] *Supra*, note 101 at paras. 34–35. CERD has the advantage of contact with the Anti-Racism Information Service (ARIS), a coordinating NGO in its field.
[106] *Supra*, note 101 at paras. 36–37.
[107] *Supra*, note 101 at para. 38.
[108] *Supra*, note 101 at paras. 39–42.
[109] *Supra*, note 101 at para. 43.

information, arranged haphazardly and impossible to verify. The treaty bodies could manage this information flow by communicating well in advance of the review the lists of issues or the topics the country rapporteur or pre-sessional working groups had selected for scrutiny at the particular session. However, rigid constraints might interfere with NGOs' ability to divert the committee's attention to emerging issues of great concern at the national level. Much more intense servicing and data management by the Secretariat is vital to maximize the benefit of this influx of factual information.

(c) A super-committee?

Organizing the overwhelming flow of factual information from IGOs, specialized agencies, NGOs, scholars and the media to enhance human rights fact-finding by the UN treaty bodies is a daunting task. The maintenance by the Secretariat of centralized databases on states is one possible step, but the need to divert resources from other tasks is a major obstacle. As Elizabeth Evatt of the Human Rights Committee has noted, highly qualified professional staff at the Secretariat, possibly assisted by interns funded from external sources, could provide the expertise to coordinate a database of this type, though state receptivity to this exposure of their human rights practices is unlikely to be uniformly enthusiastic.[110]

A more radical proposal is to centralize the implementation process in a single UN treaty body, possibly with specialized chambers. This would achieve efficiencies both for states, which would have a single recipient for compliance reports, and for the UN system, which would have a single body to service.[111] To maintain or increase the intensity of coverage, however, the members of this body should be salaried rather than "spare-timers." To prevent the loss of normative expertise and sensitivity to diverse perspectives on human rights, its membership must be selected with careful attention to non-"mainstream" human rights concerns.

(5) Conclusion

Fact-finding by the UN human rights treaty bodies follows many of the patterns outlined in this paper. Only three of the six treaty bodies have authority to adjudicate individual complaints, and only where the ratifying state has opted to accept such competence. A fourth (CEDAW), will have such authority when its Optional Protocol comes into force. The Human Rights Committee, CERD and CAT adopt rather relaxed quasi-judicial methods in handling individual communications.[112] Resource limits prevent thorough investigation of complaints (for example, through on-site visits). Judgment is reached after a review of the written submissions by the applicant and the respondent state, without oral hearings or cross-examination. In many cases, the "respondent" is silent or

---

[110] Elizabeth Evatt, "Ensuring effective supervisory procedures: The need for resources", in *The Future of UN Human Rights Treaty Monitoring*, Philip Alston and James Crawford (eds.), Cambridge University Press, 2000, 461 at 465–466.
[111] *Supra*, note 96 at para. 94.
[112] CEDAW is still at the first stages of developing procedures.

replies with unilluminating categorical denials. The treaty bodies are sometimes forced to rely upon rather underdeveloped evidentiary presumptions in order to determine their views. While each body has the capacity to draft its own rules of procedure, these rules tend not to address sophisticated evidentiary questions. To adopt stricter, quasi-criminal standards such as those employed by the *ad hoc* international tribunals does not appear advisable at the present, given resource constraints and the high rate of government non-cooperation.

CAT's inquiries under article 20 are promising. CAT transparently relies upon NGO evidence and information provided by the Special Rapporteur on Torture. In the Turkish case, a substantial on-site visit yielded important corroborating evidence. Non-cooperation by Egypt forced CAT to rely upon information that could not be verified to the same extent, but CAT appropriately placed the onus on the state by adopting reasonable evidentiary presumptions. CAT wisely decided to publish summaries of these two inquiries, placing pressure on future respondents not only to cooperate at the investigatory stage but to implement suggested reforms in a sincere manner.

Inter-state complaints concerning human rights treaty compliance by other members have never been brought under any of the UN treaties. As a result, the UN treaty bodies, unlike the human rights treaty organs of the Council of Europe, have not been required to experiment with fact-finding techniques suitable to such broad-ranging adversarial proceedings.

State reporting remains the primary device to assess compliance with human rights treaty obligations, although it is a deeply flawed means to assess human rights facts. The primary source of information is self-interested, and non-compliance with reporting obligations is rampant. The optimistic aspect of this picture is the increasing flow of information from NGOs, specialized agencies and *ad hoc* country and thematic mechanisms, as the treaty bodies take substantial steps to forge closer links with these crucial sources. Though several treaty bodies have sent delegates to the field, these travels have not been actual on-site fact-finding missions. CERD has very occasionally deployed members as a crisis response; the Child Committee has organized informal meetings in various regions, which may enhance fact-finding in the long term. The Human Rights Committee has launched a rather weakly funded initiative, with limited scope, to follow up certain individual communications at the remedial stage.

The less optimistic aspect of recent developments is that the new flow of information must be adequately managed in order to improve the accuracy of the treaty bodies' concluding observations and views. This requires the services of trained archivists and technological improvements. In addition, the treaty bodies must devise means to test the reliability of evidence supplied by a growing proliferation of NGOs, especially those at the national and local levels whose track record for accuracy cannot realistically be known.

Compared to other existing human rights mechanisms, the fact-finding methodology of the UN treaty bodies is relatively unsophisticated. Recent improvements and the bodies' eagerness to institute reforms are encouraging. But genuine enhancement of the system is impeded by severe resource constraints.

CHAPTER 7

The Role of a Human Rights Field Presence

Ian Martin

Traditionally, human rights fact-finding has been carried out through fact-finding visits, often pretentiously entitled missions, to the country of concern. Such visits have been made by non-governmental organizations (NGOs) working internationally or regionally, by intergovernmental organizations (IGOs), the United Nations special rapporteurs and working groups, regional human rights commissions such as the Inter-American Commission on Human Rights, and recently UN treaty bodies. They have drawn substantially on the investigations of in-country human rights NGOs.

(1) The development of human rights field operations

In recent years, the UN has established[1] substantial human rights field operations in a number of countries. The pioneering operation was in El Salvador. UN-brokered peace negotiations led to commitments by both government and armed opposition to respect human rights and to invite UN verification of their observance. In July 1991 la Mission d'observation des Nations Unies en El Salvador (ONUSAL) was established, with an international staff of 101, including 42 human rights observers. The huge UN Transitional Administration in Cambodia, established in February 1992, initially provided for 10 human rights officers (out of a total UN Transitional Authority in Cambodia (UNTAC) deployment of some 20,000); this was later increased, but the human rights component remained a small one. The Organization of American States (OAS) established a small International Civilian Mission under military rule in Haiti in September 1992; from February 1993 this was absorbed into a joint UN/OAS mission called the Mission Civil Internationale en Haiti (MICIVIH). The UN/OAS budget for MICIVIH provided for 280 international staff. At the mission's peak before its first evacuation in October 1993, it reached around 200, the largest human rights presence in any single country up to that time. The Guatemala peace negotiations led to a human rights verification mission (MINUGUA) being established there from November 1994, with an authorized

---

[1] In one case, it did so jointly with a regional organization.

strength of 245 international staff, including 10 military liaison officers and 60 civilian police observers.

These four human rights field presences had their origins in attempts to negotiate and oversee political transitions, and were part of a new generation of UN peace-operations. They were conceptualized out of the UN's political departments in New York, and in virtual isolation from its human rights mechanisms and supporting bureaucracy in Geneva. In the cases of El Salvador, Haiti and Guatemala, the UN Commission on Human Rights had already mandated special country rapporteurs, representatives or experts. They had no formal relationship with the field operations, and both field mission and special rapporteur were left to work out a relationship without any consistent guidance from the respective headquarters in Geneva and New York. Still less was any relationship with the Commission's thematic procedures or the treaty bodies given any consideration.

The advantages of a field presence were quickly apparent, however, to the Geneva human rights milieu. In July 1991, Amnesty International proposed that a UN human rights monitoring presence should be imposed on Iraq. The Special Rapporteur took this up on Iraq in his February 1992 report to the Commission on Human Rights, and although a presence in Iraq never became feasible, he was allocated staff able to travel more extensively and collect information in the region. The Special Rapporteur on the former Yugoslavia was provided with field staff based in the territory of his mandate from March 1993. It rapidly became *de rigueur* for special country rapporteurs to recommend that they be similarly supported.

By the time the proposal to create the post of UN High Commissioner for Human Rights was debated ahead of the 1993 World Conference on Human Rights, the disconnection between the New York initiatives and the Geneva-based system had been remarked upon frequently. Bridging that gulf was a major motivation. Amnesty International advanced the most detailed proposal for the post.[2]

The World Conference itself noted the exclusion of the then Centre for Human Rights[3] from the new operations in its Vienna Declaration:

> The World Conference on Human Rights, recognizing the important role of human rights components in specific arrangements concerning some peace-keeping operations by the United Nations, recommends that the Secretary-General take into account the reporting, experience and capabilities of the Centre for Human Rights and human rights mechanisms ...[4]

The first High Commissioner, José Ayala-Lasso, took up his post on 5 April 1994. The next day, the genocide began in Rwanda. He visited Rwanda, and called for a special session of the Commission on Human Rights, which mandated a special rapporteur on Rwanda and requested the High Commissioner "to make the necessary arrangements for the Special Rapporteur to be assisted by a team of human rights field officers." Initially a small team was envisaged, but

---

[2] Amnesty International, *Facing Up to the Failures: Proposals for Improving the Protection of Human Rights by the United Nations* (December 1992).
[3] Now Office of the High Commissioner for Human Rights.
[4] *Vienna Declaration and Programme of Action*, A/CONF.157/23 (1993) at para. 97.

subsequently the High Commissioner appealed for funding for a team of 21. During a second visit to Rwanda in late August, he agreed with the government that as many as 147 officers would be deployed, in order to cover each of the 147 communes of the country. The dependence of this Human Rights Field Operation in Rwanda (HRFOR) on voluntary funding (rather than the UN regular or peace-keeping budgets, from which the New York-run operations were funded), together with the lack of Geneva-based systems or experience for mounting a large field operation, resulted in deployment being painfully slow. The figure of 147 was never reached. By February 1995 there were 85 officers, and later that year the operation reached its peak of about 130 international staff.

HRFOR was the first large human rights field operation responsible to the High Commissioner in Geneva, rather than to the political or peacekeeping departments in New York. The High Commissioner became personally convinced, to the displeasure of the then Secretary-General and some member states, that the future of human rights lay in the field. In his February 1997 report to the Commission on Human Rights he declared (shortly before his resignation):

> A human rights field presence established with the consent of the authorities of the state concerned, is one of the major innovations introduced under the mandate of the High Commissioner for Human Rights in the implementation of the United Nations human rights programme. Experience has proved that the effective implementation of human rights is greatly facilitated by activities *in situ*. In some countries, the human rights presence has been established as an autonomous project, in others it is part of a broader United Nations involvement as in the case of the United Nations human rights programme for Abkhazia, Georgia. Some operations integrate assistance and monitoring functions, whereas others are mandated exclusively in the area of technical assistance. The flexibility of the human rights field presence is one of its strongest assets. In 1992 there were no human rights field activities; the High Commissioner/Centre for Human Rights now has offices in 11 countries in all regions.[5]

Meanwhile the case for the incorporation of human rights components in multi-dimensional UN peace operations was being pressed.[6] Other such operations, including UNAVEM III in Angola and UNTAES in Eastern Slavonia, had human rights officers included in their staffing. Elsewhere, the mandate for human rights monitoring was given to a regional organization: in addition to the joint OAS/UN mission in Haiti, the Organization for Security and Co-operation in Europe (OSCE) became responsible for human rights monitoring in Bosnia and Herzegovina, and assumed joint responsibility with the UN in Abkhazia (Georgia). UN human rights components worked alongside UN civilian police, not always without difficulty, in defining their respective roles

---

[5] *Report of the High Commissioner for Human Rights to the Commission on Human Rights: Building a Partnership for Human Rights*, E/CN.4/1997/98 (24 February 1997). The places were: Bosnia and Herzegovina, Croatia, Federal Republic of Yugoslavia and the former Yugoslav Republic of Macedonia (managed together as the Human Rights Field Operation in the former Yugoslavia, HRFOY); Abkhazia (Georgia), Burundi, Cambodia, Colombia, Gaza, Rwanda and Zaire.
[6] See Amnesty International, *Peace Keeping and Human Rights* (January 1994); and Alice Henkin (ed.), *Honoring Human Rights and Keeping the Peace: Lessons from El Salvador, Cambodia and Haiti*, Aspen Institute (1995).

and reconciling their organizational cultures, but with much to be gained from cooperation and joint action. In some UN operations where there were few or no human rights staff, UN civilian police components were recognized as having a major human rights role, as in Mozambique and Bosnia and Herzegovina.

Other UN agencies operating in the field have a human rights aspect to their own information collection. This has always been true of the United Nations High Commissioner for Refugees (UNHCR), whose work requires it to protect the human rights of refugees in the country of asylum, and gives it access to much information from refugees on human rights conditions in the country of flight. But the UNHCR's increasing emphasis on prevention and repatriation, and growing involvement with the internally displaced, has led it further into human rights monitoring and promotion in the country of origin. As the High Commissioner for Refugees, Sadako Ogata, has written:

> For many years, UNHCR and its operational partners waited for refugees to cross an international border before providing them with protection and assistance. The subsequent search for solutions to their plight focused primarily on the question of the refugees' physical location: whether they should repatriate to their homeland, integrate in the society where they had found asylum, or move on to a third country and settle down there. The limitations of these traditional solutions, coupled with the growing scale of the refugee problem and the changing nature of the international political and economic order, have prompted UNHCR to develop a new approach to the question of human displacement. This approach is proactive and preventive, rather than reactive. Instead of focusing purely on countries of asylum, it is equally concerned with conditions in actual and potential refugee-producing states. And as well as providing protection and assistance to refugees, it seeks to reinforce the security and freedom enjoyed by several other groups: internally displaced people; refugees who have returned to their own country; war-affected communities and those who are at risk of being uprooted.[7]

Thus in Tajikistan, the UNHCR mounted what was in effect a human rights field operation to monitor and intervene on behalf of returnees.

Since the Convention on the Rights of the Child (CRC)[8] came into force in 1990, the United Nations Children's Fund (UNICEF) has increasingly applied a human rights approach in its work for children. Following the creation of the UN Department of Humanitarian Affairs (now the Office of the Coordinator for Humanitarian Affairs), the designation of a UN humanitarian coordinator in a country in crisis has established a focal point for information from UN and non-governmental humanitarian agencies, including information on the human rights situation. Thus in many situations today, there are multiple UN agencies who may not have a fact-finding mandate, but whose field presence gives them access to substantial human rights information.

---

[7] Foreword by the United Nations High Commissioner for Refugees, *The State of the World's Refugees 1995*, Oxford (1995).
[8] Convention on the Rights of the Child, 1577 UNTS 3 (in force 2 September 1990).

(2) Limitations and opportunities of human rights field operations

A large in-country human rights field presence will only ever be the product of exceptional circumstances. It will not be brought into existence by the pervasiveness of human rights violations *per se*, as some might wish. Since it requires the consent of the government concerned (or, in rare cases such as Cambodia and Eastern Slavonia, acceptance of a period of transitional administration by the UN), it is a feature of the involvement of the international community in an attempted political transition. This describes the cases of El Salvador, Haiti, and Guatemala, as well as Cambodia. The case of post-genocide Rwanda is a different, and fortunately unique, one. In many of today's most serious human rights situations, from Iraq to Myanmar/Burma, it is not realistic to think in terms of a human rights field presence, and the issue of fact-finding will remain one for the traditional mechanisms.

Where, however, a human rights field presence is established, the opportunities for fact-finding are of a new order. The terms of reference of such missions have, in the best cases, included the right to receive communications from anyone and interview people freely and privately, the right to visit any place or establishment (including places of detention) freely and without prior notice, and a guarantee by the authorities of the security not only of the mission's own personnel but also of those who may have provided it with information.[9] Thus the right of access is far-reaching, and with this is coupled the personnel resources to exercise that access widely and repeatedly, from decentralized offices as well as in the capital. Difficulties in creating trust between NGOs and an international organization whose broader political role may be suspected, mean that some human rights information may be communicated to NGOs outside the country rather than to the UN presence within it. But with well-chosen direction and personnel, a substantial in-country presence should have information regarding the human rights situation unrivaled in its detail.

(3) Fact-finding within human rights field operations

It must be understood, however, that the objective of human rights field operations is not fact-finding alone. Fact-finding by NGOs, thematic mechanisms, country rapporteurs or treaty bodies is part of a process, which seeks to bring pressure to bear primarily by public reporting. The opportunity for in-country engagement to influence the human rights performance of authorities is at best an infrequent one. The potential positive influence of a continuous in-country presence is fourfold: dissuasion, intervention, assistance and reporting.

---

[9] The San José Agreement establishing the human rights verification mandate and powers of ONUSAL in El Salvador, and the terms of reference of the International Civilian Mission in Haiti (MICIVIH), are conveniently published in Alice Henkin (ed.), *Honoring Human Rights and Keeping the Peace: Lessons from El Salvador, Cambodia and Haiti*, Aspen Institute (1995). The Comprehensive Agreement on Human Rights which is the basis of verification by MINUGUA in Guatemala is in UN document A/48/928, S/1994/448 (19 April 1994). The agreement between the High Commissioner for Human Rights and the Government of Rwanda regarding HRFOR has not been published, but is summarized in Ian Martin, "After Genocide: The UN Human Rights Field Operation in Rwanda", in *Honoring Human Rights: From Peace to Justice*, Alice Henkin (ed.), Aspen Institute (1998).

The presence of human rights officers, especially in the localities, and the relationship they can develop with both the authorities and the local population, can have a dissuasive effect which prevents some violations of human rights. The same presence can permit prompt intervention when violations occur. The most sophisticated urgent action mechanisms of special rapporteurs and international NGOs do not compare with the ability of human rights officers to present themselves at a detention centre where detainees are being tortured. Personal representations can be more powerful than written ones.

Most human rights field operations have a mixed mandate, covering both monitoring/verification and technical cooperation/assistance. In most circumstances, these roles are indeed best pursued as part of an integrated mandate. An exception was the first phase of MICIVIH in Haiti, where it was inappropriate for technical cooperation to commence under an illegitimate military regime. In an integrated operation, the monitoring identifies needs for training and resources, the technical cooperation ensures that those needs can be addressed, and the monitoring again provides feedback on the effectiveness of technical cooperation projects in improving aspects of the human rights situation to which they are directed. Certainly in a situation where institutions have been destroyed or have never existed, such as post-genocide Rwanda, to point to human rights violations while offering no linkage to assistance is to invite dismissal, and to pursue technical cooperation while ignoring serious on-going violations is naive and unacceptable.

Wherever the UN has a human rights presence with a monitoring/verification mandate, there needs to be clear arrangements, understood by the government concerned, for public reporting. As a matter of good human rights practice, such arrangements should always include the prior submission of reports to the government for discussion and response within a reasonable time-frame. Operations mandated by the Security Council or the General Assembly have had their reports made public, but not always as promptly or frequently as would have been desirable. Operations undertaken by the High Commissioner have not had their reports published as formal UN documents, although their information has been made public or semi-public in other ways. Their reporting has been partly inhibited by mandates implying that the public reporting based on their fact-finding is the responsibility of the special country rapporteurs. If field operations and special country rapporteurs are to report on the same country, a policy should be established regarding the relationship between the reports of each, especially where a field office of the High Commissioner is explicitly mandated to support the special rapporteur and thus to be his/her main source of information. No one – including NGOs pressing for more public reporting by UN operations – has yet grasped this nettle, which may call into question whether there should continue to be a special rapporteur on a country where there is a substantial human rights field operation.

(4) The nature and quality of fact-finding by human rights field operations

The objective of a human rights field presence is ultimately to ensure that national institutions have both the will and the capacity to address human rights violations, not to displace or duplicate that role. The nature of the investigations carried out by such operations will depend on the extent to which this will and this capacity exists. The investigative function will differ greatly between a context in which national institutions are extremely weak, for example Haiti, and one where the judicial system is much more capable of investigations but requires monitoring such as Guatemala. Human rights field operations are not and should not be seen as capable of quasi-judicial investigations.

Human rights field operations are a new and developing area of work, and the learning curve is steep. Initially there was a limited pool of people with human rights training and experience, plus field orientation, from which to recruit. Pre-mission and in-country training has been slow to develop. A cadre of personnel able to bring experience from one operation to another is developing, and the importance of training and field guidance is increasingly recognized.[10] Large operations will continue to rely on recruiting human rights field officers with only limited human rights experience, however, and only a small proportion of their personnel can be expected to have well-developed investigative skills. A realistic approach must be taken to the nature and extent of their fact-finding.

In a field setting, it is difficult to establish the kind of procedures for controlling possible bias and maintaining quality, which have characterized the best international NGO fact-finding. When MICIVIH was deployed in Haiti, most of its observers were politically in sympathy with the overwhelming popular support for the exiled President Aristide, and the international organizations themselves were committed to his restoration and the ousting of the military. They aspired to be objective, but not neutral. Criticisms of the Mission's findings by the United States Embassy in Port-au-Prince, whose own bias was much more obvious, discredited the Embassy more than they did the Mission. In Rwanda, objectivity was subjected to the intense challenge of awareness of the scale of the genocide, on the one hand, which tended to relativize current abuses, and on the other hand, the responsibility to monitor violations in the present which were serious by any absolute standards. Not surprisingly, conflicting perspectives sometimes divided human rights officers, as they have the external NGOs. The only answer lies in the quality of supervisory staff, a strong core of human rights professionalism, a high priority given to training and field guidance, and systems to maintain standards of objective investigation and reporting. These are far from easy to achieve in the field.

An insistence on high standards, which must weigh more heavily on a UN operation than on even the most responsible of NGOs, should not be confused with political compromise. The New York-run UN human rights field operations (and the OSCE in Bosnia and Herzegovina) have reported to senior officials with political responsibilities beyond the protection of human rights. It is important that the integrity of intervention and reporting on the human rights situation be sustained, even when this may be in tension with immediate political objectives.

---

[10] See Karen Kenny, *Towards Effective Training for Field Human Rights Tasks*, International Human Rights Trust, Dublin (1996).

(5) The relationship of human rights field operations to special procedures and treaty bodies

Little thought has been given so far – on either side of the relationship – to how human rights field operations should relate to special procedures and treaty bodies, and no system has been developed for consistently communicating the fact-finding of the former to the latter. This is primarily the responsibility of the Office of the High Commissioner for Human Rights. The Office organizationally now brings together in one Activities and Programmes Branch – and on a geographical basis – the servicing of special procedures and of the High Commissioner's field presences, but the information flow must be extended to include the treaty bodies, which are serviced by another branch.

(6) Conclusion

The deployment of numerous human rights monitors throughout a state experiencing severe human rights violations will not become "an ideal means to overcome the barriers to accurate fact-finding that have long plagued the treaty bodies, IGO *ad hoc* mechanisms, and NGOs."[11] It will occur only in exceptional circumstances, not related to the severity of human rights violations alone. And when it does occur, its objectives will rightly be wider than fact-finding alone. For a limited period its own role will far outweigh that of the treaty bodies or other mechanisms in its ability to contribute to the protection and promotion of human rights. But these are not reasons to refrain from practical measures, which could ensure that the treaty system derives the maximum contribution from these human rights field operations to its own important work.

---

[11] See *supra* Joan Fitzpatrick, Chapter 6 at 82–83.

CHAPTER 8

Fact-Finding in the Inter-American System

Douglass W. Cassel, Jr.

(1) Inter-American and United Nations human rights systems compared

Fact-finding in the individual case system of the Inter-American human rights system has a number of advantages compared to the UN human rights treaty bodies. Specifically:

- All member states of the Organization of American States (OAS) are subject to the competence of the Inter-American Commission on Human Rights to receive, investigate and report on complaints in individual cases.[1] This is despite the fact that only twenty-five of the thirty-five member states of the OAS have ratified the American Convention on Human Rights[2] and twenty-one accept the contentious jurisdiction of the Inter-American Court of Human Rights,[3]
- The Inter-American system is much better known and used by non-governmental organizations (NGOs) in most countries of the Americas than the U.N. system.
- The Inter-American system is more physically accessible to western hemisphere NGOs than most sessions of the UN treaty bodies. It is much easier and less expensive for NGOs to travel to Washington, the seat of the Inter-American Commission, than to go to Geneva. There are also extensive linkages between NGOs throughout the hemisphere and those Washington-based NGOs that specialize in litigation before the Inter-American Commission.

---

[1] Statute of the Inter-American Commission on Human Rights, adopted by the OAS General Assembly by Res. 447 (October 1979), arts. 19(a) and 20(b).
[2] American Convention on Human Rights, PAUTS 36 (in force 18 July 1978). Status of ratifications is at 1 January 2000. Trinidad and Tobago, formerly a party to the Convention, withdrew effective 1999. See Douglass Cassel, "Peru Withdraws from the Court: Will the Inter-American Human Rights System Meet the Challenge?", 20 *Human Rights Law Journal* (1999) 167 at 168, 170 (1999).
[3] As at 1 January 2000. Status of ratifications and acceptance of jurisdiction of the Court is available at www.cidh.oas.org/basic.htm. In 1999 Peru purported to withdraw from the contentious jurisdiction of the Court. See generally: *ibid*. However, the Court held Peru's withdrawal ineffective. *Ivor Bronstein Case*, Jurisdiction, Judgment of 24 September 1999; *Constitutional Court Case*, Jurisdiction, Judgment of 24 September 1999; for texts of two cases, see Court's Annual Report when issued on: www.oas.org.

- Whereas UN treaty body complaint proceedings are essentially paper battles, the Inter-American Commission conducts oral hearings. While they are not full trial-type proceedings, it has been possible for a victim to appear before the Commission to give testimony and to physically demonstrate his wounds to the assembled Commissioners.[4] Such direct and visible testimony can have more of an impact on the decision-makers than a piece of paper.
- Despite the financial constraints on the Inter-American Commission and Court, the UN treaty bodies are in even worse budgetary shape. The Inter-American Commission has a dozen or so full-time staff attorneys plus visiting fellows. None of the UN bodies has this staff complement.
- There is much better dissemination of the reports of the Inter-American Commission, both in individual cases and otherwise, to NGOs in the Americas. There remains, however, much room for improvement by both the OAS and the UN. At the same time, the home pages on the Internet of both organizations have already improved dissemination dramatically.
- Finally, the Inter-American Commission makes a more intentional, sophisticated and successful use of the press than do the UN treaty bodies with respect to human rights in the Americas. For example, at the June 1997 OAS General Assembly in Peru, the Inter-American Commission held a press conference and received good coverage of its criticisms of President Fujimori's dismissal of several judges of Peru's constitutional court.

(2) Limitations on fact-finding in the Inter-American system

In theory, all a petitioner in the Inter-American Human Rights system need do is file a complaint of a violation with the Inter-American Commission on Human Rights;[5] the system will do the rest. Thus, the American Convention empowers the Commission to "examine the matter ... in order to verify the facts. If necessary and advisable, the Commission shall carry out an investigation, for the effective conduct of which it shall request, and the states concerned shall furnish to it, all necessary facilities."[6]

In reality, complainants before the Inter-American Commission are well-advised, if they can, to file a fully documented case, including sworn statements of witnesses and available documents and photographs. They should never count on the Commission to investigate or otherwise document the facts adequately on its own.

There are five main reasons for this difference between legal theory and practice:

- The Inter-American Commission generally lacks sufficient financial and human resources to conduct field investigations, that is, to go out and interview witnesses.
- Even if the Commission could do on-site investigations, it would need the

---

[4] *Carlos Ranferí Gómez v. Guatemala*, (11.303) Report 29/96, *supra* note 1 at para. 24.
[5] American Convention on Human Rights, art. 44.
[6] American Convention on Human Rights, art. 48(1)(d).

consent of states to set foot on their territory,[7] a license which states have often felt free to deny.
- Although without visiting the states concerned the Inter-American Commission "may request [them] to furnish any pertinent information ...,"[8] states have frequently refused both to supply requested information and even to participate in proceedings before the Commission. During the ten years of Commission Annual Reports from 1985–87 through 1995–96, states failed to participate in 122 of the 218 published cases, in other words, more than half.[9] Fortunately, the extent of defaults by states in their procedural obligations under the American Convention has dramatically declined. In the last five years of this period, state participation in published cases improved greatly to 80%. By the late 1990's, state participation reached nearly 100%. Still, experience shows that a state's formal participation in a case does not necessarily mean its readiness to supply information forthrightly.
- In an adversarial system resolution of disputed issues of fact would require confrontation and cross-examination. But the Inter-American Commission's lack of resources generally precludes it from holding any semblance of a trial, even if a state participates in such a case. More typically, the complainant, or at best one or two witnesses, may be allowed a few minutes to address the Commission. They answer questions not from opposing counsel but from the Commissioners. The Inter-American Commission has a budget that enables it to meet only three to four times a year, for at most three weeks per session, and scores of complainants request hearings. Hence, it simply cannot afford to conduct trial-type proceedings in most cases.
- Until the mid-1990's, even when adequate evidence was placed in the record to craft meticulous findings of fact, the Inter-American Commission neglected to do so. Its practices were aggravated by states' refusal to cooperate, by lack of resources to investigate, by political influence in the selection of its staff, and by its overburdened workload. This often led the Commission to less than fastidious habits in making findings of fact. Again, fortunately, in recent years the Inter-American Commission has been more lawyer-like in marshalling and analyzing the evidence of record.

In sum, fact-finding by the Commission has often been a contradiction in terms. Until the early 1990's, often the best it could do and the most a complainant could hope for, was a default judgement, by which the Commission "presumed" the denounced facts to be true, for want of opposition by the state.[10]

This was the state of affairs in 1986 when the Inter-American Court of Human Rights received its first contested cases, the *Honduras Disappearance Cases*, referred by the Commission. The Commission's presumption of the facts had been based on a procedural default by Honduras. This lacked the persuasive value and moral and judicial weight essential to inaugurate the Court's

---

[7] Art. 18(g) of the Commission's Statute (*supra* note 1) authorizes it "to conduct on-site observations in a state, with the consent or at the invitation of the government in question..."
[8] American Convention on Human Rights, art. 48(1)(e).
[9] Tabulation on file with author.
[10] Art. 42 of the Regulations of the Inter-American Commission on Human Rights, approved by the Commission on 8 April 1980, and as further amended, provides that the denounced facts "shall be presumed to be true if, during the maximum period... the government has not provided the requested information, as long as other evidence does not lead to a different conclusion."

contentious jurisdiction, let alone for an innovative and landmark ruling on disappearances. The Court, therefore, wisely conducted a trial *de novo*.

This it may do with wide discretion under its regulations. The regulations permit the Inter-American Court "to obtain evidence which it considers likely to clarify the facts of the case," to request the parties to provide evidence, to designate persons or offices to obtain information, express opinions or make reports, and to designate one or more of its members to conduct an inquiry.[11] In various cases the Court has availed itself of all these approaches.

The Inter-American Court thus acts more as a trial court than as an appellate tribunal. While understandable, in light of the constraints on the Inter-American Commission described above, this role has greatly reduced the Court's efficiency and output. Because of the time required to try each case, and the fact that the Court, too, has the resources for only a few brief sessions per year, cases before the Inter-American Court take years to complete. Few are decided, leading the Inter-American Commission to ration the cases it sends to the Court, and limiting the capacity of the system to redress many serious violations of human rights.

This situation cannot continue. The Inter-American Commission has repeatedly and unsuccessfully asked the Inter-American Court to accept its findings, at least presumptively. To date the Court has consistently rebuffed these requests. However, as the Court's caseload and backlog grow, and the Commission's fact-finding capacity improves due to increased state cooperation and a more juridical approach, pressures are mounting to reduce the Court's role in fact-finding.

These pressures have been made explicit during the evaluation of the effectiveness of the system conducted by direction of the OAS General Assembly. In a November 1996 working document, the OAS General Secretariat proposed, in the interest of reducing fact-finding "duplication," that the Inter-American Court not replicate the Commission's fact-finding, and instead accord Commission's findings greater deference.[12] The problem, as acknowledged by the working paper, is that Inter-American Commission fact-finding "will have to be rigorous and exhaustive if it is to be useful to the Court ... [T]his will demand additional time and resources of the [C]ommission."[13] However, even if the Commission somehow manages to reduce substantially its backlog of hundreds of cases, the Commission is unlikely to secure the resources required to conduct proper investigations and trials of very many cases each year.

What is required is some combination of increased resources, more efficient case management, greater adversary participation and evidentiary contributions by both parties before the Commission (when feasible for the petitioner), in addition to summary judgement "on the papers" where facts emerge clearly and credibly. Whatever solution emerges will benefit from the Inter-American Court's observation in the *Honduras Disappearance Cases* that the Inter-American human rights system need not meet the same evidentiary standards as criminal courts. Neither the Inter-American Commission nor Court convicts anyone of a crime, nor can either body imprison anyone. At most, the Inter-American

---

[11] Rules of Procedure of the Inter-American Court of Human Rights, art. 34 (1)-(4).
[12] OAS General Secretariat, *Towards a New Vision of the Inter-American System*, OEA/Ser.G., CP/doc.2828/96 (26 November 1996) at 9–10.
[13] *Ibid.*, at 10.

Commission can recommend and the Court can adjudge a state responsible for a violation and liable to pay damages to the victim. Accordingly, a lesser standard of proof, which can be met without full-blown trials, should suffice. Of course, in all events the Commission will have to continue its recent practice of carefully articulating and explaining its findings of fact, so that they are susceptible of reasoned review by the Court.

In short, the system must evolve. Its current fact-finding procedures and division of labour, appropriate for an earlier time, are no longer productive enough to meet the demands of a new era in which more well-prepared cases are being filed, and the emphasis of the system has shifted from situations of massive violations to individual cases.

(3) Truth commissions[14]

The purpose, mandate and methodology of truth commissions vary widely.[15] In general, however, they confront two principal constraints on their ability to conduct fact-finding while being fair to individuals implicated in their investigations: necessarily brief life spans and the need for confidentiality of witnesses.

(a) Duration of investigations

Most commissions have a short lease on life. They are generally given from six to nine months, and few more than a year,[16] although the South African model is of longer duration.[17] Short durations are likely inevitable. Following protracted conflicts, there tends to be a collective mood to deal with the past and then to move on. Once peace agreements are signed, there is a window of opportunity of heightened international interest – and hence financial and diplomatic support – for truth commissions. There is also greater good will by the parties to comply with their commitments, including their agreements to cooperate with truth commissions. If too much time passes after the peace, the public becomes impatient, the international community may lose interest, and compliance by the parties becomes less certain.

(b) Witness confidentiality

The other principal constraint affecting possibilities for due process in truth commission fact-finding is the situation of insecurity, real and perceived, prevalent in transnational regimes. Witnesses may fear to come forward, often for

---

[14] See generally: UN Commission on the Truth for El Salvador, *From Madness to Hope: The 12-Year War in El Salvador, Report of the U.N. Commission on the Truth for El Salvador*, S/25500 (1 April 1993); Thomas Buergenthal, "The United Nations Truth Commission for El Salvador", 27 *Vanderbilt Journal of Transnational Law* (1994) 497; and Douglass W. Cassel, Jr., "International Truth Commissions and Justice", 5 *Aspen Institute Quarterly* (1993) 77. The Buergenthal and Cassel articles are excerpted in *Transnational Justice: How Emerging Democracies Reckon with Former Regimes*, Neil J. Kritz (ed.), U.S. Inst. Of Peace Press (1995), vol.1 at 292 and 326, respectively.

[15] See generally: Priscilla B. Hayner, "Fifteen Truth Commissions – 1974 to 1994: A Comparative Study", 16 *Human Rights Quarterly* (1994) 597; Human Rights Program, Harvard Law School and World Peace Foundation, *Truth Commissions: A Comparative Assessment* (1996).

[16] *Ibid.*, Hayner at 640–41.

[17] See generally: Peter Parker, "The Politics of Indemnities, Truth Telling and Reconciliation in South Africa: Ending Apartheid Without Forgetting", 17 *Human Rights Law Journal* (1996) 1.

good reason. The rule of law has most likely not yet taken hold in the state. Courts and security forces may be perceived by fearful citizens more as threats than as sources of protection. The truth commission in all likelihood has no power to provide physical security for witnesses. In consequence, key attributes of normal judicial due process – including public hearings and opportunities for accused to confront the witnesses against them – may be impractical. Important witnesses must be promised anonymity and absolute confidentiality of their testimony, or they will simply refuse to testify, and the truth commission will be stymied in its pursuit of truth.[18]

Both constraints applied in the case of El Salvador. The Commission was given only six months (later effectively extended to eight months) to investigate cases of violence arising during 12 years of war.[19] And conditions in El Salvador "forced the Commission to gather its most valuable information in exchange for assurances of confidentiality."[20] The Truth Commission found in the case of El Salvador:

> It was not just that the Parties authorized the Commission, in the peace agreements, to act on a confidential basis and to receive information in private; the reality of the situation in El Salvador forced it to do so for two reasons: first, to protect the lives of witnesses and, secondly, to obtain information from witnesses who, because of the climate of terror in which they continue to live, would not have provided such information if the Commission had not guaranteed them absolute confidentiality.
>
> ...
>
> The Commission can itself testify to the extreme fear of reprisals frequently expressed, both verbally and through their behaviour, by many witnesses it interviewed. It is also important to emphasize that the Commission was not in a position to offer any significant protection to witnesses apart from this guarantee of confidentiality. Unlike the national courts, for example, the Commission did not have the authority to order precautionary measures; neither, of course, did it have police powers. Besides, it is the perception of

---

[18] Thomas M. Franck, "Current Development: The Belgrade Minimal Rules of Procedure for International Human Rights Fact-Finding Missions", 75 *American Journal of International Law* (1981) 163 at 163–164. The Belgrade Rules, developed by a special subcommittee of the International Law Association for non-governmental organizations, providing in pertinent part as follows:

   15. The fact finding mission shall in advance require the state concerned to provide adequate guarantee of non-retaliation against individual petitioners, witnesses and other relatives.

   16. In case a guarantee... is provided to the satisfaction of the fact finding mission, the latter should, on hearing witnesses, either provide an opportunity for the state concerned to be present and to question witnesses, or make available to the state concerned a record of the witnesses' testimony for comment.

   17. The fact finding mission may withhold information which, in its judgement, may jeopardize the safety or well-being of those giving testimony, or of third parties, or which in its opinion is likely to reveal sources.

   ...

   25. The Organization establishing the fact finding mission should keep under review the compliance of states with their undertaking regarding non-reprisal against petitioners, witnesses, their relatives and associates.

[19] U.N. Commission on the Truth for El Salvador, *From Madness to Hope: The 12-Year War in El Salvador, Report of the U.N. Commission on the Truth for El Salvador*, S/25500 (1 April 1993) at 12.

[20] *Ibid.*, at 23.

the public at large that the Salvadoran judicial system is unable to offer the necessary guarantees.[21]

While this relates to post-war conditions in El Salvador, similar statements could equally be made in regard to Guatemala, Haiti and many other countries. Such realities merit emphasis because, in such cases, they mean that truth commission fact-finding simply cannot be conducted in accordance with the normal due process requirements of public trial and opportunity to confront witnesses. If the truth is to be had, another way must be found.

It is not enough that identities and testimony of witnesses, once given to investigators, be kept confidential. The initial fact-finding must itself be such that it does not reveal or even suggest their identities. This lesson has been illustrated in Rwanda, where investigators for the International Criminal Court for Rwanda made the literally fatal mistake of parking their oversized vehicles, with distinctive licence plates, in front of the homes of persons they interviewed. Subsequent elaborate precautions to provide such witnesses secret routes to the Tribunal and to conceal their identities at trial were nullified by these prior give-aways. As a result, witnesses were killed.[22] Of course, much depends on whether the investigation is intended to name names, as it was in El Salvador and in the case of the Rwanda Tribunal. In such cases, for obvious reasons, retaliation by persons named by witnesses is far more likely.

A related factor is whether the witnesses are persons capable or feared to be capable of identifying perpetrators. The Salvador commission, for example, received thousands of testimonies of survivors, not all of them confidentially, who could relate the killings of their family members, but not the identities of the perpetrators. Hence the comment in the Truth Commission Report that the Commission's "most valuable information" came in exchange for promises of confidentiality.[23] Such information typically came from persons who knew the identities of the killers as well as those who gave orders, and the details of the operations. Such persons are the very ones most in need of confidentiality. In other words, the mother whose son was killed by unidentified passing soldiers may have no fear of telling all she knows. On the other hand, the junior officer at military headquarters, who actually heard the order given to commit a massacre, will almost certainly speak to the commission only in safe locations and in return for ironclad and credible assurances of confidentiality.

In short, if the purpose of the investigation includes the naming of perpetrators, then the confidentiality of key witnesses, including insiders, is indispensable. In contrast, if the investigation seeks only to identify victims or to describe broad patterns of conduct, confidentiality is less important; the testimony of the bereaved mother, which puts no perpetrator in fear of exposure, may suffice for most (if not all) purposes.

(c) Credibility of fact-finding

A truth commission has no army and, generally, no judicial powers. Its most important asset is its credibility. In part, credibility may be established by

---

[21] *Supra*, note 19 at 23–24.
[22] For example, Chris McGreal, "Witnesses Afraid to Speak", *The Guardian* (21 January, 1997) at 12; Alan Zarembo, "Rwanda's Genocide Witnesses are Killed as Wheels of Justice Slowly Begin Turning", *Christian Science Monitor* (23 January 1997) at 7.
[23] *Supra*, note 19 at 23.

judicious selection of commission members and staff. Ultimately, however, credibility depends on whether the commission's conclusions can withstand public scrutiny. If one significant finding is shown to be erroneous, the credibility of the commission's entire report, especially if it rests largely on confidential sources, is at risk.

This risk is compounded by the fact that the commission's report will be scrutinized not only by the public, but by the perpetrators. They have not only a strong motive to look for errors, but unparalleled capacity as well. After all, they were there; they know what happened. If the commission gets it wrong, they will know, and look for a way to leak contrary information, so long as it is not inculpatory.

The Salvador Commission was well aware of these risks. Consequently, it adopted a very conservative – call it prudent – approach to fact-finding. As one of the editors of its report, I recall the agony of excising long portions of draft chapters, which proposed plausible and reasonable conclusions on important issues of fact (such as the sponsors of certain death squads) for lack of sufficient corroboration; a single source, however good, was simply not enough under our rules. These excisions brought howls of protest from staff investigators who had worked hard to develop this information, but we could not afford to jeopardize the entire report by taking a risk. Clear, internal guidance and training must be provided to investigators concerning the basic rules of evidence to be applied by a truth commission. Our experience on the Salvadoran commission was that while the international investigators (deliberately, none were Salvadorans) were talented and dedicated, one could not assume their familiarity with evidentiary concepts such as the distinction between hearsay and direct evidence.

The Commission attempted to add a degree of rigour to its findings of fact by specifying three separate levels of confidence in the evidence:

1. Overwhelming evidence – conclusive or highly convincing evidence to support the Commission's finding;
2. Substantial evidence – very solid evidence to support the Commission's finding;
3. Sufficient evidence – more evidence to support the Commission's finding than to contradict it.[24]

If there was less than sufficient evidence (that is, less than a preponderance), the Commission would not make a finding on any issue of fact. Moreover, for all findings, the Commission required at least two independent, corroborating sources, of which at least one must be a primary rather than a secondary source, that is, must be a source with first-hand, specific, credible information.[25]

(d) Need for adequate resources

Truth commissions should not be attempted "on the cheap". Human rights investigations for the purpose of establishing the truth about controversial and important cases demand an intensive investment of human resources over a

---

[24] *Supra*, note 19 at 24.
[25] *Supra*, note 19 at 24. Thus, applying its degree of confidence in the Jesuits murder case, for example, the Commission found "substantial evidence" that in Colonel Rene Emilio Ponce ordered the assassination of Jesuit priest Father Ignacio Ellacuria; "sufficient evidence" that General Gilberto Rubio

period of at least months, and all the more when multiple investigations are attempted simultaneously. Official sources of the government involved are reluctant if not obstructionist. In countries like El Salvador, witnesses are fearful. Even with the best of cooperation, cases years old can be difficult to crack. Often many leads must be pursued, and returned to more than once, in order to yield precious nuggets of evidence. If solid proof is required – as it must be especially if names are to be named – prolonged work by capable investigators, with careful legal and managerial supervision, is indispensable. There will also be significant travel expense if the commission is international. All this, of course, is expensive. Without the 2.5 million dollars raised to staff, equip and support the Truth Commission for El Salvador, it could not have fielded the investigative effort required to pursue more than thirty major cases, while also receiving thousands of complaints.[26] Some commissions have been attempted "on the cheap" – Haiti, for example. The result in that case is difficult to appraise since the Haitian report appears to have been left to collect dust on a shelf without being made public. Other things being equal, you get what you pay for.[27]

(e) Fairness to the accused

If a truth commission has judicial powers, practical considerations relating to witness fears should not excuse it from meeting basic international standards of due process.[28] While the International Criminal Tribunal for the Former Yugoslavia, for example, has developed controversial procedures designed to protect witnesses, ultimately it would be troubling to deny the accused in a criminal case the opportunity to confront and cross-examine accusing witnesses.[29]

Most commissions, however, have no judicial powers. The Salvador Commission, for example, was empowered to find facts and to make recommendations, not to render legal judgments on whether particular individuals committed particular crimes. Its finding that a particular individual ordered a killing, for example, does not mean that as a matter of law, the individual was guilty of a crime; a defence of coercion, for instance, might be raised if the case were brought before a court of law.

As the Commission explained:

Rubio took steps to conceal the truth; and "full evidence" (that is, overwhelming evidence) that Colonel Guillermo Alfredo Benavides informed officers at the Military College that the order had been given: *supra* note 19 at 53.

[26] *Supra*, note 14, Cassel at 88–89.

[27] Belgrade Rules, Rule 10: "Fact finding missions should operate with staff sufficient to permit the independent collection of data and should be assisted by such independent experts as the mission may deem necessary": *supra* note 18 at 164. The South African model, of course, with hundreds of public hearings and thousands of applications for amnesty which must be decided, in addition to reporting on the truth of what happened under Apartheid, would appear to cost considerably in excess of the 2.5 million dollars spent in El Salvador.

[28] But see *Kostovski v. The Netherlands*, Series A, Volume 166 (20 November 1989) at 3.

[29] For a debate over a Yugoslav Tribunal panel's divided vote on indefinitely withholding the identities of victims and witnesses from the accused, see Monroe Leigh, "The Yugoslav Tribunal: use of Unnamed Witnesses Against the Accused", 90 *American Journal of International Law* (1996) 235; Christine M. Chinkin, "Due Process and Witness Anonymity", 91 *American Journal of International Law* (1997) 75; and Monroe Leigh, "Witness Anonymity is Inconsistent with Due Process", 91

In weighing aspects related to the need to protect the lives of witnesses against the interests of people who might be adversely affected in some way by the publication of their names in the report, the Commission also took into consideration the fact that the report is not a judicial or quasi judicial determination as to the rights or obligations of certain individuals under the law. As a result, the Commission is not, in theory, subject to the requirements of due process which normally apply, in proceedings which produce these consequences.[30]

Still, the Commission was not insensitive to the rights of those persons potentially to be named in its report as having ordered or committed certain acts of violence. Each was afforded the opportunity to explain his or her version of the events in question to the Commission. And the same evidentiary standards designed to preserve the credibility of the Commission also served as an additional safeguard of the rights of the person named.

On the other hand, José Zalaquett, the internationally respected member of Chile's Truth Commission, has expressed what appears to be a contrary view. In his introduction to the English translation of the Chilean report, he writes:

> To name culprits who had not defended themselves and were not obligated to do so would have been the moral equivalent of convicting someone without due process. This would have been in contradiction with the spirit, if not the letter, of the rule of law and human rights principles.[31]

If the Zalaquett position were to be adopted as a rigid rule for countries like El Salvador, it would virtually ensure that most perpetrators of serious human rights violations would enjoy continued impunity, not only from criminal prosecution, but even from authoritative identification and exposure. This is a high price to pay.

In conclusion, while the legal ground rules for fact finding by truth commissions remain to be settled, prudential lessons can be derived from the considerable experience with such commissions in recent years.

American Journal of International Law (1997) 80.
[30] *Supra*, note 19 at 25.
[31] *Report of the Chilean National Commission on Truth and Reconciliation*, Philip E. Berryman trans. (1993) at xxxii, quoted in Hayner, *supra* note 15 at 648 and n.114.

CHAPTER 9

Fact-finding as Part of Effective Implementation: the Strasbourg Experience

Andrew Drzemczewski

(1) Introduction

The Council of Europe was founded in 1949 as a European organization for intergovernmental and parliamentary co-operation. Geographically, it is now the most extensive European political organization, comprising 41 member states.[1] Its principal aim is to unite the peoples of Europe around the values of pluralistic democracy, human rights, the rule of law and cultural tolerance – considered to be pre-requisites for peace and stability in Europe.

All member states of the Council of Europe are required to respect their obligations under the organization's statute, the European Convention on Human Rights[2] and other conventions to which they are parties, as well as to observe a series of principles, rules, standards and values which have been elaborated over the past 50 years within the organization with regard to democratic pluralism, human rights and the rule of law.[3]

In addition to these obligations, certain states which have become members since 1989 (principally from countries of Central and Eastern Europe) have entered into specific commitments during examination of their request for membership. These commitments have been undertaken in contacts with the Committee of Ministers (the organization's executive organ) and, in particular, the Parliamentary Assembly of the Council of Europe. They are explicitly referred

---

[1] Albania, Andorra, Austria, Belgium, Bulgaria, Croatia, Cyprus, Czech Republic, Denmark, Estonia, Finland, France, Georgia, Germany, Greece, Hungary, Ireland, Iceland, Italy, Latvia, Liechtenstein, Lithuania, Luxembourg, Malta, Moldova, Netherlands, Norway, Poland, Portugal, Romania, Russian Federation, San Marino, Slovakia, Slovenia, Spain, Sweden, Switzerland, The Former Yugoslav Republic of Macedonia, Turkey, Ukraine and the United Kingdom.
  Four states have applied for membership, namely, Armenia, Azerbaijan, Belarus and Bosnia-Herzegovina.
  For a general survey on this subject consult Peter Leuprecht, "Innovations in the European System of Human Rights Protection: Is Enlargement Compatible with Reinforcement?", 8 *Transnational Law and Contemporary Problems* (1998) 313–336.
[2] Convention for the Protection of Human Rights and Fundamental Freedoms, ETS 5 (in force 3 September 1953).
[3] See in particular, Council of Europe Statute, ETS 1 (in force 3 August 1949) arts. 1, 3 and 4.

to in the relevant opinions adopted by the Assembly to which reference is often made by the Committee of Ministers when it invites states to become members of the Council of Europe. For example, signature of the European Convention upon accession and its prompt ratification thereafter is an essential undertaking which all new member states must make.[4] Prior to the entry into force of Protocol No. 11,[5] this included declarations pursuant to former Articles 25 and 46 (but see new Articles 33 and 34) of the European Convention, namely, acceptance in full of the individual and inter-state complaints system before the Strasbourg Commission and Court, as well as Protocol No. 11 itself.

Membership does not necessarily entail compliance with the requirements established by the Strasbourg European Convention control organs case-law *ab initio*; according to Article 4 of the organization's statute, states must be "willing and able" to abide by conditions of membership. The membership admission process often entails complex fact-finding, fact-gathering and 'compatibility' procedures, the importance of which should not be underestimated and require separate analysis. Note should also be taken of the 'overviews' prepared for the Committee of Ministers under its confidential monitoring procedure set-up in November 1994, the work of the Parliamentary Assembly's Monitoring Committee[6], the fact-finding work of the Congress of Local and Regional Authorities in Europe (CLRAE) and the European Commission against Racism and Intolerance, the initiatives that can be taken by the Secretary General,[7] as well as a series of procedures set-up by other control mechanisms under the auspices of the organization.[8] However, an overview of all these dimensions has not been attempted in this paper. Comments are limited to fact-finding work of the organization's three basic and yet distinct human rights treaty mechanisms presently in force, namely the European Convention, the European Social Charter[9] and the European Convention for the Prevention of Torture.[10]

---

[4] For a study on this subject, consult Heinrich Klebes and Despina Chatzivassiliou, "Problèmes d'Ordre Constitutionnel Dans le Processus d'Adhésion d'Etats de l'Europe Centrale et Orientale au Conseil de l'Europe", 8 *Revue Universelle des Droits de l'Homme* (1996) 269–286 and publications cited therein. See also Andrew Drzemczewski, "The Council of Europe's Cooperation and Assistance Programs with Central and Eastern European Countries in the Human Rights Field", 14 *Human Rights Law Journal* (1993) at 248 and Catherine Schneider, "Le Conseil de l'Europe Acteur de Recomposition du Territoire Européen", 10 *Cahier de l'Espace*, Grenoble (May 1997).
[5] Protocol No. 11 to the European Convention, ETS 155 (in force 1 November 1998).
[6] Instituted by Parliamentary Assembly of the Council of Europe Res. 1115, adopted on 29 January 1997.
[7] See for example, Committee of Ministers, Declaration on the Protection of Journalists in Situations of Conflict and Tension (3 May 1996) at para. 7.
[8] See Council of Europe, *Monitoring Compliance with Commitments Entered into by Council of Europe Member States: An Overview*, Monitor/Inf(99)2 (26 February 1999). See also *Compliance with Commitments Entered into by Member States: Vade-Mecum on the Committee of Ministers' Monitoring Procedure*, Monitor/Inf (99)3 (1 March 1999) and *Compliance with Member States' Commitments: "Decisions" taken within the Context of the Committee of Ministers' Monitoring Procedure*, Monitor/Inf (99)5 (21 September 1999) (all of which can be consulted on the Council of Europe's Internet site: www.coe.fr/cm).
[9] European Social Charter, ETS 35 (in force 26 February 1965) and the Revised European Social Charter, ETS 163 (in force 1 July 1999).
[10] European Convention for the Prevention of Torture and Inhuman or Degrading Treatment or Punishment, ETS 126 (in force 1 February 1989).

(2) European Convention on Human Rights

(a) An overview

By virtue of Article 1 of the European Convention, the states parties undertake to secure the rights and freedoms defined by the Convention for everyone within their jurisdiction. By ratifying the European Convention and its protocols, the states parties accept the double commitment resulting from Article 1 – to ensure that their domestic law is compatible with the Convention, and to remedy any violation of the rights and freedoms protected by the Convention.

Prior to the entry into force of Protocol No. 11, any state party could refer an alleged breach of the provisions of the European Convention and its Protocols by another state to the European Commission of Human Rights. This procedure was rarely used. To date, there have been 21 inter-state applications.[11] In the case of individual applications, under former Article 25 of the European Convention the state in question must have recognized the competence of the European Commission beforehand.[12] In such cases, the state undertook "not to hinder in any way the effective exercise" of the right to individual petition. The procedure developed in two stages: before the European Commission and, depending on the case, before the European Court of Human Rights or the Committee of Ministers. For a case to be put before the European Court, the defending state must have accepted the jurisdiction of the Court by virtue of former Article 46 of the European Convention. The judgments of the European Court were final and binding on the parties concerned. If a question was not referred to the European Court in accordance with Article 48 of the Convention,[13] the Committee of Ministers decided, under Article 32, whether there had been a violation of the European Convention. These decisions were,

---

[11] Two applications by Greece against United Kingdom; Austria against Italy; four applications by Denmark, Norway, Netherlands and Sweden against Greece (and one joint application by Denmark, Norway and Sweden against Greece); five applications by Cyprus against Turkey; two applications by Ireland against United Kingdom; five applications by Denmark, France, Norway, Netherlands and Sweden against Turkey, and one application by Denmark against Turkey.

[12] Prior to the entry into force of Protocol No. 11, all states parties had made declarations under Arts. 25 and 46 of the European Convention (now mandatory under new Arts. 34 and 33 respectively). The control organs have been inundated with applications. In 1985, 2,831 provisional files were opened by the Commission. In 1998, 16,353 provisional files were opened. In 1985 the Commission registered 596 applications. In 1998, 5,981 were registered. In 1985, the Commission declared 70 cases to be admissible. In 1998, 762 cases were declared admissible. In 1985, the Commission referred 12 cases to the Court. In 1997 (the last full year of operation of the Commission), the Commission referred 97 cases to the Court (plus 68, in 1996, referred by an applicant by virtue of Protocol No. 9). See Council of Europe, *European Commission of Human Rights, Survey of Activities and Statistics* 1998. In 1985, the Court delivered 11 judgments. In 1998 the Court delivered 105 judgments. In 1999 there were 20,399 provisional files opened; 8,396 applications registered; 731 applications declared admissible; 177 judgments delivered by the Court. Council of Europe, *Survey of Activities, 1999*, Information document issued by the Registrar of the European Court of Human Rights, (Provisional Version).

Note that as of 1 November 1998, the Commission operated only in the capacity of dealing with cases which had been declared admissible prior to that date. Files were then opened by the Court. The Commission ceased operation 31 October 1999.

[13] European Convention, as amended by Protocol No. 9, ETS 140 (in force 1 October 1994), where relevant. Protocol No. 9 was repealed with the entry into force of Protocol No. 11, *supra* note 5: Art. 2(8) of Protocol No.11.

like the judgments of the European Court, final and binding on member states. The Committee of Ministers supervised their execution. With the entry into force of Protocol No. 11, a full-time, single Court has now replaced the Convention's former control mechanism. This Protocol entered into force one year after all states parties to the European Convention had ratified it,[14] namely on November 1, 1998.

The European Convention control mechanism is considered to be among the most successful international human rights treaty mechanisms in existence.[15] Nevertheless, shortcomings can be pointed out. Firstly, with the exception of the "hard-core" of the European Convention – Articles 2, 3, 4 (paragraph 1) and 7, and Protocol No. 6,[16] where pertinent – states parties are entitled, under Article 15, to take measures derogating from their obligations under the Convention. These derogations can be quite substantial and are sometimes maintained for long periods of time; the Convention organs are not always seized of such matters. Secondly, while the system of control of the European Convention allows for remedying individual situations, often bringing about substantial improvements of the respect for human rights through the adoption of measures of a general nature, the system is ill-equipped to deal with serious and/or systematic violations of human rights.

In addition, the rapid enlargement of the organization poses a potentially serious threat to the Convention *acquis*: legal standards in a number of new member states from Central and Eastern Europe fall below those required by the European Convention control organs. A difficult (and daunting) balancing act is being attempted. High standards will need to be maintained in the "old" democracies, in some of which major problems have arisen, and at the same time standards will have to be substantially improved in several "new" democracies.

Furthermore, under Article 52 (former Article 57) of the European Convention, the Secretary-General has the right to request an explanation from any state party of the manner in which its internal law ensures the effective implementation of the provisions of the European Convention and its Protocols. States parties are under an obligation to furnish the requested explanations. In such instances, the Secretary-General acts on his own responsibility; his powers under new

---

[14] For further details, consult the text of Protocol No. 11 and commentary of Andrew Drzemczewski and Jens Meyer-Ladewig, "Principal Characteristics of the New ECHR Control Mechanism, as Established by Protocol No. 11, Signed on May 11, 1994", 15 *Human Rights Law Journal* (1994) 81–115. See also the appendix to the present text which is an adapted version from Andrew Drzemczewski, "A Major Overhaul of the European Human Rights Control Mechanism: Protocol No. 11", in VI(2) *Collected Courses of the Academy of European Law* (1997) 121–244. See also Andrew Drzemczewski, "The European Human Rights Convention: A New Court of Human Rights in Strasbourg as of November 1, 1998", 55(3) *Washington and Lee Law Review* (1998) 697–736.

[15] For a survey, consult Donna Gomien, David Harris and Leo Zwaak, *Law and Practice of the ECHR and the European Social Charter*, Council of Europe Publishing (1996). Also, critical comments by Menno Kamminga, "Is the European Convention on Human Rights Sufficiently Equipped to Cope with Gross and Systemic Violations?", 12 *Netherlands Quarterly on Human Rights* (1994) 153–164; Aisling Reidy, Françoise Hampson and Kevin Boyle, "Gross Violations of Human Rights: Invoking the European Convention on Human Rights in the Case of Turkey", 15 *Netherlands Quarterly on Human Rights* (1997) 161–173; and Christian Tomuschat, "Quo Vadis, Argentoratum? The Success Story of the European Convention on Human Rights – And a few Dark Stains", 13 *Human Rights Law Journal* (1992) 401–406.

[16] Protocol No. 6 to the European Convention, ETS 114 (in force 1 March 1985).

Figure 1. European Convention on Human Rights (ECHR) summary overview.

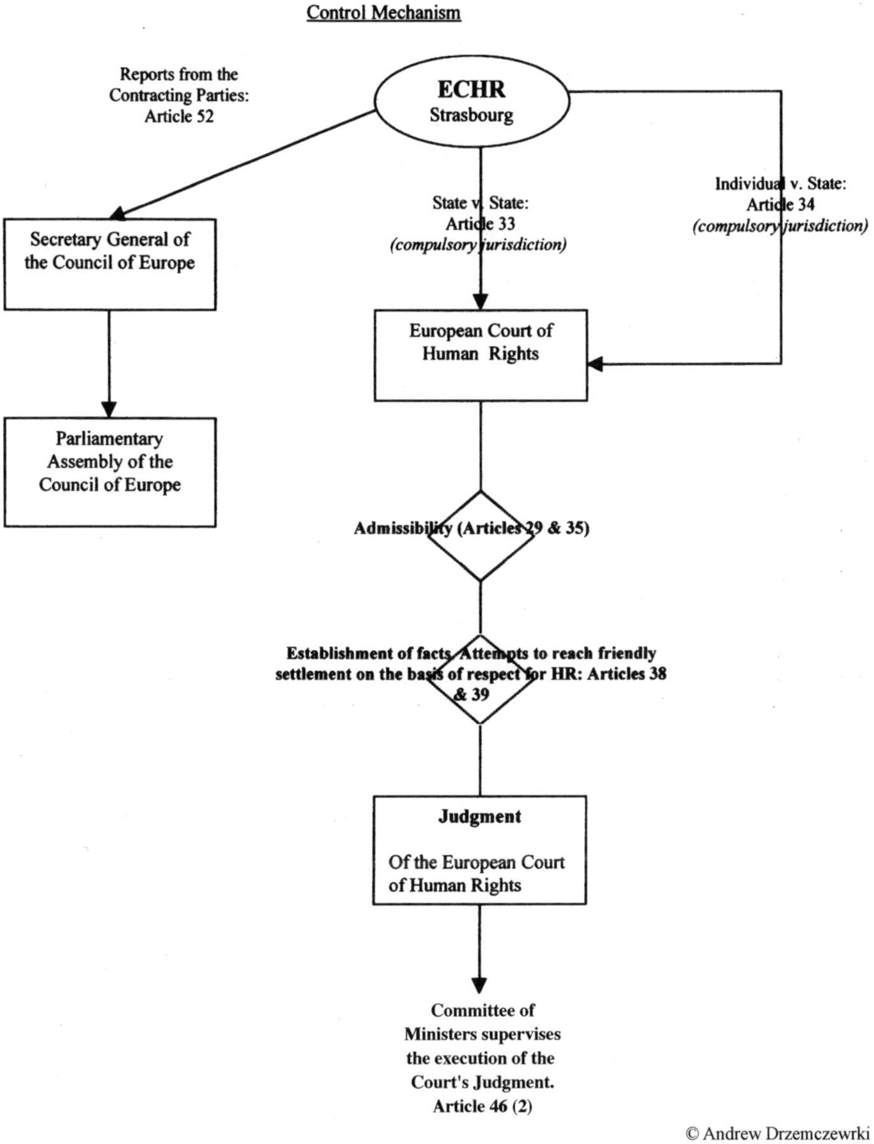

Control Mechanism

[Flowchart showing:
- ECHR Strasbourg (central node)
- Reports from the Contracting Parties: Article 52 → Secretary General of the Council of Europe → Parliamentary Assembly of the Council of Europe
- State v. State: Article 33 (compulsory jurisdiction) → European Court of Human Rights
- Individual v. State: Article 34 (compulsory jurisdiction) → European Court of Human Rights
- European Court of Human Rights → Admissibility (Articles 29 & 35) → Establishment of facts / Attempts to reach friendly settlement on the basis of respect for HR: Articles 38 & 39 → Judgment Of the European Court of Human Rights → Committee of Ministers supervises the execution of the Court's Judgment. Article 46 (2)]

© Andrew Drzemczewrki

Article 52 of the Convention are not subject to control or to instructions. To date, the Secretary-General has used this prerogative five times, in every case requesting that all states parties provide information on their legislation concerning certain provisions of the Convention. In two instances, the Secretary-General has undertaken comparative studies of the explanations provided by the governments with a view to exploring the conclusions. Until this point, however, there has been no follow-up to these studies.

Figure 2. European Convention on Human Rights (ECHR) detailed overview.
Control Mechanism

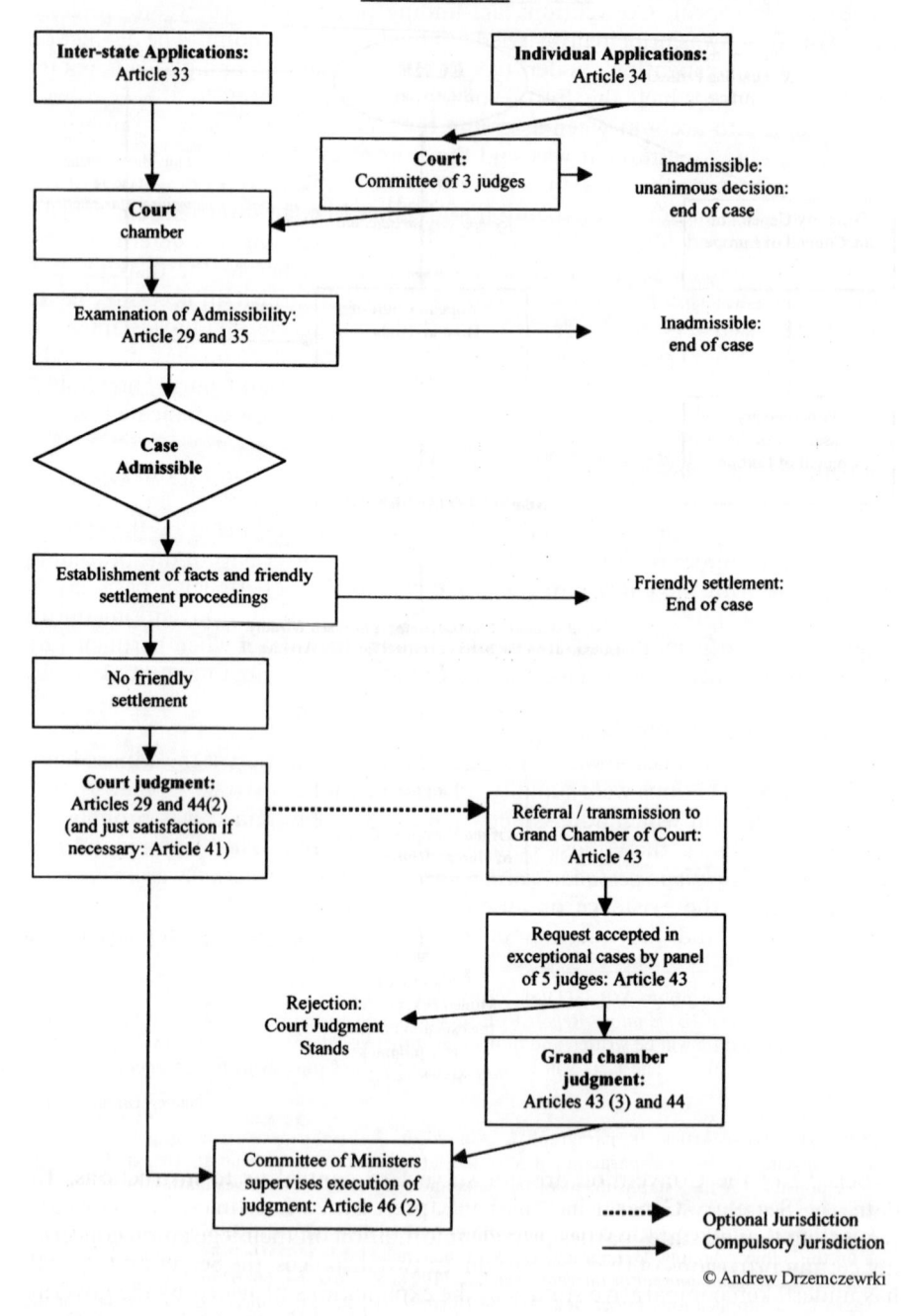

```
┌─────────────────────┐              ┌─────────────────────┐
│ Inter-state         │              │ Individual          │
│ Applications:       │              │ Applications:       │
│ Article 33          │              │ Article 34          │
└──────────┬──────────┘              └──────────┬──────────┘
           │                                    │
           │                         ┌──────────▼──────────┐      Inadmissible:
           │                         │ Court:              │ ───► unanimous decision:
           │                         │ Committee of 3      │      end of case
           │                         │ judges              │
           │                         └──────────┬──────────┘
           │            ◄───────────────────────┘
┌──────────▼──────────┐
│ Court               │
│ chamber             │
└──────────┬──────────┘
           │
┌──────────▼──────────┐                         Inadmissible:
│ Examination of      │ ──────────────────────► end of case
│ Admissibility:      │
│ Article 29 and 35   │
└──────────┬──────────┘
           │
          ╱ ╲
         ╱Case╲
        ╱Admis-╲
        ╲sible ╱
         ╲    ╱
          ╲ ╱
           │
┌──────────▼──────────┐                         Friendly settlement:
│ Establishment of    │ ──────────────────────► End of case
│ facts and friendly  │
│ settlement          │
│ proceedings         │
└──────────┬──────────┘
           │
┌──────────▼──────────┐
│ No friendly         │
│ settlement          │
└──────────┬──────────┘
           │
┌──────────▼──────────┐                        ┌─────────────────────┐
│ Court judgment:     │                        │ Referral /          │
│ Articles 29 and     │········································►│ transmission to     │
│ 44(2)               │                        │ Grand Chamber of    │
│ (and just           │                        │ Court: Article 43   │
│ satisfaction if     │                        └──────────┬──────────┘
│ necessary:          │                                   │
│ Article 41)         │                        ┌──────────▼──────────┐
└──────────┬──────────┘                        │ Request accepted in │
           │                                   │ exceptional cases   │
           │                                   │ by panel of 5       │
           │                                   │ judges: Article 43  │
           │                                   └──────────┬──────────┘
           │            Rejection:                        │
           │            Court Judgment ◄──────────────────┤
           │            Stands                            │
           │                                   ┌──────────▼──────────┐
           │                                   │ Grand chamber       │
           │                                   │ judgment:           │
           │                                   │ Articles 43 (3) and │
           │                                   │ 44                  │
           │                                   └──────────┬──────────┘
           │           ┌─────────────────────┐            │
           └──────────►│ Committee of        │◄───────────┘
                       │ Ministers           │
                       │ supervises          │
                       │ execution of        │
                       │ judgment:           │
                       │ Article 46 (2)      │
                       └─────────────────────┘
```

········► Optional Jurisdiction
─────► Compulsory Jurisdiction

© Andrew Drzemczewrki

(b) Fact-finding

Under the European Convention, fact-finding prior to the entry into force of Protocol No. 11 was principally carried out by the Commission.[17] The distinction between 'an investigation' under this provision and obtaining documentary material/evidence which the European Commission (as well as the European Court) took into account when assessing the facts in a given case is important. When accepting a petition, it was said the European Commission "shall, with a view to ascertaining the facts, undertake together with the representatives of the parties, an examination of the petition and, if need be, an investigation." This is an institutionalized form of fact-finding. The investigation was determined by the international institution itself and not by the parties to the dispute, "the effective conduct of which the states concerned shall furnish all necessary facilities." The revised version of former Article 28 (1)(a), Article 38(1)(a) (as amended by Protocol No. 11), sub-titled "examination of the case", makes no specific reference to the ascertainment of facts by the new European Court. This should, however, be considered no more than a 'tidying-up' job, as indicated in the Protocol's Explanatory Report.[18]

Furthermore, prior to the entry into force of Protocol No. 11, the European Commission's report under Article 31 stated "the facts found" and gave the Commission's opinion as to whether the facts revealed a breach by the state of its obligations under the European Convention. The latter part of this procedure disappeared with the entry into force of Protocol No. 11. Its legal basis lay in the consent of states to subject themselves to the European Convention control mechanism, and is reinforced, in certain circumstances (and when pertinent) by a separate European Agreement relating to persons participating in proceedings thereunder.[19]

Although, technically speaking, prior to entry into force of Protocol No. 11, the European Commission was not a "fact-finding" institution at the admissibility stage when applications were submitted to it under former Article 25 (new Article 34), the manner in which admissibility issues were determined was probably of greater importance than most commentators realized. The determination of incompatibility *ratione personae, ratione loci* and *ratione materiae* was an exercise in determining the existence or absence of facts, even if closely tied to legal considerations, and the question of whether the European Commission has

---

[17] See European Convention, Art. 38(1)(a) (former Art. 28(1)(a)).

[18] Paras. 44 and 93 of *Explanatory Report* to Protocol No. 11 to the European Convention specify:
   44. The procedure will be written and oral, unless otherwise decided by the Court after consultation with the parties... The facts will be established by the Court, with the co-operation of the parties...
   ...
   93. The text of Article 38, paragraph 1, is based on that of former Article 28, paragraph 1, of the Convention, although paragraph 1 a. of the latter has been somewhat shortened. The Court is responsible for the establishment of the facts and may conduct an investigation on the understanding that the parties furnish the Court with all the relevant information...

[19] For example, with respect to certain immunities and facilities afforded to witnesses and experts. See on this subject Andrew Drzemczewski, "Protocole no. 11 à la CEDH: Préparation à l'Entrée en Vigueur", 8 *European Journal of International Law* (1997) 59–76 at 64, 66–67 and references therein.

In so far as applications under new Art. 34 (former Art. 25) are concerned, the efficacy of the system hinges on the premise that states comply with their obligation not to hinder the applicant in the exercise of the right of individual petition: see *Akdivar v. Turkey*, Series A, Volume 1996-IV (16

competence to deal with an application.[20] The reasoning used by the European Commission when it considered whether applications were inadmissible as "manifestly ill-founded"[21] required the applicant to show a *prima facie* case that his or her complaint fell within the scope of the European Convention and that a preliminary examination of the merits warranted further examination of the issues raised in the application.

Although admissibility criteria remain unchanged by virtue of Protocol No. 11, concern has been expressed about the likelihood of the new European Court applying the said criteria more stringently. After all, factors such as the logistical and the physical capacity of the new European Court (in the light of the 'onslaught' of applications) may 'force' this new judicial body to be even more restrictive than the European Commission had been on questions of admissibility. It is difficult to know how the new Court, principally constituted in Chambers of at least seven judges (or committees of three), will deal with the so-called 'admissibility barrier', taking into account the need to reconcile productivity and the fair administration of justice.

This issue will arise, for example, in the application of the criteria for rejection of "manifestly ill-founded" applications. If the interpretation of the law of the European Convention by the applicant is incorrect, then the application may be declared inadmissible; the same is true where the allegation(s) appears to be wholly or clearly unsubstantiated in that there is no evidence of the alleged facts to support a claim or, even if available, is insufficient. This category comes close to being a rule of evidence, in that the facts alleged must be "proven", otherwise they are found to be untrue or inaccurate. The third category of "manifestly ill-founded" applications are those which, even if substantiated, would not or do not amount to a violation of the European Convention either because they are not of a sufficiently grave character (for example, as to amount to torture) or because certain "justified" restrictions on their use have been invoked correctly. There is also another category of "manifestly ill-founded" cases referred to as the "fourth instance formula", which deals specifically with alleged errors of law or fact committed by domestic courts, in effect, "appeals" against domestic courts' findings.

An important element in the establishment of the facts of a case is the distinction between matters which are relevant for the determination of the complaint and those which are not. This distinction is reflected in the admissibility condition of 'relevant new information' (in the French text *faits nouveaux*),[22] for an application raising the same matter as a case already examined.

In other words, in the wake of the enormous increase in applications and the potential extension of the system to countries with different kinds of human rights problems it is conceivable (and perhaps inevitable) that so-called 'less serious' cases will be declared inadmissible. Secondly, at the admissibility stage, determination of 'facts' often comes close to that of an evidential requirement with respect to both formal and substantive conditions of admissibility.

The *substance* of applications which pass the so-called 'admissibility barrier'

September 1996) at paras. 100–106. See also *Kapan v. Turkey*, (22057/93) 88 DR 17 (13 January 1997), a decision taken by the European Commission, to strike the application off of its list of cases.
[20] European Convention, Art. 35(1) (former Arts. 26 and 27(3)).
[21] European Convention, Art. 35(3) (former Art. 27(2)).
[22] European Convention, Art. 35(1)(b) (former Art. 27(1)(b)).

raises further issues of fact-finding by the new European Court. The new single full-time Court will somehow need to 'accommodate' the multi-faceted role of the European Commission, comprising at the same time quasi-judicial (determination of admissibility and the drawing-up of legal opinions) and conciliation functions, on the one hand, and the present European Court's strength in adjudication and the drafting of carefully reasoned binding judgments, on the other.

Under the pre-Protocol No. 11 regime, the European Court, in cases such as *Stocké v. Germany*,[23] *Cruz Varas and Others v. Sweden*,[24] *McCann and Others v. the United Kingdom*[25] and *Aksoy v. Turkey*,[26] recognised that the establishment and verification of the facts was primarily a matter for the European Commission, although it retained the prerogative of assessing the facts found in a different manner from the Commission.[27] The former rules of the Court[28] contained provisions for the taking of evidence, but the European Court used these powers only in exceptional circumstances. The European Court's hesitance to control the Commission's establishment and verification of facts was illustrated by the *Stocké* case. Mr. Stocké complained of collusion between the German authorities and a certain Mr. K., who had brought him back from France to Germany, where he was arrested. He requested that the European Court hear five witnesses, four of whom had not been heard by the European Commission. The European Court saw no reason to entertain this request, having considered the conclusions reached after thorough investigations by the German and French authorities, the evidence of the numerous witnesses already heard by the European Commission as set out in a summary whose accuracy had not been challenged, and the fact that the European Commission, as stated by its delegate before the Court, deemed it unnecessary to hear further evidence.[29]

The new single Court will, of course, have to readjust its working methods in order to assume the fact-finding function of the European Commission. In this connection, compare the reasoning of both the Commission and the Court in the case of *Tomasi v. France*[30] where "certain inferences could be made from the fact that Mr. Tomasi had sustained unexplained injuries during forty-eight hours spent in police custody" and the rather unusual reasoning of the Court in the case of *Klaas v. Germany*.[31] In *Klaas* the European Court, but not the

---

[23] *Stocké v. Germany*, Series A, Volume 199 (19 March 1991) at para. 53.
[24] *Cruz Varas and Others v. Sweden*, Series A, Volume 201 (20 March 1991) at para. 74.
[25] *McCann and Others v. The United Kingdom*, Series A, Volume 324 (27 September 1995).
[26] *Aksoy v. Turkey*, Series A, Volume 1996-VI (18 December 1996) at paras. 38–40.
[27] *Supra*, note 24. See also Marc-André Eissen, "La Présentation de la Preuve dans la Jurisprudence et la Pratique de la Cour Européenne des Droits de l'Homme" in, *La Présentation de la Preuve et la Sauvegarde des Libertés Individuelles*, Université Catholique de Louvain, Troisième Colloque du Département des Droits de l'Homme (1977) at 143.
[28] See, for instance, *Rules of the European Court*, Rule 43 (new Rule 42) (Measures for taking evidence), in force 1 November 1998: see http:/:www.dhcour.coe.fr.
[29] *Supra*, note 23 at paras. 52–53. Of interest to note, in this connection, is the fact that the Committee of Ministers also (implicitly) recognized the European Commission's primary competence for the establishment of facts, including the taking of evidence. It considered, in connection with rule 4 of its Rules for the Application of Art. 32 of the European Convention, that "[the Committee] is not well equipped to take evidence, etc. and ought not normally to undertake such tasks" and found that the Commission "is in its nature equipped to do so": para. 2 of the Appendix to these Rules.
[30] *Tomasi v. France*, Series A, Volume 241-A (27 August 1992).
[31] *Klaas v. Germany*, Series A, Volume 269 (22 September 1993) at para. 30.

Commission, found no "cogent elements [for it] to depart from the finding of fact of the national courts," in a situation in which the burden of proof, regarding the use of excessive force fell upon the applicant and not the police. It must be noted that until now the underlying facts have not usually been contested as disputes principally concerned the law: did the agreed facts meet European Convention standards? The European Convention organs have dealt with "the fine tuning of the democratic engine" rather than with major human rights violations. However, as the Court's Deputy Registrar mentioned at a 1997 meeting with the Bar European Group, a spate of applications against Turkey concerned serious allegations, such as destruction of villages or ill-treatment of detainees involving torture or inhuman treatment. Primary facts are now more often disputed, which obliged the European Commission – and obliges the new European Court – to undertake difficult and expensive on-site fact-finding missions.

On-site investigations have been carried out by delegates of the Commission in several inter-state cases, notably *Greece v. the United Kingdom* (the first Cyprus case),[32] the *Greek Case,*[33] the *Cyprus v. Turkey cases,*[34] *Ireland v. the United Kingdom,*[35] *France, Norway, Denmark, Sweden and the Netherlands v. Turkey*[36] and in certain individual cases. In recent years investigations *in situ* have taken place in Turkey in connection with various individual complaints.[37] In these latter cases, the European Commission actually worked as a court of first instance with regard to an increasing number of complaints concerning events in the country's south-east. Here, the subsidiary character of the European Convention was turned on its head: the Strasbourg control organs did not have the benefit of fact-finding and an initial assessment by the domestic courts. Many difficulties can be pointed to in this respect, especially concerning the European

---

[32] *Greece v. The United Kingdom,* No. 176/56, in *ECHR Yearbook II* (20 April 1958) at 176 (the investigation concerned the existence of a state of emergency).

[33] *The Greek Case,* in *ECHR Yearbook 12* (5 November 1969) at 1 (witnesses heard concerning the state of emergency and a practice of torture by the Athens Security Police).

[34] *Cyprus v. Turkey,* Nos. 6780/74 and 6950/75, DR 2 (10 July 1976) at 125 (evidence taken in Cyprus and refugee camps visited by a European Commission delegation).

[35] *Ireland v. The United Kingdom,* Series A, Volume 25 (18 January 1978) (113 witnesses heard in relation to allegations of ill-treatment and discrimination in arrest and detention procedures).

[36] *France, Norway, Denmark, Sweden and The Netherlands v. Turkey,* Nos. 9940–9944/82, DR 44 (7 December 1985) at 31 (a Commission delegation sent to gather first-hand information concerning the then current situation in Turkey).

[37] See, for example, *Sargin and Yağci v. Turkey,* Nos. 14116 and 14118/88, DR 61 (11 May 1989) (a Commission delegation sent to take evidence on complaints about, *inter alia,* ill-treatment and conditions of detention); *Çagirga v. Turkey,* No. 21895/93, DR 82A (7 July 1995) (a Commission delegation to South-East Turkey to take evidence on allegations relating to deaths resulting from the destruction of the applicant's house); *Aksoy v. Turkey,* No. 21987/93, DR 79A (19 October 1994) (a Commission delegation to take evidence on torture allegations); *Akdivar and Others v. Turkey,* No. 21893/93, unpublished (26 October 1995) (a Commission delegation to take evidence concerning allegations of the destruction of a village). The two latter cases were referred to the Court by the Turkish Government and by the Commission in December 1995: see Court judgments of *Aksoy v. Turkey,* Series A, Volume 1996-VI (18 December 1996) and *Akdivar and Others v. Turkey,* Series A, Volume 1996-IV (15 November 1996).

For a 'warning' as to implications such developments may entail for the future New Court see: Paul Mahoney, "Determination and Evaluation of Facts in Proceedings Before the Present and Future European Court of Human Rights" to be published in *Studies in Honour of J.J. Cremona* (forthcoming); Paul Mahoney "The Future of the European Court of Human Rights", paper presented at the Bar European (England and Wales) Group Conference, Strasbourg (9–10 May 1997).

II. Fact-finding as Part of Effective Implementation 125

Commission's powers of discovery of documents and its ability to compel witnesses to participate. It remains to be seen how the new European Court will now deal with such matters.[38]

Much valuable practical experience was thus gained by the European Commission and its Secretariat in this area,[39] and will somehow need to be 'taken-over' by the new Court. The fact that all or most of the staff of the European Commission and present Court have been 'transferred' to the registry of the new Court will, to a large degree, help to overcome any problems such a readjustment may cause.

In those cases where investigations have taken place, particularly inter-state cases, one can find a rich variety of examples of the types of fact-finding problems faced by the European Commission's delegates when gathering evidence. The following matters have been addressed: evidence taken in secret by delegates in the absence of the parties; drawing adverse inferences from the evidence where a contracting party refuses to participate; state objections on security grounds to hearing witnesses in a particular place; withholding the identity of witnesses for security reasons; witnesses shielded from the view of one of the parties when giving their testimony; whether proof of evidence to be called by the state at a hearing of witnesses should be made available in advance to the adverse party to facilitate cross-examination; whether a state should disclose the transcript of evidence already given to witnesses it proposes to call; and what position the European Commission should adopt towards a state that claims that certain evidence is privileged or cannot be disclosed for security reasons. The European Commission's reports and the Secretariat's case-files in the cases where these issues have arisen provide responses to these and to other questions.[40]

A related issue is the burden and standard of proof.[41] Questions of proof may arise at any stage of the European Convention proceedings. Former Article 28(1)(a) referred only to the European Commission's task of ascertaining the facts of admitted applications ("In the event of the Commission accepting a petition ..."), but as early as during the Commission's examination of the admissibility of an application, proof may have been required both for formal and for substantial conditions of admissibility. The European Court tended to avoid taking a position on these questions, holding that it would examine cases on the basis of the evidence before it or on evidence obtained of its own motion. The Commission, however, as the principal fact-finding body, was obliged to address these issues in its case-law. The new European Court will need to carry out both these functions.

In order to ease the applicant's burden of proof and/or to obtain elucidation of a point, the European Commission or its Rapporteur often requested "relevant

---

[38] In *Cruz Varas and Others v. Sweden, supra* note 24, and *Ireland v. the United Kingdom, supra* note 35, recourse was also had to expert medical testimony.
[39] See, for a more thorough study, Nicholas Bratza and Michael O'Boyle, "The Legacy of the [European] Commission to the New Court under the 11th Protocol", in *The Birth of European Human Rights Law: Studies in Honour of C.A. Nørgaard*, Michele de Salvia & Mark E. Villiger (eds.), Baden (1998) at 377–393.
[40] See, for example, the European Commission's report in *Ireland v. the United Kingdom*, Series B, Volume 23-I (25 January 1976) where many of these problems arose.
[41] For an excellent survey see Kersten Rogge "Fact-finding", in *The European System for the Protection of Human Rights*, Ronald St J. Macdonald, Franz Matscher and Herbert Petzold (eds.), Dordrecht (1993) 677 at 685–692.

information" from the applicant or the state party concerned, often even before deciding on admissibility. Prior to the admissibility stage, it was not the European Commission's role to 'establish the facts'. In certain exceptional cases, however, it actually considered it necessary to look into matters. One can cite the European Commission's decision to send delegations to visit Bobby Sands, a dying hunger-striker in the Maze Prison in Northern Ireland,[42] to verify whether he was willing to confirm an application brought in his name by his sister, and to Stammheim Prison in Germany to determine the conditions in which certain members of the Baader Meinhoff terrorist group met with their death.[43]

However, once an application was communicated to the respondent government, the burden of proving the existence of available and sufficient remedies lay with the defendant state.[44] In the *Simon-Herold* case, the European Commission, through delegated members, heard the applicant's former lawyer and a judge as witnesses "on questions of fact connected with the issue as to whether the applicant had or had not exhausted his remedies under Austrian law."[45] The evidence obtained was summarized in the European Commission's decision on the admissibility of the application,[46] in which it found that domestic remedies had not been exhausted in certain complaints.[47]

At the admissibility stage, the applicant needed only to adduce a "commencement de preuve" (beginning of proof), some evidence to substantiate the violation being alleged. At the merits stage, the applicant did not bear the burden of proving his allegations since it fell to the European Commission under former Article 28 to establish the facts. Here, the principle of the free admission and assessment of evidence was followed by the European Commission. Neither the European Convention nor the European Commission's rules of procedure prescribed a particular standard of proof; there were no fixed rules concerning illegally obtained evidence, privileged documents, or perjury. On the other hand, the Commission applied a "reasonable doubt" standard to facts constituting a violation; in expulsion or extradition cases, "substantial grounds" must have been present supporting the risk of ill-treatment. In inter-state cases, it also held that the applicant state was not required to prove its allegations at the admissibility stage, this being a matter for the merits.[48]

The former European Court accepted the approach, that the facts constituting a violation of the European Convention must be proven beyond reasonable doubt, and not a doubt based merely on a theoretical possibility or raised in order to avoid a disagreeable conclusion, but a doubt for which reasons can be

---

[42] *Sands v. The United Kingdom*, 93381/81 (unreported).
[43] *Ensslin, Baader, and Raspe v. Federal Republic of Germany* DR 14 (8 July 1978) 64 at 101–104 and 111–112.
[44] *Farrel v. The United Kingdom*, No. 9013/80, DR 30 (11 December 1982) at 96. See also the *De Weer Case*, Series A, Volume 35 (27 February 1980) at para. 26: "Where a Contracting State prays in aid the obligation to exhaust remedies, a rule essentially intended to "protect its national legal order," it is for the state to prove that there exist available remedies which have not been "utilized."
[45] *Simon-Herald v. Austria*, No. 4340/69, ECHR Yearbook XIV (2 February 1971) 352 at 378.
[46] *Ibid.*, at 386–92.
[47] *Supra*, note 45 at 378–84.
[48] See, for more details, David J. Harris, Michael O'Boyle and Chris Warbrick, *Law of the European Convention on Human Rights*, Butterworths (1995) at 598–599, and Stefan Trechsel "Article 28 § 1, a. [CEDH]" in *La Convention Européenne des Droits de l'Homme: Commentaire Article par Article*, Emmanuel Decaux, Pierre-Henri Imbert and Louis-Edmond Pettiti (eds.) Economica (1995) 649.

given drawn from the facts presented. Proof beyond reasonable doubt "may follow from the coexistence of sufficiently strong, clear and concordant inferences or of similar unrebutted presumptions of fact."[49] In this context, the conduct of the parties when evidence is being obtained has to be taken into account.

The failure by a government to provide relevant documentary evidence or to indicate the identity of public officials required as witnesses by the European Commission was given weight in the assessment of evidence in a number of individual applications brought against Turkey. Rules concerning the burden of proof with respect to the existence and adequacy of remedies have also been developed. Thus, while the state must prove the existence of domestic remedies, the burden shifts to the applicant to show that they are inadequate and/or ineffective.

Difficult questions of proof can arise in expulsion or extradition cases under Article 3 of the European Convention (torture, inhuman, degrading treatment).[50] Regarding the standard of proof at the admissibility stage, the person concerned must produce evidence to show that there is a concrete and serious risk that he will be prosecuted and exposed to treatment of the kind prohibited by Article 3.[51] The former Court, in its determination of the merits of an Article 3 complaint in an expulsion or extradition case, examined whether "substantial grounds" have been shown "for believing the existence of a real risk of treatment contrary to Article 3" in the receiving state. It considered this issue "in the light of all the material placed before it or, if necessary, material obtained *proprio motu*." Further, "since the nature of the Contracting States' responsibility under Article 3 in cases of this kind lies in the act of exposing an individual to the risk of ill-treatment, the existence of the risk must be assessed primarily with reference to those facts which were known or ought to have been known to the Contracting State at the time of expulsion;

---

[49] *Supra*, note 35, paragraph 161. Apparently this burden of proof was applied by the European Commission in Art. 2 (right to life) and Art. 3 (inhuman treatment) cases, but not expressly applied with regard to other provisions of the European Convention. Perhaps this burden of proof – established in an inter-state case before the European Court – is too stringent, hence the "nuanced" approach taken by the European Commission.

See also, for a more general discussion on this difficult subject, article by Loukis G. Loucaides, "Standards of Proof in Proceedings Under the ECHR", in *Présence du Droit Public et des Droits de l'Homme: Mélanges Offert à Jacques Velu* (1992) 1431–1443; commentary by Trechsel, *ibid.* at 656–659, and David Harris *et al.*, *supra* note 48 at 678–680.

[50] See *H.L.R. v. France*, Series A, Volume 1997-III No. 36 (29 April 1997), especially at paras. 40 to 44.

[51] A lesser degree is probably required for an interim measure under rule 39 of the European Court's Rules of Court (former rule 36 of the European Commission's Rules of Procedures; former Rule 36 of Rules of Court A, and former Rule 38 of Rules of Court B). Rule 39 specifies: "(1) The Chamber or, where appropriate, its President may, at the request of a party or of any other person concerned, or of its own motion, indicate to the parties any interim measure which it considers should be adopted in the interests of the parties or of the proper conduct of the proceedings before it." Before the Commission, the respondent state was requested to suspend the execution of the expulsion or extradition order pending the Commission's examination of the case. See Carl Aage Nørgaard and Hans-Christian Krüger, "Interim and Conservatory Measures under the European System of Protection of Human Rights", in *Progress in the Spirit of Human Rights*, Festschrift für Ermacora (1988) 109 at 112, and, for a more comprehensive analysis of both the Commission and Court practice, Gérard Cohen-Jonathan "De l'Effet Juridique des 'Mesures Provisoires' dans Certaines Circonstances et de l'Efficacité du Droit de Recours Individuel: à Propos de l'Arrêt Cruz Varas de la Cour Européenne des Droits de l'Homme", 3 *Revue Universelle des Droits de l'Homme* (1991) 205–209.

the Court is not precluded, however, from having regard to information which comes to light subsequent to the expulsion."[52]

Finally, when a respondent state refused – in the pre-Protocol No. 11 scheme – to cooperate with the European Commission or decided not to participate at all in the Commission's examination of the merits of a case, there was no possibility (as is provided for in the rules of procedure of the Inter-American Commission) for an automatic finding in favour of the other party. The European Commission considered that such a policy of non-cooperation would not hinder it in its task of ascertaining the facts: it had to satisfy itself that the information before it was sufficient to express a well-founded opinion. It certainly did not automatically find in favour of the applicant irrespective of the circumstances of the case.[53]

(2) European Social Charter

(a) An overview

The European Social Charter[54] provides for a systematic control of all of the commitments undertaken by states parties, at regular intervals (from two to four years, depending on the case). Time limits for the accomplishment of control procedures are fixed.

At regular intervals, the states parties undertake to send a report to the Secretary-General on the application of the provisions of the European Social Charter which they have accepted. The control procedure itself is implemented in three stages. The Committee of Independent Experts, composed of nine experts appointed by the Committee of Ministers and assisted by an International Labour Organization (ILO) observer, examines the reports submitted by the contracting parties and gives a legal assessment of compliance with the accepted provisions. A political evaluation – based on social, economic and other policy considerations – is then carried out within the Governmental Committee, in collaboration with social partners. The Governmental Committee presents a report to the Committee of Ministers containing a selection of situations which should, in its view, be the subject of recommendations to each contracting party. The Committee of Ministers adopts, on the basis of the report of the

---

[52] *Supra*, note 24 at para. 75. See also *D. v. United Kingdom*, Series A, Volume 1997-III (2 May 1997).
Here, as in many other cases, a distinction probably ought to be made between investigations/fact finding carried out by the European Commission by virtue of former Art. 28(1)(a) (now by the new Court under Art. 38(1)(a)) of the European Convention) and obtaining documentary evidence/material used by the Strasbourg control organs.
[53] For examples, consult David Harris *et al.*, *supra* note 48 at 597–598. In its Reports concerning cases brought by Cyprus against Turkey, the European Commission dealt at length with the procedural consequences of the respondent Government's failure to cooperate with the European Commission at the merits stage. The European Commission expressed the view that notwithstanding such failure, which contravened Art. 28 of the European Convention, it had to proceed with the case with a view to preparing a Report under Art. 31 of the European Convention on the basis of the material before it: *Cyprus v. Turkey*, Nos. 6780/74 and 6950/75, DR 2 (10 July 1978) at paras. 50–59, and *Cyprus v. Turkey*, No. 8007/77, DR 72 (4 October 1983) 5 at 19–21, paras. 48–53. See also *supra* note 49, Loucaides at 1140–1143, and *supra* note 48, Trechsel at 655–665.
[54] European Social Charter, *supra* note 9 and Additional Protocol, ETS 128 (in force 4 September 1992).

Governmental Committee, a resolution covering the entire supervision cycle and containing individual recommendations to the contracting parties concerned. The Committee of Ministers effectively started to issue individual recommendations only as of 1993. The Parliamentary Assembly is also associated with this control system, and since 1992 uses the conclusions of the Committee of Independent Experts as a basis for the organization of periodic social policy debates. Numerous amendments to legislation and adjustments of practice have been undertaken by the states parties as a result of the control exercised in accordance with this procedure.

The limits of the system reside in the fact that, besides being ratified by only 24 states, the material provisions of the European Social Charter may be accepted on a piecemeal basis subject to the acceptance of certain provisions of the "hard core" and a minimum of 10 articles.[55] This latter 'disadvantage' may in effect make it easier for several states to ratify this instrument in the next few years, as has been illustrated in the case of Poland.

Under article 22, the Committee of Ministers is also empowered to ask states parties to the European Social Charter, to produce reports on provisions they have not ratified. It has used this procedure on a few occasions.

This control procedure was modified by an Amending Protocol adopted in 1991[56] and already has been implemented partially following a decision by the Committee of Ministers in December 1991, in which the supervisory bodies were asked to apply it before its entry into force, insofar as the text of the European Social Charter allows. The modifications have now been consolidated in the Revised version of the Charter.[57]

The Additional Protocol to the European Social Charter, providing for a system of collective complaints, was adopted by the Committee of Ministers in June 1995 and opened for signature in November 1995.[58] It entered into force after five ratifications, on 1st July 1998. Its purpose is to improve the efficiency of the supervisory machinery of the European Social Charter, by enabling them to deal with collective complaints alleging violations of the Charter, in addition to examining government reports.

The following are able to submit collective complaints: international organizations of employers and trade unions which participate in the work of the Governmental Committee; other international non-governmental organizations (NGOs) with consultative status with the Council of Europe and appearing on a special list which is drawn up for this purpose by the Governmental Committee, and national organizations of employers and trade unions from the contracting party concerned. In addition, in a declaration to the Secretary-General each state is able to authorize national NGOs to lodge complaints. Collective complaints are examined by the Committee of Independent Experts which initially needs to assess their admissibility, according to criteria listed in the Protocol. Following this, the Committee collects information from the initiator of the

---

[55] See also *The Social Charter in the 21st Century* [Colloquium], Council of Europe, (Strasbourg, 14–16 May 1997).
[56] Protocol Amending the European Social Charter, ETS 142 (adopted on 21 October 1991, not yet in force).
[57] European Social Charter (Revised), ETS 163 (in force 1 July 1999).
[58] Additional Protocol to the European Social Charter Providing for a System of Collective Complaints, ETS 158 (in force 1 July 1998).

complaint, the state concerned, the other contracting parties to the European Social Charter and from the social partners. The Committee then draws up a report to the Committee of Ministers containing its opinion of whether or not the state in question has ensured the satisfactory application of the Charter as concerns the substantive issue raised in the complaint.

(b) Fact-finding

The European Social Charter's effectiveness has been hindered by four major weaknesses, in addition to the *à la carte* nature of the procedure mentioned above: its heavy and slow procedure, uncertainty as to the respective roles of the Committee of Independent Experts and of the Governmental Committee, the absence of actual participation of the social partners in the supervisory procedure, and the lack of any significant political sanction as the outcome of this procedure. The Charter's effectiveness has also been diminished by the inadequacy of certain of its provisions, overtaken by the realities and needs of modern Europe.[59] This makes procedural changes and amendments to this instrument particularly important.

The basic premise upon which the reporting system functions, namely an international control procedure based on reports submitted by states parties on the implementation of the European Social Charter, cannot – strictly speaking – be considered a "fact-finding" mechanism. The supervision of the European Social Charter's implementation is based almost entirely upon national reports from contracting parties (supplemented by information provided by the Experts themselves and the Secretariat). As yet, no party has failed to report on accepted provisions, although reports are often several months late. The Committee of Independent Experts has encountered real difficulties, however, in verifying the compliance of law and practice with accepted undertakings, despite assistance provided to it by the ILO observer.[60] Independent fact-gathering and assessment ("Conclusions") presuppose that it is possible to obtain accurate factual information on the situation in the state under examination. Although copies of state reports are sent for comments to national employers and trade union organizations (who are also entitled to be represented at the meetings of the Governmental Committee, in other words, at a later stage of proceedings), in practice very few organizations reply.[61] Indeed, the lack of interest of such organizations deprives the supervisory system of a potentially valuable source of information. Similarly, until recently no provision had been made for the participation of NGOs specializing in the social rights field. While this has now been remedied to a certain extent by the Amending Protocol *vis-à-vis* certain international NGOs, no provision exists to ensure that *national* NGOs receive reports, although they obviously possess more direct information and a vested interest in the national situation. In short, the fact-finding capacities of the supervisory bodies are substantially restricted.[62]

---

[59] For example, European Social Charter, art. 8, was updated to increase the guarantee of equality between women and men.
[60] Revised European Social Charter, art. 24(2).
[61] *Supra*, note 15, Donna Gomien *et. al.*, especially at 415–430.
[62] Council of Europe, *European Social Charter: The Charter, its Protocols, the Revised Charter* (1997). See also Regis Brillat, "La Charte Sociale Européenne du Conseil de l'Europe. Développements Récents", 12 *Droit en Quart Monde* (1996) 2–13; Regis Brillat, "A New Protocol to the European Social Charter Providing for Collective Complaints", 1 *European Human Rights Law Review* (1996)

The Amending Protocol of 1991 provides for meetings between the Committee of Independent Experts and representatives of states parties at the request of either in order to provide "additional information and clarification" to facilitate the operation of the reporting process. These meetings, like the Committee's deliberations generally, are held *in camera*.[63] In actual fact, from a meticulous reading of the Committee's *Conclusions*, it transpires that two such meetings have already been held. One took place in May 1993 with a representative of the Turkish government,[64] and the other in June 1995, when a meeting was held with a representative of the Government of Cyprus on the Cypriot situation in relation to articles 1(2) and 6(4) of the European Social Charter.[65] A similar procedure was followed with respect to other states. Positive though this development is, it might be more sensible if in future social partners actually were asked to participate in such "meetings" (hearings?) in order to be able to respond immediately to any inaccuracies or potentially controversial matters raised, rather than by doing so in a written procedure after the 'meeting."

Procedures have also started to have 'bite': witness the Committee of Ministers readiness to issue resolutions, accompanied by 'recommendations' concerning the factual situation in *individual* states parties. A growing number of such resolutions have been adopted since 1993.[66] For example,[67] 15 January 1997 the Committee of Ministers noted the Committee of Independent Experts' (now European Committee of Social Rights) "negative conclusion with regard to articles 5 (right to organize) and 6(2) (promotion of machinery for voluntary negotiations) in a case concerning Malta. Police officers were still obliged to join the Maltese Police Association and were not entitled to become affiliated to another union or similar association." After having duly endorsed a proposal by the Governmental Committee, it recommended that Malta "take account, in an appropriate manner, of the negative conclusions of the Committee of Independent Experts and requests that it provide information in its next report on the measures it has taken to this effect."[68] In 1998 Malta introduced a bill before Parliament to amend their legislation regarding the police, but it has not been enacted. Malta's seventh report on the implementation of the Social Charter in September 1999 made no mention of the issue.[69] The European Committee of Social Rights considered the report and reiterated their negative conclusions, which will again need to be considered by the Governmental Committee and

---

52–61; Markus Jaeger, "The Additional Protocol to the European Social Charter Providing for a System of Collective Complaints", 10 *Leiden Journal of International Law* (1997) 67–78, and references made in these studies. See also *supra* note 55.

[63] Revised European Social Charter, art. 24(3) (like oral hearings in the context of most UN human rights treaty bodies).

[64] Committee of Independent Experts, *Conclusions* XIII-1, 1990–91 (1994) at 23.

[65] Committee of Independent Experts, *Conclusions* XIII-3 (1996) at 23.

[66] *Supra*, note 15, Donna Gomien *et. al.* at 425–426. See also Aalt. W. Heringa, "Social Rights and the Rule of Law", paper presented at the 1997 Strasbourg colloquium, *supra* note 55.

[67] Committee of Ministers, Recommendation No. R ChS(97)1 (15 January 1997).

[68] Such recommendations are in fact adopted by the Committee of Ministers in its composition restricted only to contracting states parties to the European Social Charter.

On the same day, 15 January 1997, two other recommendations were adopted, one addressed to Turkey: No. R ChS(97)1, and another to the United Kingdom: No. R ChS(97)3.

[69] *Seventh Report on the Implementation of the European Social Charter submitted by the Government of Malta*, RAP/Cha/MA/VII(99) Or. Eng.(21 September 1999) and Addendum. RAP/Cha/MA/VII(99) Add. Or. Eng.(20 October 1999).

the Committee of Ministers. It will be important to see how the Committee of Ministers will react, in turn, in the context of a failure to take remedial steps.

The most important innovation is, of course, the collective complaints mechanism,[70] a procedure which is comparable to that which exists in the ILO, although the latter applies only in the context of freedom of association through complaints brought before the Freedom of Association Committee of the ILO's Governing Body. A complaint may allege "unsatisfactory application" of the European Social Charter (article 1), in other words, non-compliance with any of the obligations that arise under the European Social Charter. Complaints must be collective in both a substantive and procedural sense, and may be brought regarding a general legal or factual situation that raises an issue of compliance with the European Social Charter.

Concerning the admissibility of complaints, no provision is made for holding an oral hearing or for joining the question of admissibility to the merits, but presumably the Committee of Independent Experts will not be prevented from instituting such procedures. Once a complaint is declared admissible, "all relevant written explanations or information" is provided to the Committee, which may organize a hearing of the complaint on the merits, as provided in article 7 of the Additional Protocol. The role of the Committee of Ministers at the final stage of proceedings is set out in article 9.

This collective complaints procedure has the potential to provide the European Social Charter enforcement mechanism with real teeth. Indeed, at this stage one cannot exclude the possibility that this new procedure may develop its own distinctive form of quasi-judicial procedures, including the presentation of evidence and argument before the Committee of Independent Experts, akin to the former procedures of the European Commission of Human Rights.[71]

(3) European Convention for the Prevention of Torture

(a) *An overview*

By ratifying the European Torture Convention,[72] the states parties undertake to permit visits by the European Committee for the Prevention of Torture and Inhuman or Degrading Treatment or Punishment, established by the Convention, to all places within their jurisdiction where persons are or may be deprived of their liberty by a public authority. The establishment of the Committee with its strong monitoring powers is the subject of the European Torture Convention.

Under article 8(2)(c) of the European Torture Convention, the prerogatives of the European Torture Committee include the right to interview in private and without restriction persons deprived of their liberty. The Committee has the

---

[70] *Supra*, note 62, Brillat and Jaeger. See also David J. Harris "The Collective Complaints Protocol to the ESC", paper presented at the 1997 Strasbourg Colloquium, *supra* note 55 at 100–129.
[71] The fact that the Committee of Independent Experts is to be *elected* by the Parliamentary Assembly (*supra* note 62) is certainly a move in the right direction.
[72] European Convention for the Prevention of Torture and Inhuman or Degrading Treatment or Punishment, *supra* note 10, Protocol No. 1, ETS 151 (adopted in 4 November1993, not yet in force) and Protocol No. 2, ETS 152 (adopted 4 November 1993, not yet in force).

mandate to examine the treatment of persons deprived of their liberty (in prisons, police stations, military barracks, mental hospitals, and so on) with a view to making recommendations, where necessary, to strengthen the protection of such persons against ill-treatment.

The preventive mechanism is of a non-judicial character and rests on two pillars: cooperation between the European Torture Committee and the states parties, and confidentiality. After each visit, the European Torture Committee is entitled to prepare a confidential report which contains its recommendations. By transmitting it to the party concerned, the Committee initiates an "ongoing dialogue" and cooperation with that state party, and the state is expected to take measures to meet the recommendations of the Committee. According to article 11(2) of the Convention, each state party may decide to lift the confidentiality of the relevant report of the Committee. To date the vast majority of states have made use of this provision, an important development which permits the informed public to evaluate work accomplished and progress achieved. The European Torture Committee also submits a yearly general report on its activities to the Committee of Ministers under article 12 of the Convention. The report is published.

Under article 10(2) of the European Torture Convention, when a state party fails to cooperate or refuses to improve the situation in the light of the recommendations of the Committee, the latter may decide by a two-thirds majority of its members and after the party concerned has had the opportunity to present its views, to make a public statement on the subject. This is clearly an exceptional procedure which, to date, has been adopted twice by the European Torture Committee.[73]

By the end of 1999, ten years after the European Torture Committee began its activities, the Committee had undertaken a total of 96 visits, 67 of a periodic nature and 29 *ad hoc*.[74]

(b) Fact-finding

The European Torture Committee's task is, as explained in article 1 of the European Torture Convention, to "examine the treatment of persons deprived of their liberty with a view to strengthening, if necessary, the protection of such persons from torture and from inhuman and degrading treatment or punishment." States parties have undertaken to permit unlimited and uncensored access

---

[73] *Public Statement on Turkey*, CPT/Inf (93) 1 (15 December 1992) and CPT/Inf (96)34 (6 December 1996).

[74] See Annual Reports of the European Torture Committee. For statistics to the end of 1998, for example, see: the 9th Annual Report, *9th General Report on the CPT's Activities Covering the Period 1 January to 31 December 1998*, CPT/Inf(99)12 (30 August 1999). This Convention has now been ratified by 40 of the 41 member states, Georgia being the only member state not to ratify the Convention: see the European Torture Committee internet site at www.cpt.coe.fr

For commentaries on the European Torture Committee, consult, in particular, Malcolm Evans and Rod Morgan, "The European Convention for the Prevention of Torture: 1992–1997", 46 *International and Comparative Law Quarterly* (1997) 663–675; analysis by Jim Murdoch, "The European Convention for the Prevention of Torture and Inhuman or Degrading Treatment (Human Rights Survey 1996)", 21 *European Law Review* (1996) 130–137; Mark Kelly, "Preventing Ill-Treatment: The Work of the CPT", 1 *European Human Rights Law Review* (1996) 287–303; *Human Rights and the Police*, Council of Europe Publishing (1997) 46–61 and references to other literature in these publications.

to any person deprived of liberty, and to other information "which is necessary for the Committee to carry out its task."[75] The members of the Committee are expected to be independent and impartial, and to serve in their individual capacities. As explained, the European Torture Committee visits prisons and other places of detention such as police stations, military detention centres, secure mental hospitals and holding rooms for aliens. Periodic visits are conducted on a regular basis (every three to four years on average) and visits "required in the circumstances" (known as *ad hoc* visits") are made when the European Torture Committee considers this appropriate.[76]

In carrying out its functions, the European Torture Committee avails itself not only of legal standards contained in the European Convention, as interpreted by its supervisory organs, but also of other relevant legal instruments such as the European Prison Rules of 1987, which impose "powerful moral and political obligations on those member states that have accepted them".[77] The Committee uses a wide range of information sources – governmental, inter-governmental and non-governmental – in the context of deciding which countries to visit and when, and which subject areas/establishments should be given priority in the course of a visit. The European Torture Committee arrives at its own conclusions, however, and formulates its recommendations in the light of the information gathered during a visit.

The European Torture Convention obliges the European Torture Committee to draw up a report on the facts found during each visit. The report is submitted to the state concerned on a confidential basis. However, article 11(2) of the European Torture Convention stipulates that the Committee "shall publish its report, together with the comments of the Party concerned, whenever requested to do so by that Party." Of the 21 states visited in the first round of periodic visits between 1990 and 1993, with the exception of Turkey, all have authorized publication, (and all, except San Marino, have published one or more responses).

As the publication of European Torture Committee reports with detailed information concerning the way in which visits are conducted in the public domain has become the norm, only a few comments on the European Torture Committee's "fact-finding" procedures will be made here, concerning both the results produced by its work as well as the way it carries out its task. The

---

See also Parliamentary Assembly Recommendation 1323 (1997) (21 April 1997) on strengthening the machinery of the European Torture Convention (together with *Report of the Committee on Legal and Human Rights*, 7784). In this Recommendation, note is made of the fact that the ratification of the European Torture Convention by Russia and by Ukraine will more than double the prison population subject to the European Torture Committee's mandate and that an increase in human and budgetary resources of the European Torture Committee is a *sine qua non* in order to safeguard this body's effectiveness and credibility. Since the time the said Assembly Recommendation was issued both Russia and Ukraine have ratified the Convention.

[75] European Torture Convention, arts. 2 and 8(1). Art. 9(1) permits certain restrictions "in exceptional cases."

[76] It is interesting to note that as of 18 February 2000, of the 35 members of the European Torture Committee, 18 were lawyers (including 2 former parliamentarians), 6 were physicians, and 6 were psychologists. A group of 9 members (including 3 of the lawyers) have some operational experience of penal administration.

[77] *European Prison Rules*, Recommendation R (87) 3, Council of Europe: Committee of Ministers (12 February 1987); quotation taken from the introduction of the Explanatory Memorandum of the Rules.

European Torture Committee has issued only two public statements in accordance with article 10(2).[78] In December 1992, the Committee concluded in relation to Turkey that "the practice of torture and other forms of severe ill-treatment of persons in police custody remains widespread," that this is a "deep-rooted problem" and that the Turkish authorities were failing to take steps to improve the situation.[79] The same conclusions were repeated in 1996.[80]

The European Torture Committee pays particular attention to the extent to which certain basic safeguards against ill-treatment exist, especially the rights to notify a close relative or third party when a person is apprehended, to have access to and the assistance of an independent lawyer, as well as to have access to a doctor (including to a doctor of one's own choice). The Committee considers that these three rights should apply from the very outset of detention, from the moment when a person is obliged to remain with the police, and that persons deprived of their liberty by the police should be given information on their rights in a language which they understand. The possibility of lodging a complaint to an independent body about ill-treatment or conditions of detention is regarded as another essential safeguard.

The organizational aspects of visits have been well-documented in academic commentaries.[81] It suffices here to note the distinction between fact-finding undertaken by the European Commission or now Court of Human Rights[82] and that performed by the European Torture Committee. Whereas fact-finding under the European Convention was undertaken (and will continue to be under Protocol No. 11) in the context of the examination of an application, the scope of the European Torture Committee's jurisdiction is wider. It embraces regular visits of inspection which form the basis for general recommendations. In other words, as indicated in the European Torture Convention's preamble, the protection of detained persons is "strengthened by non-judicial means of a preventive nature based on visits," focussing upon institutions or practices rather than upon the individual detained. The investigation of a particular situation in the course of a visit by the European Torture Committee will not preclude an application under the European Convention or the First Optional Protocol of the UN Covenant on Civil and Political Rights.[83] There is, however, an obvious risk of overlap of the work of the European Convention mechanism with that of *ad hoc* visits by the European Torture Committee.[84]

Concerning the logistics of a visit, note should be taken of the way in which "experts" are utilized.[85] Visiting delegations require a blend of expertise and

---

[78] *Supra*, note 73.
[79] *Supra*, note 73, 1992 Statement at paras. 2, 21 and 25.
[80] *Supra*, note 73, 1996 Statement.
[81] See, in particular, Malcolm Evans and Rod Morgan, "The ECPT: Operational Practice", 41 *International and Comparative Law Quarterly* (1992) 590–614 (as well as publications referred to, *supra* note 74).
[82] Under Art. 38(1)(a) of the European Convention.
[83] First Optional Protocol to the International Covenant on Civil and Political Rights, 999 UNTS 171 (in force 23 March 1976).

As regards periodic visits, this is quite clear. But as concerns *ad hoc* visits, the position might be more controversial: see European Torture Convention, art. 17(1) and its *Explanatory Report*, CPT/Inf/C (89) 1 Part 2 (26 November 1987) at para. 71.

[84] *Supra*, note 81 at 591–593.
[85] Discussed by Evans and Morgan in both of their articles in the *International and Comparative Law Quarterly*, in 1992 and 1997, *supra* notes 74 and 81.

experience. When this blend cannot be provided by members, it is achieved by recruiting experts on an as-needed basis, many of whom have medical and psychiatric qualifications. The European Torture Committee has made frequent use of such experts, raising an issue regarding the text of the European Torture Convention. When the Convention was being drafted, the question arose as to whether visits should be made by members, or by a panel of experts on whose reports members should rely. The latter model, inspired by the International Committee of the Red Cross, was favoured by NGOs, such as the International Commission of Jurists, but the former view prevailed. Though the European Torture Convention allows the Committee to be assisted by experts when "it considers it necessary",[86] the status of experts was downgraded and their use apparently intended to be the exception rather than the rule. In fact, the reverse has proved to be the case: the European Torture Committee has consistently made use of a relatively small number of experts.[87]

Publication of the European Torture Committee's visit reports has become the norm. On occasion, however, there have been difficulties at the local level, in particular concerning the gaining of rapid access to places of detention. During second periodic visits, it appeared in some instances that persons in charge of places reviewed in the course of the first periodic visit had not been informed of earlier findings.[88]

---

[86] European Torture Convention, art. 7(2).
[87] *Supra*, note 74, Evans and Morgan, indicate that six out of the 33 experts used up to the end of 1996 have accompanied delegations on six or more occasions.
[88] *5th General Report on the CPT's Activities Covering the Period 1 January to 31 December 1994*, CPT/Inf(95)10 (3 July 1995) at paras. 4 to 6. Overall, the European Torture Committee considers its cooperation with national authorities "invariably... very good": *2nd General Report on the CPT's Activities Covering the Period 1 January to 31 December 1991*, CPT/Inf(92)3 (13 April 1992) at para. 20. See also the *3rd General Report on the CPT's Activities Covering the Period 1 January to 31 December 1992*, CPT/Inf(93)12 (4 June 1993) at para. 15, and the *5th General Report on the CPT's Activities Covering the Period 1 January to 31 December 1994*, *supra* at para. 4.

III. An Effective Individual Complaint Mechanism in an International Human Rights Context

CHAPTER 10

An Effective Complaints Procedure in the Context of International Human Rights Law

Andrew Byrnes*

(1) Introduction

One of the most striking developments in the field of international human rights in the post-World War II era has been the adoption of a range of international procedures under which individuals subject to the jurisdiction of a country can bring alleged human rights violations by that country before an international body. The proliferation of these procedures and their burgeoning use – especially in the last two decades – manifest a shift of emphasis towards the more effective implementation and enforcement of existing human rights standards rather than a continuing concentration of the formulation of additional standards (though that process has also continued).

These procedures are of various types,[1] but one significant category comprises individual complaint procedures under which a state accepts the jurisdiction of an international body to receive complaints by an individual that the state has violated the internationally guaranteed rights of that person. There are two major categories of communication procedures. The first includes those procedures available as the result of a state's membership in an international organization. The individual communications procedure of the UN Educational, Scientific and Cultural Organization (UNESCO)[2] and the complaint procedures

---

*I am grateful to Elizabeth Evatt for her comments on a draft of this chapter, as well as to Caroline Dommen for information she provided.
[1] See generally Hurst Hannum (ed.), *Guide to International Human Rights Practice 3rd ed*, Transnational (1999) and Andrew Byrnes, "Using International Procedures to Advance the Human Rights of Women", in *Women's International Human Rights, Law Volume 2*, Kelly Dawn Askin and Dorean Koenig (eds.), Transnational (1999) at 79.
[2] UNESCO EX/Decision 3.3, Doc 120 (1978) at para 14(a)(ii). See generally on the UNESCO procedure: David Weissbrodt and Rose Farley, "The UNESCO Human Rights Procedure: An Evaluation", 16 *Human Rights Quarterly* (1994) 391; Philip Alston, "UNESCO's Procedures for Dealing with Human Right Violations", 20 *Santa Clara Law Review* (1980) 665; Steven Marks, "UNESCO and Human Rights: The Implementation of Rights Relating to Education, Science, Culture and Communication Violations", 13 *Texas International Law Journal* (1997) 35; Suzanne Bastid, "La Mise en Oeuvre d'un Recours Concernant les Droits de l'Homme dans le Domaine Relevant de la Compétence de l'UNESCO", in *Völkerrecht als Rechtsordnung – Internationale*

under the International Labour Organization (ILO) Constitution (though restricted to organizations rather than being open to individuals)[3] are examples. The second type comprises the individual complaint procedures established under both United Nations and regional human rights treaties. Under this category, a state may elect to recognize the competence of a body established by the treaty (or given jurisdiction under it) to consider complaints by individuals that the state has violated the rights guaranteed in the relevant treaty. Examples include the procedure established by First Optional Protocol to the International Covenant on Civil and Political Rights (CCPR),[4] the Optional Protocol to the Convention on the Elimination of All Forms of Discrimination Against Women (CEDAW),[5] article 22 of the Convention against Torture (CAT),[6] and article 14 of the International Convention on the Elimination of All Forms of Racial Discrimination (CERD),[7] as well as the procedures available under the European Convention on Human Rights (European Convention),[8] the American Convention on Human Rights (American Convention),[9] and the African Charter on Human and Peoples' Rights (African Charter).[10] There is also a proposal to

---

Gerichtsbarkeit – Menschenrechte: Festschrift für Hermann Mosler, Rudolf Bernhardt, Wilheim Geck, Günther Jänicke & Helmut Steinberger (eds.) (1983) 47.

[3] See Klaus Samson, "The Standard-Setting and Supervisory Activities of the International Labour Organisation", in *Social Rights as Human Rights: A European Challenge*, Krzysztof Drzewicki, Catarina Krause and Allan Rosas (eds.), Finland Institute for Human Rights (1994) 115 at 142–144; and Virginia Leary, "Lessons from the Experience of the International Labour Organisation", in *Human Rights and the United Nations: A Critical Appraisal*, Philip Alston (ed.), Clarendon Press (1992) 580 at 609–611.

[4] First Optional Protocol to the International Covenant on Civil and Political Rights, 999 UNTS 171 (in force 23 March 1976). See generally Manfred Nowak, *UN Covenant on Civil and Political Rights: CCPR Commentary*, N.P. Engel (1993) at 647–723; and Dominic McGoldrick, *The Human Rights Committee: Its Role in the Development of the International Covenant on Civil and Political Rights*, Clarendon (1991) at 120–246. See also Manfred Nowak, "The Activities of the UN Human Rights Committee: Developments from 1 August 1992 to 31 July 1995", 16 *Human Rights Law Journal* (1995) 377 at 382–397.

[5] Optional Protocol to the Convention on the Elimination of all Forms of Discrimination Against Women, G.A. Res. 54/4, annex, adopted on 6 October 1999 (not yet in force). CEDAW, 1249 UNTS 14 (in force 3 September 1981).

[6] Convention Against Torture and other Forms of Cruel, Inhuman or Degrading Treatment or Punishment, 1465 UNTS 85 (in force 26 June 1987), art. 22.

[7] Convention on the Elimination of All Forms of Racial Discrimination, 660 UNTS 3 (in force 4 January 1969, art. 14.

[8] Convention for the Protection of Human Rights and Fundamental Freedoms, ETS 5 (in force 3 September 1953), as amended by Protocol No. 11, ETS 155 (in force 1 November 1998).

[9] American Convention on Human Rights, PAUTS 36 (in force 18 July 1978). Individual complaints alleging violations of the American Declaration of the Rights and Duties of Man (adopted 1948) can also be brought to the Inter-American Commission on Human Rights against all member States of the OAS. The Inter-American Convention on the Prevention, Punishment and Eradication of Violence against Women, 33 *International Legal Materials* (1994) 1535, also makes provision for individual complaints.

[10] African Charter on Human and Peoples' Rights (in force 21 October 1986). On the work of the African Commission in relation to individual communications submitted under the African Charter, see generally Rachel Murray, "Decisions by the African Commission on Individual Communications under the African Charter on Human and Peoples' Rights", 46 *International and Comparative Law Quarterly* (1997) 412; and Evelyn A. Ankumah, *The African Commission on Human and Peoples' Rights: Practice and Procedures*, Martinus Nijhoff (1996) at 51–77.

adopt an individual complaints procedure to supplement the International Covenant on Economic, Social and Cultural Rights (CESCR).[11]

These efforts are taking place at a time when major reforms have been made to the European Convention system of dealing with individual complaints and when the increasing workload of the United Nations bodies, combined with decreasing levels of resources, has stimulated efforts to find more efficient ways of dealing with that workload (including communications).[12] The recent adoption of new complaint procedures and the proposal for others evidence the belief on the part of many in the international community that these procedures provide a useful way of enhancing the enjoyment of internationally guaranteed human rights and providing remedies for their breach.

This Chapter attempts to address the question of whether the individual complaints procedures under the UN human rights treaties are effective, and seeks to identify the factors that contribute to, or detract from, the effective operation of such procedures.[13] A striking aspect of the literature relating to international human rights procedures is the dearth of comprehensive and detailed evaluations of the impact that these procedures have had in practice at the national level: one is largely reliant on anecdotal accounts of the impact of reporting procedures or complaints procedures. This is no doubt due to the fact that these procedures are still relatively young, but it is clearly time to promote such studies as part of an overall review of the system as it exists today.

(2) Criteria of effectiveness: goals and functions of an individual complaint procedure

Experience has shown that an individual complaints procedure can contribute to the effective protection of human rights in a number of ways, not all of which were necessarily contemplated or intended to be primary goals of the procedure by the drafters. While the primary motivation of such a procedure is to provide a remedy for a wronged individual, the impact of the procedure may be beneficial even in cases in which a timely and effective remedy is not afforded the individual. In practice such procedures can perform other, perhaps equally significant, functions. These functions have become an important part of the contribution of the procedure to the realization of human rights. This impact needs to be taken into account in assessing the overall contribution of the procedure (and indeed was invoked by advocates of an Optional Protocol to CEDAW and advocates of a new procedure under the CESCR as part of the reason why an individual complaint procedure is important).

An assessment of the effectiveness of an individual complaint procedure requires an identification of the goals of the procedure and an evaluation of the

---

[11] International Covenant on Economic, Social and Cultural Rights, 993 UNTS 3 (in force 3 January 1976).
[12] See generally *infra* Anne Bayefsky, Appendix 6, *International Law Association, Committee on International Human Rights Law and Practice, Report on the UN Human Rights Treaties: Facing the Implementation Crisis.*
[13] See generally Markus Schmidt, "Individual Human Rights Complaints Procedures based on United Nations Treaties and the Need for Reform", 41 *International and Comparative Law Quarterly* (1992) 645.

extent to which these goals are met. In practice, individual complaint procedures can be seen as potentially serving at least three functions:

- providing an effective and timely remedy to the person whose rights have been violated;
- bringing about changes to law and practice in the respondent state which will benefit others in a similar position to the complainant, now and in the future; and
- through the elaboration of a jurisprudence of the relevant treaty, providing guidance to states parties and others on the meaning of the guarantees contained in the treaty and the measures that are needed to protect those rights.[14]

While the first role is for most people the major reason for adopting an individual complaint procedure, in practice the others may turn out to be equally significant. In addition, if the upshot of a successful complaint is that laws and administrative practices generally need to be changed, rather than a remedy such as damages provided in an individual case, such a procedure may also benefit others in a similar situation in the same country who are not parties to the complaint. The changes may take too long or come too late for the complainant who mounted the challenge, but they may inure to the benefit of others in a similar position.

Thirdly, the process of adjudication can play an important role in showing those who are not directly involved in the litigation the scope of the obligations contained in the treaty insofar as the case law developed under the complaints procedure provides a source of precedential/quasi-authoritative interpretation of those provisions.

(3) Provision of redress for the individual

The primary motivation for the adoption of individual complaint procedures under the various UN human rights treaties was no doubt the hope that, where a person had been unable to obtain redress at the national level for an alleged human rights violation, the formal pronouncement by a treaty body that there had been a violation of the rights guaranteed by the treaty would lead to the provision of a remedy and might ensure that violations of the same sort were prevented in the future. For a complaints procedure to be viewed as effective from this perspective, one must be able to show that resort to the procedure has provided a remedy for victims of violations in some, or several cases.

---

[14] Rein Müllerson has suggested that an individual complaints procedure can in theory serve three different functions:
   First, as a result of considering such a complaint an individual, whose rights have been violated, may have a remedy against the wrong suffered by him, and the violation could be stopped and/or compensation paid, etc; second, considering a complaint may result not only in a remedy for the victim of the violation, whose complaint has been considered, but also in changes to internal legislation and practice; and third, an individual complaint (or more often, a series of complaints) may serve as evidence of systematic and/or massive violations of certain rights in a given country."
Rein Müllerson, "The Efficiency of the Individual Complaint Procedures: The Experience of CCPR, CERD, CAT and ECHR", in *Monitoring Human Rights in Europe: Comparing International Procedures and Mechanisms*, Arie Bloed et al. (eds.), Martinus Nijhoff (1993) at 25, 26.

Assessments of the effectiveness of the CCPR Optional Protocol in this regard have been mixed. Two former members of the Human Rights Committee, for example, are pessimistic about the effectiveness of the procedure in providing effective relief. One of them, Rein Müllerson, is of the opinion that in practice an individual complaint procedure serves only the second function outlined above, namely bringing about changes in laws and practices that may be of benefit to other persons rather than to the complainant.[15] Similarly, Bernhard Graefrath maintains that the individual complaints procedure "can do little" to protect an individual's rights, as it "starts too late, takes too much time, does not lead to binding results and lacks any effective enforcement."[16] Is this pessimistic assessment a fair one, or has the procedure in fact provided more by way of redress for individual complainants than these assessments suggest?[17]

An effective procedure is one that provides an accessible and relatively speedy procedure for reviewing both parties' claims of fact and law in a fair manner, that results in a determination which gives a clear indication of the basis of a finding and of the steps that need to be taken to remedy any violation, and that is acted upon by the state concerned within a reasonable time. While the ultimate criterion may be whether a remedy is actually provided to the complainant within a reasonable time, the manner in which the procedure is conducted and the quality of the decision-making may well influence that outcome.

In assessing the effectiveness of a procedure, it is useful to examine the following factors:

- *Accessibility of the procedure*: How many of those individuals who might bring complaints under the procedure avail themselves of that opportunity? Are the barriers to this a lack of knowledge about the procedure, lack of expertise or lack of funds?
- *Speed and efficiency*: How quickly and efficiently does the adjudicatory body consider a complaint once it has been submitted?
- *Interim measures*: Does the adjudicatory body have power to request interim measures of protection? Do states abide by such requests?
- *Due process concerns*: Does each party have a fair opportunity to put forward its case and permit full consideration of disputed issues of fact and law so that credible and persuasive decisions result?
- *Participation by states parties*: Do states parties participate in the consideration of complaints? What can be done where states parties do not so participate?
- *Quality of decision-making*: Does the decision of the adjudicatory body clearly indicate the reasoning on which any finding of a violation is based or indicate the appropriate remedy so that the state party can take the necessary remedial steps?

---

[15] *Ibid.*, at 27–28.
[16] Bernhard Graefrath, "Reporting and Complaint Systems in Universal Human Rights Treaties", in *Human Rights in a Changing East/West Perspective*, Allan Rosas and Jan Helgesen (eds.), Pinter Publishers (1990) 290 at 327; Bernhard Graefrath, *Menschenrechte und Internationale Kooperation: 10 Jahre Praxis des Internationalem Menschenrechtskommittees*, Akademie-Verlag (1988) at 170–171.
[17] Neither of these commentators place any special emphasis on the lawmaking role of such a procedure through the development of case law in response to complaints.

- *State compliance*: Do states comply with the decision by providing the remedy recommended within a reasonable time?
- *Follow-up*: Does the adjudicatory body have effective procedures for follow-up to monitor steps that have been taken and to ensure that reluctant or recalcitrant states give effect to the decision?

(4) Indicia of an effective complaints system

(a) Awareness and accessibility of the procedure

One measure of the effectiveness of an international complaints procedure that might be adopted is whether the procedure is really accessible to the citizens of countries which have accepted it and in which there are clearly many violations of the rights guaranteed. It has been noted on various occasions that many of the complaints lodged under the CCPR Optional Protocol have come from a small number of states, and that the vast majority of states (including a number in which it is well-known that there are serious violations of human rights) have produced few or no complaints.[18] Furthermore, many of these complaints involve "fine-tuning" of human rights concerns in countries where the protection of human rights is generally good, rather than serious or systematic violations of human rights. While this argument discounts the serious violations that have been raised under such procedures (including against countries with generally good human rights records), the distribution of complaints under the CCPR Optional Protocol is striking.[19] The question implicitly raised by such observations is whether the resources of the international system would be better directed, either through the complaints procedure or through some other mechanisms, towards addressing the much more serious violations that occur in some countries. For those committed to using complaints procedures to address violations, it raises the questions of how individuals in other countries can be empowered to make complaints.[20]

Various reasons have been suggested for this lack of utilization of international

---

[18] See, for example, *supra* note 12, *infra* Appendix 6 at 689; Elizabeth Evatt, "The Right to Individual Petition: Assessing Its Operation before the Human Rights Committee and Its Future Application to the Women's Convention on Discrimination", in *Proceedings of the 89th Annual Meeting of the American Society of International Law* (1995) 227 at 228 ("Experience with the ICCPR suggests that there is no necessary correspondence between the level of violations in a state and resort to the communications procedure."); Torkel Opsahl, "The Human Rights Committee" in *The United Nations and Human Rights: A Critical Appraisal*, Philip Alston (ed.), Oxford (1992) 369 at 422–423.

[19] A similar development has taken place under the complaints procedure established by art. 22 of CAT. A large number of complaints have been lodged by asylum-seekers in countries such as Sweden, Switzerland and Canada seeking protection under art. 3 of the Convention against return to a country where they claim they run a real risk of being subjected to torture. The number of cases claiming actual torture or inhuman treatment by the respondent state is fairly small. See generally Andrew Byrnes, "The Committee against Torture", in *Human Rights and the United Nations: A Critical Appraisal*, Philip Alston (ed.), Oxford (2nd ed, forthcoming, 2000).

[20] This assumes that an individual complaints procedure can have a positive impact on a situation where there are systematic and widespread violations of human rights, and raises the question of whether "rogue" governments are likely to heed the decisions of the Committee. While the experience of the Human Rights Committee may be somewhat disheartening in this regard, over the longer term it may be that the procedure can have an impact, even in such cases. Compare Menno T. Kamminga, "Is the European Convention on Human Rights Sufficiently Equipped to Cope with

procedures. One significant obstacle must be a high level of ignorance about the availability of the procedure and how one goes about invoking it,[21] and a lack of access to expertise that could assist in the formulation and submission of a complaint.

In theory, bringing a case before the Human Rights Committee need not involve great expense (though exhaustion of domestic remedies may well), since it is not necessary to employ a lawyer to lodge the complaint, the complainant is not required to travel to Geneva or New York for an oral hearing, and costs are not awarded against an unsuccessful complainant (as is the case in some legal systems). Nevertheless, lodging a complaint without recourse to any expert assistance may not be a practical option for many, and in order to give a complaint the best chance of success expert assistance of some sort is frequently required to ensure that it is properly formulated and supported. At present, there is no international legal aid available to finance the preparation of such cases for submission to the UN bodies, as there is within the Council of Europe for cases brought to Strasbourg. Although it appears that legal aid may be available under national legal aid schemes in some countries,[22] it is not clear how widespread this is,[23] and it is probably very much the exception. Fortunately, in many cases lawyers and human rights groups are prepared to provide this type of assistance on a pro bono basis: many of the death penalty cases brought before the Human Rights Committee from the Commonwealth Caribbean have been submitted in this manner.[24]

The challenge is to ensure that potential complainants are informed and can access this type of assistance. A number of practical steps have been taken by governments and non-governmental organizations (NGOs) to enhance awareness of such procedures. In some countries, following ratification of the Optional Protocol, seminars have been held to raise awareness among government officials and lawyers on the significance of the ratification, the procedure itself and the case law of the Committee. Canada and Nepal are two examples of this. In Australia, a CCPR Optional Protocol network was established by a group of

---

Gross and Systematic Violations?", 12(2) *Netherlands Quarterly of Human Rights* (1994) 153.

[21] See *supra* note 12, *infra* Appendix 6 at 689.

[22] See, for example, *Wellington District Legal Services Corporation v. Tangiora* (1997) 3 *Human Rights Reports of New Zealand* 136, (1997) 3 *Butterworths Human Rights Cases* 1 (New Zealand C.A.). In this case the New Zealand Court of Appeal reversed the decision of the High Court which had held that the Human Rights Committee was a "judicial authority" within the meaning of the Legal Services Act (1991) and that a person was therefore entitled to apply for legal aid to bring a case before the Committee under the Optional Protocol, provided that the person satisfied the other tests for the award of legal aid ((1996) 3 *Human Rights Reports of New Zealand* 267, [1997] *New Zealand Administrative Reports* 118). The case involved a challenge by a Maori group which, having unsuccessfully challenged provisions of the Treaty of Waitangi (Fisheries Settlement) Act under national law, wished to bring their case before the Human Rights Committee. An appeal to the Privy Council from the judgment of the Court of Appeal was subsequently dismissed: *Tangiora v. Wellington District Legal Services Corporation* [2000] 1 *Weekly Law Reports* 240, [2000] *New Zealand Law Reports* 17.

[23] See *supra* note 22, *Tangiora* at 9 (noting that, of 17 countries surveyed, only the Netherlands, and possibly Finland, provided legal aid for bringing cases to the Human Rights Committee).

[24] For example, the London law firm Simons Muirhead & Burton has provided pro bono representation to more than 50 persons sentenced to death in the Caribbean for the purpose of appealing to the Privy Council, as well as to the Human Rights Committee and the Inter-American Commission on Human Rights. The project, supported by Penal Reform International, is co-funded by the European Commission and Simons Muirhead & Burton.

interested academics and practising lawyers, and for a period the federal government provided financial support for its activities. Such actions require a certain broad-mindedness on the part of governments, many of which may well be reluctant to stir up litigation against themselves. They would also presumably lead to an increase in workload of the Human Rights Committee, something which would need to be addressed by further innovations in the manner in which the Committee considers complaints.

(b) Speed in considering and disposing of cases

From the individual complainant's point of view, a speedy determination of a complaint is obviously desirable. In most cases the requirement that the complainant first exhaust all available domestic remedies will mean that (s)he may already have been involved in litigation at the national level for a number of years. Even if the complainant succeeds at the end of the day, if the proceedings before the international forum have taken up an excessive amount of time, the victory may be of little consolation.

Various factors influence the time taken to consider and dispose of a complaint at the international level: the volume of complaints pending consideration;[25] the frequency with which the Committee meets; the need to provide adequate time to both the government and complainant to respond to submissions of the other party; the resources available within the UN Secretariat to process complaints; and the complexity of the case and the volume of material placed before the Committee.

The time taken for consideration of a complaint under the CCPR Optional Protocol varies in length, but is normally rather long. For example, in relation to the final decisions adopted by the Human Rights Committee between 1995 and 1999,[26] the average length of time from submission of the communication to the adoption of a final decision by the Committee was three and one-half years; the shortest time was 4 months, and the longest 6 years and 3 months.[27] Decisions on the initial question of admissibility generally made up 2 years of the overall time,[28] although recent reforms have permitted joining the issues of

---

[25] As of 13 December 1999, the Human Rights Committee had registered 903 cases since it commenced its work under the Optional Protocol. Of these, 167 were pending: *Statistical Survey of Individual Complaints Dealt with by the Human Rights Committee under the Optional Protocol to the International Covenant on Civil and Political Rights,* http://www.unhchr.ch/html/menu2/8/stat2.htm. The Committee deals with about 30–35 cases per year on the merits, as well as making a considerable number of decisions on inadmissibility.

[26] At the 52nd through the 66th sessions of the Committee: see *Report of the Human Rights Committee,* A/50/40 Vol.II, CCPR/C/57/1 (1995); *Report of the Human Rights Committee,* A/51/40 Vol.II (1996); *Report of the Human Rights Committee,* A/52/40 Vol.II (1997); *Report of the Human Rights Committee,* A/53/40 Vol.II (1998); *Report of the Human Rights Committee,* A/54/40 Vol.II (1999) (forthcoming).

[27] The Judicial Committee of the Privy Council expressed the hope in *Pratt v. Attorney-General for Jamaica* [1993] 2 *Appeal Cases* 1, [1993] 4 *All England Reports* 769 (P.C.) at 788 that it would be possible for the Human Rights Committee to deal with cases involving death penalty cases "at most within eighteen months" from their submission.

[28] This may be compared with the record of CAT up to April 1999 (the 1999 Annual Report). An examination of the communications contained in the annual reports of the Committee in 1995 to 1999 shows that it has generally been able to reach admissibility decisions in one year and has also generally adopted its views within a year to a year and one-half of submission of the complaint. The workload of CAT (which received 133 communications from 1987 to April 1999) is, of course, much lighter than that of the Human Rights Committee.

admissibility and merits to shorten delays. Similar delays have bedevilled the operation of the Strasbourg process.

It is difficult to know how to address this problem if one wishes to ensure that the parties are given a fair opportunity to put their case. The Human Rights Committee may need to give further consideration to imposing less generous time limits for the parties to respond at each stage of the proceedings. This is a delicate matter, since a state party which considers that it has been denied the opportunity to present its case fully is less likely to abide by the decision of the Committee than it might otherwise have been.

(c) *Interim measures (power and capacity to act quickly)*

Related to the time needed for the consideration of complaints is the availability of interim measures to protect the complainant from irreparable harm, and the extent to which requests for interim measures are heeded by states. The Human Rights Committee, CAT and CERD all have the competence to request a state party to take interim measures pending the consideration of a complaint. Such requests have been made in a number of cases, mainly in death penalty cases and deportation/expulsion cases. In general, these requests appear to have been observed by states parties, though in a couple of cases governments have not given effect to them,[29] or have taken steps that mean that a request for interim measures could not be made.[30]

---

[29] In *Ashby v. Jamaica* (580/1994), the Special Rapporteur for New Communications had requested, under Rule 86 of the Committee's Rule of Procedure, a stay of execution for Ashby pending consideration of his complaint by the Committee (the matter was also still before the Privy Council). Ashby was executed the day after the request was sent. Jamaica failed to respond to the Committee's request for an explanation, leading to the adoption by the Committee of a formal resolution on the subject: *Report of the Human Rights Committee*, A/49/40 (1994) Vol. I, at 70. In 1988, in *Lubicon Lake Band v. Canada* (167/1984), in A/45/40 Vol. II (26 March 1990) at 1, the Human Rights Committee called on the government of Canada to take immediate steps to ensure no further damage be done to Lubicon society. One writer states that, following the decision, Alberta sold almost all the trees on the Lubicon's 4000 square mile territory to Daishowa, a Japanese-based forestry company: Ed Bianchi, "The Lubicon Lake Cree: Negotiations – An Update" 2 (1) *The Ethnic News Watch* 77 (1996). In *Kandu-Bo et al. v. Sierra Leone* (840 & 841/1998), the Special Rapporteur for New Communications requested on 13–14 October 1998, that the state party stay the execution of 12 individuals while their communications were under consideration by the Committee. The individuals were executed on 19 October 1998. Sierra Leone failed to respond to the Committee's request for further information, leading to the adoption by the Committee of a formal decision on the subject: *Report of the Human Rights Committee*, A/54/40 Vol. I (1999) Annex X. In *Piandiong v. Philippines* (869/1999) the state party did not comply with the Committee's request of 23 June 1999 to stay the execution of the authors of the communication, executing them some two weeks after the request was made, A/54/40 Vol. I (1999) at para. 420(b).

Under the Torture Convention states parties have generally complied with requests not to deport or expel individuals pending consideration of a communication, though not without some protest: see the complaint of Switzerland in *K.N. v. Switzerland* (94/1997), A/53/44 (19 May 1998) at 111, paras. 5.1–5.2. However, in one case, *Singh v. Canada*, it was reported that an Indian national whose application for asylum had not been successful and who had lodged a complaint with the Committee was deported to India, even though the Committee had requested the Canadian government not to do so pending resolution of the complaint: Lorne Waldman, "Canada too hasty to deport hijacker", *Toronto Star* (28 January 1998) at A21.

[30] In the case of *Ng v. Canada* (469/1991), A/49/40 Vol. II (5 November 1993) at 189, 15 *Human Rights Law Journal* (1994) 149, Ng's attorney claimed that the Canadian government had extradited Ng to the United States while there was a case pending before the Human Rights Committee. Ng had been returned immediately after the Supreme Court of Canada had dismissed his appeal, an

(d) Due process

The consideration of communications by all three treaty bodies takes place on paper. Parties are neither entitled to appear to present oral argument or evidence, nor are they invited to do so. Nevertheless, the procedure is based on the notion of adversarial proceedings and the right of each party to put its case fully. The desirability of oral hearings has been raised by some commentators (suggesting that they would facilitate the determination of disputed issues of fact and save time in the overall process of consideration of a complaint).[31] Concern about the power of the committee(s) to consider other than written evidence and, perhaps more importantly, concern that this would not be possible for reasons of time and resources, have meant that this proposal has not progressed very far.

It may, however, be worthwhile giving further consideration to the judicious use of oral hearings in appropriate cases. Issues that may take months to be resolved in the back and forth of written submissions between the parties and the Committee may be sorted out very quickly at an oral hearing at which all parties are present. In cases in which there are disputed issues of fact, an oral hearing may be the most effective way of dealing with the issue. Oral hearings would not have to be full-scale oral hearings as in the British mold; rather the procedure used by the United States appellate courts – under which brief oral argument follows extensive written submissions – might be more appropriate. Such hearings need not be held in every case.

However, the time and resources that the use of oral hearings (even on a modest scale) would involve are likely to stymie such a proposal. The Committee would have to spend more time considering communications in which oral hearings were held, though there are ways of reducing the overall impact. For example, if the Committee were to sit in chambers,[32] this would mean that less Committee time was used for this purpose. Furthermore, if the Committee wished to hold an oral hearing for the taking of evidence, there is no reason why it could not adopt a procedure found at both the international and national level and appoint one of its members to act as fact-finder and report to the Committee.

---

event which his lawyer claimed triggered a complaint pending before the Committee and of which the Canadian government was aware: Rick Mofina, "Ng Back in U.S. to Face Charges", *Calgary Herald* (27 September 1991) A1.

[31] See *supra* note 13 at 653. Though they were not motivated by a desire to improve the functioning of the Human Rights Committee's procedures, the following comments by a former Attorney-General of Australia are revealing:

It is just as well that the United Nations committee cannot enforce directly in Australia its findings on the application of the Covenant to a particular situation. The committee's method of arriving at its views on any matter before it would breach the procedural fairness requirements of Article 14 of the Covenant which states "all persons shall be equal before the Courts and Tribunals." The committee does not sit in public (as specifically required by the Article) and it makes its decision on the basis of written submissions from the complainant and the state party concerned. In the case of a federal state, it does not receive any submission from the provincial government, even if it is the alleged offender. The committee does not receive any evidence from witnesses and therefore the allegations of fact are untested by cross-examination. Nor does it listen to any oral argument by counsel for either party. Finally, it is not obliged to give any reasons for its decision.

Peter Durack, "Do We Need an Imported Bill of Rights?", 47(3) *Institute of Public Affairs Review* (1995) 29 at 32.

[32] Some members of the Human Rights Committee have expressed doubt whether the Optional Protocol would allow the Committee to take final decisions in chambers.

Even so, the additional expense involved might be considerable; perhaps consideration could be given to having a member of the Committee hold hearings in the country concerned, though this would still entail costs for the parties in the preparation for the oral hearing.

(e) *Publicity or confidentiality?*

Under the previous practice of the Human Rights Committee[33] (and the current practice of the other Committees),[34] proceedings were confidential to the Committee and to the parties until a decision on admissibility or a final decision had been reached. This meant, in theory, that a person lodging a complaint with the Committee was not free to discuss the progress of proceedings or to make available publicly copies of either party's submissions to the Committee. This restriction had been justified on the basis that the confidentiality of proceedings may have been more conducive to a friendly settlement or constructive discussion of the case, and might ensure that media pressure is not used in an attempt to pressure one of the parties.

This situation was unduly restrictive and not in accordance with the practice in most national jurisdictions where proceedings are commenced in the courts. Using publicity to embarrass a government is, within reason, a tactic that should be available at the national level to individuals. The Human Rights Committee revisited its position on this matter and decided at its April 1997 session to lift its restrictions on publicity. This was a welcome development; presumably either party may still request that the proceedings be considered confidential if the interests of justice require it.

(f) *Decisions and reasoning*

The decision of an adjudicatory body serves a number of functions. First, it must seek to explain and justify the conclusion it has reached in a persuasive manner; this is important for the acceptance and implementation of the decision by the party affected in an individual case, as well as for establishing the legitimacy of the body more generally. Second, the decision must give a clear indication of what remedy, if any, needs to be provided and of the measures necessary to avoid future violations. Third, and ideally, the decision should give those faced with similar or analogous issues guidance as to what a particular human rights guarantee requires a government to do in practice, in order to comply with its obligations.

The record of the UN treaty committees has been somewhat mixed when measured against these criteria.[35] While the background to a case and the submissions of the parties are set out in a standard format and in detail, the reasoning which underlies the decision is often rather brief,[36] and in some cases,

---

[33] See, for example, rule 96 of the *Rules of Procedure of the Human Rights Committee*, CCPR/C/3/Rev.3 (24 May 1994). This rule has now been amended: see *infra* note 34.
[34] For the revised rule 96, see *Rules of Procedure of the Human Rights Committee*, CCPR/C/3/Rev.5 (11 August 1997).
[35] See *supra* note 12 at 689.
[36] Opsahl comments on the views of the Human Rights Committee up to the early 1990s: "The views are not reasoned in great detail, but sufficiently to explain the Committee's understanding and application of the Covenant": *supra* note 18, Opsahl, at 427. See also *Towards an Optional Protocol*

involves little more than a formulaic incantation of a justificatory mantra laid down in an earlier case. While this may satisfy the immediate needs of the case, the danger of *ex cathedra*-style pronouncements is that they tend to undermine the authority of the Committee and to limit the utility of the decisions as a source of precedent, as well as making the decision difficult to apply to other contexts. Since the decisions of an international body can be extremely persuasive at the national level, from the point of view of developing the impact of the human rights treaties nationally it is important that full opportunity be taken to produce well-reasoned and more discursive decisions.[37]

It is perhaps unfair to single out individual decisions which may be less than clear or helpful in their reasoning, when others may satisfy that test.[38] Nevertheless, for those who are seeking to apply Covenant standards at the national level, the quality of individual decisions can make an important difference. For example, the case of *Kivenmaa v Finland*[39] involved a challenge to the holding of a public meeting by the applicant and members of her organization. Curiously, the Human Rights Committee held that this meeting did not amount to an assembly within the meaning of article 21, but considered the case one involving freedom of expression under article 19 only. The Committee did consider the article 21 issue in passing, however, and appeared to hold that a notification requirement for demonstrations may be permissible under article 21 of the CCPR, concluding that "the application of Finnish legislation on demonstrations to such a gathering cannot be considered as an application of a

---

to the International Covenant on Economic, Social and Cultural Rights, Analytical Paper adopted by the Committee on Economic, Social and Cultural Rights at its Seventh session, A/CONF.157/PC/ 62/Add. 5 (26 March 1993) at para. 30 ("[T]he vast majority of commentators who have assessed the work of the Human Rights Committee have acknowledged the enormous importance of the procedure [under the (First) Optional Protocol] in terms of its contribution to an enhanced understanding of the normative implications of many of the provisions contained in the Covenant").

[37] Henry Steiner has described the decisions of the Committee in the following terms:

Throughout the Committee's life, views have been written in a form that could not be called user-friendly.... The upshot is that views are uninspiring documents, whatever their audience... They hardly summon the human rights community to debate and dialogue.... These formulaic presentations go well back in the Committee's history.... Consider the typical view.... [I]t starts with detailed descriptions of legal arguments and assertions of fact made by the parties, set forth more or less in chronological order... Most of this material turns out to be irrelevant to the Committee's conclusions, as many of the parties' arguments fall by the wayside.

Henry Steiner, "Individual claims in a world of massive violations: What role for the Human Rights Committee?", in *The Future of UN Human Rights Treaty Monitoring*, Philip Alston and James Crawford (eds.), Cambridge University Press, 2000, 15 at 43.

[38] Henry Steiner argues that these cases (in which he would include the death penalty cases, *Toonen*, and the Holocaust denial case of *Faurisson*) "constitute a small minority of the views, most of which remain terse and formulaic, often opaque as to the facts found, syllogistic in style, hardly an expounding of the Covenant": ibid. The cases referred to are *Toonen v. Australia*, (488/1992), A/49/40 vol II (31 March 1994) 226, 1(3) IHRR (1994) 97, and *Faurisson v. France* (550/1993), A/52/40 (8 November 1996) 84, 18 *Human Rights Law Journal* (1997) 40. The death penalty cases to which Steiner refers are presumably those relating to extradition to face the death penalty (*Kindler v. Canada* (470/1991), A/48/40 (30 July 1993) 138, 14 *Human Rights Law Journal* (1993) 307, *Ng v. Canada*, supra note 30, and *Cox v. Canada* (539/1993), A/50/40 (31 October 1994) 117, 15 *Human Rights Law Journal* (1994) 410: see supra note 4, Nowak at 385–387, rather than the series of cases involving the death penalty in Jamaica (see Nowak, ibid. at 384–385). To these might also be added the cases concerning the meaning of the phrase "one's own country" in art. 12 of the CCPR such as *Stewart v. Canada* (538/1993), A/52/40 (1 November 1996) 47.

[39] *Kivenmaa v. Finland* (412/1990), A/49/40 (31 March 1994) Vol II. (1994) at 85.

restriction permitted by article 21 of the Covenant."[40] Unfortunately, this gives little guidance to those seeking to determine the extent of permissible limitations on the right to freedom of assembly in the national context.[41]

There are various reasons for the style of the decisions. These include the weight of work, the role that the Secretariat plays in the preparation of drafts, the need to ensure consensus in the majority opinion, and a difference of approach between common law and civil law expectations of what a decision should contain. It has been suggested that the Committee move to majority voting rather than consensus on decisions, in the belief that this may contribute to a more extensively reasoned judgment.[42] The increasing use of separate or dissenting opinions in many of the Human Rights Committee's difficult cases has been an important and welcome development, since they often illuminate both the basis of the majority opinion and alternative approaches to the issue.[43] While it does appear that in the case of the Human Rights Committee more accessible and more fully reasoned decisions are becoming more frequent, it is important for the committees to keep in mind that they are not writing only for the parties to a particular case, but for the broader community of states parties and others interested in the jurisprudence and effective implementation of the international instruments.

(5) Compliance by the state – enforcement and follow-up

The speedy and effective implementation of a decision of an adjudicatory body is a critical indicator of the effectiveness of a complaint procedure. Whether a state will give effect to a decision depends on a number of factors: whether the state considers it is formally bound as a matter of international law by the decision of the body; whether the state considers that the procedure has been fair and has involved the impartial and full consideration of the relevant evidence and law; whether the decision of the body is persuasively reasoned; whether the decision gives a clear indication of the nature of the violation and the steps that need to be taken to remedy it; whether the domestic political situation is favourable to the implementation of the decision or militates against it; the

---

[40] *Ibid.*, at para. 9.2.
[41] For example, prior to the Committee's consideration of the report on Hong Kong, such a Committee decision provided little guidance on the legitimacy of restrictions in Hong Kong on the right to freedom of assembly (involving a requirement for notification and criminal liability for holding an assembly without having given notification). The incoming government claimed they were consistent with the CCPR. See generally Chief Executive's Office, *Civil Liberties and Social Order: Consultation Document* HKSAR, (April 1997) and Lawyers Committee for Human Rights and Hong Kong Human Rights Monitor, *Tightening the Leash: Threats to Freedom of Association and Independent Human Rights Advocacy in the New Hong Kong* (June 1997). In November 1999, the Committee's concluding observations on Hong Kong made clear they were "concerned that the Public Order Ordinance could be applied to restrict unduly enjoyment of the rights guaranteed in article 21 of the Covenant. The HKSAR should review this Ordinance and bring its terms into compliance with article 21 of the Covenant." *Concluding Observations of the Human Rights Committee: Hong Kong Special Administrative Region*, CCPR/C/79/Add.117 (4 November 1999).
[42] *Supra*, note 13 at 657–658.
[43] *Supra*, note 13 at 656–657.

government's and public's perception of the status, role, competence and legitimacy of the body and its decisions;[44] the existence of a mechanism to monitor compliance; and a state's perception of itself as a responsible international actor.

For an outsider, it is somewhat difficult to assess, other than in very general terms, the extent to which states give effect to decisions under the CCPR Optional Protocol and the factors which persuade them to do so (or not to do so). Recognizing the importance of having a formal procedure for follow-up, in 1990 the Human Rights Committee appointed a Special Rapporteur for the Follow-up of Views.

The adoption of this procedure was an important step in the effort to ensure that states give effect to the views of the Human Rights Committee. The subsequent annual reports of the Human Rights Committee give some indication of the extent of compliance and the effectiveness of the follow-up procedure. The Committee has increasingly been of the view that giving some measure of publicity to the steps taken (or not taken) by states will promote compliance with its views, though the decision to increase publicity appears to reflect a certain frustration with those states which have failed to cooperate with the Committee in the follow-up procedure or to give effect to the views of the Committee.

At the same time, the public documents of the Human Rights Committee do not give a sufficiently solid basis to identify the exact level of compliance by states parties. In its 1999 report, for example, the Human Rights Committee reported that in response to the Special Rapporteur's requests for follow-up information since 1991, replies had been received from governments in relation to 152 views, but no replies had been received in 84 cases (although complainants had submitted information in a number of them). Of the replies which had been received, "roughly 30 per cent of the replies received could be considered satisfactory in that they display the State party's willingness to implement the Committee's Views or to offer the applicant an appropriate remedy"; replies not

---

[44] There is a great deal of confusion about the status of the Human Rights Committee, for example, and the implications of its being a "UN body". Following the decision of the New Zealand High Court in *Tangiora* (*supra* note 22) that legal aid could be made available for proceedings under the Optional Protocol, one newspaper commented:

> But what should cause even greater unease is that the New Zealand legal system, without any public debate, has acquired a whole new superstructure. Justice Gallen has effectively ruled that the Human Rights Committee must now be considered part of our judicial system. The irony of this occurring just when New Zealand is preparing to sever its link with the Privy Council, on the basis that we are capable of making and interpreting our own laws without paternal interference from outside sources, should not escape anyone. At least the Privy Council could be counted on to bring some judicial rigor to bear; that is more than can be said of a quasi-judicial body of the U.N., where decisions are likely to be influenced as much by politics as by sound jurisprudence.

The Evening Post (Wellington) (4 December 1996) at 6.

Following the decision another paper commented:

> Sir Geoffrey [Palmer, counsel for the applicants] told, on the Revolution television series, how in 1989, after the Appeal Court ruled that the Crown must not transfer land and mining rights to a state-owned enterprise without safeguarding Maori interests, he had argued against appealing to the Privy Council. He said this was a peculiarly New Zealand issue which it would be inappropriate to take to London. Most would say the same logic applies to the treaty fisheries deal. The 18 members of the United Nations committee in Geneva include representatives (not necessarily lawyers) from Chile, Mauritius, Slovenia and Lebanon whose knowledge of the intricacies of Treaty of Waitangi jurisprudence must be even more questionable.

The Dominion (Wellington) (9 December 1996) at 12.

considered "fully satisfactory" were those that "either do not address the Committee's recommendations at all or merely relate to one aspect of them."[45] Other replies, for example, challenged the legal or factual basis of the Committee's findings, constituted much belated submissions on the merits of the case, stated that the states would not give effect to the Committee's views, or promised to investigate the matter.[46] In short, in only one in five cases involving a finding of a violation of the Covenant, satisfactory replies were received in the sense of acceptance of the Human Rights Committee's decision and the expression of a willingness to implement it (something different from *actually* doing so). In a number of cases, complainants had lodged new complaints, based on the failure of the state party to provide a remedy for the violation found earlier by the Committee.

The Committee has evidenced a feeling of dissatisfaction with this compliance record of states parties. This appears to be reflected in decisions to make greater use of publicity by identifying states that have failed to cooperate in the follow-up procedure, continuing to press states to provide information about the steps they have taken to implement decisions, welcoming NGO information about compliance, bringing the matter before the meetings of states parties, and seeking to conduct follow-up missions.[47]

Unfortunately, the Human Rights Committee has not published at any stage a comprehensive overview of the steps taken by states parties in response to its views on individual cases. Detailed information about the exact steps taken by states parties, if available at all in the UN records,[48] has been difficult to track

---

[45] *Report of the Human Rights Committee*, A/54/40 (1999) at paras. 458–459.

[46] *Ibid.*, at para. 460. The level of discontent of some states parties with the outcome of cases brought against them before the Committee and involving the imposition of the death penalty has led to more extreme action. Jamaica denounced the Optional Protocol with effect from 23 January 1998, and Trinidad and Tobago denounced the Optional Protocol on 26 May 1998, and re-acceded to it on 28 May 1998 with the reservation that the Committee "shall not be competent to receive and consider communications relating to any prisoner who is under sentence of death in respect of any matter relating to his prosecution, his detention, his trial, his conviction, his sentence or the carrying out of the death sentence on him and any matter connected therewith": United Nations, *Multilateral Treaties Deposited with the Secretary-General*, ST/LEG/SER.E (1998), as available on http://www.un.org.Depts/Treaty/ on 5 July 1998. Guyana denounced the Optional Protocol on 5 January 1999, and re-acceded to it on 5 January 1999 with the reservation that the "Committee shall not be competent to receive and consider communications from any persons who is under sentence of death for the offences of murder and treason in respect of any matter relating to his prosecution, detention, trial, conviction, sentence or execution of the death sentence and any matter connected therewith." United Nations, *Multilateral Treaties Deposited with the Secretary-General*, see http://www.untreaty.un.org. The Human Rights Committee held, by a majority, in *Kennedy v. Trinidad and Tobago* (845/1999), CCPR/C/67/D/845/1999 (2 November 1999) that the reservation lodged by Trinidad and Tobago was invalid. On 27 March 2000 Trinidad and Tobago denounced the Optional Protocol with effect from 27 June 2000.

[47] *Report of the Human Rights Committee*, A/50/40 (1995) at paras. 556 and 565; *Report of the Human Rights Committee*, A/54/40 (1999) at paras. 472 and 474. In the light of the record, the early assessment by the Human Rights Committee that "the overall results of the first five years of experience with the follow-up procedure are encouraging, yet they cannot be termed fully satisfactory" seemed to paint somewhat too rosy a picture. *Report of the Human Rights Committee*, A/50/40 (1995) at para. 548.

[48] Some of the positive responses to decisions of the Human Rights Committee appear in states parties' subsequent reports under article 40 or are disclosed in the dialogue with the state party, but until 1996 these were not compiled in one place. See the references to a number of cases in P.R. Ghandhi, "The Human Rights Committee and the Right of Individual Communication", 57 *British Yearbook of International Law* (1987) 201 at 245–247. From 1996, the Committee began to include

down; until relatively recently the regular progress reports on follow-up prepared for the Committee were not made public and meetings of the Committee on this subject were closed. In 1996 for the first time the Human Rights Committee provided in its annual report more detailed information about the steps that states had taken in response to the decisions of the Committee and, in particular, to follow up action on the part of the Committee.[49] While the reader still does not obtain a complete picture of the exact measures that states have taken to give effect to the decisions of the Human Rights Committee, the information shows a rather mixed record of compliance, with a significant group of states not giving effect to decisions of the Committee. The record also shows the critical importance of increasingly energetic and public follow-up measures. It is important that the Human Rights Committee make available more detail about the responses provided by states parties, both in those cases in which the state has given effect to the views of the Committee as well as in those cases in which it has not. The former, as a compendium of "best practices," may provide both information and encouragement to other states; the latter may help to put further pressure on those states which have failed to give effect to decisions of the Committee.

The UN follow-up procedure may be compared with the follow-up procedure which exists within the framework of the European Convention. Under Article 46 (former Article 54) of the European Convention, the Committee of Ministers of the Council of Europe has the responsibility for supervising the execution or implementation of judgments of the European Court. When the European Court decides that there has been a violation of the Convention, the Committee of Ministers invites the state concerned to inform it of the measures it has taken in pursuance of the judgment of the Court. The Committee of Ministers remains involved until it has taken note of the information supplied, and where any compensation has been awarded, that this has been paid.[50]

This procedure appears to be a particularly effective mechanism,[51] with nearly all judgments of the European Court being implemented in the course of time.[52] The decisions of the Committee of Ministers are readily available, so that one

---

in its annual report a cumulative listing of decisions and references to steps taken by states parties in response: see *Report of the Human Rights Committee*, A/51/40 (1996) at para. 429; *Report of the Human Rights Committee*, A/52/40 (1997) at para. 524; *Report of the Human Rights Committee*, A/53/40 (1997) at para. 486; *Report of the Human Rights Committee*, A/54/40 (1999) at para. 461.

[49] *Report of the Human Rights Committee*, A/51/40 (1996) at paras. 430–466. See also *Report of the Human Rights Committee*, A/52/40 (1997) at paras. 526–557; *Report of the Human Rights Committee*, A/53/40 (1998) at paras 488–507; *Report of the Human Rights Committee*, A/54/40 (1999) at paras. 463–471. This information is now a regular part of the annual report. No similar information is provided by CAT in its annual reports.

[50] Pieter van Dijk and Godefridus J.H. van Hoof, *Theory and Practice of the European Convention on Human Rights* 2nd ed, Kluwer (1990) at 156.

[51] A similar but much less successful mechanism existed under Art. 32 of the European Convention. Under it, the Committee of Ministers considered whether there had been a violation of the European Convention on the basis of a report of the Commission in a case that had not been referred to the Court. This mechanism has been dropped from the new scheme reorganizing the system for consideration of individual complaints: see David J. Harris, Michael O'Boyle and Chris Warbrick, *Law of The European Convention on Human Rights*, Butterworths (1995) at 691–699.

[52] "The level of state compliance with judgments of the Court is generally recognized to be exemplary": *ibid.* at 702 (noting the few occasions on which there have been extensive delays in giving effect to judgments of the Court).

can see both the extent and nature of compliance by states with judgments of the European Court.[53] A number of factors may account for the effectiveness of the procedures. The fact that the decisions of the European Court are formally binding as a matter of international law may provide states with additional impetus to give effect to judgments. The nature of the community of states that makes up the Council of Europe may be a factor (being much less diverse than the corresponding UN community). The political influence of the Committee of Ministers is also significant, and the regular meetings of the Committee keep items on the agenda on a regular basis until they are resolved.

The success of the Council of Europe's arrangement gives rise to the question of whether the UN system could in some way adopt it. The decisions of the treaty bodies on communications are not formally binding as a matter of international law; any change in that regard would require an amendment to the treaties and would likely be resisted.[54] But would it be possible for a body other than the Committee to assume the follow-up role or a complementary role to that undertaken by the Committee? The only realistic option would appear to be the states parties to the Optional Protocol. While at present the states parties meet relatively infrequently, one possibility would be for the states parties to elect a small working group on follow-up which would meet frequently to carry out scrutiny comparable to that carried out by the Committee of Ministers of the Council of Europe.

(6) Proposals for new complaint procedures

An appraisal of the successes and limitations of the existing procedures is essential for the improvement of those procedures. It is also important for the efforts to formulate new individual complaint procedures to build on the successes of the procedures that already exist and, if possible, to avoid their limitations.

The last few years have seen efforts to formulate complaint procedures under both CEDAW and the CESCR, the former resulting in the successful adoption of a new Optional Protocol in 1999. The proponents of each of these new procedures sought to follow fairly closely in many respects existing procedures and practice. However, they also sought to strengthen the existing procedures by proposing changes that would make the role of the respective Committee

---

[53] See, for example, the information available through the website of the European Court of Human Rights: "Effects of Judgments or Cases 1959–1998", http://www.echr.coe.int/eng/effects.html. Based on the resolutions of the Committee of Ministers, this provides detailed information about the steps taken in response to the judgments of the Court. There does not, however, appear to be a publicly available list of cases where a state has not yet complied with a judgment or where a state has refused to give effect to a judgment or given effect to it only in part.

[54] The proposal had been made in the context of the development of an Optional Protocol to CEDAW that views of the Committee adopted under the Optional Protocol would be binding on the state party concerned. This proposal was resisted by states, both because they did not wish to be formally bound by such decisions and because this would have changed CEDAW from a quasi-judicial body into a judicial body, something which would have had implications for its membership. The final text states: Article 7(4) "The State Party shall give due consideration to the views of the Committee, together with its recommendations, if any, and shall submit to the Committee, within six months, a written response, including information on any action taken in the light of the views and recommendations of the Committee." *Supra*, note 5.

more active and more akin to an international court. Furthermore, in relation to each proposal, innovations were suggested that, in the proponents' view, were necessary to permit the particular nature of the rights violations at issue to be addressed effectively. In the CEDAW context, some of these proposals were in fact incorporated into the CEDAW Optional Protocol.

(a) Optional Protocol to the Convention on the Elimination of All Forms of Discrimination against Women

An Optional Protocol embodying a complaints procedure was adopted on 6 October 1999 and opened for signature on 10 December 1999. On the first day it received 23 signatures. Although encouraging statements were made at the Vienna and Beijing conferences, the credit for transforming the political statements of support for a protocol into action belongs primarily to NGOs and CEDAW.[55]

The elaboration of a draft protocol[56] by an expert group meeting held at Maastricht in late 1994 was the event which started the process moving. This draft went to CEDAW in early 1995 and CEDAW forwarded to the Commission on the Status of Women (CSW) its suggestions for the form and content of a protocol;[57] these corresponded very closely to the Maastricht draft. The question was considered in general terms by an open-ended working group of the CSW in 1996[58] and discussions on a draft text[59] commenced at the Commission's session in March 1997, at which a first reading of the text was completed.[60] This was followed by further negotiations in the working group at the March 1998 session of the Commission.[61] At the March 1999 session, the working group

---

[55] For the history and content of the draft optional protocol, see generally Andrew Byrnes, "Slow and Steady Wins the Race? The Development of An Optional Protocol to the Women's Convention", in *Proceedings of the 91st Annual Meeting of the American Society of International Law* (1997) 383; Aloisia Wörgetter, "The Draft Optional Protocol to the Convention on the Elimination of All Forms of Discrimination Against Women", 2 *Austrian Review of International and European Law* (1997) 261; Andrew Byrnes and Jane Connors, "Enforcing the Human Rights of Women: A Complaints Procedure for the Convention on the Elimination of All Forms of Discrimination Against Women", 21(3) *Brooklyn Journal of International Law* (1996) 679; and *supra* note 18, Evatt.
[56] *Infra*, note 80.
[57] CEDAW, "Suggestion No. 7, Elements for an Optional Protocol to the Convention on the Elimination of All Forms of Discrimination against Women", in *Report of the Committee on the Elimination of Discrimination against Women, Fourteenth Session*, A/50/38 (1995) at 8.
[58] See "Report of the Open-Ended Working Group on the Elaboration of a Draft Optional Protocol to the Convention on the Elimination of All Forms of Discrimination against Women", in *Commission on the Status of Women: Report on the Fortieth Session*, E/1996/26 (1996) Annex III.
[59] *Draft Optional Protocol to the Convention on the Elimination of All Forms of Discrimination Against Women*, E/CN.6/1997/WG/L.1 (10 March 1997).
[60] For a review of the 1997 discussions, see "Report of the Open-ended Working Group on the Elaboration of a Draft Optional Protocol to the Convention on the Elimination of All Forms of Discrimination Against Women", in *Commission on the Status of Women: Report on the Forty-First Session*, E/1997/27 (1997) Annex III. For the text that resulted from these discussions: *ibid*. at Appendix I.
[61] At the 1998 session of the working group the overwhelming majority of states participating in the working group were supportive of the effort to move forward with the draft at the 1998 Commission. This was not to be, however. A small core of states -- of which Egypt, Algeria, Cuba, China and India were the main actors -- sought to delay the drafting process by opposing central provisions of the draft which the overwhelming majority of states supported (in the purported search for consensus), by proposing amendments to dilute or undermine the draft, and by engaging in simple filibustering.

concluded consideration of the text, which was approved by CSW on 12 March 1999.[62]

The draft optional protocol put before the Working Group of the CSW in 1997 by the Chairperson of the Working Group was significantly influenced by the Maastricht draft, though a number of the more ambitious features of that draft were not included in light of government comments on CEDAW's *Suggestion No. 7*.[63] The draft proposed an individual complaint procedure modelled closely on the existing procedures under the Optional Protocol to the CCPR, CAT, and CERD. It also included an inquiry procedure modelled on article 20 of CAT, allowing CEDAW to investigate on its own motion the situation in a state party where it receives reliable information indicating that serious or systematic violations of the Convention have taken place in that state party. Both these mechanisms were eventually incorporated into the final version of the Optional Protocol.

In the negotiations surrounding the development of the CEDAW Optional Protocol, the governments and NGOs committed to an effective protocol sought:

- to ensure that the terms of the optional protocol were no less strong than the existing procedures under the Optional Protocol to the CCPR, article 14 of CERD and articles 22 and 20 of CAT;
- to incorporate the positive developments that had developed in the practice under the other UN treaties since their adoption and, as appropriate, other international complaint procedures (for example, the power to request interim measures); and
- to support innovations which would make the protocol stronger (but which had no parallels in the other procedures) and which reflected the particular disadvantages that women might face in accessing an international complaints procedure (for example, broadened standing, and less stringent requirements relating to the exhaustion of domestic remedies).

The states which were opposed to the adoption of an effective protocol adopted a minimalist approach, advocating positions that would essentially restrict the protocol to a replica of existing procedures or, in some cases, even a weaker

---

The upshot was that not only was work on the draft not completed, but central issues were still unresolved. These included the question of standing (who may lodge a complaint), the inclusion of the inquiry procedure (and whether there should be an opt in or opt out clause), and the issue of whether reservations to the protocol should be permitted.

For a review of the 1998 discussions, see "Chairperson's Summary of Views Expressed and Comments made by Delegations During Negotiations on the Optional Protocol to the Convention on the Elimination of All Forms of Discrimination Against Women", in *Commission on the Status of Women: Report on the Forty-Second Session*, E/1998/27 (1998) Annex II, Appendix II. For the text that emerged, see *Revised Draft Optional Protocol 1998*, ibid. at Annex II, Appendix I.

[62] At the 1999 session of the working group the draft optional protocol was adopted after much discussion. A number of states made interpretive statements following its adoption. The CSW then approved a draft resolution recommending that the Economic and Social Council (ECOSOC) approve the optional protocol for adoption by the General Assembly. *Commission on the Status of Women: Report on the Forty-Third Session*, E/1999/27 (1999), Chapter I (A), adopted on 12 March 1999. For a summary of the exchange of views in the Working Group, and text of the Interpretive statements, see the Report, Annex II.

[63] For a discussion of the initial draft and the 1997 discussions by the chairperson of the Working Group, see, *supra* note 55, Wörgetter, and Byrnes.

version. For all participants in the debate, the existing procedures and practices tended to define (and limit) the options seriously canvassed.

Among the more contentious issues was the question of standing, since the draft protocol proposed the extension of standing beyond the traditional victim requirement, to include the lodging of complaints:[64]

- by an individual, group or organization claiming to have suffered from a violation of any of the rights in the Convention or claiming to be directly affected by the failure of a state party to comply with its obligations under the Convention; and
- by an individual, group or organization claiming that a state party had violated any of the rights set forth in the Convention or had failed to comply with its obligations under the Convention, if the Committee considered this person group or organization had sufficient interest in the matter.

This expansion of standing was intended to address the problems of retaliation or reprisal that may face women in some situations if they were to lodge complaints, or by allowing an organization to do so on their behalf. But the proposal proved controversial.[65] Concern about expanded standing overlapped with concerns about the justiciability of the obligations contained in CEDAW. Various states advanced traditional notions of justiciability (showing a bias in favour of traditionally formulated civil and political rights guarantees) and argued that many of the Convention's obligations were not justiciable. Nevertheless, there was an acceptance that the obligations contained in CEDAW were in general justiciable and that the extent to which obligations were justiciable could really only be determined in a particular factual context. Those who argued that many of the Convention's obligations were not justiciable sought to prepare the ground for either subjecting only some of the Convention obligations to the complaints procedure or allowing individual states to select the obligations in respect of which they would be prepared to subject themselves to the complaints procedure. Ultimately, the CEDAW Optional Protocol as adopted applied to victims of violations of any of the rights set forth in the Convention.[66]

The 1998 Chairperson's draft, like the Maastricht draft, contained both an individual communications procedure and an inquiry procedure, the former modelled closely on existing individual complaint procedures under UN human rights treaties, the latter on the inquiry procedure in article 20 of CAT. While there was general agreement that an individual complaint procedure was a necessary component of any optional protocol, among governments there was some opposition to (as well as much support for) the inclusion of an inquiry procedure. The arguments made against such a procedure were that while such a procedure might be appropriate for systematic torture, it was not appropriate for the types of human rights guaranteed in CEDAW and was, in any event, unlikely to provide much assistance in cases of serious and widespread violations. In the final analysis there was much support for an inquiry procedure – which many states saw as a potential vehicle for addressing systematic and structural

---

[64] *Supra*, note 59, art. 2.
[65] *Supra*, note 61, *Revised Draft Optional Protocol 1998*, art. 2 (and alternative).
[66] *Supra*, note 5, art. 2.

III. An Effective Individual Complaint Mechanism

violations of women's equality. The final outcome was therefore similar to the position under CAT, namely that states which become parties to the Optional Protocol were permitted to choose whether to accept the inquiry procedure, by opting out at the time of ratification.[67]

One other major innovation related to the status of the views to be adopted by CEDAW following the examination of a communication or conclusion of an inquiry. Under existing UN procedures, the views of the treaty body are not formally binding on the state party as a matter of international law, although they are generally considered to be "of high authority." The Chairperson's draft took up the Maastricht proposals under which a state party would be obliged as a matter of international law to implement recommendations made by the Committee following the conclusion of its examination of a complaint or conduct of an inquiry. Perhaps unsurprisingly, this proposal met with strong opposition from a number of delegations, and many other delegations were concerned about the implications of the proposal, which they saw as transforming the role of CEDAW from quasi-judicial to judicial, with consequences both for the procedure that might be appropriate under the protocol and the composition of the Committee. As a consequence, it was eliminated from the draft during the 1998 discussions and the Optional Protocol as adopted resembled the other treaties in this respect.[68]

The Chairperson's draft proposed that no reservations would be permitted to the Optional Protocol. The intention of this provision was twofold: first, to prevent states parties from accepting just one of the two procedures (individual complaint procedure and inquiry procedure), but rejecting the other; and secondly, to prevent states from picking and choosing among the substantive obligations in respect of which they would be subject to complaints. In the final version, this proposal was accepted and no reservations were permitted.[69]

There are many other issues of importance that gave rise to controversy. They included the appropriate test for the exhaustion of local remedies, with resistance to any relaxation of the existing requirements under general international law. The Protocol as adopted required the exhaustion of domestic remedies, unless such remedies were unreasonably prolonged or unlikely to bring effective relief.[70] The question of the Committee's power to request interim measures – a codification of existing practice that has developed under the other treaties – also gave rise to discussion. The Protocol as adopted ultimately included a provision giving the Committee power to request interim measures.[71] The proposal that the protocol expressly oblige states parties to publicize the protocol and CEDAW's decisions under it was incorporated into the final version.[72] The suggestion that the Committee have the power to visit the territory of a state, with its consent, as part of an inquiry into grave or systematic violations of rights was ultimately included in the Protocol.[73] The final text also broadly permitted the Committee to consider, in the course of its deliberations on

---

[67] *Supra*, note 5, art. 10.
[68] *Supra*, note 65, art. 7(3) and (4).
[69] *Supra*, note 5, art. 17.
[70] *Supra*, note 5, art. 4(1).
[71] *Supra*, note 5, art. 5.
[72] *Supra*, note 5, art. 13.
[73] *Supra*, note 5, art. 8(2).

complaints, "all information made available to it by or on behalf of individuals or groups of individuals and by the State Party concerned, provided that this information is transmitted to the parties concerned."[74]

Finally, on the institutional front, while concerns about overlap and duplication were expressed, some appear to have been addressed by provisions restricting the bringing of complaints to more than one body.[75] The question of the resources CEDAW will need under the Optional Protocol and how they will be obtained remains under discussion.[76]

(b) Draft Optional Protocol to the International Covenant on Economic, Social and Cultural Rights

Serious consideration of the possibility of adopting a complaints procedure under the CESCR began in the Economic, Social and Cultural Rights Committee in the early 1990s.[77] The issues and proposed drafts have been discussed intensively at a number of sessions of the Committee, as well as being the subject of a meeting convened in Utrecht in early 1995 by the Netherlands Institute of Human Rights.[78] The Economic, Social and Cultural Rights Committee finished its examination of the issues in late 1996 and forwarded its views on the form and content of a protocol, together with a draft instrument, to the Commission on Human Rights at its 1997 session.[79]

The question of justiciability of the obligations under the CESCR was a central concern addressed by the Economic, Social and Cultural Rights Committee. The Committee maintained that the dichotomy between justiciable civil and political rights, and aspirational or non-justiciable economic, social and cultural rights was a false one, and that most economic rights are justiciable in important respects, and therefore capable of being made the subject of a complaints procedure.

---

[74] *Supra*, note 5, art. 7(1).
[75] *Supra*, note 5, art.4(2)(a) states: "The Committee shall declare a communication inadmissable where: (a) The same matter has already been examined by the Committee or has been or is being examined under another procedure of international investigation or settlement."
[76] See *Ways and Means of Expediting the Work of the Committee*, CEDAW/C/1999/II/4 (6 May 1999) at para. 29; *Ways and Means of Expediting the Work of the Committee*, CEDAW/C/2000/I/4 (27 December 1999); *Report on the Optional Protocol to the Convention*, CEDAW/C/2000/I/5 (3 December 1999).
[77] For a review of the developments see *Report of the Committee on Economic, Social and Cultural Rights to the Commission on Human Rights on a Draft Optional Protocol for the Consideration of Communications Concerning Non-Compliance with the International Covenant on Economic, Social and Cultural Rights*, E/CN.4/1997/105 (18 December 1996), 5 *International Human Rights Reports* (1998) 527. In 1997, 1998 and 1999 the Commission on Human Rights requested states to submit comments on the draft optional protocol. Decision 1997/104, (3 April 1997); Resolution 1998/33, adopted on 17 April 1998; Resolution 1999/25, adopted on 26 April 1999. Comments received: *Draft Optional Protocol to the International Covenant on Economic, Social and Cultural Rights: Report of the Secretary-General*, E/CN.4/1998/84 and Add. 1 (16 January 1998); *Draft Optional Protocol to the International Covenant on Economic, Social and Cultural Rights: Note by the Secretariat*, E/CN.4/1999/112 and Add. 1 (7 January 1999); *Draft Optional Protocol to the International Covenant on Economic, Social and Cultural Rights: Report of the High Commissioner for Human Rights*, E/CN.4/2000/49 (14 January 2000).
[78] For the report of the meeting see Fons Coomans and Fried van Hoof (eds.), *The Right to Complain About Economic, Social and Cultural Rights*, Netherlands Institute of Human Rights (1995) 178–98.
[79] *Supra*, note 77.

III. An Effective Individual Complaint Mechanism 161

The concern about justiciability has given rise to the question of whether the complaints procedure should cover all, or only some, of the rights, and, if only some, whether the protocol would specify which ones or would leave individual states the option of selecting those rights in respect of which they were prepared to be subject to complaints. The majority of the Economic, Social and Cultural Rights Committee supported comprehensive coverage of all rights in the CESCR, though a significant minority took a different view.

A related issue has been who should be permitted to lodge complaints under a protocol, in particular whether the right should be confined to groups or individuals, or whether both should be permitted to lodge complaints. The question of standing has also arisen, most importantly in connection with whether the right to submit complaints should be confined to those individuals and groups who are victims of violations (and their legal or personal representatives), or whether it could be extended to any group with "a sufficient interest." The Economic, Social and Cultural Rights Committee eventually supported a compromise, suggesting that an individual or group acting on behalf of alleged victims (and with their knowledge and agreement) would be permitted to lodge a complaint.

The Committee also expressed its support for a number of proposals that were modelled on provisions in the Maastricht draft optional protocol to CEDAW,[80] in particular, the power of the Committee to conduct on-site visits (with the consent of the state concerned) as part of its consideration of a complaint. In addition, the Economic, Social and Cultural Rights Committee proposed expanding the Committee's access to sources of information beyond that provided by the parties, and left open the possibility of oral hearings. The Committee supported proposals to provide an explicit power to request interim measures, an obligation on states parties to protect complainants against reprisals, and an explicit follow-up power. The Committee did not, however, support the idea that the state party be expressly obligated to carry out any recommendations made by the Committee following its consideration of a communication.

The reception accorded the results of the Economic, Social and Cultural Rights Committee's deliberations on the question of an optional protocol has been somewhat lukewarm. The response of the Commission on Human Rights at its 1997 session was to "note[ ] with interest" the report of the Committee and to ask the Secretary-General to provide information about the reactions of states to that report.[81] There is no suggestion that the Commission is in any hurry to start examining the issue in any detail itself, or to establish a working group to commence the drafting of a text. Few states submitted comments for

---

[80] For the text of the Maastricht draft, see Byrnes and Connors, *supra* note 55 at 784–797; 44 *American University Law Review* (1995) at 1419; and Cees Flinterman, "Draft Optional Protocol to the Convention on the Elimination of All Forms of Discrimination Against Women", 13(1) *Netherlands Quarterly on Human Rights* (1995) 85.
[81] Commission on Human Rights Res. 1997/17, adopted on 11 April 1997. The Commission decided at para. 6:

(b) To request the Secretary-General to submit reports to the General Assembly at its fifty-second session and to the Commission on Human Rights at its fifty-fourth session... on progress towards the realization of the rights set forth in the International Covenant on Economic, Social and Cultural Rights, giving due reflection to:
...
(ii) Their reactions to the report of the Committee on Economic, Social and Cultural Rights on

the 1998, 1999 and 2000 sessions of the Commission,[82] and no significant progress was made at these sessions. The Commission resolved in 1998 merely to ask the High Commissioner for Human Rights to urge states to continue to submit their comments.[83] In 1999, in addition to asking states again to submit comments, the High Commissioner was asked to report to the 2000 Commission on "options relating to the proposal for a draft optional protocol."[84] In the High Commissioner's subsequent report, options were identified ranging from (a) requests for additional state comments, (b) study by an open-ended working group, and (c) discussion and eventual adoption of the draft optional protocol by the Commission. At the moment, however, it appears that sufficient political will is simply lacking to forge ahead with such an instrument.

(7) Conclusion

The critical challenge underlying most of the proposals for improving and expanding the operations of the UN individual complaint procedures is that of resources in the form of people, money and time. An increasing workload for the committees, an overburdened Secretariat, diminishing financial resources (and no prospect of any real increase in the near future), and committee members who simply may not have time, energy or resources to take on additional work make even the most enthusiastic reformers throw up their hands in dismay.

Nevertheless, the situation is not hopeless. There are a number of initiatives that might be taken if the Human Rights Committee were prepared to move away from sitting in plenary to adopt its views on communications (and decisions on inadmissibility). The measures adopted by the Human Rights Committee to join admissibility to the merits is one way of using time more efficiently. The possibility of sitting in chambers (of 5 or 7 members), with the option of referring difficult cases to the full Committee – along the lines of the practice adopted by the European Court of Human Rights – is an option that could be explored fruitfully.

The only long-term solution is to concentrate resources at the national level – in the training of judges, government officials, legislatures, lawyers and others and the development of effective national level institutions such as human rights commissions – so that an understanding of how to give effect domestically to international human rights norms can be spread more broadly. In this way accessible mechanisms attuned to human rights norms can be made available at home, where people can have more ready access to them.

---

a draft optional protocol for the consideration of communications concerning non-compliance with the International Covenant on Economic, Social and Cultural Rights.
[82] See *supra* note 77.
[83] Commission on Human Rights Res. 1998/33, adopted on 17 April 1998 at para. 7.
[84] Commission on Human Rights Res. 1999/25, adopted on 26 April 1999 at para. 6(d).

CHAPTER 11

Commentary on Complaint Processes by Human Rights Committee and Torture Committee Members

(a) The Human Rights Committee

David Kretzmer

Considering the problems with the communications system of the Human Rights Committee, there are three kinds of constraints on the Committee's work: legal, political and internal.

Legal constraints suggest a response to the suggestions that the Human Rights Committee should make its decisions on communications in chambers. The Optional Protocol[1] states that the Committee shall consider the communications and that the Committee shall forward its views to the parties. Article 39 of the International Covenant on Civil and Political Rights (CCPR)[2] stipulates that 12 members of the Committee shall constitute a quorum. It therefore seems quite clear that there is a legal constraint on establishing chambers, the views of which would be considered the final word of the Committee on communications.

An alternative approach would be to establish chambers, whose decisions would not be binding until they had received the approval of the plenary. This approach was discussed by Human Rights Committee members in an informal meeting held after July 1996. Many of the members were opposed, as they felt that even this approach was not consistent with the requirements of the CCPR and its Optional Protocol. Perhaps, as the Committee's backlog of communications grows the approach will be reconsidered.

Political constraints indicate the difficulty of reforming the system through amendments to the CCPR or its Optional Protocol. Attempts at such amendments would require a huge effort, which may well prove futile. But even if the states parties were willing to amend these instruments, the end result may be detrimental, rather than beneficial. The end product could be a weakened system. However imperfect the present legal structure may be, it is better to work within the existing legal constraints, rather than trying to change them.

---

[1] Optional Protocol to the International Covenant on Civil and Political Rights, 999 UNTS 171 (in force 23 March 1976).
[2] International Covenant on Civil and Political Rights, 999 UNTS 171 (in force 23 March 1976).

The treaty system reflects the weakness of the international system. The fact that the Optional Protocol does not state that the Human Rights Committee's views under the Protocol are legally binding, and that there are no enforcement mechanisms, was a clear policy decision by the international community. States were quite willing to lay down binding standards of human rights, provided that there was no really effective enforcement mechanism to make sure that they were adhering to the standards when they chose not to do so.

There is therefore reason for some pessimism as to the chances of states agreeing to make the enforcement mechanisms more effective. Even if the legal basis were to be strengthened (for example, by expressly stating that the Committee's views are binding), it is unlikely that the decision-makers within the United Nations, will commit significantly greater resources to the communications system.

Over 90 states have now ratified the Optional Protocol. These include many countries of the former Soviet Union. Vast numbers of individuals live in states that are parties to the Optional Protocol and in which there are serious human rights violations, but in practice they have no access to the communications process. At the same time, if one could wave some kind of magic wand that could make all persons in countries that are party to the Optional Protocol aware of their rights, the Human Rights Committee would not be able to cope in practice with the communications submitted.

At present, the Human Rights Committee deals with 30 to 35 views (in addition to several cases on inadmissability) per year. If only two individuals in every one of the 90 states that have joined the Optional Protocol were to submit a communication each year, the Committee would receive 180 new communications per annum. The system would buckle under. Resources are key to the Committee's success. Not only are these resources not being increased in order to cater to the growing case load, they are in fact being reduced. One of the proposals that may need to be considered in the future is the possibility of funding from independent, non-governmental, foundations. Such funding might increase the resources available for processing communications without impugning the Committee's independence.

Internal constraints raise the issue of the Human Rights Committee's own rules of procedure. The Committee's procedure had been based on a two-level decision-making process. First, the Committee made a formal, detailed and written decision on admissibility. If the communication was declared admissible it went back to the parties for further argument on the merits. Approximately two years after the admissibility decision, the Committee made a second decision on the merits, in which it often reviewed some of the arguments dealt with at the admissibility stage. According to the amended rules,[3] once a communication has been registered, the state party concerned is asked to respond both on admissibility and on the merits. In most cases, the questions of admissibility and merits are addressed in the same decision. The object is to shorten the proceedings and streamline the process.

The issue of oral hearings has been discussed by the Committee on a number of occasions. There is no consensus among members of the Human Rights Committee on the question of oral hearings. Some members favour allowing

---

[3] See Human Rights Committee, *Rules of Procedure*, CCPR/C/3/Rev.5 (11 August 1997).

oral hearings in certain cases. In my own view, instituting oral hearings under the present structure would create problems of equality. Those members of the Human Rights Committee who support oral hearings agree that such hearings could not be instituted unless funding were available for the authors of communications, or their counsel, to appear before the Committee.

Under the present legal structure, oral hearings would encounter legal constraints. The Optional Protocol states that the Human Rights Committee shall consider communications received in the light of all written information made available. Presumably, with the consent of both the state party and the author of a communication, the Committee could supplement the written information with an oral hearing. But this would exacerbate the equality problem, as it would apply only when there was consent by both parties. The Committee would have two levels of decisions – some in which there was consent to oral hearings (assuming that the state party would only agree when it considered it would be advantageous to it to do so), and others in which there was no consent.

Oral hearings would not necessarily make the system more efficient. They might make the decision-making process even more drawn-out. Representatives of the parties would have to come all the way to Geneva or New York for the hearing. In such circumstances it is unlikely that the Committee would hear each side for half an hour and then say: "Thank you very much. We now have all the information we need to decide this case." Judging from the experience with state reports, I think the Committee would spend at least one half-day and possibly even a full-day, on a hearing. Given the case load of the Human Rights Committee, this may not be the most efficient way of dealing with communications. Furthermore, unless the Committee were to hear witnesses, the oral pleadings of the parties would probably add little to the pleadings which are at present submitted in writing.

Given the weakness of the system as far as providing proper remedies for individuals whose rights have been violated, emphasis should be placed on the interpretative role of the Committee, and that function can best be served when there is detailed and sound reasoning in the decisions.

However, this in itself breeds problems. The Human Rights Committee is comprised of eighteen people who come from diverse legal traditions. Some come from common law countries or other countries in which the tradition is for courts to write long, reasoned decisions. Others come from countries in which the tradition is for courts to write brief decisions that rest on short statements of the law and that rely on external legal commentary to supplement the judicial decisions. In this context, note, for example, three decisions of the Human Rights Committee in which detailed legal reasoning was provided. *Errol Johnson v. Jamaica*[4] deals with the length of time on death row; *Stewart v. Canada*[5] discusses the meaning of article 12 (4) of the CCPR; and the *Faurisson v. France*[6] case discusses criminalization of Holocaust denial as a breach of freedom of expression. In the first two cases, the Human Rights Committee was split and there are a number of dissenting opinions. In the third, the Committee

---

[4] *Johnson v. Jamaica* (588/1994), A/51/40 vol. II (22 March 1996) 174.
[5] *Stewart v. Canada* (538/1993), A/52/40 vol. II (1 November 1996) 47.
[6] *Faurisson v. France* (550/1993), A/52/40 vol. II (8 November 1996) 84.

was unanimous in deciding that there had been no violation of the CCPR, but a number of members appended concurring opinions.

(b) The Committee Against Torture
Peter Burns

The Committee Against Torture (CAT) is faced with a number of significant problems in the context of communications. The first relates to the issue of resources. There are insufficient resources at the Office of the High Commissioner for Human Rights to provide CAT with the assistance which the members require. Most importantly, there is no capacity for research. In addition, there is a major backlog problem, which will increase over time.

CAT is also confronted with a particular problem: the legal issue of the appropriate burden of proof upon the author of a communication. Does the author have to raise a *prima facie* case that demands an answer on the part of the state? Committee members, emanating from different legal traditions, do not share the same answer. The common law lawyers are of the view that there is some sort of burden cast upon the author. While it may be a low burden, the author is required at least to make a case that demands an answer. Other members of the Committee, from different legal traditions, hold the view that there is no burden; if a claim is made, then the burden shifts to the state to respond and to justify its position. The answer has major implications in terms of efficiency. If indeed the Committee can rely upon the presumed legitimacy of the process which was involved in the state concerned, and the burden is upon the author to at least argue that there was an excess of jurisdiction, or bias, or a manifest failure to find facts properly, then CAT can deal with a case relatively quickly and efficiently. Otherwise, the danger arises of the Committee re-litigating the whole matter again.

It is important to emphasize the need for cogent reasons in the decision-making of the communications system. There should be a statement of facts, a statement of the principles or rules that are involved in reaching a conclusion, and a summary conclusion. Unfortunately, CAT does not always operate in this way. A rapporteur is assigned the task of reviewing a particular communication file, and the rapporteur brings the case before the Committee, presents the case, and provides a recommendation. Whether or not the desirable reasoning process is utilized, is dependent on the individual Committee rapporteur. At the same time, there is an internal dynamic of reluctance to interfere with the rapporteur's conclusions and reasoning. If members of the Committee agree with the result, their sense of propriety suggests that they will not interfere with the manner in which the result was reached. Of course if the reasoning was manifestly unreasonable or absurd, changes would be made. But for the most part, there is no interference with the rapporteur's report. As a consequence, the quality of the reasoning in communication decisions is extremely variable.

CAT has managed its processes in a relatively timely fashion, in the sense that when an original communication is dealt with and there have been interim measures taken, the Committee will meet to consider the case again in six months time. Within eighteen months a decision will usually have been rendered. The reason for the backlog in cases, therefore, relates to article 3 of the Convention.[7] Article 3 imposes an obligation on a state not to return or extradite a person to another state where there are reliable indications that person would be subjected to torture if he or she were returned. It is a legitimate and fundamental proposition. At the same time, four or five refugee-sustaining countries have ratified the individual communication provision in article 22, such as Canada, Denmark, the Netherlands, Sweden and Switzerland. The legal profession in those countries has therefore come to view CAT as a further tier of appeal in the refugee claims system. Even if their client loses, they will likely receive a reprieve of a minimum of six months. This is because when CAT has a case in which there is even a scintilla of evidence that the individual should not be sent back, then it generally recommends interim measures of protection in favour of the author. Caution is exercised. Hence, almost invariably individuals receive interim measures. Lawyers therefore believe that merely by applying to CAT, their clients will receive an extra six months stay in the country concerned at a minimum, and perhaps twelve months if the Committee is unable to reach the case at its next session. This does not mean that such cases are not legitimate. But it does suggest a significant difficulty for the Committee.

Language of communication is another problem CAT faces. For example, the Netherlands permits individual communications under article 22. But if the file is in Dutch, no one on the Committee can read it. Hence, considerable time is taken with additional translation requirements in such cases.

Most of the Committee's individual cases involve article 3 of CAT and these cases primarily relate to countries that are committed to the international human rights ethos. Hence, the record of observance of the Committee's recommendations has been good. Requests for interim measures of protection are seldom ignored by a state, although there have been a couple of instances of non-observance in very recent times.

At the moment CAT does not have the time or the resources required to introduce oral hearings.

---

[7] Convention Against Torture and Other Cruel, Inhuman or Degrading Treatment or Punishment, 1465 UNTS 85 (in force 26 June 1987).

CHAPTER 12

Reflections on the Effectiveness of the European System for the Protection of Human Rights

Michael O'Boyle*

The European system is without doubt the world's most developed regional treaty system for the protection of human rights and there is much to be learned from its experience, procedures and case law. It has made a unique contribution to the law on the international protection of human rights and has had substantial impact on national law in many areas. It is not, however, a study in perfection – far from it. It is rather one of a success story – probably unexpected and unforeseen – made up of gradual (and to many governments imperceptible) incremental advances in both case law and procedures. The system has various shortcomings and weaknesses – as well as a "few dark stains"[1] – but unlike others has benefitted from a political willingness amongst Council of Europe member states which has enabled episodic improvements to be made culminating in the radical reform creating a single Court embodied in Protocol No. 11.[2] One has the impression that the European Convention on Human Rights'[3] founders would have experienced a certain pride in reading statements of government ministers explaining to Parliament that legislation had to be amended because the European Court of Human Rights had found that it was incompatible with a provision of the European Convention and that, accordingly, the state's international obligations required the government to introduce corrective measures. This form of transparent and public compliance with European Convention obligations is certainly an indicator that the system is operating effectively. However, a more telling indicator is when the minister's statement is based not on the result of a dispute concerning his own country but on a judgment of the European Court concerning another contracting party.[4] Reliance on European

---

*This article is written in my personal capacity.
[1] See the provocative and critical appraisal by Professor Christian Tomuschat in "Quo Vadis, Argentoratum? The Success Story of the European Convention on Human Rights and a few Dark Stains", 13 *Human Rights Law Journal* (1992) 401–406; see also *infra* Leo F. Zwaak, Chapter 20.
[2] Protocol No. 11 to the Convention for the Protection of Human Rights and Fundamental Freedoms, ETS 155 (in force 1 November 1998).
[3] Convention for the Protection of Human Rights and Fundamental Freedoms, ETS 5 (in force 3 September 1953).
[4] For examples of this see David Harris, Michael O'Boyle and Chris Warbrick, *Law of the European Convention of Human Rights*, Butterworths (1995) at 31.

Convention case law by national courts when deciding issues before them also provides impressive evidence of the European Convention operating as it should.

The picture was not always so idyllic. At the beginning, following the entry into force of the European Convention, there were few cases brought before the European Commission of Human Rights and the optional clauses providing for the right of individual petition (former Article 25) and the compulsory jurisdiction of the European Court (former Article 46) were accepted by few states. There were so few cases brought before the European Court in the 1960s – because of a reticence by the European Commission and states to do so – that Judge Rolin was able to give a lecture entitled "Has the European Court of Human Rights a Future?" Judge Ross, the Danish member of the European Court, spoke at the same time about the Court being in need of employment. Their remarks are there to remind us that the achievements of the Convention are the product of almost forty-five years' evolution and development.

Today the landscape is completely transformed. There are 41 contracting parties, including Georgia, the Russian Federation and Ukraine. New member states of the Council of Europe are not only required to ratify the European Convention but also to accept the optional clauses, as well as Protocol No. 11. Prior to the coming into force of Protocol No. 11, the European Commission registered more than 3,000 cases each year. The Court delivered 177 judgments in 1999.[5]

Protocol No. 11 came into force on 1 November 1998, and the single European Court has been set up. New rules of the European Court have been adopted. Forty-one judges have been elected in respect of the 41 contracting parties. In addition to the Grand Chamber, the Court now sits in four sections of ten judges from which the Chambers of seven judges and the Committees of three are drawn. In 1999 there were 8,396 registered applications.[6]

In addition, there is an impressive corpus of Convention case law involving more than 600 judgments of the Court and many thousands of European Commission admissibility decisions. In fact, the Convention system has grown imperceptibly from an international petition system based on the concept of a collective guarantee of human rights to a fledgling constitutional system for the protection of human rights in the New Europe. An important feature of this development is that the European Convention has rooted itself so pervasively in the legal culture of many European states that withdrawal from the system would lead to significant adverse political consequences, both domestic and international.

The present commentary is primarily concerned to identify those aspects of the European Convention system which have contributed to its reputation for effectiveness. This can be examined under five heads: (1) particular features of the petition system; (2) jurisprudential developments enhancing the effectiveness of the system; (3) external indicia of effectiveness; (4) the improvements brought about by Protocol No. 11; and (5) the reasons for the success of the system.

---

[5] *Survey of Activities 1999*, Information Document Issued by the Registrar of the European Court of Human Rights at 50. Available at: "www.echr.coe.int/eng/select%20folder.html".
[6] *Ibid.*, at 51. For texts of judgments, the Rules of Court, press releases and other information, consult the European Court's web site at "www.echr.coe.int/".

(1) Features of the petition system

Initial stages of the process are easily accessible. Applicants need not be legally represented at the initial stages and incur no cost in filing an application. Formalities have been reduced to a minimum and the legal Secretariat provides advice on obvious admissibility difficulties. Legal aid at a modest level covering fees and expenses is available in respect of cases that have been communicated to the government for observations. In one contracting party (Norway) legal aid is even made available under the national legal aid and advice system.

The adversarial principle is respected throughout the procedures, the parties being given an opportunity either orally or in writing to respond to each other's submissions at every stage. During *in situ* investigations, witnesses are generally heard in the presence of the parties with the possibility of cross-examination.

Interim measures are also provided for in the rules, although not in the text of the European Convention or its Protocols.[7] However in *Cruz Varas and Others v. Sweden*[8] the European Court decided (by a vote of ten to nine) that interim measures granted by the European Commission had no binding force under the European Convention because of the absence of a specific treaty provision to this effect. Accordingly the European Convention lacks the power to require the parties to abstain from measures which could give rise to serious and irreversible harm. Fortunately, however, the practice of widespread compliance with such measures has continued. States are aware that they remain subject to a legal obligation not to "hinder in any way" the effective exercise of the right of individual petition (Article 34, former Article 25(1)) and that non-compliance with a request in a particular case gives rise to such hindrance.[9] So far there has been no indication that the states would be willing to amend the European Convention to provide for binding interim measures although the matter may come back to the European Court for reconsideration.

Other features of the European Convention procedure which are central to the question of effectiveness are the friendly settlement procedure and the power of the European Court under Article 41 (former Article 50) to make an award of just satisfaction when it finds a violation of the Convention. Settlements may occur at all stages of the procedure and may involve specific (for example, compensation awards) as well as general measures (undertakings to amend legislation or administrative practice).[10] They enable problems to be remedied "on the basis of respect for human rights" efficiently and expeditiously, usually to the satisfaction of both sides and in a manner, which takes account of the public interest, reflected in the application. As regards Article 41, the European Court will award legal costs and expenses systematically where these are actually incurred, necessarily incurred and reasonable as to quantum. It may also award both pecuniary and non-pecuniary damages payable within three months of judgment. Failure to pay leads to the imposition of default interest at a rate set out in the judgment. Although the Court frequently holds that the finding of a

---

[7] Rule 39 (former rule 36) of the *Rules of Court* (1 November 1998), adopted following the entry into force of the Protocol No. 11 on 1 November 1998.
[8] *Cruz Varas and Others v. Sweden*, Series A, Volume 201 (20 March 1991).
[9] *Ibid.*, at 37, para. 104.
[10] Most settlements occur at the preliminary stages: *supra* note 4 at 599–603.

violation is sufficient vindication of an applicant's rights and refuses to make an award, proof of a causal link between pecuniary damage sustained and breach of a Convention provision will lead to damages. On occasion, particularly in cases concerning property rights, awards have been substantial.[11]

In a series of decisions, however, the European Court has held that its judgments are of a declaratory nature and that it does not have jurisdiction under the European Convention to order consequential measures in the form of directions or recommendations to the state. Thus, for example, it has refused requests that it should order the state to bring criminal prosecution against those responsible for ill treatment in breach of Article 3. The European Court has also, so far, refused to award aggravated or exemplary damages but has not shirked from making high awards when confronted with arbitrary behaviour.[12]

Compliance with the Court's judgments is supervised by the Committee of Ministers of the Council of Europe pursuant to Article 46 (former Article 54) of the European Convention. Its role is to ensure that the state not only takes the general measures that are required by the terms of the decision but also that the amounts awarded under Article 41 have been paid. It also ensures that the terms of friendly settlements reached in proceedings before the European Court have been complied with. Details of changes in legislation and administrative practices that have been introduced following judgments of the Court appear in the published *Collection of Resolutions*. While the level of compliance with Court judgments is exemplary there have, on occasion, been delays in the introduction of remedial legislation and in the payment of compensation. The Committee of Ministers is aware that the credibility and effectiveness of the Convention system is at stake when confronted with non-compliance, and diplomatic pressure behind closed doors is brought to bear on recalcitrant governments. An example is provided by the enforcement of the judgment in the *Stran Greek Refineries* case.[13] In its judgment of 9 December 1994, the European Court made a multi-million dollar award in favour of the applicant to be paid by 9 March 1995. After the expiry of this time limit the Committee of Ministers adopted an interim resolution urging the Government of Greece to proceed without delay to pay the award and stressing Greece's obligation to safeguard the value of the amounts awarded. Since the judgment had still not been implemented, the Chairman of the Committee wrote to the Greek Foreign Minister in September 1996 underlining the fact "that the credibility and effectiveness of the mechanism ... is based on the respect of the obligations freely entered into by the Contracting Parties and in particular in respect of the decisions of the supervisory bodies." On 17 January 1997, after much diplomatic discussion in the Committee of Ministers concerning the implications for the system of a blatant refusal to execute a judgment of the European Court, the sums were paid in full and "increased in order to provide compensation for the loss of value caused by the delay in payment."[14]

---

[11] For example, *Pine Valley Development Ltd and Others v. Ireland*, Series A, Volume 246-B (9 February 1993); and *Stran Greek Refineries and Stratis Andreadis v. Greece*, Series A, Volume 301-B (9 December 1994) (more than $16 million and 116 million drachmas).
[12] For example, *Tomasi v. France*, Series A, Volume 241-A (27 August 1992); *Tsirlis and Kouloumpas v. Greece*, Reports 1997-III (29 May 1997) and *Georgiadis v. Greece*, Reports 1997-III (29 May 1997).
[13] *Supra*, note 11.
[14] Committee of Ministers Res. DH (97) 184, adopted on 20 March 1997; see also *supra* note 1, Zwaak.

Finally, mention should be made of the developing practice of the European Court to accept the filing of *amicus* briefs by non-governmental organizations (NGOs) where they can show that they have an interest in the case or special knowledge of the subject-matter involved and that their intervention would serve the administration of justice. Permission is often subject to the condition that the third party restricts itself to providing information on questions of comparative law and not address the merits of the case. The practice has developed considerably over the last decade to the point where Protocol No. 11 has amended the European Convention to provide expressly for third-party intervention. The European Court's liberal practice may not only assist it to decide the case but has important educational benefits to the third party concerned.

(2) Judicial developments

The effectiveness of the European Convention has also been enhanced by various key rulings of the European Court on both procedural and substantive questions. In its case-law, the Court has:

- given free rein to the dynamic or evolutive principle of interpretation,[15]
- emphasized time and again that the European Convention is intended to guarantee not rights "that are theoretical or illusory but rights that are practical and effective,"[16]
- given an autonomous meaning to the concepts of "civil rights" and "criminal charge" in the Convention's fair-trial provision,
- accepted that persons may complain of the existence of legislative measures and practices concerning secret measures of surveillance without being required to show that they have been the victim of them,[17]
- prepared in extradition and deportation cases to make anticipatory rulings,[18] and
- ruled that state responsibility may arise in respect of acts occurring outside the national territory.[19]

The European Court has also extensive case law on the concept of fair trial, freedom of speech, unlawful detention, privacy and family rights.[20]

---

[15] *Supra*, note 4, at 7–9.
[16] *Artico v. Italy*, Series A, Volume 37 (13 May 1980) at para. 33.
[17] *Klass and Others v. Germany*, Series A, Volume 28 (6 September 1978).
[18] *Soering v. the United Kingdom*, Series A, Volume 161 (7 July 1988).
[19] *Loizidou v. Turkey (Preliminary Objections)*, Series A, Volume 310 (23 March 1995) and *(Merits)*, Series A, Volume 1996-VI (18 December 1996).
[20] Perhaps the most significant judgment from the standpoint of effectiveness pre-Protocol No. 11 is that of *Loizidou* v. *Turkey (Preliminary Objections)* (*ibid.*), where the Court held that the formerly optional clauses (former Articles 25 and 46 of the European Convention) did not permit restrictions or limitations other than of a temporal nature. The Court specifically found that a condition limiting Turkey's acceptance of the right of individual petition and the jurisdiction of the European Court to matters occurring within the national territory was invalid. In reaching this view, the Court noted that if substantive or territorial restrictions were permissible under Articles 25 and 46, states would be free to subscribe to separate regimes of enforcement of Convention obligations depending on the scope of their acceptances. Such a system would not only weaken the role of the European Commission and Court in the discharge of their functions but would also diminish the effectiveness of the European Convention as a constitutional instrument of European public order. The importance

The European Court, in its case law, has also constantly stressed that the system of human rights protection instituted under the European Convention is subsidiary to the national system. While this philosophy has led to a strict approach to the application of the exhaustion of domestic remedies rule – unless national remedies were considered to be inadequate or ineffective[21] – it has also resulted in emphasis being placed on the legal obligation under Article 13 to provide an "effective remedy" under national law for those who have an "arguable" claim to be the victim of a violation of their rights under the European Convention. The judgment of the Court in *Aksoy v. Turkey*[22] has revitalized this important obligation as regards allegations of torture or other serious Article 3 violations. In this case, the European Court held that Article 13 imposes, without prejudice to any other remedy available under the domestic system, an obligation on states to carry out a thorough and effective investigation of incidents of torture:

> The notion of an 'effective remedy' thus entails, in addition to the payment of compensation where appropriate a thorough and effective investigation capable of leading to the identification and punishment of those responsible and including effective access for the complainant to the investigatory procedure.[23]

Mention should also be made in this context of the judgment in *Chahal v. the United Kingdom*[24] where the Court was called on to determine whether the applicant, an alleged Sikh terrorist whose extradition to India had been ordered on national security grounds by the Secretary of State, was able to have the lawfulness of his detention decided by a court as required by Article 5(4) of the European Convention. Under United Kingdom case law, the courts were not prepared to review the facts underlying the determination that a person was a threat to national security. The European Court considered that Article 5(4) required a more effective form of judicial control even in such cases. While recognizing that the use of confidential materials may be unavoidable where national security is at stake, the Court considered (with reference to Canadian practice) that national tribunals could have recourse to techniques which "both accommodate legitimate security concerns about the nature and sources of intelligence information and yet accord the individual a substantive measure of procedural justice."[25]

In the same case, the applicant also complained that the national courts did not provide an "effective remedy" in respect of his complaint under Article 3 that he would be tortured and possibly assassinated if sent back to India. In

---

of this judgment in preserving and strengthening the integrity of the Convention's supervisory machinery at a time when many eastern and central European states are joining the Convention community cannot be overemphasized. The *Loizidou (Preliminary Objections)* judgment has given a clear and uncomplicated message to states parties: governments may limit their acceptance of the optional clauses in time but they cannot under the Convention impose limitations *ratione materiae* or *loci* on the scope of supervision by the European Commission and Court.

[21] See in this connection the Court's judgment in *Akdivar and Others v. Turkey*, Reports 1996-IV, Volume 15, (16 September 1996).
[22] *Aksoy v. Turkey*, Reports 1996-VI, Volume 26, (18 December 1996).
[23] *Ibid.*, at para. 98.
[24] *Chahal v. United Kingdom*, Reports 1996-V, Volume 22, (15 November 1996).
[25] *Ibid.*, at paras. 124–133.

judicial review proceedings the national courts had assessed whether the Home Secretary had properly weighed the threat to Mr. Chahal's life or freedom in the event of deportation against the danger to national security if he were permitted to stay. For the Court this was insufficient. The notion of an "effective remedy" in respect of such a complaint "requires independent scrutiny of the claim that there exists substantive grounds for fearing a real risk of treatment contrary to Article 3. This scrutiny must be carried out without regard to what the person may have done to warrant expulsion or to any perceived threat to the national security of the expelling state."[26]

(3) External indicia of effectiveness

An effective system of human rights protection must be capable of providing remedies to the aggrieved individual leading, where necessary, to changes in legislation or administrative practices and to the development of a corpus of human rights law which provides guidance to contracting parties. It must also be seen to be working effectively in order to bring its influence to bear on national law and practice. Questions should be asked not only about systemic features – the number of cases, follow-up procedures, compliance, and so on – but also about appearances. Is the treaty regarded nationally as a system of law capable of imposing obligations? Is there respect for the pronouncements of the international body? Are policy makers who are responsible for framing legislation, Convention sensitive? Do the national courts refer to and follow the case law of these bodies? If these questions are answered in the affirmative, then the national authorities will be concerned not only to comply with pronouncements of the treaty body that concern them but also to follow developments in the case-law in order to ensure that national law and practice is in conformity with the rulings on treaty obligations. This prophylactic or deterrent effect provides an added dimension of effectiveness, which is perhaps of greater practical importance than the results in individual cases. It is in this area that the real achievement of the European Convention lies. States, confronted with a system that works, are obliged to keep their law and administrative practices under review. In this way the European Convention radiates a constant pressure for the maintenance of human rights standards and for change throughout Europe. A judgment of the European Court in a case brought by one person may thus have an impact on more than 41 national jurisdictions.

Although not a requirement of the European Convention, incorporation in national law is perhaps the single most important step that can be taken to ensure the effectiveness of Convention influence. When one considers the delays inherent in Strasbourg adjudication, it is not surprising that the European Court places so much influence on the subsidiary nature of the European Convention to national law. There can be little doubt that a national bill of rights is, at least in principle, a more rapid and secure method of protecting rights than recourse to an international tribunal. In this connection, the European Convention has been incorporated into the domestic law of most contracting parties. In addition,

---

[26] *Supra*, note 24 at paras. 140–155.

many parties have introduced Convention-proofing procedures designed to assess the compatibility of draft legislation with Convention norms.

The impact of the European Convention is also directly linked to the question of information. For this reason the European Court has a web site on the Internet to provide for easy access to its judgments.[27] In many eastern and central European countries, however, the treaty and its case law remain unknown entities. Indeed, in many western European countries Convention law appears as an inaccessible mystery to many members of the legal profession. It is clear that the European Convention will only begin to have an impact domestically in the new democracies if steps are taken to translate the leading decisions of the European Commission and judgments of the European Court into the respective languages. Judges, lawyers, academics and members of the public must have effective access to, and be properly informed about, these sources of law if the European Convention is to have any worthwhile impact. The experience of the Convention institutions demonstrates that a single case against a new contracting party which excites the attention of the media has a pedagogical impact which is far superior to the best-organized series of information meetings. Information exercises should thus target more precisely those likely to bring complaints, namely practicing lawyers and members of the NGO community.

(4) Protocol No. 11

Protocol No. 11 has established a full-time single Court to replace the European Convention's earlier enforcement machinery. It is seen as a response to the problem of the length of proceedings caused by the steadily increasing workload of the European Commission and Court over the years, and as a means of preserving and building upon the Convention's achievements in the light of the large increase in contracting parties due to developments in eastern and central Europe. Other important changes brought about by the Protocol are as follows. (1) The right of individual petition is now mandatory and the European Court has jurisdiction over all inter-state cases.[28] (2) The decision-making role of the Committee of Ministers has been abolished. Its role is limited to supervising the execution of the Court's judgments. All allegations of a violation of a Convention right are adjudicated by the European Court.[29] (3) Judges of the Court are full-time and elected for six-year terms rather than the earlier nine years. A retirement age of 70 has been introduced. There is no longer a prohibition on two judges having the same nationality. An express power of dismissal has also been introduced where a majority of two-thirds of the other judges consider that the judge has ceased to fulfil the required conditions.[30] (4) The Protocol also

---

[27] See www.dhcour.coe.fr". For the Council of Europe generally the Internet address is "www.coe.fr".
[28] European Convention, Art. 34 (former Art. 25). However, the optional character of the right of individual petition has been retained in respect of overseas territories – see Art. 56 (former Art. 63) and para. 113 of the *Explanatory Report to the Eleventh Protocol*, Council of Europe, 17 *European Human Rights Reports* (1994) 514.
[29] European Convention, Art. 46 (former Art. 54).
[30] European Convention, Art. 23 (former Art. 40). See Hans-Christian Krüger, "Procédure de Sélection des Juges de la Nouvelle Cour Européenne des Droits de l'Homme", 8 *Revue Universelle des Droits de l'Homme* (1996) at 113–116, for proposals as to the procedure for electing the new judges.

expressly provides for the possibility of third-party intervention. The President of the Court may invite contracting parties not only to submit written comments but also to take part in hearings.[31] However, the opportunity has not been taken to add a specific provision concerning the power of the European Court to order binding interim measures.[32]

The European Court sits in Committees, Chambers and a Grand Chamber comprising three, seven and seventeen judges respectively and occasionally in plenary.[33] The Plenary Court is responsible for appointing the Presidents of Chambers, constituting Chambers, adopting rules of procedure and the election of Presidents and Vice-Presidents of the Court. However it does not hear cases.[34] The new Court, in its various case-handling compositions, has responsibility for determining all aspects of the admissibility and merits of registered applications.

The extent to which the new European Court can achieve its objectives appears to depend on two crucial factors: firstly, the existence of a large measure of continuity between the new system and the former one in terms of judges, case-law, procedures and Secretariat. This is necessary if the existing case law and working methods of the former bodies (the so-called *acquis conventionnel*) are to have their proper place in the daily working habits of the new Court. In this connection it should be borne in mind that the new European Court has inherited many thousands of cases that the European Commission did not have an opportunity to examine, as well as a sizeable number of cases from the former Court to be dealt with by a seventeen-judge Grand Chamber of the Court in accordance with the transitional provisions of the Protocol. The experience of the European Commission in handling large numbers of provisional files and registered applications is especially important in this context. Secondly, the success of the new system in dealing efficiently with a large volume of cases and retaining the confidence of contracting parties depends on the quality of the new judges which have been elected to the Court. Protocol No. 11 brought with it the risk that in seeking to bring about a much needed improvement in the Strasbourg system, the new institution might find itself in conditions which make it difficult to achieve the goals of reform.[35]

(5) The reasons for the success of the system

Why has the European Convention been successful? There are four main reasons. The first is that the European Commission and Court succeeded in retaining the confidence of governments (and national courts) by carrying out their tasks in a judicial manner with the appropriate degree of detachment and objectivity. In so doing they have earned a reputation for fairness and intellectual rigour.

---

[31] European Convention, Art. 36 (2).
[32] A Swiss initiative to include such a provision modeled on rule 36 of the Commission's Rules of Procedure was unsuccessful – see Andrew Drzemczewski, "A Major Overhaul of the European Human Rights Convention Control Mechanism: Protocol No. 11", in *Collected Courses of the Academy of European Law*, volume V-2 (1994) at 45.
[33] European Convention, Art. 27 (former Art. 43).
[34] European Convention, Art. 26 (former Art. 41). It also elects the Registrar and Deputy Registrar.
[35] See generally, Nicholas Bratza and Michael O'Boyle, "The Legacy of the Commission to the New Court under the 11th Protocol", 3 *European Human Rights Law Review* (1997).

They also respected the principle of subsidiarity which recognizes the primary competence and duty of the state to protect effectively, within the domestic legal order, the rights enshrined in the European Convention. This notion has both a procedural as well as a substantive side. The former is reflected in the exhaustion of domestic remedies rule that any applicant must have referred his or her complaints to all domestic fora, which can be considered to offer an adequate and effective remedy. The latter requires that the Convention organs make due allowance in the examination of disputes for those legal and factual features which characterize the life of the society in the state concerned. The full operation of the principle of subsidiarity has several significant implications: first, it gives the Convention institutions an opportunity to learn from the legal approach of the competent national authorities in relation to those issues which the European Court may have to decide and, second, it helps to prevent an overloading of the control bodies. It also communicates the reassuring message to the national authorities that domestic legal developments and experience will not be overlooked.[36]

Second, the system has never stood still. It has been constantly aware of its impact and shortcomings and has demonstrated a capacity to adapt to changing circumstances. Thus new Protocols have been added which extended the list of rights (Protocols Nos. 1, 4, 6 and 7)[37] and introduced improvements to the procedures of the control bodies. Protocol No. 6, for example, prohibits the death penalty in times of peace. Protocol No. 9[38] enabled the individual to refer his or her case to the Court and Protocol No. 11, as noted above, provided for the creation of a single Court in place of the earlier organs.

Third, up until recent times the Convention community has been composed, as the preamble indicates, of countries which are like-minded and have a common heritage of political traditions, ideals, freedom and the rule of law. There has been thus a shared vision of the need for a collective enforcement of human rights. It is this common attachment to the rule of law that explains the high compliance rate with judgments of the European Court even when they have been greeted with hostility by the state concerned. One of the key questions for the operation of the system in the future is whether the new democratic states from eastern and central European countries will be able to maintain this tradition of compliance.

Finally, the European Convention has taken root in political and legal life in western European countries and enjoys considerable popular support. It has provided a frame of reference for national discussion of human rights issues and has contributed to the formation of a sensitized and informed public conscience on these questions. There are few governments, which would take the political risk of denouncing the European Convention.

---

[36] See Herbert Petzold, "The Convention and the Principle of Subsidiarity" in Ronald St. J. Macdonald, Franz Matscher and Hebert Petzold (eds.), *The European System for the Protection of Human Rights*, Dordrecht (1993) 41–63.
[37] For example, Protocol No. 1, ETS 9 (in force 18 May 1954); Protocol No. 4, ETS 46 (in force 2 May 1968); Protocol No. 6, ETS 114 (in force 1 March 1985); and Protocol No. 7, ETS 117 (in force 1 November 1988).
[38] Protocol No. 9, ETS 140 (in force 1 October 1994).

(6) Conclusion

The above reflections on the effectiveness of the Strasbourg system must be tempered by some mention of its weaknesses. The main shortcoming of the system – and one, which calls into question its many achievements and threatens public confidence – lies in the problem of the length of proceedings.[39] Protocol No. 11 will ultimately be judged on its capacity to reduce to acceptable levels the amount of time it takes to give judgment in individual cases. Other shortcomings are:

- The record of the Convention system in dealing with gross and systematic allegations of human rights violations has been subjected to much criticism.[40] The inter-state complaint has proved on occasions to be time-consuming, counter-productive and ultimately ineffective and has created doubts about the ability of an overcharged system to respond effectively to the most serious allegations. Nevertheless, the European Commission and Court had been able to make extensive findings in many cases involving serious allegations. In recent times, however, the European Commission had substantial institutional difficulties in carrying out extensive fact-finding in numerous individual cases concerning Turkey. Such investigations *in situ* are costly and time-consuming. The difficulties in dealing effectively with such allegations contrast strikingly with the abundance of attention devoted to issues concerning the finer points of constitutional interpretation. This may be seen as part of a wider and more general deficiency, however: the inability of international human rights bodies to react speedily and effectively to urgent situations and to torture, disappearances, summary executions and arbitrary arrests on a large scale.[41]
- There is no possibility to act *proprio motu* in the absence of a complaint filed under Articles 34 or 35 (former Articles 24 and 25) of the European Convention. Whether human rights problems can be addressed depends entirely on whether proceedings are instituted. This explains, for example, why states parties can thus derogate from the European Convention under Article 15, and maintain such derogations for lengthy periods, until the Convention bodies are provided with an opportunity to examine their compatibility with the Convention.
- The possibility of entering reservations and the fact that not all contracting parties have ratified the various Protocols means that the scope of protection afforded by the European Convention is not the same throughout Europe.

Recognition of some of these limitations has led to the European Convention for the Prevention of Torture and Inhuman or Degrading Treatment or

---

[39] Roughly two years for a decision of admissibility and five to six years from the filing of an application until judgment.
[40] See Menno Kamminga, "Is the European Convention on Human Rights Sufficiently Equipped to Cope with Gross and Systematic Violations", 12 *Netherlands Quarterly of Human Rights* (1994) 153–164, and *supra* note 1, Christian Tomuschat at 402–403.
[41] Peter Leuprecht, "Human Rights in the New Europe", in *Collected Courses of the Academy of European Law*, Volume V-2 (1994) at 173–174.

Punishment[42] and the establishment of a Committee with a broad capacity to examine conditions of detention throughout Europe.[43] Consideration is also being given to the idea of a European High Commissioner for Human Rights empowered to enter into discussions with governments about general human rights problems or situations. The failings concerning allegations of systematic and widespread violations raise the general questions whether it is at all feasible to deal with such problems by way of a petition system which will only be called on to examine specific aspects of a wider problem, and whether one can speak sensibly about "effectiveness" of human rights systems which are incapable of adequate responses to the most serious violations.

Notwithstanding the shortcomings noted above, the European system has established itself as a source of influence for legal and human rights development in a large number of European countries. Its influence has also radiated far beyond Europe.[44] With the Convention community stretching from the Atlantic to the Pacific and the coming into force of a single European Court – the largest of its kind in the world – it is clear that a new phase of development has begun. It can be predicted that with the increase of contracting parties there will be greater challenges to the authority of the European Court both in terms of the seriousness of the cases brought before it and of problems of compliance. The European Court will be called on to resist temptations to "dilute" the standards embodied in existing case law. Over the next decade we will be assessing the question of effectiveness in terms of the reception of Strasbourg case law into the legal culture of the new democracies and its contribution to the deepening of democratic security in the New Europe.

---

[42] European Convention for the Prevention of Torture and Inhuman or Degrading Treatment or Punishment, ETS 126 (in force 1 February 1989).
[43] Mark Kelly, "Preventing Ill Treatment: The Work of the CPT", 1 *European Human Rights Law Review* (1966) 287–303.
[44] The case-law of the European Court has been relied on or cited in cases decided in the national courts of many non-European states: see *supra* note 4 at 31.

IV. Defining the Role of Non-Governmental Organizations

CHAPTER 13

Defining the Role of Non-Governmental Organizations with Regard to the UN Human Rights Treaty Bodies

Andrew Clapham*

The role that non-governmental organizations (NGOs) play with regard to the United Nations treaty bodies has yet to be defined and clarified. Different actors have different views on what role NGOs should play before, during, and after the examination of the states' reports. The expert members of the treaty bodies and the government representatives are the only players with speaking parts during the formal meetings, which examine the reports. They are understandably unenthusiastic about giving NGOs the stage. On the other hand, all of the participants constantly reaffirm the important role that NGOs ought to play. This ambivalence towards NGOs can be frustrating for NGOs and confusing for governments presenting their reports to the treaty bodies. The lack of clarity concerning the NGO role points to a bigger problem surrounding the work of the treaty bodies, however. The human rights obligations are undertaken by states, the method for monitoring is designed by states, and the casting and selection of the expert monitors is reserved for states; the human rights treaties make few direct references to the role of NGOs. NGO parts have not been written into the treaties that determine the scenario for the examination of the state reports. In the end, each treaty body has found its own way to include NGOs in their work.[1]

---

*I would like to thank Liz Hodgkin, Nick Howen, Mariana Katzarova, Martin MacPherson, Guadaloupe Marengo, Florence Martin, Mona Rishmawi and Wilder Tayler who all made useful suggestions for this piece. The opinions expressed do not represent the position of Amnesty International, with whom I was employed when the original version of this paper was presented.

[1] The Convention on the Rights of the Child (CRC), 1577 UNTS 3 (in force 2 September 1990) sets out an obligation in art. 22 for states parties to cooperate with "competent... non-governmental organizations co-operating with the United Nations" to protect and assist children seeking refugee status. With regard to participation by NGOs in the hearings, the Child Committee has interpreted art. 45(a) of the CRC so that the Committee's entitlement to invite "competent bodies" as appropriate "to provide expert advice on the implementation of the Convention in areas falling within the scope of their respective activities" covers non-governmental organizations. CEDAW reviewed the practice of other treaty bodies with regard to the receipt of information from NGOs and the participation of NGOs in the work of the treaty bodies in: *Report of the Secretariat on Ways and Means of Improving the Work of the Committee*, CEDAW/C/1997/5 (6 December 1996). See also: *Report of the Committee on Economic, Social and Cultural Rights*, E/1999/22 (1999) at paras. 30–31; *Report of the Committee on the Elimination of Discrimination Against Women*, A/53/38/Rev.1 (1998), Decision 18/I at 3; *Report*

But NGOs have been shy about taking on a leading role. The awe-inspiring spectacle of a government actually being assessed on its human rights performance has produced a sort of reverence for the process and the players. As Mark Thomson points out in Chapter 16, this can be particularly important where powerful governments such as the United States, China, Germany, India, the Russian Federation and the United Kingdom are involved, as those governments are less likely to be scrutinized by the UN's political bodies such as the Commission on Human Rights. As NGOs become more familiar with the process, the dynamic is changing and some NGOs are starting to redefine their own role in their own terms. The problem with current attempts to develop the role of NGOs is that the main players have conflicting interests.

First, the governments that have chosen to ratify the treaties and report to the treaty bodies often resent the coverage which is given to information provided by human rights NGOs. This sort of information is embarrassing for governments as the meetings are held in public, and they resent having to respond to detailed questions about individual detainees or proposed legislation. Furthermore, despite the repeated suggestions by the treaty bodies that the government reports would benefit from NGO input, most governments do not yet see a role for NGOs at the time of the preparation of their report.[2] Non-governmental input during the examination therefore comes as something of a shock and surprise.

Second, expert members of the treaty bodies have different expectations. Some members feel that NGOs represent a useful resource for the treaty bodies. They would like NGOs to answer detailed questions on the legislative history of national measures. Other members are less comfortable with certain NGOs giving detailed briefings to Committee members, even in informal meetings organized by the UN Secretariat. Finally, the NGOs themselves are determined to retain their independence and their freedom to communicate their reports to Committee members. They do not want to be incorporated somehow into the governmental reporting process or incorporated selectively in the government delegation. They do not want to be given a defined role which compromises their non-governmental character.

The problem of defining the role of human rights NGOs was highlighted during a session of the Human Rights Committee. One Human Rights Committee member, who was a national of a state being examined, suggested that the NGO briefings to the Committee should include Committee members who were nationals of the state being examined, though Committee members do not normally participate or interfere in the examination of reports from their

---

of the Committee on the Elimination of Discrimination Against Women, A/54/38/Rev.1 (1999), Decision 20/I at 7.

[2] It is sometimes suggested that NGOs should be involved in the preparation of the government's report. This seems to deny the nature of NGOs as bodies which define themselves as not part of the government. The Advisory Committee on Human Rights and Foreign Policy of the Dutch Ministry of Foreign Affairs

... is of the opinion that [the preparation of country reports] is in principle an area of government responsibility, and that a clear distinction must be upheld between government responsibility and those of NGOs. The Advisory Committee therefore believes that when preparing reports, NGOs should in principle only be required to provide information.

"Advisory Report 22", *UN Supervision of Human Rights* (1996) at 10.

own country.[3] This tension and conflict of interest have been exacerbated by the fact that a proportion of elected Committee members are also serving government officials.[4] Some might argue that a treaty monitoring system set up by states will inevitably be state-centered. If the reporting mechanism is to have any relationship with the actual human rights situation in the country, however, then non-governmental voices need to be present and considered.

If one does not admit such a non-governmental role, the examination risks being seen as part of inter-state diplomacy rather than an examination by independent experts. One also risks isolating the work of the Committee from the national human rights debate and those sectors in society that are dealing day-to-day with these issues. The treaty bodies risk "splendid isolation"[5] as they remain removed from other parts of the human rights movement. The treaty bodies often fail to contact NGOs at the national level to alert them to upcoming reports, hardly any provision is made for circulating relevant NGO information to the Committee members, and no consideration is given in the scheduling to facilitating NGO participation.[6] Despite the obstacles of the lack of defined roles or the distance between the treaty bodies and relevant NGOs, however, human rights organizations have managed to develop a role with regard to the treaty bodies.

---

[3] The meeting of the Chairpersons of the Treaty Bodies recommended "that members of treaty bodies refrain from participating in any aspect of the consideration of the reports of the states of which they are nationals, or communications or inquiring concerning those states, in order to maintain the highest standards of impartiality, both in substance and in appearance": *Report of the Seventh Meeting of Persons Chairing the Human Rights Treaty Bodies*, 16–20 September 1996, A/51/482 (11 October 1996) at para. 29.

[4] In fact, in addition to those currently working for their governments, a large proportion were employed or had been recently employed by their governments at the time of their election. According to Anne Bayefsky,

"an examination of the curriculum vitae that have been submitted to the states parties for the purposes of the election of the members of the six treaty bodies reveals that approximately 45 percent to 65 percent were employed in some capacity by their nominating governments. There are also curriculum vitae that fail to indicate the individual's current job; if account is taken of these curriculum vitae and their revelation of last known jobs for those nominated for treaty body membership, approximately half to three-quarters were currently or last employed in some capacity by their nominating governments. If one isolates the individuals who were elected to the treaty bodies, between 35 percent and 65 percent were employed in some capacity by their governments."

Anne Bayefsky, "Making the Human Right Treaties Work", in *Human Rights: An Agenda for the Next Century*, Louis Henkin and John L. Hargrove (eds.), American Society of International Law (1994) 229–297 at 243–4 (footnote omitted).

[5] This phrase is apparently originally attributable to Sir George Foster (1828–1904) who used it in a speech in the Canadian House of Commons on 16 June 1896 to describe the position of Britain in Europe, "In these somewhat troublesome days when the great Mother Empire stands splendidly isolated in Europe": *Official Report of the Dominion of Canada, Volume 41 (1896)* at column 176. The speech was reported in *The Times of London* under the heading "Splendid Isolation" on 22 June 1896. (Details from the *Oxford Dictionary of Quotations*, Oxford University Press (1979)).

[6] For a series of recommendations addressed to the Secretariat on the how to enhance input from NGOs, see *infra* Anne Bayefsky, Appendix 6, *International Law Association, Committee on International Human Rights Law and Practice, Report on the UN Human Rights Treaties: Facing the Implementation Crisis*, at 692–693. Some of the problems regarding notification of upcoming reports and examinations have been ameliorated by the creation of a home page on the Internet which gives the dates of upcoming examinations as well as the concluding observations and other very useful information.

(1) Some different roles taken on by non-governmental organizations

It is quite obvious that different NGOs will have different roles. Although international NGOs have had a number of opportunities to develop their roles with the Committee when they meet in New York and Geneva, the role of national NGOs remains rather unexplored. The treaty bodies have encouraged governments to make their reports available to national NGOs for study and comment,[7] but so far, few governments have recognized this as part of their reporting obligations under the human rights treaties. The reporting process could be used to define a new role for NGOs in relation to their governments at the national level. At the international level, national NGOs have started to use the reporting process to develop some international accountability for their governments' human rights records. The obstacles associated with the development of this role are mainly issues of resources. National NGOs cannot afford to attend meetings in Geneva and New York when one considers the possible benefits that such attendance can bring. There have often been appeals for a trust fund to be set up by governments to facilitate participation by national NGOs in the work of the treaty bodies, but no such trust fund has been established as yet.

It may be useful to highlight the role which Amnesty International has played with regard to some of the treaty bodies with which it works.[8] Although this is not an exhaustive list, it does illustrate the sort of work that a large international NGO considers worthwhile in this context. When drawing up prescriptive lists of things that NGOs should do in connection with the treaty bodies, it should always be borne in mind that NGOs are not obliged to follow such prescriptions. NGOs will only participate in the work of the treaty bodies to the extent that it seems to bring rewards. In defining a role for NGOs, it is essential to remember that other priorities are never far from any NGO's field of vision.

First, with regard to legislative programmes, NGOs can play a role in ensuring that members of the treaty bodies are informed of the nuances of the application of national legislation, and, where necessary, translate the bills and laws into other languages used by the treaty bodies. This sort of work obviously lends itself to cooperation between international and national NGOs. An example of such cooperation took place in the context of the Human Rights Committee's examination of Peru. Amnesty International expressed concern about the failure of the Peruvian Congress to adopt any of the draft measures that had been filed to tackle the problem of prisoners falsely charged and convicted of terrorism-related offenses.[9] The *Coordinadora Nacional de Derechos Humanos*, an independent organization which brings together 47 non-governmental human rights groups in Peru, concentrated on another issue: the laws which grant a general

---

[7] See *supra* note 2. For an example of an exchange on this point, see the questions posed by Thomas Buergenthal to the Sri Lanka delegation, Human Rights Committee, *Summary Record of the 1436th Meeting, 24 July 1995*, CCPR/C/SR.1436 (28 July 1995) at paras. 64, 65; discussed in *Sri Lanka: Under Scrutiny by the Human Rights Committee*, Amnesty International, AI index ASA 37/21/95 (1995) at 4.

[8] I have dealt with a number of case studies in more detail elsewhere. See Andrew Clapham, "UN human rights reporting procedures: An NGO Perspective", in *The Future of UN Human Rights Treaty Monitoring*, Philip Alston and James Crawford (eds.), Cambridge University Press, 2000 at 175.

[9] *Peru: Legislative Bills for Pardoning Prisoners Unjustly Convicted of Terrorism*, Amnesty International, AI Index AMR 46/18/96 (16 July 1996).

amnesty to military, police or civilian personnel who face a complaint or conviction in relation to events related to the fight against terrorism conducted between May 1980 and June 1995.[10] The Human Rights Committee heard briefings from representatives of Amnesty International and the *Coordinadora* and members were able to ask detailed questions on points of law and receive the written briefings and translations that had been prepared. This sort of collaboration may pave the way for NGOs to be seen by members of the Committee as legal experts rather than "interest groups."[11]

Second, NGOs may take on the role of disseminators as they seek to make the provisions of the treaties better known at the national level. Amnesty International worked with local Russian NGOs to publicize the examination of that country's second report to the Committee Against Torture (CAT) within Russian prisons. Where a state has allowed for individual complaints, well-targeted publicity can be particularly valuable. More generally, NGOs may choose to publicize the examination of the state report where this could lead to improvements in the human rights situation. Arguably, the extensive publicity surrounding the discussion by CAT of the conditions of detainees in Northern Ireland led to better treatment there. Third, NGOs have the opportunity to lobby for special reports to be presented by states parties to the treaties.[12] At one stage this was considered a sort of "early warning" role. However, it is questionable whether the treaty bodies will ever be able to play a role in conflict prevention. Nevertheless, there may be cases where NGOs will want special reports in response to specific situations such as particular judicial decisions or new executive measures.

(2) Using the complaints procedures

The issue of human rights NGOs assisting victims with complaints to the treaty bodies[13] again raises the question of the costs and benefits to NGOs of using these procedures. Few NGOs can justify the intensive human resources needed to prepare and pursue complaints through the system. For larger NGOs, the problem is how to discriminate and choose which cases ought to be assisted before the treaty bodies. Current interpretations of the rules seem to exclude NGOs from *locus standi* so that they are in effect unable to represent individual

---

[10] Peru Law No. 264779, art. 1, in "Normas Legales", *Diario Oficial El Peruano* (15 June 1995). For an English translation see *Peru: UN Experts Condemn Amnesty Laws*, Amnesty International, AI Index AMR 46/20/96 (5 August 1996) at appendix 1. Law No. 26492, art. 2, in "Normas Legales" *Diario Oficial El Peruano* (2 July 1995). For an English translation see *Peru: UN Experts Condemn Amnesty Laws, Ibid.* at Appendix 2.
[11] See generally *infra* Mark Thompson, at Chapter 16.
[12] See, for example, the special report requested from Israel following NGO lobbying: *Special Report Submitted By Israel*, CAT/C/33/Add.2/Rev.1 (18 February 1997). See discussion in Connors, *infra* Chapter 1 at 19.
[13] Optional Protocol to the International Covenant on Civil and Political Rights, 999 UNTS 171 (in force 23 March 1976); Convention Against Torture and other Forms of Cruel, Inhuman or Degrading Treatment or Punishment, 1465 UNTS 85 (in force 26 June 1987), art. 22; Convention on the Elimination of All Forms of Racial Discrimination, 660 UNTS 3 (in force 4 January 1969), art. 14.

victims in the complaints procedures without becoming the *formal legal representative*.[14] Although few NGOs would admit to abundant resources, the rules do dissuade NGOs from becoming properly involved in the complaints procedures. This is how Helena Cook explained Amnesty International's unwillingness to embark on a strategy for backing individual complaints:

> Observers are sometimes surprised that Amnesty does not submit cases to the complaints procedures set up under some of these human rights treaties. These procedures generally require NGOs to act as the formal representative of the individual concerned. As a matter of policy, Amnesty has always avoided representing individuals in judicial or quasi-judicial proceedings, whether at the national or the international level. It is anyway practically impossible for Amnesty, as a global organization dealing with thousands of individual cases in all regions of the world, to take up individual cases in this way. It does, however, play an educative role in informing individuals, lawyers and others about how to use the complaints procedures and joined in efforts at the United Nations to improve their effectiveness and scope.[15]

There are other factors which have similarly discouraged attention by NGOs to the communications procedure. First, there is no provision for oral hearings before the Committees. Second, there are no provisions which allow for third party briefs or *amicus curiae* submissions. Third, the backlog of cases means that the time between the original submission and the publication of the views of the relevant Committee makes it impractical for many NGOs to invest in such procedures. These factors, taken together, mean that NGOs are unable to use the communications procedure to suggest ways in which the Committees might develop their jurisprudence or doctrine. Given these factors, it seems likely that NGOs will concentrate their efforts on cases in national courts and regional treaty bodies procedures such as those established by the European Convention on Human Rights,[16] the American Convention on Human Rights[17] and the African Charter on Human and Peoples' Rights.[18]

One idea put forward to increase the minimal NGO activity around the complaints procedure is the creation of an international network of lawyers that could take on suitable cases under the First Optional Protocol to the International Covenant on Civil and Political Rights (CCPR) and some of the other UN individual complaints procedures. Human rights organizations such as the London-based Interights have already started to consider how to encourage communications which raise certain key issues in order to develop the 'case-law' of the Human Rights Committee. As organizations concerned with economic and social rights become familiar with the new European complaints procedures

---

[14] Note that article 2 of the Optional Protocol to the Convention on the Elimination of All Forms of Discrimination Against Women (CEDAW), adopted by G.A. Res. 54/4 on 6 October 1999 (not yet in force), states that a complaint may be brought on behalf of individuals or groups of individuals with the consent of the alleged victim (unless the author can justify acting on their behalf without such consent).
[15] Helena Cook, "Amnesty International at the United Nations", in *The Conscience of the World: The Influence of NGOs in the United Nations System*, Peter Willets (ed.), Brookings Institution (1997).
[16] Convention for the Protection of Human Rights and Fundamental Freedoms, ETS 5 (in force 3 September 1953).
[17] American Convention on Human Rights, PAUTS 36 (in force 18 July 1978).
[18] African Charter on Human and Peoples' Rights (in force 21 October 1986).

in this field, one may find that NGOs start to carve out a role as 'litigators' for rights protection.[19] So far NGOs have failed to give this possibility much attention or write themselves a leading role in the area of individual complaints to the treaty bodies.

However, together with other groups, Amnesty International has used the procedure under article 20 of the Torture Convention (CAT)[20] whereby the Committee is entitled to initiate an inquiry when it receives "reliable information" which suggests "well-founded indications that torture is being systematically practiced in the territory of a state party." Under this procedure, Amnesty International made submissions on Turkey and joined with other organizations in making submissions on Egypt. The procedure makes no provision for a continuing role for NGOs beyond the submission of their original complaint. Nevertheless, NGOs have followed these investigations very closely. Both complaints led to investigation by the Committee and the results of the procedure were published in the annual report of CAT to the General Assembly.[21] CAT seriously considered the information submitted to it by NGOs and, in the case of Egypt, concluded that the information was well-founded even though the Committee was unable to visit Egypt due to that country's failure to reply to requests to visit.[22] It is interesting that CAT chose to accept the information from the NGOs and the Special Rapporteur on Torture noting that it came "from sources that have proved to be reliable in connection with other activities of the Committee."[23] By working regularly with CAT, NGOs may be able to present evidence of the systematic practice of torture and discover that the Committee is prepared to draw conclusions on the basis of this evidence. In the case of Egypt, the Committee felt it was "forced to conclude that torture is systematically practiced by the security forces in Egypt, in particular the State Security Intelligence."[24]

In the case of Turkey, the submission of information triggered a visit to Turkey by two members of CAT which resulted in a series of recommendations and a report transmitted to the Government of Turkey. The Committee considered the Government's replies and decided that publication (as part of its annual report) of a summary of the results was necessary. The Committee noted "with satisfaction" the cooperation of the Turkish authorities during the inquiry, and congratulated them on having acted on many of the recommendations. But the

---

[19] For a guide to the complaints procedure provided for in the Additional Protocol to the European Social Charter, ETS 158 (in force 1 July 1998), ETS 35 (in force 26 February 1965) see Tom Kenny *Securing Social Rights Across Europe: How NGOs Can Make Use of the European Social Charter*, Oxfam (1997).

[20] *Supra*, note 13.

[21] *Summary Account of the Results of the Proceedings Concerning the Inquiry on Turkey: Report of the Committee Against Torture*, 44A A/48/44/Add.1 (1993); "Summary Account of the Results of the Proceedings Concerning the Inquiry on Egypt, in *Report of the Committee Against Torture*, A/51/44 (1996), Chapter V at Section B. For the objection of the Egyptian Government to the way in which this summary account of the investigations was published, see A/C.3/51/17 (22 November 1996).

[22] See *Report of the Committee Against Torture* (1996), *supra* note 21 at para 217.

[23] *Ibid.*, at para. 219. The sources listed by CAT were: "(a) reports of the Special Rapporteur of the Commission on Human Rights on questions relating to torture; (b) Amnesty International; (c) the Egyptian Organizations for Human Rights; and (d) the World Organization against Torture. Other non-governmental sources have occasionally provided information during this inquiry": *Ibid.* at para. 201.

[24] *Ibid.*, at para. 220.

"final statement" continues: "the Committee remains concerned at the number and substance of allegations of torture received, which confirm the existence and systematic character of the practice of torture in this state party."[25]

These conclusions then became instrumental in a wider campaign to bring political pressure on Turkey in fora such as the Organization for Security and Cooperation in Europe (OSCE) and the UN Commission on Human Rights. The independent finding by a UN expert body turned allegations of torture into a finding which the governmental representatives in the political arena found more difficult to dismiss. Even though the non-governmental pressure for a factfinding mission by the OSCE or action in the Commission on Human Rights has not borne fruit, the finding of CAT has remained a useful campaigning tool for NGOs in the fight against torture.

(3) Working with the treaty bodies on the drafting of General Comments and the development of thematic issues

The production of General Comments on the scope of the treaties and the reporting duties of states parties has proven invaluable in giving the treaty bodies wider impact beyond the periodic examinations of states' reports. Because many constitutions either incorporate international law or draw inspiration from the international human rights instruments, national courts will often have to apply either the treaty provisions or constitutions based on language found in the UN treaties. In this context, NGOs have found it useful to be able to point to the General Comments as authoritative interpretations of the rights in question.

However, there are difficulties with over reliance on these General Comments. There is a tendency to see international law as providing the maximum protection afforded by the right in question rather than a safety net and minimum standard. This is unfortunate as the comments do not really represent a maximum attainable standard and benchmark, but rather are usually molded by consensus and are deliberately designed to be acceptable to a wide range of states and legal systems. Without NGO attention to the evolving nature of human rights law and the possibilities to adapt the comments to reflect new challenges and threats to human rights, there is a danger that international human rights law, as defined by the General Comments, will become fossilized and a brake on progressive interpretation.

The role which NGOs are invited to play varies from Committee to Committee. For example, the Economic, Social and Cultural Rights Committee has encouraged certain NGOs to become involved in its thematic work and assist with the development of its doctrine. On the other hand, NGOs have been excluded from the working groups of the Committee on the Elimination of Discrimination Against Women (CEDAW) when general recommendations have been elaborated.[26] The generation of these recommendations has sometimes

---

[25] *Supra*, note 21, *Report of the Committee Against Torture* (1993) at para. 58.

[26] "[C]ommittee members may fear undue influence or interference in the work of an expert body that does not see itself as a target for the kind of lobbying that is more commonly accepted by the governmental bodies. Moreover, most of the committees are much less open to NGO input on organizational and methodological aspects of their work. NGO input on new or revised General

frustrated NGOs as there is a sense that CEDAW is giving undue attention to the perspective of states, and that the Committee treats the issues as though they were issues of social policy rather than human rights questions. Part of the blame for this may lie with the organic link which the Committee enjoys with the UN Commission on the Status of Women (CSW). The influence of CSW, an inter-governmental policy body, is not only due to the formal origins of the Convention on the Elimination of Discrimination Against Women (CEDAW),[27] but also due to the role played by some of the expert members in the parent governmental body. The governmental culture of the Committee has often meant that there is limited opportunity for non-governmental input, although this approach to NGOs is changing.[28]

Part of the explanation for the limited profile of international NGOs in the context of CEDAW lies in the nature of the non-governmental community. International human rights organizations with country concerns have tended to concentrate on the Human Rights Committee and CAT. Women's organizations have in turn concentrated on themes (perhaps in part due to the failure of CSW to look at complaints about country situations and report only on emerging themes). The initiative by the International Women's Rights Action Watch (IWRAW) to ensure that national women's groups are aware of upcoming examinations by CEDAW has connected the work of the Committee to national women's groups,[29] but much more could be done by all of the Committees as well as by the different Secretariats in New York and Geneva to encourage greater participation and contributions by both national and international human rights NGOs.

Committees such as the Child Committee and the Economic, Social and Cultural Rights Committee have invited NGOs to contribute ideas on thematic

---

Comments is not generally sought, with the committees perhaps too jealously holding on to their role as sole guardians of the treaty."

Supra, note 14.

At the same time, there have been contacts between some members of CEDAW and NGOs relating to the drafting of General Comments outside Committee sessions. See for example, the history of the drafting of CEDAW's *General Recommendation No. 24: Article 12 of the Convention on the Elimination of All Forms of Discrimination Against Women – Women and Health, Report of the Committee on the Elimination of Discrimination Against Women*, A/53/38/Rev.1 (1998) at 7, para. 31.

Although the Human Rights Committee and the Economic, Social and Cultural Rights Committee have been more open to NGOs in this context, this has brought its own problems in some cases as there is no opportunity for open debate as to why one non-governmental opinion should be favoured over another. The chairpersons of the treaty bodies recommended in 1994 that draft general comments be circulated in advance to interested NGOs so that they can study them and make comments: *Report of the Fifth Meeting of Persons Chairing the Human Rights Treaty Bodies, 19–23 September 1994*, A/49/537 (19 October 1994) at para. 41.

[27] Convention on the Elimination of All Forms of Discrimination Against Women, 1249 UNTS 13 (in force 3 September 1981).

[28] See Roberta Jacobson, "The Committee on the Elimination of Discrimination Against Women" in *The United Nations and Human Rights: A Critical Appraisal*, Philip Alston (ed.), Oxford (1992) 444–472 at 466. In more recent years, this approach has shifted. See *supra* Jane Connors, Chapter 1 at note 63.

[29] See the impressive guide published by the IWRAW and the Commonwealth Secretariat, *Assessing the Status of Women: A Guide to Reporting Under the Convention on the Elimination of All Forms of Discrimination Against Women*, 2nd ed. (1996); see also *The Women's Convention and CEDAW: Opportunities and Challenges in Light of Beijing*, IWRAW (1996); for an example of a compilation by IWRAW of national reports see *IWRAW to CEDAW Country Reports*, IWRAW (October 1995).

issues. An example of a particularly fruitful exchange between NGOs and a committee occurred with the Child Committee on the subject of "Children in Armed Conflict." During that 1992 discussion, the representative of the Quakers suggested that the Child Committee might want to consider an in-depth study on the recruitment of children into armed conflict and their participation in hostilities.[30] The eventual recommendation to the General Assembly, for the General Assembly to request the Secretary-General to undertake a study on ways and means of improving the protection of children in armed conflict, resulted in the Graça Machel study[31] and the appointment of a Special Representative on Children in Armed Conflict. As a result of the creation of this human rights mechanism by the General Assembly (in 1996), much of the work and recommendations in the study could be followed up. The history of this thematic mechanism has meant that the Special Representative, Olara Otunnu, has continued to benefit from the role played by NGOs in this area.[32]

(4) Improving the system

Increased NGO participation is not an end in itself – but rather a means to achieving more effective implementation of the rights contained in the treaties. NGOs can help the members of the treaty bodies select the issues that they are going to take up with the government. NGOs can disseminate the results of the examination as well as the relevant General Comments and Views. NGOs can provide a committee with an alternative perception of the state's compliance with its obligations under the treaties. The treaty bodies' ambivalence about NGOs may have been born out of a fear that governments would be angry at being embarrassed by the accusations of NGOs when governmental representatives met the committee in order to engage in constructive dialogue. New efforts at constructive dialogue between the treaty bodies and NGOs could lead to more effective monitoring. This will involve both sides thinking more clearly about what sort of role NGOs are to play.

One last role for NGOs must be the role of critic. As privileged players who can participate and observe almost simultaneously, NGOs can play the roles of insiders and outsiders. Few committee members are in a position to criticize the way the treaty bodies work, their composition, the quality of the government delegations, nor do they feel comfortable proposing radical changes. Nevertheless, radical change has been on the agenda for some time. In 1988, the UN General Assembly adopted a resolution requesting a report on "enhancing the long term effectiveness of the United Nations human rights treaty system."[33]

---

[30] Child Committee, *Summary Record of the 38th Meeting, 4 October 1992*, CRC/C/SR.38 (22 January 1993) at para. 15.
[31] Graça Machel, *Impact of Armed Conflict on Children: Report of the Expert of the Secretary-General*, A/51/306 (26 August 1996) and annex to that report, A/51/306/Add.1 (9 September 1996). Graça Machel was appointed by the Secretary-General pursuant to G.A. Res. 48/157, adopted on 20 December 1993.
[32] *Protection of Children Affected by Armed Conflict: Report of the Special Representative of the Secretary-General for Children and Armed Conflict*, A/53/482 (12 October 1998); *Protection of Children Affected by Armed Conflict: Report of the Special Representative of the Secretary-General for Children and Armed Conflict*, A/54/430 (1 October 1999).
[33] G.A. Res. 43/115, adopted on 8 December 1988.

An independent expert, Philip Alston, was appointed by the Secretary-General; Alston's subsequent reports outline a number of possible changes to enhance effectiveness. The reports highlight the "chronic" non-reporting by states and the fact the current reporting system is "unsustainable" due to the increasing number of ratifications and communications set against a background of no increase in resources, either for more meetings, or for allocating more staff to the UN Secretariat.[34] Alston outlines various options for governments to consider, including urging the treaty bodies to undertake "far-reaching reforms." His suggestions for such reforms include the preparation by governments of "consolidated reports" which would cover obligations contained in more than just one treaty.[35] He also notes the possibility of a consolidation of the number of treaty bodies.[36] So far NGOs have been reluctant to take a critical look and support radical reform for fear of weakening the system. Logic suggests that, as governments are ultimately in charge of fundamental reform, they would hardly agree to something that will ensure greater enforcement, or which would more effectively expose the violations they are committing.[37] While there may be good reason to be suspicious of government-led reform, and there are considerable legal and administrative problems associated with any really radical reform of the system, it seems important to identify the weaknesses with the current system and to be idealistic about the sort of system that could remedy these problems.

From an NGO perspective, the problems relate less to the increasing burdens on government departments and the Secretariat, and more to the quality of the 'constructive dialogue' between the expert members and the government representatives. Government representatives escape real scrutiny due to the stylized legalistic nature of the members' questions. Moreover, the committee members are in effect working part-time and usually having to juggle another job. Some members even have full-time jobs as government officials in areas such as foreign affairs, thus producing a glaring conflict of interest. It would seem that moving towards a professional full-time consolidated body would ameliorate some of these problems. Experts would have the chance to study the countries they are

---

[34] See the three reports submitted by Philip Alston: the first report submitted to the General Assembly, *Long Term Approaches to Enhancing the Effective Operation of Existing and Prospective Bodies Established under the United Nations Human Rights Instruments*, A/44/668 (8 November 1989); the interim report submitted to the World Conference on Human Rights, *Interim Report on Updated Study of Mr. Philip Alston*, A/CONF.157/PC/62/Add.11/Rev.1 (22 April 1993); and the final report transmitted to the Commission on Human Rights, *Final Report on Enhancing the Long Term Effectiveness of the United Nations Human Rights Treaty System*, E/CN.4/1997/74 (27 March 1997). 35
[35] *Ibid.*, E/CN.4/1997/74 at para. 90.
[36] *Supra*, note 34, E/CN.4/1997/74 at para. 94:
(f) Towards a consolidation of the treaty bodies: Some of the arguments for and against this reform have already been explored in the independent expert's 1989 report (A/44/668, paras. 182–183). For that reason, they will not be repeated here. Given the limitations of space it must suffice to note in this context that while the legal and procedural problems inherent in such an initiative would not be negligible, the prior issue is whether there is the political will to begin exploring in any detail the contours of such a reform. If that will were manifest, the technical challenges would be resolvable. It is therefore recommended that consideration be given to the convening of a small expert group, with an appropriate emphasis upon international legal expertise, to prepare a report on the modalities that might be considered in this respect.
[37] See the response of Mark Thomson *infra* Chapter 16 at 224: "[States] won't want to introduce a system that from the outset is likely to give them a harder time about their implementation commitments, let alone their reporting obligations."

dealing with, examinations could be planned in greater detail, and members would not be working with divided loyalties. Another problem already alluded to is that the whole treaty body system seems to work in isolation from the rest of the UN, including the UN's own human rights field missions around the world. The disconnected nature of the treaty monitoring system means that their meetings are little understood by the media, or by the general public, or indeed by those government departments that are uninvolved with the preparation of the reports.

Consolidation of the reports and of the treaty bodies would address some of these problems, but one could go further and imagine a professional, permanent body which sat on a full-time basis with members appointed for non-renewable periods of seven years. This sort of reform is not currently popular with NGOs as they rightly fear that governments will not make much effort to ensure that the consolidated body is composed of truly independent experts. Furthermore, there are fears amongst NGOs, and the treaty body members themselves, that such a body would inevitably loose some of the focus currently found in the six different committees. The consolidated body would, it is feared, replicate the general bias towards core civil and political rights, and neglect issues of gender, racial discrimination, children's issues and economic and social rights.

Some guarantees could be built in to ensure that the new consolidated body retained a multi-dimensional approach to human rights – even if the consolidation would obviously mean that fewer experts would be involved. But even if the problems of balance and independent expertise could be overcome, and a near perfect consolidated body could be formed, the actual effectiveness of the treaty bodies still essentially depends on the concrete changes implemented by governments on the ground. The impact of any treaty body will depend on how seriously governments take the recommendations and how involved local NGOs can become in the work of the body. The system will not necessarily be more effective just because it has been rationalized and streamlined.[38]

On balance, it is suggested that consolidation of expertise and resources around a permanent paid body of experts would lead to a more meaningful dialogue with governments. If the transition is carefully planned, governments might see the advantages of not only having fewer overlapping reporting duties, but also having recommendations, observations and views that are more developed and of greater use at the national level. From the NGO perspective, to have such a consolidated full time body would increase the opportunities for constructing a dialogue based on real problems. In this way the national/ international divide, which currently isolates the work of the treaty bodies from the work of national NGOs trying to enhance the enjoyment of human rights around the world, could be transcended.

---

[38] The drive to rationalize and streamline the human rights machinery is recalled in the Secretary-General's programme for reform of the UN and remains at the heart of the human rights discussion at the Third Committee of the General Assembly. See *Renewing the United Nations: A Programme for Reform*, A/51/950 (14 July 1997) at recommendation 16 (a): "The Secretary-General will ask the High Commissioner for Human Rights to review the human rights machinery and develop recommendations on possible ways to streamline and rationalize it."

CHAPTER 14

Women's Human Rights NGOs and the Treaty Bodies: Some Case Studies in Using the Treaty Bodies to Protect the Human Rights of Women

Alice M. Miller*

(1) Introduction

The following can be described as fundamental principles: (1) the integration of a gendered understanding of human rights throughout the UN system, including treaty bodies, is a stated priority of the international community; (2) non-governmental organizations (NGOs) play a critical role in fulfilling this priority, (3) gender integration should be a priority for both national and international NGOs, whether or not their mandates explicitly focus on women, and (4) the protection of women's human rights belongs to all treaty bodies, and can be found in all treaties, in addition to the Convention on the Elimination of All Forms of Discrimination Against Women (CEDAW).[1]

Evaluation of the roles of NGOs must acknowledge the reality of the diversity of NGO needs and interests in the human rights treaty system. Women's NGOs, local or national NGOs, and groups which have only recently emerged internationally (such as those working for the human rights of lesbians and gay men or persons with disabilities), have different needs in relation to the treaty system, than larger, established or international NGOs. Some NGOs are still struggling to grasp the idea and meaning of the rights promised in the human rights treaties, and the role of the treaty bodies as apparent gatekeepers of universal rights. Others are standing within the gates, the rights of those on whose behalf they speak having been accepted. These differences need not, and should not, be divisive.

There is a continuing need to reaffirm the universality of human rights and to give concrete meaning to rights. In this context, global participation has an

---

*I would like to thank Susan Fried of the Centre for Women's Global Leadership, Ilama Landsberg-Lewis of UNIFEM for their comments, and the many women activists whose presence at workshops and UN sessions have generated many of the ideas contained in this chapter. In addition, Ms. Ranjana Ariaratanam Zook provided helpful support.
[1] Convention on the Elimination of All Forms of Discrimination Against Women, 1249 UNTS 13 (in force 3 September 1981).

intrinsic value, as well as a functional value to increasing the impact of the system world wide. One goal of a fully functioning treaty system should be the global participation of women. Indeed, there is a potential transformative impact for women's groups at the national level from experience with international work.

This Chapter will draw on actual projects by women's NGOs that make use of the treaty system, and the first-hand experience of the Women's Rights Advocacy Program (WRAP) (formerly the Women in the Law Project of the International Human Rights Law Group).[2] The case studies are presented from the perspective of an international NGO working at the international and national level with national NGOs. There are two different case studies of women's groups and the treaty system, one from the national level and the other at the international level. The studies assist in responding to the challenge posed by Andrew Clapham in Chapter 13 that "[a]lthough international NGOs have had a number of opportunities to develop their roles, the role of national NGOs remains rather unexplored."

(2) Background: Women's NGOs and human rights – calling on the treaty system to take into account more effectively women's human rights

One of the most dynamic aspects of the 1993 World Conference on Human Rights was its call to correct the historic marginalization of women's human rights. This has been underscored and affirmed since that time, including by the final Declaration and Platform for Action of the Fourth World Conference on Women.[3] The continuing need to take concrete steps toward integration has also been affirmed by the Commission on the Status of Women (CSW) and the Commission on Human Rights.[4]

NGOs have played a critical role in pushing the question of gender integration on to the United Nations' agenda in the context of the treaty bodies and in

---

[2] The Women's Rights Advocacy Program (WRAP) of the International Human Rights Law Group was established in the fall of 1992 to build the capacity of local and national women's groups to use human rights language, methods and mechanisms as tools in their work. By collaborating at national and international levels with women's groups, WRAP contributes to the progressive strengthening and development of standards to hold governments accountable for violations of women's civil, cultural, economic, political or social rights. The Law Group is based in Washington, D.C., USA.

[3] See generally, Strategic Objective I.1: "Promote and protect the human rights of women, through the full implementation of all human rights instruments, especially the Convention on the Elimination of All Forms of Discrimination Against Women", in *The Beijing Declaration and Platform for Action*, DPI/1766/WOM (15 September 1995) at paras. 230–231.

[4] See for example, *Mainstreaming a Gender Perspective into all the Policies and Programmes in the United Nations System*, E/CN.6/1997/L.14 (18 March 1997) in E/1997/27, and Commission on Human Rights Res. 1997/43, adopted on 11 April 1997 which states that the Commission: "Expresses concern that the implementation of the relevant recommendations of the Vienna Declaration and Programme of Action, and the Beijing Platform for Action remains far from the objectives set forth in the two documents ..." and "... welcomes the efforts of the treaty bodies to monitor more effectively the human rights of women in their activities, including such initiatives as the roundtable on human rights approaches to women's health ..." and affirms the need to "develop gender sensitive guidelines ..." as well as the need to "incorporate a gender perspective into concluding observations." See also Commission on Human Rights Res. 2000/46, adopted on 20 April 2000 at para. 17.

other mechanisms. NGOs have contributed to developing "gender-sensitive indicators"[5] or gender-specific questions for treaty body experts, and have appeared as advocates at various treaty body meetings to make this point. The on-going role of NGOs as advocates and constructive critics of treaty body practices cannot be underestimated in the context of women's human rights.

(a) Evaluating the roles of NGOs

In Chapter 13 Andrew Clapham has set out a number of concerns to be considered in evaluating the role of NGOs. These need to be reiterated and reviewed in the context of national NGOs and gender. Among these concerns is that the issue of defining NGO roles is being addressed by parties with conflicting or at least divergent interests. There are disparate ideas regarding the functions that NGOs serve best, such as publicity, outreach, documentation and information presentation. There are also questions about whether NGOs should be characterized as governmental "partners", treaty body "partners", oppositional monitors, or critics. The general lack of access by those unfamiliar with the UN to treaty information, and the knowledge of how to obtain it and use it, poses great problems. There is a need for an honest evaluation of the benefits for NGOs in participating at various levels of the treaty system as opposed to the costs (resources, time, diversion of attention to direct local activities). Overall, there is a need to identify obstacles and inherent limitations of the treaty system, including the treaty bodies' difficulties in obtaining and evaluating sophisticated country-specific information, as well as the impossibility of their becoming thorough experts on every country.

Experience supports Clapham's point that certain substantive issues would be advanced by the more effective participation of national women's groups. This greater participation should be advanced in tandem with more fully gender-integrated submissions by mainstream NGOs, both at the international and national level. In addition, with respect to the treaty bodies other than CEDAW, gendered questions on specific rights are rare. Questions concerning reported violations of the human rights of women are sporadic and incomplete. Questions and concerns about women's human rights should also be reflected in the specific recommendations and concluding comments of the treaty bodies. These have great potential for use by NGOs in domestic advocacy. In sum, a mix of normative, substantive and participatory values which could arguably be advanced by greater participation of national women's NGOs in the work of the treaty bodies, must be weighed against the negative factors and weaknesses set out by Clapham.

(b) The functional roles of NGOs in the treaty system: monitors, alternative sources of information, amplifiers

The critical differences between international and national NGO participation in the treaty system deserve serious scrutiny. National NGOs have concerns that international NGOs are co-opting their voices and information, while

---

[5] For example, The Human Rights Program of the American Association for the Advancement of Science (AAAS) has been focusing particular attention on the question of gender sensitive indicators.

controlling access to the treaty bodies. These issues can lead to damaging schisms in NGO work if left unaddressed. Similarly, national NGOs which choose to act internationally, may face distrust or hostility from within the national NGO community.[6] While both international and national NGOs are needed, and each has a particular role to play, there are differences in the values advanced by national groups. Some of the different values supported by national NGO work include increased validity of the work of the local NGO, its increased empowerment and advocacy capacity. National NGOs also advance the goal of holding governments accountable to their own people. Increased local capacity in turn can usefully amplify the impact of the work of the treaty body at the national level.

These benefits for national NGOs are dependent on a great many other factors, including the relative openness with which NGOs can operate in their own country, as well as internationally and in conjunction with international NGOs. An examination of risks and benefits to local NGO action in the national environment, should set the background for negotiating an appropriate division of labour between the "umbrella" or supportive international NGO and the national NGO. In one instance with respect to CEDAW, an NGO representative came from a country with significant areas in armed conflict, and her information covered abuses against women of an unpopular ethnic minority which the government associated with terrorism. She brought documented cases in confidence to an international NGO with the request that they be passed on to the Committee. Her name was never publicly associated with the information. Indeed, her situation, along with that of a number of other women, stimulated a discussion about monitoring returning national NGOs who might fear reprisals. While the practice of submitting information by international NGOs, without crediting local or national NGOs as sources, can be justified in a number of ways, questions were raised on when and how international NGOs should name local sources and collaborate on approaches to the treaty bodies.

(c) *Case studies on using the human rights treaty system by national level women's NGOs*

(i) *National level action*
National NGOs can engage with the human rights treaty system at home or internationally. Many women's NGOs have no interest in directly engaging internationally; they wish to use the human rights treaties ratified by their governments as tools for local accountability. The promises made by governments in ratifying these treaties can be the basis for effective public education on women's rights, for advocacy on the obligations to change discriminatory laws, or for direct litigation to find laws or practices invalid.

---

[6]The clear tensions between national and international NGOs, and among national NGOs that opt to pursue international fora for action, have been commented on by many activists involved in the preparations and participation in the Fourth World Conference for Women in Beijing. The NGOs, which focused on government activities in the formal conference were quite distanced – literally and politically – from the NGOs which focused on the events of the NGO Forum. In some countries, the splits are still being felt within national NGOs, which chose to work in the formal governmental sector as opposed to those which focused on the NGO Forum.

Because of the growing number of women's group which have begun to investigate the usefulness of treaty-based advocacy on their issues, WRAP has developed a number of activist-oriented training programs. WRAP has participated as a technical adviser or trainer at many seminars and workshops convened by the Global Alliance Against Traffic in Women (GAATW), based in Bangkok. The first five-day meeting took place in Chiang Mai, Thailand, in 1994. Over 45 women from 27 countries came together and the question of human rights protection was covered in only half a day. GAATW then identified activists with a strong interest in learning more about the international human rights framework to strengthen their domestic work against trafficking. Subsequent workshops and seminars in South-East Asia and North America have attempted to provide a human rights framework for activist women's groups.

Many local activists, often engaged in direct services to women, have turned to the international system in part because the language of women's human rights is seen as empowering. In practice, they often have no experience with the formal aspects of the system. In response, for example, in 1996 GAATW convened a ten-day intensive workshop to explore possible uses of the human rights framework to advance the protection of women's rights in the context of trafficking.[7] Activists had a wide range of experiences: direct service providers, legal advocates, medical and mental health care providers, and academics. They came with country-based case studies addressing abuses including kidnapping, false promises of marriage, false job promises, debt bondage, sale by family members, sexual slavery, concubinage, and servile marriage. The participants also considered abuses arising from consensual and non-consensual prostitution, illegal border crossing and the challenges of citizenship.

The workshop introduced the vocabulary and structures of the human rights treaties, as well as other mechanisms, to the participants. Participants learned how to determine whether their governments were bound by certain treaties, what facts they needed in order to document violations of various treaty articles, and the strategic uses of those analyses in campaigning for law reform, and change of police and immigration authority practice. In this training, WRAP stressed the need for NGOs to provide the system with documented information as an essential component of their local work, arguing that the reporting system will function only if its information is of high quality.

Because the UN human rights monitoring bodies have not consistently applied the relevant guarantees of rights protection to women's lives, the workshop provided activists with the opportunity to explore new and valid ways of applying treaty guarantees. For example, the participants in the workshop demonstrated gendered violations by India of article 9 (arbitrary detention) of the International Covenant on Civil and Political Rights (CCPR)[8] regarding women in the context of trafficking. They had documentation of women arrested in brothel raids being held in detention indefinitely in India because authorities would only release them to the custody of male relatives; these relatives, from either Bangladesh or Pakistan, will not rescue such "dishonoured" women. They then discussed how to approach the authorities with this concern.

---

[7] See Global Alliance Against Trafficking in Women, *Report on the Workshop for Activists in the Context of Trafficking in Women* (June 1996) (on file with author).
[8] International Covenant on Civil and Political Rights, 999 UNTS 171 (in force 23 March 1976).

Activists seek to use the obligations contained in the treaties as tools with which to hold their governments accountable at the national level. As yet, however, they are still unsure about sending their information on to New York or Geneva meetings of treaty bodies at the relevant times. They lack consistent information on when to do so. They fear that the information will be lost, and that they will never hear how it was treated by the treaty body or the government.

While some were interested in the formal workings of the treaty system, most activists wanted to know how to use the reporting process at home to shame or push the government forward. They discussed using the treaties as public promises not honoured by governments. Media, education and outreach to new sectors were perceived as benefitting from the use of the treaty-based human rights analysis.

In general, while participants in these national level training sessions have been interested, and often excited, they face severe obstacles to using the treaty system effectively. The scope and breadth of the reservations to CEDAW has appeared as an obstacle to raising certain abuses, such as religion or custom-based inequalities within the family. However, it is also true that the same abuses can be raised under articles in other treaties that are free of reservations, such as equality within the family contained in the CCPR. This situation reinforces the importance of spreading information on all the treaties to women's NGOs.

These and other similar workshops reaffirm some commonalities among local NGOs. Activists often have exaggerated expectations of the treaty system coupled with great skepticism about law and the state-centered nature of the system. They have few illusions, however, about the low level of state compliance with obligations, although they generally express great interest in the "public shaming" capacity of treaty review. Yet, there is some ambivalence about this publicly confrontational role; one NGO delegate felt that her work – direct services in jails and prisons – would be blocked if she participated in public actions reporting on her government's failure to act. At the same time, all were excited by the power of agreed, common, promises for women's human rights in the treaties, and saw immediate uses for their work in public education and campaigning at the domestic level. Thus, while these NGOs may never appear in New York or Geneva, their work should be supported for its power to amplify the concrete effect of the human rights system.

(ii) International level action

The idea that women's NGOs, as a particular sector of NGOs, could concretely contribute to furthering the impact of the treaty system was one factor behind an important project which was sponsored by the United Nations Development Fund for Women (UNIFEM) together with the Malaysia-based affiliate of the International Women's Rights Action Watch (IWRAW Asia-Pacific) and launched in the fall of 1996. CEDAW was perceived to lag behind the Geneva-based treaty bodies in developing formal or informal links with NGOs, both as sources of independent information and as constituents whose efforts strengthen women's human rights promotion at the national and international levels. Women's NGOs were arriving relatively late onto the UN human rights scene.

Furthermore, the bodies which address women (including CEDAW) are marginalized within the UN system.[9] CEDAW experts therefore asked UNIFEM to support increased information from, and interaction with, NGOs. While certain international NGOs, including IWRAW,[10] and more recently Amnesty International and Human Rights Watch/Women's Rights Project, had submitted alternative information on specific countries to CEDAW, few national NGOs had done so. Even fewer had the opportunity to attend CEDAW meetings and carry out informal advocacy or directly monitor and report back to their constituents about the submissions of their governments or the comments of CEDAW.

UNIFEM and IWRAW Asia-Pacific began preparations for a major program that would bring together eight women from six countries[11] whose reports were scheduled for consideration at the sixteenth session of CEDAW in New York in January of 1997. The project components included: (1) a sponsoring organization based in the South (IWRAW Asia-Pacific operates from a base in Kuala Lumpur); (2) grants of money to identified women's NGOs in those countries to enable them to form coalitions with other groups and to collect information on women's rights relevant under the Convention; (3) guidance and support in the event that the NGO was preparing an alternative report or "shadow report";[12] (4) a special, intensive two-day training session to provide background, substantive understanding of the Convention and advocacy skills; (5) a mentored stay of a week or more in New York to enable participants to observe CEDAW in action, make informal contacts and witness the dialogue with governments and the development of concluding comments; and (6) a commitment from UNIFEM to circulate follow-up information such as final concluding comments and other results of the session.

Each of these components was critical to the design of the project.[13] Indeed, participants were clear that the time spent at home before and after their tenure at CEDAW would be the real test of the usefulness of the project. The women activists were coming from radically different country contexts. Only a few had

---

[9] Andrew Clapham addresses this issue *supra* Chapter 13 at 191. See also, for example, Andrew Byrnes, "The Other Human Rights Treaty Body: The Work of the Committee on the Elimination of Discrimination Against Women", 14 *Yale Journal of International Law* (1989) 1–67; Roberta Jacobson, "The Committee on the Elimination of Discrimination Against Women", in *The United Nations and Human Rights: A Critical Appraisal*, Philip Alston (ed.), Oxford (1991) 444–72; and Shelley Wright, "Human Rights and Women's Rights: An Analysis of the United Nations Convention on the Elimination of All Forms of Discrimination Against Women", in *Human Rights in the 21st Century: A Global Challenge*, Kathleen Mahoney and Paul Mahoney (eds.), Dordrecht (1993) 75–88.

[10] The IWRAW is a global network of individuals and organizations that monitors the implementation of CEDAW. It is based at the Hubert H. Humphrey Institute of Public Affairs, University of Minnesota, USA.

[11] The countries were: Bangladesh, Canada, Morocco, Philippines, Turkey and Zaire.

[12] Guidance for creating "shadow reports" was contained in a short paper prepared by the Women's Rights Advocacy Program of the International Human Rights Law Group; it set out the reasons for producing shadow reports (alternative information to the treaty bodies as well as: coalition-building efforts; documents useful for creating benchmarks for domestic education; and activism using standards agreed upon by the government. Copies of the draft guidelines can be obtained from the Law Group at ihrlg@aol.com; tel. (+ 1 202 232 8500). *Assessing the Status of Women: A Guide to Reporting Under the Convention on the Elimination of All Forms of Discrimination Against Women*, 2nd edition, IWRAW (1999) also provides comprehensive information for reporting, supplementing the *Manual on Human Rights Reporting*, United Nations (1997).

[13] The project was subsequently reviewed and repeated by UNIFEM.

CEDAW-specific experience prior to the training. Their national information was supplemented by submissions by international NGOs. In some cases the women had used the international NGO to submit information they considered too politically charged to submit themselves.

The trainers themselves came from Malaysia, Philippines, Costa Rica, and the United States, and had a mix of national and international experience. The project implicitly stressed the importance of the exchange of skills and experiences of the trainers, and the sessions demonstrated a mixture of methodologies and expectations based on contacts with other treaty bodies. As experienced international advocates, the trainers embodied the tension between maximizing continuity or the power of an identified constituency, and opening up the access to treaty bodies to new advocates. At the same time, the goal was to use insiders to bring in new "outsiders".

The project took place at a time when CEDAW was considering revising its practices, particularly with regard to the role of NGOs.[14] The NGO participants raised a number of points that they felt would strengthen their ability to participate effectively. Advance notice was key. Notification of reporting schedules well in advance would facilitate the ability of NGOs to compile relevant information. At the same time, participants acknowledged that the reporting process is subject to the vagaries of governments.[15] The tension between the need of local NGOs for lead-time, and a fair assessment of how their resources would be used, was immediately apparent. Great difficulty in obtaining the governments own report to CEDAW was identified as a problem, as was translation into local languages.

Many participants were amazed at frequent mild questioning of governments by CEDAW members, and the fact that much detail went into questioning on some subjects, while other issues which NGO delegates considered crucial were ignored. Most had been uncertain of how to approach the Committee experts, although for the most part they found the experts interested in their information. In response, a number of experts emphasized that short, concise identification of key issues and concrete recommendations submitted well in advance would be useful. All participants clearly noted that a primary task upon their return home would be to publicize the kinds of questions asked and the governments' responses. At least one NGO representative attempted to obtain media coverage while she was in New York; others discussed media strategies to be implemented upon their return.

---

[14] See *Ways and Means of Improving the Work of the Committee*, CEDAW/C/1997/5 (6 December 1996) for a detailed and comprehensive discussion of the practice of CEDAW vis-à-vis country rapporteurs and concluding comments, relations with other treaty bodies, thematic and country specific mechanisms, and the practice of other treaty bodies in relation to NGOs. Since that time, CEDAW revised its practices and modify its working methods with respect to NGOs. Decision 18/I, *Report of the Committee on the Elimination of Discrimination Against Women*, A/53/38/Rev.1 (1998) at 3; Decision 20/I, *Report of the Committee on the Elimination of Discrimination Against Women*, A/54/38/Rev.1 (1999) at 7.

[15] Zaire (now the Democratic Republic of Congo) posed a particular problem: owing to some miscommunication, due in part to the offensive in eastern Zaire, the government initially cancelled, then sent representatives and was uncertain about whether it would report. It was then asked by CEDAW to report on an exceptional basis, but the representative proceeded with a status report on conditions in Zaire ignoring the armed conflict. This report was interrupted by experts who asked heatedly about protection of women's human rights in the crisis (a subject about which they had been briefed in English and French by the Zairian NGO present). At the same session (sixteenth session, January 1997), Argentina had been scheduled to present and withdrew.

A notable exception to the "mild" questioning and a high point of the session in many participants' eyes, came during the extensive questioning of the representatives of Morocco. Part of the experts more in-depth questioning may have been related to the NGO "shadow" report. This report was detailed, prioritized critical issues, and demonstrated sophistication in its repudiation of culture or religion as a justification for discrimination, as well as including extensive concrete recommendations.[16] The NGO representative herself was extraordinarily keen to understand and use the political space opened up by the session to approach her government, with which she had never had direct contact. She was contacted directly by the representatives of the government for a follow-up meeting. She felt strongly that this approach validated her work, and the work of the NGO coalition, and would strengthen its ability to approach the government upon its return.

(3) The framework for receiving and analyzing information

A catalogue of concrete initiatives on gender integration efforts in which NGOs play substantive roles, includes, for example, consistent advocacy at the meeting of the Chairpersons of the human rights treaty bodies,[17] participation in an expert group meeting in July 1995, and participation in a Roundtable in 1997 of the human rights treaty bodies on the "Human Rights Approaches to Women's Health with a Focus on Reproductive and Sexual Health Rights."[18]

The then Centre for Human Rights[19] and UNIFEM organized the expert group meeting in Geneva for the purpose of developing guidelines for the integration of gender perspectives into the United Nations activities and programmes.[20] In the course of setting out comprehensive recommendations for

---

[16] Association Democratique des Femmes du Maroc, *Parallel Report of Moroccan NGOs on the Application of the Convention on Eliminating All Forms of Discrimination Against Women* (December 1996) (on file with UNIFEM and author). UNIFEM has considered the possibility of putting "shadow reports" on line so that other NGOs can see various models of NGO reports.

[17] In 1994, the Chairpersons agreed to amend their guidelines to require that states parties report on the status of women with respect to the rights articulated in each treaty. *Report of the Fifth Meeting of Persons Chairing the Human Rights Treaty Bodies, 19–23 September 1994*, A/49/537 (19 October 1994) at para. 20. See also: *Report of the Sixth Meeting of Persons Chairing the Human Rights Treaty Bodies, 18–22 September 1995*, A/50/505 (4 October 1995) at paras. 34–35. *Report of the Seventh Meeting of Persons Chairing the Human Rights Treaty Bodies, 16–20 September 1996*, A/51/482 (11 October 1996) at paras. 58–61. *Report of the Eighth Meeting of Persons Chairing the Human Rights Treaty Bodies, 15–19 September 1997*, A/52/507 (21 October 1997) at paras. 62–64. *Report of the Tenth Meeting of Persons Chairing the Human Rights Treaty Bodies, 14–18 September 1998*, A/53/432 (25 September 1998) at paras. 53–54. With respect to the guidelines of the Human Rights Committee, see: *Consolidated Guidelines for State Reports under the International Covenant on Civil and Political Rights*, CCPR/C/66/GUI/Rev.1 (1 November 1999) at C.7.

[18] See *Report of the Roundtable of Human Rights Treaty Bodies on Human Rights Approaches to Women's Health, with a Focus on Reproductive and Sexual Health Rights*, jointly organized by the United Nations Division for the Advancement of Women, United Nations Population fund and the United Nations High Commissioner for Refugees (1997). (on file with author).

[19] Now the Office of the High Commissioner for Human Rights.

[20] See the *Report of the Expert Group Meeting on the Development of Guidelines for the Integration of Gender Perspectives into the United Nations Human Rights Activities and Programmes*, E/CN.4/1996/105 (20 November 1995). See also Gender Integration into the Human Rights System: Report of the Workshop, United Nations Office at Geneva, 26 to 28 May 1999, (OHCHR, UNDAW, UNIFEM).

gender integration, the experts looked specifically at the treaty bodies' working methods and procedures, and at the reporting process, including concluding comments. They called for the development of minimum standards of the enjoyment of women's rights. The expert meeting also accorded high priority to the development and application of a framework for state accountability for violations of women's human rights.[21] The meeting recognized the critically important role that local NGOs play in documenting and facilitating the flow of gendered information to the UN. It recommended more "aggressive steps to disseminate [information on human rights work of the UN which] could include media outreach, when appropriate to the mandate of the activity, using such means as radio, popular newspapers, etc."[22]

The Roundtable of the Treaty Bodies was an historic event at which representatives of all the human rights treaty bodies met together to consider a specific thematic issue, women's health, with a focus on reproductive and sexual health. The meeting emphasized a collaborative role for NGOs, treaty bodies and UN agencies, in order to transcend the divide between human rights and the development-oriented discourse which has characterized much of the divergent practice over assertions of women's human rights and men's human rights.[23]

> It was suggested that specialized agencies and NGOs could provide effective assistance to the treaty monitoring process at various stages of the reporting process [contributing to]: preparation of guidelines for reporting, ... holding pre-sessional meetings, developing questions for States, general recommendations and concluding comments.[24]

The meeting also noted a role for NGOs in monitoring compliance.

The overall tone of the meeting was one of "collaboration", with less attention paid to the potential for oppositional politics and much value placed on team playing. At the same time, NGOs face the reality that resources directed toward NGOs playing this key "partnership" role is very small. And, while the fact of the Roundtable meeting itself was groundbreaking, its significance will depend on its practical impact in each of the treaty bodies

(4) Gender integration: a role for NGOs in contributing to the normative aspects of human rights protections for women

While some steps toward integrating gender have occurred within the UN treaty system, very few institutionalized advances have taken place. This lack of progress can be attributed not only to various residual prejudices, but to an even more fundamental problem. There is very little concrete understanding of exactly what a gender analysis is in regard to any one right, or in regard to rights as a whole. The most useful contribution NGOs may make to women's human rights protection under the treaty system will be well documented, fact-based submissions, combined with carefully shaped legal analyses. NGOs can play an important role in demonstrating the real meaning of gender-specific reporting: "the

---

[21] Ibid., at paras. 38–55.
[22] Supra, note 20 at para. 71, Recommendation 6.
[23] Supra, note 20 at para. 68.
[24] Supra, note 20 at para. 72.

form which a violation takes; the circumstances in which it occurs; the consequences of the violation for the victim; and the availability and accessibility of remedies."[25]

This is not to say that the treaty body experts themselves cannot, and will not, play a critical role in developing the framework for gender analysis. It merely underscores the impact of Clapham's assessment of the need for the treaty body experts to become human rights professionals, and that one of the elements of their professionalism must be a substantive understanding of women's human rights as an area of international legal protection.

Understanding the nature of the obligation of governments to respect, protect, promote and fulfill the rights of men and women, girls and boys requires a number of different steps. It includes a gendered understanding of "classic" human rights concerns, such as the right to life. This right can be seen through the question of state responsibility for maternal mortality if the state blocks, or fails to facilitate, steps to ensure adequate access to contraception, abortion, nutritional information.[26] It can also be seen as the right to be free from torture, which requires a greater understanding of torture as directed at men and women, including the specific forms directed primarily or exclusively at women. Or it can be approached from the perspective of the nature of the harm suffered by men and women, with a view to constructing more complete and effective methods of prevention, as well as of compensation and redress.

In addition to these commonly addressed fundamental rights, the entire range of civil, cultural, economic, political and social rights as enjoyed by women must be better understood in their most concrete, fact-based terms. Such issues as women's rights to participate in the public life of their country, including issues of citizenship, political participation, culture and development, would be better articulated through increased documentation coupled with questioning of the steps taken by governments to remove gender-based obstacles faced by women in the enjoyment of such rights.

The fuller development of the analytic and factual bases for holding states internationally accountable for abuses by non-state actors, including abuses by corporate as well as individual entities, is a critical aspect of the work of the treaty bodies. Many local NGOs, especially, but not exclusively, women's NGOs, focus extensively on this issue. Major abuses and obstacles to women's enjoyment of fundamental rights arise in the private sphere, through home-based violence, unequal rights within marriage contracts, access to property or to choice in their sexual and reproductive lives.[27] NGOs are deeply concerned with failures of the state to take action. Some specific examples of concerns are: the lack of key

---

[25] Donna Sullivan, *Integration of Women's Rights into the Work of the Special Rapporteurs*, United Nations Development Fund for Women (March 1997) at 4.

[26] For a comprehensive application of the full range rights articulated in the various articles of human rights treaties to reproductive self-determination for women, see Rebecca J. Cook, "Human Rights and Reproductive Self-Determination", 44 *American University Law Review* (1995) 975.

[27] The work of the Special Rapporteur on Violence against Women has begun to synthesize a great deal of the fact-based and analytical research on violence against women, its causes and consequences. There have been four reports by the Special Rapporteur, Radhika Coomaraswamy, all entitled *Report of the Special Rapporteur on Violence Against Women, its Causes and Consequences*. The first report addressed violence against women in the family, E/CN.4/1996/53 and Add.2 (6 February 1996); the second report in 1997 examined violence against women in the community, E/CN.4/1997/47 (12 February 1997); the third report in 1998 examined violence against women in times of armed conflict,

legislation criminalizing acts of violence against women (such as the marital rape exception in Kenya), the system-wide failure to train police to investigate or prosecute allegations of domestic violence, the failure to prosecute abuses on an equal basis with other crimes of violence, or the absence of any systems of redress or structures for compensation.

The potential role of the treaty bodies in this area is vital, as they could contribute to the overall development of the critical notion of "due diligence". This notion has arisen in part through its explicit incorporation in such international standards as the UN Declaration on the Elimination of Violence against Women[28] and CEDAW's General Recommendation 19.[29] It is also closely related to theories of complicity and acquiescence, which may further develop the nature of the obligations "to ensure" the enjoyment of rights contained within the treaties.[30] The interest within the Human Rights Committee in further developing the understanding of the CCPR's article 3 obligation to "ensure the equal right of men and women to the enjoyment" of the rights contained with the Covenant, will be critical to this goal.[31]

(5) Conclusion

The global participation of women's NGOs in the treaty system is needed to give meaning to the assertion that "the human rights of women are an inalienable, integral and indivisible part of universal human rights."[32] At the same time, there needs to be an expanded understanding of NGO roles, since many NGOs are still establishing claims within the system as rights claims.

There is also a need for improved transparency, both in the workings of the UN and the actions of governments. Improved transparency can in part be furthered by NGO activity and the capacity of domestic NGOs to amplify the impact of the actions of treaty bodies, for example, through campaigning on the standards and publicizing the concluding comments at the national level. The question of resources dedicated to NGOs must be addressed if the language of "partnership", in whatever guise, is going to be used. Similarly, commitments to

---

E/CN.4/1998/54 and Add.1 (26 January 1998); and the fourth report in 1999 report once again examined the family and violence, E/CN.4/1999/68 and Adds.1–4 (10 March 1999).

[28] Art. 4(c) of the United Nations Declaration on the Elimination of Violence Against Women, adopted by G.A. Res. 48/104 on 20 December 1993 states that governments shall "exercise due diligence to prevent, investigate and in accordance with national legislation, punish acts of violence against women, whether those acts are perpetrated by the State or by private persons."

[29] CEDAW, *General Recommendation 19: Violence Against Women*, in *Report of the Committee on the Elimination of Discrimination Against Women*, A/47/38 (1992) at 5–10.

[30] See for example, discussions on the crucial question of state accountability for private actor abuses of women's human rights by Celina Romany, "State Responsibility Goes Private: A Feminist Critique of the Public/Private Distinction in International Human Rights Law", in *The Human Rights of Women: National and International Perspectives*, Rebecca Cook (ed.), University of Pennsylvania Press (1994); Rebecca Cook, "State Accountability Under the Convention on the Elimination of All Forms of Discrimination Against Women", *ibid.*; Donna Sullivan, "The Public/Private Distinction in International Human Rights Law", in *Women's Rights/Human Rights: International Feminist Perspectives*, Julie Peters and Andrea Wolper (eds.), Routledge (1995).

[31] *General Comment Number 28*, Equality Rights Between Men and Women (article 3), CCPR/C/21/Rev.1/Add.10, 29 March 2000.

[32] *Supra*, note 3, at para. 213.

increase the pool of NGOs with the capacity to operate in international fora, must be made at all levels.

The latter is contingent on the treaty bodies actions being relevant to the work of concerned NGOs. The treaty bodies must increase their understanding of obstacles faced by women. Scheduling meetings within states and facilitating the travel of treaty body experts to states, would be of great benefit to national NGOs. Knowledge of women's human rights should be a characteristic of a treaty expert, male and female. An appropriate division of labour among NGOs, based on a respect for the strengths and needs of both national and international NGOs, must be negotiated.

The experience of women's NGOs in world conferences and summits in Rio, Vienna, Cairo, Copenhagen, and Beijing, bears reiterating. Activists brought their demands to the international level so that the claim to universality of women's human rights would be concretely addressed locally, nationally, and internationally. The source of legitimacy for enforcing this claim to universality lies to a great extent in the normative power of UN treaties as well as in participatory values. Therefore, even as we discuss the implications of moving human rights activities into all the other activities of the UN for the implementation of rights, we cannot lose sight of the fact that organizations such as women's groups, recently arrived to claim "international human rights", cannot move automatically into the implementing spheres of agencies and other UN entities. They face great dangers of finding their not-yet solidified rights merged with other considerations at the programmatic level, as most agencies do not have rights protection as the basis of their activities.

In sum, there is a fertile but tricky field to negotiate for national NGOs, especially women's NGOs, before they can participate fully in the treaty system. On the one hand, there is great interest among local and national women's groups in using the treaty system for human rights protection. Much of it has emerged from the explosive growth of human rights as the language of empowerment for women in all regions, stoked by the dramatic priority given to it through the world conferences. On the other hand, this interest is tempered by justified skepticism, and in some cases active distrust, of both international structures and traditional law-based or legal-styled activity. There is limited information within women's groups about the actual nature of the work of the treaty bodies and the content of the human rights treaties themselves. This is compounded by the lack of communication between women's groups which are often based on development models, and the traditional rights groups which are often focussed on law and prioritizing civil and political rights. Recognizing that this discussion is set within the larger debate of the relationship between rights and development and the future of the nation-state, the task is to open up the space to let the NGOs define their roles for themselves.

CHAPTER 15

The NGO Role: Implementation, Expanding Protection and Monitoring the Monitors

Stefanie Grant*

Ambiguities about the nature of the relationship of non-governmental organizations (NGOs) to the UN treaty bodies have existed from the outset. When the Human Rights Committee was established in 1976, it was a contentious issue whether NGOs could play *any* role in relation to its work. Although the International Covenant on Civil and Political Rights (CCPR)[1] does not provide for any relationship, it does not, of course, deny it. So in the early years, a modest compromise was reached between some western experts and their more restrictive eastern bloc colleagues: NGOs could provide information on human rights issues to members, but only in their individual capacity, not to the Human Rights Committee as a whole, and not through the UN Secretariat. Amnesty International reports were distributed, but almost as *samizdat*, and were never referred to publicly by members. The Committee's work was limited in scope, and was little known outside the UN.

In the 20 years since then, much has changed. The specific constraints dictated by a bi-polar world have been removed. International law is no longer seen at the UN as "a quiet backwater in human affairs."[2] New areas of international human rights law have been written which radically modify traditional principles of national sovereignty, and a majority of UN member states have ratified the human rights treaties. This virtual revolution in international attitudes has been paralleled at the national level by a growth in the number of NGOs with mandates encompassing human rights protection, and which use this new international law and its interpretation by international bodies in their work. Treaty law is the standard against which national laws are increasingly measured. In those countries where treaties have primacy over domestic law, the decisions of treaty bodies can directly affect national human rights law. This means that governments no longer implement treaty obligations in isolation; implementation is a primary task of judges[3], lawyers, bar associations, and other parts of the

---

*The views expressed are those of the author solely in her personal capacity.
[1] International Covenant on Civil and Political Rights, 999 UNTS 171 (in force 23 March 1976).
[2] Brian Urquhart and Erskine Childers, *A World in Need of Leadership*, Ford Foundation (1990).
[3] *The Bangalore Principles* (1988), reproduced in 1 *Commonwealth Human Rights Digest*, Interights (1996) 126.

non-governmental sector. The relationship between this broad non-governmental sector and the treaty bodies is changing, with national non-governmental institutions becoming an agent and often the catalyst in implementation.

In this situation, it is natural that NGOs seek to expand the work of treaty bodies in order to develop the legal protection, which the committee's interpretation of treaty provisions can provide. They also have a proper concern that governments should elect members who are both independent and expert, so that the committee's comments and decisions carry authority, and cannot be impugned by defaulting governments. But despite this growing NGO dynamic there is very little actual contact between national NGOs and treaty bodies and the practical aspects of the relationship remain tentative and under-developed.

In this regard, the experience of the Lawyers Committee for Human Rights is largely the same as that of Amnesty International, and they share many of Andrew Clapham's concerns.

(1) National implementation

The defining question for NGOs, both national and international, is how the treaty system can be given effect in the national protection of human rights. Specifically, NGOs ask how the informational and geographical distance between the treaty bodies and the country situations they review can be bridged (especially since most committees make no country visits), how their country examinations can be focussed and accurate given the absence of substantive support work by the Office of the High Commissioner for Human Rights, and how their normative work (General Comments, country concluding observations, and case decisions) can be given effect in the application, implementation and enforcement of treaty law. As the number of states parties increases, the question also arises, how increasing expectations of individuals and groups in a growing number of states can be met by treaty bodies whose supervisory procedures are in large part determined by tiny and diminishing resources.

The priority now is to strengthen connections between the treaty system and national non-governmental institutions. Implementation is properly placed first in the hands of national institutions. The non-governmental human rights community is likely to have the greatest interest in importing and using international standards. NGOs need access to the decisions of the treaty bodies, in order to use them in protection work nationally. In the words of one advocate, a commonwealth civil rights lawyer working in 1987:

> Justiciable fundamental rights were introduced into our Constitution fairly recently. The whole field of international ... human rights law, the jurisprudence of Strasbourg and the Human Rights Committee was (and largely remains) unknown to us. The State, however, which defends the violation of human rights, has access to this. It is the State which attends UN meetings and gets to know what is happening in the Human Rights Committee [...]; it is the State that has the resources to stock its law officers' libraries with text books and reports on international human rights law. Decisions, which would help us therefore, remain uncited, while adverse ones are used.[4]

---

[4]Extracts from a letter written to Interights by a commonwealth lawyer (unnamed), 2:1 *Interights Bulletin*, (1987) 12.

In the last decade efforts have been made by a number of international NGOs to bridge the chronic information gap between international institutions and national NGOs. For example, Interights plays a primary role in publishing decisions of the treaty bodies, promoting the use of international human rights law by national courts, and training lawyers and judges in the use of treaty law.[5] Other international NGOs typically provide country factual and legal briefings when treaty bodies consider individual states parties reports. Often, it is they who transmit what is said in Geneva or New York, to the national institutions – media, rights groups, professions including the legal profession. Increasingly, they play a liaison and supporting role to national NGOs, by telling them when a country report is due, when it will be considered by the committee, how the committee functions, and assisting them to attend committee sessions and brief members prior to their own country's review. National NGOs play key roles at the reporting stage – either (but rarely) by contributing to the government's report, or by preparing their own, "shadow" report to a committee, and afterwards as an engine and catalyst for national implementation. It is this last function which is least visible from the "splendid isolation" (in Clapham's terms) of the treaty bodies, but most crucial to the application and enforcement of treaty-based rights.

Colombia's appearances before the Human Rights Committee illustrate the ways in which international and national NGOs support the Committee's work. The Colombian human rights situation is one of considerable complexity, which combines a high level of human rights violation, especially non-derogable security of the person rights, with serious security problems, and intense guerilla and paramilitary activity. The Colombian government operates within a rights-oriented legal framework, and uses law to prosecute a counter insurgency strategy which itself creates serious violations of rights. In preparation for the March 1997 meeting, Human Rights Committee members were given the government's 125-page report only as they arrived in New York. Some Committee members have expertise on the region, but they also took steps to expand the information they had been given by formally inviting NGOs to suggest the issues which should be addressed in questioning, and attending an informal NGO briefing on broader legal and factual areas.[6] The Committee's concluding comments were informed and accurate. This was of particular importance because there is a Colombian member of the Committee, who is also a government official, and it was inevitable that weaknesses in the Committee's assessment would have been popularly, if wrongly, attributed to her influence in the absence of any formal recusal rule.[7] The Colombian field office of the Office of the High

---

[5] See generally *Interights Bulletin* and Interights *Commonwealth Human Rights Digest*. See more specifically: *Minister for Immigration and Ethnic Affairs v. Teoh*, (High Court of Australia), reproduced in 1 *Commonwealth Human Rights Digest*, Interights (1996) 67 (holding that Australia's ratification of the Convention on the Rights of the Child, although not incorporated into Australian law, created a legitimate expectation in parents and children that any action or decision by the Commonwealth of Australia would be conducted or made in accordance with the principles of the treaty).

[6] *Comments Relating to the Fourth Periodic Report of Colombia before the Human Rights Committee: Aspects of Colombian Justice and Human Rights: States of Exception, Criminal Justice and Due Process, Military Justice and Impunity*, Lawyers Committee for Human Rights, New York (March 1997).

[7] In 1998 the Human Rights Committee did adopt guidelines which addressed the issue of the participation of members in the consideration of reports from states of which they are a citizen. "Participation in Consideration of State Report", "Guidelines for the Exercise of their Functions by

Commissioner for Human Rights is mandated to follow up on the government's implementation of the Committee's concluding comments, and Colombian human rights groups will monitor this process.

The work of the Lawyers Committee for Human Rights focuses on the CCPR and has three distinct aspects. In advance, and during the Human Rights Committee's session, the Lawyers Committee informs the members of the areas and issues on which they believe questions and examination should focus. After the session, they use the Committee's "jurisprudence" in their work both generally and on specific countries.[8] On a continuing basis, the Lawyers Committee tries to be a bridge, interpreter and translator between the Committee, its Secretariat and national human rights NGOs.[9]

Should these three areas be seen as an inherent part of the NGO role, or are they short term in nature, deriving from the UN's practical inability to provide adequate resources for the work and information for its members? The first two clearly lie at the permanent centre of the NGO role: human rights NGOs, both national and international, should act as expert witnesses, who can brief the Committee on legal and factual issues which are relevant for the review and identify the areas of breach or non compliance. They should also be advocates who use treaty law in their work.

But the third, liaison function, is not inherent to the NGO role, and has developed because of the UN's failure to create the legal, analytical, translation, and informational infrastructure needed by treaty body members, and to reach out from Geneva to national NGOs. Greater efforts are being made to do this, by use of the Internet, through international NGOs and by some direct contact with national groups. But the practice of the Child Committee, which has support staff who work with NGOs before, during and after country reviews, shows that basic information and explanation on the timetable and operation of a treaty body, is best done on behalf of a committee, rather than by international NGOs, whose efforts are likely to be piecemeal.

Furthermore, the UN should always be able to translate and provide to the treaty body members a state party's constitution and basic legal texts which are needed for the country review, together with information from national organizations in a UN official language. As well as written summary records, the UN should – ideally – produce a summary video record of each country review to give the media, NGOs and other national institutions greater access to the members' questions, the government's response, and the concluding comments.

The treaty bodies are gradually changing their procedures to give greater "standing" to NGOs, but visits to states parties remain the exception, and most

---

Members of the Human Rights Committee", in *Report of the Human Rights Committee*, A/53/40 (1998) at Annex III, paras. 4–5.

[8] For example, the Human Rights Committee, *General Comment 24*, in *Report of the Human Rights Committee*, A/50/40 (1995) at Annex V, in relation to the United States' treaty reservations; *General Comment 25*, in *Report of the Human Rights Committee*, A/51/40 (1996) at Annex V, in relation to Hong Kong legislative proposals; Committee Against Torture (CAT) case decisions on non-refoulement in relation to United States' refugee practice.

[9] The Lawyers Committees' Witness Program has produced an educational video for NGOs, which presents the Human Rights Committee's work through interviews with members, and through the review of the first United States report in 1995. Before the Human Rights Committee considered the Bolivian report, it screened video information submitted by Bolivian NGO, with the Lawyers Committee's help. This was the first use of a video by the Committee in the NGO reporting process.

deal only with the small number of human rights groups who can travel to Geneva or New York. Connections with legal and other non-governmental institutions are rare. This is in part a question of resources, and in part a question of adopting procedures which recognize qualified NGOs – including legal associations – as partners who will implement the national reform agenda which is set by the concluding country observations.

(2) Expanding treaty protection

Refugees and stateless persons inhabit a half-way house within the treaty system. Both are protected under specialized treaties, but in neither case is there a classic treaty body, which supervises states' compliance and interprets the treaties' provisions. The 1951 Convention on the Status of Refugees[10] gives the United Nations High Commissioner for Refugees (UNHCR) the supervisory role. The 1961 Convention on the Reduction of Statelessness[11] goes further – in principle – by providing in article 11 for the establishment of a "body" within the framework of the UN to which anyone claiming the benefit of the 1961 Convention may apply for an examination of his claim and for assistance in presenting it to the appropriate authority. The UNHCR is not named, but has a later mandate from the General Assembly to fulfill these functions. Perhaps because statelessness declined in the years after the 1951 Refugee Convention came into effect, no steps were taken to create the treaty body which it envisaged.

European NGOs have therefore turned to the European Convention on Human Rights[12] to provide protection to refugees and asylum seekers and, potentially, those without nationality. Although the results have so far been modest,[13] they illustrate a key role of NGOs: to use their case-based knowledge of human rights problems to expand the reach of treaty protection. Both NGOs and the UNHCR now see the European Convention system as offering a necessary complement to the supervision system established by the 1951 Refugee Convention. By contrast to the 1951 Refugee Convention, the European system offers a developed body of case law and jurisprudence to guide national courts, the requirement of an effective remedy, and the existence of a central authority to interpret and create binding and enforceable interpretations of the rights contained in the European Convention. The 1951 Refugee Convention merely obligates governments to co-operate with the UNHCR, as the supervisory authority, but creates no expert or quasi-judicial institution comparable to the UN human rights treaty bodies. Although case law on the application of the 1951 Refugee Convention exists, it comes from national courts and is comparative in nature. Interpretations of the 1951 Refugee Convention at an international level are made either through statements by the High Commissioner or in the

---

[10] Convention Relating to the Status of Refugees, 189 UNTS 137 (in force 22 April 1954).
[11] Convention on the Reduction of Statelessness, 989 UNTS 175 (in force 13 December 1975).
[12] Convention for the Protection of Human Rights and Fundamental Freedoms, ETS 5 (in force 3 September 1953).
[13] See generally "The European Convention on Human Rights and the Protection of Refugees, Asylum-Seekers and Displaced Persons", 2(3) *UNHCR European Series* (1996 Colloquy), jointly organized by the Council of Europe and UNHCR, Strasbourg, 2–3 October 1995. But see also *Chahal v. United Kingdom*, Series A, Volume 1996-V (15 November 1996).

form of decisions by UNHCR's Executive Committee. These have more of an advisory than a legal character.

Within the UN a similar development is taking place. The Convention on the Rights of the Child (CRC)[14] was drafted at a time when the need for wider treaty protection for refugees had become clear, and article 12 gives refugee and asylum seeker children full Convention rights. Refugee advocates argue that in view of the limited treaty supervision process created by the 1951 Refugee Convention, treaty bodies should interpret their jurisdiction as broadly as possible in relation to refugees and asylum seekers. The Human Rights Committee has done so in its General Comment 15,[15] and the Committee Against Torture is developing jurisprudence under article 3 of the Convention Against Torture (CAT).[16]

As the global refugee population has risen, as legal statelessness has increased with the break-up of the Soviet Union and Yugoslavia, and as the UNHCR has become the lead UN agency in providing humanitarian relief, the UNCHR's protection activities have assumed a lower priority. All these developments encourage expansive uses of the treaty body system to better protect, for example, refugees and stateless persons.

(3) Monitoring the monitors

Clapham suggests another role for NGOs: as the scrutineer of candidates put forward by governments for election to the treaty bodies. This suggestion arises from concerns about the extraneous political considerations which influence the elections, and the absence of detailed criteria for the selection of candidates. This idea is increasingly – if informally – put to NGOs by individual members of different bodies, and indicates their unease with the way in which almost all governments deal with the important task of identifying, nominating and electing members. NGOs believe it is appropriate for them to comment on candidates for treaty body membership, because they have a legitimate interest in a treaty system, which has authority and legitimacy *because* it is expert and independent.[17]

While the treaty bodies are not courts in the strict sense of the term, but rather quasi-judicial bodies, they deal with equally complex – and often more

---

[14] Convention on the Rights of the Child, 1577 UNTS 3 (in force 2 September 1990).

[15] *General Comment 15*, in *Report of the Human Rights Committee*, A/41/40 (1986) at Annex 1: "... the general rule is that each one of the rights of the Covenant must be guaranteed without discrimination between citizens and aliens".

[16] Convention Against Torture and Other Cruel, Inhuman or Degrading Treatment or Punishment, 1465 UNTS 85 (in force 26 June 1987). Article 3 prohibits the *refoulement* of any "person" to a country in which "there are substantial grounds for believing he would be in danger of being subjected to torture". This prohibition is absolute and cannot be modified – for example, for reasons of national security.

[17] "Members [of the Human Rights Committee] may simultaneously belong to other international organs in the field of the UN or regional organizations. They may also be public servants of their states, parliamentary representatives or even occupy government office. However, such a position harbours the danger of partiality, which may raise conflicts with the obligations of independence and impartiality. In the interests of the Committee, States Parties should avoid as far as possible the nomination of civil servants or government officials."

Manfred Nowak, *UN Covenant on Civil and Political Rights*, N.P. Engel (1993) at 508–9.

sensitive – matters of law and fact. Their authority depends on their possession of visible and apparent impartiality seen through the eyes of a "public" which is geographically far flung and receives little information about the treaty system. This is even truer in the case of the governments they criticize.

Several issues must be distinguished. The first is the issue of independence from government, both actual and apparent. Is any government employment incompatible with the status of independent expert, or only at a senior or political level? Although members serve in a personal capacity, this distinction will be invisible outside the treaty body where the expert is also an ambassador or senior official. Is this incompatibility reduced where the official is a distinguished human rights expert in his or her own right? The issue of independence does not arise only in relation to the country of nationality. It can be present where the state party takes strong positions on human rights in relation to its allies, neighbours and adversaries. The second, and more practical, issue concerns the difficulty which otherwise qualified candidates have in reconciling 3 or even 4 months full-time, but unpaid, work each year as a treaty body member with professional employment outside government service. This may contribute to the tendency of governments to nominate officials who receive their salaries while sitting as members.[18] If so, other solutions – ideally a trust fund – should be found which recompense members for lost time and earnings, but do so without creating an occupational or material dependency on a national government. A third issue is the need for equitable geographical or regional representation[19] as a prerequisite for a legitimate and well-functioning system of international supervision. This last issue has presented itself in acute form in the case of the Human Rights Committee, whose African members are from Tunisia and Mauritius, with no member from the many states parties of sub-Saharan Africa.

A related question is whether members should participate at any point when their own country reports or communications are considered. Practice appears to differ between different treaty bodies, with some members arguing that where the member is expert in his or her own country's legal system, it is a greater evil to exclude his expertise from the wider discussion. NGOs accept the need for expertise, but believe that participation of the national member is not the only way of obtaining it, and prefer the formal adoption of clear exclusionary rules of procedure. NGOs therefore welcomed the Chairpersons of the Treaty Bodies' 1996 recommendation that members should refrain from participating *in any aspect* "of the consideration of the reports of the states of which they are nationals, or communications or enquiries concerning those states," in order to maintain the highest standards of impartiality both in substance and appearance.[20] The Human Rights Committee subsequently adopted "Guidelines for

---

[18] See Anne Bayefsky's figures, cited *supra* Andrew Clapham, Chapter 13 at 185, note 4.
[19] In para. 28 of G.A. Res. 53/138, adopted on 9 December 1998, the General Assembly recalled:
... with regard to the election of the members of the human rights treaty bodies, the importance of giving consideration to equitable geographical distribution of membership and to the representation of the principal legal systems, and of bearing in mind that the members shall be elected and shall serve in their personal capacity and shall be of high moral character, acknowledged independence and recognized competence in the field of human rights ...
[20] See *Report of the Seventh Meeting of Persons Chairing the Human Rights Treaty Bodies, 16–20 September 1996*, A/51/482 (11 October 1996). See also: *Report of the Eighth Meeting of Persons Chairing the Human Rights Treaty Bodies, 15–19 September 1997*, A/52/507 (21 October 1997) at para. 67.

the Exercise of their Functions by Members", which specifically state that members should not participate in the examination of reports presented by their country in any manner, or in the discussion or drafting of the concluding observations, or in consultations between the Committee and NGOs or specialized agencies.[21] CEDAW adopted a decision in January 1998 confirming "that members of the Committee should refrain from participating in any aspect of the consideration of the reports of the States of which they were nationals in order to maintain the highest standards of impartiality, both in substance and appearance."[22] It is desirable that all treaty bodies also amend their rules.

The experience of regional human rights bodies shows that most have also found it necessary to tighten their procedures with time, and as the number of their *states parties* increased. Prior to the coming into force of Protocol 11[23] and the introduction of a full-time Court, the European Court of Human Rights required candidates to give an undertaking that they would resign from government office if elected.[24] In 1985 an Eighth Protocol was added to the European Convention which – *inter alia* – required European Commission on Human Rights members to hold no position "incompatible with their independence and impartiality as members of the Commission or the demands of this office."[25] In 1990, the European Committee on the Prevention of Torture adopted a rule prohibiting a member taking part in a visit to his or her own state.[26] The Inter-American human rights treaty system has clear rules on the question of incompatibility.[27] By contrast, the Statute of the International Court of Justice (ICJ)[28] gives parties the right to nominate a judge of the same nationality, thus assuming some degree of representation on the part of the national judge.[29]

NGOs are well aware that these issues are accentuated by a shortage of

---

[21] *Supra*, note 7.

[22] *Report of the Committee on the Elimination of Discrimination Against Women*, A/53/38/Rev.1 (1998), Decision 18/III at 3.

[23] Protocol No. 11 to the European Convention, ETS 155 (in force 1 November 1998).

[24] Old rule 4 (in force 1 February 1994): "A judge may not exercise his function while he holds a post or exercises a profession which is incompatible with his independence and impartiality" (but see new rules 3 and 4, in force 1 November 1998). Rule 4: "... the judges shall not during their term of office engage in any political or administrative activity or any professional activity which is incompatible with their independence or impartiality ..."

Parliamentary Assembly of the Council of Europe Recommendation 809, adopted on 29 April 1977 provides:

... Considering the weighty responsibilities which devolve upon judges... regretting that candidates put forward have sometimes been civil servants and other persons who, by the very nature of their functions, were not independent of their government... Recommends that governments of the member states... Not to put forward candidates who, by the very nature of their functions, are dependant on government, without an assurance that they will resign from their functions on election to the court.

[25] Protocol No.8 to the European Convention, ETS 118 (in force 1 January 1990), Art. 3.

[26] Rule 37(2), in *Rules of Procedure*, CPT/Inf/C/89 3 rev.1 (1997).

[27] Statute of the Inter-American Court of Human Rights, adopted by the OAS General Assembly (October 1979), OAS Res. 448 (in force 1 January 1980), art. 18.

[28] Statute of the International Court of Justice, 1 UNTS xvi (in force 24 October 1945), Annex.

[29] *Ibid.*, art. 31. See also James L. Brierly, *The Law of Nations*, Oxford University Press (1963) at 253:

A judge of the same nationality as one of the parties retains the right to sit, but if a party has no judge of its nationality on the court it may nominate one for a particular case. This provision for ad hoc 'national' judges can only be defended if it is necessary, as perhaps it is, for political reasons. It is a concession to the vicious theory that in some sense a judge ought to 'represent' the parties, and it places the 'national' judge himself in a difficult position.

qualified candidates for election. The recent growth of international legal and human rights institutions has not been matched by procedures which enable the international community to find qualified candidates to staff senior positions.[30] In the case of the treaty bodies, there is a need to agree on criteria, identify qualified candidates, ensure regional representation, and encourage governments to nominate on the basis of merit alone. Treaty bodies might find it helpful to record their own needs in terms of, for example, professional skills, as the European Torture Committee has done.[31] Before nominating judges for election to the Court, the ICJ Statute recommends that governments should consult national legal institutions, including supreme courts and law faculties.[32] Probably some screening mechanism would also be helpful, as exists in the European system. But the greatest need is for governments to raise the priority they give to identifying candidates for nomination, both from within their countries, and from other states parties.

The problem is not unique to the treaty bodies, and neither should be its resolution. Faced with similar dilemmas in 1990, Brian Urquhart and Erskine Childers reviewed the UN's procedures, or lack of procedures, for appointment to senior jobs; their recommendations were prepared after a wide consultation and are now beginning to inform UN practice.[33] This influential study is a model, which could well be used in reviewing the selection of treaty body members. NGOs should be involved in the consultation process.

---

[30] It took the Security Council over a year to appoint the first Prosecutor of the International Criminal Tribunal for the Former Yugoslavia, an appointment for which time was of the essence.
[31] See, *Report on Strengthening the Machinery of the European Convention on the Prevention of Torture and Inhuman or Degrading Treatment or Punishment*, CPT/7784 (26 March 1997) at paras. 47– 48.
[32] *Supra*, note 28 at art. 6.
[33] *Supra*, note 2. The process of selecting a new High Commissioner for Human Rights was one of the first to take place on the basis of a written and detailed job description.

CHAPTER 16

Defining the Role of Non-Governmental Organizations: Splendid Isolation or Better Use of NGO Expertise?

Mark Thomson*

Andrew Clapham gives an accurate overview of the existing role of non-governmental organizations (NGOs) along with some interesting proposals for changes to avoid the treaty bodies being confined to a state of "splendid isolation." He has also usefully reported on the contributions that NGOs can make for a more meaningful dialogue between treaty bodies and governments, when they present alternative information on the state's implementation of the international conventions. However, his views more accurately represent an Amnesty International approach to the treaty bodies, than the experiences of other international NGOs such as the International Service for Human Rights.

The International Service is a relatively small, Geneva-based, NGO that provides frank political, legal and strategic advice, information and training to hundreds of NGOs throughout the world. In our experience, regional and national NGOs, which know about the treaty bodies, have quite a different approach to using them than Amnesty International. Although these NGOs can appreciate the legal, historical and operational differences between the treaty-based and the charter-based human rights procedures of the United Nations, and governments claim that the two systems are separate, national NGOs tend not to regard the treaty bodies as being in splendid isolation. They often see the conventions and treaty bodies as a rare opportunity to put pressure on their government to conform to international norms in a public procedure of reporting, dialogue and debate that may not normally occur on the national stage, nor in other inter-governmental meetings of the United Nations. In recent years, most national NGOs who have presented shadow reports to the treaty bodies[1] have tried to make maximum use of the treaty bodies to strengthen their national and international lobbying efforts, especially at the UN Commission on Human Rights.

For a variety of reasons, NGO participation in the treaty bodies has not

---

*The commentary does not represent the official views and policy of the International Service for Human Rights. I am grateful for the comments of James Sloan.
[1] For example, from South Korea, Mexico, Nigeria, Peru, the Russian Federation, India, Algeria, Turkey, Morocco and Guatemala.

always been very fruitful and often has been a waste of scarce resources. The key challenge for an effective treaty system is how to ensure that the best use is made of the available expertise, amongst international, regional and national NGOs, existing and potential members of the treaty bodies, government officers, and staff of the Office of the High Commissioner for Human Rights.

(1) Drafting of conventions, ratifications and reservations to articles in the conventions

The most obvious role for NGOs is that of supplying information on the implementation of the conventions. At the same time, NGOs have made important other contributions in the treaty system. NGOs have made significant contributions to the drafting of the conventions and the more recent drafting of optional protocols. NGOs have pushed their legislative authorities to ratify the international conventions, such as was the case with the United States and South Africa. Furthermore, it has been NGOs, including Amnesty International, who have critically publicized the reservations that states have made when ratifying conventions. NGO expertise can be put to good effect in creating a potentially worthwhile system of international norms and monitoring.

(2) Shadow reports

An example of how NGOs can provide alternative information to a treaty body is Clapham's report on the "informal briefing" in July 1996, of members of the Human Rights Committee, by an Amnesty International researcher and a representative of the Coordinadora Nacional de Derechos Humanos of Peru. The lunch time briefing took place the day before Peru was due to present its report to the Human Rights Committee. It was an example of a joint lobby of the treaty body by an international NGO and a national NGO. Andrew Clapham explains how this briefing led to the Human Rights Committee members asking some tough questions of the Peruvian delegation. One might add to this account of how these NGOs were able to work successfully with Committee members.

The two representatives were both Latin American and they spoke Spanish, English and French. The Amnesty International researcher was supported by the well-earned credibility of her organization and the Coordindora representative came with the backing of the 47 Peruvian human rights NGOs which made up the association. He also introduced himself as a human rights lawyer. These credentials helped, but what was important for the Committee members present was whether the representatives could answer their questions (including on the written information they had received from these two NGOs) and whether they knew in detail the new amnesty laws of Peru and its Constitution. They could. At one point, for example, Lord Colville asked a complicated legal question about the difference in one aspect of the two Amnesty laws in Peru. The representative of the Coordindora calmly explained the difference and the significance of this for human rights in Peru, and the Amnesty International representative circulated the two laws in the original Spanish and in English translation. It is rare to see such a perfect division of labour in the expertise and resources of international and national NGOs. The Committee members were visibly impressed and spent the rest of the briefing competing to ask their questions, so much so that they had to be reminded to return to the formal session of the Committee. Furthermore, any written information they lacked, including copies of Peruvian laws and press reports were distributed, by the two NGOs, to the Committee members either that afternoon or the next morning before the session.

The main lesson of this experience was that the Human Rights Committee members wanted not only written information that they could rely upon, but also appreciated the opportunity to double-check written submissions and ask questions on issues which were not clear. The joint lobby by an international NGO and national NGO proved to be a welcome combination. The fact that they were represented by two very knowledgeable and competent persons, from the region and well-supported by their UN representatives, impressed the Committee members. The positive result of all of this was the subsequent tough questioning of the Minister of Justice of Peru by the Committee members.[2] The Committees can therefore benefit from well-prepared and reliable NGO expertise, from both well-known international NGOs and national organizations.

Yet more questions should be asked about the background to this "success story" because although Amnesty International and other international NGOs have presented some good written reports, they do not always arrange these briefings in such coordination with NGOs from the state reporting to the treaty body. It is significant that the researcher from Amnesty International was from a department of their international Secretariat that clearly has fewer qualms about associating itself publicly with reliable national NGOs. Secondly, although the International Service for Human Rights did not advise the NGOs making up the Coordinadora to link up specifically with Amnesty International, in a July 1995 meeting with two of their representatives, one of whom was their representative at the Human Rights Committee briefing a year later, the International Service suggested that they make fuller use of the treaty bodies because at that stage it was unlikely that the Human Rights Commission would adopt a country-specific procedure on Peru. Thirdly, during March and April 1996, in Geneva, the International Service trained two other representatives of Peruvian NGOs that make up the Coordinadora, on the effective use of international human rights procedures. Finally, it should be added that the Secretary of this treaty body was exceptionally cooperative in facilitating briefings between NGOs and members of the Human Rights Committee.

(3) Further advantages of national NGOs presenting their alternative reports

National NGO expertise can also prove to be extremely useful in other contexts. For example, when Morocco's second periodic report was due to be examined by the Committee Against Torture (CAT) on 16 November 1994, the International Service assisted the Moroccan Organization for Human Rights to present its "shadow report" by financing the participation of their representative,

---

[2] See Human Rights Committee, *Summary Records of the 1519th Meeting, 18 July 1996*, CCPR/C/SR.1519 (14 November 1996); *1520th Meeting, (19 July 1996*, CCPR/C/SR.1520 (25 July 1996); and the *1521st Meeting, 19 July 1996*, CCPR/C/SR.1521 (23 October 1996).

Mr. Driss Benziker, in the session. Mr. Benziker had been a political prisoner for 19 years in the notorious Derb Moulay Chérif prison of Casablanca. His participation proved to be useful not only because he presented their report and discussed its contents with Committee members, but also because he recognized a member of the government delegation, Mr. Kaddour, as one of the torturers in Derb Moulay Chérif prison during the 1970s and 1980s.

Two other Moroccans who were alerted to this news, one an officer of the (then) UN Centre for Human Rights, and the other a representative of another NGO, the Moroccan Association of Human Rights, who also identified Mr. Kaddour as being an official in the prison during that period. The experts of the Committee and the press were informed, and although the Geneva and Moroccan Press published the story, the Committee chose not to react at the time. However, it later became apparent that CAT did contact the Moroccan Ministry of Foreign Affairs about the "incident." The shocking revelation of the identity of a member of the delegation demonstrated clearly the lack of respect of the Moroccan government for the Convention[3] and the Committee. After such a discovery how could anything the government delegation said about implementing the Convention be taken as sincere? The act of identifying Mr. Kaddour, by a national NGO representative and former political prisoner, proved to be the most significant part of the presentation of Morocco's second periodic report.

This example supports the point made by Clapham about NGO use of the press. For instance, Amnesty International and Russian NGOs made good use of the Russian media when Russia presented its report to CAT in November 1996. NGO-generated media interest in the United Kingdom's report to CAT, pushed the Committee members in November 1995 to ask more difficult questions than expected of the United Kingdom delegation.[4]

It must be pointed out that although the Chairpersons of the Treaty Bodies have recommended that NGOs be allowed to participate in the press conferences of treaty bodies, this is still not standard practice.[5]

(4) Political significance of shadow reports from NGOs

It can be an exceptional occasion in the United Nations for NGOs to be able to criticize a state's poor record in fully implementing a ratified convention when a state party is due to report to a treaty body. This is particularly true for those states which have avoided any country specific procedure in other UN bodies such as the Commission on Human Rights. This is the case, for example, with the reports of China to CAT (May 1996), the United Kingdom (especially regarding Hong Kong, October, 1996), the United States of America to the Human Rights Committee (March-April 1995), and India to the Human Rights Committee in July 1997. When the Human Rights Committee, for example,

---

[3] Convention Against Torture and Other Cruel, Inhuman or Degrading Treatment or Punishment, 1465 UNTS 85 (in force 26 June 1987).
[4] See CAT, *Summary Records of the 234th Meeting, 17 November 1995*, CAT/C/SR.234 (22 November 1995) and the *235th Meeting, 17 November 1995*, CAT/C/SR.235 (27 November 1995).
[5] See for example *Report of the Seventh Meeting of Persons Chairing the Human Rights Treaty Bodies, 16–20 September 1996*, A/51/482 (11 October 1996).

produces critical conclusions on human rights in India, this assists those NGOs who lobby the state members of the Commission on Human Rights to take action on the situation in India. Normally this is a fruitless task as India, is such an important player on the international scene. Like China, it warns other member states that any criticisms will not be acceptable and will come with a high price. However, if the treaty bodies as well as NGOs are voicing their concerns, it can be easier to have a country specific resolution adopted. This assumes that governments have the political will to raise the issues which is not always the case. For instance, with respect to Turkey, despite all the reports and concerns of CAT and NGOs, no government has been prepared to take any action at the level of the Commission on Human Rights.

(5) Creating a government expertise to improve reporting and implementation

Regarding the problems of the overload and overlapping of reports, and the poor quality of some of the reports and those sent to present them, governments should create expertise within one specific department. The department should have responsibility to produce comprehensive reports. This is the most convincing solution for the correct use of available resources in the preparation and presentation of reports. It would not only increase the chances of better quality reports being presented by government experts, but would also facilitate the dialogue between governments and NGOs (especially useful at a national level), and offer more assurances that someone at a national level (identifiable by NGOs) was responsible for overseeing the implementation of the variety of conventions to which the state was a party. In fact, the second meeting of the Chairpersons of the Treaty Bodies proposed in 1991 "that a specific unit be designated at the national level as being responsible for the preparation of the reports to all of the treaty bodies by that State."[6] At the 53rd session of the Commission on Human Rights, the Brazilian delegation made a statement developing this idea:

> Rationalization, which is a term and a trend typical of this period within the United Nations, should also encompass the task of monitoring human rights. An important step in that direction could be a decision of the appropriate bodies to allow states to consolidate their information in just one or two periodic reports, to be examined accordingly by each of the various treaty bodies. An integrated, comprehensive report, instead of six or seven different ones, could save precious time and resources at a national level as well as at the level of the treaty bodies making it possible to apply these savings to enhance the implementation at the national level.[7]

Such an approach would also make better use of the annual training for governments on their reporting obligations, offered every year in Turin by the

---

[6] See Philip Alston, *Interim Report on Updated Study by Mr. Philip Alston*, A/CONF.157/PC/62/Add.11/Rev.1 (22 April 1993) at para. 153.
[7] The statement was made at the 13th meeting, held on 18 March 1997. The original statement was made in English and was distributed at the meeting. The representative spoke under agenda items 14 (Status of the International Covenants on Human Rights), and 15, (Effective functioning of bodies established pursuant to United Nations human rights instruments).

Office of the High Commissioner for Human Rights and the International Labour Organization (ILO). As an NGO, the International Service shares its expertise by providing training to these annual courses of government representatives. It would be more worthwhile for the International Service to continue with this training if it knew that the training was being put to better use at a national level, rather than having former trainees given junior postings in their Permanent Missions in Geneva and rarely seen at the treaty bodies.

This solution is also preferable to the proposal of a single professional treaty body. One overall and professional treaty body is unrealistic and a potential obstacle. After all, states parties will be interested in reforms that make their reporting obligations easier, and for which they can apply for assistance. They will not want to introduce a system that from the outset is likely to give them a harder time about their implementation commitments, let alone their reporting obligations. Furthermore, the single professional body runs the real risk of producing one poor quality treaty body, as the best experts are unlikely to be attracted to such a seven year full-time ordeal as suggested by Clapham. Even if they are, what are the chances they will be elected? As in other inter-governmental negotiations, other criteria based on politics, rather than quality, will determine the outcome.

(6) Wider use of concluding observations, general comments

Clearly, better use could be made of the concluding observations and General Comments of the treaty bodies if they were better known. This is an obvious point for the NGOs of the country concerned, but it can also apply to NGOs who may use a precedent concerning one country to strengthen their defense of a case in another state which might not even be party to the particular convention. For example, the International Service received a letter from the Korean network of human rights NGOs, (KOHRNET), in which they informed the International Service that they were fighting a case of *non-refoulment* of a Zairian (now Democratic Republic of Congo) political refugee. They were immediately sent information about how CAT, in 1994, had succeeded in persuading the Swiss government not to deport another asylum-seeker back to Zaire because of the danger he faced of being tortured in his country. The International Service was informed that the information proved useful.

(7) NGO input into and response to state party meetings

NGOs often complain about the level of expertise and commitment of some members of the treaty bodies, yet very little appears to have been done either to propose suitable candidates or to comment on the candidates due to be elected. There is scope for NGOs to have input, albeit confidential, into this key process of states parties' elections of members. The International Service has been approached by state party members prior to elections for advice on candidates, and following consultations with other NGOs, the advice of the Service has helped ensure that at least better new candidates have been elected. However, the International Service is not always approached for advice and when it is, it is normally at very short notice before the election during the states parties meetings.

NGOs must keep an eye on the closed meetings of the states parties as they can have an effect on the operations of the treaty bodies. In the November 1993 state party meeting, for example, Turkey, Egypt, Yemen and Morocco wanted to discuss the role of CAT and specific cases instead of the election of officers and financial matters. This was after the Committee had used article 20 of CAT to conduct a confidential investigation in Turkey and announced a similar procedure for Egypt. At the states parties meeting, Egypt opposed such enquiries by CAT and expressed its solidarity with Turkey by criticizing the visit of CAT as an "unfortunate precedent."[8] Fortunately, enough other states parties did not agree with Egypt and company, but warning bells should be rung.

The Russian Federation Representative at the 1997 session of the Commission on Human Rights indicated they were not happy with what most observers have regarded as improvements in the treaty bodies. Mr. Gorkun-Voevoda stated[9]:

> We consider that during the past years the treaty bodies at times went beyond the scope of their mandate, though acting for the best and trying to improve their functions. Russia believes that it is high time to seriously analyze the activities of treaty bodies during meetings of states parties. Unfortunately, when the treaty bodies attempted to tighten their schedule and [tried] to examine as many states reports as possible during a single session, the constructive dialogue between state and the bodies wasn't there any more. The treaty bodies simply did not have enough time to listen to what the states' representative had to say. Thus, the concluding remarks by the Committee could no longer be considered to be objective.[10]

This strong criticism is ironic, when one considers how many of the government statements during the presentation of its report to the treaty bodies make an art form out of using up the time, to say nothing of avoiding meaningful substance.

(8) Conclusions

In defining the role of NGOs in an effective international human rights treaty system, focus should be placed on the issue of the expertise of all those involved. The most obvious challenges for international and national NGOs will be: to continue to make expert interventions in the drafting of optional protocols or new conventions; to make well-prepared and accurate written and oral interventions on a state party's implementation of a convention (which need not be

---

[8] *Meeting of the States Parties to the Convention Against Torture: Summary Record of the 5th Meeting, 24 November 1993*, CAT/SP/SR.5 (29 November 1993) at para. 83.
[9] The statement was made at the 13th meeting, held on 18 March 1997. The representative was speaking under agenda items 14 (Status of the International Covenants on Human Rights), and 15 (Effective functioning of bodies established pursuant to United Nations human rights instruments).
[10] The original statement, made at the 13th meeting, held on 18 March 1997 was in Russian. This quote is from the translation by the Russian delegation of the points made in the presentation by Mr. Gorkun-Voevoda, under agenda items 14 and 15, on behalf of the delegation of the Russian Federation to the 53rd session of the UN Commission on Human Rights (1997).

extensive and may only apply to one article); to make fuller and more imaginative use of the concluding observations and General Comments of the treaty bodies (with the press as well as in their international and national campaigning and lobbying); to co-ordinate, where appropriate, their efforts to ensure that the committee members are receiving the best possible alternative information, which should not contradict other NGO reports; to share experiences of using the treaty bodies, with international NGOs providing training, advice and assistance to national NGOs in the presentation of crucial local expertise; finally, to be alert to the politics and tactics of those states which seek to undermine the importance of the treaty bodies. Such actions by states to block positive developments indicate that, from a political perspective, they clearly do not see that the committees are in "splendid isolation."

Such NGO input will only be worthwhile, however, if all those concerned with having an effective system consider realistic ways of improving and sustaining the quality of the expertise of: the members of the treaty bodies, the government officers responsible for reporting and implementation, and the UN staff, who continue to appear to focus on servicing artificially constructed divisions within the Office of the High Commissioner for Human Rights rather than on building up expertise on themes and countries that could be better used throughout all the mechanisms, procedures, bodies and programmes which they service and operate on behalf of the UN.

CHAPTER 17

The Committee on Economic, Social and Cultural Rights and Non-Governmental Organizations

Virginia Dandan

(1) Background

The non-governmental community plays a major role in the work of the Economic, Social and Cultural Rights Committee. It is a role which was fostered even in the Committee's early days. The Economic, Social and Cultural Rights Committee was established in 1985 by the United Nations Economic and Social Council (ECOSOC). It meets twice a year at the United Nations Office in Geneva. It is composed of eighteen independent experts who serve in their individual capacities, and although nominated by governments, are not themselves governmental representatives. They are elected for four-year terms by ECOSOC and are eligible for re-election if nominated. Equitable geographical distribution applies in the election procedure.

The primary function of the Committee is to monitor the extent to which states parties have complied with their obligations under the International Covenant on Economic, Social and Cultural Rights (CESCR).[1] Presently, there are 142[2] states parties to the CESCR and all are obliged to submit periodic reports every five years to the Economic, Social and Cultural Rights Committee. In these reports, states parties provide information on the legislative, administrative and other measures they have undertaken in compliance with their obligations to ensure the enjoyment by their citizens of the rights set forth in the CESCR. In particular, states parties are required to describe the application and implementation of such measures, the progress made over a given period of time, the difficulties encountered, and the problems that remain unresolved.

Once a state party submits its report to the Economic, Social and Cultural Rights Committee, the report is translated by UN staff and is reviewed by the Committee's five-member pre-sessional working group meeting six months prior to the full Committee's consideration of the report. The pre-sessional working group draws up a list of issues based on gaps and disparities in the report, as

---

[1] International Covenant on Economic, Social and Cultural Rights, 993 UNTS 3 (in force 3 January 1976).
[2] As of 31 December 1999.

well as on information coming from other sources. This list is then transmitted to the state party, which is required to respond in writing. The written response by a state party must be received by the Committee prior to its consideration of the report at a succeeding session.

Representatives of the state party formally present their report to the Economic, Social and Cultural Rights Committee and engage in an extensive discussion with Committee members who may comment and ask further questions in relation to the report. At the end of this dialogue, the Committee concludes its consideration of the report by adopting a set of concluding observations regarding the status of the CESCR in the state party. Concluding observations, which will comprise part of the Committee's annual report to ECOSOC, are sent to the state's Permanent Mission in the last afternoon of the Committee session.

Five to six reports, scheduled well in advance, are considered by the Economic, Social and Cultural Rights Committee during each session. This provides some time for the Committee to receive relevant information from various sources on the status of economic, social and cultural rights in states parties whose reports are scheduled for consideration.

(2) Non-governmental organization participation

The importance of the role of the non-governmental community in the work of the Economic, Social and Cultural Rights Committee is a fact that the Committee has always recognized and acknowledged. The Economic, Social and Cultural Rights Committee was the first treaty body to welcome written and oral statements from non-governmental organizations (NGOs) regarding the status of economic, social and cultural rights in specific countries. As early as its first session in 1987, the Committee asked the Economic and Social Council that ECOSOC Resolution 1296 be considered applicable to the Committee so that NGOs in consultative status with the United Nations would be able to submit written reports. In its eighth session in May 1993, the Committee went a step further in its working relationship with NGOs when it adopted a formal procedure for NGO participation in its activities. The Committee reiterated its longstanding invitation to NGOs to submit written information at any time regarding any aspect of its work. The first afternoon of each session has since been set aside for receiving oral information from NGOs. In addition, a short period of time at the beginning of each session of the pre-sessional working group has been made available for the submission of relevant oral information by NGOs.

The Committee adopted this procedure to make the process of receiving NGO information more transparent, among other reasons. The NGO presentations in the first afternoon are open and interpretation is available, although these presentations are not covered by summary records. Information provided to the Economic, Social and Cultural Rights Committee in writing, and referred to in questions posed by Committee members to the state party is available for consultation by the government concerned, as well as by any other interested party. On a number of occasions, concerned government representatives have been present during the NGO presentations. NGOs are encouraged to submit materials in other forms in addition to oral and written statements. Photo and video documentation are particularly effective sources of information, and are a welcome respite from the vast quantities of documents that must be read by Committee members.

Since this procedure was adopted, the Committee's pre-sessional working groups have received only a small number of NGO submissions during the time reserved for such purposes. In contrast, NGOs flock to every session's first afternoon. The low turnout at the pre-sessional working groups may be because it is not widely known that there is a time set aside for submissions during the pre-sessional meetings, and because limited financial resources may make it impossible for organizations to travel to Geneva twice, the first time for the pre-sessional working group and the second six months later for the first afternoon of the following session. Most opt to be present on the first afternoon of the session and then stay on for the presentation and consideration of state party reports, and attend the day of general thematic discussion on the third Monday of the session. They then often wait for the release of the Committee's concluding observations on the last afternoon of the session, which is almost always on the Friday of the third week.

Country-specific information is received by the Economic, Social and Cultural Rights Committee from a number of diverse sources and it is not uncommon for disparities to occur in this data. The Committee must be able to analyze such information and draw its own conclusions. It is most effective when it has a clear picture of economic, social and cultural rights situations in practice, in real terms, and on the ground. It can arrive at this only if it is able to elicit the answers it needs during the dialogue with representatives of states parties. Clearly then, the Committee must ask the right questions to get the information it wants.

In this sense, the cooperation of international and national NGOs has been invaluable. They provide information on the current situation and assist Committee members to formulate questions to delegations during the dialogue. The answers elicited form an important part of the basis from which the Committee will analyze and draw its conclusions as to how states are complying with their obligations under the CESCR. Food First Information and Action Network (FIAN) and Habitat International Coalition (HIC) have shown remarkable consistency in their support for the work of the Economic, Social and Cultural Rights Committee, particularly of article 11 of the CESCR, the right to an adequate standard of living which in turn defines the right to food and to adequate housing. The American Association for the Advancement of Science has likewise been supportive. The International Women's Rights Action Watch (IWRAW) has more recently involved itself in the work of the Committee even as IWRAW continues to work mainly with the Committee on the Elimination of Discrimination Against Women (CEDAW).[3] These international NGOs have also been assisting national counterparts to travel to Geneva to submit oral statements and to call the attention of Committee members to violations of economic, social and cultural rights in their countries. It is largely through the efforts of these international and national NGOs that the Committee has been able to focus on specific issues affecting the realization of rights provided for in the CESCR.

---

[3] See for instance, the IWRAW Newsletter, *The Women's Watch*, Humphrey Institute of Public Affairs, University of Minnesota, USA.

NGO experts have contributed significantly to other aspects of the Committee's work. They actively participate during days of general thematic discussion. These days focus on particular provisions of the CESCR, or other themes that are directly relevant to the Committee and its mandate of monitoring implementation of the CESCR.

The contribution of NGOs has made a world of difference to the work of human rights treaty-monitoring bodies, but there is a need to ensure that this state of affairs is maintained and improved. For instance, many of the large international human rights organizations have focussed primarily on civil and political rights, paying lip service to economic, social and cultural rights but continuing to ignore them and the work of the Economic, Social and Cultural Rights Committee.

It has been said that the CESCR is the poor cousin of the International Covenant on Civil and Political Rights (CCPR)[4]. One of the reasons for this unfortunate situation may be the fact that economic, social and cultural rights are not spectacular and do not sell newspapers. These rights have to do with humdrum existence – family, work, social security, food, housing, health, education, culture – and we often forget that these are the most basic and essential elements of what it means to be a human being. There is a low level of awareness among civil society of these rights, let alone of the CESCR itself.

This is a reality that challenges the Economic, Social and Cultural Rights Committee to continue to evolve creative, and even non-traditional, methods of work in order to establish goodwill and cooperation with states parties and to encourage them along the difficult path towards the realization of economic, social and cultural rights. It seeks, therefore, to continue its work with NGO partners who are committed to the cause of all human rights.

---

[4] International Covenant on Civil and Political Rights, 999 UNTS 171 (in force 23 March 1976).

V. Follow-up of Treaty Body Conclusions

CHAPTER 18

Follow-Up Mechanisms Before UN Human Rights Treaty Bodies and the UN Mechanisms Beyond

Markus G. Schmidt*

One, if not *the*, major lacuna of UN individual complaints procedures in the field of human rights remains the absence of binding and thus legally enforceable decisions. While the UN human rights treaty bodies recommend specific remedies to be given to victims of human rights violations when they find that a state has violated provisions of the International Covenant on Civil and Political Rights (CCPR),[1] the International Convention on the Elimination of All Forms of Racial Discrimination (CERD)[2] or the Convention Against Torture (CAT),[3] they have little leverage to ensure that states comply with these recommendations.

UN human rights treaty bodies have been acutely aware of this situation which, at least as far as the European level is concerned, explains why the vast majority of individuals prefer to lodge their complaints with the European Convention on Human Rights[4] organs in Strasbourg. A judgment of the European Court of Human Rights constitutes an enforceable title. Under Article 41 (former Article 50) of the European Convention, the European Court may award the victim equitable monetary compensation which the state party is obligated to pay. Under the European system, there is an undeniable psychological pressure upon states to comply with judgments of the European Court since, pursuant to Article 46 (former Article 54) of the European Convention, the issue of the implementation of the judgment remains on the agenda of the Committee of Ministers as long as there has been no compliance.[5]

---

*The views expressed in this article are personal and do not necessarily reflect those of the United Nations.
[1] International Covenant on Civil and Political Rights, 999 UNTS 171 (in force 23 March 1976).
[2] Convention on the Elimination of All Forms of Racial Discrimination, 660 UNTS 195 (in force 4 January 1969).
[3] Convention Against Torture and Other Cruel, Inhuman or Degrading Treatment or Punishment, 1465 UNTS 85 (in force 26 June 1987).
[4] Convention for the Protection of Human Rights and Fundamental Freedoms, ETS 5 (in force 3 September 1953).
[5] Considerable efforts are sometimes necessary to persuade Council of Europe member states to implement judgments of the European Court; it took eight years for the Government of Belgium to change its legislation after the Court's judgment in the case of *Marckx v. Belgium*, Series A, Volume 31 (13 June 1979).

In the context of the International Labour Organization (ILO), follow-up mechanisms have a long tradition, in the form of a systematic exchange of communications between the Committee on Freedom of Association, which primarily examines complaints, and the Committee of Experts on the Application of the ILO Conventions and Recommendations, which examines state reports. By contrast, follow-up to the decisions of UN human rights treaty bodies is a relatively new phenomenon. Until 1990, treaty bodies were provided with little information from states parties as to what the latter had done to give effect to the treaty bodies' decisions. Only rarely did states parties volunteer the information they had, in response to a decision of the Human Rights Committee or CERD, concerning amended domestic legislation deemed to be in violation of the CCPR or CERD.[6] With increasing frequency, however, individuals wrote to the Committee complaining that states parties had failed to take any measures to implement the Committee's views.

(1) Follow-up to views adopted under the Optional Protocol to the CCPR

The Human Rights Committee was the first to conceptualize follow-up activities. In 1982, the issue of follow-up to views adopted under the Optional Protocol[7] to the CCPR was discussed for the first time, but without any results.[8] Against the background of Cold War polarization, which bedeviled the work of some treaty bodies until well into the 1980s, this should hardly come as a surprise. But the dynamics slowly changed, and attitudes among Committee members gradually evolved. Late in 1989, the Human Rights Committee commissioned a working paper from the UN Secretariat on possible approaches to monitor compliance with its views under the Optional Protocol. This paper was discussed and refined by the Committee.

Some members expressed the view that the Human Rights Committee had no competence to engage in further exchanges with the state party concerning communications after views had been transmitted to the state party. If anything, the Committee could register a follow-up request from a complainant as a new communication under the Optional Protocol, if a new or continued violation of CCPR rights had been alleged. In most instances, however, authors merely alleged that the state party had failed to observe the Committee's views and thus denied that there had been an effective remedy for the violations suffered.

Other Committee members considered that *some* follow-up competence was an inherent part of the effective performance of the Committee's functions. Even if views under the Optional Protocol are not legally binding judgments and the Committee thus cannot ensure their enforcement, it must at least have the authority to monitor the effect of its views. This authority can be derived from the doctrine of *implied powers*.[9] Every international organ must be deemed to

---

[6] See for example *Selected Decisions of the Human Right Committee under the Optional Protocol*, Vol. II, CCPR/C/OP/2 (1988) at 224–226 (follow-up information provided by the Governments of Canada, Mauritius and Finland).
[7] Optional Protocol to the CCPR, 999 UNTS 171 (in force 23 March 1976).
[8] See *Report of the Human Rights Committee* A/38/40 (1983) at 100–101.
[9] See Advisory Opinion of the International Court of Justice, "Reparation for Injuries Suffered in the Service of the United Nations", *International Court of Justice Reports* (1949) at 174–188.

have certain implied powers; every procedure of international investigation or settlement must necessarily have the means of determining whether a settlement has been reached and whether it is being observed. States parties that submit voluntarily to the Optional Protocol do so in good faith, intending to respect the Committee's views. Accordingly, even if the Optional Protocol is silent on the issue of the Committee's powers subsequent to the adoption and transmittal of views, the Human Rights Committee would not exceed its authority by monitoring implementation. A follow-up competence could also be derived from article 1 of the Optional Protocol, which provides that the Committee may "consider" complaints. It would not be unreasonable to interpret the competence to "consider" communications as encompassing a mandate to consider the measures adopted by a state party to remedy CCPR violations found in the course of the examination of a communication.[10]

After another thorough debate on the Human Rights Committee's competence to engage in follow-up activities, it was the second view which prevailed, and in July 1990, the Committee created the mandate of a Special Rapporteur for Follow-Up on views.[11] The Committee further adopted follow-up guidelines and spelled out the Special Rapporteur's competencies in its annual report for 1990.[12] The latter can be summarized as follows. The Special Rapporteur on Follow-Up will:

- recommend to the Committee action on complaints from individuals who were held to be victims of violations of the CCPR and who contend that no appropriate remedy has been provided;
- communicate with the parties in respect of such letters already received by the Committee;
- provide information on any action taken by states parties in relation to views adopted by the Committee when such information has not otherwise been made available. He/she will communicate with all states parties and, where appropriate, with victims in respect of whom findings of violations have been made, to ascertain what action, if any, has been taken;
- assist the Rapporteur of the Committee in the preparation of the sections of the annual report that will contain detailed information on follow-up activities;
- advise the Committee on the appropriate deadlines for the receipt of information on remedial measures adopted by states parties found to have violated CCPR provisions; and

---

[10] The working paper of March 1990 was not made public; on the background of Committee discussions of the follow-up mandate, see Markus Schmidt, "Portée et suivi des Constatations du Comité des Droits de l'Homme des Nations Unies", in: *La Protection des Droits de l'Homme par le Comité des Droits de l'Homme: Les Communications Individuelles*, Actes du Colloque de Montpellier (6–7 March 1995) 157–69, at 159–160.

[11] In July 1990, the Committee designated the late Mr. Janosz Fodor as Special Rapporteur; from March 1993 to the end of 1996, Mr. Andreas Mavrommatis acted as Special Rapporteur; from March 1997 to the end of 1998, Justice Prafullachandra N. Bhagwati acted as Special Rapporteur. Mr. Fausto Pocar acted as Special Rapporteur from March 1999 to March 2000. In March 2000 Ms. Christine Chanet was appointed Special Rapporteur.

[12] See *Report of the Human Rights Committee*, A/45/40 (1990), Vol. I, at 144–145 and Vol. II, Appendix XI.

- make regular recommendations to the Committee on possible ways of making the follow-up procedure more effective.

Since the spring of 1991, the Special Rapporteur on Follow-Up has issued numerous requests for detailed information from states parties as to the measures they have taken to implement the Committee's views. Notes verbales are regularly addressed to all states parties in respect of whom decisions of a finding of a violation of the CCPR have been adopted. If states parties do not reply within the deadlines, reminders are addressed to them. Furthermore, the Special Rapporteur prepares, with the assistance of the UN Secretariat, regular "follow-up progress reports" for the benefit of the Committee. These provide a detailed overview of the state of implementation of the Committee's views.[13]

In the spring of 1993, the Human Rights Committee first took stock of the effectiveness of the follow-up procedure. By that time, a considerable number of states parties had indeed sent follow-up information in reply to the Special Rapporteur's request for detailed information. While the rate of return of replies was considered satisfactory on the whole, the Committee noted that some states parties had not responded at all to requests for follow-up information,[14] whereas others had done so only with regard to *some* of the views adopted in their respect.[15] The Special Rapporteur noted that only a small percentage of follow-up replies received by that time – approximately 20% – could be deemed "satisfactory," in the sense that they both addressed the Committee's recommendations **and** offered the applicant an appropriate remedy. Far too many replies simply provided general information that was not tailored either to the specific factual circumstances of the case or to the recommendations formulated in the Committee's views.

A number of follow-up replies, for example, from Colombia[16] and from Jamaica[17] criticized the Committee's views and challenged them on either factual or legal grounds. Some follow-up replies constituted, in reality, much belated government submissions on the merits of the complaint. There has been – and continues to be – unanimity among Committee members that such belated submissions on the merits cannot be accepted under any circumstances.

The Human Rights Committee further noted that even states parties which did not challenge the views sometimes argued that as there was no domestic legal basis for the implementation of the Committee's decisions or for granting compensation to the victim, the Committee's recommendations could not be

---

[13] Until the spring of 1997, these progress reports remained internal Committee documents and were not made public. On 10 April 1997, the Committee decided that all future follow-up progress reports should be made public: see the 1586th meeting of the Human Rights Committee (11 April 1997). However, availability of these reports is limited to those in attendance at the Committee sessions, since they are not produced as UN documents. A summary of these reports is produced in the annual report. In the 1998 annual report, the Committee noted limitations concerning what was made available through the annual reports: *Report of the Human Rights Committee* A/53/40 (1998) at para. 486.
[14] This was, for example, the case for Panama, Suriname and Zaire.
[15] This was, for example, the case for Jamaica, Bolivia and the Netherlands.
[16] Follow-up replies on the views in *Páez v. Colombia* (195/1985), A/45/40 (12 July 1990) 43 and *Arevalo et al. v. Colombia* (181/1984), A/45/40 (3 November 1989) at 31.
[17] Follow-up reply from the Government of Jamaica on the views in *Campbell v. Jamaica* (248/1987), A/47/40 (30 March 1992) at 240.

acted upon.[18] Other follow-up replies displayed a marked reluctance to consider the Committee's views as binding but indicated that compensatory payments to the victim(s) had been made *ex gratia*, or that other forms of remedy had been offered *ex gratia*. This was, for instance, the argument of the government of the Netherlands in its follow-up replies on the views in respect of communications *Hugo van Alphen v. The Netherlands* and *Coeriel and Aurick v. The Netherlands*.[19]

While Committee members have emphasized the need to endow the Special Rapporteur with all the necessary powers to perform his/her mandate effectively, in fact it took until the summer of 1994 before the Special Rapporteur's powers were spelled out formally in the Committee's rules of procedure. Rule 95, paragraph 2, stipulates that the "Special Rapporteur may make such contacts and take such action as appropriate for the due performance of the follow-up mandate," and that he/she may make "such recommendations for further action as may be necessary." The formulation of paragraph 2 was deliberately left wide and elastic enough to also cover potential fact-finding missions of the Special Rapporteur under the follow-up mandate. Rule 95, paragraph 4, stipulates that the Committee "shall include information on follow-up activities in its annual report."[20] Rule 99 stipulates that all information received in the context of follow-up activities shall not be subject to confidentiality, "unless the Committee decides otherwise."[21] In its past practice, the Human Rights Committee placed some important limitations on the publicity of follow-up information, especially in cases where direct informal contacts with governments may yield better results for the victims of violations of the CCPR than highly publicized follow-up activities. Thus, the so-called 'follow-up progress reports,' which contain a detailed survey of the status of implementation of the Committee's decisions, were not made public until the spring of 1997.[22]

Parallel to the inclusion of the Special Rapporteur's mandate in the rules of procedure, the Human Rights Committee discussed further measures to make follow-up activities more effective. A detailed conference room paper prepared for the Committee's 51st session in July 1994 outlined the options available to the Committee, taking into account the unanimity among Committee members on the necessity to enhance publicity for follow-up activities.[23] After thorough debates in the spring and summer of 1994, the Committee formally adopted a number of decisions designed to enhance the effectiveness and publicity of the follow-up procedure. They cover both publicity and contacts with governments and Permanent Missions to the UN, and include the following:

(a) Every form of publicity will be given to follow-up activities;

---

[18] This was the reply of the Government of Austria concerning the views on communication *Pauger v. Austria* (415/1990), A/47/40 (26 March 1992) at 333.
[19] For the commentary on the follow-up replies in these cases, see *Report of the Human Rights Committee* A/51/40 (1996) at para. 431. For the text of views, see *Coriel and Aurik v. The Netherlands* (453/1991), A/50/40 (31 October 1994) 23; and *van Alpen v. The Netherlands* (305/1988), A/45/40 (23 July 1990) 108.
[20] See *Report of the Human Rights Committee*, A/49/40 (1994) Vol. I, annex VI at 111.
[21] After the amendment of the rules of procedure during the 59th session in April 1997, rule 99 has now become rule 97: see *Rules of Procedure of the Human Rights Committee*, CCPR/C/3/Rev.5 (11 August 1997).
[22] See *supra* note13.
[23] It is a matter of regret that this Secretariat Working Paper has remained a confidential document.

(b) Annual reports will include a separate chapter on follow-up activities. This should clearly, and in a highly visible format, convey the names of states parties which have cooperated or which have failed to cooperate with the Special Rapporteur on Follow-Up;
(c) Reminders will be sent to all those states parties which have failed to provide follow-up information;
(d) Press communiqués will be issued once a year after the summer session of the Committee, highlighting both positive and negative developments concerning follow-up activities of the Committee and the Special Rapporteur on Follow-Up;
(e) The Committee welcomes information which non-governmental organizations (NGOs) may wish to submit as to what measures states parties have taken, or failed to take, in respect of the implementation of the Committee's views;
(f) The Special Rapporteur and Committee members are encouraged to establish contacts with particular governments and Permanent Missions to the UN, to inquire further about implementation of the Committee's views; and
(g) The Committee should draw the attention of states parties, at their bi-annual meetings, to the failure of certain states to implement the Committee's views and to cooperate with the Special Rapporteur in providing information on the implementation of views.[24]

Of these decisions, points (b) and (f) are arguably the most appropriate to exert direct and effective pressure upon states parties. No country, be it a superpower or a small landlocked developing state, appreciates the publication of its name in what may amount to annual "black lists" in the annual report of a human rights treaty body submitted to the UN General Assembly. Accordingly, the Human Rights Committee has emphasized the desirability of preparing comprehensive follow-up chapters for its annual reports, with lists clearly highlighting those states, which have failed to cooperate with the Special Rapporteur on Follow-Up. After some experimentation with the format of the follow-up chapter for the annual report, the first chapter was included in the Report for 1995.[25] A more detailed follow-up chapter was included in the Report for 1996.[26] That the lists of uncooperative states under the follow-up mandates *do* have an effect was demonstrated after the publication of the 1995 and 1998 annual reports: two states parties promptly reacted, both forwarded follow-up replies and provided victims with remedies.[27]

Direct contacts with governments or Permanent Missions to the UN are another appropriate device for soliciting cooperation on follow-up issues from states parties. Since the end of 1994, the Special Rapporteur has held regular follow-up consultations during Committee sessions or inter-sessionally, either in

---

[24]These decisions can be found in the *Report of the Human Rights Committee*, A/51/40 (1996) at para. 437.
[25]*Report of the Human Rights Committee*, A/50/40 (1995) Vol. I, chapter IX at paras. 544–565.
[26]*Supra*, note 24 at paras. 424–466.
[27]The states were France and Ecuador. In the case of France (in reply to the 1995 annual report), see *supra* note 24 at para.459. In the case of Ecuador, (in reaction to the 1998 annual report), see *Report of the Human Rights Committee*, A/54/40 (1999) at paras. 461, 466 and Annex IX.

Geneva or in New York. At each session between 1995 and 1998, he has been able to meet with representatives of between three and ten states parties, frequently at the ambassadorial level, to remonstrate about non-cooperation under the follow-up procedure, to explain the purpose and modalities of the follow-up mandate, or to recommend specific remedial action.[28] The "educational value" of such direct consultations is particularly important: as most state party representatives have little or no information about treaty body procedures, including follow-up activities, they are not likely to react and to report back to their capitals until the costs of non-cooperation are explained to them in more graphic detail. The follow-up chapter of the annual report now gives detailed information about these follow-up consultations.[29] More recently and regrettably, these meetings have taken place with much less frequency.[30]

The frequency with which certain states parties are solicited for follow-up consultations is in itself an indicator of the problems with the implementation of the Committee's recommendations. Between the end of 1994 and the end of 1997, the Special Rapporteur has met with representatives of the following states parties:

- *once*: Bolivia (spring 1997); Cameroon (summer 1997); Central African Republic (spring 1996); Czech Republic (autumn 1997); Ecuador (spring 1997); France (autumn 1995); Madagascar (spring 1997); Nicaragua (spring 1997); Panama (summer 1996); Uruguay (summer 1996); Zambia (spring 1995).
- *twice*: Dominican Republic (summer 1996, spring 1997); Equatorial Guinea (spring 1996 and 1997); Peru (1995, summer 1996); Republic of Korea (spring 1996 and summer 1997).
- *three times or more*: Colombia (1995, 1996, and 1997); Jamaica (on several occasions since October 1994); Suriname (spring 1995, 1996, and 1997); Trinidad and Tobago (spring 1996 and 1997).

It should also be acknowledged that some states parties such as the Democratic Republic of the Congo have not responded to repeated requests for follow-up consultations, or have opted for delaying tactics, arguing that consultations are better left to a subsequent Committee session. Other state party representatives have tended to display rather defensive attitudes vis-à-vis the Special Rapporteur's explanations and recommendations. When asked about the follow-up to the views adopted in a case in which the state party had failed to provide detailed information at the merits stage, the representative of Equatorial Guinea doubted whether the Human Rights Committee had any justification to condemn his government on the basis of allegations he considered to be uncorroborated.[31]

Direct contacts with governments may involve, where appropriate, on-site follow-up fact-finding missions. It is obvious that follow-up fact finding missions will be reserved for the most serious instances of non-cooperation under the

---

[28] See *supra* note 24, *Report of the Human Rights Committee*, A/52/40 (1997) at paras. 518–557, and *Report of the Human Rights Committee*, A/53/40 (1998) at paras. 480–510.
[29] See *supra* note 24 at paras. 438–454.
[30] *Report of the Human Rights Committee*, A/53/40 (1998) at para. 510; *Report of the Human Rights Committee*, A/54/40 (1999) at para. 474.
[31] *Ibid.*, at para. 442.

follow-up procedure. After all, the Optional Protocol procedure itself does not provide for fact-finding, and it could be argued that fact-finding under the follow-up procedure overly stretches the meaning of *implied powers*. Notwithstanding, the first follow-up fact-finding mission took place in Jamaica in the summer of 1995, with the consent and full cooperation of the government. It remains a matter of regret that the Special Rapporteur's detailed report on his mission to Jamaica was not made public and continues to be a restricted document, and that the mission's results were only summarized in the Committee's annual report for 1995.[32]

Several general conclusions can be derived from this first follow-up mission. First, *in situ* investigations and consultations enable the treaty body concerned and its Special Rapporteur to check and verify certain facts and legal issues, which are difficult to ascertain with the requisite certainty in written proceedings. Second, follow-up missions help to explain to the governments concerned, and to those directly concerned with international reporting obligations and complaints procedures (usually civil servants in the foreign and justice ministries), the binding nature of international obligations. Such obligations necessitate the creation of a special machinery for the expeditious enforcement of international resolutions and decisions. Third, follow-up missions may help the treaty body concerned to formulate an "implementable" recommendation for remedial action if a violation of the CCPR, CERD or CAT has been found. It has been argued, for instance, that the recommendation for release of individuals under sentence of death in circumstances where procedural guarantees were found to have been violated while on trial could not be followed by the government of Jamaica in the vast majority of cases. Fourth, follow-up missions may have indirect and unintended spin-offs, in that they prompt improvements in some of the areas that are the subject of consultations with the government(s) concerned, such as the prison conditions in general or the state party's legal aid system. Finally, the Human Rights Committee has endeavored to strengthen the legal authority of its decisions by adding a paragraph (designed to remind all states of their obligation to implement in good faith the Committee's recommendations), to all decisions in which a violation of the CCPR has been found:

> Bearing in mind that, by becoming a state party to the Optional Protocol, the state party has recognized the competence of the Committee to determine whether there has been a violation of the Covenant or not and that, pursuant to Article 2 of the Covenant, the state party has undertaken to ensure to all individuals within its territory and subject to its jurisdiction the rights recognized in the Covenant to provide an effective and enforceable remedy in case a violation has been established, the Committee wishes to receive from the state party, within ninety days, information about the measures taken to give effect to its views.[33]

Clearly, a three month deadline to inform the Human Rights Committee of the measures taken to comply with its recommendations is too short. In states parties with a federal structure such as Australia or Canada, where the federal

---

[32] See *supra* note 25 at paras. 557–562.
[33] This formulation was first used in the views on *Koné v. Senegal* (386/1989), in *Report of the Human Rights Committee*, in A/50/40 (21 October 1994) Vol. II, 1 at para. 11.

government must consult with provincial or state governments about the most appropriate means of implementing a treaty body's decisions, this deadline is seldom met. Thus, the follow-up reply of the Australian Government on the Human Rights Committee's views in the case of *Toonen v. Australia* was received two years after the transmittal of the views.[34] Nor are the deadlines met by smaller developing countries with limited foreign service resources. In the future, therefore, treaty bodies may wish to set more realistic deadlines – say between at least six and a maximum of twelve months – for the receipt of follow-up information.

Any attempts to categorize follow-up replies are inherently imprecise, as the Human Rights Committee itself has noted.[35] By the beginning of the Human Rights Committee's 66th session in July 1999, roughly one third of the follow-up replies received were considered satisfactory in that they displayed a willingness, on the part of the state party, to implement the Committee's recommendations, generally but not exclusively, in the future or to offer the complainant an appropriate remedy. Another category of replies could not be considered satisfactory, in that they either did not address the Committee's recommendations at all or merely related to one aspect thereof.[36]

While the majority of states parties *have* replied to the Special Rapporteur's requests for information,[37] others have remained silent, in spite of numerous follow-up *reminders* addressed to them, or have challenged the Committee's recommendations on factual and/or legal grounds.[38] Many replies simply indicate that the victim has failed to file a claim for compensation within the statutory deadlines established by domestic legislation, and that, accordingly, no compensation can be paid to the victims(s).[39] Some requests for direct consultations were followed by direct contacts and fruitful exchanges of views, whereas other requests were ignored. Some follow-up replies have been extremely positive, promising for example a legislative review on the basis of the Committee's findings, or indicating that compensation will be paid to the victim(s). A number of countries have enacted or are in the process of enacting so-called "enabling laws," under which the decisions of UN human rights treaty bodies and regional human rights instances are given legal status. Peru was the first to enact such an enabling law in 1985, which unfortunately was rescinded by the government of President Alberto Fujimori in 1996.[40] The Government

---

[34] Views on *Toonen v. Australia* (No.488/1992) were adopted in March 1994: for text see: *Report of the Human Rights Committee*, A/49/40 (31 March 1994) 226. The state party's follow-up reply was dated 3 May 1996: see *Report of the Human Rights Committee*, A/51/40 (1996) at para. 456.
[35] See *supra* note 24 at para. 427.
[36] *Report of the Human Rights Committee*, A/54/40 (1999) at para. 459.
[37] *Ibid.*, at para. 458.
[38] Thus, in January 1995, the Government of Jamaica informed the Committee that it was not prepared to follow the recommendations in the views on *Hamilton v. Jamaica* (333/1988), A/49/40 (23 March 1994) 37, which recommended that the author, who was sentenced to death after a trial considered to have been unfair, should be released.
[39] This argument has, for example, been advanced by the Government of Uruguay in a number of follow-up replies.
[40] See articles 39 and 40 of Peru Law 23.506 (1985), pursuant to which Peru undertakes to cooperate with the Committee and to implement its recommendations; this law was rescinded in the autumn of 1996.

of Colombia enacted an enabling law in the summer of 1996, and recommendations for the compensation of individuals who obtained positive decisions of the Human Rights Committee were made by a Ministerial Committee in September 1996.[41]

It must be conceded that the number of states with specific enabling legislation remains infinitesimal compared to the total number of states parties to the various UN human rights instruments. It is not surprising therefore, that a significant number of follow-up replies display a marked reluctance on the part of states parties to recognize the Human Rights Committee's views as binding. If only for that reason, any Special Rapporteur for Follow-Up on Views must carry out his or her mandate with vigour yet circumspection, and the Human Rights Committee, or any other treaty body, must keep the follow-up procedure under review and refine it whenever appropriate.

The experience of the follow-up procedure under the Optional Protocol to the CCPR over the past decade permits the formulation of a number of recommendations and suggestions for improvements.

First, the publicity of the follow-up procedure should be guaranteed and strengthened whenever possible. While the rules of procedure of the Human Rights Committee stipulate that follow-up information is in principle public, the publicizing of follow-up "progress reports" was not made the rule until the Committee's 59th session in April 1997.[42] *All* future follow-up progress reports and all follow-up mission reports should be made public and widely disseminated without delay.

Second, follow-up activities should be properly budgeted by the Committee's Secretariat and in particular in the Office of the High Commissioner for Human Rights. The Human Rights Committee's annual reports for 1995 through 1999 recommend that at least *one* follow-up mission be budgeted per year by the Office.[43] However, no funds were earmarked for the purpose in 1996–97 or 1998–1999. Nor have funds been earmarked for the biennium budget 2000–2001.[44] While it is correct that the UN human rights program has to service all of its mandates "from within existing resources" and is under constant budgetary constraints, this should not result in *some* of the treaty bodies' activities simply being placed on the back burner. Conversely, it is incumbent upon treaty bodies to insist that *all* of their activities be serviced properly.

Third, follow-up activities should be acknowledged as an integral and important part of treaty body activities, and therefore serviced appropriately by the UN Secretariat of the treaty bodies. This would require, at a minimum, the assignment of one full-time professional staff member to follow-up activities. In the absence of such a staff person, it becomes impossible to dispatch all follow-up requests and reminders in as timely a manner as possible, and the preparation

---

[41] The enabling legislation is Colombia Law No.288 (1996); the recommendations of the Colombian Ministerial Committee which approves compensation of the victims of human rights violations on the basis of views of the Human Rights Committee are resolutions 8/96 to 17/96, adopted on 11 September 1996.
[42] See Human Rights Committee, *Summary Record of the 1586th Meeting, 11 April 1997*, CCPR/C/SR.1586. But see *supra* note 13.
[43] See *supra* note 25 at para. 565; *supra* note 36 at para. 474.
[44] *Proposed Programme Budget for the Biennium, 2000 – 2001*, Vol. III, A/54/6/Rev.1 (1999) section 22 at paras. 22.15 to 22.25

V. Follow-up of Treaty Body Conclusions 243

of follow-up progress reports and follow-up missions will inevitably suffer. It is also primarily due to a lack of staff resources that the annual press release on follow-up activities, which in principle should be issued after each summer session of the Human Rights Committee (the conclusion of the annual reporting cycle for the General Assembly), has not been prepared. The Committee has complained about the lack of adequate staff resources on numerous occasions and has expressed the hope that the specialized staff assigned to service the Committee's activities both under the state reporting and the Optional Protocol procedure would be increased.[45] A Plan of Action for the treaty bodies which was discussed at the Eleventh Chairperson's Meeting (1999) addresses the addition of staff to deal with follow-up activities.[46] Recently, the Office of the High Commissioner on Human Rights has launched an annual appeal which incorporates a request for funds for follow-up activities.[47]

Fourth, the format of the annual report's chapter dealing with follow-up activities should be reviewed and modified. Under the present format, the Committee characterizes as "satisfactory" follow-up replies which respond in substance to the Committee's recommendations or represent substantial compliance. Replies which do not respond to the Committee's recommendations, fail to address a recommendation to grant compensation, or constitute less than substantial compliance are termed "unsatisfactory". The country-by-country list that follows only indicates that a given country had submitted or failed to submit follow-up replies, without clearly identifying whether or not the replies received were or were not satisfactory.[48] As a result, the reader is left guessing in which instances there has been substantial compliance and in which there has not. Future annual reports should indicate, on a case-by-case basis, instances of compliance and non-compliance. In addition, the follow-up chapter should be issued as a separate Committee document and be given the widest possible circulation.

Fifth, a schedule for direct follow-up consultations should be prepared at least one year in advance and governments concerned should be given sufficient notice so as to enable states parties with whom the Special Rapporteur wishes to consult to prepare their responses. Past scheduling of direct follow-up consultations has been *ad hoc* and haphazard, primarily due to insufficient staff resources.

Sixth, the Committee should do more to highlight instances of non-compliance with its recommendations under the Optional Protocol in its concluding observations on periodic state reports examined under article 40 of the CCPR. When such non-compliance has been put to states parties on past occasions, this has been done in overly diplomatic and muted language.

Seventh, states parties should be encouraged to enact enabling legislation pursuant to which decisions of UN treaty bodies are given legal force. One

---

[45] *Supra*, note 25 at para. 18.
[46] *Draft Proposal for a Plan of Action to strengthen the Implementation of the International Covenant on Civil and Political Rights, the International Convention on the Elimination of All Forms of Racial Discrimination and the Convention Against Torture and Other Forms of Cruel, Inhuman or Degrading Treatment or Punishment*, HRI/MC/1999/Misc.3 (28 May 1999) at 13.
[47] *Annual Appeal 2000: Overview of Activities and Financial Requirements*, United Nations High Commissioner for Human Rights (2000) at 94.
[48] See, in particular the *Report of the Human Rights Committee*, A/54/40 (1999) at para. 461.

should not forget that the most effective mechanisms for the implementation of international human rights standards are domestic ones.

(2) Follow-up to concluding observations and periodic reports

The implementation of periodic reporting procedures is arguably the most visible and effective activity of UN human rights treaty bodies. Over the past twenty years, treaty bodies have issued detailed reporting guidelines to help states discharge their reporting obligations in a timely and efficient way.[49] All the treaty bodies now formulate concluding observations after the conclusion of the examination of a periodic report. These observations pinpoint both positive and negative aspects in the implementation of Convention or Covenant guarantees by states parties, and ideally formulate recommendations on how best to bring domestic legislation or practice into line with international obligations. The experience since 1992 suggests that states *are* mindful of such concluding observations and do take them into consideration when preparing their next periodic report; some have used them as a basis for amendments to domestic legislation. However, there are those states parties, which either do not follow-up on the treaty bodies' recommendations or studiously ignore them.[50]

Of the treaty bodies, only the Child Committee has conceptualized a structured follow-up procedure to its concluding observations on periodic reports. *The Revised Plan of Action to Strengthen the Implementation of the Convention on the Rights of the Child* makes provision for follow-up activities:

> [12] ... [D]uring the periods between reports, the Committee wishes to keep in touch with the developments in the country concerned to encourage progress in putting its recommendations into practice. States on their own initiative are providing information to the Committee on the progress made in implementing Committee recommendations and on any need for assistance for that purpose. The provision of such information forms part of an on-going dynamic process of interaction between the Committee, the

---

[49] For example, *General Guidelines Regarding the Form and Contents of Initial Reports to be Submitted by States Parties under Article 19, Paragraph 1, of the Convention*, CAT/C/4/Rev.2 (18 June 1991); *General Guidelines Regarding the Form and Contents of Periodic Reports to be Submitted by States Parties under Article 19, Paragraph 1, of the Convention*, CAT/C/14/Rev.1 (2 June 1998); *General Guidelines Regarding the Form and Content of Initial Reports to be Submitted by States Parties Under Article 44, Paragraph 1(a) of the Convention*, CRC/C/5 (30 October 1991); *General Guidelines Regarding the Form and Contents of Periodic Reports to be Submitted by States Parties Under Article 44, Paragraph 1(b) of the Convention*, CRC/C/58 (20 November 1996); *Consolidated Guidelines for State Reports Under the International Covenant on Civil and Political Rights*, CCPR/C/66/GUI/Rev.1 (1 November 1999); *Revised General Guidelines Regarding the Form and Contents of Reports to be Submitted by States Parties under Articles 16 and 17 of the International Covenant on Economic, Social and Cultural Rights*, E/C.12/1991/1 (17 June 1991); *Guidelines for Preparation of Reports by States Parties*, CEDAW/C/7/Rev.3 (26 July 1996); *General Guidelines Regarding the Form and Contents of Reports to be Submitted by States Parties*, CERD/C/70/Rev.4 (14 December 1999); *Preparation of the Initial Parts of State Party Reports ("Core Documents") under the Various International Human Rights Instruments*, HRI/CORE/1 (24 February 1992), Annex.

[50] On developments in the procedure under article 40 CCPR, see Sarah Joseph, "New Procedures Concerning the Human Rights Committee's Examination of State Reports", 13 *Netherlands Quarterly of Human Rights* (1995) 5–23.

Government concerned, civil society and international partners leading up to the presentation of the subsequent report.[51]

The *Revised Plan of Action* provides for an additional support team of four professional staff members who would back up the Child Committee's (regular) Secretariat, and one of the support team's principal tasks would be to "collect and analyze information on the follow-up of the Committee's recommendations in general," and to assist the Child Committee in following up recommendations and establishing a continued dialogue with governments.[52] The 'continued dialogue' with states parties would include follow-up missions.

Particularly with respect to the other human rights treaty bodies, there is still much scope for the conceptualization of activities and formulation of specific guidelines. It remains a fact that in the course of the examination of periodic reports, some questions asked by treaty body experts remain unanswered, and the state party representatives provide evasive replies to others or refuse to answer.[53] Faced with such evasive or incomplete answers, treaty bodies generally request that these issues be addressed in more detail in the state party's next periodic report, thereby literally letting the state party "off the hook" for between two to five years, depending on the periodicity of reporting requirements under the various instruments. At most, the state party is requested to return to the next session of the Committee and reply to the questions left unanswered, to submit its next periodic report within a shorter deadline, or in rare cases to submit an *ad hoc* report focusing on the issues left in limbo during the examination of the previous report. And even if states parties return to the Committee's following session to resume a dialogue considered unsatisfactory at an earlier session, they have been known to display utter disregard for the treaty body's interim recommendations which were formulated after the end of the first part of the dialogue. For example, at the end of the consideration of the third periodic report of Peru, the Human Rights Committee regretted

> ... the fact that Peru has not only failed to take measures in response to the recommendation made in para. 25 of the observations [sc: after examination of the first part of the report], but has on the contrary extended, only a few days before the second part of the report was considered, the system of "faceless judges". The Committee expresses its profound concern at this situation, which undermines the judicial system and will again lead to the conviction of innocent persons without a proper trial.[54]

---

[51] See, *Revised Plan of Action to Strengthen the Implementation of the Convention on the Rights of the Child*, CRC/SP/26 (21 January 1999) at para. 12.

[52] *Ibid.*, at para. 19 (b). The staff members are now in place and commencing in June 1999 follow-up projects have been organized for three states: Haiti, Uganda and Benin. These entail the identification of one of the recommendations in the Committee's concluding observations for that state, and the design of a follow-up project intended to implement that recommendation in partnership with national or local actors. It is envisaged that there will be three such projects per year.

[53] An example would be some of the replies given by the representative of Lebanon during consideration of the second periodic report of Lebanon in April 1997: see Human Rights Committee, *Summary Record of the 1578th Meeting, 7 April 1997*, CCPR/C/SR.1578 and *Summary Record of the 1579th Meeting, 7 April 1997* CCPR/C/SR.1579, and *Concluding Observations of the Human Rights Committee: Lebanon, 10 April 1997*, CCPR/C/79/Add.78 (5 May 1997) (regarding the second periodic report of Lebanon), especially at paras. 12 and 15.

[54] See *Concluding Observations of the Human Rights Committee: Peru, 6 November 1996*, CCPR/C/79/Add.72 (18 November 1996) at para. 11 (regarding the third periodic report of Peru); the initial observations are reprinted in the *Report of the Human Rights Committee*, A/51/40 (1996)

There may of course be many reasons for such behavior, but one undoubtedly is the absence of any effective sanction for non-compliance with a treaty body's recommendations.

There is now general concern among treaty bodies that the follow-up to concluding observations and recommendations is seriously deficient and must be remedied. This concern was reflected in General Assembly Resolutions 51/87, 52/118, and 53/138 which "urges all states parties whose reports have been examined by treaty bodies to provide adequate follow-up to the observations and final comments of the treaty bodies on their reports."[55]

The Human Rights Committee, in particular, has been mindful of the necessity to improve the follow-up to its activities under article 40 of the CCPR. In the spring of 1996, it decided that the members of its Bureau[56] should observe, during each session, how the situation with regard to serious violations of human rights had changed in order to determine the desirability and possibility of adopting a special decision by the Committee's plenary. The Bureau was further given the responsibility of assessing, wherever the examination of a report reveals a particularly serious human rights situation, whether the Human Rights Committee could ask the state party concerned to receive a mission of one or more of its members "in order to re-establish dialogue with it, explain the situation ... and formulate appropriate ... recommendations."[57] At the Committee's Bureau meeting of 1 April 1997, the Committee's Working Group on article 40 was instructed to examine the issue of follow-up in more detail during its July 1997 session. Further action on this issue has not yet been taken and no Committee member has been designated as a Follow-up Rapporteur specifically for article 40 and the reporting procedure.

Comprehensive procedures should be developed as an integral part of the periodic reporting process. This would include several options, depending on whether the treaty body concerned is following up on its own concluding observations, or whether it seeks to ensure there is compliance with its request for further information (or an *ad hoc* report) addressed to a state party. In the latter situation, procedures should ensure compliance with a request from treaty bodies to states parties to file further information, ensure that the information had indeed been provided, and that it has been examined by the treaty body.

Follow-up on a treaty body's concluding observations should be made the responsibility of a Special Rapporteur for Follow-Up on Concluding Observations. Follow-up to a request for additional information or for an *ad hoc* report might be left under the authority of the country Rapporteur concerned.[58]

First, the mandate of a Special Rapporteur for Follow-Up on Concluding

---

at paras. 339–364; the system of "faceless judges" is severely criticized in para. 350. It has since been abandoned by the government of Peru: See *Report of the UN Working Group on Arbitrary Detention on its Visit to Peru*, E/CN.4/1999/63/Add.2 (11 January 1999) at paras. 65 and 173.

[55] G.A. Res. 51/87, adopted on 12 December 1996 at para. 14; G.A. Res. 52/118, adopted on 12 December 1997 at para. 17, G.A. Res. 53/138, adopted on 9 December 1998 at para. 22.

[56] Namely, the Chairperson, the three Vice Chairpersons and the Committee's Rapporteur.

[57] *Supra*, note 24 at para. 33.

[58] Some of these ideas are developed by Elizabeth Evatt, "Ensuring effective supervisory procedures: The need for resources", in *The Future of UN Human Rights Treaty Monitoring*, Philip Alston and James Crawford (eds.), Cambridge University Press, 2000, 461 at 468.

Observations should draw, *mutatis mutandis*, on the experience of the Special Rapporteur for Follow-Up on Views. The Special Rapporteur may not need to present sessional follow-up progress reports to the Human Rights Committee – one progress report per year, drafted with the assistance of the Secretariat, would be sufficient. As for the follow-up on communications, the annual report of each treaty body should include a separate chapter on follow-up to concluding observations. In order to exert additional pressure on recalcitrant states parties and to ensure the necessary publicity, states parties which do not follow-up on concluding observations should be included in a highly visible "black list."

Second, the procedure for requesting follow-up information on periodic reports from states parties must be both firm and flexible. States parties should routinely be requested to provide information on the measures they have taken to translate the concluding observations or treaty body recommendations into concrete action at the domestic level, as well on the response of the authorities directly concerned by the recommendations. Obviously, the deadlines for requesting such information must be realistic and cannot be the same as those for follow-up to Optional Protocol decisions. One simply cannot expect a state party to effect legislative changes or change administrative practices within a few weeks or months. A deadline of between eighteen months and two years would appear to be more appropriate. If the state party encounters difficulties with the implementation of the treaty body's recommendations, the Special Rapporteur for Follow-Up on Concluding Observations may offer his/her assistance or good offices. If good offices still do not yield a satisfactory solution, the state party concerned should benefit from advisory services or technical assistance under the Program for Technical Cooperation of the Office of the High Commissioner for Human Rights.

Third, provision for follow-up missions is even more important for follow-up in the reporting process than it is for follow-up to decisions under the Optional Protocol. It should be envisaged that the possibility of a follow-up mission be mentioned, *in the concluding observations themselves*. This need not be done in every concluding observation, but only in those instances in which the examination of the report has revealed serious problems with the implementation of Covenant and/or Convention guarantees.

Fourth, it is highly desirable that all follow-up information on periodic reports and concluding observations be public, easily accessible in document form, and disseminated as widely as possible. States parties should be asked to confirm that publicity was given to the treaty body's concluding observations at the domestic level. The Special Rapporteur's annual progress report on his/her activities should, of course, also be made public.

Fifth, serious consideration should be given to incorporating all concluding observations produced by the UN treaty bodies into the UN system-wide common country assessment and country strategy framework. This would mean that all concluding observations should be addressed to the Resident Coordinators as expeditiously as possible; this practice is now being implemented, albeit slowly and not always consistently. These Resident Coordinators are often in a much better position than the treaty body's Special Rapporteur to intercede with the state party's authorities with a view to requesting remedial action for serious human rights violations, or following up the treaty body's concluding observations.

Sixth, there is a serious case for incorporating all information on so-called **"best practices"** into any follow-up activities on periodic reports. For this objective to be realized in an effective manner, the Office of the High Commissioner for Human Rights should collate its own information on "best practices" and share it with other organizations. The Consultative Committee on Program and Operational Questions (CCPOQ), a sub-body of the Advisory Committee on Co-ordination (ACC),[59] has devoted considerable attention to the Resident Coordinator system and to the issue of "best practices", and established working groups on both subjects. The participation of the Office of the High Commissioner for Human Rights in these Working Groups was practically non-existent until early 1997.[60] Since the beginning of High Commissioner Mary Robinson's mandate, it has participated actively in both groups. Once the identification of "best practices" has been completed, these practices should be included in any of the treaty bodies' program(s) designed to follow up on concluding observations on periodic state reports.[61]

Seventh, to the extent that concluding observations of a treaty body concern a state party in which the UN human rights program maintains a field presence,[62] they should come to the attention of the Officer-in-Charge of the field office immediately, with a view to monitoring the state party's compliance with the treaty body's recommendations. It is important that this information is sent to field officers. Current concluding observations are available on the Office of the High Commissioner for Human Rights website soon after their adoption and the March 1998 memorandum of understanding between the Office of the High Commissioner and the United Nations Development Programme (UNDP) facilitates their transmission to UNDP country offices.

Eighth and finally, the treaty bodies' rules of procedure should be amended as appropriate to formalize all follow-up activities in respect of periodic reports and concluding observations.

It is obvious that all of these proposals would have considerable financial implications over which the treaty bodies themselves have little control. For follow-up activities to state reports to be effective, however, adequate UN Secretariat staff resources must be made available to the treaty bodies' Special Rapporteur(s). In a context of scarce resources, the Secretariat should consider the discontinuation of the preparation of country profiles and comparative analyses for each periodic state report, as no more than a small percentage of treaty body experts regularly consult such analyses.[63] The resources thus freed should be made available to follow-up on periodic reports and on concluding

---

[59] ACC is the UN system's supreme coordinating body, chaired by the UN Secretary-General and attended by the directors-general of all specialized agencies.
[60] Although a staff member of the Center *did* accompany the Working Group on Best Practices on a mission to Malawi.
[61] See *Report of the Consultative Committee on Programme and Operational Questions on its Tenth Session*, ACC/1997/7 (23 June 1997).
[62] Field Offices of the UN High Commissioner for Human Rights are currently in place in Angola, Bosnia and Herzegovina, Burundi, Cambodia, Central African Republic, Colombia, Croatia, Democratic Republic of The Congo, El Salvador, Georgia (Abkhazia), Guatemala, Indonesia, Liberia, Malawi, Mongolia, Palestine-Occupied Territories, Sierra Leone, South Africa, The Former Yugoslavia (Serbia and Montenegro), and the former Yugoslav Republic of Macedonia.
[63] See Markus Schmidt, "Servicing and Financing Supervisory Procedures in a Context of Diminishing Resources", in *The Future of the UN Human Rights Treaty System, supra* note 58.

observations. Alternatively, comprehensive country analyses could be prepared by a section of the Office other than the section responsible for the servicing of treaty bodies, provided that it is in a format that is radically different from the country profiles made available to treaty body experts at present.[64]

Follow-up to the decisions of the treaty bodies under individual complaints procedures and periodic state reporting mechanisms clearly must be further developed. In the absence of legally binding decisions, which could trigger other forms of compliance and implementation, follow-up information represents one of the few reliable indicators of the effectiveness of the treaty bodies' activities. If only for that reason, the UN human rights treaty bodies should continue to strengthen and periodically review follow-up mechanisms.

If there is no effective follow-up to decisions under the complaints procedures and concluding observations on periodic reports, states parties will be tempted to take a benign view of non-compliance with the recommendations of treaty bodies. Were this to become the general view of the effectiveness of treaty body mechanisms, the *raison d'être* of the entire treaty body system would be open to question, and its effectiveness eroded. If, on the contrary, follow-up mechanisms are pursued with vigour and imagination by the treaty bodies and their special rapporteurs, and backed up with the appropriate resources by the UN Secretariat, the message to states parties would be altogether different – that non-compliance with treaty body recommendations has serious consequences and political costs.

---

[64] Under the current organizational structure of the High Commissioner's Office, it has been envisaged to assign to the Branch Unit responsible for Research and the Right to Development the responsibility for such detailed country analyses, but this Branch does not currently have the personnel resources required to conduct such detailed country analyses.

CHAPTER 19

The UN High Commissioner for Human Rights: A Link Between Decisions of Expert Monitoring Bodies and Enforcement by Political Bodies

Manfred Nowak

Markus Schmidt addresses the issue of the enforcement of decisions of treaty-monitoring bodies. He states, that in general, "[i]t cannot be denied that one if not *the* major lacuna of UN individual complaints procedures in the field of human rights remains the absence of binding and thus legally enforceable decisions."[1] It would, of course, be desirable if the decisions of UN treaty monitoring bodies were legally binding as are, for example, the judgments of the European Court of Human Rights. But, in my view, this is not the major lacuna. The decisions of the Human Rights Chamber for Bosnia and Herzegovina are legally binding, but the authorities do not seem to take them particularly seriously. If states tend to show higher respect *vis-a-vis* judgments of the European Court than, for example, final views of the Human Rights Committee, the legally binding nature of these judgments is not the decisive factor. A more important issue seems to be the fact that European states in general are more open towards individual complaints procedures and have more experience with this type of treaty-monitoring than most of the states parties to the first Optional Protocol.[2] Moreover, the European Convention on Human Rights,[3] in contrast to the first Optional Protocol, contains an explicit follow-up procedure in Article 46 (former Article 54) and entrusts the major political decision-making body of the Council of Europe, the Committee of Ministers, with the supervision of states' compliance. In addition, it is doubtful whether the member states of the Council of Europe actually *do* comply much more faithfully with the legally binding judgments of the European Court than with the non-binding views of the Human Rights Committee. A number of good examples indicate that countries such as Finland or the Netherlands changed their laws in reaction to views of the Human Rights Committee. At the same time there are quite a few judgments of the European

---

[1] See *supra* Markus Schmidt, Chapter 18 at 233.
[2] First Optional Protocol to the International Covenant on Civil and Political Rights, 999 UNTS 171 (in force 23 March 1976).
[3] Convention for the Protection of Human Rights and Fundamental Freedoms, ETS 5 (in force 3 September 1953).

Court which still await implementation by the respective governments. This is the case not only with respect to ongoing systematic human rights violations in Turkey, but also with respect to the judgments of the European Court in relation to other countries, including for example, Austria.

International law has moved from the promotion to the protection of human rights, but not yet to effective enforcement. Just as the best domestic legal system would not function without law enforcement powers, international human rights law does not function without proper enforcement. In the long run, the creation of comprehensive standards and monitoring procedures without effective enforcement mechanisms might even prove to be counterproductive. If governments and the public at large get used to the fact that international human rights standards and decisions by monitoring bodies may be ignored or even deliberately violated without any sanction, states that hitherto have complied with their international obligations may be induced to behave less faithfully. This is the experience with domestic legal systems lacking effective enforcement measures. International human rights law is in this respect more comparable to domestic criminal or administrative law than to other fields of international law. Traditional international law, similar to domestic civil law, developed on the basis of mutual interests and the principle of reciprocity. Non-compliance of one party, therefore, usually leads to non-compliance or even retaliation by the other party. However, this system does not function in the case of human rights law, which is intended to protect the interests of individuals rather than those of states. Effective enforcement by collective action, by inter-governmental or supranational organizations is, therefore, a necessary element of international protection of human rights.

Follow-up mechanisms by the treaty monitoring body itself are only the first step of enforcement. The UN human rights treaties are particularly weak in this respect, as they do not even provide for a modest follow-up competence of the respective treaty monitoring bodies. As Schmidt indicates, such a competence can be derived from the doctrine of implied powers, both in the reporting and the complaints procedures.[4] The establishment of Special Rapporteurs for Follow-up by the treaty monitoring bodies is, therefore, a welcome first step in order to put pressure on governments by publishing "black lists," carrying out follow-up missions, and so on.

Further follow-up and enforcement measures must, however, not be left to the treaty-monitoring bodies, bodies composed of independent experts. These bodies lack any enforcement power, and broader attempts to have their own decisions respected by governments would in fact undermine their authority as a quasi-judicial and final decision-making body. One might think of a domestic judge knocking at the door of a party in order to enforce his or her judgment. Effective international protection of human rights should be based instead on a well-balanced division of labour between non-governmental organizations (NGOs), independent experts (treaty bodies, special rapporteurs, working groups, and so on) and the political decision-making bodies of inter-governmental organizations. One of the major shortcomings of UN human rights treaties

---

[4]See also: Optional Protocol to the Convention on the Elimination of All Forms of Discrimination Against Women, adopted by G.A. Res. 54/4 on 6 October 1999 (not yet in force), art. 7(5): "The Committee may invite the State Party to submit further information about any measures the State Party has taken in response to its views or recommendations, if any, including as deemed appropriate by the Committee, in the State Party's subsequent reports under article 18 of the Convention."

is the missing link between independent expert bodies and political decision-making bodies. Decisions and recommendations by treaty monitoring bodies usually are not even taken up by the UN Human Rights Commission, not to mention the Economic and Social Council (ECOSOC), the General Assembly, or the Security Council. The unsatisfactory follow-up provided by political bodies to decisions and recommendations of individual experts seems to go far beyond UN treaty monitoring bodies and constitutes, in my opinion, one of the major problems of contemporary human rights. In order to react to public pressure and perhaps ease their troubled consciences, governments today tend to create highly sophisticated systems with independent experts as the major players. If these experts actually carry out their mandate in an independent, impartial and non-political manner, and arrive at critical conclusions and recommendations, they often lose the political support of governments. Bosnia and Herzegovina provides an excellent example for this type of hypocrisy. Having independent experts is not a goal in itself but a tool for assisting governments to establish the truth and to recommend appropriate actions.

Article 46 (former Article 54) of the European Convention is in this respect a much better model as it leaves the follow-up and enforcement not to the European Court but to the major political decision-making body. Apart from political and diplomatic pressure and the ultimate sanction of expelling a state from the Council of Europe, the Committee of Ministers lacks, however, effective enforcement powers as compared to, for example, the decision-making bodies of the European Union.

In principle, the United Nations seems to be in a stronger position than the Council of Europe since the Security Council, under chapter VII of the UN Charter[5], can invoke a wide range of collective enforcement measures including economic sanctions and military action. This power relates, however, exclusively to threats to peace, breaches of the peace and acts of aggression, whereas human rights have been traditionally perceived as a matter essentially within the domestic jurisdiction of states pursuant to article 2 (7) of the UN Charter. At least with respect to gross and systematic violations of human rights, this doctrine of "domestic jurisdiction" and "no power to take action" has been gradually eroded. In recent years the Security Council has taken a number of enforcement measures against governments responsible for serious human rights violations such as Somalia, Rwanda, Haiti, and the former Yugoslavia. Until now the Security Council has lacked the competence to enforce individual decisions or recommendations of treaty-monitoring bodies. If a given state, however, were to be found by an independent expert body to have seriously violated human rights and consistently ignored decisions and recommendations by that body, the situation might change.

The two stages of judicial or quasi-judicial monitoring and fact-finding by independent experts, and enforcement measures by political bodies should be conceptually separated from each other and at the same time procedurally linked in order to improve the efficiency of both. The UN High Commissioner for Human Rights might provide this link. On the basis of decisions and recommendations by independent treaty monitoring bodies, the Office of the High

---

[5] United Nations Charter, 1 UNTS xvi (in force 24 October 1945).

Commissioner should be encouraged to determine those situations which warrant urgent preventive or enforcement action and should make recommendations to the Human Rights Commission and other political bodies, including the Security Council.

Other proposals for a more effective treaty monitoring system in the 21st century include: the establishment of a permanent Human Rights Court with the power to decide on individual complaints relating to all respective human rights treaties; of a permanent Human Rights Committee with the task of considering periodic state reports relating to a variety of treaties; the strengthening of the power of follow-up special rapporteurs to carry out on-the-spot missions; the obligation of states to enact enabling legislation for the domestic implementation of decisions by international bodies; and finally, the authorization of the necessary financial means and staff resources to carry out effectively all of these independent judicial, monitoring, fact finding, follow-up and enforcement tasks.

The lack of adequate financial resources for the work of UN treaty monitoring bodies, and the lack of political will to support and confirm their decisions and recommendations, reveals a certain hypocritical attitude of governments towards the international protection of human rights. Judicial or quasi-judicial monitoring by independent experts without proper enforcement by political bodies is in the long run counter-productive, as the persistent non-compliance by governments with judicial or quasi-judicial decisions tends to undermine the authority of these expert bodies. The modest follow-up procedures developed so far by the treaty-monitoring bodies themselves cannot solve this problem, but can only remind governments once more of their obligation to comply and collectively enforce the decisions of treaty bodies. Further follow-up action by independent experts would again become counterproductive. Enforcement is the responsibility of those who establish independent monitoring mechanisms and who have the actual power to enforce, that is, governments and political bodies of intergovernmental or transnational organizations.

CHAPTER 20

The Effects of Final Decisions of the Supervisory Organs Under the European Convention on Human Rights

Leo F. Zwaak

(1) Introduction[1]

Before considering the effects and execution of the judgments of the European Court of Human Rights, the decisions of the European Commission of Human Rights and the resolutions of the Committee of Ministers of the Council of Europe, it should be noted that the European Convention on Human Rights leaves a certain discretion to the contracting parties to limit the effectiveness of the European Convention. The international application of the European Convention is based on the assumption that national legal systems differ. The purpose is not to attain a strict homogeneity but to ensure that minimum European standards are interpreted and applied throughout the territories of the contracting parties in such a way that those standards are protected, at least at a common minimum level. Also, the wording of Article 53 (former Article 60) of the European Convention presupposes that the protection of human rights that states parties agree upon is a minimum standard.[2] The effectiveness of the European Convention depends not only on the legal obligations arising out of the European Convention but equally on the status of the European Convention and the decisions of the Strasbourg organs in the domestic legal order. Within the member states of the Council of Europe, there is great variation in how effect has been given to Article 1 of the European Convention under which the parties "undertake to secure the rights and freedoms" in the European Convention of individuals within their jurisdiction. Thus, although Articles 1 and 53, and indeed the entire legal regime of the European Convention, are

---

[1] All references to Articles of the European Convention on Human Rights (Convention for the Protection of Human Rights and Fundamental Freedoms, ETS 5 (in force 3 September 1953)) are to the Articles as renumbered, due to the entry into force of Protocol No. 11 (Protocol No.11 to the European Convention, ETS 155 (in force 1 November 1998)), unless otherwise specified. The first reference to an Article (as renumbered) will be followed by the number of the former Article.
[2] Art. 53 (former Art. 60) of the European Convention states:
   Nothing in this Convention shall be construed as limiting or derogating from any of the human rights and fundamental freedoms which may be ensured under the laws of any High Contracting Party or under any other agreements to which it is a party.

based upon state acceptance of the obligation to secure human rights for all, there are several means by which the state can limit the effectiveness of the system.

(2) The possibility of limiting the effectiveness of the European Convention

Only a few of the rights and freedoms enshrined in the European Convention are absolute; all others may be restricted on well-defined grounds and in accordance with procedures described by law. According to the European Court,

> some compromise between the requirements for defending democratic society and individual rights is inherent in the system of the Convention...As the Preamble to the Convention states, "Fundamental freedoms"...are best maintained on the one hand by an effective political democracy and on the other by a common understanding and observance of the Human Rights upon which (the contracting states) depend...this means that a balance must be sought between the exercise by the individual of the right guaranteed to him under paragraph 1...and the necessity under paragraph 2...for the protection of the democratic society as a whole.[3]

This balancing of state and individual interests, particularly in the context of restrictions has occupied the European Commission and Court in important cases. Using the doctrine of the "margin of appreciation," the European Court and the Commission sought the proper balance between the interests of the state and those of the individual.

There are also provisions to limit the applicability of the European Convention. Article 56 (former Article 63) of the European Convention contains the possibility of limiting the territorial scope of the European Convention. Still, the fact that the European Convention applies only to the territory of the contracting states does not imply that a contracting state cannot be responsible under the European Convention for acts that its organs commit outside its territory.[4] Another possibility which limits the applicability of the European Convention, and thus the scope of its supervisory mechanism, has more far-reaching implications. Under Article 15 of the European Convention, a state may limit the application of some of the substantive rights of the European Convention in certain exceptional circumstances. The second paragraph of this article prohibits derogations from Articles 2, 3, 4 and 7 of the European Convention. This prohibition is absolute as regards Article 3 (torture, inhuman and degrading treatment or punishment) and paragraph 1 of Article 4 (slavery or servitude). As is appropriate to a serious matter such as derogation from a human rights treaty, paragraph 1 of Article 15 prescribes a very strict standard for states wishing to derogate from the Convention.

Finally, under the Convention, a state may limit the operation and effect of articles protecting specific substantive rights by lodging reservations to the relevant article. Article 57 (former Article 64) lays down two main conditions for the admissibility of reservations: (a) the reservation must be the direct

---

[3] *Klass v. Germany*, Series A, Volume 28 (6 September 1978) 28 at para. 59.
[4] *X v. Federal Republic of Germany* (1611/62), ECHR Yearbook VIII (25 September 1965) at 158 (163); *Loizidou v. Turkey*, Series A, Volume 310 (23 March 1995) 24.

consequence of a national law that is not in conformity with a provision of the European Convention (it being understood that the law must be in force when the reservation is made) and, (b) the reservation must be made in respect of a particular provision of the European Convention. Reservations have been made by most of the parties to the European Convention.[5] They have been invoked successfully in several cases to prevent a claim being examined.[6]

Considering the possibilities of limitations to the applicability of the European Convention, one might well question whether there exists a minimum standard. According to the preamble to the European Convention, the parties have a "common heritage of political traditions, ideals, freedom and the rule of law." Some means, however, such as reservations or interpretative declarations, affect those provisions of the European Convention that guarantee substantive rights, and some, such as derogations, suspend the operation of certain substantive provisions for a given period under specific circumstances. This possibility of limitations through derogations and reservations is one of the great weaknesses of the European Convention on Human Rights. According to Johann Frowein, the fact that vast parts of the protective system may be cut out by unilateral acts of states may seriously jeopardize the possibility of attaining a minimum standard. This minimum standard is in fact not the minimum at all.[7] The more recent members of the Council of Europe have been able to make their reservations subject to the extensive and well-established case law of the European Commission and Court, which the earlier members have not been able to do.[8] It is therefore not surprising that there is a tendency towards a growing number of reservations being made by states which have joined the European Convention system recently. Frowein warns that this inequality may lead to a situation where some states will consider withdrawing from the European Convention so that they may ratify again, subject to more accommodating reservations.[9]

(3) The impact of decisions of the supervisory organs

The importance of the individual right of complaint for the functioning of the supervisory system under the European Convention is apparent from the large number of individual applications submitted to the European Commission. Until 1 January 1999, a total of 45,028 applications had been registered at the Secretariat of the Commission, and the Commission had taken a decision with respect to admissibility in 37,544 cases. It should be borne in mind, however, that a great many cases (29,734) were declared inadmissible at once. Of the remaining cases, the majority (2,883) were declared inadmissible after having been transmitted to the government concerned for its observations. In the course

---

[5] See in this respect *European Convention on Human Rights: Collected Texts*, Council of Europe (1995).
[6] See, for example *Chorrherr v. Austria*, Series A, Volume 266-B (25 August 1993).
[7] See in this respect Johann A. Frowein, "Reservations to the European Convention on Human Rights", in *Protecting Human Rights: The European Dimension, Studies in Honour of Gerard J. Wiarda*, Franz Matscher, Herbert Petzold (eds.), Köln (1988) 193–200.
[8] Ronald St. J. Macdonald, "Reservations under the European Convention on Human Rights", 21(2) *Revue de Belge de Droit International* (1988) 432.
[9] *Supra* note 7 at 199.

of the examination of the merits, another twelve cases were rejected for inadmissibility in accordance with Article 29. Only a total of 4,923 cases, therefore, were ultimately declared admissible.[10]

In 1999, 8,396 applications were registered by the Convention system, compared to 5,981 in 1998.[11] In 1999, the European Court delivered 177 judgments, declared inadmissible or struck off 3,519 applications and declared admissible 731 applications.[12]

Without any doubt, it can be said that the decisions of the Strasbourg organs have had not only a profound influence on the situation of individuals who complain about human rights violations, but these decisions have had a far-reaching impact on the legal situation of the contracting parties to the European Convention.

In most cases, proceedings before the European Court conclude with a decision in the form of a judgment. Article 41 (former Article 50) of the European Convention provides that if a high contracting party is in breach of its obligations under the European Convention, and if its domestic law does not provide for adequate reparation of that breach, then "the decision of the Court shall, if necessary, afford just satisfaction to the injured party." At the outset, it is important to understand that the notion of "just satisfaction" encompasses pecuniary compensation only. Neither the European Court, nor the Committee of Ministers, has the power to order a state to take a particular action in response to the finding of a violation.

Article 41 appears to imply that the decision on an award of compensation must be given together with the judgment on the merits. Rule 75 (former Rule 54) of the Rules of Court, however, leaves the moment of the decision on an award of compensation entirely open. If the Chamber of the European Court which deals with the case finds that there is a violation of the European Convention, it rules on the application of Article 41 (former Article 50) in the same judgment only if the question, after being raised under Rule 60 (former Rule 50), is ready for decision. Reference can be made to the judgment in the *Golder v. The United Kingdom* case, for example, in which the European Court, after having found that there had been a violation of Articles 6(1) and 8, decided unanimously "that the preceding findings amount in themselves to adequate just compensation under Article 50 [new Article 41]."[13] On the other hand, in a few cases the European Court has awarded substantial sums of money.[14] Decisions

---

[10] See Council of Europe, *European Commission of Human Rights, Survey of Activities and Statistics 1998*. These figures include two months after the entry into force of Protocol No. 11, *supra* note 1, on 1 November 1998, during which time the Commission operated only in the capacity of dealing with cases which had been declared admissible prior to that date.

[11] Protocol No.11 to the European Convention, *supra* note 1, replaced the two-tier system of a part-time European Court and Commission with a single, full-time Court. Under transitional arrangements, the European Commission continued to function until 31 October 1999. Council of Europe, *Survey of Activities, 1999*, Information document issued by the Registrar of the European Court of Human Rights, (Provisional Version).

[12] *Ibid.*

[13] *Golder v. The United Kingdom*, Series A, Volume18 (21 February 1975) at 2; in others that a token amount of money is sufficient, for instance: 100 Dutch guilders; see, *Engel and Others v. The Netherlands*, Series A, Volume 22 (23 November 1976).

[14] *Sunday Times v. The United Kingdom*, Series A, Volume 38 (6 November 1980); *Guincho v. Portugal*, Series A, Volume 81 (10 July 1984).

concerning Article 41 which were made simultaneously with the judgment on the merits are also to be found, as in *De Weer v. Belgium*,[15] *Artico v. Italy*,[16] *Schönenberger and Durmaz v. Switzerland*,[17] *Berrehab v. The Netherlands*[18] and *Karakaya v. France*.[19] If the question of compensation has been raised, but is not yet ready for decision, the Chamber reserves it in whole or in part and fixes the further procedure. If the question of the compensation has not been raised, the Chamber lays down a time limit within which this may be done by the original applicant (Rule 75(1) (former Rule 54(1)) of the Rules of Court).[20]

Reparation under Article 41 is intended to place the applicant as close as possible to the position in which he would have been had the violation of the European Convention not taken place.[21] Whether, and to what extent, satisfaction will be awarded by the European Court depends on the circumstances of the case.

The European Court also considers whether the finding of a violation has an effect beyond the confines of a particular case. The respondent state is then under the obligation to take the necessary measures in its domestic legal system to ensure the performance of its obligations under Article 46(1) (former Article 53) of the European Convention.

Until recently, the European Court did not cite any time limit within which the government was required to reimburse costs and expenses incurred, or satisfy the claim which it afforded for "just satisfaction". The European Court now specifies the period, usually three months, within which the specified sum must have been paid to the individual.[22] It is then up to the Committee of Ministers under Article 46(2) (former Article 54) to determine if the sum has been paid within the time limit set by the Court.

According to the terms of Article 44 (former Article 52) of the European Convention, "the judgment of the Court shall be final." As the European Court has already underlined, "the sole object" of this provision "is to make the Court's judgments not subject to any appeal to another authority."[23] A request for interpretation or revision of a judgment may be addressed to the Court, however.[24] The text of the judgment is submitted to the Committee of Ministers for the purpose of the supervision of its execution under Article 46(2) of the European Convention.[25]

---

[15] *Deweer v. Belgium*, Series A, Volume 35 (27 February 1980) at 31–32.
[16] *Artico v. Italy*, Series A, Volume 37 (13 May 1980) at 19–22.
[17] *Schönenberger and Durmaz v. Switzerland*, Series A, Volume 137 (20 June 1988) at 14–16.
[18] *Berrehab v. The Netherlands*, Series A, Volume 138 (21 June 1988) at 17.
[19] *Karakaya v. France*, Series A, Volume 289-B (26 August 1995).
[20] See, for example, *König v. Germany*, Series A, Volume 27 (28 June 1978) at 40–41.
[21] *Piersack v. Belgium*, Series A, Volume 85 (23 October 1984) at 15–16.
[22] *Moreira De Azevedo v. Portugal*, Series A, Volume 208-C (28 August 1991) at 30; *Kremzow v. Austria*, Series A, Volume 268-B (21 September 1993) at 34; *Dombo Beheer B.V. v. The Netherlands*, Series A, Volume 274 (27 October 1993) at 41.
[23] *Ringeisen v. Austria*, Series A, Volume 15 (22 June 1972) at 7.
[24] Rule 77 (former Rule 57 of the Rules of Court "A" and former Rule 59 of the Rules of Court "B") deals with the possibility to request the European Court for the interpretation of a judgment. The procedure to be followed in connection with a request for revision is also to be found in Rule 80 (former Rule 58 of the Rules of Court "A" and former Rule 60 of the Rules of Court "B").
[25] Rule 77(3) (former Rule 55(3)) of the Rules of Court.

(4) The legal basis of the execution of the decisions of the Strasbourg organs

In accordance with Article 46(1), "The High Contracting Parties undertake to abide by the decision of the Court in any case in which they are parties." In *Marckx v Belgium*, the Court held that its "judgment is essentially declaratory and leaves to the state the choice of the means to be utilized in its domestic legal system for performance of its obligation under Article 53 [new Article 46(1)]" and "cannot of itself annul or repeal" inconsistent national law or judgments.[26] The contracting parties must execute the judgments of the Court. Article 46(2) of the European Convention provides that the Committee of Ministers supervises the execution of the judgments.

The Court has had to declare repeatedly that it lacked jurisdiction to direct states to take certain measures, for instance to rectify the violation found by the European Court, or to repay costs and other expenses.[27] In *Marckx v Belgium*, the Court added that its judgments leave to the state the "choice of the means to be utilized in its domestic legal system for performance of its obligation under Article 53 [new Article 46(1)]."[28] This seems to imply that, according to the European Court, the Committee of Ministers cannot indicate which measures the respondent state must take. *Soering v The United Kingdom*, however, points in the opposite direction. In this case, the applicant submitted that "just satisfaction of his claims would be achieved by effective enforcement of the Court's ruling"[29] and he invited the European Court to give directions in relation to the operation of its judgment to the governments which were concerned in his case. The Court responded that it was not empowered under the European Convention to make accessory directions of the kind requested by the applicant: "By virtue of Article 54 [new Article 46], the responsibility for supervising execution of the Court's judgments rests with the Committee of Ministers of the Council of Europe."[30] Thus, the European Court seems to emphasize the relation between its own competence and that of the Committee of Minister's and might indicate that according to the Court, the Committee of Ministers is empowered to give directions to the governments concerned.

In the case of *Ireland v. United Kingdom*,[31] the Irish government requested that the European Court recommend to the British government that it lay criminal or disciplinary charges against members of the security forces who had taken actions in violation of Article 3 of the European Convention. The European Court did not explicitly answer the question of whether such a recommendation was possible; it simply held that it did not have to consider whether its functions

---

[26] *Marckx v. Belgium*, Series A, Volume 31 (13 June 1979) at 25–26, para. 58.
[27] In contrast, see art. 63(1) of the American Convention on Human Rights, PAUTS 36 (in force 18 July 1978) which confers extensive powers on the Inter-American Court.
[28] *Marckx v. Belgium*, supra note 26 at para. 58. See also *Pakelli v. Federal Republic of Germany*, Series A, Volume 64 (25 April 1983) at 19–20; *Albert and Le Compte v. Belgium*, Series A, Volume 68 (24 October 1983) at 6; *McGoff v. Sweden*, Series A, Volume 83 (26 October 1984) at 28; *Pauwels v. Belgium*, Series A, Volume135 (26 May 1985) at 19; and *B. v. United Kingdom*, Series A, Volume 136-D (9 June 1988) at 35.
[29] *Soering v. The United Kingdom*, Series A, Volume 161 (7 July 1989) at para. 125.
[30] *Ibid.*, at para. 127.
[31] *Ireland v. The United Kingdom*, Series A, Volume 25 (18 January 1978).

extended, in certain circumstances, to addressing consequential orders to contracting states. The European Court found that the sanctions available to it did not include the power to direct one of those states to institute criminal or disciplinary proceedings in accordance with its domestic law.[32] One might be inclined to assume that the nature of the requested measure prevented the European Court from complying with the request. However, in its later case law the Court has shown that it is not willing to recommend concrete measures other than financial satisfaction.

In *Corigliano v. Italy*, the European Court declared it beyond its jurisdiction to order the state to make certain articles of its penal code inapplicable to "political and social trials," claiming that this "falls outside the scope of the case brought before the Court."[33] The request to publish a summary of the Court's judgment in local newspapers or to remove any reference to the applicant's conviction in the central criminal records, also was held to fall outside the scope of the jurisdiction of the European Court.[34]

In *Bozano v. France*, the applicant requested that the European Court recommend to the French government that it approach the Italian authorities through diplomatic channels, with a view to securing either a "presidential pardon" – leading to his "rapid release" – or a reopening of the criminal proceedings against him in Italy from 1971 to 1976. The government argued that the European Court did not have power to recommend such a course of action. It maintained further that such a recommendation would in any case be unconnected with the subject matter of the dispute, since it would amount to recommending that France intervene in the enforcement of final decisions of the Italian courts. The Court did not go into these arguments. It merely pointed out that Mr. Bozano's complaints against Italy were not at issue before it, as the European Commission had declared them inadmissible.[35] One cannot escape the impression that the European Court did not want to enter into the issue, whether or not it had power to make a recommendation as requested by the applicant. It might be argued that in cases where *restitutio in integrum* is impossible, as in this case, the Court had nothing left but to award just satisfaction. However, what Mr. Bozano had requested was only a *recommendation* and such a recommendation should, in general, not be deemed inappropriate. It would seem to be comparable to the recommendation of provisional measures, for which there is also no express basis in the European Convention.

As discussed above, however, the European Court leaves the choice of the means to be utilized in a domestic legal system for the performance of obligations under Article 46(1) to the domestic authorities. On occasion, however, there have been significant delays in the introduction of remedial legislation, delays which have threatened to bring the enforcement system into disrepute. For example, it took the Belgian authorities almost eight years to introduce legislation amending "various legal provisions relating to affiliation" in response to the *Marckx v. Belgium*[36] judgment. In the meantime, a further application based

---

[32] *Ibid.*, at para. 186.
[33] *Corigliano v. Italy*, Series A, Volume 57 (10 December 1982) at 17.
[34] *Manifattura F.L. and others v. Italy*, Series A, Volume 230-B (27 February 1992) at 21; *Castells v. Spain*, Series A, Volume 236 (23 April 1992) at 25.
[35] *Bozano v. France*, Series A, Volume 111 (18 December 1986) at 28.
[36] *Marckx v. Belgium*, *supra* note 26.

on the previous legislation was lodged with the European Commission, culminating in the European Court's judgment in *Vermeire v. Belgium*[37] in which another violation was found. The European Court allowed the Belgian government's claim that the inheritance law revised subsequent to the judgment in the *Marckx v. Belgium* case could not be applied retroactively, but rejected its claim that the judgment could not be given effect until the completion of domestic legislative reform. The Court stated that

> The freedom of choice allowed to a state as to the means of fulfilling its obligation under Article 53 [new Article 46(1)] cannot allow it to suspend the application of the Convention while waiting for such a reform to be completed, to the extent of compelling the Court to reject in 1991, with respect to a succession which took effect on 22 July 1980, complaints identical to those which it upheld on 13 June 1979.[38]

In a lengthy article, Judge Sibrand Martens has presented another perspective on the supervision of the execution of the judgments by the European Court.[39] In the case of *Olsson v. Sweden (No. I)*,[40] the main issue was whether the decision of the Swedish authorities to take the children of the applicants into care had given rise to a violation of Article 8 of the European Convention. The European Court found a violation of that provision and awarded the applicants just satisfaction under Article 41 of the European Convention. In the case of *Olsson v. Sweden (No. II)*,[41] the applicants complained that despite the Court's *Olsson v. Sweden (No. I)* judgment, the Swedish authorities had still denied their reunion with their children. The applicants had not been allowed to meet the children under circumstances which would have enabled them to re-establish parent-child relationships. In their view, Sweden had continued to act in breach of Article 8 and had thereby failed to comply with its obligations under Article 46(1) of the European Convention. The European Court referred to Resolution DH (88)18,[42] adopted on 26 October 1988, concerning the execution of the *Olsson v. Sweden (No. I)* judgment, in which the Committee of Ministers, "having satisfied itself that the Government of Sweden has paid to the applicants the sums provided for in the judgment," declared that it had "exercised its functions under Article 54 [new Article 46(2)] of the European Convention." The European Court noted that the facts and circumstances underlying the applicants' complaint under Article 46(1) raised a new issue which was not determined by the *Olsson v. Sweden (No. I)* judgment and was essentially the same as those considered above under Article 8, with respect to which no violation was found.[43] The European Court thus left open the possibility that there might be circumstances under which a complaint under Article 46(1) of the European Convention could be examined by it. Judge Martens questions whether the Committee of

---

[37] *Vermeire v. Belgium*, Series A, Volume 214-C (29 November 1991).
[38] *Ibid.*, at para. 26.
[39] Sibrand K. Martens, "Individual Complaints under Article 53 of the European Convention on Human Rights", in *The Dynamics of the Protection of Human Rights in Europe: Essays in Honour of Henri G. Schermers*, Rick Lawson and Mathijs de Blois (eds.), Dordrecht (1994) at 252–292.
[40] *Olsson v. Sweden (No. 1)*, Series A, Volume 130 (24 March 1988).
[41] *Olsson v. Sweden (No. 2)*, Series A, Volume 250 (27 November 1992).
[42] Committee of Ministers Res. DH 88(18), adopted on 26 October 1988.
[43] *Supra*, note 41.

Ministers' competence under Article 46(2) of the European Convention was exclusive. He gives two persuasive reasons for taking the view that complaints under Article 46(1) should not be decided by the Committee of Ministers but by the European Court. First, the interpretation of its own judgments is better left to the Court than to a gathering of professional diplomats who are not necessarily trained lawyers possessing the qualifications laid down in the European Convention. Second, the members of the Committee of Ministers are under the direct authority of their national administrations and cannot be considered a "tribunal" in the sense of the European Convention.[44] Judge Martens has raised a very important question: the Committee of Ministers, being a political body composed of representatives of member states, is not the best equipped or motivated body to question whether the steps taken go far enough. It is therefore to be hoped that the application of Article 46(1) will be more successful in the future.

(5) Failure to abide by the decisions of the Strasbourg organs

(a) Supervision of the execution of the judgments of the European Court

Article 46(2) provides that "The final judgment of the Court shall be transmitted to the Committee of Ministers, which shall supervise its execution." This supervision may take the form of monitoring legislative or administrative reforms instituted by states in response to a finding of a violation, or, in the case of judgments for "just satisfaction" under Article 41, ensuring that the state has made its payment to the individual. Under this Article, the Committee of Ministers deals only with judgments of the European Court finding a violation of the European Convention and with judgments striking a case from the Court's list if the parties have agreed to a friendly settlement.

The Committee of Ministers adopted a number of rules in 1976 with a view to its supervisory function under Article 46(2).[45] These rules outline that when the European Court has decided that there has been a violation of the European Convention and/or when it has afforded just satisfaction to the injured party, the Committee of Ministers is to invite the state concerned to inform it of the measures it has taken in pursuance of the judgment of the Court (Rule 2). The Committee of Ministers does not regard its function under Article 46(2) as having been exercised until it has taken note of the information supplied and, when just satisfaction has been awarded, until it has convinced itself that this has actually been afforded. If a state fails to execute a judgment of the European Court, by a two-thirds majority of the representatives casting a vote and a majority of the representatives entitled to sit on the Committee, the Committee of Ministers may decide on the measure to be taken.[46]

---

[44] *Supra*, note 39 at 285.
[45] Rules adopted by the Committee of Ministers for the application of Art. 46(2) (former Art. 54) of the European Convention: *Collection of Resolutions Adopted by the Committee of Ministers in Application of Articles 32 and 54 of the European Convention on Human Rights; Supplement 1986–87*, Council of Europe (1989).
[46] The European Convention is silent on the voting procedure with respect to decisions under Art. 46(2) (former Art. 54). The Rules of Procedure of the Committee of Ministers refer in general to Art. 20 of the Statute of the Council of Europe (Rule 10). It appears from Art. 20 that decisions

(b) Sanctions in the Statute of the Council of Europe

In the worst cases, there are more serious sanctions not established by the European Convention itself. For example, article 3 of the Statute of the Council of Europe provides that respect for human rights is a fundamental principle underlying participation in the Council. Article 8 of the same Statute empowers the Committee of Ministers to suspend or even to expel from the Council of Europe any member state guilty of serious human rights violations. In the *Greek case*[47] (which arose under an Article of the European Convention permitting decisions on the merits to be made by the Committee of Ministers, and no longer operative with the coming into force of Protocol 11), the Committee of Ministers considered that a great many Articles of the European Convention had been violated. Before the Committee of Ministers adopted its resolution in this case, however, Greece withdrew from the Council of Europe and denounced the European Convention. Had the Greek government not denounced the European Convention and withdrawn from the Council of Europe, it is quite possible that the Committee of Ministers would have exercised its authority to suspend or expel Greece from the Council.

(6) The monitoring system

The record of states in executing European Court judgments has been described as "remarkably good."[48] This is true of the payment of compensation and costs, the restitutive steps taken to remedy a wrong done to an individual applicant and the amendment of legislative and administrative practices found contrary to the European Convention. There is as yet no case in which the Committee of Ministers, which is seized with the task of supervising the execution of judgments and decisions, has found that a state has not complied with its obligations.[49] The practice of the European Convention shows that the decisions of the Strasbourg organs have acquired a highly persuasive status in the domestic legal order. Therefore the need for a monitoring system has been discussed only rarely. It has to be said, however, that more and more states are becoming reluctant to execute judgments against them.

Consider the *Brogan v. United Kingdom* case.[50] In its judgment, the European Court held that the government of the United Kingdom had violated Article 5 of the European Convention by detaining without charge or procedural protections persons suspected of participating in "terrorist" activities. Following this judgment, the United Kingdom lodged a derogation on 23 December 1988, stating that the government found it necessary to continue to exercise its powers

---

concerning a number of expressly mentioned matters require unanimity or a simple majority. Decisions on all other matters, including therefore decisions under Art. 46(2) (former Art. 54) of the European Convention, are taken with a two-thirds majority of the representatives casting a vote and a majority of the representatives entitled to sit on the Committee.

[47] *The Greek Case*, ECHR Yearbook XII (5 November 1969) 1.

[48] Peter Leuprecht, "The Execution of Judgments and Decisions", in *The European System for the Protection of Human Rights*, Ronald St. J. Macdonald, Franz Matscher and Herbert Petzold (eds.), Dordrecht (1993) at 791–800.

[49] David J. Harris, Michael O'Boyle and Chris Warbrick, *Law of the European Convention on Human Rights*, Butterworths (1995) at 30.

[50] *Brogan and Others v. The United Kingdom*, Series A, Volume 145-B (29 November 1988).

under the Prevention of Terrorism Act to detain individuals without charge for several days, on the authority of the Secretary of State. It stated that the possibility of exercising such discretion was strictly required by the exigencies of the situation to enable necessary enquiries and investigations to be completed properly in order to decide whether criminal proceedings should be instituted.[51] During the examination of this case by the Committee of Ministers, the British government informed the Committee of Ministers that it would make use of the possibility of derogation as long as it was necessary in the circumstances. In its resolution, the Committee of Ministers stated that it was not for the Committee of Ministers to take a position on the validity of a derogation. It decided, having taken note of the information supplied by the government, to discontinue its examination of the case.[52] In a later decision, the validity of this derogation was challenged by arguing *inter alia* that the lodging of the derogation was not a genuine response to an emergency situation, but was intended merely to circumvent the effects of the judgment in *Brogan v. The United Kingdom*. The European Court, however, did not follow this argument and held that the British government had acted within its margin of appreciation in lodging a derogation in regard to Article 46(2).[53]

It has also been pointed out that the theoretical and practical difficulties of transposing the decisions of the European Court into domestic law may escalate if the European Court continues to develop a dynamic jurisprudence. The more the European Court focuses its attention on the particular facts of a case and on a specific social development, the greater the danger that the domestic courts will be inclined to see each case through a national law perspective and thus ignore the Strasbourg Court's rulings.[54] This may be a valid concern, but it is to be hoped that the European Court will continue to conceive of its function as the guardian of human rights in a dynamic and probing way. At the same time, this leaves the Court with the difficult task of trying to respect the rich diversity in the legal systems of the contracting parties without losing touch with common European values.

During the Council of Europe Summit in Vienna in October 1993, one of the points discussed was the implications of the geographical enlargement of the Council of Europe as a result of the political changes which had taken place in Central and Eastern Europe from 1989. On that occasion, the Heads of State and Government of the Member States of the Council of Europe stated that:

> ... the Council is the pre-eminent European political institution capable of welcoming, on an equal footing and in permanent structures, the democracies of Europe freed from communist oppression. For that reason the accession of those countries to the Council of Europe is a central factor in the process of European construction based on our Organisation's values. Such accession presupposes that the applicant country has brought its institutions and legal system into line with the basic principles of democracy, the rule of law and respect of human rights.[55]

---

[51] Council of Europe, *Information Sheet No. 24* (November 1988–5 May 1989) at 73.
[52] Committee of Ministers Res. DH (90) 23, adopted on 24 September 1990.
[53] *Brannigan and McBride v. The United Kingdom*, Series A, Volume 258-B (26 May 1993) at 50–51.
[54] Georg Ress, "The Effects of Judgments and Decisions in Domestic Law", in *The European System for the Protection of Human Rights, supra* note 48 at 848.
[55] Council of Europe Summit, Vienna (9 October 1993); see *Vienna Declaration of Human Rights*, at 11(4) *Netherlands Quarterly on Human Rights* (1993) 513.

In that context, the Committee of Ministers has repeatedly expressed the view that opening up to Central and Eastern European countries cannot take place at the cost of lowering the norms and standards of human rights protection established by the Council of Europe. In connection with the requests for accession of new member states, the question arose, how to determine whether the state concerned fulfilled the requirements for membership. Apart from the procedure of Article 52 (former Article 57) of the European Convention, the Council of Europe lacks a mechanism under which the member states can be kept under constant surveillance on their compliance with the commitments accepted within the Council of Europe.

Against this background and inspired by the Vienna Summit, on 10 November 1994 the Committee of Ministers adopted a declaration on compliance with these commitments.[56] The 1994 Declaration envisages a political mechanism under which the member states of the Council of Europe, its Secretary-General or its Parliamentary Assembly may refer questions of implementation of commitments concerning the situation of democracy, human rights and the rule of law to the Committee of Ministers. On 20 April 1995, the Committee of Ministers adopted the procedure for implementing the 1994 Declaration. When considering issues referred to it, the Committee of Ministers will take account of all relevant information available from different sources such as the Parliamentary Assembly and the Organization for Security and Cooperation in Europe (OSCE). The mechanism will not effect the existing procedures arising from statutory or conventional control mechanisms.

The monitoring procedure of the Committee of Ministers was put into operation in 1996. It consists of political monitoring based on a confidential, non-discriminatory approach. It supplements other statutory and convention-based monitoring procedures such as that of the European Convention and those of the Parliamentary Assembly and the Congress of Local and Regional Authorities in Europe.[57] This procedure was set up as a result of the Vienna Summit. The Heads of State and Government of the Council of Europe member countries declared then that they were "... resolved to ensure full compliance with the commitments accepted by all member states within the Council of Europe."[58] In contrast to the Parliamentary Assembly's practice, the Committee of Ministers' monitoring focuses on specific themes selected by the Committee of Ministers: the reports prepared for the Committee of Ministers by the Secretary General's Monitoring Unit describe the situation with regard to a given theme in all member states. Since the procedure was introduced, six "themes" (initially called "areas of concern"), have been under consideration: freedom of expression and information, functioning and protection of democratic institutions, functioning of the judicial system, local democracy, capital punishment, and police and security forces.

On the basis of a decision taken by the Committee of Ministers (Ministers'

---

[56] Declaration of the Committee of Ministers on the Compliance with Commitments Accepted by Member States of the Council of Europe, adopted on 10 November 1994, in *ECHR Yearbook* XXXVII (1994) 461–462.
[57] For an overview, see *Monitoring of Compliance with Commitments Entered into by Council of Europe Member States: An Overview*, Monitor/Inf (99)2 (26 February 1999).
[58] *Supra*, note 56, Preamble.

Deputies) in April 1998,[59] the monitoring procedure now operates as follows. The first stage of the preparatory phase consists of the preparation and presentation of a country-by-country overview, drawn up by the Monitoring Unit. It is based on national contributions of between 5 and 10 pages in length, established in accordance with the "outline of basic issues." These are supplemented by short comments prepared by the Secretariat, in which the latter identifies issues which might merit further consideration. In preparing these comments, the Monitoring Unit relies on national contributions provided by the member states and on all relevant information it has been able to obtain. A provisional text containing national contributions and comments made by the Monitoring Unit are distributed to member states. Each state receives only the sections concerning it. Bilateral contacts then take place between delegations of member states and the Monitoring Unit. The relevant authorities in each member state are able to propose corrections and updates to the provisional texts before a specific deadline. The final overview drawn up by the Monitoring Unit, containing national contributions and the short comments made by the Secretariat through the Monitoring Unit, are then released – as a confidential document – according to a schedule approved by the Committee of Ministers at the outset.

Circulation of the overview is followed by the second stage, which consists of debate on compliance, by member states, with commitments entered into. At least three meetings of the Ministers' Deputies must be devoted every year to the question of monitoring. The preparatory phase comes to a close after those discussions. The Chairman of the Ministers' Deputies then has the possibility to present a summary. The first stage of the operational phase takes the form of conclusions. Any Chairman's summary is supplemented by a set of conclusions agreed upon by the Deputies, which take the form of "decisions." After the Committee of Ministers' conclusions comes the final stage in the procedure, consisting of follow-up. This can take a number of forms, such as adjustments to intergovernmental work, review of the cooperation programmes on the "Activities for the Development and Consolidation of Democratic Stability", and "specific action" as envisaged in paragraph 4 of the 1994 Declaration.[60] The

---

[59] Decision to Re-Adjust and Streamline the Committee of Ministers' Monitoring Procedure, taken by the Ministers' Deputies at their 630th meeting on 29–30 April 1998. For background information, consult documents *Compliance with Commitments Entered into by Member States: Information Concerning the Committee of Ministers' Monitoring Procedure, Document Prepared by the Secretary-General's Monitoring Unit*, Monitor/Inf (97)2 rev. (26 June 1997) and *Compliance with Commitments Accepted by Member States of the Council of Europe: Committee of Ministers' Monitoring Procedures Instituted in November 1994, Chairman's Conclusions Following the 591st Meeting of the Ministers' Deputies, 30 April 1997*, CM Misc(97)15 rev. (13 May 1997). A detailed description of how the procedure operated up to April 1998 is provided in *Compliance with Commitments Entered into by Member States: Development of the Committee of Ministers' Monitoring Procedure*, Monitor/Inf (98)2 (23 November 1998). See also: *Monitoring of Compliance with Commitments Entered into by Council of Europe Member States: An Overview*, Monitor/Inf(99)2 (26 February 1999).

[60] *Supra*, note 56. Paragraph 4 of the 1994 Declaration states that:
The Committee of Ministers, in cases requiring specific action, may decide to: request the Secretary General to make contacts, collect information or furnish advice; issue an opinion or recommendation; forward a communication to the Parliamentary Assembly; take any other decision within its statutory powers.

The procedure laid down in paragraph 4 has not yet been used.

Parliamentary Assembly is informed of any decision regarding follow-up.[61]

It is premature to draw conclusions from this initiative because the greater part of these activities are not made public. The only documents in the public domain are the documents issued separately by the Monitoring Unit, by the Secretariat of the Committee of Ministers, or those transmitted, for information, to the Parliamentary Assembly.[62] The "confidential" documents, with a strictly limited distribution, consist of comments issued by the Monitoring Unit and summary records of the Ministers' Deputies' discussions on the subject of monitoring, as well as additional comments received from member states. Although they are classified, as most other "confidential" documents of the Committee of Ministers, they are in fact distributed – in sealed envelopes – to a limited number of persons who are directly involved in the Committee of Ministers monitoring exercise. All other documents concerning the Committee of Ministers monitoring procedure, which include observations and suggestions made by delegations on how monitoring should be undertaken and which subjects should be dealt with, proposals made by the Secretariat, as well as all other pertinent documents issued on this subject by the Secretariat of the Committee of Ministers, such as Chairman's summing-up of discussions, and records are confidential.[63] Apart from this, the monitoring system does not provide the Committee of Ministers with more powers than it already had. It also may result in even less willingness on the part of the member states to make use of the inter-state complaint mechanism under Article 24 of the European Convention. The new mechanism has, however, the advantage that it may create a platform for the Committee of Ministers and the member states to discuss and examine on a structural basis the human rights situation in all member states of the Council of Europe. It also provides a more convenient tool for the member states to employ a kind of "early warning system" when there are indications that one of the member states does not fulfil its obligations. If the member states are fully aware of their responsibilities concerning the collective enforcement of human rights, the new mechanism may add a new dimension to the protection of human rights in Europe. In the more than 50 years of its existence, there have been situations in which silent diplomacy might have had a better result than the existing complaint procedures.

---

[61] For detailed information see: *Compliance with Commitments Entered into by Member States: Vademecum on the Committee of Minsters' Monitoring Procedure*, Monitor/Inf (99)3 (1 March 1999).
[62] To date, only two such document has been issued, *Compliance with Commitments Accepted by Member States of the Council of Europe: Committee of Ministers' Monitoring Procedures Instituted in November 1994, Chairman's Conclusions Following the 591st Meeting of the Ministers' Deputies, 30 April 1997*, CM Misc(97)15 rev. (13 May 1997) and *Compliance with Member States' Commitments, Committee of Ministers Declaration of 10 November 1994, Capital Punishment: Information Submitted by State, Secretariat Memorandum Prepared by the Secretary-General's Monitoring Unit*, AS/Inf (1999)2 (26 April 1999) and "decisions adopted" by the Ministers' Deputies, which can also be consulted on the Internet (i.e., the texts of decisions adopted at meetings of the Deputies: Committee of Ministers Web site: http://www.coe.fr/cm). These decisions include a number of replies to Parliamentary Assembly Recommendations concerning monitoring.
[63] See for more information: *Compliance with Member States' Commitments: "Decisions" Taken within the Context of the Committee of Ministers' Monitoring Procedure*, Monitor Inf/(99)5, (21 September 1999).

(7) What makes the European system work?

The answer is not to be found in the hierarchical structure of the European supervisory mechanism and the supervisory role of the Committee of Ministers. The encouraging result of the European Convention's mechanism is, in my opinion, mainly the result of the status given to the European Convention in the hierarchy of domestic laws. This is mainly true for those states where the European Convention has direct effect.[64] Even in states where the provisions of the European Convention are not directly applicable, the European Convention may produce effect via the judgments of national courts if, and insofar as, the latter gives a certain "reflex effect" to the European Convention. This means that if national courts cannot apply the European Convention directly and are unable to refrain from applying any rules of national law contrary thereto, they will interpret those rules in such a way that they are consistent with the European Convention. This has been pointed out by Andrew Drzemczewski in his study on the domestic effect of the European Convention, in which he states with respect to the United Kingdom, for example, "the operative provisions of the decisions of the European Court of Human Rights in cases in which the United Kingdom is a party bind the authorities on the international plane under Article 53 [new Article 46(2)] of the Convention."[65] Another reason may be that the decision-making organs and the courts of the member states are willing to comply with the rulings of the European Convention in order to prevent any future finding by the European Court of a violation of the Convention. In general, the domestic authorities of the parties to the European Convention cooperate faithfully with the Strasbourg organs.

Although a judgment of the European Court binds only the state which is a party to the case, it frequently happens that states which are not directly affected by a Court judgment draw legislative or other consequences from it. They are aware that they too risk a conviction by the European Court if they allow similar situations to continue. Proceedings will therefore also be followed closely by states other than those directly involved. In that respect, the decisions of the Strasbourg organs have, apart from a corrective affect, also a preventive effect. For example, the Supreme Court of the Netherlands addressed the question of custody of infants. The Supreme Court held that legislation in matters of custody of infants, although originally intended to apply in cases of legitimate children only, had to be interpreted as applying equally to cases of illegitimate children.[66] The Supreme Court held that the circle of relatives eligible for appointment to guardianship should be widened to include members of the "illegitimate family." The decision did not overrule the statutory provision, but was presented as an interpretation adapted to social change. It nevertheless deviated distinctly from the prevailing practice. The Supreme Court argued that views regarding the difference between legitimate and illegitimate children recently had changed

---

[64] *Supra*, note 54 at 848.
[65] Andrew Drzemczewski, *European Human Rights Convention in Domestic Law: A Comparative Study*, Oxford (1983) at 316. Note that in 1998 the United Kingdom passed *The Human Rights Act, 1998*, 1998 Chapter 42 "to give further effect to rights and freedoms guaranteed under the European Convention on Human Rights" (preamble).
[66] Netherlands Judgment No. 463 (1980) (Netherlands Supreme Court).

greatly. To support its argument, the Supreme Court referred to the judgment of 13 June 1979 in *Marckx v. Belgium*[67] and the interpretation given there of Article 8 of the European Convention in conjunction with Article 14. On that ground it annulled a decision of the District Court rendered before the *Marckx v. Belgium* judgment was even delivered. The Supreme Court did not find it necessary to wait for the amendment of the national law, which was in progress. Another example is *Brogan v. The United Kingdom*[68] concerning detention on remand and the right to be brought promptly before a judge or officer authorized by law to exercise judicial power in order to decide on the lawfulness of the deprivation of liberty. Although the United Kingdom was found to be in violation, Dutch authorities realized that their legislation also needed to be amended.

It should also be stressed that sometimes governments found to have been in violation of the provisions of the European Convention react in a less constructive and cooperative way. The answer of the government of the United Kingdom to the above-mentioned *Brogan v The United Kingdom* case is one example. Turkey has been found in violation of several provisions of the European Convention, including the prohibition of torture and inhuman treatment.[69] The Turkish government reacted by making furious statements that the European Court had overstepped its competence. There is also *Loukanov v. Turkey*, the first case from East and Central Europe to reach the European Court. The European Court found unanimously that there has been a violation of the European Convention. This judgment is significant for the judicial interpretation of the term "reasonable suspicion" and the power of the prosecutor to detain anyone in Bulgaria.[70] Following the judgment, the National Television of Bulgaria showed the public statement of the Prosecutor General of Bulgaria concerning the decision. He stated that the judgment might not have the force of a validly pronounced judicial act, that it was inadmissible from the point of view of the procedure, and that the judgment was unlawful. Further, he declared that the European Court had gone beyond its jurisdiction by assessing whether a detention was lawful or not under the Bulgarian law, and that the judgment constituted an infringement of the basic principle of independence of Bulgarian judicial power. He called it a judicial absurdity. Too much weight should not be attributed to such reactions. Statements such as those of the Prosecutor General are made mainly for political reasons on the home front. It should be noted that the Bulgarian government has stated that it will abide by the European Court decision. In the long run, defaulting states will take the measures necessary to execute the Court's judgments because unless they do, they will be found in violation in the near future, when similar complaints are lodged by applicants in analogous situations.

(8) Concluding remarks

In the 1990's fifteen Central and Eastern European states joined the Council of Europe. Their requests for membership have been accepted, notwithstanding the

---

[67] *Marckx v. Belgium, supra* note 26.
[68] *Brogan v. The United Kingdom, supra* note 50.
[69] See in this respect, *Loizidou v. Turkey*, Series A, Volume 310 (23 March 1995); *Yagci and Saragin v. Turkey*, Series A, Volume 319 (8 June 1995); *Akdivar and Others v. Turkey*, Series A, Volume 1996-IV (16 September 1996); and *Aksoy v. Turkey*, Series A, Volume 1996-VI (18 December 1996).
[70] *Lukanov v. Bulgaria*, Series A, Volume 1997-II (20 March 1997).

fact that some member states occasionally expressed doubts about their ability to meet the standards of the Council of Europe. Some of these new democracies have also ratified the European Convention.[71] This will increase the workload of the Strasbourg organs dramatically, and will lead inevitably to delays in the hearing of cases on the merits. It can take two years for a decision as to admissibility to be reached and it will usually be five years before the various stages of proceeding are completed and a final decision given. Such delays are unacceptable and may undermine public confidence in the system of the European Convention. There is some doubt that the reform of the supervisory mechanism under Protocol No. 11 will provide a sufficient remedy in this respect.[72]

When the enforcement machinery under the European Convention was reformed, it was the appropriate moment to pay attention to some of the above-mentioned weaknesses of the European Convention. Under Article 15 of the European Convention, a state may limit the application of many of the substantive rights of the European Convention in certain well-defined and exceptional circumstances. Although states may choose to make use of these possibilities, this rarely happens. With the enlargement of the membership of the Council of Europe, there are indications that the situation is becoming worse. Both the former supervisory mechanism and the reformed system under Protocol No. 11 do not provide a means to control reservations or derogations when they are made. This possibility only occurs once a complaint has been lodged.

The supervisory role entrusted to the Secretary-General of the Council of Europe under Article 52 of the European Convention has hardly been exploited. Under this provision, it is possible to request that any contracting party "furnish an explanation of the manner in which its internal law ensures the effective implementation of any of the provision of [the] Convention."[73] In comparison with most other treaties on human rights which include the obligation that contracting states submit reports, the provision of Article 52 of the European Convention is very brief and leaves a great number of questions unanswered. Contracting states have been invited five times to submit reports on the application of the rights laid down in the European Convention, in October 1964, in July 1970, in April 1975, in March 1983 and in July 1988. The Secretary-General of the Council of Europe should make use of his competence under Article 52 of the European Convention much more frequently.

It is clear that the Council of Europe lacks a mechanism under which the member states can be kept under constant surveillance to ensure their compliance with the commitments accepted within the Council of Europe. On 10 November 1994, the Committee of Ministers tried to fill this gap and adopted the 1994 Declaration. This declaration envisages a political mechanism under which the Members of the Council of Europe, its Secretary-General or its Parliamentary Assembly may refer questions of implementation of commitments concerning

---

[71] The European Convention has now been ratified by Albania, Bulgaria, Croatia, the Czech Republic, Estonia, Georgia, Hungary, Latvia, Lithuania, Poland, Republic of Moldova, Romania, Russian Federation, Slovenia, Slovakia, The Former Yugoslav Republic of Macedonia, and Ukraine.
[72] *Supra*, note 49 at 34–36.
[73] See in this respect Paul Mahoney, "Does Article 57 of the European Convention on Human Rights Serve Any Useful Purpose?", in *Protecting Human Rights: The European Dimension – Studies in Honour of Gerard Wiarda*, supra note 7, 373–393.

the situations of democracy, human rights and the rule of law to the Committee of Ministers. On 20 April 1995, the Committee of Ministers adopted the procedure for implementing the 1994 Declaration. When considering issues, the Committee of Ministers will take account of all relevant information available from different sources such as the Parliamentary Assembly and the OSCE. This mechanism will not affect the existing procedures arising from statutory or conventional control mechanisms. At least three scheduled meetings per year of the Ministers' Deputies at A level will be devoted to this question. At the first meeting and again every second year, unless decided otherwise, the Secretary-General will present a factual overview of compliance with the commitments. The discussions will be confidential and held in camera "with a view to ensuring compliance with commitments, in the framework of a constructive dialogue."[74] Finally, in cases requiring specific action, the Committee of Ministers may decide to request that the Secretary-General make contacts, collect information or furnish advice; issue an opinion or recommendation; forward a communication to the Parliamentary Assembly or take any other decision within its statutory powers.[75] Whatever the effect of this mechanism may be, it does not provide the Committee of Ministers with more powers than it had previously.

Improvement in the enforcement of the Strasbourg decisions can be achieved by taking steps on the domestic level. In this respect, attention should be drawn to the possibility that review proceedings at the national level could be instituted to facilitate compliance with the Strasbourg decisions. Certain countries have express provisions relating to review,[76] while there are others where there might be possibilities for review.[77] The arguments for and against the possibility have been discussed in a study prepared by the Committee of Experts regarding the improvement of procedures for the protection of human rights.[78]

Many who have commented upon the UN Covenant on Civil and Political Rights[79] have pointed to the fact that this instrument is lacking a provision like Article 46 of the European Convention, in which a political body oversees the execution of a judicial body's decisions. This is a lacuna and efforts should be made to fill this gap. However, in the long run success depends on the willingness of the parties to cooperate in good faith with the supervisory organs. The success of the European system may be attributed in large part to the fact that there were more "good guys" than "bad guys."

---

[74] *Supra*, note 56 at para. 5.
[75] *Supra*, note 56 at para. 4.
[76] Review is possible in Austria, Luxembourg, Malta, Norway and Switzerland.
[77] These countries are Belgium, Cyprus, Denmark, Finland, France, Greece, Turkey and Hungary.
[78] See Council of Europe, "Study Prepared by the Committee of Experts for the Improvement of the Procedure for the Protection of Human Rights", 113(11–12) *Human Rights Law Journal* (1992) at 71.
[79] International Covenant on Civil and Political Rights, 999 UNTS 171 (in force 23 March 1976).

CHAPTER 21

Follow-Up in the ILO Context

Jane Hodges

The International Labour Organization (ILO) has no direct role concerning follow-up to the UN treaty bodies concluding observations. However, the ILO Committee of Experts on the Application of Conventions and Recommendations does use relevant concluding observations when it examines ratifying states' reports on the ILO human rights conventions such as Convention No. 87 on freedom of association;[1] No. 98 on collective bargaining;[2] No. 29 on forced labour;[3] No. 105 on the abolition of forced labour;[4] and particularly Convention No. 111 on the elimination of discrimination in employment and occupation.[5] An example is the observation made by the Committee of Experts concerning the Islamic Republic of Iran's application of Convention No. 111.[6] The Observation noted a concordance of several treaty bodies looking at Iranian reports plus resolutions adopted by the UN's functional commissions. The Committee of Experts used this ammunition from the treaty bodies and the functional commissions to add to its own assessment that the government was not complying with its obligations in the field of sex discrimination and religious minority discrimination. That made it a very powerful convergence of views. We can judge its impact by the Iranian government's angry reaction. It criticized the fact that the Committee of Experts, working in the field of labour and employment, had been exposed to the decisions of the treaty bodies. Its statement in the 1996 ILO conference discussion of its application of the ILO Convention objected to the politicization of certain UN bodies.[7] The ILO is part of the UN

---

[1] ILO Convention No. 87, Freedom of Association and Protection of the Right to Organize Convention, 48 UNTS 17 (in force 4 July 1950).
[2] ILO Convention No. 98, Right to Organize and Collective Bargaining Convention, 96 UNTS 257 (in force 18 July 1951).
[3] ILO Convention No. 29, Forced Labour Convention, 39 UNTS 55 (in force 1 May 1932).
[4] ILO Convention No. 105, Abolition of Forced Labour Convention, 320 UNTS 291 (in force 17 January 1959).
[5] ILO Convention No. 111, Discrimination (Employment and Occupation) Convention, 362 UNTS 31 (in force 15 June 1960).
[6] ILO Committee of Experts on the Application of Conventions and Recommendations, *Observations*, 1997. See also *Committee on Application of Standards Cites Labour Abuses in Iran, Myanmar, Morocco, Nigeria, Sudan and Swaziland*, ILO Press Release ILO/97/18 (19 June 1997).
[7] Statement by the government of Iran at the International Labour Conference, 84th session (1996).

system and the various ILO supervisory bodies will use all available public information, and in turn make it accessible to the various UN human rights expert bodies.

The ILO annual conference in June 1997 provides another example of follow-up of other human rights bodies' conclusions, albeit not those of the treaty bodies. The ILO Conference Committee on the Application of Standards, referring to work by the ILO Committee of Experts which were in turn based on decisions of the Special Rapporteur on the situation of human rights in Sudan, arrived at a decision concerning Convention No. 29's non-application in that country.[8] The Provisional Record to the decisions of UN bodies of the ILO's Conference Committee is an example of follow-up.

As regards follow-up of the ILO's own supervisory bodies' decisions, consider the Committee on Freedom of Association, which is the best known of the supervisory bodies. It has fast administration of justice and the benefit of tripartite practitioners – that is, workers' representatives, employers' representatives and government representatives – examining day-to-day practical freedom of association problems. The Committee prepares a publicly identifiable and well-publicized part of a report – called *Cases in Which the Committee Requests to be Kept Informed of Developments*, commonly known as "follow-up" cases. This follow-up procedure involves situations where a violation has been found, but either some form of settlement is underway, or there is an admission from the state that it has to remedy the problem and an undertaking to do so, and the Committee closes the case but wishes to be kept informed of what finally happens. It follows the case in a dogged, and very systematic, way. When information is provided from the government concerned on what has happened, it is published in the introduction to the Committee reports, under the heading "Effect Given to the Recommendations of the Committee on the Freedom of Association and the Governing Body."

There are between 20 and 30 separate paragraphs describing follow-up action on cases in any one session. There are three sessions per year, hence, considerable follow-up information is being fed back into the system. While it is true that not every one of those 20 to 30 paragraphs represents a perfect solution of the identified problem, it is a good sign that member states do send in the information requested and, more often than not, do respond positively to the recommendations made.

The information may concern legislative improvements – that is, laws that have been criticized or administrative practices that have been found lacking, have been repealed or ceased operating, or practical situations where individuals have been reinstated following findings of unfair dismissal. The sad part, of course, in any of these follow-up cases, is that you cannot bring back to life trade unionists or employer's representatives who have been killed because they tried to exercise their freedom of association rights.

A good example of how meticulous the tripartite Committee on Freedom of Association is on follow-up cases is Case No. 1074 against the United States. It concerned the 1981 strike, and subsequent dismissal of over 11,000 air traffic

---

[8] See the Provisional Record of the International Labour Conference, 85th session (1997). See also *Committee on Application of Standards Cites Labour Abuses in Iran, Myanmar, Morocco, Nigeria, Sudan and Swaziland*, at *supra* note 6.

controllers. The Committee, apart from its actual finding on the legality of the strike ban, asked the government to give information on all those dismissed air traffic controllers. The Committee stuck at it for over seven years until it was able to note that 460 reinstatements had been ordered, and until the last batch were able to have their appeals heard by the Merits Appeal Tribunal.

The Committee of Experts, the second standing body of the supervisory system of the ILO, also places much store in making public its follow-up actions and recommendations. Since the mid-1960's it has been publishing, in the introduction to its annual report, a list entitled "Cases of Progress." There are usually about 30 per session, and most often are linked to legislative progress, that is, repeal of non-complying legislation or amendment or cessation of administrative practices. To date over 2,100 such cases of progress have been registered, which is an impressive amount when compared to follow-up in the other international treaty systems.

Like the tripartite committee, the ILO Committee of Experts is extremely persistent in insisting that its proposals be followed-up. At its 1997 session, the Committee of Experts examined a problem regarding compensation for occupational diseases that had been looked at for almost 30 years. This was not exactly shining success, but the Committee of Expert's persistence led the government of New Zealand to request technical assistance so as to successfully resolve the question.

The third standing body, the ILO Conference Committee on the Application of Standards, is also very careful about follow-up to its findings and its procedures enjoy the additional weight of being able to have public hearings. In a public tripartite setting, the heads of delegations – who usually are the ministers of labour or secretaries of state for labour, or of an equally high political level – are invited in the few most serious cases, to come in person and explain the case. The procedure is not a litigious one, but represents an opportunity for government representatives to explain why a law has been drafted in such a way or why a practice is the way it is. Despite at times political or technical sensibilities, the procedure works. The ministers do come to engage in dialogue with the Conference Committee. At the 1997 session, out of the small number of extremely serious cases, seven ministers came and spoke, and had questions put to them from the workers' benches and the employers' benches and fellow governments. The 1997 Conference Committee provides an excellent example of follow-up. The Conference Committee adopted a record six "special paragraphs" which is a particular type of sanction in the ILO's system, the cases being highlighted in the general report indicating non-compliance with a particular convention. They receive a great deal of publicity and in this case were adopted with respect to Myanmar, Morocco, Nigeria, the Islamic Republic of Iran, Sudan, and Swaziland. Moreover, of the six special paragraphs, three were singled out, Myanmar, Sudan, and Nigeria, for the ultimate "sanction" in ILO terms. They were named as cases of continued failure to implement a ratified convention, again in a special section of the Conference Committee's general report. When the Conference Committee's report was adopted, the public gallery was full of persons representing the press, interested non-governmental organizations (NGOs), pressure groups, and students, taking note of the ILO's calls for follow-up action.

Another set of procedures, which includes similar, successful follow-up proposals, is the article 24 "representation" and article 26 "complaint" procedures.

These are two articles of the ILO Constitution[9] allowing different groups to allege violations of specific ratified conventions. The findings of both of those types of procedures are fed back into the normal reporting system for follow-up by the Committee of Experts.

Overall, these different bodies carry out systematic and very persistent follow-up of their recommendations. Follow-up does not end after one particular procedure is closed. The procedures dovetail together to give extra strength to the follow-up.

Perhaps the most important element of the follow-up action carried out by all three bodies, whether it be the Committee on Freedom of Association, the Committee of Experts, or the Conference Committee, is the use of technical cooperation: the offer of assistance through the ILO's operational activities to resolve the particular violation which has been identified.

Some, particularly from the workers' benches, and the occupational NGOs, feel that this takes the sting out of the supervisory system, but the ILO believes that the use of technical cooperation has in fact given strength to the whole system. It is not a system based on blacklists or condemnations. On the contrary, the aim of the ILO system is to improve the implementation of specific ratified instruments and to be capable of backing up findings of non-compliance with offers of assistance.

Lastly, the point should be made that the Secretariat has, under the ILO's Director-General, stepped up publicity and public awareness of the supervisory systems, their working methods and decisions, and, follow-up proposals. The Office has a computerized database (ILOLEX), where all these decisions appear in the three working languages of the ILO.

Publicity is also encouraged through the field structure. The ILO has fourteen multidisciplinary teams, as distinguished from the regional offices. These are teams comprising specialists in various areas, one of which is international standards and labour law. Whenever a supervisory body comes to a decision, the field staff receives copies of those decisions immediately after the relevant meeting. They might not have to make specific reference to each such finding, but they are clearly informed about what the expert bodies have said, so that they can assist, if requested, in follow-up action.

Similarly, successful follow-up requires cooperation between all the human rights bodies of the UN system. For example, whenever the United Nations Development Programme country teams are looking at a specific country's needs and problems, the ILO participants will have the most up-to-date information about that country's implementation of ratified instruments in the labour field. The ILO has had both successes and failures of its follow-up procedures, although ultimately its only "sanctions" are the mobilization of international embarrassment and public pressure.

---

[9] Constitution of the International Labour Organization, Treaty of Versailles, Part XIII, UKTS 4 (in force 10 January 1920).

CHAPTER 22

Follow-Up of Treaty Body Conclusions by the Treaty Bodies and the UN Mechanisms Beyond

Bert G. Ramcharan*

(1) Law

The organization with the most extensive experience to date in dealing with the implementation of international norms is the International Labour Organization (ILO). In a review of its first 50 years of efforts to promote the application of international labour standards, the ILO Committee of Experts on the Application of Standards insisted on the obligation of all states, regardless of their political, economic, or social system, or of their level of development, to implement their treaty obligations faithfully.[1] This is the essential starting point in considering the obligations of states to respect their commitments under international human rights treaties and in addressing issues of follow-up action.

The duty of states to implement treaty obligations may entail obligations of result or obligations of conduct. The former may give rise to situations in which a result obligatory under an international human rights treaty has not been achieved, or there has been a finding of breach in respect of a particular right. The latter may arise in respect of the duty to pursue a course of action for the progressive implementation of a particular right or rights. Obligations of result and obligations of conduct may need different types of follow-up action.

In considering the issue of follow-up action, legal considerations such as the following, must be borne in mind:

- Supervisory organs under human rights conventions may deal with violations of human rights in their respective treaties not only in the light of the applicable treaty provisions but also in the light of the international customary law of state responsibility. The specific implementation machinery established under each treaty does not exclude the application of the regime of state responsibility provided for by international customary law. While the latter cannot supplant treaty-based implementation machinery, it can reinforce and complement it.

---
*The views expressed are those of the author solely in his personal capacity.
[1] See the *Report of the ILO Committee of Experts on the Application of Standards*, 50th session of the ILO Conference, Report 3 (1966).

- If a state party has been found in breach of its obligations under a human rights treaty, other states parties may take appropriate individual or collective measures to encourage the defaulting state to bring its breach to an end and to discharge its ensuing responsibilities.
- Issues of international criminal responsibility may also be involved in the follow-up stage.

There is thus much legally, that may be involved by way of follow-up action. What course of action is actually pursued will be influenced by the particular circumstances of each state party.

(2) Practicality

States which have ratified international human rights treaties fall broadly into four categories: those well advanced on the road to implementing their treaty obligations; those somewhat advanced; those at the starting point; and those only preparing to approach the starting point. This places a premium on cooperation, persuasion, capacity-building and technical assistance – while maintaining, as a point of departure, the principle that the duty of states is to fulfil the obligations which they have signed. In practice, therefore, legal considerations pertaining to the obligations of states and the nature of follow-up action may have to be adjusted in light of what states can do realistically.[2]

(3) Policy

Follow-up action may take a number of forms. In addition to the suggestions of Markus Schmidt, reference could also be made to two experiments tried in the late 1970's and the mid-1980's: follow-up efforts in the Third Committee of the United Nations General Assembly in respect of views handed down by the Human Rights Committee under the Optional Protocol to the International Covenant on Civil and Political Rights;[3] and follow-up efforts in the meeting of states parties to the International Covenant on Civil and Political Rights (CCPR).[4] Broader follow-up action, could also entail: the designation of regional advisers for human rights standards, follow-up by non-governmental organizations (NGOs), and follow-up by the development agencies of the United Nations system.

---

[2] See in general: Charles de Visscher's connection between theory and reality: *Theory and Reality in Public International Law*, Princeton University Press (1968).
[3] First Optional Protocol to the International Covenant on Civil and Political Rights, 999 UNTS 171 (in force 23 March 1976). See *Letter dated 1 November 1979 from the Permanent Representative of Panama to the United Nations Secretary-General*, A/C3/34/6 (1 November 1979); and Bert G. Ramcharan, "State Responsibility for Violations of Human Rights Treaties", in *Contemporary Problems of International Law: Essays in Honour of Georg Schwarzenberger on his Eightieth Birthday*, Bin Cheng and Edward D. Brown (eds.), Steven & Sons (1988) 242–261.
[4] International Covenant on Civil and Political Rights, 999 UNTS 171 (in force 23 March 1976). See Bert G. Ramcharan (ed.), *The Principle of Legality in International Human Rights Institutions*, Martinus Nijhoff (1997).

(a) *Regional advisers for international human rights standards*

The evolution of models for the promotion and protection of human rights from the mid-1970s to the mid-1990s involves the methodical development of efforts to: broaden fact-finding through the use of special rapporteurs and direct contacts; promote human rights awareness through education and the dissemination of information; deal with post-violation reconstruction; and develop technical assistance related to the application of international standards. This was the reason the trust fund for advisory services was established in 1987. Such efforts were also directed at the establishment of the Office of the High Commissioner for Human Rights.[5]

One part of the strategic thrust in the creative period of the late-1970s to the mid-1980s that was not successfully implemented for financial reasons, was the establishment of a system of regional advisors for international human rights standards. The model in mind at the time was the ILO system of regional advisors for international labour standards, through which ILO specialists on international labour standards were deployed in different regions of the world. Relying on studies done within the Norms and Standards Department on what was needed in each state to follow-up on the ratification and implementation of international labour standards, the regional advisors kept in regular touch with governments, advised them on legislation, consulted with them on problems encountered, and were generally available to each country to help it move along the path towards implementation.

The then Centre for Human Rights (now Office of the High Commissioner for Human Rights) proposed the establishment of such a system of regional advisors for international human rights standards to the leadership of the United Nations in the mid-1980s, but was asked to hold back the idea because the United Nations was then undergoing financial problems. The idea was never resurrected. In the Centre's view, the establishment of a system of regional advisors for international human rights standards was one of the key policy options for future follow-up action.

The ILO has since modified its system, and specialists in international labour standards are now part of ILO regional multi-disciplinary teams. In 2000 they are present in all of the 13 multi-disciplinary teams: Abidjan, Addis Ababa, Bangkok, Beirut, Dakar, Harare, Lima, Manila, Moscow, New Delhi, Port of Spain, San José and Santiago. They assist their national constituents in fulfilling their standards-related obligations and ensuring that all due consultations take place among governments, employers and workers. They also contribute to the work of the teams by promoting the integration of standards' considerations into the formulation of country objectives and the elaboration and execution of technical cooperation projects and programmes.

The International Labour Standards Department assists in this process by supplying the necessary technical back-up to the standards specialists, enabling headquarters officials to undertake missions where standards specialists are not available to deal with particular problems, and by systematically contributing to the country objectives papers drafted by the teams or by ILO area offices.

---

[5] For an account of the emplacement of this strategy, see "Courage and Conviction. One Man's Crusade for Human Rights", 4 *Human Rights Tribune* (1997) 15–17.

This helps to ensure that the necessary attention is given to problems in the application of ratified conventions and to the need to promote other relevant conventions, particularly those identified as a priority by the ILO Governing Body, including those on fundamental workers' rights. In addition, the department holds national workshops for team members and other ILO field staff designed to ensure familiarity with the standard-setting and supervisory procedures and to explain their importance to the overall work of the teams.

The United Nations programme of advisory services is less focused in this sense than that of the ILO. Some technical assistance is targeted at follow-up activities required under international human rights conventions. There are also some field offices in the particular countries, but their focus is more general than in the case of the ILO specialists on standards. The broad scope of the UN programme of advisory services comes out in the following statement of United Nations objectives in its proposed budget document for 1998–1999:

> In the area of advisory services and technical cooperation, the objectives are to assist countries, at their request, in developing comprehensive national plans of action to promote and protect human rights, to provide advice and to support specific projects to promote respect for human rights; to develop a comprehensive and coordinated United Nations programme to help States in building and strengthening national structures for human rights promotion and protection; and to raise awareness and promote specialized knowledge about human rights through the organization of training courses, seminars and workshops, and the production of a wide range of educational, training and information material.[6]

When the then Centre for Human Rights launched the idea of a voluntary fund for advisory services in 1987, the central strategic idea was to monitor the consideration of states' reports in treaty bodies, such as the Human Rights Committee and, together with members of the Committee, identify countries in need which could be approached discretely. The main reason for launching the voluntary fund was to link it with follow-up action related to the implementation of human rights conventions. It was the Centre's view that this should be the central focus of United Nations programmes of advisory services and technical assistance and that it is precisely the area of follow-up action where more focused attention should be given.

(b) Follow-up by the development agencies of the United Nations system

In the 1970's when the then Centre for Human Rights approached the United Nations Development Programme (UNDP) and the Director-General for Development and International Economic Cooperation to integrate human rights considerations into their work, it was politely signaled to desist. These days, however, agencies of the United Nations system, such as UNDP, have come to realize that unless they address issues of governance, democratization, the rule of law and respect for human rights, they are pouring money down the drain. UNDP, in particular, is placing emphasis increasingly on issues of governance. When the United Nations Secretary-General launched the Special

---

[6] *United Nations Proposed Programme Budget for the Biennial 1998–1999*, A/52/6/Rev.1 (30 May 1997) Vol. 1, at item 22.

Initiative for Africa in 1996, governance was identified as one of the four core themes in recognition of the fact that the strengthening of both the public sector and civil society is fundamental to much of the development process. The issue of governance has occupied centre stage in UNDP's strategy in the post-Cold War period. UNDP organized its first forum on Governance in Africa in Addis Ababa in July 1997. A UNDP paper prepared for the forum conceptualized governance in the following terms:

> 21. Governance should indeed be seen in a much broader perspective than government and its system. It should encompass the overall direction and management of a country's affairs in accordance with its established constitution, its institutions, its established procedures and practices, and its cultural and historical background. The dimension of cultural values and historical experiences cannot be discounted in favour of a monolithic and universally applicable format.
> 22. In conceptualizing Governance therefore, the view is taken that it should be seen as the totality of the exercise of authority in the management of a country's affairs, comprised of the complex mechanisms, processes, and institutions through which citizens and groups articulate their interests, exercise their legal rights and mediate their differences. It encompasses the political, economic, legal, judicial, social, technological and administrative authority and therefore comprises the government, the private sector and the civil society. The private sector and to a larger extent civil society have important roles to play since the consent to govern is derived primarily from these two sectors.[7]

In the future, the UNDP and other development agencies of the United Nations system intend to deploy more and more of their resources to programmes of governance. As the UNDP country offices go about the implementation of governance programmes, the core human rights conventions should be at the heart of their work and follow-up activities related to capacity-building and structural issues of governance should be an integral part of their activities.

Every UNDP country office should have either an officer specializing in international human rights standards or should be regularly visited by one of the regional advisers on international human rights standards suggested in the preceding section. The core international human rights treaties, such as the two Covenants[8] on human rights, indicate human rights strategies of governance that should be at the heart of the activities of governments themselves, and of agencies such as UNDP. It is hard to see how an agency like UNDP could address issues of governance, within the framework of its own conceptualization as related above, without proceeding from the starting point of the international Covenants. As part of this reasoning, when recommendations for follow-up action are made by treaty bodies, the governance sectors of UNDP country offices must be mobilized and put to service.

---

[7] United Nations Development Programme, *The African Governance Forum: A Conceptual Framework* (3 December 1998) at paras. 21 and 22. Available on the Internet at www.undp.org/rba/special/framewrk.htm.
[8] The CCPR, *supra* note 4, and the International Covenant on Economic, Social and Cultural Rights (CESCR), 993 UNTS 3 (in force 3 January 1976).

(c) NGO follow-up activities

Within the international human rights community – consisting of governments, international organizations, regional organizations, non-governmental organizations, and educational institutions – the NGOs are by far the most dynamic sector, operating within the normative framework they helped to shape. The NGOs are closest to the peoples of the world and push the most insistently for human rights compliance. When the CCPR came into force, the NGOs had to struggle to demonstrate that they could provide members of the Human Rights Committee with information on conditions within states whose reports were being considered. It has since come to be understood by all concerned that without NGO information, supervisory bodies would hardly be able to go about the consideration of states' reports in a meaningful manner.

NGO activities with respect to follow-up actions have not kept pace with their efforts to provide information to members of monitoring bodies. In the earlier days, NGOs did try to provide information within countries, on reports submitted by their governments, as well as on the results of their consideration in human rights bodies, and decisions handed down in particular cases. This was not sustained in a systematic way over the years, however. It often happens that a state report is considered in a treaty body, significant comments and recommendations are made, and this remains largely unknown within the country concerned. This situation needs to change and it is the NGOs which must help to effect that change. NGOs will need to consider how they can facilitate or contribute to arrangements whereby, for each country considered by a human rights monitoring body, the reports submitted, comments and recommendations made, and follow-up action required, are disseminated within the country itself.

This is not an easy task in view of the multiplicity of human rights instruments – including those of the ILO and the UN Economic, Social and Cultural Organization (UNESCO) – and the multiplicity of supervisory bodies. It will undoubtedly be a burdensome enterprise to inform the population of each country about the findings and recommendations of treaty bodies and it may be necessary, in the future, to address the issue of the great number of reporting requirements and of supervisory bodies. For the immediate future, it may be necessary to concentrate on the core instruments. The point remains, though, that unless the NGOs get involved, follow-up action will not proceed adequately or effectively.

(4) Concluding observations

Policies and strategies for follow-up action are part of the same problematique involved in advancing the implementation of international human rights conventions generally. The organizing principle must be the centrality of human rights, their integration in all parts of the activities of governments, international organizations and regional organizations, and the need to pursue strategies of governance inspired in their conception and guided in their application by the International Bill of Human Rights[9] and other international human rights

---

[9] The International Bill of Human Rights consists of three documents: the CCPR, *supra* note 4; the CESCR, *supra* note 8; and the Universal Declaration of Human Rights, G.A. Res. 217 A (III), adopted on 10 December 1948.

treaties. From this perspective, the integration of human rights components within governance programmes is key to implementation as well as to follow-up. The presence of specialists on international human rights standards in all regions of the world, available to all governments on an on-going basis, is crucial to implementation as well as to follow-up. The role of NGOs in informing and mobilizing the populace in each country is basic and crucial to efforts for follow-up action. The mobilization of NGOs on behalf of human rights is crucial to the human rights endeavour, to the entrenchment of a universal culture of human rights, to the promotion and protection of human rights, and to the corrective action that is the essence of any follow-up.

VI. The Future of the Human Rights Treaty System: Forging Recommendations

CHAPTER 23

The Future of the Human Rights Treaty System: Forging Recommendations

Elizabeth Evatt

(1) Introduction

For a system that was intended to last indefinitely, the UN human rights treaty system was not well planned. It has grown haphazardly, in response to different needs and pressures and its outcomes are often disappointing. Most agree that major reforms are essential. But first, it should be asked what the system is for and whether it is still needed. Should it be scrapped, leaving human rights to regional systems or to national action?

My preferred answer to that question is that human rights as envisaged in the UN Charter[1] imply universal standards. The UN system was intended to provide a legal framework in which to pursue the ideals of the Charter. Universality of rights was reaffirmed by the World Conference in 1993 in Vienna.[2] To be meaningful, the universality of rights needs to be supported by an effective global human rights treaty system. Whether regional human rights systems could, in the long run, displace the need for a global system is open to doubt. In the foreseeable future, however, regional mechanisms are not a practical alternative.

As for leaving human rights to individual states, it seems hardly necessary to belabour the point that it is the abuse and neglect of rights by so many of their number which has forced states to accept, at least on paper, collective responsibility to ensure respect for human rights standards. Unfortunately, the factors that make it necessary to have international mechanisms, namely the extent of state violations, also work against the effectiveness of the system. While states will agree that there are violations, they are reluctant to create an effective system that may condemn them or their allies by name.

The realities are that, despite their many ratifications, most states are indifferent to the international human rights system, and do not want it to have effective power. Many do not take their obligations seriously; they do not report,

---

[1] United Nations Charter, 1 UNTS xvi (in force 24 October 1945) arts. 1(3), 55(c), 62(2).
[2] *Vienna Declaration and Programme of Action*, A/CONF.157/23 (12 July 1993) at para.1.

report late or in a perfunctory manner; they do not cooperate in the communications procedure; they pay no attention to the recommendations of the treaty body in regard to reports or communications. They are unwilling to ensure that the system has sufficient resources to carry out its functions,[3] despite the obvious importance of human rights in the UN Charter. Further, states do not particularly care whether another state is or is not fulfilling its obligations, though there are some exceptions. Their lack of real concern is reflected in the tired language of the human rights resolutions passed year after year by the UN Commission on Human Rights and the General Assembly.

The defects in the system do not rest entirely with states. There are flaws in the procedures of the treaty bodies. The reporting procedures are drawn out, ineffective and repetitive and the recommendations are often too vague or impractical. The communications procedures are too prolonged to provide real redress for serious violations, and there is a relatively low level of compliance with the determinations of the treaty bodies.

The financial crisis, for which member states are largely responsible, has imposed severe resource restraints on the UN Secretariat and consequently on the treaty bodies themselves.[4] Ironically, the reporting system is saved from seizing up only by the fact that many states have not fulfilled their reporting obligations. The effectiveness of the system is further undermined by the proliferation of instruments and standards.

Other failings are that the system as a whole is inaccessible to the community; most people whose rights are at issue do not even know of the existence of the instruments, let alone the treaty bodies. Even non-governmental organizations (NGOs) do not use the system to the extent that could be expected. The communications procedures are not used by many who would have grounds to do so.

(2) Is change possible?

It is clear enough that change is needed. The real question is whether there is any will to overcome the current problems. Major reforms would require commitment and action from those with the power to affect outcomes, primarily the states themselves. Ultimately the states would have to agree on amendments to the instruments to give the treaty bodies effective power, to ensure that they had

---

[3] International Covenant on Civil and Political Rights, 999 UNTS 171 (in force 23 March 1976) (CCPR), art. 36: The Secretary-General of the United Nations shall provide the necessary staff and facilities for the effective performance of the functions of the Committee under the present Convention. See also, Convention on the Elimination of All Forms of Discrimination Against Women, 1249 UNTS 13 (in force 3 September 1981) (CEDAW) art.17(9); and the Convention on the Rights of the Child, 1577 UNTS 3 (in force 2 September 1990) (CRC) art. 43(11). Different arrangements have applied to the other bodies: Convention on the Elimination of All Forms of Racial Discrimination, 660 UNTS 195 (in force 4 January 1969) (CERD) arts. 8(6), 10(3); and the Convention Against Torture and Other Cruel, Inhuman or Degrading Treatment or Punishment, 1465 UNTS 85 (in force 26 June 1987) (CAT) arts. 17(7), 18(5).

[4] For instance, in recent times staff has been reassigned from time to time, meetings have been cancelled, interpretation has been restricted, summary records not prepared and there have been delays in translation of reports. See also *Report of the Human Rights Committee*, A/52/40 (1997) at paras. 19 and 463–465; *Report of the Human Rights Committee*, A/53/40 (1998) at paras. 22 and 429–432; and *Report of the Human Rights Committee*, A/54/40 (1999) at paras.28 and 395–397.

the resources and independence to use that power effectively. There is little evidence of the states bringing their collective will to bear upon these problems.

Since the system and its ideals are worth preserving, it seems that it will be left largely to the treaty bodies to carry out their own reforms, individually or, preferably, in conjunction with each other and with the support of NGOs and the few sympathetic and supportive states. But will the efforts of the treaty bodies be worthwhile if the states ultimately do not take seriously their own obligations, those of other states or the recommendations of the supervisory bodies?

The treaty bodies must take seriously all issues which bear upon the effectiveness of their work. Consistently with that obligation, the treaty bodies must do their utmost to ensure that the states fulfil their treaty obligations, and they must do so conscientiously and with full commitment to the principles of impartiality.[5] The integrity of the committees, their own acceptance of high ethical standards and their insistence on quality in all their work are the only real weapons they have. They must use them, even in the knowledge that states have the power to nominate and elect members and are willing to do so without regard to the needs of the treaty bodies or their effective functioning.

The challenge to the treaty bodies is not a simple one. It extends from their internal rules and codes of conduct, necessary to maintain the transparency and integrity of their proceedings, through all aspects of their mandate, to cooperation with other bodies and with NGOs. Inevitably, the treaty bodies must act together to strengthen their effectiveness. To achieve their goals, they will have to beg for resources from within the system or act on their own initiative to secure resources from outside the system.[6]

Improvements are needed in virtually all aspects of the system – in the reporting processes, in the communications procedures and in liaison with NGOs.

(3) How can the reporting process be made effective?

The reporting system is common to all treaty bodies, and offers opportunities for cooperation between them, and with NGOs. My comments draw upon the work of the Human Rights Committee, and hence what is said may not apply in precisely the same way to other treaty bodies.

(a) Objectives of reporting

The reporting process provides an opportunity to assess the progress made by states in implementing their obligations to respect and to ensure rights. Though not expressly provided for in the instruments, the treaty bodies have developed this process as an open dialogue with the state in which they make (hopefully) constructive criticisms and recommendations. The aim is to persuade states to

---

[5] For example, CCPR, art. 38.
[6] The treaty bodies could seek funding for projects carried out under their direction. See Elizabeth Evatt, "Ensuring effective supervisory procedures: The need for resources", in *The Future of UN Human Rights Treaty Monitoring*, Philip Alston and James Crawford (eds.), Cambridge University Press, 2000, 461 at 472.

make changes in their laws and practices to give full effect to rights. The importance of the dialogue is that it brings senior representatives of the state in question into direct contact with the committees in public session.

There has always been doubt as to whether the reporting system has any effect in persuading states to make the changes necessary to fulfil their treaty obligations. The committees responded to this perceived lack of effectiveness, and to the need for order and structure in the process, by introducing written concluding observations, adopted by the committee as a whole. This provides at least some sort of benchmark against which to measure a state's progress. There is no provision, however, to check whether states do in fact take any steps or make any changes as a result of the process, or whether any changes which were made had beneficial effects. Nor do the committees make any contact with NGOs to discover whether their recommendations were of use in NGO efforts to lobby for change. The matter is usually left until the next report is presented.

If the purpose of the reporting process is not just to engage in an encounter and to produce concluding observations, but to have a real influence on states, greater emphasis must be put on the preparation for the dialogue and on the follow-up. The better the preparation, the better the analysis of state law and practice, the more accurate and precise the observations, the greater will be the value of those observations to agents for change, and the easier it will be to verify whether any change has in fact occurred. The objective of the reporting process should be quality analysis and continuity of the process in terms of verification, follow-up and further analysis.

(b) Need for analysis and continuity

The Human Rights Committee often embarks on the dialogue with states without adequate information. Of course, there is often a great deal of material, including the previous reports of the state, the discussions and conclusions of the Committee, reports to other committees, material from specialized agencies and material from NGOs. However, despite its bulk, this material may be deficient, or lacking in detail. Members may not receive it until close to the date of the dialogue. Regrettably, despite the work that is done in the reporting process by individual members and by the committees collectively, the process does not result in an analytical study by the Human Rights Committee as a whole of the extent of compliance by states.

As the reports from any one state accumulate, and in the case of the Human Rights Committee some states have put in their fourth reports, the need for a comprehensive, progressive analysis of the situation in each state should be recognized as a priority.

With further commitment from committee members and support from the UN Secretariat, the process could begin with the preparation of a written study by a country rapporteur, (a committee member charged with drafting suggested questions for the state party and the first draft of the committee's concluding observations with respect to that state). While a comprehensive study using material from all sources would be the ideal, the essential minimum would be to outline the matters on which information is inadequate and to summarize the significant issues which arise and which should be included in the dialogue. This analytical study should be before a working group of the committee (in the case of the Human Rights Committee at a meeting prior to committee sessions), and before the committee at least one session before the consideration of the report (in the case of the Human Rights Committee three or four months).[7] The committee could then approve the request for information and the list of issues or questions to be put to the state party in connection with the examination of their report, and these should then go to the state with a request for a written response. The state's responses could lead to an updating of the rapporteur's study at a working group before the session at which the report is to be considered. In this way, matters of information could be separated from issues of compliance.[8]

The committee would, as a result of this procedure, have its own analytical study to work with in the dialogue. While many changes are called for to make the so-called "dialogue" effective and meaningful, one significant improvement would be the possibility of concentrating on key issues already identified and agreed to by the committee.[9] The committee's study, as illuminated by the dialogue, would also provide a framework on which to base the concluding observations.

If analytical studies of the kind outlined above were undertaken, the later reports and any other new material could be incorporated into a revision of the earlier study. This would overcome the lack of continuity in dealing with the reports from a particular state and improve coordination between the treaty

---

[7] Another option would be to invite a representative of the state to meet with the working group for a brief explanation of what information is being asked for, and what key issues are proposed as the focus of discussions.

[8] The Human Rights Committee, CEDAW, the Child Committee and the Economic, Social and Cultural Rights Committee all formulate lists of issues at working group meetings, a session in advance of the state-committee dialogue. CEDAW, the Child Committee and the Economic, Social and Cultural Rights Committee send the list of issues to states parties well in advance to enable the state to provide the Committee with written answers. With respect to the Human Rights Committee, the list of issues is adopted at the session prior to the examination of a report, but the state party is not expected to submit written answers to the Committee. See *Committee on Economic, Social and Cultural Rights: Report of the Eighteenth and Nineteenth Sessions*, E/1999/22 (1998) at para. 26; *Report of the Committee on the Elimination of Discrimination Against Women*, A/54/38/Rev.1 (1999) at paras. 412–413; CERD and CAT do not have pre-sessional working groups and do not prepare lists of issues in advance of the dialogue for states parties.

[9] *Report of the Special Working Group on Procedures*, unpublished (July 1996) at paras. 8 – 12, and *Report on the Informal Meeting on Procedures*, CCPR/C/133 (28 July 1996) at paras. 9–12.

Some treaty bodies are now attempting to focus questions on a more limited range of issues than are raised by the convention as a whole, either by asking states parties to focus their next report on issues raised in the concluding observations of the previous report, or by restricting the scope of the lists of issues. The Human Rights Committee's most recent reporting guidelines provide that the Committee's concluding observations should be the starting point of a state's next report: *Consolidated Guidelines for States Reports under the International Covenant on Civil and Political Rights*, CCPR/C/66/GUI/Rev.1 (1 November 1999) at 4. The Economic, Social and Cultural Rights Committee may take note that specific matters should be addressed in detail in the next report: *Committee on Economic, Social and Cultural Rights: Report of the Eighteenth and Nineteenth Sessions*, ibid. note 8 at para. 39(a). CERD, has been implementing the concept of focussed reports on an *ad hoc* basis in its concluding observations: see for example, *Report of the Committee on the Elimination of Racial Discrimination*, A/54/18 (1999), at 60 (Korea), 84–85 (Finland), 102–103 (Portugal), 131–132 (Italy), 164 (Peru), 267 (Haiti) and 309 (Antigua and Barbuda). CEDAW is in the process of considering the question of focussed periodic reports, and postponed the consideration of this issue at its last session: *Report of the Committee on the Elimination of Discrimination Against Women*, supra note 8, at 40, para. 420.

bodies. The concluding observations provide a benchmark of sorts, but they cover only certain issues and are not backed up by any commentary. By extending its functions to the preparation of analytical studies, the committee could use the reporting process to produce a clear (and reasonably comprehensive) analysis of the current state of human rights under the Covenant or relevant instrument in the reporting country. In time, this approach would open the way to a more selective examination of some states, focusing on one or more issues and avoiding unnecessary repetition.

In the long run, by their collective efforts the treaty bodies should aim to develop an authoritative analysis of the application of standards in each state party, from the independent perspective of the treaty bodies. Such an analysis would build up a comprehensive picture of the human rights situation in that state. It would show the extent to which the instruments were implemented, what their influence was, where the shortcomings were, the committees' concerns, and what kinds of changes the committees have recommended. Cooperation between the treaty bodies would be essential to achieve this goal.

The practical steps needed for this approach include setting the program of work at least two sessions ahead,[10] nominating a country rapporteur, and allocating a brief in-session period for the committee to adopt the questions and issues to go to the state. There would need to be a high-level research capability. The material on which to base such an analysis would seldom be found in the state report alone, nor would the NGO material usually be adequate or reliable enough to fill the gap. The state party would also have to be asked to provide copies of laws and decisions and other information.

(c) Delinquent states, late reports, no reports

The regularity with which a state reports and the quality of its reports are a test of the state's commitment to fulfilling its treaty obligations. Regrettably, too many states are late with their reports or fail to report. Too often their reports consist of lists of laws and bland reassurances without any information to show how, if at all, the law and practice of the state have been brought into line with the relevant treaty.

In those cases where states encounter genuine difficulties in meeting their reporting commitments because they do not have the resources or expertise necessary to prepare adequate reports, technical assistance should be made available. If this were done in an imaginative way, it could create opportunities for members of the committees to visit the states and to meet with NGOs and government agencies.

The treaty bodies must find a way to deal with those states that do not report.

---

[10] The Human Rights Committee moved to set the states for consideration two sessions ahead, in October 1995, see *Report of the Special Working Group on Procedures*, supra note 9 at paras. 4 and 7. See also *Report on the Informal Meeting on Procedures*, supra note 9 at para. 7. The Office of the High Commissioner for Human Rights website lists each committee's schedules for the consideration of states parties reports: for the Human Rights Committee, the reporting schedule is set two sessions ahead; for the Economic, Social and Cultural Rights Committee, the reporting schedule is set three sessions ahead; and for the Child Committee the reporting schedule is set five sessions ahead. The other three committees have only released their reporting schedule for the next session: see the Office of the High Commissioner web site at www.unhchr.ch.

Otherwise non-cooperating states gain an unfair advantage over others and the system falls into disrepute. One approach would be to prepare a study, similar to those mentioned above, for any state that has not reported for a number of years. Such a study, which could be based on the material available from a wide range of UN and NGO sources, would open the way for the committee to invite the state to provide particular information or to respond on specific issues. In this way, the analysis could in effect be a substitute for a report, which had not eventuated. The committee could thus get into dialogue with the state and persuade it to cooperate with the system. If the state did not respond, the committee could make appropriate observations in its annual report.

(d) Follow-up to the examination of state reports

Since the ultimate goal of the treaty system is to promote compliance, the work of the treaty bodies should not end when their concluding observations are drafted, to be resumed only when several years have passed. True, the committee's observations do not have legally binding force; nevertheless, if treaty obligations are taken seriously, the state should respond to the committee, and the committee should have its own procedures to find out whether states have acted upon its recommendations. The question of follow-up to the reporting process needs to be developed. Otherwise, it will remain far too easy for states to ignore what the committee has said without fear of repercussions.

If the treaty body has made a specific request for the state to provide information, it should ensure that this information is provided, or that the failure to provide it is dealt with by further request or by comment. It should note in its annual report whether states have responded to such requests for information. Where the committee has made specific recommendations, it should ask the state to inform it at the end of an appropriate period what action has been taken in respect of those recommendations. If publicity has been requested for its observations, states should be asked to provide information about this publicity. If the state responds to the concluding observations of the committee, this response should be considered by the committee[11], and should be mentioned in the committee's annual report.[12]

The committees should accept information from NGOs or other sources as to the action or non-action of the state following the presentation of its report and the committee's observations. In this regard it should invite comments from NGOs as to whether the committee's concluding observations have played a useful role in the process of change, and in particular whether they were given any publicity.

Whether or not the state or NGOs publicize the outcome of the reporting process, the treaty bodies could explore ways of persuading the media to publicize the outcome of the dialogue.[13] Knowledge about the system may raise the expectations of the community and encourage it to press for change.

---

[11] See *Report of the Human Rights Committee*, A/51/40 (1996) paras. 34 and 41 (referring to observations by Sri Lanka); *Report of the Human Rights Committee*, A/52/40 (1997) also includes a reference to observations by Colombia and Georgia on the Committee's concluding observations. These were referred to the pre-session Working Group in October 1997.
[12] *Report of the Special Working Group on Procedures, supra* note 9 at paras. 66–69.
[13] *Ibid.*, at para. 70.

Treaty bodies should offer states further advice and assistance with regard to implementation, where it appears appropriate. For example, after the presentation of the report one or more members of a treaty body could visit a state, with its agreement, to take part in further discussions about implementation of the instrument, preparation of reports, establishing local mechanisms, and so on.[14] If such a procedure were successful, it could be extended by giving the country rapporteur an extended mandate to visit the state on a fact-finding mission before the presentation of that state's report to the committee. It is envisaged that in the first instance such a mission would take place by agreement with the state. The mandate for such visits would need to be clearly defined. It should include an opportunity to meet with NGOs, as well as government agencies.

(e) Better coordination between the treaty bodies

Human rights are said to be indivisible, and yet the treaty system itself divides them in a haphazard manner. A state has one part of its human rights obligations examined in detail by one committee and another part, including some of the same issues, looked at by a totally different committee. There are examples of states that have entered reservations to a provision in one instrument, which has substantially the same effect as a provision of another instrument to which there is no reservation. The treaty bodies set up under all of these instruments act largely in isolation from each other. One of the treaty bodies, the Committee on the Elimination of Discrimination Against Women (CEDAW), is separated institutionally from the other five, even though many of the issues it deals with overlap the work of those other bodies. Without coordination between the supervisory bodies, there is a real risk of inconsistency. This would not be in the interests of the system as a whole.

In addition, some states have problems meeting all their reporting obligations and preparing reports under several treaties which have overlapping provisions. This multiplicity of instruments and standards contributes to late or inadequate reports. States could minimize the effects of overlapping obligations by ensuring that the preparation of reports is under a single national agency responsible for coordinating the work under each instrument.[15] The lead for co-ordination should come from the treaty bodies, however.

The need for cooperation between the treaty bodies was recognized with the establishment of the Meeting of Chairpersons of Treaty Bodies. In practice, however, the treaty bodies have not always given proper weight to the work of that body. There is an urgent need for effective coordination between the treaty bodies on substantive issues, in a manner compatible with the mandate of each committee under its own instrument.

One proposal already on the table is to establish a single treaty body to

---

[14] Country visits are rare for the Human Rights Committee. The Chairperson and Rapporteur visited Hong Kong in 1995 at the invitation of the Hong Kong administration, prior to the presentation by the United Kingdom of its report on Hong Kong. The Child Committee conducted informal visits until 1997, funded by UNICEF, but such visits have not taken place since that time: see *supra* Fitzpatrick, Chapter 6 at 83–84, Schmidt, Chapter 18 at 245.

[15] Reporting under major International Labour Organization Conventions could also be covered where relevant.

receive all reports from a state under all instruments, thus enabling the whole human rights situation in that state to be considered. Such a body would, almost inevitably, require full-time membership with appropriate expertise to cover the whole range of issues. It may be premature to think of such a monolithic outcome when the treaty bodies still have a great deal to do in developing approaches to the interpretation of their instruments. In any event, the amendments to the instruments necessary to bring this about are unlikely to be achieved until there is universal ratification of the instruments.[16] With respect to some of the treaties, this could be a long time in coming. Other options could include greater use of common membership of the treaty bodies,[17] and arrangements for members of one body to observe another, especially when they have reports pending from the same state. None of these solutions would deal effectively with the overlap in the instruments and the problem of multiple reports.

One way for states to avoid the multiplicity of reporting obligations could be by preparing a single report covering all their treaty obligations. To meet the needs of each of the treaty bodies, such a report would have to follow closely guidelines adopted by those bodies. It would, inevitably, be lengthy and unwieldy. The sheer difficulty of compiling it might lead to further delays.

As an alternative, or even as a possible step towards preparing guidelines for a single mega-report, treaty bodies could, in cooperation with each other, prepare reporting guidelines for each of the instruments. The guidelines could indicate what material prepared for the purposes of an instrument might satisfy the requirements for information under particular articles of other instruments. These guidelines could describe "modules" of information, which would meet the needs of more than one committee. Once prepared by the state, each of these modules could be included in the reports to any relevant treaty body. Examples might include:

- Information on freedom of expression and on incitement to racism, relevant to CCPR, articles 19, 20; CRC, articles 12, 13, 17; and CERD, articles 4 and 5 (d)(viii);
- Information on the right to work, relevant to CESCR, article 6 (1); CERD, article 5 (e)(i); and CEDAW, articles 11(1)(a-c), 11(2);
- Information on marriage and family, relevant to CESCR, articles 10(1) and (2); CCPR, article 23; CEDAW, articles 5(b), 16; and CRC, articles 5, 18(1), 27(4), 37(c).

Joint Working Groups could be established immediately by the committees to work through the instruments progressively. Drafts prepared by the committees' working groups would be adopted by each treaty body in accordance with its own mandate. The ultimate goal of this exercise would be a comprehensive series of modules covering the provisions of all instruments. They could be used to make separate reports or ultimately, if agreement could be reached, one mega-report.

---

[16] The CRC is near universal ratification at this stage. CEDAW is 24 states away from universal ratification.
[17] See CAT, art. 17 (2): "... States parties shall bear in mind the usefulness of nominating persons who are also members of the Human Rights Committee established under the International Covenant on Civil and Political Rights and who are willing to serve on the Committee Against Torture."

(f) Other changes

In regard to the communications procedure, the Human Rights Committee is seeking ways to use current resources more effectively in order to avoid delays in dealing with matters. However, problems remain. The outcomes of the procedure are not outstanding and some states still fail to cooperate. Recourse to the procedure is not at the level which could be expected, especially from countries where the Human Rights Committee is aware of extensive violations. It appears that people do not know about the procedure, or they are reluctant to use it. Consistent with its mandate, the Human Rights Committee should insist on public education and information programmes. Any significant increase in the number of communications, however, would put an even greater burden on already stretched resources and lead to intolerable delays.

An unexpressed, but essential, element in the work of the treaty bodies is the contribution of NGOs. Like the treaty system itself, they lack resources. The effect of changes in the structure of the treaty bodies or the reports should be the subject of consultation, and carefully considered, especially in regard to those bodies, which are grouped around a particular constituency, such as children or women.[18]

The human rights system generates a vast amount of paper, some of ephemeral value, some which could be of value if readily accessible. The computerization of relevant material at the Office of the High Commissioner for Human Rights, together with provision for access to that material for members of treaty bodies through the Internet, saves time and money.[19] Literacy in computer-generated information and access to the Internet and e-mail should be incorporated fully into the skills of everyone involved. Computerization has opened the way to receive up-to-date material from NGOs, and from other treaty bodies, at comparatively little cost.

(4) Conclusions: limits to reform

The treaty bodies carry a weight of responsibility to make the system more effective, to insist that states respect the international obligations they have undertaken voluntarily, and to ensure that there is a coherent and effective system of international accountability to assess the level of compliance. They must continue to seek ways to bring about commitment and action by the states parties. If there is no impetus for change within the treaty bodies themselves, and within the UN Secretariat, reforms will be hard to achieve.

But there are limits to what the treaty bodies can achieve themselves without the support of states. Many of the weaknesses in the human rights system arise from the fact that the states have given limited mandates to the treaty bodies, no effective legal powers and few resources. The treaty bodies are *ad hoc* bodies and their work is largely honorary. Most reform proposals would, if implemented,

---

[18] For example, Defence of Children International (DCI) organizes national groups preparing alternative reports under the CRC. International Women's Rights Action Watch (IWRAW) coordinates the preparation of "shadow" reports for most states reporting to CEDAW.

[19] See web site of the Office of the High Commissioner for Human Rights, and the information concerning the treaty bodies at: www.unhchr.ch

inevitably widen the functions performed by the treaty bodies and thereby impose greater burdens on the members and the secretariat, without the support of additional resources. Those members who have other full-time commitments are not easily able to give more time to committee work. The efficiency and effectiveness of the treaty bodies will, in these circumstances, become more dependent on the ability of the members to cooperate among themselves, to delegate tasks to each other, and to maintain a level of trust and commitment which makes this possible. But the treaty bodies do not have control over their membership, and current trends suggest that there may be more rapid changes in membership. If the states do not exercise their electoral powers carefully, and there is not much evidence of their willingness to do this, they could undermine the collegiate spirit and continuity of approach that is necessary to the success of the bodies.

Unless a sufficient number of states support change and stand behind the treaty bodies in their efforts to make the system effective, the current impasse will remain. This leaves the treaty bodies in an unenviable position. They are encouraged to become more and more outspoken and effective in their supervisory roles. At the same time, they must ask states whose actions they vigorously condemn, to streamline the treaty system and make it stronger and more effective by giving them wider legal power and more resources. It is a dilemma which treaty body members themselves cannot resolve.

CHAPTER 24

A Court and Two Consolidated Treaty Bodies

Thomas Buergenthal

There is no disagreement among those who have studied the work of the United Nations treaty bodies that today these institutions are facing a serious crisis. In my opinion, the crisis is largely organizational in character. Of course, it is also true that a good number of the problems confronting the treaty bodies could be solved with adequate financial resources. It is ironic that the financial crisis of the UN began in earnest just as the Cold War was ending, impeding the implementation of many innovative reforms in the human rights area for which there was political support in the euphoria of the immediate post-Cold War period. That support has gradually eroded.

There seems to be general agreement that significant additional financial resources will not be made available to UN human rights treaty bodies in the foreseeable future. Hence, focus should be on ways to improve their working methods and on institutional reorganization. Others have addressed the first point – the improvement of the working methods of the treaty bodies, but most are stopgap measures that in the long run will not solve the problems confronting these bodies. It is therefore important to address the question of long-term reforms.

Firstly, the six existing treaty bodies should be replaced by two consolidated committees.[1] One committee would assume the function of reviewing state reports under all six treaties and the other would deal with individual and inter-state communications under the treaties that confer this competence. Secondly, a court should be established which would initially have jurisdiction only to render advisory opinions rather than binding judgments in contentious cases.

The six existing treaty committees all require and review periodic state reports. This means that the states parties to these treaties now have to prepare separate reports for each of these bodies. Since a large number of states have ratified all six treaties, they have to file an equal number of reports every few years. Of course, there is some overlap as far as the rights that these treaties guarantee –

---

[1] This idea was adopted by the American Bar Association at its annual meeting in 1998:
  ... the American Bar Association recommends that the United States Government and the United Nations work toward consolidating into two committees the six United Nations standing committees currently monitoring compliance with the United Nations human rights treaties: one committee to review all State reports, and the other to examine inter-State and individual communications.

for example, both the Torture Convention[2] and the Covenant on Civil and Political Rights[3] guarantee the right not to be tortured; similarly, the principle of non-discrimination is proclaimed in a number of these instruments. The fact remains nevertheless, that each treaty proclaims a series of discrete rights that need to be separately analyzed for each committee. Hence, a country not only has to prepare six separate reports over a relatively short period of time, it also has to appear before six different committees to explain and defend these reports. This is a considerable burden for any country; it is so especially for smaller, poorer countries.

The resulting administrative and bureaucratic burden could be lightened somewhat were one to permit countries to submit one single consolidated report to be reviewed by all six committees. This approach would not overcome the problem that would result from outdated consolidated reports. That is to say, since it is unlikely that each committee could take up a country's report within roughly the same time frame, supplemental reports would have to be prepared to account for subsequent developments relevant to the work of the other committees. These reports would in turn have to be updated the more time elapsed between different committee hearings, gradually nullifying the intended purpose of consolidated reports. Consolidated reports also place greater burdens on individual committee members who will have to work their way through much more material extraneous to the concerns of their own committee in order to find information of particular interest to them. In theory, although such work could be performed by staff, staff cuts make that increasingly unlikely.

Over the years, the caseload of treaty bodies with optional jurisdiction to receive individual communications has increased dramatically as more and more states subject themselves to that jurisdiction. This places an additional burden on these committees with the result that some of them, the Human Rights Committee for example, accumulate an ever-increasing backlog. Part of the problem here is that members of the Committee must divide their time between the review of state reports and the examination of individual communications. Quorum requirements applicable to both functions, and limited resources, for the most part prevent the Committee from performing these tasks in smaller groups. Moreover, the professional qualifications needed to deal with communications – principally legal experience – are not necessarily right for the review of state reports. The latter raises issues that are not exclusively, or even predominantly, legal in character. Here economists, sociologists, anthropologists, criminologists, psychologists, historians, and political scientists probably have a greater contribution to make than lawyers.

Hence, it would make sense to establish two consolidated treaty bodies, instead of the existing six, one for state reports and the other for communications. The latter would consist principally of lawyers having a good background in human rights and constitutional law, the former of individuals representing a mix of different professions. The communications panel might number twenty-one members, enabling it to work in three panels of seven, or even four panels of five,

---

American Bar Association, *Report of Action Taken at 1998 Annual Meeting*, Toronto (1998), Recommendation 118.
[2] Convention Against Torture and Other Forms of Cruel, Inhuman or Degrading Treatment or Punishment, 1465 UNTS 85 (in force 26 June 1987).
[3] International Covenant on Civil and Political Rights, 999 UNTS 171 (in force 23 March 1976).

members. The increased number of panels would permit this committee to keep pace with the growing case law. It would also enable it to deal with cases that involve violations of more than one of the six treaties. That possibility does not exist today.

The committee on state reports could be somewhat larger, but it too should be able to work in at least two panels. The reports reviewed by the committee on state reports would be consolidated reports, although the new committee can be expected to develop working methods that would permit the subject-matter focus of the review to vary from reporting period to reporting period or from country to country, depending on the application of a previously determined set of standards. Such a consolidated review would enable the committee to engage in a comprehensive examination of the application of all six treaties in a given country instead of the piecemeal approach in effect today.

Apart from the fact that the above reforms would permit a more rational development of the law codified in the six treaties than is possible today under the six-committee system, it makes a great deal of administrative sense as well. It would, of course, also make for a much more efficient use of scarce resources.

My proposal also calls for the establishment of a court – the United Nations Court for Human Rights. Its function would be to render advisory opinions interpreting the six human rights treaties at the request of the two consolidated committees and the states parties to these treaties. Individuals would not have standing to request such opinions. The court would also not have contentious jurisdiction, that is, the power to decide cases. Of course, subsequent protocols could enlarge the court's jurisdiction and give individuals standing to appeal specific cases to it. To overcome objections to the establishment of yet another UN court and the added costs involved in such a venture, one could envisage conferring the above-described jurisdiction on a special chamber of the International Court of Justice or of the forthcoming permanent International Criminal Court.

The reason for limiting the court's power to render only advisory opinions and not to give individuals standing to appeal to it, is based on the assumption that a court with more extensive powers would have no chance of obtaining the needed state support for a long time to come. Even a court with the limited jurisdiction proposed will encounter serious opposition, but its chances are certainly much better, precisely because its jurisdiction would be limited and because it would give states an opportunity to challenge the legality of any decision of the consolidated committees they found objectionable. From a human rights perspective, it is important to recognize that despite its limited powers, the court would make an important contribution to the development and strengthening of universal human rights law. Bodies that are not courts cannot do so as effectively. Once the court is established, it will also be easier over time to expand its jurisdiction.

There will be state support for the idea of two consolidated treaty bodies, if only because the proposed reorganization would reduce the bureaucratic and financial burden on states parties. Of course, there is likely to be state opposition to a court, regardless of the limits imposed on its jurisdiction. But even if for the time being there should be little support for a court, it is important to begin to promote the idea now. I have no doubt whatsoever that there will eventually be a UN human rights court. The sooner the subject is discussed, the sooner a court will be created.

Lastly, the current concept of the Meetings of Chairpersons of the Treaty Bodies needs to be expanded if there is to be effective coordination and cooperation between the different treaty bodies. The Meetings of Chairpersons as an institution should be expanded by inter-committee working groups dealing with different subjects of concern to the treaty bodies. For example, there might be a working group on state reports, on individual communications, on follow-up, and so on. These working groups would be composed of selected members of the different treaty bodies who would report regularly to their respective committees. Members of all committees would thus gain a much greater awareness of developments of common interest in the other bodies, enabling them to benefit from the experience and working methods of these bodies. The current system does not contribute in a meaningful way to the sense of commonality between the existing treaty bodies that is needed for the most effective discharge of their respective mandates.

VII. The Role of National Courts: A Canadian Example

CHAPTER 25

Enforcing International Human Rights Law: The Treaty System in the 21st Century

Rt. Hon. Antonio Lamer, P.C., Chief Justice of Canada

As the 20th Century draws to a close, it is abundantly clear that treaties have become the primary source of legal norms in the international legal order. This is particularly true in the realm of international human rights law. The history of the modern international human rights movement begins with the reference to human rights in article 1(3) of the UN Charter of 1945,[1] an international treaty which has been referred to by some as an embryonic constitution for the global legal order. From the UN Charter, the course of this movement can be traced, through the adoption in 1948 of the Universal Declaration of Human Rights[2] by the General Assembly, to the various international human rights treaties that form the backbone of the United Nations human rights system, and of other regional human rights systems that can now be found throughout the world.

As a Canadian jurist, I feel a special affinity for the international human rights movement. I say that in part because of the involvement of a great many Canadians in it, beginning, of course, with former Professor John Humphrey of McGill University who was so important to the drafting of the Universal Declaration of Human Rights. But I say it also because that Declaration, and the treaties which followed it, provided much of the inspiration for the adoption of the legal instruments which protect human rights in Canada – our federal and provincial human rights statutes, the federal statutory *Bill of Rights* of 1960[3] and finally, and most importantly, the *Canadian Charter of Rights and Freedoms*.[4] The history of the legal protection of human rights within Canada, in an important sense, can be understood as part of the larger history of the struggle for human rights worldwide.

I wish to reflect on some of the institutional aspects of international human rights treaties. International human rights law now appears to be facing – to

---
[1] United Nations Charter, 1 UNTS xvi (in force 24 October 1945).
[2] Universal Declaration of Human Rights, G.A. Res. 217 A (III), Annex, adopted on 10 December 1948.
[3] *Canadian Bill of Rights*, S.C. 1960 c.44, part I (1960).
[4] *Canadian Charter of Rights and Freedoms*, Part I of the *Constitution Act, 1982*, being Schedule B to the *Canada Act 1982* (U.K.), 1982, c. 11.

borrow a term devised by others – "a historical moment." A historical moment, as I understand it, is a critical juncture in the life of a system or order, at which fundamental changes must be accepted and implemented if that system or order is to survive and move forward. As I see it, this "historical moment" for international human rights law can be aptly described as the "institutional moment" of international human rights law.

I am, of course, not alone in viewing international human rights law as being at something of a crossroads. A number of distinguished commentators, such as the UN High Commissioner for Human Rights, Mary Robinson, have written in recent years that the moment is ripe for momentous change in the promotion and protection of international human rights, and have suggested a number of institutional reforms to achieve that end.

From my perspective, this "institutional moment" has two particularly significant aspects: first, recognition of the importance of a human rights culture to the effective enforcement of international human rights law; and second, the growth of institutional dialogue between international human rights bodies and national courts to strengthen the international protection of human rights. I begin with the importance of a human rights culture.

There are six major international human rights treaties administered by the United Nations – the International Covenant on Civil and Political Rights (CCPR),[5] the International Covenant on Economic, Social, and Cultural Rights (CESCR),[6] the Convention on the Elimination of All Forms of Racial Discrimination (CERD),[7] the Convention on the Elimination of All Forms of Discrimination Against Women (CEDAW),[8] the Convention Against Torture and Other Cruel, Inhuman or Degrading Treatment or Punishment (CAT),[9] and the Convention on the Rights of the Child (CRC).[10]

Despite slow beginnings, these conventions have now been ratified by a great many nation states. A full 75% of the member states of the United Nations have ratified at least five of the six major treaties.[11] However, in recent years, commentators have contrasted the apparent breadth of the international community's commitment to these treaties with what they describe as the rather shallow depth of that commitment. For example, Anne Bayefsky has written that international human rights law is facing an "implementation crisis."[12] She and other commentators typically focus on what might be termed the institutional pathologies, which beset the enforcement of international human rights treaties. I do not wish to rehearse those pathologies here, other than to say that they extend

---

[5] International Covenant on Civil and Political Rights, 999 UNTS 171 (in force 23 March 1976).
[6] International Covenant on Economic, Social and Cultural Rights, 993 UNTS 3 (in force 3 January 1976).
[7] Convention on the Elimination of All Forms of Racial Discrimination, 660 UNTS 195 (in force 4 January 1969).
[8] Convention on the Elimination of All Forms of Discrimination Against Women, 1249 UNTS 13 (in force 3 September 1981).
[9] Convention Against Torture and Other Cruel, Inhuman or Degrading Treatment or Punishment, 1465 UNTS 85 (in force 26 June 1987).
[10] Convention on the Rights of the Child, 1577 UNTS 3 (in force 2 September 1990).
[11] This figure relates to the following five treaties: CERD, CCPR, CESCR, CEDAW and CRC.
[12] See *infra*, Anne Bayefsky, Appendix 6, *International Law Association, Committee on International Human Rights Law and Practice, Report on the UN Human Rights Treaties: Facing the Implementation Crisis*, at 689.

to the whole process of human rights enforcement. Some of the more serious problems that have been identified include the lack of detailed information provided by states parties regarding their compliance with the human rights treaties to the committees which monitor their implementation, and the lack of resources at the disposal of those committees to enable them properly to fulfill their monitoring functions.

These institutional pathologies have generated a broad range of proposals for institutional reform – the development of an independent machinery based at the United Nations to investigate state compliance with treaty provisions, the greater use of individual petitions, and so on. Important as such reforms would no doubt be, my sense is that the problems which they would be designed to correct run deeper than the reforms might suggest, and accordingly require a more comprehensive – perhaps one might say, a more subtle – approach.

The effectiveness of international human rights law ultimately depends, in my view, not only on the existence and operation of effective institutions, but also on the willingness of all of the actors within the system – the persons who hold rights, the states which are obliged to respect those rights, and the bodies which enforce those rights – to regard the norms laid down in the human rights treaties as being authoritative and worthy of respect. For international human rights law to be effective, therefore, it must be supported by what I would term "a human rights culture," by which I mean a culture in which there is a firm and deep-seated commitment to the importance of human rights in our world.

The development of such a culture worldwide is, of course, an exceedingly challenging task, and one that is likely to take a great many years if not decades to achieve, if in fact it is ever achieved. There are many countries in which, for historical, social as well as political reasons, the development and entrenchment of a human rights culture will be very difficult. However, from my vantage point at least, there are reasons for some optimism now on this front. Within the last five to ten years, a great many countries have committed themselves some for the first time, others anew – to democratic forms of self-governance and to the rule of law, both of which are integral to any coherent system for protecting individual human rights.

If these countries are to succeed in these endeavours, they will, of course, require assistance from others, including various international organizations and entities. I believe that judges too can play a role in this regard, particularly judges from countries in which a human rights culture already exists. And in fact, members of the judiciary from some of these countries are already playing such a role. In this regard, it may be of interest to you to hear about some recent developments in this area involving the Canadian judiciary.

In my capacity as Chief Justice of Canada, I have been receiving a growing number of requests from the kinds of countries of which I have been speaking to provide assistance to the judges and judicial systems of those countries in their efforts to enhance the rule of law and the protection of human rights there. Some of the requests that I have received – for example, for bibliographies of Canadian materials on such topics – can easily be met on the basis of the resources of my own Chambers. The majority, however, cannot be so easily accommodated. They entail the expenditure of considerable amounts of money and require, not only a pool of volunteers from within the Canadian judiciary to provide the requested assistance, but also an administrative infrastructure to plan and carry out the assistance programs.

In order for us to be able to accede to these more substantial requests, I have therefore been obliged to enlist the support of others. I have now had a number of meetings with Madame Huguette LaBelle, President of the Canadian International Development Agency, to see whether or not that agency might be able to assist in providing funding. Those meetings have gone very well, and I am optimistic that, with this agency's help, the necessary funds will soon be in place. I have also generated a list of some 75–80 Canadian judges who have indicated a willingness to participate in foreign judicial assistance programs. Most of these judges, I should note, come from a special category of judges that we have and that we call "supernumerary." Judges in this category have satisfied the requirements for retirement on full pension, but rather than retire, have opted to remain on the bench, drawing full salary but sitting approximately half time. The time that the volunteers from this category will be giving to these programs will be drawn from their non-sitting periods – in other words, from their free time (with the result, I note, that their involvement will not have any adverse effect on the administration of justice in Canada, particularly insofar as the right of litigants to have their cases heard in a timely manner is concerned). Moreover, as true volunteers, they will not be receiving any remuneration for their efforts. I might add that it gives me considerable pride to be able to tell people that so many Canadian judges have stepped forward in this manner to contribute to what I consider to be the fulfillment of one of this country's many moral responsibilities in the international sphere.

Finally, I have designated the Office of the Commissioner for Federal Judicial Affairs as the body with primary responsibility for coordinating the participation of the Canadian judiciary in foreign support programs. It is through that office that requests for support that I receive are now processed. That office has also become involved on its own initiative in several projects, for example, a major one relating to Ukraine. That project, which extended over many months, was designed to assist Ukraine both in enhancing understanding of and developing mechanisms to protect judicial independence, and in improving the day-to-day functioning of the Ukrainian court system. An important element of this project was a visit to Canada – that took place in February 1997 – by some 21 Ukrainian judges and court officials for five weeks. During the course of their visit, the participants took a course on judicial independence under the auspices of the National Judicial Institute, the main provider of judicial education in Canada. Each of them also spent two weeks in one of Edmonton, Winnipeg or Toronto, studying the operations of the courts in these various cities and "shadowing" a Canadian judge. All in all, some 27 Canadian judges from across the country and from various different levels of our court system were involved in one way or another in this part of the project.

Granted, the kind of judicial education in which these and other members of the Canadian judiciary have been involved has been directed at national courts, whose work is largely directed at the entrenchment within their respective countries of the rule of law and, where human rights are protected by national constitutions and other legislation, at the interpretation, application, and enforcement of those rights. However, the disjunction between the domestic and international protection of human rights should not be over-emphasized. The development of effective judicial responses to the violation of human rights under national law can only facilitate and nourish the growth of a human rights culture within a nation. As that culture becomes ingrained, it will, one has to hope, percolate up to the international realm.

I turn now to the second aspect of what I have termed the "institutional moment" of international human rights law, the growth of institutional dialogue between international human rights bodies and national courts. Like any true dialogue, this dialogue depends on the willing participation of both parties. My focus here is on the involvement of national courts in this dialogue. In particular, I want to focus on the growing tendency of national courts to rely on international human rights treaties, and by implication, on the decisions that interpret those treaties, as aids to interpreting and applying the human rights which are protected under national law.

The experience of the Supreme Court of Canada in this regard is instructive. Since 1982, Canada has afforded constitutional protection to human rights through the *Canadian Charter of Rights and Freedoms*, or as we now customarily refer to it, the Charter. Unlike the South African Constitution, the Canadian Charter does not contain a provision requiring or even encouraging Canadian courts to look at international law as an aid to construing its provisions. Nevertheless, the Supreme Court of Canada has frequently looked to the provisions of international human rights treaties to which Canada is a signatory as an aid to interpreting the Canadian Charter. The Court has cited at least one of the six human rights treaties in twenty-two of its Charter decisions. The treaty that has been referred to most frequently is, not surprisingly, the CCPR – it has been cited in eighteen cases. The Child Convention has been referred to in three decisions; the Economic, Social and Cultural Rights Covenant and CERD have been cited in two cases each; and CAT has been cited in one case. CEDAW has yet to be referred to in a Charter case although it has been cited in one non-Charter case.

International human rights law has been relied on at a number of different stages of Charter analysis and, at each stage, in a number of different ways. First and foremost, the Court has relied on human rights treaties to define the content of Charter rights. In some instances, this reliance has resulted in Charter rights being given a broad scope. This has occurred, for example, when the Court has read the specific language used in a human rights treaty into the more general language used in the Canadian Charter. Hence, in *R. v. Brydges*,[13] the issue before the Court was whether the right to counsel protected by s. 10(b) of the Charter, which imposes a duty on police officers to inform arrested persons of that right, also imposes a duty to give a person information about the availability of free duty counsel and means-tested Legal Aid. Speaking for the court, I held that s. 10(b) did impose such a requirement, and in support referred to article 14(3)(d) of the CCPR, which grants to accused persons similar entitlements to those set out in s. 10(b), and which specifically provides that an accused has the right to legal assistance without payment if he or she is without sufficient means. Other examples of this form of reliance can be found in judgments relating to the protection of the right to privacy under the Canadian Charter, the interpretation of the prohibition against cruel and unusual punishment, and the meaning of freedom of association.

On one occasion, the Court has held that the Canadian Charter afforded

---

[13] *R. v. Brydges* [1990] 1 *Supreme Court Reports* 190.

more protection than the CCPR, because the right in question had been framed more broadly than its counterpart in the treaty. In that decision, *United States of America v Cotroni*,[14] the Court held that the right of a citizen "to remain in" Canada was violated by extradition. The Court contrasted the broad wording of the Canadian Charter provision with the much narrower terms used in the corresponding provision in the Covenant. It drew the inference that, had the Charter provision been intended to be narrow in scope and, therefore, to exclude protection against extradition, it would have been framed in similar terms to those used in the Covenant. In other words, the CCPR was used to broaden the protection afforded by the Canadian Charter by negative implication.

The Court, however, has not always used comparisons with corresponding treaty provisions to broaden the scope of Charter rights. Hence, in *R. v Milne*,[15] the Court rejected a claim, based on the CCPR, that indeterminate detention for an offence that, subsequent to the passing of sentence had been removed from the list of offences for which indeterminate detention was available, amounted to arbitrary imprisonment or cruel and unusual punishment. Although article 15 of the Covenant may have been favourable to the accused in such circumstances, the Court held that the benefits of a reduced sentence in these circumstances had been dealt with exhaustively by a specific provision of the Charter, s. 11(i), which limits those benefits to the time period between the commission of an offence and the passing of sentence.

Using similar reasoning, in *R. (B.) v. Children's Aid Society of Metropolitan Toronto*,[16] I held that the liberty interest protected by s. 7 of the Canadian Charter should be confined to physical liberty. In support of that conclusion, I took note of the fact that the analogous provision, s. 9, of the CCPR had not been interpreted as protecting liberty interests beyond the right to physical liberty. Likewise, in *R. v L.(D.O.)*,[17] the Court held that the right of an accused not to be deprived of his liberty except in accordance with the principles of fundamental justice was not violated by a provision in the Criminal Code[18] which allows victims of sexual offences to adopt, while testifying, the content of a videotape made within a reasonable time after the alleged offence had been committed. The accused in that case had argued that the provision in question was arbitrary, because it only applied to complainants below the age of 18. In her concurring opinion, Madame Justice L'Heureux-Dubé based her conclusion that the age limit was not arbitrary on the fact that the age of 18 had been accepted by the Child Convention as the default age of majority.

International human rights treaties have also been used by the Supreme Court of Canada in determining whether or not a limitation on a Charter right can be justified on the basis that it is reasonable and can be "justified in a free and democratic society."[19] That language, I note, has been interpreted by the Court

---

[14] *United States of America v. Cotroni* [1989] 1 *Supreme Court Reports* 1469.
[15] *R. v. Milne* [1987] 2 *Supreme Court Reports* 512.
[16] *R. (B.) v. Children's Aid Society of Metropolitan Toronto* [1995] 1 *Supreme Court Reports* 315.
[17] *R. v. L. (D.O.)* [1993] 4 *Supreme Court Reports* 419.
[18] *Criminal Code of Canada*, R.S.C. 1985, c. C-46, as amended.
[19] *Supra*, note 4, section 1: "The *Canadian Charter of Rights and Freedoms* guarantees the rights and freedoms set out in it subject to only to such reasonable limits prescribed by law as can be demonstrably justified in a free and democratic society."

to generate a test of justification with two distinct components. First, the offending governmental action must be shown to be in furtherance of a pressing and substantial objective; and second, there must be proportionality between that objective and the means used to pursue it.

The Supreme Court of Canada understands human rights treaties to be relevant to both of these components. Thus, international human rights law has been used to establish the significance of a governmental objective. In *R. v Keegstra*,[20] involving a challenge to the hate propaganda provisions of the Criminal Code, the Court referred to provisions in both the CCPR and CERD obliging states parties to prohibit such propaganda, to support the conclusion that the purpose of the Code provision was particularly important. The importance of that objective was also relied upon at the proportionality stage of the analysis to support the conclusion that the Criminal Code provision was proportional in the relevant sense to the achievement of that objective.

Why has the Supreme Court of Canada been prepared to rely in these different ways on international human rights law as an aid to Canadian Charter interpretation? I think it is possible to identify several different rationales. One is that the adoption of the Charter should be, and has been, understood as part of the international human rights movement. My predecessor, Chief Justice Brian Dickson, invoked this rationale in his reasons in a case involving freedom of association, when he stated that, "the Charter conforms to the spirit of ... [the] contemporary international human rights movement, and it incorporates many of the policies and prescriptions of the various international documents pertaining to human rights."[21] Embedded in that rationale is, of course, a hidden premise – that Canada is a signatory to many international human rights treaties and, as a result, the Canadian Charter can be viewed in an important sense as the domestic analogue of those instruments. In other words, the Charter can be understood to give effect to Canada's international legal obligations, and should therefore be interpreted in a way that conforms to those obligations.

Another rationale for our reliance on international human rights law is that it assists the Court to fulfill an important purpose of the Charter which is, again to borrow from former Chief Justice Dickson, to "secure for individuals the full benefit of the Charter's protection."[22] On this account, international human rights treaties serve as a benchmark against which to measure the protection provided by Charter rights. In this vein, former Chief Justice Dickson stated that, "the Charter should generally be presumed to provide protection at least as great as that afforded by similar provisions in international human rights documents which Canada has ratified."[23]

Finally, and most importantly, Canada's international human rights obligations are relevant to Charter interpretation because they reflect the values of free and democratic societies. That phrase is found in the first section of the Charter, which both introduces the rights in the Charter and states that those

---

[20] *R. v Keegstra* [1990] 3 *Supreme Court Reports* 697.
[21] *Reference Re: Public Service Employee Relations Act (Alberta)*, [1987] 1 *Supreme Court Reports* 313 at 348.
[22] *Ibid.*, at 349.
[23] *Supra*, note 21 at 349. See also: *Slaight Communications Inc. v. Davidson*, [1989] 1 *Supreme Court Reports* 1038 at 1056.

rights may be subject to reasonable limits.[24] Accordingly, the Court has held that the values of a free and democratic society underlie both the rights in the Charter and their limitation. International human rights law, as a reflection of what it means to live in a free and democratic society, is part of the background of principle, which informs the interpretation of Charter rights and their limitation.

In conclusion, it appears from my vantage point as Chief Justice of a country in which a human rights culture exists and, I would say, is flourishing, that there is reason to be optimistic about the role that international legal instruments play in fostering greater protection of human rights around the world. I believe the judiciary can do much in this regard, as I think the Canadian judiciary has done, by looking to international treaties and the jurisprudence of international human rights bodies in the interpretation of domestic human rights norms. By doing so, judges raise the profile of those international treaties and further the creation of a human rights culture. In addition, as I have described, judges from countries like Canada can have a direct influence on the legal culture of other states. They can assist the judiciary and the legal systems of those states in protecting judicial independence and giving primacy to the rule of law which are essential to the recognition of human rights in the law.

---

[24] *Supra*, note 19.

VIII. Conference: Discussion and Recommendations

VII. Conference Discussion and Recommendations

CHAPTER 26

Discussion

The following are points made during three days of discussion by Conference participants. Proceedings were recorded and transcribed. The remarks have been organized by theme by the Rapporteur, Anne Bayefsky. The speakers have not been identified, in accordance with the Conference procedures. For a list of conference participants see Chapter 27, note 1. The text closely follows the actual comments made, and individual comments are not necessarily congruent.

General Comments

- The treaty monitoring system is in crisis.
- It is an important and positive trend to focus on enforcement and not the creation of new standards.
- Solutions should concentrate on what can be done quickly within the existing system. The difficulty of amending treaties should not be underestimated.
- The Cold War had a tremendous effect on the working methods of the treaty bodies. Treaty bodies' internal procedures are changing slowly, but we are still living with the Cold War legacy.
- To some extent universality is a product of failure. When you have a system of compliance or implementation which is not very effective, it does not cost very much to ratify. But what is the good of ratifications with many reservations, or ratifications without compliance?
- For the Torture Convention a large number of states have yet to ratify. Since ratification is a necessary first step for implementation of human rights treaties we still need to press for universal ratification.
- If the United Nations is effective or non-effective, it is because member states want it to be so. With respect to the treaty system, it is the states parties that have more responsibility than the treaty bodies for effective implementation.
- States need to be reminded that the treaty obligations were freely assumed. They were not forced to ratify the human rights treaties.
- The United Nations human rights treaty system addresses two very different situations:
  (a) isolated violations from countries which have a decent national domestic supervisory system,
  (b) violations committed or perpetrated in states in which this is not the case and in which there is no human rights culture.

In the first case the international human rights system serves a corrective purpose. In the latter context, a secondary or subsidiary role of international law (which is generally the case) may not be appropriate.
- In judging the benefits of the treaty system we ought to be careful about the standard of efficacy invoked. We tend to study efficacy in a specific context – there is a report on jail conditions, it is critical of those conditions, and then three years later you ask whether jail conditions have improved. This approach does not gauge well the contribution of the whole process to the culture of human rights. The general effect has to be considered, as well as the result in specific cases.
- There have been some achievements of the treaty system. These frequently relate to states parties that are now in transition from a totalitarian regime to democracy. There have been constitutions that have been amended, legislation amended, new legislation drafted, programs initiated for magistrates, law enforcement officials, police, security forces in order to encourage them – in the performance of their duties – to take into consideration basic human rights and fundamental freedoms.
- Key goals are:
  (a) The ultimate goal is to have the human rights treaties incorporated into national legal systems and directly applied. But only a handful of states have incorporated the treaties.
  (b) The goal should be to teach people about the human rights treaties, to train people about them and to make it known that there are instruments that they can use. A right to know your rights is one that has been neglected. We should find ways of implementing the right to know your rights.
- There is clearly a problem of the remoteness of the treaty monitoring system from the national level. Effective monitoring requires that the treaty bodies get out of Geneva and New York, and get into the field for purposes of accessibility, public education, publicity, effectiveness and follow-up.
- Follow-up to concluding observations and decisions in individual complaints depends to a large extent on national non-governmental organizations (NGOs), and training should be available to assist them to conduct this role effectively.
- Sweeping reservations that effectively render ratification meaningless should be objected to by all other states parties.

Reporting

State reporting has a number of benefits:
- The examination of reports elucidates the interdependency of rights. It provides an understanding of how rights interact and by concentrating on one right, protection of another may be improved. This systemic understanding may not be evident in the context of individual complaints.
- In the examination of reports, the questions of the treaty body members clarify and expand upon the extent, the scope and the contents of a right.
- The treaty bodies, in a formal setting, ask probing questions of states parties, and through their concluding observations make judgments about overall

situations. These may probe very sensitive areas of life within states. The questioning and judging in these areas for many states parties is often unique.
- There is a value in making states write their reports, regardless of whether they do so honestly or not. The exercise itself forces the states parties to rethink the issues, and this can have a useful effect.

On the other hand,

- The state report itself cannot be taken as representing an accurate statement of the human rights facts in that state. Relying on state reports for information is fundamentally flawed because of the inherent reluctance, the natural reluctance, to report negatively on oneself to an international body.
- The report itself is frequently a tedious document of little interest to the reader.
- State reporting, from the state perspective, is often a very difficult process. Particular people are charged with consolidating information from many different government agencies, many of which ignore repeated requests for information.

The reports themselves are government documents, and non-governmental (NGO) information and participation should be distinguishable:

- The Committee on Economic, Social and Cultural Rights used to ask the state party whether NGOs had input into the state reports. The Committee discontinued their practice of posing that question because they concluded the report was a government document and it was the states' responsibility to write it. They do however, ask whether individuals from outside government were given an opportunity to comment on the government report.
- National NGOs are advised by international NGOs not to do joint reports with the government, but to submit their own, separate information. It is suggested to national NGOs to have meetings with government and to comment on the state report, but not to participate in the drafting of the report.
- Similarly, national NGOs are advised by international NGOs not to serve as members of government delegations to the treaty bodies meetings.

Thematic Reporting

There are advantages to focused or thematic reports:

- For states that have already presented one or more reports it is more productive to focus on specific issues, or themes, or to address specific questions.
- Some treaty bodies have decided to identify a range of questions and issues which relate to a specific state, and to ask them to focus on them for the next state report.
- The article-by-article approach which repeats the same questions for states with very different human rights records is not productive.
- Focused or thematic reports allow for flexibility and allow the committees to take account of, or be guided by, the type, nature and seriousness of violations.

On the other hand,
- To say that the committees should tailor their questioning to only certain issues or to specialize, requires considerable knowledge of a country situation. Currently, the committees do not have that degree of expertise on country situations.
- Focusing risks making mistakes about the range of questions to be posed on the human rights conditions in the state party.
- An important argument in advancing compliance with the treaties is the emphasis on the equality of all states, and the fact that all states are subject to the same dialogue process. The equality of states in the reporting process needs to be maintained.

Consolidated Reports

Consolidated reports are a good idea, because:
- States are tired of writing so many reports, particularly when they are examined only after significant delays following submission. States are therefore interested in consolidating the number of reports they are required to produce.
- Consolidated reports are a good first step on the way to a single consolidated committee to examine those reports.
- Consolidated reports could be accomplished through the use of guidelines for producing modules which would address the substantive elements of different treaties, but be combined in a single report.

On the other hand,
- Consolidation and consolidated reporting should not become a vehicle of eliminating important features of the monitoring process. Consolidation should not be used as a means of "rationalizing" or "streamlining" without concomitant benefits for human rights protection.

The Reporting Period

The reporting period for different states parties should be flexible:
- States can be treated equally and still have different reporting periods by applying the same principles for determining the reporting period for all states; in other words, for example, if a state (any state) did not cooperate in a follow-up process, they might have to come back to the committee or produce the next report earlier. If they did cooperate, they might not need to report for a longer period.
- After each report, the committee should decide when to request the next report from that state.
- A flexible reporting period is possible with respect to the Human Rights Committee because Article 40 of the Covenant only requires the initial report, and has no requirement for periodic reports. The subsequent reports are at the discretion of the Committee.

On the other hand,

- The reporting period between state reports should not be much longer than five years because there may be major changes in such a length of time.
- Having different reporting periods for different states detracts from the principle embedded in the treaties that all states parties are equal and should be treated equally.
- Decisions concerning when to require the next state report, if not made immediately following consideration of the report in hand, would require some means of monitoring the ongoing human rights conditions in that state – in order to determine when to request a report. Currently, the committees have no such means.
- The ILO manages to ask for a report from states every two years for its ten core treaties. The periodicity has been extended to five years for every other convention.

On-going Monitoring in the Form of Follow-up to Reports

In the case of states with very poor compliance with the treaty, the reporting process is not meaningful without ongoing monitoring and the flexibility to ask for further information at variable intervals, in addition to the time of the regular reporting dialogue itself. An ongoing process, or a process of follow-up on state reports, may take the form of:

(a) asking for further information,
(b) making sure it comes in,
(c) writing reminders if it does not come in,
(d) publishing the information when it does come in,
(e) asking a state to come back to the committee if necessary.

Special Reports

Special reports requested outside the regular reporting system, or outside the follow-up of a state report, are not helpful because:

- Special reports requested in emergency situations or exceptional circumstances waste a lot of valuable time, and duplicate unnecessarily the work of other UN bodies more effective in this context than the treaty bodies.
- The value of the state reporting system is that it treats all states equally, and special reports encourage the treaty bodies to be selective. This jeopardizes the non-selectivity of the entire process, which is a primary strength.

Failure to Report

States parties which fail to produce reports should be considered by the treaty body in the absence of a report, because:

- The failure to report is a failure to comply with the states' international obligations.

- Scheduling a state for consideration in the absence of a report, often results in the report being submitted in advance of the dialogue.
- A state which is scheduled for consideration in the absence of a report, will usually send a state representative to the dialogue even without a report.
- Even without a report the state party's compliance with the treaty should be considered, (preferably in the presence of a state party representative but if necessary without a state party representative).
- Some of the treaty bodies do schedule non-reporting states for consideration.

On the other hand,

- In the absence of a state report, or state representative at the dialogue, the impact of the committee's comments and their ability to make an impression on the state at the national level is considerably reduced.
- The value depends on considerable research and initiative by part-time treaty body members, which is currently impractical and unrealistic.
- The quality and level of detail of the concluding observations tends to be reduced.

Quality of the Dialogue

The quality of the dialogue is often very poor, because:

- Committee members frequently repeat the same questions.
- Committee members show little ability to agree among themselves in advance of the dialogue about the major, most serious problems in a state party and to restrict themselves to those issues.
- The committee members often ask irrelevant questions, or have a particular interest in a subject and have a tendency to raise that issue for every country, whether or not it is significant in that context.
- Committee members speak for too long.
- Committee members often ask very detailed questions that governments could not possibly answer, and which require too much information than is possible to provide in the course of the time allowed for discussion.
- The government representative is often permitted to give a speech or oral presentation of written information at great length, even an entire session, without interruption.

The quality of the dialogue could be improved if:

- The chair restricted the time allotted for presentations by government.
- The committee agreed prior to the dialogue about what issues to deal with and abided by that agreement.
- Committee members did not ask questions as if they were making speeches for the summary record, and did not repeat questions of previous members.
- The oral dialogue was focused through effective use of written questions and answers exchanged well in advance.

The Usefulness of the Dialogue

The dialogue is not a necessary feature of the examination of every state report:

- The dialogue is unnecessary after the first report and the committees should conduct the dialogue with states selectively, but on the basis of clear, reasonable and transparent criteria.
- The dialogue is pointless for states in which there is no respect for the rule of law.
- The usefulness of the dialogue depends on the degree to which it is followed-up at the national level, and at the moment it is not. It does not begin or stimulate a dialogue at the national level, for instance between governments and NGOs.

On the other hand,

- The dialogue about the states' human rights conditions and treaty compliance, as a requirement for all states parties, is one of the major contributions of the treaty bodies to the UN system.
- The dialogue does resonate at the national level and open lines of communication.
- Even in the case of governments which have little respect for the rule of law, citizens who have otherwise little opportunity to observe their government criticized and examined, are encouraged and inspired by witnessing the government's questioning in an international fora.
- Concluding observations of the committees would be less effective if they were not the product of the dialogue between the committee and state representatives.
- The dialogue forces governments to respond. State representatives experiencing the dialogue process will think about the consequences for their next appearance of their activities at the national level.
- Some of the government representatives give the clear impression that they want the committee to raise problematic issues, or to push such issues forward, because they are having difficulty doing so alone at the national level.

The Usefulness of the Concluding Observations

The concluding observations need to be considerably improved:

- Resources and methodologies to produce good concluding observations are required.
- Concluding observations would be much more useful for government officials if they were more in-depth and more focused.
- The impact of the concluding observations, or follow-up, is limited at the national level because of their lack of specificity. It is not enough, for example, to say "eliminate child poverty".
- The distribution of the concluding observations also has to be considerably improved. In the case of the Committee on the Rights of the Child, the Committee adopts the concluding observations at 1:00 p.m. on the final day

of the session and an hour or so later, the national level NGOs that submitted information on a state party receive the concluding observations. This is not the case with other committees.

On the other hand,

- The treaty bodies often do not have sufficient knowledge of the national circumstances to be more specific, and risk making mistakes in fact or law the more specific concluding observations become.
- The treaty body members have before them much of the human rights record of a given state and concluding observations are a few pages long. The treaty body members do not feel they have enough understanding of the specific facts about states to be reach very specific conclusions.

Monitoring the Treaty Bodies and Accessibility of the Treaty Body Process

- National NGOs have limited ability in terms of resources to attend or provide information to the treaty bodies both at the pre-sessional meetings of treaty bodies during which treaty bodies determine questions to be asked of states parties, and during the dialogue itself months later.
- The Geneva and New York meetings are remote from the actors at the national level, or members of civil society.
- Regional, sub-regional, and even national meetings of the committees, perhaps on a consolidated basis would improve access.
- Visits by some members of the committees to a state party will generate more interest on the part of NGOs, the media, and other members of civil society, than meetings in Geneva and New York.
- Media interest at the national level is impeded by the lack of access of local media to meetings – process or outcome – held in Geneva and New York.
- An in-country dialogue can strengthen treaty body linkages to civil society and NGO communities.
- The Inter-American experience is that going to a country and holding press conferences at the national/local level has a significant impact on coverage of the treaty (body) work in all its dimensions.
- The impact of NGOs and their information on the treaty body process is greater if the NGO can attend the meeting prior to the dialogue during which the treaty body formulates the list of questions it wishes the state party to answer during the dialogue.
- Some NGOs have found that they are empowered by being present during the dialogue in which their governments are asked questions in public about their human rights record.

Fact-finding

An accurate assessment of a states' human rights record is the primary essential element of an effective monitoring regime. The treaty bodies have limited resources and procedures for assessing the facts with a high degree of accuracy.

The problem is:
- The state report itself cannot be taken as representing an accurate statement of the human rights facts in that state. Relying on state reports for information is fundamentally flawed because of the inherent reluctance, the natural reluctance, to report negatively on oneself to an international body. [see also under reporting].
- The central question for the treaty bodies is, therefore, how do they prepare for the analysis of a state report. How should they inform themselves of a country situation? How do they get enough information about a state to ensure valid and accurate concluding observations? How are they able to assess the accuracy and reliability of information which comes to them from a variety of sources?
- The related question is: is a treaty body only a secondary source, operating at a secondary level, relying on special rapporteurs and others for their information, or is there a place for the treaty bodies to go and get the information themselves? Should the treaty bodies develop a fact-finding capacity, (for example, similar to the Inter-American Commission on Human Rights)?
- Furthermore, often the treaty bodies are lacking the laws of a state, the laws in a language the members can understand, the social facts and conditions beyond the laws.

The role of the Office of the High Commissioner for Human Rights:
- Overall, ongoing familiarity with country situations ought to be a responsibility of the Office of the High Commissioner for Human Rights and the Secretariat servicing the treaty bodies. They should be producing country files and building up information on a country-by-country basis independently of both NGOs and government reports.
- Treaty bodies should be provided with all the human rights information gathered from UN agencies and sources. This should include (a) information from UN agencies such as UNHCR, (b) information drawn from those UN agencies and operations with an ongoing field presence, (c) UN thematic and country-specific rapporteurs should routinely provide factual information on states parties prior to their consideration by a treaty body.
- At the same time, the treaty bodies must protect sources of fact, IGOs or UN agencies involved in humanitarian aid (recognizing that there may be a conflict between human rights advocacy and dispensing relief or humanitarian aid).
- There ought to be a clearly division of labour between the Office of the High Commissioner for Human Rights and other UN agencies involved in various dimensions of human rights field operations or which are in circumstances where they become especially informed of human rights situations.
- Factual information about human rights situations from NGOs needs to be prepared for the treaty bodies in a manner which is easily digested, and related to the treaty rights. The treaty bodies cannot digest very large numbers of NGO reports. The Office of the High Commissioner for Human Rights should have sufficient staff resources to be able to prepare the incoming material.
- On the other hand, at the moment many NGOs are wary of the capacity of

the Secretariat to summarize and present or highlight the important issues contained in NGO information to the treaty bodies, and would prefer the members read their material in its original form.

The role of the treaty bodies:

Re: secondary-level fact-finding:

- should do a better job of actively soliciting information from a whole range of sources, including national NGOs, UN agencies, UN field operations at the national level.
- they should also solicit the help of UN agencies in particular states to identify national NGOs and other sources of information.

Re: primary-level fact finding:

The treaty bodies should engage in primary-level fact-finding:

- If the treaty bodies do not have an independent fact finding capacity, then they are very dependent upon others. The others tend to be NGOs, and this raises questions of who is setting the priorities in terms of implementation of treaty rights.
- Treaty bodies (or their secretariat) should be able to make on-site visits in order to determine facts, particularly in the context of systemic violation of human rights in a particular state.
- Treaty bodies should pursue private funding sources in order to finance visits to states parties.
- Treaty body on-site visits can serve a number of purposes simultaneously, including fact-finding (education or raising general awareness of the treaty requirements in civil society, accessibility, publicity, follow-up).
- Treaty bodies should act as fact-finders themselves, at least in the cases of those states where the facts are not otherwise available, that is, where
    (a) there are no UN special rapporteurs
    (b) there is no information available from UN agencies
    (c) the reliability of the NGO information is at issue.

On the other hand,

- In the case of most states, primary fact-finding in the form of on-site visits will not be necessary in order to obtain sufficient information.
- Missions are a huge drain on resources and require an enormous amount of time and money.

NGO information:

- NGO material is more credible and useable for the treaty bodies if it comes from coalitions of national NGOs, who have worked together prior to the presentation of information to the treaty bodies in order to present the material in an organized, succinct, and non-repetitive manner.
- On the other hand, NGOs should not act as gatekeepers for other NGOs.
- NGO material should not have to be factually proven prior to being used to question governments, since it is not used to assert factual conclusions in advance of asking the state party for comments or responses.
- International NGOs should assist national NGOs in preparing material

which is suitable, accessible and timely, to the treaty bodies. This may entail keeping national NGOs informed about the timetable of committee sessions, any guidelines for the preparation of information, distributing their documents to the treaty body members, distributing state reports to the national NGOs, sending national NGOs concluding observations, and where necessary in order to protect the confidentiality of national sources, presenting the national NGO information to the treaty body.

Follow-up

The failure on the part of the treaty monitoring system to follow-up the many dimensions of the state reporting process is a key shortcoming.
- There is no proper follow-up to the work of the treaty bodies in the dialogue with states.

The role of the treaty bodies:
- The implementation of specific recommendations of the treaty bodies in the concluding observations is not monitored until the next state report. The hiatus is detrimental. Information sent to the committee in between reports relating specifically to concluding observations, is simply filed until the next report – when appropriate action may no longer be possible.
- When the committee requests a state to submit additional information between reports, it is not considered until the next report. If the additional information is received, it is not published or accessible. There is no official document even indicating whether or not the information was received for any treaty body other than the Committee on the Rights of the Child. The fact of submission of additional information should be published and the additional information submitted, if substantive, should also be published.
- Failure to submit additional information requested in the course of the dialogue should also be followed-up by some effort to ensure that it comes in.
- The treaty body members themselves should assist in writing press releases concerning their work, in effective language for civil society.
- In cases where the treaty body has a Rapporteur following a particular state, that individual's name might be released to the general public and that person assigned a Follow-up role with respect to that particular state. An internet site should be made available which would permit the information flow to the Committee to continue with respect to that state after the concluding observations were adopted, and as follow-up to the impact of the concluding observations.

The role of the Office of the High Commissioner for Human Rights:
- Although the Office of the High Commissioner for Human Rights prepares a document which summarizes all of the recommendations from all of the treaty bodies on advisory services and technical assistance, on a state-by-state basis, the document is not made public. This inhibits follow-up. No document is prepared which contains recommendations made by the treaty bodies on other issues. Such a published summary on a state-by-state basis would also encourage follow-up.

- The Office should prepare a list for each country of the names and addresses of every known, identifiable major NGO in the human rights field, human rights ombudsman in each country, major newspapers, televisions and radio stations. Press releases concerning the treaty bodies work and concluding observations should be disseminated to sources directly at the national level.

The role of states parties:

- Meetings of states parties are not the appropriate venue for follow-up of concluding observations or treaty body recommendations because:
  (a) the states parties will refuse to do this,
  (b) making states parties meetings anything other than procedural meetings for election purposes only risks states parties which are unhappy with the monitoring process attempting to use the fora to restrict the treaty bodies' work,
  (c) follow-up should be done by the normal political bodies of the UN, since it is their responsibility to ensure implementation.
- Suggestion: the states parties should create some sort of subcommittee whose job it is to follow up, in the political context, the recommendations of the treaty bodies.

The role of the Human Rights Commission and the General Assembly:

- Although the Human Rights Commission and the General Assembly ought to follow-up the recommendations of the treaty bodies, in most cases they do and will not, since their tendency is to target only a very limited number of states by name. Their resolutions on the treaties and treaty bodies have been general, and of little value as a follow-up vehicle.

The role of NGOs:

- NGOs, bar associations, law reform bodies, parliamentary committees, should each follow-up the work of the treaty bodies, by calling on governments and asking them what has been done in response to the committee's conclusions or requests.
- National NGOs are the key participant in an effective follow-up process, and need training to perform that function better.

Individual Complaints

In the United Nations context the individual complaint system operates in the context of both isolated violations from states with decent national domestic supervisory systems, and violations committed in states in which there is no human rights culture. The general premise of the subsidiary nature of international law to domestic law is challenged in the latter context. This has implications for the scope and effectiveness of the treaty bodies procedures and decisions.

The task of the international monitor, however, is not simply to decide what is palatable at the given national level.

Overall, the status of the UN treaty body decisions in individual cases has been minimal:

- National courts make little reference to the decisions of the Human Rights

Committee, the Committee Against Torture (CAT) or the Committee on the Elimination of Racial Discrimination (CERD).
- The procedures for arriving at those decisions detract from their authority.
- In general, the individual complaints have not led to major changes in laws or practice.
- There have only been a small number of cases. After twenty years, thousands more cases would have been expected. For example, there are only 50 cases a year on average in the 1990's registered by the Human Rights Committee from a potential complainant population of over a billion people, and the numbers awaiting registration do not significantly change the order of magnitude. Forty percent of states parties have never been the subject of a single complaint, even states with very poor human rights records.
- There is a significant delay in the proceedings, for example, the Human Rights Committee takes approximately four years to resolve cases.

Some solutions to this problem:

The role of NGOs:

- Individuals need to be encouraged to file cases in appropriate circumstances; they need to be informed of the potential remedy; this requires training, education, publicity which in part could be undertaken by national NGOs, or by the Office of the High Commissioner.
- Communications are frequently poorly presented and incoherent. NGOs and others should assist authors in submitting communications.

The role of the Office of the High Commissioner for Human Rights:

- Complaints received by the High Commissioner's office need to be channeled to the appropriate body and full use made of the potential of the treaty bodies in the case of individuals writing from states parties to the Optional Protocol or under the relevant provisions of the Convention against Torture and Other Cruel, Inhuman or Degrading Treatment or Punishment (CAT) or the Convention on the Elimination of All Forms of Racial Discrimination (CERD).
- Complaints which are not properly before any UN body should at least be acknowledged and directed elsewhere if possible.
- Press releases on the individual communications decided at each session of the Human Rights Committee, CAT and CERD should be issued.

The role of the treaty bodies (HRC, CAT, CERD):

- Should institute a summary procedure when essentially the same facts come again to the committee, so that the treaty body does not have to repeat unnecessarily a complete discussion in the working group and in the plenary.
- A working group should be given the power to adopt decisions on admissibility, and also on inadmissibility. Inadmissibility decisions could be given to the plenary on the first day of the meeting, and if no one objects to the decision declaring a case inadmissible, then it would mature into a decision of the plenary.
- Where appropriate, the committee should not substitute its own judgment for that of local courts which have specifically considered all aspects.

- Deference should be given to the findings of local courts where they are independent and impartial tribunals.
- On the merits, the committee should institute a chamber system; the views adopted by a chamber will on the whole normally be accepted by the full committee without debate.
- The committee should abolish the summary record for the confidential sittings of the committee leading to individual decisions. Those records are embargoed, and the committee should avoid wasting time letting members speak to the record.
- Avoid any individual rapporteur decision-making method.
- The reasoning behind decisions needs to be clearer and expanded, and a consistent and reasoned jurisprudence developed in order:
  (a) that other potential complainants can be guided accordingly and further cases are not taken unnecessarily.
  (b) to provide guidance to states parties in implementing those rights
  (c) to increase the usefulness of decisions for national courts who may be able to make greater use of the treaties at the national level.
- Oral hearings in the long run are necessary.
- On the other hand, oral hearings would compound the problem of length of time in the consideration of cases, or the delay in decision-making.

Qualifications of Committee Members

- The Committee on the Elimination of Discrimination Against Women (CEDAW) is primarily comprised of non-lawyers from different countries and the few lawyer-members are not international lawyers; there is concern that CEDAW members lack the qualifications to deal with individual cases in a quasi-judicial setting.
- Treaty body members must be completely independent of government and impartial.
- Governments should be encouraged to nominate only appropriate candidates.

General Comments/Recommendations

General comments are useful contributions to the development and understanding of the treaties. More could be done in this respect with the help of external assistance (for example, researchers, NGO conferences).

Cooperation Between Treaty Bodies

Cooperation among the treaty bodies needs to be improved and should include:

- Follow-up as a joint exercise.
- Sharing country information; sharing information on action taken, particularly where mandates overlap.
- Comparing/discussing working methods.

- A few members from each treaty body should collaborate on particular cross-cutting themes, for example, in the context of general comments.
- Meetings should be coordinated, so that a country with a very problematic human rights record might be scheduled to appear before different committees on a basis which maximized the effectiveness of the reporting process.
- CEDAW should move to Geneva.

A Consolidated Committee for Reports

Overall, a consolidated committee is needed to consider state reports. This committee would consider consolidated reports for all treaties ratified by each state, and would be a permanent body.

Consolidation through the creation of a permanent body is required in order to:

- reduce overlapping and redundant processes within states parties for writing many reports.
- avoid the duplication in the dialogue and questioning of the state party.
- increase the ability to follow-up in terms of the reporting process (requests for additional information, and so on).
- ensure coherent and planned scheduling of reports.
- develop enhanced, specialized expertise on the human rights conditions in each state.
- develop consistent interpretation of human rights.

Contrary to criticism,

- There is no reason why a permanent treaty body which dealt with reports could not include experts in the rights of specific vulnerable groups or thematic rights, such as, children, women, torture, race.
- The last holdouts or the strongest voices against consolidation in the European human rights convention system were the members of the institutions themselves, that is, those with a vested interest.

On the other hand,

- A consolidated committee would not be effective unless the qualifications for membership ensured independence, impartiality and the requisite expertise.
- Special groups or rights may suffer by consolidation, such as women, children, race and torture; the thrust of the work might be only civil and political rights.
- The positive impact of having committee members in a large number of states (now 97) would be lost.

Consolidated Committee for Complaints

A consolidated full-time committee is needed for hearing individual complaints from all the treaties which permit such complaints. Such consolidation might require the development of a protocol for each of the instruments to provide for the communication or complaint procedures to be transferred to the consolidated committee.

A consolidated committee to consider complaints would:

- have the time to consider individual complaints, thereby improving the quality and depth of decisions
- develop jurisprudence in a way which would allow national institutions to take the decisions of the committee seriously
- deal with cases more quickly
- develop adequate dissemination techniques and enhanced publicity for individual cases
- develop and implement adequate follow-up techniques
- generate additional cases through improvements to the quality of the jurisprudence, dissemination, increased references in national institutions, timeliness.

Ultimately, a consolidated committee will develop through a step-by-step approach into an international court of human rights dealing with individual complaints. Such a step-by-step approach could take the following form:

1. an international human rights court with only advisory jurisdiction
2. the development of appropriate procedures
3. the move to a full-time body
4. an international human rights court with the capacity to deal with individual applications and to render legally-binding decisions; an optional protocol to all the treaties establishing such a full-time court would be required.

CHAPTER 27

Conclusions and Recommendations

*Enforcing International Human Rights Law:
The Treaty System in the Twenty-First Century
York University, Toronto, Canada
June 22–24, 1997*

Professor Anne F. Bayefsky
Conference Rapporteur

I. Introduction

The conclusions and recommendations are the Rapporteur's impressions, from the Conference as a whole, of some of the important issues and solutions which ought to occupy the international human rights community into the twenty-first century. They were drafted, discussed and then circulated at the conclusion of the Conference. This is not a consensus document or a set of recommendations which were endorsed by all participants.[1] Rather, it reflects the Rapporteur's

---

[1] Conference Participants: **Professor Anne Bayefsky**, York University, Toronto, Canada; **Ms. Rachel Brett**, Fellow, Human Rights Centre, University of Essex, Associate Representative, Quaker United Nations Office (Geneva); **Professor Tom Buergenthal**, Member, Human Rights Committee, Former President, Inter-American Court of Human Rights, George Washington University, Washington, DC; **Professor Peter Burns**, Member, Committee against Torture, Faculty of Law, University of British Columbia, British Columbia; **Professor Andrew Byrnes**, Faculty of Law, University of Hong Kong, Hong Kong; **Mr. Douglass Cassel Jr.**, Executive Director, International Human Rights Law Institute, DePaul University, College of Law, Chicago, Illinois; **Ms. Christina M. Cerna**, Senior Specialist in Human Rights, Inter-American Commission on Human Rights, Organization of American States, Washington, DC; **Mr. Andrew Clapham**, Representative of Amnesty International to the United Nations, New York; **Dr. Thomas Clark**, Coordinator, Inter-Church Committee for Refugees, Toronto (Canada); **Dr. Jane Connors**, Chief, Women's Rights United, United Nations Division for the Advancement of Women; **Mr. Crispin Conroy**, First Secretary, Australian Permanent Mission to the United Nations (Geneva); **Professor Virginia B. Dandan**, Rapporteour, Committee on Economic, Social and Cultural Rights, College of Fine Arts, University of Philippines, Manilla; **Mr. Alfred de Zayas**, Senior Human Rights Officer, Support Services Branch, Office of the High Commissioner for Human Rights (Geneva); **Ms. Adèle Dion**, Director, Human Rights Division, Department of Foreign Affairs and International Trade, Ottawa (Canada); **Mr. Andrew Drzemczewski**, Head of Secretary General's Monitoring Unit, Council of Europe, Strasbourg, France; **Judge Elizabeth Evatt**, Rapporteur, Human Rights Committee, Australia; **Professor Joan Fitzpatrick**, School of Law, University of Washington, Seattle, Washington; **Professor Thomas Franck**, Director,

summary of many of the ideas for constructive change, both short-term and long-term, which were voiced at the Conference either in the background papers or in the discussion at the Conference itself.

Centre for International Studies, School of Law, New York University, New York; **Mr. Claude Francoeur**, Director General, Institutional Cooperation Division, Canadian Partnership Branch, Canadian International Development Agency, Ottawa (Canada); **Ms. Felice Gaer**, Director, Jacob Blaustein Institute for the Advancement of Human Rights, New York; **Mr. Ivan Garvalov**, Vice-Chairperson, Committee on the Elimination of Racial Discrimination, Bulgaria; **Ms. Stefanie Grant**, Director of Program and Policy, Lawyers' Committee for Human Rights, New York; **Professor Hurst Hannum**, Fletcher School of Law and Diplomacy, Tufts University, Massachusetts; **Mr. Arthur C. Helton**, Director, Forced Migration Projects, Open Society Institute, New York; **Mr. Jean-Marie Henckaerts**, Legal Advisor, International Committee of the Red Cross, Geneva; **Professor Louis Henkin**, School of Law, Columbia University, New York; **Ms. Jane Hodges**, Equality and Human Rights Coordination Branch, International Labour Office, Geneva; **Mrs. Judith Karp**, Member, Committee on the Rights of the Child, Jerusalem, Israel; **Mrs. Helga Klein-Bidmon**, Chief a.i., Support Services Branch, United Nations Centre for Human Rights, Geneva; **Professor David Kretzmer**, Member, Human Rights Committee, Director, Centre for Human Rights, Faculty of Law, The Hebrew University, Jerusalem, Israel; **Mr. Daniel Lack**, Legal Counsel, United Nations Watch, Geneva; **Ms. Johanne Levasseur**, Counsel, Human Rights Law Section, Department of Justice, Ottawa (Canada); **Ms. Lori Mann**, Programme Assistant, Human Rights and International Cooperation, Peace and Social Justice Program, The Ford Foundation, New York; **Ms. Janice Marshall**, Legal Officer (Human Rights Liaison), Promotion of Refugee Law Unit, Office of the High Commissioner for Refugees, Geneva; **Mr. Ian Martin**, Former Director, Human Rights/Deputy Executive Director, U.N./O.A.S. International Civilian Mission in Haiti, Former Chief, United Nations Human Rights Field Operation in Rwanda, Fellow, Human Rights Centre, University of Essex, United Kingdom; **Mrs. Nurjehan Mawani**, Chairperson, Immigration and Refugee Board, Ottawa (Canada); **Professor Cecilia Medina**, Member, Human Rights Committee, Universidad Diego Portales (Chile); **Ms. Alice M. Miller**, Director, Women's Rights Advocacy Program, International Human Rights Law Group Washington, DC; **Professor Manfred Nowak**, Director, Boltzman Institute of Human Rights, Judge of the Human Rights Chamber for Bosnia-Herzegovina, Vienna, Austria; **Mr. Michael O'Boyle**, Head of Division, European Court of Human Rights, Council of Europe, Strasbourg, France; **Ms. Heather Olson**, Counsel, Human Rights Law Section, Department of Justice, Ottawa (Canada); **Mr. Bert Ramcharan**, United Nations Director, Africa 1 Division, Department of Political Affairs, United Nations, New York; **Professor Nigel Rodley**, United Nations Special Rapporteur on Torture, School of Law, University of Essex, United Kingdom; **Ms. Françoise Roy**, Senior Officer, Education and Promotion, Human Rights Directorate, Department of Canadian Heritage, Ottawa; **Ms. Anne Lise Ryel**, Member, Committee on the Elimination of Discrimination Against Women, Gender Equality Ombudsman (Norway); **Mr. Bruno Scheire**, Manager, Human Rights Program, Citizen's Participation Directorate, Department of Canadian Heritage, Ottawa; **Dr. Markus G. Schmidt**, Office of the High Commissioner for Human Rights, Geneva; **Mr. John Scratch**, Senior General Counsel, Specialized Legal Advisory Services, Department of Justice, Ottawa (Canada); **Dr. Carmel Shalev**, Member, Committee on the Elimination of Discrimination Against Women, Jerusalem, Israel; **Mr. James Sloan**, Legal Advisor, International Service for Human Rights (Geneva); **Mr. Peter Splinter**, First Secretary, Permanent Mission of Canada to the United Nations, Geneva; **Mr. David Stewart**, Assistant Legal Advisor, U.S. Department of State, Washington, DC; **Ms. Laura Theytaz-Bergman**, Liaison Officer, NGO Group for the Convention on the Rights of the Child, Geneva; **Mr. Mark Thomson**, Deputy-Director, International Service for Human Rights, Geneva; **Ms. Irit Weiser**, Senior Counsel, Human Rights Law Section, Department of Justice, Ottawa (Canada); **Mr. Doug Williams**, Senior Policy Advisor, Human Rights and Democracy, Canadian International Development Agency, Ottawa (Canada); **Mr. Maxwell Yalden**, Member, Human Rights Committee, Ottawa (Canada); **Dr. Leo Zwaak**, Lecturer, Utrecht University, Researcher, Netherlands Institute of Human Rights (SIM), Netherlands.

II. Underlying Principles

While international human rights standards and their ratification have greatly proliferated, serious problems of compliance remain. The papers and discussions, which focused on the problem of implementation, evidenced a number of underlying principles and assumptions.

1. Human rights are universal, and their universality is reflected in the principal human rights treaties.
2. Universality is diluted to the extent that the treaties are subject to widespread and radical reservations, and by failures to comply. Ratification is not an end in itself, but must be linked to performance.
3. There is an essential relationship between the adequate protection of human rights and the institution of democracy, good governance and the rule of law.
4. The non-discriminatory application of human rights standards to all UN member states is a fundamental strength of the treaty system, all UN member states having ratified at least one of the six major treaties.
5. International human rights law and institutions are designed to complement national human rights systems and to make them more effective.
6. Access by victims to the process of state reporting and to the potential for individual complaint is a necessary element of successful implementation.
7. The credibility and effectiveness of the treaty regime depends upon the treaty bodies obtaining accurate, current information on compliance.
8. Non-governmental organizations play a vital role in the treaty enforcement system.

III. Recommendations

The treaty system is confronted with a number of specific implementation problems: large numbers of overdue reports, significant backlogs of reports and individual communications, inadequate meeting time for the treaty bodies, inadequate access to procedures for victims of human rights violations, and poor follow-up of the conclusions of the treaty bodies by the political organs of the United Nations. Furthermore, the resources available to institute substantial improvements in implementation are seriously inadequate.

(A) RATIFICATION

While universal ratification of human rights treaties is desirable, ratification is marred by widespread and radical reservations, and by failures to comply.

1. States should refrain from diluting their obligations through reservations incompatible with the object and purpose of the treaties.

(B) STATE RESPONSIBILITY

The human rights treaties embody obligations of, and between, state parties. States parties have the right, and the responsibility, to call violators to account by appropriate means.

2. States parties should exercise their capacity, where available, to lodge complaints that other states parties are not fulfilling their obligations under the treaty.
3. States parties should exercise their capacity to object to reservations which are incompatible with the object and purpose of the treaty.

(C) THE REPORTING PROCESS

The state reporting process is intended to encourage a comprehensive review by a state of its national legislation, administrative rules, and procedures and practices in relation to the treaty. It should result in the integration of international human rights obligations into domestic policy-making.

(i) *States parties should*

Preparation of the Report:
4. Develop adequate national machinery for the preparation of reports, including coordination mechanisms between governmental departments.
5. Ensure that the preparation of national reports provides the occasion for public discussion and debate of the issues covered by the treaty.
6. Make reports available to the public in local languages.

The dialogue:
7. Ensure that the delegations which appear before the treaty bodies have appropriate seniority and expertise to undertake a dialogue with the treaty body.
8. Publicize the fact of the consideration of the state report by the treaty bodies.

Concluding observations:
9. Disseminate widely, in local languages, the concluding observations of the treaty bodies.

Resources:
10. Ensure that the treaty system is provided the necessary funding and resources required for the operation of effective enforcement machinery.

(ii) *Treaty bodies should*

Co-operation:
11. Take steps to ensure greater co-operation among the treaty bodies, including the development of joint general comments.
12. Develop modular guidelines which group similar or related articles under the different treaties, and which allow states to repeat information in their reports which is common to these modular groupings.
13. Nominate individual treaty body members to serve a liaison function in respect of other UN entities and treaty bodies.
14. Develop close collaboration with the relevant country specific or thematic rapporteurs or mechanisms.

Adequacy of reports:
15. Adopt general guidelines for reporting.

Information gathering:
16. Develop a data base of NGOs at the national and international level; inform them of submissions of state reports; provide copies of state reports; indicate a willingness to receive written information; inform them of the timetable of

consideration of the list of issues to be asked of the state party and the oral dialogue; provide guidelines for NGO reporting.
17. Invite representatives of specialized agencies to attend pre-sessional meetings. Formulate guidelines for their contributions.
18. Produce a schedule for the consideration of reports at least one year in advance.
19. Consider the possibility of identifying specific areas of concern which should be addressed in a state report in lieu of comprehensive reports on compliance with the treaty. Apply flexibility in the range and nature of questions to be addressed to state parties.
20. Schedule the pre-sessional working group at the end of the previous session, or sufficiently far in advance of the dialogue to enable the identification of issues on which they require further information.
21. Invite NGOs to attend the pre-sessional working group and present country-specific information directly related to the treaty on states scheduled to appear at the forthcoming session.
22. Require written responses from states parties to the list of issues in advance of the dialogue.
23. Reconsider the practice of requesting exceptional reports, which open the treaty bodies to charges of abuse for political bias or discriminatory and unjustified selection of targeted states, have been applied without clear guidelines on their use, are of questionable value in crisis situations, do not serve a significant preventive function, and are a comparatively poor allocation of treaty body resources in view of the activities and capacities of other UN bodies in these circumstances.

Examination of reports:
24. Improve the use of country rapporteurs. Charge country rapporteurs with the responsibility of: studying a particular report; preparing, with the assistance of the secretariat, a written comprehensive study; identifying inadequacies; summarizing the significant issues.
25. Ensure the best use of time during the dialogue: limit the length of time for introductory remarks of state parties, avoid repetitious questioning by members, and ensure time is allotted to follow-up questions or comments.
26. Focus the dialogue on key issues and themes identified by the country rapporteur, the pre-sessional working group and the state's written responses to the list of issues.
27. Schedule meetings, where appropriate, in the country concerned.
28. Schedule for review all states which have failed to report for considerable lengths of time.

Concluding observations:
29. Disseminate concluding observations immediately after their adoption, including to all relevant UN agencies. Send concluding observations to NGOs which have exhibited an interest in the state report.
30. Adopt concluding observations which clearly identify circumstances which are inconsistent with the requirements of the treaty, and which are sufficiently specific to be useful to domestic legislators, policy-makers and citizens.

(iii) *The Office of the High Commissioner for Human Rights and the Division for the Advancement of Women should*

Information gathering:
31. Develop a country profile consisting of all the country-specific information within the UN system which could be updated and supplied to the treaty bodies. Utilize, where appropriate, the assistance of the UN specialized agencies.
32. To the extent possible, assist in providing NGOs with resources to participate in the treaty monitoring process.
33. Facilitate field missions for the treaty body members, where appropriate.

Co-operation:
34. Encourage co-operation between the treaty bodies.
35. Schedule treaty body sessions simultaneously to encourage co-operation.
36. Schedule the meeting of special rapporteurs and other human rights mechanisms, and the meeting of the chairpersons of the treaty bodies at the same time.

Access:
37. Take steps to ensure public access to state reports.
38. Ensure that the deliberations of treaty bodies, and in particular their concluding observations, are disseminated to other parts of the UN system with a human rights mandate or function. Take steps to ensure that the work of the treaty bodies is disseminated at the national level in the country concerned.
39. Ensure that the various websites of the Secretariat are fully integrated and cross-referenced.
40. Encourage the hosting of roundtables between the treaty bodies, members of the UN system and NGOs to identify gaps in information collection and to explore ways of collecting and sharing information and the identification of benchmarks for the enjoyment of human rights.
41. Ensure adequate attention is given to educating, interesting, and informing the media about the work of the treaty bodies.

(iv) *The Annual Meeting of the Chairpersons of the Treaty Bodies should*
42. Allocate time for sustained discussion of treaty body working methods.
43. Allocate time for discussion of a common substantive theme arising under several treaties, with a view to developing common guidelines on that theme, so that portions of state reports might satisfy the requirements of more than one treaty body.
44. Create a sub-committee of chairpersons to address and to prepare a public report on the issues of: increased cooperation among the treaty bodies, treaty body working methods, and common substantive themes under the treaties.

(v) *NGOs should*

Education and access:
45. Conduct national, regional and international training with respect to the human rights treaty system.
46. Develop a data base of national NGOs which should be kept informed of the treaty processes.

47. Encourage, where appropriate, national coalitions of NGOs to cooperate with the treaty bodies and to monitor the implementation of treaty obligations.
48. Facilitate access by national NGOs to the treaty bodies, where necessary, through the experience and assistance of international NGOs.
49. Inform the media about all stages of the treaty body process, and encourage their interest in the dialogue with state parties and the concluding observations of the treaty bodies.

Information gathering and input:
50. Provide credible and reliable information to treaty bodies to be used in the review of national reports.
51. Host expert group meetings to provide input to the development of general comments and recommendations by the treaty bodies.

(*vi*) *Private bodies and foundations should*

52. Facilitate the production of educational materials publicizing the work of the treaty bodies.
53. Establish funds to facilitate the attendance by NGOs to the sessions of the treaty bodies.
54. Facilitate national, sub-regional, regional and international meetings between treaty body members.

(D) POST-REPORTING FOLLOW-UP

(*i*) *Treaty bodies should*

55. Publicize the concluding observations.
56. Request states parties to translate the concluding observations into local languages, and disseminate them.
57. Request the state party, where the committee has made specific recommendations, to inform the committee within a specified period of time what action has been taken to give effect to the recommendations.
58. Appoint a special rapporteur for follow-up of state reports with a mandate to seek information from the state party or from other sources, such as NGOs and relevant national institutions, to request meetings with representatives of the state, to request visits to states where appropriate, and to report to the committee at regular intervals on the progress of follow-up activities and the extent of state party compliance with the requests of the committee.
59. Publish the results of follow-up procedures and include them in the annual report, giving special prominence to states parties which fail to respond to requests for information.

(*ii*) *The Office of the High Commissioner for Human Rights and the Division for the Advancement of Women should*

60. Budget adequately for follow-up activities.
61. Acknowledge that follow-up activities are an integral and important part of treaty body activities and must be serviced accordingly.
62. Create a team of professionals to collect and analyze information on the

follow-up of the treaty bodies' recommendations, and to establish a continued dialogue with governments. This team could be a group of specialists on international human rights standards in all regions of the world, available to governments on an on-going basis.
63. Incorporate all the concluding observations produced by all the treaty bodies into a UN system-wide country assessment.
64. Transmit the concluding observations of treaty bodies to UN human rights field missions, and UN agencies, with a view to monitoring the state party's compliance with the treaty body's recommendations.
65. Encourage UNDP country offices to consider having an officer specializing in international human rights standards. Encourage the governance sectors of UNDP country offices to consider assistance and the provision of services designed to give effect to recommendations of the treaty bodies.
66. Provide advisory services and technical assistance to states parties, in cooperation with field offices of UN agencies, which are directed at encouraging implementation of treaties at the national level. Assist in the development of programs of action in states parties for implementing concluding observations.
67. Prepare annual press releases on follow-up activities.

(iii) Other UN bodies should

68. The General Assembly, ECOSOC, the Human Rights Commission, and the Commission on the Status of Women, should take up and reinforce the concluding observations, decisions and recommendations of the treaty bodies.

(iv) NGOs should

69. Encourage the use at the national level, including in domestic litigation, of the results of the treaty body process such as: undertakings in state reports, General Comments and Recommendations.

(v) Private bodies and foundations should

70. Sponsor research into the impact of the work of the treaty bodies at the national level, specifically, documentation and analysis of the impact of the treaties and the operation of the treaty bodies, and collections of case studies on the use of the treaty regime by individuals, and national and international NGOs.

(E) INDIVIDUAL COMMUNICATIONS

Given the limitations, inherent and otherwise, of the state reporting system of implementation, an ability to implement the legal standards through individual complaints and remedies offers an important alternative.

The international complaint process is activated following an exhaustion of domestic remedies. International machinery cannot replace the obligation and capacity of national institutions and courts to implement human rights standards.

The objectives of an individual complaint procedure are to provide individual victims with an effective and timely remedy; to bring about systemic changes to law and practice which will benefit others in a similar position, and to provide guidance to states parties, national institutions and courts on the requirements of the treaty through the elaboration of the meaning of the treaty provisions.

(i) States parties should

71. Translate decisions relating to the state party, and summaries of other decisions, into local languages.

(ii) Treaty bodies should

Quality of decisions:
72. In view of the important educational and preventive potential of individual cases, provide full, reasoned decisions on the merits.

Procedures:
73. Join the admissibility and merits of a case wherever possible.
74. Take provisional measures to protect complaints from irremediable damage.
75. Impose short time limits for state responses.
76. Adopt evidentiary presumptions to facilitate determinations in the absence of submissions or complete information.
77. Sit in chambers in routine cases to make draft determinations, which would be adopted by the plenary, normally without debate.
78. Review the viability of conducting oral hearings where appropriate, in circumstances where legal aid is available to the complainant, and with strictly enforced time limits on oral presentations by the parties.

(iii) The Office of the High Commissioner for Human Rights and the Division for the Advancement of Women should

79. Organize seminars on communications procedures and jurisprudence at both the international and national level.
80. Provide advice to complainants on admissibility problems and procedures.
81. Publicize decisions of treaty bodies.

(iv) NGOs should

82. Explore the viability of creating a network of international human rights lawyers to act for complainants.
83. Make use of The Torture Convention's Article 20.
84. International NGOs should consider assisting in those instances where national NGOs are reluctant to be publicly associated with a case.

(F) POST-INDIVIDUAL COMPLAINT FOLLOW-UP

(i) States parties should

85. Ensure that there is a recourse to domestic remedies for violation of the human rights treaties. Take the view of the treaty bodies concerning violations, seriously.

(ii) Treaty bodies should

86. Appoint a special rapporteur on follow-up to the views of the committee.
87. Produce regular, detailed progress reports on a state-by-state basis, which should be discussed in public session and published.

88. Identify states which do not cooperate in the follow-up process in the annual report.
89. Undertake follow-up missions to state parties, where appropriate.
90. Formulate a model of enabling legislation, for consideration by states parties, which would permit claims before domestic courts for non-compliance with the views of the committee on an individual communication.

(G) MEMBERSHIP AND CODES OF CONDUCT FOR TREATY BODIES

(i) States parties should

91. Nominate and elect individuals to membership on the treaty bodies who are genuinely independent, impartial and have the necessary international human rights expertise. Ensure that individuals on treaty bodies which deal with individual complaints are well-qualified to handle the procedure.
92. Take into account regional and gender balance in nominating and electing members to the treaty bodies.
93. Respect the codes of conduct for members which are developed by the treaty bodies.

(ii) Treaty bodies should

94. Develop codes of conduct for members which would address such matters as independence and impartiality, the relationship of members with their government and NGOs, and the involvement of members in any aspect of the consideration of reports or communications relating to their own countries.

(iii) NGOs should

95. Encourage the identification and election of qualified treaty body experts.

(H) INSTITUTIONAL CHANGE

In addition to the preceding shorter term recommendations, some specific suggestions for **step-by-step** change directed at the longer term were introduced. These have been set out below as a contribution to the field and the shared goal of strengthening the enforcement of international human rights law in the twenty-first century.

96. The treaty bodies should introduce into the state reporting process, joint modular guidelines which group similar or related articles under the different treaties thematically, and which allow states to repeat information in their reports common to these modular groupings.
97. The treaty bodies should ask states parties to produce a single, consolidated report on the six human rights treaties. Compliance should be addressed by grouping articles of the treaties together on a thematic basis.
98. The treaty bodies should engage in joint examinations of reports; the treaty bodies should conduct, where appropriate, examinations in the country concerned.
99. The six treaty bodies should be merged into a single, permanent, full-time body which would consider state reports.
100. The potential for insensitivity or disregard of some rights, should be

addressed by paying special attention to these categories of rights which have suffered from past neglect, such as many dimensions of sex discrimination. In particular, the clear demarcation of key thematic issues and the selection of members with insight, understanding and expertise on these subjects, should be ensured.
101. States parties should ensure the identification, development and application of obligatory qualifications for treaty-body membership. The membership qualifications of a consolidated committee charged with the task of considering state reports should give rise to an interdisciplinary body oriented towards engendering a culture of human rights in states parties.
102. Provision for individual complaint mechanisms should be extended to all six human rights treaties, through the elaboration of additional optional protocols.
103. A single, permanent, full-time body should be created which would consider individual complaints under all six human rights treaties. Such a committee would be of a quasi-judicial nature. The membership qualifications of a consolidated committee charged with the task of considering individual complaints should include legal experience.
104. A permanent international court of human rights should be created that could handle individual complaints arising from all six, or portions of all six, of the human rights treaties.
105. The court should be given only advisory jurisdiction to render non-binding decisions at the behest of states parties or treaty bodies, but not individuals.
106. Significant rules and processes should be developed which when instituted, would warrant making the court accessible to individuals, and potentially groups, and rendering determinations of the court legally binding.

Appendix 1: The Text of the Treaties

International Convention on the Elimination of All Forms of Racial Discrimination

Adopted and opened for signature and ratification by General Assembly Resolution 2106 (XX) of 21 December 1965

entry into force 4 January 1969

The States Parties to this Convention,

Considering that the Charter of the United Nations is based on the principles of the dignity and equality inherent in all human beings, and that all Member States have pledged themselves to take joint and separate action, in co-operation with the Organization, for the achievement of one of the purposes of the United Nations which is to promote and encourage universal respect for and observance of human rights and fundamental freedoms for all, without distinction as to race, sex, language or religion,

Considering that the Universal Declaration of Human Rights proclaims that all human beings are born free and equal in dignity and rights and that everyone is entitled to all the rights and freedoms set out therein, without distinction of any kind, in particular as to race, colour or national origin,

Considering that all human beings are equal before the law and are entitled to equal protection of the law against any discrimination and against any incitement to discrimination,

Considering that the United Nations has condemned colonialism and all practices of segregation and discrimination associated therewith, in whatever form and wherever they exist, and that the Declaration on the Granting of Independence to Colonial Countries and Peoples of 14 December 1960 (General Assembly resolution 1514 (XV)) has affirmed and solemnly proclaimed the necessity of bringing them to a speedy and unconditional end,

Considering that the United Nations Declaration on the Elimination of All Forms of Racial Discrimination of 20 November 1963 (General Assembly resolution 1904 (XVIII)) solemnly affirms the necessity of speedily eliminating racial discrimination throughout the world in all its forms and manifestations and of securing understanding of and respect for the dignity of the human person,

Convinced that any doctrine of superiority based on racial differentiation is scientifically false, morally condemnable, socially unjust and dangerous, and that there is no justification for racial discrimination, in theory or in practice, anywhere,

Reaffirming that discrimination between human beings on the grounds of race, colour or ethnic origin is an obstacle to friendly and peaceful relations among nations and is capable of disturbing peace and security among peoples and the harmony of persons living side by side even within one and the same State,

Convinced that the existence of racial barriers is repugnant to the ideals of any human society,

Alarmed by manifestations of racial discrimination still in evidence in some areas of the world and by governmental policies based on racial superiority or hatred, such as policies of apartheid, segregation or separation,

Resolved to adopt all necessary measures for speedily eliminating racial discrimination in all its forms and manifestations, and to prevent and combat racist doctrines and practices in order to promote understanding between races and to build an international community free from all forms of racial segregation and racial discrimination,

Bearing in mind the Convention concerning Discrimination in respect of Employment and Occupation adopted by the International Labour Organisation in 1958, and the Convention against Discrimination in Education adopted by the United Nations Educational, Scientific and Cultural Organization in 1960,

Desiring to implement the principles embodied in the United Nations Declaration on the Elimination of All Forms of Racial Discrimination and to secure the earliest adoption of practical measures to that end,

Have agreed as follows:

PART I

Article 1

1. In this Convention, the term "racial discrimination" shall mean any distinction, exclusion, restriction or preference based on race, colour, descent, or national or ethnic origin which has the purpose or effect of nullifying or impairing the recognition, enjoyment or exercise, on an equal footing, of human rights and fundamental freedoms in the political, economic, social, cultural or any other field of public life.
2. This Convention shall not apply to distinctions, exclusions, restrictions or preferences made by a State Party to this Convention between citizens and non-citizens.
3. Nothing in this Convention may be interpreted as affecting in any way the legal provisions of States Parties concerning nationality, citizenship or naturalization, provided that such provisions do not discriminate against any particular nationality.
4. Special measures taken for the sole purpose of securing adequate advancement of certain racial or ethnic groups or individuals requiring such protection as may be necessary in order to ensure such groups or individuals equal enjoyment or exercise of human rights and fundamental freedoms shall not be deemed racial discrimination, provided, however, that such measures do not, as a consequence, lead to the maintenance of separate rights for different racial groups and that they shall not be continued after the objectives for which they were taken have been achieved.

Article 2
1. States Parties condemn racial discrimination and undertake to pursue by all appropriate means and without delay a policy of eliminating racial discrimination in all its forms and promoting understanding among all races, and, to this end:
   (a) Each State Party undertakes to engage in no act or practice of racial discrimination against persons, groups of persons or institutions and to ensure that all public authorities and public institutions, national and local, shall act in conformity with this obligation;
   (b) Each State Party undertakes not to sponsor, defend or support racial discrimination by any persons or organizations;
   (c) Each State Party shall take effective measures to review governmental, national and local policies, and to amend, rescind or nullify any laws and regulations which have the effect of creating or perpetuating racial discrimination wherever it exists;
   (d) Each State Party shall prohibit and bring to an end, by all appropriate means, including legislation as required by circumstances, racial discrimination by any persons, group or organization;
   (e) Each State Party undertakes to encourage, where appropriate, integrationist multiracial organizations and movements and other means of eliminating barriers between races, and to discourage anything which tends to strengthen racial division.
2. States Parties shall, when the circumstances so warrant, take, in the social, economic, cultural and other fields, special and concrete measures to ensure the adequate development and protection of certain racial groups or individuals belonging to them, for the purpose of guaranteeing them the full and equal enjoyment of human rights and fundamental freedoms. These measures shall in no case entail as a consequence the maintenance of unequal or separate rights for different racial groups after the objectives for which they were taken have been achieved.

Article 3
States Parties particularly condemn racial segregation and apartheid and undertake to prevent, prohibit and eradicate all practices of this nature in territories under their jurisdiction.

Article 4
States Parties condemn all propaganda and all organizations which are based on ideas or theories of superiority of one race or group of persons of one colour or ethnic origin, or which attempt to justify or promote racial hatred and discrimination in any form, and undertake to adopt immediate and positive measures designed to eradicate all incitement to, or acts of, such discrimination and, to this end, with due regard to the principles embodied in the Universal Declaration of Human Rights and the rights expressly set forth in article 5 of this Convention, *inter alia*:
(a) Shall declare an offence punishable by law all dissemination of ideas based on racial superiority or hatred, incitement to racial discrimination, as well as all acts of violence or incitement to such acts against any race or group of persons of another colour or ethnic origin, and also the provision of any assistance to racist activities, including the financing thereof;

(b) Shall declare illegal and prohibit organizations, and also organized and all other propaganda activities, which promote and incite racial discrimination, and shall recognize participation in such organizations or activities as an offence punishable by law;
(c) Shall not permit public authorities or public institutions, national or local, to promote or incite racial discrimination.

Article 5
In compliance with the fundamental obligations laid down in article 2 of this Convention, States Parties undertake to prohibit and to eliminate racial discrimination in all its forms and to guarantee the right of everyone, without distinction as to race, colour, or national or ethnic origin, to equality before the law, notably in the enjoyment of the following rights:
(a) The right to equal treatment before the tribunals and all other organs administering justice;
(b) The right to security of person and protection by the State against violence or bodily harm, whether inflicted by government officials or by any individual group or institution;
(c) Political rights, in particular the right to participate in elections-to vote and to stand for election-on the basis of universal and equal suffrage, to take part in the Government as well as in the conduct of public affairs at any level and to have equal access to public service;
(d) Other civil rights, in particular:
    (i) The right to freedom of movement and residence within the border of the State;
    (ii) The right to leave any country, including one's own, and to return to one's country;
    (iii) The right to nationality;
    (iv) The right to marriage and choice of spouse;
    (v) The right to own property alone as well as in association with others;
    (vi) The right to inherit;
    (vii) The right to freedom of thought, conscience and religion;
    (viii) The right to freedom of opinion and expression;
    (ix) The right to freedom of peaceful assembly and association;
(e) Economic, social and cultural rights, in particular:
    (i) The rights to work, to free choice of employment, to just and favourable conditions of work, to protection against unemployment, to equal pay for equal work, to just and favourable remuneration;
    (ii) The right to form and join trade unions;
    (iii) The right to housing;
    (iv) The right to public health, medical care, social security and social services;
    (v) The right to education and training;
    (vi) The right to equal participation in cultural activities;
(f) The right of access to any place or service intended for use by the general public, such as transport hotels, restaurants, cafes, theatres and parks.

Article 6
States Parties shall assure to everyone within their jurisdiction effective protection and remedies, through the competent national tribunals and other State

institutions, against any acts of racial discrimination which violate his human rights and fundamental freedoms contrary to this Convention, as well as the right to seek from such tribunals just and adequate reparation or satisfaction for any damage suffered as a result of such discrimination.

Article 7
States Parties undertake to adopt immediate and effective measures, particularly in the fields of teaching, education, culture and information, with a view to combating prejudices which lead to racial discrimination and to promoting understanding, tolerance and friendship among nations and racial or ethnical groups, as well as to propagating the purposes and principles of the Charter of the United Nations, the Universal Declaration of Human Rights, the United Nations Declaration on the Elimination of All Forms of Racial Discrimination, and this Convention.

PART II

Article 8
1. There shall be established a Committee on the Elimination of Racial Discrimination (hereinafter referred to as the Committee) consisting of eighteen experts of high moral standing and acknowledged impartiality elected by States Parties from among their nationals, who shall serve in their personal capacity, consideration being given to equitable geographical distribution and to the representation of the different forms of civilization as well as of the principal legal systems.
2. The members of the Committee shall be elected by secret ballot from a list of persons nominated by the States Parties. Each State Party may nominate one person from among its own nationals.
3. The initial election shall be held six months after the date of the entry into force of this Convention. At least three months before the date of each election the Secretary-General of the United Nations shall address a letter to the States Parties inviting them to submit their nominations within two months. The Secretary-General shall prepare a list in alphabetical order of all persons thus nominated, indicating the States Parties which have nominated them, and shall submit it to the States Parties.
4. Elections of the members of the Committee shall be held at a meeting of States Parties convened by the Secretary-General at United Nations Headquarters. At that meeting, for which two thirds of the States Parties shall constitute a quorum, the persons elected to the Committee shall be nominees who obtain the largest number of votes and an absolute majority of the votes of the representatives of States Parties present and voting.
5. (a) The members of the Committee shall be elected for a term of four years. However, the terms of nine of the members elected at the first election shall expire at the end of two years; immediately after the first election the names of these nine members shall be chosen by lot by the Chairman of the Committee;
   (b) For the filling of casual vacancies, the State Party whose expert has ceased to function as a member of the Committee shall appoint another expert from among its nationals, subject to the approval of the Committee.

6. States Parties shall be responsible for the expenses of the members of the Committee while they are in performance of Committee duties.

Article 9
1. States Parties undertake to submit to the Secretary-General of the United Nations, for consideration by the Committee, a report on the legislative, judicial, administrative or other measures which they have adopted and which give effect to the provisions of this Convention:
   (a) within one year after the entry into force of the Convention for the State concerned; and
   (b) thereafter every two years and whenever the Committee so requests. The Committee may request further information from the States Parties.
2. The Committee shall report annually, through the Secretary General, to the General Assembly of the United Nations on its activities and may make suggestions and general recommendations based on the examination of the reports and information received from the States Parties. Such suggestions and general recommendations shall be reported to the General Assembly together with comments, if any, from States Parties.

Article 10
1. The Committee shall adopt its own rules of procedure.
2. The Committee shall elect its officers for a term of two years.
3. The secretariat of the Committee shall be provided by the Secretary General of the United Nations.
4. The meetings of the Committee shall normally be held at United Nations Headquarters.

Article 11
1. If a State Party considers that another State Party is not giving effect to the provisions of this Convention, it may bring the matter to the attention of the Committee. The Committee shall then transmit the communication to the State Party concerned. Within three months, the receiving State shall submit to the Committee written explanations or statements clarifying the matter and the remedy, if any, that may have been taken by that State.
2. If the matter is not adjusted to the satisfaction of both parties, either by bilateral negotiations or by any other procedure open to them, within six months after the receipt by the receiving State of the initial communication, either State shall have the right to refer the matter again to the Committee by notifying the Committee and also the other State.
3. The Committee shall deal with a matter referred to it in accordance with paragraph 2 of this article after it has ascertained that all available domestic remedies have been invoked and exhausted in the case, in conformity with the generally recognized principles of international law. This shall not be the rule where the application of the remedies is unreasonably prolonged.
4. In any matter referred to it, the Committee may call upon the States Parties concerned to supply any other relevant information.
5. When any matter arising out of this article is being considered by the Committee, the States Parties concerned shall be entitled to send a representative to take part in the proceedings of the Committee, without voting rights, while the matter is under consideration.

Article 12
1. (a) After the Committee has obtained and collated all the information it deems necessary, the Chairman shall appoint an ad hoc Conciliation Commission (hereinafter referred to as the Commission) comprising five persons who may or may not be members of the Committee. The members of the Commission shall be appointed with the unanimous consent of the parties to the dispute, and its good offices shall be made available to the States concerned with a view to an amicable solution of the matter on the basis of respect for this Convention;
   (b) If the States parties to the dispute fail to reach agreement within three months on all or part of the composition of the Commission, the members of the Commission not agreed upon by the States parties to the dispute shall be elected by secret ballot by a two-thirds majority vote of the Committee from among its own members.
2. The members of the Commission shall serve in their personal capacity. They shall not be nationals of the States parties to the dispute or of a State not Party to this Convention.
3. The Commission shall elect its own Chairman and adopt its own rules of procedure.
4. The meetings of the Commission shall normally be held at United Nations Headquarters or at any other convenient place as determined by the Commission.
5. The secretariat provided in accordance with article 10, paragraph 3, of this Convention shall also service the Commission whenever a dispute among States Parties brings the Commission into being.
6. The States parties to the dispute shall share equally all the expenses of the members of the Commission in accordance with estimates to be provided by the Secretary-General of the United Nations.
7. The Secretary-General shall be empowered to pay the expenses of the members of the Commission, if necessary, before reimbursement by the States parties to the dispute in accordance with paragraph 6 of this article.
8. The information obtained and collated by the Committee shall be made available to the Commission, and the Commission may call upon the States concerned to supply any other relevant information.

Article 13
1. When the Commission has fully considered the matter, it shall prepare and submit to the Chairman of the Committee a report embodying its findings on all questions of fact relevant to the issue between the parties and containing such recommendations as it may think proper for the amicable solution of the dispute.
2. The Chairman of the Committee shall communicate the report of the Commission to each of the States parties to the dispute. These States shall, within three months, inform the Chairman of the Committee whether or not they accept the recommendations contained in the report of the Commission.
3. After the period provided for in paragraph 2 of this article, the Chairman of the Committee shall communicate the report of the Commission and the declarations of the States Parties concerned to the other States Parties to this Convention.

Article 14
1. A State Party may at any time declare that it recognizes the competence of the Committee to receive and consider communications from individuals or groups of individuals within its jurisdiction claiming to be victims of a violation by that State Party of any of the rights set forth in this Convention. No communication shall be received by the Committee if it concerns a State Party which has not made such a declaration.
2. Any State Party which makes a declaration as provided for in paragraph I of this article may establish or indicate a body within its national legal order which shall be competent to receive and consider petitions from individuals and groups of individuals within its jurisdiction who claim to be victims of a violation of any of the rights set forth in this Convention and who have exhausted other available local remedies.
3. A declaration made in accordance with paragraph 1 of this article and the name of any body established or indicated in accordance with paragraph 2 of this article shall be deposited by the State Party concerned with the Secretary-General of the United Nations, who shall transmit copies thereof to the other States Parties. A declaration may be withdrawn at any time by notification to the Secretary-General, but such a withdrawal shall not affect communications pending before the Committee.
4. A register of petitions shall be kept by the body established or indicated in accordance with paragraph 2 of this article, and certified copies of the register shall be filed annually through appropriate channels with the Secretary-General on the understanding that the contents shall not be publicly disclosed.
5. In the event of failure to obtain satisfaction from the body established or indicated in accordance with paragraph 2 of this article, the petitioner shall have the right to communicate the matter to the Committee within six months.
6. (a) The Committee shall confidentially bring any communication referred to it to the attention of the State Party alleged to be violating any provision of this Convention, but the identity of the individual or groups of individuals concerned shall not be revealed without his or their express consent. The Committee shall not receive anonymous communications;
    (b) Within three months, the receiving State shall submit to the Committee written explanations or statements clarifying the matter and the remedy, if any, that may have been taken by that State.
7. (a) The Committee shall consider communications in the light of all information made available to it by the State Party concerned and by the petitioner. The Committee shall not consider any communication from a petitioner unless it has ascertained that the petitioner has exhausted all available domestic remedies. However, this shall not be the rule where the application of the remedies is unreasonably prolonged;
    (b) The Committee shall forward its suggestions and recommendations, if any, to the State Party concerned and to the petitioner.
8. The Committee shall include in its annual report a summary of such communications and, where appropriate, a summary of the explanations and statements of the States Parties concerned and of its own suggestions and recommendations.
9. The Committee shall be competent to exercise the functions provided for in

this article only when at least ten States Parties to this Convention are bound by declarations in accordance with paragraph I of this article.

Article 15
1. Pending the achievement of the objectives of the Declaration on the Granting of Independence to Colonial Countries and Peoples, contained in General Assembly resolution 1514 (XV) of 14 December 1960, the provisions of this Convention shall in no way limit the right of petition granted to these peoples by other international instruments or by the United Nations and its specialized agencies.
2. (a) The Committee established under article 8, paragraph 1, of this Convention shall receive copies of the petitions from, and submit expressions of opinion and recommendations on these petitions to, the bodies of the United Nations which deal with matters directly related to the principles and objectives of this Convention in their consideration of petitions from the inhabitants of Trust and Non-Self-Governing Territories and all other territories to which General Assembly resolution 1514 (XV) applies, relating to matters covered by this Convention which are before these bodies;
   (b) The Committee shall receive from the competent bodies of the United Nations copies of the reports concerning the legislative, judicial, administrative or other measures directly related to the principles and objectives of this Convention applied by the administering Powers within the Territories mentioned in subparagraph (a) of this paragraph, and shall express opinions and make recommendations to these bodies.
3. The Committee shall include in its report to the General Assembly a summary of the petitions and reports it has received from United Nations bodies, and the expressions of opinion and recommendations of the Committee relating to the said petitions and reports.
4. The Committee shall request from the Secretary-General of the United Nations all information relevant to the objectives of this Convention and available to him regarding the Territories mentioned in paragraph 2 (a) of this article.

Article 16
The provisions of this Convention concerning the settlement of disputes or complaints shall be applied without prejudice to other procedures for settling disputes or complaints in the field of discrimination laid down in the constituent instruments of, or conventions adopted by, the United Nations and its specialized agencies, and shall not prevent the States Parties from having recourse to other procedures for settling a dispute in accordance with general or special international agreements in force between them.

PART III

Article 17
1. This Convention is open for signature by any State Member of the United Nations or member of any of its specialized agencies, by any State Party to the Statute of the International Court of Justice, and by any other State which has been invited by the General Assembly of the United Nations to become a Party to this Convention.

2. This Convention is subject to ratification. Instruments of ratification shall be deposited with the Secretary-General of the United Nations.

Article 18
1. This Convention shall be open to accession by any State referred to in article 17, paragraph 1, of the Convention.
2. Accession shall be effected by the deposit of an instrument of accession with the Secretary-General of the United Nations.

Article 19
1. This Convention shall enter into force on the thirtieth day after the date of the deposit with the Secretary-General of the United Nations of the twenty-seventh instrument of ratification or instrument of accession.
2. For each State ratifying this Convention or acceding to it after the deposit of the twenty-seventh instrument of ratification or instrument of accession, the Convention shall enter into force on the thirtieth day after the date of the deposit of its own instrument of ratification or instrument of accession.

Article 20
1. The Secretary-General of the United Nations shall receive and circulate to all States which are or may become Parties to this Convention reservations made by States at the time of ratification or accession. Any State which objects to the reservation shall, within a period of ninety days from the date of the said communication, notify the Secretary-General that it does not accept it.
2. A reservation incompatible with the object and purpose of this Convention shall not be permitted, nor shall a reservation the effect of which would inhibit the operation of any of the bodies established by this Convention be allowed. A reservation shall be considered incompatible or inhibitive if at least two thirds of the States Parties to this Convention object to it.
3. Reservations may be withdrawn at any time by notification to this effect addressed to the Secretary-General. Such notification shall take effect on the date on which it is received.

Article 21
A State Party may denounce this Convention by written notification to the Secretary-General of the United Nations. Denunciation shall take effect one year after the date of receipt of the notification by the Secretary General.

Article 22
Any dispute between two or more States Parties with respect to the interpretation or application of this Convention, which is not settled by negotiation or by the procedures expressly provided for in this Convention, shall, at the request of any of the parties to the dispute, be referred to the International Court of Justice for decision, unless the disputants agree to another mode of settlement.

Article 23
1. A request for the revision of this Convention may be made at any time by any State Party by means of a notification in writing addressed to the Secretary-General of the United Nations.
2. The General Assembly of the United Nations shall decide upon the steps, if any, to be taken in respect of such a request.

Article 24
The Secretary-General of the United Nations shall inform all States referred to in article 17, paragraph 1, of this Convention of the following particulars:
(a) Signatures, ratifications and accessions under articles 17 and 18;
(b) The date of entry into force of this Convention under article 19;
(c) Communications and declarations received under articles 14, 20 and 23;
(d) Denunciations under article 21.

Article 25
1. This Convention, of which the Chinese, English, French, Russian and Spanish texts are equally authentic, shall be deposited in the archives of the United Nations.
2. The Secretary-General of the United Nations shall transmit certified copies of this Convention to all States belonging to any of the categories mentioned in article 17, paragraph 1, of the Convention.

International Covenant on Civil and Political Rights

Adopted and opened for signature, ratification and accession by
General Assembly Resolution 2200A (XXI) of 16 December 1966

entry into force 23 March 1976

Preamble

The States Parties to the present Covenant,

Considering that, in accordance with the principles proclaimed in the Charter of the United Nations, recognition of the inherent dignity and of the equal and inalienable rights of all members of the human family is the foundation of freedom, justice and peace in the world,

Recognizing that these rights derive from the inherent dignity of the human person,

Recognizing that, in accordance with the Universal Declaration of Human Rights, the ideal of free human beings enjoying civil and political freedom and freedom from fear and want can only be achieved if conditions are created whereby everyone may enjoy his civil and political rights, as well as his economic, social and cultural rights,

Considering the obligation of States under the Charter of the United Nations to promote universal respect for, and observance of, human rights and freedoms,

Realizing that the individual, having duties to other individuals and to the community to which he belongs, is under a responsibility to strive for the promotion and observance of the rights recognized in the present Covenant,

Agree upon the following articles:

PART I

Article 1
1. All peoples have the right of self-determination. By virtue of that right they freely determine their political status and freely pursue their economic, social and cultural development.
2. All peoples may, for their own ends, freely dispose of their natural wealth and resources without prejudice to any obligations arising out of international economic co-operation, based upon the principle of mutual benefit, and international law. In no case may a people be deprived of its own means of subsistence.
3. The States Parties to the present Covenant, including those having responsibil-

ity for the administration of Non-Self-Governing and Trust Territories, shall promote the realization of the right of self-determination, and shall respect that right, in conformity with the provisions of the Charter of the United Nations.

PART II

Article 2
1. Each State Party to the present Covenant undertakes to respect and to ensure to all individuals within its territory and subject to its jurisdiction the rights recognized in the present Covenant, without distinction of any kind, such as race, colour, sex, language, religion, political or other opinion, national or social origin, property, birth or other status.
2. Where not already provided for by existing legislative or other measures, each State Party to the present Covenant undertakes to take the necessary steps, in accordance with its constitutional processes and with the provisions of the present Covenant, to adopt such laws or other measures as may be necessary to give effect to the rights recognized in the present Covenant.
3. Each State Party to the present Covenant undertakes:
   (a) To ensure that any person whose rights or freedoms as herein recognized are violated shall have an effective remedy, notwithstanding that the violation has been committed by persons acting in an official capacity;
   (b) To ensure that any person claiming such a remedy shall have his right thereto determined by competent judicial, administrative or legislative authorities, or by any other competent authority provided for by the legal system of the State, and to develop the possibilities of judicial remedy;
   (c) To ensure that the competent authorities shall enforce such remedies when granted.

Article 3
The States Parties to the present Covenant undertake to ensure the equal right of men and women to the enjoyment of all civil and political rights set forth in the present Covenant.

Article 4
1. In time of public emergency which threatens the life of the nation and the existence of which is officially proclaimed, the States Parties to the present Covenant may take measures derogating from their obligations under the present Covenant to the extent strictly required by the exigencies of the situation, provided that such measures are not inconsistent with their other obligations under international law and do not involve discrimination solely on the ground of race, colour, sex, language, religion or social origin.
2. No derogation from articles 6, 7, 8 (paragraphs I and 2), 11, 15, 16 and 18 may be made under this provision.
3. Any State Party to the present Covenant availing itself of the right of derogation shall immediately inform the other States Parties to the present Covenant, through the intermediary of the Secretary-General of the United Nations, of the provisions from which it has derogated and of the reasons by which it

was actuated. A further communication shall be made, through the same intermediary, on the date on which it terminates such derogation.

Article 5
1. Nothing in the present Covenant may be interpreted as implying for any State, group or person any right to engage in any activity or perform any act aimed at the destruction of any of the rights and freedoms recognized herein or at their limitation to a greater extent than is provided for in the present Covenant.
2. There shall be no restriction upon or derogation from any of the fundamental human rights recognized or existing in any State Party to the present Covenant pursuant to law, conventions, regulations or custom on the pretext that the present Covenant does not recognize such rights or that it recognizes them to a lesser extent.

PART III

Article 6
1. Every human being has the inherent right to life. This right shall be protected by law. No one shall be arbitrarily deprived of his life.
2. In countries which have not abolished the death penalty, sentence of death may be imposed only for the most serious crimes in accordance with the law in force at the time of the commission of the crime and not contrary to the provisions of the present Covenant and to the Convention on the Prevention and Punishment of the Crime of Genocide. This penalty can only be carried out pursuant to a final judgement rendered by a competent court.
3. When deprivation of life constitutes the crime of genocide, it is understood that nothing in this article shall authorize any State Party to the present Covenant to derogate in any way from any obligation assumed under the provisions of the Convention on the Prevention and Punishment of the Crime of Genocide.
4. Anyone sentenced to death shall have the right to seek pardon or commutation of the sentence. Amnesty, pardon or commutation of the sentence of death may be granted in all cases.
5. Sentence of death shall not be imposed for crimes committed by persons below eighteen years of age and shall not be carried out on pregnant women.
6. Nothing in this article shall be invoked to delay or to prevent the abolition of capital punishment by any State Party to the present Covenant.

Article 7
No one shall be subjected to torture or to cruel, inhuman or degrading treatment or punishment. In particular, no one shall be subjected without his free consent to medical or scientific experimentation.

Article 8
1. No one shall be held in slavery; slavery and the slave-trade in all their forms shall be prohibited.
2. No one shall be held in servitude.
3. (a) No one shall be required to perform forced or compulsory labour;
   (b) Paragraph 3(a) shall not be held to preclude, in countries where imprisonment with hard labour may be imposed as a punishment for a crime, the

performance of hard labour in pursuance of a sentence to such punishment by a competent court;
(c) For the purpose of this paragraph the term "forced or compulsory labour" shall not include:
  (i) Any work or service, not referred to in subparagraph (b), normally required of a person who is under detention in consequence of a lawful order of a court, or of a person during conditional release from such detention;
  (ii) Any service of a military character and, in countries where conscientious objection is recognized, any national service required by law of conscientious objectors;
  (iii) Any service exacted in cases of emergency or calamity threatening the life or well-being of the community;
  (iv) Any work or service which forms part of normal civil obligations.

Article 9
1. Everyone has the right to liberty and security of person. No one shall be subjected to arbitrary arrest or detention. No one shall be deprived of his liberty except on such grounds and in accordance with such procedure as are established by law.
2. Anyone who is arrested shall be informed, at the time of arrest, of the reasons for his arrest and shall be promptly informed of any charges against him.
3. Anyone arrested or detained on a criminal charge shall be brought promptly before a judge or other officer authorized by law to exercise judicial power and shall be entitled to trial within a reasonable time or to release. It shall not be the general rule that persons awaiting trial shall be detained in custody, but release may be subject to guarantees to appear for trial, at any other stage of the judicial proceedings, and, should occasion arise, for execution of the judgement.
4. Anyone who is deprived of his liberty by arrest or detention shall be entitled to take proceedings before a court, in order that court may decide without delay on the lawfulness of his detention and order his release if the detention is not lawful.
5. Anyone who has been the victim of unlawful arrest or detention shall have an enforceable right to compensation.

Article 10
1. All persons deprived of their liberty shall be treated with humanity and with respect for the inherent dignity of the human person.
2. (a) Accused persons shall, save in exceptional circumstances, be segregated from convicted persons and shall be subject to separate treatment appropriate to their status as unconvicted persons;
   (b) Accused juvenile persons shall be separated from adults and brought as speedily as possible for adjudication.
3. The penitentiary system shall comprise treatment of prisoners the essential aim of which shall be their reformation and social rehabilitation. Juvenile offenders shall be segregated from adults and be accorded treatment appropriate to their age and legal status.

Article 11
No one shall be imprisoned merely on the ground of inability to fulfil a contractual obligation.

Article 12
1. Everyone lawfully within the territory of a State shall, within that territory, have the right to liberty of movement and freedom to choose his residence.
2. Everyone shall be free to leave any country, including his own.
3. The above-mentioned rights shall not be subject to any restrictions except those which are provided by law, are necessary to protect national security, public order (ordre public), public health or morals or the rights and freedoms of others, and are consistent with the other rights recognized in the present Covenant.
4. No one shall be arbitrarily deprived of the right to enter his own country.

Article 13
An alien lawfully in the territory of a State Party to the present Covenant may be expelled therefrom only in pursuance of a decision reached in accordance with law and shall, except where compelling reasons of national security otherwise require, be allowed to submit the reasons against his expulsion and to have his case reviewed by, and be represented for the purpose before, the competent authority or a person or persons especially designated by the competent authority.

Article 14
1. All persons shall be equal before the courts and tribunals. In the determination of any criminal charge against him, or of his rights and obligations in a suit at law, everyone shall be entitled to a fair and public hearing by a competent, independent and impartial tribunal established by law. The press and the public may be excluded from all or part of a trial for reasons of morals, public order (ordre public) or national security in a democratic society, or when the interest of the private lives of the parties so requires, or to the extent strictly necessary in the opinion of the court in special circumstances where publicity would prejudice the interests of justice; but any judgement rendered in a criminal case or in a suit at law shall be made public except where the interest of juvenile persons otherwise requires or the proceedings concern matrimonial disputes or the guardianship of children.
2. Everyone charged with a criminal offence shall have the right to be presumed innocent until proved guilty according to law.
3. In the determination of any criminal charge against him, everyone shall be entitled to the following minimum guarantees, in full equality:
   (a) To be informed promptly and in detail in a language which he understands of the nature and cause of the charge against him;
   (b) To have adequate time and facilities for the preparation of his defence and to communicate with counsel of his own choosing;
   (c) To be tried without undue delay;
   (d) To be tried in his presence, and to defend himself in person or through legal assistance of his own choosing; to be informed, if he does not have legal assistance, of this right; and to have legal assistance assigned to him, in any case where the interests of justice so require, and without payment

by him in any such case if he does not have sufficient means to pay for it;
  (e) To examine, or have examined, the witnesses against him and to obtain the attendance and examination of witnesses on his behalf under the same conditions as witnesses against him;
  (f) To have the free assistance of an interpreter if he cannot understand or speak the language used in court;
  (g) Not to be compelled to testify against himself or to confess guilt.
4. In the case of juvenile persons, the procedure shall be such as will take account of their age and the desirability of promoting their rehabilitation.
5. Everyone convicted of a crime shall have the right to his conviction and sentence being reviewed by a higher tribunal according to law.
6. When a person has by a final decision been convicted of a criminal offence and when subsequently his conviction has been reversed or he has been pardoned on the ground that a new or newly discovered fact shows conclusively that there has been a miscarriage of justice, the person who has suffered punishment as a result of such conviction shall be compensated according to law, unless it is proved that the non-disclosure of the unknown fact in time is wholly or partly attributable to him.
7. No one shall be liable to be tried or punished again for an offence for which he has already been finally convicted or acquitted in accordance with the law and penal procedure of each country.

Article 15
1. No one shall be held guilty of any criminal offence on account of any act or omission which did not constitute a criminal offence, under national or international law, at the time when it was committed. Nor shall a heavier penalty be imposed than the one that was applicable at the time when the criminal offence was committed. If, subsequent to the commission of the offence, provision is made by law for the imposition of the lighter penalty, the offender shall benefit thereby.
2. Nothing in this article shall prejudice the trial and punishment of any person for any act or omission which, at the time when it was committed, was criminal according to the general principles of law recognized by the community of nations.

Article 16
Everyone shall have the right to recognition everywhere as a person before the law.

Article 17
1. No one shall be subjected to arbitrary or unlawful interference with his privacy, family, home or correspondence, nor to unlawful attacks on his honour and reputation.
2. Everyone has the right to the protection of the law against such interference or attacks.

Article 18
1. Everyone shall have the right to freedom of thought, conscience and religion. This right shall include freedom to have or to adopt a religion or belief of his choice, and freedom, either individually or in community with others and

in public or private, to manifest his religion or belief in worship, observance, practice and teaching.
2. No one shall be subject to coercion which would impair his freedom to have or to adopt a religion or belief of his choice.
3. Freedom to manifest one's religion or beliefs may be subject only to such limitations as are prescribed by law and are necessary to protect public safety, order, health, or morals or the fundamental rights and freedoms of others.
4. The States Parties to the present Covenant undertake to have respect for the liberty of parents and, when applicable, legal guardians to ensure the religious and moral education of their children in conformity with their own convictions.

Article 19
1. Everyone shall have the right to hold opinions without interference.
2. Everyone shall have the right to freedom of expression; this right shall include freedom to seek, receive and impart information and ideas of all kinds, regardless of frontiers, either orally, in writing or in print, in the form of art, or through any other media of his choice.
3. The exercise of the rights provided for in paragraph 2 of this article carries with it special duties and responsibilities. It may therefore be subject to certain restrictions, but these shall only be such as are provided by law and are necessary:
   (a) For respect of the rights or reputations of others;
   (b) For the protection of national security or of public order (ordre public), or of public health or morals.

Article 20
1. Any propaganda for war shall be prohibited by law.
2. Any advocacy of national, racial or religious hatred that constitutes incitement to discrimination, hostility or violence shall be prohibited by law.

Article 21
The right of peaceful assembly shall be recognized. No restrictions may be placed on the exercise of this right other than those imposed in conformity with the law and which are necessary in a democratic society in the interests of national security or public safety, public order (ordre public), the protection of public health or morals or the protection of the rights and freedoms of others.

Article 22
1. Everyone shall have the right to freedom of association with others, including the right to form and join trade unions for the protection of his interests.
2. No restrictions may be placed on the exercise of this right other than those which are prescribed by law and which are necessary in a democratic society in the interests of national security or public safety, public order (ordre public), the protection of public health or morals or the protection of the rights and freedoms of others. This article shall not prevent the imposition of lawful restrictions on members of the armed forces and of the police in their exercise of this right.
3. Nothing in this article shall authorize States Parties to the International Labour Organisation Convention of 1948 concerning Freedom of Association

and Protection of the Right to Organize to take legislative measures which would prejudice, or to apply the law in such a manner as to prejudice, the guarantees provided for in that Convention.

Article 23
1. The family is the natural and fundamental group unit of society and is entitled to protection by society and the State.
2. The right of men and women of marriageable age to marry and to found a family shall be recognized.
3. No marriage shall be entered into without the free and full consent of the intending spouses.
4. States Parties to the present Covenant shall take appropriate steps to ensure equality of rights and responsibilities of spouses as to marriage, during marriage and at its dissolution. In the case of dissolution, provision shall be made for the necessary protection of any children.

Article 24
1. Every child shall have, without any discrimination as to race, colour, sex, language, religion, national or socialorigin, property or birth, the right to such measures of protection as are required by his status as a minor, on the part of his family, society and the State.
2. Every child shall be registered immediately after birth and shall have a name.
3. Every child has the right to acquire a nationality.

Article 25
Every citizen shall have the right and the opportunity, without any of the distinctions mentioned in article 2 and without unreasonable restrictions:
(a) To take part in the conduct of public affairs, directly or through freely chosen representatives;
(b) To vote and to be elected at genuine periodic elections which shall be by universal and equal suffrage and shall be held by secret ballot, guaranteeing the free expression of the will of the electors;
(c) To have access, on general terms of equality, to public service in his country.

Article 26
All persons are equal before the law and are entitled without any discrimination to the equal protection of the law. In this respect, the law shall prohibit any discrimination and guarantee to all persons equal and effective protection against discrimination on any ground such as race, colour, sex, language, religion, political or other opinion, national or social origin, property, birth or other status.

Article 27
In those States in which ethnic, religious or linguistic minorities exist, persons belonging to such minorities shall not be denied the right, in community with the other members of their group, to enjoy their own culture, to profess and practise their own religion, or to use their own language.

PART IV

Article 28
1. There shall be established a Human Rights Committee (hereafter referred to in the present Covenant as the Committee). It shall consist of eighteen members and shall carry out the functions hereinafter provided.

2. The Committee shall be composed of nationals of the States Parties to the present Covenant who shall be persons of high moral character and recognized competence in the field of human rights, consideration being given to the usefulness of the participation of some persons having legal experience.
3. The members of the Committee shall be elected and shall serve in their personal capacity.

Article 29
1. The members of the Committee shall be elected by secret ballot from a list of persons possessing the qualifications prescribed in article 28 and nominated for the purpose by the States Parties to the present Covenant.
2. Each State Party to the present Covenant may nominate not more than two persons. These persons shall be nationals of the nominating State.
3. A person shall be eligible for renomination.

Article 30
1. The initial election shall be held no later than six months after the date of the entry into force of the present Covenant.
2. At least four months before the date of each election to the Committee, other than an election to fill a vacancy declared in accordance with article 34, the Secretary-General of the United Nations shall address a written invitation to the States Parties to the present Covenant to submit their nominations for membership of the Committee within three months.
3. The Secretary-General of the United Nations shall prepare a list in alphabetical order of all the persons thus nominated, with an indication of the States Parties which have nominated them, and shall submit it to the States Parties to the present Covenant no later than one month before the date of each election.
4. Elections of the members of the Committee shall be held at a meeting of the States Parties to the present Covenant convened by the Secretary General of the United Nations at the Headquarters of the United Nations. At that meeting, for which two thirds of the States Parties to the present Covenant shall constitute a quorum, the persons elected to the Committee shall be those nominees who obtain the largest number of votes and an absolute majority of the votes of the representatives of States Parties present and voting.

Article 31
1. The Committee may not include more than one national of the same State.
2. In the election of the Committee, consideration shall be given to equitable geographical distribution of membership and to the representation of the different forms of civilization and of the principal legal systems.

Article 32
1. The members of the Committee shall be elected for a term of four years. They shall be eligible for re-election if renominated. However, the terms of nine of the members elected at the first election shall expire at the end of two years; immediately after the first election, the names of these nine members shall be chosen by lot by the Chairman of the meeting referred to in article 30, paragraph 4.
2. Elections at the expiry of office shall be held in accordance with the preceding articles of this part of the present Covenant.

Article 33
1. If, in the unanimous opinion of the other members, a member of the Committee has ceased to carry out his functions for any cause other than absence of a temporary character, the Chairman of the Committee shall notify the Secretary-General of the United Nations, who shall then declare the seat of that member to be vacant.
2. In the event of the death or the resignation of a member of the Committee, the Chairman shall immediately notify the Secretary-General of the United Nations, who shall declare the seat vacant from the date of death or the date on which the resignation takes effect.

Article 34
1. When a vacancy is declared in accordance with article 33 and if the term of office of the member to be replaced does not expire within six months of the declaration of the vacancy, the Secretary-General of the United Nations shall notify each of the States Parties to the present Covenant, which may within two months submit nominations in accordance with article 29 for the purpose of filling the vacancy.
2. The Secretary-General of the United Nations shall prepare a list in alphabetical order of the persons thus nominated and shall submit it to the States Parties to the present Covenant. The election to fill the vacancy shall then take place in accordance with the relevant provisions of this part of the present Covenant.
3. A member of the Committee elected to fill a vacancy declared in accordance with article 33 shall hold office for the remainder of the term of the member who vacated the seat on the Committee under the provisions of that article.

Article 35
The members of the Committee shall, with the approval of the General Assembly of the United Nations, receive emoluments from United Nations resources on such terms and conditions as the General Assembly may decide, having regard to the importance of the Committee's responsibilities.

Article 36
The Secretary-General of the United Nations shall provide the necessary staff and facilities for the effective performance of the functions of the Committee under the present Covenant.

Article 37
1. The Secretary-General of the United Nations shall convene the initial meeting of the Committee at the Headquarters of the United Nations.
2. After its initial meeting, the Committee shall meet at such times as shall be provided in its rules of procedure.
3. The Committee shall normally meet at the Headquarters of the United Nations or at the United Nations Office at Geneva.

Article 38
Every member of the Committee shall, before taking up his duties, make a solemn declaration in open committee that he will perform his functions impartially and conscientiously.

Article 39
1. The Committee shall elect its officers for a term of two years. They may be re-elected.
2. The Committee shall establish its own rules of procedure, but these rules shall provide, *inter alia*, that:
   (a) Twelve members shall constitute a quorum;
   (b) Decisions of the Committee shall be made by a majority vote of the members present.

Article 40
1. The States Parties to the present Covenant undertake to submit reports on the measures they have adopted which give effect to the rights recognized herein and on the progress made in the enjoyment of those rights:
   (a) Within one year of the entry into force of the present Covenant for the States Parties concerned;
   (b) Thereafter whenever the Committee so requests.
2. All reports shall be submitted to the Secretary-General of the United Nations, who shall transmit them to the Committee for consideration. Reports shall indicate the factors and difficulties, if any, affecting the implementation of the present Covenant.
3. The Secretary-General of the United Nations may, after consultation with the Committee, transmit to the specialized agencies concerned copies of such parts of the reports as may fall within their field of competence.
4. The Committee shall study the reports submitted by the States Parties to the present Covenant. It shall transmit its reports, and such general comments as it may consider appropriate, to the States Parties. The Committee may also transmit to the Economic and Social Council these comments along with the copies of the reports it has received from States Parties to the present Covenant.
5. The States Parties to the present Covenant may submit to the Committee observations on any comments that may be made in accordance with paragraph 4 of this article.

Article 41
1. A State Party to the present Covenant may at any time declare under this article that it recognizes the competence of the Committee to receive and consider communications to the effect that a State Party claims that another State Party is not fulfilling its obligations under the present Covenant. Communications under this article may be received and considered only if submitted by a State Party which has made a declaration recognizing in regard to itself the competence of the Committee. No communication shall be received by the Committee if it concerns a State Party which has not made such a declaration. Communications received under this article shall be dealt with in accordance with the following procedure:
   (a) If a State Party to the present Covenant considers that another State Party is not giving effect to the provisions of the present Covenant, it may, by written communication, bring the matter to the attention of that State Party. Within three months after the receipt of the communication

the receiving State shall afford the State which sent the communication an explanation, or any other statement in writing clarifying the matter which should include, to the extent possible and pertinent, reference to domestic procedures and remedies taken, pending, or available in the matter;

(b) If the matter is not adjusted to the satisfaction of both States Parties concerned within six months after the receipt by the receiving State of the initial communication, either State shall have the right to refer the matter to the Committee, by notice given to the Committee and to the other State;

(c) The Committee shall deal with a matter referred to it only after it has ascertained that all available domestic remedies have been invoked and exhausted in the matter, in conformity with the generally recognized principles of international law. This shall not be the rule where the application of the remedies is unreasonably prolonged;

(d) The Committee shall hold closed meetings when examining communications under this article;

(e) Subject to the provisions of subparagraph (c), the Committee shall make available its good offices to the States Parties concerned with a view to a friendly solution of the matter on the basis of respect for human rights and fundamental freedoms as recognized in the present Covenant;

(f) In any matter referred to it, the Committee may call upon the States Parties concerned, referred to in subparagraph (b), to supply any relevant information;

(g) The States Parties concerned, referred to in subparagraph (b), shall have the right to be represented when the matter is being considered in the Committee and to make submissions orally and/or in writing;

(h) The Committee shall, within twelve months after the date of receipt of notice under subparagraph (b), submit a report:
  (i) If a solution within the terms of subparagraph (e) is reached, the Committee shall confine its report to a brief statement of the facts and of the solution reached;
  (ii) If a solution within the terms of subparagraph (e) is not reached, the Committee shall confine its report to a brief statement of the facts; the written submissions and record of the oral submissions made by the States Parties concerned shall be attached to the report. In every matter, the report shall be communicated to the States Parties concerned.

2. The provisions of this article shall come into force when ten States Parties to the present Covenant have made declarations under paragraph I of this article. Such declarations shall be deposited by the States Parties with the Secretary-General of the United Nations, who shall transmit copies thereof to the other States Parties. A declaration may be withdrawn at any time by notification to the Secretary-General. Such a withdrawal shall not prejudice the consideration of any matter which is the subject of a communication already transmitted under this article; no further communication by any State Party shall be received after the notification of withdrawal of the declaration has been received by the Secretary-General, unless the State Party concerned has made a new declaration.

Article 42
1. (a) If a matter referred to the Committee in accordance with article 41 is not resolved to the satisfaction of the States Parties concerned, the Committee may, with the prior consent of the States Parties concerned, appoint an ad hoc Conciliation Commission (hereinafter referred to as the Commission). The good offices of the Commission shall be made available to the States Parties concerned with a view to an amicable solution of the matter on the basis of respect for the present Covenant;
   (b) The Commission shall consist of five persons acceptable to the States Parties concerned. If the States Parties concerned fail to reach agreement within three months on all or part of the composition of the Commission, the members of the Commission concerning whom no agreement has been reached shall be elected by secret ballot by a two-thirds majority vote of the Committee from among its members.
2. The members of the Commission shall serve in their personal capacity. They shall not be nationals of the States Parties concerned, or of a State not Party to the present Covenant, or of a State Party which has not made a declaration under article 41.
3. The Commission shall elect its own Chairman and adopt its own rules of procedure.
4. The meetings of the Commission shall normally be held at the Headquarters of the United Nations or at the United Nations Office at Geneva. However, they may be held at such other convenient places as the Commission may determine in consultation with the Secretary-General of the United Nations and the States Parties concerned.
5. The secretariat provided in accordance with article 36 shall also service the commissions appointed under this article.
6. The information received and collated by the Committee shall be made available to the Commission and the Commission may call upon the States Parties concerned to supply any other relevant information.
7. When the Commission has fully considered the matter, but in any event not later than twelve months after having been seized of the matter, it shall submit to the Chairman of the Committee a report for communication to the States Parties concerned:
   (a) If the Commission is unable to complete its consideration of the matter within twelve months, it shall confine its report to a brief statement of the status of its consideration of the matter;
   (b) If an amicable solution to the matter on tie basis of respect for human rights as recognized in the present Covenant is reached, the Commission shall confine its report to a brief statement of the facts and of the solution reached;
   (c) If a solution within the terms of subparagraph (b) is not reached, the Commission's report shall embody its findings on all questions of fact relevant to the issues between the States Parties concerned, and its views on the possibilities of an amicable solution of the matter. This report shall also contain the written submissions and a record of the oral submissions made by the States Parties concerned;
   (d) If the Commission's report is submitted under subparagraph (c), the States Parties concerned shall, within three months of the receipt of the report,

notify the Chairman of the Committee whether or not they accept the contents of the report of the Commission.
8. The provisions of this article are without prejudice to the responsibilities of the Committee under article 41.
9. The States Parties concerned shall share equally all the expenses of the members of the Commission in accordance with estimates to be provided by the Secretary-General of the United Nations.
10. The Secretary-General of the United Nations shall be empowered to pay the expenses of the members of the Commission, if necessary, before reimbursement by the States Parties concerned, in accordance with paragraph 9 of this article.

Article 43
The members of the Committee, and of the ad hoc conciliation commissions which may be appointed under article 42, shall be entitled to the facilities, privileges and immunities of experts on mission for the United Nations as laid down in the relevant sections of the Convention on the Privileges and Immunities of the United Nations.

Article 44
The provisions for the implementation of the present Covenant shall apply without prejudice to the procedures prescribed in the field of human rights by or under the constituent instruments and the conventions of the United Nations and of the specialized agencies and shall not prevent the States Parties to the present Covenant from having recourse to other procedures for settling a dispute in accordance with general or special international agreements in force between them.

Article 45
The Committee shall submit to the General Assembly of the United Nations, through the Economic and Social Council, an annual report on its activities.

PART V

Article 46
Nothing in the present Covenant shall be interpreted as impairing the provisions of the Charter of the United Nations and of the constitutions of the specialized agencies which define the respective responsibilities of the various organs of the United Nations and of the specialized agencies in regard to the matters dealt with in the present Covenant.

Article 47
Nothing in the present Covenant shall be interpreted as impairing the inherent right of all peoples to enjoy and utilize fully and freely their natural wealth and resources.

PART VI

Article 48
1. The present Covenant is open for signature by any State Member of the United Nations or member of any of its specialized agencies, by any State Party to the Statute of the International Court of Justice, and by any other

State which has been invited by the General Assembly of the United Nations to become a Party to the present Covenant.
2. The present Covenant is subject to ratification. Instruments of ratification shall be deposited with the Secretary-General of the United Nations.
3. The present Covenant shall be open to accession by any State referred to in paragraph 1 of this article.
4. Accession shall be effected by the deposit of an instrument of accession with the Secretary-General of the United Nations.
5. The Secretary-General of the United Nations shall inform all States which have signed this Covenant or acceded to it of the deposit of each instrument of ratification or accession.

Article 49
1. The present Covenant shall enter into force three months after the date of the deposit with the Secretary-General of the United Nations of the thirty-fifth instrument of ratification or instrument of accession.
2. For each State ratifying the present Covenant or acceding to it after the deposit of the thirty-fifth instrument of ratification or instrument of accession, the present Covenant shall enter into force three months after the date of the deposit of its own instrument of ratification or instrument of accession.

Article 50
The provisions of the present Covenant shall extend to all parts of federal States without any limitations or exceptions.

Article 51
1. Any State Party to the present Covenant may propose an amendment and file it with the Secretary-General of the United Nations. The Secretary-General of the United Nations shall thereupon communicate any proposed amendments to the States Parties to the present Covenant with a request that they notify him whether they favour a conference of States Parties for the purpose of considering and voting upon the proposals. In the event that at least one third of the States Parties favours such a conference, the Secretary-General shall convene the conference under the auspices of the United Nations. Any amendment adopted by a majority of the States Parties present and voting at the conference shall be submitted to the General Assembly of the United Nations for approval.
2. Amendments shall come into force when they have been approved by the General Assembly of the United Nations and accepted by a two-thirds majority of the States Parties to the present Covenant in accordance with their respective constitutional processes.
3. When amendments come into force, they shall be binding on those States Parties which have accepted them, other States Parties still being bound by the provisions of the present Covenant and any earlier amendment which they have accepted.

Article 52
Irrespective of the notifications made under article 48, paragraph 5, the Secretary-General of the United Nations shall inform all States referred to in paragraph I of the same article of the following particulars:

(a) Signatures, ratifications and accessions under article 48;
(b) The date of the entry into force of the present Covenant under article 49 and the date of the entry into force of any amendments under article 51.

Article 53
1. The present Covenant, of which the Chinese, English, French, Russian and Spanish texts are equally authentic, shall be deposited in the archives of the United Nations.
2. The Secretary-General of the United Nations shall transmit certified copies of the present Covenant to all States referred to in article 48.

Optional Protocol to the International Covenant on Civil and Political Rights

Adopted and opened for signature, ratification and accession by General Assembly Resolution 2200A (XXI) of 16 December 1966

entry into force 23 March 1976

The States Parties to the present Protocol,

Considering that in order further to achieve the purposes of the International Covenant on Civil and Political Rights (hereinafter referred to as the Covenant) and the implementation of its provisions it would be appropriate to enable the Human Rights Committee set up in part IV of the Covenant (hereinafter referred to as the Committee) to receive and consider, as provided in the present Protocol, communications from individuals claiming to be victims of violations of any of the rights set forth in the Covenant.

Have agreed as follows:

Article 1

A State Party to the Covenant that becomes a Party to the present Protocol recognizes the competence of the Committee to receive and consider communications from individuals subject to its jurisdiction who claim to be victims of a violation by that State Party of any of the rights set forth in the Covenant. No communication shall be received by the Committee if it concerns a State Party to the Covenant which is not a Party to the present Protocol.

Article 2

Subject to the provisions of article 1, individuals who claim that any of their rights enumerated in the Covenant have been violated and who have exhausted all available domestic remedies may submit a written communication to the Committee for consideration.

Article 3

The Committee shall consider inadmissible any communciation under the present Protocol which is anonymous, or which it considers to be an abuse of the right of submission of such communications or to be incompatible with the provisions of the Covenant.

Article 4

1. Subject to the provisions of article 3, the Committee shall bring any communications submitted to it under the present Protocol to the attention of the State Party to the present Protocol alleged to be violating any provision of the Covenant.

2. Within six months, the receiving State shall submit to the Committee written explanations or statements clarifying the matter and the remedy, if any, that may have been taken by that State.

Article 5
1. The Committee shall consider communications received under the present Protocol in the light of all written information made available to it by the individual and by the State Party concerned.
2. The Committee shall not consider any communication from an individual unless it has ascertained that:
    (a) The same matter is not being examined under another procedure of international investigation or settlement;
    (b) The individual has exhausted all available domestic remedies. This shall not be the rule where the application of the remedies is unreasonably prolonged.
3. The Committee shall hold closed meetings when examining communications under the present Protocol.
4. The Committee shall forward its views to the State Party concerned and to the individual.

Article 6
The Committee shall include in its annual report under article 45 of the Covenant a summary of its activities under the present Protocol.

Article 7
Pending the achievement of the objectives of resolution 1514(XV) adopted by the General Assembly of the United Nations on 14 December 1960 concerning the Declaration on the Granting of Independence to Colonial Countries and Peoples, the provisions of the present Protocol shall in no way limit the right of petition granted to these peoples by the Charter of the United Nations and other international conventions and instruments under the United Nations and its specialized agencies.

Article 8
1. The present Protocol is open for signature by any State which has signed the Covenant.
2. The present Protocol is subject to ratification by any State which has ratified or acceded to the Covenant. Instruments of ratification shall be deposited with the Secretary-General of the United Nations.
3. The present Protocol shall be open to accession by any State which has ratified or acceded to the Covenant.
4. Accession shall be effected by the deposit of an instrument of accession with the Secretary-General of the United Nations.
5. The Secretary-General of the United Nations shall inform all States which have signed the present Protocol or acceded to it of the deposit of each instrument of ratification or accession.

Article 9
1. Subject to the entry into force of the Covenant, the present Protocol shall enter into force three months after the date of the deposit with the Secretary-General of the United Nations of the tenth instrument of ratification or instrument of accession.

2. For each State ratifying the present Protocol or acceding to it after the deposit of the tenth instrument of ratification or instrument of accession, the present Protocol shall enter into force three months after the date of the deposit of its own instrument of ratification or instrument of accession.

Article 10
The provisions of the present Protocol shall extend to all parts of federal States without any limitations or exceptions.

Article 11
1. Any State Party to the present Protocol may propose an amendment and file it with the Secretary-General of the United Nations. The Secretary-General shall thereupon communicate any proposed amendments to the States Parties to the present Protocol with a request that they notify him whether they favour a conference of States Parties for the purpose of considering and voting upon the proposal. In the event that at least one third of the States Parties favours such a conference, the Secretary-General shall convene the conference under the auspices of the United Nations. Any amendment adopted by a majority of the States Parties present and voting at the conference shall be submitted to the General Assembly of the United Nations for approval.
2. Amendments shall come into force when they have been approved by the General Assembly of the United Nations and accepted by a two-thirds majority of the States Parties to the present Protocol in accordance with their respective constitutional processes.
3. When amendments come into force, they shall be binding on those States Parties which have accepted them, other States Parties still being bound by the provisions of the present Protocol and any earlier amendment which they have accepted.

Article 12
1. Any State Party may denounce the present Protocol at any time by written notification addressed to the Secretary-General of the United Nations. Denunciation shall take effect three months after the date of receipt of the notification by the Secretary-General.
2. Denunciation shall be without prejudice to the continued application of the provisions of the present Protocol to any communication submitted under article 2 before the effective date of denunciation.

Article 13
Irrespective of the notifications made under article 8, paragraph 5, of the present Protocol, the Secretary-General of the United Nations shall inform all States referred to in article 48, paragraph I, of the Covenant of the following particulars:
(a) Signatures, ratifications and accessions under article 8;
(b) The date of the entry into force of the present Protocol under article 9 and the date of the entry into force of any amendments under article 11;
(c) Denunciations under article 12.

Article 14
1. The present Protocol, of which the Chinese, English, French, Russian and Spanish texts are equally authentic, shall be deposited in the archives of the United Nations.
2. The Secretary-General of the United Nations shall transmit certified copies of the present Protocol to all States referred to in article 48 of the Covenant.

Second Optional Protocol to the International Covenant on Civil and Political Rights, aiming at the abolition of the death penalty

Adopted and proclaimed by General Assembly Resolution 44/128
of 15 December 1989

entry into force 11 July 1991

The States Parties to the present Protocol,

Believing that abolition of the death penalty contributes to enhancement of human dignity and progressive development of human rights,

Recalling article 3 of the Universal Declaration of Human Rights, adopted on 10 December 1948, and article 6 of the International Covenant on Civil and Political Rights, adopted on 16 December 1966,

Noting that article 6 of the International Covenant on Civil and Political Rights refers to abolition of the death penalty in terms that strongly suggest that abolition is desirable,

Convinced that all measures of abolition of the death penalty should be considered as progress in the enjoyment of the right to life,

Desirous to undertake hereby an international commitment to abolish the death penalty,

Have agreed as follows:

Article 1
1. No one within the jurisdiction of a State Party to the present Protocol shall be executed.
2. Each State Party shall take all necessary measures to abolish the death penalty within its jurisdiction.

Article 2
1. No reservation is admissible to the present Protocol, except for a reservation made at the time of ratification or accession that provides for the application of the death penalty in time of war pursuant to a conviction for a most serious crime of a military nature committed during wartime.
2. The State Party making such a reservation shall at the time of ratification or accession communicate to the Secretary-General of the United Nations the relevant provisions of its national legislation applicable during wartime.
3. The State Party having made such a reservation shall notify the Secretary-General of the United Nations of any beginning or ending of a state of war applicable to its territory.

Article 3
The States Parties to the present Protocol shall include in the reports they submit to the Human Rights Committee, in accordance with article 40 of the Covenant, information on the measures that they have adopted to give effect to the present Protocol.

Article 4
With respect to the States Parties to the Covenant that have made a declaration under article 41, the competence of the Human Rights Committee to receive and consider communications when a State Party claims that another State Party is not fulfilling its obligations shall extend to the provisions of the present Protocol, unless the State Party concerned has made a statement to the contrary at the moment of ratification or accession.

Article 5
With respect to the States Parties to the first Optional Protocol to the International Covenant on Civil and Political Rights adopted on 16 December 1966, the competence of the Human Rights Committee to receive and consider communications from individuals subject to its jurisdiction shall extend to the provisions of the present Protocol, unless the State Party concerned has made a statement to the contrary at the moment of ratification or accession.

Article 6
1. The provisions of the present Protocol shall apply as additional provisions to the Covenant.
2. Without prejudice to the possibility of a reservation under article 2 of the present Protocol, the right guaranteed in article 1, paragraph 1, of the present Protocol shall not be subject to any derogation under article 4 of the Covenant.

Article 7
1. The present Protocol is open for signature by any State that has signed the Covenant.
2. The present Protocol is subject to ratification by any State that has ratified the Covenant or acceded to it. Instruments of ratification shall be deposited with the Secretary-General of the United Nations.
3. The present Protocol shall be open to accession by any State that has ratified the Covenant or acceded to it.
4. Accession shall be effected by the deposit of an instrument of accession with the Secretary-General of the United Nations.
5. The Secretary-General of the United Nations shall inform all States that have signed the present Protocol or acceded to it of the deposit of each instrument of ratification or accession.

Article 8
1. The present Protocol shall enter into force three months after the date of the deposit with the Secretary-General of the United Nations of the tenth instrument of ratification or accession.
2. For each State ratifying the present Protocol or acceding to it after the deposit of the tenth instrument of ratification or accession, the present Protocol shall

enter into force three months after the date of the deposit of its own instrument of ratification or accession.

Article 9

The provisions of the present Protocol shall extend to all parts of federal States without any limitations or exceptions.

Article 10

The Secretary-General of the United Nations shall inform all States referred to in article 48, paragraph 1, of the Covenant of the following particulars:

(a) Reservations, communications and notifications under article 2 of the present Protocol;
(b) Statements made under articles 4 or 5 of the present Protocol;
(c) Signatures, ratifications and accessions under article 7 of the present Protocol:
(d) The date of the entry into force of the present Protocol under article 8 thereof.

Article 11

1. The present Protocol, of which the Arabic, Chinese, English, French, Russian and Spanish texts are equally authentic, shall be deposited in the archives of the United Nations.
2. The Secretary-General of the United Nations shall transmit certified copies of the present Protocol to all States referred to in article 48 of the Covenant.

International Covenant on Economic, Social and Cultural Rights

Adopted and opened for signature, ratification and accession by General Assembly Resolution 2200A (XXI) of 16 December 1966

entry into force 3 January 1976

Preamble

The States Parties to the present Covenant,

Considering that, in accordance with the principles proclaimed in the Charter of the United Nations, recognition of the inherent dignity and of the equal and inalienable rights of all members of the human family is the foundation of freedom, justice and peace in the world,

Recognizing that these rights derive from the inherent dignity of the human person,

Recognizing that, in accordance with the Universal Declaration of Human Rights, the ideal of free human beings enjoying freedom from fear and want can only be achieved if conditions are created whereby everyone may enjoy his economic, social and cultural rights, as well as his civil and political rights,

Considering the obligation of States under the Charter of the United Nations to promote universal respect for, and observance of, human rights and freedoms,

Realizing that the individual, having duties to other individuals and to the community to which he belongs, is under a responsibility to strive for the promotion and observance of the rights recognized in the present Covenant,

Agree upon the following articles:

PART I

Article 1
1. All peoples have the right of self-determination. By virtue of that right they freely determine their political status and freely pursue their economic, social and cultural development.
2. All peoples may, for their own ends, freely dispose of their natural wealth and resources without prejudice to any obligations arising out of international economic co-operation, based upon the principle of mutual benefit, and international law. In no case may a people be deprived of its own means of subsistence.
3. The States Parties to the present Covenant, including those having responsibility for the administration of Non-Self-Governing and Trust Territories, shall

promote the realization of the right of self-determination, and shall respect that right, in conformity with the provisions of the Charter of the United Nations.

PART II

Article 2
1. Each State Party to the present Covenant undertakes to take steps, individually and through international assistance and co-operation, especially economic and technical, to the maximum of its available resources, with a view to achieving progressively the full realization of the rights recognized in the present Covenant by all appropriate means, including particularly the adoption of legislative measures.
2. The States Parties to the present Covenant undertake to guarantee that the rights enunciated in the present Covenant will be exercised without discrimination of any kind as to race, colour, sex, language, religion, political or other opinion, national or social origin, property, birth or other status.
3. Developing countries, with due regard to human rights and their national economy, may determine to what extent they would guarantee the economic rights recognized in the present Covenant to non-nationals.

Article 3
The States Parties to the present Covenant undertake to ensure the equal right of men and women to the enjoyment of all economic, social and cultural rights set forth in the present Covenant.

Article 4
The States Parties to the present Covenant recognize that, in the enjoyment of those rights provided by the State in conformity with the present Covenant, the State may subject such rights only to such limitations as are determined by law only in so far as this may be compatible with the nature of these rights and solely for the purpose of promoting the general welfare in a democratic society.

Article 5
1. Nothing in the present Covenant may be interpreted as implying for any State, group or person any right to engage in any activity or to perform any act aimed at the destruction of any of the rights or freedoms recognized herein, or at their limitation to a greater extent than is provided for in the present Covenant.
2. No restriction upon or derogation from any of the fundamental human rights recognized or existing in any country in virtue of law, conventions, regulations or custom shall be admitted on the pretext that the present Covenant does not recognize such rights or that it recognizes them to a lesser extent.

PART III

Article 6
1. The States Parties to the present Covenant recognize the right to work, which includes the right of everyone to the opportunity to gain his living by work which he freely chooses or accepts, and will take appropriate steps to safeguard this right.

2. The steps to be taken by a State Party to the present Covenant to achieve the full realization of this right shall include technical and vocational guidance and training programmes, policies and techniques to achieve steady economic, social and cultural development and full and productive employment under conditions safeguarding fundamental political and economic freedoms to the individual.

Article 7
The States Parties to the present Covenant recognize the right of everyone to the enjoyment of just and favourable conditions of work which ensure, in particular:
(a) Remuneration which provides all workers, as a minimum, with:
  (i) Fair wages and equal remuneration for work of equal value without distinction of any kind, in particular women being guaranteed conditions of work not inferior to those enjoyed by men, with equal pay for equal work;
  (ii) A decent living for themselves and their families in accordance with the provisions of the present Covenant;
(b) Safe and healthy working conditions;
(c) Equal opportunity for everyone to be promoted in his employment to an appropriate higher level, subject to no considerations other than those of seniority and competence;
(d) Rest, leisure and reasonable limitation of working hours and periodic holidays with pay, as well as remuneration for public holidays

Article 8
1. The States Parties to the present Covenant undertake to ensure:
   (a) The right of everyone to form trade unions and join the trade union of his choice, subject only to the rules of the organization concerned, for the promotion and protection of his economic and social interests. No restrictions may be placed on the exercise of this right other than those prescribed by law and which are necessary in a democratic society in the interests of national security or public order or for the protection of the rights and freedoms of others;
   (b) The right of trade unions to establish national federations or confederations and the right of the latter to form or join international trade-union organizations;
   (c) The right of trade unions to function freely subject to no limitations other than those prescribed by law and which are necessary in a democratic society in the interests of national security or public order or for the protection of the rights and freedoms of others;
   (d) The right to strike, provided that it is exercised in conformity with the laws of the particular country.
2. This article shall not prevent the imposition of lawful restrictions on the exercise of these rights by members of the armed forces or of the police or of the administration of the State.
3. Nothing in this article shall authorize States Parties to the International Labour Organisation Convention of 1948 concerning Freedom of Association and Protection of the Right to Organize to take legislative measures which would prejudice, or apply the law in such a manner as would prejudice, the guarantees provided for in that Convention.

Article 9
The States Parties to the present Covenant recognize the right of everyone to social security, including social insurance.

Article 10
The States Parties to the present Covenant recognize that:
1. The widest possible protection and assistance should be accorded to the family, which is the natural and fundamental group unit of society, particularly for its establishment and while it is responsible for the care and education of dependent children. Marriage must be entered into with the free consent of the intending spouses.
2. Special protection should be accorded to mothers during a reasonable period before and after childbirth. During such period working mothers should be accorded paid leave or leave with adequate social security benefits.
3. Special measures of protection and assistance should be taken on behalf of all children and young persons without any discrimination for reasons of parentage or other conditions. Children and young persons should be protected from economic and social exploitation. Their employment in work harmful to their morals or health or dangerous to life or likely to hamper their normal development should be punishable by law. States should also set age limits below which the paid employment of child labour should be prohibited and punishable by law.

Article 11
1. The States Parties to the present Covenant recognize the right of everyone to an adequate standard of living for himself and his family, including adequate food, clothing and housing, and to the continuous improvement of living conditions. The States Parties will take appropriate steps to ensure the realization of this right, recognizing to this effect the essential importance of international co-operation based on free consent.
2. The States Parties to the present Covenant, recognizing the fundamental right of everyone to be free from hunger, shall take, individually and through international co-operation, the measures, including specific programmes, which are needed:
   (a) To improve methods of production, conservation and distribution of food by making full use of technical and scientific knowledge, by disseminating knowledge of the principles of nutrition and by developing or reforming agrarian systems in such a way as to achieve the most efficient development and utilization of natural resources;
   (b) Taking into account the problems of both food-importing and food-exporting countries, to ensure an equitable distribution of world food supplies in relation to need.

Article 12
1. The States Parties to the present Covenant recognize the right of everyone to the enjoyment of the highest attainable standard of physical and mental health.
2. The steps to be taken by the States Parties to the present Covenant to achieve the full realization of this right shall include those necessary for:
   (a) The provision for the reduction of the stillbirth-rate and of infant mortality and for the healthy development of the child;

(b) The improvement of all aspects of environmental and industrial hygiene;
(c) The prevention, treatment and control of epidemic, endemic, occupational and other diseases;
(d) The creation of conditions which would assure to all medical service and medical attention in the event of sickness.

Article 13
1. The States Parties to the present Covenant recognize the right of everyone to education. They agree that education shall be directed to the full development of the human personality and the sense of its dignity, and shall strengthen the respect for human rights and fundamental freedoms. They further agree that education shall enable all persons to participate effectively in a free society, promote understanding, tolerance and friendship among all nations and all racial, ethnic or religious groups, and further the activities of the United Nations for the maintenance of peace.
2. The States Parties to the present Covenant recognize that, with a view to achieving the full realization of this right:
    (a) Primary education shall be compulsory and available free to all;
    (b) Secondary education in its different forms, including technical and vocational secondary education, shall be made generally available and accessible to all by every appropriate means, and in particular by the progressive introduction of free education;
    (c) Higher education shall be made equally accessible to all, on the basis of capacity, by every appropriate means, and in particular by the progressive introduction of free education;
    (d) Fundamental education shall be encouraged or intensified as far as possible for those persons who have not received or completed the whole period of their primary education;
    (e) The development of a system of schools at all levels shall be actively pursued, an adequate fellowship system shall be established, and the material conditions of teaching staff shall be continuously improved.
3. The States Parties to the present Covenant undertake to have respect for the liberty of parents and, when applicable, legal guardians to choose for their children schools, other than those established by the public authorities, which conform to such minimum educational standards as may be laid down or approved by the State and to ensure the religious and moral education of their children in conformity with their own convictions.
4. No part of this article shall be construed so as to interfere with the liberty of individuals and bodies to establish and direct educational institutions, subject always to the observance of the principles set forth in paragraph I of this article and to the requirement that the education given in such institutions shall conform to such minimum standards as may be laid down by the State.

Article 14
Each State Party to the present Covenant which, at the time of becoming a Party, has not been able to secure in its metropolitan territory or other territories under its jurisdiction compulsory primary education, free of charge, undertakes, within two years, to work out and adopt a detailed plan of action for the

progressive implementation, within a reasonable number of years, to be fixed in the plan, of the principle of compulsory education free of charge for all.

Article 15
1. The States Parties to the present Covenant recognize the right of everyone:
   (a) To take part in cultural life;
   (b) To enjoy the benefits of scientific progress and its applications;
   (c) To benefit from the protection of the moral and material interests resulting from any scientific, literary or artistic production of which he is the author.
2. The steps to be taken by the States Parties to the present Covenant to achieve the full realization of this right shall include those necessary for the conservation, the development and the diffusion of science and culture.
3. The States Parties to the present Covenant undertake to respect the freedom indispensable for scientific research and creative activity.
4. The States Parties to the present Covenant recognize the benefits to be derived from the encouragement and development of international contacts and co-operation in the scientific and cultural fields.

PART IV

Article 16
1. The States Parties to the present Covenant undertake to submit in conformity with this part of the Covenant reports on the measures which they have adopted and the progress made in achieving the observance of the rights recognized herein.
2. (a) All reports shall be submitted to the Secretary-General of the United Nations, who shall transmit copies to the Economic and Social Council for consideration in accordance with the provisions of the present Covenant;
   (b) The Secretary-General of the United Nations shall also transmit to the specialized agencies copies of the reports, or any relevant parts therefrom, from States Parties to the present Covenant which are also members of these specialized agencies in so far as these reports, or parts therefrom, relate to any matters which fall within the responsibilities of the said agencies in accordance with their constitutional instruments.

Article 17
1. The States Parties to the present Covenant shall furnish their reports in stages, in accordance with a programme to be established by the Economic and Social Council within one year of the entry into force of the present Covenant after consultation with the States Parties and the specialized agencies concerned.
2. Reports may indicate factors and difficulties affecting the degree of fulfilment of obligations under the present Covenant.
3. Where relevant information has previously been furnished to the United Nations or to any specialized agency by any State Party to the present Covenant, it will not be necessary to reproduce that information, but a precise reference to the information so furnished will suffice.

Article 18
Pursuant to its responsibilities under the Charter of the United Nations in the field of human rights and fundamental freedoms, the Economic and Social Council may make arrangements with the specialized agencies in respect of their reporting to it on the progress made in achieving the observance of the provisions of the present Covenant falling within the scope of their activities. These reports may include particulars of decisions and recommendations on such implementation adopted by their competent organs.

Article 19
The Economic and Social Council may transmit to the Commission on Human Rights for study and general recommendation or, as appropriate, for information the reports concerning human rights submitted by States in accordance with articles 16 and 17, and those concerning human rights submitted by the specialized agencies in accordance with article 18.

Article 20
The States Parties to the present Covenant and the specialized agencies concerned may submit comments to the Economic and Social Council on any general recommendation under article 19 or reference to such general recommendation in any report of the Commission on Human Rights or any documentation referred to therein.

Article 21
The Economic and Social Council may submit from time to time to the General Assembly reports with recommendations of a general nature and a summary of the information received from the States Parties to the present Covenant and the specialized agencies on the measures taken and the progress made in achieving general observance of the rights recognized in the present Covenant.

Article 22
The Economic and Social Council may bring to the attention of other organs of the United Nations, their subsidiary organs and specialized agencies concerned with furnishing technical assistance any matters arising out of the reports referred to in this part of the present Covenant which may assist such bodies in deciding, each within its field of competence, on the advisability of international measures likely to contribute to the effective progressive implementation of the present Covenant.

Article 23
The States Parties to the present Covenant agree that international action for the achievement of the rights recognized in the present Covenant includes such methods as the conclusion of conventions, the adoption of recommendations, the furnishing of technical assistance and the holding of regional meetings and technical meetings for the purpose of consultation and study organized in conjunction with the Governments concerned.

Article 24
Nothing in the present Covenant shall be interpreted as impairing the provisions of the Charter of the United Nations and of the constitutions of the specialized agencies which define the respective responsibilities of the various organs of the

United Nations and of the specialized agencies in regard to the matters dealt with in the present Covenant.

Article 25
Nothing in the present Covenant shall be interpreted as impairing the inherent right of all peoples to enjoy and utilize fully and freely their natural wealth and resources.

PART V

Article 26
1. The present Covenant is open for signature by any State Member of the United Nations or member of any of its specialized agencies, by any State Party to the Statute of the International Court of Justice, and by any other State which has been invited by the General Assembly of the United Nations to become a party to the present Covenant.
2. The present Covenant is subject to ratification. Instruments of ratification shall be deposited with the Secretary-General of the United Nations.
3. The present Covenant shall be open to accession by any State referred to in paragraph 1 of this article.
4. Accession shall be effected by the deposit of an instrument of accession with the Secretary-General of the United Nations.
5. The Secretary-General of the United Nations shall inform all States which have signed the present Covenant or acceded to it of the deposit of each instrument of ratification or accession.

Article 27
1. The present Covenant shall enter into force three months after the date of the deposit with the Secretary-General of the United Nations of the thirty-fifth instrument of ratification or instrument of accession.
2. For each State ratifying the present Covenant or acceding to it after the deposit of the thirty-fifth instrument of ratification or instrument of accession, the present Covenant shall enter into force three months after the date of the deposit of its own instrument of ratification or instrument of accession.

Article 28
The provisions of the present Covenant shall extend to all parts of federal States without any limitations or exceptions.

Article 29
1. Any State Party to the present Covenant may propose an amendment and file it with the Secretary-General of the United Nations. The Secretary-General shall thereupon communicate any proposed amendments to the States Parties to the present Covenant with a request that they notify him whether they favour a conference of States Parties for the purpose of considering and voting upon the proposals. In the event that at least one third of the States Parties favours such a conference, the Secretary-General shall convene the conference under the auspices of the United Nations. Any amendment adopted by a majority of the States Parties present and voting at the conference shall be submitted to the General Assembly of the United Nations for approval.

2. Amendments shall come into force when they have been approved by the General Assembly of the United Nations and accepted by a two-thirds majority of the States Parties to the present Covenant in accordance with their respective constitutional processes.
3. When amendments come into force they shall be binding on those States Parties which have accepted them, other States Parties still being bound by the provisions of the present Covenant and any earlier amendment which they have accepted.

Article 30
Irrespective of the notifications made under article 26, paragraph 5, the Secretary-General of the United Nations shall inform all States referred to in paragraph I of the same article of the following particulars:
(a) Signatures, ratifications and accessions under article 26;
(b) The date of the entry into force of the present Covenant under article 27 and the date of the entry into force of any amendments under article 29.

Article 31
1. The present Covenant, of which the Chinese, English, French, Russian and Spanish texts are equally authentic, shall be deposited in the archives of the United Nations.
2. The Secretary-General of the United Nations shall transmit certified copies of the present Covenant to all States referred to in article 26.

Convention on the Elimination of All Forms of Discrimination against Women

Adopted and opened for signature, ratification and accession by General Assembly Resolution 34/180 of 18 December 1979

entry into force 3 September 1981

The States Parties to the present Convention,

Noting that the Charter of the United Nations reaffirms faith in fundamental human rights, in the dignity and worth of the human person and in the equal rights of men and women,

Noting that the Universal Declaration of Human Rights affirms the principle of the inadmissibility of discrimination and proclaims that all human beings are born free and equal in dignity and rights and that everyone is entitled to all the rights and freedoms set forth therein, without distinction of any kind, including distinction based on sex,

Noting that the States Parties to the International Covenants on Human Rights have the obligation to ensure the equal rights of men and women to enjoy all economic, social, cultural, civil and political rights,

Considering the international conventions concluded under the auspices of the United Nations and the specialized agencies promoting equality of rights of men and women,

Noting also the resolutions, declarations and recommendations adopted by the United Nations and the specialized agencies promoting equality of rights of men and women,

Concerned, however, that despite these various instruments extensive discrimination against women continues to exist,

Recalling that discrimination against women violates the principles of equality of rights and respect for human dignity, is an obstacle to the participation of women, on equal terms with men, in the political, social, economic and cultural life of their countries, hampers the growth of the prosperity of society and the family and makes more difficult the full development of the potentialities of women in the service of their countries and of humanity,

Concerned that in situations of poverty women have the least access to food, health, education, training and opportunities for employment and other needs,

Convinced that the establishment of the new international economic order based on equity and justice will contribute significantly towards the promotion of equality between men and women,

Emphasizing that the eradication of apartheid, all forms of racism, racial discrimination, colonialism, neo-colonialism, aggression, foreign occupation and domination and interference in the internal affairs of States is essential to the full enjoyment of the rights of men and women,

Affirming that the strengthening of international peace and security, the relaxation of international tension, mutual co-operation among all States irrespective of their social and economic systems, general and complete disarmament, in particular nuclear disarmament under strict and effective international control, the affirmation of the principles of justice, equality and mutual benefit in relations among countries and the realization of the right of peoples under alien and colonial domination and foreign occupation to self-determination and independence, as well as respect for national sovereignty and territorial integrity, will promote social progress and development and as a consequence will contribute to the attainment of full equality between men and women,

Convinced that the full and complete development of a country, the welfare of the world and the cause of peace require the maximum participation of women on equal terms with men in all fields,

Bearing in mind the great contribution of women to the welfare of the family and to the development of society, so far not fully recognized, the social significance of maternity and the role of both parents in the family and in the upbringing of children, and aware that the role of women in procreation should not be a basis for discrimination but that the upbringing of children requires a sharing of responsibility between men and women and society as a whole,

Aware that a change in the traditional role of men as well as the role of women in society and in the family is needed to achieve full equality between men and women,

Determined to implement the principles set forth in the Declaration on the Elimination of Discrimination against Women and, for that purpose, to adopt the measures required for the elimination of such discrimination in all its forms and manifestations,

Have agreed on the following:

PART I

Article 1

For the purposes of the present Convention, the term "discrimination against women" shall mean any distinction, exclusion or restriction made on the basis of sex which has the effect or purpose of impairing or nullifying the recognition, enjoyment or exercise by women, irrespective of their marital status, on a basis of equality of men and women, of human rights and fundamental freedoms in the political, economic, social, cultural, civil or any other field.

Article 2

States Parties condemn discrimination against women in all its forms, agree to pursue by all appropriate means and without delay a policy of eliminating discrimination against women and, to this end, undertake:

(a) To embody the principle of the equality of men and women in their national constitutions or other appropriate legislation if not yet incorporated therein and to ensure, through law and other appropriate means, the practical realization of this principle;
(b) To adopt appropriate legislative and other measures, including sanctions where appropriate, prohibiting all discrimination against women;
(c) To establish legal protection of the rights of women on an equal basis with men and to ensure through competent national tribunals and other public institutions the effective protection of women against any act of discrimination;
(d) To refrain from engaging in any act or practice of discrimination against women and to ensure that public authorities and institutions shall act in conformity with this obligation;
(e) To take all appropriate measures to eliminate discrimination against women by any person, organization or enterprise;
(f) To take all appropriate measures, including legislation, to modify or abolish existing laws, regulations, customs and practices which constitute discrimination against women;
(g) To repeal all national penal provisions which constitute discrimination against women.

Article 3
States Parties shall take in all fields, in particular in the political, social, economic and cultural fields, all appropriate measures, including legislation, to en sure the full development and advancement of women, for the purpose of guaranteeing them the exercise and enjoyment of human rights and fundamental freedoms on a basis of equality with men.

Article 4
1. Adoption by States Parties of temporary special measures aimed at accelerating de facto equality between men and women shall not be considered discrimination as defined in the present Convention, but shall in no way entail as a consequence the maintenance of unequal or separate standards; these measures shall be discontinued when the objectives of equality of opportunity and treatment have been achieved.
2. Adoption by States Parties of special measures, including those measures contained in the present Convention, aimed at protecting maternity shall not be considered discriminatory.

Article 5
States Parties shall take all appropriate measures:
(a) To modify the social and cultural patterns of conduct of men and women, with a view to achieving the elimination of prejudices and customary and all other practices which are based on the idea of the inferiority or the superiority of either of the sexes or on stereotyped roles for men and women;
(b) To ensure that family education includes a proper understanding of maternity as a social function and the recognition of the common responsibility of men and women in the upbringing and development of their children, it being understood that the interest of the children is the primordial consideration in all cases.

Article 6
States Parties shall take all appropriate measures, including legislation, to suppress all forms of traffic in women and exploitation of prostitution of women.

PART II

Article 7
States Parties shall take all appropriate measures to eliminate discrimination against women in the political and public life of the country and, in particular, shall ensure to women, on equal terms with men, the right:
(a) To vote in all elections and public referenda and to be eligible for election to all publicly elected bodies;
(b) To participate in the formulation of government policy and the implementation thereof and to hold public office and perform all public functions at all levels of government;
(c) To participate in non-governmental organizations and associations concerned with the public and political life of the country.

Article 8
States Parties shall take all appropriate measures to ensure to women, on equal terms with men and without any discrimination, the opportunity to represent their Governments at the international level and to participate in the work of international organizations.

Article 9
1. States Parties shall grant women equal rights with men to acquire, change or retain their nationality. They shall ensure in particular that neither marriage to an alien nor change of nationality by the husband during marriage shall automatically change the nationality of the wife, render her stateless or force upon her the nationality of the husband.
2. States Parties shall grant women equal rights with men with respect to the nationality of their children.

PART III

Article 10
States Parties shall take all appropriate measures to eliminate discrimination against women in order to ensure to them equal rights with men in the field of education and in particular to ensure, on a basis of equality of men and women:
(a) The same conditions for career and vocational guidance, for access to studies and for the achievement of diplomas in educational establishments of all categories in rural as well as in urban areas; this equality shall be ensured in pre-school, general, technical, professional and higher technical education, as well as in all types of vocational training;
(b) Access to the same curricula, the same examinations, teaching staff with qualifications of the same standard and school premises and equipment of the same quality;
(c) The elimination of any stereotyped concept of the roles of men and women at all levels and in all forms of education by encouraging coeducation and other types of education which will help to achieve this aim and, in particular,

by the revision of textbooks and school programmes and the adaptation of teaching methods;
(d) The same opportunities to benefit from scholarships and other study grants;
(e) The same opportunities for access to programmes of continuing education, including adult and functional literacy programmes, particulary those aimed at reducing, at the earliest possible time, any gap in education existing between men and women;
(f) The reduction of female student drop-out rates and the organization of programmes for girls and women who have left school prematurely;
(g) The same Opportunities to participate actively in sports and physical education;
(h) Access to specific educational information to help to ensure the health and well-being of families, including information and advice on family planning.

Article 11
1. States Parties shall take all appropriate measures to eliminate discrimination against women in the field of employment in order to ensure, on a basis of equality of men and women, the same rights, in particular:
    (a) The right to work as an inalienable right of all human beings;
    (b) The right to the same employment opportunities, including the application of the same criteria for selection in matters of employment;
    (c) The right to free choice of profession and employment, the right to promotion, job security and all benefits and conditions of service and the right to receive vocational training and retraining, including apprenticeships, advanced vocational training and recurrent training;
    (d) The right to equal remuneration, including benefits, and to equal treatment in respect of work of equal value, as well as equality of treatment in the evaluation of the quality of work;
    (e) The right to social security, particularly in cases of retirement, unemployment, sickness, invalidity and old age and other incapacity to work, as well as the right to paid leave;
    (f) The right to protection of health and to safety in working conditions, including the safeguarding of the function of reproduction.
2. In order to prevent discrimination against women on the grounds of marriage or maternity and to ensure their effective right to work, States Parties shall take appropriate measures:
    (a) To prohibit, subject to the imposition of sanctions, dismissal on the grounds of pregnancy or of maternity leave and discrimination in dismissals on the basis of marital status;
    (b) To introduce maternity leave with pay or with comparable social benefits without loss of former employment, seniority or social allowances;
    (c) To encourage the provision of the necessary supporting social services to enable parents to combine family obligations with work responsibilities and participation in public life, in particular through promoting the establishment and development of a network of child-care facilities;
    (d) To provide special protection to women during pregnancy in types of work proved to be harmful to them.
3. Protective legislation relating to matters covered in this article shall be reviewed periodically in the light of scientific and technological knowledge and shall be revised, repealed or extended as necessary.

Article 12
1. States Parties shall take all appropriate measures to eliminate discrimination against women in the field of health care in order to ensure, on a basis of equality of men and women, access to health care services, including those related to family planning.
2. Notwithstanding the provisions of paragraph I of this article, States Parties shall ensure to women appropriate services in connection with pregnancy, confinement and the post-natal period, granting free services where necessary, as well as adequate nutrition during pregnancy and lactation.

Article 13
States Parties shall take all appropriate measures to eliminate discrimination against women in other areas of economic and social life in order to ensure, on a basis of equality of men and women, the same rights, in particular:
(a) The right to family benefits;
(b) The right to bank loans, mortgages and other forms of financial credit;
(c) The right to participate in recreational activities, sports and all aspects of cultural life.

Article 14
1. States Parties shall take into account the particular problems faced by rural women and the significant roles which rural women play in the economic survival of their families, including their work in the non-monetized sectors of the economy, and shall take all appropriate measures to ensure the application of the provisions of the present Convention to women in rural areas.
2. States Parties shall take all appropriate measures to eliminate discrimination against women in rural areas in order to ensure, on a basis of equality of men and women, that they participate in and benefit from rural development and, in particular, shall ensure to such women the right:
(a) To participate in the elaboration and implementation of development planning at all levels;
(b) To have access to adequate health care facilities, including information, counselling and services in family planning;
(c) To benefit directly from social security programmes;
(d) To obtain all types of training and education, formal and non-formal, including that relating to functional literacy, as well as, *inter alia*, the benefit of all community and extension services, in order to increase their technical proficiency;
(e) To organize self-help groups and co-operatives in order to obtain equal access to economic opportunities through employment or self employment;
(f) To participate in all community activities;
(g) To have access to agricultural credit and loans, marketing facilities, appropriate technology and equal treatment in land and agrarian reform as well as in land resettlement schemes;
(h) To enjoy adequate living conditions, particularly in relation to housing, sanitation, electricity and water supply, transport and communications.

PART IV

Article 15
1. States Parties shall accord to women equality with men before the law.
2. States Parties shall accord to women, in civil matters, a legal capacity identical

to that of men and the same opportunities to exercise that capacity. In particular, they shall give women equal rights to conclude contracts and to administer property and shall treat them equally in all stages of procedure in courts and tribunals.
3. States Parties agree that all contracts and all other private instruments of any kind with a legal effect which is directed at restricting the legal capacity of women shall be deemed null and void.
4. States Parties shall accord to men and women the same rights with regard to the law relating to the movement of persons and the freedom to choose their residence and domicile.

Article 16
1. States Parties shall take all appropriate measures to eliminate discrimination against women in all matters relating to marriage and family relations and in particular shall ensure, on a basis of equality of men and women:
   (a) The same right to enter into marriage;
   (b) The same right freely to choose a spouse and to enter into marriage only with their free and full consent;
   (c) The same rights and responsibilities during marriage and at its dissolution;
   (d) The same rights and responsibilities as parents, irrespective of their marital status, in matters relating to their children; in all cases the interests of the children shall be paramount;
   (e) The same rights to decide freely and responsibly on the number and spacing of their children and to have access to the information, education and means to enable them to exercise these rights;
   (f) The same rights and responsibilities with regard to guardianship, wardship, trusteeship and adoption of children, or similar institutions where these concepts exist in national legislation; in all cases the interests of the children shall be paramount;
   (g) The same personal rights as husband and wife, including the right to choose a family name, a profession and an occupation;
   (h) The same rights for both spouses in respect of the ownership, acquisition, management, administration, enjoyment and disposition of property, whether free of charge or for a valuable consideration.
2. The betrothal and the marriage of a child shall have no legal effect, and all necessary action, including legislation, shall be taken to specify a minimum age for marriage and to make the registration of marriages in an official registry compulsory.

PART V

Article 17
1. For the purpose of considering the progress made in the implementation of the present Convention, there shall be established a Committee on the Elimination of Discrimination against Women (hereinafter referred to as the Committee) consisting, at the time of entry into force of the Convention, of eighteen and, after ratification of or accession to the Convention by the thirty-fifth State Party, of twenty-three experts of high moral standing and competence in the field covered by the Convention. The experts shall be elected by States Parties from among their nationals and shall serve in their personal

capacity, consideration being given to equitable geographical distribution and to the representation of the different forms of civilization as well as the principal legal systems.
2. The members of the Committee shall be elected by secret ballot from a list of persons nominated by States Parties. Each State Party may nominate one person from among its own nationals.
3. The initial election shall be held six months after the date of the entry into force of the present Convention. At least three months before the date of each election the Secretary-General of the United Nations shall address a letter to the States Parties inviting them to submit their nominations within two months. The Secretary-General shall prepare a list in alphabetical order of all persons thus nominated, indicating the States Parties which have nominated them, and shall submit it to the States Parties.
4. Elections of the members of the Committee shall be held at a meeting of States Parties convened by the Secretary-General at United Nations Headquarters. At that meeting, for which two thirds of the States Parties shall constitute a quorum, the persons elected to the Committee shall be those nominees who obtain the largest number of votes and an absolute majority of the votes of the representatives of States Parties present and voting.
5. The members of the Committee shall be elected for a term of four years. However, the terms of nine of the members elected at the first election shall expire at the end of two years; immediately after the first election the names of these nine members shall be chosen by lot by the Chairman of the Committee.
6. The election of the five additional members of the Committee shall be held in accordance with the provisions of paragraphs 2, 3 and 4 of this article, following the thirty-fifth ratification or accession. The terms of two of the additional members elected on this occasion shall expire at the end of two years, the names of these two members having been chosen by lot by the Chairman of the Committee.
7. For the filling of casual vacancies, the State Party whose expert has ceased to function as a member of the Committee shall appoint another expert from among its nationals, subject to the approval of the Committee.
8. The members of the Committee shall, with the approval of the General Assembly, receive emoluments from United Nations resources on such terms and conditions as the Assembly may decide, having regard to the importance of the Committee's responsibilities.
9. The Secretary-General of the United Nations shall provide the necessary staff and facilities for the effective performance of the functions of the Committee under the present Convention.

Article 18
1. States Parties undertake to submit to the Secretary-General of the United Nations, for consideration by the Committee, a report on the legislative, judicial, administrative or other measures which they have adopted to give effect to the provisions of the present Convention and on the progress made in this respect:
   (a) Within one year after the entry into force for the State concerned;
   (b) Thereafter at least every four years and further whenever the Committee so requests.

2. Reports may indicate factors and difficulties affecting the degree of fulfilment of obligations under the present Convention.

Article 19
1. The Committee shall adopt its own rules of procedure.
2. The Committee shall elect its officers for a term of two years.

Article 20
1. The Committee shall normally meet for a period of not more than two weeks annually in order to consider the reports submitted in accordance with article 18 of the present Convention.
2. The meetings of the Committee shall normally be held at United Nations Headquarters or at any other convenient place as determined by the Committee.

Article 21
1. The Committee shall, through the Economic and Social Council, report annually to the General Assembly of the United Nations on its activities and may make suggestions and general recommendations based on the examination of reports and information received from the States Parties. Such suggestions and general recommendations shall be included in the report of the Committee together with comments, if any, from States Parties.
2. The Secretary-General of the United Nations shall transmit the reports of the Committee to the Commission on the Status of Women for its information.

Article 22
The specialized agencies shall be entitled to be represented at the consideration of the implementation of such provisions of the present Convention as fall within the scope of their activities. The Committee may invite the specialized agencies to submit reports on the implementation of the Convention in areas falling within the scope of their activities.

PART VI

Article 23
Nothing in the present Convention shall affect any provisions that are more conducive to the achievement of equality between men and women which may be contained:
(a) In the legislation of a State Party; or
(b) In any other international convention, treaty or agreement in force for that State.

Article 24
States Parties undertake to adopt all necessary measures at the national level aimed at achieving the full realization of the rights recognized in the present Convention.

Article 25
1. The present Convention shall be open for signature by all States.
2. The Secretary-General of the United Nations is designated as the depositary of the present Convention.

3. The present Convention is subject to ratification. Instruments of ratification shall be deposited with the Secretary-General of the United Nations.
4. The present Convention shall be open to accession by all States. Accession shall be effected by the deposit of an instrument of accession with the Secretary-General of the United Nations.

Article 26
1. A request for the revision of the present Convention may be made at any time by any State Party by means of a notification in writing addressed to the Secretary-General of the United Nations.
2. The General Assembly of the United Nations shall decide upon the steps, if any, to be taken in respect of such a request.

Article 27
1. The present Convention shall enter into force on the thirtieth day after the date of deposit with the Secretary-General of the United Nations of the twentieth instrument of ratification or accession.
2. For each State ratifying the present Convention or acceding to it after the deposit of the twentieth instrument of ratification or accession, the Convention shall enter into force on the thirtieth day after the date of the deposit of its own instrument of ratification or accession.

Article 28
1. The Secretary-General of the United Nations shall receive and circulate to all States the text of reservations made by States at the time of ratification or accession.
2. A reservation incompatible with the object and purpose of the present Convention shall not be permitted.
3. Reservations may be withdrawn at any time by notification to this effect addressed to the Secretary-General of the United Nations, who shall then inform all States thereof. Such notification shall take effect on the date on which it is received.

Article 29
1. Any dispute between two or more States Parties concerning the interpretation or application of the present Convention which is not settled by negotiation shall, at the request of one of them, be submitted to arbitration. If within six months from the date of the request for arbitration the parties are unable to agree on the organization of the arbitration, any one of those parties may refer the dispute to the International Court of Justice by request in conformity with the Statute of the Court.
2. Each State Party may at the time of signature or ratification of the present Convention or accession thereto declare that it does not consider itself bound by paragraph I of this article. The other States Parties shall not be bound by that paragraph with respect to any State Party which has made such a reservation.
3. Any State Party which has made a reservation in accordance with paragraph 2 of this article may at any time withdraw that reservation by notification to the Secretary-General of the United Nations.

Article 30
The present Convention, the Arabic, Chinese, English, French, Russian and Spanish texts of which are equally authentic, shall be deposited with the Secretary-General of the United Nations.

Optional Protocol to the Convention on the Elimination of All Forms of Discrimination against Women

Adopted and opened for signature, ratification and accession by General Assembly Resolution 54/4 of 6 October 1999

The States Parties to the present Protocol,

Noting that the Charter of the United Nations reaffirms faith in fundamental human rights, in the dignity and worth of the human person and in the equal rights of men and women,

Also noting that the Universal Declaration of Human Rights Resolution 217 A (III). proclaims that all human beings are born free and equal in dignity and rights and that everyone is entitled to all the rights and freedoms set forth therein, without distinction of any kind, including distinction based on sex,

Recalling that the International Covenants on Human Rights Resolution 2200 A (XXI), annex. and other international human rights instruments prohibit discrimination on the basis of sex,

Also recalling the Convention on the Elimination of All Forms of Discrimination against Women[4] ("the Convention"), in which the States Parties thereto condemn discrimination against women in all its forms and agree to pursue by all appropriate means and without delay a policy of eliminating discrimination against women,

Reaffirming their determination to ensure the full and equal enjoyment by women of all human rights and fundamental freedoms and to take effective action to prevent violations of these rights and freedoms,

Have agreed as follows:

Article 1
A State Party to the present Protocol ("State Party") recognizes the competence of the Committee on the Elimination of Discrimination against Women ("the Committee") to receive and consider communications submitted in accordance with article 2.

Article 2
Communications may be submitted by or on behalf of individuals or groups of individuals, under the jurisdiction of a State Party, claiming to be victims of a violation of any of the rights set forth in the Convention by that State Party. Where a communication is submitted on behalf of individuals or groups of individuals, this shall be with their consent unless the author can justify acting on their behalf without such consent.

Article 3
Communications shall be in writing and shall not be anonymous. No communication shall be received by the Committee if it concerns a State Party to the Convention that is not a party to the present Protocol.

Article 4
1. The Committee shall not consider a communication unless it has ascertained that all available domestic remedies have been exhausted unless the application of such remedies is unreasonably prolonged or unlikely to bring effective relief.
2. The Committee shall declare a communication inadmissible where:
   (a) The same matter has already been examined by the Committee or has been or is being examined under another procedure of international investigation or settlement;
   (b) It is incompatible with the provisions of the Convention;
   (c) It is manifestly ill-founded or not sufficiently substantiated;
   (d) It is an abuse of the right to submit a communication;
   (e) The facts that are the subject of the communication occurred prior to the entry into force of the present Protocol for the State Party concerned unless those facts continued after that date.

Article 5
1. At any time after the receipt of a communication and before a determination on the merits has been reached, the Committee may transmit to the State Party concerned for its urgent consideration a request that the State Party take such interim measures as may be necessary to avoid possible irreparable damage to the victim or victims of the alleged violation.
2. Where the Committee exercises its discretion under paragraph 1 of the present article, this does not imply a determination on admissibility or on the merits of the communication.

Article 6
1. Unless the Committee considers a communication inadmissible without reference to the State Party concerned, and provided that the individual or individuals consent to the disclosure of their identity to that State Party, the Committee shall bring any communication submitted to it under the present Protocol confidentially to the attention of the State Party concerned.
2. Within six months, the receiving State Party shall submit to the Committee written explanations or statements clarifying the matter and the remedy, if any, that may have been provided by that State Party.

Article 7
1. The Committee shall consider communications received under the present Protocol in the light of all information made available to it by or on behalf of individuals or groups of individuals and by the State Party concerned, provided that this information is transmitted to the parties concerned.
2. The Committee shall hold closed meetings when examining communications under the present Protocol.
3. After examining a communication, the Committee shall transmit its views on the communication, together with its recommendations, if any, to the parties concerned.

4. The State Party shall give due consideration to the views of the Committee, together with its recommendations, if any, and shall submit to the Committee, within six months, a written response, including information on any action taken in the light of the views and recommendations of the Committee.
5. The Committee may invite the State Party to submit further information about any measures the State Party has taken in response to its views or recommendations, if any, including as deemed appropriate by the Committee, in the State Party's subsequent reports under article 18 of the Convention.

Article 8
1. If the Committee receives reliable information indicating grave or systematic violations by a State Party of rights set forth in the Convention, the Committee shall invite that State Party to cooperate in the examination of the information and to this end to submit observations with regard to the information concerned.
2. Taking into account any observations that may have been submitted by the State Party concerned as well as any other reliable information available to it, the Committee may designate one or more of its members to conduct an inquiry and to report urgently to the Committee. Where warranted and with the consent of the State Party, the inquiry may include a visit to its territory.
3. After examining the findings of such an inquiry, the Committee shall transmit these findings to the State Party concerned together with any comments and recommendations.
4. The State Party concerned shall, within six months of receiving the findings, comments and recommendations transmitted by the Committee, submit its observations to the Committee.
5. Such an inquiry shall be conducted confidentially and the cooperation of the State Party shall be sought at all stages of the proceedings.

Article 9
1. The Committee may invite the State Party concerned to include in its report under article 18 of the Convention details of any measures taken in response to an inquiry conducted under article 8 of the present Protocol.
2. The Committee may, if necessary, after the end of the period of six months referred to in article 8.4, invite the State Party concerned to inform it of the measures taken in response to such an inquiry.

Article 10
1. Each State Party may, at the time of signature or ratification of the present Protocol or accession thereto, declare that it does not recognize the competence of the Committee provided for in articles 8 and 9.
2. Any State Party having made a declaration in accordance with paragraph 1 of the present article may, at any time, withdraw this declaration by notification to the Secretary-General.

Article 11
A State Party shall take all appropriate steps to ensure that individuals under its jurisdiction are not subjected to ill treatment or intimidation as a consequence of communicating with the Committee pursuant to the present Protocol.

Article 12
The Committee shall include in its annual report under article 21 of the Convention a summary of its activities under the present Protocol.

Article 13
Each State Party undertakes to make widely known and to give publicity to the Convention and the present Protocol and to facilitate access to information about the views and recommendations of the Committee, in particular, on matters involving that State Party.

Article 14
The Committee shall develop its own rules of procedure to be followed when exercising the functions conferred on it by the present Protocol.

Article 15
1. The present Protocol shall be open for signature by any State that has signed, ratified or acceded to the Convention.
2. The present Protocol shall be subject to ratification by any State that has ratified or acceded to the Convention. Instruments of ratification shall be deposited with the Secretary-General of the United Nations.
3. The present Protocol shall be open to accession by any State that has ratified or acceded to the Convention.
4. Accession shall be effected by the deposit of an instrument of accession with the Secretary-General of the United Nations.

Article 16
1. The present Protocol shall enter into force three months after the date of the deposit with the Secretary-General of the United Nations of the tenth instrument of ratification or accession.
2. For each State ratifying the present Protocol or acceding to it after its entry into force, the present Protocol shall enter into force three months after the date of the deposit of its own instrument of ratification or accession.

Article 17
No reservations to the present Protocol shall be permitted.

Article 18
1. Any State Party may propose an amendment to the present Protocol and file it with the Secretary-General of the United Nations. The Secretary-General shall thereupon communicate any proposed amendments to the States Parties with a request that they notify her or him whether they favour a conference of States Parties for the purpose of considering and voting on the proposal. In the event that at least one third of the States Parties favour such a conference, the Secretary-General shall convene the conference under the auspices of the United Nations. Any amendment adopted by a majority of the States Parties present and voting at the conference shall be submitted to the General Assembly of the United Nations for approval.
2. Amendments shall come into force when they have been approved by the General Assembly of the United Nations and accepted by a two-thirds majority of the States Parties to the present Protocol in accordance with their respective constitutional processes.

3. When amendments come into force, they shall be binding on those States Parties that have accepted them, other States Parties still being bound by the provisions of the present Protocol and any earlier amendments that they have accepted.

Article 19
1. Any State Party may denounce the present Protocol at any time by written notification addressed to the Secretary-General of the United Nations. Denunciation shall take effect six months after the date of receipt of the notification by the Secretary-General.
2. Denunciation shall be without prejudice to the continued application of the provisions of the present Protocol to any communication submitted under article 2 or any inquiry initiated under article 8 before the effective date of denunciation.

Article 20
The Secretary-General of the United Nations shall inform all States of:
(a) Signatures, ratifications and accessions under the present Protocol;
(b) The date of entry into force of the present Protocol and of any amendment under article 18;
(c) Any denunciation under article 19.

Article 21
1. The present Protocol, of which the Arabic, Chinese, English, French, Russian and Spanish texts are equally authentic, shall be deposited in the archives of the United Nations.
2. The Secretary-General of the United Nations shall transmit certified copies of the present Protocol to all States referred to in article 25 of the Convention.

Convention against Torture and Other Cruel, Inhuman or Degrading Treatment or Punishment

Adopted and opened for signature, ratification and accession by General Assembly Resolution 39/46 of 10 December 1984

entry into force 26 June 1987

The States Parties to this Convention,

Considering that, in accordance with the principles proclaimed in the Charter of the United Nations, recognition of the equal and inalienable rights of all members of the human family is the foundation of freedom, justice and peace in the world,

Recognizing that those rights derive from the inherent dignity of the human person,

Considering the obligation of States under the Charter, in particular Article 55, to promote universal respect for, and observance of, human rights and fundamental freedoms,

Having regard to article 5 of the Universal Declaration of Human Rights and article 7 of the International Covenant on Civil and Political Rights, both of which provide that no one shall be subjected to torture or to cruel, inhuman or degrading treatment or punishment,

Having regard also to the Declaration on the Protection of All Persons from Being Subjected to Torture and Other Cruel, Inhuman or Degrading Treatment or Punishment, adopted by the General Assembly on 9 December 1975,

Desiring to make more effective the struggle against torture and other cruel, inhuman or degrading treatment or punishment throughout the world,

Have agreed as follows:

PART I

Article 1

1. For the purposes of this Convention, the term "torture" means any act by which severe pain or suffering, whether physical or mental, is intentionally inflicted on a person for such purposes as obtaining from him or a third person information or a confession, punishing him for an act he or a third person has committed or is suspected of having committed, or intimidating or coercing him or a third person, or for any reason based on discrimination of any kind, when such pain or suffering is inflicted by or at the instigation of

or with the consent or acquiescence of a public official or other person acting in an official capacity. It does not include pain or suffering arising only from, inherent in or incidental to lawful sanctions.
2. This article is without prejudice to any international instrument or national legislation which does or may contain provisions of wider application.

Article 2
1. Each State Party shall take effective legislative, administrative, judicial or other measures to prevent acts of torture in any territory under its jurisdiction.
2. No exceptional circumstances whatsoever, whether a state of war or a threat of war, internal political in stability or any other public emergency, may be invoked as a justification of torture.
3. An order from a superior officer or a public authority may not be invoked as a justification of torture.

Article 3
1. No State Party shall expel, return ("refouler") or extradite a person to another State where there are substantial grounds for believing that he would be in danger of being subjected to torture.
2. For the purpose of determining whether there are such grounds, the competent authorities shall take into account all relevant considerations including, where applicable, the existence in the State concerned of a consistent pattern of gross, flagrant or mass violations of human rights.

Article 4
1. Each State Party shall ensure that all acts of torture are offences under its criminal law. The same shall apply to an attempt to commit torture and to an act by any person which constitutes complicity or participation in torture.
2. Each State Party shall make these offences punishable by appropriate penalties which take into account their grave nature.

Article 5
1. Each State Party shall take such measures as may be necessary to establish its jurisdiction over the offences referred to in article 4 in the following cases:
   (a) When the offences are committed in any territory under its jurisdiction or on board a ship or aircraft registered in that State;
   (b) When the alleged offender is a national of that State;
   (c) When the victim is a national of that State if that State considers it appropriate.
2. Each State Party shall likewise take such measures as may be necessary to establish its jurisdiction over such offences in cases where the alleged offender is present in any territory under its jurisdiction and it does not extradite him pursuant to article 8 to any of the States mentioned in paragraph I of this article.
3. This Convention does not exclude any criminal jurisdiction exercised in accordance with internal law.

Article 6
1. Upon being satisfied, after an examination of information available to it, that the circumstances so warrant, any State Party in whose territory a person alleged to have committed any offence referred to in article 4 is present shall

take him into custody or take other legal measures to ensure his presence. The custody and other legal measures shall be as provided in the law of that State but may be continued only for such time as is necessary to enable any criminal or extradition proceedings to be instituted.
2. Such State shall immediately make a preliminary inquiry into the facts.
3. Any person in custody pursuant to paragraph 1 of this article shall be assisted in communicating immediately with the nearest appropriate representative of the State of which he is a national, or, if he is a stateless person, with the representative of the State where he usually resides.
4. When a State, pursuant to this article, has taken a person into custody, it shall immediately notify the States referred to in article 5, paragraph 1, of the fact that such person is in custody and of the circumstances which warrant his detention. The State which makes the preliminary inquiry contemplated in paragraph 2 of this article shall promptly report its findings to the said States and shall indicate whether it intends to exercise jurisdiction.

Article 7
1. The State Party in the territory under whose jurisdiction a person alleged to have committed any offence referred to in article 4 is found shall in the cases contemplated in article 5, if it does not extradite him, submit the case to its competent authorities for the purpose of prosecution.
2. These authorities shall take their decision in the same manner as in the case of any ordinary offence of a serious nature under the law of that State. In the cases referred to in article 5, paragraph 2, the standards of evidence required for prosecution and conviction shall in no way be less stringent than those which apply in the cases referred to in article 5, paragraph 1.
3. Any person regarding whom proceedings are brought in connection with any of the offences referred to in article 4 shall be guaranteed fair treatment at all stages of the proceedings.

Article 8
1. The offences referred to in article 4 shall be deemed to be included as extraditable offences in any extradition treaty existing between States Parties. States Parties undertake to include such offences as extraditable offences in every extradition treaty to be concluded between them.
2. If a State Party which makes extradition conditional on the existence of a treaty receives a request for extradition from another. State Party with which it has no extradition treaty, it may consider this Convention as the legal basis for extradition in respect of such offences. Extradition shall be subject to the other conditions provided by the law of the requested State.
3. States Parties which do not make extradition conditional on the existence of a treaty shall recognize such offences as extraditable offences between themselves subject to the conditions provided by the law of the requested State.
4. Such offences shall be treated, for the purpose of extradition between States Parties, as if they had been committed not only in the place in which they occurred but also in the territories of the States required to establish their jurisdiction in accordance with article 5, paragraph 1.

Article 9
1. States Parties shall afford one another the greatest measure of assistance in connection with criminal proceedings brought in respect of any of the offences referred to in article 4, including the supply of all evidence at their disposal necessary for the proceedings.
2. States Parties shall carry out their obligations under paragraph I of this article in conformity with any treaties on mutual judicial assistance that may exist between them.

Article 10
1. Each State Party shall ensure that education and information regarding the prohibition against torture are fully included in the training of law enforcement personnel, civil or military, medical personnel, public officials and other persons who may be involved in the custody, interrogation or treatment of any individual subjected to any form of arrest, detention or imprisonment.
2. Each State Party shall include this prohibition in the rules or instructions issued in regard to the duties and functions of any such person.

Article 11
Each State Party shall keep under systematic review interrogation rules, instructions, methods and practices as well as arrangements for the custody and treatment of persons subjected to any form of arrest, detention or imprisonment in any territory under its jurisdiction, with a view to preventing any cases of torture.

Article 12
Each State Party shall ensure that its competent authorities proceed to a prompt and impartial investigation, wherever there is reasonable ground to believe that an act of torture has been committed in any territory under its jurisdiction.

Article 13
Each State Party shall ensure that any individual who alleges he has been subjected to torture in any territory under its jurisdiction has the right to complain to, and to have his case promptly and impartially examined by, its competent authorities. Steps shall be taken to ensure that the complainant and witnesses are protected against all ill-treatment or intimidation as a consequence of his complaint or any evidence given.

Article 14
1. Each State Party shall ensure in its legal system that the victim of an act of torture obtains redress and has an enforceable right to fair and adequate compensation, including the means for as full rehabilitation as possible. In the event of the death of the victim as a result of an act of torture, his dependants shall be entitled to compensation.
2. Nothing in this article shall affect any right of the victim or other persons to compensation which may exist under national law.

Article 15
Each State Party shall ensure that any statement which is established to have been made as a result of torture shall not be invoked as evidence in any proceedings, except against a person accused of torture as evidence that the statement was made.

Article 16
1. Each State Party shall undertake to prevent in any territory under its jurisdiction other acts of cruel, inhuman or degrading treatment or punishment which do not amount to torture as defined in article I, when such acts are committed by or at the instigation of or with the consent or acquiescence of a public official or other person acting in an official capacity. In particular, the obligations contained in articles 10, 11, 12 and 13 shall apply with the substitution for references to torture of references to other forms of cruel, inhuman or degrading treatment or punishment.
2. The provisions of this Convention are without prejudice to the provisions of any other international instrument or national law which prohibits cruel, inhuman or degrading treatment or punishment or which relates to extradition or expulsion.

PART II

Article 17
1. There shall be established a Committee against Torture (hereinafter referred to as the Committee) which shall carry out the functions hereinafter provided. The Committee shall consist of ten experts of high moral standing and recognized competence in the field of human rights, who shall serve in their personal capacity. The experts shall be elected by the States Parties, consideration being given to equitable geographical distribution and to the usefulness of the participation of some persons having legal experience.
2. The members of the Committee shall be elected by secret ballot from a list of persons nominated by States Parties. Each State Party may nominate one person from among its own nationals. States Parties shall bear in mind the usefulness of nominating persons who are also members of the Human Rights Committee established under the International Covenant on Civil and Political Rights and who are willing to serve on the Committee against Torture.
3. Elections of the members of the Committee shall be held at biennial meetings of States Parties convened by the Secretary-General of the United Nations. At those meetings, for which two thirds of the States Parties shall constitute a quorum, the persons elected to the Committee shall be those who obtain the largest number of votes and an absolute majority of the votes of the representatives of States Parties present and voting.
4. The initial election shall be held no later than six months after the date of the entry into force of this Convention. At least four months before the date of each election, the Secretary-General of the United Nations shall address a letter to the States Parties inviting them to submit their nominations within three months. The Secretary-General shall prepare a list in alphabetical order of all persons thus nominated, indicating the States Parties which have nominated them, and shall submit it to the States Parties.
5. The members of the Committee shall be elected for a term of four years. They shall be eligible for re-election if renominated. However, the term of five of the members elected at the first election shall expire at the end of two years; immediately after the first election the names of these five members shall be chosen by lot by the chairman of the meeting referred to in paragraph 3 of this article.

6. If a member of the Committee dies or resigns or for any other cause can no longer perform his Committee duties, the State Party which nominated him shall appoint another expert from among its nationals to serve for the remainder of his term, subject to the approval of the majority of the States Parties. The approval shall be considered given unless half or more of the States Parties respond negatively within six weeks after having been informed by the Secretary-General of the United Nations of the proposed appointment.
7. States Parties shall be responsible for the expenses of the members of the Committee while they are in performance of Committee duties.

Article 18
1. The Committee shall elect its officers for a term of two years. They may be re-elected.
2. The Committee shall establish its own rules of procedure, but these rules shall provide, *inter alia*, that:
   (a) Six members shall constitute a quorum;
   (b) Decisions of the Committee shall be made by a majority vote of the members present.
3. The Secretary-General of the United Nations shall provide the necessary staff and facilities for the effective performance of the functions of the Committee under this Convention.
4. The Secretary-General of the United Nations shall convene the initial meeting of the Committee. After its initial meeting, the Committee shall meet at such times as shall be provided in its rules of procedure.
5. The States Parties shall be responsible for expenses incurred in connection with the holding of meetings of the States Parties and of the Committee, including reimbursement to the United Nations for any expenses, such as the cost of staff and facilities, incurred by the United Nations pursuant to paragraph 3 of this article.

Article 19
1. The States Parties shall submit to the Committee, through the Secretary-General of the United Nations, reports on the measures they have taken to give effect to their undertakings under this Convention, within one year after the entry into force of the Convention for the State Party concerned. Thereafter the States Parties shall submit supplementary reports every four years on any new measures taken and such other reports as the Committee may request.
2. The Secretary-General of the United Nations shall transmit the reports to all States Parties.
3. Each report shall be considered by the Committee which may make such general comments on the report as it may consider appropriate and shall forward these to the State Party concerned. That State Party may respond with any observations it chooses to the Committee.
4. The Committee may, at its discretion, decide to include any comments made by it in accordance with paragraph 3 of this article, together with the observations thereon received from the State Party concerned, in its annual report made in accordance with article 24 If so requested by the State Party concerned, the Committee may also include a copy of the report submitted under paragraph I of this article.

Article 20
1. If the Committee receives reliable information which appears to it to contain well-founded indications that torture is being systematically practised in the territory of a State Party, the Committee shall invite that State Party to co-operate in the examination of the information and to this end to submit observations with regard to the information concerned.
2. Taking into account any observations which may have been submitted by the State Party concerned, as well as any other relevant information available to it, the Committee may, if it decides that this is warranted, designate one or more of its members to make a confidential inquiry and to report to the Committee urgently.
3. If an inquiry is made in accordance with paragraph 2 of this article, the Committee shall seek the co-operation of the State Party concerned. In agreement with that State Party, such an inquiry may include a visit to its territory.
4. After examining the findings of its member or members submitted in accordance with paragraph 2 of this article, the Commission shall transmit these findings to the State Party concerned together with any comments or suggestions which seem appropriate in view of the situation.
5. All the proceedings of the Committee referred to in paragraphs I to 4 of this article shall be confidential, and at all stages of the proceedings the co-operation of the State Party shall be sought. After such proceedings have been completed with regard to an inquiry made in accordance with paragraph 2, the Committee may, after consultations with the State Party concerned, decide to include a summary account of the results of the proceedings in its annual report made in accordance with article 24.

Article 21
1. A State Party to this Convention may at any time declare under this article that it recognizes the competence of the Committee to receive and consider communications to the effect that a State Party claims that another State Party is not fulfilling its obligations under this Convention. Such communications may be received and considered according to the procedures laid down in this article only if submitted by a State Party which has made a declaration recognizing in regard to itself the competence of the Committee. No communication shall be dealt with by the Committee under this article if it concerns a State Party which has not made such a declaration. Communications received under this article shall be dealt with in accordance with the following procedure;
   (a) If a State Party considers that another State Party is not giving effect to the provisions of this Convention, it may, by written communication, bring the matter to the attention of that State Party. Within three months after the receipt of the communication the receiving State shall afford the State which sent the communication an explanation or any other statement in writing clarifying the matter, which should include, to the extent possible and pertinent, reference to domestic procedures and remedies taken, pending or available in the matter;
   (b) If the matter is not adjusted to the satisfaction of both States Parties concerned within six months after the receipt by the receiving State of

the initial communication, either State shall have the right to refer the matter to the Committee, by notice given to the Committee and to the other State;

(c) The Committee shall deal with a matter referred to it under this article only after it has ascertained that all domestic remedies have been invoked and exhausted in the matter, in conformity with the generally recognized principles of international law. This shall not be the rule where the application of the remedies is unreasonably prolonged or is unlikely to bring effective relief to the person who is the victim of the violation of this Convention;

(d) The Committee shall hold closed meetings when examining communications under this article;

(e) Subject to the provisions of subparagraph (c), the Committee shall make available its good offices to the States Parties concerned with a view to a friendly solution of the matter on the basis of respect for the obligations provided for in this Convention. For this purpose, the Committee may, when appropriate, set up an ad hoc conciliation commission;

(f) In any matter referred to it under this article, the Committee may call upon the States Parties concerned, referred to in subparagraph (b), to supply any relevant information;

(g) The States Parties concerned, referred to in subparagraph (b), shall have the right to be represented when the matter is being considered by the Committee and to make submissions orally and/or in writing;

(h) The Committee shall, within twelve months after the date of receipt of notice under subparagraph (b), submit a report:
  (i) If a solution within the terms of subparagraph (e) is reached, the Committee shall confine its report to a brief statement of the facts and of the solution reached;
  (ii) If a solution within the terms of subparagraph (e) is not reached, the Committee shall confine its report to a brief statement of the facts; the written submissions and record of the oral submissions made by the States Parties concerned shall be attached to the report.
  In every matter, the report shall be communicated to the States Parties concerned.

2. The provisions of this article shall come into force when five States Parties to this Convention have made declarations under paragraph 1 of this article. Such declarations shall be deposited by the States Parties with the Secretary-General of the United Nations, who shall transmit copies thereof to the other States Parties. A declaration may be withdrawn at any time by notification to the Secretary-General. Such a withdrawal shall not prejudice the consideration of any matter which is the subject of a communication already transmitted under this article; no further communication by any State Party shall be received under this article after the notification of withdrawal of the declaration has been received by the Secretary-General, unless the State Party concerned has made a new declaration.

Article 22

1. A State Party to this Convention may at any time declare under this article that it recognizes the competence of the Committee to receive and consider

communications from or on behalf of individuals subject to its jurisdiction who claim to be victims of a violation by a State Party of the provisions of the Convention. No communication shall be received by the Committee if it concerns a State Party which has not made such a declaration.
2. The Committee shall consider inadmissible any communication under this article which is anonymous or which it considers to be an abuse of the right of submission of such communications or to be incompatible with the provisions of this Convention.
3. Subject to the provisions of paragraph 2, the Committee shall bring any communications submitted to it under this article to the attention of the State Party to this Convention which has made a declaration under paragraph I and is alleged to be violating any provisions of the Convention. Within six months, the receiving State shall submit to the Committee written explanations or statements clarifying the matter and the remedy, if any, that may have been taken by that State.
4. The Committee shall consider communications received under this article in the light of all information made available to it by or on behalf of the individual and by the State Party concerned.
5. The Committee shall not consider any communications from an individual under this article unless it has ascertained that:
   (a) The same matter has not been, and is not being, examined under another procedure of international investigation or settlement;
   (b) The individual has exhausted all available domestic remedies; this shall not be the rule where the application of the remedies is unreasonably prolonged or is unlikely to bring effective reliefto the person who is the victim of the violation of this Convention.
6. The Committee shall hold closed meetings when examining communications under this article.
7. The Committee shall forward its views to the State Party concerned and to the individual.
8. The provisions of this article shall come into force when five States Parties to this Convention have made declarations under paragraph 1 of this article. Such declarations shall be deposited by the States Parties with the Secretary-General of the United Nations, who shall transmit copies thereof to the other States Parties. A declaration may be withdrawn at any time by notification to the Secretary-General. Such a withdrawal shall not prejudice the consideration of any matter which is the subject of a communication already transmitted under this article; no further communication by or on behalf of an individual shall be received under this article after the notification of withdrawal of the declaration has been received by the SecretaryGeneral, unless the State Party has made a new declaration.

Article 23

The members of the Committee and of the ad hoc conciliation commissions which may be appointed under article 21, paragraph I (e), shall be entitled to the facilities, privileges and immunities of experts on mission for the United Nations as laid down in the relevant sections of the Convention on the Privileges and Immunities of the United Nations.

Article 24
The Committee shall submit an annual report on its activities under this Convention to the States Parties and to the General Assembly of the United Nations.

PART III

Article 25
1. This Convention is open for signature by all States.
2. This Convention is subject to ratification. Instruments of ratification shall be deposited with the Secretary-General of the United Nations.

Article 26
This Convention is open to accession by all States. Accession shall be effected by the deposit of an instrument of accession with the SecretaryGeneral of the United Nations.

Article 27
1. This Convention shall enter into force on the thirtieth day after the date of the deposit with the Secretary-General of the United Nations of the twentieth instrument of ratification or accession.
2. For each State ratifying this Convention or acceding to it after the deposit of the twentieth instrument of ratification or accession, the Convention shall enter into force on the thirtieth day after the date of the deposit of its own instrument of ratification or accession.

Article 28
1. Each State may, at the time of signature or ratification of this Convention or accession thereto, declare that it does not recognize the competence of the Committee provided for in article 20.
2. Any State Party having made a reservation in accordance with paragraph I of this article may, at any time, withdraw this reservation by notification to the Secretary-General of the United Nations.

Article 29
1. Any State Party to this Convention may propose an amendment and file it with the Secretary-General of the United Nations. The SecretaryGeneral shall thereupon communicate the proposed amendment to the States Parties with a request that they notify him whether they favour a conference of States Parties for the purpose of considering and voting upon the proposal. In the event that within four months from the date of such communication at least one third of the States Parties favours such a conference, the SecretaryGeneral shall convene the conference under the auspices of the United Nations. Any amendment adopted by a majority of the States Parties present and voting at the conference shall be submitted by the Secretary-General to all the States Parties for acceptance.
2. An amendment adopted in accordance with paragraph I of this article shall enter into force when two thirds of the States Parties to this Convention have notified the Secretary-General of the United Nations that they have accepted it in accordance with their respective constitutional processes.
3. When amendments enter into force, they shall be binding on those States

Parties which have accepted them, other States Parties still being bound by the provisions of this Convention and any earlier amendments which they have accepted.

Article 30
1. Any dispute between two or more States Parties concerning the interpretation or application of this Convention which cannot be settled through negotiation shall, at the request of one of them, be submitted to arbitration. If within six months from the date of the request for arbitration the Parties are unable to agree on the organization of the arbitration, any one of those Parties may refer the dispute to the International Court of Justice by request in conformity with the Statute of the Court.
2. Each State may, at the time of signature or ratification of this Convention or accession thereto, declare that it does not consider itself bound by paragraph I of this article. The other States Parties shall not be bound by paragraph I of this article with respect to any State Party having made such a reservation.
3. Any State Party having made a reservation in accordance with paragraph 2 of this article may at any time withdraw this reservation by notification to the Secretary-General of the United Nations.

Article 31
1. A State Party may denounce this Convention by written notification to the Secretary-General of the United Nations. Denunciation becomes effective one year after the date of receipt of- the notification by the Secretary-General.
2. Such a denunciation shall not have the effect of releasing the State Party from its obligations under this Convention in regard to any act or omission which occurs prior to the date at which the denunciation becomes effective, nor shall denunciation prejudice in any way the continued consideration of any matter which is already under consideration by the Committee prior to the date at which the denunciation becomes effective.
3. Following the date at which the denunciation of a State Party becomes effective, the Committee shall not commence consideration of any new matter regarding that State.

Article 32
The Secretary-General of the United Nations shall inform all States Members of the United Nations and all States which have signed this Convention or acceded to it of the following:
(a) Signatures, ratifications and accessions under articles 25 and 26;
(b) The date of entry into force of this Convention under article 27 and the date of the entry into force of any amendments under article 29;
(c) Denunciations under article 31.

Article 33
1. This Convention, of which the Arabic, Chinese, English, French, Russian and Spanish texts are equally authentic, shall be deposited with the Secretary-General of the United Nations.
2. The Secretary-General of the United Nations shall transmit certified copies of this Convention to all States.

Convention on the Rights of the Child

Adopted and opened for signature, ratification and accession by
General Assembly Resolution 44/25 of 20 November 1989

entry into force 2 September 1990

Preamble

The States Parties to the present Convention,

Considering that, in accordance with the principles proclaimed in the Charter of the United Nations, recognition of the inherent dignity and of the equal and inalienable rights of all members of the human family is the foundation of freedom, justice and peace in the world,

Bearing in mind that the peoples of the United Nations have, in the Charter, reaffirmed their faith in fundamental human rights and in the dignity and worth of the human person, and have determined to promote social progress and better standards of life in larger freedom,

Recognizing that the United Nations has, in the Universal Declaration of Human Rights and in the International Covenants on Human Rights, proclaimed and agreed that everyone is entitled to all the rights and freedoms set forth therein, without distinction of any kind, such as race, colour, sex, language, religion, political or other opinion, national or social origin, property, birth or other status,

Recalling that, in the Universal Declaration of Human Rights, the United Nations has proclaimed that childhood is entitled to special care and assistance,

Convinced that the family, as the fundamental group of society and the natural environment for the growth and well-being of all its members and particularly children, should be afforded the necessary protection and assistance so that it can fully assume its responsibilities within the community,

Recognizing that the child, for the full and harmonious development of his or her personality, should grow up in a family environment, in an atmosphere of happiness, love and understanding,

Considering that the child should be fully prepared to live an individual life in society, and brought up in the spirit of the ideals proclaimed in the Charter of the United Nations, and in particular in the spirit of peace, dignity, tolerance, freedom, equality and solidarity,

Bearing in mind that the need to extend particular care to the child has been stated in the Geneva Declaration of the Rights of the Child of 1924 and in the

Declaration of the Rights of the Child adopted by the General Assembly on 20 November 1959 and recognized in the Universal Declaration of Human Rights, in the International Covenant on Civil and Political Rights (in particular in articles 23 and 24), in the International Covenant on Economic, Social and Cultural Rights (in particular in article 10) and in the statutes and relevant instruments of specialized agencies and international organizations concerned with the welfare of children, '

Bearing in mind that, as indicated in the Declaration of the Rights of the Child, "the child, by reason of his physical and mental immaturity, needs special safeguards and care, including appropriate legal protection, before as well as after birth",

Recalling the provisions of the Declaration on Social and Legal Principles relating to the Protection and Welfare of Children, with Special Reference to Foster Placement and Adoption Nationally and Internationally; the United Nations Standard Minimum Rules for the Administration of Juvenile Justice (The Beijing Rules); and the Declaration on the Protection of Women and Children in Emergency and Armed Conflict,

Recognizing that, in all countries in the world, there are children living in exceptionally difficult conditions, and that such children need special consideration,

Taking due account of the importance of the traditions and cultural values of each people for the protection and harmonious development of the child,

Recognizing the importance of international co-operation for improving the living conditions of children in every country, in particular in the developing countries,

Have agreed as follows:

PART I

Article 1

For the purposes of the present Convention, a child means every human being below the age of eighteen years unless under the law applicable to the child, majority is attained earlier.

Article 2

1. States Parties shall respect and ensure the rights set forth in the present Convention to each child within their jurisdiction without discrimination of any kind, irrespective of the child's or his or her parent's or legal guardian's race, colour, sex, language, religion, political or other opinion, national, ethnic or social origin, property, disability, birth or other status.
2. States Parties shall take all appropriate measures to ensure that the child is protected against all forms of discrimination or punishment on the basis of the status, activities, expressed opinions, or beliefs of the child's parents, legal guardians, or family members.

Article 3

1. In all actions concerning children, whether undertaken by public or private social welfare institutions, courts of law, administrative authorities or legislative bodies, the best interests of the child shall be a primary consideration.

2. States Parties undertake to ensure the child such protection and care as is necessary for his or her well-being, taking into account the rights and duties of his or her parents, legal guardians, or other individuals legally responsible for him or her, and, to this end, shall take all appropriate legislative and administrative measures.
3. States Parties shall ensure that the institutions, services and facilities responsible for the care or protection of children shall conform with the standards established by competent authorities, particularly in the areas of safety, health, in the number and suitability of their staff, as well as competent supervision.

Article 4
States Parties shall undertake all appropriate legislative, administrative, and other measures for the implementation of the rights recognized in the present Convention. With regard to economic, social and cultural rights, States Parties shall undertake such measures to the maximum extent of their available resources and, where needed, within the framework of international co-operation.

Article 5
States Parties shall respect the responsibilities, rights and duties of parents or, where applicable, the members of the extended family or community as provided for by local custom, legal guardians or other persons legally responsible for the child, to provide, in a manner consistent with the evolving capacities of the child, appropriate direction and guidance in the exercise by the child of the rights recognized in the present Convention.

Article 6
1. States Parties recognize that every child has the inherent right to life.
2. States Parties shall ensure to the maximum extent possible the survival and development of the child.

Article 7
1. The child shall be registered immediately after birth and shall have the right from birth to a name, the right to acquire a nationality and. as far as possible, the right to know and be cared for by his or her parents.
2. States Parties shall ensure the implementation of these rights in accordance with their national law and their obligations under the relevant international instruments in this field, in particular where the child would otherwise be stateless.

Article 8
1. States Parties undertake to respect the right of the child to preserve his or her identity, including nationality, name and family relations as recognized by law without unlawful interference.
2. Where a child is illegally deprived of some or all of the elements of his or her identity, States Parties shall provide appropriate assistance and protection, with a view to re-establishing speedily his or her identity.

Article 9
1. States Parties shall ensure that a child shall not be separated from his or her parents against their will, except when competent authorities subject to judicial review determine, in accordance with applicable law and procedures, that

such separation is necessary for the best interests of the child. Such determination may be necessary in a particular case such as one involving abuse or neglect of the child by the parents, or one where the parents are living separately and a decision must be made as to the child's place of residence.
2. In any proceedings pursuant to paragraph 1 of the present article, all interested parties shall be given an opportunity to participate in the proceedings and make their views known.
3. States Parties shall respect the right of the child who is separated from one or both parents to maintain personal relations and direct contact with both parents on a regular basis, except if it is contrary to the child's best interests.
4. Where such separation results from any action initiated by a State Party, such as the detention, imprisonment, exile, deportation or death (including death arising from any cause while the person is in the custody of the State) of one or both parents or of the child, that State Party shall, upon request, provide the parents, the child or, if appropriate, another member of the family with the essential information concerning the whereabouts of the absent member(s) of the family unless the provision of the information would be detrimental to the well-being of the child. States Parties shall further ensure that the submission of such a request shall of itself entail no adverse consequences for the person(s) concerned.

Article 10
1. In accordance with the obligation of States Parties under article 9, paragraph 1, applications by a child or his or her parents to enter or leave a State Party for the purpose of family reunification shall be dealt with by States Parties in a positive, humane and expeditious manner. States Parties shall further ensure that the submission of such a request shall entail no adverse consequences for the applicants and for the members of their family.
2. A child whose parents reside in different States shall have the right to maintain on a regular basis, save in exceptional circumstances personal relations and direct contacts with both parents. Towards that end and in accordance with the obligation of States Parties under article 9, paragraph 1, States Parties shall respect the right of the child and his or her parents to leave any country, including their own, and to enter their own country. The right to leave any country shall be subject only to such restrictions as are prescribed by law and which are necessary to protect the national security, public order (ordre public), public health or morals or the rights and freedoms of others and are consistent with the other rights recognized in the present Convention.

Article 11
1. States Parties shall take measures to combat the illicit transfer and non-return of children abroad.
2. To this end, States Parties shall promote the conclusion of bilateral or multilateral agreements or accession to existing agreements.

Article 12
1. States Parties shall assure to the child who is capable of forming his or her own views the right to express those views freely in all matters affecting the child, the views of the child being given due weight in accordance with the age and maturity of the child.

2. For this purpose, the child shall in particular be provided the opportunity to be heard in any judicial and administrative proceedings affecting the child, either directly, or through a representative or an appropriate body, in a manner consistent with the procedural rules of national law.

Article 13
1. The child shall have the right to freedom of expression; this right shall include freedom to seek, receive and impart information and ideas of all kinds, regardless of frontiers, either orally, in writing or in print, in the form of art, or through any other media of the child's choice.
2. The exercise of this right may be subject to certain restrictions, but these shall only be such as are provided by law and are necessary:
   (a) For respect of the rights or reputations of others; or
   (b) For the protection of national security or of public order (ordre public), or of public health or morals.

Article 14
1. States Parties shall respect the right of the child to freedom of thought, conscience and religion.
2. States Parties shall respect the rights and duties of the parents and, when applicable, legal guardians, to provide direction to the child in the exercise of his or her right in a manner consistent with the evolving capacities of the child.
3. Freedom to manifest one's religion or beliefs may be subject only to such limitations as are prescribed by law and are necessary to protect public safety, order, health or morals, or the fundamental rights and freedoms of others.

Article 15
1. States Parties recognize the rights of the child to freedom of association and to freedom of peaceful assembly.
2. No restrictions may be placed on the exercise of these rights other than those imposed in conformity with the law and which are necessary in a democratic society in the interests of national security or public safety, public order (ordre public), the protection of public health or morals or the protection of the rights and freedoms of others.

Article 16
1. No child shall be subjected to arbitrary or unlawful interference with his or her privacy, family, home or correspondence, nor to unlawful attacks on his or her honour and reputation.
2. The child has the right to the protection of the law against such interference or attacks.

Article 17
States Parties recognize the important function performed by the mass media and shall ensure that the child has access to information and material from a diversity of national and international sources, especially those aimed at the promotion of his or her social, spiritual and moral well-being and physical and mental health. To this end, States Parties shall:
(a) Encourage the mass media to disseminate information and material of social and cultural benefit to the child and in accordance with the spirit of article 29;

(b) Encourage international co-operation in the production, exchange and dissemination of such information and material from a diversity of cultural, national and international sources;
(c) Encourage the production and dissemination of children's books;
(d) Encourage the mass media to have particular regard to the linguistic needs of the child who belongs to a minority group or who is indigenous;
(e) Encourage the development of appropriate guidelines for the protection of the child from information and material injurious to his or her well-being, bearing in mind the provisions of articles 13 and 18.

Article 18
1. States Parties shall use their best efforts to ensure recognition of the principle that both parents have common responsibilities for the upbringing and development of the child. Parents or, as the case may be, legal guardians, have the primary responsibility for the upbringing and development of the child. The best interests of the child will be their basic concern.
2. For the purpose of guaranteeing and promoting the rights set forth in the present Convention, States Parties shall render appropriate assistance to parents and legal guardians in the performance of their child-rearing responsibilities and shall ensure the development of institutions, facilities and services for the care of children.
3. States Parties shall take all appropriate measures to ensure that children of working parents have the right to benefit from child-care services and facilities for which they are eligible.

Article 19
1. States Parties shall take all appropriate legislative, administrative, social and educational measures to protect the child from all forms of physical or mental violence, injury or abuse, neglect or negligent treatment, maltreatment or exploitation, including sexual abuse, while in the care of parent(s), legal guardian(s) or any other person who has the care of the child.
2. Such protective measures should, as appropriate, include effective procedures for the establishment of social programmes to provide necessary support for the child and for those who have the care of the child, as well as for other forms of prevention and for identification, reporting, referral, investigation, treatment and follow-up of instances of child maltreatment described heretofore, and, as appropriate, for judicial involvement.

Article 20
1. A child temporarily or permanently deprived of his or her family environment, or in whose own best interests cannot be allowed to remain in that environment, shall be entitled to special protection and assistance provided by the State.
2. States Parties shall in accordance with their national laws ensure alternative care for such a child.
3. Such care could include, *inter alia*, foster placement, kafalah of Islamic law, adoption or if necessary placement in suitable institutions for the care of children. When considering solutions, due regard shall be paid to the desirability of continuity in a child's upbringing and to the child's ethnic, religious, cultural and linguistic background.

Article 21
States Parties that recognize and/or permit the system of adoption shall ensure that the best interests of the child shall be the paramount consideration and they shall:
(a) Ensure that the adoption of a child is authorized only by competent authorities who determine, in accordance with applicable law and procedures and on the basis of all pertinent and reliable information, that the adoption is permissible in view of the child's status concerning parents, relatives and legal guardians and that, if required, the persons concerned have given their informed consent to the adoption on the basis of such counselling as may be necessary;
(b) Recognize that inter-country adoption may be considered as an alternative means of child's care, if the child cannot be placed in a foster or an adoptive family or cannot in any suitable manner be cared for in the child's country of origin;
(c) Ensure that the child concerned by inter-country adoption enjoys safeguards and standards equivalent to those existing in the case of national adoption;
(d) Take all appropriate measures to ensure that, in inter-country adoption, the placement does not result in improper financial gain for those involved in it;
(e) Promote, where appropriate, the objectives of the present article by concluding bilateral or multilateral arrangements or agreements, and endeavour, within this framework, to ensure that the placement of the child in another country is carried out by competent authorities or organs.

Article 22
1. States Parties shall take appropriate measures to ensure that a child who is seeking refugee status or who is considered a refugee in accordance with applicable international or domestic law and procedures shall, whether unaccompanied or accompanied by his or her parents or by any other person, receive appropriate protection and humanitarian assistance in the enjoyment of applicable rights set forth in the present Convention and in other international human rights or humanitarian instruments to which the said States are Parties.
2. For this purpose, States Parties shall provide, as they consider appropriate, co-operation in any efforts by the United Nations and other competent intergovernmental organizations or non-governmental organizations co-operating with the United Nations to protect and assist such a child and to trace the parents or other members of the family of any refugee child in order to obtain information necessary for reunification with his or her family. In cases where no parents or other members of the family can be found, the child shall be accorded the same protection as any other child permanently or temporarily deprived of his or her family environment for any reason, as set forth in the present Convention.

Article 23
1. States Parties recognize that a mentally or physically disabled child should enjoy a full and decent life, in conditions which ensure dignity, promote self-reliance and facilitate the child's active participation in the community.
2. States Parties recognize the right of the disabled child to special care and

shall encourage and ensure the extension, subject to available resources, to the eligible child and those responsible for his or her care, of assistance for which application is made and which is appropriate to the child's condition and to the circumstances of the parents or others caring for the child.
3. Recognizing the special needs of a disabled child, assistance extended in accordance with paragraph 2 of the present article shall be provided free of charge, whenever possible, taking into account the financial resources of the parents or others caring for the child, and shall be designed to ensure that the disabled child has effective access to and receives education, training, health care services, rehabilitation services, preparation for employment and recreation opportunities in a manner conducive to the child's achieving the fullest possible social integration and individual development, including his or her cultural and spiritual development
4. States Parties shall promote, in the spirit of international cooperation, the exchange of appropriate information in the field of preventive health care and of medical, psychological and functional treatment of disabled children, including dissemination of and access to information concerning methods of rehabilitation, education and vocational services, with the aim of enabling States Parties to improve their capabilities and skills and to widen their experience in these areas. In this regard, particular account shall be taken of the needs of developing countries.

Article 24
1. States Parties recognize the right of the child to the enjoyment of the highest attainable standard of health and to facilities for the treatment of illness and rehabilitation of health. States Parties shall strive to ensure that no child is deprived of his or her right of access to such health care services.
2. States Parties shall pursue full implementation of this right and, in particular, shall take appropriate measures:
   (a) To diminish infant and child mortality;
   (b) To ensure the provision of necessary medical assistance and health care to all children with emphasis on the development of primary health care;
   (c) To combat disease and malnutrition, including within the framework of primary health care, through, *inter alia*, the application of readily available technology and through the provision of adequate nutritious foods and clean drinking-water, taking into consideration the dangers and risks of environmental pollution;
   (d) To ensure appropriate pre-natal and post-natal health care for mothers;
   (e) To ensure that all segments of society, in particular parents and children, are informed, have access to education and are supported in the use of basic knowledge of child health and nutrition, the advantages of breastfeeding, hygiene and environmental sanitation and the prevention of accidents;
   (f) To develop preventive health care, guidance for parents and family planning education and services.
3. States Parties shall take all effective and appropriate measures with a view to abolishing traditional practices prejudicial to the health of children.
4. States Parties undertake to promote and encourage international co-operation

with a view to achieving progressively the full realization of the right recognized in the present article. In this regard, particular account shall be taken of the needs of developing countries.

Article 25
States Parties recognize the right of a child who has been placed by the competent authorities for the purposes of care, protection or treatment of his or her physical or mental health, to a periodic review of the treatment provided to the child and all other circumstances relevant to his or her placement.

Article 26
1. States Parties shall recognize for every child the right to benefit from social security, including social insurance, and shall take the necessary measures to achieve the full realization of this right in accordance with their national law.
2. The benefits should, where appropriate, be granted, taking into account the resources and the circumstances of the child and persons having responsibility for the maintenance of the child, as well as any other consideration relevant to an application for benefits made by or on behalf of the child.

Article 27
1. States Parties recognize the right of every child to a standard of living adequate for the child's physical, mental, spiritual, moral and social development.
2. The parent(s) or others responsible for the child have the primary responsibility to secure, within their abilities and financial capacities, the conditions of living necessary for the child's development.
3. States Parties, in accordance with national conditions and within their means, shall take appropriate measures to assist parents and others responsible for the child to implement this right and shall in case of need provide material assistance and support programmes, particularly with regard to nutrition, clothing and housing.
4. States Parties shall take all appropriate measures to secure the recovery of maintenance for the child from the parents or other persons having financial responsibility for the child, both within the State Party and from abroad. In particular, where the person having financial responsibility for the child lives in a State different from that of the child, States Parties shall promote the accession to international agreements or the conclusion of such agreements, as well as the making of other appropriate arrangements.

Article 28
1. States Parties recognize the right of the child to education, and with a view to achieving this right progressively and on the basis of equal opportunity, they shall, in particular:
   (a) Make primary education compulsory and available free to all;
   (b) Encourage the development of different forms of secondary education, including general and vocational education, make them available and accessible to every child, and take appropriate measures such as the introduction of free education and offering financial assistance in case of need;

(c) Make higher education accessible to all on the basis of capacity by every appropriate means;
(d) Make educational and vocational information and guidance available and accessible to all children;
(e) Take measures to encourage regular attendance at schools and the reduction of drop-out rates.
2. States Parties shall take all appropriate measures to ensure that school discipline is administered in a manner consistent with the child's human dignity and in conformity with the present Convention.
3. States Parties shall promote and encourage international cooperation in matters relating to education, in particular with a view to contributing to the elimination of ignorance and illiteracy throughout the world and facilitating access to scientific and technical knowledge and modern teaching methods. In this regard, particular account shall be taken of the needs of developing countries.

Article 29
1. States Parties agree that the education of the child shall be directed to:
    (a) The development of the child's personality, talents and mental and physical abilities to their fullest potential;
    (b) The development of respect for human rights and fundamental freedoms, and for the principles enshrined in the Charter of the United Nations;
    (c) The development of respect for the child's parents, his or her own cultural identity, language and values, for the national values of the country in which the child is living, the country from which he or she may originate, and for civilizations different from his or her own;
    (d) The preparation of the child for responsible life in a free society, in the spirit of understanding, peace, tolerance, equality of sexes, and friendship among all peoples, ethnic, national and religious groups and persons of indigenous origin;
    (e) The development of respect for the natural environment.
2. No part of the present article or article 28 shall be construed so as to interfere with the liberty of individuals and bodies to establish and direct educational institutions, subject always to the observance of the principle set forth in paragraph 1 of the present article and to the requirements that the education given in such institutions shall conform to such minimum standards as may be laid down by the State.

Article 30
In those States in which ethnic, religious or linguistic minorities or persons of indigenous origin exist, a child belonging to such a minority or who is indigenous shall not be denied the right, in community with other members of his or her group, to enjoy his or her own culture, to profess and practise his or her own religion, or to use his or her own language.

Article 31
1. States Parties recognize the right of the child to rest and leisure, to engage in play and recreational activities appropriate to the age of the child and to participate freely in cultural life and the arts.
2. States Parties shall respect and promote the right of the child to participate

fully in cultural and artistic life and shall encourage the provision of appropriate and equal opportunities for cultural, artistic, recreational and leisure activity.

Article 32
1. States Parties recognize the right of the child to be protected from economic exploitation and from performing any work that is likely to be hazardous or to interfere with the child's education, or to be harmful to the child's health or physical, mental, spiritual, moral or social development.
2. States Parties shall take legislative, administrative, social and educational measures to ensure the implementation of the present article. To this end, and having regard to the relevant provisions of other international instruments, States Parties shall in particular:
   (a) Provide for a minimum age or minimum ages for admission to employment;
   (b) Provide for appropriate regulation of the hours and conditions of employment;
   (c) Provide for appropriate penalties or other sanctions to ensure the effective enforcement of the present article.

Article 33
States Parties shall take all appropriate measures, including legislative, administrative, social and educational measures, to protect children from the illicit use of narcotic drugs and psychotropic substances as defined in the relevant international treaties, and to prevent the use of children in the illicit production and trafficking of such substances.

Article 34
States Parties undertake to protect the child from all forms of sexual exploitation and sexual abuse. For these purposes, States Parties shall in particular take all appropriate national, bilateral and multilateral measures to prevent:
(a) The inducement or coercion of a child to engage in any unlawful sexual activity;
(b) The exploitative use of children in prostitution or other unlawful sexual practices;
(c) The exploitative use of children in pornographic performances and materials.

Article 35
States Parties shall take all appropriate national, bilateral and multilateral measures to prevent the abduction of, the sale of or traffic in children for any purpose or in any form.

Article 36
States Parties shall protect the child against all other forms of exploitation prejudicial to any aspects of the child's welfare.

Article 37
States Parties shall ensure that:
(a) No child shall be subjected to torture or other cruel, inhuman or degrading treatment or punishment. Neither capital punishment nor life imprisonment

without possibility of release shall be imposed for offences committed by persons below eighteen years of age;
(b) No child shall be deprived of his or her liberty unlawfully or arbitrarily. The arrest, detention or imprisonment of a child shall be in conformity with the law and shall be used only as a measure of last resort and for the shortest appropriate period of time;
(c) Every child deprived of liberty shall be treated with humanity and respect for the inherent dignity of the human person, and in a manner which takes into account the needs of persons of his or her age. In particular, every child deprived of liberty shall be separated from adults unless it is considered in the child's best interest not to do so and shall have the right to maintain contact with his or her family through correspondence and visits, save in exceptional circumstances;
(d) Every child deprived of his or her liberty shall have the right to prompt access to legal and other appropriate assistance, as well as the right to challenge the legality of the deprivation of his or her liberty before a court or other competent, independent and impartial authority, and to a prompt decision on any such action.

Article 38
1. States Parties undertake to respect and to ensure respect for rules of international humanitarian law applicable to them in armed conflicts which are relevant to the child.
2. States Parties shall take all feasible measures to ensure that persons who have not attained the age of fifteen years do not take a direct part in hostilities.
3. States Parties shall refrain from recruiting any person who has not attained the age of fifteen years into their armed forces. In recruiting among those persons who have attained the age of fifteen years but who have not attained the age of eighteen years, States Parties shall endeavour to give priority to those who are oldest.
4. In accordance with their obligations under international humanitarian law to protect the civilian population in armed conflicts, States Parties shall take all feasible measures to ensure protection and care of children who are affected by an armed conflict.

Article 39
States Parties shall take all appropriate measures to promote physical and psychological recovery and social reintegration of a child victim of: any form of neglect, exploitation, or abuse; torture or any other form of cruel, inhuman or degrading treatment or punishment; or armed conflicts. Such recovery and reintegration shall take place in an environment which fosters the health, self-respect and dignity of the child.

Article 40
1. States Parties recognize the right of every child alleged as, accused of, or recognized as having infringed the penal law to be treated in a manner consistent with the promotion of the child's sense of dignity and worth, which reinforces the child's respect for the human rights and fundamental freedoms of others and which takes into account the child's age and the desirability of

promoting the child's reintegration and the child's assuming a constructive role in society.
2. To this end, and having regard to the relevant provisions of international instruments, States Parties shall, in particular, ensure that:
   (a) No child shall be alleged as, be accused of, or recognized as having infringed the penal law by reason of acts or omissions that were not prohibited by national or international law at the time they were committed;
   (b) Every child alleged as or accused of having infringed the penal law has at least the following guarantees:
      (i) To be presumed innocent until proven guilty according to law;
      (ii) To be informed promptly and directly of the charges against him or her, and, if appropriate, through his or her parents or legal guardians, and to have legal or other appropriate assistance in the preparation and presentation of his or her defence;
      (iii) To have the matter determined without delay by a competent, independent and impartial authority or judicial body in a fair hearing according to law, in the presence of legal or other appropriate assistance and, unless it is considered not to be in the best interest of the child, in particular, taking into account his or her age or situation, his or her parents or legal guardians;
      (iv) Not to be compelled to give testimony or to confess guilt; to examine or have examined adverse witnesses and to obtain the participation and examination of witnesses on his or her behalf under conditions of equality;
      (v) If considered to have infringed the penal law, to have this decision and any measures imposed in consequence thereof reviewed by a higher competent, independent and impartial authority or judicial body according to law;
      (vi) To have the free assistance of an interpreter if the child cannot understand or speak the language used;
      (vii) To have his or her privacy fully respected at all stages of the proceedings.
3. States Parties shall seek to promote the establishment of laws, procedures, authorities and institutions specifically applicable to children alleged as, accused of, or recognized as having infringed the penal law, and, in particular:
   (a) The establishment of a minimum age below which children shall be presumed not to have the capacity to infringe the penal law;
   (b) Whenever appropriate and desirable, measures for dealing with such children without resorting to judicial proceedings, providing that human rights and legal safeguards are fully respected.
4. A variety of dispositions, such as care, guidance and supervision orders; counselling; probation; foster care; education and vocational training programmes and other alternatives to institutional care shall be available to ensure that children are dealt with in a manner appropriate to their well-being and proportionate both to their circumstances and the offence.

Article 41
Nothing in the present Convention shall affect any provisions which are more

conducive to the realization of the rights of the child and which may be contained in:
(a) The law of a State party; or
(b) International law in force for that State.

PART II

Article 42
States Parties undertake to make the principles and provisions of the Convention widely known, by appropriate and active means, to adults and children alike.

Article 43
1. For the purpose of examining the progress made by States Parties in achieving the realization of the obligations undertaken in the present Convention, there shall be established a Committee on the Rights of the Child, which shall carry out the functions hereinafter provided.
2. The Committee shall consist of ten experts of high moral standing and recognized competence in the field covered by this Convention. The members of the Committee shall be elected by States Parties from among their nationals and shall serve in their personal capacity, consideration being given to equitable geographical distribution, as well as to the principal legal systems.
3. The members of the Committee shall be elected by secret ballot from a list of persons nominated by States Parties. Each State Party may nominate one person from among its own nationals.
4. The initial election to the Committee shall be held no later than six months after the date of the entry into force of the present Convention and thereafter every second year. At least four months before the date of each election, the Secretary-General of the United Nations shall address a letter to States Parties inviting them to submit their nominations within two months. The Secretary-General shall subsequently prepare a list in alphabetical order of all persons thus nominated, indicating States Parties which have nominated them, and shall submit it to the States Parties to the present Convention.
5. The elections shall be held at meetings of States Parties convened by the Secretary-General at United Nations Headquarters. At those meetings, for which two thirds of States Parties shall constitute a quorum, the persons elected to the Committee shall be those who obtain the largest number of votes and an absolute majority of the votes of the representatives of States Parties present and voting.
6. The members of the Committee shall be elected for a term of four years. They shall be eligible for re-election if renominated. The term of five of the members elected at the first election shall expire at the end of two years; immediately after the first election, the names of these five members shall be chosen by lot by the Chairman of the meeting.
7. If a member of the Committee dies or resigns or declares that for any other cause he or she can no longer perform the duties of the Committee, the State Party which nominated the member shall appoint another expert from among its nationals to serve for the remainder of the term, subject to the approval of the Committee.
8. The Committee shall establish its own rules of procedure.
9. The Committee shall elect its officers for a period of two years.

10. The meetings of the Committee shall normally be held at United Nations Headquarters or at any other convenient place as determined by the Committee. The Committee shall normally meet annually. The duration of the meetings of the Committee shall be determined, and reviewed, if necessary, by a meeting of the States Parties to the present Convention, subject to the approval of the General Assembly.
11. The Secretary-General of the United Nations shall provide the necessary staff and facilities for the effective performance of the functions of the Committee under the present Convention.
12. With the approval of the General Assembly, the members of the Committee established under the present Convention shall receive emoluments from United Nations resources on such terms and conditions as the Assembly may decide.

Article 44

1. States Parties undertake to submit to the Committee, through the Secretary-General of the United Nations, reports on the measures they have adopted which give effect to the rights recognized herein and on the progress made on the enjoyment of those rights:
    (a) Within two years of the entry into force of the Convention for the State Party concerned;
    (b) Thereafter every five years.
2. Reports made under the present article shall indicate factors and difficulties, if any, affecting the degree of fulfilment of the obligations under the present Convention. Reports shall also contain sufficient information to provide the Committee with a comprehensive understanding of the implementation of the Convention in the country concerned.
3. A State Party which has submitted a comprehensive initial report to the Committee need not, in its subsequent reports submitted in accordance with paragraph 1 (b) of the present article, repeat basic information previously provided.
4. The Committee may request from States Parties further information relevant to the implementation of the Convention.
5. The Committee shall submit to the General Assembly, through the Economic and Social Council, every two years, reports on its activities.
6. States Parties shall make their reports widely available to the public in their own countries.

Article 45

In order to foster the effective implementation of the Convention and to encourage international co-operation in the field covered by the Convention:
(a) The specialized agencies, the United Nations Children's Fund, and other United Nations organs shall be entitled to be represented at the consideration of the implementation of such provisions of the present Convention as fall within the scope of their mandate. The Committee may invite the specialized agencies, the United Nations Children's Fund and other competent bodies as it may consider appropriate to provide expert advice on the implementation of the Convention in areas falling within the scope of their respective mandates. The Committee may invite the specialized agencies, the United Nations Children's Fund, and other United Nations organs to submit reports

on the implementation of the Convention in areas falling within the scope of their activities;
(b) The Committee shall transmit, as it may consider appropriate, to the specialized agencies, the United Nations Children's Fund and other competent bodies, any reports from States Parties that contain a request, or indicate a need, for technical advice or assistance, along with the Committee's observations and suggestions, if any, on these requests or indications;
(c) The Committee may recommend to the General Assembly to request the Secretary-General to undertake on its behalf studies on specific issues relating to the rights of the child;
(d) The Committee may make suggestions and general recommendations based on information received pursuant to articles 44 and 45 of the present Convention. Such suggestions and general recommendations shall be transmitted to any State Party concerned and reported to the General Assembly, together with comments, if any, from States Parties.

PART III

Article 46
The present Convention shall be open for signature by all States.

Article 47
The present Convention is subject to ratification. Instruments of ratification shall be deposited with the Secretary-General of the United Nations.

Article 48
The present Convention shall remain open for accession by any State. The instruments of accession shall be deposited with the Secretary-General of the United Nations.

Article 49
1. The present Convention shall enter into force on the thirtieth day following the date of deposit with the Secretary-General of the United Nations of the twentieth instrument of ratification or accession.
2. For each State ratifying or acceding to the Convention after the deposit of the twentieth instrument of ratification or accession, the Convention shall enter into force on the thirtieth day after the deposit by such State of its instrument of ratification or accession.

Article 50
1. Any State Party may propose an amendment and file it with the Secretary-General of the United Nations. The Secretary-General shall thereupon communicate the proposed amendment to States Parties, with a request that they indicate whether they favour a conference of States Parties for the purpose of considering and voting upon the proposals. In the event that, within four months from the date of such communication, at least one third of the States Parties favour such a conference, the Secretary-General shall convene the conference under the auspices of the United Nations. Any amendment adopted by a majority of States Parties present and voting at the conference shall be submitted to the General Assembly for approval.
2. An amendment adopted in accordance with paragraph 1 of the present article

shall enter into force when it has been approved by the General Assembly of the United Nations and accepted by a two-thirds majority of States Parties.
3. When an amendment enters into force, it shall be binding on those States Parties which have accepted it, other States Parties still being bound by the provisions of the present Convention and any earlier amendments which they have accepted.

Article 51
1. The Secretary-General of the United Nations shall receive and circulate to all States the text of reservations made by States at the time of ratification or accession.
2. A reservation incompatible with the object and purpose of the present Convention shall not be permitted.
3. Reservations may be withdrawn at any time by notification to that effect addressed to the Secretary-General of the United Nations, who shall then inform all States. Such notification shall take effect on the date on which it is received by the Secretary-General

Article 52
A State Party may denounce the present Convention by written notification to the Secretary-General of the United Nations. Denunciation becomes effective one year after the date of receipt of the notification by the Secretary-General.

Article 53
The Secretary-General of the United Nations is designated as the depositary of the present Convention.

Article 54
The original of the present Convention, of which the Arabic, Chinese, English, French, Russian and Spanish texts are equally authentic, shall be deposited with the Secretary-General of the United Nations.

Optional Protocols to the Convention on the Rights of the Child on the Involvement of Children in Armed Conflict and on the Sale of Children, Child Prostitution and Child Pornography

Adopted and opened for signature, ratification and accession by
General Assembly Resolution 54/263 of 25 May 2000

Not yet in force

The General Assembly,

Recalling all its previous resolutions on this topic, and in particular its resolution 54/149, in which it strongly supported the work of the open-ended inter-sessional working groups and urged them to finalize their work before the tenth anniversary of the entry into force of the Convention on the Rights of the Child,

Expressing its appreciation to the Commission on Human Rights for having finalized the texts of the two draft optional protocols to the Convention on the Rights of the Child on involvement of children in armed conflict and on the sale of children, child prostitution and child pornography,

Conscious of the tenth anniversaries, in the year 2000, of the World Summit for Children and the entry into force of the Convention on the Rights of the Child and of the symbolic and practical importance of the adoption of the two draft optional protocols to the Convention on the Rights of the Child before the special session of the General Assembly for the follow-up to the World Summit for Children, to be convened in 2001,

Adhering to the principle that the best interests of the child are to be a primary consideration in all actions concerning children,

Reaffirming its commitment to strive for the promotion and protection of the rights of the child in all avenues of life,

Recognizing that the adoption and implementation of the two draft optional protocols to the Convention on the Rights of the Child on involvement of children in armed conflict and on the sale of children, child prostitution and child pornography will make a substantial contribution to the promotion and protection of the rights of the child,

1. *Adopts and opens for signature and ratification or accession* the two optional protocols to the Convention on the Rights of the Child on involvement of children in armed conflict and on the sale of children, child prostitution and child pornography, the texts of which are annexed to the present resolution;
2. *Invites* all States, which have signed or ratified or acceded to the Convention

on the Rights of the Child, to sign and ratify or accede to the annexed optional protocols as soon as possible in order to facilitate their early entry into force;

3. *Decides* that the two optional protocols to the Convention on the Rights of the Child will be open for signature:

At the special session of the General Assembly, entitled "Women 2000: gender equality, development and peace for the twenty-first century, to be convened from 5 to 9 June 2000 in New York; and thereafter

At United Nations Headquarters including

At the special session of the General Assembly, entitled "World Summit for Social Development and beyond: achieving social development for all in a globalized world", to be convened from 26 to 30 June 2000 in Geneva; and

At the Millennium Summit of the United Nations, to be convened from 5 to 8 September 2000, in New York;

4. *Requests* the Secretary-General to include information on the status of the two optional protocols in his regular report to the General Assembly on the status of the Convention on the Rights of the Child."

Annex

A

OPTIONAL PROTOCOL TO THE CONVENTION ON THE RIGHTS OF THE CHILD ON INVOLVEMENT OF CHILDREN IN ARMED CONFLICT

The States Parties to the present Protocol,

Encouraged by the overwhelming support for the Convention on the Rights of the Child, demonstrating the widespread commitment that exists to strive for the promotion and protection of the rights of the child,

Reaffirming that the rights of children require special protection and calling for continuous improvement of the situation of children without distinction, as well as for their development and education in conditions of peace and security,

Disturbed by the harmful and widespread impact of armed conflict on children and the long-term consequences this has for durable peace, security and development,

Condemning the targeting of children in situations of armed conflict and direct attacks on objects protected under international law, including places generally having a significant presence of children, such as schools and hospitals,

Noting the adoption of the Statute of the International Criminal Court and, in particular, the inclusion in the Statute of conscripting or enlisting children under the age of 15 years or using them to participate actively in hostilities as a war crime in both international and non-international armed conflicts,

Considering therefore that to strengthen further the implementation of rights recognized in the Convention on the Rights of the Child, there is a need to increase the protection of children from involvement in armed conflict,

Noting that article 1 of the Convention on the Rights of the Child specifies that, for the purposes of that Convention, a child means every human being below the age of 18 years unless, under the law applicable to the child, majority is attained earlier,

Convinced that an optional protocol to the Convention, raising the age of possible recruitment of persons into armed forces and their participation in hostilities, will contribute effectively to the implementation of the principle that the best interests of the child are to be a primary consideration in all actions concerning children,

Noting that the twenty-sixth international Conference of the Red Cross and Red Crescent in December 1995 recommended, *inter alia*, that parties to conflict take every feasible step to ensure that children under the age of 18 years do not take part in hostilities,

Welcoming also the unanimous adoption, in June 1999, of ILO Convention No. 182 on the Prohibition and Immediate Action for the Elimination of the Worst Forms of Child Labour, which prohibits, *inter alia*, forced or compulsory recruitment of children for use in armed conflict,

Condemning with the gravest concern the recruitment, training and use within and across national borders of children in hostilities by armed groups distinct from the armed forces of a State, and recognizing the responsibility of those who recruit, train and use children in this regard,

Recalling the obligation of each party to an armed conflict to abide by the provisions of international humanitarian law,

Stressing that this Protocol is without prejudice to the purposes and principles contained in the Charter of the United Nations, including Article 51, and relevant norms of humanitarian law,

Bearing in mind that conditions of peace and security based on full respect of the purposes and principles contained in the Charter of the United Nations and observance of applicable human rights instruments are indispensable for the full protection of children, in particular during armed conflicts and foreign occupation,

Recognizing the special needs of those children who are particularly vulnerable to recruitment or use in hostilities contrary to this Protocol owing to their economic or social status or gender,

Mindful also of the necessity to take into consideration the economic, social and political root causes of the involvement of children in armed conflicts,

Convinced of the need to strengthen international cooperation in implementation of this protocol, as well as physical and psychosocial rehabilitation and social reintegration of children who are victims of armed conflict,

Encouraging the participation of the community and, in particular, children and child victims in the dissemination of information and education programmes concerning the implementation of the Protocol,

Have agreed as follows:

Article 1
State Parties shall take all feasible measures to ensure that members of their armed forces who have not attained the age of 18 years do not take a direct part in hostilities.

Article 2
State Parties shall ensure that persons who have not attained the age of 18 years are not compulsorily recruited into their armed forces.

Article 3
1. States Parties shall raise the minimum age in years for the voluntary recruitment of persons into their national armed forces from that set out in article 38.3 of the Convention on the Rights of the Child, taking account of the principles contained in that article and recognizing that under the Convention persons under 18 are entitled to special protection.
2. Each State Party shall deposit a binding declaration upon ratification of or accession to this Protocol which sets forth the minimum age at which it will permit voluntary recruitment into its national armed forces and a description of the safeguards that it has adopted to ensure that such recruitment is not forced or coerced.
3. States Parties which permit voluntary recruitment into their national armed forces under the age of 18 shall maintain safeguards to ensure, as a minimum, that:

    Such recruitment is genuinely voluntary;
    Such recruitment is done with the informed consent of the person's parents or legal guardians;
    Such persons are fully informed of the duties involved in such military service; and
    Such persons provide reliable proof of age prior to acceptance into national military service.

4. Each State Party may strengthen its declaration at any time by notification to that effect addressed to the Secretary-General of the United Nations, who shall inform all States Parties. Such notification shall take effect on the date on which it is received by the Secretary-General.
5. The requirement to raise the age in paragraph 1 does not apply to schools operated by or under the control of the armed forces of the States Parties, in keeping with articles 28 and 29 of the Convention on the Rights of the Child.

Article 4
1. Armed groups, distinct from the armed forces of a State, should not, under any circumstances, recruit or use in hostilities persons under the age of 18 years.
2. States Parties shall take all feasible measures to prevent such recruitment and use, including the adoption of legal measures necessary to prohibit and criminalize such practices.
3. The application of the present article under this Protocol shall not affect the legal status of any party to an armed conflict.

Article 5
Nothing in the present Protocol shall be construed as precluding provisions in the law of a State Party or in international instruments and international humanitarian law which are more conducive to the realization of the rights of the child.

Article 6
1. Each State Party shall take all necessary legal, administrative and other measures to ensure the effective implementation and enforcement of the provisions of this Protocol within its jurisdiction.
2. States Parties undertake to make the principles and provisions of the present Protocol widely known and promoted by appropriate means, to adults and children alike.
3. States Parties shall take all feasible measures to ensure that persons within their jurisdiction recruited or used in hostilities contrary to this Protocol are demobilized or otherwise released from service. States Parties shall, when necessary, accord to these persons all appropriate assistance for their physical and psychological recovery, and their social reintegration.

Article 7
1. States Parties shall cooperate in the implementation of the present Protocol, including in the prevention of any activity contrary to the Protocol and in the rehabilitation and social reintegration of persons who are victims of acts contrary to this Protocol, including through technical cooperation and financial assistance. Such assistance and cooperation will be undertaken in consultation among concerned States parties and relevant international organizations.
2. States Parties in a position to do so shall provide such assistance through existing multilateral, bilateral or other programmes, or, *inter alia*, through a voluntary fund established in accordance with the General Assembly rules.

Article 8
1. Each State Party shall submit, within two years following the entry into force of the Protocol for that State Party, a report to the Committee on the Rights of the Child providing comprehensive information on the measures it has taken to implement the provisions of the Protocol, including the measures taken to implement the provisions on participation and recruitment.
2. Following the submission of the comprehensive report, each State Party shall include in the reports they submit to the Committee on the Rights of the Child in accordance with article 44 of the Convention any further information with respect to the implementation of the Protocol. Other States Parties to the Protocol shall submit a report every five years.
3. The Committee on the Rights of the Child may request from States Parties further information relevant to the implementation of this Protocol.

Article 9
1. The present Protocol is open for signature by any State which is a party to the Convention or has signed it.
2. The present Protocol is subject to ratification or open to accession by any State. Instruments of ratification or accession shall be deposited with the Secretary-General of the United Nations.
3. The Secretary-General of the United Nations, in his capacity as depositary of the Convention and the Protocol, shall inform all States Parties to the Convention and all States which have signed the Convention of each instrument of declaration pursuant to article 3, ratification or accession to the Protocol.

Article 10
1. The present Protocol shall enter into force three months after the deposit of the tenth instrument of ratification or accession.
2. For each State ratifying the present Protocol or acceding to it after its entry into force the present Protocol shall enter into force one month after the date of the deposit of its own instrument of ratification or accession.

Article 11
1. Any State Party may denounce the present Protocol at any time by written notification to the Secretary-General of the United Nations, who shall thereafter inform the other States Parties to the Convention and all States which have signed the Convention. Denunciation shall take effect one year after the date of receipt of the notification by the Secretary-General of the United Nations. If, however, on the expiry of that year the denouncing State Party is engaged in armed conflict, the denunciation shall not take effect before the end of the armed conflict.
2. Such a denunciation shall not have the effect of releasing the State Party from its obligations under the present Protocol in regard to any act which occurs prior to the date at which the denunciation becomes effective. Nor shall such a denunciation prejudice in any way the continued consideration of any matter which is already under consideration by the Committee prior to the date at which the denunciation becomes effective.

Article 12
1. Any State Party may propose an amendment and file it with the Secretary-General of the United Nations. The Secretary-General shall thereupon communicate the proposed amendment to States Parties, with a request that they indicate whether they favour a conference of States Parties for the purpose of considering and voting upon the proposals. In the event that, within four months from the date of such communication, at least one third of the States Parties favour such a conference, the Secretary-General shall convene the conference under the auspices of the United Nations. Any amendment adopted by a majority of States Parties present and voting at the conference shall be submitted to the General Assembly for approval.
2. An amendment adopted in accordance with paragraph 1 of the present article shall enter into force when it has been approved by the General Assembly of the United Nations and accepted by a two-thirds majority of States Parties.
3. When an amendment enters into force, it shall be binding on those States Parties which have accepted it, other States Parties still being bound by the provisions of the present Protocol and any earlier amendments which they have accepted.

Article 13
1. The present Protocol, of which the Arabic, Chinese, English, French, Russian and Spanish texts are equally authentic, shall be deposited in the archives of the United Nations.
2. The Secretary-General of the United Nations shall transmit certified copies of the present Protocol to all States Parties to the Convention and all States which have signed the Convention.

B.

OPTIONAL PROTOCOL TO THE CONVENTION ON THE RIGHTS OF THE CHILD ON THE SALE OF CHILDREN, CHILD PROSTITUTION AND CHILD PORNOGRAPHY

The States Parties to the present Protocol,

Considering that in order further to achieve the purposes of the Convention on the Rights of the Child and the implementation of its provisions, especially articles 1, 11, 21, 32, 33, 34, 35 and 36, it would be appropriate to extend the measures that States Parties should undertake in order to guarantee the protection of the child from the sale of children, child prostitution and child pornography,

Considering also that the Convention on the Rights of the Child recognizes the right of the child to be protected from economic exploitation and from performing any work that is likely to be hazardous or to interfere with the child's education, or to be harmful to the child's health or physical, mental, spiritual, moral or social development,

Gravely concerned at the significant and increasing international traffic of children for the purpose of the sale of children, child prostitution and child pornography,

Deeply concerned at the widespread and continuing practice of sex tourism to which children are especially vulnerable, as it directly promotes the sale of children, child prostitution and child pornography,

Recognizing that a number of particularly vulnerable groups, including girl children, are at greater risk of sexual exploitation, and that girl children are disproportionately represented among the sexually exploited,

Concerned about the growing availability of child pornography on the Internet and other evolving technologies and recalling the International Conference on Combating Child Pornography on the Internet (Vienna, 1999) and, in particular, its conclusion calling for the worldwide criminalization of the production, distribution, exportation, transmission, importation, intentional possession and advertising of child pornography, and stressing the importance of closer cooperation and partnership between Governments and the Internet industry,

Believing that the elimination of the sale of children, child prostitution and child pornography will be facilitated by adopting a holistic approach addressing the contributing factors, including underdevelopment, poverty, economic disparities, inequitable socio-economic structure, dysfunctioning families, lack of education, urban-rural migration, gender discrimination, irresponsible adult sexual behaviour, harmful traditional practices, armed conflicts and trafficking of children,

Believing that efforts to raise public awareness are needed to reduce consumer demand for the sale of children, child prostitution and child pornography, and in the importance of strengthening global partnership among all actors, and of improving law enforcement at the national level,

Noting the provisions of international legal instruments relevant to the protection of children, including the Hague Convention on the Protection of Children and Co-operation with Respect to Intercountry Adoption, the Hague Convention on the Civil Aspects of Child Abduction, the Hague Convention on Jurisdiction, Applicable Law, Recognition, Enforcement and Co-operation in Respect of Parental Responsibility and Measures for the Protection of Children and ILO Convention No. 182 Concerning the Prohibition and Immediate Action for the Elimination of the Worst Forms of Child Labour,

Encouraged by the overwhelming support for the Convention on the Rights of the Child, demonstrating the widespread commitment that exists for the promotion and protection of the rights of the child,

Recognizing the importance of the implementation of the provisions of the Programme of Action for the Prevention of the Sale of Children, Child Prostitution and Child Pornography and the Declaration and Agenda for Action of the 1996 Stockholm Congress against the Commercial Sexual Exploitation of Children and the other relevant decisions and recommendations of pertinent international bodies,

Taking due account of the importance of the traditions and cultural values of each people for the protection and harmonious development of the child,

Have agreed as follows:

Article 1
States Parties shall prohibit the sale of children, child prostitution and child pornography as provided for by this Protocol.

Article 2
For the purpose of the present Protocol:

SALE OF CHILDREN

(a) Sale of children means any act or transaction whereby a child is transferred by any person or group of persons to another for remuneration or any other consideration;

CHILD PROSTITUTION

(b) Child prostitution means the use of a child in sexual activities for remuneration or any other form of consideration;

CHILD PORNOGRAPHY

(c) Child pornography means any representation, by whatever means, of a child engaged in real or simulated explicit sexual activities or any representation of the sexual parts of a child, the dominant characteristic of which is depiction for a sexual purpose.

Article 3
1. Each State Party shall ensure that, as a minimum, the following acts and activities are fully covered under its criminal or penal law, whether these offences are committed domestically or transnationally or on an individual or organized basis:
   (a) In the context of sale of children as defined in article 2(a):

(i) The offering, delivering, or accepting by whatever means a child for the purpose of:

Sexual exploitation of the child;
Transfer of organs of the child for profit;
Engagement of the child in forced labour;

(ii) Improperly inducing consent, as an intermediary, for the adoption of a child in violation of applicable international legal instruments on adoption;

(b) Offering, obtaining, procuring or providing a child for child prostitution, as defined in article 2(b); and
(c) Producing, distributing, disseminating, importing, exporting, offering, selling, or possessing for the above purposes, child pornography as defined in article 2(c).

2. Subject to the provisions of a State Party's national law, the same shall apply to an attempt to commit any of these acts and to complicity or participation in any of these acts.
3. Each State Party shall make these offences punishable by appropriate penalties which take into account their grave nature.
4. Subject to the provisions of its national law, each State Party shall take measures, where appropriate, to establish the liability of legal persons for offences established in paragraph 1 of this article. Subject to the legal principles of the State Party, this liability of legal persons may be criminal, civil, or administrative.
5. States Parties shall take all appropriate legal and administrative measures to ensure that all persons involved in the adoption of a child act in conformity with applicable international legal instruments.

Article 4
1. Each State Party shall take such measures as may be necessary to establish its jurisdiction over the offences referred to in article 3.1, when the offences are commited in its territory or on board a ship or aircraft registered in that State.
2. Each State Party may take such measures as may be necessary to establish its jurisdiction over the offences referred to in article 3.1 in the following cases:
   (a) When the alleged offender is a national of that State or a person who has his habitual residence in its territory;
   (b) When the victim is a national of that State.
3. Each State Party shall also take such measures as may be necessary to establish its jurisdiction over the above-mentioned offences when the alleged offender is present in its territory and it does not extradite him to another State Party on the ground that the offence has been committed by one of its nationals.
4. This Protocol does not exclude any criminal jurisdiction exercised in accordance with internal law.

Article 5
1. The offences referred to in article 3.1 shall be deemed to be included as extraditable offences in any extradition treaty existing between States Parties, and shall be included as extraditable offences in every extradition treaty

subsequently concluded between them, in accordance with the conditions set forth in these treaties.
2. If a State Party which makes extradition conditional on the existence of a treaty receives a request for extradition from another State Party with which it has no extradition treaty, it may consider this Protocol as a legal basis for extradition in respect of such offences. Extradition shall be subject to the conditions provided by the law of the requested State.
3. States Parties which do not make extradition conditional on the existence of a treaty shall recognize such offences as extraditable offences between themselves subject to the conditions provided by the law of the requested State.
4. Such offences shall be treated, for the purpose of extradition between States Parties, as if they had been committed not only in the place in which they occurred but also in the territories of the States required to establish their jurisdiction in accordance with article 4.
5. If an extradition request is made with respect to an offence described in article 3.1 and if the requested State Party does not or will not extradite, on the basis of the nationality of the offender, that State shall take suitable measures to submit the case to its competent authorities for the purpose of prosecution.

Article 6
1. States Parties shall afford one another the greatest measure of assistance in connection with investigations or criminal or extradition proceedings brought in respect of the offences set forth in article 3.1, including assistance in obtaining evidence at their disposal necessary for the proceedings.
2. States Parties shall carry out their obligations under paragraph 1 of the present article in conformity with any treaties or other arrangements on mutual legal assistance that may exist between them. In the absence of such treaties or arrangements, States Parties shall afford one another assistance in accordance with their domestic law.

Article 7
States Parties shall, subject to the provisions of their national law:
(a) Take measures to provide for the seizure and confiscation, as appropriate, of:
   (i) Goods such as materials, assets and other instrumentalities used to commit or facilitate offences under the present protocol;
   Proceeds derived from such offences;
(b) Execute requests from another State Party for seizure or confiscation of goods or proceeds referred to in subparagraph (i);
(c) Take measures aimed at closing on a temporary or definitive basis premises used to commit such offences.

Article 8
1. States Parties shall adopt appropriate measures to protect the rights and interests of child victims of the practices prohibited under the present Protocol at all stages of the criminal justice process, in particular by:
   (a) Recognizing the vulnerability of child victims and adapting procedures to recognize their special needs, including their special needs as witnesses;
   (b) Informing child victims of their rights, their role and the scope, timing and progress of the proceedings and of the disposition of their cases;
   (c) Allowing the views, needs and concerns of child victims to be presented

and considered in proceedings where their personal interests are affected, in a manner consistent with the procedural rules of national law;
    (d) Providing appropriate support services to child victims throughout the legal process;
    (e) Protecting as appropriate the privacy and identity of child victims and taking measures in accordance with national law to avoid the inappropriate dissemination of information that could lead to the identification of child victims;
    (f) Providing, in appropriate cases, for the safety of child victims, as well as that of their families and witnesses on their behalf, from intimidation and retaliation;
    (g) Avoiding unnecessary delay in the disposition of cases and the execution of orders or decrees granting compensation to child victims.
2. States Parties shall ensure that uncertainty as to the actual age of the victim shall not prevent the initiation of criminal investigations, including investigations aimed at establishing the age of the victim.
3. States Parties shall ensure that, in the treatment by the criminal justice system of children who are victims of the offences described in the present Protocol, the best interest of the child shall be a primary consideration.
4. States Parties shall take measures to ensure appropriate training, in particular legal and psychological, for the persons who work with child victims of the offences prohibited under the present Protocol.
   States Parties shall, in appropriate cases, adopt measures in order to protect the safety and integrity of those persons and/or organizations involved in the prevention and/or protection and rehabilitation of child victims of such offences.
5. Nothing in this article shall be construed as prejudicial to or inconsistent with the rights of the accused to a fair and impartial trial.

Article 9
1. States Parties shall adopt or strengthen, implement and disseminate laws, administrative measures, social policies and programmes, to prevent the offences referred to in the present Protocol. Particular attention shall be given to protect children who are especially vulnerable to these practices.
2. States Parties shall promote awareness in the public at large, including children, through information by all appropriate means, education and training, about the preventive measures and harmful effects of the offences referred to in the present Protocol. In fulfilling their obligations under this article, States Parties shall encourage the participation of the community and, in particular, children and child victims, in such information and education and training programmes, including at the international level.
3. States Parties shall take all feasible measures with the aim of ensuring all appropriate assistance to victims of such offences, including their full social reintegration, and their full physical and psychological recovery.
4. States Parties shall ensure that all child victims of the offences described in the present Protocol have access to adequate procedures to seek, without discrimination, compensation for damages from those legally responsible.
5. States Parties shall take appropriate measures aimed at effectively prohibiting the production and dissemination of material advertising the offences described in the present Protocol.

Article 10
1. States Parties shall take all necessary steps to strengthen international cooperation by multilateral, regional and bilateral arrangements for the prevention, detection, investigation, prosecution and punishment of those responsible for acts involving the sale of children, child prostitution, child pornography and child sex tourism.
    States Parties shall also promote international cooperation and coordination between their authorities, national and international non-governmental organizations and international organizations.
2. States Parties shall promote international cooperation to assist child victims for their physical and psychological recovery, social reintegration and repatriation.
3. States Parties shall promote the strengthening of international cooperation in order to address the root causes, such as poverty and underdevelopment, contributing to the vulnerability of children to the practices of sale, prostitution, pornography and child sex tourism.
4. States Parties in a position to do so shall provide financial, technical or other assistance through existing multilateral, regional, bilateral or other programmes.

Article 11
Nothing in the present Protocol shall affect any provisions which are more conducive to the realization of the rights of the child and which may be contained in:
(a) The law of a State Party; or
(b) International law in force for that State.

Article 12
1. Each State Party shall submit, within two years following the entry into force of the Protocol for that State Party, a report to the Committee on the Rights of the Child providing comprehensive information on the measures it has taken to implement the provisions of the Protocol.
2. Following the submission of the comprehensive report, each State Party shall include in the reports they submit to the Committee on the Rights of the Child in accordance with article 44 of the Convention any further information with respect to the implementation of the Protocol. Other States Parties to the Protocol shall submit a report every five years.
3. The Committee on the Rights of the Child may request from States Parties further information relevant to the implementation of this Protocol.

Article 13
1. The present Protocol is open for signature by any State which is a party to the Convention or has signed it.
2. The present Protocol is subject to ratification or open to accession by any State which is a party to the Convention or has signed it. Instruments of ratification or accession shall be deposited with the Secretary-General of the United Nations.

Article 14
1. The present Protocol shall enter into force three months after the deposit of the tenth instrument of ratification or accession.
2. For each State ratifying the present Protocol or acceding to it after its entry

into force, the present Protocol shall enter into force one month after the date of the deposit of its own instrument of ratification or accession.

Article 15
1. Any State Party may denounce the present Protocol at any time by written notification to the Secretary-General of the United Nations, who shall thereafter inform the other States Parties to the Convention and all States which have signed the Convention. Denunciation shall take effect one year after the date of receipt of the notification by the Secretary-General of the United Nations.
2. Such a denunciation shall not have the effect of releasing the State Party from its obligations under this Protocol in regard to any offence which occurs prior to the date at which the denunciation becomes effective. Nor shall such a denunciation prejudice in any way the continued consideration of any matter which is already under consideration by the Committee prior to the date at which the denunciation becomes effective.

Article 16
1. Any State Party may propose an amendment and file it with the Secretary-General of the United Nations. The Secretary-General shall thereupon communicate the proposed amendment to States Parties, with a request that they indicate whether they favour a conference of States Parties for the purpose of considering and voting upon the proposals. In the event that, within four months from the date of such communication, at least one third of the States Parties favour such a conference, the Secretary-General shall convene the conference under the auspices of the United Nations. Any amendment adopted by a majority of States Parties present and voting at the conference shall be submitted to the General Assembly for approval.
2. An amendment adopted in accordance with paragraph 1 of the present article shall enter into force when it has been approved by the General Assembly of the United Nations and accepted by a two-thirds majority of States Parties.

When an amendment enters into force, it shall be binding on those States Parties which have accepted it, other States Parties still being bound by the provisions of the present Protocol and any earlier amendments which they have accepted.

Article 17
1. The present Protocol, of which the Arabic, Chinese, English, French, Russian and Spanish texts are equally authentic, shall be deposited in the archives of the United Nations.
2. The Secretary-General of the United Nations shall transmit certified copies of this Protocol to all States Parties to the Convention and all States which have signed the Convention.

A/RES/47/111
UNITED NATIONS GENERAL ASSEMBLY

Effective implementation of international instruments on human rights, including reporting obligations under international instruments on human rights

General Assembly Resolution 47/111
adopted on 16 December 1992

The General Assembly,

Recalling its resolution 46/111 of 17 December 1991, as well as its other relevant resolutions,

Reaffirming that the effective implementation of United Nations instruments on human rights is of major importance to the efforts of the Organization, pursuant to the Charter of the United Nations and the Universal Declaration of Human Rights, to promote universal respect for and observance of human rights and fundamental freedoms,

Reaffirming its responsibility to ensure the proper functioning of treaty bodies established pursuant to instruments adopted by the General Assembly and, in this connection, also reaffirming the importance of:

(a) Ensuring the effective functioning of systems of periodic reporting by States parties to these instruments;
(b) Securing sufficient financial resources to overcome existing difficulties with the effective functioning of treaty bodies;
(c) Addressing questions of reporting obligations and financial implications whenever elaborating any further instruments on human rights,

Recalling the conclusions and recommendations of the second meeting of persons chairing the human rights treaty bodies, held at Geneva from 10 to 14 October 1988, and the endorsement of the recommendations aimed at streamlining, rationalizing and otherwise improving reporting procedures by the General Assembly in its resolution 46/111 and the Commission on Human Rights in its resolution 1992/15 of 21 February 1992,

Taking particular note of the conclusions and recommendations of the third and fourth meetings of persons chairing the human rights treaty bodies, held at Geneva from 1 to 5 October 1990, and from 12 to 16 October 1992, respectively,

Expressing concern about the increasing backlog of reports on implementation by States parties to United Nations instruments on human rights and about delays in consideration of reports by the treaty bodies,

Taking note of the reports of the Secretary-General on progress achieved in enhancing the effective functioning of the treaty bodies,

Recalling the study on possible long-term approaches to enhancing the effective operation of existing and prospective bodies established under United Nations instruments on human rights, prepared by an independent expert, and aware of the need to update the study,

Welcoming the decision taken at the Fourteenth Meeting of States Parties to the International Convention on the Elimination of All Forms of Racial Discrimination on 15 January 1992 to amend paragraph 6 of article 8 of the Convention and to add a new paragraph, as paragraph 7 of article 8, by which the members of the Committee established under the Convention shall henceforth receive emoluments from United Nations resources on such terms and conditions as may be decided by the General Assembly,

Welcoming also the decision taken at the Conference of the States Parties to the Convention Against Torture and Other Cruel, Inhuman or Degrading Treatment or Punishment, on 9 September 1992, to delete paragraph 7 of article 17 and paragraph 5 of article 18 of the Convention, to insert a new paragraph, as paragraph 4 of article 18, by which the members of the Committee established under the Convention shall receive emoluments from United Nations resources on such terms and conditions as may be decided by the General Assembly, and to recommend that the Assembly take action for the implementation of the proposed amendment at its forty-seventh session.

Welcoming the reports of the Secretary-General examining the financial, legal and other implications of providing full funding for the operation of all human rights treaty bodies,

1. Endorses the conclusions and recommendations of the meetings of persons chairing the human rights treaty bodies aimed at streamlining, rationalizing and otherwise improving reporting procedures, and supports the continuing efforts in this connection by the treaty bodies and the Secretary-General within their respective spheres of competence;
2. Expresses its satisfaction with the study by the independent expert on possible long-term approaches to enhancing the effective operation of existing and prospective bodies established under United Nations instruments on human rights, which contains several recommendations on reporting and monitoring procedures, servicing and financing of supervisory bodies and long-term approaches to human rights standard-setting and implementation mechanisms, and which was presented to the Commission on Human Rights for detailed consideration at its forty-sixth session, and, in the light of the conclusions and recommendations contained in the report of the fourth meeting of persons chairing the human rights treaty bodies, requests that the report of the independent expert be updated for submission to the Commission at its fiftieth session and that an interim report be presented to the General Assembly at its forty-eighth session and be made available to the World Conference on Human Rights in June 1993;
3. Requests the Secretary-General to give high priority to establishing a computerized database to improve the efficiency and effectiveness of the functioning of the treaty bodies;

4. Again urges States parties to make every effort to meet their reporting obligations and to contribute, individually and through meetings of States parties, to identifying and implementing ways of further streamlining and improving reporting procedures as well as enhancing coordination and information flow between the treaty bodies and with relevant United Nations bodies, including specialized agencies;
5. Welcomes the emphasis placed by the meetings of persons chairing the human rights treaty bodies and by the Commission on Human Rights on the importance of technical assistance and advisory services and, further to this end:
    (a) Endorses the request of the Commission to the Secretary-General to report regularly to it on possible technical assistance projects identified by the treaty bodies;
    (b) Invites the treaty bodies to give priority attention to identifying such possibilities in the regular course of their work of reviewing the periodic reports of States parties;
6. Endorses the recommendations of the meetings of persons chairing the human rights treaty bodies on the need to ensure financing and adequate staffing resources for the operations of the treaty bodies and, with this in mind:
    (a) Reiterates its request to the Secretary-General to provide adequate resources with regard to the various treaty bodies;
    (b) Requests the Secretary-General to report on this question to the Commission on Human Rights at its forty-ninth session and to the General Assembly at its forty-eighth session;
7. Calls upon all States parties to meet fully and without delay their financial obligations under the relevant instruments on human rights, and requests the Secretary-General to consider ways and means of strengthening collection procedures and making them more effective;
8. Emphasizes that any administrative and budgetary measures shall be taken without prejudice to the duty of States parties under United Nations human rights instruments to meet all their current and outstanding financial obligations pursuant to such instruments;
9. Endorses the amendments to the International Convention on the Elimination of All Forms of Racial Discrimination and the Convention Against Torture and Other Cruel, Inhuman or Degrading Treatment or Punishment and requests the Secretary-General:
    (a) To take the appropriate measures to provide for the financing of the committees established under those conventions from the regular budget of the United Nations, beginning with the budget for the biennium 1994–1995;
    (b) To take the necessary measures to ensure that the two committees meet as scheduled until the amendments enter into force;
10. Requests the Secretary-General to take the appropriate steps in order to finance the biennial meetings of persons chairing the human rights treaty bodies from the resources available from the regular budget of the United Nations;
11. Also requests the Secretary-General, in the light of the views expressed at the forty-ninth session of the Commission on Human Rights and the thirty-seventh session of the Commission on the Status of Women, to submit to the General Assembly at its forty-eighth session a report examining the

conclusions and recommendations of the fourth meeting of persons chairing the human rights treaty bodies, held in October 1992;
12. Decides to give priority consideration at its forty-eighth session to the conclusions and recommendations of the meetings of persons chairing human rights treaty bodies under the item entitled "Human rights questions".

A/RES/50/155

UNITED NATIONS GENERAL ASSEMBLY

Conference of States Parties to the Convention on the Rights of the Child

General Assembly Resolution 50/155
adopted on 21 December 1995

The General Assembly,

Recognizing the importance of the Committee on the Rights of the Child and the valuable contribution of its members to the evaluation and monitoring of the implementation of the Convention on the Rights of the Child[1] by its States parties,

Noting with satisfaction that there are now 182 States parties to the Convention on the Rights of the Child, a figure approaching universal ratification,

Noting that the amendment to article 43, paragraph 2, of the Convention was adopted by the Conference of States Parties to the Convention,

1. Approves the amendment to article 43, paragraph 2, of the Convention on the Rights of the Child, replacing the word "ten" with the word "eighteen";
2. Urges States parties to take appropriate measures so that acceptance by a two-thirds majority of the States parties can be reached as soon as possible in order for the amendment to enter into force.

---

[1] Resolution 44/25, annex.

Appendix 2: Status of Ratifications

Office of the United Nations High Commissioner for Human Rights

STATUS OF RATIFICATIONS OF THE PRINCIPAL INTERNATIONAL HUMAN RIGHTS TREATIES as of 15-May-00*

The international human rights treaties of the United Nations which establish committees of experts (often referred to as "treaty bodies") to monitor their implementation are the following:

(1) the International Covenant on Economic, Social and Cultural Rights (CESCR) which is monitored by the Committee on Economic, Social and Cultural Rights;
(2) the International Covenant on Civil and Political Rights (CCPR), which is monitored by the Human Rights Committee;
(3) the International Convention on the Elimination of All Forms of Racial Discrimination (CERD) which is monitored by the Committee on the Elimination of Racial Discrimination;
(4) the Convention on the Elimination of All Forms of Discrimination against Women (CEDAW), which is monitored by the Committee on the Elimination of Discrimination against Women;
(5) the Convention against Torture and Other Cruel, Inhuman or Degrading Treatment or Punishment (CAT), which is monitored by the Committee against Torture;
(6) the Convention on the Rights of the Child (CRC), which is monitored by the Committee on the Rights of the Child;
(7) the Optional Protocol to the International Covenant on Civil and Political Rights (OPT), which is supervised by the Human Rights Committee; and
(8) the Second Optional Protocol to the International Covenant on Civil and Political Rights, aimed at the abolition of the death penalty (OPT2).

The following chart of States shows which are a party (indicated by the date of adherence) or signatory (indicated by an "s" and the date of signature) to the United Nations human rights treaties listed above. Self-governing territories that have ratified any of the treaties are also included in the chart.

As of 15-May-00, all 188 Member States of the United Nations and 5 non-member States were a party to one or more of those instruments.

---

*Can be updated online at http://www.unhchr.ch/html/menu2/convmech.htm

STATE	CCPR	CESCR	CAT	CERD	CEDAW	CRC	OPT	OPT2
Afghanistan	23-Jan-83[a]	23-Jan-83[a]	01-Apr-87	05-Jul-83[a]	s:14-Aug-80	28-Mar-94		
Albania	03-Oct-91[a]	03-Oct-91[a]	10-May-94[a]	10-May-94[a]	10-May-94	27-Feb-92		
Algeria	11-Sep-89	11-Sep-89	12-Sep-89*	13-Feb-72*	21-May-96[a]	16-Apr-93	11-Sep-89[a]	
Andorra					15-Jan-97[a]	02-Jan-96		
Angola	09-Jan-92[a]	09-Jan-92[a]			16-Sep-86[a]	05-Dec-90	09-Jan-92[a]	
Antigua & Barbuda			19-Jul-93[a]	24-Oct-88[d]	31-Jul-89[a]	05-Oct-93		
Argentina	07-Aug-86	07-Aug-86	24-Sep-86*	01-Oct-68	14-Jul-85	04-Dec-90	07-Aug-86[a]	
Armenia	22-Jun-93[a]	12-Sep-93[a]	12-Sep-93	22-Jun-93[a]	12-Sep-93[a]	23-Jun-93	22-Jun-93	
Australia	12-Aug-80	09-Dec-75	07-Aug-89[a]	29-Sep-75*	27-Jul-83	17-Dec-90	24-Sep-91[a]	01-Oct-90[a]
Austria	09-Sep-78	09-Sep-78	28-Jul-87[a]	08-May-72	31-Mar-82	06-Aug-92	09-Dec-87	01-Mar-93
Azerbaijan	12-Aug-92[a]	12-Aug-92[a]	16-Aug-96[a]	16-Aug-96[a]	09-Jul-95[a]	13-Aug-92[a]		22-Jan-99[a]
Bahamas				04-Aug-75[d]	05-Oct-93[a]	20-Feb-91		
Bahrain			06-Mar-98[a]	27-Mar-90[a]		13-Feb-92[a]		
Bangladesh		05-Oct-98[a]	05-Oct-98[a]	10-Jun-79[a]	05-Nov-84[a]	03-Aug-90		
Barbados	04-Jan-73[a]	04-Jan-73[a]		07-Nov-72[a]	15-Oct-80	09-Oct-90	04-Jan-73[a]	
Belarus	11-Nov-73	11-Nov-73	12-Mar-87	07-Apr-69	03-Feb-81	01-Oct-90	29-Sep-92[a]	
Belgium	20-Apr-83	20-Apr-83	25-Jun-99	06-Aug-75	09-Jul-85	16-Dec-91	16-May-94[a]	08-Dec-98
Belize	09-Jun-96[a]		16-Mar-86[a]		15-May-90	02-May-90		
Benin	11-Mar-92[a]	11-Mar-92[a]	11-Mar-92[a]	s:02-Feb-67	11-Mar-92	03-Aug-90	11-Mar-92[a]	
Bhutan				s:26-Mar-73	30-Aug-81	01-Aug-90		
Bolivia	11-Aug-82[a]	11-Aug-82[a]	12-Apr-99[a]	21-Sep-70	07-Jun-90	26-Jun-90	11-Aug-82[a]	
Bosnia and Herzegovina	31-Aug-93[a]	03-Mar-92[d]	31-Aug-93	15-Jul-93[d]	31-Aug-93[d]	01-Sep-93[d]	28-Feb-95	
Botswana				19-Feb-74[a]	13-Aug-96[a]	14-Mar-95[a]		
Brazil	23-Jan-92[a]	23-Jan-92[a]	27-Sep-89	26-Mar-68	31-Jan-84	24-Sep-90		
Brunei Darussalam						27-Dec-95[a]		
Bulgaria	20-Sep-70	20-Sep-70	15-Dec-86*	07-Aug-66*	07-Feb-82	03-Jun-91	25-Mar-92[a]	10-Aug-99
Burkina Faso	04-Jan-99[a]	04-Jan-99[a]	04-Jan-99[a]	17-Jul-74[a]	13-Oct-87[a]	31-Aug-90	04-Jan-99[a]	
Burundi	08-May-90[a]	08-May-90[a]	17-Feb-93[a]	26-Oct-77	07-Jan-92	19-Oct-90		
Cambodia	25-May-92[a]	25-May-92[a]	14-Oct-92[a]	27-Nov-83	14-Oct-92[a]	15-Oct-92		
Cameroon	26-Jun-84[a]	26-Jun-84[a]	18-Dec-86[a]	23-Jun-71	22-Aug-94	11-Jan-93	26-Jun-84[a]	
Canada	18-May-76[a]	18-May-76[a]	23-Jun-87*	13-Oct-70	09-Dec-81	13-Dec-91	18-May-76[a]	

Appendix 2: Status of Ratification 453

Cape Verde	05-Aug-93ª	05-Aug-93ª	03-Jun-92ª	02-Oct-79ª	04-Dec-80ª	04-Jun-92ª
Central African Republic	07-May-81ª	07-May-81ª		15-Mar-71	20-Jun-91ª	23-Apr-92	07-May-81ª
Chad	08-Jun-95ª	08-Jun-95ª	08-Jun-95ª	16-Aug-77ª	08-Jun-95ª	02-Oct-90	08-Jun-95ª
Chile	09-Feb-72	09-Feb-72	29-Sep-88	19-Oct-71*	06-Dec-89	13-Aug-90	27-May-92ª
China	s:05-Oct-98	s:27-Oct-97	03-Oct-88	28-Dec-81ª	03-Nov-80	02-Mar-92	
Colombia	28-Oct-69	28-Oct-69	07-Dec-87	01-Sep-81	18-Jan-82	28-Jan-91	28-Oct-69	05-Aug-97ª
Comoros					30-Oct-94ª	22-Jun-93	
Congo	04-Oct-83ª	04-Oct-83ª		10-Jul-88ª	25-Jul-82	14-Oct-93ª	04-Oct-83ª
Cook Islands						06-Jun-97ª	
Costa Rica	28-Nov-68	28-Nov-68	10-Nov-93	15-Jan-67*	04-Apr-86	21-Aug-90	28-Nov-68	05-Jun-98
Cote d'Ivoire	25-Mar-92ª	25-Mar-92ª	17-Dec-95ª	03-Jan-73ª	19-Dec-95	04-Feb-91	05-Mar-97ª
Croatia	11-Oct-92ᵈ	08-Oct-91ᵈ	11-Oct-92ᵈ*	11-Oct-92ᵈ	08-Sep-92ᵈ	12-Oct-92ᵈ	11-Oct-95ª	11-Oct-95ª
Cuba			16-May-95	14-Feb-72	16-Jul-80	21-Aug-91	
Cyprus	02-Apr-69	02-Apr-69	17-Jul-91*	20-Apr-67*	22-Jul-85ª	07-Feb-91	14-Apr-92
Czech Republic	21-Feb-93ᵈ	01-Jan-93ᵈ	01-Jan-93ᵈ*	21-Feb-93ᵈ	21-Feb-93ᵈ	22-Feb-93ᵈ	21-Feb-93ᵈ	10-Sep-99ª
Democratic People's Republic of Korea	13-Sep-81ª	13-Sep-81ª				21-Sep-90	
Democratic Republic of the Congo	31-Oct-76ª	31-Oct-76ª	17-Mar-96	20-Apr-76ª	16-Oct-86	27-Sep-90	31-Oct-76ª
Denmark	05-Jan-72	05-Jan-72	26-May-87*	08-Dec-71*	20-Apr-83	19-Jul-91	05-Jan-72	23-Feb-94
Djibouti					02-Dec-98ª	06-Dec-90	
Dominica	16-Jun-93ª	16-Jun-93ª			14-Sep-80	13-Mar-91	
Dominican Republic	03-Jan-78ª	03-Jan-78ª	s:04-Feb-85	24-May-83ª	01-Sep-82	11-Jun-91	03-Jan-78ª
Ecuador	05-Mar-69	05-Mar-69	30-Mar-88*	21-Sep-66**	08-Nov-81	23-Mar-90	05-Mar-69	22-Feb-93ª
Egypt	13-Jan-82	13-Jan-82	24-Jun-86ª	30-Apr-67	17-Sep-81	06-Jul-90	
El Salvador	29-Nov-79	29-Nov-79	16-Jun-96ª	29-Nov-79ª	18-Aug-81	10-Jul-90	05-Jun-95
Equatorial Guinea	24-Sep-87ª	24-Sep-87ª			22-Oct-84ª	15-Jun-92ª	24-Sep-87ª
Eritrea					04-Sep-95ª	03-Aug-94	
Estonia	20-Oct-91ª	20-Oct-91ª	20-Oct-91ª	20-Oct-91ª	20-Oct-91ª	21-Oct-91ª	20-Oct-91ª
Ethiopia	10-Jun-93ª	10-Jun-93ª	13-Mar-94ª	22-Jun-76ª	09-Sep-81	14-May-91ª	
Fiji				10-Jan-73ᵈ	27-Aug-95	13-Aug-93	
Finland	18-Aug-75	18-Aug-75	29-Aug-89*	13-Jul-70*	03-Sep-86	20-Jun-91	18-Aug-75	04-Apr-91
France	03-Nov-80ª	03-Nov-80ª	17-Feb-86*	27-Jul-71*	13-Dec-83	07-Aug-90	16-Feb-84ª
Gabon	20-Jan-83ª	20-Jan-83ª	s:21-Jan-86	28-Feb-80	20-Jan-83	09-Feb-94	

STATE	CCPR	CESCR	CAT	CERD	CEDAW	CRC	OPT	OPT2
Gambia	21-Mar-79[a]	28-Dec-78[a]	s:22-Oct-85	28-Dec-78[a]	15-Apr-93	08-Aug-90	08-Jun-88[a]	
Georgia	02-May-94[a]	02-May-94[a]	25-Oct-94[a]	02-Jun-99[a]	25-Oct-94[a]	02-Jun-94[a]	02-May-94[a]	22-Mar-99[a]
Germany	16-Dec-73	16-Dec-73	30-Sep-90	15-May-69	09-Jul-85	06-Mar-92	24-Aug-93[a]	17-Aug-92
Ghana				07-Sep-66	01-Jan-86	05-Feb-90		
Greece	05-May-97[a]	15-May-85[a]	05-Oct-88*	17-Jun-70	06-Jun-83	11-May-93	05-May-97[a]	05-May-97[a]
Grenada	05-Sep-91[a]	05-Sep-91[a]		s:17-Dec-81	29-Aug-90	05-Nov-90		
Guatemala	06-May-92[a]	18-May-88[a]	04-Jan-90[a]	17-Jan-83	11-Aug-82	06-Jun-90		
Guinea	23-Jan-78	23-Jan-78	09-Oct-89	13-Mar-77	08-Aug-82	13-Jul-90[a]	16-Jun-93	
Guinea-Bissau		01-Jul-92[a]			22-Aug-85	20-Aug-90		
Guyana	14-Feb-77	14-Feb-77	18-May-88	14-Feb-77	16-Jul-80	14-Jan-91	09-May-93[a]	
Haiti	05-Feb-91[a]			18-Dec-72	19-Jul-81	08-Jun-95		
Holy See				30-Apr-69		20-Apr-90		
Honduras	25-Aug-97	16-Feb-81	05-Dec-96[a]		02-Mar-83	10-Aug-90	s:19-Dec-66	s:09-May-90
Hungary	16-Jan-74	16-Jan-74	14-Apr-87*	01-May-67*	21-Dec-80	07-Oct-91	06-Sep-88[a]	23-Feb-94[a]
Iceland	21-Aug-79	22-Nov-79	23-Oct-96*	12-Mar-67*	17-Jun-85	28-Oct-92	21-Aug-79[a]	02-Apr-91[a]
India	09-Apr-79[a]	09-Apr-79[a]	s:14-Oct-97	02-Dec-68	08-Jul-93	11-Dec-92[a]		
Indonesia			28-Oct-98	25-Jun-99[a]	12-Sep-84	05-Sep-90		
Iran (Islamic Republic of)	23-Jun-75	23-Jun-75		28-Aug-68		13-Jul-94		
Iraq	24-Jan-71	24-Jan-71		13-Jan-70	12-Aug-86[a]	15-Jun-94[a]		
Ireland	07-Dec-89	07-Dec-89	s:27-Sep-92	s:21-Mar-78	22-Dec-85[a]	28-Sep-92	08-Dec-89	17-Jun-93[a]
Israel	02-Oct-91	02-Oct-91	02-Oct-91	02-Jan-79	02-Oct-91	03-Oct-91		
Italy	14-Sep-78	14-Sep-78	11-Jan-89*	04-Jan-76*	09-Jun-85	05-Sep-91	14-Sep-78	14-Feb-95
Jamaica	03-Oct-75	02-Oct-75		03-Jun-71	18-Oct-84	14-May-91		
Japan	20-Jun-79	20-Jun-79	29-Jun-99[a]	14-Dec-95[a]	24-Jun-85	22-Apr-94		
Jordan	27-May-75	27-May-75	12-Nov-91	29-May-74[a]	30-Jun-92	24-May-91		
Kazakhstan			26-Aug-98[a]	26-Aug-98[a]	26-Aug-98[a]	12-Aug-94		
Kenya	01-May-72[a]	30-Apr-72[a]	21-Feb-97[a]		08-Mar-84[a]	30-Jul-90		
Kiribati						11-Dec-95[a]		
Kuwait	20-May-96[a]	20-May-96[a]	07-Mar-96[a]	14-Oct-68[a]	01-Sep-94[a]	21-Oct-91		
Kyrgyzstan	06-Oct-94[a]	06-Oct-94[a]	05-Sep-97[a]	05-Sep-97[a]	10-Feb-97[a]	07-Oct-94[a]	07-Oct-95[a]	
Lao people's Democratic Republic				21-Feb-74[a]	13-Aug-81	08-May-91[a]		

Appendix 2: Status of Ratification 455

Latvia	13-Apr-92[a]	13-Apr-92[a]	13-Apr-92[a]	13-Apr-92[a]	14-Apr-92[a]	21-Jun-94[a]
Lebanon	02-Nov-72[a]	02-Nov-72[a]		11-Nov-71[a]	21-Apr-97[a]	
Lesotho	08-Sep-92[a]	08-Sep-92[a]		03-Nov-71[a]	21-Aug-95[a]	
Liberia	[s]18-Apr-67	[s]18-Apr-67		04-Nov-76[a]	16-Jul-84	
Libyan Arab Jamahiriya	14-May-70[a]	14-May-70[a]	15-May-89[a]	02-Jul-68[a]	15-Apr-93[a]	16-May-89[a]
Liechtenstein	10-Dec-98[a]	10-Dec-98[a]	01-Nov-90*	01-Mar-00[a]	22-Dec-95	10-Dec-98[a]	10-Dec-98[a]
Lithuania	19-Nov-91[a]	19-Nov-91[a]	31-Jan-96	10-Dec-98	31-Jan-92[a]	19-Nov-91[a]
Luxembourg	17-Aug-83	17-Aug-83	28-Sep-87*	30-Apr-78[a]	07-Mar-94	17-Aug-83[a]	11-Feb-92
Madagascar	21-Jun-71	21-Sep-71		06-Feb-69	01-Feb-89	19-Mar-91	20-Jun-71
Malawi	21-Dec-93[a]	21-Dec-93[a]	10-Jun-96[a]	10-Jun-96[a]	16-Mar-89	02-Jan-91[a]	10-Jun-96
Malaysia					11-Mar-87[a]	17-Feb-95[a]	
Maldives				04-Jul-95	11-Feb-91	
Mali	15-Jul-74[a]	15-Jul-74[a]	26-Feb-99[a]	23-Apr-84[a]	30-Jun-93[a]	20-Sep-90
Malta	12-Sep-90[a]	12-Sep-90	12-Sep-90*	15-Jul-74[a]	09-Sep-85	30-Sep-90	28-Dec-94[a]
-Mar-shall Islands				26-May-71*	07-Mar-91[a]	04-Oct-93	
Mauritania				12-Dec-88		16-May-91	
Mauritius	12-Dec-73[a]	11-Dec-73[a]	08-Dec-92[a]	29-May-72[a]	08-Jul-84[a]	26-Jul-90[a]	11-Dec-73[a]
Mexico	22-Mar-81[a]	22-Mar-81[a]	22-Jan-86	19-Feb-75	22-Mar-81	21-Sep-90	
Micronesia (Federated States of)						05-May-93[a]	
Monaco	28-Aug-97	28-Aug-97	05-Dec-91[a]*	26-Sep-95[a]		21-Jun-93[a]	28-Mar-00[a]
Mongolia	17-Nov-74	17-Nov-74		05-Aug-69	19-Jul-81	05-Jul-90	15-Apr-91[a]
Morocco	02-May-79	02-May-79	20-Jun-93	17-Dec-70	20-Jun-93[a]	21-Jun-93	
Mozambique	20-Jul-93[a]	20-Jul-93[a]	14-Sep-99[a]	17-Apr-83[a]	16-Apr-97[a]	26-Apr-94	20-Jul-93[a]
Myanmar					22-Jul-97[a]	15-Jul-91[a]	
Namibia	27-Nov-94[a]	27-Nov-94[a]	27-Nov-94[a]	10-Nov-82[a]	22-Nov-92[a]	30-Sep-90	27-Nov-94[a]	27-Nov-94[a]
Nauru						27-Jul-94[a]	
Nepal	13-May-91[a]	13-May-91[a]	13-May-91[a]	29-Jan-71[a]	21-Apr-91	14-Sep-90	13-May-91[a]	04-Mar-98[a]
Netherlands	10-Dec-78	10-Dec-78	20-Dec-88*	09-Dec-71*	22-Jul-91	06-Feb-95	10-Dec-78	25-Mar-91
New Zealand	27-Dec-78	27-Dec-78	09-Dec-89*	21-Nov-72	09-Jan-85	06-Apr-93	25-May-89[a]	21-Feb-90
Nicaragua	11-Mar-80[a]	11-Mar-80[a]	[s]15-Apr-85	14-Feb-78[a]	26-Oct-81	05-Oct-90	11-Mar-80[a]	[s]21-Feb-90
Niger	06-Mar-86[a]	06-Mar-86[a]	05-Oct-98[a]	26-Apr-67	08-Oct-99[a]	30-Sep-90	06-Mar-86[a]	
Nigeria	28-Jul-93[a]	28-Jul-93[a]	[s]28-Jul-88	15-Oct-67[a]	12-Jun-85	19-Apr-91		
Niue						20-Dec-95[a]		

STATE	CCPR	CESCR	CAT	CERD	CEDAW	CRC	OPT	OPT2
Norway	12-Sep-72	12-Sep-72	08-Jul-86*	05-Aug-70*	20-May-81	08-Jan-91	12-Sep-72	04-Sep-91
Oman						09-Dec-96[a]		
Pakistan				20-Sep-66	11-Mar-96[a]	12-Nov-90		
Palau						04-Aug-95[a]		
Panama	07-Mar-77	08-Mar-77[a]	23-Aug-87	15-Aug-67	28-Oct-81	12-Dec-90	07-Mar-77	20-Jan-93[a]
Papua New Guinea				26-Jan-82[a]	11-Jan-95[a]	01-Mar-93		
Paraguay	09-Jun-92	09-Jun-92[a]	11-Mar-90		05-Apr-87[a]	25-Sep-90	09-Jan-95[a]	
Peru	27-Apr-78	27-Apr-78	06-Jul-88	28-Sep-71*	12-Sep-82	04-Sep-90	02-Oct-80[a]	
Philippines	22-Oct-86	06-Jul-74	17-Jun-86[a]	14-Sep-67	04-Aug-81	21-Aug-90	21-Aug-89[a]	
Poland	17-Mar-77	17-Mar-77	25-Jul-89*	04-Dec-68	29-Jul-80	07-Jun-91	06-Nov-91[a]	s 21-Mar-00
Portugal	14-Jun-78	30-Jul-78	08-Feb-89*	23-Aug-82[a]	29-Jul-80	21-Sep-90	02-May-83	16-Oct-90
Qatar			11-Jan-00[a]	21-Jul-76[a]		03-Apr-95		
Republic of Korea	09-Apr-90[a]	09-Apr-90[a]	08-Jan-95[a]	04-Dec-78*	26-Dec-84	19-Nov-91	09-Apr-90[a]	
Republic of Moldova	25-Jan-93[a]	25-Jan-93[a]	27-Nov-95	25-Jan-93[a]	30-Jun-94[a]	26-Jan-93[a]		
Romania	08-Dec-74	08-Dec-74	17-Dec-90[a]	14-Sep-70[a]	06-Jan-82	28-Sep-90	19-Jul-93[a]	26-Feb-91
Russian Federation	15-Oct-73	15-Oct-73	02-Mar-87*	03-Feb-69*	22-Jan-81	16-Aug-90	30-Sep-91[a]	
Rwanda	15-Apr-75[a]	15-Apr-75[a]		15-Apr-75[a]	01-Mar-81	24-Jan-91		
Saint Kitts and Nevis					24-Apr-85[a]	24-Jul-90		
Saint Lucia				13-Feb-90[d]	07-Oct-82[a]	16-Jun-93[a]		
Saint Vincent and the Grenadines	08-Nov-81[a]	08-Nov-81[a]		08-Nov-81[a]	03-Aug-81[a]	26-Oct-93	08-Nov-81[a]	
Samoa					24-Sep-92[a]	29-Nov-94		
San-Mar-ino	17-Oct-85[a]	17-Oct-85[a]				25-Nov-91[a]	17-Oct-85[a]	
Sao Tome and Principe	s 31-Oct-95	s 31-Oct-95			s 31-Oct-95	14-May-91[a]		
Saudi Arabia			23-Sep-97[a]	23-Sep-97[a]		26-Jan-96[a]		
Senegal	12-Feb-78	12-Feb-78	20-Aug-86*	18-Apr-72*	04-Feb-85	31-Jul-90	12-Feb-78	
Seychelles	04-May-92[a]	04-May-92[a]	04-May-92[a]	06-Mar-78[a]	04-May-92[a]	07-Sep-90[a]	04-May-92[a]	14-Dec-94[a]
Sierra Leone	23-Aug-96[a]	23-Aug-96[a]	s 18-Mar-85	01-Aug-67	10-Nov-88	18-Jun-90	23-Aug-96[a]	
Singapore					04-Oct-95[a]	05-Oct-95[a]		
Slovakia	27-May-93[d]	27-May-93[d]	27-May-93[d]	27-May-93[d]	27-May-93[d]	28-May-93[d]	27-May-93	22-Jun-99
Slovenia	05-Jul-92[d]	05-Jul-92[d]	15-Jul-93[a]*	05-Jul-92[d]	05-Jul-92[d]	06-Jul-92[d]	15-Jul-93[a]	09-Mar-94

Appendix 2: Status of Ratification 457

Solomon Islands	23-Jan-90[a]					
Somalia	10-Dec-98	16-Mar-82[d]		16-Mar-82[d]		
South Africa		23-Jan-90[a]	23-Jan-90[a]	25-Aug-75		23-Jan-90[a]
Spain	26-Apr-77	s:03-Oct-94	10-Dec-98*	10-Dec-98*	14-Dec-95	10-Apr-95[a]
Sri Lanka	10-Jun-80[a]	26-Apr-77	20-Oct-87[a]	12-Sep-68*,[a]	04-Jan-84	16-Jun-95	24-Jan-85[a]	10-Apr-91
Sudan	17-Mar-76[a]	10-Jun-80[a]	02-Jan-94[a]	17-Feb-82[a]	04-Oct-81	06-Dec-90	03-Oct-97[a]
Suriname	27-Dec-76[a]	17-Mar-86[a]	s:04-Jun-86	20-Mar-77[a]		12-Jul-91	
Swaziland		27-Dec-76[a]		14-Mar-84[d]	28-Feb-93[a]	03-Aug-90	27-Dec-76[a]
Sweden	05-Dec-71			06-Apr-69[a]		01-Mar-93	
Switzerland	17-Jun-92[a]	05-Dec-71	07-Jan-86*	05-Dec-71*	01-Jul-80	07-Sep-95	05-Dec-71	10-May-90
Syrian Arab Republic	21-Apr-69[a]	17-Jun-92[a]	01-Dec-86*	28-Nov-94[a]	27-Mar-97	29-Jun-90		15-Jun-94[a]
Tajikistan	05-Jan-99[a]	20-Apr-69[a]		20-Apr-69[a]		24-Feb-97	04-Jan-99[a]
Thailand	29-Oct-96[a]	04-Jan-99[a]	10-Jan-95[a]	10-Jan-95[a]	25-Oct-93[a]	15-Jul-93	
The Former Yugoslav Republic of Macedonia	17-Jan-94[d]	05-Sep-99[a]			08-Aug-85[a]	26-Oct-93[a]	11-Dec-94[a]	25-Jan-95
		17-Jan-94[d]	11-Dec-94[a]	17-Jan-94[d]	17-Jan-94[d]	27-Mar-92[a]	
Togo	23-May-84[a]					02-Dec-93[d]	
Tonga		23-May-84[a]	17-Nov-87*	31-Aug-72[a]	25-Sep-83[a]	01-Aug-90	30-Mar-88[a]
Trinidad and Tobago	20-Dec-78[a]			15-Feb-72[a]		06-Nov-95[a]	
Tunisia	17-Mar-69	07-Dec-78[a]	22-Sep-88*	03-Oct-73	11-Jan-90	05-Dec-91	26-May-98[a]
Turkey		17-Mar-69	01-Aug-88*	12-Jan-67	19-Sep-85	30-Jan-92	
Turkmenistan	01-May-97[a]		25-Jun-99[a]	s:12-Oct-72	19-Dec-85[a]	04-Jan-95	01-May-97[a]	11-Jan-00[a]
Tuvalu		01-May-97[a]		28-Sep-94[a]	01-May-97[a]	20-Sep-93[a]	
Uganda	20-Jun-95[a]		02-Nov-86[a]	20-Nov-80[a]	06-Oct-99[a]	22-Sep-95[a]	13-Nov-95
Ukraine	11-Nov-73	20-Jan-87[a]	23-Feb-87	06-Mar-69*	21-Jul-85	17-Aug-90	24-Jul-91[a]
United Arab Emirates		11-Nov-73		19-Jun-74[a]	11-Mar-81	28-Aug-91	
United Kingdom of Great Britain and Northern Ireland	19-May-76		07-Dec-88	06-Mar-69	06-Apr-86	04-Jan-97[a]	15-Dec-91	10-Dec-99
		19-May-76				15-Dec-91	
United Republic of Tanzania	10-Jun-76[a]			26-Oct-72[a]	19-Aug-85	10-Jun-91	
		10-Jun-76[a]					
United States of America	07-Jun-92	s:05-Oct-77	20-Oct-94	20-Oct-94	s:17-Jul-80	s:16-Feb-95	
Uruguay	01-Apr-70		23-Oct-86*	29-Aug-68*	08-Oct-81	20-Nov-90	01-Apr-70	20-Jan-93
Uzbekistan	27-Sep-95[a]	01-Apr-70	27-Sep-95[a]	27-Sep-95[a]	18-Jul-95[a]	29-Jun-94[a]	27-Sep-95[a]
		27-Sep-95[a]					

STATE	CCPR	CESCR	CAT	CERD	CEDAW	CRC	OPT	OPT2
Vanuatu						07-Jul-93		
Venezuela	09-May-78	09-May-78	28-Jul-91*	09-Oct-67	01-May-83	13-Sep-90	09-May-78	21-Feb-93
Viet Nam	24-Sep-82[a]	23-Sep-82[a]		08-Jun-82[a]	16-Feb-82	28-Feb-90		
Yemen	08-Feb-87[a]	08-Feb-87[a]	04-Nov-91[a]	17-Oct-72[a]	29-May-84[a]	01-May-91		
Yugoslavia	01-Jun-71	01-Jun-71	09-Sep-91*	01-Oct-67	26-Feb-82	03-Jan-91	s:14-Mar-90	
Zambia	09-Apr-84[a]	09-Apr-84[a]	07-Oct-98[a]	03-Feb-72	20-Jun-85	05-Dec-91	09-Apr-84[a]	
Zimbabwe	12-May-91[a]	12-May-91[a]		12-May-91[a]	12-May-91[a]	11-Sep-90		
TOTAL STATES PARTIES	144	142	119	156	165	191	95	43
TOTAL SIGNATORIES (non-States parties)	3	5	9	5	3	1	2	3

Notes

a accession
d succession
* indicates that the State party has recognized the competence to receive and process individual communications of the Committee on the Elimination of Racial Discrimination under article 14 of the CERD (total 27 states parties) or of the Committee against Torture under article 22 of CAT (total 41 states parties).

Appendix 3: Status of Individual Communications

Statistical survey of individual complaints dealt with by the Human Rights Committee under the Optional Protocol to the International Covenant on Civil and Political Rights

(updated on 19 May 2000)*

State	Living cases Pre-admissible	Living cases Admissible	Concluded cases Inadmissible	Concluded cases Discontinued	Views (1)/(2)	Total
Algeria	–	–	–	–	–	–
Angola	1	0	–	–	1/2	2
Argentina	–	–	4	–	1/0	5
Armenia	–	–	–	–	–	–
Australia	10	–	11	4	2/2	29
Austria	2	–	3	–	2/0	7
Barbados	–	–	3	–	–	3
Belarus	5	–	–	–	1/0	5
Belgium	1	–	–	–	–	1
Benin	–	–	–	–	–	–
Bolivia	–	–	–	–	2/0	2
Bosnia and Herzegovina	–	–	–	–	–	–
Bulgaria	–	–	2	–	–	2
Burkina Faso	–	–	–	–	–	–
Cameroon	–	1	–	–	1/0	2
Canada	5	2	44	22	9/8	90
Cap Verde #5	–	–	–	–	–	–
Central African Republic	–	–	–	–	1/0	1
Chad	–	–	–	–	–	–
Chile	2	–	4	–	–	6
Colombia	3	2	3	5	9/0	22
Congo	–	–	–	–	–	–
Costa Rica	1	–	1	1	–	3
Côte d'Ivoire	–	–	–	–	–	–
Croatia	–	1	1	–	–	2
Cyprus	1	–	–	–	–	1
Czech Republic	3	3	5	–	2/0	13
Democratic Republic of the Congo	1	1	4	2	10/0	18

*Can be updated online at http://www.unhchr.ch/html/menu2/8/stat2.htm

| | Living cases | | Concluded cases | | | |
State	Pre-admissible	Admissible	Inadmissible	Discontinued	Views (1)/(2)	Total
Denmark	–	–	7	1	–	8
Dominican Republic	–	–	–	–	3/0	3
Ecuador	–	–	–	4	5/0	9
El Salvador	–	–	–	–	–	–
Equatorial Guinea	–	–	–	–	2/0	2
Estonia	–	–	–	–	–	–
Finland	1	–	14	2	4/7	28
France	4	3	23	9	3/7	49
Gambia	–	–	–	–	–	–
Georgia	–	–	–	–	4/0	4
Germany	2	–	2	–	–	4
Greece	1	–	–	–	–	1
Guinea	–	–	–	–	–	–
Guyana	7	1	–	1	1/0	10
Hungary	1	–	4	2	2/1	10
Iceland	–	–	1	1	–	2
Ireland	1	–	1	–	–	2
Italy	–	–	8	3	1/1	13
Jamaica #2	8	3	39	14	94/19	177*
Kyrgyzstan	–	–	–	–	–	–
Latvia	2	–	–	1	0/1	4
Liechtenstein	–	–	–	–	–	–
Lithuania	2	–	–	–	–	2
Libyan Arab Jamahiriya	–	–	1	–	1/0	2
Luxembourg	–	–	–	–	–	–
Macedonia (former Yugoslav Republic of)	–	–	–	–	–	–
Madagascar	–	–	–	2	4/0	6
Malawi	–	–	–	–	–	–
Malta	–	–	–	–	–	–
Mauritius	2	–	2	–	1/0	5
Mongolia	–	–	–	–	–	–
Namibia	1	1	–	–	–	2
Nepal	–	–	–	–	–	–
Netherlands	5	–	42	–	5/15	67
New Zealand	12	2	4	1	0/1	20
Nicaragua	–	–	1	3	1/0	5
Niger	–	–	–	–	–	–

Appendix 3: State of Individual Communications

	Living cases		Concluded cases			
State	Pre-admissible	Admissible	Inadmissible	Discontinued	Views (1)/(2)	Total
Norway	–	–	8	–	1/3	12
Panama	–	–	4	7	2/0	13
Paraguay	–	–	–	–	–	–
Peru	2	1	–	4	6/0	13
Philippines	3	–	–	1	–	4
Poland	2	–	–	–	0/1	3
Portugal	–	–	–	–	–	–
Republic of Korea	2	–	–	1	3/1	7
Romania	–	–	–	–	–	–
Russian Federation	12	3	1	–	–	16
Saint Vincent and the Grenadines	1	–	–	–	–	1
San Marino	–	–	–	–	–	–
Senegal	–	–	–	–	1/0	1
Seychelles	–	–	–	–	–	–
Sierra Leone	3	–	–	–	–	3
Slovak Republic	1	–	1	–	–	2
Slovenia	–	–	–	–	–	–
Somalia	–	–	–	–	–	–
Spain	8	1	7	3	2/2	23
Sri Lanka	2	–	–	–	–	2
Suriname	–	–	–	–	8/0	8
Sweden	–	–	3	1	0/6	10
Tajikistan	–	–	–	–	–	–
Togo	1	–	–	–	4/0	5
Trinidad and Tobago #4	4	7 #3	15	5	12/2	45
Turkmenistan	–	–	–	–	–	–
Uganda	–	–	–	–	–	–
Ukraine	6	2	–	–	–	8
Uruguay	–	–	5	28	45/1	79
Uzbekistan	5	–	–	–	–	5
Venezuela	–	–	1	–	1/0	2
Zambia	6	–	–	1	4/0	11
95	143	34	279	129	261/78 (339)	924 #1

177 living cases.

(1) Disclose a violation.
(2) Disclose no violation.

1. 924 registered communications with respect to 64 countries.
2. Denunciation by Jamaica of the Optional Protocol took effect on 23 January 1998. Therefore, only 95 States are still part to it. However, the cases relating to Jamaica, still under consideration at the time the denunciation became effective, are still to be considered by the Human Rights Committee.
3. The Human Rights Committee decided at its 67th session to make public an admissibility decision concerning Trinidad and Tobago. This decision is reproduced in document CCPR/C/67/D/845/1999 available in the Treaty Body database.
4. Denunciation by Trinidad and Tobago of the Optional Protocol will take effect on 27 June 2000. Therefore on that day, there will be 94 States still part to it. However, the cases relating to Trinidad and Tobago, still under consideration at the time the denunciation will become effective, was still to be considered by the Human Rights Committee.
5. The Optimal Protocol enters into force on 19 August 2000.

Statistical survey of individual complaints dealt with by the Committee against Torture under the procedure governed by article 22 of the Convention against Torture and Other Cruel, Inhuman or Degrading Treatment or Punishment

(updated on 3 February 2000)*

	Living cases		Concluded cases				
State*	Pre-adm.	Admissible	Suspend	Inadm.	Discont.	Views (1)/(2)	Total
Algeria	–	–	–	–	–	–	–
Argentina	–	–	–	3	–	–	3
Australia	7	–	–	–	2	1/1	11
Austria	0	1	–	1	–	1/0	3
Belgium	–	–	–	–	–	–	–
Bulgaria	–	–	–	–	–	–	–
Canada	11	2	1	8	5	1/1	29
Croatia	–	–	–	–	–	–	–
Cyprus	–	–	–	–	–	–	–
Czech Republic	–	–	–	–	–	–	–
Denmark	2	–	–	–	1	–	3
Ecuador	–	–	–	–	1	–	1
Finland	–	–	–	–	–	–	–
France	1	–	–	5	18	1/0	25
Greece	–	–	–	–	–	0/1	1
Hungary	–	–	–	1	–	–	1
Iceland	–	–	–	–	–	–	–
Italy	–	–	–	–	–	–	–
Liechtenstein	–	–	–	–	–	–	–
Luxembourg	–	–	–	–	–	–	–
Malta	–	–	–	–	–	–	–
Monaco	–	–	–	–	–	–	–
Netherlands	3	–	–	1	1	1/2	8
New Zealand	–	–	–	–	–	–	–
Norway	–	–	–	2	–	–	2
Poland	–	–	–	–	–	–	–
Portugal	–	–	–	–	–	–	–
Russian Federation	1	–	–	–	–	–	1

*Can be updated online at http://www.unhchr.ch/html/menu2/8/stat3.htm

	Living cases		Concluded cases				
State*	Pre-adm.	Admissible	Suspend	Inadm.	Discont.	Views (1)/(2)	Total
Senegal	–	–	–	–	–	–	–
Slovakia	–	–	–	–	–	–	–
Slovenia	–	–	–	–	–	–	–
South Africa	–	–	–	–	–	–	–
Spain	–	–	–	3	–	1/1	5
Sweden	5	–	–	3	3	7/5	23
Switzerland	8	–	–	4	8	3/9	32
Togo	–	–	–	–	–	–	–
Tunisia	–	–	–	1	1	1/0	3
Turkey	–	–	–	1	–	–	1
Uruguay	–	–	–	–	–	–	–
Venezuela	–	–	–	–	–	1/0	1
Yugoslavia	1	–	–	–	–	–	1
41	39	3	1	33	40	18/20	155

43 living cases.
[154 registered communications with respect to 19 countries].
(1) Disclose a violation.
(2) Disclose no violation.
* States Parties which have accepted the competence of the Committee under article 22 of the Convention.

Statistical survey of individual complaints considered under the procedure governed by article 14 of the International Convention on the Elimination of All Forms of Racial Disrimination

(updated on 6 April 2000)*

	Living cases		Concluded cases			
State*	Pre-adm.	Admissible	Inadm.	Discont.	Views(1)/(2)	Total
Algeria	–	–	–	–	–	–
Australia	1	–	1	–	0/2	4
Bulgaria	–	–	–	–	–	–
Chile	–	–	–	–	–	–
Costa Rica	–	–	–	–	–	–
Cyprus	–	–	–	–	–	–
Denmark	–	–	1	–	2/1	4
Ecuador	–	–	–	–	–	–
Finland	–	–	–	–	–	–
France	–	–	–	–	0/1	1
Hungary	–	–	–	–	–	–
Iceland	–	–	–	–	–	–
Italy	–	–	–	–	–	–
Luxembourg	–	–	–	–	–	–
Malta	–	–	–	–	–	–
Macedonia	–	–	–	–	–	–
Netherlands	1	–	–	–	2/0	3
Norway	–	–	–	–	1/0	1
Peru	–	–	–	–	–	–
Poland	–	–	–	–	–	–
Republic of Korea	–	–	–	–	–	–
Russian Fed.	–	–	–	–	–	–
Senegal	–	–	–	–	–	–
Slovakia	–	2	–	–	–	2
South Africa	–	–	–	–	–	–
Spain	–	–	–	–	–	–
Sweden	1	–	1	–	–	2
Ukraine	–	–	–	–	–	–
Uruguay	–	–	–	–	–	–
29	3	2	3	–	5/4	17

5 living cases.

*Can be updated online at http://www.unhchr.ch/html/menu2/8/stat4.htm

(1) Disclose a violation.
(2) Disclose no violation.
* States Parties which have accepted the competence of the Committee under article 22 of the Convention.

Appendix 4: Draft Amendments to the Treaties

E/CN.4/1997/105 — 18 December 1996

COMMISSION ON HUMAN RIGHTS
Fifty-third session

STATUS OF THE INTERNATIONAL COVENANTS ON HUMAN RIGHTS

Draft Optional Protocol to the International Covenant on Economic, Social and Cultural Rights

Note by the Secretary-General

1. At its fifty-second session, the Commission on Human Rights took note of the measures taken by the Committee on Economic, Social and Cultural Rights towards the elaboration of a draft optional protocol to the International Covenant on Economic, Social and Cultural Rights granting the right of individuals or groups to submit communications concerning non-compliance with the Covenant, as recommended by the World Conference on Human Rights, and requested the Committee to submit a report on the matter to its fifty-third session (resolution 1996/16, para. 10).
2. The Committee on Economic, Social and Cultural Rights continued and concluded its consideration of a draft optional protocol at its fifteenth session (E/C.12/1996/SR.44–49 and 54). The report of the Committee on Economic, Social and Cultural Rights to the Commission on Human Rights on a draft optional protocol for the consideration of communications in relation to the International Covenant on Economic, Social and Cultural Rights is annexed to the present note.

ANNEX

Report of the Committee on Economic, Social and Cultural Rights to the Commission on Human Rights on a draft optional protocol for the consideration of communications in relation to the International Covenant on Economic, Social and Cultural Rights

Introduction

1. In the Vienna Declaration and Programme of Action the World Conference on Human Rights "encourage[d] the Commission on Human Rights, in cooperation with the Committee on Economic, Social and Cultural Rights, to continue the examination of optional protocols to the International

Covenant on Economic, Social and Cultural Rights" (Part II), para. 75). Although the reference is to "protocols" (in the plural) the only specific proposal before the Conference related to an optional communications procedure. This commitment was reiterated by the Commission on Human Rights which, in paragraph 6 of its resolution 1994/20, took note of the "steps taken by the Committee ... for the drafting of an optional protocol ... granting the right of individuals or groups to submit communications concerning non-compliance with the Covenant, and invite[d] the Committee to report thereon to the Commission ..." A brief progress report (E/CN.4/1996/96) on these deliberations was submitted to the Commission on Human Rights at its fifty-second session. The Commission, in paragraph 5 of its resolution 1996/11, welcomed the information and took note of the steps taken by the Committee.

2. The preparation of an optional protocol was first discussed in the Committee in 1990 and the matter has been formally under consideration by the Committee since its sixth session.[1]

In the following year the adoption of such a protocol was expressly recommended by Mr. Danilo Türk, the Special Rapporteur of the Sub-Commission on Prevention of Discrimination and Protection of Minorities on the realization of economic, social and cultural rights, in his final report (E/CN.4/Sub.2/1992/16, para. 211). Subsequently, four separate reports were prepared at the Committee's request by Mr. Philip Alston and provided the basis for extensive discussions within the Committee.[2]

3. The present report reflects the outcome of the discussions held by the Committee over the course of a number of sessions. In particular, the Committee conducted in-depth discussions based on a specific set of draft proposals from its eleventh to its fifteenth sessions.[3] It adopted the present report at its fifteenth session. In doing so the Committee decided that while it would prefer wherever possible to adopt a consensus position in relation to the issues under consideration, its report would also reflect divergent viewpoints whenever these could not be brought together in a consensus position. In the course of the Committee's discussions one of its members – Mr. Grissa – indicated that he was opposed to the proposal to draft an optional protocol. His views are reflected in the summary records, in particular E/C.12/1996/SR.42.

4. The present report provides an analysis of the issues that will need to be examined by the Commission on Human Rights in its consideration of the proposed optional protocol. It takes account of the comments made by members of the Committee in the course of its various discussions and, in particular, reflects the outcome of the Committee's deliberations at its fifteenth session. Careful note was taken in the course of those deliberations of very helpful oral and written submissions by the International Labour Organization, the United Nations Division for the Advancement of Women and the representatives of various non-governmental organizations, as well

---

[1] See E/1992/23 – E/C.12/1991/4, paras. 360–366.
[2] E/C.12/1991/WP.2, E/C.12/1992/WP.9, E/C.12/1994/12, and E/C.12/1996/CRP.2/Add.1.
[3] See E/C.12/1994/SR.42, 45 and 56; E/C.12/1995/SR.5 and 50; E/C.12/1996/SR.19 and 20; and E/C.12/1996/SR.42–47.

as of the report of an expert meeting convened in Utrecht by the Netherlands Institute for Human Rights in January 1995 to discuss the draft protocol.[4]

5. Before considering the issues that arise in relation to the content of a draft optional protocol to the Covenant, it is appropriate to consider briefly the broader setting in relation to which such an examination must take place.

I. PARALLEL DEVELOPMENTS IN RELATION TO THE CONVENTION ON THE ELIMINATION OF ALL FORMS OF DISCRIMINATION AGAINST WOMEN

6. The World Conference on Human Rights called upon the Commission on the Status of Women and the Committee on the Elimination of Discrimination against Women to "quickly examine the possibility of introducing the right of petition through the preparation of an optional protocol to the Convention on the Elimination of All Forms of Discrimination against Women" (Part II, para. 40). Subsequently, an expert meeting was convened under independent auspices at the University of Maastricht in the Netherlands from 29 September to 1 October 1994 and which adopted a comprehensive draft optional protocol. The general lines of this draft were subsequently endorsed by the Committee on the Elimination of Discrimination against Women (CEDAW) at its fourteenth session.[5]

7. At its fortieth session, in March 1996, the Commission on the Status of Women established an open-ended sessional working group to examine the issue. The working group held a general exchange of views, followed by an in-depth consideration of the major issues arising from the proposal. The Commission recommended the renewal of the working group's mandate for 1997 and requested the Secretary-General to prepare two reports dealing respectively with a comparative survey of other comparable international procedures and a synthesis of the views expressed on the issue by Governments and inter-governmental and non-governmental organizations.[6]

II. SIMILAR DEVELOPMENTS IN RELATION TO REGIONAL HUMAN RIGHTS TREATIES

8. In the context of the Organization of American States, the Additional Protocol to the American Convention on Human Rights in the Area of Economic, Social and Cultural Rights (the Protocol of San Salvador, of 1988), which provides for a limited complaints procedure, has now been ratified or acceded to by six States and will enter into force upon acceptance by five more.

---

[4] F. Coomans and G.J.H. van Hoof (eds.), *Right to Complain About Economic and Social Rights* (Utrecht, Netherlands Institute for Human Rights, 1995).
[5] *Official Records of the General Assembly, Fiftieth Session, Supplement No. 38* (A/50/38), chap. I Sect. B, suggestion 7. For a comprehensive analysis see A. Byrnes and J. Connors, "Enforcing the Human Rights of Women: A complaints Procedure for the Women's Convention", 21 *Brooklyn Journal of International Law* (1996) 679–797.
[6] See *Official Records of the Economic and Social Council, 1996, Supplement No. 6* (E/1996/26) – E/CN.6/1996/15), annex III.

Pursuant to Article 19(6):

"Any instance in which [the right to organize trade unions and the right to education] are violated by action directly attributable to a State Party to this Protocol may give rise, through participation of the Inter-American Commission on Human Rights and, when applicable, of the Inter-American Court of Human Rights, to application of the system of individual petitions governed by Articles 44 through 51 and 61 through 69 of the American Convention on Human Rights."

9. Of even greater direct relevance is the adoption in June 1995 by the Council of Europe of an Additional Protocol to the European Social Charter Providing for a System of Collective Complaints.[7] As with the proposed optional protocol to the International Covenant on Economic, Social and Cultural Rights, the new procedure is viewed only as a supplement to the reporting mechanism, which remains the primary means of supervising compliance with the Charter. Complaints alleging "unsatisfactory application of the Charter" cannot be submitted by individuals in their own right. Instead, they must be submitted by one of the following groups: (1) designated "international organizations of employers and trade unions"; (2) "other international non-governmental organizations which have consultative status with the Council of Europe and have been put on a list established for this purpose" by a Governmental Committee; (3) "representative national organizations of employers and trade unions" within the State against whom the complaint is directed (art. 1); and (4) "any other representative non-governmental organization" designated by the Government concerned to lodge complaints against it (art. 2). Groups in categories (2) and (4) may only submit complaints in respect of matters regarding which "they have been recognized as having particular competence" (art. 3). The complainant is required to indicate "in what respect the [Contracting Party] has not ensured the satisfactory application" of a specified provision of the Charter (art. 4).

10. The complaint is initially examined by the Committee of Independent Experts, established under the Charter. Having determined that the complaint is admissible, the Committee calls for observations from both sides as well as from other Parties to the Protocol and category (1) organizations (art. 7). It then reports on whether or not the State's application of the relevant provision of the Charter has been "satisfactory" (art. 8). The report is sent confidentially to the parties concerned, all Parties to the Charter and the Council of Europe's Committee of Ministers. Within four months thereafter it must be sent to the Parliamentary Assembly and made public. On the basis of the report, the Committee of Ministers adopts a resolution and, if the conclusions of the Committee of Independent Experts are negative, addresses a recommendation to the State concerned (art. 9). The latter is required to report "on the measures it has taken to give effect to the ... recommendation" (art. 10). The Protocol will enter into force upon acceptance of 5 member States of the Council of Europe, of which there are currently 40.

---

[7] See Council of Europe document H (95) 8 of 5 July 1995.

III. PRELIMINARY CONSIDERATIONS

11. At its seventh session the Committee adopted a consolidated "analytical paper" which it submitted to the World Conference on Human Rights (A/CONF.157/PC/62/Add.5, annex II). In addition to that analysis, the Committee made the following submission in its general statement to the Conference:

    "The Committee believes that there are strong reasons for adopting a complaints procedure (in the form of an optional protocol to the Covenant) in respect of the economic, social and cultural rights recognized in the Covenant. Such a procedure would be entirely non-compulsory and would permit communications to be submitted by individuals or groups alleging violations of the rights recognized in the Covenant. It might also include an optional procedure for the consideration of inter-State complaints. Various procedural safeguards designed to guard against abuse of the procedure would be adopted. They would be similar in nature to those applying under the first Optional Protocol to the International Covenant on Civil and Political Rights" (A/CONF.157/PC/62/Add.5, annex I, para. 18).

12. In its "analytical paper" the Committee emphasized the following aspects of the proposed optional protocol:
    (a) Any protocol to the Covenant will be strictly optional and will thus only be applicable to those States parties which specifically agree to it by way of ratification or accession;
    (b) The general principle of permitting complaints to be submitted under an international procedure in relation to economic, social and cultural rights is in no way new or especially innovative, given the precedents that exist within the International Labour Organization, United Nations Education Scientific and Cultural Oganization, the resolution 1503 procedure of the Economic and Social Council, the Additional Protocol to the American Convention on Human Rights in the Area of Economic, Social and Cultural Rights (the Protocol of San Salvador, of 1988), and proposals currently under consideration within the Council of Europe;
    (c) Experience to date with a wide range of existing international petition procedures indicates that there is no basis for fears that an optional protocol will result in a vast number of complaints;
    (d) Under an optional protocol procedure the State party concerned retains the final decision as to what will be done in response to any views adopted by the Committee; and
    (e) That if the principle of the indivisibility, interdependence and interrelatedness of the two sets of rights is to be upheld in the work of the United Nations, it is essential that a complaints procedure be established under the International Covenant on Economic, Social and Cultural Rights, thereby redressing the imbalance that presently exists.

IV. AN ANALYSIS OF THE POSSIBLE PROVISIONS OF AN OPTIONAL PROTOCOL

13. The following analysis is based primarily on the Committee's deliberations at its fifteenth session while also drawing upon its earlier discussions between

1991 and 1996. It also draws heavily on the approach adopted in existing communications procedures under United Nations human rights treaties, and particularly the first Optional Protocol to the International Covenant on Civil and Political Rights.

14. After a lengthy discussion the Committee decided not to recommend the inclusion of an inter-State complaints procedure within the proposed optional protocol. It was noted that such a procedure is included in various of the other core human rights treaties such as the International Covenant on Civil and Political Rights, the International Convention on the Elimination of All Forms of Racial Discrimination and the Convention against Torture and Other Cruel, Inhuman or Degrading Treatment or Punishment. All such procedures apply only between States which have mutually accepted the relevant procedure. The report submitted to the Committee at its fifteenth session summarized the different perspectives on this issue in the following terms:

"In principle, there are good reasons to include such a procedure within the optional protocol. It would increase the options available for dealing with economic, social and cultural rights and it would put those rights on a par with those dealt with in the instruments listed above. In practice, however, there are also strong reasons that militate against the inclusion of such a procedure. Those that already exist under comparable United Nations human rights treaties have never been used and Governments have consistently been wary of what has been referred to as 'a Pandora's Box, which all parties prefer to keep shut'.[8]

Even in the ILO the two procedures for inter-State complaints (under art. 26 of the Constitution and under the freedom of association procedure) have only been used four times and once, respectively. This explains why such a procedure has not been proposed in relation to the draft optional protocol to the Convention on the Elimination of All Forms of Discrimination against Women."

A. *Preamble*

15. The Preamble to the first Optional Protocol to the International Covenant on Civil and Political Rights consists of a single paragraph. For present purposes it would seem appropriate not to depart significantly from the basic simplicity of this approach. However, since the proposed protocol is not being adopted at the same time as the Covenant (as was the case in relation to the first Optional Protocol to the International Covenant on Civil and Political Rights), it is desirable to indicate some of the reasons for establishing an additional procedure. These relate to the interdependence of the two sets of rights, the contribution of the World Conference on Human Rights, the role of the Committee on Economic, Social and Cultural Rights, the importance of recourse procedures in relation to these rights, the relationship between this protocol and the international community's broader economic and social development objectives, and the nature of the obligations specified in article 2 (1) of the Covenant.

---

[8] Rosalyn Higgins, "Encouraging Human Rights", 2 *London School of Economics Quarterly* (1988) 249.

16. The proposed text of the Preamble is:
    "*The States Parties to the present Protocol,*
    "[a] *Emphasizing* that social justice and development, including the realization of economic, social and cultural rights, are essential elements in the construction of a just and equitable national and international order,
    "[b] *Recalling* that the Vienna Declaration and Programme of Action recognized that 'all human rights are universal, indivisible and interdependent and interrelated',
    "[c] *Emphasizing* the role of the Economic and Social Council, and through it the Committee on Economic, Social and Cultural Rights (hereinafter referred to as the Committee) in developing a better understanding of the International Covenant on Economic, Social and Cultural Rights (hereinafter referred to as the Covenant) and in promoting the realization of the rights recognized therein,
    "[d] *Recalling* the provision of article 2(1) of the Covenant pursuant to which 'Each State Party to the present Covenant undertakes to take steps, individually and through international assistance and co-operation, especially economic and technical, to the maximum of its available resources, with a view to achieving progressively the full realization of the rights recognized in the present Covenant by all appropriate means, including particularly the adoption of legislative measures',
    "[e] *Noting* that the possibility for the subjects of economic, social and cultural rights to submit complaints of alleged violations of those rights is a necessary means of recourse to guarantee the full enjoyment of the rights,
    "[f] *Considering* that, in order further to achieve the purposes of the Covenant and the implementation of its provisions, it is appropriate to enable the Committee to receive and examine, in accordance with the provisions of this Protocol, communications alleging violations of the Covenant,
    "*Have agreed* as follows: ..."

B. *The scope of the Committee's competence*

1. *Questions of terminology*

17. In communications procedures generally the first article contains the undertaking pursuant to which a State party recognizes the competence of the Committee to receive communications. It is traditional in such texts to distinguish between the *receipt* of a communication (which does not necessarily imply that it will subsequently be examined) and the *consideration*, or *examination*, phase (which occurs once the various procedural requirements have been met). The first Optional Protocol to the International Covenant on Civil and Political Rights uses both the latter verbs – "consider" and "examine" – without implying any clear distinction. Given the Human Rights Committee's practice of referring to the "examination" of communications, that verb is used in the following draft proposals.

18. The Committee recommends that the Protocol should refer to a "violation ... of ... the rights set forth in the International Covenant", thereby following the wording of article 1 of the first Optional Protocol to the International Covenant on Civil and Political Rights. The report submitted to the Committee at its fifteenth session also noted various other options which had been put forward:

"[One option is to] refer to a failure by the State party to give effect to its obligations under the Covenant (as proposed in the Maastricht draft referred to in para. 4 above, and which amounts to a hybrid version of the different forms of terminology used in article 41 of the Covenant on Civil and Political Rights in relation to inter-State complaints). Other options are to follow the wording of the Additional Protocol to the European Social Charter and refer to a failure to ensure the satisfactory application of a provision or to adopt a formulation proposed by the ILO which would refer to those 'who allege failure by that State party to secure the observance of any of the rights'. In the case of the Covenant, all but the first of these formulations might be read as applying not only to the rights recognized in articles 1 to 15 but also to the procedural obligations contained in Part IV of the Covenant relating to reporting, etc. It is not clear, however, that it is desirable for individuals to be able to bring a communication against a State party on the grounds that it has failed to report in a timely fashion, or at all. While such behaviour clearly constitutes a violation of the State's obligations, there are alternative means by which the Committee has sought to address such problems.

"A requirement that a 'violation' be alleged would not have the effect of exposing a State party to a successful complaint solely by virtue of its failure to ensure to a specific complainant the full realization of a given right. The obligation of the State under the Covenant, and thus the question of whether a violation had occurred, would still depend upon the facts of the case and a consideration of the implications of the terminology used both in the substantive provision recognizing the right and in article 2 (1) of the Covenant defining the nature of the obligation. There would thus seem to be no reason not to follow the approach used in the first Optional Protocol to the Covenant on Civil and Political Rights of referring to a violation. The only qualification would be to use the term 'recognized' rather than 'set forth', in view of the different terminology used in each of the Covenants."

2. *Individuals and/or groups as complainants*

19. The next question dealt with by the Committee was whether an individual should be permitted to submit a communication. In this regard it was noted that the Additional Protocol to the European Social Charter had excluded this possibility and adopted a restrictive list of group-based complainants. In the course of a full discussion of this option, all members of the Committee who contributed to the debate agreed that the inclusion of an individual right to petition was essential. It was also recalled in this regard that, already at its seventh session, the Committee had indicated a "strong and clear preference for an individual" focus (A/CONF.157/PC/62/Add.5, annex II, para. 66).

20. A related issue was whether groups, one or more of whose members claimed to be a victim of a violation, should also be permitted to submit complaints. In this regard the Committee recalled the reference in Commission on Human Rights resolution 1994/20 to "granting the right of individuals or groups to submit communications" (para. 6), and noted that the Human Rights Committee has, in practice, dealt with many communications submitted by individuals on behalf of affected groups and vice versa. It was thus agreed that groups should be included among those alleged victims entitled to submit complaints.

21. The proposed text of article 1, based on the decisions reflected in the preceding analysis is:

"A State Party to the Covenant that becomes a Party to the present Protocol recognizes the competence of the Committee to receive and examine communications from any individuals or groups subject to its jurisdiction in accordance with the provisions of this Protocol."

C. Right to submit a communication

1. Third parties acting "on behalf of" alleged victims

22. The next issue is whether "standing" to submit a communication should be extended to "third parties", or, in other words, individuals and groups who, although not themselves victims of a violation, have what is deemed "a sufficient interest" in the matter (to use the phrase used in the CEDAW draft). The report submitted to the Committee at its fifteenth session noted in this regard that:

"This broad approach is not necessary merely in order to permit a communication to be submitted by another person or group on behalf of an individual claiming to be a victim of a violation. The Human Rights Committee has consistently interpreted article 1 of the first Optional Protocol [to the International Covenant on Civil and Political Rights] to accommodate that situation – an approach which is clearly reflected in rule 90 (1)(b) of the Committee's rules of procedure. The broader formulation would therefore seem to envisage a situation in which a public interest group or some other type of non-governmental organization might be authorized by the protocol to bring a complaint without having to identify and act with, or on behalf of, an individual or group claiming to be a victim of a violation. While this would have the advantage of permitting complaints which sought to anticipate violations, whether imminent or merely possible, it would also broaden considerably the scope of the obligation assumed by States parties and would potentially open the door to speculative complaints.

"During discussions in the Committee it has been argued that any 'NGOs and other organizations' should be authorized to submit complaints. This would eliminate all requirements such as 'consultative status', links to the country concerned, or special knowledge or particular competence in relation to the issues raised. It would thus make the procedure much more easily accessible than is the case under the European Social Charter and the ILO procedures. Even the non-treaty-based procedure under resolution 1503 has some limits in theory, although not in practice. The proposal would eliminate any need for a nexus between the complainant and the alleged violation. While it is clear that a 'wide open' approach to standing would increase the capacity of the procedure to address every possible issue of relevance, it would seem to come at the price of opening up the procedure to a vast number of complaints which do not have to satisfy any minimum requirements designed to filter out ill-informed or gratuitous complaints.

"... It should also be noted that the requirement to exhaust domestic remedies before lodging a complaint with an international body, which is a standard provision in relation to all comparable human rights complaints procedures (except that of the ILO), would make it somewhat illusory to eliminate the nexus between the complainant(s) and the State party."

23. In light of these considerations the Committee recommends that the right to submit a complaint should be extended also to individuals or groups who act on behalf of alleged victims. The Committee noted, however, that this formulation should be interpreted only to embrace individuals and groups who, in the view of the Committee, are acting with the knowledge and agreement of the alleged victim(s).

2. *The range of rights covered*

24. The next issue is whether the procedure should apply to all of the rights recognized in the Covenant or only to some of them. The report submitted to the Committee at its fifteenth session noted in this regard that:

"After canvassing four different options, the Committee's analytical paper submitted to the World Conference opted for an inclusive rather than a restrictive approach. However, in order to exclude the reporting obligations contained in part IV of the Covenant it is proposed to restrict the coverage of the procedure to the rights recognized in articles 1 to 15 of the Covenant. This approach has been supported by the Committee in its deliberations to date, except in relation to questions raised in relation to the right to self-determination recognized in article 1 and in relation to the rights recognized in article 15. It has been suggested that the inclusion of the former could involve a grave danger of the procedure being misused. It may be noted that the right to self-determination is recognized in exactly the same terms in article 1 of the International Covenant on Civil and Political Rights and that it is subject to complaints under the first Optional Protocol to that Covenant. In practice, however, the Human Rights Committee has adopted a cautious or restrictive approach to its application. In relation to article 15, it would seem difficult to single it out for exclusion while retaining other formulations of equivalent generality."

25. The Committee recommends that the optional protocol should apply in relation to all of the economic, social and cultural rights set forth in the Covenant and that this would include all of the rights contained in articles 1 to 15. The Committee noted, however, that the right to self-determination should be dealt with under this procedure only in so far as economic, social and cultural rights dimensions of that right are involved. It considered that the civil and political rights dimensions of the right should remain the

preserve of the Human Rights Committee in connection with article 1 of the International Covenant on Civil and Political Rights.

26. Another issue, closely related to the previous one, is whether provision should be made to enable States to accept the procedure provided for in the optional protocol either in relation to all of the provisions of articles 1 to 15 (a "comprehensive" approach) or only in relation to particular elements of the Covenant (a "selective" approach). The latter approach, sometimes referred to as a *smörgasbörd* or *à la carte* approach, could take either of two forms. The first would require States parties to indicate which provisions of the Covenant would *not* be covered by the procedure they have accepted by becoming a party to the optional protocol. Each State would thus have to "opt out" in relation to specified provisions if it wished to avoid the application of the optional protocol in relation to all of the rights recognized in the Covenant. The second would require them to "opt in" to the procedure in relation to provisions of the Covenant which they would specify upon becoming a party to the protocol. A further distinction was also noted in the report submitted to the Committee at its fifteenth session which observed that each of these selective approaches:

"could apply either to articles of the Covenant or, in an even more specific fashion, to specific rights. Thus, for example, under the first approach, a State could identify article 11 as one in relation to which it would accept the complaints procedure (thus covering all of the elements – adequate standard of living, food, clothing, housing, etc. – dealt with in that article). Under the second approach it could identify a specific right such as the right to adequate food in relation to which it would accept the procedure. It should be noted that the adoption of a more restrictive coverage in the optional protocol would in no way diminish or otherwise affect the full range of obligations already applicable to every State party to the Covenant."

27. The same report noted the following advantages and disadvantages of permitting any type of selective approach:

"Its principal advantages are: (i) it enables States to tailor the extent of the obligations that they accept to fit the situation within the country, thus making it more feasible to accept the principle of a complaints procedure; (ii) it would facilitate a progressive acceptance of a wider range of rights over time; (iii) it would partly resolve the question of which rights are justiciable and to what extent by enabling States to resolve that issue for themselves and expanding their approach as the content of individual rights evolves with greater clarity; and (iv) it would make the procedure as a whole more manageable, and thus more acceptable, to a broader range of States.

"This option also has some clear disadvantages: (i) the approach might be perceived from a practical viewpoint, although not from a theoretical perspective, to challenge the principle that all rights are equally important; (ii) the approach would differ from the holistic one reflected in the first Optional Protocol to the International Covenant on Civil and Political Rights, although it would be consistent with the options given to States to accept some provisions, but not others, when ratifying the European Social Charter; and (iii) there is a risk States might initially opt to accept the procedure only in relation to an unduly narrow range of rights.

"Whatever approach is adopted in this regard, it would have to be assumed, given the fundamental importance of articles 2–5 of the Covenant, that they would always be fully applicable in relation to the interpretation of the meaning of any of the specific rights recognized in articles 6–15."

28. After a long debate over this issue the majority of the members of the Committee who participated expressed a clear preference for a comprehensive approach which would require any State becoming a party to the optional protocol to accept the relevant procedure in relation to all of the rights recognized in the Covenant. On the other hand, a strong minority favoured the adoption of a selective approach which would permit States to accept obligations only in relation to a specified range of rights. The minority considered that this could be achieved either through requiring States expressly to "opt out" of provisions that they would need to identify at the time of becoming a party to the protocol or through enabling them to "opt in" in relation to provisions which they would specify.

3. Protecting access to the procedure

29. A related issue concerns protection of the right to submit a complaint. The report submitted to the Committee at its fifteenth session put the issue in the following terms:

"It is appropriate to include a provision which not only affirms the right of an individual or group to submit a written communication alleging a violation of the rights recognized in the Covenant, but also obliges States parties to do whatever is necessary to enable potential complainants to submit communications. The importance of this aspect of a complaints procedure has consistently been highlighted by the Commission on Human Rights in a series of resolutions since 1990. Based on a report of the Secretary-General [E/CN.4/1994/42], the Commission, in its resolution 1994/70, requested the treaty bodies to take urgent steps, in conformity with their mandates, to help prevent the hampering of access to United Nations human rights procedures in any way. The Commission also urged Governments to refrain from all acts of intimidation or reprisal against, *inter alia*, those who submit or have submitted communications under procedures established by human rights instruments. It therefore seems appropriate for a specific provision of this nature to be included in the protocol."

30. The Committee agreed that such a provision should be included.
31. The proposed text of article 2, based on the decisions reflected in the preceding analysis, is:
    "1. Any individual or group claiming to be a victim of a violation by the State party concerned of any of the economic, social or cultural rights recognized in the Covenant, or any individual or group acting on behalf of such claimant(s), may submit a written communication to the Committee for examination.
    "2. States Parties to this Protocol undertake not to hinder in any way the effective exercise of the right to submit a communication and to take all steps necessary to prevent any persecution or sanctioning of any person or group submitting or seeking to submit a communication under this Protocol."

D. *Receivability and admissibility*

32. Bringing together the various provisions relating to receivability and admissibility within a single article of the draft protocol would seem to be the most convenient approach. For the most part, these various procedural rules are based directly upon the formulations used in the first Optional Protocol to the International Covenant on Civil and Political Rights. For the purposes of this draft they have been reorganized slightly but the wording remains almost identical in its key provisions.
33. The proposed text of article 3 is:
    "1. No communication shall be received by the Committee if it is anonymous or is directed at a State which is not a party to this Protocol.
    "2. The Committee shall declare a communication inadmissible if it:
       "(a) does not contain allegations which, if substantiated, would constitute a violation of rights recognized in the Covenant;
       "(b) constitutes an abuse of the right to submit a communication; or
       "(c) relates to acts and omissions which occurred before the entry into force of this Protocol for the State Party concerned, unless those acts or omissions:
          "(i) continue to constitute a violation of the Covenant after the entry into force of the Protocol for that State party; or
          "(ii) have effects which continue beyond the entry into force of this Protocol and those effects themselves appear to constitute a violation of a right recognized in the Covenant.
    "3. The Committee shall not declare a communication admissible unless it has ascertained:
       "(a) that all available domestic remedies have been exhausted; and
       "(b) that a communication submitted by or on behalf of the alleged victim which raises essentially the same issues of fact and law is not being examined under another procedure of international investigation or settlement. The Committee may, however, examine such a communication where the procedure of international investigation or settlement is unreasonably prolonged."

E. *Substantiation of complaints*

34. In any complaints procedure there is an onus placed upon the complainant to provide information which gives substance to the allegations that have been made. Moreover, it is appropriate to provide the Committee with the opportunity to re-examine a communication if new information is provided to it after it has already taken a decision to declare the communication inadmissible on the basis of its first examination.
35. The proposed text of article 4 is:
    "1. The Committee may decline to continue to examine a communication if the author, after being given a reasonable opportunity to do so, fails to provide information which would sufficiently substantiate the allegations contained in the communication.
    "2. The Committee may, upon the request of the author of the complaint,

recommence examination of a communication which it has declared inadmissible under article 3 if the circumstances which led to its decision have changed."

F. *Interim measures*

36. Although the first Optional Protocol to the International Covenant on Civil and Political Rights does not contain a specific provision dealing with interim measures, procedures which have been adopted subsequently by the Human Rights Committee have addressed this important issue. While the Committee does not consider it necessary or desirable to adopt a blanket provision which would apply in all cases, it considers it should be given the discretion, to be used in potentially serious cases involving the possibility of irreparable harm, to request that interim measures be taken.
37. The proposed text of article 5 is:

"If at any time after the receipt of a communication, and before a determination on the merits has been reached, a preliminary study gives rise to a reasonable apprehension that the allegations, if substantiated, could lead to irreparable harm, the Committee may request the State Party concerned to take such interim measures as may be necessary to avoid such irreparable harm."

G. *Reference to State party and friendly settlement*

38. The great majority of communications procedures provide for the possibility of reaching a friendly settlement with the State party concerned. Particularly in view of the nature of economic, social and cultural rights, it would seem especially appropriate to provide for a procedure of friendly settlement in the draft protocol. For this purpose the Committee would specifically indicate its preparedness to facilitate such a settlement, provided only that the resulting arrangement is based upon respect for the rights and obligations contained in the Covenant.
39. Another matter is whether to include a provision comparable to that contained in the International Convention on the Elimination of All Forms of Racial Discrimination (art. 14 (6)(a)) according to which "the identity of the individual or groups of individuals concerned shall not be revealed without his or their express consent". In the view of the Committee the possible need to protect the identity of the alleged victim(s) is a matter best taken care of in the relevant rules of procedure.
40. The other matter in this regard is the setting of a time-limit within which a State must respond to information received from the Committee. The first Optional Protocol to the International Covenant on Civil and Political Rights provides for a period of six months. Consideration was given in the Committee's earlier deliberations to setting a time-limit of three months. It was suggested that that would be conducive to achieving a prompt and equitable solution. The ILO and other sources made it clear, however, that three months would, in their experience, be too short a time for Governments to respond. The Committee therefore recommends that six months be retained.

41. The proposed text of article 6 is:
    "1. Unless the Committee considers that a communication should be declared inadmissible without reference to the State party concerned, the Committee shall confidentially bring to the attention of the State party any communication referred to it under this Protocol.
    "2. Within six months, the receiving State shall submit to the Committee explanations or statements and the remedy, if any, that may have been afforded by that State.
    "3. During its examination of a communication, the Committee shall place itself at the disposal of the parties concerned with a view to facilitating settlement of the matter on the basis of respect for the rights and obligations set forth in the Covenant.
    "4. If a settlement is reached, the Committee shall prepare a report containing a statement of the facts and of the solution reached."

H. *Examination of communications*

42. The first Optional Protocol to the International Covenant on Civil and Political Rights specifies that the Committee shall base itself upon "all written information made available to it by the individual and by the State Party concerned" (art. 5(1)). In practice this is a generous provision since it does not exclude information from any source provided only that it is specifically submitted by one party or the other. Nevertheless, it seems unduly restrictive and counterproductive for the Committee not to be able to take into account information which it has obtained for itself from other sources. The Committee recommends the inclusion of authorization for such action to be undertaken by it, on condition that any such information would also be provided to the parties concerned for comment.
43. Article 5 of the first Optional Protocol to the International Covenant on Civil and Political Rights does not specify the procedures to be used by the Committee in examining communications, other than to state that its consideration shall take place in closed meetings. It is unnecessary for the draft protocol to be any more detailed and it would seem to be sufficient to indicate that the Committee is empowered to adopt its own procedures for the consideration of communications and that such consideration should take place in private session. The only significant additional element recommended by the Committee concerns including the possibility of a visit to the territory of a State party as part of the Committee's examination of a communication. By providing such an option, to be employed only if the State party concerned wishes to exercise it, the procedure would have the flexibility required to enable the Committee, in cooperation with the State party, to tailor the best approach under the circumstances.
44. It is also proposed to indicate that the final views of the Committee will be made public at the same time as they are communicated to the parties directly involved. This is consistent with the existing practice of the Human Rights Committee.
45. The proposed text of article 7 is:
    "1. The Committee shall examine communications received under this Protocol in the light of all information made available to it by or on

behalf of the author in accordance with paragraph 2, and by the State party concerned. The Committee may also take into account information obtained from other sources, provided that this information is transmitted to the parties concerned for comment.

"2. The Committee may adopt such procedures as will enable it to ascertain the facts and to assess the extent to which the State party concerned has fulfilled its obligations under the Covenant.

"3. As part of its examination of a communication, the Committee may, with the agreement of the State Party concerned, visit the territory of that State Party.

"4. The Committee shall hold closed meetings when examining communications under this Protocol.

"5. After examining a communication, the Committee shall adopt its views on the claims made in the communication and shall transmit these to the State party and to the author, together with any recommendations it considers appropriate. The views shall be made public at the same time."

I. *Results of examination*

46. While the first Optional Protocol to the International Covenant on Civil and Political Rights provides only that the Committee shall forward its views to the two concerned parties, the practice of the Human Rights Committee, as well as of other comparable complaints procedures, has developed very significantly in recent years in relation to the various follow-up procedures. It would therefore seem appropriate in drafting a protocol in the late 1990s to be more specific as to the recommendations that the Committee might make with a view to remedying any violation which it has identified. This approach would be entirely consistent with the importance attached by the International Covenant on Civil and Political Rights to the provision of an appropriate remedy for violations, and with the approach proposed in the study prepared for the Sub-Commission on Prevention of Discrimination and Protection of Minorities concerning "the right to restitution, compensation and rehabilitation for victims of gross violations of human rights and fundamental freedoms" (E/CN.4/Sub.2/1993/8).

47. Following the Committee's discussions, it is not recommended, however, to include a provision which would expressly obligate the State party concerned to implement the Committee's recommendations, to provide an appropriate remedy or to ensure the provision of adequate compensation where appropriate. While there is much to be said in policy terms for such measures, it is correct, as pointed out during the debates, that making such measures legally mandatory would transform the nature of the procedure from a quasi-judicial to a judicial one. In the latter case, more complex procedures in general would be necessary, including a greater variety of procedural safeguards for the parties concerned.

48. In paragraph 2 it is proposed to extend the relevant time-limit to six months for the same reasons cited in relation to article 6(2) in paragraph 40 above.

49. The proposed text of article 8 is:

"1. Where the Committee is of the view that a State Party has violated its obligations under the Covenant, the Committee may recommend that the State Party take specific measures to remedy the violation and to prevent its recurrence.

"2. The State Party concerned shall, within six months of receiving notice of the decision of the Committee under paragraph 1, or such longer period as may be specified by the Committee, provide the Committee with details of the measures which it has taken in accordance with paragraph 1 above."

J. *Follow-up procedures*

50. Once again, while the first Optional Protocol to the International Covenant on Civil and Political Rights does not spell out the procedures which will be used in relation to following up on the adoption of views in particular cases, the Human Rights Committee has developed an extensive procedure for this purpose. The Committee therefore recommends that such a procedure be reflected in the provisions contained in the proposed draft protocol.

51. The proposed text of article 9 is:

"1. The Committee may invite a State Party to discuss with it, at a mutually convenient time, the measures which the State Party has taken to give effect to the views or recommendations of the Committee.

"2. The Committee may invite the State Party concerned to include in its reports under article 17 of the Covenant details of any measures taken in response to the Committee's views and recommendations.

"3. The Committee shall include in its annual report an account of the substance of the communication and its examination of the matter, a summary of the explanations and statements of the State Party concerned, of its own views and recommendations, and the response of the State Party concerned to those views and recommendations."

K. *Rules of procedure, servicing, etc.*

52. In view of the fact that the text of the Covenant itself does not contain specific provisions relating to the adoption of rules of procedure, the meetings of the Committee or the responsibility of the Secretary-General for the servicing of the Committee, it is recommended that this lack be remedied in relation to the communications procedure provided for in the draft protocol. The Committee therefore proposes provisions comparable to those contained in other major human rights treaties.

53. The proposed text of article 10 is:

"The Committee may make rules of procedure prescribing the procedure to be followed when it is exercising the functions conferred on it by this Protocol."

54. The proposed text of article 11 is:

"1. The Committee shall meet for such period as is necessary to carry out its functions under this Protocol.

"2. The Secretary-General of the United Nations shall provide the

Committee with the necessary staff, facilities and finances for the performance of its functions under this Protocol, and in particular shall ensure that expert legal advice is available to the Committee for this purpose."

L. Final articles

55. For the most part, the final articles recommended for inclusion in the present draft protocol follow closely those already contained in the first Optional Protocol to the International Covenant on Civil and Political Rights. Changes have been made only where this would seem necessary or appropriate for an instrument which may be adopted in the late 1990s rather than in 1966. In particular, the provisions requiring the Secretary-General to circulate the various documents and other information would seem to be superfluous today in view of the regular notification of States parties of all such developments.
56. The proposed text of the final articles is reproduced below. No commentary is offered at this stage in view of the fact that they are reasonably self-explanatory and that the Commission will need to resolve the more substantive matters dealt with in the earlier articles before finalizing these provisions.
57. The Committee discussed at some length the question of whether reservations to the optional protocol should be permitted or excluded, or whether the protocol should be silent in relation to that matter. The Committee agreed to recommend that it would be appropriate for the Commission to consider providing for the lodging of reservations if it opts for a comprehensive approach in relation to the range of rights, as described in paragraph 28 above.
58. The proposed text of the final articles is:

"Article 12

"1. This Protocol is open for signature by any State Party to the Covenant.
"2. This Protocol is subject to ratification or accession by any State Party to the Covenant. Instruments of ratification or accession shall be deposited with the Secretary-General of the United Nations.

"Article 13

"1. This Protocol shall enter into force three months after the date of the deposit with the Secretary-General of the United Nations of the fifth instrument of ratification or accession.
"2. For each State ratifying this Protocol or acceding to it after its entry into force, this Protocol shall enter into force three months after the date of the deposit of its own instrument of ratification or accession.

"Article 14

"1. This Protocol will be binding upon each State Party in respect of all territories subject to its jurisdiction.
"2. The provisions of this Protocol shall extend to all parts of federal States without any limitations or exceptions.

"*Article 15*

"1. Any State Party to this Protocol may propose an amendment and file it with the Secretary-General of the United Nations. The Secretary-General shall thereupon communicate any proposed amendments to the States Parties to this Protocol with the request that they notify him or her whether they favour a conference of State Parties for the purpose of considering and voting upon the proposal. If within four months from the date of such communication at least one third of the States Parties favour such a conference, the Secretary-General shall convene such a conference under the auspices of the United Nations. Any amendment adopted by majority of the State parties present and voting at the conference shall be submitted to the General Assembly of the United Nations for approval.
"2. Amendments shall come into force when they have been approved by the General Assembly of the United Nations and accepted by a two-thirds majority of the States Parties to this Protocol in accordance with their respective constitutional processes.
"3. When amendments come into force, they shall be binding on those States Parties which have accepted them, other States Parties still being bound by the provisions of this Protocol and any earlier amendment which they have accepted.

"*Article 16*

"1. Any State Party may denounce this Protocol at any time by written notification addressed to the Secretary-General of the United Nations. Denunciation shall take effect one year after the date of receipt of the notification by the Secretary-General.
"2. Denunciations shall be without prejudice to the continued application of
"3. Following the date at which the denunciation of a State Party becomes effective, the Committee shall not commence consideration of any new matters regarding that State.

"*Article 17*

"This Protocol, of which the Arabic, Chinese, English, French, Russian and Spanish texts are equally authentic, shall be deposited in the archives of the United Nations."

E/CN.4/2000/58 — 2 December 1999

COMMISSION ON HUMAN RIGHTS
Fifty-sixth session

CIVIL AND POLITICAL RIGHTS, INCLUDING THE QUESTIONS OF TORTURE AND DETENTION

Report of the Working Group on the Draft Optional Protocol to the Convention Against Torture and Other Cruel, Inhuman or Degrading Treatment or Punishment on its eighth session

Chairman-Rapporteur: Ms. Elizabeth Odio Benito (Costa Rica)

CONTENTS

	Paragraphs
Introduction	1–2
I. ORGANIZATION OF THE SESSION	3–16
A. Opening of the session and election of officers	3–4
B. Attendance	5–9
C. Documentation	10
D. Organization of work	11–16
II. GENERAL DISCUSSION	17–53
A. Prevention mechanism	17–23
B. Dialogue and cooperation between the Subcommittee and States parties	24–34
C. Different aspects of cooperation and framework of cooperation	35–50
D. Proposals for future work	51–53
III. CONSIDERATION AND DRAFTING OF PARAGRAPHS AND ARTICLES OF THE DRAFT OPTIONAL PROTOCOL	54–73
A. Preamble and articles 1, 8, 12 and 13	54–61
B. Particular views expressed by some delegations	62–73
IV. FUTURE WORK	74–76
V. ADOPTION OF THE REPORT	77

A.F. Bayefsky (ed.), *The UN Human Rights Treaty System in the 21st Century*, 490–512.
© 2000 Kluwer Law International. Printed in Great Britain.

ANNEXES

I. Text of the articles which constitute the outcome of the second reading at the fifth, sixth and seventh sessions
II. Text of the articles which constitute the basis for future work

Introduction

1. The Commission on Human Rights, in its resolution 1999/30, took note of the report of the working group on the draft optional protocol to the Convention against Torture and Other Cruel, Inhuman or Degrading Treatment or Punishment (E/CN.4/1999/59 and Add.1) and requested the working group, in order to continue its work, to meet prior to the fifty-sixth session of the Commission for a period of two weeks, with a view to completing expeditiously a final and substantive text, and to report to the Commission at its fifty-sixth session.
2. The Economic and Social Council, in its decision 1999/237, authorized an open-ended working group of the Commission to meet for a period of two weeks prior to its fifty-sixth session.

I. ORGANIZATON OF THE SESSION

A. *Opening of the session and election of officers*

3. The working group held its eighth session from 4 to 15 October 1999. It was opened by the United Nations High Commissioner for Human Rights, Ms. Mary Robinson, who made an introductory statement.
4. At its first meeting, on 4 October 1999, the working group elected Ms. Elizabeth Odio Benito (Costa Rica) as Chairman-Rapporteur.

B. *Attendance*

5. Representatives of the following States members of the Commission on Human Rights attended the meetings of the working group, which were open to all members of the Commission: Argentina, Austria, Canada, China, Colombia, Cuba, Ecuador, El Salvador, France, Germany, Guatemala, Ireland, Italy, Japan, Mexico, Morocco, Norway, Poland, Republic of Korea, Russian Federation, South Africa, United Kingdom of Great Britain and Northern Ireland, United States of America, Uruguay and Venezuela.
6. The following States non-members of the Commission on Human Rights were represented by observers at the meetings of the working group: Algeria, Australia, Bahrain, Belgium, Brazil, Bulgaria, Costa Rica, Croatia, Denmark, Egypt, Estonia, Finland, Georgia, Hungary, Iran (Islamic Republic of), Lithuania, Netherlands, Slovakia, Spain, Sweden, Saudi Arabia, Syrian Arab Republic, Turkey and Ukraine.
7. The Holy See and Switzerland were also represented by observers.
8. The International Committee of the Red Cross and the following non-governmental organizations were represented by observers at the meetings of the

working group: Amnesty International, Association for the Prevention of Torture, International Federation of ACAT (Action of Christians for the Abolition of Torture) and Human Rights Watch.
9. The Committee against Torture was represented by an observer.

C. *Documentation*

10. The working group had before it the following texts and documents:

E/CN.4/1999/WG.11/1	Provisional agenda
E/CN.4/1999/59 and Add.1	Report of the working group on its seventh session
E/CN.4/1999/WG.11/WP.1	Working paper submitted by the secretariat
E/CN.4/1998/42 and Corr.1	Report of the working group on its sixth session
E/CN.4/1997/33	Report of the working group on its fifth session
E/CN.4/1996/28 and Corr.1	Report of the working group on its fourth session
E/CN.4/1991/66	Letter dated 15 January 1991 from the Permanent Representative of Costa Rica to the United Nations Office at Geneva addressed to the Under-Secretary-General for Human Rights

D. *Organization of work*

11. At its first meeting, on 4 October 1999, the working group adopted its agenda as contained in document E/CN.4/1999/WG.11/1.
12. At the same meeting, the working group agreed with the proposal of the Chairman-Rapporteur to hold, during the first week of its session, a general discussion on the following issues:
    (a) Prevention mechanism: the protocol as a preventive and not a punitive instrument;
    (b) Dialogue and cooperation between the Subcommittee and States parties as the main principles of the protocol;
    (c) Different aspects of cooperation:
        (i) Confidentiality and standing invitations to the Subcommittee;
        (ii) Cooperation of States parties with the Subcommittee in the course of missions and visits;
        (iii) Cooperation between the Subcommittee and States parties to implement recommendations of the Subcommittee;
    (d) Framework of cooperation:
        (i) Different missions;
        (ii) Modalities;
        (iii) Places to visit;
        (iv) Organization and conduct of missions;
        (v) Follow-up (reports and recommendations);
        (vi) Follow-up visits;
    (e) Proposals for future work.

13. The working group also considered it appropriate that this general discussion be linked to texts of articles of the draft optional protocol proposed at previous sessions.
14. At the eighth meeting, on 7 October 1999, the working group decided, with regard to organizing its work on the consideration and drafting of various articles of the optional protocol during the second week of the session, to alternate, as needed, informal discussions with plenary meetings. Subsequently, a small drafting group was set up to speed up the drafting process (see also paragraph 50 below).
15. At its seventh meeting on 7 October 1999, at the request of the working group, the observer for the Association for the Prevention of Torture informed the participants about the contents and results of the discussion at the workshop entitled "Visits under international law: verification, monitoring and prevention". The workshop had been organized by the Association for the Prevention of Torture in cooperation with the Verification Research, Training and Information Centre (VERTIC), the International Commission of Jurists, the Quakers United Nations Office and the Foundation for International Environmental Law (FIELD) and held at Geneva on 23 and 24 September 1999. The objective of the workshop was to explore and discuss the subject of visits and missions as emerging standards of preventive, monitoring and verification procedures in international law, including human rights law. It provided a broad overview of the subject and explored similarities and differences between the experiences from different fields of international law (environmental law, human rights, humanitarian law and disarmament).
16. At the ninth meeting, on 12 October 1999, the observer for the Committee against Torture addressed the working group. He made comments on some of the new proposals relating to draft article 1 which the working group had before it and answered the questions put by participants regarding various aspects of the work of the Committee against Torture and the European Committee for the Prevention of Torture and Inhuman or Degrading Treatment or Punishment (CPT).

II. GENERAL DISCUSSION

A. *Prevention mechanism*

17. At the first and second plenary meetings, on 4 October 1999, the working group discussed the issue of the optional protocol as an instrument of prevention. The discussion was held with reference to the preamble, article 3 (confidentiality) and article 18 (reservations) of the draft optional protocol (see E/CN.4/1997/33, annex I; E/CN.4/1996/28, annex I).
18. It was generally felt that the optional protocol would have a preventive rather than punitive character since its goal was not to sanction but to create an effective system of preventive visits in order to help States parties to improve the protection of persons deprived of their liberty. Prevention, cooperation and confidentiality were referred to as fundamental principles to achieve the main goals of the optional protocol.
19. With regard to confidentiality, several delegations considered this element

to be a modus operandi; a methodology to be used in the implementation of the optional protocol. They felt that observing confidentiality was not an end in itself but a tool to facilitate confidence and to ensure that States would cooperate. Confidentiality was therefore important but not a core issue. According to another view shared by several delegations, confidentiality was one of the important principles on which the optional protocol was based and which could promote its acceptability by States. Reference was made in this connection to article 3(3) stating that the principle of confidentiality was one of the guiding principles for the Subcommittee. The Chairman-Rapporteur subsequently proposed to consider confidentiality as a principle having a complementary, facilitating function; she also proposed that a reference to confidentiality, as well as to the principle of cooperation, be included in the preambular part of the optional protocol.

20. On the issue of reservations, several delegations felt that the text of the draft optional protocol should include the possibility of making reservations. It was argued that in accordance with the Vienna Convention on the Law of Treaties, any legal instrument could allow reservations. Since the optional protocol contained not only procedural but also substantive provisions imposing obligations on States parties, they should be entitled to make reservations. A reference was made to the Second Protocol to the Hague Convention of 1954 on the Protection of Cultural Property in the Event of Armed Conflict which was adopted in March 1999 and which does allow reservations. It was also pointed out that the possibility of making reservations would guarantee wider acceptance of the optional protocol. Alternatively it was proposed that those articles or concepts on which reservations would not be allowed be mentioned in the text of the optional protocol.

21. Another view, shared by several speakers, held that reservations could undermine the whole purpose of the optional protocol and the impartial functioning of its monitoring mechanism. It was crucial that no reservations to the optional protocol be allowed. It was also pointed out that draft article 13 already contained a "negotiated reservation" and that other(s) could be discussed if necessary. A reference was made to the Statute of the International Criminal Court which does not allow any reservations. Some delegations considered that since the optional protocol was to be mainly institutional and procedural, it would be illogical to permit reservations to it.

22. The Chairman-Reporter concluded that in the absence of consensus, further discussion was needed on the issue of reservations.

23. As part of the effort to prevent torture, it was important to provide technical assistance to developing countries in the training of relevant personnel at places of detention. It was proposed to include a reference to such international assistance and cooperation in article 17 relating to the establishment of a special fund for such a purpose (see E/CN.4/1999/59, annex I). In this regard, it was also proposed to use as a model the wording of article 2 of the International Covenant on Economic, Social and Cultural Rights.

B. *Dialogue and cooperation between the Subcommittee and States parties*

24. At the third plenary meeting, on 5 October 1999, the working group held a discussion on the issue of dialogue and cooperation between the Subcommittee and States parties as the main principles of the optional

protocol. Articles 1 (purpose and scope of the protocol) and 8 (types of missions and their notification) were considered to be of direct relevance to this discussion (see E/CN.4.1998/42, annex II).

25. There was general support for the statement that dialogue and cooperation were essential to ensuring the effectiveness of the optional protocol. It was emphasized that international cooperation and technical assistance were needed in order to improve conditions in prisons and other places of detention, in particular in developing countries; this was to be financed by the special fund envisaged in article 17, referred to in paragraph 23 above. It was felt appropriate to include in the text of the optional protocol the idea of a State-to-State dimension of such international cooperation.

26. With regard to draft article 1 and related issues, the following main questions were raised.

27. The view was expressed that the wording of article 1(1) permitting visits to any place in any territory under a State party's jurisdiction might lead to a conflict of law or have a potential impact on non-State parties, particularly in cases when access would be sought to diplomatic missions or foreign military installations. In this connection, it was pointed out that article 2 of the European Convention for the Prevention of Torture and Inhuman or Degrading Treatment or Punishment also refers to any place within a State party's jurisdiction and that no exceptions were made to this provision nor had any problems been encountered in its implementation.

28. According to another opinion, visits "to any place" could not in practice be permitted because they might infringe some existing domestic regulations, or might conflict with national security concerns in general. In this regard, it was argued that if national security concerns were to be invoked, this should be done in the context of visits by the Subcommittee rather than in the context of article 1.

29. It was also felt by some delegations that the meaning of the phrase "at its instigation or with its consent or acquiescence" in article 1(1) was not clear enough since it could have a bearing on the categories of places to be open to visits. It was also suggested that this wording should be deleted because it provided wide scope for controversy in its interpretation. Others pointed out that this was the wording used in article 1 of the Convention against Torture.

30. Several delegations found that the notion of places where the persons deprived of their liberty "may be held" as stated in article 1(1) was too broad and imprecise. Other speakers supported this wording and argued that in order to prevent torture, visits to all de facto places of detention should be allowed. Other delegations noted that the words were derived from article 1 of the Convention against Torture and argued that the optional protocol should not have a narrower scope than the Convention. An analysis was also offered that the notion of "may be held" would cover not only de facto places of detention but also places intended to serve as places of detention, such as prisons under construction.

31. With regard to the places that could be visited by the Subcommittee, a question was raised as to whether this referred only to those affiliated with the Government or also to those that were privately owned. The view was expressed that the links to acts or orders of public authorities should in all cases be clearly established.

32. With regard to the formula "in accordance with applicable international law and relevant international standards", as contained in article 1(2), it was suggested that specific references should be added in the text to make national obligations more clear. A view was also expressed that the notion of "international standards" was undefined and problematic in application and should therefore be deleted. Another proposal was to replace this wording with "applicable international instruments and international law". Other delegations found the formula used in article 1(2) sufficiently clear and therefore fully acceptable. In their view, relevant international standards included both binding (universal and regional) instruments as well as pertinent recommendatory documents ("soft law").

33. On the issue of periodic and other missions as envisaged in article 8(1), some delegations expressed concern with regard to a lack of precision as to the grounds on which such ad hoc visits could take place. It was also pointed out that the obligation of States to accept visits which were "triggered" by allegations of torture had to be in line with their constitutional provisions protecting privacy and private property.

34. The scope of application suggested in draft articles 1 and 8 was found by some speakers to be wider than the corresponding standards of the European Convention for the Prevention of Torture. The view was expressed that the optional protocol could not go beyond the standards of the European Convention. It was also pointed out that in some developing countries resources might not be available to implement higher standards. Other speakers disagreed and insisted that it should be possible to establish new and improved standards in a new legal document.

C. Different aspects of cooperating and framework of cooperation

35. At the 4th, 5th and 6th meetings, on 5 and 6 October 1999, the working group discussed different aspects and the framework of cooperation with reference to articles 1 and 8 (see above), 12 (modalities of conducting a mission and visits – see E/CN.4/1996/28, annex I), 13 (exceptional circumstances in which a visit could be postponed – see E/CN.4/1999/59), annex II) and 14 (reporting and publicity – see E/CN.4/1996/28, annex I).

36. In this connection, the following main issues were discussed:
    (a) Whether the ratification of the protocol by a State party implied that a standing invitation was extended to the Subcommittee or whether the Subcommittee should receive prior consent from the State party before each mission (arts. 1 and 8);
    (b) Cooperation between the Subcommittee and the State party during a mission (art. 12);
    (c) Exceptional circumstances in which a visit could be postponed (art. 13);
    (d) Reporting and publicity (art. 14).

37. No agreement was reached in the working group on the first issue. The view was expressed that the principle of a standing invitation was necessary for the efficacy of the optional protocol. If the Subcommittee were to be obligated to enter into long negotiations with States parties prior to missions, it would have negative implications on the efficiency and the continuity of the Subcommittee's activities. It was emphasized that in the absence of a standing

invitation, the optional protocol would bring no or limited added value to the Convention since article 20 of the Convention already allows the Committee against Torture to undertake confidential missions with the prior consent of the State party. Further, in view of earlier discussions on the subject, several delegations added that the principle of a standing invitation was in full conformity with the principle of national sovereignty, since the ratification of the protocol was optional and since the decision to ratify was itself an act of national sovereignty. It was also pointed out that standing invitations were a sign of continuity and long-term cooperation and favoured constructive dialogue with States.

38. Other delegations expressed the opinion that in view of the broad scope of draft article 1 in terms of the places and territories the Subcommittee was to be allowed to visit, a standing invitation would basically enable the Subcommittee to go anywhere at any time. Such far-reaching competence would be an infringement on the sovereignty of States and thus unacceptable. The concern was also expressed that including a standing invitation in the optional protocol would result in it being ratified by very few States.

39. Several speakers mentioned the possibility of having different standards relating to different types of missions, i.e. standing invitations for regular missions and another standard if the mission was occasioned by special circumstances and/or allegations of torture.

40. On the second issue, the working group concentrated on the scope of the cooperation envisaged between the States parties and the Subcommittee. Some delegations pointed out that their constitutional requirements and/or their national legislation, in particular on the right to privacy and private property, safety requirements, witness protection, etc., could prevent them from giving the Subcommittee free access to all types of information or places. Restrictions in national legislation could also limit the possibility of the Subcommittee to require testimony from detained persons or to interview prisoners "without witnesses".

41. It was emphasized by some delegations that it was a prerequisite to establish a framework for the normal work of the Subcommittee, including such elements as freedom of movement and access to all relevant information, places and persons.

42. On the third issue, it was strongly felt that representations against visits should be strictly limited, and only made for urgent and compelling reasons, which should be narrowly defined in the text; the general rule should be unhindered access for the Subcommittee. It was also suggested that any such representations should lead only to the postponement of a visit, not its cancellation.

43. Additional grounds for postponing a visit were proposed by some speakers, including the urgent interrogation of persons to be visited and the health problems of such persons. It was pointed out, with regard to the former, that under article 9 of the European Convention for the Prevention of Torture, urgent interrogation could only be an acceptable excuse when it was actually in progress, but not in relation to the whole process of criminal investigation. Doubts were also expressed concerning the acceptability of health problems as a valid ground for refusing access to the person in question. It was pointed out in this regard that as a result of torture or

other cruel treatment or punishment, such persons were normally in very bad physical condition.

44. On the fourth issue, relating to the nature and implementation of recommendations, there was a general discussion on whether article 14 should basically be of a technical nature. It was proposed that two types of recommendations could normally be addressed to States parties by the Subcommittee: (a) those for more or less speedy implementation by the States parties themselves; and (b) those which were supposed to be progressively implemented by the States parties through technical assistance and cooperation financed by the special fund to be set up pursuant to article 17. The improvement of national legislation or the reform of penitentiary systems were mentioned as examples of the second type of recommendation. It was felt that the concept of technical assistance and cooperation should be duly highlighted in article 14.

45. According to another opinion, shared by some delegations, the missions of the Subcommittee should be of short duration (a few days only); the Subcommittee should comply with the principle of non-interference with the domestic affairs of States and its recommendations should be technical, realistic (feasible) and objective. Thus, recommendations should not relate to such issues as the penalty to be imposed or to substantive matters of national legislation which are exclusively within the sovereign competence of States. It was emphasized that in no case should the Subcommittee be acting as a supranational body.

46. On the question of public statements by the Subcommittee or the publication of its reports, it was widely felt that such "going public" would be an exceptional measure; the reports would normally be confidential unless the State concerned manifestly refused to cooperate.

47. While a public statement by the Subcommittee as a last resort in cases of a failure or refusal to cooperate was acceptable to many speakers, a view was expressed that this provision of draft article 14 still needed precision and that major amendments had to be made. Particular emphasis was placed on the need to arrive at a definition of the concept of the "failure to cooperate" or to identify the specific circumstances of non-cooperation and to determine who was to decide whether a State had been cooperative or not, and how this determination was to be made.

48. The view was expressed that the public statement and the publication of a report should not be seen as a punishment. In this regard, it was felt that according to the draft provision concerned, it was up to the Subcommittee to judge whether a State was cooperative or not and consequently to decide whether to publicize or not. It was argued that the Subcommittee would therefore become a de facto arbitrator and that this was incompatible with the nature of the Subcommittee and the optional protocol.

49. With reference to the question of publishing the reports of the Subcommittee, several delegations considered of particular importance the provision of article 14(5) stating that no personal data should be published without the express consent of the person concerned.

50. Other issues raised in connection with article 14 included the contents of the reports of the Subcommittee; the feasibility of implementing its recommendations; the relationship between the Subcommittee and the Committee against Torture; the time-frame for the (progressive) implementation of the

recommendations of the Subcommittee; and the question of how the special fund to be established under article 17 would be informed of the Subcommittee's recommendations.

D. *Proposals for future work*

51. At the seventh and eighth meetings, on 7 October 1999, the working group discussed the organization of its work during the second week of the session. It was decided to set up three "baskets" of issues on which drafting would continue on the basis of the texts proposed during previous sessions and any new proposals received. The first basket contained the preambular part and articles 1, 8, 12 and 13. The second basket contained article 18, and the third basket was composed of articles 14, 16 and 17. Delegations wishing to present new or modified texts were requested to submit them in writing before the established deadline.

52. The written contributions received from the delegations of Australia, Canada, Egypt (also on behalf of Algeria, China, Cuba, Saudi Arabia, the Sudan and the Syrian Arab Republic) and Japan were before the working group on 11 October 1999 when it met in informal session and began its consideration and drafting of articles relating to the first basket of issues. A small drafting group consisting of authors or coordinators of written contributions as well as other interested delegations was established to speed up the drafting process.

53. In the course of informal meetings held on 12, 13 and 14 October 1999, the working group discussed the preliminary texts of the preamble and some of the articles relating to the first basket of issues which were prepared by the drafting group.

III. CONSIDERATION AND DRAFTING OF PARAGRAPHS AND ARTICLES OF THE DRAFT OPTIONAL PROTOCOL

A. *Preamble and articles 1, 8, 12 and 13*

54. At the tenth plenary meeting, on 14 October 1999, the working group had before it the consolidated texts of various proposals relating to the preamble and articles, 8, 12 and 13 as submitted by the informal drafting group (see annex II).

55. In introducing the proposals on behalf of the drafting group, the observer for Australia explained that disagreements which could not be resolved in the group were reflected in square brackets in the text. He pointed out that some delegations took the view that articles 8, 12 and 13 should only refer to visits and that a distinction between missions and visits should not be maintained in the text. Other delegations noted that the working group had already adopted a number of articles (e.g. art. 11) which reflected a distinction between missions and visits, a concept found in the first draft of the optional protocol (E/CN.4/1991/66). No agreement could therefore be reached on this issue, and the words "missions" and "visits" appeared as alternatives within brackets in draft articles 8, 12 and 13. The observer for Australia felt

that this problem might be solved once the concerned delegations had had the time to review the implications of the distinction.
56. With regard to article 13, the observer for Australia indicated that many delegations agreed that this article should apply only to particular visits in the context of a mission to a country. The text reproduced in paragraph 66 of the report of the working group on its last session (E/CN.4/1999/59) was referred to in this regard. Other delegations argued that article 13 should apply to a mission to a country and not just to a visit which comprised part of a mission to a particular country, i.e. a decision whether to go to a country at all. Views were divided as to whether the grounds for postponing a visit contained in article 13(1) should be limited to the grounds found in the European Convention for the Prevention of Torture. Some delegations argued that "the medical condition of a person" should not be included as a ground for postponement. In article 13(2), a reference to transferring a person to be visited to another place was considered to be redundant given the reference to "arrangements to enable the Committee to exercise its functions" and therefore was deleted.
57. With regard to article 8, the observer for Australia explained that the draft text included in brackets the proposal of one group of countries for the optional protocol to provide only for regular and not follow-up or ad hoc visits. In paragraph 1 (b), the term "reliable information" had been incorporated so as to be consistent with the language used in the Convention against Torture and the Convention on the Elimination of All Forms of Discrimination against Women. Some delegations argued that the Subcommittee, in making a notification under paragraph 2(a), should be required to include a definitive list of places to be visited. Other delegations argued that this was too restrictive and that it might be appropriate for the Subcommittee, e.g. in relation to a regular mission, first to send a notification which would propose timing, with more details to be worked out during the period of consultation leading up to the mission. It was also explained that the words ["six months"] in paragraph 3(a) reflected the view of some delegations that: (i) a maximum time-limit should be imposed for the carrying out of a visit/mission beginning at the time of the notification so that a notification was not left without being acted upon; and (ii) a minimum period of prior notification should be required before any mission/visit took place. Many other delegations held the view that the protocol should not prescribe in detail the operating rules of the Subcommittee. The observer for Australia also pointed out that there was no agreement on the prior consent requirement contained in bracketed paragraph 2(b).
58. In connection with article 12, it was explained that the first paragraph reflected closely the language found in draft article 12 as reproduced in paragraph 20 of the report of the working group on its last session (E/CN.4/1999/59). The drafting group ran out of time before it could fully consider the issue of whether an article X on national legislation should be included in the protocol and, if included, what content it should have. Some delegations insisted that if an article X on national legislation were included in the protocol, they might be able to accept article 12(1) as drafted. Other delegations indicated that they opposed a separate article X on national legislation and, depending on the final form of paragraph 2 of article 12,

they might be able to accept paragraph 1 as drafted. A number of other delegations stated that they could not accept at all a separate article X on national legislation as it would undermine the objectives of the protocol. All delegations agreed that paragraph 2 of article 12 required further development. In light of these divergent views the whole of article 12 was put in square brackets. In addition, the whole text of article X was also put in brackets.

59. With regard to the preamble, the observer for Australia noted that views were divided on whether to include the term "detained" or "deprived of their liberty". Many delegations pointed out that the term "deprived of their liberty" was more commonly used in the human rights arena and that the term "detained" could be too narrow. He also pointed out that there was no agreement on whether to include paragraph 3 of article 1. A number of delegations felt that the issues covered in that paragraph would be more appropriately addressed in article 13. Many delegations also expressed the view that the language of paragraph 3, if accepted, would provide for an excessively wide exclusion to the scope of the protocol.

60. The representative of Cuba suggested, with regard to article 8(1)(b), that the concept of "reliable information" should be given further consideration to make it clearer by establishing precise criteria.

61. Following the proposal by the Chairman-Rapporteur, the working group agreed to include the text of the preamble and articles 1, 8, 12 and 13 as submitted to the plenary by the drafting group in annex II to the report of the working group to serve as a basis for future discussion.

B. *Particular views expressed by some delegations*

62. At the same meeting, several delegations expressed their particular views on the first basket of articles and related issues. These are given below.

63. The representative of Cuba, speaking also on behalf of the delegations of Algeria, China, Egypt, Saudi Arabia, the Sudan and the Syrian Arab Republic, made a joint statement on their position paper submitted to the Chair regarding the preamble and articles 1, 8, 12, 13 and X. They stated that starting from the preamble the content of the draft protocol should reflect clearly its cooperative, preventive, confidential, non-duplicative and advisory nature. It was also stated that it was possible to balance the sovereignty and legitimate concerns of States and the effectiveness of the protocol through the prior consent of the State to a visit. In this connection, the words "may" and "any place", as well as "deprived of their liberty", were too wide, controversial and undefined, and raised many problems relating to national security and domestic affairs.

64. Regarding the visits, the above delegations emphasized that while defining the word "visits", the protocol should be based on non-discriminatory regular visits to all States parties, avoiding any possibility of selectivity. They also pointed out that paragraph 1 of article 12 might be acceptable on the understanding that there would be an article X on national legislation. They underlined that the objections mentioned in article 13 were to be decided by the State party and should apply to a particular part of a visit but also, as appropriate, to a whole visit.

65. The representative of China, referring to the question of "visits" and "missions", stated that since the drafting process had been conducted in English only, the interpretation of those terms in other languages might appear to be quite different. Therefore, he felt it advisable to use one term only to avoid possible controversies in the future. He also reaffirmed the importance which his delegation attached to the provision that all missions or visits should be conducted only with the prior consent of the State concerned.
66. The representative of China also reiterated the importance of referring to national legislation in the optional protocol and recalled the understanding reached on this issue last year according to which article 12 had a close relationship with article X dealing with national legislation.
67. The observer for Denmark stated that her delegation would continue to show flexibility in the negotiations with a view to creating an effective mechanism of preventive visits providing the Subcommittee with a reasonable framework for its work. Her delegation hoped that the principle of cooperation would prevail and that the negotiations would continue in that spirit.
68. The observer for Switzerland said that his delegation had taken note of the remarks made by the representative of Cuba on behalf of a number of delegations. Although his Government did not share the concerns expressed, it would continue to negotiate in good faith, constructively and in a spirit of compromise so that an effective protocol could be adopted as soon as possible.
69. The observer for Australia, supported by several other delegations, suggested that a link be made between draft article 8(3) and the arrangements referred to in article 12(2).
70. The representative of the United States of America stated that his delegation would be hesitant to agree to such a link since that would imply that any arrangements mentioned in article 12(2) should be worked out in advance of a visit. That, however, could be problematic since the circumstances on the ground could change.
71. The representative of Poland stated that although not much progress had been made during the current session of the working group, some small steps had been taken and the group should continue to move forward.
72. The observer for Costa Rica referred to the original text of the draft optional protocol as submitted by her Government in 1991 and expressed the hope that an effective system of preventive visits to places of detention would soon be established in order to strengthen the protection of persons deprived of their liberty.
73. The observer for the Association for the Prevention of Torture referred to the clear distinctions between "missions" and "visits" which had already been clearly settled at the previous sessions of the working group and reflected throughout the text of the optional protocol. The observer also pointed out that the optional protocol had always been intended to apply to "persons deprived of liberty", as opposed to the narrower concept of "detained persons". She expressed the concerns of her organization with regard to the attempts to reopen the debate on agreed language on these issues. She stated that the Subcommittee should be able to apply modalities in the conduct of a mission to everybody in order to promote its impartial

and non-selective functioning and to ensure the universality of the protocol. She also reiterated that there had been no consensus in the working group with regard to the inclusion of a separate provision (article X) on national legislation in the optional protocol since it was not needed in an international instrument and could only limit the scope of its application.

IV. FUTURE WORK

74. At its eleventh plenary meeting, on 15 October 1999, the representative of Guatemala proposed, on behalf of the Latin American group, to recommend to the Commission on Human Rights that the Chairman-Rapporteur of the working group should again be requested to continue her informal consultations in the period between the sessions of the working group on any remaining outstanding issues. The proposal was also supported by the delegations of Switzerland, Denmark, Georgia, Finland (on behalf of the European Union), Sweden, Canada, Australia, the United Kingdom of Great Britain and Northern Ireland and Turkey.
75. The representative of Cuba pointed out in this regard that when organizing her informal consultations, the Chairman-Rapporteur should bear in mind the heavy workload of various delegations.
76. The observer for Georgia proposed to recommend to the Commission on Human Rights to authorize the working group to hold an additional session of several days to speed up the drafting process. The representative of Cuba stated that his delegation did not agree to additional time for the working group which should remain within the time normally allocated to other important working groups which perform similar tasks.

V. ADOPTION OF THE REPORT

77. The report of the working group was adopted ad referendum at the eleventh plenary meeting, on 15 October 1999. The details of the adoption will be included, if necessary, in an addendum to the present report.

Annex I

TEXT OF THE ARTICLES WHICH CONSTITUTE THE OUTCOME OF THE SECOND READING AT THE FIFTH, SIXTH AND SEVENTH SESSIONS*

Article 2
There shall be established a Subcommittee for the Prevention of Torture and Other Cruel, Inhuman or Degrading Treatment or Punishment of the Committee against Torture which shall carry out the functions laid down in the present Protocol (hereinafter referred to as the Subcommittee); the Subcommittee shall

---

*As contained in document E/CN.4/1999/59, annex I. The number in brackets refers to the number of the article in the first-reading text (E/CN.4/1996/28, annex I).

be responsible for organizing missions to the States Parties to the present Protocol for the purposes stated in article 1.

Article 3
1. In the application of this Protocol the Subcommittee and the State Party concerned shall cooperate with each other.
2. The Subcommittee shall conduct its work within the framework of the Charter of the United Nations and be guided by the purposes and principles therein.
3. The Subcommittee shall also be guided by the principles of confidentiality, impartiality, universality and objectivity.

Article 4
1. The Subcommittee shall consist of 10 members. After the fiftieth accession to the present Protocol, the number of members of the Subcommittee shall increase to 25.
2. The members of the Subcommittee shall be chosen from among persons of high moral character, having proven professional experience in the field of the administration of justice, in particular in criminal law, prison or police administration or in the various medical fields relevant to the treatment of persons deprived of their liberty or in the field of human rights.
3. No two members of the Subcommittee may be nationals of the same State.
4. The members of the Subcommittee shall serve in their individual capacity, shall be independent and impartial and shall be available to serve the Subcommittee effectively.

Article 5
1. Each State Party may nominate, in accordance with paragraph 2, up to two candidates possessing the qualifications and meeting the requirements set out in article 4, and in doing so shall provide detailed information on the qualifications of the nominees.
2. (a) Nominees of the Subcommittee shall have the nationality of a State Party to the present Protocol.
   (b) At least one of the two candidates shall have the nationality of the nominating State Party.
   (c) Not more than two nationals of a State Party shall be nominated.
   (d) Before a State Party nominates a national of another State Party, it shall seek and obtain the written consent of that State Party.
3. At least five months before the date of the meeting of the States Parties during which the elections will be held, the Secretary-General of the United Nations shall address a letter to the States Parties inviting them to submit their nominations within three months. The Secretary-General shall submit a list in alphabetical order of all persons thus nominated, indicating the States Parties which have nominated them.

Article 6
The members of the Subcommittee shall be elected in the following manner:
1. Elections of the members of the Subcommittee shall be held at biennial meetings of States Parties convened by the Secretary-General of the United Nations. At those meetings, for which two thirds of the States Parties shall constitute a quorum, the persons elected to the Subcommittee shall be those

who obtain the largest number of votes and an absolute majority of the votes of the representatives of the States Parties present and voting.
2. The initial election shall be held no later than six months after the date of entry into force of the present Protocol.
3. The States Parties shall elect the members of the Subcommittee by secret ballot.
4. In the election of the members of the Subcommittee, primary consideration shall be given to the fulfilment of the requirements and criteria of article 4. Furthermore, due consideration shall be given to a proper balance among the various fields of competence referred to in article 4, to equitable geographical distribution of membership and to the representation of different forms of civilization and legal systems of the States Parties.
5. Consideration shall also be given to balanced representation of women and men on the basis of the principles of equality and non-discrimination.
6. If, during the election process, two nationals of a State Party have become eligible to serve as members of the Subcommittee, the membership of the Subcommittee shall be resolved in the following manner in conformity with article 4, paragraph 3:
    (a) The candidate receiving the higher number of votes shall serve as the member of the Subcommittee.
    (b) Where the nationals have received the same number of votes, the following procedure applies:
        (i) Where only one has been nominated by the State Party of which he or she is a national, that national shall serve as the member of the Subcommittee;
        (ii) Where both nationals have been nominated by the State Party of which they are nationals, a separate vote by secret ballot shall be held to determine which national shall be the member;
        (iii) Where neither national has been nominated by the State Party of which he or she is a national, a separate vote by secret ballot shall be held to determine which national shall be the member.

Article 7
If a member of the Subcommittee dies or resigns or for any other cause can no longer perform the member's Subcommittee duties, the State Party which nominated the member shall nominate another eligible person possessing the qualifications and meeting the requirements set out in article 4, taking into account the need for a proper balance among the various fields of competence, to serve until the next meeting of the States Parties, subject to approval of the majority of the States Parties. The approval shall be considered given unless half or more of the States Parties respond negatively within six weeks after having been informed by the Secretary-General of the United Nations of the proposed appointment.

Article 9 [6]
The members of the Subcommittee shall be elected for a term of four years. They shall be eligible for re-election once if renominated. The term of half of the members elected at the first election shall expire at the end of two years; immediately after the first election the names of these members shall be chosen by lot by the Chairman of the meeting referred to in article 6, paragraph 1.

Article 10 [7]
1. The Subcommittee shall elect its officers for a term of two years. They may be re-elected.
2. The Subcommittee shall establish its own rules of procedure, but these rules shall provide, *inter alia*, that:
   (a) Half plus one members shall constitute a quorum;
   (b) Decisions of the Subcommittee shall be made by a majority vote of the members present;
   (c) The Subcommittee shall meet in camera.
3. The Secretary-General of the United Nations shall convene the initial meeting of the Subcommittee. After its initial meeting, the Subcommittee shall meet at such times as shall be provided in its rules of procedure.

Article 11 [9]
1. The Subcommittee may decide to postpone a mission to a State Party if the State Party concerned has agreed to a scheduled visit to its territory by the Committee against Torture, pursuant to article 20, paragraph 3 of the Convention. The dates of the rescheduled mission shall be determined taking into account the provisions of articles 1 and 8.
2. The Subcommittee, while respecting the principles set out in article 3, is encouraged to cooperate for the prevention of torture in general with the relevant United Nations organs and mechanisms as well as international, regional and national institutions or organizations working towards strengthening the protection of persons from torture and other cruel, inhuman or degrading treatment or punishment.
3. If, on the basis of a regional convention, a system of visits to places of detention similar to the one under the present Protocol is in force for a State Party, the Subcommittee shall still be responsible for missions to such a State Party under this Protocol, assuring its universal application. However, the Subcommittee and the bodies established under such regional conventions are encouraged to consult and cooperate with a view to the efficient promotion of the objectives of this Protocol, including on the matter of duplication of work.
   Such cooperation may not exempt the States Parties belonging also to such conventions from cooperating fully with the Subcommittee.
4. The provisions of the present Protocol do not affect the obligations of States Parties to the four Geneva Conventions of 12 August 1949 and their Additional Protocols of 8 June 1997, or the possibility for any State Party to authorize the International Committee of the Red Cross to visit places of detention in situations not covered by international humanitarian law.

Article 13 [consolidated 10 and 11]
1. Missions should be carried out by at least two members of the Subcommittee, assisted by interpreters if necessary. If needed, the Subcommittee may be assisted by experts.
2. The Subcommittee shall upon deciding the composition of the mission take into account the particular objectives of the mission.
3. (a) The Subcommittee shall consult confidentially the State Party concerned, in particular regarding the composition and size of the mission other than with regard to the participating members of the Subcommittee.

(b) The State Party concerned may oppose the inclusion of an expert or interpreter in the mission to the territory under its jurisdiction, whereupon the Subcommittee shall propose alternatives.
4. No member of the delegation, with the exception of interpreters, may be a national of the State to be visited. The conduct of the delegation and of all of its members shall be bound by the criteria of independence, impartiality, objectivity and confidentiality.
5. Experts shall be subordinate to and assist the Subcommittee. With regard to a mission, they shall in all respects act on the instruction of and under the authority of the Subcommittee. They shall in no case undertake any missions by themselves under the present Protocol.

Article 14
1. In order to establish a list of experts available for the Subcommittee, each State Party may propose no more than five national experts, qualified in the areas covered by the present Protocol, giving due consideration to gender balance.
2. As needed, the United Nations and specialized agencies may also propose experts to be included on that list.
3. The Subcommittee will annually notify the States Parties of the comprehensive list of experts.
4. In special cases, where specific knowledge or experience is required for a particular mission, and such knowledge or experience is not available on the list of experts, the Subcommittee may include in a mission an expert who is not on the list.
5. In selecting experts for a mission, the Subcommittee shall give primary consideration to the professional knowledge and skills required, taking into account regional and gender balance.

Article 15 [12 bis]
Each State Party shall disseminate information about the present Protocol, the tasks of the Subcommittee and the facilities to be provided to the Subcommittee during a mission to all concerned authorities and ensure the inclusion of such information in the training of relevant personnel, civil, police and military, who are involved in the custody, interrogation or treatment of persons in situations referred to in article 1.

Article 16 [16]
1. The expenditure incurred by the implementation of the present Protocol, including missions, shall be borne by the United Nations.
2. The Secretary-General of the United Nations shall provide the necessary staff and facilities for the effective performance of the functions of the Subcommittee under the present Protocol.

Article 17 [16 bis]
1. A Special Fund shall be set up in accordance with General Assembly procedures, to be administered in accordance with the financial regulations and rules of the United Nations, to help finance the implementation of the recommendations made by the Subcommittee to a State Party expressing the need for additional assistance for its ongoing efforts to improve the protection of persons deprived of their liberty.

2. This Fund may be financed through voluntary contributions made by Governments, intergovernmental and non-governmental organizations as well as other private or public entities.

Article 18 [17]
1. The present Protocol is open for signature by any State which has signed the Convention.
2. The present Protocol is subject to ratification by any State which has ratified or acceded to the Convention. Instruments of ratification shall be deposited with the Secretary-General of the United Nations.
3. The present Protocol shall be open to accession by any State which has ratified or acceded to the Convention.
4. Accession shall be effected by the deposit of an instrument of accession with the Secretary-General of the United Nations.
5. The Secretary-General of the United Nations shall inform all States which have signed the present Protocol or acceded to it of the deposit of each instrument of ratification or accession.

Article 19 [18]
1. The present Protocol shall enter into force on the thirtieth day after the date of deposit with the Secretary-General of the United Nations of the twentieth instrument of ratification or accession.
2. For each State ratifying the present Protocol or acceding to it after the deposit with the Secretary-General of the United Nations of the twentieth instrument of ratification or instrument of accession, the present Protocol shall enter into force on the thirtieth day after the date of the deposit of its own instrument of ratification or accession.

Article 20 [18 bis]
The provisions of the present Protocol shall extend to all parts of federal States without any limitations or exceptions.

Article 21 [19]
1. Any State Party may denounce the present Protocol at any time by written notification addressed to the Secretary-General of the United Nations, who shall thereafter inform the other States Parties to the present Protocol and the Convention. Denunciation shall take effect one year after the date of receipt of the notification by the Secretary-General.
2. Such a denunciation shall not have the effect of releasing the State Party from its obligations under the present Protocol in regard to any act or situation which occurs prior to the date at which the denunciation becomes effective, or to the actions that the Subcommittee has decided or may decide to adopt with respect to the State Party concerned, nor shall denunciation prejudice in any way the continued consideration of any matter which is already under consideration by the Subcommittee prior to the date at which the denunciation becomes effective.
3. Following the date at which the denunciation of the State Party becomes effective, the Subcommittee shall not commence consideration of any new matter regarding that State.

Article 22 [19 bis]
1. Any State Party to the present Protocol may propose an amendment and file it with the Secretary-General of the United Nations. The Secretary-General shall thereupon communicate the proposed amendment to the States Parties to the present Protocol with a request that they notify him whether they favour a conference of States Parties for the purpose of considering and voting upon the proposal. In the event that within four months from the date of such communication at least one third of the States Parties favour such a conference, the Secretary-General shall convene the conference under the auspices of the United Nations. Any amendment adopted by a majority of two thirds of the States Parties present and voting at the conference shall be submitted by the Secretary-General of the United Nations to all States Parties for acceptance.
2. An amendment adopted in accordance with paragraph 1 of the present article shall come into force when it has been accepted by a two-thirds majority of the States Parties to the present Protocol in accordance with their respective constitutional process.
3. When amendments come into force, they shall be binding on those States Parties which have accepted them, other States Parties still being bound by the provisions of the present Protocol and any earlier amendment which they have accepted.

Article 23 [20]
Members of the Subcommittee and of missions authorized under the present Protocol shall be accorded such privileges and immunities as are necessary for the independent exercise of their functions. In particular, they shall be accorded the privileges and immunities specified in section 22 of the Convention on Privileges and Immunities of the United Nations of 13 February 1946, subject to the provisions of section 23 of that Convention.

Article 24
In the conduct of missions, all members shall without prejudice to the provisions and purposes of the present Protocol and such privileges and immunities as they may enjoy:
(a) Respect the laws and regulations of the visited State; and
(b) Refrain from any action or activity incompatible with the impartial and international nature of their duties.

Article 25 [21]
1. The present Protocol, of which the Arabic, Chinese, English, French, Russian and Spanish texts are equally authentic, shall be deposited with the Secretary-General of the United Nations.
2. The Secretary-General of the United Nations shall transmit certified copies of the present Protocol to all States.

Annex II

TEXT OF THE ARTICLES WHICH CONSTITUTE THE BASIS FOR FUTURE WORK

Preamble

The States Parties to the present Protocol,

Considering that in order to further achieve the purpose of the Convention against Torture and Other Cruel, Inhuman or Degrading Treatment or Punishment (hereafter referred to as the Convention) it is appropriate to strengthen the protection of [persons deprived of their liberty from torture and other cruel, inhuman or degrading treatment or punishment] [the detained persons],

Considering that the protection of persons deprived of their liberty against torture and other cruel, inhuman or degrading treatment or punishment could be strengthened by non-judicial means of a preventive character based on visits,

Bearing in mind also the principles of cooperation and confidentiality as basic principles of the present Protocol,

[Affirming that non-judicial, non-selective, non-duplicative and technical consultative visits can lead to the realization of the provisions of the present Protocol, and complement the functions of the Convention against Torture and other human rights mechanisms related to torture,]

Have agreed as follows:

Article 1
1. The objective of this Protocol is to establish a preventive visiting mechanism to examine the treatment of persons [deprived of their liberty] [detained] with a view to recommending means for strengthening, if necessary, the protection of such persons from torture and other cruel, inhuman or degrading treatment or punishment [as defined under international law applicable to the State Party] [and relevant international standards].
2. Each State Party agrees to permit visits, [in principle,] in accordance with this Protocol, to [any place] [places of detention] [on any territory] under its jurisdiction [and control] where persons (may, based on reliable information [as determined by a competent and independent judicial authority of the State Party concerned] be deprived or) are [deprived of their liberty] [detained] [including structures intended or used to house or transport such persons] by [or pursuant to an order of] a public authority [or at its instigation or with its consent or acquiescence].

[3. Nothing in this Protocol will be interpreted as allowing:
   (a) Visits to any civil or military facility that the State considers related to strategic national interest; or
   (b) Interference in the domestic affairs of Member States in a manner which exceeds the provisions of the present Protocol.]

Article 8
1. The Subcommittee:
   (a) Shall establish, on the basis of a transparent and impartial procedure, a

programme of regular [missions] [visits] to all States Parties [A reasonable frequency for the [missions] [visits] shall be decided by agreement with State[s] Party[ies];
[these regular [missions] [visits] include follow-up missions;
(b) Shall also undertake such other [missions] [visits] as appear to it to be required in the circumstances and based on reliable information, [determined as described in article 1 of the Protocol] with a view to furthering the aims of this Protocol];
2. (a) The Subcommittee shall send a written notification to the Government of the State Party concerned of its [intention] [request] to organize a [mission] [visit], [followed by] [including] a list of places to be visited and the composition of the delegation. [The Subcommittee may also visit other places as needed during its mission];
[(b) Those [missions] [visits] shall be conducted after the consent of the State concerned and shall be mutually agreed upon between the Subcommittee and the State Party in a spirit of cooperation];
(c) [Missions] [visits] shall be organized and carried out in accordance with the principles set out in article 3 of the Protocol;
3. [(a)]
[Six months] Before a [mission] [visit] is carried out, the Subcommittee and the State Party concerned shall, [if either of them so requests,] enter into consultations with a view to agreeing [without delay on the practical arrangements] [on the modalities] of the [mission] [visit];
[(b) Such consultations on the practical arrangements for the [mission] [visit] may not include negotiations on the obligations of a State Party under article 1 of the Protocol].

Article 12
[1. The Subcommittee and the State Party shall cooperate with a view to the effective fulfilment of the [mission] [visit]. In particular, the State Party shall provide:
   (c) The delegation with access to, and freedom of movement within, any territory under its jurisdiction [and control] for the conduct of the [mission] [visit];
   (d) The Subcommittee or its delegations with all information relevant to the effective conduct of the [mission] [visit], including in particular on any person or places referred to in article 1 of the Protocol;
   (e) The delegation with access to and within any place referred to in article 1 of the Protocol;
   (f) The delegation with access to persons referred to in article 1 of the Protocol, and the opportunity for private interviews with them;
   (g) The Subcommittee and its delegation with the opportunity to communicate freely with any other person who is in a position to supply relevant information.
[2. The obligations referred to above shall be subject to any arrangements that the State Party concerned considers necessary for:
   [(a) The protection of sensitive areas [equipment] or information [based on imperative grounds of national security] [or economic, technological or scientific secrets];]

[(b) The protection of any constitutional obligations the State Party concerned may have with regard to proprietary rights, searches and seizures, or other constitutional rights [of individuals];]
[(c) The physical protection and safety of persons, including the members of the Subcommittee; and]
[(d) The protection of personal data of individuals as required by national legislation [consistent with human rights principles]].

If the State Party is unable to provide full access to places, information or persons, the State Party shall make every reasonable effort to demonstrate to the Subcommittee, through alternative means, its compliance with this Protocol.]]

[Article X
The provisions of this Protocol shall be applied in accordance with domestic legislation consistent with the Charter of the United Nations and other international obligations of the State.]

Article 13
1. In exceptional circumstances, [in the context of a mission,] the competent authorities of the State Party concerned may make objections to the Subcommittee [or its delegation] against a particular visit [or a mission]. Objections may only be made on [urgent and compelling] grounds of national defence, public [or individual] safety, natural disasters, serious disorder in [the place to be visited] [places where persons are detained,] [the medical condition of a person] [or that an urgent interrogation relating to a serious crime is in progress] [which temporarily prevent the carrying out of a visit. The existence of a state of emergency as such should not be invoked by a State Party as a reason to object to a visit].
2. Following any such objections, the Subcommittee and the State Party shall [immediately] enter into consultations regarding those circumstances and seek agreement on arrangements to enable the Committee to exercise its functions [expeditiously]. [Until the [mission or] visit takes place, the State Party shall provide information to the Subcommittee about persons or places relevant to its [mission or] visit.]

Appendix 5: Report of the Independent Expert on Enhancing the Long-Term Effectiveness of the United Nations Human Rights Treaty System

A/CONF.157/PC/62/Add.11/Rev.1 (22 April 1993)
WORLD CONFERENCE ON HUMAN RIGHTS

STATUS OF PREPARATION OF PUBLICATIONS, STUDIES AND DOCUMENTS FOR THE WORLD CONFERENCE

Note by the Secretariat
Addendum

Interim report on updated study by Mr. Philip Alston

1. In paragraph 15(a) of its resolution 43/115 of 8 December 1988, the General Assembly requested the Secretary General "to consider entrusting, within existing resources, an independent expert with the task of preparing a study on possible long-term approaches to the supervision of new instruments on human rights, taking into account the conclusions and recommendations of the meeting of persons chairing the treaty bodies, the deliberations of the Commission on Human Rights and other relevant materials, to be submitted to the General Assembly at its forty-fourth session".
2. Pursuant to the resolution, the Commission on Human Rights adopted resolution 1989/47, paragraph 5 of which requested the Secretary-General "to entrust an independent expert with the task of preparing a study, within existing resources, on possible long-term approaches to enhancing the effective operation of existing and prospective bodies established under United Nations human rights instruments taking into account the conclusions and recommendations of the meeting of persons chairing the human rights treaty bodies", and requested that the report be submitted to the General Assembly at its forty-fourth session and the Commission on Human Rights at its forty-sixth session.
3. In accordance with the foregoing resolutions, the Secretary-General appointed Mr. Philip Alston to carry out the study in question. The study was transmitted to the General Assembly at its forty-fourth session in document A/44/668 and was subsequently made available to the Commission on Human Rights at its forty-sixth session.
4. In paragraph 2 of its resolution 47/111 of 16 December 1992, the General Assembly expressed "its satisfaction with the study by the independent expert" and, "in the light of the conclusions and recommendations contained in the report of the fourth meeting of persons chairing the human rights treaty bodies, request[ed] that the report of the independent expert be updated for submission to the fiftieth session of the Commission on Human Rights and that an interim report be presented to the General Assembly at its forty-eighth session, and be made available to the World Conference on Human

Rights in June 1993". The Commission on Human Rights also expressed its satisfaction with the study and made the same request for an updated version in paragraph 6 of its resolution 1993/16 of 26 February 1993.

5. The annex to the present document contains the interim report on the updated study. It has been prepared by Mr. Philip Alston, Professor of International Law and Director of the Centre for International and Public Law at the Australian National University, currently Visiting Professor of Law at Harvard Law School and Chairman of the Committee on Economic, Social and Cultural Rights.

ANNEX

Interim report on study on enhancing the long-term effectiveness of the United Nations human rights treaty regime

CONTENTS

	Paragraphs
SUMMARY OF CONCLUSIONS AND RECOMMENDATIONS	
I. INTRODUCTION	1–22
A. Mandate	1–3
B. Approach adopted and issues examined	4–14
C. Situating treaty body reform within a broader context	15–22
II OVERVIEW OF THE RAPIDLY CHANGING ENVIRONMENT WITHIN WHICH THE TREATY BODIES ARE FUNCTIONING	23–90
A. The evolution of the human rights treaty system over time	23–41
B. Implications for the treaty system of the general expansion of multilateral human rights activities	42–52
C. The treaty system as the cornerstone of the United Nations human rights programme	53–71
D. Towards universality of membership in the treaty regime	72–90
III REPORTING BY STATES PARTIES	91–182
A. The importance and functions of reporting procedures	91–102
B. Current problems of reporting procedures	103–108
C. Responding to the non-submission of reports	109–122
D. The burden of coexisting reporting systems	123–138
E. Reducing overlapping reporting requirements	139–155
F. Enhancing the capacity of the treaty system as a whole to address specific themes	156–163
G. Possible long-term options involving fundamental change	164–182
IV FUNCTIONING OF TREATY BODIES: FINANCIAL AND ADMINISTRATIVE ISSUES	183–206
A. Financial arrangements	183–184
B. Length and frequency of Committee sessions	185–193

C. Conditions of service for experts 194–196
D. Secretariat servicing 197–206

V. FUNCTIONING OF TREATY BODIES: SUBSTANTIVE ISSUES 207–254
   A. Towards more effective monitoring of compliance 207–237
   B. Promoting normative consistency 238–244
   C. Relationships with the principal regional human rights mechanisms 245–254

VI. OTHER SELECTED LONG-TERM ISSUES *
    A. A long-term consolidation of the existing network of treaty bodies *

SUMMARY OF CONCLUSIONS AND RECOMMENDATIONS

1. This is an interim report on a thoroughly revised and updated version of a study originally prepared at the request of the General Assembly in 1989. Since that time many of the recommendations contained in the original report have been acted upon. Those matters are therefore not dealt with again in the present version of the study.

2. The treaty regime (along with the Universal Declaration of Human Rights) constitutes the cornerstone of international human rights endeavours (paras. 53–71). Its development is one of the great achievements of the United Nations.

3. That regime has reached a critical crossroads. Its successful future evolution demands that the magnitude and urgency of existing challenges be recognized, that the vital importance of the treaty regime as a whole be reaffirmed and that the quest for creative and effective solutions be pursued with energy and commitment. In doing so, care must be taken to ensure that the integrity of the system, and particularly its ability to safeguard human rights, are not sacrificed to illusory notions of streamlining and efficiency (paras. 7–13).

4. At the time of the Teheran Conference in 1968 not a single human rights treaty body existed. Only a quarter of a century later there are seven. Over the last decade the complexity, reach and potential significance of the treaty regime have expanded enormously. Between 1989 and 1992 alone, the number of States parties to the principal treaties increased by 27 per cent. By the year 2000 there could well be an average of 160 States parties to each of the six treaties, thus generating almost 1,000 reports per reporting cycle and up to 2,000 pages of annual committee reports containing an extensive array of materials of jurisprudential significance (paras. 23–41).

5. In at least some respects, reform of the treaty regime is closely linked to reform of the overall human rights programme. That programme has grown

---

*To be issed as an addendum to this document.

exponentially over the past decade through a process of cumulative incrementalism rather than planned evolution. The question arises as to whether an overview study of selected aspects of the long-term development of the Charter-based system should be undertaken, either by the Secretary-General or one or more independent experts (paras. 15–22).
6. The existing heavy demands upon the Centre for Human Rights seem certain to grow even more rapidly in the years ahead. Already the disparity between demands made and resources provided has exacerbated the situation. Of the many areas affected by these problems, the present study focuses in particular upon four which are in urgent need of overall review: advisory services, public information, collaboration with other United Nations bodies and agencies, and the relationship between United Nations human rights bodies and their regional counterparts (paras. 15–22).
7. The treaty bodies have becoming increasingly intertwined with the overall human rights programme of the United Nations. While this phenomenon is greatly to be welcomed, there is a difficult line that must be maintained between, on the one hand, promoting the most effective degree of interaction and, on the other hand, ensuring that the distinctive characteristics of the committees' treaty supervisory functions are not inappropriately blurred or even lost (paras. 53–71).
8. For many reasons, including the possibility to pursue the complex question of the role of cultural factors in the application of human rights norms, universal participation by all countries of the six principal treaties is a goal of the utmost importance (paras. 72–75).
9. The existing level of participation is only around 60 per cent for the Covenants and as low as 40 per cent for the Convention against Torture. Efforts to date to improve this record have been piecemeal, excessively reliant upon repeated exhortation, and lacking in depth as well as resources (paras. 76–80).
10. The United Nations should immediately adopt a three-point programme designed to achieve universality:
    (a) Universal acceptance of the package of six core treaties should be identified as one of the foundation stones of the human rights programme. In addition, the six States which are parties to only one of the two International Human Rights Covenants should be urged to ratify the other as soon as possible (para. 82).
    (b) The programme should target specific issues to be pursued and develop effective strategies for addressing them. For example, attention should be paid to the specific problems and concerns of the 30 States with a population of two million or less which have not ratified either Covenant. If measures could be devised to enable these States to ratify or access the total number of parties to the Covenants could rise by some 25 per cent (paras. 83–88).
    (c) A target date for achieving universality should be set (the year 2000) and a strategy devised for achieving it. Implementation of the programme should be overseen by specialists and resources should be earmarked for related activities (paras. 89–90).
11. Reporting procedures are of central importance to the international human rights regime. Reporting should be viewed as a multi-faceted undertaking

Appendix 5: Long-Term Effectiveness of the UN Human Rights Treaty System 519

that serves a variety of objectives both domestically and internationally (paras. 91–94).
12. The role of the international treaty bodies is essentially catalytic. The primary role in the reporting process belongs to the relevant actors at the national level. Ideally the treaty bodies major function should be to monitor the domestic monitors. The treaty bodies should focus more systematically on the following issues: (a) dissemination, in local languages, of the text of the relevant instrument; (b) the modalities of preparation of the State report; (c) the submission of information to the treaty body from diverse sources in connection with the examination of State reports; and (d) national level discussion of the results of the Committee-State party dialogue (paras. 95–102).
13. The current level of overdue reports (in excess of 1,000) is chronic and entirely unacceptable. As long as it is tolerated, the credibility of the entire regime is threatened, Governments become accustomed to ignoring their obligations, and the criticisms of those who portray the reporting system as toothless or ineffectual are partly vindicated (paras. 103–111).
14. Ironically, the treaty system is able to function at present by relying upon the continuing delinquency of States parties. Once this problem is resolved, however, major reforms of the present system will be unavoidable (para. 106).
15. Rather than seeking to identify appropriate incentives and disincentives to address this issue, both the treaty bodies and the political organs have tended simply to exhort States to report. It is imperative that this problem now be addressed with determination and imagination.
16. Four steps should be considered: (a) The provision of advisory services, of a very different kind to those presently on offer, to States parties whose reports are more than two years overdue; (b) the immunity from scrutiny, currently enjoyed by non-reporting States, must be removed by scheduling the situation in those States for examination, even in the absence of a report; (c) States parties whose reports are long overdue should be listed by name in resolutions adopted by the Charter-based organs; and (d) States parties should be provided with a positive incentive to report by virtue of the availability of *additional* technical assistance (paras. 109–122).
17. States are currently subject to an excessive number of demands for information on human rights matters. At a certain point, additional demands might be counter-productive given the available capacity. Many of the demands are essential, but some could be reduced or avoided. Any solution must satisfy the twin criteria of (i) minimizing the burden placed on States and (ii) maximizing the effectiveness of measures to ensure respect for human rights (paras. 123–125).
18. Requests based on treaty obligations or emanating from special procedures established by the Charter-based organs should be distinguished from other demands and the principal focus of endeavours to reduce the burden should concentrate on requests emanating from sources other than these two (paras. 126–135).
19. In particular, measures should be taken to reduce the paper warfare against States and non-governmental organizations that currently characterizes the process of preparing much of the documentation sought by the Charter-based organs from the secretariat (para. 134).

20. The consolidation of reporting guidelines with respect to a country profile, which has recently been achieved, is a valuable initiative but serves to address only a part of the much larger problem of overlapping reporting requirements (para. 139).
21. As a result of extensive overlapping in the competences of different treaty bodies, States may be required to report on virtually the same issue to five or more different bodies. In an effort to reduce such duplication each State party should be encouraged to identify for its own purposes the instances in which cross-referencing can be used effectively and appropriately in preparing its reports. If necessary, and if resources are available, interested States should be assisted in that task through the Advisory Services Programme. Each of the treaty bodies might also consider providing some guidance to States parties in this respect (para. 152).
22. States might also consider designating a specific administrative unit at the national level to coordinate the preparation of all reports to treaty bodies (para. 152).
23. Given the need to better understand existing overlap between ILO and United Nations treaty standards the International Labour Office should be asked to consider updating and expanding for informational purposes the analysis it prepared in 1969, which compares the provisions of relevant ILO Conventions with the standards contained in the United Nations human rights treaties. This could be linked to a more concerted effort by the treaty bodies to take full account of instances in which a State party has already reported to the ILO on the same subject-matter (paras. 142–143 and 155).
24. The meeting of chairpersons should be specifically mandated to consider, on the basis of policy options submitted by the secretariat, how the various committees might reduce overlapping or duplication in respect to specific issues such as the rights of the child (para 146–148).
25. The overlapping competences of different treaty bodies can result in a situation in which a State may be required to report on virtually the same issue to several different treaty bodies. In an effort to reduce such duplication each State party should be encouraged to identify for its own purposes the instances in which cross-referencing can effectively and appropriately be used in preparing its reports. Other measures might include designating a specific administrative unit to coordinate the preparation of all such reports. The treaty bodies and the ILO should also contribute to the development of more effective approaches (paras. 149–155).
26. Given the increasing number of specific themes, such as the rights of women, the disabled, the ageing etc., to which all treaty bodies are being asked to pay particular attention, it should be considered whether flexible modalities can be found for allocating primary responsibility for addressing a given dimension of an issue to one body or another (paras. 156–163).
27. Long-term options for reducing reporting burdens should be considered. They include: (i) reducing the number of treaty bodies and hence the number of reports required (paras. 164–166); (ii) encouraging States to produce a single "global" report to be submitted to all relevant treaty bodies (paras. 167–173); and (iii) replacing the requirement of comprehensive periodic reports with specifically-tailored reports (paras. 174–182).
28. Reform of the financing arrangements relating to the treaty bodies is one of

Appendix 5: Long-Term Effectiveness of the UN Human Rights Treaty System 521

the major achievements of recent years. States parties to the two treaties concerned should be urged to ratify the amendments as soon as possible (paras. 183–184).

29. The meeting time available to the treaty bodies as a whole has been expanding steadily, although still insufficiently, and is likely to reach 34 weeks with six weeks of working groups in 1993. That figure may need to be doubled when the system is working effectively (paras. 185–193).

30. Members of all committees should be provided with honoraria, rather than only three out of six as at present (paras. 194–196).

31. The existing levels of secretariat servicing provided to the treaty bodies is entirely inadequate. Computerization needs to be expedited; a documentation unit established; an inventory of committee needs should be drawn up; CEDAW should be serviced by the Centre for Human Rights; specialist expertise must be developed within the secretariat, in the context of a major restructuring of existing servicing arrangements; and greatly increased resources need to be made available (paras. 197–206).

32. The various intergovernmental agencies need to be involved in the work of the treaty bodies, but on a much more discerning basis than current approaches might imply. Overall, effective and targeted coordination needs to be put on the inter-agency agenda in a far more substantive way than hitherto (paras. 209–217).

33. Relations between the treaty bodies and non-governmental organizations are badly in need of review. A non-governmental liaison office needs to be established within the Centre for Human Rights (paras. 218–237).

34. Every effort should be made to maximize normative consistency. As standards proliferate and new treaty bodies are created the risks of inconsistency will continue to grow. Confusion and diminished credibility could result. In the longer term the implications of creating additional treaty bodies need to be very carefully weighed. In the short term, the desirability of seeking normative consistency should be reiterated and every effort made to ensure that any potential inconsistency is brought to the attention of the body concerned by the secretariat (paras. 238–241).

35. The Secretary-General might consider revising or supplementing *United Nations Action in the Field of Human Rights* so as to provide a more accessible record of the jurisprudence emerging under the various bodies. The development of more specialized expertise within the secretariat should also be considered (paras. 242–243).

36. At present the United Nations and regional human rights treaty bodies pay very little attention to one another's jurisprudence. In order to improve the chances of a coherent overall international human rights regime evolving, and to reduce the likelihood of widely diverging and even directly incompatible approaches and interpretations, efforts need to be made to encourage cross-fertilization. The treaty bodies should be kept informed of developments elsewhere, interaction between the universal and regional systems should become less superficial and more substantive, the respective treaty bodies or their representatives should get together occasionally, and data bases should be developed to enable the jurisprudence of each body to be available to the others (paras. 245–254).

Request for comments to be reflected in the final study

37. The present report is an interim one, as requested by the General Assembly. The final version of the report will be submitted to the Commission on Human Rights at its fiftieth session, in 1994. It should be noted that that version will deal with several other issues not included here, including in particular, public information and advisory services.
38. That version will also take full account of any comments received by the independent expert in the intervening period. Any such comments are warmly invited.

I. INTRODUCTION

A. *Mandate*

1. The focus of the present updated and significantly revised study is on long-term approaches to enhancing the effective operation of existing and prospective bodies established under United Nations human rights instruments. The independent expert was requested to take account, in the preparation of the study, of the conclusions and recommendations contained in the report of the fourth meeting of persons chairing the human rights treaty bodies (A/47/628, Annex).
2. In addition account has been taken of recent discussions held under relevant agenda items in the General Assembly, the Economic and Social Council, the Commission on Human Rights and the Sub-Commission on Prevention of Discrimination and Protection of Minorities. Extensive reference has also been made to the reports of the various United Nations human rights treaty bodies and to a range of other relevant literature.
3. In addition, in view of the General Assembly's request that this interim version of the study be made available to the World Conference on Human Rights, a particular effort has been made to bear in mind the provisional agenda for the Conference (General Assembly resolution 47/122, Annex) which, *inter alia*, calls for it to make recommendations for:
   (a) Strengthening international cooperation in the field of human rights in conformity with the Charter of the United Nations and with international human rights instruments;
   (b) Ensuring the universality, objectivity and non-selectivity of the consideration of human rights issues;
   (c) Enhancing the effectiveness of United Nations activities and mechanisms;
   (d) Securing the necessary financial and other resources for United Nations activities in the area of human rights.

B. *Approach adopted and issues examined*

4. It may reasonably be assumed that the present study has been entrusted to an independent expert in order to facilitate the task of addressing some of the more difficult and far-reaching issues raised by the problems currently facing the human rights treaty bodies as well as some of those which may reasonably be expected to arise over the next decade or so. Moreover, the quest for enhanced effectiveness inevitably requires consideration of issues on

which no consensus may immediately be discernible. An expert study is thus a useful means by which to shed further light on issues that require continuing reflection and debate. It may also be an appropriate mechanism for dealing with issues relating to the functioning of a diverse and somewhat disparate range of bodies that are not subject to the overall authority of any one body and that do not fit easily into any particular organizational structure or hierarchy.

5. The present revised study deals with a variety of issues raised in discussions within the relevant United Nations organs and in the deliberations of the treaty bodies themselves. It does not, however, purport to be comprehensive or to deal with each of the issues exhaustively.

6. In preparing the revised version of this study, the author has endeavoured to keep two rather different objectives in mind. The first is to place the issues in their wider context and to stimulate reflection on approaches that, in the short term, may seem impracticable or even unnecessary but, in the long term, may be unavoidable. Given the centrality of the treaty bodies within the global human rights regime and the speed at which the environment in which they are operating is changing, it is essential to undertake such long-term analysis at some point and it is clear that the General Assembly and the Commission on Human Rights are the bodies best situated to do so. Thus, while some of the issues raised here may not be of immediate and pressing concern, they must nevertheless be factored into any overall analysis today if the human rights regime is to be made both more effective and more efficient tomorrow.

7. The second objective of the revised study is to present an overview and analysis of a number of issues that are of very immediate concern and have a direct bearing on the effective functioning of the existing treaty bodies. An indication of those issues emerges very clearly from recent resolutions adopted by the General Assembly and the Commission on Human Rights as well as from the problems identified by the 1992 meeting of persons chairing the human rights treaty bodies (see A/47/628). They include the following:

   (a) The importance of moving closer to universal ratification of, or accession to, the principal international human rights treaties;
   (b) The problem of responding to an increasing number of reservations which appear to be incompatible with the object and purpose of the treaty in question;
   (c) The growing burden imposed on many States by the expansion and overlapping of reporting obligations under different instruments;
   (d) Excessive delays by some States parties in the submission of their reports and the difficulties encountered by the treaty bodies in seeking to induce such States to submit their overdue reports;
   (e) The problem of inadequate reports submitted by some States parties;
   (f) Insufficient resources to enable the treaty bodies to function effectively;
   (g) The inability of the secretariat, for reasons of inadequate staffing levels, to provide the treaty bodies with the administrative and technical support they require;
   (h) The need to continue to explore the use of more innovative procedures if the various treaty bodies are to operate both effectively and efficiently;
   (i) The need to make more effective use of public information activities;

(j) Concern that the creation of additional treaty bodies will exacerbate existing problems; and

(k) The need to ensure that recent amendments to two of the treaties, designed to ensure regular budget funding of their operations, are endorsed by States parties and enter into force as soon as possible.

8. It has been suggested that all of this adds up to a crisis situation and that there is an "impending deadlock affecting international procedures for monitoring compliance with United Nations human rights conventions" (A/C.3/43/5, p. 6). Other commentators have conceded that United Nations "bodies dealing with human rights ... need to be reorganized on the basis of ... new thinking".[1] Similarly, a member of the Human Rights Committee warned in 1989 that "there comes a critical moment in the life of successful international institutions, a moment at which they can go forward or begin to disintegrate. And among all the generous words [praising the achievements of the Human Rights Committee] see dangers for the International Covenant on Civil and Political Rights".[2]

9. While some observers have been more critical than others, there appears to be a consistent recognition of the need for sustained reform. It is therefore appropriate, by way of background, to note some of the diagnoses that have recently been made. One study of the reporting procedure under the Covenant on Civil and Political Rights, prepared by a group of experts with extensive experience as members of the Human Rights Committee, observed that "[a]n increasing number of States are finding their reporting duties to have become too onerous, and the whole procedure in danger of becoming a ritualistic routine".[3] The report concluded that, "[i]f new approaches are not found, support might decline".[4] The same report then identifies a range of problems which are also reflected in other assessments. Thus, for example, a recently published, comprehensive review of the Committee's work noted the following problems:

"inadequate guidelines for the preparation of reports; inadequate and incomplete reports which do not deal with the realities ...; the absence of procedures to determine the adequacy of the reports submitted; delays in the submission of State reports; the absence of agreement on procedures for requesting [additional reports]; the absence of any formal role for specialized agencies or non-governmental organizations in the reporting procedure; the duplication of questions and the pressures placed on State representatives; the absence of any clear 'Committee view' of the human rights performance in a particular State ...; the disagreement within the [Human Rights Committee] ... which has resulted in no country specific reports ...; and the limited roles played by ECOSOC, and the General Assembly."[5]

---

[1] Alexei Glukhov, "A Two-Way Street", *International Affairs*, July 1988, 31 at 34.
[2] Rosalyn Higgins, "The United Nations: Still a Force for Peace", 52 *Modern Law Review* 1 at 20 (1989). The title of the article was subsequently corrected to read "The United Nations: Some Questions of Integrity".
[3] *Making the Reporting Procedure under the International Covenant on Civil and Political Rights More Effective* (Oslo, Norwegian Institute of Human Rights, Publication No. 8, 1991), at 4.
[4] *Ibid.*
[5] Dominic McGoldrick, *The Human Rights Committee: Its Role in the Development of the International Covenant on Civil and Political Rights* (Oxford, Clarendon Press, 1991), at 499.

10. Although this list is long, an observer who follows the work of the Human Rights Committee closely could not help but be struck by the extent to which the Committee has moved to address many of the issues within the past couple of years.[6] The same is true, although to varying degrees, of the preparedness of each of the other treaty bodies to innovate in order to respond to perceived problems and to enhance effective functioning.
11. Nevertheless, the innovations that have been implemented so far have been insufficient to satisfy many observers. The General Assembly and the Commission on Human Rights have continued to call for improvements within the system and other observers have continued to make even more critical appraisals of the treaty regime as a whole. One recent assessment, for example, suggests that States parties to the various treaties have contributed significantly to the system's ineffectiveness:

    "In large numbers they fail to produce timely reports, do not engage in reform activities in the course of producing reports, author inadequate reports, send uninformed representatives to the examination of reports by the treaty bodies, fail to respond to questions during the examinations, discourage greater media attention of the examination of reports, fail to disseminate reports and the results of the examinations within the State, elect non-independent/government employees to treaty body membership, fail to object to reservation, and fail to challenge reservations by additional means."[7]

12. Whatever terms may be used to characterize the present situation, however, it is generally agreed that the United Nations human rights treaty monitoring system has reached a critical crossroads. Its successful future evolution demands that the magnitude and urgency of existing challenges be recognized, that the vital importance of the treaty regime as a whole be reaffirmed and that the quest for creative and effective solutions be pursued with energy and commitment. By the same token, that quest must not be embarked upon without acknowledging the very considerable achievements to date and the importance of proceeding with sensitivity and sophistication in order to ensure that the fundamental integrity of the system, and particularly its ability to safeguard human rights, are not sacrificed to illusory notions of streamlining and efficiency.
13. The paradox is, that while far-reaching and even radical reforms may be necessary, they can best, and perhaps only, be achieved through measures that are both carefully conceived and formulated and painstakingly implemented. In other words, a time of crisis or challenge should also be seen as a time of opportunity for constructive reform and improvement.
14. Before proceeding to examine the overall context in which these issues need to be considered, it is appropriate and important to re-state the fact that the attention devoted over the past four years (since the first version of the present study was prepared) to the need to promote the more effective functioning of the treaty supervisory system has given rise to some important

---

[6] See, for example, Manfred Nowak, "The Activities of the UN Human Rights Committee: Developments from 1 August 1989 through 31 July 1992", 14 *Human Rights Law Journal* 9–19 (1993).
[7] Anne Bayefsky, "Making Human Rights Treaties Work", unpublished manuscript, University of Ottawa, 1993, at 37.

achievements. Leaving aside for the moment the many reforms introduced by each of the treaty bodies, perhaps the most important general initiative has been the major reforms initiated by the General Assembly, and acted upon by the relevant meetings of States parties, in the financing arrangements relating to the Committee for the Elimination of Racial Discrimination and the Committee against Torture. While this matter has not yet been definitively resolved,[8] the steps that have been taken are of fundamental importance in affirming that the financing of the activities of supervisory bodies in the human rights field cannot be left dependent upon the preparedness to pay of those States parties which might well have an incentive to paralyse the procedures by not paying.[9]

C. Situating treaty body reform within a broader context

15. The United Nations stands poised on the threshold of a new era. It is an era that has been ushered in by the end of the Cold War, by the reinvigorated movement towards democracy in many countries, and by a renewed sense of the importance of the Charter principle of respect for human rights and of its far-reaching implications for both the domestic and international orders. It is also an era in which the magnitude and severity of a range of gross and often recurrent abuses of human rights has removed from the Organization and its Member States any option they might once have had to remain unresponsive to those violations, whatever the reasons proffered. Within the Organization's human rights forums the removal of many of the ideological barriers that had artificially prevented progress on so many issues, combined with the emergence of a realization that institutional renewal and reform are not only possible but indispensable, have created opportunities as well as challenges.

16. While the immediate focus of the present study is confined to the treaty regime, the analysis that follows is predicated upon the assumption that the treaty regime has become an integral part of the overall human rights program within the United Nations system. That assumption inevitably raises the question of whether a comparable overview study of the long-term development of the Charter-based system for the promotion and protection of human rights is desirable and perhaps even necessary.

17. Over the past decade the overall United Nations human rights program has grown at an exponential rate. This is the result of various factors that have combined to place far greater demands on the United Nations than seemed likely, or even possible, only a decade ago. Those factors include: the rapidity of changes in the international system, a growing recognition of the interdependence of human rights with peace, security, development and other issues, the ever-increasing capacity of new communications technologies to bring

---

[8] Thus the fourth meeting of chairpersons noted: (i) that "it is imperative that individual States parties act as rapidly as possible to ratify the [relevant] amendments to the two treaties; and (ii) that "in the period prior to the entry into force of those amendments there will continue to be a critical need to assure adequate funding to the two committees concerned to enable them to fulfil adequately their supervisory functions". A/47/628, paras. 47–48.

[9] This issue was discussed at length in the first version of this study (A/44/668, paras. 54–99) but will not be further examined in the present report.

instant news of developments throughout the world at virtually the same time as they are occurring, the growth in expectations on the part of all concerned (governments, non-governmental organizations, and the victims of human rights violations), and the preparedness of governments to authorize activities that had previously been blocked for ideological or other reasons.

18. But the resulting increased workload has not been matched by the availability of adequate personnel or financial resources within the secretariat and particularly within the Centre for Human Rights. The resulting gross disparity between the demands being made and resources being made available has meant, among other things, that time and opportunities for reflection on the ways in which the system could best be expanded, consolidated and reformed have simply not been available. While the need for reflection on these matters has recently been raised by the Commission on Human Rights in relation to special procedures (resolution 1993/58), such reflection would seem to be even more essential in relation to many of the activities that are of vital concern to the treaty bodies. This conclusion emerges clearly from the report of the fourth chairpersons meeting, which concluded that "many of the urgent needs experienced by the treaty bodies cannot be satisfactorily dealt with in the absence of more far-reaching financial, personnel and administrative reforms" (A/47/628, para. 49).

19. By the same token, there is also a need for some sustained management and policy analysis of the results in specific areas of activities which have been subjected to a process of virtually unrestrained incremental growth. The process has, in some ways, resembled that of placing ever more building blocks on top of one another in a vertical structure, until eventually the whole structure topples over because nothing has been done to ensure a solid foundation or to reinforce it as it grows. In the context of the present study, several such areas stand out. They include: the provision of advisory services; the arrangements for disseminating public information; the possibilities of constructive collaboration with other United Nations bodies and agencies; and the relationship between United Nations human rights bodies and their regional counterparts.

20. Although each of these issues is dealt with in some detail later in this study, particularly in so far as they concern the treaty bodies, it is appropriate to flag them at this point. Thus, although the advisory services program has developed under very significant financial and other limitations, requests that such services be made available for one purpose or another have proliferated to the point where they have become an almost automatic component of any resolution dealing with a host of diverse issues. The same situation would seem to apply in relation to public information.

21. In terms of collaboration between the United Nations human rights organs and relevant United Nations agencies, such as the ILO, UNESCO, UNDP or the World Bank, the potential has grown in recent years. At the same time, however, requests have proliferated to such an extent, and are so lacking in coordination or the setting of priorities that it is perhaps not surprising that so little response has generally been elicited. In relation to the regional human rights bodies, the unremitting expansion of both universal and regional regimes with minimal consultation between them risks

leading to a situation in which even very modest forms of coordination will come to appear too complicated to contemplate. In at least some of these areas it is possible that a continuation of the existing approach might result either in the paralysis of the relevant activity or in the adoption of resolutions and decisions in response to which very little will, or can, be done.

22. It would thus seem desirable for steps to be taken to re-evaluate existing approaches and for more coherent strategies to be developed in each area.[10] It seems unlikely, however, that either the Commission on Human Rights or any of the principal organs will be well placed to undertake such a re-evaluation in the absence of detailed technical analyses of the policy needs and options that exist in each domain. Consideration should thus be given to the commissioning of such analyses, either by the Secretary-General or by one or more independent experts.

II. OVERVIEW OF THE RAPIDLY CHANGING ENVIRONMENT WITHIN WHICH THE TREATY BODIES ARE FUNCTIONING

23. One of the enduring paradoxes of the United Nations human rights treaty system is that while each treaty regime must be considered on its own merits and in the light of its own specific norms and procedures, for some purposes the various regimes cannot realistically be viewed in isolation either from one another or from the broader human rights programme of which they are but a part. Indeed, one of the problems with some of the analyses that have been undertaken in the past is a tendency to compartmentalize each of the treaty bodies as though they existed solely within entirely self-contained regimes. Thus, in order to identify potentially effective, acceptable and enduring solutions to some of the challenges currently facing the treaty system, it is necessary to consider (briefly) the evolution of that system over time and to situate it in relation to the development of the human rights programme as a whole.

A. *The evolution of the human rights treaty system over time*

24. By most standards, the existing human rights treaty system is a remarkably recent creation. Less than a quarter of a century ago, at the time of the 1968 World Conference on Human Rights held in Teheran, not a single treaty body was functioning. Since that time the system has mushroomed and its rapid growth has brought with it a range of problems that could perhaps have been foreseen without great difficulty. The process of evolution and growth is perhaps best illustrated by comparing the broad contours of the situation in 1993 with that which prevailed in 1970 and 1980 respectively.

1. *The treaty system in 1970*

25. In 1970, less than two decades ago, there was only one United Nations human rights treaty body in existence, the Committee on the Elimination of Racial Discrimination. It met for the first time in January 1970. The

---

[10] See, in this regard, the San José Declaration adopted by the Regional Meeting for Latin America

Committee's first annual report to the General Assembly was less than 40 pages in length and related largely to procedural matters.[11] The Convention under which the Committee had been established, the International Convention on the Elimination of All Forms of Racial Discrimination, adopted by the General Assembly in resolution 2106 A (XX) of 21 December 1965, had attracted only 41 States parties and the optional petition system that it established would not receive sufficient declarations to enter into force for another 13 years (on 3 December 1982). There were, at the time, no other treaty-based communications procedures in the human rights field. The International Covenants on Human Rights had been adopted by the General Assembly in its resolution 2200 A (XXI) of 16 December 1966 but would not enter into force until a decade later.

2. The treaty system in 1980[12]

26. Only a decade later, four different treaty bodies were in existence. They were, in addition to the Committee on the Elimination of Racial Discrimination: the Group of Three established under the Convention on the Suppression and Punishment of the Crime of *Apartheid* (resolution 3068 (XXVIII), annex); the Sessional Working Group on the Implementation of the International Covenant on Economic, Social and Cultural Rights; and the Human Rights Committee. The Committee on the Elimination of Racial Discrimination produced a 135 page report[13] relating to a Convention that by then had 104 States parties. The Group of Three was concerned with a Convention that had 49 States parties but only five reports were before it at its 1979 session. It submitted a six-page report to the Commission on Human Rights (E/CN.4/1328). The Sessional Working Group, which was assisting the Economic and Social Council to monitor a Covenant that then had 56 States parties, met for the first time in 1979 and presented the Council with a six-page report (E/1979/64).

27. In 1980, the Human Rights Committee was barely four years old and was monitoring a Covenant that then had 58 States parties, almost a quarter of which had only ratified the Covenant in the preceding two years. Only 21 of them had ratified the Optional Protocol and 10 had made the declaration under article 41 (concerning inter-State communications). The latter procedure had only just entered into force (in March 1979), and the Committee had only registered a total of 53 communications (relating to 9 States) under the Optional Protocol. More than four fifths (a total of 43) of those communications related to only 2 States. By the end of 1979 the Committee had adopted only one set of final views under article 5 (4) of the Optional Protocol. The adoption of General Comments (under article 40 (4)), an activity which is now regular and of major importance, had not yet begun and there was not even any agreement as to the method that might be

---

and the Caribbean of the World Conference on Human Rights, which stated that "an evaluation of the United Nations human rights system is needed ...", A.CONF.157/PC/58, para. 8.

[11] *Official Records of the General Assembly, Twenty-fifth Session, Supplement No. 27* (A/8027).

[12] The statistics used in this section actually relate to 1979 rather than 1980. They will be revised to reflect the 1980 statistics in the final version of this updated study.

[13] *Ibid., Thirty-fourth Session, Supplement No. 18* (A/34/18).

followed in doing so. The report of the Committee for 1979 was 130 pages in length.[14]

28. Thus by 1979 the General Assembly was receiving annual reports directly from only two treaty bodies (the two Committees), although it was also taking note in its resolutions of the work of the other two bodies (the Group of Three and the Sessional Working Group). It thus had a total of 276 pages of reports to consider. Those reports contained no General Comments (adopted by the Human Rights Committee), no decisions or general recommendations on matters other than procedural ones (adopted by the Committee on the Elimination of Racial Discrimination), and only one set of final views in response to communications by individuals. There were a total of 267 States parties to the 4 treaties, making an average of 67 per instrument.

3. The treaty system in 1993

29. By 1993 the human rights treaty system had undergone a major transformation in comparison with the situation in 1980. Briefly stated, there are now seven treaty bodies (with the addition, since 1980, of the Committee on the Elimination of Discrimination against Women (1982), the Committee against Torture (1988), and the Committee on the Rights of the Child (1991), as well as the replacement of the Sessional Working Group by the Committee on Economic, Social and Cultural Rights (1987). There are (at 1 January 1993) a total of 678 States parties to the 6 instruments (at an average of 113 per treaty).[15] The Optional Protocol has been ratified by three times the number of States that had accepted it at the beginning of the previous decade. In so far as delegates to the General Assembly or the Commission endeavoured to read the annual reports of all 6 treaty bodies they were confronted (on the basis of 1992 reports) with a total of 939 pages, a 50 per cent increase from three years earlier.[16]

30. Thus, in quantitative terms, the General Assembly at its forty-seventh session was, by comparison with its work-load only a little over a decade earlier, expected to consider the reports of 50 per cent more treaty bodies (from 4 to 6), to deal with instruments that have more than two and one-half times the number of States parties (from 267 to 678) and to read three and one-half times the amount of documentation (from 276 to 939 pages). The comparison between the figures at the beginning of 1993 and those used in the first version of this study only three years earlier are equally revealing in showing the rate of growth of the treaty regime. The number of States parties increased by 27 per cent (from 533 to 678) and the average number of parties per treaty went from 90 to 113. Thus, in overall terms, the potential workload of each committee increased by more than 25 per cent within a three year period.

---

[14] *Ibid., Supplement No. 40* (A/34/40).
[15] Status of International Instruments: Chart of Ratifications as at 1 January 1993, ST/HR/4/Rev.7.
[16] This figure is actually significantly lower than it will be in the years ahead because the Committee on the Rights of the Child had not considered any States reports by the end of 1992 and the Committee on the Elimination of Racial Discrimination was able to meet for only two weeks instead of the scheduled six weeks.

31. It is in the qualitative rather than the quantitative realm, however, that the greatest change has taken place. By comparison with a little over a decade ago the annual reports are generally less procedurally oriented and contain far more information of substantive relevance beyond the confines of the treaty regime itself. In 1980 none of the treaty bodies had adopted any general comments. By January 1993, the Human Rights Committee had adopted 21 such comments (two of which replaced earlier ones), the Economic, Social and Cultural Rights Committee had adopted four and foreshadowed others, the Committee against Torture is empowered by the relevant Convention to adopt general comments, the Committee on the Elimination of Discrimination against Women had adopted 20 general recommendations and 3 suggestions, and the Committee on the Elimination of Racial Discrimination had adopted 10 general recommendations and a significant number of decisions.

32. It is not so much the overall number of these types of statements nor their length that are most significant. Their true relevance lies in the importance that the respective committees attach to them and the extent to which they assume that States parties and other interested observers will take account of their content and implications in interpreting or applying the relevant treaty provisions. They are therefore of cumulative relevance, in the sense that a full appreciation of the work of a particular Committee in 1993 might require an understanding of a range of general comments it has adopted in previous years but which are not reprinted in its current annual report.[17]

33. In addition to general comments and other similar statements, all of the committees now adopt substantive, evaluative "general observations" at the conclusion of their consideration of individual State party reports. As the transition has been made from the consideration of initial reports to that of periodic reports and as the Committees have become more specific and more sophisticated in their requests for detailed information, these concluding observations have also become more detailed and precise and more significant in jurisprudential terms. For that reason, their relevance is increasingly perceived not to be restricted solely to the State party concerned. They too must thus be taken into account by observers wishing to obtain a full understanding of the Committees' approach in matters of both normative (substantive) and procedural import.

34. Finally, the situation in 1993 differs dramatically from that of 1980 in terms firstly of the sheer volume of individual communications being received by the Human Rights Committee in particular and secondly of the jurisprudential significance and complexity of many of the relevant decisions. In its 1988 report, the Committee noted that there had been "an exponential growth in the number of communications submitted to it" and observed that while it had had 33 pending cases before it at the end of 1986, the figures for the following two years were 49 and 116 respectively.[18] By July 1992 the Committee had 153 cases pending.[19]

---

[17] All of the general comments and general recommendations have recently been issued in a single compilation, contained in HRI/GEN/1 (1992).
[18] Ibid., Forty-third Session, Supplement No. 40 (A/43/40), para. 642.
[19] Official Records of the General Assembly, Forty-seventh Session, Supplement No. 40 (A/47/40), para. 615.

35. Moreover, in its early years, many of the Committee's decisions on the merits dealt with cases of physical and psychological abuse where the facts rather than the law were principally in dispute. Procedural rather than substantive matters were also often the major focus. In recent years, the range of issues dealt with has increased considerably and the jurisprudential interpretations adopted by the Committee have sometimes had a significance ranging far beyond the immediate case in hand. In the Committee's 1992 report, for example, important decisions in response to communications dealt with matters such as the right to take part in the conduct of public affairs, the right to a fair trial, the double jeopardy rule, the right of an accused person to communicate with counsel, procedural safeguards in relation to extradition, what constitutes trial within a "reasonable time", the principle of non-discrimination in relation to social security benefits, and reasonable conditions of detention.[20] The approach adopted in each of these decisions is therefore of direct relevance to specific matters being dealt with in other United Nations human rights forums.

4. *The treaty system in the year 2000: a glimpse into the future*

36. A few bare facts must suffice to provide an indication of the likely shape of the treaty system seven years from now. In the first place, current proposals for the creation of at least one more treaty body (dealing with the rights of migrant workers) might have reached fruition by that time, bringing the total to eight. Moreover, it seems very likely that these treaties will, by the year 2000, have been supplemented by a significant number of optional protocols, some but not all of which will involve additional procedural as well as substantive obligations for States parties (the draft optional protocol to the Convention against Torture and Other Cruel, Inhuman or Degrading Treatment or Punishment (E/CN.4/1993/28) being a prime example in this regard).

37. Secondly, the number of States parties is likely to have continued growing at a steady pace and the total extent of reporting obligations will have grown accordingly as well as being further extended by the entry into force of the new treaty on migrant workers and some of the optional protocols. If we assume that each of the six principal treaties will have 160 States parties by the year 2000, there will be almost 1,000 separate reports required. The ramifications for all concerned of such a workload are potentially immense. If existing procedures are retained, and if reports are submitted on schedule, each of the treaty bodies will need a radical increase in the amount of meeting time available to them (this issue is explored in more detail below).

38. In addition, all of the treaty bodies have now indicated that they are prepared to set special procedures in train where it seems essential to respond to urgent situations pertaining to the rights recognized in the relevant treaty. It can be assumed that the use of these procedures will have been considerably developed by the year 2000 and that a significant number of States parties will, each year, be requested to furnish information which is additional

---

[20] *Ibid.*, Annex IX.

Appendix 5: Long-Term Effectiveness of the UN Human Rights Treaty System 533

to that contained in their scheduled periodic reports under each of the treaties. In total then, the overall amount of information required to be processed will have increased very significantly and the extent of secretariat servicing needed will have expanded accordingly.

39. The number of communications being processed will probably have risen dramatically as the Human Rights Committee's work becomes even better known, as the procedure of the Committee on the Elimination of Racial Discrimination outlined in article 14 of the relevant Convention moves well beyond its current rather embryonic stage and as the Committee against Torture begins to attract a sizeable number of communications.

40. In addition, proposed optional protocols permitting communications to be lodged might by that time have been adopted in connection with both the Convention on the Elimination of All Forms of Discrimination against Women and the Covenant on Economic, Social and Cultural Rights. There is also good reason to expect that the rate of acceptance by States of the arrangements relating to communications will accelerate in the years ahead, even when compared to the impressive rate achieved in recent years. As communications procedures become more widespread, and as the issues raised become more complex and more far-reaching in their implications, the pressure will increase further for staff to process the applications and to prepare initial legal analyses of the issues raised.

41. Finally, it is very clear that the various treaty bodies will be making extensive use of the technique of adopting general comments and similar statements. This in turn will give rise to an even greater need for coordination and consultation and for an increasingly voluminous jurisprudence under each treaty to be taken into account. If all of these trends are confirmed, it seems reasonable to predict that the total volume of the 8 annual reports could easily double its 1992 level, to reach 2,000 pages by the year 2000.

B. *Implications for the treaty system of the general expansion of multilateral human rights activities*

42. The past two decades have witnessed a major expansion not only in the human rights treaty system but also in the United Nations human rights programme as a whole. A similar expansion has also occurred within the framework of other multilateral groupings. While these developments are clearly to be welcomed, it is also necessary to acknowledge that they have helped to render the challenges facing the treaty bodies considerably more complex than they might otherwise have been. In the present context it must suffice to note four areas in which particular expansion has taken place.

1. *The increasing number, and degree of detail, of standards*

43. The first area is human rights standard-setting, which is generally recognized as one of the most impressive achievements of the United Nations human rights programme. This activity has yielded not only the treaties on the basis of which the various treaty supervisory bodies have been established but also a wide range of other international standards. Thus for example the

1988 edition of the United Nations *Compilation of International Instruments*[21] contains the texts of 65 different instruments adopted between 1948 and 1986 (as well as 2 others adopted in 1926 and 1930, respectively). While the average rate of adoption of new standards has remained relatively constant over this period, the result of 40 years of consistent activity is an extensive accumulation of standards, which are, in most cases, of direct relevance to the work of one or more of the treaty bodies. Although the treaty bodies are not called upon to apply, and much less to interpret, any standards other than those contained in their respective constitutive instruments, a familiarity on the part of members of the Committees with all relevant international standards is clearly desirable in order to avoid potential inconsistency and confusion. As the total number of instruments continues to grow, the difficulty of mastering the relevant body of international legal provisions also increases.

2. *The expansion of the activities of the Charter-based organs*

44. The second area of expansion of direct relevance to the work of the treaty bodies concerns the range of activities undertaken by the principal Charter-based organs and in particular the Commission on Human Rights and the Sub-Commission on Prevention of Discrimination and Protection of Minorities. Over the past decade, there has been a major expansion in the work of these bodies, particularly in the context of thematic procedures, country-specific procedures, advisory service activities and studies and standard-setting activities of general relevance. In monitoring States parties' compliance with their treaty obligations it is clearly desirable that each Committee be adequately informed of relevant developments in these other contexts. This entails, however, the continuing review of an increasingly voluminous documentation. In addition, there is a growing tendency for the Commission, the Sub-Commission and the Commission on the Status of Women, as well as various other bodies (in addition, of course, to the General Assembly and the Economic and Social Council), to address the activities of the treaty bodies directly in their respective resolutions. Whatever the formal status of such resolutions *vis-a-vis* the individual treaty bodies, the more or less explicit policy suggestions they contain clearly need to be taken into account.

3. *The increasing range of international policies of direct relevance*

45. The third area of expansion concerns the broad range of United Nations activities about which the treaty bodies should be reasonably well informed if they are to be fully effective in their own work. Obvious examples include the desirability of an awareness on the part of the members of the treaty bodies of the current position in relation to the drafting of new standards in the field of human rights. Moreover, not all such activities are taking place within the specialist human rights organs. Thus, certain aspects of the work of the Commission on Social Development, the Commission on the

---

[21] United Nations publication, Sales No. E.88.XIV.1.

Appendix 5: Long-Term Effectiveness of the UN Human Rights Treaty System 535

Status of Women and the Commission on Crime Prevention and Criminal Justice may be of direct relevance to the treaty bodies.

46. The less obvious examples include the relevance to the work of the Committee on the Elimination of Discrimination against Women, for instance, of the activities of a vast array of United Nations bodies dealing with women's issues. Thus, a "cross-organizational programme analysis of the activities of the United Nations system for the advancement of women" prepared by the Secretary-General identified over 500 "legislative instruments" (resolutions and decisions, etc.) adopted primarily during the period 1975 to 1988 (E/1989/19, para. 17). While Committee members clearly do not require a detailed knowledge of all of these instruments (or of the programmes to which they have given rise) in order to carry out the tasks entrusted to them by the Convention, a certain level of awareness is obviously desirable.

47. In addition, reference can also be made to the relevance of the work of the committees of experts of the International Labour Organisation (ILO) and the United Nations Educational, Scientific and Cultural Organization (UNESCO) that are responsible for monitoring States parties' compliance with a range of relevant human rights-related treaty obligations. The work of these bodies is of direct importance for at least three reasons. In the first place, the standards that are set within these organisations are often very directly related to the standards being dealt with by the different treaty bodies. This is true, for example, in relation to a wide range of anti-discrimination provisions, to the rights of women, indigenous peoples and various vulnerable groups, as well as in relation to specific rights such as freedom of association, the right to join trade unions and the right to education.

48. Secondly, the jurisprudence generated by these supervisory committees is of potentially major relevance to the work of the treaty bodies, in much the same way as is the jurisprudence generated by the principal regional bodies (see the discussion below). Thirdly, it is likely that at least some of the issues considered in relation to a given State party's report by a United Nations treaty body will already have been examined within the context of the work of either the ILO or the UNESCO supervisory committee's work. While previous consideration of the issue in those contexts does not in any way deprive the relevant United Nations treaty body of either its jurisdiction or its responsibility to examine the issue, it is desirable that the latter be aware of, and indeed well-informed about, the latter.

4. Developments at the regional level

49. The final area of expansion concerns human rights activities being undertaken in other multilateral contexts, and particularly by the principal regional organizations. The General Assembly has consistently emphasized the importance that it attaches to regional human rights initiatives as a complement to United Nations activities, most recently in its resolution 47/125. Similarly, the Commission on Human Rights has regularly received information from, and heard interventions by, representatives of the Council of Europe, the Organization of African Unity (OAU) and the Organization of American States (OAS) and by representatives of their respective human rights organs.

50. Over the past decade, in particular, both the Inter-American Commission and Court of Human Rights and the European Commission and Court of Human Rights have built up an impressive human rights jurisprudence in interpreting instruments that contain many provisions similar to those contained in United Nations human rights treaties. The gradual expansion of the activities of the African Commission on Human and Peoples' Rights will, in time, contribute further to building up this body of jurisprudence. In addition, other specialist bodies are likely to be created at the regional level. The European Committee for the Prevention of Torture and Inhuman or Degrading Treatment or Punishment is an example of such a body that has already been set up. Others are certain to follow, such as the African Committee of Experts on the Rights and Welfare of the Child whose creation is already envisaged under the African Charter on the Rights and Welfare of the Child.

51. While it must be emphasized that it would be entirely inappropriate to assume that the approach adopted by a regional organ on the basis of a regional treaty could simply be transposed automatically to the international level (or vice versa), the growing maturity of the three separate regional mechanisms, the organs of which often operate in parallel to their United Nations counterparts, raises important issues which have yet to be adequately addressed. Some of these matters are addressed in a later part of this study in connection with the consideration of initiatives that might be desirable in order to promote normative consistency.

52. In addition, reference must be made in this context to the activities of other regional bodies which may well be of direct relevance to the work of the United Nations human rights treaty bodies. In particular, the range of activities now being conducted under the auspices of the Conference on Security and Co-operation in Europe has grown dramatically in recent years.

C. *The treaty system as the cornerstone of the United Nations human rights programme*

53. As noted earlier, it is true in a strict legal sense that the output of each treaty body is of direct applicability only in connection with the performance of the specific tasks accorded to it in the relevant treaty. Thus, it can be argued that the approaches that it adopts and the jurisprudence that emerges from its various activities are of direct relevance only to those States which have ratified the treaty and then only in situations in which the treaty regime is clearly applicable. However, such a narrow, legalistic characterization of the role of the treaty bodies is artificial at best, and misleading at worst. Taken to its logical extreme it could, for example, be used to justify the conclusion that the effective functioning of a given treaty body is of no particular concern to the policy-making organs or that the interpretation accorded to a particular norm by the appropriate treaty body should not necessarily affect, in any way, the approach to an identical or very similar norm by another body (whether a policy-making organ or another treaty body). However, propositions such as these have been consistently contradicted by the policy and practice of virtually all of the relevant bodies.

54. Indeed, in a number of different ways the treaty bodies have come to be

Appendix 5: Long-Term Effectiveness of the UN Human Rights Treaty System 537

seen as an indispensable cornerstone for the activities of the United Nations human rights programme as a whole. Over the past few years the nature and extent of the interaction between the policymaking organs and the treaty bodies has increased very significantly. This interaction has manifested itself in a number of different contexts as the following illustrative survey indicates.

1. *Reference to the work of the treaty bodies in matters of interpretation*

55. In an address to the General Assembly on the occasion of the twentieth anniversary of the adoption of the Covenants, the Secretary-General noted that the Human Rights Committee had contributed significantly to the further elaboration of international human rights law in key areas (A/41/PV.54, p. 5). This comment has subsequently been borne out by various rapporteurs of the Commission on Human Rights, and other similar sources. Thus, for example, the then Special Rapporteur on summary or arbitrary executions observed in his 1992 report that:

"The General Comments adopted by the Committee on Human Rights [sic], as well as the decisions adopted in cases considered under the Optional Protocol, have been cited frequently by the Special Rapporteur as a guide to the interpretation of international standards concerning summary and arbitrary executions." (E/CN.4/1992/30, para. 645).

56. In a similar vein, the Commission on Human Rights specifically requested the Special Rapporteur, to bear in mind, as appropriate, the Human Rights Committee's comments "in its interpretation of article 6" of the Covenant (resolution 1993/71, para. 9).

57. Similarly, the then Special Rapporteur on torture and other cruel, inhuman or degrading treatment or punishment cited the relevant general comments of the Human Rights Committee at considerable length in his 1993 report. In his conclusion he notes:

"If all Governments would take to heart the views and opinions of the Committee and would scrutinize their national system [sic] to see whether it is in conformity with these views and opinions and would start to introduce the necessary reforms, the campaign against torture would gain new momentum. The Human Rights Committee is a highly authoritative body ... Its views should ... be taken with the greatest possible seriousness." (E/CN.4/1993/26, para. 594).

58. The assumption that the work of the Committee is of major and direct relevance to the United Nations programme as a whole is perhaps most clearly expressed in Economic and Social Council resolution 1987/4, in which, *inter alia*, it welcomed the continuing efforts of the Human Rights Committee to strive for uniform standards in the implementation of the Covenant and appealed to other bodies dealing with similar questions of human rights to respect those uniform standards, as expressed in the General Comments of the Human Rights Committee. Given the Council's specific co-ordination mandate in the field of human rights, such an expression of policy is of particular significance.

59. However, the Committee itself has acknowledged that its influence should

extend beyond the United Nations system by defining the prospective audience of its decisions under the Optional Protocol broadly. In its view, their ready availability has been of great value to government departments, researchers and the general public.[22] Other commentators have been less optimistic. One expert group has estimated that the influence of the Committee's general comments on States parties has been "insignificant, even when reference to [them] is put on the list of issues for the consideration of a report".[23]

60. The work of the Committee on the Elimination of Discrimination against Women has assumed major significance far beyond the immediate confines of the relevant treaty regime, in the context of a broad range of international activities touching on the issue of non-discrimination against women. As the Director of the Division for the Advancement of Women noted at the opening of the Committee's eighth session, the Committee's work has come to have an extremely important multiplier effect in the definition of global policies.[24] The important relationship between the work of the Committee and that of other relevant bodies has also been noted by the Commission on the Status of Women, which has indicated in its resolution 33/3 that it shares the concern expressed by the Committee that its recommendations be consistent with recommendations adopted by intergovernmental bodies dealing with the advancement of women or human rights issues.

2. Enhanced efforts to ensure coordination between treaty and Charter bodies

61. Various of the treaty bodies have been actively engaged in efforts to coordinate, to the extent appropriate, certain aspects of their work with that of one or other of the Charter-based organs. Of the many examples that could be cited, reference may be made to: the joint meeting between the Sub-Commission on Prevention of Discrimination and Protection of Minorities and the Committee on the Elimination of Racial Discrimination in 1991; the dialogue between the Committee on the Rights of the Child and the Commission's Special Rapporteur on the sale of children, child prostitution and child pornography; the opportunities provided by the Committee on Economic, Social and Cultural Rights for various Special Rapporteurs of the Sub-Commission (including, on different occasions, Messrs. Turk, Despouy, Eide and Sachar) to engage in a dialogue with it: and the exchanges of views held between the members of the Committee against Torture and the Special Rapporteur of the Commission on Human Rights on questions relating to torture.

62. The question of coordination assumes special significance in a context in which suggestions have been made that there are now too many mechanisms addressing the same issues. Although this is a theme to which this study returns in relation to the need for enhanced coordination among the treaty bodies themselves, it should be noted that the treaty bodies and thematic

---

[22] *Official Records of the General Assembly, Forty-second Session, Supplement No. 40* (A/42/40), para. 28.
[23] *Making the Reporting Procedure under the International Covenant on Civil and Political Rights More Effective*, op cit., at 25.
[24] *Ibid., Forty-fourth Session, Supplement No. 38* (A/44/38) Para. 8.

mechanisms are designed to fulfill significantly different functions. Indeed they can, and often seek to, complement one another rather than to duplicate. The differences in this regard have been carefully set down by the Special Rapporteur on torture and other cruel, inhuman or degrading treatment or punishment in his most recent report to the Commission on Human Rights (E/CN.4/1993/26, paras. 6–18). While the case made therein for the continuation of complementary mechanisms is very strong, it will be less so if both the treaty bodies and the other relevant mechanisms do not remain vigilant in their efforts to ensure appropriate coordination.[25] A major difficulty in this regard, however, is that such coordination must rely heavily upon appropriate secretariat advice and analysis which, largely but not solely for reasons of inadequate resources, is not always available to the treaty bodies.

3. *The submission of specific proposals for the consideration of the treaty bodies*

63. In theory, with the exception of the International Covenant on Economic, Social and Cultural Rights, no provision is made for any direct relationship between the treaty bodies and organs such as the Commission on Human Rights and its Sub-Commission. Yet despite this lacuna, in recent years the Commission has, as a matter of course, addressed itself on a regular basis to the various treaty bodies. Similarly, Special Rapporteurs of both the Commission and the Sub-Commission have regularly made suggestions to the treaty bodies as to the conduct of their work.

64. A few examples from the Commission's forty-ninth session are sufficient to illustrate this point. Thus, the Commission: invited the treaty bodies to pay particular attention to the rights of persons infected with HIV or AIDS and those around them (resolution 1993/53; para. 4); invited the Committee on the Rights of the Child to study the possibility of bearing the Programme of Action for the Elimination of the Exploitation of Child Labour in mind when considering reports (resolution 1993/79, para. 5); requested the treaty bodies to include in their reports a reference to allegations of intimidation or reprisal and of hampering access to United Nations human rights procedures, as well as an account of action taken by them in this regard (resolution 1993/64, para. 4); encouraged the Committee on Economic, Social and Cultural Rights and the Committee on the Rights of the Child to pay particular attention to the question of extreme poverty (resolution 1993/13, paras. 3 and 4); requested the committees to give particular attention to matters related to contemporary forms of slavery (resolution 1993/27, para. 14); and requested the treaty bodies to provide the relevant Commission mechanisms with all relevant and accurate information in their possession on the human rights situations creating or affecting refugees and displaced persons within their mandates (resolution 1993/70, para. 4).

65. For the most part, this treatment of the committees as being an integral part of the overall United Nations human rights regime is to be strongly welcomed. It may be, however, that careful consideration needs to be given to

---

[25] It is significant in this context that the Commission on Human Rights has welcomed "the importance that the Working Group [on Arbitrary Detention] attaches to coordination with other mechanisms of the commission as well with treaty-monitoring bodies". Resolution 1993/36, para. 7.

the limits that might be appropriate in this regard. Thus, for example, while information contained in reports submitted to, and adopted by, the treaty bodies is in the public domain and should certainly be taken into account by other mechanisms, it might not necessarily be appropriate to ask the treaty bodies to submit thematic reports to the Commission.

4. *Communications from the treaty bodies to the Charter-based organs*

66. The treaty bodies have on many occasions communicated their views on certain issues to the Charter-based organs. This has happened especially in relation to the World Conference on Human Rights and is likely to continue in relation to events such as the proposed World Summit on Social Development and the 1994 International Conference on Population and Development. Similarly, the Committee on the Elimination of Racial Discrimination has contributed to the formulation of the draft Programme of Action for the Third Decade to Combat Racism and Racial Discrimination.[26]

67. In a related development, some of the treaty bodies have also communicated with Charter-based mechanisms in relation to situations of particular concern. Thus, for example, in August 1992 the Committee on the Elimination of Racial Discrimination expressed its grave concern at developments taking place in the former Yugoslavia and expressed its 'trust' that the Commission on Human Rights "would take expeditious and effective measures" at a Special Session scheduled in that regard. The Committee also expressed "its readiness to cooperate in this endeavour within the framework of [its] mandate".[27] In relation to the same situation the Committee on the Elimination of Discrimination against Women, at its twelfth session, in 1993, wrote to the Special Rapporteur of the Commission on Human Rights to express its concern over violent acts taking place in the former Yugoslavia.

68. In a similar vein, the Secretary-General has suggested that ways should be explored "of empowering the Secretary-General and expert human rights bodies to bring massive violations of human rights to the attention of the Security Council, together with recommendations for action".[28] This proposal subsequently received the full support of the fourth meeting of chairpersons (A/47/628, para. 43). The fact that each of the treaty bodies has, within the past year or so, decided to take special action in response to exceptional, or emergency, situations may be seen as an indispensable step towards responding to the need identified by the Secretary-General in relation to the Security Council. It also, and perhaps more importantly, is a way of responding to the view that the treaty bodies will lose their credibility unless they are seen to be responsive to massive violations or other emergency situations relating to matters that fall directly within their mandates.

69. But while this development is to be very warmly welcomed, it would seem to raise a number of important and complex questions of coordination which should be specifically addressed by the various treaty bodies, perhaps on

---

[26] Commission on Human Rights resolution 1993/11, Annex, Part II.
[27] *Official Records of the General Assembly, Forty-seventh Session, Supplement No. 18* (A/47/18)., Annex VII.
[28] *Official Records of the General Assembly, Forty-seventh Session, Supplement No. 1* (A/47/1), para. 101.

the basis of an analytical paper prepared for them by the secretariat. The meeting of chairpersons should also have a role to play in this regard.

5. *Proposals for new functions to be assumed by the treaty bodies*

70. In principle, only the Committee on Economic, Social and Cultural Rights (because it is a creation of the Economic and Social Council, which therefore has the authority to determine its mandate) can be formally entrusted with new functions by the Charter-based organs. In practice, however, the inability of the Charter-based organs to expand the formal functions of the other treaty bodies (a measure which would require an amendment of the relevant treaty in accordance with the procedures provided for therein) has not deterred them from suggesting ways in which existing mandates might be applied in a different, or more expansive, manner. Thus, for example, the Commission has invited the treaty bodies "to monitor the compliance of States with their commitments under the relevant human rights instruments in order to ensure the full enjoyment of those rights by disabled persons" (resolution 1993/29, para. 7). Along similar lines, a recent report by the Secretary-General relating to Declaration on the Right to Development suggested that both the Human Rights Committee and the Committee on Economic, Social and Cultural Rights might be requested to "take into consideration the Declaration ... when examining States parties' reports", and that the latter Committee could also be asked, "when dealing with reports of both developing and developed States, bear in mind their obligation under Article 56 of the Charter" (E/CN.4/1993/16, paras. 53–54).
71. These various examples, which are by no means exhaustive, demonstrate the extent to which the work of the treaty bodies has becoming increasingly intertwined with the overall human rights programme of the United Nations. For the most part, this phenomenon is greatly to be welcomed since it underscores the fact that both the treaty- and Charter-based bodies are engaged in a common endeavour to promote and protect human rights. By the same token, it must be recognized that there is a difficult line that must be maintained between, on the one hand, promoting the most effective degree of interaction and, on the other hand, ensuring that the distinctive characteristics of the committees' treaty supervisory functions are not inappropriately blurred or even lost. It is important, therefore, that all concerned should bear in mind the need to strike an appropriate balance in this regard.

D. *Towards universality of membership in the treaty regime*

72. The attainment of universal membership in the international human rights treaty regime is, in very many ways, central to the effective long-term functioning of that regime. It is thus an essential focus of consideration in the present study.
73. The term "universality" is used to connote two rather different, but nonetheless related, concepts. The first usage refers to the quest to achieve universal ratification of, or accession to, the principal international human rights treaties. The second usage refers to the extent to which the concept of human rights is universally consonant with diverse cultural, religious and other

traditions. In this second context the concept of universality is sometimes contrasted to the assertion that all values, including rights, are culturally relative in the sense of being specific to the culture or society in question (and thus not susceptible to authentic universalization).

74. All too often these concepts are confused or combined with one another in ways that are not helpful. Acceptance of the view that culture has an appropriate role in the approach to, and manner of application of, universal standards need not in any way undermine the quest to achieve universal membership of the human rights treaty regime. Indeed, in many ways, the contrary position is by far the most persuasive. That is, that universal membership and active participation by all countries in the global human rights regime would provide the most constructive context in which to pursue the complex question of the role of culture in the application of human rights standards. The importance of this dialogue has been emphasized in the conclusions adopted by the Interregional meeting organised by the Council of Europe in advance of the World Conference on Human Rights:

"We must go back to listening. More thought and effort must be given to enriching the human rights discourse by explicit reference to other non-Western religions and cultural traditions. By tracing the linkages between constitutional values on the one hand and the concepts, ideas and institutions which are central to Islam or the Hindu-Buddhist tradition or other traditions, the base of support for fundamental rights can be expanded and the claim to universality vindicated. The Western world has no monopoly or patent on basic human rights. We must embrace cultural diversity but not at the expense of universal minimum standards."[29]

75. There could be no better forum, or context, in which to pursue this dialogue in a structured, thoughtful and constructive manner than that provided by the treaty bodies. Universal membership is thus a goal of the utmost importance.

76. Both the General Assembly and the Commission on Human Rights have appealed to States, on innumerable, occasions to become parties to one treaty or another. In recent years, it would seem that this approach has been at least partly successful if measured by the increasing number of parties to many of the treaties. Although this picture of success needs to be tempered by acknowledgment of the fact that many of the new parties are newly independent States which were previously part of another State party to the relevant treaties, it remains the case that several States of very major importance, in all regions of the world, have extended their participation in the treaty regime significantly in recent years. Nevertheless, the fact remains that the two International Human Rights Covenants had been ratified by only slightly more than 60 per cent of the community of States as at 1 January 1993. The Convention against Torture and Other Cruel, Inhuman or Degrading Treatment or Punishment had achieved acceptance by only about 40 per cent of States.

---

[29]"Conclusions by the General Rapporteur, Mary Robinson, President of Ireland", Human Rights at the Dawn of the 21st Century, Council of Europe doc. CE/CMDH (93) 16 of 30 January 1993, at 3.

Appendix 5: Long-Term Effectiveness of the UN Human Rights Treaty System 543

77. The principal challenge then is how universality can most effectively be promoted by the United Nations. It is clear that there are limits to the extent to which the international community can go in "insisting" that States accept any particular international treaty obligations; such acceptance remains entirely a sovereign decision for each State to take in accordance with its own constitutional and other procedures. By the same token, however, it is important not to overstate this point to such a degree that it renders United Nations bodies unwilling to pursue the quest for universality with appropriate vigour.

78. In essence, three different approaches have been explored so far. The first consists largely of exhortation by each of the Charter-based organs and the various mechanisms established under them, including thematic rapporteurs and special rapporteurs. Similarly, both the Secretary-General and the Under-Secretary-General for Human Rights have frequently urged States to ratify or accede to international human rights instruments (HRI/MC/1992/2, para. 8).

79. The second approach, undertaken primarily by the Sub-Commission on Prevention of Discrimination and Protection of Minorities, has been to request States to indicate the reasons why they have chosen not to become parties to the relevant treaties. But one such request for information elicited no replies at all (E/CN.4/Sub.2/1992/27, para. 7). More recently the Commission on Human Rights has invited States that have not ratified or acceded to the treaties dealing with slavery "to explain in writing, if they so wish, why they feel unable to do so ..." (resolution 1993/27, para. 4). But while a similar approach has been effective in relation to the standard-setting activities of the International Labour Organization, this would seem to be more a function of the constitutional basis of the procedure in the ILO's case rather than of any general preparedness on the part of Governments to respond to such queries.

80. The third approach has been to offer advisory services to States with a view to assisting them to become parties to the principal instruments. Although it has most recently found expression in paragraph 3 of Commission resolution 1993/15, the link between advisory services and the encouragement of universal membership has long been drawn. While there is probably no satisfactory basis on which the effectiveness of this strategy could be evaluated, it is difficult to point to instances in which the type of services currently available have made a crucial difference in this respect.

81. In general, it seems fair to conclude that, despite the best intentions of all concerned, the strategy pursued to date has, for the most part, been piecemeal and lacking in depth as well as resources. What is needed now is for the United Nations to adopt a more sustained and carefully planned programme designed to achieve universality. Such a programme should consist of three principal elements:

(a) *Universal membership in the treaty regime should be identified as one of the foundation stones of the human rights programme*

82. It should be portrayed as the best means of consolidating the universal foundations of the regime and of facilitating more sensitive and constructive consideration of the cultural dimensions of human rights implementation.

This element of the programme should also involve treating the six instruments which are, in effect the focus of the present study, as constituting the fundamental core of the United Nations human rights system. They should, to the greatest extent possible, be treated as part of a package so that States which have formally adhered to only some of the six should be urged in the strongest possible terms to complete their acceptance of the basic package. In particular, States which are parties to only one of the two International Human Rights Covenants should, in the interests not only of universality but of upholding the fundamental principle of the equality of the two sets of rights, be urged to ratify the other half of the basic package as soon as possible. As of 1 January 1993 there were six States which had ratified only one or other but not both of the Covenants.[30]

(b) *The universality strategy should identify specific issues to be pursued and obstacles to be targeted*

83. There is no doubt that a lack of political will explains the failure of some Governments to have ratified the principal treaties. By the same token, however, there are also various other reasons why Governments might have been unable to ratify. In some cases those reasons might be of a rather mundane bureaucratic, administrative or financial nature. For the most part, these are not reasons which Governments are likely to want to set down in writing nor are the underlying issues likely to be addressed by the type of regional or sub-regional meetings that have been held so far within the framework of the advisory services programme.

84. Among the reasons that might well be impeding ratification or accession in some countries are the following: a lack of understanding of the implications of the instrument on the part of mid-level officials who would need to prepare the ground before the Government could act; a lack of trained personnel who could explain the implications of ratification with the necessary sophistication and detail to the relevant Government Minister; the existence of an element of confusion between the treaty body procedures and the special procedures of the Commission on Human Rights; a low budget priority for the measures needed to precede or accompany ratification or accession, such as the undertaking of a survey of existing law and practice, the drafting of necessary legislation or regulations, the training of officials etc.; the lack of an informed domestic constituency which would support Government proposals to ratify or accede to an instrument; and a fear that the reporting obligations would be too onerous for the country concerned.

85. Each of these difficulties, which are of an eminently practical nature, could perhaps best be addressed with the assistance of an expert who visits all countries concerned as a matter of course and who is able to mobilize a limited amount of resources to address specific problems that he or she identifies. Moreover, the programme itself could begin by identifying some

---

[30] See ST/HR/4/Rev.7. States which have ratified only the Covenant on Civil and Political Rights are: Haiti: and the United States of America. States which have ratified only the Covenant on Economic, Social and Cultural Rights are: Greece; Guinea Bíssau: Honduras; Solomon Islands; and Uganda.

of the characteristics that appear to be common to countries that have not accepted certain instruments, and then devise appropriate strategies to address the relevant issues.

86. To take but one example, it is apparent from a list of States which have not become parties to either of the International Covenants that there is a predominance of those with relatively small populations. Indeed, as of 1 January 1993, there were 30 States with a population of two million or less in this category. Of those, 21 countries have a population of 500,000 people or less. Fourteen of those 21 can be classified as small island countries. Two-thirds of the 30 countries had an annual Gross National Product per capita of less than $2,000.[31]

87. Provided that the usual caveats in relation to such generalizations are kept in mind, several conclusions might reasonably be drawn from this data. Firstly, at least some of these small States are probably concerned that the legal, bureaucratic and administrative requirements involved are too onerous given the size of their population. Secondly, the reporting requirements might well act as a significant deterrent in such cases. Thirdly, the 20 States with very low populations and low per capita GNP might be strongly influenced by the resource implications of ratification. The addition of these States as parties to the Covenants might thus be facilitated by explaining carefully the various ways in which the ensuing obligations could best be handled, training domestic personnel, making technical assistance available in relation to the preparation of necessary legislation and of reports, or offering assistance to enable Government officials to present their reports in person to the relevant treaty bodies.

88. If measures such as these were successful, the rate of participation in the core regime based on the two Covenants could rise by some 25 per cent very rapidly. At a time when virtually every other major treaty regime, operating under United Nations auspices, goes out of its way to take special account of the specific circumstances of many of these States, it would seem to make little sense for the human rights treaty regime to insist that no such arrangements are warranted.

(c) *A target date for achieving universality should be set and a strategy devised for achieving it. Implementation of the programme should be overseen by a specialist and resources should be earmarked for related activities*

89. The Executive Director of UNICEF recently proposed setting the year 1995 for achieving universal ratification of, or accession to, the Convention on the Rights of the Child.[32] A similar approach should be applied to each of the other five basic treaties. The World Conference should set the year 2000 as the year by which to ensure that all States have become full-fledged members of the international human rights treaty regime. Such a target

---

[31] This data is based on a comparison of the Chart of Ratifications, as at 1 January 1993, contained in ST/HR/4/Rev.7 and statistics provided in UNDP, *Human Development Report 1992* (New York, Oxford University Press, 1992). See Table 22 – Demographic Change – listing the estimated population for 1990; and Table 2 – Profile of Human Development – listing GNP per capita for 1989.

[32] "From Madness to Hope", Address by Mr James P. Grant at the Consultation on the Role of the United Nations and NGOs in the Implementation of the Convention on the Rights of the Child, UNICEF House, 24 March 1993, at 5.

would provide an important domestic goal and would greatly assist the task of those at the national level who are advocates of ratification. Moreover, it would provide the occasion for the Commission on Human Rights to undertake periodic reviews of progress achieved.

90. Finally, an effective ratification programme can only be implemented effectively by individuals who are thoroughly well versed in all of the relevant issues, have the appropriate linguistic and other skills and are able to devote themselves to the programme on a full-time basis. Expert members of the Committees cannot be relied upon for this purpose, except in a supplementary capacity. Similarly, resources must be specifically earmarked for this programme rather than being part of a general fund which may or may not be able to be used for this purpose. In other words, the ratification programme needs to be treated as if it is a serious priority concern.

III. REPORTING BY STATES PARTIES

A. *The importance and functions of reporting procedures*

91. The development of reporting systems lies at the very heart of the international system for the promotion and protection of respect for human rights. The establishment of such a system, related to the provisions of the Universal Declaration of Human Rights, was proposed within the United Nations as early as 1951 (see E/CN.4/517, p. 2). A comprehensive periodic reporting system was subsequently established within the framework of the Commission on Human Rights in 1956 by its resolution 1 (XII). The objectives sought to be achieved by this system were not narrowly conceived. On the contrary, they included, in addition to establishing an embryonic form of accountability by States in connection with their responsibilities under Articles 55 and 56 of the Charter of the United Nations the goals of providing an incentive to Governments' efforts; constituting a source of information for United Nations human rights activities in general; helping States to identify areas in which they might benefit from the provision of advisory services by the Secretary-General; and facilitating an exchange of information and ideas in the human rights area.

92. Nevertheless despite the widespread support in principle for the *ad hoc* reporting system, it did not function especially well in practice. As a consequence, the former Director of the United Nations Division of Human Rights concluded with deep regret in the early 1970s that the reporting system had "been allowed to wither away without having been given a fair chance".[33] In effect, however, that system has subsequently been replaced by the various reporting procedures established within the context of the treaties that have entered into force beginning in the late 1960s. The central importance of the new procedures has frequently been affirmed by the General Assembly including most recently in its resolution 43/115, in the preamble of which it recognized that:

---

[33] John Humphrey, "The International Law of Human Rights in the Middle Twentieth Century", in M. Bos (ed.), *The Present State of International Law and other Essays* (Deventer, Kluwer, 1973) 75 at 91.

Appendix 5: Long-Term Effectiveness of the UN Human Rights Treaty System 547

"The effective implementation of instruments on human rights, involving periodic reporting by States parties to the relevant treaty bodies and the efficient functioning of the treaty bodies themselves, not only enhances international accountability in relation to the protection and promotion of human rights but also provides States parties with a valuable opportunity to review policies and programmes affecting the protection and promotion of human rights and to make any appropriate adjustments".

93. It is noteworthy that even States parties that have experienced difficulties in complying with their reporting obligations have acknowledged the value of the procedure. Thus as one such Government told the Human Rights Committee in 1988, the system has the merit of encouraging the carrying out of "a kind of examination of conscience demanded by the international community".[34]

94. In an attempt to shed additional light on the various functions performed by reporting systems, the first General Comment adopted by the Committee on Economic, Social and Cultural Rights sets out a variety of objectives, which, in the view of the Committee, should be served by reporting.[35] To a large extent these objectives would seem to be applicable to all of the reporting systems covered by the present study. The following excerpts from the General Comment provide an indication of its content:

"2. A *first objective*, which is of particular relevance to the initial report required to be submitted within two years of the Covenant's entry into force for the State party concerned, is to ensure that a comprehensive review is undertaken with respect to national legislation, administrative rules and procedures, and practices in an effort to ensure the fullest possible conformity with the Convenant ...

3. A *second objective* is to ensure that the State party monitors the actual situation with respect to each of the rights on a regular basis and is thus aware of the extent to which the various rights are, or are not, being enjoyed by all individuals within its territory or under its jurisdiction ...

4. While monitoring is designed to give a detailed overview of the existing situation, the principal value of such an overview is to provide the basis for the elaboration of clearly stated and carefully targeted policies, including the establishment of priorities which reflect the provisions of the Covenant. Therefore, a *third objective* of the reporting process is to enable the Government to demonstrate that such principled policy-making has in fact been undertaken ...

5. A *fourth objective* of the reporting process is to facilitate public scrutiny of government policies with respect to economic, social and cultural rights and to encourage the involvement of the various economic, social and cultural sectors of society in the formulation, implementation. and review of the relevant policies ...

6. A *fifth objective* is to provide a basis on which the State party itself, as well as the Committee, can effectively evaluate the extent to which progress has been made towards the realization of the obligations contained in the Covenant ...

---

[34] *Official Records of the General Assembly, Forty-third Session, Supplement No. 40* (A/43/40), para. 486.
[35] *Official Records of the Economic and Social Council, 1989, Supplement No. 4* (E/1989/22), annex III.

7. A *sixth objective* is to enable the State party itself to develop a better understanding of the problems and shortcomings encountered in efforts to realize progressively the full range of economic, social and cultural rights ...
8. A *seventh objective* is to enable the Committee, and the States parties as a whole, to facilitate the exchange of information among States and to develop a better understanding of the common problems faced by States and a fuller appreciation of the type of measures which might be taken to promote effective realization of each of the rights contained in the Covenant ..."

95. If there is any one element that runs through each of these functions like a thread it is the importance attached to the role of national level institutions in virtually all phases of the reporting process. It is all too often forgotten (or ignored) that the monitoring role played by the international treaty bodies is, for the most part, only a secondary or catalytic one. The primary role in the procedure should, and indeed must if the process is to be truly effective, be that played by all of the relevant actors at the national level. After all, the best promoters and protectors of human rights are those with the strongest stake in the outcome and the best knowledge and understanding of the situation – the citizens and residents of the country in question. As noted in the Tunis Declaration "[t]he component institutions, organizations and structures of society also play an important role in safeguarding and disseminating these rights; they should therefore be strengthened and encouraged" (A/CONF.157/PC/57, para. 4). Ideally then the treaty bodies principal role would be to monitor the domestic monitors and to make sure that the process of implementation and monitoring in which the Government and its various social partners are cooperating is functioning effectively.

96. It is clear, however, that the current situation in many, if not most, countries falls considerably short of this model. But that is no reason for the treaty bodies to pay less attention to the need to encourage the evolution of appropriate domestic procedures. Such arrangements are, at least potentially, an indispensable prelude, accompaniment and follow-up to the actual examination of a State party's report. While the precise modalities of the best process at the national level will vary significantly from one country to another, there are certain basic issues to which the treaty bodies should in future be encouraged to pay greater attention. Although most of these issues have surfaced at one time or another in the work of each committee, there has been no systematic or persistent endeavour to ensure that they are addressed in relation to every State participating in the treaty regime. Those issues include the following.

1. Dissemination of the text of the relevant instrument

97. This involves full information as to the languages in which the treaty is available, the number of copies printed in each language, the extent to which those copies have been freely and widely disseminated and the means used for that purpose. Efforts to ensure the protection of the rights of individuals and peoples cannot be deemed adequate in the absence of a concerted effort

Appendix 5: Long-Term Effectiveness of the UN Human Rights Treaty System 549

to ensure that the holders of those rights are informed of the content of the rights as well as the means by which they may be vindicated.

2. The modalities of preparation of the State report

98. It has been suggested that Governments should "ensure popular participation" in the preparation of initial and periodic reports (Commission on Human Rights resolution 1993/14, para. 3) and that national human rights institutions should contribute to the preparation of State party reports.[36] In practice, such approaches are, as one recent expert report concluded, rather rare:

"Little [information] is available on the extent to which NGOs actually influence [the drafting] process in various countries, but it is assumed that officially approved, active NGO involvement in the preparation of State reports must be a rarity".[37]

99. But, in any event, although such contributions may be of great value, it will not always be appropriate for either "popular" groups or national institutions to be directly involved in the preparation of what is, both legally and in practical terms, a quintessentially governmental report. What is essential, however, is for the text of the report itself to be readily available at the domestic level (which is often not the case), and for opportunities to have been presented for national debate or discussion of the content of the report. In situations in which no such discussion has occurred, it is probably safe to assume that the report is either so anodyne and detached as to generate no interest or that the appropriate forums have not been used. Governments should be encouraged to schedule their own reports for debate in the national legislature, for consideration by committees of experts or by nationally active non-governmental groups and should report to the treaty bodies on any such discussions.

100. At present the consolidated reporting guidelines ask States to indicate how their reports have been prepared, but this request seems to have elicited very little information of particular relevance. Thus in addition to each treaty body indicating that it attaches major importance to this issue, it may also be appropriate for the next meeting of chairpersons to address the issue in relation to the consolidated reporting guidelines.

3. The submission of information to the treaty body in connection with the examination of the State party report

101. This issue is dealt with below in relation to the question of sources of information.

---

[36] Report of the Regional Meeting for Africa of the World Conference on Human Rights, Tunis, 2–6 November 1992, A/CONF.157/PC/57, resolution AFRM/2, para. 4 (d); and the "Principles relating to the Status of Commissions and Their Advisory Role", adopted by the International Workshop on National Institutions for the Promotion and Protection of Human Rights, Paris, 7–9 October 1991, reprinted in A/CONF.157/PC/42, para. 82 at para. 3 (d).

[37] *Making the Reporting Procedure under the International Covenant on Civil and Political Rights More Effective, op cit.*, at 35.

4. Discussion, at the national level, of the results of the dialogue between the State party representatives and the Committee

102. This issue is also dealt with, in part, below in relation to the question of public information. It needs to be emphasized at this point, however, that no matter how probing, constructive and insightful the examination of a State party report is, it counts for very little unless there is some effective follow-up at the national level to the concluding observations adopted by the relevant treaty body. While it is too early to conclude that this follow-up is inadequate (because the treaty bodies have only quite recently begun to adopt meaningful conclusions of this type), it is not clear that very many States have effective follow-up procedures in place at this stage.

B. Current problems of reporting procedures

103. As noted in the introduction to the present study, a variety of problems have been encountered in recent years in the operation of the various reporting procedures. Since these have been described in some detail in the report of the fourth meeting of chairpersons (A/47/628) and in the reports of each of the relevant Committees, it is unnecessary to cover the same ground here. It must suffice to note that the principal manifestations of the problems are (a) inadequate or unsatisfactory reports; (b) the non-submission of reports; and (c) the inability of the treaty bodies to cope under existing circumstances if States parties were to honour their reporting obligations. While the first of these problems has been the subject of frequent comments in the various committees, its magnitude cannot readily be measured. The other problems, however, can be quantified.

104. The situation in relation to overdue reports has continued to deteriorate steadily in recent years. Thus, as at 1 June 1988, when 146 States were parties to one or more of 6 treaties covered by the present study, the number of overdue reports totalled 626 (leaving aside the Convention against Torture, under which reports were not yet due as at that date). This compared to a total of 460 overdue reports 2 years earlier (when only 3 less States were involved).[38] By 15 March 1993, however, this number had grown to 971 reports and, if the Convention against Torture is included, the total was 1,009 overdue reports owed by 499 States parties. On that date the situation in relation to each treaty was as follows:[39]

105. While it must be acknowledged that these totals could be reduced somewhat if a calculation was made to distinguish reports that are a few months overdue from those that are clearly delinquent, this would still not reduce significantly the dimension of the problem that currently exists. Moreover, the number of States parties whose *initial* reports are overdue, in some instances for as long as 17 years, is extraordinarily high. Leaving aside the

---

[38] These figures were given in document HR1/MC/1988/L.2, prepared for the second meeting of the persons chairing the human rights treaty bodies.
[39] Information provided by the Centre for Human Rights, as at 15 March 1993. It may be noted that, in relation to the Covenant on Economic, Social and Cultural Rights the real number of overdue reports is significantly fewer than it would have been before the Committee amended its periodicity from 2 or 3 years (depending on the type of report) to 5 years.

Appendix 5: Long-Term Effectiveness of the UN Human Rights Treaty System 551

Table 1. Current status of overdue reports at 15 March 1993

Treaty	Parties	Parties with overdue reports	Total overdue reports
ICCPR	115	64	83
ICESCR	119	65	65
CAT	71	36	38
CERD	132	112	342
CEDAW	118	78	127
CRC	126	59	59
Apartheid	95	85	295
TOTAL	775	499	1009

Convention against Apartheid and the Convention on the Rights of the Child (because of its relatively recent entry into force) a total of 108 initial reports are due under the remaining five treaties. While the substantive consequences of non-reporting are potentially grave (see discussion below), the procedural consequences are also significant.

106. Indeed in this regard one of the most problematic aspects of the current situation is that the treaty bodies actually rely very heavily upon the continuing delinquency of a great number of parties in order to be able to fulfill their obligations within the meeting time currently at their disposal. According to a calculation of the length of time it would take the different treaty bodies to review all of the reports due if they were to be submitted, based on 1992 statistics and on the number of annual meetings currently scheduled, an additional 32 years would be required.[40]

107. In the next section of the study some of the specific problems confronting the treaty bodies at present are examined. They should be read in the light of two caveats. The first is that the reporting system, for all its shortcomings or weaknesses, has developed very rapidly in only a little more than two decades. In many respects, this rapid evolution might not have been possible if the system had been more carefully planned from the outset. Overall, the system has, in a number of respects, surpassed the expectations that might reasonably have been held out for it originally. Thus, while far-reaching reforms might now be required this does not necessarily mean that the principles underlying the system have lost their validity.

108. The second caveat is that there is evidence to support the existence of positive correlation between the efficiency and effectiveness of reporting systems and the extent to which States parties take their reporting obligations seriously. The most important implications of this proposition are that the treaty bodies themselves can play an important part in resolving some of the existing problems and that one of the best ways of doing so is to demonstrate that the results achieved by the process justify the efforts made by States parties to comply fully with their obligations. Seen from a different angle, this also implies that any measures designed to

---

[40] This chart is taken from Bayefsky, *op cit.*, at 16.

Table 2. The length of time it would take to review all State reports currently due if they were to be submitted

	No. of meetings required*	Average no. of meetings per year	Average no. of meetings per year devoted to consideration of reports	No. of years required**
CERD	189	48 (6 weeks)	33	6
CEDAW	110	19 (2 weeks)	12	9
CAT***	22	31 (4 weeks)	19	1
CCPR	241	82 (9 weeks)	42	6
CESCR	156	26 (3 weeks)	15	10

*This figure has been calculated using the different average times spent considering each kind of report (initial, second periodic, third periodic, etc.), and by identifying the number of overdue reports in each category (initial, second, third, etc.).
**This number has generally been rounded off to the nearest year.
***For CAT this figure will change considerably with the 1993 annual report because quite a number of first supplementary reports came due in June of 1992 (after the 1992 annual report was produced), many of which have not been submitted to March 1993.

make the system more effective by being less demanding may well be counterproductive.

C. Responding to the non-submission of reports

109. The consequences of non-reporting and of significantly overdue reports are immense. Failure to provide an initial report is particularly disturbing since it constitutes prima facie evidence that the State concerned has failed to undertake the initial comprehensive review of law, policy and practice that should enable it to identify the panoply of measures required to bring the situation into conformity with the treaty. As noted above, there are currently some 108 such initial reports overdue a good many of which are well beyond the stage of merely being delayed. Failure to produce subsequent periodic reports is also very troubling because such failure may well reflect the fact that major problems do indeed exist and that Governments are anxious to avoid a dialogue with the relevant treaty body.

110. All parties concerned suffer from a failure to report. For the treaty body the price is relatively mild, although in the longer term its credibility is inevitably diminished. In the short-term it may well be receiving a somewhat distorted picture of the situation in the world. For the State party itself, the price is much higher. Government officials may justifiably come to assume that ratification or accession to a human rights treaty is an act that brings much sought after kudos but is otherwise of little consequence. The standards contained in the treaty are unlikely to be taken seriously in the context of domestic law and policy-making if the obligation to report to

the treaty body, which in many respects is one of the less onerous implications of becoming a party, is ignored. Finally, any fears on the part of non-governmental organizations or of political and other interest groups that the treaty system is toothless and even irrelevant are reinforced.

111. But perhaps the highest price is extracted from the system itself. The treaty regime must inevitably lose some of its precious credibility if a State can ostentatiously signal its acceptance of a significant range of obligations and then thumb its nose at the committee. Acceptance of such a situation also leads to a system of double standards whereby some States parties regularly subject themselves to monitoring and to the probing of the treaty bodies while others are not subjected to any such scrutiny, even though their records may be far less satisfactory. This concern led the fourth meeting of chairpersons to note "that a persistent and long-term failure to report should not result in the State party concerned being immune from supervision while others, which had reported, were subject to careful monitoring" (A/47/628, para. 71). In effect, the failure of the treaty bodies to insist upon carrying out their monitoring responsibilities can only encourage other States parties to delay, or entirely neglect, their own reporting obligations.

112. Rather than seeking to identify appropriate incentives and disincentives to address this issue, the treaty bodies have, for far too long, contented themselves with seeking ever more inventive ways to exhort States to report. In some cases these appeals have been effective, but in overall terms they have clearly not succeeded in preventing a situation in which more than 1,000 individual reports are overdue. It is imperative, therefore, that the treaty bodies, as well as the political organs, address this issue with determination and imagination.

113. There are four steps that should be considered in order to address this problem:

(a) *The provision of advisory services to States parties whose reports are more than two years overdue*

114. This suggestion has several dimensions. In the first place, it is essential to bear in mind the possibility that a failure to report (like a failure to ratify) will sometimes be due in significant part to mundane bureaucratic reasons. A lack of expertise at the national level, a failure on the part of the bureaucrats or politicians concerned to understand what is really required, the assumption that the task is so large as to be beyond a small ministry's capacity, etc., may all help to explain a failure to report.

115. Secondly, it should not be assumed that a routine offer of advisory services for this purpose will elicit a positive response, even from a State party with relatively minor problems and considerable goodwill towards the system. The system of advice in the preparation of overdue reports thus needs to be made more routine and less dependent upon the country concerned taking the initiative. The reasons for this are that: (i) the bureaucratic inertia responsible for the failure to report is very likely to apply equally to the request for assistance; and (ii) such requests are, often for no good reason, still seen to amount to an acknowledgment of failure in some way.

116. This is not to suggest that assistance should in any way be mandatory. It

should certainly not be, since the decision on whether to honour its treaty-derived international legal obligation to report remains a sovereign matter for the Government concerned. Making such assistance more routine would, however, be very much in line with approaches already adopted in other contexts. Thus, for example, the United Nations Framework Convention on Climate Change specifically provides that one of the functions of the relevant secretariat is "[t]o facilitate assistance to the Parties, particularly developing country Parties, on request, in the compilation and communication of information required in accordance with the provisions of the Convention".[41]

117. One approach then might be to appoint one or more individuals whose sole responsibility would be to assist States to fulfill their reporting obligations. That person would have the necessary expertise, would develop a relationship of trust with Governments, would be able to operate in a low-key manner, and would be able to initiate direct contacts with the Governments concerned at the request of the treaty bodies.

118. Thirdly, following from the previous proposal, the relevant part of the United Nations advisory services programme needs to be radically revised in order to be able to respond to the needs of the treaty system. This is dealt with in more detail below.

(b) *The immunity from scrutiny. currently enjoyed by non-reporting States must be removed by scheduling the situation in those States for examination, even in the absence of a report*

119. This approach has already been endorsed by the fourth meeting of chairpersons which recommended "that each treaty body follow, as a last resort, and to the extent appropriate, the practice ... of scheduling for consideration the situation in States parties that have consistently failed to report or whose reports are long overdue" (A/47/628, para. 71). One treaty body (the Committee on Economic, Social and Cultural Rights) has already adopted this approach and its action has been welcomed by the Commission on Human Rights (resolution 1993/14, para. 4). Another (the Committee on the Elimination of Racial Discrimination) has done so with respect to States which have at least submitted an initial report. There is, however, no sound reason why the approach should be restricted to such States. Initial reports may be virtually irrelevant to the current situation, either because they were prepared long ago or because of fundamental changes which have occurred in the intervening period. In any event, importance should not be attached in the context of gross delinquency in reporting to whether the overdue report is initial or periodic in character.

120. The procedures adopted so far in developing this approach make it clear that the consideration of a situation in the absence of a report is purely a last resort. Even when a situation is scheduled the preferred option is for the State party to notify the committee that a report will be submitted within a specified (and short) time-frame and for that report to provide the basis for a dialogue of the established kind between the Committee and representatives of the State party. Even if the examination does proceed in

---

[41] Reprinted in 31 *International Legal Materials* (1992), at 851, art. 8. 2(c).

the absence of a report it should be made clear to the State party concerned that its representatives are very welcome to participate in the proceedings. The committee should under these circumstances make a special effort to ensure that it obtains adequate information on the situation from all appropriate sources. Because of the need to maintain the reporting system's integrity and credibility all treaty bodies should consider adopting this approach as soon as possible.

(c) *States parties whose reports are long overdue should be listed by name in resolutions adopted by the Charter-based organs*

121. The various organs concerned have so far avoided setting particular "tolerance" levels in relation to overdue reports for fear that acceptance of any such level would only encourage delays. Taken to its present extreme, however, this approach is counter-productive. While any delay is to be frowned upon, the treaty bodies should consider proposing, for adoption by the relevant Charter-based organ, a list of those States parties whose reports are beyond two years overdue. Once a report is more than three years overdue the treaty body should automatically decide to proceed with its examination and schedule the State concerned accordingly.

(d) *States parties should be provided with a positive incentive to report by virtue of the availability of additional technical assistance*

122. This issue is dealt with below in relation to the advisory services programme. For present purposes, however, it needs to be stressed that such assistance would need to be additional to that which is currently available if it is to constitute a genuine incentive. The present situation completely lacks this element of "additionality".

D. *The burden of coexisting reporting systems*

123. It has been suggested with increasing frequency in recent years that one of the most significant problems facing States parties is the cumulative impact of the demands placed upon them for reporting on human rights matters. Thus, for example, one report submitted to the World Conference on Human Rights has called for reform of "what are now cumbersome and repetitious reporting duties".[42] In a similar vein, the sixth preambular paragraph of a resolution adopted by the Commission on Human Rights at its forty-ninth session (resolution 1993/58, adopted by a vote of 33 to 16 with 3 abstentions) stated that "in view of the substantial increase in recent years in the number of mechanisms created in this sphere, many countries, particularly developing countries, have to prepare numerous periodic reports and answer a wide range of requests for information on facts or situations said to exist in these countries, requests that cannot be fully met as required or within the requisite time-limits".
124. In tackling this issue, several general propositions should be kept in mind.

---

[42] Report of Nordic Seminar on Human Rights (Laugarvatn, Iceland, 9–10 June 1991), A/CONF.157/PC/7, para. 56.

First of all, problems of proliferation are by no means limited to the human rights field.[43] As the extent of international interdependence grows inexorably, and as it becomes increasingly apparent in more and more fields of action that international cooperation is indispensable, so too will the demands placed upon States expand. Secondly, the indispensability of reporting mechanisms of various kinds should not blind us to the need to maintain under constant review the possibilities of streamlining and coordinating the demands placed upon States. Thirdly, in this context it seems reasonable to assume that there is a point at which additional demands become counter-productive, particularly if the status and importance of the relevant requests remain undifferentiated. Finally, it may also be assumed that new and rapidly evolving information systems offer important opportunities which have not so far even been explored.

125. While the focus of the present study is limited in scope, the issue of reporting obligations within the treaty regime cannot productively be examined in complete isolation from the closely related issue affecting the overall human rights system. For this purpose, it is essential to distinguish the different component parts of the problem before seeking to identify some solutions which might satisfy the twin criteria of (a) minimizing the burden placed on States and (ii) maximizing the effectiveness of measures to ensure respect for human rights.

126. The problem of proliferating requests for human rights reports is a multifaceted one. Viewed from the perspective of a specific State, requests may emanate from any or all of the following sources: (a) United Nations treaty bodies; (b) United Nations policy-making organs and most notably the Commission on Human Rights and the Sub-Commission on Prevention of Discrimination and Protection of Minorities and their respective subsidiary bodies; (c) specialized agencies and in particular ILO and UNESCO; (d) regional human rights treaty bodies; and (e) regional human rights policy-making organs. A variety of other, less formally institutionalized sources of requests for information could also be cited.

127. For purposes of the present analysis, five different categories of request for information can be distinguished. They are: (a) requests based on treaty obligations;[44] (b) requests based on special procedures established by the Charter based organs; (c) requests relating to the implementation of non-treaty-based standards: (d) requests relating to studies and surveys; and (e) requests emanating from non-United Nations sources. Problems of duplication and over-reach can arise both within and among these categories. But while it would therefore be appropriate in the context of a study of the problem as a whole to examine each category in detail, the present study must confine itself primarily to category (a) while also making a few

---

[43] See, for example, Benedetto Conforti, "Proliferation organique, proliferation normative et crise des Nations Unies: reflexions d'un juriste", in D. Bardonnet (ed.), *The Adaptation of Structures and Methods at the United Nations* (Dordrecht, Martinus Nijhoff for the Hague Academy of International Law, 1986), at 153.

[44] This category does not, however, include requests based on the fact that a State has ratified the United Nations Charter, since that basis might be used to justify a far broader range of requests.

pertinent remarks in relation to categories (b) to (e) in so far as they relate to the treaty regime.

(a) *Requests based on treaty obligations*

128. This category is dealt with below.

(b) *Requests based on special procedures established by the Charter-based organs*

129. While it may seem logical to an observer who is not fully versed in the legal and other details of the system as a whole to equate requests for reports from the treaty bodies with requests from Special Rapporteurs, thematic Rapporteurs, Working Groups and other such special procedures, it is essential that the fundamental distinctions between the two categories of request be borne in mind. Those distinctions arise at a number of levels. In terms of their legal foundations, the obligation to report under a given treaty is derived from the specific provisions of that treaty. It is not therefore within the competence of the Commission on Human Rights or any other poltical organ to contemplate any "arrangement" which would reduce those obligations on condition, for example, that States cooperate more fully with the special procedures. In terms of the nature of the information sought, the treaty reporting arrangements are by definition comprehensive, and their periodicity is more or less settled. In terms of urgency, the treaty bodies seek information of an urgent nature only in very exceptional circumstances and thus do not purport in any way to perform the same function in relation to alleged violations as do the special procedures. Finally, the treaty bodies cover only a limited number of States, whereas the special procedures are, by virtue of the provisions of the United Nations charter, universal in scope.

(c) *Requests relating to the implementation of non-treaty based standards*

130. Some of the non-treaty-based procedures are in effect quite formal. Perhaps the best example is the procedures for the effective implementation of the Standard Minimum Rules for the Treatment of Prisoners, adopted by the Economic and Social Council in its resolution 1984/47 and endorsed by the General Assembly in resolution 39/118 of 14 December 1984. Under those procedures, Governments are requested, *inter alia*, to respond to the Secretary-General's periodic inquiries on the implementation of the Rules and on difficulties encountered.

131. In addition, new proposals for similar procedures relating to non-binding standards continue to be made in various contexts. Several such examples must suffice. In relation to the Slavery Conventions, the Commission on Human Rights (in paragraph 7 of resolution 1993/27) recently encouraged the Sub-Commission on Prevention of Discrimination and Protection of Minorities "to elaborate recommendations on the ways and means of establishing an effective mechanism for [their] implementation". Similarly, in establishing a thematic working group on the right to development, with a view to the implementation of the Declaration on the Right to Development, the Commission noted that its work would be based on information "furnished by Member States and other appropriate sources".

Finally, in the drafting of a declaration on the rights of indigenous populations, the need for an effective implementation mechanism has frequently been stressed in the Working Group on Indigenous Populations.

132. The information sought in connection with these and various other reporting initiatives inevitably overlaps, albeit to varying degrees, with information required to be submitted to the treaty bodies. There is, therefore, at least in principle, significant scope for seeking to avoid the resulting duplication. An effort to do so would require at least two changes in existing procedures. The first would be to permit States which have reported on the precise matter in question to a treaty body to do no more than refer to the relevant paragraphs in reporting in response to the *ad hoc* request. The second would be to insist on improved reporting under the relevant treaties so as to ensure that the issues of concern in the *ad hoc* procedure are dealt with adequately.

(d) *Requests relating to studies and surveys*

133. This is an area which, in recent years, has witnessed a particular proliferation of requests to States for information. As in the case of category (c) there is considerable scope for making use of information already provided in reports to the treaty bodies. Such an approach would also, however, need to be premised on the changes noted in the preceding paragraph.

134. Another initiative, which could serve to reduce enormously the burden of these requests would be to authorize the secretariat to seek information already available in the public domain before making a formal request in a *note verbale* to all Governments. This alternative approach could readily be adopted provided that the secretariat is able to develop the Resource and Documentation Centre that has long been lacking. Thus, for example, a study on a specific issue could draw upon legislative texts, and analytical works already available within the Centre for Human Rights, as well as specific and carefully-targeted requests for information when necessary, rather than giving rise to the paper warfare that currently characterizes the process of preparing much of the documentation sought by the Charter-based organs from the secretariat.

(e) *Requests emanating from non-United Nations sources*

135. While it is clearly not within the jurisdiction of the United Nations organs to determine the approach adopted within the relevant regional and other organizations, a greater effort could be made to coordinate relevant activities and to exchange information rather than requesting it twice. This is linked to the broader issue of relations with the regional organizations which is dealt with below.

(f) *Requests based on treaty obligations*

136. In the first version of this study (A/44/668, Annex) it was noted that extending the periodicity of reporting under the various treaty instruments would help to reduce the burden. Appropriate measures have now been adopted in this regard by virtually all of the treaty bodies. As a result, reporting under the two Covenants is now required at five-year intervals and under each of the other four conventions at four-year intervals.

Appendix 5: Long-Term Effectiveness of the UN Human Rights Treaty System   559

137. In time, considerable advantages may be expected to flow from this less demanding and more closely co-ordinated periodicity. In drafting future treaties, however, consideration should be given to vesting a degree of discretion in the treaty body as to the periodicity of reporting. This would ensure that the system has a built-in element of flexibility while at the same time not simply permitting the meetings of States parties to determine for themselves how frequently (or infrequently) they might wish to report.

138. Two other measures were also proposed in the first version of the study. One, which was designed to reduce the burden on States, or at least to spread it more evenly over time, would be to seek to ensure that the due date for a given State party's reports under the different treaties is staggered as far as possible. Once the treaty system has begun to make effective use of computerization it should be relatively easy to work out a co-ordinated schedule for each State. The other related to the possibility of reducing the extent of overlapping reporting requirements, an issue to which we now turn.

E. *Reducing overlapping reporting recruitements*

139. The problem of overlapping competences among the various treaty bodies is an inevitable consequence of the approach adopted by the United Nations compared to that of, for example, the Council of Europe. While the latter started with a single core treaty (the European Convention on Human Rights) and has subsequently expanded its scope by adding concentric circles around the core,[45] the United Nations chose instead to supplement its two principal Covenants with a series of independent and increasingly narrowly focused instruments dealing in more detail, or with greater specificity, with issues that, to a significant extent, are also dealt with in the Covenants. Moreover, since each instrument is designed so that a State could become a party to it without necessarily being a party to any of the other treaties and since each treaty body is entirely separate from the others, overlapping competences are effectively ensured.

140. Perhaps the most important, but also the most difficult way of reducing the overall reporting burden on States is to encourage the respective treaty bodies as well as the States parties themselves to adopt measures designed to reduce the overlapping of existing reporting demands.

1. *The core document or country profile*

141. The easiest way of doing this is through the harmonization and consolidation of the reporting guidelines. However, this is only feasible in any comprehensive sense with respect to the country profile or what has come to be called the "core document". The system whereby each State party is requested to submit a single core document, to be used by each of the relevant treaty bodies in conjunction with the State party's substantive report relating specifically to the instrument in question, has now been

---

[45] Although it should be noted that the European system is not unitary *per se* since it also includes the Committee of Independent Experts under the European Social Charter and the European Committee for the Prevention of Torture.

approved by all of the treaty bodies. A number of States has now submitted such a report, although the great majority has not yet done so.[46] But while the introduction of such core documents can be expected to save time for the reporting State and to ensure that each committee is presented with a reasonably comprehensive general profile of the State party, it does not go very far, however, in tackling the larger problem of duplication.

2. The possibilities for more broadly-based coordination

142. The nature and extent of the broader problem are best illustrated by taking a couple of examples. Many different rights could be used for the purpose but the right to freedom of association is probably as good as any. The right is recognized in six of the seven treaties covered by the present study. It is also contained in the International Convention on the Protection of the Rights of All Migrant Workers and Members of Their Families. Moreover, the two principal ILO Conventions dealing with that right have (as at 1 January 1992) been ratified by 98 States (in the case of Convention No. 87 of 1948 on Freedom of Association and Protection of the Right to Organize) and 113 States (in the case of Convention No. 98 of 1949 on the Right to Organize and Collective Bargaining).[47] Thus any State that is a party to all or most of these treaties is obligated to submit periodic reports under each and every one of them detailing the situation with respect to, *inter alia*, the right to freedom of association.

143. The principle of non-discrimination is dealt with by an even larger number of treaties and gives rise to even more complex questions relating to the overlapping competences of different treaty bodies. Some indication of the overall extent of overlapping among the six United Nations treaty bodies is provided by an analysis undertaken by the Secretary-General (E/C.12/1989/3) in response to a request by the Committee on Economic, Social and Cultural Rights, endorsed by the Economic and Social Council in its resolution 1988/4, that a report be prepared "showing clearly the extent and nature of any overlapping of issues dealt with in the principal human rights treaties, with a view to reducing, as appropriate, duplication in the different supervisory bodies of issues raised with respect to any given State party".

3. The development of a system of cross-referencing

144. Tackling the problem of overlapping competences is however far more difficult than ascertaining its extent. The principal difficulty is that, in formal terms, each treaty constitutes a separate legal regime with its own precise obligations, its own specific normative formulations, its own set of States parties and its own monitoring body. Thus, for example, in response to a suggestion that it should not be necessary to provide information to

---

[46] Thus, as at 31 July 1992, 13 of a total of 112 States parties to the Covenant on Civil and Political Rights had submitted core documents. *Official Records of the General Assembly, Forty-seventh Session Supplement No 40* (A/47/40), Annex V.F.

[47] Jean-Bernard Marie, "International Instruments Relating to Human Rights: Classification and Status of Ratifications as of 1 January 1992", 13 *Human Rights Law Journal* (1992), at 55 para. 62.

Appendix 5: Long-Term Effectiveness of the UN Human Rights Treaty System 561

the Human Rights Committee on matters on which a report will be made to another treaty body, a member of the Committee has recently written:

"How can it be right, as a matter of law or otherwise, that States enter into an obligation to provide information and submit to examination under Treaty A, but declare that unnecessary in part because of new arrangements entered into with certain other States under Treaty B? Even were the monitoring and compliance provisions in the later treaty equally effective (which is not generally the case) the suggestion is unacceptable. States will find a rather firm response from the Committee on Human Rights to this proposal as to how future reporting should be handled: the integrity of the Covenant implementing procedures would seem to be at stake."[48]

145. Yet this response would seem to be based upon a misunderstanding of the proposals that have been made and that do, in fact, appear to offer the best medium-term solution to the problem. The proposal is not that States parties should be exempted from their reporting obligations under one treaty because they have already reported under a different treaty. Rather it is that where a State has already provided information in a report to one treaty body that it believes should also be taken into account by another treaty body, the relevant information need not be submitted and reproduced twice (or even several times). Instead a reference to the other report should suffice. Such a procedure in no way challenges or undermines the authority of a treaty body to request whatever additional information it requires and nor does the consideration of the information by one treaty body in any way prejudice the approach that another treaty body might adopt towards the same information. It is thus fully compatible with the preservation of the autonomy of each treaty body.[49]

146. A comparable cross-referencing procedure is even expressly provided for in article 17(3) of the International Covenant on Economic, Social and Cultural Rights (see General Assembly resolution 2200 (XXI), annex), which states that:

"Where relevant information has previously been furnished to the United Nations or to any specialized agency by any State Party to the present Covenant, it will not be necessary to reproduce that information, but a precise reference to the information so furnished will suffice."

147. The appropriateness of moving towards a more concerted cross-referencing system may be illustrated by the case of children's rights. Since its entry into force in 1990 the Convention on the Rights of the Child has, as of 1 January 1993, been ratified by some 128 States. Of those, States which are also parties to the two Covenants will be expected to report to three different treaty bodies on very similar issues. Indeed, the Human Rights Committee's General Comment No. 17(35) on article 24 of the International Covenant on Civil and Political Rights raises many of the same issues that are specifically addressed in the Convention. Under the circumstances, it would seem unnecessary, having first required a State to report in considerable detail to the Committee on the Rights of the Child,

---

[48] Rosalyn Higgins, *op. cit.*, at 9.
[49] See the summary of the presentation by Mr. Pocar in document CCPR/C/SR.859, para. 8.

to then require that it reproduce much the same information in a different report to the Human Rights Committee. Moreover, similar information could also be requested by the Committee on Economic, Social and Cultural Rights under article 10 of the International Covenant on Economic, Social and Cultural Rights, as well as by the Committee on the Elimination of Discrimination against Women.

148. In an effort to determine how best to approach this potential overlap, the Committee on Economic, Social and Cultural Rights proposed that a meeting should be held with one or two representatives each of the Committee on the Rights of the Child, the Human Rights Committee, the Committee on the Elimination of Discrimination against Women and the Committee on Economic, Social and Cultural Rights with a view to discussing how best to manage the supervision of overlapping treaty obligations. In endorsing this proposal the fourth meeting of chairpersons noted that the meeting had not been held because of lack of resources and called upon the General Assembly to consider making available the resources required (A/47/628, para. 88).The fact that any such endeavour, designed both to ease the burden imposed upon States and to improve the efficiency of the relevant treaty bodies, cannot be pursued without specific financial arrangements being made at the highest level (which, in this case, has already taken some three years) surely indicates a defect in the system which would warrant being repaired.

149. In some respects at least, the procedures which currently need to be followed in order to pursue initiatives designed to enhance the effective functioning of the overall treaty system are not only cumbersome and time-consuming but may even act as a deterrent. There is a need to seek to introduce greater flexibility into the system, in both financial and bureaucratic terms. It may be that the decision to regularize the holding of the chairpersons meeting on a biennial basis and to ensure its financing from the regular budget (General Assembly resolution 47/111, para. 10), will enable that forum to serve such coordinating functions in the future. But if that is to happen, more sustained consideration should be given in the future by each treaty body to the specific issues that it would wish to see addressed by the Meeting.

150. The same issue of duplication also arises in connection with some of the human rights treaties adopted under the auspices of ILO. A good example is the general recommendation No. 13 (eighth session 1989) adopted by the Committee on the Elimination of Discrimination against Women, in which it recommended in paragraph 1 that:

"In order to implement fully the Convention on the Elimination of All Forms of Discrimination against Women, those States parties that have not yet ratified ILO Convention No. 100 should be encouraged to do so".[50]

151. Having thus encouraged ratification of ILO Convention No. 100 (which concerns Equal Remuneration for Men and Women Workers for Work of Equal Value), the Committee could reasonably be expected to consider

---

[50] *Official Records of the General Assembly, Forty-fourth Session, Supplement No. 38* (A/44/38), para. 392.

permitting States parties that have ratified both Conventions to refer to the information already provided to ILO in those parts of their reports to the Committee on the Elimination of Discrimination against Women that deal with equal remuneration for work of equal value. Such an approach has already been adopted by the Committee on Economic, Social and Cultural Rights in connection with ILO Conventions that are of direct relevance to the rights contained in articles 6 to 9 of the Covenant (dealing with the rights to work, to just and reasonable conditions of work and to social security, as well as with trade union rights). Thus, the reporting guidelines adopted by the Committee indicate, in relation to article 6 of the Covenant for Example:

"If your State is a party to any of the following [ILO] Conventions: ... and has already submitted reports to the supervisory committee(s) concerned which are relevant to the provisions of article 6, you may wish to refer to the respective parts of those reports rather than repeat the information here. However, all matters which arise under the present Covenant and are not fully covered in those reports should be dealt with in the present report".[51]

152. The difficult part of this proposal to encourage cross-referencing is how best to facilitate its implementation. Appropriate efforts can be made at three different levels. Probably the most important level is that of the States parties themselves. Each State should, on the basis of the instruments that it has ratified or proposes to ratify in the near future, seek to identify the instances in which cross-referencing can be used effectively and appropriately and draw up its reports accordingly.[52] While some States have already begun to do this it is inevitably going to be difficult to achieve for those States which have very limited resources available to devote to reporting. This might therefore be an area in which advisory services provided by the Centre for Human Rights could be of particular relevance. In broad terms the principle that "the specific takes priority over the general" (A/C.3/43/5, annex, p. 12) is an appropriate rule of thumb to guide efforts to reduce duplication. Care must nevertheless be taken to avoid elevating such a rule of thumb to the status of a hard and fast rule. Moreover, as noted above, the use of cross-referencing must not be interpreted as eliminating the need (i.e. the obligation) to report to a particular body but simply as providing a less burdensome means of doing so.

153. Another initiative that might be considered at the national level is to follow the suggestion made by the second meeting of chairpersons to the effect that a specific administrative unit be designated at the national level as being responsible for the preparation of the reports to all of the treaty bodies by that State. Such a centralization of the principal reporting function would make far greater coordination possible than is the case where

---

[51] Committee on Economic, Social and Cultural Rights, Report on the Fifth Session, *Official Records of the Economic and Social Council, Supplement No. 3*, (E/1991/23), Annex IV, part B. 1.
[52] It may be noted in this regard that the Human Rights Committee has expressed the view that "efforts towards harmonization and unification may also find an appropriate solution within a State party, particularly through the creation of a co-ordination mechanism" (*Official Records of the General Assembly, Forty-third Session Supplement No. 40* (A/43/40), para 28 (4)).

several different units submit reports in an uncoordinated fashion. A comparable approach has also been endorsed in relation to environment and development matters in Agenda 21 which provides that:

"States may wish to consider setting up a national coordination structure responsible for the follow-up of Agenda 21. Within this structure, which would benefit from the expertise of non-governmental organizations, submissions and other relevant information could be made to the United Nations" (A/CONF.151/26 (Vol. III), Chap. 38, para. 40).

154. The second level at which action may be taken is that of the treaty bodies. Each Committee could be asked to consider providing some guidance to States parties with respect to appropriate instances of cross-referencing that might be taken into account. In this respect the possible computerization of the work of the treaty bodies would obviously greatly facilitate any efforts in this direction. It should be acknowledged, however, that this would require a degree of coordination and consultation for which the different treaty bodies have yet to demonstrate their capacity. Again, the role of the meeting of chairpersons is vital. That forum in turn, however, is unlikely to make significant progress in the absence of a list of clearly stated options provided by the secretariat.

155. The third level is that of the specialized agencies and, in particular, ILO. In 1969 the International Labour Office undertook a detailed and precise "Comparative Analysis of the International Covenants on Human Rights and International Labour Conventions and Recommendations".[53] That analysis could be of great assistance in guiding the approach adopted by each of the treaty bodies to the use of ILO standards and information provided by States parties thereto. The Office should therefore be encouraged to consider the preparation of an updated and expanded analysis that would take account of all of the six United Nations treaties covered by the present study. Other relevant agencies could undertake similar analyses to the extent that it is felt that duplication in reporting could ultimately be reduced as a result.

F. *Enhancing the capacity of the treaty system as a whole to address specific themes*

156. An issue which raises questions of coordination but has not been adequately recognized, let alone addressed, concerns the possibility of an informal division of primary competences among the different treaty bodies. The issue arises because of the overlap between different treaties, as illustrated above in relation to the rights of the child, freedom of association and non-discrimination. The absence of coordination would seem to be at least partly to blame for the fact that certain issues have been neglected by at least some of the committees, despite the clear mandate they have in relation to those issues.

157. The most prominent, and in some ways the most difficult issue in this context concerns the rights of women. It is now widely acknowledged that

---

[53] ILO, 52 *Official Bulletin* 181–216 (1969).

United Nations human rights bodies have tended to marginalize this fundamentally important issue, at least in part because of the assumption that it is being dealt with elsewhere (such as by the Commission on the Status of Women or the Committee on the Elimination of Discrimination against Women). At a certain level this assumption is accurate, but many observers would argue that it is essential for each and every human rights body to seek to promote the rights of women within the scope of its activities and mandate. There is, according to this reasoning, no justification for any particular treaty body, whose mandate clearly includes the elimination of discrimination on the grounds of sex, to assume that that part of its own work is being, or even could be, done by any other body. In line with this approach the Commission on the Status of Women, as well as the various regional preparatory conferences for the World Human Rights Conference, have all urged that greater attention be paid to women's human rights issues.[54]

158. In relation specifically to the work of the treaty bodies, the Committee on the Elimination of Discrimination against Women, has recommended to the World Conference that "gender-specific information and analysis should be fully integrated into the implementation of all human rights instruments".[55] There can be no question that this approach is correct. Nor can it readily be denied that some of the treaty bodies have devoted relatively few of their energies to these concerns. The proposal does, however, raise the question of whether there is an informal division of labour that might more effectively and efficiently ensure that women's human rights issues are examined systematically and comprehensively to a far greater extent than is currently the case. Implicit in the question is the suspicion that asking all five treaty bodies to focus on the issue in a broad and unrestricted manner has not led to any of them actually doing very much, whereas the development of clearer proposals as to what more precisely ought to be done by which body might be more productive.

159. An illustration may help to demonstrate that it is not especially helpful to adopt a purely legalistic approach to this issue by pointing to the fact that the competence of each committee is different and is clearly defined in the relevant instrument. Concern to protect the economic rights of women arises squarely within the context of both the Convention on the Elimination of Discrimination against Women and the Covenant on Economic, Social and Cultural Rights and to a lesser extent in the Convention on the Rights of the Child. There is therefore full scope for the issue to be pursued in depth in each context, as well as in relation to the Covenant on Civil and Political Rights non-discrimination provisions and the relevant provisions of the Convention on the Elimination of All Forms of Racial Discrimination.

160. Before proceeding with this analysis it is essential to emphasize that, while the women's human rights dimension of this issue is very important, it is

---

[54] See, for example, resolution AFRM/13 entitled "protection of the rights of women", adopted by the Regional Meeting for Africa of the World Conference on Human Rights, A/CONF.157/PC/57.
[55] Paragraph 1 (a) of Suggestion 4, adopted by the Committee on the Elimination of Discrimination against Women at its twelfth session, reproduced in E/CN.6/1993/CRP.2, Annex I.

by no means the only one which gives rise to the present concern. Indeed, some of the other issues would appear to have been subject to even more pervasive benign neglect under current arrangements. Many discrimination related issues could be cited in this regard. The plight of the ageing and elderly has not been addressed systematically by any of the committees, although the Committee on Economic, Social and Cultural Rights is beginning to do so. The situation of disabled peoples has also received very little attention, despite the fact that it arises in relation to the concerns of all of the relevant treaty bodies. The same might be said in relation to indigenous peoples, migrant workers, HIV/AIDS victims and various other such groups. In addition to these partly discrimination-related matters, there are many substantive rights issues that also cut across the mandates of the different treaty bodies, which tend sometimes to fall between the cracks.

161. As the Charter-based organs become more aware of the central role of the treaty bodies in the overall human rights regime, they are tending to address more and more requests to them to focus on specific concerns. These requests have sometimes been addressed to specific bodies and sometimes not. Thus, for example, at its forty-ninth session the Commission on Human Rights:
    - invited the Human Rights Committee, the Committee on Economic, Social and Cultural Rights "and other similar bodies" to address relevant HIV/AIDS-related issues (resolution 1993/53, para. 4);
    - invited "the human rights treaty bodies, notably the Committee on Economic, Social and Cultural Rights and the Human Rights Committee" to monitor disability-related issues (resolution 1993/29, para. 7);
    - recommended that "the Human Rights Committee, the Committee on Economic, Social and Cultural Rights, the Committee on the Elimination of Discrimination against Women and the Committee on the Rights of the Child" to give particular attention to matters pertaining to contemporary forms of slavery (resolution 1993/27, para. 14); and
    - in relation to child labour, noted that "the United Nations human rights bodies should continue to be concerned with this question (resolution 1993/79, Annex, para. 29).

162. This list could be extended but it would serve little purpose. The point is that the treaty bodies in general are increasingly being asked to give their attention to particular attention, although there is little evidence to show that their approach to their work has been significantly affected by such requests to date. It is submitted that this is, to a large extent, a matter in relation to which a much greater coordination effort is required.

163. Perhaps in recognition of this fact, the Commission on Human Rights has recently encouraged closer cooperation between, *inter alia*, "the Committee on the Elimination of Discrimination against Women and other treaty bodies" in the "promotion, protection and implementation of the rights of women" (resolution 1993/46, para. 5) and has invited the Secretary-General "to consult with all United Nations human rights bodies, including the treaty bodies, on the implementation" of the resolution (*ibid.*, para. 7). This would seem to present an opportunity for the treaty bodies to consider whether some modalities can be worked out among them to allocate

primary responsibility for addressing a given dimension of an issue to one body or another (in cases where the State party in question is a party to several treaties). Such arrangements would need to be flexible, subject to change and reflected in the reporting guidelines.

G. *Possible long-term options involving fundamental change*

164. There are at least three possible long-term options that might be considered with a view to decreasing the reporting burden upon States which are parties to all, or at least several, of the treaties dealt with in this study. It needs to be stressed at the outset of this discussion, however, that it is based on four premises. The first is that the method of monitoring States parties compliance with their treaty obligations by means of reporting is an essential part of the regime and remains not only a viable, but a potentially very effective, technique. No consideration should be given to its elimination. The second premise is that the rapid, uncoordinated growth of the overall treaty regime, in all its dimensions, will eventually demand that consideration be given to approaches which involve more fundamental changes than have been discussed in the preceding sections of this study.
165. The third premise is that the burden which prompts consideration of these options is that borne by a State which is a party to at least several treaties. States which are a party to only one or two would seem to have far less cause to complain of an undue burden. The fourth premise is that States have voluntarily accepted the reporting obligations contained in each treaty; it should not therefore be thought that there is anything inherently unfair in seeking to hold them to those legal commitments.

(a) *Reducing the number of treaty bodies and hence the number of reports required*

166. Against this background, the first (and most radical) long-term option is to consolidate the treaty regime so as to reduce the number of treaty bodies and, accordingly, the number of reports required of a State which is a party to several treaties. Such a consolidation could be limited in scope so that two or three committees would replace six and the number of reports reduced to the same number, or it could be comprehensive so that only a single report (perhaps as well as specific supplementary reports) submitted to a single committee would be required. This option is explored in greater detail in the final chapter of this study.

(b) *A single 'global' report*

167. The second option is, in some ways, linked to the first. It would involve the preparation of a single 'global' report by each State which would then be submitted to each of the relevant treaty bodies to which that State is legally required to report. This proposal has been put forward at both the third and fourth meetings of chairpersons, but not developed in any detail. It is not possible within the confines of the present study to analyze all of the issues raised by this approach but it is useful to at least touch upon some of the main ones.
168. At one level it might be objected that such an approach is inconsistent with the provisions of each of the treaties. There is, however, no reason

why this need be the case. Indeed, it would seem to be possible today, at least in principle, for a particular State to adopt such an approach unilaterally by preparing a single comprehensive report and submitting it to several treaty bodies at about the same time. Provided that the reporting guidelines relevant to each treaty were met and that the report was submitted within a time frame acceptable to each of the committees, no formal difficulties would seem to arise. Nevertheless, if such an approach were to be specifically endorsed by the various treaty bodies there would be good reason for a major effort to be made to coordinate reporting requirements somewhat and to seek to synchronize reporting schedules for each State. Ultimately, the relevant treaties could be amended accordingly, but this would not seem to be urgent or even essential.

169. Thus the practical dimensions of the proposal warrant more attention than the legal dimensions. In this regard, it would clearly have major advantages as well as some clear disadvantages. Whether the former convincingly outweigh the latter, or not, is a matter for States to decide. To begin with the advantages, a global report would give effect to the doctrine of the equality of the various rights in a singularly compelling way. Each committee would be presented with a truly comprehensive picture of the overall situation in the State party and be enabled to appreciate more fully the context in which particular issues are situated. A global report would also resolve, definitively, the otherwise unavoidably complex question of how different committees could avoid overlapping in terms of the issues dealt with (this issue is discussed again below). From the perspective of the State party the main advantage would be in the need to produce only one report in a five year period. While that one report would clearly be considerably more time-consuming to prepare, there would inevitably be significant economies of scale in not having to produce a series of often overlapping reports at different times.

170. The State would also have a much stronger incentive to produce a detailed and thorough stock-taking of the human rights situation than is currently the case when none of the six reports that might be required over a five-year reporting cycle will be seen to be especially definitive or comprehensive. From the perspective of the most important constituency of all – the local community in the State concerned – it is much easier to focus upon a single report on the state of human rights in that country than to make sense of a bewildering array of reports, each with a different emphasis, each submitted to a different international body at different times, subject to significantly different procedures when being considered, and so on. The possibilities for developing a genuine national dialogue would seem far higher in relation to one such report than to a series of them. Finally, the preparation of a global report would be more likely to involve high-level policy-makers and to constitute a process in relation to which advisory services would be both more relevant and more sought after.

171. On the other side of the balance sheet there are some significant disadvantages. In the first place the State party would only be required to report once every five years which, in human rights terms, is a long time. One of the factors that made an extension of reporting periodicity appropriate in recent years was the assumption that most States would be reporting to

more than one committee and would thus be under scrutiny of one kind or another by an international body several times in a single five year period. Nevertheless, this concern is less compelling in light of the increasingly common practice of committees to call for special or supplementary reports when circumstances so warrant, regardless of the regular reporting schedule. Thus, even though a formal, comprehensive report would only be required every five years, additional, more narrowly focused reports could be called for as required.

172. Another disadvantage is that the global report would probably need to be very lengthy. But while its preparation would thus be demanding, it might still represent a significant saving of time by comparison with the present system. From the point of view of a particular committee there would be far more to read, but the broader context covered by the report might make many questions of the type currently asked unnecessary. Moreover, each committee would, in practice, be primarily concerned only with a particular part of the report, such as that relating to children, women, torture, etc.

173. The resulting reporting guidelines would inevitably be very extensive. A single report would, however, provide a context in which duplication in reporting guidelines could be dealt with far more effectively than is ever likely to be possible under the present system. If there is significant interest on the part of States in this option it is suggested that a detailed feasibility study be requested to be prepared by the secretariat as an aid to further consideration of the issue.

(c) *Replacing comprehensive periodic reports with specifically-focused reports*

174. One possibility which has been raised but not explored in the Committee on Economic, Social and Cultural Rights is to replace the existing approach whereby a State party is required to submit a periodic report covering the entire gamut of issues covered in the relevant treaty, by the requirement of a report that addresses only a limited range of specific issues identified in advance by the responsible committee.

175. There are two principal rationales for considering this option. The first is simply the extent of the reporting burden currently imposed on States that are parties to all six of the principal treaties. While some States might not, in fact, feel unduly burdened at present, it has to be acknowledged that this might be more a reflection of the inadequacy of the reports currently being submitted than of the manageability of the overall demands if.they were to be satisfied in the manner sought by each committee.

176. The second rationale is that existing reporting requirements are so extensive that it is difficult at best, and impossible at worst, for some States to satisfy them entirely. The example of the Committee on economic, Social and Cultural Rights is instructive in this regard. When it first met, in 1907, its work was based on existing guidelines that had been drawn up a decade earlier. Their approach is best illustrated by taking an example. Article 7(b) relates to the relatively minor issue of "safe and healthy working conditions". The guidelines requested each State to submit, *inter alia*, all of its "principal laws, administrative regulations, collective agreements and court decisions" along with details of the "principal arrangements and procedures

(including inspection services and various bodies at the national, industry, local, or undertaking level entrusted with the promotion or supervision of health and safety at work) to ensure that these provisions are effectively respected in individual work-places" (E/C.12/1987/2). As the present writer has observed elsewhere: "[o]nly the arrival of semi-trailer loads of documents at the Palais des Nations in Geneva could have signified that a medium-sized industrialized State was taking such a reporting requirement seriously".[56]

177. When it decided to revise its reporting guidelines the Committee was faced with two alternatives. The first was to be highly selective and to seek only a limited amount of information from States, thus making the reporting process manageable and potentially increasing the likelihood of receiving detailed and comprehensive reports. The principal objection to this approach was that many issues that are of major importance would thereby be ignored by the guidelines and States would, in effect, not be held to account in relation to such matters.

178. The other alternative, for which the Committee eventually opted, was to draft detailed and lengthy guidelines covering all of the issues raised in the guidelines and requesting disaggregation of information to reflect the specific status of a range of different "vulnerable and disadvantaged groups". The result is that a State party would need to present a vast amount of information in order faithfully to comply with all of the requests posed. One of the resulting risks is that reports end up covering a large array of issues but do so in only a fairly superficial manner. The Committee is then in a position where it is difficult, if not impossible, for it to probe into a matter of concern in sufficient depth to enable it to get to the heart of the matter. When dealing with reports from federal States the problem is further compounded.

179. It is true that this problem is particularly acute in relation to economic, social and cultural rights but it should be noted that three of the other treaties (dealing with children, women and race) all have a large component of such rights and thus all face a similar dilemma.

180. How then might an alternative approach work? In effect, the existing system would be reversed. Instead of beginning with a State report and then drawing up a list of specific issues to be the principal focus of the Committee's examination, the process would begin with the identification by a Committee (or its designated Working Group) of the key issues in relation to which the State party is requested to report. The Committee would determine these issues on the basis of all information available to it and would not generally require information on matters in relation to which there appeared to be no significant problems or difficulties. This would mean that a State party would not have to present a comprehensive report but would be expected to report in detail only on the issues identified. Thus, the overall reporting burden would, in most cases, be greatly reduced but the specificity and timeliness of information provided would be specifically enhanced.

---

[56] Philip Alston, "The Committee on Economic, Social and Cultural Rights", in P. Alston (ed.), *The United Nations and Human Rights: A Critical Appraisal* (Oxford, Clarendon Press, 1992), at 497.

181. This approach would also enable States parties to choose the composition of the delegation to appear before the Committee with much more attention to the specialist expertise required. As long as questions are liable to be asked on a very wide range of issues States will continue to send generalists. If a State party knows in advance that the principal concentration will be on, for example, prison conditions, the justice system, the electoral system or social security arrangements, appropriate experts can be designated. A dialogue with such experts would, at least potentially, be far more productive than are many of the dialogues taking place under the existing arrangements.

182. Such an approach would not, of course, apply to initial reports due under any of the treaties since a comprehensive initial review of the situation is an important dimension of the process as a whole. Nor would this approach preclude individual committee members from raising issues other than those identified for primary consideration. In addition, the approach would not need to be applied in an identical manner by all committees. Thus, for example, it might make sense for the Human Rights Committee and perhaps the Committee against Torture to continue to require regular periodic reports while the other committees might opt to adapted their existing approaches to some extent along the lines proposed.

IV. FUNCTIONING OF TREATY BODIES: FINANCIAL AND ADMINISTRATIVE ISSUES

A. *Financing arrangements*

183. When the first version of this study was submitted, in 1989, the problem of ensuring adequate financing arrangements to enable two of the existing treaty bodies to function effectively, as well as two other potential bodies, was of very major importance. It was, in fact, the issue dealt with at the greatest length. In the intervening period, effective diplomatic initiatives have taken place and amendments to both the Convention on the Elimination of All Forms of Racial Discrimination and the Convention against Torture have been adopted. As a result the Secretary-General has been requested to take the appropriate measures to provide for the financing of the two committees from the regular budget of the United Nations, beginning with the budget for the biennium 1994–1995 (General Assembly resolution 47/111).

184. These developments are to be very warmly welcomed since they ensure that the funding of the sessions of the relevant treaty bodies can no longer be put in jeopardy by the financial delinquency of a few States. It is now of the utmost importance that all States parties to those two treaties should move to ratify the amendments so that they can take effect at the earliest possible moment.

B. *Length and frequency of Committee sessions*

185. Another issue of considerable importance in the future concerns the adequacy or otherwise of existing arrangements with respect to the length and frequency of the sessions of the various bodies. At present, there is substantial variation from one body to another. Thus, for example, while the

Human Rights Committee meets for nine weeks a year with an additional three weeks for working groups, the Committee on Economic, Social and Cultural Rights generally meets for only one third of that time (i.e. three weeks plus one week for a single working group). This discrepancy exists despite the fact that each Covenant has virtually the same number of States parties. As an exceptional measure the Economic and Social Council has authorized the Committee on Economic, Social and Cultural Rights to hold an additional three week session in May 1993 to deal with the existing backlog of reports.

186. The Committee on the Elimination of Discrimination against Women, in accordance with article 20 of the relevant Convention "shall normally meet for a period of not more than two weeks annually". This has proven to be clearly inadequate and the General Assembly has, on several occasions, authorized a limited extension of meeting time. Most recently, in its resolution 47/94, the Assembly endorsed the Committee's request that its twelfth and thirteenth sessions should be of three weeks each. Subsequently, at its twelfth session the Committee recommended amendment of the Convention "to provide adequate meeting time by eliminating the limitation set out in article 20" (E/CN.6/1993/CRP.2, Annex I, para. 6(b)).

187. The newest of the treaty bodies – the Committee on the Rights of the Child – has also found the time available to it initially to be inadequate. Accordingly, the General Assembly recently approved the recommendation of the meeting of the States parties to the Convention on the Rights of the Child that the Committee should have up to two three week sessions each year with a week long pre-sessional working group well in advance of each session (resolution 47/112, para. 10). It is notable, however, that even after this decision had been taken the Commission on Human Rights expressed its "concern at the increasingly heavy workload of the Committee ... and the resulting difficulties faced by it in the fulfilment of its functions" (resolution 1993/78, para. 15).

188. Partly as a result of the different time spans available, the time allotted for the examination of each State party report varies significantly from one treaty body to another. Thus, the Human Rights Committee generally devotes between three and four meetings (the equivalent of one and a half to two days) to each periodic report while the Committee on the Elimination of Discrimination against Women and the Committee on the Elimination of Racial Discrimination have recently spent less than a single meeting (i.e. less than three hours) on each report. For example, at its thirty-fourth session, the latter Committee created a record by examining 26 reports in the space of 14 working days.[57] The Committee on Economic, Social and Cultural Rights currently devotes a little more than two meetings to each report.

189. The time available to the Human Rights Committee inevitably enables a much more detailed and thorough examination to be undertaken. A member of that Committee has written that "while wordiness is no guarantee of worth, a serious report must necessarily be of a certain length: as

---

[57] *Official Records of the General Assembly, Forty-second Session, Supplement No. 18* (A/42/18), para. 60.

must a serious examination. Ten page reports and two hour examinations are simply pointless".[58] Similarly, at the second meeting of chairpersons, it was noted that "a thorough examination of a report and a genuinely constructive dialogue with a State party required at least two meetings" (A/44/98, para. 40). But while the difficulties of conducting a comprehensive examination in the space of three hours are not to be underestimated, the present reality is that several of the treaty bodies presently have no choice but to try. Each of them has, at one time or another, expressed the view that more time would be desirable but, for a variety of reasons, it has not been forthcoming.

190. In recent years the Committees concerned have recognized the problems and have sought to deal with them through procedural innovations designed to maximize the effective use of available time. There is, however, a limit to the amount of streamlining and simplification that can be undertaken without at the same time damaging or even destroying the effectiveness of the reporting system.

191. In the medium term, it will be necessary to devote more systematic attention to the need for extended, or more frequent, sessions (or both) for some of the existing treaty bodies. As more and more States become parties to the relevant instruments, as reporting guidelines become more precise and sophisticated (and probably more demanding) and as the quality of reports improves, the need for more time will become too pressing to ignore. That is not to suggest that all treaty bodies should seek to emulate the Human Rights Committee in every way or that they should be given exactly the same meeting time as it has. In fact there is, and should be, considerable room for variations in procedure and emphasis from one treaty body to another.

192. The first version of this report listed three measures that could be taken in the short-term to enable some of the committees to make maximum use of available time and resources. To a very considerable extent, each of these three measures has been employed extensively in recent years. The first measure, as specifically endorsed by the second meeting of chairpersons, is to encourage "each treaty body [to] consider how best to make use of the expertise of its members during the periods between sessions" (A/44/98, para 100). This technique is particularly pertinent to the preparation of General Comments or comparable analyses and the analysis of issues that are of general concern to the relevant committee. The second is to determine that the "normal" meeting period for the Committee shall not apply when an abnormal number of reports is awaiting examination. Thus, if a specific threshold number is exceeded the General Assembly could, as a matter of course, authorize an extraordinary session in an attempt to return the situation to normal. The third is to provide the resources to enable a working group or groups of the Committee to meet either on an intersessional or pre-sessional basis.

193. However, despite the additional productivity achieved through the use of these measures, the fact remains in 1993 that many of the treaty bodies are only able to function within their existing allocations of meeting time

---

[58] Rosalyn Higgins, *op. cit.*, at 19.

because of the enormous rate of overdue and unsubmitted reports, and because they are devoting a clearly inadequate amount of time to the consideration of each report. Once the various committees begin to schedule for consideration the situation in States parties which have not submitted a report, the amount of total meeting time required will jump considerably. Based on anticipated 1993 sessions the six committees between them will meet for 34 weeks with at least seven weeks of pre-sessional working group meetings. If this schedule is to be expanded to reflect: (i) a reasonable amount of time per report; (ii) a significant increase in the number of States parties; and (iii) a greatly improved rate of submission of reports on time, the total could probably be doubled without difficulty. This again points to the need for either greatly increased resources to be made available or for some major innovations to be introduced into the system as a whole, or both.

C. *Conditions of service for experts*

194. An issue which has not been faced up to by the General Assembly to date concerns the payment of honoraria to members of the treaty bodies. The 18 members of the Human Rights Committee have received such payments ($5,000 to the Chairman and $3,000 to the other members per year) since 1981.[59] When the payment was originally proposed, an analogy was made to the International Law Commission whose members also receive an honorarium. The practice raises two questions. The first is why the members of the other human rights treaty bodies do not receive any such sum. One answer is that article 35 of the Covenant expressly allows for honoraria, so too do the relevant provisions of the Convention on the Elimination of All Forms of Discrimination against Women and the Convention on the Rights of the Child. That leaves three committees whose members receive no honoraria. But it is entirely unclear how such a distinction can be justified when the various Committees are charged with comparable tasks.

195. The second is why the honorarium is so small, given that each member of the Human Rights Committee spends almost three months a year in Committee meetings while the amount received is around two weeks salary for a mid- to junior-level Professional Officer in the Centre for Human Rights. The easy answer is that most, if not all, of the members are already receiving an annual salary from their regular employers. But this takes for granted a problem that is built into the present system, which is that few experts other than government officials, university professors or retired persons could afford to devote so much time to the work of a treaty body without receiving any significant remuneration. The situation will become even more problematic as the Human Rights Committee's total annual meeting time is extended. It may be noted that the expert members of the European Commission on Human Rights (who currently meet for 14 weeks a year, only 2 more than most of their Human Rights Committee counterparts) are automatically "appointed in the service of the Council of Europe for two thirds of their working time", and remunerated accordingly.[60]

---

[59] Pursuant to General Assembly resolution 35/218.
[60] Henry-G. Schermers, "Has the European Commission on Human Rights Got Bogged Down?", 9 *Human Rights Law Journal* p. 175 at 179 (1988).

196. A final matter which relates in some way at least to the present topic is the fact that absolutely no working facilities are provided to members of the treaty bodies when they are in Geneva to perform their committee functions. While the matter can easily be made to sound petty, it is not. A member needing to prepare a report, to consult available information, to work on a draft general comment, or merely to read background materials, must do so in the coffee lounge or the Library. In the latter he or she has no automatic borrowing privileges and is by no means necessarily assured of a desk at which to work. There are absolutely no office facilities at the disposal of experts, such as a word processor or a fax machine. In part this reflects the "primitive" (to use the term chosen by the fourth meeting of chairpersons – A/47/628, para. 49) working conditions under which officials in the Centre for Human Rights have been compelled to work. It is essential, however, that efforts to improve the latter, which are already under way, should also include consideration of the inappropriate situation of committee members.

D. *Secretariat servicing*

197. A consistent theme that has continued to emerge from recent reports of the various treaty bodies is the need for more significant and sustained secretariat servicing. In 1988, the second meeting of chairpersons noted that the level and amount of such services is "an important determinant of how efficiently and effectively" the various Committees were able to function (A/44/98, para. 72). Four years later the fourth meeting of chairpersons noted that the resources available were still grossly inadequate. They noted that:

[t]his inadequacy has ... led to a situation in which requests for assistance by the various treaty bodies are sometimes unable to be met, despite the fact that such requests have been kept at an artificially low level in recognition of the impossibility of greater assistance being provided from existing resources" (A/47/628, para. 50).

198. In essence, the chairpersons comments are little more than a distillation of the statements made on a regular basis by each of the committees to the effect that the servicing each receives is inadequate and an impediment to more effective functioning. For present purposes it must suffice to note that the Human Rights Committee, which has always received the highest level of service (not only in terms of the number of staff allocated to it, but also of functions performed for it) of any of the treaty bodies, observed in its 1992 report that "a substantial increase" was required "in the specialized staff assigned to service the Committee both in relation to the monitoring of States' reports and the Optional Protocol".[61] The level of assistance currently provided to most of the other bodies, includes little other than the routine compilation and sometimes perfunctory analysis of a limited, and entirely inadequate, range of materials. This situation is in direct contrast with the now commonly held view that "the composition of lists

---

[61] *Official Records of the General Assembly, Forty-seventh Session, Supplement No. 40* (A/47/40), para. 22.

of issues and the compilation of other background documentation by a competent and adequately staffed secretariat [is] essential if the committees are to function optimally".[62]

199. Although comparisons can be used only with great caution (given the different mandates and structures involved), the same report notes that the ILO Committee of Experts on the Application of Conventions and Recommendations, which monitors compliance with ILO Conventions, is assisted by a secretariat with a staff of 20–25 legally trained persons. Similarly, the European Commission and the European Court of Human Rights have 32 and 10 lawyers at their disposal respectively.[63] By comparison, the International Instruments Section of the Centre for Human Rights consists of only about eight staff members to deal with all of the reporting functions under the six principal human rights treaties.

200. The fourth meeting of chairpersons recommended that "a thorough study be undertaken, preferably by an independent expert, of the full range of measures that would be required at the secretariat level if adequate servicing is to be provided" (A/47/628, para. 50). While such a study is well beyond the scope of the present report, a number of propositions may be identified as starting points. The first is that progress has been unduly slow in relation to the essential task of developing a computerized database to underpin the work of the treaty bodies. Very little progress has been made on plans endorsed by the Commission on Human Rights over three years ago (E/CN.4/1990/39). A principal reason for this problem is the absence of an expert on the development and use of databases within the secretariat. As long as the Centre for Human Rights relies *entirely* upon either external assistance (including from other parts of the secretariat) or upon officials with a casual interest in, but no clear mandate in relation to, databases, little if any progress may be expected.

201. A second priority need, to which the chairpersons and various individual committees have been calling attention since 1988, is the establishment of a resource, or documentation, unit within the Centre for Human Rights. It is extremely gratifying that this issue is finally, as of 1993, beginning to receive the attention it so urgently demands. It is imperative that this new initiative be strongly supported by States and that funding be made available to develop an adequate database and a basic collection of reference materials, as well as to cover the salary of a skilled documentalist.

202. A third issue, which is a prerequisite to the much-needed restructuring described below, concerns the need to ascertain precisely what services each committee would wish to have performed for it by the secretariat. At present the Human Rights Committee, for example, receives the following specific services: preparation of analytical studies; preparation of draft lists of issues for country rapporteurs; preparation of varios notes (for example on the submission of reports, states of emergency, country reservations and reporting profile); research and other assistance in connection with the

---

[62] Letter dated 29 September 1988 from the Minister for Foreign Affairs of the Netherlands addressed to the Secretary-General, enclosing an advisory report of the Netherlands Human Rights and Foreign Policy Advisory Committee on the functioning of the human rights conventions under United Nations auspices (A/C.3/43/5), at 17.
[63] Schermers, *op. cit.*

formulation of general comments; dispatch of previous reports and of other reports under various human rights instruments; solicitation of country-specific information from ILO and relevant NGOs; and dispatch of Committee's comments to States parties concerned.[64] Other committees receive varying, but in any event significantly less, services of this kind. A realistic overview of the total demand for secretariat services cannot be obtained unless each committee is specific as to its own needs.

203. Fourthly, the Committee on the Elimination of Discrimination against Women should be serviced by the Centre for Human Rights so as to underscore its status as a human rights treaty body, to enable it to benefit from the services and facilities that will be developed for the other treaty bodies, and to facilitate effective interaction between its members and those of the other human rights bodies. This proposal has been endorsed by the third and fourth meetings of chairpersons. At its twelfth session the Committee itself advocated that it be serviced by both the Centre for Human Rights and the Division for the Advancement of Women (E/CN.6/1993/CRP.2, Annex I, para. 6(c)). The latter part of the proposal would seem unnecessary if another important need were to be addressed. We turn now to that issue.

204. The fifth issue concerns the need for the development of specialist expertise within the secretariat. The current arrangements reflect an approach which was developed, and may well have been appropriate, at a time when the role of the secretariat of the then Human Rights Division was conceived of in terms of a glorified post office and conference organizer. There was neither the need, nor the political support, nor the resources, for the development of specialist expertise in particular fields. Today, at least in the case of some of the treaty bodies, this approach is no longer tenable. As has been noted elsewhere in relation to economic, social and cultural rights:

"The possibility of developing an effective programme for the promotion of economic, social and cultural rights in the context of United Nations activities is deeply undermined by the absence of a single official with any particular expertise in these rights. Special [thematic] Rapporteurs, country Rapporteurs, advisory services experts, members of treaty bodies, officials of other UN agencies, and non-governmental experts, have not even one single person within the Centre [for Human Rights] to whom they can turn for expert advice or assistance in relation to these rights. Similarly, the Centre has no meaningful collection of materials, books or documents relating to these issues".[65]

205. The situation is similar, although not identical, in relation to the rights of the child, political rights, women's rights, racism, and torture. Thus, at its third session, the Committee on the Rights of the Child called for the

---

[64] This list is taken directly from a document prepared by the secretariat at the request of the fourth meeting of chairpersons and circulated at that meeting.

[65] Philip Alston, "The Importance of the Inter-play Between Economic, Social and Cultural Rights and Civil and Political Rights", paper presented to the Interregional meeting organised by the Council of Europe in advance of the World Conference on Human Rights, Strasbourg, 28–30 January 1993, Council of Europe doc. CE/CMDH (93) 7, para. 33.

establishment of a specialist unit within the secretariat to deal with the broad range of children's rights issues. While it cannot be pretended that the development of appropriate arrangements designed to provide such substantive expertise to the treaty bodies will be an easy matter in bureaucratic terms, it is clear that a restructuring of the existing arrangements within the secretariat is an essential starting point. The present system of separate servicing for each and every committee ensures that no economies of scale are derived, that many functions are replicated several times over, that cross-fertilization is obstructed and that opportunities for the performance of substantive, as opposed to bureaucratic tasks, is effectively eliminated.

206. The sixth, and final issue, in this regard concerns the need for more staff and financial resources to be devoted to the servicing of the treaty bodies. This is an issue which goes far beyond the scope of the present analysis. Suffice it to say that the present, grossly inadequate, level of available resources, virtually condemns the treaty bodies to function at a level of efficiency and effectiveness that is far below what could readily be achieved if less short-sighted policies were adopted in this regard by the Member States of the Organization as a whole. Ironically, it is often the Member States themselves who pay the penalty of the resulting inefficiency.

V. FUNCTIONING OF TREATY BODIES: SUBSTANTIVE ISSUES

A. *Towards more effective monitoring of compliance*

207. It has been correctly observed in a speech to the General Assembly that "setting standards cannot protect human rights if the standards laid down are then blatantly disregarded ... Ratification is not enough. Implementation is the essential task before us" (A/41/PV.54, p. 11). In that regard, as noted above, action at the national level is clearly of pre-eminent importance. At the same time, however, the various treaty bodies also have a vital role to play in giving substance to the concept of international accountability, the importance of which has been recognized on many occasions by the General Assembly. The key to ensuring such accountability is the development and application of effective procedures for monitoring the extent of States parties' compliance with their treaty obligations.

208. In the first version of this study a variety of issues was raised in this regard (A/44/668, Annex, paras. 112–122). Although some of those matters, such as the adoption of measures to facilitate effective and appropriate use by the treaty bodies of statistical indicators, or the effective use of outside expertise, have drawn only a limited response, they will not be repeated in this updated version. Rather, the focus will be on three issues of overriding importance in terms of ensuring that the treaty bodies have access to adequate sources of information, without which their work cannot possibly be effective. Those three issues concern the role of intergovernmental agencies, the role of non-governmental organizations and the need for country files.

1. The role of intergovernmental agencies

209. The history of the relationship between the United Nations and its specialized agencies is, perhaps inevitably, much more complex and convoluted than is generally acknowledged.[66] Different priorities, different political majorities, different assumptions, jurisdictional jealousies and empire-building, structural deficiencies, a desire for independence or autonomy, and personalities have all played a part. In the very early years of the evolution of the treaty body system some of these factors probably contributed to arrangements which resulted in the specialized agencies being accorded, at best, a peripheral role in relation to the work of most of the committees. The issue was also very significantly complicated by the implications of the Cold War.

210. In recent years, most of the reasons for avoiding close cooperation between the treaty bodies and the specialized agencies have disappeared. The current state of play is thus best reflected in the most recent of the treaties under consideration. Thus, the Convention on the Rights of the Child provides that the relevant treaty body may invite specialized agencies, UNICEF and other competent bodies to provide expert advice and reports to it as appropriate. In the same spirit, the Commission on Human Rights has noted the importance of "enhancing coordination and information flow between the treaty bodies and with relevant United Nations bodies, including the specialized agencies" (resolution 1993/16, para. 8).

211. Ironically, this new spirit of cooperation has yielded rather little, except in relation to the Committee on the Rights of the Child. While there may be a number of reasons for this phenomenon, one in particular warrants consideration in the present context. It concerns the dramatic contrast between the pre-existing situation and the current one. In terms of the former, United Nations bodies and agencies, including the specialized agencies, were (with a limited number of obvious exceptions, such as the ILO) for many years reticent about any effective involvement in human rights matters within the United Nations. It was assumed that such matters would involve them in a part of the political arena in which they did not belong, or did not wish to be involved. Whatever the merits or otherwise of that position in the past, it is now widely recognized that human rights concerns are appropriately reflected in all of the Organization's activities, and that no areas can simply be cordoned off and deemed to be "human rights-free zones".

212. This evolution in thinking, however, has led to what might be described as an avalanche of requests directed to the various agencies for contributions to human rights activities of one kind or another. While in some narrowly-defined areas these requests have met with a constructive response, for the most part the response is either non-existent or formalistic in the extreme. It is thus not uncommon for inter-agency liaison officials to attend relevant United Nations meetings, put formal statements of the most general kind on the record, and depart with a sense of having accomplished their

---

[66] But see K.T. Samson, "Human Rights Co-ordination within the UN System", in Alston (ed.), *op. cit.*, at 620–675.

missions. But such exercises actually contribute little, if anything, to better coordination or to an exchange of expertise or useful information.

213. It is, however, too simple to place all of the blame for this state of affairs upon the agencies. They are, in fact, receiving a mass of undifferentiated requests from United Nations human rights mechanisms of all varieties, including each of the treaty bodies[67] and, while disappointing, it is hardly surprising that their response is often formalistic or none at all.

214. None of the foregoing analysis, should be interpreted, however, as in any way underestimating the potentially immense benefits that could flow to the treaty bodies from effective, coordinated, collaboration with the relevant agencies. The point has been perfectly illustrated in the following plea by the Executive Director of UNICEF about the need to get "the entire UN system on board" in relation to the work of the Committee on the Rights of the Child:

> If, for example, the ILO provided data about child labour and hazardous working conditions ... if UNDP reported on the impact on children of development programmes around the world ... if UNFPA supplied critical data about population trends and family planning in the context of children's well-being ... if UNESCO provided data on basic education ... if UNEP and the Commission on Sustainable Development helped the Committee explore the linkages between the environmental crisis and children in the development process ... if the Department for Disarmament Affairs would show the effects of bloated military budgets on children ... if the World Bank and the IMF provided "child impact statements" corresponding to their major loans ... if the Department of Humanitarian Affairs and UNHCR reported on children caught up in wars and natural disasters ... in short, if a more policy-coherent and operationally-coordinated United Nations system worked more closely with the Committee on the Rights of the Child in order to better support the efforts of governments, there's no doubt that we would see a real acceleration of progress.[68]

215. The need for "getting the agencies on board" applies equally to some of the other treaty bodies. It is, for example, in some ways almost ludicrous that three of the different committees whose mandate includes careful monitoring of a significant range of economic and social rights (the Committee on Economic, Social and Cultural Rights, the Committee on the Elimination of Racial Discrimination and the Committee on the

---

[67] A not atypical example is to be found in a recent resolution on the work of the Sub-Commission's Working Group on Contemporary Forms of Slavery in which the Commission on Human Rights invited:
"intergovernmental organizations, relevant organizations of the United Nations system, including the United Nations Children's Fund, the United Nations Development Programme, the United Nations University, the International Labour Organisation, the Food and Agriculture Organization of the United Nations, the United Nations Educational, Scientific and Cultural Organization, the World Health Organization, the World Bank, the International Monetary Fund and the World Tourism Organization, as well as the International Criminal Police Organization and non-governmental organizations concerned, to continue to supply relevant information to the Working Group".
Commission on Human Rights resolution 1993/27, para. 5.
[68] Grant, op. cit., at 7.

Elimination of Discrimination against Women) have virtually no access whatsoever to the voluminous, highly detailed and directly relevant expert analyses of issues prepared on a regular basis by a range of United Nations agencies. Instead, such documentation is completely unavailable to the committees in their deliberations. In their place, reports from non-governmental organizations or the press must suffice and observers wonder why the level of analysis, as well as the resulting impact, is often so limited.

216. In part, the reluctance of most intergovernmental agencies to cooperate with the treaty bodies may be due to nothing more subtle than traditional inter-agency rivalry. But it is unacceptable to dismiss the matter on that basis. Ignorance of the role and methods of work of the committees is almost certainly another factor. In addition, there is probably a perception on the part of the agencies that the treaty bodies are ineffectual and that efforts made to contribute to their work would not be repaid in results. Such a perception can best be dispelled by the committees themselves.

217. The issue of cooperation with intergovernmental agencies urgently needs to be addressed in an open and forthright manner. It is therefore suggested that consideration be given by the treaty bodies to examining carefully the type of cooperation which they would most value from the agencies and for these requests to be discussed with agency representatives. This needs to take place not only in the context of the meeting of chairpersons, which would allow the issue to be seen in some overall perspective, but also on a case by case basis. For that purpose each committee should designate an individual member to hold direct, substantive discussions with the relevant agencies to determine what, if any, cooperation is genuinely feasible. By the same token, however, this is an issue that also needs to be addressed in a framework that goes well beyond the specific and immediate concerns of the treaty bodies. Effective and targeted coordination in the human rights domain therefore needs to be put on the inter-agency agenda in a far more substantive way than has hitherto been the case.

2. Relations with non-governmental organizations

218. In the early days of the United Nations human rights programme it was sometimes argued that the only information that should be taken into account was that which emanated directly (and even officially) from the Government concerned. However, this proposition has been so consistently rejected in practice by each and every one of the human rights bodies that it is now rarely, if ever, suggested, let alone pursued. Nevertheless, in the first version of this study the treaty bodies were taken to task for the reticence or timidity that, it was suggested, had sometimes characterized their approach to the sources of information to which reference could be made. It was noted that:

"[s]uch an approach would seem to be entirely out of step with the evolution of international practice generally and to result in an unnecessarily self-denying policy, which deprives the treaty body of information that is indispensable to its efforts to obtain a balanced and comprehensive picture of situation prevailing in the territory of any given State party. As a matter of principle, efforts by the treaty bodies to undertake effective monitoring can thus be facilitated by the adoption of procedures that help to provide each body with access to diverse but none the less well-informed sources of information" (E/44/668, para. 114).

219. Since that passage was written, the treaty bodies have risen to the challenge in many respects and are now making effective use of a variety of information sources (although, the possibilities in this respect remain artificially constrained by the inadequate secretariat servicing available). The one area which remains to be addressed systematically by virtually all of the treaty bodies is their relationship with non-governmental organizations.

220. In recent years the role of non-governmental organizations within the international community, both in the human rights field and elsewhere, has evolved very significantly. There are various reasons for this phenomenon. They include the growth in membership of such organizations, and the fact that they have become more professional, better organized, more closely linked into networks that bring national and international actors together, and more adept at maximizing the opportunities offered by international conferences and agencies. The communications revolution has made it extremely difficult for governments to prevent information from being disseminated beyond national borders or to content themselves with issuing blanket denials of allegations. The end of the Cold War has removed much of the tension that surrounded the relations between particular governments and specific non-governmental organizations.

221. Moreover, the triumph of democratic systems of government in many countries has brought increased recognition of the importance of freedom of association and has demonstrated that non-governmental organizations can be important partners with governments in many endeavours. Finally, the inherently transnational dimension of many issues has been increasingly recognized and along with that recognition has come a realization that non-governmental organizations have strengths and potentials which cannot readily be matched by governments, whether acting alone or together with others.

222. These developments have given rise to a vastly more open attitude to the role of non-governmental organizations in many international forums. This is perhaps best illustrated by the case of the 1992 United Nations Conference on Environment and Development. As the Secretary-General has noted, "non governmental organizations contributed greatly to the success of the Conference" (A/47/598, para. 31). As a result, it was agreed in Agenda 21 that:

The United Nations system ... should, in consultation with non-governmental organizations, take measures to:
(a) Design open and effective means to achieve the participation of non-governmental organizations ... in the process established to review and evaluate the implementation of Agenda 21 at all levels ...'
(b) take into account the findings ... of non-governmental organizations in relevant reports of the Secretary-General (A/CONF.151/26 (Vol. III), Chap. 38, para. 43).

223. This approach is also reflected in an increasing number of resolutions of

the Commission on Human Rights which recognize the key role of non-governmental organizations in a wide range of contexts. In the case of the treaty bodies, however, there remains significant uncertainty not only on the part of the bodies themselves but also of commentators as to the appropriate, or most desirable, role that should formally be accorded to those organizations. Thus for example, while one recent report noted that "caution has been expressed about inviting just any group to send in their reports or to approach the [Human Rights] Committee",[69] another urged that "[p]rocedures should be developed and additional doors opened for non-governmental ... organizations to channel information" to the treaty bodies. [70]

224. At present, the approach to non-governmental organizations varies significantly from one treaty body to another. It is unnecessary to review those arrangements in detail here. Suffice it to note that: (i) the flow of information from such groups to the members of all treaty bodies is now largely open; (ii) formal procedures have generally not been adapted to reflect the *de facto* situation; (iii) the arrangements that do exist are not transparent, although this does not inhibit the use by committee members of any information they might receive; (iv) State party representatives are probably not aware, in the majority of instances, of precisely what has been said, or by whom, about their Government's compliance in information made available to the committees; (v) small, or grass-roots, non-governmental organizations, and especially those from developing countries, are inevitably badly placed under the existing rather informal arrangements in terms of their access to the treaty bodies; (vi) the opportunities that do exist for groups other than the large ones to channel information to the treaty bodies are not well known, and as a result, poorly used.

225. All of this adds up to the need for each treaty body to seek to develop a more open, rational, transparent and balanced approach to dealing with information from non-governmental organizations. While the present study is in no position to suggest any specific model in this regard, it is appropriate to canvas some of the options that might be available.

226. In the first place, the importance of receiving reliable information from non-governmental organizations might be officially confirmed by each committee. This would remove much of the uncertainty and ambiguity which still exists and would ensure that the message reaches beyond those organizations large or wealthy enough to be active at the international level in New York, Geneva or Vienna. Such confirmation could be contained in a general comment, a recommendation, or some other "official" committee statement.

227. The principal issue which needs to be addressed in this regard is whether the information sought should be restricted to information from non-governmental organizations in consultative status with the Economic and Social Council. There is, in many respects, no formal reason why the treaty

---

[69] Making the Reporting Procedure under the International Covenant on Civil and Political Rights More Effective, *op. cit.*, at 37.
[70] Nordic Seminar on Human Rights (Laugarvatn, Iceland, 9–10 June 1991), A/CONF.157/PC/7, para. 61.

bodies should feel themselves bound by rules devised for an entirely different purpose. Indeed, the Economic and Social Council approach is intrinsically inappropriate from the treaty bodies perspective, since organizations which are active only within one country are effectively precluded from being accorded status under the rules contained in Economic and Social Council resolution 1296 (XLIV). The principal argument in favour of the consultative status approach is that it should enhance the likelihood that reliable information will be received because organizations which do not abide by the rules can be disciplined in some way. But this does not reflect adequately the realities confronting the treaty bodies. Groups operating at the national level only (and thus not holding consultative status) are in fact likely to be the best placed, and potentially the most effective and constructive partners of all, in shedding light upon the human rights situation within a given State party's territory.

228. The principal remaining practical reason for privileging organizations with consultative status is to deter a flood of information from an excessive number of sources. But the approach is not well tailored to achieve that objective. It must, in any event, be asked whether, at least at this stage, there is either an actual or potential problem in this regard. The experience of most committees to date (with the sole possible exception of the Human Rights Committee) is that there is currently all too little information coming from such sources, rather than too much.

229. The next rationale for imposing such a restriction concerns the cost of reproducing documents submitted by such groups. This is not, however, even an issue for most committees at present. Of those that already provide for such submissions, the approach adopted by the Committee against Torture is adequate to deal with any potential problem in this regard. Rule 62 of that Committee's rules of procedure provides that "[t]he Committee shall determine the form and the manner in which such information, documentation and written statements may be made available to members of the Committee."[71]

230. One possible approach would therefore be to: (i) indicate that reliable information from all sources will be received by the secretariat and made available to the treaty bodies; and (ii) provide that a brief statement (perhaps four pages or less) from each group with consultative status will be reproduced in the committee's documentation (perhaps only in whichever working language it is received) and that the chairperson, rapporteur, or pre-sessional working group of the committee will scrutinize statements from groups not holding consultative status with a view to authorizing their reproduction. This would be seen solely as a safeguard against patently inappropriate information being processed.

231. The most difficult issue for the committees to decide is whether any opportunities should be provided at which they can listen to submissions by non-governmental organizations and probe or challenge the evidence submitted

---

[71] *Official Records of the General Assembly, Forty-third Session, Supplement No. 46* (A/43/46), annex III. See also, in the report of the Committee to the forty-fourth session *(Official Records of the General Assembly, Forty-fourth Session, Supplement No. 46* (A/44/46), annex IV), rule 76 (4) (pertaining to proceedings under article 20 of the Convention).

Appendix 5: Long-Term Effectiveness of the UN Human Rights Treaty System 585

to them. According to one such proposal the treaty bodies should dedicate part of a meeting "to formal hearings in which national and international NGOs would be invited to present public testimony. These hearings should be held on each country just prior to the Committee's formal consideration of that country's report".[72] Variations on this theme could easily be envisaged. Such participation could be limited, for example, to groups authorized for this purpose by the government concerned, or to groups not specifically vetoed by the government, or to groups with consultative status, or to groups chosen by the committee itself etc.

232. There would seem to be very good reasons to fear, however, that the essential nature of the constructive dialogue which characterizes the work of the treaty bodies could be irreparably harmed by such a procedure if it were to degenerate into a "slinging match" between a government and those critical of its policies. While this would not always be the case, it is difficult to see how it could be avoided in many situations. Moreover, such confrontations would seem more appropriate to the Charter-based organs, in which they already occur on a regular basis. It would thus not seem appropriate to go as far as to incorporate non-governmental organizations as full participants in the actual dialogue.

233. If it is accepted then that they should be excluded from the formal proceedings involving governments, the question that remains is whether there are other options in relation to oral presentations that might still deserve to be explored. The answer would seem to be in the affirmative for several reasons. They include the need to open up the system and make it more transparent from the perspective of governments as well as non governmental organizations, the need to make a greater effort to accommodate groups from the national level, and, perhaps most importantly, the need to ensure that all points of view are available to the committees to enable them to reach well-founded and insightful conclusions.

234. The principal options then would seem to be: (i) providing an opportunity at the beginning of each committee session for groups to present any information of direct relevance; (ii) limiting such an opportunity to the committee's pre-sessional working group; or (iii) scheduling informal sessions, without summary records and with only essential interpretation, outside of the committee's regular meetings. The first of these options is the strongest but would still seem to entail the risk that inflammatory, as opposed to constructive, contributions might divert the focus of the entire dialogue between the committee and the State party. There are, in fact, both good and bad consequences flowing from the fact that, once such allegations are on the record, it would be essential for the government concerned to respond in detail.

235. The second option would seem attractive in some respects, but may be less necessary if it is assumed that all relevant written information will, in any event, be provided to the sessional working groups charged with responsibility for drawing up the list of specific questions to be posed to each govern-

---

[72] Michael Posner, "The Establishment of the Right of Non-Governmental Human Rights Groups to Operate", paper presented to American Society of International Law's Project on an International Human Rights Agenda for the Post-Cold War World, Washington DC, March 1993, at 15.

ment. The third option is appealing in a number of respects. If there were very few groups wanting to place their views before the committee, a single informal session could be held at the beginning of the committee's session. Thus, for example, the Monday afternoon of the first week could be set aside for that purpose. Alternatively, one hour meetings might be scheduled in relation to an individual country report, at either 9 a.m. or 2 p.m. the day before the country is scheduled to report. Such meetings could be open to all concerned groups and individuals and to all interested committee members. At the very least, the committee could ask one of its members to report back to it, perhaps informally, on the outcome of such a session.

236. In conclusion, it must be observed that these issues are as important as they are complex. They should no longer simply be ignored, whatever the outcome of each committee's discussions. In the meantime, the general arrangements for liaison between the committees and non-governmental organizations are in dire need of reform. At present, notification of the reports scheduled at each session is inadequate and the possibilities for groups, particularly at the national level, to obtain the relevant documentation are very slight indeed. As long as this situation persists, urging by the treaty bodies that more groups at the national level should follow their deliberations will be largely in vain. Suggestions that the United Nations Information Centres be relied upon for this purpose may be appealing in theory (to those who do not know the *modus operandi* of most such Centres), but they are very misplaced in practice. Indeed, one would hardly expect such Centres to play the sort of role envisaged in this regard.

237. What is clearly needed is for the Centre for Human Rights to develop its own non-governmental liaison office which would be in a position to develop a carefully planned strategy for reaching out to the key groups whose inputs would greatly assist the work of the treaty bodies as well as other mechanisms. Virtually all United Nations agencies, such as UNDP, UNICEF, UNHCR etc. have such offices, but the United Nations Office in Geneva has only one person to do that job across the entire gamut of activities. Although that office has been extraordinarily effective it is inconceivable that it could, on its own, do an adequate job in relation to all of the non-governmental organization-related needs of the human rights programme.

B. *Promoting normative consistency*

238. In addressing the General Assembly on the occasion of the twentieth anniversary of the adoption of the International Covenants, the Secretary-General noted that "we must be constantly vigilant that nothing is done to detract from their provisions" (A/41/PV.54, p. 6). Yet the introductory part of the present study (paras. 9–30) provides a clear illustration of the extent to which factors such as the recent proliferation of standards (both binding and non-binding), the increasing range and depth of the activities of the policy-making organs and the expanding number of treaty bodies can combine in such a way as to render ever more difficult the maintenance of a reasonable degree of normative consistency. A recent manifestation of concern over this problem is reflected in the Economic and Social Council's

appeal in paragraph 8 of its resolution 1987/4 to bodies dealing with similar questions of human rights to respect the Human Rights Committee's uniform standards.

239. Because of the uniqueness of each of the different treaty regimes, the quest to achieve normative consistency is subject to certain clear limitations. It is generally accepted, however, that the interpretation accorded to a given norm by one united Nations human rights body should, as far as possible, be consistent with that adopted by another body. In so far as complete consistency is neither possible nor appropriate for reasons inherent in the relevant treaty provisions. a principled explanation for the resulting differences should be available. But although these principles are unproblematic, at least in the abstract, the existence of a significant range of different treaty bodies, and the proposed creation of several new ones, inevitably gives rise to certain problems. They have recently been formulated in the following terms by a member of the Human Rights Committee:

"Does the interpretation under the prior or later treaty prevail? Does interpretation given under a one topic treaty have greater authority than interpretation given of a specific right under a more general treaty? Is the integrity of each treaty to be protected by each body carefully not looking beyond its own jurisprudence in any given subject area? Is the authority and standing of any one interpreting body to be weighted against the authority and standing of any other interpreting body?"[73]

240. The problems that have already arisen in this domain[74] can be expected to become even more frequent and troublesome as a phenomenon that has been called "permeability" becomes more widespread.[75] Permeability refers to the process by which the norms contained in one instrument are used in connection with the interpretation of norms contained in another instrument. Thus, for example, economic rights contained in the International Covenant on Economic, Social and Cultural Rights might be taken into account by the Human Rights Committee, especially when deciding cases brought to it under the Optional Protocol to the International Covenant on Civil and Political Rights. This situation actually arose in several recent cases in which the Human Rights Committee held that article 26 of the latter Covenant, which provides for equal protection of the law, was applicable to social security legislation (an issue dealt with under article 9 of the other Covenant).[76]

241. In the longer term, it seems inevitable that instances of normative inconsistency will multiply and that significant problems will result. Among the possible worst-case consequences, mention may be made of the emergence-of significant confusion as to the "correct" interpretation of a given right, the undermining of the credibility of one or more of the treaty

---

[73] Higgins, *op. cit.*, at 8.
[74] *Ibid.*, at 8–11.
[75] Craig Scott, "The Interdependence and Permeability of Human Rights Norms: Towards a Partial Fusion of the International Covenants on Human Rights", 27 *Osgoode Hall Law Journal* 769–878 (1989).
[76] *Official Records of the General Assembly Forty-second Session, Supplement No. 40* (A/42/40), annex VIII, views B, C and D.

bodies and eventually a threat to the integrity of the treaty system. While it is to be hoped that none of these scenarios will eventuate, the possibility exists that they might be sufficient to cause the international community to hesitate before creating new treaty bodies beyond those already in the pipeline. It is also an important reason to consider long-term measures towards the rationalization of the present system (see chap. VI below).

242. In the short term questions of credibility and integrity will also probably arise. In addition, the transparency of the overall system (i.e. the ease with which Governments and their citizens can comprehend both the normative and institutional dimensions of the system) may well be threatened. The principal short-term solutions are twofold. The first is the recognition of the problem and of its potential seriousness by both the treaty bodies and the policy-making organs. Unless the problem is clearly recognized its solution will not be found. The second solution is to develop procedures designed to ensure that as much relevant information as possible is brought to the attention of any United Nations human rights body in connection with its consideration of a specific issue. In particular, the secretariat should be mandated to draw the attention of the body in question (whether a treaty body or a policy-making organ) to any proposal it believes involves or might involve normative inconsistency. The decision-making responsibility, of course, rests with the body concerned but its deliberations should at least be based on full information, and efforts to avoid inconsistency should he facilitated as far as possible.

243. The principal practical difficulty with this solution is the burden it imposes upon an already under-staffed secretariat. While that problem is beyond the confines of the present study, two suggestions may be offered. The first is that consideration be given to re-conceptualizing or supplementing the publication *United Nations Action in the Field of Human Rights*,[77] which has retained essentially the same format since it was first produced in preparation for the International Conference on Human Rights held at Tehran in 1968. It currently constitutes an extremely valuable record of institutional developments and provides, in effect, an indispensable institutional memory. Nevertheless, it does not provide any sort of integrated or synthetic overview of the approaches or interpretation adopted by the various treaty bodies with respect to specific norms. For example, if information were to be sought as to the normative content of the prohibition of discrimination on the grounds of status or social origin, the publication would offer little, if any, direct assistance. An alternative course of action would be to begin work on an entirely new publication (perhaps in loose leaf format), which would seek to provide the sort of information that States parties, the human rights organs and expert members of the treaty bodies could consult as required.

244. Another suggestion is that consideration be given by the secretariat to trying to build up a greater degree of specialist expertise on the basis of different topics or subject areas rather than allocating all human resources on a functional or institutional basis. As long as the latter approach is applied almost exclusively there is little likelihood of any officials developing

---

[77] United Nations publication, Sales No. E.88.XIV.2

a detailed knowledge of all of the activities relevant to specific subjects whether undertaken by a treaty body, a policy-making organ, a specialized or other agency or a regional human rights organization.

C. Relationships with the principal regional human rights mechanisms

245. While the norms being applied by each of the three principal regional mechanisms (the African, the European and the Inter American) are, as noted earlier,[78] by no means identical, either to one another or to the relevant United Nations norms, there is, in addition to a very great number of comparably formulated standards, an underlying presumption that the various organs are all engaged in a common endeavour to promote understanding of, and respect for, internationally recognized human rights principles. This is not to suggest an absolute identity of standards: indeed among the rationales sometimes cited for a regional system are: (i) the desire to have more demanding standards; or (ii) the quest for standards which are formulated in such a way as to more precisely reflect the specific cultural and other traditions within the region concerned than is possible in the case of universal standards. Nevertheless, it is generally accepted that "regional instruments should complement the universally accepted human rights standards" and "that certain inconsistencies between provisions of international instruments and those of regional instruments might raise difficulties with regard to their implementation".[79]

246. The most effective way of promoting an appropriate complementarity of approach among the organs at the different levels is to ensure the development of effective channels of communication, both in terms of the individuals concerned and of the jurisprudence. This is, however, very far indeed from the existing situation, despite the number of occasions on which the General Assembly and the Commission on Human Rights have affirmed the importance of greater interaction. Thus, to take but one such example, the General Assembly reaffirmed in its resolution 47/125 that "regional arrangements ... may make a major contribution to the effective enjoyment of human rights and fundamental freedoms and that the exchange of information and experience in this field ... may be improved" (8th preambular para.).

247. At present, however, there is no regular (or even occasional) forum in which the members of the United Nations treaty bodies can become acquainted with their regional counterparts or can exchange views on issues of common concern.[80] Moreover, and ultimately much more problematic, there is no way of ensuring that doctrinal approaches being adopted at either the

---

[78] See the discussion above in Chap. II.
[79] General Assembly resolution 47/125, ninth preambular para.
[80] The exceptions in this regard have generally been fortuitous rather than a result of a particular policy decision. Thus, for example, the Committee against Torture has been briefed on the activities of its regional counterpart the European Convention for the Prevention of Torture and Inhuman or Degrading Treatment or Punishment. But the briefing was carried out by one of its own members who is also a member of the European Committee. See *Official Records of the General Assembly, Forty-seventh Session, Supplement No.44* (A/47/44), paras. 13–14.

United Nations or regional levels take account of directly relevant approaches already adopted at the other level.

248. This is not to imply that the jurisprudence of, for example, the Inter-American Commission or Court of Human Rights would be in any way determinative of the approach to be adopted in relation to a particular matter by a United Nations treaty body such as the Human Rights Committee. Nevertheless, based on the premise that there is a shared commitment to the building of a jurisprudence of international human rights norms which is as generally coherent and consistent as possible, every effort should be made to ensure that the jurisprudence of each of the treaty systems is not only readily available to each of the bodies, but is specifically taken into account whenever it is relevant. Even if such a process leads on occasion, as it almost inevitably often will, and probably sometimes should, to the rejection, or significant modification, of another body's approach, such an explicit acknowledgment of what is being done would help to contribute to the development of a better, and more sophisticated, international human rights jurisprudence.

249. It may be objected that the treaty bodies actually spend rather little of their time exploring what might be termed jurisprudential issues in the sense of developing a better understanding of the legal and policy implications of a particular norm in relation to a given fact situation. Indeed the most explicit context in which this process takes place, that of considering communications submitted under one of the optional procedures, is confined largely to the Human Rights Committee and, on a significantly smaller scale, to the procedures applied under the Convention on the Elimination of All Forms of Racial Discrimination and the Convention against Torture and Other Cruel, Inhuman or Degrading Treatment or Punishment. However, such an objection risks under-estimating the extent to which use of these procedures seems likely to grow in the years ahead, as well neglecting the fact that proposals have already been made for the adoption of new communications procedures in relation to both the Convention on the Elimination of All Forms of Discrimination against Women and the International Covenant on Economic, Social and Cultural Rights.[81]

250. Moreover, while jurisprudential issues do not present themselves quite as clearly or explicitly in connection with the other principal concerns of the treaty bodies they are still in fact of major relevance. Thus, for example, as the examination of States reports becomes more sophisticated and nuanced there will be a greater need for committee members to spell out in some detail the legal analysis on the basis of which they are suggesting that a given law or practice is incompatible with, or inadequate, to satisfy, the obligations reflected in a particular treaty norm. Similarly, as the importance attributed to the drafting of general comments grows, and as they become more influential in legal, academic, governmental and non-governmental contexts, the treaty bodies will need to re-double their efforts to

---

[81] *CEDAW Committee Report; Official Records of the Economic and Social Council, 1993, Supplement No. 3* (E/1993/22), Annex IV. Although, it should be noted that the Committee on the Elimination of Discrimination against Women rejected one specific proposal for the adoption of an optional protocol in response to the problem of violence against women. See *Official Records of the General Assembly, Forty-seventh Session, Supplement No.38* (A/47/38), para. 464.

Appendix 5: Long-Term Effectiveness of the UN Human Rights Treaty System 591

ensure that the normative interpretations that they are helping to shape take into account the jurisprudence already existing at the regional level. Failure to do so can only contribute to confusion and ultimately to undermining the authority of the jurisprudence generated at both the universal and regional levels.

251. The need which already exists in this regard is by no means only a one way street. It seems highly likely, to take but one of several possible examples, that a careful search of the jurisprudence generated by the European system would reveal extremely few references to, for example, the final views or general comments of the Human Rights Committee. The converse is certainly also true. Over the longer term, one *potential* result of this lack of interaction is the development of very significantly different, and perhaps ultimately incompatible, interpretations and assumptions in relation to norms that are virtually identical in their basic formulations. While many such differences might reasonably be explained by reference to concepts such as the margin of appreciation applied by the different organs in an effort to reflect appropriate specificities, there is also a strong risk that an unarticulated or unacknowledged element of cultural relativism will enter into normative interpretations unless an endeavour is made to justify differences of approach and interpretation when they are deemed necessary.

252. In considering specific policy recommendations that follow from this analysis four approaches should be explored. The first is to draft a programme of action designed solely to ensure that the United Nations treaty bodies and the relevant regional bodies are kept reasonably well informed of one another's activities. The second is for the Secretary-General to devise appropriate means by which to respond to the request directed to him by the General Assembly "to continue to strengthen exchanges between the United Nations and regional intergovernmental organizations dealing with human rights" (resolution 47/125, para. 6). It must be acknowledged, however, that most of the exchanges that have taken place so far have resulted in very little genuine interaction between the two levels. Rather they have been predominantly concerned with the holding of meetings of one kind or another on a regional or sub-regional basis, in which the relevant regional bodies have, almost coincidentally, been marginally involved (such as through the provision of premises or the coordination of some of the administrative arrangements).

253. A third possible approach is to explore the possibility of regular, even if rather infrequent, meetings between representatives of the United Nations treaty bodies and their regional counterparts. Such meetings should involve (but by no means be limited to) the provision of detailed briefings on the work of the host organs. Thus, for example, if a meeting were to be held in Banjul, at the headquarters of the African Commission, the representatives of the United Nations treaty bodies would gain an invaluable opportunity to learn at first hand what is being done by that Commission, what the principal problems are that have been encountered and what the opportunities might be for joint iniatives in the future.

254. The fourth possible approach is both the most important and the most challenging. It will become increasingly urgent for the members of the

different United Nations and regional bodies to have full and reasonably easy access to the jurisprudence generated by the other bodies. Ideally, this will be achieved in part through the increasing sophistication of data bases being developed in some areas, although it must be noted that the United Nations Centre for Human Rights has barely even begun to implement the rather basic programme of activities identified for it three and a half years ago (as of June 1993) by a Task Force on Computerization appointed by the Commission on Human Rights (E/CN.4/1990/39). It is clear, however, that the availability, exchange and accessibility of such information will not be achieved either accidentally or inevitably over time. Rather, what is required, is the appointment of an expert group comprised of appropriate experts from the regional and United Nations systems (including, in this case, the ILO, in view of the considerable progress it has already made in this regard), with a mandate to develop a range of specific recommendations for future action.

E/CN.4/1997/74 — 27 March 1997
COMMISSION ON HUMAN RIGHTS
Fifty-third session

EFFECTIVE FUNCTIONING OF BODIES ESTABLISHED PURSUANT TO UNITED NATIONS HUMAN RIGHTS INSTRUMENTS

Final report on enhancing the long-term effectiveness of the United Nations human rights treaty system

Note by the Secretary-General

The Secretary-General has the honour to transmit to the Commission on Human Rights the final report on enhancing the long-term effectiveness of the United Nations human rights treaty system, prepared by an independent expert, Mr. Philip Alston.

CONTENTS BY PARAGRAPH

I. INTRODUCTION
   A. Background — 1–3
   B. Progress achieved since the previous reports by the independent expert — 4–6
   C. A thumbnail sketch of the present situation — 7–8
   D. The premises upon which this report is based — 9–13

II. MAJOR CURRENT POLICY ISSUES
   A. Towards universal ratification — 14–36
   B. Responding to the problem of significantly overdue reports — 37–47
   C. The inadequacy of the current system to deal with the timely submission of reports — 48–52
   D. Problems in relation to documentation — 53–59
   E. The development and use of electronic databases — 60–66
   F. Public information — 67–71
   G. Advisory services — 72–77
   H. Special reports — 78–79

III. MEDIUM-TERM AND LONG-TERM REFORM ISSUES
   A. Introduction — 80
   B. The nature of the emerging challenge — 81–84
   C. A review of options — 85–89

	D. Consolidated reports	90
	E. Elimination of comprehensive periodic reports in their present form	91–93
	F. Towards a consolidation of the treaty bodies	94
	G. The desirability of additional proactive measures	95–97
	H. Amending the treaties	98–101
IV.	OTHER ISSUES	
	A. The unmentionable language question	102–106
	B. Cooperation with the specialized agencies and other bodies	107–108
	C. The quality of concluding observations	109
V.	PRINCIPAL RECOMMENDATIONS	110–122

I. INTRODUCTION

A. Background

1. This report is submitted by the independent expert, Mr Philip Alston, appointed by the Secretary-General pursuant to General Assembly resolution 43/115 of 8 December 1988 and Commission on Human Rights resolution 1989/47 of 6 March 1989. A first report was submitted to the General Assembly at the forty-fourth session (A/44/668) and an interim report was submitted to the World Conference on Human Rights (A/CONF.157/PC/62/Add.11/Rev.1); both the Assembly and the Commission have subsequently requested the completion of the report. The aim of the study is to identify, in as concise a way as possible, some of the key measures that might be taken to improve the effective functioning of the United Nations human rights treaty system.

2. The report builds upon the two previous reports. For the most part, neither the analysis of nor the recommendations in those reports are repeated herein. The purpose of the present report is to update the previous analyses in light of recent developments and to present specific recommendations in relation to a selected range of issues for consideration by the relevant bodies.

3. The independent expert is currently Chairperson of the Committee on Economic, Social and Cultural Rights, and served as Chairman-Rapporteur of the meeting organized at the time of the World Conference on Human Rights which, for the first time ever, brought together the presidents, chairpersons or their representatives of the African Commission of Human and Peoples' Rights, the European Court of Human Rights and the European Commission on Human Rights, the Inter-American Court of Human Rights and the Inter-American Commission on Human Rights, the six United Nations treaty bodies and the Committee of Experts on the Application of Conventions and Recommendations of the International Labour Organization. He has participated in five of the seven meetings of persons chairing the United Nations human rights treaty bodies that have been held

Appendix 5: Long-Term Effectiveness of the UN Human Rights Treaty System 595

to date (in 1988, 1990, 1992, 1994 and 1996). He also served as Chairman-Rapporteur of the Task Force on Computerization established by the Commission on Human Rights in 1989. Discussions in these various contexts have been invaluable as a source of information in the preparation of the present report.

B. *Progress achieved since the previous reports by the independent expert*

4. Many of the recommendations contained in the earlier reports have been put into effect. From the 1989 report, they include: the preparation of a study on overlapping provisions of the different treaties and the potential for the use of cross-referencing in reporting; the amendment of the Convention against Torture and Other Cruel, Inhuman or Degrading Treatment or Punishment and the Convention on the Elimination of All Forms of Racial Discrimination to provide for regular budget funding and the adoption of interim measures to assure the necessary funding; extension of the meeting time available to several of the treaty bodies; advance preparation by most committees of a list of written questions to facilitate the dialogue with the State party; acceptance of all sources of information as being potentially relevant; the adoption of substantive and focused conclusive observations; and the regular publication of an inventory of all international human rights standard-setting activities.
5. From the 1993 report, reference can be made to: the adoption of specific target dates for the achievement of universal ratification of at least some of the treaties; the continuing search for effective responses to the non-submission of reports, including, if necessary, consideration of the situation in the absence of a report; a diminution in the number of requests directed to States for reports outside the convention-based reporting system; the provision of minimal office facilities for one or two members of the treaty bodies in Geneva; the move towards establishing a documentation facility within the Centre; greater emphasis upon electronic information sources; and other more minor reforms.
6. By the same token, many of the recommendations have remained unaddressed. Some of these are taken up again in the present report.

C. *A thumbnail sketch of the present situation*

7. Despite the progress that has been achieved in recent years, the principal characteristics of the situation have not changed fundamentally since the independent expert's interim report in 1993. The following elements are significant in this regard:
   (a) Since 1993 the number of ratifications has grown by some 26 per cent with the most notable increases occurring in relation to the Convention on the Rights of the Child and the Convention on the Elimination of All Forms of Discrimination against Women. Nevertheless, 31 per cent of States are not parties to either of the International Covenants and almost 50 per cent of States have not become parties to the Convention against Torture;
   (b) The operation of the International Convention on the Suppression and Punishment of the Crime of Apartheid has been suspended. This is a blessing for the system as a whole since the delinquency in submitting

reports under that Convention was so great that one very experienced observer characterized the situation as a "fiasco";

(c) No new treaty bodies have been created and no new treaties providing for the establishment of monitoring bodies have entered into force. The approved meeting time of three of the committees has, however, increased notably;

(d) The number of overdue reports has increased by 34 per cent and the delays experienced by States parties between the submission and examination of their reports have increased to the point where some States will wait almost three years before their reports are examined;

(e) The number of communications being processed under the various complaints procedures has greatly increased and existing backlogs are unacceptably high. At the same time, there is a clear need to create additional complaints systems in order to ensure that due attention is paid to economic, social and cultural rights and to the full range of women's rights. Specific proposals in relation to both the Convention on the Elimination of All Forms of Discrimination against Women and the International Covenant on Economic, Social and Cultural Rights are currently under consideration;

(f) The resources available to service this sizeable expansion in the system have actually contracted rather than expanded and there have been consistent calls, escalating in volume and intensity, by the various committees, and especially by the meetings of chairpersons, for increased resources and improved servicing to be made available;

(g) At the same time, conference servicing officials in Geneva have proposed that a limit of an average of 50 pages per State party report be imposed. The production of summary records is now confined to two languages (English and French) and the translation into the second language (whichever one it might be) is generally significantly delayed.

8. The extent of the shortcomings inherent in the treaty monitoring system has led some observers to propose radical solutions. Thus, for example, in 1994 one commentator proposed, *inter alia*, that States which do not satisfy a set of minimum requirements drawn from the relevant treaties should be expelled from the treaty regime; the system of State reporting should be discontinued; the treaty bodies should undertake on-site fact-finding in every State party; and acceptance of a right to petition under all six treaties should be made mandatory. Writing in August 1996, in a report for the International Law Association, the same commentator considered there to be an "implementation crisis ... of dangerous proportions". In her view, "the treaty regime has been depreciated by chronic levels of non-compliance, both with the substantive terms of the treaties, and with existing enforcement mechanisms". Other observers have been much more optimistic about the potential of the supervisory system to achieve its objectives.

D. *The premises upon which this report is based*

9. The present report is based upon several premises. The first is that the basic assumptions of the treaty supervisory system are sound and remain entirely valid. In other words, the principle of holding States accountable for non-

Appendix 5: Long-Term Effectiveness of the UN Human Rights Treaty System 597

compliance with their treaty obligations by means of an objective and constructive dialogue, on the basis of comprehensive information and inputs from all interested parties, has been vindicated in practice and has the potential to be an important and effective means by which to promote respect for human rights. The potential contribution that it can make has not in any way been superseded by other approaches or mechanisms that have been created. The second premise is that considerable achievements have been recorded by all of the treaty bodies in recent years, although there has been significant unevenness in that regard. The third is that progress, both in improving the quality and effectiveness of monitoring and in reforming the procedures and institutions, is inevitably a gradual process and there are no "miracle cures" to be found.

10. The fourth premise is that the present system is unsustainable and that significant reforms will be required if the overall regime is to achieve its objectives. This is a function of several developments including the immense expansion of the human rights treaty system in a period of less than two decades, the expanding reach and increasing demands of regional human rights systems, the proliferation of reporting obligations in other contexts, especially in the environmental field, and the increasing pressures upon Governments and the United Nations system to reduce their budgetary outlays and streamline their programmes. The treaty bodies cannot, and nor should they seek to, remain immune to these pressures.

11. Indeed, predictions as to likely future levels of resource availability are critical to any assessment of what needs to be done in relation to the treaty system. While firm predictions are difficult at best, there is very little cause to think that there will be a dramatic increase in existing resource levels in the years ahead. In part this is a reflection of global budgetary pressures and their impact on the United Nations as a whole. But, more significantly, it reflects the perhaps inevitable, although nonetheless short-sighted and regrettable, reluctance of Governments to provide adequate resources for the development of mechanisms which might be able to monitor their human rights performance more effectively.

12. In many respects, this is the key issue both for those who are persuaded of the need to reform the system and for those who are not. In considering the future of the treaty supervisory system, much depends upon the assumptions that are made as to the future availability of resources. If it is assumed that, over time, even if not in the immediate future, considerably more resources will be made available, then the focus should be upon seeking to perfect, or at least improve, the system in the form in which it is currently developing. But if the assumption is that the existing level of funding is unlikely to be increased in the years ahead, then the current system is simply not sustainable and we will witness a steady diminution in the support available to each treaty body and in the ability of each to function in a meaningful way.

13. Before examining specific reform proposals, it is appropriate to recall the cautionary comment made earlier by the independent expert in his interim report that the quest for reform "must not be embarked upon without acknowledging the very considerable achievements to date and the importance of proceeding with sensitivity and sophistication in order to ensure that the fundamental integrity of the system, and particularly its ability to

safeguard human rights, are not sacrificed to illusory notions of streamlining and efficiency" (A/CONF.157/PC/62/Add.11/Rev.1, para. 12).

II. MAJOR CURRENT POLICY ISSUES

A. *Towards universal ratification*

14. Universal ratification of the six core United Nations human rights treaties would establish the best possible foundations for international endeavours to promote respect for human rights. In his interim report in 1993 the independent expert recommended that the year 2000 be set as a target date for achieving that objective. In the event, the World Conference on Human Rights, in the Vienna Declaration and Programme of Action, endorsed three sets of measures in relation to ratification:
   (a) it set the following goals: the year 1995 as the target date for universal ratification of the Convention on the Rights of the Child (Part I, para. 21), the year 2000 as the target date in relation to the Convention on the Elimination of All Forms of Discrimination against Women (Part II, para. 39) and, in relation to the others, urged "the universal ratification of human rights treaties" (Part I, para. 26);
   (b) it "strongly recommend[ed] that a concerted effort be made to encourage and facilitate the ratification of and accession or succession to international human rights treaties and protocols adopted within the framework of the United Nations system with the aim of universal acceptance. The Secretary-General, in consultation with treaty bodies, should consider opening a dialogue with States not having acceded to these human rights treaties, in order to identify obstacles and to seek ways of overcoming them" (Part II, para. 4);
   (c) it also recommended that when the five-year review of the implementation of the Vienna Declaration and Programme of Action is undertaken in 1998 "[s]pecial attention should be paid to assessing the progress towards the goal of universal ratification ..." (Part II, para. 100).
15. Since the Vienna Conference there has been a very significant improvement in the ratification rate of the principal treaties. On 1 January 1993 there were 678 States parties to the six treaties. By 30 June 1996 this figure had risen to 853, an increase of 175 or 26 per cent. This constitutes an impressive achievement but there is also another side to the coin which is illustrated by the fact that 31 per cent of States (59 out of 193) have not become a party to either of the two International Covenants on Human Rights, despite their centrality to the overall human rights regime.
16. Equally surprising is the fact that almost 50 per cent of States (95 out of 193) have not become parties to the Convention against Torture. When it is recalled that the Convention on the Rights of the Child contains a comprehensive prohibition against torture in the case of all persons covered by that treaty (in essence, all persons below the age of 18), it is not clear why so many States can accept that obligation but not the equivalent obligation in the Convention against Torture. Similarly, there are 36 States which have accepted the obligation not to torture under the International

Appendix 5: Long-Term Effectiveness of the UN Human Rights Treaty System 599

Covenant on Civil and Political Rights but have not yet ratified the Convention against Torture.

17. The increase in the total number of ratifications also needs to be viewed in the light of three important factors which partly account for the success. The first is that a number of new States succeeded to the treaties during this period, thus expanding the number of total ratifications but not thereby reducing the number of States which had not become parties to the various treaties by the time of the Vienna Conference. The second factor is the impact of the Fourth World Conference on Women, both before and after the event, in terms of encouraging States to ratify the Convention on the Elimination of All Forms of Discrimination against Women. Ratifications of the Convention went from 114 on 1 January 1993 to 153 on 30 June 1996, an increase of 39 States parties, or 34 per cent. The Beijing Platform for Action called for universal ratification of the Convention by the year 2000.

18. The third factor is the extraordinary success of efforts to promote ratification of the Convention on the Rights of the Child. As a result, 30 per cent of the overall increase in ratifications during this three and a half year period (53 ratifications) was attributable exclusively to that Convention, the number of States parties to which went from 134 to 187. Taken together those two conventions accounted for 92 of the new ratifications, or some 53 per cent.

19. There are some important lessons to be learned from the successes achieved in relation to the two conventions which have attracted so many new ratifications in recent years. The first concerns the importance of political will, whether expressed through the holding of international conferences which place appropriate emphasis upon the convention in question or through consistent efforts by international organizations. In contrast, the lead-up to international conferences focusing on social development (Copenhagen) and human settlements (Istanbul) saw no attention at all to efforts to promote ratification of the relevant human rights treaties. The second lesson concerns the importance of mobilizing domestic constituencies (in this case, women's and children's non-governmental organizations) in support of the goals and mechanisms reflected in the treaty, thus making it easier for Governments to undertake ratification.

20. The third lesson, and in the case of the Convention on the Rights of the Child the most important, concerns the provision of assistance and advice by an international agency, which in this instance was the United Nations Children's Fund. Such agencies can, whenever requested, assist Governments and the principal social partners in various ways, including: by explaining the significance of the treaty as a whole and of its specific provisions; by promoting an awareness of the treaty which facilitates domestic consultations and discussions; by shedding light upon the requirements of the treaty in the event of ratification; by providing assistance to enable any necessary pre-ratification measures to be identified and implemented; by assisting in relation to the preparation of reports, both indirectly through the agency's own situation analyses, and directly through the provision of expert assistance where appropriate; and by reassuring developing countries in particular that ratification should bring with it enhanced access to at least some of the expert or financial resources needed to implement key provisions of the treaty.

21. In this respect the success of the effort to promote ratification of the Convention on the Rights of the Child indicates that there is no (or at least no longer) deep-rooted resistance to the principle of participation in human rights supervisory arrangements. Given the relative comprehensiveness of the Convention, along with the integral links between respect for children's rights and those of the rest of the community, it might be thought that the reasons which had previously led various States not to ratify all six of the core human rights treaties are no longer compelling and that there will be a new openness to increased participation in the overall treaty regime. Indeed, there is something odd about a situation in which all States but four have become parties to such a far-reaching Convention while almost one State in every three has not become a party to either of the two International Covenants.

22. The success of the Convention on the Rights of the Child, and the factors that contributed to that success, would also seem to vindicate the following analysis contained in the independent expert's interim report to the Vienna Conference:

"Among the reasons that might well be impeding ratification or accession in some countries are the following: a lack of understanding of the implications of the instrument on the part of mid-level officials who would need to prepare the ground before the Government could act; a lack of trained personnel who could explain the implications of ratification with the necessary sophistication and detail to the relevant government minister; the existence of an element of confusion between the treaty body procedures and the special procedures of the Commission on Human Rights; a low budget priority for the measures needed to precede or accompany ratification or accession, such as the undertaking of a survey of existing law and practice, the drafting of necessary legislation or regulations, the training of officials, etc.; the lack of an informed domestic constituency which would support government proposals to ratify or accede to an instrument; and a fear that the reporting obligations would be too onerous for the country concerned" (A/CONF.157/PC/62/Add.11/Rev.1., para. 84).

23. The emphasis upon promoting universal ratification is an essential one in order to strengthen and consolidate the universalist foundations of the United Nations human rights regime. Despite the fears of some critics, the quest for universal ratification need not have any negative consequences for the treaty regime as a whole. One such critic, Professor Bayefsky, has argued that the "implementation crisis" which she perceives to exist is due in part to "a deliberate emphasis on ratification" which for many States, has "become an end in itself, a means to easy accolades for empty gestures". In her view, ratification is often "purchased at a price, namely, diminished obligations, lax supervision, and few adverse consequences from non-compliance". But such an analysis would seem to confuse two processes which should remain, and for the most part have remained, separate. It is difficult to accept the proposition that the treaty bodies have been lax in their supervision in order to entice more States to accept the obligations in question. Indeed, the experience of the Convention on the Rights of the Child would seem clearly incompatible with such an analysis. The Committee on the Rights of the

Child has, to date, been one of the most demanding and conscientious of the treaty bodies, but this has in no way impeded the dramatic movement towards the achievement of near-universal ratification of the Convention. In the view of the independent expert more, rather than less, should be done to explore ways in which to overcome the legitimate, as opposed to the inappropriate, concerns of certain identifiable groups of countries that have so far been reluctant to ratify.

24. Perhaps the most obvious such group consists of those States with a population of 1 million or less. Twenty-nine such States have not ratified either of the two International Covenants on Human Rights. As of 1996, 21 of those were estimated to have a Gross National Product per capita of below US$ 5,000 per annum, and with 11 of them being below the $2,000 per annum level. In relation to those States the independent expert recalls the analysis contained in his interim report:

"Provided that the usual caveats in relation to such generalizations are kept in mind, several conclusions might reasonably be drawn from this data. Firstly, at least some of these small States are probably concerned that the legal, bureaucratic and administrative requirements involved are too onerous given the size of their population. Secondly, the reporting requirements might well act as a significant deterrent in such cases. Thirdly, the ... States with very low populations and low per capita GNP might be strongly influenced by the resource implications of ratification" (A/CONF.157/PC/62/Add.11/Rev.1, para. 87).

25. This in turn raises the question of whether the international community should be providing resources to facilitate the ratification of treaties by such States and to assist them in meeting the subsequent reporting burden, at least initially. Curiously, it has yet to be acknowledged that such activities, which are essential to laying the foundations for a stable and peaceful world in which human rights are respected, should be funded adequately within the United Nations framework. It almost seems to be thought that efforts to promote the acceptance of human rights norms would somehow be tainted if progress were purchased at a price, in terms of the necessary technical assistance. In contrast, the principle was recognized long ago in the environmental area in which many of the arrangements made in relation to key treaties provide for financial and other forms of assistance to help States to undertake the necessary monitoring, to prepare reports and to implement some of the measures required in order to ensure compliance with treaty obligations.

26. Thus the principal question in the present context is what measures might be taken in order to facilitate achievement of the oft-confirmed goal of universal ratification of the six core treaties? Following the World Conference on Human Rights, the General Assembly, in resolution 48/121 of 20 December 1993, endorsed the Vienna Declaration and Programme of Action (para. 2) and requested the Secretary-General to implement the relevant recommendations (para. 9). At that time, provision was made to undertake a study on the encouragement of ratifications, as well as a study on questions relating to reservations, and for two regional meetings to be held around these issues. In the intervening three years neither of these studies has been

commissioned and only one of the regional seminars has been held. It took place in Addis Ababa in May 1996 and focused on the African region. The four-day meeting did not produce any official report, but informal reports indicate that the significance of the various elements identified above was strongly affirmed.

27. Before examining specific measures that might be taken to promote universal ratification it is appropriate to consider the existing and potential contribution made in this regard by bodies other than the High Commissioner for Human Rights. One of the major consequences of the ending of the Cold War has been the greatly increased attention given to the human rights dimensions of their activities by intergovernmental bodies which are not per se part of the human rights framework as narrowly defined. This is specifically reflected in the coordination mandate given to the High Commissioner for Human Rights by the General Assembly in resolution 48/141. Similarly, agencies such as the United Nations Development Programme (UNDP) and the World Bank have acknowledged the importance of respect for human rights (and of intimately related issues such as democratization, governance and the rule of law) in the broad context of their own programmes. Curiously, however, those agencies have never viewed the commitment to promote the universal ratification of the core treaties as something of direct relevance to their own work. Yet, to take one example, the centrality of the rights recognized in the Convention on the Elimination of All Forms of Discrimination against Women to the programmes of those agencies is such that it might reasonably be expected that they would have adopted some active measures aimed at encouraging ratification. The same applies in relation to the two International Covenants on Human Rights.

28. The vital importance of the role that might potentially be played by these agencies in promoting the achievement of universal ratification has been recognized by the chairpersons of the treaty bodies. At their sixth meeting, in 1995, the chairpersons recommended that such a role be played and in that regard recommended that, at their seventh meeting, "a dialogue [should] take place with senior officials of key organizations and agencies, to include, *inter alia*", the UNDP (A/50/505, para. 18). Yet, at the seventh meeting, UNDP, the World Bank and FAO were not represented, and the WHO and UNESCO representatives were present only briefly and did not speak. In other words, there was no dialogue at a senior level, and indeed no dialogue at all on the contribution that might be made by the agencies to the promotion of universal ratification. Similarly, although a UNDP senior official addressed the sixteenth session of the Committee on the Elimination of Discrimination against Women (in January 1997) and was asked about the potential role of that agency in encouraging ratifications or assisting States in the preparation of reports, the relevant press release (WOM/948) records no response.

29. A related question that should also be addressed is whether those agencies which have played an active role in the promotion of specific human rights treaties – most notably UNICEF in relation to the Convention on the Rights of the Child and ILO in relation to ILO conventions – could not also take it upon themselves to explicitly encourage the ratification of key treaties such as the two International Covenants and the Convention on the Elimination of All Forms of Discrimination against Women.

30. Regional organizations might also be asked to contribute to the effort to encourage universal ratification. The Organization for Security and Cooperation in Europe (OSCE) is particularly relevant in that regard. Since its considerable human rights-related activities are not based on formally binding instruments its various normative and other pronouncements have relied extensively upon the International Covenants and other treaties. It would seem especially appropriate, therefore, for a joint effort to be made by the OSCE and the United Nations in regard to ratification of the six core United Nations treaties.
31. A variety of recommendations relating to universal ratification follow from the foregoing analysis.
32. The High Commissioner on Human Rights should be requested to consult specifically with the relevant international agencies, including UNDP, the World Bank, UNESCO, WHO and FAO, with a view to ascertaining what initiatives, if any, they might be prepared to take in order to encourage States with which they are dealing to ratify any of the six core treaties to which they are not already a party. The High Commissioner should be asked to report in writing to the eighth meeting of chairpersons, expected to be held in September 1997.
33. The dialogue recommended by the World Conference on Human Rights for the purpose of identifying "obstacles and to seek ways of overcoming them" must be undertaken. It should be approached in a systematic, even-handed and constructive manner. Given the resource constraints, which partly explain the absence of any organized or systematic dialogue to date, it is recommended that a specific trust fund be established for the purpose of employing two advisers to the High Commissioner on ratification and reporting. Their tasks would be to assist States in the ways outlined above. One of these persons would be a political adviser and the other a technical expert with the capacity to undertake or oversee pre-ratification surveys as well as the preparation of initial reports. This unit should be established for a three-year period with sufficient earmarked funding to enable assistance to be provided in national capitals rather than in Geneva. The special advisers on ratification should be urged to adopt clear priority groups of countries in order to maximize the effectiveness of their activities.
34. Specific funding should be earmarked from the advisory services programme to support the preparation of initial reports by newly-ratifying developing countries. Since the preparation of subsequent reports is, in most respects, considerably less demanding, and would be greatly facilitated by the experience gained in connection with the initial report, the subsequent reporting burden would not be unduly onerous.
35. The meeting of chairpersons should be asked to consider various ways in which the reporting process might be streamlined and made less burdensome in relation to all States with populations of 1 million or fewer people.
36. The special advisers on ratification and reporting should explore and report on the most appropriate methodology by which to enable those 32 States which have ratified either the International Convention on the Rights of the Child alone or that Convention and only one other treaty (in most cases either the International Convention on the Elimination of All Forms of Racial Discrimination or the Convention on the Elimination of All Forms

of Discrimination against Women) to prepare a consolidated report which, by building upon the one or two reports they are already obliged to prepare, would enable them to become parties to the remaining treaties without thereby significantly increasing their reporting burden.

B. Responding to the problem of significantly overdue reports

37. Most of the committees continue to express concern over the consequences of the large number of significantly overdue reports. Table 1, below, shows the extent of the problem at the time of the independent expert's interim report in 1993 in comparison with the situation at the end of 1996.

38. In its 1996 annual report (A/51/44) the Committee against Torture noted in paragraph 1 that there were 96 States parties and in paragraph 21 that there were 55 States with overdue reports. The Committee went on to deplore the failure of those States whose reports were more than four years overdue and recounted how numerous reminders had been sent by the Secretary-General and various letters sent by the Chairman of the Committee. The Committee took two measures in response. The first was to issue a separate document listing overdue reports. The second was to give wide publicity to the list at its end of session press conferences.

39. In its 1996 annual report (A/51/40) the Human Rights Committee expressed "its serious concern" that "more than two thirds of all States parties ... were in arrears with their reports", and noted that this "state of affairs seriously impedes [its] ability to monitor the implementation of the Covenant" (para. 45). The Committee has continued to seek new means by which to encourage delinquent States parties to submit reports. In addition to the regular sending of reminders and the holding of meetings between members of the Bureau of the Committee with the permanent representatives of the relevant States, the Committee began in 1994 to include a separate list in the main part of its annual report indicating those States that have more than one report overdue. In its 1996 report the Committee went further and "reserved the right to make public a list of [those States] during the press conference convened at the end of each session of the Committee" (para. 32).

40. Measures such as those resorted to by these two committees show an

Table 1. The trend in relation to overdue reports, 1993–1996

Treaty	State parties 1993	State parties 1996	Parties with overdue reports 1993	Parties with overdue reports 1996	Total overdue reports 1993	Total overdue reports 1996
ICESCR	119	134	65	97	65	115
ICCPR	115	134	64	84	83	114
CERD	132	147	112	126	342	401
CEDAW	118	153	78	115	127	189
CAT	71	98	36	61	38	67
CRC	126	187	59	71	59	71
Total	680	853	414	554	714	957

admirable faith in the extent of the readership of annual reports by committees and in the newsworthiness of delinquency by a State in its reporting to a United Nations body. Nevertheless, it is difficult to avoid the conclusion that they are unlikely to have a significant impact upon the behaviour of the States concerned. Thus, for example, in the case of the Human Rights Committee, five States have each received 20 or more reminders over a period of 10 years or more and have failed to respond (A/51/40, para. 45).

41. Other responses might include an easing of the reporting requirements under certain circumstances. Thus, at its sixteenth session, the Committee on the Elimination of Discrimination against Women considered an oral report presented by one State party. The Committee emphasized, however, that it had done so on an exceptional basis and as a matter of courtesy to the delegation and insisted that the presentation of a written report be scheduled. The Human Rights Committee decided in 1996 that, "under very exceptional circumstances", when a report is overdue "because of material difficulties", the State party could be invited to send a delegation to discuss those difficulties or be asked to submit a provisional report dealing only with certain aspects of the Covenant (A/51/40, para. 32). Such initiatives raise two types of questions. The first is whether, from a pragmatic perspective, they are likely to succeed in enabling more States to report. Only time will provide a definitive answer, but it seems that a significant response rate could only come as a result of important, case-by-case, concessions in relation to the principle that all States parties must report in accordance with the general guidelines. That leads to the second question, which is whether real concessions (of the type that will act as an incentive to otherwise recalcitrant States) can be made without undermining the central tenets of the reporting system.

42. Another approach, which would be applicable across the board, rather than on an ad hoc basis, but at the same time permit a more tailored and flexible approach to reporting, would be to eliminate the obligation to provide comprehensive periodic reports, in the form in which they presently exist. This option is discussed below.

43. Broadly stated, there are two reasons why States do not report: administrative incapacity including a lack of specialist expertise or lack of political will, or a combination of both. In the first situation, repeated appeals are, almost by definition, unlikely to bear fruit. Instead, the solution lies in a more serious, more expert and more carefully targeted advisory services programme in relation to reporting. This is discussed briefly below.

44. In the second situation, a lack of political will translates essentially into a calculation by the State concerned that the consequences, both domestic and international, of a failure to report are less important than the costs, administrative and political, of complying with reporting obligations. In that case, the only viable approach on the part of the treaty bodies and/or the political organs is to seek to raise the "costs" of non-compliance. A failure to devise appropriate responses of this nature has ramifications which extend well beyond the consequences for any individual State party. Large-scale non-reporting makes a mockery of the reporting system as a whole. It leads to a situation in which many States are effectively rewarded for violating their obligations while others are penalized for complying (in the sense of

subjecting themselves to scrutiny by the treaty bodies), and it will lead to a situation in which a diminishing number of States will report very regularly and others will almost never do so.

45. The key question, however, is what types of measures designed to raise the costs of non-compliance might be appropriate, potentially productive in terms of upholding the integrity of the system, consistent with the legal framework of the relevant treaty, and politically and otherwise acceptable. Various palliatives are available and have been canvassed elsewhere in this report. They include: the elimination of reporting and its replacement by detailed questions to which answers must be given; the preparation of a single consolidated report to satisfy several different requirements; and the much wider use of a more professional advisory services programme designed to assist in the preparation of reports. Ultimately, however, none of these might make a difference in hard-core cases. Under those circumstances the only viable option open to the treaty bodies is to proceed with an examination of the situation in a State party in the absence of a report. This has been done for a number of years by the Committee on Economic, Social and Cultural Rights and the Committee on the Elimination of Racial Discrimination has adopted a very similar approach. The situation has not yet become chronic for either the Committee on the Rights of the Child, because it is still much younger than the others, or for the Committee against Torture which has many fewer States parties than the other committees. And the Committee on the Elimination of Discrimination against Women has had so little meeting time, until very recently, that it was unlikely to take any steps that would increase its workload.

46. It seems inevitable, however, that each of these committees, and certainly the Human Rights Committee, will have to contemplate taking such a step sooner or later. While the precise legal basis for such measures will need to be rooted in the text of each of the relevant treaties, the principal foundation is to be found in a teleological approach to interpretation which acknowledges that any other outcome is absurd in that it enables a delinquent State party to defeat the object and purpose of the implementation provisions. In that regard, it is pertinent to recall that the General Assembly, in its resolution 51/87, specifically "encourage[d] the efforts of the human rights treaty bodies to examine the progress made in achieving the fulfilment of human rights treaty undertakings by all States parties, without exception" (emphasis added).

47. In implementing such an approach, the experience of the Committee on Economic, Social and Cultural Rights is instructive. Ample notice has been given to the States concerned and, in a majority of the cases taken up so far, reports which had been dramatically overdue have suddenly materialized. For the rest, it is particularly important that the Committee is in a position to undertake detailed research work and to be able to base its examination upon a wide range of sources of information. The resulting "concluding observations" must be detailed, accurate and comprehensive. If they are not, States can again be rewarded for a failure to report by a routine or mechanistic response which fails to establish genuine accountability in any way. In this respect it is not clear that the conclusions adopted to date in such cases by the Committee on the Elimination of Racial Discrimination meet such criteria.

C. The inadequacy of the current system to deal with the timely submission of reports

1. Inability to process reports due to be submitted

48. The present supervisory system can function only because of the large-scale delinquency of States which either do not report at all, or report long after the due date. This is hardly a satisfactory foundation upon which to build an effective and efficient monitoring system. Thus, for example, the Committee on the Elimination of Discrimination against Women noted in its 1994 annual report (A/49/38, para. 12) that if States parties reported on schedule it would need to consider 30 reports per session.

49. In brief, the picture that emerges from table 2 is that if every State party with a report overdue under either of the Covenants were to submit that report tomorrow, the last to be received could not be considered, on the basis of existing arrangements, before the year 2003. At that point, the relevant committee would be considering an eight-year-old report and would have a huge backlog of subsequent reports pending.

50. An even more compelling way of looking at the situation is to assume that every State party to the Convention on the Rights of the Child were to submit a periodic (as opposed to initial) report, as required, every five years. In theory, this would require the Committee on the Rights of the Child to examine 187 reports over five years. At its present rate of examining reports it would require 3 meetings per report, or a total of 561 meetings. Divided over a five-year period, that would require 112 meetings per year devoted to reports. Currently, on the basis of meeting for nine weeks in plenary session and three weeks in working groups, it is able to devote 54 meetings per year to the examination of reports. Thus, its meeting time would need to be at least doubled, making 18 weeks of meetings plus 6 weeks of working groups. At least half of the Committee of 10 members would thus need to spend 24 weeks a year in session, quite apart from all of the additional activities that that Committee has so far undertaken outside of its official

Table 2. Length of time required to review all State reports currently due, if they were to be submitted at the end of 1996

	Average No. of meetings per report	Meetings required to consider reports	Average No. of meetings per year	Average No. of meetings per year devoted to examining reports	No. of years required
ICESCR	3	3 × 115 = 345	58	45	7.6
ICCPR	3	3 × 114 = 342	85	45	7.6
CERD	2	2 × 401 = 802	55	33	24.3
CEDAW	2	2 × 189 = 378	49	18	21
CAT	2.2	2.2 × 67 = 134	36	20	6.7
CRC	3	3 × 71 = 213	85	54	3.9

meeting times. The resulting burden on the Secretariat, on conference servicing facilities and on translation, interpretation and editing services would be immense.

2. *The problem of delays between submission and examination of reports*

51. In its 1994 annual report the Committee on the Elimination of Discrimination against Women observed that there was "an average of three years between the time a State party submits its report and its consideration by the Committee". The Committee went on to observe that such a situation provides "a disincentive to report and leads to the need for the State to present additional information to update the report which, in turn, increases the volume of documentation that must be considered by the Committee" (A/49/38, para. 12). This analysis is still applicable in relation to most committees. Thus, on the basis of available figures, a report submitted in December 1996 to the Committee on the Rights of the Child would not be examined until January 1999. For the Human Rights Committee and the Committee on Economic, Social and Cultural Rights, the respective dates would probably be July 1998 and May 1999.

52. The options available for responding to a situation which is clearly unacceptable to the committees and the States concerned, as well as to those whose human rights are the focus of attention, are examined later in this report. At this point, it is sufficient to observe that one option which is clearly unsatisfactory is to schedule a large number of reports for consideration in a very short time, so that each report receives only superficial consideration. Unless such an approach is preceded by very detailed preliminary work and demonstrates that it is still able to achieve convincing and accurate results, it risks going through the motions for their own sake and abandoning the raison d'être of the whole system, which is to promote respect for human rights and ensure genuine accountability.

D. *Problems in relation to documentation*

1. *A fifty-page limit on State reports?*

53. As noted at the beginning of this report, it has been proposed by conference servicing officials in Geneva, in addressing both the seventh meeting of chairpersons and individual committees in the course of 1996, that a limit of an average of 50 pages be imposed on the length of State party reports to be processed and translated. To the extent that such a limitation would apply to processing (copy-editing, clean typing and reproduction) as well as translating, it would even eliminate the option for a committee to be prepared to consider a longer report in the original language in which it is submitted. This proposal has yet to be fully implemented but its effects are already being felt in various ways. Although it is beyond the scope of this report to address the possible implications of the proposal, two procedural matters are worthy of note since they bear on the modalities of future treaty body-related reform processes. The first is that both the chairpersons' meeting and the treaty bodies themselves have been provided with very little solid statistical information to substantiate the need for draconian measures of the type

proposed. Indeed the message has, for the most part, been conveyed orally rather than in the form of a detailed written analysis which would provide a basis for careful consideration of alternative responses. The second is that the Centre for Human Rights has not provided any analysis of the alternatives that might be considered. Given the difficulty of obtaining information about the functioning of the system and the costs involved, the absence of such an analysis, or briefing paper, would seem to increase considerably the prospects for ill-informed and uncreative responses.

54. The incongruity of the proposed limitation is perhaps best illustrated by the fact that the general guidelines for the submission of periodic reports (CRC/C/58), adopted by the Committee on the Rights of the Child in October 1996, are 49 pages long. In other words, States parties would be asked to respond to 49 pages of questions and of lists of issues in relation to which information is required in the course of a report of precisely the same length. This is clearly impossible, and it is doubly so in the case of federal States which must report on the situation in relation to the different laws and practices applying in each of their constituent territories. Moreover, the suggestion that reports could be confined to 50 pages is entirely at odds with the trend in most of the committees to request ever more precise and detailed information in order to enable the experts to obtain a clearer picture of the situation. On the other hand, two committees (the Committee against Torture and the Committee on the Elimination of Racial Discrimination) have generally managed with comparatively brief reports. This is, however, primarily a function of the more restricted nature of their focus rather than of their greater frugality.

2. *Ephemeral or unrecorded documentation*

55. Another problem which is worthy of note concerns the increasing proportion of documentation which, although central to the dialogue in many cases, is of an ephemeral or officially unrecorded nature. In other words, governmental representatives submit detailed information, sometimes in the form of materials already published (and thus, in principle, available elsewhere) but more often in the form of specifically targeted information in response to questions raised or issues signalled in advance by the respective treaty bodies. Since this information is neither contained in the State party report itself nor reflected, except indirectly and in passing, in the summary records, it is effectively lost and is not part of any enduring or accessible record of the dialogue. Although it might have had a determinative influence upon the Committee's response, it is not available to any person who was not both present at the time and was privileged to gain access to the documentation.

56. As with many of the issues dealt with in this report, devising appropriate responses is rather more difficult than identifying the issues. The first step is for the materials included in the annual report to be more systematic and detailed in indicating the principal reference materials relied upon in the examination of the report. The second step would be to develop a more systematic documentary archive to be maintained at least until the examination of the subsequent report of the same State party. But again, in the context of a treaty body secretariat which employs not a single skilled

documentalist, has no satisfactory facilities for maintaining archives and has yet to focus at all on issues of this type, it is not clear that there is much use in making very detailed recommendations, beyond calling attention to the problem.

3. *Delays in the production of summary records*

57. Another problem confronting the treaty bodies is that the summary records are now produced in only two languages (English and French) and the translation into the second language (whichever one it might be) is generally significantly delayed. This is of particular significance for several reasons. The first is that, in response to budgetary and other concerns, each of the treaty bodies has eliminated from its annual reports the summary of the dialogue with each State party which was a consistent feature of the annual reports until quite recently. This could be done on the basis that there was no need to duplicate information which was any event provided, and in a more systematic fashion, by the summary records. The second is that the summary records constitute one of the most important elements in the process of accountability which provides the principal rationale for the process of dialogue. If the records are not accessible within a reasonably short period of time after the examination of the report and the adoption of the concluding observations, a significant part of the value of the undertaking may be lost.

58. By the same token, it is not clear that there is sufficient value-added by the publication, in the case of the Human Rights Committee, of a set of official records (previously known as the Committee's Yearbooks) reproducing all of the summary records and other already issued documentation. The Committee on the Elimination of Discrimination against Women has requested that further yearbooks be issued for it, in addition to those produced some years ago, and similar proposals have been made in relation to the Committee on the Rights of the Child. In a context of the generous availability of resources such undertakings are certainly desirable since they make the records more accessible for historical and related purposes. However, at a time of the utmost financial stringency when neither paper nor pencils can be provided in conference rooms for the use of expert members of the treaty bodies, such expenditures are surely not a priority.

59. In any event, their value has been radically reduced by the increased importance of electronic sources of information, especially through the Internet. While summary records of the treaty bodies are not yet available in that form, it is surely only a matter of time. Priority should therefore be accorded to that enterprise. For the reasons noted below, the advantages make the investment in the electronic form of the records far more rewarding than the production of prestigious dinosaurs such as the Yearbooks (official records). The first step should therefore be the transfer of the existing Yearbooks onto the electronic databases, and the second step should consist of a concerted effort to achieve the timely publication, again in electronic form, of the summary records as soon as they are available.

E. *The development and use of electronic databases*

1. *The home page of the Centre for Human Rights*

60. The approach advocated in relation to summary records is entirely consistent with one of the most encouraging recent developments overseen by the High Commissioner for Human Rights. On 10 December 1996 a major electronic database of human rights documentation was made available on the World Wide Web and is thus accessible through the Internet. In such form, the concluding observations, reports by States, and eventually the summary records will all be made available to literally millions of potential users. This contrasts dramatically with the situation in relation to both the mimeographed documents in their original form and the printed official records (Yearbook) volumes. All of these documents have a small print run and a very limited distribution network that rarely includes national-level NGOs, scholars in places outside the industrialized countries, and other key potential users. The costs of upkeep of a hard copy collection of treaty body documents is considerable and there are only a handful of libraries around the world which devote the resources necessary for the maintenance of an accessible and functional collection of such documentation. Moreover, the utility of the hard copy documents is very limited by comparison with that of the electronic versions which can be comprehensively searched, organized and selectively printed out in very little time.

61. Concern has justifiably been expressed that an emphasis on new technology will not necessarily cater for the needs of those with limited resources or living in countries which do not have ready or reliable access to the Internet. Such concerns need to be addressed, but it must also be recalled that the accessibility of printed ("hard copy") documents in such countries and to such individuals is currently close to zero and that even elites in such countries, whether governmental, academic or activist, invariably have difficulty getting access to printed United Nations documents. In this respect, far from reinforcing existing disparities in access to information, the Internet and its equivalents offer a unique opportunity to democratize access and to ensure the systematic availability of documentation which has hitherto been extremely difficult to obtain.

62. But the full potential of these developments, in terms of those currently without ready access, will only be realized if a deliberate strategy is devised for that purpose. This in turn will require the adoption of a more systematic, consultative and transparent process than has hitherto been developed. In that respect, the Centre for Human Rights could learn from two recent initiatives. The first is the "WomenWatch" project, undertaken jointly by the Division for the Advancement of Women, the United Nations Development Fund for Women (UNIFEM) and the International Research and Training Institute for the Advancement of Women (INSTRAW), which aims to conceptualize, design and implement a joint Internet space on global information on women, accessible through World Wide Web, gopher and e-mail technology. The project's aims include identifying best current practices, improving access, providing training, and developing cooperative links with other actors.

63. The Centre for Human Rights should convene an expert seminar for similar purposes in relation to human rights information and documentation. Adequate resources should be devoted to ensure that the newly created Web site is developed further and kept fully up to date. Consideration should also be given to the appointment of an external expert advisory group to assist in relation to the development of electronic information activities, especially as they relate to the treaty bodies.
64. The second initiative from which the Centre should explore the lessons to be learned is the provision, by UNICEF, of notebook computers to all members of the Committee on the Rights of the Child. The computers are programmed to provide e-mail access and access to the key databases and documentation sources needed by members in carrying out their monitoring functions. If the experiment is a success, comparable measures should be taken in respect of members of the five other treaty bodies.

2. *Broader access to ILO and UNHCR electronic databases*

65. One of the curious features of current information technology developments which directly concern the treaty bodies is that one of the agencies which has moved the most rapidly and achieved some of the best results – the ILO – has persisted with a strategy which is no longer optimum and which now does a considerable disservice to the constituencies the organization aims to serve. It has developed an extensive and very sophisticated database, of major and direct relevance to various aspects of the work of the treaty bodies and the human rights field generally. But it has chosen only to make it available to external users by means of a CD-ROM which must be purchased and for which separate equipment, beyond a computer and an Internet connection, must be acquired. One result, for example, is that the database is unavailable to any members of the treaty bodies, to NGOs or scholars unless they make an individual purchase at considerable expense.
66. There also seems to be a significant time lag in relation to the availability of data generated by UNHCR, which is produced first for its CD-ROM ("Refworld") and subsequently, but rather more slowly, made available on its Web site. The income generated by this "user-pays" strategy may not be insignificant but the costs, in terms of unnecessarily restricted access to information and the resulting diminution of the reliance placed upon the work of the organizations, would seem to be considerable. It is to be hoped that both agencies, but the ILO in particular, will reconsider their existing strategy and make their very valuable resources available in as timely a fashion as possible to a far broader public.

F. *Public information*

67. The need for improved public information materials to be devoted to the work of the treaty bodies has been a constant theme of recommendations adopted in recent years. However, given the budgetary restraints upon the Secretariat, the cumbersome and costly procedures followed and the lack of the necessary human and other resources, it is not surprising that relatively little information about the treaty bodies has been produced. The Human

Appendix 5: Long-Term Effectiveness of the UN Human Rights Treaty System 613

Rights Committee, for example, has been calling for a number of years for the publication of a third volume of Selected Decisions of the Human Rights Committee under the Optional Protocol, without success. Volume 2 covers the period October 1982 to April 1988. A second volume of Human Rights: A Compilation of International Instruments has been under preparation since 1992, and although the Department of Public Information reports that it "is now being updated", it has in fact never been published. Apart from the extremely valuable United Nations Action in the Field of Human Rights, published every five years, there is relatively little in print which is of direct relevance to the treaty bodies. The Professional Training Series is potentially the most serious and valuable set of publications. The 25 Fact Sheets issued to date may have been printed in large numbers but their overall utility, and the effectiveness of their distribution, would be unlikely to be rated highly by external experts.

68. Without wishing to underestimate the difficulties faced by those who labour with very few resources and much more limited political support than is usually acknowledged, it would seem that the publicity provided for the work of the various treaty bodies is usually unimaginative and not especially informative. It is far beyond the mandate of the independent expert to review in any detail the various alternative approaches that might be considered in the future. It must suffice to say that three avenues would seem worth exploring. The first is giving the treaty bodies a direct input into how a specified public information budget, earmarked for that purpose, should be spent. For that purpose an options paper should be prepared and discussed by the meeting of chairpersons on the basis of discussions in individual committees. The second is to acknowledge that the greatest need is for information to be made available at the grass-roots level, rather than in Geneva and New York where it seems likely the great majority of existing materials are disseminated. But this does not mean simply that there should be a more extensive distribution of brochures by the United Nations information centres. Rather, it means that a public information budget should be available to support grass-roots initiatives designed to disseminate information about the treaty bodies in culturally appropriate and more popular formats and media.

69. The third avenue is to explore the extent to which the preparation of publications, such as the Selected Decisions, can be entrusted to academic and other external institutions that are prepared to take them on. The publication could then be achieved commercially, at a cost which would be substantially less than having either the editorial or printing work done within the United Nations. This approach would also respond to calls by the Advisory Committee on Administrative and Budgetary Questions to explore alternative and less costly approaches to the publication of United Nations materials. The treaty body concerned could still insist on appropriate standards in relation to content and the publication process would be potentially much faster and certainly less costly.

70. In general, there would seem to be good reason to convene, from time to time, an external advisory group to review the human rights-related publications programme and make recommendations in relation to it. At present, the system is singularly lacking in transparency and opportunities for inputs

from informed sources. The nature and quality of the resulting output faithfully reflects the closed and bureaucratic character of the process.

71. One minor matter that warrants attention concerns the request by the General Assembly in resolution 50/170 that the United Nations information centre in each country should make available a copy of the following: recent reports to the treaty bodies by that State, the summary records reflecting the examination of those reports and the relevant concluding observations adopted by the treaty bodies. While the Secretary-General has reported that a procedure has been put in place for this purpose (see A/51/45), he should be asked to submit a follow-up report describing the situation in practice. From informal reports by non-governmental organizations there is no reason to believe that an active programme of dissemination has been undertaken in relation to this material at the country level.

G. *Advisory services*

72. It has been suggested in a number of places in this report that the provision of "advisory services", or technical cooperation in the field of human rights, has a vital role to play in relation to those States which do not have the administrative capacity, technical expertise or financial resources required to prepare the reports they are legally obligated to provide under the relevant treaties. Equally, similar needs hamper the quest to move towards universal ratification.

73. One of 20 "substantive themes" identified for the advisory services programme is "treaty reporting and international obligations" (E/CN.4/1996/90, para. 23), but the independent expert has not been able to identify from the available documentation any case in which assistance has been provided specifically for either the undertaking of a survey of the necessary measures to be taken prior to ratification of a human rights treaty or the preparation of a report to a treaty body. The principal exceptions would seem to relate to situations such as Cambodia or Haiti in which a small part of a large assistance package has been devoted to such activities. While this assessment probably underestimates the extent of assistance provided for such purposes, it is clear that the programme as a whole does not accord sufficient priority to these activities. It may be replied that the initiative in such matters must rest with Governments and if they choose not to make requests there is little more that the programme can do. But the situation is one of "chicken and egg". In the absence of a well-resourced fund for this purpose, along with the identification of experts who are technically competent, and targeted suggestions that particular States should avail themselves of the assistance, there are likely to continue to be few requests. As a result, the advisory services programme will not make a significant contribution to the goals of reducing the incidence of non-reporting or improving the quality of reporting.

74. One activity which has been funded in the context of the advisory services programme is the organization of regional or subregional training courses in relation to reporting. It is not at all clear, however, that this approach is likely to be cost-effective. To take but one example, a regional training course on reporting obligations for countries of a particular region, held

over five days in November 1996, cost the United Nations $143,800. The budget provided for the involvement of 30 government representatives, along with 6 consultants and 3 staff members. If each of the Governments in the region sent one representative, the achievement of an impact in each country concerned would depend upon the relevant individual having benefited significantly from the project, being in a job which gives him or her responsibility for reporting, being kept in the same job long enough for the benefits to take effect, and having the time, commitment and skills required to convey some expertise or insights to others involved in reporting at the national level. While there may be some individuals who satisfy all these requirements, it seems unlikely to be the case in the majority of instances. The "multiplier effect" of a substantial expense is thus extremely limited. By contrast, a specially trained official (or consultant) could spend an entire month in the field providing carefully tailored training and advice to a wide range of individuals (both governmental and non-governmental) in a particular country at a cost of less than $15,000. Thus, concentrated assistance could have been supplied for one month each in ten different countries for the same amount of money, or probably less.

75. The problem of expertise has also yet to be addressed. It seems often to be assumed that members of the treaty bodies will have the necessary technical competence, pedagogical and drafting skills, and the availability to carry out such functions. Leaving aside the question of whether some conflict of interest might arise in such situations, there is clearly much to be said for hiring or training individuals with the requisite skills than relying upon the inevitably very uneven capacities of any given treaty body member. Given that the International Labour Organization has long had programmes involving regional advisers in the provision of such expert advice, it would be appropriate for the Centre for Human Rights to draw directly upon that experience and to explore the possibilities for cooperative training and advisory activities.

76. The High Commissioner for Human Rights should thus be requested to draw up a specific project designed to provide the necessary resources, both financial and technical, for the preparation of reports for those States which clearly lack the necessary resources to do so for themselves. The project should reflect lessons to be learned from the experience of the ILO and canvas the possibility of collaboration, as appropriate, with that body.

77. The Board of Trustees for the Voluntary Fund for Technical Cooperation should be requested to include the preparation of reports to the treaty bodies as a specific priority project. It is not clear that it falls within the priorities endorsed by the Board to date (see E/CN.4/1996/90, para. 47).

H. *Special reports*

78. A defining characteristic of the work of some of the treaty bodies in recent years has been an emphasis upon "special reports" or "urgent procedures". The Human Rights Committee and the Committee on the Elimination of Racial Discrimination, respectively, have made significant use of these procedures aimed, in the words of the latter "at responding to problems requiring immediate attention to prevent or limit the scale or number of serious

violations" (A/51/18, para. 26(b)). These initiatives can be traced back to a proposal made by the Secretary-General in 1992 that ways should be explored "of empowering the Secretary-General and expert human rights bodies to bring massive violations of human rights to the attention of the Security Council together with recommendations for action" (A/47/1, para. 101). Subsequently the fourth meeting of chairpersons noted the important role of the treaty bodies in seeking to prevent, as well as to respond to, human rights violations. They then stated that:

"It is thus appropriate for each treaty body to undertake an urgent examination of all possible measures that it might take, within its competence, both to prevent human rights violations from occurring and to monitor more closely emergency situations of all kinds arising within the jurisdiction of States parties. Where procedural innovations are required for this purpose, they should be considered as soon as possible" (A/47/628, para. 44).

79. The independent expert participated actively in the consensus on that statement, which has since been endorsed by the General Assembly and subsequent meetings of chairpersons. Today, however, the expert questions the wisdom of the manner in which this mandate has been applied. It is frustrating for a treaty body to have to remain inactive in the face of massive violations and it risks sending a signal of impotence, perhaps disdain and certainly marginality. On the other hand, the invocation of relatively formalist and inflexible procedures directed at States in which chronic violations are occurring in a context of crisis or major armed conflict would seem unlikely to achieve a great deal. Experience to date seems largely to confirm this conclusion. While there should not and probably could not be any hard and fast rules in this regard, and while the treaty bodies should retain appropriate flexibility, there is much to be said for maintaining what has been referred to as "a division of labour ... whereby the special rapporteurs, representatives or experts [of the Commission on Human Rights, etc.] would remain responsible for urgent appeals, whereas the treaty bodies would focus mainly on State party reports" (E/CN.4/1997/3, para. 43).

III. MEDIUM-TERM AND LONG-TERM REFORM ISSUES

A. *Introduction*

80. It is now almost eight years since the independent expert first suggested that consideration might be given to the preparation of consolidated reports to the treaty bodies as well as to the eventual consolidation of the existing treaty bodies into "one or perhaps two new treaty bodies". He also called for "a sustained exchange of views" on these proposals (A/44/668, paras. 179 and 182). Since that time, academic and other observers have taken up the challenge while the treaty bodies themselves, the meetings of chairpersons and the policy organs have all remained virtually silent. There is good reason for the silence of the treaty bodies. Their members are in the process of investing considerable time and energy into making the existing procedures work and they can hardly be expected to be enthusiastic about the elimination of either the procedures they are struggling to perfect or of those

Appendix 5: Long-Term Effectiveness of the UN Human Rights Treaty System 617

committees as they currently exist. It is less clear why the policy organs have remained reluctant to engage in the debate. It is suggested that the trends documented in this report have already made such debate urgent and that, in any event, the unsustainability of the existing system will have compelled radical changes of one type or another within less than a decade. The only real question is whether they will be of an ad hoc, reactive and incomplete nature or whether they will have been planned logically and systematically.

B. *The nature of the emerging challenge*

81. The information and analysis contained in this report support a number of conclusions as to the future evolution of the treaty body system. Over the course of the next decade, close to universal ratification of the six core treaties is likely to be achieved. States will be under increased pressure to honour their reporting obligations and significant technical and financial assistance will be made available to help them to do so. States which do not report will often be subject to review anyway. States will be expected to produce six reports, to engage in six separate "constructive dialogues", to answer to additional ad hoc requests from six committees, and to respond to complaints emanating from perhaps four or more separate communications procedures. They will also be expected to take full account of general comments (or their equivalents) emanating from six different committees and to respond to increasingly detailed concluding observations from the same number of committees.

82. In addition to these obligations, within a decade a significant number of countries may well be required to report under the International Convention on the Protection of the Rights of All Migrant Workers and Members of Their Families. That would add a seventh reporting procedure and yet another committee and will require States parties to report in relation to the most complex, detailed and lengthy of all of the human rights treaties.

83. But a growing burden upon States will not be the only consequence. The treaty bodies will need to at least double their existing meeting time so that the Committee on the Rights of the Child alone would be meeting for close to six months of every year. Committees which already have a very large backlog of unexamined communications will be joined by others in the same situation and together they will need to find the time and the expertise to deal with the more and more complex issues which, in the nature of things, will inevitably be brought before them. The size of the secretariat servicing the treaty bodies would need at least to be doubled just in order to maintain existing levels of service (which almost every treaty body has condemned as entirely inadequate). The costs of conference servicing (especially translation of documents and interpretation) will rise exponentially, thus making major additional demands upon resources that are presently subject to dramatic cuts. Domestic non-governmental organizations would rapidly lose interest in reporting to a different treaty body every year and their international counterparts will be unable to keep up with the demands emanating every year from one treaty body or another in relation to every country. The media, both national and international, are likely to become even less interested than is currently the case in relation to such frequent, and most likely superficial, procedures.

84. The members of the treaty bodies would be required to spend between one third and one half of their time in Geneva or New York, for which some (members of the Human Rights Committee, the Committee on the Elimination of Discrimination against Women and the Committee on the Rights of the Child) will receive US$ 3,000 per year (apart from their daily allowances) and the others (members of the Committee on Economic, Social and Cultural Rights, the Committee on the Elimination of Racial Discrimination and the Committee against Torture) will receive nothing (apart from the same allowances). In light of such demands, committee membership will be feasible only for governmental officials paid by their national authorities (a situation unlikely to guarantee either independence or expertise), academics subsidized by their Governments (since in today's climate of budget cuts and a user-pays approach most universities are unlikely to be prepared to subsidize international service for half the year), or retirees.

C. *A review of options*

85. In essence, there would seem to be four options available to States in dealing with such a scenario. The first is to dismiss the concern as alarmist and misplaced on the ground that the situation will not in fact evolve in this way. States will not move towards universal ratification; they will continue to be chronically overdue in reporting; and they will become increasingly blasé in their dealings with the treaty bodies. The response by the latter will remain essentially as it is today and, somehow, existing resources will be used more efficiently in order to enable the maintenance of the status quo. The number of complaints procedures will not increase and the number of communications will stabilize. And the migrant workers convention will not enter into force. Over time, this option will lead to a reporting system that will have become little more than a costly charade, since it will be unable to cope in any meaningful way with the various functions entrusted to it.

86. The second option would amount to the fulfilment of the dreams of some reformers and of most budget-cutters: the treaty bodies will undertake far-reaching reforms of their existing procedures, and will manage from within existing resources. Extensive authority will be delegated to the Secretariat to undertake preliminary report processing. The latter will be staffed largely by interns, junior professional officers (JPOs) paid for on a voluntary basis by the industrialized countries, and by individuals from other countries sponsored by foundations or their own Governments. Individual committee members will be responsible for drafting assessments which will be reviewed in small working groups and, except in especially controversial cases, will be rapidly endorsed in plenary. Any "dialogue" will take place largely in writing. No report would be considered in plenary for more than one or two hours and each expert would be limited to five minutes' speaking time (thus making a total of 90 minutes in the case of the two Covenant-related committees, for example). Communications will be processed in a similar manner. Summary records will be dispensed with, and translation will only be available for the final products of the committees. Interpretation will be

available only for plenary sessions and the remaining work will be done by heterogeneous language groups working overwhelmingly in English.

87. Apart from the difficulty of achieving any of these reforms, the main problem with this option is that it would require a radical change in many of the assumptions on the basis of which the current system has been developed. For the most part, States have shown no preparedness to make such changes. Moreover, the quality of the resulting outcomes, as well as their ability to command respect and generate the desired domestic responses, is unlikely to be high.

88. The third option is the provision of greatly enhanced budgetary resources to support all aspects of the procedures with a view to more or less maintaining the status quo. Funding would be provided for increased Secretariat staffing, translation and interpretation facilities, and a large technical cooperation budget would be allocated to fund an extensive array of advisory services designed to enable States to meet their extensive reporting obligations. Even leaving aside the question of whether this would be a workable approach in practice, current as well as foreseeable future budget trends would seem to be moving in the opposite direction to that required.

89. The fourth option is a more complex one, drawing on elements of the other options, and based primarily upon the adoption of some or all of the reforms canvassed below.

D. *Consolidated reports*

90. The interim report by the independent expert outlined a proposal for the preparation of a single consolidated report by each State party, which would then be submitted in satisfaction of the requirements under each of the treaties to which the State is a party. That proposal is for individual States to consider and act upon. It does not require endorsement or other formal action by any United Nations body or the treaty bodies. The detailed analytical study called for by the General Assembly in resolution 51/87 will, when completed, assist in the preparation of any such consolidated reports. Ultimately, the questions and concerns that have been raised can only be answered definitively on the basis of concrete efforts to produce and work on the basis of such reports.

E. *Elimination of comprehensive periodic reports in their present form*

91. Another proposal, previously foreshadowed by the independent expert but not developed in any detail, would be to eliminate the requirement that States parties' periodic reports should be comprehensive. Such an approach would clearly not be appropriate in relation to initial reports. Similarly, it might be better suited to the situation of some treaty bodies than others, and might not be applied in all cases. The broader the scope of a treaty, the more appropriate it would seem to be to seek to limit the range of issues which must be addressed in a report. In effect, the reporting guidelines would be tailored to each State's individual situation. In many respects, it is a logical extension of an approach followed by the Human Rights Committee since 1989.

92. Since there are various formulas which might be adopted, the following process is only indicative. It would begin with a decision by the committee at session A to draw up a list of questions at session B. In the intervening period it would invite submissions of information from all relevant sources and would request the Secretariat to prepare a country analysis. The pre-sessional working group could then meet, perhaps immediately before or during session B, and draft a specific and limited list of questions. After endorsement by the Committee at session B the list would be forwarded immediately to the State party with a request for a written report to be submitted in advance (in sufficient time to enable translation) of session C or D. Such a procedure would: focus the dialogue on a limited range of issues; entirely eliminate the need to produce a lengthy report covering many issues of little particular import in relation to the country concerned; ensure that issues of current importance are the principal focus; guarantee that a report would be examined on schedule; enable individuals with expertise in the matters under review to participate in the delegation; reduce the number of ministries directly involved in report preparation; enhance the capacity of expert members of the committees to be well prepared for the dialogue; and provide a strong foundation for more detailed and clearly focused concluding observations.

93. It is therefore recommended that each committee should consider the extent to which all or some of its principal supervisory functions could be conducted on the basis not of general reports based on universally applicable reporting guidelines but of more limited and specially tailored requests for reports as described above.

F. Towards a consolidation of the treaty bodies

94. Some of the arguments for and against this reform have already been explored in the independent expert's 1989 report (A/44/668, paras. 182–183). For that reason, they will not be repeated here. Given the limitations of space it must suffice to note in this context that while the legal and procedural problems inherent in such an initiative would not be negligible, the prior issue is whether there is the political will to begin exploring in any detail the contours of such a reform. If that will were manifest, the technical challenges would be resolvable. It is therefore recommended that consideration be given to the convening of a small expert group, with an appropriate emphasis upon international legal expertise, to prepare a report on the modalities that might be considered in this respect.

G. The desirability of additional proactive measures

95. In addition to examining the possibility of steps to reduce the existing number of treaty bodies, it is important for United Nations organs which are involved in the design of new procedures to bear in mind the desirability of limiting the number of additional bodies to be created. Viewed in isolation, and on their individual merits, proposals to establish new, and improved, mechanisms are inevitably attractive. This attraction should, however, be balanced against the impact on the system as a whole of new bodies competing for scarce resources and perhaps, in some respects at least, unnecessarily

duplicating the demands upon States parties. At least two current endeavours might be relevant in this respect.

96. The first concerns a procedure which has already been finalized and enshrined in a treaty. Article 72 of the International Convention on the Protection of the Rights of All Migrant Workers and Members of Their Families provides for the election of a Committee on the Protection of the Rights of All Migrant Workers and Members of Their Families within six months of the Convention's entry into force. This occurs when there are 20 States parties. Although it was adopted six years ago (in December 1990), as at 1 November 1996 there were only seven States parties. By acting now to amend the treaty so as to provide that the supervisory functions which the Convention entrusts to a new committee would instead be performed by one of the existing committees (presumably either the Committee on Economic, Social and Cultural Rights or the Human Rights Committee) the United Nations could avoid the expense of establishing an entire new supervisory apparatus, States parties could avoid increasing the number of committees to which they must report and the number of occasions on which reports must be presented and evaluated, and the number of States which would have to ratify the amendment would be minimal. A failure to act now will only result in exacerbating a situation that most States already consider to be unwieldy. Moreover, one of the major obstacles to reform in all such matters is the resistance of those (including experts, Secretariat officials, Governments, NGOs, etc.) with a vested interest in the maintenance of the status quo. Action taken at this stage would encounter comparatively very little resistance from such sources. But if delayed, it will probably become impossible.

97. The second example concerns the draft optional protocol to the Convention against Torture and Other Cruel, Inhuman or Degrading Treatment or Punishment, the drafting of which is currently being undertaken by a working group of the Commission on Human Rights. The protocol would, *inter alia*, provide for visits to places of detention by an expert body entrusted with that function. At its most recent session the working group took note of two different views as to the relationship, on the one hand between the new instrument and the existing Convention, and on the other hand between the proposed new subcommittee and the existing Committee against Torture. Persuasive arguments were put forward in favour of the instrument being kept quite separate from the Convention and of the sub-committee being entirely independent of the Committee (see E/CN.4/1997/33, paras. 14, 16, 19). But whatever the undoubted merits of those proposals, they would contribute very significantly to the further proliferation of instruments and committees, while doing nothing to ameliorate the present situation. A more appropriate solution would seem to be to arrive at a formula by which States which accepted the new procedures would be exempted from most, if not all, of their reporting obligations under the Convention and to explore all possible formulas by which the members of the Committee could serve on the new mechanism as well. This would seem to be a case in which the Secretariat should be requested to prepare an analytical paper exploring different options in a creative rather than mechanistic fashion.

H. *Amending the treaties*

98. Since the submission of the first report on treaty body reform, in 1989, amendments to three of the six treaties have been approved by the respective Meetings of the States Parties and endorsed by the General Assembly. They seek to ensure that the activities of both the Committee on the Elimination of Racial Discrimination and the Committee against Torture are financed from the regular budget of the United Nations (rather than wholly or partly by the States parties as currently provided for in the respective treaties) and to permit the Committee on the Elimination of Discrimination against Women to meet for longer than the two weeks annually specified in the Convention. A fourth proposed amendment would expand the membership of the Committee on the Rights of the Child from 10 to 18. The fact that both the respective Meetings of States Parties, as well as the General Assembly, have approved these amendments is an indication of the need for reform and of the preparedness of Governments to endorse such reforms.

99. Despite this clear consensus none of the amendments has yet entered into force and the prospects that they will do so in the foreseeable future must be considered slight. Thus, for example, over a period of four years only 20 of the 148 (as at 19 February 1997) States parties to the International Convention on the Elimination of All Forms of Racial Discrimination had accepted the amendments. In the case of the Convention against Torture and Other Cruel, Inhuman or Degrading Treatment or Punishment 20 of 101 States parties had done so (see E/CN.4/1997/73, para. 7). The problem is not that States parties are opposed to the amendment or that they are reluctant to see them brought into force. This is illustrated by the fact that every State party stands to gain financially from the amendments, since the costs involved will then be spread among the entire membership of the United Nations, rather than falling only on the parties to the relevant treaty. It is thus the non-States parties that would have a financial incentive to oppose such amendments, but they have chosen not to do so when called upon to vote in the General Assembly. Rather, the problem lies in the process of satisfying all of the domestic legal and political requirements needed to approve an amendment to a treaty. It is apparent that they are considered by many Governments, all of whom are confronted with an ever-increasing volume of international agreements to "process", to be too time-consuming and cumbersome to be worth the effort.

100. To the extent possible, the General Assembly has, in each instance, authorized temporary measures to ameliorate the situation in the intervening period. Such flexibility is indispensable, even though it might have the unintended consequence of further discouraging States parties from taking the domestic steps required to effect their legal acceptance of the amendments.

101. Several recommendations emerge from this situation:
    (a) All future human rights treaties should provide for a simplified process to be followed in order to amend the relevant procedural provisions. While the specific endorsement of this proposal by the Commission on Human Rights could not be binding in the context of any future

negotiations it would constitute a clear policy guideline and help to facilitate the adoption of such flexibility in the future;
(b) A report should be requested from the Legal Counsel which would explore the feasibility of devising more innovative approaches in dealing with existing and future amendments to the human rights treaties;
(c) The General Assembly should request the Meetings of the States Parties to the relevant treaties to discuss means by which the States concerned might be encouraged to attach a higher priority to ratification of the amendments already approved;
(d) Consideration should be given immediately to amending the International Convention on the Protection of the Rights of All Migrant Workers and Members of Their Families in line with the recommendation made below;
(e) In view of the agreement of the Meeting of States Parties and of the General Assembly in 1992 to amend article 8, paragraph 6, of the International Convention on the Elimination of All Forms of Racial Discrimination to eliminate the responsibility of the States parties for the expenses of the Committee members, action should now be taken to write off the continuing backlog of contributions owed for that purpose. At present, 57 States parties owe a total of US$225,506, or an average of just under $4,000 each (see A/51/430, annex II). Given that these assessments are now anachronistic and that the cost incurred by the United Nations of calculating, updating and reporting on their non-payment will soon exceed the amount involved, agreement should be sought to cover the outstanding amount from the regular budget and close the file. For legal and policy reasons, it should be indicated that no precedent of broader application is thereby created.

IV. OTHER ISSUES

A. *The unmentionable language question*

102. The question of languages has gone largely unaddressed in this report. For the most part, this is merely an accurate reflection of the inability of the United Nations and its Member States to come to grips with one of the most controversial and enduring issues confronting the Organization as a whole. Unfortunately, it is also one which is of particular importance to the treaty bodies. Any attempt by the independent expert to resolve the dilemmas would be both presumptuous and doomed to failure. Nevertheless, it is appropriate to proffer a few pertinent observations.

103. In the first place, the treaty bodies have been compelled by resource constraints and decisions taken elsewhere to privilege the two principal working languages of the Secretariat. This is reflected in the production of summary records and press releases, and in the vast majority of drafting exercises. Simultaneous interpretation into languages other than Spanish, unless specifically requested, seems to be increasingly less common in the day-to-day work of the treaty bodies. Secondly, the de facto dominance of English as the main working language of the committees has increased very significantly in the past few years. While this may be regrettable in terms

of the maintenance of linguistic equality and diversity it is largely a reflection of national trends which are outside the control of the treaty bodies. These trends seem likely to accelerate in the years ahead as a result of the emphasis upon English in business, information technology, science, media and other spheres of activity. Thirdly, for a variety of reasons well beyond the control of the United Nations, English language materials tend to predominate in the rapidly growing volume of information which makes up the background materials available to the treaty bodies in their examination of individual State reports.

104. Official responses within the United Nations to these trends have been somewhat contradictory. On the one hand, the General Assembly has reaffirmed its strong commitment to the principle of linguistic diversity, and the Secretariat has attached renewed emphasis to an old rule by which a document cannot be issued in any language until it is available in all. At the same time, various policies and practices encourage the treaty bodies to operate with as few languages as possible. The very rapidly increasing number of individuals, groups and agencies obtaining access to the documentation of international organizations by electronic means are, and are virtually certain to continue to be, significantly advantaged if they can work in English rather than in any other language.

105. The official rules are appropriate reflections of a commitment to multilingualism and would, in a context of adequate resources, help to maintain an appropriate balance. But in a situation of dire financial stringency the resulting inflexibility will, on the one hand, wreak havoc and on the other, provoke resort to ever more creative and devious strategies to circumvent unworkable rules. Such strategies invariably add to overall costs and, at least in the longer term, generate a range of inefficient, opaque and counter-productive practices. Understandable resentment of the extent to which extraneous factors have tended to undermine the policy of language equality has tended to stifle efforts to identify a range of medium-term and long-term strategies which might respond to emerging realities in a more nuanced manner.

106. In the context of the treaty bodies the importance of maintaining linguistic diversity is, for many reasons, beyond doubt. By the same token, in the absence of a substantial increase in funds for interpretation, there is a clear need for the different committees to explore ways in which working groups and other non-plenary meetings can be held without official translation. Greater emphasis should be attached to the ability of nominees for election to the treaty bodies to work in at least one, and preferably two, of the three major languages. Ways will have to be found in which the content of materials available in only one language can be drawn upon more efficiently for the benefit of the whole committee. Consideration will need to be given to delegating certain responsibilities to working groups capable of working without translation. While these and other more innovative and flexible steps will probably be considered only reluctantly, necessity will have its way sooner rather than later.

B. *Cooperation with the specialized agencies and other bodies*

107. Cooperation between the specialized agencies and the treaty bodies remains more problematic than is generally recognized. There are several outstand-

ing examples of such cooperation, most notably between the Committee on the Rights of the Child and UNICEF, ILO, UNESCO and UNHCR, and between the ILO and several of the other treaty bodies. The overall situation remains unsatisfactory, however. There have been many calls for consultation in order to identify the most productive and sustainable forms of cooperation, but little has resulted. As noted above, a request by the sixth meeting of chairpersons for such a discussion to take place at a high level at the seventh meeting (in 1996) resulted in the active involvement of very few agencies and an inability to take any measures of consequence in relation to this issue. Similarly, repeated requests by the Commission on Human Rights, contained in resolutions adopted since 1993, calling for an expert seminar to be organized in conjunction with the international financial institutions have resulted in no action by the Centre for Human Rights despite the willingness of the World Bank to proceed. While the High Commissioner for Human Rights held a meeting in July 1996 with the President of the World Bank, this has not led to any concrete results in relation to the work of the treaty bodies. As a result, important opportunities are being missed.

108. In order to remedy this situation it is recommended that the Commission on Human Rights should request the High Commissioner to convene a high-level meeting over a period of two days between senior representatives of the key specialized agencies and other bodies (including ILO, WHO, FAO, UNESCO, UNICEF, UNHCR, UNDP, UNFPA and the World Bank), senior staff of the Centre and the chairpersons of the six treaty bodies. In order to minimize costs and capitalize on other coordination efforts, the meeting should take place immediately before or after one of the annual meetings of the chairpersons. The purpose should be to explore the most constructive, appropriate, cost-effective, and mutually rewarding means of cooperation between these bodies and the human rights committees.

C. *The quality of concluding observations*

109. In 1990, the Committee on Economic, Social and Cultural Rights pioneered the practice of adopting concluding observations which reflected the views of the Committee as a whole, were structured in a systematic fashion and sought to be as specific as possible. Although it was the Human Rights Committee which, in 1984, had first made use of the phrase "concluding observations", it was not until 1992 that that Committee began to adopt collective evaluations of the report of each State. The Committee on the Elimination of Racial Discrimination followed the example in 1993. Prior to this development all of the effort required on the part of the relevant Government, the United Nations, the treaty body and other interested parties culminated in little more than a few disparate, sometimes inconsistent, observations made in the name of individual members of the committees. While the present approach thus constitutes a major step forward there is still considerable room for improvement in the quality of concluding observations, especially in terms of their clarity, degree of detail, level of accuracy and specificity. This will require, *inter alia*, a more sustained expert

contribution to the process by the Secretariat. A marked improvement in the level of sophistication of concluding observations is indispensable if the reporting process is ultimately going to justify the expense and effort involved.

V. PRINCIPAL RECOMMENDATIONS

110. This section summarizes some of the recommendations made in the report.
111. The goal of achieving universal ratification of the six core treaties has been affirmed frequently. Concrete measures aimed at making it a reality are needed. They should include: (a) consultations with the leading international agencies to explore their potential involvement in a ratification campaign (para. 32); (b) the appointment of special advisers on ratification and reporting and the earmarking of funds for those purposes (paras. 33–34); (c) special measures should be explored to streamline the reporting process for States with small populations (para. 35); and (d) particular attention should be paid to other substantial categories of non-parties.
112. Non-reporting has reached chronic proportions. In addition to considering reforms to the overall system (noted below), a new specially tailored project for the provision of advisory services should be implemented. In responding to cases of persistent delinquency, all treaty bodies should be urged to adopt procedures which lead eventually to the examination of situations even in the absence of a report (paras. 37–45). Such an approach should reflect thorough research and lead to detailed, accurate and comprehensive "concluding observations" (para. 47).
113. The present reporting system functions only because of the large-scale delinquency of States which either do not report at all, or report long after the due date. If many were to report, significant existing backlogs would be exacerbated, and major reforms would be needed even more urgently (paras. 48–52).
114. Proposed documentation limits are unworkable within the context of existing procedures. The issue needs to be dealt with in a far more transparent manner than has so far been the case and full justification for any cuts need to be provided. The Secretariat should draw up a detailed options paper to enable the committees to consider measured and innovative responses (paras. 53–54).
115. The extent of documentation which is central to the dialogue but which is nowhere officially recorded is an important problem and calls for appropriate measures to be devised by the Secretariat (para. 55). The preparation of summary records is an indispensable element in the system and their timely preparation should be accorded priority. The continued production of bound and edited volumes of Official Records of the Human Rights Committee (previously known as Yearbooks) is difficult to justify at a time of financial stringency (para. 58). Priority should be accorded to transferring the existing data on to electronic databases and ensuring the timely publication, including in electronic form, of all summary records as soon as they are available (para. 59).
116. The new home page of the High Commissioner/Centre for Human Rights

Appendix 5: Long-Term Effectiveness of the UN Human Rights Treaty System 627

constitutes an unduly delayed but very welcome development. It should be maintained and expanded and a strategy to widen access should be devised. Future development of the database should reflect a more systematic, consultative and transparent process than has hitherto been the case. An expert seminar should be convened for that purpose and an external advisory group appointed (paras. 60–64). The ILO should consider making its very valuable database available on the Web to the human rights community and others (para. 65).

117. The public information materials relating to the work of the treaty bodies are highly inadequate. The treaty bodies should be given a direct input into future decision-making in this regard. A public information budget should be made available to support grass-roots initiatives designed to disseminate information about the treaty bodies in culturally appropriate and more popular formats and media. Partnerships with academic and other external institutions should be explored in order to enhance the publications programme. An external advisory group should be asked to review the human rights-related publications programme and make recommendations (paras. 66–70). The Secretary-General should report on the actual availability of treaty body-related materials at United Nations information centres (para. 71).

118. The advisory services programme has not provided sufficient support for surveys required prior to ratification of a human rights treaty or for the preparation of reports by States in need of assistance. Regional and subregional training courses in relation to reporting are unlikely to produce results commensurate with their cost. A specially designed programme should be devised to address the needs in this area and it should be accorded priority (paras. 72–77).

119. The effectiveness of "special reports" and "urgent procedures" should be carefully evaluated by the committees concerned. At present, the value they add seems low. In general, the division of labour between the treaty bodies and special mechanisms should be maintained (paras. 78–79).

120. In light of current trends the existing reporting system is unsustainable (paras. 81–84). Four options are available to States: (a) to dismiss the concern as alarmist and take no action; (b) to urge the treaty bodies to undertake far-reaching reforms and adapt to cope with existing and new demands from within existing resources; (c) to provide greatly enhanced budgetary resources to sustain the status quo; (d) to combine some elements of (b) and (c) with the adoption of some far-reaching reforms (paras. 85–89). The latter could include: the preparation of "consolidated reports" (para. 90); elimination of comprehensive periodic reports in their present form and replacement by reporting guidelines tailored to each State's individual situation (paras. 91–93); and a consolidation (reduction) of the number of treaty bodies (para. 94). If the political will exists in relation to the latter, a small expert group should be convened to examine modalities. Proactive measures should also be considered, including amending the migrant workers convention to entrust the supervisory functions to an existing committee and giving more systematic consideration to the institutional implications of the proposed optional protocol to the Convention against Torture (paras. 96–98).

121. The procedural provisions of human rights treaties need to be made more susceptible to amendment. Various recommendations are suggested (para. 101). Constructive attention needs to be given to the taboo subject of working languages (paras. 102–106). Existing arrangements for cooperation with the specialized agencies and other bodies have been improved in some respects but remain very inadequate. The High Commissioner should convene a high-level meeting to explore better means of cooperation with the treaty bodies (para. 108).
122. Treaty bodies must strive to further improve the quality of their "concluding observations", in terms of their clarity, degree of detail, level of accuracy and specificity (para. 109).

E/CN.4/1998/85 — 4 February 1998

COMMISSION ON HUMAN RIGHTS
Fifty-fourth session

EFFECTIVE FUNCTIONING OF BODIES ESTABLISHED PURSUANT TO THE UNITED NATIONS HUMAN RIGHTS INSTRUMENTS

Report of the Secretary-General

CONTENTS

I. INTRODUCTION

II. SUMMARY OF THE RECOMMENDATIONS OF THE INDEPENDENT EXPERT, COMMENTS RECEIVED AND VIEWS OF THE SECRETARY-GENERAL THEREON
  A. Towards universal ratification
  B. The problem of significantly overdue reports
  C. Dealing with the timely submission of reports
  D. Problems in relation to documentation
  E. Development and use of electronic databases
  F. Public information
  G. Advisory services
  H. Special reports
  I. Consolidation of reports and treaty bodies
  J. Amending the treaties
  K. The language question
  L. Cooperation with the specialized agencies and other bodies
  M. The quality of concluding observations
  N. Other issues

I. INTRODUCTION

The original study on the effective operation of existing and prospective bodies established under United Nations human rights instruments was initiated pursuant to General Assembly resolution 43/115 of 8 December 1988 and Commission on Human Rights resolution 1989/47, carried out by Mr. Philip Alston during the period 1989 to 1992 and transmitted to the General Assembly in document A/44/668, annex.

In its resolution 47/111 of 16 December 1992, the General Assembly requested that the report be updated for submission to the fiftieth session of the Commission on Human Rights and that an interim report be presented to the General Assembly at its forty-eighth session, and be made available to the World Conference on Human Rights in June 1993. Pursuant to that resolution, as well as Commission on Human Rights resolution 1993/16 of 26 February 1993, Mr. Alston undertook to update his original study, submitting an interim report thereon in document A/CONF.157/PC/62/Add.11/Rev.1 and a final report in document E/CN.4/1997/74, which was submitted to the fifty-third session of the Commission on Human Rights in 1997. By its decision 1997/105, the Commission on Human Rights invited the Secretary-General to solicit the views of United Nations bodies, Governments, specialized agencies, intergovernmental and non-governmental organizations and interested persons on the report of the independent expert and to submit a report thereon, including the Secretary-General's own views on the legal, administrative and other implications of the report's recommendations, to the Commission on Human Rights at its fifty-fourth session.

The present report contains a summary of the comments and observations provided by those consulted pursuant to decision 1997/105, as well as the Secretary-General's own views on the legal, administrative and other implications of the report's recommendations, where appropriate. In order to facilitate discussion, the present report presents the issues raised and recommendations made by the independent expert and summarizes the responses received with respect to each. Comments were received from the Governments of Australia, Canada, Cyprus, Finland, Israel, the Netherlands, Norway and the Republic of Korea. The United Nations departments and specialized agencies that submitted comments were: the Crime Prevention and Criminal Justice Division, the United Nations Children's Fund (UNICEF), the Office of the United Nations High Commissioner for Refugees (UNHCR), and the International Labour Organization (ILO). The following non-governmental organizations submitted their views: Inter-Church Committee for Refugees, Grand Council of the Crees (of Quebec), North-South XXI and the NGO Group for the Convention on the Rights of the Child. Comments have also been received from a number of "interested persons", in the meaning of Commission on Human Rights decision 1997/105: Mr. Leo Zwaak and Ms. Ineke Boerefijn, both researchers at the Netherlands Institute of Human Rights (SIM); Mr. Michael O'Flaherty, specialist/author on human rights treaty bodies; Mr. Craig Scott, professor of law at the University of Toronto. The full texts of all comments received are available for consultation in the files of the Secretariat. In addition, the seventh meeting of persons chairing the human rights treaty bodies, held in September 1996, discussed in detail the improvement of the operation of the human rights treaty bodies. At their eighth meeting, in September 1997, the chairpersons addressed the recommendations contained in the final report of the independent expert. Their conclusions are available in the annexes to documents A/51/482 and A/52/507, respectively, and should be read together with the present report.

II. SUMMARY OF THE RECOMMENDATIONS OF THE INDEPENDENT EXPERT, COMMENTS RECEIVED AND VIEWS OF THE SECRETARY-GENERAL THEREON

A. *Towards universal ratification*

Recommendations of the independent expert
According to the independent expert, universal ratification of the six core United Nations human rights treaties would establish the best possible foundation for international endeavours to promote respect for human rights. In his final report, he made four specific recommendations: (a) consultations with the leading international agencies to explore their potential involvement in a ratification campaign; (b) appointment of special advisers on ratification and reporting and the earmarking of funds for those purposes; (c) examination of special measures to streamline the reporting process for States with small populations; and (d) granting particular attention to other substantial categories of non-parties (E/CN.4/1997/74, paras. 14, 31-35, 111).

Government comments
The Government of Australia stated that the provision of assistance to States wishing to ratify one or more of the six core treaties was an important part in the promotion of universal ratification. In this context, further consideration should be given to the role of the advisory services programme of the Office of the High Commissioner for Human Rights, ways and means to increase resources and how best to utilize them. The Government of Canada agreed that assistance to States that were willing to ratify human rights instruments but were encountering practical difficulties in doing so was an important element in promoting universal ratification. Such assistance should be pursued within the limits of available resources. Special thought should be given to the role of the advisory services programme in that regard, and avenues should be explored by which additional sources of funding for such action could be tapped. Canada believed that the reporting process for States with small populations should be streamlined in order to facilitate ratification.

The Government of Cyprus took note of the independent expert's recommendations for more innovative approaches to deal with existing and future amendments to the human rights treaties. Pending adoption of any such approaches, Cyprus presented a suggestion that might assist those Governments that are confronted with the need to constantly "process" international agreements. The Office of the High Commissioner for Human Rights should, in each case where an amendment or a new protocol has been approved, submit a standardized reasoned memorandum for use by each State's executive and legislature, as well as a model draft statute enacting the relevant amendment or protocol. Provision of such model statutes would assist States whose legal systems require that enabling legislation be enacted before international treaties can become operative; this would facilitate ratifications by small States.

The Government of Finland expressed concern about the gap between standard-setting and implementation in the field of human rights. The six core United Nations human rights treaties and their protocols formed a solid and comprehensive legal basis for the promotion and protection of all human rights.

It was most important to achieve universal acceptance of those treaties, as was strongly recommended by the World Conference on Human Rights in the Vienna Declaration and Programme of Action.

The Government of the Netherlands supported the recommendation to appoint special advisers to the High Commissioner for Human Rights who could provide invaluable assistance to States experiencing difficulties relating to ratification. The Netherlands suggested that an expert on legal issues also be appointed. A political adviser and a technical adviser alone would not be sufficient to address the complex legal issues involved in accession to or ratification of international treaties. The addition of a legal adviser could ensure adequate expert support to States willing to ratify the conventions but needing advice on national implementation measures.

Comments by United Nations agencies and bodies
UNICEF indicated that since the adoption by the General Assembly in 1989 of the Convention on the Rights of the Child, it has actively promoted the universal ratification of the Convention. To that end, UNICEF initiated a wide range of actions at the global, regional and national levels in order to generate the necessary political support for the Convention. This involved collaborating with a number of partners, particularly non-governmental organizations and intergovernmental organizations in different regions of the world, such as the Organization of African Unity, the Commonwealth, the European Union, the Organization of the Islamic Conference and others. Country offices carried out advocacy and social mobilization activities in order to increase national support for ratification by reaching out to parliamentarians, religious leaders, mayors and municipal leaders, youth groups and many others.

The ILO has been coordinating a campaign for universal ratification of its fundamental human rights conventions. Since the Director-General launched his appeal in May 1995, there have been 80 ratifications of these 7 conventions, and some 30 countries had now ratified all of them. A large number of further ratifications were expected shortly.

In addition, at its two hundred and sixty-ninth session in June 1997, the Governing Body of the International Labour Organization decided to consider the possibility of including on the agenda of the eighty-sixth session of the International Labour Conference in 1998 – which marks the fiftieth anniversary of the Universal Declaration of Human Rights and the ILO's Freedom of Association and Protection of the Right to Organize Convention, 1948 (No. 87) – an additional item relating to a declaration on fundamental rights, including an appropriate follow-up mechanism. The purpose of a declaration on fundamental rights would be to recognize explicitly, through a solemn statement approved by the International Labour Conference, the consensus which the international community has reached regarding the special significance of a number of fundamental rights in the present global context, and to express the commitment of its constituents to strengthening their universal application by the ILO.

The concept of fundamental rights may be traced to the ILO Constitution, in which the High Contracting Parties affirmed that there are methods and principles for regulating labour conditions which all industrial communities should endeavour to apply, so far as their special circumstances will permit, and that among them, some seemed to be of special and urgent importance.

Comments by non-governmental organizations
North-South XXI noted that certain permanent members of the Security Council were not parties to the principal legal instruments, which acted as a disincentive to smaller States.

Comments by interested persons
Mr. Zwaak and Ms. Boerefijn noted that the recent announcements of withdrawal by the Democratic People's Republic of Korea from the International Covenant on Civil and Political Rights and by Jamaica from the Optional Protocol thereto went counter to the Vienna Declaration and Programme of Action and undermined the entire international machinery developed for the promotion and protection of human rights. The recently adopted General Comment No. 26(6) of the Human Rights Committee on issues relating to the continuity of obligations to the Covenant constituted a basis for further actions by the appropriate bodies.

In the same context, Mr. O'Flaherty suggested that the High Commissioner for Human Rights should use her good offices and resources for technical cooperation to assist States in addressing their concerns by means other than denunciation. He also felt that it would be fruitful to address the relationship between the treaty system and non-State entities (NSEs), particularly in regard to the role and responsibility that the treaty bodies could perhaps assume in appropriate circumstances. The experience with rebel groups and with the parties in Bosnia and Herzegovina to the Dayton Agreement who had undertaken a commitment to respect the substantive provisions of human rights instruments could have held some useful lessons in the foregoing regard, he thought.

Mr. O'Flaherty also drew attention to the ratification-related concerns arising with regard to the individual petition procedures. States sometimes attested an unwillingness to embrace the Optional Protocol to the International Covenant on Civil and Political Rights or other United Nations complaints procedures because of their participation in the mechanisms under the European Convention on Human Rights. Some States which ratified the Optional Protocol sometimes argued that acceptance of the complaints procedures under the International Convention on the Elimination of All Forms of Racial Discrimination and under the Convention against Torture and Other Cruel, Inhuman or Degrading Treatment or Punishment were also rendered superfluous for the same reason. On such matters, it might be worthwhile to consider the deployment of technical cooperation resources aimed at disabusing States of such misplaced ideas.

Comments by the Secretary-General
The Secretary-General reaffirms his commitment to promote universal ratification of the international human rights treaties and welcomes the recommendations of the independent expert toward this end. The United Nations departments and specialized agencies which are cooperating with the Office of the High Commissioner for Human Rights on activities relating to the fiftieth anniversary of the Universal Declaration of Human Rights and the five-year review of the Vienna Declaration and Programme of Action are being consulted regarding their contribution to the promotion of universal ratification. Information on these initiatives will be included in the report on the five-year Review to be submitted to the General Assembly at its fifty-third session. In marking the start of the fiftieth anniversary year, which the High Commissioner referred to in her

report to the General Assembly as "Human Rights Year", the Secretary-General and the High Commissioner for Human Rights addressed appeals to all Governments, suggesting that they consider ratifying the core treaties to which they were not already a party.

B. *The problem of significantly overdue reports*

Recommendations of the independent expert
The independent expert pointed out that non-reporting had reached chronic proportions. He suggested that, in addition to considering reforms to the overall system, a new specially tailored project for the provision of advisory services should be designed and implemented. In responding to cases of persistent delinquency, all treaty bodies should be urged to adopt procedures which would eventually lead to the examination of country situations even in the absence of a report. Such an approach should reflect thorough research and lead to detailed, accurate and comprehensive concluding observations (ibid., paras. 37–45, 47, 112)

Government comments
The Government of Canada expressed support for the adoption by treaty bodies of appropriate procedures which would allow them to consider the situation of persistently delinquent States parties in the absence of a report. It would be inequitable and contrary to the basic purpose of the conventions if States parties could evade scrutiny from the treaty bodies by neglecting to fulfil their reporting obligations, while States that submit reports are held accountable for implementation of their commitments.

The Government of Finland stressed that all States parties should be on an equal footing regarding regular monitoring. Finland supports the development of methods for treaty bodies to examine the situation in a State party even when it fails to fulfil its reporting obligation.

The Government of Israel agreed that non-submission of reports was a result of either technical difficulties or lack of political will, neither of which would be overcome by unilateral steps or repeated reminders on the part of treaty bodies. A more constructive way to address the problem would be to make the reporting system less daunting to States.

In Israel's view there was no established legal basis for the examination of a situation in a State in the absence of a report. While acknowledging that consideration of a situation in the absence of a report could serve as an incentive in cases where States had the means but chose not to report, the current policy did not distinguish between cases where the problem was lack of means rather than will. In addition, Israel believed that to base an entire examination on non-governmental sources in the absence of a government report would be contrary to the letter, purposes and principles of the treaties.

Israel also noted that while there was a significant delay in the submission of State party reports, treaty bodies maintained a rigid schedule in demanding future reports, without taking into account the date of examination of previous reports. This observation was especially relevant where special reports were involved which often covered the same matters as regular reports. Therefore, all reports submitted, whether regular or special, should be taken into account when calculating due dates.

Comments by United Nations agencies and bodies
UNICEF indicated that, through its presence in 161 countries and in cooperation with its 38 National Committees, it regularly monitored the submission of State party reports under the Convention on the Rights of the Child. It also encouraged the timely submission of reports and provided Governments with technical assistance in the preparation of reports. UNICEF supported the monitoring role of the Committee on the Rights of the Child and participated in meetings where States parties' reports were considered by the Committee.

Comments by non-governmental organizations
North-South XXI welcomed the practice developed by the Human Rights Committee since 1994 to identify those States parties that do not fulfil their reporting obligations despite numerous reminders, but the Committee should take care not to penalize the States parties that respected their obligations and de facto reward those States parties that did not. It was logical that the conventional organs of the United Nations should, in the absence of a State report, proceed to examine through all possible means the situation in that State. Non-governmental organizations could participate in such action.

Comments by interested persons
Mr. Zwaak and Ms. Boerefijn considered it of great importance that some sort of sanction be developed for States parties which do not comply with their reporting obligations. So-called "blacklists" in the treaty bodies' annual reports did not seem to persuade States to submit overdue reports. Mr. Zwaak and Ms. Boerefijn agreed with the independent expert that the treaty bodies had no other option but to consider the "situation" in a State in the absence of a report from delinquent States parties. This should be the ultimate remedy and particularly wide distribution of the concluding comments had to be ensured in such instances.

Comments by the Secretary-General
The Secretary-General notes with deep concern the serious situation with respect to overdue reports. The existence of a large number of States that do not comply with their reporting obligations detracts significantly from the capacity of the treaty system to be of service to the international community.

Participants in programmes on the preparation of State reports to treaty bodies have consistently expressed satisfaction at the skills and insights gained during those training courses. The Secretary-General will continue those programmes and will continue to urge that countries sending participants provide the necessary opportunities for them to train their colleagues when returning from such courses.

The Secretary-General calls upon all States parties to fulfil their reporting obligations, which are the cornerstone of the international human rights treaty system. He encourages treaty bodies to continue to undertake creative initiatives to address the problems posed in respect of States parties whose reports are chronically late or who fail to submit reports at all.

C. Dealing with the timely submission of reports

Recommendations of the independent expert
The independent expert noted that the present reporting system functioned only because of the large-scale delinquency of States which either did not report at

all, or reported long after the due date. If many were to report, significant existing backlogs would be exacerbated, and major reforms would be needed even more urgently (ibid., paras. 48–52).

Government comments
The Government of Finland noted that, according to the statistics presented in the final report of the independent expert, the system was faltering seriously. When a State report was scheduled for consideration one to three years after its submission, much of its contents were rendered obsolete. Another consequence of this situation was that those three treaty bodies which at present examined individual complaints had difficulty finding enough time to deal with complaints. This unfortunate situation compromised the entire human rights monitoring system. Finland supported the proposals to widen complaints procedures to other conventions although they would, as a result, increase the existing workload.

The Government of the Republic of Korea considered that, in view of the chronic delays between the submission and examination of reports, the current report-reviewing mechanism needed to be reformed. The Government supported the second option proposed by the independent expert in paragraph 86 of his final report, whereby the treaty bodies should undertake far-reaching reforms of their existing procedures. Extensive authority should be delegated to the Secretariat to undertake a preliminary review of State reports. The Secretariat staff would be complemented by interns and junior professional officers (JPOs). The results of that review by the Secretariat should be reported to small working groups composed of individual committee members who would offer their assessments. The conclusions reached at the small groups should then be endorsed by the Committee in plenary.

D. *Problems in relation to documentation*

Recommendations of the independent expert
The independent expert suggested that the proposed limits on documentation were unworkable within the context of existing procedures. He expressed the view that the issue needed to be dealt with in a far more transparent manner than has so far been the case and full justification for any cuts needed to be provided. The Secretariat should draw up a detailed options paper to enable the committees to consider measured and innovative responses (ibid., paras. 53–54, 114).

In addition, the independent expert drew attention to the large volume of documentation furnished to treaty bodies that was not recorded officially and called for appropriate measures to be devised by the Secretariat. He considered the preparation of summary records to be an indispensable element in the system and recommended that their timely preparation should be accorded priority. The continued production of bound and edited volumes of Official Records of the Human Rights Committee (previously known as Yearbooks) was difficult to justify at a time of financial stringency. Priority should be accorded to transferring the existing data onto electronic databases and ensuring the timely publication, including in electronic form, of all summary records as soon as they are available (ibid., paras. 55, 58–59, 115).

Government comments
The Government of Australia welcomed the establishment of the Office of the High Commissioner for Human Rights homepage on the World Wide Web and encouraged wide use of electronic forms of publication and dissemination of documentation, although it acknowledged that not all States had ready access to the Internet. The Australian Government also encouraged every effort being made to ensure that human rights information was more widely accessible and better targeted, particularly at the grass-roots level.

The Government of Canada recognized the importance of having adequate documentation available during the review of reports by States parties, and the difficulties that resulted when limits were imposed on the length of those reports. It also recognized the need to respect financial constraints and to ensure that committee members were not burdened with a greater volume of documentation than they could reasonably be expected to assimilate. It therefore supported a more focused approach to reporting as a way to reconcile these different priorities. With respect to summary records, Canada considered them to be an important tool in following up on reports by States parties and encouraged their prompt publication in electronic form.

The Government of Finland affirmed that access to information from various sources and cooperation with other United Nations bodies must be guaranteed.

The Government of Israel agreed that a 50-page limit on a report was impracticable, in view of the wide range of issues which reports had to address. Moreover, it would give rise to situations where a State was required to limit the information it submitted and was later reprimanded for not having reported on certain issues. A solution to the difficulty of processing extensive reports should not compromise the integrity of the report.

Comments by United Nations agencies and bodies
UNICEF reported that it regularly disseminated worldwide a wide range of publications and information materials on the Convention on the Rights of the Child in numerous languages. It also supported efforts to disseminate copies of States parties' reports and concluding observations in the countries concerned.

Comments by non-governmental organizations
The NGO Group for the Convention on the Rights of the Child expressed its view that, in the short term, better information-sharing among treaty bodies could enhance the reporting system. Although the treaty body database had helped to ensure the sharing of official United Nations information, there was a weak system within the United Nations and none within the NGO community for ensuring that NGO information that already existed was transmitted to other treaty bodies that may have the same State party under consideration.

Comments by interested persons
Mr. O'Flaherty drew attention to the important role played by the practice of tape-recording committee meetings. He made reference to instances where the tapes were transcribed and used effectively as lobbying tools by national non-governmental organizations subsequent to the examination by a treaty body of that State's report. He suggested that the practice of tape-recording should continue and that access to the recordings should be facilitated.

Comments by the Secretary-General
The financial crisis of the United Nations has also affected the production of documentation, which has affected the functioning of treaty bodies. The delays in the processing of the reports, summary records and other documents of treaty bodies are due in large part to the overload of the Languages Service, the capacities of which have been drastically reduced. Late submission and excessive volume of documents have hampered the normal processing of documents. There is an inherent difficulty in forecasting the volume of State reports to be processed, given the difficulty in knowing when States will submit their reports and how long they will be. Since 1995, the number of pages of country reports submitted to the five treaty bodies serviced in Geneva has increased by over 30 per cent, from 4,512 pages to 5,926 pages in 1997.

While observing the rules established by the General Assembly regulating control and limitation of documentation, treaty bodies must be able to fulfil their monitoring function. Requesting focused rather than comprehensive reports and limiting agenda items to be covered by summary records may lead to a reduction in the volume of documentation. As soon as they are issued, all official documents are regularly loaded onto the treaty body database, which is linked to the United Nations human rights Website.

E. Development and use of electronic databases

Recommendations of the independent expert
The independent expert considered the new homepage of the Office of the High Commissioner for Human Rights to be an unduly delayed but very welcome development. He recommended that it be maintained and expanded and that a strategy to widen access be devised. Future development of the database should reflect a more systematic, consultative and transparent process than had hitherto been the case. An expert seminar should be convened for that purpose and an external advisory group appointed. UNHCR and the ILO should consider making their valuable databases available on the Web to the human rights community and others (ibid., paras. 60–66, 116).

Comments by United Nations agencies and bodies
UNICEF welcomed the information retrieval and database system developed for the Convention on the Rights of the Child and favoured its expansion to include other human rights treaties. UNICEF supported and participated in those initiatives in cooperation with the Office of the High Commissioner for Human Rights.

UNHCR noted the concerns of the independent expert about the time lag in relation to the availability of country-specific and other data generated by UNHCR on the Internet. UNHCR affirmed its policy of placing priority on the collection and production of legal and country specific information for its CD-Rom ("RefWorld"), which is updated every six months. This strategy was chosen in view of the fact that the primary audience of the CD-Rom, namely the field offices of UNHCR, did not enjoy access or had such intermitted access to the Internet that it could not be relied on as a research tool. The "RefWorld" CD-Rom has been purchased by many Governments, judiciaries, refugee advocates, libraries and research centres throughout the world. In addition, some treaty body experts who had expressed an interest in using the CD-Rom had been provided with their own copies; others indicated that they had access through a library or university. UNHCR thus believed that the information on "RefWorld" was readily available to those who needed it and that the cost was not a prohibiting factor in its use by the treaty body system.

Comments by the Secretary-General
The Secretary-General welcomes the positive responses received about the United Nations human rights Website, which was designed to be one of the most comprehensive sources of public information on the United Nations human rights programme and features a full-text database on treaty body information capable of easy retrieval. Since its inauguration on 10 December 1996, the Website has been visited, on average, 3,000 times per week and treaty body experts have been given the opportunity to be briefed on the use of the Website and database. Their comments or suggestions for improvements will continue to be welcome.

F. Public information

Recommendations of the independent expert
The independent expert considered the public information materials relating to the work of the treaty bodies to be highly inadequate. He recommended that the treaty bodies be given a direct input into future decision-making in this regard. He further recommended that a public information budget be made available to support grass-roots initiatives designed to disseminate information about the treaty bodies in culturally appropriate and more popular formats and media. Partnerships with academic and other external institutions should be explored in order to enhance the publications programme. An external advisory group should be asked to review the human rights-related publications programme and make recommendations. The Secretary-General should report on the actual availability of treaty body-related materials at United Nations information centres (ibid., paras. 66–71, 117).

Government comments
The Government of Canada suggested that a public information campaign to promote awareness of the treaty bodies should be considered as an element of, or as follow-up to the fiftieth anniversary of the Universal Declaration of Human Rights.

Comments by non-governmental organizations
North-South XXI expressed interest in the recommendation to entrust to academic and other external institutions the preparation of certain publications, with a reservation that Governments should not be able to exercise influence over the process. As it may be difficult to select truly "independent" universities, the best alternative might be to entrust the same functions to various institutions in countries in the South as well as the North that came from different cultural environments, as done in the selection of judges for the International Court of Justice.

Comments by interested persons
Mr. Zwaak and Ms. Boerefijn agreed that the extent to which publications could be entrusted to other institutions needed to be explored. Some institutions, including the Netherlands Institute of Human Rights (SIM), had already taken

initiatives to make relevant material more easily accessible. Without the support of the Office of the High Commissioner for Human Rights, the continuity of such projects could not be ensured. Although it might be necessary to explore commercial approaches to this question, this should never be to the detriment of the widest possible distribution of materials.

Mr. O'Flaherty expressed doubt as to whether primacy of importance should be given to involvement by treaty body members in development of public information campaigns. That was not their area of expertise. Instead, he suggested an approach whereby the work would be undertaken by carefully recruited specialists. He further suggested that the Office of the High Commissioner for Human Rights should develop training and educational materials to be disseminated on the Internet. An excellent model in that regard was provided by the Council of Europe, including most recently the Website of the European Commission against Racism and Intolerance.

Comments by the Secretary-General
The Secretary-General notes the recommendation that the treaty bodies be given a direct input into future decision-making about public information materials relating to their work. In this regard, he draws attention to the close cooperation already existing between the human rights-related publications programme and the treaty bodies. All publications relating to the work of treaty bodies are developed in consultation with them and relevant sections are often drafted by their members, including the *Manual on Human Rights Reporting* and the Fact Sheet series on the treaty bodies.

The Secretary-General notes the suggestion that a public information budget be made available to support grass-roots initiatives designed to disseminate information about the treaty bodies in culturally appropriate and more popular formats and media and agrees that the challenge is in the implementation at the grass-roots level. Additional effort has been made in recent years to engage the attention of United Nations Information Centres to promote the work of the treaty bodies. This includes, when the report of a State party comes before a treaty body, ensuring that the relevant UNIC receives a copy of the report, following up with press releases on specific meetings of the relevant treaty body and transmitting to the UNIC the concluding observations adopted on the report. The success of this strategy has depended on a number of factors. The first is the capacity of the UNIC to respond to the additional workload and the receptiveness of the local media to such information. A second factor is the relevance and interest of the proceedings in the treaty body. Another is the quality of the concluding observations. While the results have been mixed, in a number of instances, UNICs have been able to generate considerable local interest in the proceedings of treaty bodies relating to the countries in which they are situated.

The Secretary-General encourages the treaty bodies to reflect on ways to present their findings that may be easier to comprehend by a non-specialist public. The establishment of a public information budget should be undertaken together with such efforts by the treaty bodies.

G. *Advisory services*

Recommendations of the independent expert
The independent expert considered that the advisory services programme had not provided sufficient support for surveys required prior to ratification of a

human rights treaty or for the preparation of reports by States in need of assistance. Regional and subregional training courses in relation to reporting were unlikely to produce results commensurate with their cost. He recommended that a specially designed programme be devised to address the needs in this area and that it be accorded priority (ibid., paras. 72–77, 118).

Comments by United Nations agencies and bodies
The Convention on the Rights of the Child assigned UNICEF a legal obligation in the promotion and protection of the rights of children. Article 45 made specific reference to UNICEF's responsibility in: participating in the consideration of States parties' reports; providing expert advice on the implementation of the Convention; submitting reports to the Committee on the Rights of the Child on the implementation of the Convention; and responding to requests by the Committee for technical advice or assistance to a State party. The reporting process provided UNICEF with a special opportunity to enhance the efforts made at the national and local levels to implement the Convention. UNICEF fostered a reporting process that was participatory and transparent and that promoted the involvement of all sectors of society in the rights of the child. It was an important initiative to enhance the capacity-building of government officials, non-governmental organizations and UNICEF staff.

UNICEF organized a number of national and regional workshops to familiarize the above-mentioned personnel on the reporting process related to the Convention on the Rights of the Child and the Convention on the Elimination of All Forms of Discrimination against Women. The programmes included information about the human rights treaties and treaty bodies. In 1997, workshops were held in, *inter alia*, Swaziland, the United Republic of Tanzania, South Africa, Cote d'Ivoire and Turkey.

Comments by the Secretary-General
A concentrated effort has been made in recent years to strengthen national capacities in the area of national reporting to treaty bodies. Since 1993, the Office of the High Commissioner for Human Rights has been requested to train approximately 134 officials from more than 81 Member States. The suggestions offered by the independent expert provide a welcome opportunity to reflect on lessons learned from this experience.

One of the most important advances made recently is the development of a complete treaty-system reporting package, comprising the *Manual on Human Rights Reporting*, a *Trainers' Guide on Human Rights Reporting* and a *Pocket Guide on the Basic Human Rights Instruments*. They were developed in cooperation with the United Nations Staff College Project in Turin and are now available to all Member States.

Training activities are organized regularly at the regional and subregional levels, as well as at the national level. With respect to the former, the training approach and methodology are focused on "training the trainers" to enable them to design and implement training programmes at the national level. This approach emphasizes national capacity-building instead of direct assistance and takes into account effective follow-up at the national level by the participants. The intensive training of trainers has been designed to enable reporting officers to conduct training activities at the national level after having followed the course, drawing on the experience of practitioners from the field. Participants benefit from preparing a plan of action before returning to their countries, which enables them to reflect on the organization of training activities at the national level to ensure a "multiplier effect". What remains to be done, to guarantee the multiplier effect, rests at the national level with the concerned Governments. Many of the constructive comments made by the participants during the training sessions highlighted a need for follow-up at the national level by the trainer of the Office. In view of current financial constraints, post-training requirements must be addressed through extrabudgetary resources.

"Cooperative training" with the United Nations Staff College Project in Turin is an on-going practice; since 1994, three training programmes have been conducted with the support of UNSCP and, in addition, training activities were also held in Addis Ababa in July 1997 and Antananarivo in December 1997, financed with resources from the United Nations Staff College Project.

The number of State party reports that have been submitted by States since participating in a training programme on reporting might be a fair indication of the effectiveness of these programmes. In 1994, representatives from 19 countries were trained by the Office of the High Commissioner for Human Rights on the preparation of their State reports. As of December 1997, 12 of those countries have submitted a total of 27 reports. The 1995 training programme was attended by representatives from 28 countries[1], 18 of which subsequently submitted a total of 38 reports due under the treaties. In 1996, representatives from 13 countries[2] attended the training programme, of which 4 countries submitted 5 reports. In 1997, representatives from 26 more countries[3] participated in one of the training sessions organized by the Office of the High Commissioner for Human Rights or by the United Nations Staff College Project.

At the national level, several training courses have been organized in countries where there is an acute lack of capacity in the field of reporting. In the experience of the Office of the High Commissioner for Human Rights, national training programmes require post-training follow-up, as do the regional or subregional programmes, which also involves resources. If resources were plentiful, national training programmes attended by a wide range of national officers would undoubtedly be more effective than regional programmes attended by only one or two national officers from each participating State. Concentrated assistance, however, could not satisfy the needs of the same number of countries with the same available resources as does the present regional and subregional approach.

The idea of regional advisers based on the ILO model, as cited in paragraph 75 of the report of the independent expert, is worth exploring. UNDP has also established programmes involving regional advisers to provide continuous *in situ* substantive support in UNDP priority areas of focus. The main issue will again be the availability of resources; at least four posts would have to be created for this function. States may wish to discuss the modalities for implementing this recommendation.

It may be noted that in southern Africa, a joint UNDP-OHCHR project will

---

[1] Not including three countries from the 1994 programme that also participated in the 1995 programme. The total number of participating countries in 1995 was 31.
[2] Not including eight countries from the 1994 or 1995 programmes that also participated in the 1996 programme. The total number of participating countries in 1995 was 21.
[3] Not including 19 countries from the 1994, 1995 or 1996 programmes that also participated in one of the 1997 programmes. The total number of participating countries in 1995 was 45.

be implemented in 1998 which foresees the establishment of a regional adviser position. A human rights regional programme adviser will work closely with Governments and United Nations Resident Coordinators in the subregion to provide on-site support, advice and assistance on human rights matters, including reporting under the treaty bodies.

H. *Special reports*

Recommendations of the independent expert
The independent expert recommended that the effectiveness of "special reports" and "urgent procedures" should be carefully evaluated by the committees concerned. At present, the value they added seemed low. In general, the division of labour between the treaty bodies and special mechanisms should be maintained (ibid., paras. 78–79, 119).

Government comments
While recognizing that the treaty bodies should not attempt to duplicate the work of the United Nations human rights special procedures, the Government of Canada continued to believe that there was a role for them in giving expert attention, on a timely basis, to emerging issues of concern. By virtue of their regular review of the performance of States parties, the treaty bodies were in a position to follow trends which might foreshadow a deterioration in a given human rights situation. They were also well placed to follow up on human rights concerns identified by United Nations special procedures. Canada attached particular importance to encouraging United Nations agencies to make greater use of reports by treaty bodies.

The Government of Cyprus recognized the difficulties for the independent expert to consider in any detail the relationship between the human rights treaty system and the system of special rapporteurs, representatives and experts of the Commission on Human Rights. Nevertheless, it noted that if the "division of labour" between the two systems in relation to urgent appeals is to be maintained, the Commission on Human Rights should make procedural provision for thorough consideration of the reports received from its special rapporteurs, etc. It should also consider procedures as to how best to channel reports reflecting urgent appeals.

Israel was of the view that there should be a clear distinction between the functions of treaty bodies and special reports. First, the treaty bodies could not provide an efficient framework to deal with pressing emergency situations. Second, special reports would be examined at the expense of regular reports from States. Finally, the vague criteria for urgent procedures opened the possibility of manipulation by treaty bodies, who could resort to them whenever they were dissatisfied with a State. Treaty bodies should justify in writing and in detail why the urgent procedures mechanism was resorted to.

Comments by interested persons
Mr. Zwaak and Ms. Boerefijn agreed with the independent expert that an examination should be made into the results of the treaty bodies' practice of requesting special reports over the past five years. They observed that, for outsiders, it was entirely unclear what were the criteria for requesting a special report. It did not become clear, for example, whether the proclamation of a state

of emergency, or a de facto existence of a state of emergency played any role. Many special rapporteurs of the Commission on Human Rights were concerned with countries which were States parties to, *inter alia*, the International Covenant on Civil and Political Rights; it was not clear whether the existence of such mandates played any role. It should be examined what additional value emanated from a special report and the consideration thereof. States parties might regard the opportunity to submit special reports as the only way for them to present their side of the story before an international forum. Their cooperation could also be attributed to the fact that the treaty bodies, generally speaking, were believed to be unpoliticized and consequently States might expect a "fair hearing".

Mr. O'Flaherty expressed disagreement with regard to the role of the treaty bodies regarding complex emergency situations. He pointed out that the final report of the independent expert did not contain verifiable indicators in support of the conclusion that the involvement of treaty bodies was only marginally useful, nor did it distinguish between the report-based and other special procedures. References to the role of Charter-based mechanisms should, in a context where there was urgent need to develop an effective mutuality between them and treaty bodies, focus on means of collaboration and cooperation rather than on "division of labour". He further noted that a remarkable role had been accorded to the treaty bodies in the Dayton Agreement (annex 6, article XIII; see also the Constitution of the Federation of Bosnia and Herzegovina, contained in the Washington Agreement of March 1994). The invitation contained therein for ongoing involvement by treaty bodies in the implementation of the peace agreement was an exceptional opportunity to advance committee practice.

I. Consolidation of reports and treaty bodies

Recommendations of the independent expert
The independent expert contended that in light of current trends the existing reporting system was unsustainable. He presented four options that were available to States: (a) to dismiss the concern as alarmist and take no action; (b) to urge the treaty bodies to undertake far-reaching reforms and adapt to cope with existing and new demands from within existing resources; (c) to provide greatly enhanced budgetary resources to sustain the status quo; (d) to combine some elements of (b) and (c) with the adoption of some far-reaching reforms. The latter could include: the preparation of "consolidated reports"; elimination of comprehensive periodic reports in their present form and replacement by reporting guidelines tailored to each State's individual situation; and a consolidation (reduction) of the number of treaty bodies. If the political will existed in relation to the last, a small expert group should be convened to examine modalities (ibid., paras. 81–97, 120).

Government comments
The Government of Australia supported reforms to the reporting procedures with the object of streamlining the reporting obligations on States parties, the production of shorter and more focused reports, and encouraging the greater coordination and sharing of information between the treaty bodies. Australia saw great potential for the streamlining of reports. Of the two options presented by the independent expert – consolidation of reports under all the treaties in

Appendix 5: Long-Term Effectiveness of the UN Human Rights Treaty System

one report or elimination of the requirement to produce comprehensive periodic reports – Australia endorsed the second option. While the initial report should be comprehensive, subsequent periodic reports should focus on a limited range of issues identified well in advance and tailored to the situation of each State party.

An alternative approach would be to draft reports which focused on particular issues. Those issues would be identified by reference to the comments and concluding observations of a committee on an earlier report. A State party could also provide information to the Committee on significant developments which had occurred in the reporting period. Cross-referencing to relevant material contained in other periodic reports would avoid unnecessary duplication.

The Australian Government believed that further careful consideration was needed as to the suggestion to consolidate the six treaty bodies into one. Priority should be given to those reforms to the treaty system that could be achieved in the short to medium term.

The Government of Canada expressed caution as to any suggestion that the treaty bodies be consolidated. The fact that not all States had ratified the same range of conventions was merely the most obvious in a wide range of practical difficulties that would afflict this scheme. The risk that particular issues, such as children's or women's rights, would not receive adequate attention in a comprehensive report would also pose difficulties. More importantly, Canada was not confident that amalgamation would significantly lower the reporting burden on States parties. Canada considered that consolidated reports, providing input to more than one treaty body in a single submission, would pose practical difficulties, although not insurmountable ones. While interested States should have the option of pursuing this approach if they judged it to be appropriate in their specific case, Canada expressed doubt that consolidated reports would produce the dramatic improvement in efficiency necessary to restore the treaty body system to good health.

In Canada's view, the single most important step that could be taken to improve the functioning of the United Nations human rights treaty system would be a move away from submission of comprehensive reports and towards reporting focused on specific issues of concern. Although this would not be an advisable approach for initial reports by States parties, for subsequent periodic reports it would radically enhance the efficiency and effectiveness of the reporting system. Managed properly, issue-specific reporting would accomplish a number of goals: it would reduce the amount of work required to prepare reports, reduce duplication between reports, and identify with more precision points on which follow-up is required by States parties. Canada believed that each individual treaty body should consider how best to implement such a system.

The factors which Canada considered the essential elements of issue-specific reporting were as follows: (a) the issues which a State is asked to address in its report should be selected using all available sources of information, but special attention should be given to previous recommendations made by the treaty body; (b) the list of issues should be focused and should not attempt to cover more than a limited number of priority themes or areas; (c) the State party should be advised what issues will be raised well in advance of the proposed dates of examination to allow adequate time to prepare a written report; and (d) the State party would have a responsibility to provide its report to the treaty body a specified minimum length of time before consideration by the Committee, to allow Committee members sufficient preparation time.

Canada encouraged each treaty body to develop a flexible approach or policy for issue-specific reporting, and to make States parties aware of their decisions in this regard. Even in the absence of such a policy, Canada was of the view that issue-specific reporting could proceed immediately in any case in which the treaty body and State party concerned were in agreement on the procedure to be followed. In cases where no report had been submitted in recent years, treaty bodies might, as in the case of initial reports, prefer submission of a comprehensive report.

The Government of Cyprus expressed support for the recommendation in paragraph 120 that a small expert group be convened to examine modalities to consolidate the treaty bodies. It also supported the view that there could be consolidated reports even before other measures were taken. Such reports would reduce the heavy burden on small States of preparing six reports, which in many respects overlapped. If, owing to differences in the dates on which reports to the various treaty bodies were due, the consolidated report was submitted more than 18 months before a report to the relevant treaty body was due, States should be encouraged to submit a brief updating report on matters specifically related to the competence of that treaty body.

The Government of Finland agreed with the assessment of the independent expert that the present system was unsustainable and that significant reforms would be required. A significant number of States reports were overdue, partly because many States lacked adequate resources. The preparation of reports and their consideration by the treaty bodies involved a great deal of work. The final report of the independent expert proposed several measures which could address the problem. Finland considered especially valuable, *inter alia*, an easing of the reporting requirements. A more tailored and flexible approach to reporting, including the replacement of extensive reports by reports on a limited range of issues possibly based on the concluding observations on the previous report, could be an option.

The Government of Israel supported consolidation of reports prepared for the different treaty bodies. A single comprehensive report would be more coherent than an artificial separation into different reports. It noted that a reform in the contents of periodic reports had already been implemented by the Committee on the Elimination of Racial Discrimination, pursuant to which one in two reports may be limited to an update. Broadening this approach could help alleviate the current situation, especially if clear guidance were given as regards the difference in scope between comprehensive reports and updates. Israel welcomed the proposal of the independent expert to convene a small expert group to examine modalities for the consolidation of the treaty bodies.

The Government of the Netherlands indicated that national reports tended to reveal only that information which the State concerned was willing to divulge, the underlying principle being that the States themselves provided information about their measures to implement human rights standards. This often led to a paradoxical situation in which States in which little or no human rights violations occurred submitted reports critical of those problems that did exist, while States in which human rights violations were more prevalent were less inclined to submit comprehensive reports. The Netherlands suggested, as a way to address this issue, the provision to States of questionnaires, containing specific questions tailored to the State's situation. Specific reports could be submitted on the basis of these questions. States parties might therefore begin to relate treaty obligations to national practice, which ultimately might lead to an improvement in the human rights situation.

The Government of the Republic of Korea observed that the proliferation of requests for reports under a growing number of human rights instruments had placed increasingly heavy burdens on States parties in general and on developing countries in particular. The Republic of Korea believed that such burdens had been magnified by duplication and a lack of coordination among the different procedures and mechanisms of various treaty bodies. The Republic of Korea agreed that the existing reporting system was unsustainable, owing to the large number of significantly overdue reports and the serious delays between submission and examination of reports.

In view of these significant problems, the Republic of Korea considered it inevitable that the administrative burdens associated with State reporting be alleviated, both on States parties and on the treaty bodies. The Republic of Korea supported reforms that would streamline the process and observed that the single consolidated report proposed by the independent expert could be a practical solution. As the reports due under the respective human rights treaty bodies often required similar elements, the Republic of Korea was of the view that the reports could be integrated into one, with a five-year reporting cycle, thus eliminating duplication of administrative demands on States parties.

The Republic of Korea suggested that the treaty bodies, in cooperation with the Office of the High Commissioner for Human Rights, prepare a set of guidelines for the preparation of a consolidated report. The report could be categorized into two parts: the first part describing universally common subjects applicable to all the States parties, the second dealing with specific items specially tailored to the different States parties.

Comments by United Nations agencies and bodies
With reference to the proposal for the submission of a single consolidated report by each State party, UNICEF maintained that there was a need for specific information on various areas, in particular children. The submission of a single report ran the risk of diluting important issues and neglecting both their consideration and the formulation of specific recommendations.

Comments by non-governmental organizations
The NGO Group for the Convention on the Rights of the Child presented its views on the problems facing the reporting system. The backlog of reports was two years long for the Convention on the Rights of the Child and other treaty bodies were faced with similar delays. By the time of the examination of a State report, not only was it out of date but NGOs were also likely to produce information that became out of date and the momentum of the reporting process was lost. Radical solutions were necessary to deal with these problems and the consolidation of the treaty bodies or consolidation of the reports due to them appeared to be the only viable long-term option. The overlaps in the system were obvious and created a burden on both the States parties and those contributing to the monitoring of the implementation of the treaties.

The Inter-Church Committee for Refugees addressed the recommendation for a single unified professional salaried treaty monitoring body. In view of the problems of "normative consistency" and relationships with regional human rights mechanisms, as discussed in the interim report of the independent expert, the Inter-Church Committee for Refugees saw value in a single complaint mechanism. This would seem possible and desirable in the short term. It also favoured the establishment of a Court of Human Rights with non-threatening "advisory" jurisdiction. Such jurisdiction had proven useful for the Inter-American Court of Human Rights.

The Inter-Church Committee for Refugees expressed doubt that the treaties would be more effectively implemented by collapsing the various examinations of State reports by treaty bodies into one. While recognizing the problems of meeting time for experts who essentially served on a volunteer basis, it did not appear that alternative ways of working had been exhausted. It was difficult to envisage the distinctive perspectives of women, children, prevention of torture, etc. without specialist treaty bodies.

The Inter-Church Committee for Refugees welcomed the proposal for a consolidated State report. It did not view this recommendation as inconsistent with the suggestion of preserving distinct examination processes from the perspectives mentioned above. A general report could potentially provide a strong basis for examination by the various treaty bodies on their respective concerns.

Comments by interested persons
Mr. Zwaak and Ms. Boerefijn noted that, although the reports of State parties constituted the major source of their dialogue with treaty bodies, additional information from official and unofficial sources were currently being used by all the treaty bodies. The State reports therefore no longer constituted the only source of information and in due time may not even be the most important source. Moreover, many reports rarely provided information beyond legislative measures. Information on practice was hardly ever provided in the reports, although it had on occasion been more forthcoming during the dialogue with representatives of State parties.

Mr. Zwaak and Ms. Boerefijn suggested that it might be worthwhile to explore whether the major efforts of States parties should be shifted. States could prepare one report composed of several sections which dealt with the various treaties to which it was a party. This could only work if Governments sent well-briefed delegations to the committees when their reports were being discussed. Further study would be required into adjusting the guidelines for reporting in order to ensure that the information which needed to be submitted under the specialized treaties would not be lost, i.e. the consolidated report should not be merely a combination of a report under the two Covenants but should take fully into account all aspects of the other relevant treaties. An important side-effect of consolidated reports might be that the interdependence of civil and political rights and economic, social and cultural rights is strengthened.

Mr. Craig Scott commented that the recommendation to study modalities for consolidation, including a possible reduction in the number of human rights treaty bodies, may not, upon reflection and in the context of evolving financial realities, prove desirable. In particular, consolidation of the treaty bodies could jeopardize the principle of interactive diversity of expertise, of experience and of normative focus – the maintenance of which was central to the functioning of collective decision-making bodies. Mr. Scott also proposed the establishment of an international candidate identification process that could be set in motion prior to the election of candidates at meetings of States parties.

Comments by the Secretary-General
While recognizing the need to streamline the reporting process and supporting the discussion on this critical issue, the Secretary-General draws attention to the need for further reflection by the treaty bodies as to the objective of focused reports and how the main issues would be selected with respect to each State party. The treaty bodies are invited to give careful thought as to the objective of focused reports and to propose concrete ways in which the issues would be selected.

J. Amending the treaties

Recommendations of the independent expert
The independent expert highlighted the need to make procedural provisions of human rights treaties more susceptible to amendment. His recommendations were as follows (ibid., paras. 101, 121):

(a) All future human rights treaties should provide for a simplified process to be followed in order to amend the relevant procedural provisions. While the specific endorsement of this proposal by the Commission on Human Rights could not be binding in the context of any future negotiations it would constitute a clear policy guideline and help to facilitate the adoption of such flexibility in the future;

(b) A report should be requested from the Legal Counsel which would explore the feasibility of devising more innovative approaches in dealing with existing and future amendments to the human rights treaties;

(c) The General Assembly should request the Meetings of the States Parties to the relevant treaties to discuss means by which the States concerned might be encouraged to attach a higher priority to ratification of the amendments already approved;

(d) Consideration should be given immediately to amending the International Convention on the Protection of the Rights of All Migrant Workers and Members of Their Families in line with the recommendation made below;

(e) In view of the agreement of the Meeting of States Parties and of the General Assembly in 1992 to amend article 8, paragraph 6, of the International Convention on the Elimination of All Forms of Racial Discrimination to eliminate the responsibility of the States parties for the expenses of the Committee members, action should now be taken to write off the continuing backlog of contributions owed for that purpose. Agreement should be sought to cover the outstanding amount from the regular budget and close the file. For legal and policy reasons, it should be indicated that no precedent of broader application is thereby created.

Existing arrangements for cooperation with the specialized agencies and other bodies had been improved in some respects but remained very inadequate. The High Commissioner should convene a high-level meeting to explore better means of cooperation with the treaty bodies (ibid., paras. 108, 121).

Government comments
The Government of Australia agreed that there should be steps taken to simplify the procedure for amending technical or procedural provisions in respect of future and current treaties. It endorsed the recommendation that an option be sought from the Legal Counsel on more innovative approaches to dealing with existing and future amendments to the technical or procedural provisions of the human rights treaties.

The Government of Canada agreed that the process of amending the procedural provisions of human rights treaties should be simplified and that options in this regard should be considered.

Comments by United Nations agencies and bodies
UNICEF expressed support for the proposed amendment to the Convention on the Rights of the Child that would expand the membership of the Committee on the Rights of the Child from 10 to 18 experts.

K. The language question

Recommendations of the independent expert
The independent expert considered that the importance of maintaining linguistic diversity in the treaty bodies was, for many reasons, beyond doubt. However, in the absence of a substantial increase in funds for interpretation, he believed there was a clear need for the different committees to explore ways in which working groups and other non-plenary meetings could be held without official translation. He suggested that greater emphasis should be attached to the ability of nominees for election to the treaty bodies to work in at least one, and preferably two, of the three major languages: English, French and Spanish. Ways would have to be found in which the content of materials available in only one language could be drawn upon more efficiently for the benefit of the whole committee. Consideration would need to be given to delegating certain responsibilities to working groups capable of working without translation (ibid., para. 106).

Government comments
The Government of Finland indicated that reports should be available to the members of the treaty bodies in good time but noted that this had not always been the case, as a report cannot be distributed before it has been translated into all official languages.

The Government of the Republic of Korea viewed the suggestion that English be used as a single working language of the treaty bodies as a constructive suggestion to reduce the burdens on the Secretariat. It maintained, however, that final official documents should continue to be published in English, French and other official languages of the United Nations at the request of the States parties concerned, as is currently the practice.

Comments by non-governmental organizations
The NGO Group for the Convention on the Rights of the Child stated that it did not have the capacity to translate NGO documents and the United Nations would not do so. Therefore, NGO documents submitted in a language other than English were not taken fully into consideration by the Committee. In order

to combat these weaknesses, the NGO Group recommended that international NGOs working at the national level translate, or provide funds to translate, NGO documents into English.

North-South XXI expressed regret that budgetary restrictions should give rise to non-respect for the principle of linguistic diversity. The predominance of the English language was but one of the forms of domination exercised around the world in the fields of the hard sciences and was closely linked to the question of economic domination. In the field of human rights, linguistic domination carried with it controversial conceptions of human rights. In certain languages, the vocabulary of the "great powers in human rights" did not exist, while in contrast, in some languages of the South, there existed certain humanist concepts that were unknown in the languages of Northern countries. This diversity reflected different cultures and different values which the United Nations should respect. The reaffirmation of the General Assembly of the importance of linguistic diversity was actively supported by many non-governmental organizations, notably North-South XXI.

L. Cooperation with the specialized agencies and other bodies

Recommendations of the independent expert
The independent expert recommended that the Commission on Human Rights should request the High Commissioner to convene a high-level meeting over a period of two days if senior representatives of the key specialized agencies and other bodies (including ILO, WHO, FAO, UNESCO, UNICEF, UNHCR, UNDP, UNFPA and the World Bank), senior staff of the Office of the High Commissioner for Human Rights and the chairpersons of the six treaty bodies. In order to minimize costs and capitalize on other coordination efforts, the meeting should take place immediately before or after one of the annual meetings of the chairpersons. The purpose should be to explore the most constructive, appropriate, cost-effective, and mutually rewarding means of cooperation between these bodies and the human rights committees (ibid., para. 108).

Comments by United Nations agencies and bodies
UNICEF highlighted its close relationship with the Committee on the Rights of the Child. It supported the work of the Committee in a number of ways, including by providing technical assistance and ensuring that members of the Committee had the opportunity, through field visits, to consult with a number of actors at the country level. UNICEF also regularly supported the participation of Committee members in relevant conferences, seminars and workshops at the global, regional and national levels. It continuously promoted cooperative efforts aimed at involving the specialized agencies in the implementation of the Convention on the Rights of the Child and in supporting the monitoring function of the Committee on the Rights of the Child, particularly in the follow-up to concluding observations at the national level.

UNICEF encouraged other United Nations agencies to support the work of human rights treaty bodies as a means to a more effective implementation of human rights treaties and to promote a constructive dialogue on human rights between the treaty bodies and States parties.

Comments by non-governmental organizations
North-South XXI considered the recommendation for strengthened cooperation with ILO to be judicious.

M. *The quality of concluding observations*

Recommendations of the independent expert
The independent expert recommended that treaty bodies should strive to further improve the quality of their concluding observations, in terms of their clarity, degree of detail, level of accuracy and specificity (ibid., paras. 109, 122).

Government comments
The Government of Australia agreed on the need to further improve the quality of concluding observations to ensure that they were precise, clear and detailed. This would become even more of an issue if periodic reports were to be based essentially on the comments and concluding observations of a committee.

Comments by United Nations and bodies
UNICEF concurred with the view that it was imperative for the concluding observations to be based on the most accurate and comprehensive information available on the situation of children in each country. The quality of the concluding observations was essential in order for recommendations to be effectively implemented at the national level and to enhance the dialogue with States parties. Treaty bodies should strive to improve the quality of the concluding observations in terms of their clarity, degree of detail, level of accuracy and specificity, which would enable a more effective follow-up at the national level by all concerned.

Comments by interested persons
Mr. Zwaak and Ms. Boerefijn noted that recent developments with respect to the adoption of country-based concluding observations had strengthened the reporting procedure as a method of supervision, particularly as it allowed for follow-up measures at both the national and international levels. Follow-up to the recommendations of treaty bodies needed to be more solidly imbedded in the practice of treaty bodies and States. Especially when the reporting cycle was relatively long, additional measures needed to be taken by the treaty bodies to monitor compliance with recommendations. This could be done, for example, by requesting a short interim report on the measures taken, comparable to the Human Rights Committee's practice with the follow-up of views under the Optional Protocol. Domestic NGOs were also provided with an important tool to hold Governments accountable for non-compliance with treaty obligations and they would be more inclined to take part in the reporting procedure if there were a tangible outcome.

Mr. Zwaak and Ms. Boerefijn noted that concluding observations dealt with violations of treaty obligations, concerns as well as positive aspects, and suggestions and recommendations. In so doing, the treaty bodies kept intact an important feature of the reporting procedure, the constructive character, while adding a new component, namely expressions of concern by the treaty body as a whole. It was of great importance that the concluding observations be widely published and made accessible by the States parties concerned in domestic languages and distributed to the relevant national authorities. NGOs could also play a role in this respect. They fully agreed with the recommendation of the independent expert for concluding observations to be detailed, accurate and comprehensive.

Mr. O'Flaherty noted the need for development of effective methodologies for follow-up of concluding observations. One issue which could be addressed in this context is that of the manner in which the programming of technical cooperation activities could be better linked to the content and implementation of concluding observations. In that regard, he believed it would be helpful to assess the evolving experience of the Committee on the Rights of the Child and UNICEF.

N. *Other issues*

A number of responses raised issues that were not the subject of recommendations in the final report of the independent expert. Those views are summarized in this section.

1. *The role of non-governmental organizations*

Comments by non-governmental organizations
The NGO Group for the Convention on the Rights of the Child emphasized the need to develop methods for sound national monitoring in order to provide the strongest possible basis for effective international monitoring. Although the primary responsibility for implementation of the human rights treaties rested with Governments, NGOs had a significant role to play in monitoring the extent to which compliance was being achieved. In order to fulfil this role, NGOs had to become partners in the monitoring process from the beginning.

The NGO Group outlined how a role for non-governmental organizations in the reporting process had slowly emerged. Reports were often prepared at the national level by one or more civil servants, normally in the Ministry of Foreign Affairs, with little or no consultation with other government offices or NGOs directly implicated in the implementation of the relevant treaty. Civil society was usually not informed when reports were scheduled for consideration by a treaty body, when they had been examined or when conclusions had been adopted.

The NGO Group for the Convention on the Rights of the Child noted that the Committee on the Rights of the Child had considerably involved NGOs in the reporting and monitoring process, which had been beneficial to both the Committee and to the NGO community. The positive relationship between this Committee and NGOs benefited from the support of the NGO Group for the Convention on the Rights of the Child. The NGO Group aimed at facilitating the flow of information between the Committee and NGOs as well as promoting full implementation of the Convention. At a time when the level of servicing for the treaty bodies was limited and the workload of the treaty bodies was growing, NGO cooperation with the treaty bodies should relieve pressure from the Secretariat and not add to its work. For example, the request of the Committee on Economic, Social and Cultural Rights to send copies of reports pending consideration to a range of national NGOs in each State party would place an undue burden on the Secretariat.

A primary concern of all treaty bodies was how to ensure that the information before them was reliable and objective. The NGO Group had promoted the development of national coalitions of NGOs working with children which reflected the full range of issues raised by the Convention. With the specialist knowledge of its members and the diversity of perspectives that were brought together, coalitions enabled more effective monitoring of the Convention at the national level. While admittedly in need of refinement, the cooperation achieved between the Committee on the Rights of the Child and NGOs could nevertheless serve as a model to other treaty bodies.

The Inter-Church Committee for Refugees expressed strong support for preserving the role which non-governmental organizations had been allowed to play by submitting information in respect of the State reporting process. It raised concerns for the way in which NGO information could be abused and suggested, for example, that if NGO information was repudiated by a Government, the NGO should have an opportunity to defend itself. In addition to such technical adjustments in procedures, ways must be found to engage NGOs in a meaningful way around issues of common concern to them and to treaty body experts. In this regard, the Inter-Church Committee for Refugees suggested that a worldwide consultation process of treaty body members and staff and with domestic as well as international NGOs could be held on topics of current international concern. The PARINAC (PARtnership IN ACtion) project of UNHCR was a successful example of such an approach. The Inter-Church Committee for Refugees further suggested that a general hearing be organized on a country-, region- or issue-specific basis to enable treaty bodies and NGOs to share insights and information. The Inter-Church Committee for Refugees had participated in a General Hearing of the Inter-American Commission on Human Rights on a country, in which the Government concerned was invited to participate. Such activities could prove useful to treaty bodies in the preparation of general comments.

The Inter-Church Committee for Refugees pointed out that domestic NGOs had a role to play in encouraging States to assume their responsibilities to promote treaty rights at the domestic level. Domestic NGOs should therefore be used as a medium for promoting treaty rights in a State party. The establishment of an independent domestic agency to promote and articulate rights and jurisprudence credibly among relevant professional groups in the country, including civil servants, lawyers and judges, would also be helpful. A national human rights commission or ombudsperson that conformed to the Principles relating to the status of national institutions ("Paris Principles") could be an attractive way for States to promote treaty rights. Such institutions should complement and draw on the work of domestic human rights NGOs.

The Grand Council of the Crees (of Quebec) expressed concern regarding the process of examining State reports, which did not allow for indigenous peoples in those countries or other groups mentioned in them to review the contents of the reports before they were submitted to the United Nations. The Grand Council of the Crees proposed that countries sending periodic reports on the implementation of human rights instruments be advised to review the contents of those reports with the concerned parties, including organizations for women, indigenous peoples, etc., and that their comments be reflected in the content of the reports. The secretariats of the treaty bodies should make special efforts to hear from concerned groups when reports were examined. In that way, the reporting process would better serve its original purpose: to determine to what extent the instruments are being respected and to correct problems where identified. At present, the submission of reports is nothing but an exercise of States in self-praise and obfuscation.

Comments by interested persons
Mr. Zwaak and Ms. Boerefijn suggested that States parties should be encouraged to make available their reports to NGOs immediately after submission to the Secretary-General, so NGOs would have ample time to prepare their comments. It would encourage NGOs if the treaty bodies would make it clear that they use information submitted by NGOs. As it was often not clear which information was actually used by members, it would be worthwhile if the treaty bodies would include a list of NGO reports they had received and/or consulted during the examination of State reports. The current openness of the treaty bodies towards NGOs, while warmly welcomed, could be further expanded. NGOs also had an important role to play in the reporting procedure. However, NGOs must maintain their distance from the Government. They should not be involved in drafting the State party's report; that must remain entirely a government responsibility.

Mr. O'Flaherty noted that the role of NGOs was adverted to in the interim report of the independent expert but not dealt with in his final report. It would be useful to clarify the continuing advances made in the practice of treaty bodies, such as the development of excellent and paradigmic NGO support for the work of the Committee on the Rights of the Child, and to revisit the question of whether NGO access to the treaty body system should be regulated.

2. Other comments

General comments
The Australian Government noted that little attention was paid in the report to the communications procedures, despite the importance of these procedures and the increasing communications workload of the Human Rights Committee, the Committee against Torture and the Committee on the Elimination of Racial Discrimination, as well as the proposals for optional protocols to provide for individual communications procedures under the International Covenant on Economic, Social and Cultural Rights and the Convention on the Elimination of All Forms of Discrimination against Women. The decisions of treaty bodies in respect of individual communications could be improved. Often, issues raised in a communication were dealt with in a cursory fashion or not at all and, on occasion, little reasoning or justification was advanced for a particular view reached by a committee. The lack of adequate reasoning or justification made it difficult for States parties to review their individual laws and practices. The Australian Government welcomed the efforts of committees with individual communications procedures to improve their working methods. It also sought to pursue further reform proposals of the procedures through direct dialogue with the committees concerned.

The Government of Australia also stated that adequate resources were essential if the human rights treaty body system is to function effectively and if improvements are to be made to the treaty bodies' existing procedures and practices.

The Government of Canada considered that any significant overhaul of the treaty body system should be accompanied by a commitment on the part of the treaty bodies to adopt more flexible and efficient working methods. Areas which Canada considered worthwhile pursuing included:

(a) Expanded use of working groups or chambers, to enable each treaty body to hold parallel sessions;
(b) Focusing the list of questions circulated to each State party in advance of presentation of its report – at present, the lists were cumbersome and ineffective, and few of the questions posed could be dealt with during the presentation;
(c) Adoption of guidelines on time-saving practices, such as those suggested in the report of the eighth meeting of persons chairing the human rights treaty bodies; and
(d) Increased coordination between treaty bodies, to ensure that when a specific situation was considered by more than one treaty body, successive discussions of the issue were complementary and mutually reinforcing.

The Government of Israel noted that on occasion the treaty bodies offered interpretations of the various conventions that were at odds with those of States parties. These differences of opinion often related to questions of scope and competency, but they could also involve points of principle, frequently with far-reaching implications. The treaty bodies tended to interpret the conventions in a self-interested way. With regard to the present method of considering reports, the Government of Israel would recommend that the practice adopted by some treaty bodies of providing States with a detailed list of questions well before the consideration of their reports should be adopted by all the treaty bodies.

Comments by interested persons
Mr. O'Flaherty raised several matters that were not dealt with in the final report of the independent expert but which might benefit from further examination, *inter alia*, the fundamental issue of whether the treaty bodies were actually effective in bringing about improvements in the protection of human rights – an evaluation of this aspect of their performance must precede any profound reflection on their future direction. A systematic overview was urgently required. Second, on the role of the United Nations High Commissioner for Human Rights, there seemed to be a lack of concerted reflection on the implications for treaty body practice of the nature of the mandate of the High Commissioner. While there were many references to the need for cooperation, these were not located within the fundamentally changed environment which had emerged subsequent to the publication of the interim report. Third, the process by which members were elected to serve on treaty bodies was unsatisfactory and led to the not infrequent appointment of unsuitable experts. In addition, the meetings of chairpersons were a potentially useful but underdeveloped channel of communication. Among the issues which should be considered is the extent to which recommendations emanating from the meetings were actually implemented. Fifth it would be valuable to reflect on the appropriateness of the preliminary decision of the Preparatory Committee on the Establishment of an International Criminal Court to exclude from the jurisdiction of the proposed new Court human rights treaty-based crimes, such as those deriving from the Convention against Torture

Appendix 5: Long-Term Effectiveness of the UN Human Rights Treaty System 657

and Other Cruel, Inhuman or Degrading Treatment or Punishment. The drafting process of the Courts Statute also raised familiar problems of human rights treaty-related issues being determined without input from the treaty bodies themselves.

E/CN.4/1998/85/Corr.1 — 4 February 1998

COMMISSION ON HUMAN RIGHTS
Fifty-fourth session

EFFECTIVE FUNCTIONING OF BODIES ESTABLISHED PURSUANT TO THE UNITED NATIONS HUMAN RIGHTS INSTRUMENTS

Report of the Secretary-General

Corrigendum

"Under section F "Public information", in the subsection entitled "comments by the Secretary-General", please replace paragraph 56 by the following three paragraphs renumbered 56, 56 *bis* and 56 *ter*.

"56. With respect to print materials issued by the Department of Public Information, DPI should be allowed a certain autonomy in the production of its print materials as these are not for the record. They are produced primarily to create awareness and understanding of the human rights work of the United Nations, including the work of the treaty bodies, and to generate media interest in covering it. Materials produced by DPI on the work of the treaty bodies, such as special press releases, normally feature articles or background material and highlight the meeting's main issues or recommendations. In this regard, the secretariat of the treaty body and DPI staff should cooperate to identify specific issues that might provide journalists with information on which they could base stories. Such information would have greater impact if it is communicated to the press in advance and not after the meeting has taken place. DPI press releases are useful to the media but are mainly produced for delegations, staff and others. At New York and Geneva, press conferences and media outreach to national, regional and international press are also an important aspect of promoting the work of the treaty bodies.

"56 *bis*. The Secretary-General notes the suggestion that a public information budget be made available to support grass-roots initiatives designed to disseminate information about the treaty bodies in culturally appropriate and more popular formats and media and agrees that the challenge is in the implementation at the grass-roots level. A pro-active strategy, in promoting the work of the treaty bodies in the field is used by relevant United Nations Information Centres (UNICs) when the report of a State party is submitted to a treaty body. UNICs generate interest in the national media and in grass-roots organizations by disseminating information about the work of treaty bodies through briefings, press conferences, organization of interviews and meetings with grass-roots organizations.

"56 *ter*. Additional effort has been made in recent years to engage the attention of UNICs to promote the work of the treaty bodies. This includes, when the report of a State party comes before a treaty body, ensuring that the relevant UNIC receives a copy of the report, following up with press releases on specific meetings of the relevant treaty body and transmitting to the UNIC the concluding observations adopted on the report. The success of this strategy has depended on a number of factors. The first is the capacity of the UNIC to respond to the additional workload and the receptiveness of the local media to such information. A second factor is the relevance and interest of the proceedings in the treaty body. Another is the quality of the concluding observations. While the results have been mixed, in a number of instances, UNICs have been able to generate considerable local interest in the proceedings of treaty bodies relating to the countries in which they are situated."

E/CN.4/1998/85/Add.1 — 16 March 1998

COMMISSION ON HUMAN RIGHTS
Fifty-fourth session

EFFECTIVE FUNCTIONING OF BODIES ESTABLISHED PURSUANT TO THE UNITED NATIONS HUMAN RIGHTS INSTRUMENTS

Report of the Secretary-General

Addendum

The present addendum contains comments by the Governments of New Zealand and Sweden on the report of the independent expert of the Commission on Human Rights on enhancing the functioning of the United Nations human rights treaty system (E/CN.4/1997/74) which were received subsequent to the publication of the main report.

A. *Towards universal ratification*

The Government of New Zealand expressed strong support for the goal of universal ratification of the six core human rights treaties. It concurred with the finding of the independent expert that the administrative burden of acceding to and reporting under the treaties, as well as associated resource implications, could present a barrier to ratification for many States. It therefore endorsed the recommendations of the independent expert on measures to assist States in developing the capacity to ratify the core treaties, including the development of improved technical cooperation programmes and the involvement of the specialized agencies in providing advisory services.

The Government of Sweden drew attention to the fact that the aim of achieving universal ratification of the six core treaties had been frequently affirmed, including at the 1993 World Conference on Human Rights. It agreed that concrete measures aimed at encouraging and facilitating ratification of the treaties were needed, *inter alia*, by providing technical cooperation.

B. *The problem of significantly overdue reports*

The Government of New Zealand agreed with the assessment that reporting obligations represented a substantial burden, particularly for States that had ratified all six of the core treaties and on small and developing States. It considered it important that adequate advisory services and technical cooperation be made available to such States, particularly when reports were overdue, and welcomed the suggestion that the Office of the High Commissioner for

Human Rights provide special assistance to developing countries with a population of less than 1 million, including with the process of ratification and the preparation of initial reports. The Government of New Zealand expressed support, as a short-term measure when reports were excessively overdue, for the possibility that States might be examined in the absence of a report, as was the practice with some treaty bodies.

The Government of Sweden believed that the rise in the number of overdue reports and cases of non-reporting was partly due to the lack of the necessary technical, administrative or financial resources by many States. It considered the possibility of easing the reporting requirements under certain circumstances to merit further exploration. It drew attention to the option of eliminating comprehensive periodic reports in their present form and replacing them, under certain circumstances, by reporting guidelines tailored to each State's individual situation and focusing on certain human rights obligations of particular interest. When a situation so warrants, the treaty bodies could request an additional report from a State party to address questions of implementation in a more flexible and focused manner.

The Government of Sweden agreed that the technical cooperation programme for the preparation of reports, for those States in need of assistance, should be accorded priority. In cases of non-reporting, Sweden stressed that it found unacceptable the possibility that some States escaped scrutiny by not fulfilling their reporting obligations, while those that were conscientious were held to account. It therefore agreed that all treaty bodies should develop a practice whereby the situation in a non-reporting State party could be examined in the absence of a report.

D. *Problems in relation to documentation*

The Government of New Zealand agreed with the independent expert that further work must be done on the question of documentation. The Government expressed the view that the body of reports should be limited to approximately 30 to 40 pages and that States parties should be encouraged to present more detailed information, including relevant statistics, in an annex to their reports. Initial reports could be excluded from this limit. The Government expressed particular support for the suggestion that special measures should be adopted to streamline reporting procedures for small States.

I. *Consolidation of reports and treaty bodies*

The Government of New Zealand suggested that, as a short-term measure, periodic reports should focus principally on addressing comments made during the consideration of the preceding report, as well as significant new developments. This would not affect the reporting obligations for initial reports, which should continue to be comprehensive. It invited treaty bodies to provide guidance on the issues that they wished to see reflected in the next periodic report. While this could be reflected in its concluding observations, additional guidance would be useful to ensure that the issues of most interest are addressed as a priority. The Government indicated that its delegations would seek such guidance in the future.

As another short-term measure, the Government of New Zealand suggested that the harmonization of reporting dates and cycles for States parties to a number of treaties could assist in the identification and elimination of duplication of effort. This might enable a more comprehensive picture of the human rights environment in a particular State to be presented. It could be accompanied by the development of a thorough system of cross-referencing of information provided in reports, a more comprehensive core document, or consolidation in one document of information common to a number of reports. The Government considered a useful model for other treaty bodies the practice of the Committee of the Rights of the Child of allowing reports to address common themes by clusters of related articles.

While it therefore considered some degree of consolidation in national reporting to be desirable, the Government of New Zealand expressed concern that the consolidation of reports due under all the treaties would make it difficult to ensure a meaningful review of the provisions of individual treaties. Similarly, in examining the possibility of consolidating the treaty bodies into one, it considered that the ability of one body to address effectively the wide range of human rights issues covered by the core treaties should be a primary consideration. The Government expressed support for the recommendation that a small expert group meeting be convened to examine the modalities for further reforms of the treaty system, including possibilities for consolidation of the treaty bodies.

J. Amending the treaties

The Government of New Zealand agreed that more flexible amendment procedures for procedural elements of the six treaties were required to enable the treaty bodies to respond to the need for reform.

M. The quality of concluding observations

The Government of Sweden expressed the view that treaty bodies must strive to further improve the quality of their concluding observations. Concluding observations should be formulated so as to be detailed, accurate and comprehensive: if they are not, the treaty bodies risk losing credibility and the political will to have them implemented will diminish.

N. Other issues

The Government of Sweden expressed deep concern at the high number of communications that were pending examination by the treaty bodies. It considered that an increase of staff composed of experienced skillful lawyers within the Office of the High Commissioner for Human Rights was necessary to remedy the situation.

E/CN.4/2000/98 — 20 January 2000

COMMISSION ON HUMAN RIGHTS
Fifty-sixth session

EFFECTIVE FUNCTIONING OF HUMAN RIGHTS MECHANISMS: TREATY BODIES

Report of the Secretary-General on the consultations conducted in respect of the report of the independent expert on enhancing the long-term effectiveness of the United Nations human rights treaty system

CONTENTS

	Paragraphs
I. INTRODUCTION	1–4
II. SUMMARY OF THE RECOMMENDATIONS OF THE INDEPENDENT EXPERT AND COMMENTS RECEIVED THEREON	5–56
A. Towards universal ratification	5–7
B. The reporting process: the problem of significantly overdue reports, dealing with the timely submission of reports and and consolidation of reports	8–23
C. Problems in relation to documentation	24–26
D. Development and use of electronic databases	27–28
E. Public information	29–30
F. Advisory services	31–33
G. Special reports	34–35
H. Consolidation of treaty bodies	36–37
I. Amending the treaties	38–39
J. The language question	40–41
K. Cooperation with the specialized agencies and other bodies	42–48
L. The quality of concluding observations	49–50
M. Other issues	51–56
III. OBSERVATIONS	57–65

I. INTRODUCTION

1. The original study on the effective operation of existing and prospective bodies established under United Nations human rights instruments was initi-

ated pursuant to General Assembly resolution 43/115 of 8 December 1988 and Commission on Human Rights resolution 1989/47, carried out by Mr. Philip Alston during the period 1989 to 1992 and transmitted to the General Assembly in document A/44/668, annex.
2. In its resolution 47/111 of 16 December 1992, the General Assembly requested that the report be updated for submission to the fiftieth session of the Commission on Human Rights and that an interim report be presented to the General Assembly at its forty-eighth session, and be made available to the World Conference on Human Rights in June 1993. Pursuant to that resolution, as well as Commission on Human Rights resolution 1993/16 of 26 February 1993, Mr. Alston undertook to update his original study, submitting an interim report thereon in document A/CONF/157/PC/62/Add.11/Rev.1 and a final report in document E/CN.4/1997/74, which was submitted to the fifty-third session of the Commission on Human Rights in 1997. By its decision 1997/105, the Commission on Human Rights invited the Secretary-General to solicit the views of Governments, United Nations bodies, specialized agencies, intergovernmental and non-governmental organizations and interested persons on the report of the independent expert and to submit a report thereon, including the Secretary-General's own views on the legal, administrative and other implications of the report's recommendations, to the Commission on Human Rights at its fifty-fourth session. That report was submitted in document E/CN.4/1998/85 and Add.1 and Corr.1.
3. In its resolution 1998/27, the Commission on Human Rights invited the Secretary-General to continue to solicit the views of Governments, United Nations bodies, specialized agencies, intergovernmental and non-governmental organizations and interested persons on the report of the independent expert and to submit a further report thereon, including the Secretary-General's own views on the legal, administrative and other implications of the report's recommendations, to the Commission on Human Rights at its fifty-sixth session. The General Assembly, in its resolution 53/138, also invited the Secretary-General to continue to solicit views on the report of the independent expert. The present report contains a summary of the comments and observations provided by those consulted pursuant to the above resolutions and relates additional views of the Secretary-General on the implications of the report's recommendations. The present report therefore updates the comments contained in documents E/CN.4/1998/85 and Add.1 and Corr.1 and should be read together with them.
4. Comments were received from the Governments of Cuba and New Zealand. Comments were also received from the Joint United Nations Programme on HIV/AIDS (UNAIDS) and the United Nations Educational, Scientific and Cultural Organization (UNESCO). Comments have been received from the following "interested person", in the meaning of Commission on Human Rights resolution 1998/27: Mr. Ion Diaconu, member of the Committee on the Elimination of Racial Discrimination. The full texts of these comments are available for consultation in the files of the Secretariat.

II. SUMMARY OF THE RECOMMENDATIONS OF INDEPENDENT EXPERT AND COMMENTS RECEIVED THEREON

A. Towards universal ratification

Recommendations of the independent expert

5. According to the independent expert, universal ratification of the six core United Nations human rights treaties would establish the best possible foundation for international endeavours to promote respect for human rights. In his final report, he made four specific recommendations: (a) consultations with the leading international agencies to explore their potential involvement in a ratification campaign; (b) appointment of special advisers on ratification and reporting and the earmarking of funds for those purposes; (c) examination of special measures to streamline the reporting process for States with small populations; and (d) granting particular attention to other substantial categories of non-parties (E/CN.4/1997/74, paras. 14, 31-35, 111).

Government comments

6. The Government of Cuba was of the view that efforts to achieve universal ratification of the human rights treaties should not be limited to the six that are referred to as the "principal" human rights treaties, in the view of the Government erroneously so. It expressed concern that the reorientation of technical cooperation programmes of the United Nations in the field of human rights towards promotion of ratification would mean a diversion of scarce funds away from the priorities established by the countries requesting assistance.

Comments by United Nations agencies and bodies

7. UNAIDS acknowledged the importance of respect for human rights in the context of its policy and programmes, as well as those of its co-sponsors. UNAIDS had long emphasized that the fulfilment of human rights, in addition to its own inherent value, was crucial to combating the spread of the virus and lessening the impact on those already infected. While welcoming the activities of one of its co-sponsors, UNICEF, in promoting the universal ratification of the Convention on the Rights of the Child, UNAIDS agreed that agencies should be further encouraged to promote ratification of the core treaties that have not yet been as widely ratified as that Convention. UNAIDS expressed support for the suggestion of the independent expert that the High Commissioner for Human Rights should consult with the agencies to ascertain what initiatives, if any, agencies were prepared to undertake in order to encourage States with which they were dealing to ratify the core treaties.

B. *The reporting process: the problem of significantly overdue reports, dealing with the timely submission of reports and consolidation of reports*

Recommendations of the independent expert

8. The independent expert pointed out that non-reporting had reached chronic proportions. He suggested that, in addition to considering reforms to the overall system, a new specially tailored project for the provision of advisory services should be designed and implemented. In responding to cases of

persistent delinquency, all treaty bodies should be urged to adopt procedures which would eventually lead to the examination of country situations even in the absence of a report. Such an approach should reflect thorough research and lead to detailed, accurate and comprehensive "concluding observations" (ibid., paras. 37–45, 47, 112).
9. The independent expert noted that the present reporting system functioned only because of the large-scale delinquency of States which either did not report at all, or reported long after the due date. If many were to report, significant existing backlogs would be exacerbated, and major reforms would be needed even more urgently (ibid., paras. 48–52).
10. The independent expert presented several options that were available to States to address the problems of the reporting system (ibid, para. 120 and para. 36 of the present report). Among the steps suggested towards far-reaching reform were the preparation of "consolidated reports" or the elimination of comprehensive periodic reports in their present form and replacement by reporting guidelines tailored to each State's individual situation.

Government comments
11. The Government of Cuba agreed that the present system was unsustainable. It stressed, however, that constructive, frank and transparent dialogue was the only way to guarantee the climate of cooperation necessary for the effective implementation of international treaties. The Government considered the practice of some treaty bodies of examining States parties' reports in the absence of representatives of the State concerned to violate basic norms of due process and turn the constructive dialogue into a punitive process. According to the Government, strengthening of the reporting process in a meaningful way could only be done through its rationalization and simplification.
12. The Government of Cuba considered that the main source of information to be considered by treaty bodies should be that provided by States parties, whether in their periodic reports or in the additional information often provided at the request of a treaty body. When committees made use of other sources of information, the Government believed that it should be, as a minimum, transmitted to the State party concerned. Transparency in the processing of information and the public scrutiny of such sources were of vital importance in preventing political manipulation of the activities of treaty bodies and in fostering a climate of cooperation and mutual confidence in relations with States parties. It called upon the treaty bodies to embark, with urgency, on the elaboration of clear guidelines concerning the admissibility of information provided by sources other than States parties.
13. The Government of Cuba agreed on the need to improve the methodology for the preparation of periodic reports by establishing as far as possible common guidelines among the various bodies and avoiding duplication on the matters on which States were required to report. The Government was opposed to the possibility that treaty bodies should elaborate selective criteria that differentiated among States parties when reports were requested from them. It also opposed the recommendation for consolidation of reports before the various treaty bodies, as the special competencies of each body in concrete areas of human rights would be lost.

Appendix 5: Long-Term Effectiveness of the UN Human Rights Treaty System 667

14. The Government of Cuba suggested that the average periodicity of reports due under the treaties of four years could be extended. That would not only alleviate the heavy burden facing States parties and treaty bodies today in preparing and examining reports, respectively, but would also allow more time in which the policies and programmes adopted upon recommendations of treaty bodies could bear fruit.
15. The Government of New Zealand identified overdue or non-reporting by States parties as a problem to be addressed as a matter of priority. It considered that the delays in the examination of reports by treaty bodies not only undermined the effectiveness of the reporting system, which relied on timely and regular consideration of reports and feedback to Governments, but also served as a disincentive to compliance with reporting deadlines. In some cases, especially in small and developing States, it believed the key difficulty in complying with reporting obligations was administrative incapacity. There was also concern that the reporting burden might act as a disincentive to ratification and was therefore a barrier to achieving universal ratification of the human rights treaties. The Government stressed that urgent steps needed to be taken to address the difficulties facing States in meeting their current reporting obligations, and to encourage non-reporting States to report. Procedural and substantive reforms to improve the effectiveness and efficiency of the treaty bodies, particularly those aimed at ensuring timely consideration of reports once submitted, would encourage compliance with reporting obligations and deadlines. The Government suggested that urgent attention be given to the following areas: reducing the reporting burden by streamlining periodic reporting requirements and reducing duplication; improving the working methods of the treaty bodies; and providing adequate resources and administrative support from the regular budget of the United Nations.
16. With respect to the first matter, the Government of New Zealand supported moves towards shorter and more focused reports concentrating on significant new developments, themes of interest and concerns identified by the treaty bodies. It also considered that harmonization of reporting dates and cycles could contribute to reducing duplication and facilitate presentation of the comprehensive situation. In addition, the Government encouraged adoption of the following additional steps: consistent application of a policy of examining the situation in non-reporting States parties in the absence of a report (as was the practice of the Committee on Economic, Social and Cultural Rights) and accommodation of consolidated reporting when more than one report was owed.
17. With respect to its suggestion for improvement of the working methods of the treaty bodies, the Government of New Zealand acknowledged the ongoing efforts of the treaty bodies to improve their working methods, including through delegation of work to pre-sessional working groups and refinement of rules of procedure, and recognized that there was little meeting time available for treaty bodies to deliberate on ways of improving working methods in addition to discharging their core functions. It nevertheless believed that the treaty bodies had a key role to play in identifying ways of overcoming the problems facing them and encouraged the chairpersons to take initiatives in producing coordinated plans for reform and improvements that could be speedily and uniformly implemented.

18. Finally, the Government of New Zealand highlighted the need for provision of adequate resources and administrative support to the treaty bodies to enable them to adequately discharge their functions. While it welcomed the increased allocation of funding to OHCHR, which serviced the Geneva-based treaty bodies, the Government stressed that the treaty bodies were at the centre of the United Nations human rights machinery and that the necessary additional resources should therefore be provided from the regular budget of the United Nations.
19. Other areas identified by the Government of New Zealand as requiring priority attention are dealt with elsewhere under the relevant sections of the present report.

Comments by United Nations agencies and bodies
20. UNAIDS agreed that large-scale non-reporting undermined the purpose of the reporting system. It thus supported the proposal that advisory assistance in the preparation of reports be provided to States parties. It also supported the approach, for States parties persistently failing to report, of treaty bodies determining, on a case-by-case basis, whether to proceed with the examination of the situation in those States in the absence of a report. Further, UNAIDS welcomed the suggestion to eliminate the requirement for comprehensive States parties' reports. To this end, it agreed that States parties should be requested to submit an initial comprehensive report but that subsequent reports could be specifically tailored in accordance with the particular situation in each country. In this way, the dialogue between treaty bodies and States parties could be focused on specific issues, such as HIV/AIDS, and the time required by States parties to prepare periodic reports could be reduced.

Comments by interested persons
21. Mr. Diaconu stated that the number of reports due under the treaties, as presented in table 1 of the report of the independent expert, misrepresented the reports due under the International Convention on the Elimination of All Forms of Racial Discrimination. Since several overdue reports could be combined in a single submission under this treaty, each State party would only need to submit a single report to be up to date. In effect, as there were approximately 100 States parties with reports overdue in 1998, the number of reports overdue should be counted at about 100. He further noted that the Committee on the Elimination of Racial Discrimination was managing to examine States parties' reports within one year of submission, on average.
22. Mr. Diaconu considered the proposal for consolidation of reports due under all treaties impractical. Such an approach would make the processes of preparation and examination of reports cumbersome for both States parties and treaty bodies. The specific, specialized focus of the dialogue that treaty bodies and States parties now engage in would also be diminished.
23. Mr. Diaconu suggested that one useful approach could be to generalize the practice of requesting from States parties updating reports in place of comprehensive reports. Exceptions to this practice would be initial and special reports. He favoured requesting reports that focused on issues determined by treaty bodies, which would limit themselves to problems specific to each

State party. Such issues could be those raised as concerns in concluding observations, or they could be specially formulated by treaty bodies.

C. *Problems in relation to documentation*

Recommendations of the independent expert

24. The independent expert suggested that the proposed limits on documentation were unworkable within the context of existing procedures. He expressed the view that the issue needed to be dealt with in a far more transparent manner than has so far been the case and full justification for any cuts needed to be provided. The Secretariat should draw up a detailed options paper to enable the committees to consider measured and innovative responses (ibid., paras. 53–54, 114).

25. In addition, the independent expert drew attention to the large volume of documentation furnished to treaty bodies that was not recorded officially and called for appropriate measures to be devised by the Secretariat. He considered the preparation of summary records to be an indispensable element in the system and recommended that their timely preparation should be accorded priority. The continued production of bound and edited volumes of Official Records of the Human Rights Committee (previously known as Yearbooks) was difficult to justify at a time of financial stringency. Priority should be accorded to transferring the existing data onto electronic databases and ensuring the timely publication, including in electronic form, of all summary records as soon as they are available (ibid., paras. 55, 58–59, 115).

26. No comments were received on this subject.

D. *Development and use of electronic databases*

Recommendations of the independent expert

27. The independent expert considered the new home page of the Office of the High Commissioner for Human Rights to be an unduly delayed but very welcome development. He recommended that it be maintained and expanded and that a strategy to widen access be devised. Future development of the database should reflect a more systematic, consultative and transparent process than had hitherto been the case. An expert seminar should be convened for that purpose and an external advisory group appointed. UNHCR and the ILO should consider making their valuable databases available on the Web to the human rights community and others (ibid., paras. 60–66, 116).

28. No comments were received on this subject.

E. *Public information*

Recommendations of the independent expert

29. The independent expert considered the public information materials relating to the work of the treaty bodies to be highly inadequate. He recommended that the treaty bodies should be given a direct input into future decision-making in this regard. He further recommended that a public information budget be made available to support grass-roots initiatives designed to disseminate information about the treaty bodies in culturally appropriate

and more popular formats and media. Partnerships with academic and other external institutions should be explored in order to enhance the publications programme. An external advisory group should be asked to review the human rights-related publications programme and make recommendations. The Secretary-General should report on the actual availability of treaty body-related materials at United Nations information centres (ibid., paras. 66–71, 117).

30. No comments were received on this subject.

F. *Advisory services*

Recommendations of the independent expert

31. The independent expert considered that the advisory services programme had not provided sufficient support for surveys required prior to ratification of a human rights treaty or for the preparation of reports by States in need of assistance. Regional and subregional training courses in relation to reporting were unlikely to produce results commensurate with their cost. He recommended that a specially designed programme be devised to address the needs in this area and that it be accorded priority (ibid., paras. 72–77, 118).

Comments by Governments

32. The Government of New Zealand agreed on the importance of providing technical assistance to States, especially small developing countries, in meeting their reporting requirements, both in respect of preparing and presenting reports. It believed that greater priority should be given to enhancing coordination of efforts to provide technical assistance to States in this area and encouraged greater information-sharing and cooperation among the various intergovernmental, governmental and non-governmental organizations involved in providing such assistance.

Comments by United Nations agencies and bodies

33. UNAIDS welcomed the independent expert's suggestion that advisory services or technical cooperation in the field of human rights could be provided to States that did not have the administrative capacity, technical expertise or financial resources required to prepare the reports. UNAIDS proposed that such courses be integrated into comprehensive technical cooperation projects and programmes at the national level. In this connection, UNAIDS and its co-sponsors, in collaboration with the Office of the High Commissioner for Human Rights, could explore possibilities of developing cooperative training and advisory activities in the field of HIV/AIDS-related human rights. Such cooperation would contribute to integrating HIV/AIDS in human rights programmes and vice versa. This in turn would reduce overlap of activities in the United Nations system and maximize available human and financial resources.

G. *Special reports*

Recommendations of the independent expert

34. The independent expert recommended that the effectiveness of "special reports" and "urgent procedures" should be carefully evaluated by the committees concerned. At present, the value they added seemed low. In general,

the division of labour between the treaty bodies and special mechanisms should be maintained (ibid., paras. 78–79, 119).

Comments by interested persons
35. Mr. Diaconu stated that while each treaty body should decide on its own procedure for requesting special reports, such a procedure should be used only in exceptional circumstances and in a way that did not duplicate the examination of periodic reports.

H. *Consolidation of treaty bodies*

Recommendations of the independent expert
36. The independent expert contended that in light of current trends the existing reporting system was unsustainable. He presented four options that were available to States: (a) to dismiss the concern as alarmist and take no action; (b) to urge the treaty bodies to undertake far-reaching reforms and adapt to cope with existing and new demands from within existing resources; (c) to provide greatly enhanced budgetary resources to sustain the status quo; (d) to combine some elements of (b) and (c) with the adoption of some far-reaching reforms. The latter could include: the preparation of "consolidated reports" (see section B of this report); elimination of comprehensive periodic reports in their present form and replacement by reporting guidelines tailored to each State's individual situation (see section B of this report); and a consolidation (reduction) of the number of treaty bodies. If the political will existed in relation to the last, a small expert group should be convened to examine modalities (ibid., paras. 81–97, 120).
37. No comments were received on this subject.

I. *Amending the treaties*

Recommendations of the independent expert
38. The independent expert suggested that it would be helpful for the procedural provisions of human rights treaties to be made more susceptible to amendment. A number of recommendations were suggested in his report on particular areas that could be simplified through amendment (ibid., para. 101).
39. No comments were received on this subject.

J. *The language question*

Recommendations of the independent expert
40. The independent expert considered that the importance of maintaining linguistic diversity in the treaty bodies was, for many reasons, beyond doubt. However, in the absence of a substantial increase in funds for interpretation, he believed there was a clear need for the different committees to explore ways in which working groups and other non-plenary meetings could be held without official translation. He suggested that greater emphasis should be attached to the ability of nominees for election to the treaty bodies to work in at least one, and preferably two, of the three major languages: English, French and Spanish. Ways would have to be found in which the

content of materials available in only one language could be drawn upon more efficiently for the benefit of the whole committee. Consideration would need to be given to delegating certain responsibilities to working groups capable of working without translation (ibid., para. 106).

Government comments
41. The Government of Cuba maintained that only through respect for diversity could universality be achieved. It held the view that linguistic plurality should therefore also be guaranteed, in all stages of the work of treaty bodies.

K. Cooperation with the specialized agencies and other bodies

Recommendations of the independent expert
42. The independent expert recommended that the Commission on Human Rights should request the High Commissioner to convene a high-level meeting over a period of two days of senior representatives of the key specialized agencies and other bodies (including ILO, WHO, FAO, UNESCO, UNICEF, UNHCR, UNDP, UNFPA and the World Bank), senior staff of the Office of the High Commissioner for Human Rights and the chairpersons of the six treaty bodies. In order to minimize costs and capitalize on other coordination efforts, the meeting should take place immediately before or after one of the annual meetings of the chairpersons. The purpose should be to explore the most constructive, appropriate, cost-effective, and mutually rewarding means of cooperation between these bodies and the human rights committees (ibid., para. 108).

Government comments
43. The Government of Cuba, while acknowledging that some treaties contain provisions establishing ties between the expert bodies monitoring their implementation and certain operational parts of the United Nations system working on questions of development, expressed the view that in the majority of treaties those ties were intended to limit the possibility that the agencies, funds and programmes of the United Nations would, at the request of the treaty bodies, present information on their activities. The Government considered it a concern for countries from the South that the nature of those ties could be altered.
44. In particular, the Government of Cuba drew attention to the possibility that the so-called "rights-based approach" might change the priorities of the agencies, funds and programmes to the detriment of the long-term structural needs of developing countries. Bearing in mind that the human rights treaties essentially address the relationship between the individual and the State, new demands would be placed upon Governments of countries from the South without any guarantee that additional financial resources would be mobilized for international efforts for their development needs, which was necessary for the full realization of the rights enunciated in the treaties. The Government further suggested that, as the activities of the agencies, funds and programmes were concentrated in developing countries, should there be established an efficient system for following up on the recommendations of the treaty bodies, the system should be established in such a way as to exert equal influence in countries of the North as on those of the South.

45. The Government of Cuba stated that the intention of conferring upon the concluding observations and recommendations of the treaty bodies a nature that served as valid directives for the activities of the agencies, funds and programmes in the field amounted in practice to questioning the authority of their intergovernmental governing bodies to direct those organizations. Finally, the Government stated that concluding observations of the treaty bodies held no automatic relevance for the work of other components of the United Nations system. For that, explicit endorsement from a resolution or decision of the General Assembly was necessary.

46. The Government of New Zealand considered the benefits of improved cooperation between the treaty bodies and other parts of the United Nations system to be entirely appropriate where different bodies were working towards the same objective, namely the promotion and protection of human rights as established by international law. Mechanisms for regular dialogue, both among treaty bodies and between them and other United Nations bodies, needed to be developed and sustained. In this regard, the Government of New Zealand attached importance to the useful role that the regular coordinating meetings of the chairpersons of human rights treaty bodies could play in promoting debate on ways in which the system could be improved.

Comments by United Nations agencies and bodies

47. UNAIDS endorsed the proposal that the High Commissioner convene high-level meetings of senior representatives of the key specialized agencies and other bodies, including UNAIDS and its co-sponsors, and the chairpersons of the six treaty bodies. Such meetings could prove useful in, *inter alia*, exploring possible cooperation between agencies and the treaty bodies as a means to streamline and enhance the work of the treaty bodies in this area. Furthermore, UNAIDS considered it particularly important that agencies and non-governmental organizations provide input to the pre-sessional working groups of the treaty bodies. Additional information could be presented in oral or written form on States parties' reports, thereby enhancing the focus on specific areas of concern, including on issues related to HIV/AIDS.

48. The United Nations Educational, Scientific and Cultural Organization (UNESCO) expressed support for the organization of a high-level meeting of senior representatives of the key specialized agencies and other bodies, including UNESCO, and senior staff of the Office of the High Commissioner for Human Rights, with a view to strengthening inter-agency cooperation in the field of human rights.

L. *The quality of concluding observations*

Recommendations of the independent expert

49. The independent expert recommended that treaty bodies should strive to further improve the quality of their concluding observations, in terms of their clarity, degree of detail, level of accuracy and specificity (ibid., paras. 109 and 122).

Comments by United Nations agencies and bodies
50. UNAIDS agreed that concluding observations needed to be more focused, specific and accurate. Such concluding observations would be invaluable in ensuring effective implementation of recommendations at national level and enhancing dialogue with States parties on issues such as HIV/AIDS.

M. *Other issues*

51. Several responses raised issues that were not the subject of recommendations in the final report of the independent expert. Those views are summarized in this section.

Government comments
52. With respect to the question of geographical distribution of membership in the treaty bodies, the Government of Cuba drew attention to the alarming over-representation of the Western and Other Group in most of the treaty bodies. It invited the States parties to the various international instruments, as well as all States Members of the United Nations, to consider measures to establish a system of quotas based on equitable geographical distribution of the membership, based on the geographical distribution of the States parties to the various treaties. The quotas established under such a system could be periodically reviewed to reflect any changes in the composition of States parties that may arise.

Comments by United Nations agencies and bodies
53. UNAIDS noted the importance of the general comments and recommendations made by treaty bodies, which served to interpret or elaborate further the various treaty provisions, provided guidance to States parties when reporting, summarized the current practices of the treaty bodies, and clarified language and definitions relating to the various rights. In this connection, UNAIDS suggested that treaty bodies be encouraged to undertake the elaboration and adoption of general comments or recommendations in relation to HIV/AIDS.
54. UNAIDS noted with satisfaction that a number of relevant general comments and recommendations had already been adopted by treaty bodies on such topics as the right to non-discrimination, the right to privacy, freedom of expression, freedom of movement, the right to education and the right to health. These all have a bearing on HIV/AIDS. It encouraged treaty bodies to adopt further general comments that may be useful in this regard, such as on the right to work, the right to enjoy the benefits of scientific progress, the right to liberty and security of person and the right to freedom of assembly and association, to assist States in clarifying major prevention and care issues relating to HIV/AIDS.
55. UNAIDS welcomed the initiative of the Committee on the Rights of the Child of holding a day of general discussion on "Children and young people living in a world with HIV/AIDS". This day of general discussion, held on 5 October 1998, contributed to raising awareness of issues pertaining to children infected by, affected by and vulnerable to HIV/AIDS, and led to the adoption of recommendations by the Committee on the Rights of the Child on ways in which States can better report on this issue and further

integrate HIV/AIDS-related strategies into their national policies and programmes. UNAIDS encouraged other treaty bodies to engage in similar discussions on HIV/AIDS-related rights in order to promote understanding of their content and implications.

Comments by interested persons

56. Mr. Diaconu suggested several improvements in relation to the examination of States parties' reports that could be undertaken immediately. First, all treaty bodies could improve their methods of work, reduce repetition and make better use of available meeting time. Second, the conclusions and recommendations could be prepared in a more succinct manner, while maintaining expressions of concern where appropriate and relevant recommendations thereon. More numerous and better prepared staff in the secretariat could assist the treaty bodies to better fulfil their responsibilities. A non-governmental organization could be entrusted with collecting and presenting the necessary information to members of treaty bodies in an impartial manner. Mr. Diaconu considered that it would be difficult to accept that the secretariat be entrusted with the task of preliminary examination of reports, or that the role of experts and the dialogue with States parties be limited to a written procedure, at the risk of losing the most valuable tool at the disposal of the treaty bodies today, namely direct and effective dialogue.

III. OBSERVATIONS

57. The achievement of universal ratification of the main international human rights treaties remains a top priority of the United Nations. The High Commissioner for Human Rights is committed to achieving universal ratification by 2003 and, in collaboration with the Secretary-General, has periodically appealed to States to ratify those treaties to which they are not already a party.

58. The question of ratification has received high priority in discussions undertaken between the Office of the High Commissioner for Human Rights and its key partner agencies and departments in the United Nations system. A noteworthy example was the memorandum of understanding concluded in 1997 between the Office and the United Nations Development Programme (UNDP), in which the promotion of ratification of the human rights treaties featured prominently as a common objective. A programme entitled "Human Rights Strengthening" (or "HURIST") has been developed jointly by the Office and UNDP to make available practical tools for the implementation of the memorandum of understanding during the period 1999–2001. Through "window 3" of HURIST, a series of workshops is foreseen, to be held at the regional, subregional or national level with the participation of representatives of States that are not parties to most of the principal treaties. The workshops would aim at enabling in-depth discussion among participants on the obstacles to ratification and formulation of concrete strategies to overcome them, in keeping with the request of the 1993 World Conference

on Human Rights[1] for the Secretary-General to initiate a dialogue with non-States parties.
59. In addition, the High Commissioner for Human Rights has been working to elaborate a regional strategy for each major geographic region. One of the main elements of such a strategy is the nomination of regional advisers. Justice P.N. Bhagwati is assisting as regional adviser to the High Commissioner for Asia and the Pacific. Among the principal responsibilities of the regional advisers is to engage in a high-level policy dialogue with senior officials of countries in the region on all areas relating to human rights, including the question of ratification of the human rights instruments.
60. The situation with respect to overdue reports has remained a serious issue. In the most extreme case, over 40 per cent of the States parties to the International Covenant on Economic, Social and Cultural Rights have failed to submit even their initial reports. The existence of a large number of States that do not comply with their reporting obligations detracts significantly from the capacity of the treaty-monitoring system to serve its intended purpose.
61. While no clear consensus has yet been reached on the desirability of consolidating reports due under the various treaties, a number of treaty bodies have moved towards a more focused examination of States parties' reports. This is most apparent in the lists of issues or questions formulated by most treaty bodies requesting clarification on specific parts of States parties' reports or on specific rights. Practical difficulties, however, remain in reducing the reporting burden on States parties at the point where it would be most useful, namely *before* the preparation of their reports. There is, therefore, a need for further reflection on ways to streamline the reporting process.
62. To make the requirements of the reporting process as clear as possible, the secretariat has, at the request of various bodies, begun to produce several compilations of basic information from the treaty bodies of relevance to that process. Pursuant to General Assembly resolution 53/138, a compilation of reporting guidelines of the six human rights treaty bodies is being prepared and is to be issued by the time of the fifty-sixth session of the Commission as document HRI/GEN/2. The compilation of general comments has been updated and will soon be issued as document HRI/GEN/1/Rev.4. In accordance with a request emanating from the 11th meeting of chairpersons of the human rights treaty bodies, a new document outlining the recent reporting history of all States parties to all the treaties is to be prepared annually that would list the last periodic report submitted under each treaty and either the next report due or, if the State party was not up to date with its obligations, any outstanding periodic reports. These documents should clarify the situation of all States parties with respect to the reports due from them under the treaties, not only for States parties but also for the interested public. In addition, a compilation of the rules of procedures of all the treaty bodies is also being prepared.
63. These documents will soon be accessible to the general public through the United Nations Human Rights Website (www.unhchr.ch), as are a large

---

[1] Vienna Declaration and Programme of Action (A/CONF.153/24) (Part I), chap. III, sect. II.A, para. 4.

number of documents issued by and submitted to the treaty bodies. Considerable progress has been made in recent years in relation to the Website and the treaty bodies database which is linked to the Website. Information on that subject is contained in the report of the Secretary-General to the fifty-sixth session of the Commission on the implementation of resolution 1998/27 of the Commission (E/CN.4/2000/106).

64. Concerning the advisory services provided by the United Nations, training programmes on the preparation of States parties' reports to treaty bodies are aimed at imparting skills and insights helpful to fulfilling their reporting obligations. Countries sending participants are encouraged to provide the necessary opportunities for their representatives to train colleagues working in areas of relevance to the reporting process upon their return from such programmes. In addition, a number of training workshops and programmes on reporting have been or are being undertaken at the national level within the framework of the technical cooperation programme of the United Nations in the field of human rights and the Plan of Action to strengthen implementation of the Convention on the Rights of the Child. While the main purpose of such workshops is training the relevant domestic audience, including representatives of all ministries and agencies that would eventually be involved in the reporting process, they also have a secondary effect of already contributing to the formation of a domestic network for the preparation of reports. For the countries that participated in such training workshops, the "concentrated assistance" recommended by the independent expert has proven to be quite beneficial. Details on those projects is contained in document E/CN.4/2000/105.

65. Finally, most treaty bodies are seeking to strengthen their cooperation with their partners in the United Nations system. In addition to the already close cooperation between the Committee on the Rights of the Child and the United Nations Children's Fund, strong progress has been made recently between the Committee on Economic, Social and Cultural Rights and UNDP. A number of other specialized agencies also contribute regularly or occasionally to the work of the treaty bodies on specific matters of direct relevance to their own work. The chairpersons of treaty bodies have regularly discussed with representatives of United Nations departments, bodies and specialized agencies the state of cooperation between them and the treaty bodies at their annual meetings. The meetings of chairpersons could be used as the forum for the type of discussions recommended by the independent expert.

Appendix 6: International Law Association Report on the Treaty System

Reproduced below is the First Report of the International Law Association's Committee on International Human Rights Law and Practice, submitted to the Helsinki Conference, 11-17 August 1996. The Committee was established after the Buenos Aires Conference to replace the former Committee on the Enforcement of Human Rights Law.[1] The study was prepared by the Committee's Canadian member, Professor Anne F. Bayefsky, York University, Canada.

INTERNATIONAL LAW ASSOCIATION

HELSINKI CONFERENCE (1996)

COMMITTEE ON INTERNATIONAL HUMAN RIGHTS LAW AND PRACTICE

REPORT ON THE UN HUMAN RIGHTS TREATIES: FACING THE IMPLEMENTATION CRISIS

INTRODUCTION

The United Nations inspires the hope of so many of the world's downtrodden. Every year thousands of individuals and groups appeal to UN bodies for help. On their behalf a myriad of non-governmental organizations attempt to place their cases on the international agenda. When national institutions fail, when governments are unresponsive, millions of the tortured, the repressed, the hungry, turn to the UN.

In response to those pleas, and in the knowledge that the protection of human rights can fare poorly in political fora where improvement of the human condition is not the primary aim, there has been a 50 year effort at the UN to set universal legal standards. At the center of this endeavor stands the system of human rights treaties, legally-binding norms which attach to all ratifying states. The treaties have now been ratified by a large proportion of the UN community. To a large extent the standards are in place, broad legal responsibility is assured.

The spectre of the needy however, has not faded away. Their voices make clear that somewhere along the path the international legal response to the protection of human rights has lost its way. Half a century after the project of

---

[1] *Members of the Committee:* Professor Richard B. Lillich (USA) *Chairman*, Professor Yuji Iwasawa (Japan) *Rapporteur*, Professor Anne Bayefsky (Canada), Mr. Percy Bratt (Sweden), Mr. Andrew Byrnes (HQ/Hong Kong), Professor Thomas M. Franck (USA), *Alternate:* Professor Hurst Hannum, Chief Justice A.R. Gubbay (HQ/Zimbabwe), Mr. Christof Heyns (South Africa), *Alternate:* Professor John Dugard, Professor Menno Kamminga (Netherlands), Professor Eckart Klein (Germany), *Alternate:* Professor Matthias Herdegen, Justice Dennis Mahoney (Australia/New Zealand), *Alternate:* Dr. Keith Suter, Dr. Ernest Petric (Slovenia), Chief Justice Sajjad Ali Shah (Pakistan).

developing and adopting human rights treaties began, the ultimate goal of alleviating human suffering remains elusive. What happened? What distances the legal undertaking from its objectives?

The international lawyer does not operate in a vacuum. Norms are not intended to be drafted for their own sake. Ratification of human rights treaties was not meant to be an end in itself. Yet the record reveals a serious rift between standard-setting and implementation.

Conceptual agreement has been reached on the interdependence of peace and security and the adequate protection of human rights. The dividends in terms of increased enforcement of human rights standards, however, have not been realized. This report seeks to identify the major deficiencies of the human rights treaty system and to identify detailed recommendations for improving implementation.

THE HUMAN RIGHTS TREATY SYSTEM

At the heart of the UN's legal system for the protection of human rights lie the six major human rights treaties, adopted between 1965 and 1989. The treaty system, of course, is optional. Obligations are dependent upon ratification. Nevertheless, today participation in the treaty system is extensive. More than three-quarters of the world's states have ratified five of the treaties, while 50 percent have ratified a sixth.[2]

The treaties relate to a broad range of human rights concerns: racial discrimination, economic, social and cultural rights, civil and political rights, discrimination against women, torture, and children.

Implementation is monitored by six treaty bodies or committees. These monitoring bodies have been in operation for between five and 25 years. During that time they have met for between 25 and 160 weeks. They have considered between 40 and 675 state reports.[3]

In light of the broad participation in the treaty system and the considerable length of time in which the monitoring bodies have operated, an assessment of the efficacy of the regime now can be based on a significant degree of experience.

Successful implementation depends both on the substantive or normative quality of the rules, and on their accompanying procedural or enforcement methodologies.

On a substantive level, the treaties themselves embody certain concepts which diminish the capacity for effective implementation. In particular, the Cold War context of the drafting exercise had a number of negative consequences for the content of the treaties. To make ratification more palatable they contain broad limitation clauses, by which rights and freedoms can be avoided on the basis of public order, morality and health, and national security. In the past these clauses frequently were invoked by states parties in defense of their policies and practices. The limitation clauses still are summoned occasionally. For example, in July of 1993 Iran appeared before the Human Rights Committee, a body which monitors the Covenant on Civil and Political Rights.

---

[2] The Torture Convention has the lowest number of ratifications.
[3] These statistics are based on the 1995 annual reports to the UN General Assembly, and in the case of the Committee on the Rights of the Child, the ninth session in June 1995.

The Iranian representative stated:

> With reference to the freedoms of opinion and expression ... Iran conformed strictly to the Covenant, whereby the exercise of those freedoms was subject to certain restrictions necessary "for respect of the rights or reputations of others" and "for the protection of national security or of public order ... or of public health or morals". ... The Islamic decrees thus imposed restrictions on the exercise of those freedoms only in the interests of maintaining social cohesion.[4]

This statement notwithstanding, the monitoring bodies now question and criticize directly such spurious references to the limitation provisions.[5]

More importantly, on a procedural level the enforcement regime associated with the treaties is seriously flawed. It operates in the following way. States parties are required to produce reports on how their laws and practices adhere to the terms of the treaty. These reports are written for each treaty generally every four to five years. Once produced, state representatives appear before the respective treaty body and answer questions concerning the report. These question and answer sessions are public. Upon conclusion of the so-called "constructive dialogue," the treaty body formulates and releases concluding observations on the report and the state's record of compliance with the treaty obligations.

The success of the scheme depends on many factors, in particular: the extent to which states comply with their reporting obligations and submit reports; the amount of time the treaty bodies have to question state representatives; the amount of independent information on a state's human rights record available to the treaty body members; the accessibility of many aspects of the process to non-governmental organizations (NGOs) and individuals; the drafting of state reports, the dialogue, information flow to the treaty bodies; the ability of treaty bodies to follow-up inadequate reports or oral replies; the quality of the treaty body's concluding observations; the extent to which the questioning and conclusions of the treaty bodies is followed by the media.

On each of these different points, the system falters. Forty-five to 80 percent of states parties to the six treaties have overdue reports. About half of this number are initial reports. Eighty-one states, or an average of 60 percent of states parties to all the treaties, have five or more overdue reports. In fact, the system relies on this degree of non-compliance. On the basis of the meeting time currently allotted to the treaty bodies, if all the overdue reports actually were submitted it would take the treaty bodies an average of eight years just to expunge the backlog.

The treaty bodies meet for varying lengths of time annually, from two weeks for the Women's Discrimination Convention to nine weeks for the Human Rights Committee and the Child Committee. Within that time frame, the treaty bodies spend between three hours to ten and a half hours on each state report. The shortest period relates to the Racial Discrimination Committee and the Women's

---

[4] CCPR/C/SR.1252, para. 45.
[5] With respect to the response to these remarks of the representative of Iran and the comments of the Human Rights Committee, see A/48/40 (Part I), Report of the Human Rights Committee, para. 262.

Discrimination Committee, and the longest to the Human Rights Committee.[6] These few hours are only repeated generally once every four to five years. In that space of time, a country presents its report; questions are put by ten to 23 treaty body members (depending upon the Committee); the state responds; there are sometimes follow-up questions and subsequent responses; and final comments are made by the treaty body members. Obviously, the ability to have a frank discussion, or at least one in which the treaty body members are able to expose the shortfalls in a state's record, is severely limited by the restrictions on meeting time. The treaty body members are not full-time. Beyond expenses during meetings, they receive only a small honorarium and no other support. The treaty bodies are serviced by a permanent UN secretariat, which involves only the equivalent of one full-time professional per committee. Information relating to human rights from a multitude of sources is not organized in the UN on a state-by-state basis. For all these reasons, it is difficult for the UN staff or treaty body members themselves to gather comprehensive, reliable material relating to all the states parties. To a considerable extent the treaty bodies rely on information provided by NGOs. In the early years, many Eastern-bloc treaty body members impeded the use of information from non-UN sources. Although such interference still occurs, in general the information is welcomed and used.

The flow of information, however, depends on the access which NGOs have to the process. The treaty bodies mainly meet in Geneva and occasionally in New York. Their schedules of country reports, the actual dates at which they will be considered, usually are not known well in advance. The UN and the treaty body members generally do not take it upon themselves to inform NGOs of the forthcoming meeting times. Neither do most states parties. Public access to UN premises is difficult. Even obtaining a country's report, or the subsequent concluding comments on a state, is frequently arduous.

At the same time, in the case of the Child Committee and the Women's Discrimination Committee, NGOs have taken it upon themselves to institute an NGO coordinator or create a focal point for NGO submissions, and they make contact with those persons having information on forthcoming reports. International NGOs also are familiar with the UN and the processes, and are able to interact with the treaty bodies. Furthermore, two of the treaty bodies specifically have set aside meeting times in order to have an oral exchange with NGOs about the human rights conditions in states which they are due to consider.

The "constructive dialogue" between representatives of the state party and the treaty body members frequently amounts to a series of unclear, incomplete, misleading, or dishonest representations, on the one hand, and a series of polite, but skeptical responses, on the other hand.

For example, state parties appearing before the various treaty bodies have made some of the following statements. The representative of Tunisia told the Human Rights Committee:

> With regard to freedom of the press ... [w]hile it was true that two French newspapers, *Le Monde* and *Libération*, were still banned, that was because

---

[6]Three hours is the time the Women's Discrimination Committee spends on subsequent, periodic reports. It spends approximately five hours on initial reports.

both had published articles disparaging Tunisia and had denied the authorities the possibility of publishing a rejoinder in their pages.[7]

The Algerian representative told the Economic, Social and Cultural Rights Committee that:

> "The only requirement for setting up an NGO was to apply for registration,"[8]" ... the State strongly encouraged NGOs, which could operate in total freedom."[9]

The Mexican representative told the Racial Discrimination Committee:

> In Mexico the indigenous population ... was not regarded as a minority that was in some way excluded from society. Most Mexicans were of mixed race and the indigenous population formed the whole basis and essence of the nation.[10]

The Nigerian representative told the Racial Discrimination Committee in August 1995:

> Nigeria was participating in the worldwide process of political democratization and economic liberalization and would continue to promote the principles of the dignity and equality of all human beings.[11]

At the same time, there are sometimes some candid admissions by states about human rights deficiencies. For example, before the Child Committee the Jamaican representative said:

> Jamaica was an unusually violent society, in which guns were a common means of coping with conflict.[12]

Senegal told the same Committee:

> While investigations to determine a mother's identity were legal, similar efforts to establish paternity were prohibited ... A child born out of wedlock received only half of the inheritance entitlements of a legitimate child. That, of course, was a form of discrimination.[13]

In many instances, state party representatives are not prepared to answer the questions posed. For example, during the report of Pakistan to the Child Committee, the Pakistan representative said:

> [T]he delegation ... could not respond to the majority of specific points raised some of which, in any event, needed replies from a more qualified source.[14]

The treaty bodies generally recognize the inadequacies. In a typical remark, for example, one member of the Human Rights Committee told the representative

---

[7] CCPR/C/SR.1361. para. 18, Summary Record of discussion of 18 Oct. 1994.
[8] E/C.12/1995/SR46. para. 33, Summary Record of discussion of 30 Nov. 1995.
[9] E/C.12/1995/SR48. para. 83, Summary Record of discussion of 1 Dec. 1995.
[10] CERD/C/SR.1105. para. 30, Summary Record of discussion of 3 Aug. 1995.
[11] CERD/C/SR.1116. para. 22, Summary Record of discussion of 11 Aug. 1995.
[12] CRC/C/SR. 197, para 93, Summary Record of discussion of 18 Jan. 1995.
[13] CRC/C/SR. 248, para 66, Summary Record of discussion of 9 Nov. 1995.
[14] CRC/C/SR.132, para. 31, Summary Record of discussion held 5 Apr. 1994.

of Togo bluntly that "he considered the report a bad one"[15] A member of the Human Rights Committee told the Libyan representative:

> [N]o one could reasonably harbour any illusions about the degree to which Libyan citizens in reality enjoyed the basic rights guaranteed under the Covenant, many articles of which appeared to be routinely violated.[16]

Having recognized the inadequacies of reports and oral replies, however, the important issue becomes what the treaty bodies then do. They have a wide range of responses to these shortfalls. Usually, they simply ask the state party to include responses to their queries in the next report., normally years hence. Sometimes they ask for the information to be submitted in writing prior to the consideration of the next report. Very infrequently, they set deadlines for the receipt of written responses and follow-up non-compliance. Even more rarely do they insist that a state representative return to answer queries on new information received. Normally, the information is used in the course of considering the next report. While the whole process of follow-up to inadequate reports or inadequate oral responses is evolving, and is handled differently by each committee,[17] in general it is a fundamental failing of the entire system. The treaty bodies do not have the practical capacity in terms of resources, staff or meeting time, to insist on answers and to follow through on their requests. The basic plan of state reports and evaluations for a few hours every four or five years remains the vehicle of implementation.

The final evaluation of the state's compliance with the treaty, issued as "concluding observations," is published in reports of the treaty bodies. These evaluations are of widely varying quality. Three of the treaty bodies issue concluding observations on states of between one to two pages in length and containing only a handful of specific recommendations for changes to laws or practices. On the other hand, the other treaty bodies issue longer concluding observations, and two of them routinely specify for each state at least 20 laws or practices which should be addressed. Brief, general conclusions are of very little value either to states or human rights advocates interested in reform.

The impact of forceful and detailed concluding observations will depend, however, on public interest in these conclusions and the extent of media attention. Yet another major shortcoming of the system is the fact that there generally is very little interest in the work of the treaty bodies. Attendance

---

[15] CCPR/C/SR.1325, para. 34, Summary Record of discussion of 7 July 1994.

[16] CCPR/C/SR.1377, para. 72, Summary Record of discussion of 28 Oct. 1994. The Libyan representative had told the Human Rights Committee:

[A]rticle 13 of the Constitutional Declaration guaranteed freedom of opinion within the limits of public interest and the principles of the Revolution. Article 8 of the Promotion of Freedom Act also guaranteed freedom of expression. However, publication of any opinion incompatible with the interests of society was prohibited. (CCPR/C/SR.1377, para. 21. Summary Record of discussion of 28 Oct. 1994).

He also said:

"All citizens were equal before the law and social harmony reigned." (CCPR/C/SR.1377, para. 25, Summary Record of discussion of 28 Oct. 1994), and "Libya fully respected the rights of minorities, but it had none of its own." (CCPR/C/SR.1377, para. 55, Summary Record of discussion of 28 Oct. 1994).

[17] The Committee on the Rights of the Child is much more advanced than the other committees in this regard, even publishing a separate document on "follow-up" of special requests for additional information and responses. See CRC/C/27 Rev.3 (1 Aug. 1995).

during the state reporting exercise is sparse. While dozens of people may attend the reports of the United States, the United Kingdom or Japan, there is often a sole representative of Amnesty International or one or two other persons from international NGOs watching the reports of developing countries. The treaty bodies make virtually no attempt to develop media links. Media coverage is almost entirely the work of the in-house UN press office. It issues routine, mundane press releases which are ignored.Even though, for example, the United States presented its first report to the Human Rights Committee in New York (in March 1995), there was no mention of the Committee's questioning or conclusions in the New York press. Media coverage is extremely important because states often do not distribute disparaging concluding observations to their nationals. Non-governmental women's groups in Japan, for example, obtained the January 1995 concluding observations of the Women's Discrimination Committee from outside the country and then translated it themselves.[18] The Columbian reports to the Human Rights Committee never have been circulated inside the country.

The process of state reporting does not end there. The concluding observations of the treaty bodies are sent to the UN General Assembly. They identify the states which do not meet their substantive treaty obligations. The annual reports also name states which fail to submit reports. In addition, the chairs of all the treaty bodies meet annually and adopt recommendations which are forwarded to the General Assembly. This same material also goes to the UN Commission on Human Rights or the Commission on the Status of Women. Through these vehicles, the treaty bodies request, for example, more meeting time, more staff, better documentation. The treaty body routinely appeal to the frequent ad-hoc meetings of all the states parties to each treaty, and ask them to take up issues like the large number of overdue reports.

The response is minimalist at best. The meetings of states parties simply refuse to deal with substantive issues. They will not take up questions like overdue reports since so many of them are culpable. They recently have refused to increase the Women's Discrimination Committee's grossly inadequate meeting time.[19] The primary response of the General Assembly and the Commission on Human Rights is a resolution, adopted annually, on "Effective Implementation of International Instruments on Human Rights." This resolution is carried by consensus but at the price of accepting a very limited text. At the Commission on Human Rights session in March 1995, for example, India insisted on the deletion of a paragraph which would have endorsed the following recommendation of the meetings of treaty body chairpersons to:

> identify common obstacles to the implementation of the human rights treaties, develop strategies aimed at achieving progress in the application

---

[18] Information from the Yokohama Women's Association for Communication & Networking.
[19] A state party meeting in May 1995 refused the direct request to increase the meeting time to six weeks annually, or a general recommendation to allow increases as necessary. Instead it adopted a formula which stymied the increase in the immediate future (and left the Women's Discrimination Committee with no increase in 1996) by making it subject to future determinations, and additional meetings of states parties.

of the treaties, and, in particular, exchange views on guidelines for monitoring more effectively the rights of women.[20]

The result is a weak resolution, which at the 1995 General Assembly "urges States parties to make every effort to meet their reporting obligations,"[21] concentrates on reducing the burden upon states faced with producing multiple reports to different treaty bodies, and emphasizes technical assistance. Technical assistance is supposed to help, for instance, states which are apparently "unable to comply with the requirements to submit their initial report."[22]

In sum, the system of implementation of human rights treaties through voluntary state reports on compliance, followed by questioning of state representatives by an independent body of experts, is riddled with major deficiencies.

However, state reports are not the only vehicle for enforcing the human rights treaties. The right of individual petition is an optional feature of the Civil and Political Covenant, the Racial Discrimination and the Torture Convention. Where states accept these optional provisions, individual victims of violations of these treaties can complain to the treaty bodies.

It might be thought that, in contrast to the reluctance of states to admit human rights violations and encourage a thorough analysis by the treaty bodies, individual victims would force breaches more vigorously onto the public stage. The results to date, though, have been disappointing. Firstly, many states that ratify the treaties refuse to permit individual complaints. The number of states parties to the respective treaties that do not allow such complaints are 35 percent in the case of the Civil and Political Covenant, 85 percent in the case of the Racial Discrimination Convention, and 60 percent in the case of the Torture Convention.[23]

Secondly, the potential to lodge complaints is seriously underutilized. The Racial Discrimination Committee has decided the merits of only four cases, with a further two pending.[24] The Torture Committee has made four decisions on the merits, found another 18 to be inadmissible and have only an additional 12 active cases.[25] With respect to the most widely used mechanism, the Optional Protocol to the Civil and Political Covenant, an average of 44 cases per year have been registered since 1990 from states having a combined population of over one billion people. This number has remained fairly constant.[26] Forty-three percent of states parties to the Protocol have never been the subject of a single communication, including states like Angola and Chad.

The reason for the failure to lodge complaints is not that the success rate is discouragingly low. In fact, roughly 50 percent of cases submitted to the Human

---

[20] See the draft resolution E/CN.4/1995/L.28, operative paragraph 17 (21 Feb. 1995); India's draft amendment E/CN.4/1995/L.119, point 14 proposing to delete paragraph 17; and the resolution as adopted, which omits the proposed paragraph. Commission on Human Rights Res. 1995/92, adopted 8 Mar. 1995, E/1995/23.
[21] A/50/635/Add.I. Report of the Third Committee, Draft Resolution II, para. 11.
[22] A/50/635/Add.1. Report of the Third Committee, Draft Resolution II, para.12.
[23] These statistics are from Dec. 1, 1995.
[24] Statistics are from Nov. 16, 1995.
[25] Statistics date from Dec. 13, 1995.
[26] In 1995 the Committee registered 49 cases. In 1994 the Committee registered 35 cases. In 1993 the Committee registered 37 cases. In 1992 the Committee registered 46 cases. In 1991 the Committee registered 50 cases. In 1990 the Committee registered 47 cases.

Rights Committee are admissible, and of that number 75 percent have revealed violations of the Covenant. Clearly the process remains largely inaccessible; victims are ignorant of the possibility of lodging a complaint or they are reluctant to come forward.

Thirdly, considering the primary procedure of the Optional Protocol, the process has been of little assistance in the context of the human rights problems of Western democratic states. Forty percent of the caseload of the Human Rights Committee has come from states within one of the five UN regional groups that is known as the Western European and Other groups. Yet, only 12 percent of violations of the Covenant come from these states. The Committee has not handled more subtle human rights issues, such as those raising questions of discriminatory benefits from facially neutral rules, as well as it has gross violations of human rights, like infringements of the right to life.

The processes associated with the Optional Protocol's complaint mechanism are not conducive to improving this situation. There are no oral hearings. All exchanges are conducted in writing. The Committee spends much of its time on state reports and has resisted recent attempts to focus its energies on individual complaints.[27] There is also sufficient divergence of opinion among the 18 members of the Committee to impede development of a common and sophisticated jurisprudence.

For the remaining three human rights treaties the potential of lodging a complaint does not exist. Drafting of a right of petition has begun in the case of the Covenant on Economic, Social and Cultural Rights, and the Women's Discrimination Convention.[28] However, these developments remain at a preliminary state and adoption is many years away. The idea that individuals should be able to complain of violations of economic, social and cultural rights is contested by many states. The idea of lodging complaints of violations of the Women's Discrimination Convention is met by general, widespread reluctance to bolster any implementation mechanism associated with this treaty.

IDENTIFYING REMEDIES

The implementation crisis facing the principle UN human rights legal standards is now of dangerous proportions. For a great many states ratification has become an end in itself, a means to easy accolades for empty gestures.

The problem has arisen in part because of a deliberate emphasis on ratification. The primary goal of the UN community has been to achieve universal ratification of the human rights treaties. The underlying belief is that once universal ratification is realized, the implementation techniques can be strengthened. Once committed to participation, states will find it difficult to pull out and will find themselves ensnared in an ever-expanding network of international supervision and accountability.

In the meantime, ratification by human rights adversaries is purchased at a

---

[27] CCPR/C/SR.1458, suggestion is at para. 1, Summary Record of discussion of 24 Oct. 1995.
[28] The issue is currently before the Economic Rights Committee, which is formulating a draft instrument. In the case of the Women's Convention, the issue is before a working group of the Commission on the Status of Women which has been instructed to draft such an instrument.

price, namely, diminished obligations, lax supervision, and few adverse consequences from non-compliance. The cost of membership has been deliberately minimized. One significant example of this phenomenon is the acceptance into the treaty regime of states that ratify only with broad reservations. These reservations purport to limit the obligations assumed. For example, many Islamic and Asian states only ratify the treaties with the caveat that any obligation sustained must first be compatible with Islamic law or a similar broad reservation.[29] Such reservations are inconsistent with international law which requires reservations to conform to the object and purpose of the treaty, and in the case of human rights treaties means identifying and applying overriding, universal standards. Nevertheless, few states are prepared to challenge other states on the legitimacy of their reservations, and some important states like the United States and the United Kingdom currently are resisting attempts by the treaty bodies themselves to challenge reservations.[30]

The treaty regime has been depreciated by chronic levels of non-compliance, both with the substantive terms of the treaties, and with existing enforcement mechanisms. Stronger implementation machinery would mean, for example, expanding rights and procedures of individual petition, and adequate funding to allow greater familiarity with country situations, better investigation, and missions to states parties. Clearly such fortifications to the implementation machinery will be met with significant resistance. In itemizing the following specific recommendations, the report therefore has focused on various improvements which the treaty bodies themselves can make without seeking state approval. It also includes other proposals which are intended to be forward-looking strategies, and which would require somewhat of a revolution in political will.

RECOMMENDATIONS

STATE REPORTING PROCEDURE

(i) *Producing State Reports*

The treaty bodies should support involvement of NGOs in the process of preparing the report. Treaty bodies should ask questions about NGO involvement. Treaty bodies should recommend that governments create a permanent mechanism to monitor implementation of the Convention, and that monitoring involve the cooperation of non-governmental organizations.

(a) *Failure to Report*

The treaty bodies should publish a separate document on overdue reports. It should highlight state-by-state the worst transgressors. It should be sent to meetings of state parties with requests for action. It should be sent to all other

---

[29] Indonesia's reservation to the Convention on the Rights of the Child says: "The ratification of the Convention ... does not imply the acceptance of ... any obligation to produce any right beyond those prescribed under the Constitution." The Malaysian reservation to the Child Convention says: "The Government of Malaysia accepts the provisions of the Convention on the Rights of the Child but expresses reservations with respect to Article 1, 2, 7, 13, 14, 15, 22, 28, 37, 40 para. 3 and 4, 44 and 45 of the Convention and declares that the said provisions shall be applicable only if they are in conformity with the Constitution, national laws and national policies of the Government of Malaysia."

[30] See 1995 annual report of the Human Rights Committee, A/50/40, at 131–39.

human rights mechanisms, such as the special rapporteurs and the High Commissioner for Human Rights, who should be asked to raise the subject at contacts with state representatives or while on country visits.

The treaty bodies should not agree to combine overdue reports in a single document. Receipt of the first overdue report may give rise to a rescheduling of the due dates for subsequent reports.

(b) *Quality of Reports*
The treaty bodies should request states parties to redo significantly unsatisfactory reports in accordance with treaty body guidelines prior to examination.

The treaty bodies should ask states to quote directly in their reports from important national laws to which they refer.

The General Assembly should provide the treaty bodies with enough time and resources to ensure that reports are taken up soon after they are submitted. A large backlog of submitted reports is unacceptable.

(i) *Examining State Reports*

(a) *Caliber of State Representatives appearing before the Treaty Bodies*
The treaty bodies should set guidelines that indicate the qualities or expertise of state representatives that will be most useful for the dialogue.

(b) *Quality of the Dialogue*
The treaty bodies should insist that states parties adhere to their undertakings made during the dialogue to provide answers in writing at a later date.

The treaty bodies should be encouraged to offer direct and forceful criticism of the accuracy of state reports.

The treaty bodies should support and encourage governments that submit honest analyses of their countries' situations.

The treaty bodies should give states written questions several months in advance of the dialogue and request written answers in advance of the dialogue.

The treaty bodies should conduct the examination of state reports, and the adoption and release of concluding observations, in the state concerned, or at least in the region.

(c) *Quality of the Members of the Treaty Bodies: Political Independence*
States parties should not nominate individuals to the treaty bodies who are not wholly independent of the government. Guidelines should be formulated by the Center for Human Rights, or the High Commissioner for Human Rights, that indicate that individuals nominated should not be government employees, and should meet criteria such as the ones set out in the Covenant on Civil and Political Rights, namely, of high moral character, recognized competence in the field of human rights, and preferably (particularly where rights of individual petition exists) having legal experience. States parties should insist that these guidelines be followed when elections to the treaty bodies are held.

(d) *Time Allotted for the Dialogue*
The treaty bodies should place time limits on each stage of the dialogue, including the government's opening statement and Committee questions.

Treaty body members should not duplicate each other's questions. Treaty body members should decide in advance what issues are most important for a given state, and be governed in their questioning accordingly.

The treaty bodies should spend the time necessary to conduct the dialogue properly; at least three meetings should be spent per state party.

The treaty bodies should keep a running calculation of the backlog of meeting time if all reports were to be submitted and the appropriate amount of time was spent in the examination of each report. This figure should be indicated in their annual report, and sent to states parties meetings, and raised at every appropriate opportunity.

In the long term, the General Assembly should consolidate the reporting systems of all the human rights treaties and create one permanent body for the consideration of state reports on subjects covered by all six treaties.

(e) *Information Beyond the State Reports Available to the Treaty Bodies*

(1) *The United Nations*

The Center for Human Rights should ensure that there is a systematic accumulation of human rights information from all UN sources on a country-by-country basis.

The General Assembly should provide the necessary resources for the systematic accumulation of human rights information from all UN sources on a country-by-country basis.

(2) *NGOs*

The treaty bodies should develop guidelines for information submitted by NGOs, which NGOs should then be encouraged to use. The treaty bodies should indicate what information is most useful, and suggest the manner in which it should be presented, including focusing on specific laws and practices.

The treaty bodies should insist that NGO information which is distributed by the Committee staff, or upon which oral presentations or submissions are permitted, is related to the respective treaty.

The Center for Human Rights should employ individuals who have responsibility for NGO relations.

The Center for Human Rights should acknowledge information received from NGOs.

The Center for Human Rights should distribute treaty body material relating to the state that is of interest to NGOs making submissions to the treaty bodies as it becomes available.

The treaty bodies should insist that the staff develop mailing lists of NGOs in the states parties.

The treaty bodies should insist that national and international NGOs are informed of relevant information, including: due dates of state reports, receipt of state reports by the UN, and dates of forthcoming dialogues.

The treaty bodies should ensure that national and international NGOs are encouraged to send any relevant information on the country concerned to the treaty bodies.

The treaty bodies should invite NGOs to make oral presentations on states that are due to be considered at the same session. The treaty bodies should select NGOs to participate on the basis of prior written submissions. These written submissions should be used to evaluate the quality and usefulness of the material to be presented.

The treaty bodies should insist that all oral presentations relate to a state report due to be considered and to the provisions of the respective treaty. The treaty bodies should be concerned to ensure that the process of commentary is not abused for political purposes.

The treaty bodies, prior to the dialogue with the state, should send NGO information which has been submitted to the state party concerned (unless exceptional, clear issues of safety of individuals arise).

The treaty bodies should develop their schedules for considering reports one year in advance.

The treaty bodies should ensure that the days for the consideration of a single state report are consecutive, including the time for the adoption and release of the concluding observations on the state just considered.

(3) *Fact-Finding*

The treaty bodies should visit states parties in order to engage in fact-finding prior to the scheduled consideration of state reports. Fact-finding for every state party should be carried out on a routine, non-discriminatory basis. It would not be necessary for all members of the treaty bodies to visit every state.

The treaty bodies should visit states parties which have not reported for an unreasonable length of time, in order to both engage in fact-finding and facilitate the production of a report or solicit alternative sources of information.

The General Assembly should ensure that the treaty bodies have sufficient resources and administrative support to engage in fact-finding.

(iii) *Implementing Concluding Observations*

The treaty bodies should include the list of questions given in advance to states parties in their annual reports.

The treaty bodies should include a summary of the state's responses to their questions in their annual reports.

The treaty bodies should insist that summary records are produced wholly in one language in a timely fashion.

The General Assembly should ensure that the treaty bodies have sufficient resources to facilitate the production of summary records wholly in one language in a timely fashion.

(a) *Quality of Concluding Observations*

The treaty bodies should adopt more detailed and lengthier concluding observations. This recommendation is directed particularly to the Racial Discrimination Committee, the Torture Committee and CEDAW.

The treaty bodies should include references to as many specific laws and practices in their concluding observations as possible.

The treaty bodies should adopt concluding observations which are direct and do not avoid criticism where it is due. Concluding observations should not seek primarily to mollify states, or lay stress on the willingness of states merely to participate.

(b) *Access to Concluding Observations*
The treaty bodies should adopt concluding observations on a particular state following the dialogue and release those observations immediately, without waiting until the end of the session.

The treaty bodies should issue concluding observations as separate documents.

The treaty bodies should distribute concluding observations to NGOs and the press immediately following their adoption.

The treaty bodies should develop much greater links with the media, including: sending notices of news conferences to both national and international media, calling specific media contacts prior to news conferences, meeting the media for the purposes of explaining the process and the significance of particular concluding observations both informally and formally. The treaty bodies should ensure that where the dialogue and the release of the concluding observations is conducted in the state concerned, the ability of the media to attend is a prerequisite for the occasion.

(c) *Follow-up of Concluding Observations*

(1) *The Treaty Bodies*

The treaty bodies should include in their concluding observations any requests for additional information.

The treaty bodies should set deadlines for the receipt of additional information.

The treaty bodies should publish additional information which is submitted.

The treaty bodies should follow-up failures to provide additional information that has been requested.

The treaty bodies should publish a separate document containing the following information on a state-by-state basis: any follow-up measure requested such as a request for additional information, the deadline for receipt of the additional information, an indication whether the information was received, the UN document number in which additional information was published.

The treaty bodies should publish a document containing information on a state-by-state basis which indicates all references in the concluding observations to areas in need or technical assistance and advisory services. The document also should indicate the state response to these observations.

The treaty bodies should transmit the publication containing specific recommendations on a state-by-state basis and the responses received to: the Commission on Human Rights, the Commission on the Status of Women and the General Assembly.

The treaty bodies should publish a document containing information on a state-by-state basis which indicates all references in the concluding observations to areas in need of technical assistance and advisory services. The document also should indicate the state response to these observations.

The treaty bodies should ask state representatives to attend the next session in order to consider additional information that is submitted following the dialogue, where that information is significant or identifies likely violations of the Covenant.

The treaty bodies should publish a separate document containing a list of the offenders in relation to different categories of compliance with the treaty. The categories should be: overdue reports, inappropriate state representatives, non-compliance with specific recommendations made in the concluding observations.

(2) The Commission on Human Rights, the Commission on the Status of Women, the General Assembly

The Commission on Human Rights and the General Assembly should coordinate current resolutions which deal in whole or in part with the treaty bodies, namely, the resolutions on women, children, torture, race, effective implementation, and the status of the covenants. A combined resolution on all aspects of the treaty bodies is preferable.

The Commission on Human Rights and the General Assembly should pass a coordinated global resolution on the treaty bodies which contains the following elements:

- emphasis on the independence of treaty body members
- emphasis on the importance of submitting information that has been requested (either in response to questions put prior to the dialogue or in the form of additional information following the dialogue)
- support for field missions by the treaty bodies in the context of fact-finding, examining state reports and following-up recommendations
- emphasis on the importance of sending qualified state representatives to the dialogue
- support for direct treaty body involvement on reservations
- support for optional protocols extending the right of individual petition to the Women's Convention, the Economic Covenant and the Child Convention
- the names of the worst offenders on overdue reports, non-compliance of requests for information, and non-compliance with recommendations.

The Commission on Human Rights, the Commission on the Status of Women and the General Assembly should pay due attention to the individual concluding observations of the treaty bodies on each state.

The Commission on Human Rights, the Commission on the Status of Women and the General Assembly should pass country-specific resolutions on states parties to the human rights treaties where the concluding observations of the treaty bodies indicate significant cause for concern.

The Commission on Human Rights, the Commission on the Status of Women and the General Assembly should create further investigative procedures such as country rapporteurs, or request detailed country-specific reports from the Secretary-General where violations of the human rights treaties are serious. The threshold for appointing such additional investigative mechanisms should be the same for every UN member.

The General Assembly should support legitimate requests for expert studies made by the treaty bodies.

The General Assembly should ensure that sufficient resources are provided for CEDAW to have nine weeks of meeting time annually.

(3) Meetings of States Parties

Meetings of states parties should take up substantive issues, such as: overdue reports, reservations, and serious substantive non-compliance with the treaty.

Meetings of states parties should recommend increasing the meeting time allotted to CEDAW to nine weeks, the equivalent of the time allotted to the Child Committee and the Human Rights Committee (which has fewer ratifications).

(d) Reservations

The treaty bodies should decide the issue of the compatibility of reservations with the object and purpose of the treaty.

States parties should accept that the treaty bodies should decide the issue of the compatibility of reservations with the object and purpose of the treaty.

States parties should withdraw reservations that are incompatible with the object and purpose of the treaty.

All states parties should object to reservations that are incompatible with the object and purpose of the treaty.

States parties should support moves by the treaty bodies to conduct a dialogue with a state party that has made reservations that are incompatible with the object and purpose of the treaty, and moves to extend questions to areas covered by such reservations.

(i) Moving Beyond State Reports

(a) Examining States that have Failed to Report

The treaty bodies should examine states that have failed to report for a considerable length of time.

The treaty bodies should ensure that in circumstances where they have examined a state in the absence of a report, that concluding observations are of an equivalent quality to those observations adopted when a state has produced a report.

(b) Urgent Situations

(1) Regular State Reports

The treaty bodies should keep states under examination for more than one session where the human rights conditions warrant greater scrutiny.

(2) Exceptional Reports

The treaty bodies should adopt clear non-discriminatory guidelines for selecting states for consideration outside the framework of the regular reporting mechanism.

The treaty bodies should request exceptional reports in urgent situations provided that states are selected in accordance with guidelines. The treaty bodies should ensure that any decision to request an exceptional report should not be based on political motivations.

The treaty bodies should utilize such an irregular reporting procedure only very exceptionally, so as to preserve the unique capacity of the treaty bodies to address adequately human rights situations in the vast majority of the UN states.

GENERAL COMMENTS AND RECOMMENDATIONS

The treaty bodies should elaborate general comments on the interpretation of treaty provisions.

The treaty bodies should ensure that elaboration of general comments is confined to subjects within the purview of their respective instruments.

The treaty bodies should ask for expert assistance in elaborating general comments. The treaty bodies should convene meetings of experts prior to finalizing general comments.

INDIVIDUAL COMMUNICATIONS

(i) *Accepting the Right of Petition*

The states parties and the General Assembly should amend the human rights treaties, or draft an optional protocol, which makes ratification of the human rights treaty conditional upon acceptance of a right of individual petition.

(ii) *Shortage of complaints*

The treaty bodies should make it a priority to attract more individual communications. The treaty bodies should use the media to publicize the right of individual petition in states where it is available.

The Human Rights Committee should immediately drop its "gag rule" on speaking publicly about communications that are before it.

All treaty bodies having a right of individual petition should hold regional meetings with lawyers and local human rights defenders in order to explain the petition process.

(iii) *Quality of Decisions*

The Human Rights Committee should spend a greater amount of time on individual communications.

The Human Rights Committee should develop more detailed reasoning on decisions taken on the merits of communications. The Committee should vote if necessary, rather than adopt concluding observations without adequate rationale.

The Torture Committee should spend the amount of time necessary to handle individual communications properly, even if at the expense of time spent on state reports.

The treaty bodies should conduct public hearings on communications.

The treaty bodies should conduct public hearings on communications within the state concerned.

The treaty bodies should take the issue of admissibility and the merits together in circumstances that indicate no serious impediment to admissibility.

The treaty bodies should monitor closely circumstances of potential intimidation of authors of communications or potential authors. They also should monitor the potential for intimidation in states that do not have, or have very few, communications.

The General Assembly and the Human Rights Commission should encourage the Torture Committee's determination to publish Article 20 decisions in circumstances where states refuse to cooperate. The Torture Committee should ensure that the inquiry and publication should take place at a faster rate than the five and a half year process evident in the first case in which the Committee took this step.

The Torture Committee should send the results of Article 20 inquiries to the individuals or NGOs which originated the complaint, and any other individual or NGO directly affected by the outcome, or who has expressed an interest in the subject.

(iv) *Follow-up*

The Human Rights Committee, the Committee Against Torture and the Racial Discrimination Committee should request follow-up information from the state party on implementation of the Committees' views on all individual communications. The relevant treaty body should insist on precise replies, including the details of relevant legislation, and financial terms, to their requests for follow-up information.

The Human Rights Committee should immediately publish a separate document containing all follow-up information that has been received on individual communications, on a state-by-state and case-by-case basis. Such a publication should be updated regularly.

The Torture Committee and the Racial Discrimination Committee should institute the practice of collating and publishing follow-up information.

The treaty bodies should not permit political considerations to affect decisions to publish follow-up information. It should be routine and compulsory.

The relevant treaty bodies should indicate whether the remedy indicated by the follow-up information was satisfactory.

The treaty bodies should undertake follow-up missions to individual states where replies for follow-up information on communications has been unsatisfactory.

The treaty bodies should publish full accounts of any follow-up mission taken in connection with individual communications.

(v) *Expanding the Right of Petition*

(a) *Setting priorities*

In the short term, the Human Rights Committee and the Torture Committee should place greater emphasis on the proper handling of individual communications.

States parties should nominate to the treaty bodies individuals having the capacity to handle individual communications, namely, persons with legal qualifications.

In the long term, the General Assembly should consolidate the optional protocol procedures for individual communications and the procedures for handling state reports. Such a consolidation should move to the creation of a permanent international court of human rights to deal with individual petitions arising from all of the six treaties.

(b) *The other treaty bodies*

The General Assembly should immediately adopt optional protocols permitting the right of individual petition for the Women's Discrimination Convention, the Economic Covenant, and the Child Convention.

The General Assembly should be concerned to omit rights from new optional protocols containing rights of petition which are clearly non-justiciable. The determination of non-justiciability should depend on factors such as the impossibility of required factual determinations, or the inadequacy of the expertise of treaty body members.

AMENDMENTS TO THE HUMAN RIGHTS TREATIES

The Sub-Commission on Prevention of Discrimination and Protection of Minorities, the Commission on Human Rights and the General Assembly should not seek to add substantive protocols to the human rights treaties unless it is clear that the subject-matter of the proposed protocol is not covered by the existing treaties. Every effort should be made not to diminish the reach of existing treaty provisions by instituting another round of ratifications.

The Sub-Commission on Prevention of Discrimination and Protection of Minorities, the Commission on Human Rights and the General Assembly should consult the respective treaty bodies on proposed areas of potential substantive protocols.

The Commission on Human Rights should cancel the working groups on a protocol on the sale of children, child prostitution and child pornography, and the right to a fair trial, on the grounds of unnecessary duplication with existing provisions of the human rights treaties.

The Sub-Commission on Prevention of Discrimination and Protection of Minorities, the Commission on Human Rights and the General Assembly should place a priority on drafting new procedural amendments to the treaties directed at improving implementation, such as providing additional rights of petition, rather than increasing substantive standards.

Appendix 7: Meetings of Chairpersons of the Treaty Bodies

A/39/484 — 20 September 1984

UNITED NATIONS GENERAL ASSEMBLY
Thirty-ninth session

INTERNATIONAL COVENANTS ON HUMAN RIGHTS

Reporting obligations of States parties to the International Covenants on Human Rights and the International Convention on the Elimination of All Forms of Racial Discrimination

Note by the Secretary-General

In accordance with paragraph 6 of General Assembly resolution 38/117 of 16 December 1983, the Secretary-General transmits to the Assembly herewith the report of the meeting of chairmen of the Commission on Human Rights, the Human Rights Committee, the Sessional Working Group of Governmental Experts on the Implementation of the International Covenant on Economic, Social and Cultural Rights and the Committee on the Elimination of Racial Discrimination convened pursuant to paragraph 5 of the above-mentioned resolution.

ANNEX

Report of Meeting of Chairpersons of the Commission on Human Rights, the Human Rights Committee, the Sessional Working Group of Governmental Experts on the Implementation of the International Covenant on Economic, Social and Cultural Rights and the Committee on the Elimination of Racial Discrimination, held at Geneva on 16 and 17 August 1984 pursuant to General Assembly resolution 38/117.

CONTENTS

	Paragraphs
I. INTRODUCTION	1–3
II. ORGANIZATION OF THE MEETING	4–9
III. REVIEW OF PROBLEMS EXPERIENCE	10–19
A. Human Rights Committee	12
B. Committee on the Elimination of Racial Discrimination	13
C. Sessional Working Group of Governmental Experts on the Implementation of the International Covenant on Economic, Social and Cultural Rights	14
D. General problems	15–19

IV. REVIEW OF THE RECENT EXAMINATION OF THE 20–26
PROBLEMS BY THE ORGANS CONCERNED
   A. Committee on the Elimination of Racial Discrimination   21
   B. Human Rights Committee   22–24
   C. Sessional Working Group of Governmental Experts on the   25
      Implementation of the International Covenant on
      Economic, Social and Cultural Rights
   D. Commission on Human Rights   26
V. VIEWS AND SUGGESTIONS   27–40
   A. Exchange of information   28
   B. Co-ordination of guidelines   29
   C. Advisory services and assistance   30–32
   D. Other matters   33–40

I. INTRODUCTION

1. At its thirty-eighth session the General Assembly had before it a report it had requested of the Secretary-General on various issues concerning the functioning of reporting procedures under international conventions in the field of human rights as well as questions regarding their rationalization and co-ordination in the future (A/38/393). By its resolution 38/20 of 20 November 1983, the General Assembly requested the Secretary-General to transmit that report to the ninth meeting of the States parties to the Convention on the Elimination of All Forms of Racial Discrimination for consideration. The General Assembly also invited the Committee on the Elimination of Racial Discrimination to consider the analysis and recommendations contained in the report of the Secretary-General, taking into account the various suggestions made in the General Assembly and at the ninth meeting of the States parties to the Convention, and to transmit its views and recommendations to the Assembly at its thirty-ninth session.

2. In resolution 38/117, the General Assembly asked the Secretary-General to transmit the above-mentioned report to the Economic and Social Council and requested the Council and its Sessional Working Group of Governmental Experts on the Implementation of the International Covenant on Economic, Social and Cultural Rights to consider the suggestions contained therein, with a view to improving the situation regarding the submission of reports under the Covenant.

3. Furthermore, the General Assembly requested the Secretary-General to consider the possibility of convening, in accordance with a suggestion made by the Human Rights Committee – and within existing resources – a meeting of the chairmen of the bodies entrusted with the consideration of reports under the relevant human rights instruments, in order to consider the report of the Secretary-General, taking into account the results of General Assembly resolutions 38/20 and 38/117.

II. ORGANIZATION OF THE MEETING

4. Following consultations, the Secretary-General organized a meeting of the following chairmen at Geneva, on 16 and 17 August 1984: the Chairman of the Commission on Human Rights (Mr. Peter H. Kooijmans), the Chairman of the Human Rights Committee (Mr. Andreas V. Mavrommatis), the Chairman of the Committee on the Elimination of Racial Discrimination (Mr. Luis Valencia Rodriguez) and the Chairman of the Sessional Working Group of Governmental Experts on the Implementation of the International Covenant on Economic, Social and Cultural Rights (Mr. Michael Bendix).
5. The following documentation was made available to the participants in the meeting:

General Assembly resolutions 38/20 and 38/117;
Report of the Committee on the Elimination of Racial Discrimination, 1983 (A/38/18);
Report of the Human Rights Committee, 1983 (A/38/40);
Report of the Secretary-General on the reporting obligations of States parties under the International Convention on the Elimination of All Forms of Racial Discrimination and other relevant human rights instruments (A/38/393);
Decision 1 (XXIX) of the Committee on the Elimination of Racial Discrimination (A/39/18, chap ... .
General guidelines of the Human Rights Committee regarding the form and contents of reports from States parties under article 40, paragraph 1(b), of the Covenant (CCPR/C/5 and CCPR/C/20);
Revised general guidelines of the Committee on the Elimination of Racial Discrimination concerning the form and contents of reports by States parties under article 9, paragraph 1, of the Convention (CERD/C/70/Rev.1);
Reporting obligations of States parties under the International Convention on the Elimination of All Forms of Racial Discrimination and other human rights instruments: analytical summary of the discussion of the report of the Secretary-General (A/38/393) by the General Assembly at its thirty-eighth session. Note by the Secretary-General (CERD/SP/20);
General guidelines for reports by States parties under article 16 of the International Covenant on Economic, Social and Cultural Rights, prepared by the Secretary-General in accordance with Economic and Social Council resolution 1988 (LX) (arts. 6–9, E/1978/8, annex; arts. 10–12, E/1980/6, annex; arts. 13–15, E/1982/3, annex);
Report of the Commission on Human Rights, 1984 (E/1984/14);
Commission on Human Rights resolutions 1984/18 and 1984/44;
Report of the Sessional working Group of Governmental Experts on the Implementation of the International Covenant on Economic, Social and Cultural Rights (E/1984/83);
Report of the Sub-Commission on Prevention of Discrimination and Protection of Minorities, 1983 (E/CN.4/1984/3);
Seminar on the experience of different countries in the implementation of international standards on human rights (ST/HR/SER.A/15).

6. The meeting was opened by Mr. Kurt Herndl, Assistant Secretary-General for Human Rights, who outlined some of the problems which had risen, the

objectives of the meeting, the activities of the organs concerned and suggestions from various sources.
7. Mr. A. Mavrommatis was elected to preside over the meeting.
8. The chairmen noted that the General Assembly had requested that the meeting be convened so as to enable the chairmen of the bodies entrusted with the consideration of reports under human rights instruments "to consider the report of the Secretary-General" (A/38/393). Furthermore, the Secretary-General had been requested to inform the General Assembly at its thirty-ninth session of "the views and suggestions" expressed at the meeting. Accordingly, they decided first to proceed to a review of the problems experienced in the functioning of reporting procedures and then to attempt to draw up views and suggestions.
9. The chairmen engaged in general exchange of views on the issues facing their respective organs which proved to be quite useful and constructive. It emerged from the discussion that there was a convergence of views among the chairmen on the issues and problems facing their respective organs. They also provided clarifications and responded to questions raised at the meeting. The above-mentioned exchange of views took into account issues raised in the report of the Secretary-General to the General Assembly (A/38/393) as well as issues raised by the chairmen concerning the reporting procedures of their respective organs and other problems encountered by those organs.

III. REVIEW OF PROBLEMS EXPERIENCED

10. Reviewing the problem encountered, the chairmen identified the following as the most important: failure of some States parties to submit reports; delays in complying with the obligations assumed by States parties to submit reports; the varying quality of the reports submitted; the burden which several co-existing reporting systems placed on States parties; lack of qualified staff to prepare reports in some States parties; and the need to enhance the implementation of the provisions of international conventions.
11. The chairmen discussed the specific problems arising in each of their organs and were of the opinion that the foundations should be laid for co-operation amongst the various organs and appropriate modalities for such co-operation should be established.

A. *Human Rights Committee*

12. It was reported that the principal problem encountered by the Human Rights Committee related to the sparse content of some reports; delays in submission of some reports: non-submission of reports by very few States parties; failure to submit supplementary information promised; and non-submission of reports once the initial report had been examined. The Committee had also remarked on the lack of sufficient lawyers or other suitably qualified persons to prepare reports in some countries which had experienced difficulties.

B. *Committee on the Elimination of Racial Discrimination*

13. The meeting was informed that, with a few exceptions, most States parties had submitted their initial reports to the Committee on the Elimination of Racial Discrimination, and that the main problem was the late submission or non-submission of subsequent reports. In some instances, however, States parties had never submitted a report, not even an initial report, notwithstanding repeated reminders (in some instances more than a dozen reminders had been sent) from the Secretary-General on behalf of the Committee. It was felt that that might indicate a lack of political will on the part of the State party concerned. The Committee had also remarked on the lack of qualified personnel in some States parties to draft reports.

C. *Sessional Working Group of Governmental Experts on the Implementation of the International Covenant on Economic, Social and Cultural Rights*

14. The Sessional Working Group had drawn attention to delays in submission of reports, non-submission of reports in some instances and the late receipt of reports, which did not enable the experts to study them carefully. The meeting was also informed that the Sessional Working Group was facing a unique problem due to the nature of its composition and the timing of its sessions. As a body of governmental experts meeting only one week before the session of the Economic and Social Council, the Sessional Working Group experienced difficulties in reaching a quorum and in carrying out its responsibilities satisfactorily since some of the governmental experts expected to participate in the meetings also had other responsibilities. These difficulties had been compounded by vacancies in the membership of the Sessional Working Group and by the failure of some States parties to designate experts. It was therefore felt that consideration might be given to the possibility of electing the members of the Sessional Working Group in the same way as those of the Human Rights Committee and the Committee on the Elimination of Racial Discrimination and of holding the meetings of the Working Group at a more convenient time, giving members sufficient time to cope with the expected workload. If the present system was retained, however, it might be necessary to envisage the election of alternates, as had been done for the Sub-Commission on Prevention of Discrimination and Protection of Minorities, so as to avoid the problems stemming from the lack of a quorum.

D. *General problems*

15. The chairmen also discussed the ways in which the different organs had attempted to deal with the above-mentioned problems. They included the sending of reminders to States parties; the delegation of a member of the organ to engage in contacts with a representative of the State party concerned; inviting a representative of the State party concerned to attend informal meetings with the organ concerned; sending an expert to visit the country concerned for discussions with the Government; and citing the States parties which had not submitted reports in the annual report to the General Assembly. The chairmen felt that the General Assembly could

consider the role it might be able to play when it was informed that several reminders had been sent to a State party, but that the State party had nevertheless not submitted its report.
16. The chairmen also raised a number of general issues which they felt would require consideration in the future. Among them were the burden of several co-existing reporting systems upon Governments, particularly Governments with limited qualified personnel; the structural problems posed for national administrations due, for example, to the fact that the preparation of a report might require the participation and approval of several ministries of Government. In that regard reference was made to the report of the Seminar on the experience of different countries in the implementation of international standards on human rights (ST/HR/SER.A/15) at which participants had advanced various suggestions for the development of the human rights infrastructure which could enable States parties to comply with their reporting and other obligations. The short periodicity of reports in some organs and the lack of qualified personnel to prepare and present reports in some States parties were also mentioned.
17. The chairmen also felt that it would be necessary to consider, in the future, ways and means of improving general publicity for the activities of the various organs. Publicity could be particularly important in the event of non-compliance by a State party with its reporting obligations.
18. Finally, the chairmen felt that consideration could be given to granting the specialized agencies a more substantial role in the operation of the reporting procedures, when appropriate.
19. The factors giving rise to the above-mentioned problems were then discussed. The chairmen noted that, in the report of the Secretary-General to the thirty-eighth session of the General Assembly, several States parties had indicated that the burden placed upon small countries, in particular, was one of the main reasons for non-compliance with reporting obligations. Some States parties had also mentioned the fact that parties to various human rights instruments were required to prepare simultaneous reports to different organs.

IV. REVIEW OF THE RECENT EXAMINATION OF THE PROBLEMS BY THE ORGANS CONCERNED

20. The chairmen then exchanged information on the discussions which had recently taken place on the above-mentioned issues in their respective organs. They noted that they were engaged in an initial discussion of issues which might require further discussion in their respective organs.

A. *Committee on the Elimination of Racial Discrimination*

21. It was noted that, at its 673rd meeting, on 22 March 1984, the Committee on the Elimination of Racial Discrimination had concluded certain States parties had failed to submit the required report under article 9 of the International Convention on the Elimination of All Forms of Racial

Discrimination owing to difficulties resulting, *inter alia*, from unavailability of the skilled personnel needed to enable them to fulfill their obligations under the Convention. The Committee also felt that there might be a problem of overloading in the reporting system as a result of the obligations of States parties under several international instruments in the field of human rights. However, in all three instances, a change in the periodicity of the reporting obligations would not be a solution because the reporting system was the most decisive element in the monitoring process with which the Committee was charged, and was the principal means by which pressure was brought to bear upon States parties to fulfill their substantive obligation to eliminate racial discrimination in all its forms. Therefore the Committee was not in favour of a longer period for reporting under the International Convention on the Elimination of All Forms of Racial Discrimination, or of amending the Convention. On the contrary, it felt that the necessary assistance in terms of training and advisory services should be provided and it would wholeheartedly support any action to be initiated by the Secretary-General in that respect. The Committee also gave its full support to the suggestion of co-ordinating meetings of the chairmen of the supervisory bodies operating under the various human rights instruments.

B. *Human Rights Committee*

22. It was recalled that, in its report to the General Assembly at its thirty-eighth session, members of the Human Rights Committee had noted the concern voiced in the Third Committee over the difficulties encountered by States parties in submitting reports in view of the lack of resources and the proliferation of reporting procedures under various instruments. Members of the Committee had emphasized the importance of co-ordinating among United Nations organs and had considered that the best way to achieve it was for the Centre for Human Rights to bring together representatives of those organs for short meetings, with a view to considering the matter in the light of the experience of their respective organs.
23. In the same report, the Committee had referred to the question of technical assistance, mainly in the legal field, that might be requested from or given to States parties where the lack of expertise had made it difficult for them to implement their obligations under the International Covenant on Civil and Political Rights. The Committee had requested the Secretary-General to find out how technical assistance could be provided to States parties which requested it.
24. The chairmen noted with appreciation that, at its recently concluded twenty-second session, the Human Rights Committee had adopted a decision authorizing one of its members to visit a State party with a view to placing his expertise and advice at the disposal of the Government of that State party, in order to enable it to discharge its reporting obligations under the Covenant. A similar offer had previously been made to another country but it had not been taken up. The chairmen considered that procedure a very useful development and looked forward to its extension to other cases in the future.

C. Sessional Working Group of Government Experts on the Implementation of the International Covenant on Economic, Social and Cultural Rights

25. The meeting noted, that in its report to the first regular session of the Economic and Social Council for 1984, the Group had expressed the opinion that the prolongation of the biennial intervals in the submission of reports by one year would not be a useful means of improving the situation. Rather, realizing the difficulties a number of States parties experienced in submitting initial and/or periodic reports on time, the Group had supported the suggestion that technical assistance and co-operation should be extended, through the United Nations or its affiliated organizations, to those States parties which might need and might formally request such assistance. Attention was specifically drawn to the expertise and assistance which relevant specialized agencies could be called upon to furnish in accordance with articles 22 and 23 of the Covenant.

D. Commission on Human Rights

26. It was noted that in resolution 1984/18, adopted on 6 March 1984, the Commission on Human Rights had requested the Secretary-General to consider ways and means of assisting States parties to the International Covenants in the preparation of their reports, including the awarding of fellowships to government officials engaged in the preparation of such reports, regional training courses and other possibilities available under the programme of advisory services. In resolution 1984/44 on advisory services in the field of human rights, the Commission had expressed its appreciation to the Secretary-General for his efforts to provide assistance in the field of human rights to Governments, at their request, under the programme of advisory services in the field of human rights and had invited the Secretary-General to report to the Commission at its forty-first session on the progress made in the provision of such expert assistance to Governments in the field of human rights, and to outline suggestions for a long-term programme of action in that field.

V. VIEWS AND SUGGESTIONS

27. The chairmen noted that a number of suggestions had already been put forward by Governments, the organs concerned and the Secretary-General. Those suggestions were reviewed by the chairmen who then agreed to focus on the following main issues: (a) exchange of information; (b) co-ordination of guidelines; (c) advisory services and assistance; and (d) other matters.

A. Exchange of information

28. The chairmen took note of the fact that, pursuant to resolutions adopted by the General Assembly, the annual reports of the Commission on Human Rights, the Human Rights Committee, the Sessional Working Group of Experts, the Committee on the Elimination of Racial Discrimination and

the Sub-Commission on Prevention of Discrimination and Protection of Minorities were being exchanged on a regular basis. The chairmen considered that exchange of documentation to be useful and encouraged its continuation. They also felt that it would be useful if the exchange of information could be enhanced in the future through the following measures:
(a) The guidelines and rules of procedure of the various organs could be included in a single document and made available for easy reference to the members of the different organs;
(b) General comments, decisions or views of the various organs could similarly be assembled in a single document and made available on an ongoing basis to the members of the various organs;
(c) In respect of each State party to the International Covenants and the International Convention on the Elimination of All Forms of Racial Discrimination, a summary table should be prepared listing all the reports submitted by a State party under the various instruments as well as reports which were still outstanding. A reference file containing all the reports submitted by a State party under the different instruments could be assembled in the working languages and made available to the members of the various organs for consultation whenever the report of that State party came up for consideration within any of the supervising organs;
(d) Consolidated tables showing the state of ratification of the International Covenants and the International Convention on the Elimination of All Forms of Racial Discrimination should be submitted at each session of the Human Rights Committee, the Sessional Working Group and the Committee on the Elimination of Racial Discrimination.

B. *Co-ordination of guidelines*

29. The chairmen took note of the guidelines for the submission of reports which had been drawn up within the respective organs. While conscious of the distinctiveness of each instrument and each supervisory organ, the chairmen nevertheless felt that the introductory part of each guideline could eventually be streamlined and that States parties could be assisted in the submission of the general information on their country needed under the various treaties to which they were parties. The chairmen were therefore of the opinion that the following measures could be considered with a view to assisting States parties.
(a) The guidelines drawn up under the different instruments could each contain an identical part requiring the State party to provide information on matters such as: geographical and demographic characteristics of the country and its basic economic and social conditions; its constitutional structure including the legislative, executive and judicial organs of Government; basic legislation dealing with civil and political rights, equality and non-discrimination, measures against racial discrimination, and economic, social and cultural rights;
(b) The Secretary-General could request each State party to the Covenants and to the Convention on the Elimination of All Forms of Racial Discrimination to prepare a composite picture (country profile) using

the information indicated under (a) above and to update that information as necessary. Once such a composite picture had been prepared by the country concerned it could be made available to each of the organs concerned whenever that organ had to consider a report by a State party. To enable the State party to draw up a composite picture along the lines suggested above, the Secretariat, in its note to each State party, could draw attention to, and provide copies of, materials already submitted by that State party in previous reports under the instruments in question;

(c) In addition to the composite picture of each State party, the Secretariat could progressively assemble and maintain, in various working languages, reference copies of the texts of the basic constitutional and legal provisions of each State party, preceded by a summary fact sheet of the geographical and demographic features of the country in question. Over a period of time the country profiles could facilitate the task of the various supervisory organs;

(d) Attention could be given in the future to ways and means of dealing with factors and difficulties experienced by States parties in their efforts to implement international conventions in the field of human rights. Similarly, efforts should be made to avoid duplication among the reporting systems. It was recommended that those matters be discussed at future meetings of chairmen.

C. *Advisory services and assistance*

30. In their review of the problems encountered in the operation of reporting procedures, their causes, and possible ways and means of assisting States parties, the chairmen noted that there was general agreement among the supervisory organs themselves, Governments and the Secretary-General that one of the most effective ways of assisting States parties would be for the Secretary-General to devise and implement a programme of advisory services and technical assistance to enable States parties better to comply with their obligations under the International Covenants on Human Rights. The chairmen noted, for example, that, in the report of the Secretary-General to the thirty-eighth session of the General Assembly, some Governments had recommended that experts could be sent on short missions to States parties facing difficulties and requesting technical assistance in that area. The Secretary-General himself had suggested that consideration could be given to ways and means of providing technical assistance, through the United Nations or its affiliated organizations to those States parties which needed or requested it. The Committee on the Elimination of Racial Discrimination had expressed the view that assistance in terms of training and advisory services should be provided. The Human Rights Committee had referred to the need for technical assistance to States parties, while the Sessional Working Group of Governmental Experts had supported the suggestion that technical assistance and co-operation should be extended, through the United Nations and the relevant specialized agencies, to those States parties in need of such assistance. The Commission on Human Rights had specifically requested the Secretary-General to develop expert assistance to

Governments in the field of human rights and to consider ways and means of assisting States parties in the preparation of their reports, including the awarding of fellowships to government officials engaged in the preparation of such reports.

31. In view of this concurrence of views in favour of the provision of advisory services and technical assistance to States parties in need of such advice and assistance, the chairmen strongly recommend to the General Assembly that the Secretary-General be invited to carry out such a programme of advice and assistance in an effective manner and provided with the means which would enable him to do so. In the development of such a programme, the ideas which have already been advanced by the various organs, some of which are referred to above, have the full support of the chairmen and should be given priority attention. The chairmen would also recommend that the following suggestions be implemented as part of a future programme of advisory services and assistance:

(a) A manual providing practical advice on the preparation and submission of reports, and consideration of such reports, could be prepared by the Secretary-General, drawing upon the reporting procedures and experience of the different supervisory organs. Such a manual could also include specimen reports for the guidance of those drafting and presenting reports;

(b) As recommended by the Commission on Human Rights, a proportion of the human rights fellowships awarded each year could be allocated to government officials who need to develop their skills in the operation of the reporting procedures, particularly those who are called upon to prepare and present such reports. In the communication to Governments inviting nominations for fellowships it could be brought to their attention that they may nominate persons for fellowships who are called upon to prepare or present reports;

(c) A programme of regional training courses for persons engaged in the preparation or presentation of reports could be implemented, in co-operation with UNITAR, on an ongoing basis. The members of supervisory organs could usefully be drawn upon as lecturers at such training courses;

(d) More seminars under the programme of advisory services in the field of human rights could be devoted to the discussion of issues affecting the implementation of international conventions in the field of human rights and their reporting procedures. In this regard the chairpersons noted that a successful seminar was organized in 1983 on the experience of different countries in the implementation of international standards on human rights (ST/HR/SER.A/15);

(e) The development of a system of regional advisors on international human rights standards could be envisaged to visit countries, advise on legislation, discuss problems encountered by Governments and make available to Governments the collective international experience in the implementation of international standards;

(f) The dispatch of experts, from the membership of the organs or from the Centre for Human Rights, on short missions to advise Governments, at their request, could be envisaged. In this regard the commendable example set by the Human Rights Committee in sending one of its members

to be available to a Government for advice and assistance could be followed for other countries in the future;
31. Under the programme of advisory services in the field of human rights, the Secretary-General could develop, within the Centre for Human Rights, a facility specializing in the provision of advice and assistance to Governments in the implementation of international conventions in the field of human rights. This facility could be drawn upon by Governments in need of advice or assistance and could even be gradually extended to the development, where necessary, of the kind of draft legislation required by the international instruments in question for sample legislation on selected human rights problems. Precedents for national institutions for the promotion and protection of human rights could be collected and made available to Governments in case of need.
32. The chairmen realized that implementation of the above-mentioned suggestions would entail some financial implications and suggested that, in order to limit costs as far as possible, existing academic or related institutions could be used where appropriate. The possibility of promoting bilateral assistance could also be envisaged.

D. *Other matters*

33. The chairmen were of the unanimous view that the opportunity provided by the meeting to exchange views and discuss matters common to the various organs was very valuable. They felt that such meetings should be held regularly in the future, possibly on an annual or biennial basis.
34. The chairmen recognized that their first meeting had been devoted to issues arising in the Human Rights Committee, the Sessional Working Group, the Committee on the Elimination of Racial Discrimination and the Commission on Human Rights, because the reporting procedures of those organs had been operational for some years and problems were therefore now coming to light. It could be anticipated, however, that, as the reporting procedure under the Convention on the Elimination of All Forms of Discrimination against Women developed and as experience was gained with that procedure, issues might arise within the Committee on the Elimination of Discrimination against Women which might need to be taken into account at future meetings. The chairmen therefore requested the Secretary-General to examine the possibility of arranging for the participation of the Chairman of the Committee on the Elimination of Discrimination against Women at any forthcoming meetings of chairmen. They noted that issues relating to the reporting procedure under the International Convention on the Suppression and Punishment of the Crime of *Apartheid* were covered by the participation of the chairmen of the Commission on Human Rights.
35. The chairmen also felt that the Secretary-General could assist greatly in encouraging States which had not already done so to ratify the International Covenants and the International Convention on the Elimination of All Forms of Racial Discrimination. In that regard they suggested that the Secretary-General could raise the question of ratifications when he met heads of State, Foreign Ministers or other high level officials during the sessions of the General Assembly or other organs or might in the course of

his visits to capitals. The Centre for Human Rights and the Assistant Secretary-General for Human Rights could also undertake similar activities to promote ratifications.
36. The chairmen felt that a very practical way of facilitating the tasks of States parties which were called upon to submit reports might be to invite them to send an official to the Centre for Human Rights for consultations, well before their report was due, and at a time when one of the supervisory organs was meeting. The official would then have an opportunity to speak to the experts in the Centre and the members of the supervisory organ concerned and to witness the proceedings of the latter. In cases of need, it might be envisaged that the travel costs of such a national official be borne, in part, by the United Nations.
37. The chairmen also felt that it might be useful for the Centre for Human Rights to examine the possibility of maintaining a list of qualified experts who could be made available to Governments at their request to assist them in preparing or presenting their reports.
38. The chairmen were of the view that it was especially important for the report of a State party to be examined in the presence of a representative of that State party in order to ensure that an ongoing and flexible dialogue was maintained between the supervisory organs and the States parties of their respective instruments.
39. The chairmen were also of the opinion that, at future meetings, consideration could be given to how the procedures and methods for considering reports could be improved with a view to assisting States parties in complying with their reporting obligations as well as in coping with the increasing burdens stemming from reporting obligations under various international conventions.
40. The chairmen also felt that the members of their respective organs could use whatever opportunities arose in the future to inform themselves of the activities of the other supervisory organs as well as to develop their understanding of the activities of those organs.

A/44/98 — 3 February 1989

UNITED NATIONS GENERAL ASSEMBLY
Forty-fourth session

REPORTING OBLIGATIONS OF STATES PARTIES TO THE UNITED NATIONS INSTRUMENTS ON HUMAN RIGHTS

Note by the Secretary-General

The Secretary-General transmits to the General Assembly herewith the report of the meeting of Chairpersons of human rights treaty bodies convened pursuant to General Assembly resolution 42/105 of 7 December 1987.

ANNEX

Report of the meeting of Chairpersons of human rights treaty bodies

CONTENTS

	Paragraphs
I. INTRODUCTION	1–3
II. ORGANIZATION OF THE MEETING	4–9
III. IDENTIFICATION AND REVIEW OF PROBLEMS	10–45
A. Human Rights Committee	10–18
B. Committee on Economic, Social and Cultural Rights	19–24
C. Committee on the Elimination of Racial Discrimination	25–35
D. Committee on the Elimination of Discrimination against Women	36–40
E. Group of Three established under the International Convention on the Suppression and Punishment of the Crime of *Apartheid*	41–42
F. Committee against Torture	43–45
IV. REMEDIAL ACTION	46–62
A. Harmonization and consolidation of reporting guidelines	46–53
B. Co-ordination of periodicity of reporting under the various United Nations instruments	54–56
C. Measures for expediting consideration of periodic reports	57–59

D. Projects for technical assistance and advisory services with   60–62
       a view to assisting States parties to fulfil their reporting
       obligations

V. CO-ORDINATION OF FUTURE ACTIVITIES   63–69
    A. Exchange of information and documentation   63–66
    B. Enhancing co-operation with specialized agencies   67
    C. Communication among Chairpersons   68–69

VI. OTHER MATTERS   70–77
    A. Financing   70–71
    B. Secretariat servicing   72–74
    C. Publicity   75
    D. Composition of the committees   76
    E. More effective use of time between sessions   77

VII. CONCLUSIONS AND RECOMMENDATIONS   78–100
    A. Matters requiring urgent action   79–85
    B. Other matters requiring attention   86–100

I. INTRODUCTION

1. At its thirty-eighth session, the General Assembly had before it a report of the Secretary-General on the functioning of reporting procedures under international conventions in the field of human rights as well as questions regarding the rationalization and co-ordination of those procedures in the future (A/38/393). After considering that report, the General Assembly, in its resolution 38/117 of 16 December 1983, requested the Secretary-General, *inter alia*, to consider the possibility of convening a meeting of the Chairmen of the bodies entrusted with the consideration of reports submitted under the relevant human rights instruments. The results of the first meeting of the Chairmen of the Commission on Human Rights, the Human Rights Committee, the Sessional Working Group of Governmental Experts on the Implementation of the International Covenant on Economic, Social and Cultural Rights and the Committee on the Elimination of Racial Discrimination, which was held at Geneva on 16 and 17 August 1984, were presented by the Secretary-General to the General Assembly at its thirty-ninth session (A/39/484, annex) and were noted by the Assembly with interest in its resolution 39/138 of 14 December 1984.

2. Since 1984, the General Assembly has continued to consider the problems relating to the reporting obligations of States parties at each of its succeeding sessions. The problems have also received attention during the various sessions of the treaty bodies, at some of the meetings of States parties, and at meetings of such other organs as the Economic and Social Council and the Commission

on Human Rights. However, many of the problems are still unresolved and the number of overdue reports has continued to grow.
3. Pursuant to General Assembly resolutions 41/121 of 4 December 1986 and 42/105 of 7 December 1987, the Secretary-General convened a second meeting of the Chairpersons of the bodies entrusted with the consideration of reports under the relevant human rights instruments.

II. ORGANIZATION OF THE MEETING

4. The meeting was held at the United Nations Office at Geneva from 10 to 14 October 1988 and was attended by the following participants: the Chairman of the Commission on Human Rights (Mr. Alioune Sène), the Chairman and Vice-Chairman of the Human Rights Committee (Mr. Julio Prado Vallejo and Mr. Fausto Pocar), the Rapporteur of the Committee on Economic, Social and Cultural Rights (Mr. Philip Alston), the Chairman of the Committee on the Elimination of Racial Discrimination (Mr. George O. Lamptey), the representative of the Committee on the Elimination of Discrimination against Women (Ms. Zagorka Ilic), the Chairman of the Group of Three established under the Convention on the Suppression and Punishment of the Crime of *Apartheid* (Mr. Gustavo-Adolfo Vargas) and the Chairman of the Committee against Torture (Mr. Joseph Voyame).
5. Dr. Jonathan Mann, Director of the Global Programme on acquired immunodeficiency syndrome (AIDS) of the World Health Organization, and Mr. Huu Tuong Dao, Co-ordinator for Human Rights Questions of the International Labour Organisation, also participated in one of the meetings.
6. The agenda f or the meeting was as follows:
   1. Opening of the meeting.
   2. Election of the Chairman.
   3. Adoption of the agenda.
   4. Identification and review of problems encountered in the operation of the reporting systems, in particular those relating to the preparation, submission and consideration of States parties' reports.
   5. Remedial actions:
      (a) Harmonization and consolidation of reporting guidelines;
      (b) Co-ordination of periodicity of reporting under the various United Nations instruments;
      (c) Measures for expediting consideration of periodic reports;
      (d) Projects for technical assistance and advisory services with a view to assisting States parties to fulfil their reporting obligations.
   6. Co-ordination of future activities:
      (a) Exchange of information and documentation;
      (b) Enhancing co-operation with specialized agencies;
      (c) Communication among chairmen.
   7. Other matters.
   8. Conclusions and recommendations.
7. The following documentation was made available to participants:
Provisional agenda (HRI/MC/1988/L.1)
Report of the Secretary-General (HRI/MC/1988/L.2)

- Updated information on the general situation of overdue reports (1 June 1988)

Report of the Secretary-General (HRI/MC/1988/L.3)
- List of articles showing the nature and extent of overlapping under six international human rights instruments.

Background documents
Report of the Secretary-General (A/39/484)
- Meeting of chairmen of treaty bodies in 1984

Report of the Secretary-General (A/40/600)
- Updated information on the general situation of the submission of reports (1 June 1985)

Report of the Secretary-General (A/40/600/Add.1)
- Compilation of guidelines under five human rights instruments.

Report of the Secretary-General (A/41/510)
- Updated information on the general situation of overdue reports (1 June 1986)

General Assembly resolutions relating to reporting obligations
- 40/116 of 13 December 1985; 41/121 of 4 December 1986; and 42/105 of 7 December 1987

Economic and Social Council resolutions
- International Covenant on Economic, Social and Cultural Rights 1988/4 of 24 May 1988
- Effective implementation of international instruments on human rights 1988/42 of 27 May 1988

Report of the Secretary-General to the Commission on Human Rights at its forty-fourth session (E/CN.4/1988/40)
- Advisory services in the field of human rights

Report of the Netherlands human rights and Foreign Policy Advisory Committee
- Human Rights conventions under United Nations supervision.

8. The meeting was opened by the representative of the Secretary-General (Mr. Enayat Houshmand, Chief, International Instruments Section, Centre for Human Rights).
9. The following officers were elected:
Chairman: Mr. Julio Prado Vallejo
Vice-Chairman: Mr. George O. Lamptey
Rapporteur: Mr. Philip Alston

III. IDENTIFICATION AND REVIEW OF PROBLEMS

A. *Human Rights Committee*

10. The Chairman of the Human Rights Committee said that, unlike some of the other treaty bodies, the Human Rights Committee had not yet accumulated a backlog of reports. Nevertheless, it had sought to expedite the consideration of reports by encouraging the representatives of States parties to keep their introductory remarks, as well as their oral responses to questions, as germane and concise as possible.

11. The representatives of the Human Rights Committee also explained that the Committee had encountered very serious delays in the submission of reports by States parties. That was partly due to the fact that the International Covenant on Civil and Political Rights covered many wide-ranging rights, which rendered the preparation of the report more difficult than for some of the other Conventions. The situation had worsened over the years, particularly since second periodic reports had become due, and the total number of overdue reports had reached 54 as at 1 June 1988. The fact that third periodic reports had also started to become due in February 1988 was expected to lead to a further increase in overdue reports.
12. Regarding remedial action to improve compliance by States parties with their reporting obligations, it was stated that the Human Rights Committee had already resorted to such measures as dispatching written reminders to States parties whose reports were overdue, inviting the permanent representatives of States parties to discuss their countries' reporting difficulties, with the Committee, designating members of the Bureau to contact permanent representatives on the Committee's behalf, and arranging for the Chairman of the Committee to dispatch special letters to the Foreign Ministers of States parties whose reports had been overdue for a long period. It was also mentioned that a member of the Committee had visited one of the States parties to provide expertise and advice, with a view to facilitating its discharge of its reporting obligations.
13. Turning to possible remedial action in the future, the representatives explained that, in the Committee's view, efforts aimed at harmonizing and consolidating reporting guidelines should remain within reasonable limits. They pointed out that, if reporting guidelines were to be fully standardized, the treaty bodies would undoubtedly receive a great deal of information of little or no relevance to their concerns, whereas States parties would not be relieved of the necessity of providing additional specific information. In their view, such problems could not be avoided, even if only the introductory parts of reports of State parties were consolidated. They also recalled that the reporting guidelines under the International Covenant on Civil and Political Rights covered a broad range of human rights and had already been well tested. Nevertheless, the Committee remained open to new approaches for harmonizing reporting guidelines, provided such proposals were compatible with the considerations mentioned.
14. It was also the Committee's belief that efforts to achieve harmonization might find an appropriate solution within a State party, particularly through the creation of a co-ordination mechanism. It also felt that the establishment of a repository of basic legal documents of the States parties within the Secretariat would be highly desirable.
15. Referring to the co-ordination of periodicity, the representatives stated that, in the Committee's view, it would help States parties that had acceded to or ratified instruments at different times to avoid having to submit reports each year if a five-year periodicity were applied by all treaty bodies. Compliance by States parties with their periodic reporting obligations would be further facilitated if duplication were reduced through such means as utilizing in one report information submitted in reports to other treaty bodies, provided that the Committee's competence was not restricted in any way.

16. In connection with the consideration of periodic reports, the Committee was of the view that the Chairpersons should appeal to States parties to adhere closely to reporting guidelines so that the consideration of reports could be conducted in an orderly and efficient manner. The length of reports had not presented major problems in itself, but it was important to emphasize the need to present information that was both relevant and complete. It would also be helpful if State party delegations could keep their introductory remarks and oral responses to questions as relevant and concise as possible.

17. Concerning the possibilities for providing assistance to States parties, the Committee considered that technical assistance efforts should be expanded, including subregional and national training courses on reporting and, where reporting problems were particularly serious, missions by experts to furnish practical assistance in areas such as the preparation of reports and the elaboration of a human rights infrastructure, and that a manual on report writing should be prepared and distributed to States parties.

18. Finally, the representatives suggested, in respect of co-ordination, that the Secretariat should make State party reports submitted to the other supervisory bodies available to each supervisory body, as it was already doing in the case of the Human Rights Committee. More frequent exchanges and contacts between members of the various treaty bodies, as well as between the secretariat of the Centre for Human Rights and the Centre for Social Development and Humanitarian Affairs, should also be encouraged.

B. *Committee on Economic, Social and Cultural Rights*

19. The representative of the Committee pointed out that some of the problems that had been encountered were due to the fact that the Committee had so far held only two sessions, while others were due to the specific nature of the rights with which it was dealing. Although the Committee had "inherited" the considerable experience of its predecessor (the Working Group of Governmental Experts), he said, it had proved necessary to revise most procedures followed previously, tailoring them to reflect the unique nature of the Committee's task. Thus, in the course of its two sessions to date, the Committee had agreed to relatively strict time-limits on oral statements and had encouraged representatives of States parties who wished to submit very detailed introductory information or to respond to questions at great length to consider doing so in writing. The Committee had also sought to minimize duplication in questioning and had established a pre-sessional working group to identify in advance those questions that might most usefully be discussed with the representatives of States parties. In addition, the Committee had recommended to the Economic and Social Council (which had subsequently endorsed the request in its resolution 1988/4) that the periodicity of reporting be changed so that States parties would henceforth be required to submit only one report every five years. Finally, the Committee had agreed to revise and simplify its reporting guidelines so as to reduce the burden on States parties and provide them with a clearer and more precise indication of what was required.

20. The representative also informed the meeting that the Committee had decided to undertake the preparation of general comments, based on specific

provisions of the Covenant. Their purpose would be to make available to all States parties the experience gained so far through the examination of reports in order to promote more effective further implementation of the Covenant, to draw the attention of the States parties to insufficiencies present in a large number of reports, and to suggest to the States parties and the relevant international organizations and specialized agencies measures designed to promote the full realization of the rights recognized in the Covenant.

21. The Committee also decided that, at each of its future sessions, it would devote one day to a general discussion of one specific right or of a particular article of the Covenant, in order to develop in greater depth its understanding of the relevant issues. At its third session, the focus would be on the rights contained in article 11 of the Covenant. That would also provide the Committee with an opportunity to review and discuss various relevant reports and studies prepared by intergovernmental as well as non-governmental organizations. The representative of the Committee noted in that regard that, as a subsidiary body of the Economic and Social Council, the Committee on Economic, Social and Cultural Rights had encouraged non-governmental organizations in consultative status to submit written statements on issues of relevance to the work of the Committee.

22. At each of its sessions, the Committee had expressed its serious concern about the failure to submit, and extended delays in the submission of, reports by States parties to the Covenant. The meeting was informed that, as of 1 October 1988, there were 139 overdue reports. Accordingly, the Committee had recommended that the Council request the Secretary-General to send appropriate reminders to those States parties that had failed to meet their reporting obligations under the Covenant. The Committee had also decided to continue to mention in its own reports those States parties that had failed to submit reports or had submitted them late.

23. In that connection, and in view of the difficulties a number of States parties might be experiencing in submitting reports on a timely basis, the Committee emphasized the need for the Secretary-General to devise and implement a programme of advisory services and technical assistance that would be available on request.

24. It was also emphasized that the Committee attached particular importance to problems relating to the adequacy of State party reports. In that connection, the Council, upon the recommendation of the Committee, invited State parties to the Covenant to review the process followed in the preparation of their periodic reports on the implementation of the Covenant, including such steps as consultation and co-ordination with appropriate governmental departments and agencies, compilation of data and training of staff and consultations with interested non-governmental organizations.

C. *Committee on the Elimination of Racial Discrimination*

25. The Chairman of the Committee on the Elimination of Racial Discrimination pointed out that, during the 18 years that the Committee had met for six weeks a year, it had handled all the reports submitted by the States parties under article 9 of the Convention on time. He stated that the recent backlog

was due solely to the fact that the duration and frequency of meetings of the Committee had been drastically curtailed. The thirty-fifth session, in August 1987, had been reduced to one week instead of three, and in 1988, the Committee had had only one reduced session of two weeks, instead of two sessions of three weeks each as scheduled.

26. He further pointed out that one of the main problems facing the Committee was the failure to submit reports, and stressed that a number of States parties had not submitted a single report since becoming a party to the Convention. That was probably due to a lack of political will on the part of the States parties concerned. In an effort to resolve the problem, the Committee had listed the defaulting States parties in its reports to the General Assembly, had delegated some of its members to raise the matter with the representatives of the States parties concerned and had requested the Secretary-General to send reminders on behalf of the Committee to those States that had not satisfied their reporting obligations.

27. The Chairman of the Committee informed the meeting that another problem encountered by the Committee was that of late submission of reports. However, he stressed that the problem was probably not due to a lack of political will but rather to the burden of complying with the increased number of human rights instruments involving reporting obligations. To overcome that problem, the Committee had adopted the practice of requesting the submission of multiple overdue reports in one consolidated report. Although that practice had helped some of the States parties, the problem had not yet been solved.

28. He informed the meeting that the Committee had found some of the reports submitted to it inconsistent with the guidelines and inadequate in content. In its early years, the Committee had followed the practice of pronouncing itself on the adequacy or otherwise of the reports submitted by States parties, but that had not been well received in the Third Committee of the General Assembly because States parties did not want to be criticized. As the practice might also have discouraged some States parties from presenting reports regularly, it had eventually been discontinued. It was pointed out that the provision of advisory services to assist States parties unable to submit adequate reports had been pioneered by the Committee on the Elimination of Racial Discrimination. The members of that Committee had also indicated their willingness to assist in seminars and workshops to train officials responsible for the preparation of human rights reports.

29. In that context, the Chairman of the Committee informed the meeting, it had been proposed that the drafters of reports be invited to a special session to observe the work of the Committee in the consideration of reports. Unfortunately, due to financial problems, the proposal – although still worth pursuing – had never been implemented.

30. On the question of periodicity, he informed the meeting that the issue had been raised very early in the work of the Committee, which had, however, long been reluctant to vary the periodicity called for in the Convention. In the Committee's view, such a step would have required an amendment and, in any event, it was crucial to have frequent and regular reports since the problem of racial discrimination was so critical. However, with the subsequent establishment of a number of other Committees, the reporting obligations of States parties to several of the instruments had become a heavy

burden for them. As a result, the Committee had decided to vary the periodicity of submission of comprehensive reports such that after the submission of a comprehensive initial report States parties would need to submit further comprehensive reports only on every second occasion thereafter when reports were due (i.e. every four years), presenting brief updating reports on each intervening occasion.

31. The Chairman informed the meeting that, except in connection with matters falling under article 15 of the Convention, the Committee on the Elimination of Racial Discrimination had up to now been working in plenary sessions. However, due to the curtailment and cancellation of some of its meetings as a result of the failure by a number of States parties to pay their assessed contributions (see the Convention, art. 8, para. 6), the Committee had decided to rationalize and streamline its work by instituting a system of rapporteurs on a trial basis beginning at its next session. He pointed out that that step had been taken despite the fact that the method used by the Committee on the Elimination of Racial Discrimination in consideration of reports to date had been very successful.

32. The Chairman of the Committee pointed out that many States had been uneasy about the reporting procedure when the Convention was adopted. In the Committees early years, however, its members had recognized that fact and had dealt with the reports in a cautious and prudent fashion, with the result that the earlier fears were soon allayed. The procedure had later been followed in other Committees, and the Convention had become the one with the highest number of ratifications.

33. The Chairman informed the meeting that the financial problems the Committee faced due to the failure by a number of States parties to pay assessed contributions had affected its ability to discharge its monitoring functions under the Convention. He said that such financial problems were likely to be experienced by other self-financing committees as well, such as the Committee against Torture. When the International Convention on the Elimination of All Forms of Racial Discrimination was being drafted, the prevailing view had been that the Committee should be self-financing so as to maintain its independence.

34. The Chairman stated that since the human rights programme was one of the major responsibilities of the United Nations and since the international human rights instruments were adopted by the General Assembly, in which all the States Members of the United Nations took part in the consideration of reports from the human rights treaty bodies, the financing of such bodies should come under the regular budget of the United Nations. That view currently prevailed in many Member States of the United Nations. In his view, unless a solution to the financing problem was found, the human rights programme would disintegrate.

35. At its last session, the Committee had adopted a decision requesting the General Assembly to authorize the Secretary-General, on a temporary basis, to ensure the financing of the expenses of the Committee members from the United Nations regular budget until such time as a more permanent solution to the problem was found.

D. Committee on the Elimination of Discrimination against Women

36. During the general debate, the representative of the Committee referred to a list of issues that the Committee wished to bring to the attention of the meeting, which were included in its annual report to the General Assembly at its forty-third session.[1] With regard to problems encountered in its activities, the Committee had felt that it was necessary, in particular: to strengthen its secretariat, especially with regard to technical and legal advice; to improve the level of servicing provided to the Committee and to bring it to the level of servicing of other treaty bodies; to consider ways and means to expedite the work of the Committee and improve the reporting system; to take measures in respect of delays in the submission by States parties of initial reports and second periodic reports to the Committee; and to assist States parties that appeared to experience difficulties in fulfilling their reporting obligations.

37. The representative emphasized that certain problems were common to all reporting procedures under human rights instruments, while other problems were specific to a particular reporting procedure, and that the latter should also be taken into account in the formulation of final recommendations by the meeting.

38. She explained that the main problems specifically concerning the reporting procedure under the Convention on the Elimination of All Forms of Discrimination against Women could be classified in two categories: (1) difficulties encountered by States parties in preparing their reports; and (2) difficulties encountered by the Committee in its consideration of reports submitted by States parties.

39. Regarding the first issue, she pointed out that in many cases States parties to the Convention were also parties to many other human rights instruments with reporting obligations. Furthermore, various United Nations resolutions and programmes requested Governments to report or provide information on numerous issues, and the work-load imposed on Governments by all the reporting procedures was one of the main causes of delay in submitting reports. In addition, when preparing their reports under the Convention, States parties had to take into account the information provided by their national machineries or institutions dealing with the problems of discrimination against women and of the advancement of their status, and had to provide the relevant demographic statistics essential to understanding the role of women in society. It was emphasized that such demographic and other statistics should be broken down according to sex. The co-ordination or compilation of different inputs often caused a further delay in the submission of government reports. The experience of the Committee had shown that Governments were willing to co-operate with the Committee. However, the lack of experience or training in international procedures on the part of many officials made it necessary to provide for technical assistance and advisory services from the United Nations Secretariat.

40. Regarding the second issue, she pointed out that under the terms of the Convention the Committee could meet only once a year for two weeks (10

---

[1] *Official Records of the General Assembly, Forty-second session, Supplement No. 38* (A/42/38).

working days) and that, as a result, the time available to the Committee to consider States parties' reports was insufficient. A thorough examination of a report and a genuinely constructive dialogue with a State party required at least two meetings of the Committee. A backlog in the consideration of reports by the Committee was thus created, as a result of which the Committee might well find itself in the position of considering initial reports which had already become obsolete because they had been submitted a long time earlier. Additional meeting time would be necessary to enable the Committee to carry out its obligations under the Convention. It was pointed out that the Committee and the Secretariat had already adopted a number of measures designed to improve the Committee's methods of work.

E. *Group of Three established under the International Convention on the Suppression and Punishment of the Crime of Apartheid*

41. The Chairman of the Group of Three stated that the main problem facing the Group was that of non-submission of reports. As at 1 June 1988, there were 87 States parties to the Convention and 176 overdue reports. Moreover, it was considered significant that 38 States parties had not yet submitted their initial reports and that 12 of those had been overdue for 10 years or more. In view of the paucity of reports received, the Group had not built up a backlog, although it met for only one week a year. In addition, the reports submitted by States parties did not adhere to the general guidelines and contained insufficient information.

42. The Chairman of the Group of Three said that the high rate of non-submission of reports no doubt resulted from the view of many States parties that the "crime of *apartheid*" was not likely to arise in their territories. He emphasized that it was important to submit reports nevertheless, particularly in order to monitor the activities of transnational corporations, which operated in all countries. He suggested that to overcome the problem the Group of Three should in future follow the practice of the Committee on the Elimination of Racial Discrimination (i.e., after having provided initial reports, States parties should be requested to submit further comprehensive reports only on every second occasion thereafter when reports were due – every four years – and to present brief updating reports on each intervening occasion when reports were due under the Convention).

F. *Committee against Torture*

43. The Chairman of the Committee stated that it was premature to try to identify problems relating to the reporting procedure established under article 19 of the Convention against Torture and Other Cruel, Inhuman or Degrading Treatment or Punishment, since States parties to the Convention had been requested to submit their initial reports for the first time in the course of 1988 or 1989, and the Committee against Torture could not begin its consideration of those initial reports until its second session in April 1989.

44. However, the Committee had already encountered a problem that would arise again in its future activities and might also affect the operation of the reporting system under the Convention: the lack of financial resources. He

recalled that States parties were responsible for expenses relating to the implementation system of the Convention, as provided in its article 17, paragraph 7, and article 18, paragraph 5. The activities of the Committee thus required that the contributions of States parties be set at appropriate levels and be paid in good time. The financial decisions of the first meeting of States parties held in November 1987 had prevented the Committee from meeting for a second session in 1988, thus creating a situation in which reports submitted by States parties in June 1988 could not be considered by the Committee until April 1989.

45. He stated that the attention of States parties should be drawn to the fact that without their co-operation in faithfully discharging their financial obligations the long-term viability of all the activities envisaged under the Convention, including its reporting procedures, could not be guaranteed.

IV. REMEDIAL ACTION

A. *Harmonization and consolidation of reporting guidelines*

46. It was noted that the possibility of achieving some consolidation of the various reporting guidelines had already been discussed at the meeting of Chairmen held in 1984. In the course of the discussion, it was stressed that the reporting procedure under each of the human rights instruments had its own specific requirements and that it would therefore not be possible fully to harmonize and consolidate all of the reporting guidelines. However, general basic information and data on each country, which would be of common interest to all treaty bodies, could be requested. It was suggested that such a "core document" should contain relevant background information on each State party and be available to the members of the committees during the consideration of the report of the State concerned. Particular attention should be paid in such a document to information concerning the political system, the main features of the legal order, the legal status of international instruments within the national legal system, the recourse procedures for the protection of human rights, demographic data and other relevant economic, social and cultural data that the State party believed to be important.

47. Various suggestions were put forward as to how such a core document might best be prepared. One proposal was that the document should be prepared by each State party and submitted to the Centre for Human Rights so that it could be made available, as appropriate, to each of the treaty bodies. The document could be updated every five years or more frequently, at the discretion of the State concerned. A related suggestion called for the relevant information to be contained in the initial part of any report sent for consideration to a treaty body and then updated in each subsequent report to that body. A third suggestion was that a questionnaire could be submitted to all States parties indicating the information needed by the Centre for Human Rights, which would then be responsible for the preparation and production of the document.

48. It was noted that several of the committees had requested that relevant statistical data, drawn from authoritative sources, should be made available

to them in connection with their consideration of States parties' reports. The importance of the availability of such data was generally recognized, and it was suggested that the committees should have available to them at least the relevant data contained in the *Statistical Yearbook* of the United Nations and the annual statistical report of the International Monetary Fund, entitled *"International Financial Statistics"*, as well as all of the statistical tables appended to the *World Development Report* of the World Bank and *The State of the World's Children* of the United Nations Children's Fund (UNICEF), each of which were updated annually. It was also noted that as far as possible, and whenever appropriate, use should be made of statistics and other information available from relevant international organizations, including agencies such as the International Labour Organisation (ILO), the United Nations Educational, Scientific and Cultural Organization (UNESCO), the World Health Organization (WHO) and the Food and Agriculture Organization of the United Nations (FAQ).

49. With particular reference to the Committee on Economic, Social and Cultural Rights, it was observed that the existing reporting guidelines were excessively complicated and demanding and accordingly very difficult, if not impossible, to comply with. For that reason, the Committee had agreed to their revision and simplification. However, it was suggested that, in carrying out such a revision, the Committee might need to consult experts from the specialized agencies and elsewhere.

50. Another suggestion, which was prefaced by an acknowledgement that it would require considerably more reflection and refinement before being acted upon, was that consideration should be given in the longer term to the possibility of each State party preparing a single overall report. Each body would then have to deal with that part of the report which fell within its competence. The preparation of the report could, if so requested, be undertaken with the assistance of experts from the Centre for Human Rights.

51. Support was expressed for the preparation of a manual to assist States parties in fulfilling their reporting obligations, and it was noted that the Centre for Human Rights, in collaboration with the United Nations Institute for Training and Research (UNITAR), was currently working towards that goal. While it would be desirable to consult with each of the relevant treaty bodies in the process of drafting the manual, it was noted that the committees themselves were ultimately responsible for determining the adequacy or otherwise of reports and that the manual should not be considered to be a definitive, or in any way binding, statement as to the relevant requirements.

52. It was also suggested that greater uniformity in reporting might be achieved by each State party if it were to establish a unit for the preparation of all of the reports submitted to the international human rights treaty bodies. Such an initiative would render the technical assistance provided by the Centre for Human Rights more effective and would help to reduce duplication in the submission of information.

53. It was generally agreed that whenever a State party had dealt with an issue in considerable detail in reporting to one committee, it need not reproduce exactly the same information in reporting to another committee. Rather, it was preferable to include a cross-reference to the original document on the assumption that the Secretariat would have made available to committee

members copies of all of the relevant reports. Such a practice was already followed by some States in their reporting to the Human Rights Committee and could achieve considerable savings of time and materials.

B. *Co-ordination of periodicity of reporting under the various United Nations instruments*

54. The meeting took note of the fact that significant changes had recently taken place in respect to the timing and nature of the reporting requirements under both the International Covenant on Economic, Social and Cultural Rights and the International Convention on the Elimination of All Forms of Racial Discrimination. It was generally agreed that those changes would reduce the burden imposed on reporting States and would further enable States that were parties to several of the principal treaties to arrange the preparation of their reports so as to distribute the burden more evenly over time. It was also agreed that each treaty body should keep the matter under review in the hope that further improvements might be identified in the future.
55. The problem of the non-submission, or excessively late submission, of reports was underlined. It was noted that the failure to report significantly undermined the objectives of the treaties and that every effort should be made by the States parties concerned to fulfil the reporting obligations that they had undertaken. The discussion on positive measures of assistance that might be provided to States is reflected in section D below. It was generally agreed that the treaty bodies should explore all possible means to promote the submission of overdue reports. In that regard, it was said that consideration might be given to the following measures, for example, which had already been used by the Human Rights Committee:
    (a) Dispatching written reminders (twice yearly);
    (b) Calling attention to the problem through personal contacts by individual members (from the relevant region) with representatives of the States parties concerned;
    (c) Listing in the committees' annual reports to the General Assembly the names of States parties with overdue reports;
    (d) Inviting the permanent representatives of the States parties concerned to discuss with the committee (in closed meetings) their countries' difficulties in respect of reporting;
    (e) Designating members of the Bureau to contact the permanent representatives of the States parties concerned;
    (f) Dispatching special letters from the Chairman to the Foreign Ministers of States parties with long-overdue reports;
    (g) Arranging for a visit by a member of the committee to a State party to provide expertise and advice.
56. Mention was also made of the possibility of the committees establishing a "special list" that would serve to highlight the names of those States parties that had been particularly unresponsive to repeated requests to submit overdue reports.

C. *Measures for expediting consideration of periodic reports*

57. In order to expedite the consideration of reports, there was general agreement on the potential usefulness of the increasingly widely used practice of nomi-

nating rapporteurs, co-ordinators or a working group to undertake a preliminary analysis of the reports or of certain issues to be discussed during the consideration of a report, and to prepare a list of principal issues to be raised with the reporting State.
58. It was also noted that most, if not all, of the committees had, on occasion, experienced difficulties with delegations speaking at undue length, either when introducing a report or when responding to questions. One committee had adopted relatively strict time-limits, but it was generally agreed that the appropriate limits would have to be decided by each committee in the light of its own circumstances and that, in any event, there would always be instances where additional time was required to ensure adequate presentation and discussion of a report. Particular emphasis was placed on the need for committee members to exert self-restraint and to pose questions as precisely and concisely as possible.
59. There was some discussion as to whether the completion by the various committees of the consideration of initial reports by States parties would lead to a reduction or an increase in the amount of time required for their consideration of follow-up reports. Some speakers expressed the hope that less time would be necessary, while others felt that the discussion would require more time as the committees began to tackle issues in greater depth and with more sophistication.

D. *Projects for technical assistance and advisory services with a view to assisting States parties to fulfil their reporting obligations*

60. It was generally agreed that the provision of technical assistance and advisory services to States parties having acknowledged difficulties in preparing their reports was highly desirable. In that regard, the meeting welcomed the proposals contained in the relevant report by the Secretary-General to the Commission on Human Rights (E/CN.4/1988,40). It was felt that the regional and subregional training courses on reporting issues had been of great value and should be continued on a regular basis. For that purpose, it would be desirable for the Centre for Human Rights to obtain the appropriate expertise for undertaking training activities. It was asked whether individual fellowships were a cost-efficient way of providing training for reporting purposes in view of their cost and the high rotation of the national officials concerned.
61. Another dimension of advisory services to which reference was made concerned the possibility of the committees being encouraged to make recommendations for specific activities to be funded on the basis of their examination of a State's report. Thus, for example, assistance could be recommended for the drafting of necessary human rights legislation, for particular educational activities or for the establishment of appropriate national institutions. It was pointed out, however, that the latter activity should be undertaken only with great care since in some cases national human rights institutions had been created mainly in order to conceal continuing violations by the Government concerned.
62. It was suggested that consideration might be given to establishing a board of trustees to administer the Voluntary Fund for Advisory Services and Technical Assistance in the Field of Human Rights, to ensure appropriate

expert input and to protect the Secretary-General from political pressures. Were such an initiative taken, it would seem appropriate to include one or two members drawn from any of the committees on the board. In any event, the hope was expressed that in future there would be greater consultation with the committees on the question of the provision of advisory services in treaty-related matters.

V. CO-ORDINATION OF FUTURE ACTIVITIES

A. *Exchange of information and documentation*

63. In general terms, it was noted that the number of relevant bodies and the amount of documentation in the human rights field had increased dramatically in the past decade. As a result, the treaty bodies should not be viewed in isolation, but as part of an overall system that included not only other United Nations organs, such as the Commission on Human Rights and the Sub-Commission on Prevention of Discrimination and Protection of Minorities, but also the principal regional bodies. While there was no question of seeking to impose "uniformity" on the different bodies, it was nevertheless important for the treaty bodies to be aware of the activities and approaches of other relevant bodies. Thus, with respect to the regional organizations, it was suggested that occasional meetings should be arranged between the persons chairing the African, European and Inter-American commissions and those chairing the United Nations treaty bodies. It was also suggested that each member of the various treaty bodies should receive a copy of the annual report of the Inter-American Commission on Human Rights and of the annual publication entitled *Stock-taking on the European Convention on Human Rights*, issued by the Council of Europe. Similarly, occasional exchanges should be arranged at the working level of the relevant secretariats.

64. With respect to the Commission on Human Rights and the Sub-Commission on Prevention of Discrimination and Protection of Minorities, it was noted that special rapporteurs were sometimes engaged in activities that were of direct and immediate relevance to the work of the treaty bodies. Examples cited included the Commission's Special Rapporteur on torture and the Sub-Commission's Special Rapporteur on economic, social and cultural rights. It was suggested that, if possible and appropriate, an effort should be made to facilitate an exchange of views between the relevant entities, perhaps on an informal basis (i.e. with interpretation but without summary records).

65. It was noted that the greatly increased number of reports by States parties, together with the enormous volume of other relevant documentation, already made it very difficult for committee members to keep track of, let alone synthesize, the diverse sources of information. That problem would probably be further compounded in the future as more ratifications were received and new instruments entered into force. For those reasons, it was said to be essential to make use of the opportunities provided by computerization in order to reduce unnecessary work, increase efficiency and assist States parties in their own endeavours. While it was recognized that a greater use of computers would entail costs, it was suggested that considerable savings in

money and staff time could result in the long term. It was proposed that a small task force be established, consisting of an expert from one of the committees, a computer expert and a Secretariat member to be appointed by the Secretary-General, to explore the costs and benefits of making greater use of computers to assist the committees in their work.
66. Another proposal was to establish a "committee resource room" in the Centre for Human Rights in which the principal documentation of the relevant committees could be kept, along with copies of the constitutions and other basic legislation of States parties. In addition, relevant reports from other United Nations bodies and other sources could be made available for the information of experts. Such a facility would also encourage greater interaction among committee members, which was considered highly desirable. It was noted that virtually all of the documents could be obtained free of charge and that interns could be responsible for arranging and cataloguing the materials so as not to incur additional staffing costs.

B. *Enhancing co-operation with specialized agencies*

67. It was noted that on many occasions the various specialized agencies, particularly ILO and UNESCO, had provided considerable assistance to the various treaty bodies. It was agreed that enhanced co-operation was desirable and it was suggested that it might help if requests for information were made in as precise terms as possible. It was also suggested that experts from the agencies might occasionally be asked in future to appear before one or other of the committees in order to provide a technical briefing on a specific issue, perhaps in private session (i.e. without summary records), if that would facilitate a more productive dialogue. Similarly, committees could delegate one of their members to spend a day or two in consultations with relevant agency officials and report back to their committee on a particular issue. It was thought that such procedures might be useful in connection with preparing general comments or revising guidelines.

C. *Communication among Chairpersons*

68. It was generally agreed that the meetings of Chairpersons should be convened on a regular basis every one or two years. It was also suggested that consideration be given to inviting the persons chairing the principal regional commissions, the Sub-Commission on Prevention of Discrimination and Protection of Minorities, the ILO and UNESCO committees on conventions and recommendations and other competent bodies. It was agreed that the chairpersons should seek to remain in contact with one another as appropriate.
69. In order to enhance communication among the different committees, it was suggested that consideration be given to scheduling sessions to allow overlapping so that the members of one committee could interact with their counterparts on another committee.

VI. OTHER MATTERS

A. *Financing*

70. There was considerable discussion of the difficulties that had arisen as a result of factors such as the financial crisis of the United Nations, the non-payment of assessed dues by States parties to the International Convention on the Elimination of All Forms of Racial Discrimination, and the method of "self-financing" provided for in the Convention against Torture and Other Cruel, Inhuman or Degrading Treatment or Punishment. it was strongly emphasized that all of the existing treaty bodies were indispensable components in the overall international system for the promotion and protection of human rights, and that any action that jeopardized or actually prevented their effective functioning must be countered by appropriate measures on the part of the United Nations. It was said that the failure of a limited number of States parties to fulfil their financial obligations under the relevant treaties must not be permitted to obstruct or otherwise undermine the work of the committees. To accept such unilateral interference would be tantamount to providing a right of veto to any State party that, for whatever reason, wished to paralyse an entire committee. That would be contrary to the fundamental assumptions on which the provisions of the Charter of the United Nations on human rights, as well as the various treaty obligations, are predicated. It was noted that the United Nations, above all the Commission on Human Rights (as the relevant functional organ) and the General Assembly (as the highest organ), had a responsibility to ensure the efficient functioning of the mechanisms established under the human rights instruments, in which the Organization had invested considerable effort and financial resources and which had been adopted by the General Assembly. The experience with the Committee on the Elimination of Racial Discrimination and the Committee against Torture suggested that the self-financing system did not contribute to ensuring the effective operation of those mechanisms or to promoting the acceptance of the obligations inherent in the instruments. It was therefore agreed that the General Assembly should, as a matter of the highest priority, ensure the financing of the committees from the United Nations regular budget or make other financial arrangements as necessary in order to enable each of the committees to operate effectively.

71. By the same token, it was acknowledged that the possible creation of additional committees in the future, as a result of the entry into force of new treaties, would have potentially significant financial implications. It was suggested that the General Assembly might consider entrusting one or two experts with the task of preparing a study on possible long-term approaches to the supervision of new instruments in the light of all relevant considerations.

B. *Secretariat servicing*

72. It was agreed that the level and amount of services that the Secretariat was able to provide to the various committees was an important determinant of how efficiently and effectively they were able to function. While the meeting

was fully aware of the financial difficulties currently facing the United Nations, it was noted that the Committee on the Elimination of Discrimination against Women had not even been able to adopt its report during its last session because of inadequate Secretariat services in New York. As a result, the report had had to be adopted by correspondence, an entirely unsatisfactory arrangement. In addition, that Committee had, in the report on its seventh session,[2] requested the current meeting to note the need to strengthen the secretariat of the Committee in general, especially with regard to technical and legal advice.

73. It was generally agreed that, in order to maintain the current high level of Secretariat services, Secretariat services should be strengthened in both the Centre for Human Rights and the Branch for the Advancement of Women. It was emphasized that that was not an attempt to undermine efforts to limit or reduce United Nations staffing levels, but a request that appropriate consideration be given to the rapidly expanding work-load of the various committees as a result of increasing numbers of ratifications and accessions and a major increase in the number of communications being submitted to the relevant bodies.

74. In the course of the discussions, it was proposed that the Committee on the Elimination of Discrimination against Women meet occasionally in Geneva to facilitate interaction with other committees, the specialized agencies and the extensive Geneva-based community of non-governmental organizations. It was also suggested that consideration be given to merging the secretariat of that Committee with the Centre for Human Rights to save costs and to facilitate and enhance co-ordination among all of the human rights treaty bodies. Alternatively, it was suggested that the relevant parts of the United Nations Secretariat should provide the necessary assistance to enable the secretariat of the Branch for the Advancement of Women to provide the Committee with the level of services it requires.

C. *Publicity*

75. It was agreed that every effort should be made to enhance media coverage of the work of the treaty bodies. It was noted with regret, however, that the deliberately unsensational nature of their work made them comparatively uninteresting to much of the media. It was suggested that, whenever the report of a State party was under consideration, the text of the report and a summary of the committee proceedings should be disseminated as widely as possible by the United Nations information centre, if any, located in the State concerned. Holding press conferences at the end of committee sessions, writing in academic journals and the issuing of press releases were all supported as publicity options. In addition, emphasis was placed on the need for widespread dissemination of all relevant instruments at the national level, on the importance of human rights teaching at all levels (including in police and military training schools) and on the vital role of non-governmental organizations in such endeavours.

---

[2] *Ibid., Forty-third session. Supplement No. 38* (A/43/38), para. 53(a).

D. Composition of the committees

76. It was noted that all the members of the Committee on the Elimination of Discrimination against Women were female. By contrast, only seven of a total of 64 members in the other four expert committees were female. The view was expressed that a better balance, in terms of gender, was desirable in the membership of all the committees. It was noted that that was, of course, a matter for individual Governments to take into account when making nominations and casting votes in elections.

E. More effective use of time between sessions

77. It was observed that one of the most valuable resources of the committees was the expertise of their members. For that reason, it was suggested that greater use should be made of members' expertise by assigning tasks to be performed between committee meetings. It was noted that several of the committees were already making use of such opportunities and that they essentially entailed no costs to the United Nations. It was suggested, for example, that an individual committee member could be designated to prepare the first draft of proposed general comments, to undertake the revision of guidelines or to brief a committee on a topic of general interest. His or her work would not in any way commit the Committee to a particular position, but it would ensure an active and continuing role for members, relieve time pressures during sessions, enhance the quality of inputs and avoid the need for interpretation and travel costs incurred when a working group was involved.

VII. CONCLUSIONS AND RECOMMENDATIONS

78. The following conclusions and recommendations are respectfully submitted to the General Assembly for its consideration in accordance with its resolutions 41/121 and 42/105. Some concern action that might be taken by the General Assembly itself or by other appropriate organs of the United Nations, while others fall within the competence of the respective treaty bodies or of the States parties to the treaties. However, no distinction is drawn in this regard for the purposes of the present report, since the mandate of the meeting is to propose diverse means to improve the functioning of the treaty supervisory system.

A. Matters requiring urgent action

79. The respective treaty bodies should be required to consider, on the basis of a proposal prepared by the Secretariat (see A/40/600, para. 21), a possible consolidation of their respective guidelines governing the initial part of each State party's report.
80. Each treaty body should use all appropriate means to promote the submission of overdue reports. For this purpose, the Secretary-General should consider instituting a regularly scheduled consultation with the representatives of States concerned while they are in attendance at the annual session

of the Commission on Human Rights and the General Assembly or other appropriate occasions.

81. Technical assistance and advisory services should be provided on a regular basis by the Secretary-General to assist States parties in fulfilling their reporting obligations. Regional and subregional training courses in the preparation and submission of reports by States parties are of particular value in this regard. Priority should also be given to the provision of assistance, upon request, to States contemplating ratification of the relevant instruments.

82. A task force on computerization should be appointed by the Secretary-General to explore the costs and benefits of computerizing the work of the committees. A member of one of the expert committees should be a part of the task force.

83. The General Assembly, in carrying out its responsibility relating to the proper functioning of the human rights treaty bodies established to monitor the implementation of instruments adopted by the Assembly itself, and as a matter of the highest priority, should ensure the financing of each of the committees from the United Nations regular budget or make any other financial arrangements that may be necessary to enable each of the committees to operate effectively.

84. The General Assembly should entrust one or two experts with preparing a study on possible long-term approaches to the supervision of new instruments in the light of all relevant considerations.

85. More adequate staffing resources should be provided immediately to service the Committee on the Elimination of Discrimination against Women and, as soon as the overall financial situation permits, additional resources should be provided to the other committees to enable them to discharge all of their responsibilities.

B. *Other matters requiring attention*

86. The Secretariat should provide the members of each committee with relevant statistical information whenever it is readily available from an intergovernmental body. Committee members should have access to at least a copy of the *Statistical Yearbook* of the United Nations and the annual statistical report of the International Monetary Fund, entitled 'International financial statistics", and should each receive annually a copy of the statistical tables appended to the *World Development Report* of the World Bank and *The State of the World's Children* by UNICEF.

87. The detailed reporting manual intended to assist States in the fulfilment of their reporting obligations, which is being prepared by the Centre for Human Rights in collaboration with UNITAR, should be given high priority. Each of the committees should be given an opportunity to comment on a draft of the manual.

88. Each Government should be encouraged to consider establishing a unit that would prepare all of the reports submitted by that State to the treaty bodies.

89. In drafting their reports, States parties are urged to refer, whenever appropriate, to information contained in reports submitted to other treaty bodies, rather than repeating the same information.

90. Each treaty body should continue to review the possibility of revising its requirements as to the periodicity of reporting, taking into account the burden on States and the need for an effective reporting procedure.
91. Treaty bodies should consider how best to make use of individual rapporteurs or co-ordinators and working groups, in order to expedite the timely and effective consideration of periodic reports.
92. Each treaty body should consider imposing some general time-limits on speakers, while acknowledging that exceptions will have to be made in particular cases.
93. The treaty bodies should be consulted when drawing up the relevant parts of the advisory services programme and, if a board of trustees is established to advise the Secretary-General on the functioning of the Voluntary Fund for Advisory Services and Technical Assistance in the Field of Human Rights, consideration should be given to including one or more experts from the treaty bodies.
94. In order to facilitate a more efficient exchange of information and documentation, occasional meetings should be convened between the Chairpersons of the United Nations treaty bodies and those of the relevant regional commissions and the ILO and UNESCO committees on conventions and recommendations and other competent bodies.
95. The treaty bodies should consider establishing procedures designed to facilitate regular meetings with special rapporteurs of the Commission on Human Rights or the Sub-Commission on Prevention of Discrimination and Protection of Minorities who are working on directly relevant subjects, whenever this would be useful.
96. Requests for information directed to the specialized agencies by the treaty bodies should be as precise as possible. Efforts should also be made to develop direct dialogue with competent officials from the agencies concerned, where appropriate.
97. The meetings of Chairpersons should be scheduled regularly on an annual or biennial basis with a view to exchanging experience and improving the implementation of the different instruments.
98. Continuing efforts should be made to ensure publicity for the work of the treaty bodies at both international and national levels. The United Nations information centre in each country should be directed to distribute copies of the report itself, along with details of the Committee's consideration of it, whenever a report of a particular State party is considered.
99. A better gender balance in the composition of the various committees would be desirable.
100. Each treaty body should consider how best to make use of the expertise of its members during the periods between sessions.

A/45/636 — 30 October 1990

UNITED NATIONS GENERAL ASSEMBLY
Forty-fifth session

EFFECTIVE IMPLEMENTATION OF UNITED NATIONS INSTRUMENTS ON HUMAN RIGHTS AND EFFECTIVE FUNCTIONING OF BODIES ESTABLISHED PURSUANT TO SUCH INSTRUMENTS

Note by the Secretary-General

The Secretary-General transmits herewith to the General Assembly the report of the third meeting of persons chairing the human rights treaty bodies convened pursuant to General Assembly resolution 44/135 of 15 December 1989.

ANNEX

Report of the third meeting of persons chairing the human rights treaty bodies

I. INTRODUCTION

1. Since the adoption of resolution 37/44 on 3 December 1982, the General Assembly has continuously kept under review the problems relating to the reporting obligations of States parties to various human rights instruments. Those problems have also received careful attention during the various sessions of the treaty bodies, at some of the meetings of States parties, and at meetings of such other organs as the Economic and Social Council and the Commission on Human Rights.
2. Pursuant to General Assembly resolution 38/117 of 16 December 1983, the Secretary-General convened a first meeting of the persons chairing the bodies entrusted with the consideration of State party reports in August 1984. The report of that meeting was presented to the General Assembly at its thirty-ninth session (A/39/484, annex). A second meeting was convened by the Secretary-General in October 1988, pursuant to General Assembly resolution 42/105 of 7 December 1987, and the report of that meeting was presented to the General Assembly (A/44/98, annex).
3. In its resolution 44/135 of 15 December 1989, the General Assembly endorsed the recommendations of the meeting aimed at streamlining, rationalizing and otherwise improving reporting procedures and invited the persons chairing the human rights treaty bodies to maintain communication and dialogue with each other on common issues and problems. To that end, the Secretary-General was requested to convene a third meeting in 1990. In its resolution

1990/25 of 27 February 1990, the Commission on Human Rights invited the meeting to discuss the range of problems affecting the effective implementation of human rights treaties and further requested that the third meeting be convened in time to allow for the consideration of its conclusions and recommendations by the General Assembly at its forty-fifth session.
4. The third meeting of the persons chairing the human rights treaty bodies was convened by the Secretary-General pursuant to General Assembly resolution 44/135 and Commission on Human Rights resolution 1990/25.

II. ORGANIZATION OF THE MEETING

5. The meeting was held at the United Nations Office at Geneva from 1 to 5 October 1990 and involved the following participants: the Chairman and the Rapporteur of the Human Rights Committee (Mr. Rajsoomer Lallah and Mr. Fausto Pocar), the Rapporteur of the Committee on Economic, Social and Cultural Rights (Mr. Philip Alston), the Chairman of the Committee on the Elimination of Racial Discrimination (Mr. Agha Shahi), the Chairman of the Committee on the Elimination of Discrimination against Women (Ms. Elizabeth Evatt), a member of the Group of Three established under the International Convention on the Suppression and Punishment of the Crime of *Apartheid* (Ms. Lourdes Vallarino)[1] and the Chairman of the Committee against Torture (Mr. Joseph Voyame).
6. Mrs. Christine A. Brautigam, United Nations Institute for Training and Research (UNITAR) Fellow, also participated in one of the meetings. Comments were also made, at the invitation of the meeting, by representatives of Amnesty International and the International Service for Human Rights.
7. The agenda for the meeting was as follows:
  1. Opening of the meeting.
  2. Election of the Chairman.
  3. Adoption of the agenda.
  4. Review of follow-up to the conclusions and recommendations adopted at the second meeting of Chairpersons.
  5. Review of recent developments relating to the work of the treaty bodies.
  6. Matters requiring special consideration:
     (a) Study on the possible long-term approaches to enhancing the effective operation of existing and prospective treaty bodies (A/44/668);
     (b) Draft reporting manual to assist States in fulfilling their reporting obligations;
     (c) Identification of possible technical assistance projects by the treaty bodies;
     (d) Report of the Secretary-General on logistical and human resources support (E/1990/50).
  7. Other matters.
  8. Conclusions and recommendations.
8. The following documentation was made available to participants:
  (a) Provisional agenda (HRI/MC/1990/L.1);

---

[1] Owing to unforseen circumstances Ms. Lourdes Vallarino was unable to participate in the meeting.

(b) Report of the Secretary-General on progress achieved in improving the operation of the reporting system and review of proposed additional measures (HRI/MC/l990/L. 2);
(c) Study on possible long-term approaches to enhancing the effective operation of existing and prospective treaty bodies (A/44/668);
(d) Draft reporting manual to assist States in fulfilling their reporting obligations;
(e) Report of the Secretary-General concerning the situation and developments regarding the logistical and human resources support for the activities of the Centre for Human Rights (E/1990/50);
(f) Background documents, including the note by the Secretary-General (A/44/98), to which was annexed the report of the second meeting; the report of the Secretary-General on the study on computerizing the work of the human rights treaty monitoring bodies (E/CN.4/1990/39); the report of the Secretary-General containing a list of articles showing the nature and extent of overlapping under six international human rights instruments (HRI/MC/1988/L.3); General Assembly resolutions 44/135 of 15 December 1989 and 43/115 of 8 December 1988; Economic and Social Council resolution 1990/47 of 25 May 1990; and Commission on Human Rights resolutions 1990/21 and 1990/25 of 27 February 1990.

9. The meeting was opened by the Under-Secretary-General for Human Rights. In his introductory statement the Under-Secretary-General drew attention to the Secretary-General's most recent report on the activities of the Organization and reviewed some of the issues and documentation that were before the meeting. He spoke in particular about the challenge of enhancing information flows both to and from the treaty bodies and suggested a number of initiatives which might be considered by the meeting. Reference was made to the difficult financial situation of the Organization and to the need for greater resources to be made available to the human rights sector. The Under-secretary-General also reviewed the significance of recent developments in the world and observed that, while denouncing was a necessary condition for the recognition of human rights, it was not in itself sufficient in order to ensure the actual enjoyment of those rights.

10. Mr. Philip Alston was elected Chairman/Rapporteur of the meeting.

III. REVIEW OF RECENT DEVELOPMENTS RELATING TO THE WORK OF THE TREATY BODIES

11. Under this item, the various participants provided a brief oral review of some of the problems and factors that were of special concern to the respective treaty bodies. In particular, problems relating to the following areas were highlighted: (a) financing and logistical support, including the reduction of the number of sessions owing to the lack of resources, insufficient secretariat support and lack of adequate publicity for the work of the committees; (b) consideration of reports, including the adequacy of reports, the provision of technical assistance to States parties and maximization of the use of time during sessions; (c) information, including the need to develop

co-operation with specialized agencies, regional organs and non-governmental organizations; and (d) universalization of the applicability of the human rights treaties, including the need for more ratifications and greater consistency between the obligations imposed by the conventions.

12. The participants noted with special concern the persistence of the problem of overdue reports, which affected all of the treaty bodies and which now amounted to a total of 767 reports.

IV. MATTERS REQUIRING SPECIAL CONSIDERATION

A. *Financial situation of human rights treaty bodies*

13. Reference was made, in particular, to the financial crisis which had adversely affected the activities of the Committee on the Elimination of Racial Discrimination since 1986. It was recalled that the non-compliance of a significant number of States parties with their financial obligations under article 8, paragraph 6, of the Convention on the Elimination of All Forms of Racial Discrimination had resulted in the reduction or cancellation of several sessions of the Committee and consequently in a backlog of reports to be considered. It was pointed out that a similar situation might occur in respect of the Committee against Torture, whose activities were entirely dependent, under article 17, paragraph 7, and article 18, paragraph 5, of the Convention against Torture and Other Cruel, Inhuman or Degrading Treatment or Punishment, on the financial contributions of States parties. It was noted that States parties to that Convention, at their second meeting on 28 November 1989, had expressed concern that the accumulation of arrears in the payment of assessed contributions might ultimately have a paralysing effect on the monitoring of the Convention's implementation.

14. The meeting drew attention to remedial measures envisaged in several resolutions of the General Assembly and the Commission on Human Rights with regard to the financing of the Committee on the Elimination of Racial Discrimination and, in particular, to the measures envisaged by Commission on Human Rights resolution 1990/25. In paragraph 10 of that resolution, the Commission had recommended that a "contingency reserve fund" be established with the concurrence of concerned States parties to the Convention to make it possible to regularize the meeting schedule of the Committee on the Elimination of Racial Discrimination.

15. While endorsing the measure recommended in paragraph 10 of resolution 1990/25, the persons chairing the human rights treaty bodies were of the view that such a measure had to be considered as a temporary arrangement. They reiterated the conclusion reached at their second meeting, in October 1988, that the General Assembly was responsible for the proper functioning of the human rights treaty bodies established to monitor the implementation of instruments that had been adopted by the Assembly itself and once again recommended that the Assembly should ensure the financing of each of the committees from the United Nations regular budget or make other appropriate financial arrangements that may be necessary to enable each of the committees to operate effectively on a permanent basis.

16. The persons chairing the human rights treaty bodies also stated that, notwithstanding the principle that States parties to the International Convention on the Elimination of All Forms of Racial Discrimination and to the Convention against Torture and Other Cruel, Inhuman or Degrading Treatment or Punishment must fulfil their financial obligations, and that every effort had to be made by the United Nations to promote respect for those obligations, strong consideration should be given by the General Assembly to the possibility of amending those human rights instruments in order to guarantee the long-term viability of their monitoring mechanisms. In this connection, they expressed their support for the various proposals to deal with the actual or potential financial problems of certain treaty bodies contained in paragraphs 97 to 99 of the study on effective implementation of international instruments on human rights, including reporting obligations under these instruments (A/44/668).

B. Servicing and resources available to human rights treaty bodies

17. With regard to this issue, the persons chairing the human rights treaty bodies recalled that at their second meeting they had recommended that more adequate staffing resources should be provided immediately to service the Committee on the Elimination of Discrimination against Women and, as soon as the overall financial situation permitted, additional resources should be provided to the other committees to enable them to discharge all of their responsibilities. Reference was made, in that connection, to the report on the situation regarding the logistical and human resources support for the increasing activities of the Centre for Human Rights (E/1990/50), which, *inter alia*, provided explanations on the basic needs of the Centre to ensure adequate services to all human rights bodies with particular attention being given to the servicing of treaty bodies as emphasized by the Commission on Human Rights in its resolution 1990/25.
18. Considerable attention was devoted at the meeting to the present arrangements devoted to the servicing of the Committee on the Elimination of Discrimination against Women. The importance of ensuring that that Committee remain in close contact with the other treaty bodies and that it is fully informed in its work of the activities of the other principal human rights organs, such as the Commission on Human Rights and the Sub-Commission on Prevention of Discrimination and Protection of Minorities, was clearly recognized. It was noted that those needs would become even more crucial in the future as the number of treaty bodies increased, as the possibilities for duplicative activities grew, and as the quest to promote normative consistency became even more challenging.
19. It was observed, however, that the present institutional arrangements, whereby the Committee alone was serviced from Vienna (by the Centre for Social Development and Humanitarian Affairs), while all of the other treaty bodies are serviced from Geneva (by the Centre for Human Rights), were not at all conducive to facilitating the type and level of interaction that was necessary. The difficulties caused by geographical separation were further exacerbated by the inadequate secretariat resources available to Committee members at Vienna. While conference servicing needs had generally been satisfied and

improvements made as to the Committee's New York sessions, no significant research, analytical or informational services were provided. Moreover, while the Secretariat provided help with its limited resources, the specialist expertise of the Vienna Centre did not extend to a close knowledge of the activities of all of the human rights organs and treaty bodies of the United Nations system. In addition, the benefits that the Committee had derived from proximity to the secretariat of the Commission on the Status of Women had been minimal as there were no formal links between these bodies. The fear was expressed that the present system could lead to the Committee becoming isolated from the United Nations human rights system as a whole.

20. For those reasons, the meeting agreed that strong and active consideration should be given to relocating the functions relating to the Convention on the Elimination of All Forms of Discrimination against Women to the United Nations Office at Geneva. It was observed that while this proposal might be seen as an attempt by the Geneva secretariat to expand its coverage (albeit minimally) at the expense of that in Vienna, such an interpretation would be entirely unwarranted. The dominant consideration in this regard had to be the best interests of the Committee itself and of the human rights treaty regime as a whole. It was suggested that the best way to proceed might be for the General Assembly to request that the Chairman of the Committee discuss the matter with the Committee at its next session and prepare without financial implications a brief evaluation of the advantages and disadvantages of the proposal, to be forwarded to the General Assembly in due course.

21. On the broader question of secretariat servicing for the treaty bodies, the meeting again drew attention to the fact that the work of the Centre for Human Rights had increased very greatly in recent years but that resources had failed to keep pace with the work-load and the increase in responsibilities. They generally agreed that it was necessary to increase the logistical and human resources of the Centre, especially to assist the treaty bodies in carrying out their mandates.

C. *Cross-referencing in the reporting procedures*

22. The persons chairing the human rights treaty bodies noted that the term "cross-referencing" would be understood to mean the incorporation in a report to a treaty body of material included in a report to another treaty body by annexure, quotation or reference. They agreed that the practice of making cross-references in the reports to be submitted by States parties to more than one international human rights instrument was necessary to alleviate the task of States parties, which frequently had to provide comprehensive information to each of the treaty bodies, as well as to avoid duplication in the information submitted. This practice was increasingly justified by the entry into force of new instruments and new reporting procedures, such as the Convention on the Rights of the Child, which contained matters already covered by other instruments. However, the meeting was of the view that a methodology had to be found to avoid depriving treaty bodies of the information they needed in the overall context of the implementation of a particular instrument, especially where interrelated rights and inconsistencies could be at issue.

23. Most participants felt that cross-referencing could not be systematic and its acceptability had to be left for determination by each treaty body on a case by case basis. It was recommended that, in the future, treaty bodies should share information with each other about their practices in the foregoing regard.
24. Furthermore, the view was expressed that a detailed technical analysis of the provisions of various human rights instruments would enable treaty bodies to identify not only the overlapping of provisions but also the differences in formulation and content between texts of certain international legal provisions. Cross-references to these provisions would also be useful to avoid competing interpretations with regard to their application.
25. In addition, it was suggested that similarities among provisions of different human rights instruments could be indicated in the reporting manual to assist States in fulfilling their reporting obligations and that specific proposals with respect to cross-referencing could be included in the general guidelines for the submission of reports by States parties. It was also noted that those issues could be addressed more fully in the context of seminars that should be organized for those persons in governmental service who materially prepared reports to be submitted to treaty bodies.
26. It was also suggested that each treaty body could appoint members who would establish liaison with each of the other treaty bodies and would be in regular contact with them with a view to solving specific problems, including those relating to cross-referencing. Those members could be invited to participate in meetings of the relevant treaty bodies and could brief the members of those bodies about important matters of mutual concern.

D. *Normative consistency*

27. The persons chairing the human rights treaty bodies noted that certain inconsistencies in the provisions of international instruments and, in particular, between provisions of international instruments and those of regional instruments might raise difficulties with regard to their implementation. Furthermore, they felt that a degree of consistency should be sought among the general comments that treaty bodies were preparing with regard to the interpretation and application of provisions of various human rights instruments. In this connection, they reiterated the view that increased contacts on a permanent basis among treaty bodies, and not only among chairmen of treaty bodies, would avoid inconsistencies and promote knowledge and harmonization of the work of each treaty body. They were of the view that for that purpose the appointment of a member of a treaty body who would establish liaison with the other treaty bodies on these and other matters, as mentioned above, was a very useful suggestion. It was also recalled that the secretariat had the important role of advising on inconsistencies or overlapping of legal provisions especially when new international human rights instruments were under elaboration.

E. *Computerization*

28. The meeting took note with interest of the study on computerizing the work of the human rights treaty monitoring bodies (E/CN.4/1990/39). The suggestion was made that regular contacts be established between the secretariat

of the Committee on the Elimination of Discrimination against Women and the Centre for Human Rights in order to share information relating to the programme of computerization.

F. The development of new international human rights instruments and its implications

29. With regard to this issue, differing views were expressed as to whether preference should be given in the future to non-binding instruments over binding instruments. The opinion was expressed that possibilities of elaborating both binding and non-binding human rights instruments should be left open. Often, in the United Nations, a declaration on a particular human rights issue was followed by the elaboration of a convention on the same issue. It was agreed, however, that whenever possible the supervisory or monitoring functions established under new human rights treaties should be assigned to appropriate existing treaty bodies that were felt to possess the necessary competence. New instruments should be adopted, to the extent possible, in the form of protocols to existing instruments. Should such new responsibilities be contemplated, the relevant monitoring bodies should be consulted and appropriate arrangements, including for staff and financial support, be made. Equally, however, it was pointed out that if the subject-matter of a new instrument required particular expertise, a specific body of experts might need to be established to monitor that instrument.

G. New international human rights instruments and the desirability of taking into account existing provisions in drafting new instruments

30. As noted above, the meeting generally agreed that it would be preferable to elaborate new instruments in the form of protocols to existing instruments. However, if this was not possible, certain basic points should be taken into account in drafting the text of new instruments.

31. The persons chairing the human rights treaty bodies were of the view that new international human rights instruments should not specify the periodicity of reporting by States parties, but should simply indicate that the periodicity should not exceed five years. They also agreed that new instruments should not indicate the maximum duration of the sessions of their supervisory organs and that a thorough review of existing international provisions should be made before drafting flew instruments. At every stage in the drafting process the possibility of overlap and the need for consistency in standards should be given close attention. Similarly, a comprehensive "technical review" should always be carried out before a new instrument is finally adopted. In addition, whenever new instruments were being drafted, every effort should be made to ensure that adequate *travaux préparatoires* were made.

32. The persons chairing the human rights treaty bodies also raised the question of difficulties in monitoring the implementation of international legal provisions which might be caused by the confidentiality of certain procedures established under other international instruments. They agreed that confidentiality should not preclude contacts among treaty bodies that would be essential to ensure the respect of the legal provisions concerned. Furthermore,

they agreed that new human rights instruments should make provision for the financing of their monitoring mechanisms through the regular budget.

33. They also felt that a briefing for newly elected members of treaty bodies about the work of the treaty bodies, United Nations organs, specialized agencies, and other relevant matters would be useful. It was suggested that such a briefing would be in addition to that given informally by other members and should be arranged in an appropriate manner with the assistance of the secretariat.

H. *Technical assistance*

34. It was recalled that the General Assembly, in its resolution 44/135, had invited the treaty bodies to give priority attention to identifying, in the regular course of their work of reviewing State reports, possibilities for technical assistance projects. The Commission on Human Rights, in its resolution 1990/58, had also called upon the treaty bodies to take action in that sense.

35. The meeting agreed that assistance to States parties in preparing reports at the national level was a high priority area for the United Nations Advisory Services and Technical Assistance Programme. Seminars and training courses at the national level were considered as the only cost-effective means to tailor the relevant assistance programmes to local circumstances and needs. It was for each treaty body in the process of consideration of State party reports to identify such needs. Reference was made in this connection to an earlier suggestion by the Committee on the Elimination of Discrimination against Women that resources should be sought to set up specific country programmes to enable an expert to be sent at the request of a State party to provide assistance to that State party in the preparation of its national reports. Additionally, participants reiterated that each Government should once again be encouraged to consider establishing a unit that would prepare all of the reports submitted by that State party to the treaty bodies.

36. It was further agreed that advisory services and technical assistance should also be directed at involving those who had a direct bearing on the implementation of human rights policies, such as members of the judiciary and lawyers, in seminars or colloquia to discuss the relevance of international human rights standards to their work. It was further noted that it would be desirable for the Centre for Human Rights to obtain more specialist expertise in the training field and that training courses in the field of human rights for officials of some of the major United Nations development agencies (the United Nations Development Programme, World Bank, etc.) should be envisaged. It was noted that the International Labour Organisation already undertook such training programmes on a regular basis for its own staff.

37. The meeting expressed regret that no training courses or workshops devoted primarily to the preparation and submission of reports had been held during the past two years by the Centre for Human Rights.

I. *Sources of information available to the treaty bodies*

38. Participants noted with appreciation that several non-governmental organizations had systematically provided background information to individual members of treaty bodies whenever State reports were considered and had

undertaken other activities directly related to the enhancement of public awareness of international human rights instruments. The material provided by non-governmental organizations was considered valuable and had, consequently, contributed to the effective fulfilment by the treaty bodies of their responsibilities regarding the consideration of State reports. In this regard particular mention was made of the valuable contribution made by the International Women's Rights Action Watch to the work of the Committee on the Elimination of Discrimination against Women. It was generally felt that each committee should decide in the light of its own circumstances the extent and the form of the co-operation with non-governmental organizations. Non-governmental organizations, in particular at the national level, were further encouraged to devote appropriate attention to the work of the treaty-bodies under the reporting system. It was also noted that the Centre for Human Rights had initiated consultations with the Department of Public Information concerning the distribution through United Nations information centres of State reports, press releases and summary records concerning the consideration of such reports, and views adopted on individual communications. Participants regretted, however, that those consultations had so far proved unproductive and that non-governmental organizations and the public at large had not yet benefitted from a regular flow of information of that type. It was therefore once again emphasized that urgent efforts should be undertaken for such basic material to be disseminated as widely as possible through the United Nations information centres and by the secretariats of the relevant committees.

39. With regard to co-operation with specialized agencies, it was noted that on many occasions the various specialized agencies, particularly the International Labour Organisation, the World Health Organization and the United Nations Educational, Scientific and Cultural Organization had provided useful assistance to the various treaty bodies. The Committee on Economic, Social and Cultural Rights, in particular, had established an extensive set of procedures whereby specialized agencies had been invited to take part in the consideration of State reports and in discussions on particular topics. It was agreed that extensive co-operation with specialized agencies should continue to be encouraged through various means.

40. With reference to the activities undertaken by treaty bodies, it was suggested that each committee might wish to request the secretariat to make available to it, in addition to the annual reports of the other treaty bodies, copies of reports of relevant States parties submitted under other instruments. Any relevant documentation of the General Assembly, the Security Council and other United Nations organs should also be made available to the treaty bodies when deemed pertinent to their activities.

41. Reference was also made to a recommendation by the second meeting relating to the establishment of a committee resource room in which documentation of the relevant committees could be kept along with copies of constitutions, basic reports and legislation and other relevant and useful information. It was generally felt that despite a shortage of available space within the Centre for Human Rights, major efforts should be undertaken towards providing such a room, which could contribute very significantly to the work of the individual committee members. It was noted that materials

for inclusion in such a resource room would probably be donated by various groups and agencies and that use could be made of interns to undertake the initial organization of the materials.

42. It was pointed out that each treaty body should have access to all the sources of information it deemed necessary to fulfil its functions effectively. It was, however, agreed that the type of information needed and the way to handle it would have to be decided by each committee in the light of its own requirements and circumstances.

J. Public information

43. With regard to the issue of public information, it was noted that the activities of the various treaty bodies should be publicized as widely as possible so that the affected individuals were made aware of their rights under the international human rights instruments and could take an appropriate role in the process of the preparation of State reports. It was underlined that the holding of press conferences at the end of committee sessions and the issuing of press releases had not always led to significant coverage by the media of the activities of the treaty bodies. It was agreed that it would be helpful if the annual report of committees could be synthesized from time to time and made available in more readable form for distribution to the general public. However, it was also generally agreed that to some extent public information on the activities of the committees, including views expressed in individual cases, should be specifically targeted to the potentially most interested groups, such as lawyers, judges and teachers. To that end, participants suggested the award of fellowships by the Centre for Human Rights specifically for the purpose of disseminating information regarding the activities of the treaty bodies.

44. Lastly, it was agreed that the most effective public information activities were those undertaken at the national and local levels and, in that connection, it was reiterated that United Nations information centres and non-governmental organizations should he more actively involved in alerting the public to the activities of the treaty bodies.

K. Long-term rationalization of the existing system of treaty bodies

45. With regard to the long-term rationalization of the existing system of treaty bodies, the meeting agreed that the relevant issues could profitably be raised in the overall context of the preparation of the proposed world conference on human rights. For that purpose consideration could be given to the appointment of an expert to prepare a study.

V. OTHER MATTERS

46. The participants took note with satisfaction of the revised text of the consolidated guidelines for the initial part of State party reports as approved by the various treaty bodies (appended to this report) and agreed that the guidelines should be disseminated to the States parties as soon as possible.

47. The participants reviewed the draft reporting manual that had been prepared by UNITAR in co-operation with the Centre for Human Rights. They considered that the manual would be extremely useful to the States parties in the preparation of their reports as well as in orienting newly elected members of the treaty bodies. They noted that the views expressed in the different contributions contained in the manual were those of their authors and did not necessarily represent those of the relevant committees or of any United Nations body. The participants agreed that the manual should be published in its present form as soon as possible and disseminated to States parties as widely as possible. They also expressed their warm appreciation of the work of the UNITAR Fellow in bringing the preparation of the manual to a successful conclusion.
48. The participants expressed strong support for the proposal addressed in General Assembly resolution 44/156 to convene a world conference on human rights. They stressed the importance of making thorough preparations for such a conference and urged that the treaty bodies should be associated with the conference and should be closely consulted, through their chairmen and where possible directly, in the course of its preparation.

VI. CONCLUSIONS AND RECOMMENDATIONS

49. The following conclusions and recommendations are respectfully submitted to the General Assembly for its consideration in accordance with its resolution 44/135. Some concern action that might be taken by the Assembly itself or by other appropriate organs of the United Nations, while others fall within the competence of the respective treaty bodies or of the States parties to the treaties. However, no distinction is drawn in this regard for the purposes of the present report, since the mandate of the meeting is to propose diverse means to improve the functioning of the treaty supervisory system.
50. In view of the very large number of overdue reports owed to the treaty bodies as a whole, the General Assembly should continue to emphasize the importance of adequate and timely reporting by all States parties to the various treaties.
51. The treaty bodies themselves should continue to use all appropriate means to promote the submission of overdue reports. Where possible, efforts should be made to develop a dialogue with the representatives in New York, Geneva or Vienna of the States parties concerned with a view to emphasizing the importance of reporting and to exploring possible means of assisting them. In cases where a number of overdue reports are involved, the Under-Secretary-General for Human Rights should raise the matter in the course of his regular consultations with the representatives of States parties.
52. While noting with satisfaction the steadily growing number of States parties to the various instruments, the meeting stressed that there was no cause for complacency in that regard. The goal of achieving the universal applicability of the principal instruments remained far from being achieved. States which have not yet ratified those instruments should be urged to reconsider their position and to take appropriate measures to seek to remove any remaining obstacles to ratification or accession.

53. The financial situation of the treaty bodies warrants continuing attention by the General Assembly and the States parties. In particular, the meeting urged that action be taken by States parties to the International Convention on the Elimination of All Forms of Racial Discrimination to establish a "contingency reserve fund" as proposed by the Commission on Human Rights in paragraph 10 of its resolution 1990/25. In any event, the General Assembly should as a matter of the highest priority take appropriate measures to ensure the financing of each of the committees from the United Nations regular budget or to make such other financial arrangements as may be necessary to enable each of the committees to operate effectively.
54. Consideration should also be given to amending the relevant provisions of the International Convention on the Elimination of All Forms of Racial Discrimination and the Convention against Torture and Other Cruel, Inhuman or Degrading Treatment or Punishment to provide full funding for the relevant treaty bodies from the regular budget of the United Nations.
55. Adequate secretariat servicing should be provided to each of the treaty bodies to enable them to function effectively. At present, the combination of diminishing resources and rapidly expanding demands on the available resources had left most of the treaty bodies without the appropriate level of secretariat servicing. The Secretary-General and the General Assembly should do their utmost to ensure that more resources are provided specifically for this purpose.
56. As recommended in the report of the second meeting (A/44/98, annex, para. 89), States parties, in drafting their reports, may refer, annex or incorporate, whenever appropriate, information contained in reports submitted to other treaty bodies, rather than repeat the same information.
57. In general terms, the effective development of the human rights treaty system as a whole would be significantly enhanced by the promotion of greater interaction among the treaty bodies. Each of the committees should thus seek to keep well informed of developments within the others. For that purpose consideration should be given to the appointment of several members, each of whom should be responsible for following as closely as possible the developments in one of the other treaty bodies and reporting thereon to his or her committee. Other innovative arrangements should also be explored, such as the holding of joint sessions of working groups of two or more committees to explore a specific issue. Advantage should also be taken of any opportunities to provide a briefing to one committee on relevant current developments by a member of another committee.
58. The General Assembly should take appropriate action to institutionalize the meeting of persons chairing the human rights treaty bodies and to ensure that it is held at least once every two years.
59. In preparing "general comments", "general recommendations" or "suggestions" on topics that are of potentially major relevance to the provisions of an instrument that is supervised by another body, the committee concerned should consider undertaking some appropriate form of consultation before the finalization of the text in question.
60. The process of establishing a computerized data base to improve the efficiency and effectiveness of the functioning of the treaty bodies should be accorded a high priority by the Secretary-General and every effort should

be made to implement fully the recommendations of the relevant task force on this issue (see E/CN.4/1990/39). The Committee on the Elimination of Discrimination against Women and its secretariat should be kept fully informed of developments within the Centre for Human Rights in this regard.
61. As far as possible and appropriate, the supervision of new human rights treaty obligations should be entrusted to one or other of the existing treaty bodies. Similarly, careful consideration should always be given to the drafting of protocols to existing instruments in preference to entirely new treaties, whenever appropriate. When such protocols are under preparation the relevant treaty body should be consulted prior to their final adoption.
62. When new treaties are drafted, the periodicity of reporting should be left open provided that a report is required at least once every five years. Similarly, new treaties should not stipulate a maximum duration for the sessions of the relevant supervisory body. They should always provide for the financing of the supervisory mechanisms from the regular budget.
63. Whenever new human rights instruments are being drafted, adequate "travaux préparatoires" should be made and a thorough technical review be undertaken prior to the final adoption of the text.
64. Prior to the first session of any new treaty body, every effort should be made to provide a detailed technical background briefing to the members of the new committee. The briefing should deal with matters such as the relationship of the different treaty bodies to one another, the relationship of the treaty bodies to the other human rights organs, the nature of the work of any other United Nations bodies or agencies in so far as it is of direct relevance to the work of the new committee, and any other pertinent matters. Newly elected members of the existing treaty bodies should also be provided with such briefings if they so request.
65. The consolidated guidelines for the initial part of State party reports under the various treaties, as drawn up in consultation with all of the treaty bodies, should be added to the relevant guidelines as soon as possible.
66. The manual on reporting drawn up by UNITAR in co-operation with the Centre for Human Rights, approved by the meeting on the advice of the Editorial Board, should be published as soon as possible and be widely disseminated.
67. The proposed world conference on human rights could, if adequately prepared, make a major contribution to furthering the overall objectives of the United Nations in the human rights field. The work of the treaty bodies should be fully reflected in the agenda, the preparation of which should be done in consultation with those bodies as far as possible. A detailed evaluation of the work of each of the treaty bodies should be prepared by individual experts as part of the background documentation for the Conference.
68. To assist it in the fulfilment of its responsibilities, each of the treaty bodies should have access to all of the sources of information that it feels it needs in order to be effective. In this regard, information provided by non-governmental organizations can be of major importance. The treaty bodies should also take full advantage of the expertise and experience of the specialized agencies and other United Nations bodies whenever appropriate.
69. Particular importance should be attached to the dissemination at the national level of he report of the relevant State party and details of its

examination by the committee, especially to those sectors which have direct responsibility for the implementation of human rights, such as the judiciary, the legal profession, appropriate ministries and national human rights bodies. For that reason, each United Nations information office should, on a routine basis, make available all reports submitted to the treaty bodies by the State in whose territory it is located, along with the summary records relating to the examination of the reports. The Secretary-General should be requested to report on the implementation of this recommendation in due course.
70. The secretariat of each of the treaty bodies should seek to enhance the means by which copies of the relevant documentation can be made available to non-governmental organizations, particularly those active at the national level.
71. As already requested by the General Assembly on several occasions, the relevant secretariats should ensure that each member of each of the treaty bodies receives the annual report of each of the other treaty bodies in a regular and timely fashion.
72. The Secretary-General should continue to publicize the activities of the treaty bodies as effectively as possible and should consider allocating a specific number of fellowships to be available especially to academics, journalists or others proposing to write on the work of any of the treaty bodies.
73. In the context of technical assistance and advisory services programmes organized by the United Nations, a series of seminars or workshops should be organized at the national level for the purpose of training those involved in the preparation of State party reports. Such workshops, if carefully tailored to the needs of the individual State, could reach many more people in each State than regional seminars and be far more cost-effective.
74. Regional and sub-regional seminars and training programmes should be directed particularly at those individuals, such as judges, lawyers and administrators who have an actual or potential substantive involvement in the implementation of the obligations assumed by their States. The Centre for Human Rights should seek to develop professional training expertise to assist in the management of such programmes.
75. Training programmes should also be arranged, on a regular basis, for the officials of United Nations bodies and agencies involved in technical co-operation programmes. The purpose of such programmes would be to familiarize the relevant officials with the standards contained in the principal human rights treaties and to develop a better understanding of the means by which those standards can be reflected in the day-to-day activities of the agencies.

APPENDIX

Consolidated guidelines for the initial part of the reports of States parties

Land and people
1. This section should contain information about the main ethnic and demographic characteristics of the country and its population, as well as such socio-economic and cultural indicators as per capita income, gross national

product, rate of inflation, external debt, rate of unemployment, literacy rate and religion. It should also include information on the population by mother tongue, life expectancy, infant mortality, maternal mortality, fertility rate, percentage of population under 15 and over 65 years of age, percentage of population in rural areas and in urban areas and percentage of households headed by women. As far as possible, States should make efforts to provide all data disaggregated by sex.
2. This section should describe briefly the political history and framework, the type of government and the organization of the executive, legislative and judicial organs.

General legal framework within which human rights are protected

3. This section should contain information on:
   (a) Which judicial, administrative or other competent authorities have jurisdiction affecting human rights;
   (b) What remedies are available to an individual who claims that any of his rights have been violated; and what systems of compensation and rehabilitation exist for victims;
   (c) Whether any of the rights referred to in the various human rights instruments are protected either in the constitution or by a separate bill of rights and, if so, what provisions are made in the constitution or bill of rights for derogations and in what circumstances;
   (d) How human rights instruments are made part of the national legal system;
   (e) Whether the provisions of the various human rights instruments can be invoked before, or directly enforced by, the courts, other tribunals or administrative authorities or whether they must be transformed into internal laws or administrative regulations in order to be enforced by the authorities concerned;
   (f) Whether there exist any institutions or national machinery with responsibility for overseeing the implementation of human rights.

Information and publicity

4. This section should indicate whether any special efforts have been made to promote awareness among the public and the relevant authorities of the rights contained in the various human rights instruments. The topics to be addressed should include the manner and extent to which the texts of the various human rights instruments have been disseminated, whether such texts have been translated into the local language or languages, what government agencies have responsibility for preparing reports and whether they normally receive information or other inputs from external sources, and whether the contents of the reports are the subject of public debate.

A/47/628 — 10 November 1992

UNITED NATIONS GENERAL ASSEMBLY
Forty-seventh session

EFFECTIVE IMPLEMENTATION OF INTERNATIONAL INSTRUMENTS ON HUMAN RIGHTS, INCLUDING REPORTING OBLIGATIONS UNDER INTERNATIONAL INSTRUMENTS ON HUMAN RIGHTS

Note by the Secretary-General

The Secretary-General transmits herewith to the General Assembly the report of the fourth meeting of persons chairing the human rights treaty bodies convened pursuant to General Assembly resolution 46/111 of 17 December 1991.

ANNEX

Report of the fourth meeting of persons chairing the human rights treaty bodies

I. INTRODUCTION

1. Since the adoption of resolution 37/44 on 3 December 1982, the General Assembly has continuously kept under review the problems relating to the effective implementation of international instruments on human rights, including reporting obligations under international instruments on human rights. Those problems have also received careful attention during the various sessions of the treaty bodies, at some of the meetings of States parties, and at meetings of such other organs as the Economic and Social Council and the Commission on Human Rights.
2. Pursuant to General Assembly resolution 38/117 of 16 December 1983, the Secretary-General convened a first meeting of the persons chairing the bodies entrusted with the consideration of State party reports in August 1984. The report of that meeting was presented to the General Assembly at its thirty-ninth session (A/39/484, annex). A second meeting was convened by the Secretary-General in October 1988, pursuant to General Assembly resolution 42/105 of 7 December 1987, and the report of that meeting was presented to the General Assembly at its forty-fourth session (A/44/98, annex). A third meeting was convened by the Secretary-General in October 1990, pursuant to General Assembly resolution 44/135 of 15 December 1989, and the report

of that meeting was presented to the General Assembly at its forty-fifth session (A/45/636, annex).
3. In its resolution 46/111 of 17 December 1991, the General Assembly endorsed the conclusions and recommendations of the meetings of persons chairing the human rights treaty bodies aimed at streamlining, rationalizing and otherwise improving reporting procedures: requested the Secretary-General to take appropriate steps in order to finance the biennial meetings of persons chairing the human rights treaty bodies from resources available from the regular budget of the United Nations; and decided to give priority consideration at its forty-seventh session to the conclusions and recommendations of the meetings of persons chairing treaty bodies, in the light of the deliberations of the Commission on Human Rights. In its resolution 1992/15 of 21 February 1992, the Commission on Human Rights endorsed the recommendation in the report of the third meeting of persons chairing the human rights treaty bodies to institutionalize the meetings and requested the General Assembly to take appropriate action to enable those meetings to be held on a biennial basis; and requested that the meeting of persons chairing the human rights treaty bodies in 1992 include on its agenda the question of the extent of reservations to human rights instruments.
4. The fourth meeting of persons chairing the human rights treaty bodies was convened by the Secretary-General pursuant to General Assembly resolution 46/111 and Commission on Human Rights resolution 1992/15.

II. ORGANIZATION OF THE MEETING

5. The meeting was held at the United Nations Office at Geneva from 12 to 16 October 1992. The following persons chairing the human rights treaty bodies attended: Mr. Philip Alston (Committee on Economic, Social and Cultural Rights), Mr. Fausto Pocar (Human Rights Committee), Mr. Luis Valencia Rodriguez (Committee on the Elimination of Racial Discrimination), Mrs. Mervat Tallawy (Committee on the Elimination of Discrimination against Women), Mr. Joseph Voyame (Committee against Torture) and Mrs. Hoda Badran (Committee on the Rights of the Child). Mr. Hector Villarroel, a member of the Group of Three established under the International Convention on the Suppression and Punishment of the Crime of Apartheid, also participated in the meeting.
6. Representatives of the International Labour Organisation (ILO), Amnesty International and the International Service for Human Rights also attended the meeting.
7. The agenda for the meeting was as follows:
    1. Opening of the meeting.
    2. Election of the Chairperson.
    3. Adoption of the agenda.
    4. Review of recent developments relating to the work of the treaty bodies and follow-up to the conclusions and recommendations adopted at the third meeting of chairpersons.
    5. Matters requiring special consideration:
        1. General situation of overdue reports;

2. Identification of possible technical assistance projects by the treaty bodies;
3. Question of the extent of reservations to human rights instruments;
4. Comments and recommendations to the preparatory Committee for the World Conference on Human Rights;
5. Developments relating to the Centre for Human Rights, including support for the work of the treaty bodies.
6. Other matters.
7. Conclusions and Recommendations.
8. The following documentation was made available to the participants:
   (a) Provisional agenda (HRI/MC/1992/1);
   (b) Report of the Secretary-General on progress achieved in improving the operation of the treaty bodies (HRI/MC/1992/2);
   (c) Report of the Secretary-General on the status of the international human rights instruments and the general situation of overdue reports (HRI/MC/1992/3);
   (d) Working paper prepared by the secretariat on the question of the extent of reservations to human rights instruments;
   (e) Compilation of general comments and general recommendations adopted by human rights treaty bodies (HRI/GEN/1);
   (f) Background documents, including the notes by the Secretary-General to which were annexed the reports of the first second and third meetings of the chairpersons (A/39/484, A/44/98 and A/45/636); a study by Mr. Philip Alston on possible long-term approaches to enhancing the effective operation of the human rights treaty bodies (A/44/668); relevant reports of the Secretary-General to the Commission on Human Rights and to the Subcommission on Prevention of Discrimination and Protection of Minorities (E/CN.4/1992/44, E/CN.4/1992/75 and E/CN.4/Sub.2/1992/27 and Corr.1); General Assembly resolutions 45/85 45/115 and 46/111; Commission on Human Rights resolutions 1991/20 and 1992/15; and various reports and other documents relating to the meetings of the Preparatory Committee of the World Conference on Human Rights.
9. The meeting was opened by Mr. Enayat Houshmand. Chief of the Implementation of International Instruments and Procedures Branch of the Centre for Human Rights, on behalf of the Under-Secretary-General for Human Rights. In his introductory statement, Mr. Houshmand noted, *inter alia*, that there had been a significant increase in the numbers of States parties to each of the human rights instruments since the third meeting of chairpersons in 1990 and that, at present, more than 160 States were party to one or more of those instruments.
10. He drew particular attention to two issues that needed to be addressed by the meeting. The first concerned the question of the extent of reservations to the various human rights conventions, which had been considered by a number of human rights treaty bodies, as well as by the Subcommission on Prevention of Discrimination and Protection of Minorities. Those bodies had expressed concern that certain reservations could have the effect of undermining the human rights treaties. In its resolution 1992/15, the Commission on Human Rights had requested that the issue be included in

the agenda of the fourth meeting of chairpersons. The second issue concerned the suggestion made by two members of treaty bodies that the meeting of chairpersons should examine the possibility of undertaking preventive action against human rights violations, within the scope of the activities of the human rights treaty bodies. Additionally, in his report to the forty-seventh session of the General Assembly on the work of the Organization, the Secretary-General had identified the need to consider ways to empower him and the expert human rights bodies to bring massive violations of human rights to the attention of the Security Council, together with recommendations for action.
11. Mrs. Mervat Tallawy was elected Chairperson of the meeting and Mr. Philip Alston was elected Rapporteur.
12. On 15 and 16 October 1992, the chairpersons considered the draft report on their fourth meeting. The report, as amended during the course of the discussion, was adopted unanimously by the chairpersons.

III. REVIEW OF RECENT DEVELOPMENTS RELATING TO THE WORK OF THE TREATY BODIES AND FOLLOW-UP TO THE CONCLUSIONS AND RECOMMENDATIONS ADOPTED AT THE THIRD MEETING OF CHAIRPERSONS AND MATTERS REQUIRING SPECIAL CONSIDERATION

13. Consideration of agenda items 4 and 5 began with a brief oral overview by each of the participants of recent developments of special concern to the respective treaty bodies. Participants noted that the significant increase in the number of States parties to each of the instruments meant that many of the long-standing problems of the treaty bodies needed to be addressed immediately if the treaty body system were to carry out its functions effectively. Chief among those problems were the precarious financial situation of some of the committees and the general need for increased servicing from the secretariat on the part of all committees. Additionally, a reliable information infrastructure was needed to ensure that the members of the various committees were informed of all relevant developments and that the work of the treaty bodies was sufficiently publicized.
14. Throughout their discussions, the chairpersons emphasized the importance of the promotion and protection of human rights within the scope of the activities of the United Nations. Recent developments had demonstrated the close connection between human rights and national stability and development as well as international peace and security. If United Nations action in the field of human rights was to be responsive to both the increased demands being placed upon it by Governments and the rising expectations of the general public, a significantly greater commitment of resources to United Nations human rights programmes would be necessary. Although the human rights treaty bodies were at the centre of the efforts to implement the international human rights standards adopted by the United Nations, their effective functioning could not be considered in isolation from the support provided under other activities of the Centre for Human Rights, particularly activities relating to information and technical assistance. If

greater resources were not forthcoming, the United Nations human rights programme as a whole risked losing credibility.

Timely submission of overdue reports

15. The chairpersons emphasized that the timely submission of reports was essential for the effective discharge by the treaty bodies of their duties under the various instruments. Since the reports formed the basis of the dialogue between the committees and the States parties, overdue reports constituted a serious interruption of the implementation process envisaged under such instruments. While a large number of States parties were overdue in meeting their reporting obligations, it was noted that a small number of States accounted for a disproportionate number of the overdue reports for all of the instruments. Some of the committees had taken initiatives to focus attention on those States and invited them to submit relevant information in accordance with their reporting obligations. It would be helpful if all of the treaty bodies would, at the very least, identify those States whose reports were long overdue so that steps could be taken to re-establish cooperation between the committees and the States concerned. This would also facilitate the identification of factors and difficulties experienced by those States with regard to their reporting obligations. The need to establish an ongoing regular dialogue was particularly important in the case of the few States whose initial reports were long overdue. By failing to fulfil their obligations under the respective instruments to which they were a party, such States threatened the credibility of the monitoring process as a whole. A range of alternative approaches to deal with this grave situation and encourage the closer cooperation of all States parties was discussed by the participants.

16. It was also noted that the long delay in some cases between the submission of a report and its actual consideration by the committee concerned was a disincentive for States to submit their reports on time. The primary reason cited for such delays was the lack of sufficient time available to those treaty bodies for the consideration of reports. This was particularly problematic for those committees which were only able to meet annually and then often for an insufficient period of time. Significant backlogs in the consideration of reports resulted in various detrimental effects, including the fact that reports lost their timeliness and necessitated the provision of substantial supplementary reporting by the State party.

Universalization of the human rights instruments

17. Participants welcomed the appreciable increase in the number of States parties to the various instruments that had taken place since the 1990 meeting of chairpersons. Although none of the treaties was close to having universal adherence, the treaty system as a whole included the vast majority of Member States of the United Nations. It was particularly important for the treaty bodies to meet the challenge of effectively supervising the implementation of human rights standards in the large number of new States parties. In that regard, the need for an improved information base supporting the work of the treaty bodies was stressed. It was also pointed out that an integrated – and not a fragmented – approach was needed with regard to the promotion of adherence to the various human rights instruments as well as in monitoring their implementation.

18. Concern was expressed that a number of States had adhered to only one or the other of the two International Covenants. This had the effect of undermining the principle that the two sets of rights covered in the Covenants – economic, social and cultural rights on the one hand and civil and political rights on the other – were complementary and indivisible. The States parties concerned should be urged to consider ratifying or acceding to the other Covenant as soon as possible. It was also pointed out that there were a number of new States that had previously been constituent parts of other States parties to some of the human rights treaties. All appropriate measures should be taken to ensure that the people living in those successor States would continue to benefit from the protection afforded by the human rights instruments.

Financial situation of the treaty bodies
19. The participants welcomed the amendments to the funding provisions of the International Convention on the Elimination of All Forms of Racial Discrimination and the Convention against Torture and Other Cruel, Inhuman or Degrading Treatment or Punishment, which had been recently adopted by the meeting of States parties to those instruments. However, serious concern was expressed over the amount of time that would likely be required for those amendments to enter into force: at least two years would be required to obtain the accord of the necessary two thirds of States parties to the International Convention on the Elimination of All Forms of Racial Discrimination. In the meantime, the Committee on the Elimination of Racial Discrimination would continue to run the risk of having its sessions curtailed or cancelled. This had happened in five of the past six years, including 1992. Under such circumstances, it was impossible for the Committee to discharge its responsibilities effectively under the Convention. This was particularly worrisome in view of the rise in racial violence and ethnic strife in many parts of the world. The Committee against Torture also faced a similarly uncertain financial situation. The States parties concerned should act as speedily as possible to approve the amendments that had been adopted. The General Assembly and the Secretary-General should also take all necessary action to ensure the financial stability of those two treaty bodies until the proposed amendments entered into force.

Adequate secretariat resources for servicing the treaty bodies
20. The chairpersons underlined the close link between adequate secretariat resources and the effective functioning of the treaty body system. Reference was made to the critical need for additional staffing in view of the large number of new States parties to the various instruments and the significantly increased workload that would result. At the same time, each of the treaty bodies was requesting additional services from the secretariat. In particular, more staff time was needed to process and analyse the large amount of relevant information originating from the various United Nations bodies and agencies as well as from intergovernmental and non-governmental sources. It was only with a higher level of secretariat support and a more comprehensive documentary basis that the treaty bodies would be able to ensure that the suggestions and recommendations they adopted would be of consistently high quality.

21. The participants agreed that the question of adequate servicing for the work of the treaty bodies was related to the overall priority given in the United Nations to human rights questions. Within this context, it was pointed out that the various committees needed to reassess their objectives and identify the staffing and other servicing resources needed to achieve those goals. It was emphasized that, in the short term, it was vital for the work of all of the treaty bodies that the Committee on the Elimination of Discrimination against Women, which was serviced by the United Nations Office at Vienna, be kept regularly apprised of developments concerning the activities of the Centre for Human Rights. In the medium term and, indeed, as soon as possible, responsibility for the servicing of the Committee on the Elimination of Discrimination Against Women should be assumed by the Centre for Human Rights.

22. Attention was also drawn to the question of a committee resource room within the Centre for Human Rights. This measure had been recommended by the chairpersons at both their second and third meetings and had subsequently been endorsed on a number of occasions by various treaty bodies. In its resolutions 1991/20 and 1992/15, the Commission on Human Rights had requested that the Secretary-General give consideration to the establishment of such an area for the purpose of facilitating access to the various sources of information that were indispensable to the effective functioning of the treaty bodies. It was pointed out that, in the present situation, documentation from United Nations bodies was not readily accessible to members of the treaty bodies and that other sources of information were available on an entirely unsatisfactory basis. In view of the fact that four years had passed since the need for the facility was first identified, the Secretary-General was urged to take action on the matter, particularly in view of the projected restructuring of the United Nations Office at Geneva.

Computerization of the work of the treaty bodies

23. With respect to that issue, the chairpersons noted with regret that only three States had responded to the request of the Secretary-General to contribute to the one-time start-up costs of the computerized information system proposed in the report of the Secretary-General (E/CN.4/1990/39). The contributions that had been received fell far short of the amount projected as the initial cost of the system. One way to facilitate progress would be to solicit contributions actively from corporate sponsors, particularly from the computer industry. It was pointed out, however, that, should such an initiative be undertaken, due consideration would have to be given to ensure compatibility with the long-term computerization planned for the Centre for Human Rights. The computerization of the treaty body system would ultimately form the basis for the human rights information base needed by the Centre for Human Rights and would greatly assist other United Nations bodies and agencies whose work concerned human rights.

Improving the effectiveness of the reporting process with special reference to adequate information

24. It was pointed out that, for the consideration of a State party's report, each of the treaty bodies needed to have access not only to the past reports of that State under the instrument concerned, but also to pertinent information

contained in the reports submitted by that State to other treaty bodies. Taken together, the information received by each of the treaty bodies comprised an impressive and important resource. The chairpersons also emphasized the importance of having relevant information from non-governmental organizations at their disposal. At present, this was only the case for some of the committees.
25. Participants welcomed the compilation of general comments and general recommendations of the various treaty bodies (HRI/GEN/1), which had recently been prepared by the secretariat. It was suggested that future revisions of the document should include a subject index.

Promoting interaction among the treaty bodies
26. The chairpersons discussed the system of designating certain members of each committee to follow developments in other committees and human rights bodies. That system, which had been recommended at the 1990 meeting of chairpersons, was generally regarded as unsatisfactory in practice. The view was expressed that the preparation of a short analytical summary of each session of the various committees would provide a more effective and consistent solution to the problem of keeping members of the various treaty bodies informed of developments in the treaty body system. It was pointed out that such a service would require additional secretariat resources in order to be implemented. It was suggested that one way to minimize the added burden on the secretariat would be to entrust the drafting of the analytical summaries to certain members of the treaty bodies. However; it was more widely felt that only the secretariat had the necessary expertise and was in the best position to provide the required information.
27. With regard to the recommendation of the Committee on Economic, Social and Cultural Rights that members of that Committee should meet jointly with members of the Human Rights Committee, the Committee on the Elimination of Discrimination against Women and the Committee on the Rights of the Child to consider approaches to supervising overlapping treaty obligations, it was noted with regret that no meeting had yet been scheduled. Strong support was expressed for the initiative, which was still considered important and valuable. Support was also expressed for any similar meetings or occasions when members from different committees would be able to meet in order to discuss issues of common concern.
28. On a related issue, the chairpersons discussed the importance of providing a background briefing for all new members of the treaty bodies. It was suggested that such a briefing could be coordinated by the chairperson of the treaty body concerned and could be carried out in cooperation with the secretariat.

Information and publications on the work of the treaty bodies
29. The chairpersons underlined the importance they attached to strengthening the human rights information programme to make it more coherent and effective. It was pointed out that the human rights publications budget of the United Nations was not sufficiently large to ensure that the work of the treaty bodies was adequately or regularly publicized. Given the high degree of interest in human rights on the part of government officials, intergovernmental and non-governmental organizations, academic and research institutions and the general public, the chairpersons agreed that a higher priority

should be given to the production, translation and distribution of human rights publications and documentation. It was pointed out, for example, that the *Manual on Human Rights Reporting*, which was considered a valuable tool to assist States parties with their reporting obligations, had been published thus far only in English and Chinese.

30. The participants welcomed the publication of the fact sheets on the various treaty bodies, although it was pointed out that, before such publications were produced, the chairperson of the committee concerned should be consulted and his or her comments obtained with regard to content and presentation. It was also suggested that the *Human Rights Newsletter*, which was not published by the Centre for Human Rights on a regular schedule, should be given a new format and a major role in informing the human rights community of the latest developments in the numerous United Nations human rights bodies and mechanisms. The view was expressed that the format and publishing schedule of the *Bulletin of Human Rights* would also benefit from a thorough review. Support was given to the various human rights training manuals being drafted by the Centre for Human Rights. However, the chairpersons underlined that there should be a comprehensive review of the distribution strategy for those and other human rights publications to ensure their availability to the specialists concerned as well as to the general public.

Regional meetings of the treaty bodies

31. Reference was made to the recent informal regional consultation of the Committee on the Rights of the Child held at Quito. The meeting, which was organized by the United Nations Children's Fund (UNICEF) in cooperation with the Centre for Human Rights, had provided a valuable opportunity to promote greater awareness of the Convention on the Rights of the Child and to publicize the work of the Committee. The chairpersons expressed strong support for such meetings and suggested that ways should be explored to organize similar meetings for the various committees in the regions, where they could have direct contact with the officials, agencies and organizations responsible for the implementation of the various human rights treaties.

World Conference on Human Rights

32. With regard to the World Conference, attention was drawn to the letter addressed to Mr. Antoine Blanca, Under-Secretary-General for Human Rights and Secretary-General of the World Conference on Human Rights, by the four representatives of the treaty bodies to the third session of the Preparatory Committee. In their letter, the treaty body representatives pointed out that they had been placed at a disadvantage and thereby unable to make a full contribution to the preparatory process. The representatives suggested that, pursuant to General Assembly resolution 45/155, a special working group should be established to examine the issues relevant to the implementation of existing human rights standards and instruments, evaluate the effectiveness of United Nations methods and mechanisms, and formulate concrete recommendations for improving the effectiveness of United Nations mechanisms aimed at promoting, encouraging and monitoring respect for human rights and fundamental freedoms.

33. The chairpersons noted that the World Conference on Human Rights had been discussed in each of the treaty bodies and a number of constructive recommendations had been adopted as a result. Additionally, provision had been made by the United Nations for representatives of the treaty bodies to attend the sessions of the Preparatory Committee. Participants expressed their regret at the difficulties that had been encountered in the past and strongly urged that the treaty body representatives should, in the future, be provided with every opportunity to participate effectively in the preparatory process. They also strongly supported the establishment of a special working group at the Preparatory Committee and at the World Conference, as proposed in the letter, as an important means to facilitate the realization of the objectives of the Conference, as set out in General Assembly resolution 45/155. It was also agreed that the treaty bodies should be represented at the regional meetings that were to be held as part of the preparatory process, as well as at the satellite meetings, as appropriate.

Identification by the treaty bodies of possible technical assistance and advisory services

34. The participants were informed by the secretariat that training courses had been organized in the past by the Centre, in cooperation with the United Nations Institute for Training and Research (UNITAR) initially, and later with the support of the Voluntary Fund for Technical Cooperation in the Field of Human Rights, for state officials in regions or subregions on the reporting obligations under all treaties in force. It was suggested that it might be useful to evaluate how that training had helped to improve the reporting by the States parties concerned. The treaty bodies might then envisage recommending the organization of training courses on a regional or subregional level.
35. The chairpersons were further informed that the programme had recently focused on providing ad hoc advisory services to the States parties upon request and when an organ such as the Commission on Human Rights had so recommended. It was, however, more expensive to provide assistance on a national basis than on a regional one, and such service could not be provided to all States parties. Accordingly, assistance should be provided to those countries whose needs were of a priority nature. In that connection, it was suggested that priority should be placed on providing assistance to developing countries having already demonstrated consistent problems with reporting under various human rights treaties and that officials of national human rights institutions and of non-governmental organizations should be included. International training institutions should also be invited to include the reporting systems in their programmes.

Extent of reservations to human rights treaties

36. Each chairperson presented the situation of reservations with regard to the respective treaty. The situation was felt to be very alarming concerning the Convention on the Elimination of All Forms of Discrimination against Women since a number of reservations were thought by the Committee on the Elimination of Discrimination against Women to be incompatible with the object and purpose of the Convention and should not have been permitted. The same question was also raised with regard to the Convention on

the Rights of the Child. It was agreed that the States parties concerned should be urged to withdraw the reservations and that other States parties should not hesitate to object to such reservations as appropriate. The treaty bodies should systematically review reservations made when considering a report and include in the list of questions to be addressed to reporting Governments a question as to whether a given reservation was still necessary and whether a State party would consider withdrawing a reservation that might be considered by the treaty body concerned as being incompatible with the object and purpose of the treaty. The chairpersons also discussed the feasibility of a comparative study on the reservations made to the seven existing treaties. It was suggested that such a study could be prepared, without financial implications, by the Subcommission on Prevention of Discrimination and Protection of Minorities.

Massive violations of human right

37. The chairpersons examined the suggestion made by the Secretary-General[1] that ways should be explored of empowering the Secretary-General and expert human rights bodies to bring massive violations of human rights to the attention of the Security Council together with recommendations for action. The chairpersons fully endorsed this suggestion. The definition of "massive" violations was discussed in particular. It was agreed that the identification by expert bodies of "massive" violations should not be limited to assessing the quantity of violations committed. The gravity of violations committed with respect to a limited number of victims could suffice to qualify a violation as "massive". A situation in a country where the human rights of thousands of persons were persistently violated could also be considered as a "massive" violation. All human rights should be taken into consideration in that respect. Each organ could decide which situation required forwarding to the Security Council.

Prevention of human rights violations and urgent action

38. The chairpersons agreed to the suggestions of some members of the treaty bodies that it would be useful to examine how violations of human rights could be effectively prevented and recommended that the treaty bodies give further consideration to the subject as appropriate.
39. Urgent action was felt to be necessary in order to monitor emergency situations and to allow the treaty bodies to intervene rapidly in such situations.

Agenda of the fifth session

40. The chairpersons approved a tentative list of issues that should be reflected in the draft agenda for the fifth meeting of the chairpersons.

IV. CONCLUSIONS AND RECOMMENDATIONS

41. The following conclusions and recommendations are submitted to the General Assembly for its consideration in accordance with resolution 46/111. Some concern action that might be taken by the Assembly itself or by other

---

[1] *Official Records of the General Assembly, Forty-seventh Session, Supplement No. 1* (A/47/1), para. 101.

appropriate organs of the United Nations, while others fall within the competence of the Secretary-General, of the respective treaty bodies or of the States parties to the treaties. However, no distinction is drawn in this regard for the purposes of the present report, since the mandate of the meeting is to propose diverse means to improve the functioning of the treaty supervisory system within the overall framework of the United Nations.

Role of the Security Council and development of effective responses in emergency situations

42. In relation to the work of the Security Council, the chairpersons consider that human rights issues need to be accorded appropriate priority, on a continuing basis, at all times. In this regard, the chairpersons welcomed the recognition by the Security Council, at its January 1992 meeting at the level of heads of State and Government, that "the absence of war and military conflicts amongst States does not in itself ensure international peace and security. The non-military sources of instability in the economic, social, humanitarian and ecological fields have become threats to peace and security".[2] Similarly, as noted by the Secretary-General in his 1992 annual report, "respect for human rights is clearly important in order to maintain international peace and security".[3]

43. Accordingly, the chairpersons recommend that the Security Council should be encouraged to take full account, in its deliberations and in its decisions and resolutions, of the obligations of States concerned pursuant to the principal human rights treaties. The chairpersons also express their full support for the proposal made by the Secretary-General that ways should be explored "of empowering the Secretary-General and expert human rights bodies to bring massive violations of human rights to the attention of the Security Council, together with recommendations for action".[4] In that regard, the chairpersons urge the treaty bodies to take all appropriate measures in response to such situations. They note that the term "massive", as used in this context, should be interpreted in the light of the January 1992 statement of the Security Council and should therefore encompass the persistence of massive structural violations of the full range of human rights.

44. The chairpersons note that the treaty bodies have an important role in seeking to prevent as well as to respond to human rights violations. It is thus appropriate for each treaty body to undertake an urgent examination of all possible measures that it might take, within its competence, both to prevent human rights violations from occurring and to monitor more closely emergency situations of all kinds arising within the jurisdiction of States parties. Where procedural innovations are required for this purpose, they should be considered as soon as possible.

45. The chairpersons recommend that, whenever ad hoc expert groups are being established by United Nations bodies or by the Secretary-General for any purpose that has a significant human rights objective, consideration be given to drawing upon the expertise of members of the human rights treaty bodies.

---

[2] S/23500, at 3.
[3] *Official Records of the General Assembly, Forty-seventh Session Supplement No. 1* (A/47/1), para. 109.
[4] *Ibid.*, para. 101.

In that regard, the chairpersons considered that it might be appropriate for a member of one of the treaty bodies to be included as part of the commission of experts appointed pursuant to Security Council resolution 780 (1992) to consider evidence of grave breaches of international humanitarian law in the territory of the former Yugoslavia.

More effective integration of human rights into the totality of United Nations activities

46. The chairpersons wish to emphasize the need for the United Nations as a whole, and the General Assembly in particular, to ensure that human rights concerns are fully integrated into the overall range of activities of the Organization. For this purpose, it would seem appropriate that consideration be given to undertaking an overall review of the system with a view to identifying the necessary innovations and reforms.

Financing

47. In relation to the financing of the work of the treaty bodies, the chairpersons express their wholehearted support for the initiatives endorsed by the respective meetings of the States parties to the International Convention on the Elimination of All Forms of Racial Discrimination and the Convention against Torture designed to provide assured funding from the regular budget of the United Nations. The chairpersons note that it is imperative that individual States parties act as rapidly as possible to ratify the resulting amendments to the two treaties.

48. In the period prior to the entry into force of those amendments there will continue to be a critical need to assure adequate funding to the two committees concerned to enable them to fulfil adequately their supervisory functions. The chairpersons note that, especially in the case of the Committee on the Elimination of Racial Discrimination, this might entail the need for the provision of contingency funds by the Secretary-General to enable the Committee to meet as scheduled until such time as the amendment to the Convention receives the necessary number of ratifications.

Secretariat servicing

49. The chairpersons note that, in the light of the greatly increased recognition of the need for human rights concerns to permeate the entire range of international endeavours, the resources available to the Centre for Human Rights are grossly inadequate, despite recent improvements, to enable it to fulfil the manifold and constantly growing number of tasks entrusted to it. In the view of the participants, existing working conditions of the secretariat, especially in terms of the facilities and information technology available at Geneva, can best be described as primitive. While the ramifications of the issue extend well beyond the immediate mandate of the meeting of chairpersons, it must be noted that many of the urgent needs experienced by the treaty bodies cannot be satisfactorily dealt with in the absence of more far-reaching financial, personnel and administrative reforms. The chairpersons urge that the broader situation be taken fully into account in the context of the ongoing restructuring of the social and economic activities of the United Nations.

50. The chairpersons consider that, despite the best efforts of the available staff

within the Centre for Human Rights and the Branch for the Advancement of Women, the resources of the secretariat required to ensure adequate servicing of each of the treaty bodies are not available. This inadequacy has, in turn, led to a situation in which requests for assistance by the various treaty bodies are sometimes unable to be met, despite the fact that such requests have been kept at an artificially low level in recognition of the impossibility of greater assistance being provided from existing resources. It is therefore recommended that a thorough study be undertaken, ideally by an independent expert, of the full range of measures that would be required at the secretariat level if adequate servicing is to be provided.

Information sources
51. In view of the fact that an adequate information base is an essential prerequisite for the effective functioning of the supervisory system, the chairpersons believe that a number of major reforms are urgently required. In general, it is apparent that the problems encountered by the treaty bodies in obtaining access to information are closely linked to the broader information challenges facing the Centre for Human Rights. The chairpersons believe that there is a desperate need for the development of a coherent and comprehensive information policy within the Centre as a whole.
52. The starting-point for reform should be the creation of a centralized information and documentation unit within the Centre. While such a unit will require space and the services of a trained documentalist and others, it is essential to the work of the Centre as a whole and to the satisfactory servicing of the treaty bodies. It is recommended that the General Assembly should request the Secretary-General to take appropriate steps to establish such a unit. In the meantime, until such a unit is established, the chairpersons wish to reiterate, for the third time, the need for the immediate establishment of a committee resource room, which would enable the members of each committee to obtain access to the basic documentation required for the effective discharge of their functions. An effort should also be made to provide committee members with access to on-line information databases that contain information of direct relevance to their work.
53. The chairpersons note that the process of requesting voluntary contributions to enable the computerization of the information relating to the work of the treaty bodies was begun in February 1992. Member States, as well as the private sector, foundations and other appropriate entities are urged to consider contributing to the fund. The Secretary-General is requested to report regularly to the treaty bodies on the progress made in implementing the programme of work identified by the Computer Task Force appointed by the Secretary-General at the request of the Commission on Human Rights. Immediate measures should be taken, on the basis of the funds already available, to begin implementation of some of the Task Force's recommendations.
54. The chairpersons request the secretariat to ensure that one copy of a comprehensive country dossier is available to each committee in respect of each State party whose report is under consideration at any given session. The dossier should be as comprehensive as possible in terms of the sources of information reflected. In addition to the full range of directly relevant United

Nations documentation, the dossier should contain all available information from non-governmental sources and relevant press reports.
55. In order to ensure an adequate flow of information from non-governmental organizations, each treaty body should consider formally inviting such groups to submit written documentation and, wherever appropriate, to do so in the form of official submissions. The chairpersons also strongly urge all non-governmental organizations in the human rights field, at both the international and national levels, to seek to provide as much relevant information as possible to the treaty bodies and to do so on a systematic and timely basis. At a minimum, a regular flow of all available information for inclusion in country dossiers should be assured.

Public information
56. In terms of public information activities relating to the work of the treaty bodies, the chairpersons are firmly convinced that there is a need for an integrated and comprehensive public information strategy for the Centre for Human Rights as a whole. The present approach is haphazard, under-resourced and lacking in priorities. Publicity for the work of the treaty bodies has suffered as a result. It is recommended that an expert group, from outside the secretariat, be constituted with a view to undertaking a comprehensive review of the existing information programme. It should be requested to make recommendations, taking full account of existing policy guidelines, for the development of an entirely new strategy that seeks to integrate the needs of the various sectors within the human rights programme, including the treaty bodies. Consultation with the latter should be part of the process and particular attention should be focused on the needs of the general public, throughout the world, rather than only on those already involved in the system in Geneva, New York and Vienna.
57. At the very least, means need to be identified for the more effective conveying of information about the activities of one organ to the other principal organs within the overall system. This includes both Charter-based and treaty-based organs. As an interim measure, the participants decided that the chairperson of each committee should, immediately after each session and with the assistance of the secretariat, prepare a brief (1–3 pages) account of the significant developments that have taken place at that session and circulate it, at least to the other chairpersons, and if possible to all committee members.
58. The chairpersons note with satisfaction that the report of each State party along with the summary records of the consideration of that report by the relevant treaty body are now being made available through the United Nations information centre located in the country concerned. It considers, however, that the treaty bodies themselves, the Governments concerned, the secretariat and non-governmental organizations should all consider further ways of disseminating that information effectively at the national level.
59. In terms of specific information issues, the chairpersons commend the publication of the *Manual on Reporting* and request that the remaining language versions be printed as soon as possible; recommend that consideration be given to producing the *Manual* in loose-leaf format to facilitate regular updating; recommend that, in future, the very useful compilation of general comments, general recommendations and so on be published with an index

to improve its usefulness; and recommend that future fact sheets dealing with the work of any of the treaty bodies be submitted to that body, or at least its chairperson, for review prior to being finalized.

Reservations

60. The chairpersons consider that the number, nature and scope of the reservations that have been made to the principal human rights treaties are cause for alarm. While recognizing that there is an important and legitimate role for reservations to treaties, they note that some of the reservations that have been lodged would appear to give rise to serious questions as to their compatibility with the object and purpose of the treaties in question. For this reason, and because of the extent to which such reservations have the potential to undermine the goals of the treaty system, the chairpersons believe that a number of measures are required to be taken.

61. In relation to reservations that, in the view of the relevant treaty body, give rise to significant questions in terms of their apparent incompatibility with the object and purpose of the treaty, that treaty body should consider requesting the Economic and Social Council or the General Assembly, as appropriate, to request an advisory opinion on the issue from the International Court of Justice.

62. The General Assembly is requested to consider giving a mandate to the Commission on Human Rights to authorize the preparation of an analytical study of issues of incompatibility arising out of the reservations that have been made to the principal treaties, to be undertaken by the Subcommission on Prevention of Discrimination and Protection of Minorities.

63. Each State that is considering ratification of a treaty should be urged to give the most careful consideration to any proposed reservation thereto and should do its utmost to keep the number and scope of such reservations to a minimum. Such reservations should be as specific as possible. Once a reservation has been made the State party should undertake a regular review of the continuing need for, and desirability of, all such reservations. The results of those reviews should be reflected in each report submitted by the State party to the treaty body concerned. That treaty body should always seek to address the issue of reservations in its dialogue with the State party.

64. The chairpersons believe that it is essential, if the present system relating to reservations is to function adequately, that States that are already parties to a particular treaty should give full consideration to lodging an objection on each occasion when that may be appropriate.

65. Whenever a new human rights treaty is being drafted the most careful consideration should be given to the inclusion of a provision permitting the relevant treaty body to request an advisory opinion from the International Court of Justice in relation to any reservation that it considers might be incompatible with the object and purpose of the treaty. Similarly, consideration should be given to the identification of certain provisions as being non-derogable (as in the case of the International Covenant on Civil and Political Rights) and they should also be identified as not being subject to reservations.

Succession in relation to human rights obligations

66. In view of the increasing number of new States that were previously part of States that had accepted various human rights treaty obligations, consideration should be given to the most appropriate and effective means by which

the provisions of such treaties can be treated as applying, on a continuing basis, to the people within the territories concerned. In addition, the General Assembly should urge all new States to confirm formally their acceptance of any pre-existing obligations or to accede to, or ratify, all of the principal human rights treaties. They should do so as a matter of urgency, in order to assure to all persons within their jurisdiction the highest possible level of protection.

New instruments
67. As far as possible and appropriate, the supervision of new human rights treaty obligations should be entrusted to one or other of the existing treaty bodies. Similarly, careful consideration should always be given to the drafting of protocols to existing instruments in preference to entirely new treaties, whenever appropriate. When such protocols are under preparation the relevant treaty body should be consulted prior to their final adoption
68. In the event, however, that the drafting of new treaties cannot be avoided, the periodicity of reporting should be left open provided that a report is required at least once every five years. Similarly, new treaties should not stipulate a maximum duration for the sessions of the relevant supervisory body. They should always provide for the financing of the supervisory mechanisms from the regular budget.
69. Whenever new human rights instruments are being drafted, adequate *travaux preparatoires* should be undertaken along with a thorough technical review prior to the final adoption of the text.

Overdue and non-submitted reports
70. The problem of excessively overdue reports and of the failure to submit initial reports continues to give rise to concern. It is suggested that each treaty body follow the practice of the Committee on the Elimination of Racial Discrimination in listing States whose reports are overdue or who have failed to submit reports in order of the length of time involved. This practice helps to identify those States parties which are the most overdue and in respect of which a particular effort is needed to encourage the submission of the necessary reports. Treaty bodies might also consider the approach, already employed by the Committee on Economic, Social and Cultural Rights, of adopting a specific decision identifying those States parties whose reporting record is especially unsatisfactory.
71. The chairpersons recommend that each treaty body follow, as a last resort and to the extent appropriate, the practice, already adopted by some committees, of scheduling for consideration the situation in States parties that have consistently failed to report or whose reports are long overdue. They note that a persistent and long-term failure to report should not result in the State party concerned being immune from supervision while others, which had reported, were subject to careful monitoring. Even in the absence of a report, adequate information exists from other appropriate sources on the basis of which an examination, ideally in the form of a dialogue, could be undertaken.
72. It is recommended that a number of steps be explored in order to encourage timely reporting by all States parties. They include an effort to make the

purpose of the reports and the nature of the supervisory process as transparent as possible to all concerned in the process, and especially to government officials; holding, at the national level, seminars and workshops on reporting; and the provision of specifically tailored advisory services, as appropriate.

Global reports
73. Consideration should be given, at least in the longer term, to the feasibility of permitting States that are parties to more than one of the treaties to prepare a single, comprehensive, global report, which would be used to satisfy its reporting obligations under each of the treaties.

Language versions of instruments
74. The chairpersons note that full and effective implementation of human rights treaty obligations, on a continuing bass, is dependent in part upon a knowledge and understanding of the relevant rights by the residents of the State concerned. For this reason, it is imperative that every effort be made to translate the test of the relevant instruments into as many local languages as possible and, in any event, into all of the major languages used in the country concerned. Each treaty body should therefore request all States parties to provide it with details of the different language versions available, those not available and plans for future translations. Wherever possible, a copy of the available translations should be provided in order to enable an appropriate collection to be built up by the United Nations.

Advisory services and technical assistance
75. The chairpersons recommend that, especially in relation to the work of the treaty bodies, a greater effort should be made to integrate and harmonize activities in the fields of public information, advisory services and national institutions. Training provided within the framework of the advisory services programme should, in so far as it concerns reporting and the work of the treaty bodies, accord priority to the organization of low-cost training workshops at the national level designed to cater for the needs of a diverse range of government officials, representatives of the various social partners, including workers and employers, and of relevant non-governmental organizations. It should not be assumed that the need for training in relation to reporting systems is confined to one or two government officials directly involved at a given moment.
76. The secretariat, in consultation with the treaty bodies, should draw up a list of priority countries whose reporting record would seem to indicate the need for advisory services to assist the preparation of long overdue reports. A letter offering specific types of assistance should then be dispatched to the Governments concerned and the responses, if any, brought to the attention of the relevant treaty bodies. The chairpersons also recognize that it is essential for advisory services to be provided wherever possible in order to assist States to fulfil their human rights obligations.

World Conference on Human Rights
77. In relation to the work of the Preparatory Committee for the World Conference on Human Rights, the chairpersons consider that the representatives of the treaty bodies have not so far been accorded an adequate, or

appropriate, opportunity to contribute to, and participate in, the discussions. In view of the central position of the treaty bodies within the overall United Nations human rights system, this situation is a matter of serious concern. Moreover, it completely contradicts the pertinent recommendation made by the last meeting of chairpersons and subsequently endorsed by the General Assembly. The chairpersons therefore recommend that, at all future meetings as well as at the Conference itself, provision should be made for the full participation of the treaty body representatives to enable advantage to be taken of their expert input. In order to achieve this objective fully, and in recognition of the fact that the treaty bodies are an integral part of the United Nations human rights system, the General Assembly should recommend that the group of chairpersons be constituted as a special advisory body to the World Conference.

78. The chairpersons are also concerned that discussions concerning the agenda for the World Conference have so inadequately reflected the priority accorded to issues relating to the treaty bodies as stated in paragraphs 1(c) to (e) of General Assembly resolution 45/155 of 18 December 1990. It is therefore recommended that efforts be made to ensure that sustained consideration be given to those issues in the agenda. Moreover, the chairpersons recommend that a special working group be established at the World Conference to examine issues relevant to the implementation of existing human rights standards and instruments, to formulate concrete recommendations for improving the effectiveness of United Nations mechanisms aimed at promoting, encouraging and monitoring respect for human rights, and to review the progress made in the implementation of the recommendations contained herein.

79. Regional preparatory meetings for the World Conference should also involve representatives of the treaty bodies and consideration should similarly be given to working groups examining the issues described in the preceding paragraph.

80. The chairpersons recommend that consideration be given to the holding of a meeting, within the framework of the World Conference, of the persons chairing the United Nations human rights treaty bodies and those chairing (or holding an equivalent position on) each of the principal regional and other human rights organizations, including the African Commission on Human and Peoples' Rights, the European Commission on Human Rights, the European Court of Human Rights, the Inter-American Commission on Human Rights, the Inter-American Court of Human Rights, the Committee on the Application of Conventions and Recommendations of ILO and the Committee on Conventions and Recommendations of the United Nations Educational, Scientific and Cultural Organization (UNESCO).

81. The chairpersons recommend that the General Assembly request that an updated version of the independent expert's study on possible long-term approaches to enhancing the effective operation of existing and prospective treaty bodies (A/44/668), the preparation of which was originally requested by General Assembly resolution 43/115 of 8 December 1988, be submitted to the World Conference on Human Rights.

82. The secretariat should include one or more members of the treaty bodies within the group of persons who will be reviewing the content of the "prototype" studies to be submitted to the World Conference.

Other matters

83. In view of the central importance of the principle of the indivisibility of the two sets of rights, as reflected in the preamble to each of the International Covenants, any State that has ratified only one of the International Covenants should be urged to give very careful consideration to the possibility of ratifying the other Covenant as soon as possible.
84. The chairpersons strongly reiterate the recommendation made in the report on their third session to the effect that the servicing by the secretariat of the Committee on the Elimination of Discrimination against Women should be provided from the Centre for Human Rights at Geneva. It is essential that a unified approach to servicing be put in place in order to ensure that that Committee has access to the same services and facilities as the other committees and to achieve the full and effective integration of the Committee into the overall human rights treaty regime.
85. It is recommended that at the next meeting of the chairpersons representatives of non-governmental organizations be invited to address the meeting and to submit appropriate recommendations for consideration by the meeting.
86. The chairpersons wish to emphasize the value of holding meetings of the treaty bodies outside of Geneva, New York and Vienna. They note, however, that existing financial and other requirements tend to make the cost of any such meeting prohibitive. For this reason, they request the Secretary-General to explore innovative ways and means (such as an agreed reduction in the number of languages in which interpretation is required, a limit on the volume of in-session documents to be translated, etc.) that would increase the likelihood of such meetings being organized.
87. It is recommended that, in future, all new members of the treaty bodies should be given a comprehensive background briefing on the work of the committee, and of the treaty bodies as a whole. The briefing should be undertaken by the chairperson or his or her delegate and by a senior secretariat official.
88. The chairpersons recall the proposal made by the Committee on Economic, Social and Cultural Rights, and subsequently endorsed by the Committee on the Rights of the Child, to the effect that a meeting should be held with one or two representatives each of the Human Rights Committee, the Committee on the Rights of the Child, the Committee on the Elimination of Discrimination against Women and the Committee on Economic, Social and Cultural Rights with a view to discussing matters of interest relating to the rights of the child, including the most appropriate approaches to the supervision of overlapping treaty obligations. That proposal has not been implemented owing to resource constraints. The chairpersons accordingly recommend that the General Assembly consider making resources available for such a meeting.

A/49/537 — 19 October 1994
UNITED NATIONS GENERAL ASSEMBLY
Forty-ninth session

EFFECTIVE IMPLEMENTATION OF INTERNATIONAL INSTRUMENTS ON HUMAN RIGHTS, INCLUDING REPORTING OBLIGATIONS UNDER INTERNATIONAL INSTRUMENTS ON HUMAN RIGHTS

Note by the Secretary-General

The Secretary-General has the honour to transmit to the members of the General Assembly the report of the fifth meeting of persons chairing the human rights treaty bodies, convened pursuant to General Assembly resolution 48/120 of 20 December 1993.

ANNEX

Report of the fifth meeting of persons chairing the human rights treaty bodies

I. INTRODUCTION

1. Since the adoption of resolution 37/44 on 3 December 1982, the General Assembly has continuously kept under review the problems relating to the effective implementation of international instruments on human rights, including reporting obligations under international instruments on human rights. Those problems have also received careful attention during the various sessions of the treaty bodies, at some of the meetings of States parties and at meetings of such other organs as the Economic and Social Council and the Commission on Human Rights.

2. Pursuant to General Assembly resolution 38/117 of 16 December 1983, the Secretary-General convened a first meeting of the persons chairing the bodies entrusted with the consideration of State party reports in August 1984. The report of that meeting was presented to the General Assembly at its thirty-ninth session (A/39/484, annex). A second meeting was convened by the Secretary-General in October 1988, pursuant to Assembly resolution 42/105 of 7 December 1987, and the report of that meeting was presented to the Assembly at its forty-fourth session (A/44/98, annex). A third meeting was convened by the Secretary-General in October 1990, pursuant to Assembly resolution 44/135 of 15 December 1989, and the report of that meeting was

presented to the Assembly at its forty-fifth session (A/45/636, annex). A fourth meeting was convened by the Secretary-General in October 1992, pursuant to Assembly resolution 46/111 of 17 December 1991, and the report of that meeting was presented to the Assembly at its forty-seventh session (A/47/628, annex).
3. In its resolution 48/120 of 20 December 1993, the General Assembly endorsed the conclusions and recommendations of the meetings of persons chairing the human rights treaty bodies aimed at streamlining, rationalizing and otherwise improving reporting procedures; requested the Secretary-General to take the appropriate steps in order to finance the biennial meetings of persons chairing the human rights treaty bodies from resources available from the regular budget of the United Nations; and decided to give priority consideration, at its forty-ninth session, to the conclusions and recommendations of the meetings of persons chairing human rights treaty bodies, in the light of the deliberations of the Commission on Human Rights. In its resolution 1994/19 of 25 February 1994, the Commission on Human Rights urged the treaty bodies to examine ways of reducing the duplication of reporting required under the different instruments and of generally reducing the reporting burden on Member States and welcomed the emphasis placed by the meeting of persons chairing the human rights treaty bodies on the importance of technical assistance and advisory services.
4. The fifth meeting of persons chairing the human rights treaty bodies was convened by the Secretary-General pursuant to General Assembly resolution 48/120 and Commission on Human Rights resolution 1994/19.

II. ORGANIZATION OF THE MEETING

5. The meeting was held at the United Nations Office at Geneva from 19 to 23 September 1994. The following representatives of the human rights treaty bodies attended: Mrs. Hoda Badran (Chairperson, Committee on the Rights of the Child), Mrs. Virginia Bonoan-Dandan (Rapporteur, Committee on Economic, Social and Cultural Rights), Mrs. Ivanka Corti (Chairperson, Committee on the Elimination of Discrimination against Women), Mr. Vojin Dimitrijevic (Vice-Chairperson, Human Rights Committee), Mr. Ivan Garvalov (Chairperson, Committee on the Elimination of Racial Discrimination) and Mr. Alexis Dipanda-Mouelle (Chairperson, Committee against Torture).
6. Representatives of the International Labour Organization (ILO), the United Nations Children's Fund (UNICEF) and the Office of the United Nations High Commissioner for Refugees attended the meeting. Representatives of the following non-governmental organizations also attended the meeting: American Association for the Advancement of Science, Amnesty International, Anti-Racism Information Service, Baha'i International Community, Friends World Committee for Consultation (Quakers), International Service for Human Rights, International Womens' Rights Action Watch and the NGO Group for the Convention on the Rights of the Child.
7. The agenda for the meeting was as follows:
   1. Opening of the meeting.

2. Election of the officers of the meeting.
3. Adoption of the agenda.
4. Organizational and other matters.
5. Review of recent developments relating to the work of the treaty bodies.
6. Improving the operation of the human rights treaty bodies.
7. Adoption of the report.
8. The following documentation was made available to the participants:
   (a) Provisional agenda (HRI/MC/1994/1);
   (b) Report of the Secretary-General on improving the operation of the human rights treaty bodies (HRI/MC/1994/2);
   (c) Report of the Secretary-General on the status of the international instruments and the general situation of overdue reports (HRI/MC/1994/3);
   (d) Informal note by the Secretariat containing a compilation of the recommendations concerning the functioning of the treaty bodies formulated by non-governmental organizations within the framework of preparatory activities for and during the World Conference on Human Rights;
   (e) Report of the fourth meeting of persons chairing the human rights treaty bodies (A/47/628);
   (f) Conclusions and recommendations of the fourth meeting of persons chairing the human rights treaty bodies: report of the Secretary-General (A/48/508 and Corr.1);
   (g) Financing and adequate staff resources for the operations of the human rights treaty bodies: report of the Secretary-General (A/48/560);
   (h) Convention on the Elimination of All Forms of Discrimination against Women: report of the Secretary-General (A/49/308);
   (i) Interim report on the updated study of the independent expert on enhancing the long-term effectiveness of the United Nations human rights treaty regime (A/CONF.157/PC/62/Add.11/Rev.1);
   (j) Vienna statement of the international human rights treaty bodies (A/CONF.157/TBB/4 and Add.1);
   (k) Vienna Declaration and Programme of Action adopted by the World Conference on Human Rights on 25 June 1993 (A/CONF.157/23);
   (l) Relevant resolutions of the General Assembly: resolutions 47/111 of 16 December 1992 and 48/120 on effective implementation of international instruments on human rights, including reporting obligations under international instruments on human rights; resolution 48/119 of 20 December 1993 on the international covenants on human rights; and resolution 48/141 of 20 December 1993 on the High Commissioner for the promotion and protection of all human rights;
   (m) Economic and Social Council resolution 1994/7 of 21 July 1994 on the Convention on the Elimination of All Forms of Discrimination against Women;
   (n) Relevant resolutions of the Commission on Human Rights, including resolutions 1993/16 of 26 February 1993 and 1994/19 on effective functioning of bodies established pursuant to United Nations human rights instruments; resolution 1994/15 of 25 February 1994 on the status of the international covenants on human rights; and resolution 1994/16 of 25

February 1994 on the succession of States in respect of international human rights treaties;
(o) Compilation of general comments and general recommendations adopted by human rights treaty bodies (HRI/GEN/1/Rev.1);
(p) Letter dated 29 August 1994 from the Assistant Secretary-General for Human Rights to the chairpersons;
(q) Letter dated 19 September 1994 from the Coordinator for the International Year for the Family to the chairpersons.
9. The meeting was opened by Mr. Ibrahima Fall, Assistant Secretary-General for Human Rights, who addressed the chairpersons. The United Nations High Commissioner for Human Rights addressed the meeting on 21 September 1994 and discussed a number of issues with the chairpersons.
10. Mr. Ivan Garvalov was elected Chairperson-Rapporteur of the meeting.
11. On 23 September 1994, the chairpersons considered the draft report of their fifth meeting. The report, as amended during the course of the meeting, was adopted unanimously by the chairpersons.

III. REVIEW OF RECENT DEVELOPMENTS RELATING TO THE WORK OF THE TREATY BODIES AND IMPROVING THE OPERATION OF THE HUMAN RIGHTS TREATY BODIES

12. Consideration of agenda items 5 and 6 began with a brief oral overview by each of the participants. Among other developments, participants noted that following the recommendation of the fourth meeting of chairpersons, a number of treaty bodies had taken steps towards elaborating early warning measures and urgent procedures with a view to preventing the occurrence, or recurrence, of serious human rights violations. In that connection, the chairpersons welcomed the establishment of the post of United Nations High Commissioner for Human Rights, whose mandate included the prevention of human rights violations around the world. The treaty bodies would be able to provide expert knowledge and advice relating to specific situations as well as detailed recommendations which could be of significant value to the High Commissioner in the discharge of his mandate.
13. Throughout their discussions, the chairpersons emphasized that the work of the treaty bodies was not only one of the fundamental pillars of the United Nations human rights programme and policy, but indeed at the core of the international human rights order. The United Nations human rights treaties were universal in nature and in application. The treaty bodies which monitored the application of the human rights treaties constituted an integrated system in which the broad spectrum of human rights – civil, cultural, economic, political and social – were dealt with as an indivisible and interdependent whole. No human rights standards were to be ignored in favour of others. The chairpersons emphasized that those standards were to guide and inform the United Nations in its diverse activities. In addition, the work of the treaty bodies constituted an invaluable guide to the application of those human rights standards in 176 of the 184 States Members of the United Nations and in 4 non-member States.

IV. CONCLUSIONS AND RECOMMENDATIONS

14. The following conclusions and recommendations are submitted to the General Assembly for its consideration in accordance with resolution 48/120. Some actions might be taken by the Assembly itself or by another appropriate organ of the United Nations, while others fall within the competence of the Secretary-General, of the respective treaty bodies or of the States parties to the treaties. However, no distinction is drawn in this regard for the purposes of the present report, since the mandate of the meeting is to propose diverse means to improve the functioning of the treaty supervisory system within the overall framework of the United Nations.

Priority objective of the United Nations

15. The chairpersons emphasize that the promotion and protection of all human rights and fundamental freedoms must be considered a priority objective of the United Nations, as stated in the Vienna Declaration and Programme of Action adopted by the World Conference on Human Rights. They pledge their full support and cooperation to realize that objective. At the same time, they believe that this commitment should be accompanied by important budgetary reallocations in favour of United Nations activities related to human rights, including the servicing of the treaty bodies.

Achieving universal acceptance of the human rights treaties

16. The chairpersons note with satisfaction that 176 of the 184 States Members of the United Nations and 4 non-member States are now parties to one or more of the six principal human rights instruments monitored by the treaty bodies. Concern is expressed, however, that no instrument has yet achieved universal ratification. With this in mind, the chairpersons welcome the recent initiative taken by the Secretary-General personally to address a communication to all heads of State urging that their Governments ratify, accede or succeed to those principal human rights treaties to which they are not yet a party. The chairpersons also welcome indications by the High Commissioner for Human Rights that he intends to follow up with a similar initiative in the near future. The chairpersons consider it of the utmost importance that the issue of ratification be brought regularly to the attention of non-States parties whenever possible in contacts between Governments and senior officials of the United Nations. They, however, reiterate their position that adherence by States to international human rights instruments is not sufficient unless it is accompanied by full compliance with their provisions, including those relating to reporting obligations.

Overdue and non-submitted reports

17. The chairpersons reiterate the views expressed in their Vienna statement that full and effective compliance with international treaty obligations is an essential component of an international order based on the rule of law. Failure to comply, including a failure to report as required, constitutes a violation of international law. They urge the States parties to the human rights treaties to deal with this matter at their regular meetings. These meetings should not only be devoted to elections of members of treaty bodies, but should consider general problems relating to the implementation

of the treaties. They also urge States parties whose reports are overdue to request the assistance of the advisory services programme of the Centre for Human Rights to fulfil their reporting obligations.
18. The chairpersons also reiterate the recommendation made at their fourth meeting that each treaty body should follow, as a last resort, the practice already adopted by some committees of considering the situation in States parties whose reports are long overdue, in the absence of a report.

More effective integration of human rights into the totality of United Nations activities
19. The chairpersons emphasize that all human rights contained in the international human rights instruments apply fully to women and that the equal enjoyment of those rights should be closely monitored by each treaty body within the competence of its mandate. A common strategy should be developed by the treaty bodies in that regard and discussed at the meeting of chairpersons.
20. The chairpersons note with concern that reports submitted by States parties often do not contain adequate information on the actual enjoyment by women of their human rights, nor has such information been forthcoming from other sources. In this regard, the chairpersons recommend that each treaty body consider amending, where appropriate, its guidelines for the preparation of State party reports to request information, including disaggregated statistical data, from States parties on the situation of women under the terms of each instrument. The chairpersons express the wish for similar information from non-governmental organizations, intergovernmental organizations, specialized agencies and from United Nations offices.
21. Furthermore, the chairpersons deplore a growing tendency in the United Nations on the part of bodies concerned with some aspects of human rights in their activities steadfastly to ignore the standards codified in the international human rights treaties and, in some cases, to attempt to redefine those standards by adopting a different vocabulary, assigning different priorities and creating additional monitoring mechanisms. This tendency has been most recently manifested in the preparatory process for the World Summit for Social Development, which has not reflected the relevant standards contained in the International Covenant on Economic, Social and Cultural Rights and in the Convention on the Elimination of All Forms of Discrimination Against Women.
22. The chairpersons draw the attention of the High Commissioner for Human Rights to this and similar problems and request that they be addressed within his mandate to coordinate human rights promotion and protection activities throughout the United Nations system. In that connection, the chairpersons also welcome the recommendation, contained in the Vienna Declaration and Programme of Action (sect. II, para. 7), that human rights training for international civil servants who are assigned to work relating to human rights should be organized. The chairpersons affirm that human rights should have a high profile in all relevant United Nations activities and, *inter alia*, must be clearly identified with, and understood in the context of, the United Nations human rights instruments and the work of the treaty monitoring bodies.

23. The chairpersons emphasize the importance of more effective cooperation at all levels with the specialized agencies, other organizations of the United Nations system and United Nations bodies. In this connection, the chairpersons welcome the participation of the High Commissioner for Human Rights in the April 1994 session of the Administrative Committee on Coordination (ACC) and the addition, for the first time, of human rights to the agenda of that body. The chairpersons express the hope that a human rights focus in ACC will continue in the future.

Education in the field of human rights
24. The chairpersons recommend that treaty bodies include the issue of education in the field of human rights among their priority activities. They should, in particular, encourage States parties to include human rights teaching and education in school curricula, in the light of the essential role they play in the promotion of human rights. Efforts in this respect should be intensified in view of the proposed decade for human rights education.
25. States parties are also urged to encourage and support the media in the production of imaginative programmes on human rights which are accessible to the wider public and adapted to the local cultural environment.

Prevention of human rights violations, including early warning and urgent procedures
26. The chairpersons welcome the initiative taken by a number of treaty bodies to develop, within the scope of their respective mandates, procedures aimed at preventing human rights violations. Further efforts in this regard are warmly encouraged. Such procedures should include early warning aimed at preventing existing problems from escalating into conflicts and urgent procedures aimed at responding to problems requiring immediate attention to prevent or limit the scale and number of violations. Consideration should be given to developing a systematic and consistent approach to identifying problem areas and developing a range of possible courses of action which might be taken.
27. The chairpersons reiterate the recommendation made at their fourth meeting that the Security Council should be encouraged to take full account, in its deliberations and in its decisions and resolutions, of the obligations of the States concerned pursuant to the principal human rights treaties. The chairpersons urge the treaty bodies to take all appropriate measures in response to situations of massive violations of human rights, including the possibility of bringing those violations to the attention of the High Commissioner for Human Rights as well as the Secretary-General and the competent organs and bodies of the United Nations, including the Security Council. The chairpersons believe that it would be most effective if more than one treaty body were to take concerted action in this regard.
28. The chairpersons also recommend that increased attention be given by the Security Council to violations of human rights, which are a first indication of national and international instabilities and a threat to peace. To this end, early warning measures adopted by treaty bodies and information provided by them on human rights violations should be taken into consideration by the Council in deciding on a course of action.
29. The chairpersons suggest a meeting in 1995 with the Secretary-General to

discuss the role of the treaty bodies in bringing urgent matters relating to human rights violations to his attention and, through him, to the Security Council.

Reservations
30. The chairpersons believe that treaty bodies should be insistent in seeking explanations from States parties regarding the reasons for making and maintaining reservations to the relevant human rights treaties. They recommend that treaty bodies state clearly that certain reservations to international human rights instruments are contrary to the object and purpose of those instruments and consequently incompatible with treaty law. Treaty bodies should also bring this to the attention of the States parties to the relevant treaties.

Successions
31. The chairpersons note with concern that a number of successor States to former States parties to the human rights treaties have not yet formally confirmed to the Secretary-General their succession to the human rights treaties. The chairpersons urge all successor States, if they have not already done so, to confirm as soon as possible their succession to those treaties. The chairpersons welcome the initiatives taken by some of the treaty bodies to bring this matter of urgency to the attention of successor States. Similar initiatives by other treaty bodies are warmly encouraged.
32. The chairpersons are, however, of the view that successor States are automatically bound by obligations under international human rights instruments from their respective date of independence and that the respect of their obligations should not depend on a declaration of confirmation made by the new Government of the successor State.

New instruments
33. The chairpersons welcome the elaboration by United Nations bodies of optional protocols to international human rights instruments. They encourage, in particular, the elaboration of provisions which have a preventive character as well as provisions relating to recourse or inquiry procedures.

Multiple reporting requirements
34. The chairpersons support the recommendation made by the World Conference on Human Rights that the treaty monitoring bodies should include the status of women and the human rights of women in their deliberations and findings, making use of gender-specific data, and that States parties should be encouraged to supply information on the situation of women, – *de jure* and *de facto*, in their reports to treaty monitoring bodies. States parties should also be encouraged to supply information on the situation of children.

Reducing the burden of reporting
35. With reference to the question of reducing the reporting burden of States, the chairpersons took note of the suggestions made by the independent expert, Mr. Philip Alston, in his interim report on the updated study on enhancing the long-term effectiveness of the United Nations human rights treaty regime.

Reducing delays in the consideration of reports
36. The chairpersons note that an increasing backlog of State party reports pending consideration is becoming a serious problem for a number of treaty bodies and invites those treaty bodies to give due consideration to ways of reducing that backlog.

Cooperation with the specialized agencies and other United Nations bodies
37. The chairpersons welcome the contribution to the work of the treaty bodies made by the specialized agencies and other United Nations bodies. The chairpersons express the hope that such cooperation will continue and increase in the future, particularly with a view to ensuring consistency in the application of related provisions of the human rights treaties and other international instruments. The chairpersons recommend that representatives of the specialized agencies and other organizations within the United Nations system be invited to their future meetings.
38. The chairpersons encourage each human rights treaty body to review its practices concerning the participation of representatives from the specialized agencies and other United Nations bodies so as to enhance that participation and the exchange of pertinent information. To that end, the treaty bodies may wish to consider issuing information obtained from the specialized agencies as documents or working papers, referring, where appropriate, to the work of other monitoring bodies (such as the ILO Committee of Experts) and drawing the attention of the reporting State, where appropriate, to the availability of technical assistance from the specialized agencies.
39. In order to give greater prominence to human rights in the work of the organs, organizations and bodies of the United Nations system, the chairpersons suggest that those agencies consider inviting one or more representatives of the human rights treaty bodies to address their general conferences on pertinent trends and developments. Alternatively, meetings with representatives of treaty bodies could be organized by specialized agencies and United Nations organs when treaty bodies are in session.
40. The chairpersons also suggest that the specialized agencies and other organizations of the United Nations system supply the treaty bodies annually with information relevant to human rights issues, such as the situation of refugees, human rights of women, the right to strike, poverty, etc., that those agencies and organizations would like to be considered by treaty bodies.

Enhancing the role of non-governmental organizations
41. The chairpersons recommend that each treaty body examine the possibility of changing its working methods or amending its rules of procedure to allow non-governmental organizations to participate more fully in its activities. Non-governmental organizations could be allowed, in particular, to make oral interventions and to transmit information relevant to the monitoring of human rights provisions through formally established and well-structured procedures. In order to facilitate the participation of non-governmental organizations, the chairpersons recommend that information about States parties' reporting, including scheduling and document numbers of the reports, be made available at a single point in the Centre for Human Rights. Similarly, advance information on the topics of proposed general comments should be made available to encourage non-governmental organizations to

provide input to the drafts and to promote further discussion. Attention should be given by treaty bodies and non-governmental organizations to securing a stronger, more effective and coordinated participation of national non-governmental organizations in the consideration of States parties' reports.
42. The chairpersons welcome the contribution made at their fifth meeting by non-governmental organizations and recommend that at future meetings representatives of non-governmental organizations again be invited to address the chairpersons and to submit appropriate recommendations for consideration by the meeting.

Public information activities
43. The chairpersons are of the view that concluding observations and comments that treaty bodies adopt at the end of their consideration of States parties reports should be given more publicity, especially at the national level. To this end, the texts should be transmitted to the appropriate United Nations information centre and made available to the public. In addition, local non-governmental organizations should be encouraged and, if possible, financially supported to translate the concluding observations on the State party where they operate or other basic decisions of treaty bodies into local languages.
44. Each treaty body should urge States parties to translate, publish and make available to the media the full text of the concluding observations on their reports. The Department of Public Information of the Secretariat should, at the end of each year, publish as a separate volume a compilation of all concluding observations adopted during that year by treaty bodies.

Adequate Secretariat resources for servicing the treaty bodies
45. The chairpersons strongly support the recommendation made by the World Conference on Human Rights that sufficient human, financial and other resources should be provided to the Centre for Human Rights to enable it to carry out its activities effectively, efficiently and expeditiously. The chairpersons reiterate the view expressed in their Vienna statement that for the treaty supervisory system to function efficiently and effectively the number of relevant Professional staff should be tripled.
46. Attention was also drawn by the chairpersons to the question of a committee resource room within the Centre for Human Rights. This measure had been recommended by the chairpersons at their second, third and fourth meetings and had been endorsed on a number of occasions by various treaty bodies. In view of the fact that six years had passed since the need for the facility was first identified, the chairpersons urge the High Commissioner for Human Rights to take action on the matter.

Financing of the treaty bodies
47. The chairpersons welcome the endorsement by the General Assembly of the amendments to the funding provisions of the International Convention on the Elimination of All Forms of Racial Discrimination and the Convention Against Torture and Other Cruel, Inhuman or Degrading Treatment or Punishment, which occurred since their last meeting, and request that the necessary measures be taken to ensure that the two committees meet as scheduled until the amendments enter in force. The chairpersons note that

individual States parties should act as rapidly as possible to notify the Secretary-General of their acceptance of the amendments.
48. In addition, the chairpersons strongly recommend that the regular budget of the United Nations providing for the functioning of the treaty bodies include a fund specifically devoted to the activities of their members relating to emergency situations, as well as to information, coordination and human rights training, which are often requested by United Nations organs and specialized agencies.

Providing adequate resources for the effective functioning of the Committee on the Elimination of Discrimination against Women

49. The chairpersons note with serious concern that the ability of the Committee on the Elimination of Discrimination against Women (CEDAW) to discharge its duties effectively under the Convention on the Elimination of All Forms of Discrimination against Women continues to be severely constrained by the lack of sufficient meeting time to examine State party reports. Owing to the resulting large backlog of reports pending consideration, State party reports may not be examined until three years after their submission, a situation which the chairpersons consider wholly unacceptable. The chairpersons strongly recommend that this deplorable situation be addressed by the addition of significantly increased meeting time until the backlog of pending reports has been eliminated. They also strongly recommend that consideration be given to the suggestion of CEDAW that the Convention be amended as necessary.
50. In addition, the chairpersons are seriously concerned at the lack of resources, including adequate Secretariat support, which continues to affect the activities of CEDAW. The chairpersons are strongly of the view that CEDAW should no longer be separated from the mainstream of the other human rights activities and that it should be based, like all the other human rights treaty bodies, at the United Nations Office at Geneva. In this connection, the chairpersons strongly reiterate the recommendation contained in the reports of their third and fourth sessions to the effect that the servicing of CEDAW by the Secretariat should be provided from the Centre for Human Rights at Geneva. They also note the difficulties encountered by CEDAW in exchanging information with other treaty bodies due to its location at Headquarters, while all the other treaty bodies are based at the United Nations Office at Geneva. It is essential that a unified approach to servicing be put in place in order that CEDAW may have access to the same services and facilities as the other committees and in order to achieve the full and effective integration of CEDAW into the overall human rights treaty regime.
51. The chairpersons recommend that, at its next session in January 1995, CEDAW give consideration to the proposed relocation of its sessions and its secretariat and take a decision on this matter.

Computerizing the work of the treaty bodies

52. The chairpersons take note of the repeated efforts made by the Centre for Human Rights to secure adequate resources for automation and urge that further and immediate action be taken to secure the required resources for the long overdue computerization of the entire Centre for Human Rights, in particular the work of the treaty bodies, both through the regular budget

of the United Nations and by means of voluntary contributions. Immediate measures should also be taken, on the basis of the funds already available, to begin implementation of some of the recommendations of the task force on computerization of the work of the treaty bodies.[1] The chairpersons are of the view that delay in the computerization of the work of treaty bodies would seriously affect their effectiveness.
53. The chairpersons deplore the fact that the recommendations contained in the report of the task force still have not been implemented despite the repeated strong support expressed for computerization of the work of the treaty bodies each year in the resolutions of the Commission on Human Rights and the General Assembly.
54. The chairpersons note with interest the proposal by the American Association for the Advancement of Science (AAAS), a non-governmental organization with consultative status in the Economic and Social Council, to provide logistical and other support to the treaty bodies in relation to the development of an electronic database. In view of the desirability of obtaining contributions towards the overall goals of the Centre for Human Rights in this area from as many sources as possible, they express the hope that the proposal would succeed in gaining funding from a private foundation or other comparable source.
55. The chairpersons note, however, that the AAAS project cannot be seen as a substitute for, and must in any event not delay in any way, the Centre's own programme to provide full electronic access to the documentation sources required by the treaty bodies, the States parties, non-governmental organizations and other users. Given the long delays that have already occurred since the task force of the Commission on Human Rights reported in late 1989, the chairpersons also request that immediate steps be taken to ensure that as much of the treaty body documentation as possible is made available immediately, particularly on Internet. For this purpose, consideration should be given to the possibility of working through Togethernet to ensure accessibility of the documentation as soon as possible.
56. Noting that some specialized agencies, academic and other institutions have already produced or are in the process of producing relevant databases, the chairpersons recommend that those efforts be coordinated so that the databases may be used without delay in the work of the treaty bodies.

Manual on Human Rights Reporting
57. Owing to the need to include a new chapter relating to the Convention on the Rights of the Child and the operations of the Committee on the Rights of the Child, as well as to reflect the numerous procedural and other changes that have been adopted by the various committees since its publication, the chairpersons recommend that the *Manual on Human Rights Reporting* (HRI/PUB/91/1) be revised prior to its issuance in loose-leaf format.

Facilitating greater coordination and interaction among the treaty bodies
58. The chairpersons note that it is imperative for the effective functioning of the treaty bodies that steps be taken to facilitate greater coordination and interaction among them. To this end, the chairpersons recommend that a

---
[1] E/CN.4/1990/39.

meeting of chairpersons be scheduled in 1995 in order to identify common obstacles to the implementation of the human rights treaties and to develop strategies aimed at achieving progress in their application. The meeting would also serve as an opportunity to exchange views on elaborating guidelines on specific topics of common concern. At the 1995 meeting, that topic will be ways to monitor more effectively the human rights of women. In preparation for that meeting, the chairpersons invite each treaty body to consider, within the competence of its mandate, how the monitoring of the human rights of women may be enhanced.

Periodicity of the meetings of chairpersons
59. In the light of the numerous issues of common interest and concern to all treaty bodies which need to be discussed and coordinated more frequently than is done at present, the chairpersons strongly recommend that henceforth their meetings be held annually instead of biennially.
60. In the future, a conference of all treaty bodies could be envisaged to discuss issues of common interest and common problems.

A/50/505 — 4 October 1995

UNITED NATIONS GENERAL ASSEMBLY
Fiftieth session

EFFECTIVE IMPLEMENTATION OF INTERNATIONAL INSTRUMENTS ON HUMAN RIGHTS, INCLUDING REPORTING OBLIGATIONS UNDER INTERNATIONAL INSTRUMENTS ON HUMAN RIGHTS

Note by the Secretary-General

The Secretary-General has the honour to transmit to the General Assembly the report of the sixth meeting of persons chairing the human rights treaty bodies, convened pursuant to General Assembly resolution 49/178 of 23 December 1994.

ANNEX

Report of the sixth meeting of persons chairing the human rights treaty bodies

I. INTRODUCTION

1. Since the adoption of resolution 37/44 on 3 December 1982, the General Assembly has continuously kept under review the problems relating to the effective implementation of international instruments on human rights, including reporting obligations under international instruments on human rights. Those problems have also received careful attention during the various sessions of the treaty bodies, at some of the meetings of States parties and at meetings of other organs such as the Economic and Social Council and the Commission on Human Rights.
2. Pursuant to General Assembly resolution 38/117 of 16 December 1983, the Secretary-General convened the first meeting of the persons chairing the bodies entrusted with the consideration of State party reports in August 1984. The report of that meeting was presented to the General Assembly at its thirty-ninth session (A/39/484, annex). The second, third, fourth and fifth meetings were convened by the Secretary-General in October 1988, October 1990, October 1992 and September 1994. The reports of those meetings were presented to the Assembly at its forty-fourth, forty-fifth, forty-seventh and forty-ninth sessions (in the annexes of documents A/44/98, A/45/636, A/47/628 and A/49/537, respectively).
3. In its resolution 49/178 of 23 December 1994, the General Assembly welcomed the submission of the report of the fifth meeting of persons chairing the

human rights treaty bodies, held at Geneva from 19 to 23 September 1994, and took note of the conclusions and recommendations in the report; welcomed the continuing efforts by the treaty bodies and the Secretary-General, within their respective spheres of competence, aimed at streamlining, rationalizing and otherwise improving reporting procedures; requested that the Secretary-General take the appropriate steps in order to finance, as of 1995, annual meetings of persons chairing the human rights treaty bodies from the available resources of the regular budget of the United Nations; and decided to continue giving priority consideration, at its fiftieth session, to the conclusions and recommendations of the meetings of persons chairing human rights treaty bodies, in the light of the deliberations of the Commission on Human Rights, under the item entitled "Human rights questions". The Commission on Human Rights, in its resolution 1995/92, welcomed the request by the General Assembly to the Secretary-General to take appropriate steps to finance, as of 1995, annual meetings of persons chairing the human rights treaty bodies from available resources of the regular budget of the United Nations.
4. The sixth meeting of persons chairing the human rights treaty bodies was convened by the Secretary-General pursuant to General Assembly resolution 49/178.

II. ORGANIZATION OF THE MEETING

5. The meeting was held at the United Nations Office at Geneva from 18 to 22 September 1995. The following representatives of the human rights treaty bodies attended: Mr. Philip Alston (Chairperson, Committee on Economic, Social and Cultural Rights), Ms. Akila Belembaogo (Chairperson, Committee on the Rights of the Child), Ms. Ivanka Corti (Chairperson, Committee on the Elimination of Discrimination against Women), Mr. Alexis Dipanda-Mouelle (Chairperson, Committee against Torture), Mr. Omran El Shafei (Vice-Chairperson, Human Rights Committee) and Mr. Ivan Garvalov (Chairperson, Committee on the Elimination of Racial Discrimination).
6. Representatives of the following United Nations bodies and specialized agencies attended the meeting: the United Nations Children's Fund (UNICEF), the Office of the United Nations High Commissioner for Refugees (UNHCR), the International Labour Organization (ILO), the United Nations Educational, Scientific and Cultural Organization (UNESCO) and the World Health Organization (WHO). The Council of Europe was represented by the President of the European Commission on Human Rights and a judge of the European Court of Human Rights. The Latin American Institute for the Prevention of Crime and the Treatment of Offenders was also represented. In addition, representatives of the following non-governmental organizations attended: American Association for the Advancement of Science, Amnesty International, Article 19, Association for the Prevention of Torture, Baha'i International Community, International Commission of Jurists, International Women's Rights Action Watch, NGO Group on the Convention of the Rights of the Child, World Organization against Torture/SOS Torture.

7. The agenda for the meeting was as follows:
   1. Opening of the meeting.
   2. Election of the officers of the meeting.
   3. Adoption of the agenda.
   4. Organizational and other matters.
   5. Review of recent developments relating to the work of the treaty bodies.
   6. Improving the operation of the human rights treaty bodies.
   7. Gender perspectives in the work of the treaty bodies.
   8. Prevention of human rights violations, including early warning and urgent procedures.
   9. Assistance to States in implementing Committee recommendations.
   10. Adoption of the report.
8. The following documentation was made available to the participants:
   (a) Provisional agenda and annotations (HRI/MC/1995/1);
   (b) Report of the Secretary-General on improving the operation of the human rights treaty bodies (HRI/MC/1995/2);
   (c) Report of the Secretary-General on the status of the international instruments and the general situation of overdue reports (HRI/MC/1994/3);
   (d) Reports of the fourth and fifth meetings of persons chairing the human rights treaty bodies (A/47/628, annex and A/49/537, annex);
   (e) Report by the Committee on the Elimination of Discrimination against Women to the Fourth World Conference on Women (A/CONF.177/7);
   (f) Report of the Main Committee containing the draft Platform for Action of the Fourth World Conference on Women (A/CONF.177/L.5 and addenda and corrigenda);
   (g) Interim report on the updated study by the independent expert on enhancing the long-term effectiveness of the United Nations human rights treaty regime (A/CONF.157/PC/62/Add.11/Rev.1);
   (h) Vienna statement of the international human rights treaty bodies (A/CONF.157/TBB/4 and Add.1);
   (i) Vienna Declaration and Programme of Action adopted by the World Conference on Human Rights on 25 June 1993 (A/CONF.157/24 (Part I), chap. III);
   (j) Compilation of general comments and general recommendations adopted by human rights treaty bodies (HRI/GEN/1/Rev.1);
   (k) Preparation of a plan of action for a United Nations decade for human rights education: report of the Secretary-General (A/49/261 and Add.1-E/1994/110 and Add.1);
   (l) Report of an expert group meeting on the development of guidelines for the integration of gender perspectives into United Nations human rights activities and programmes, held at Geneva from 3 to 7 July 1995 (to be issued as a United Nations document);
   (m) General Assembly resolution 49/178;
   (n) Commission on Human Rights resolutions 1995/18, 1995/22, 1995/80 and 1995/92.
9. The following informal working documents were also made available to the participants:
   (a) Recommendations for advisory services and technical assistance by treaty bodies: compilation prepared by the Secretariat;

(b) Actions being taken regarding recommendations made by treaty bodies for advisory services and technical assistance in the field of human rights: compilation prepared by the Secretariat;
(c) Status of the international human rights instruments: compilation prepared by the Secretariat;
(d) Status of State party reports to be submitted to the principal international human rights instruments: compilation prepared by the Secretariat;
(e) Incorporation of a gender perspective into the work of the United Nations human rights regime: working paper prepared by the Secretariat;
(f) Recommendations on human rights education: note by the Independent Commission on Human Rights Education.

10. The meeting was opened by Mr. Ibrahima Fall, Assistant Secretary-General for Human Rights, who addressed the chairpersons. On 21 September 1995, Mr. Jose Ayala-Lasso, the United Nations High Commissioner for Human Rights, addressed the meeting.
11. Ms. Akila Belembaogo was elected Chairperson-Rapporteur of the meeting.
12. On 22 September 1995, the chairpersons considered the draft report of their sixth meeting. The report, as amended during the course of the meeting, was adopted unanimously by the chairpersons.

III. REVIEW OF DEVELOPMENTS RELATING TO THE WORK OF THE TREATY BODIES

13. Under this agenda item, the chairpersons provided information on recent activities of the treaty bodies they represented. Among other developments, the chairpersons referred to their meeting with the Secretary-General on 19 June 1995 and expressed satisfaction regarding its outcome.
14. Regarding State party reports, it was noted that improvements had been seen in the quality of a number of reports submitted as well as in the methods for the formulation of concluding observations adopted by the treaty bodies following their consideration of those reports. It was also noted that, due to the increasing workload facing the treaty bodies, requests for additional meeting time had been made to the General Assembly by the Committee on Economic, Social and Cultural Rights and the Committee on the Elimination of Discrimination against Women. The Chairperson of the Committee on the Rights of the Child informed the other chairpersons that increased meeting time for the Committee on the Rights of the Child had been approved by the General Assembly in December 1994.
15. The chairpersons discussed developments in the working methods of the treaty bodies to monitor the implementation of their respective treaties by States parties. It was noted that the Committee on the Elimination of Racial Discrimination has had success in encouraging States parties to comply with their reporting obligations through the procedure developed by the Committee to examine the situations in States whose reports were seriously overdue. It was also reported that the Committee on Economic, Social and Cultural Rights had recently begun to examine, on the basis of all available information, the implementation of the International Covenant on Economic, Social and Cultural Rights in States parties that had submitted

no reports to the Committee. Participants were also informed that as from 1995, UNICEF, after consultation with the Committee on the Rights of the Child, would make public the extent of compliance with the Convention on the Rights of the Child by States parties in a special chapter of its annual report entitled "The progress of nations".

16. The chairpersons unanimously affirmed the important role of non-governmental organizations in the monitoring function of the treaty bodies. Several chairpersons also reported strengthened cooperation and improved exchanges of information with specialized agencies and various special rapporteurs of the Commission on Human Rights.

IV. SUGGESTIONS AND RECOMMENDATIONS

Improving the operation of the human rights treaty bodies

17. *Promotion of the international human rights instruments.* The chairpersons welcome the ongoing efforts of the Secretary-General and the United Nations High Commissioner for Human Rights to promote universal ratification of international human rights instruments and, in particular, the preparations for the holding of regional conferences to promote ratification and the drafting of a major study on the matter. They recommend that States which are considering ratification avoid making it subject to wide reservations. The chairpersons deplore the recent increase in the number and breadth of reservations made upon ratification of certain instruments and observe that the practice undermines the spirit and the letter of these legal texts. In this regard they both welcome and endorse the Human Rights Committee's General Comment 24 on the matter. The chairpersons also welcome the initiative of the Secretary-General, pursuant to the Vienna Declaration and Programme of Action, in proposing the preparation of a major study on the extent of reservations and on strategies to promote their withdrawal.

18. The chairpersons have noted with satisfaction the important role played by UNICEF in the promotion of universal ratification of the Convention on the Rights of the Child. They recommend that specialized agencies and international organizations should consider carrying out similar activities with regard to international human rights instruments and they look forward to exploring modalities for such action at their seventh meeting. They recommend that at that meeting a dialogue take place with senior officials of key organizations and agencies, to include, *inter alia*, the United Nations Development Programme.

19. The chairpersons suggest that those States which have not yet ratified the principal human rights instruments be given assurances that, in case of need, they will be provided with appropriate advisory services in relation to their reporting and other obligations once they become parties to the instruments.

20. The chairpersons draw attention to the importance of the human rights treaty bodies contributing fully to the achievement of the Plan of Action for the United Nations Decade for Human Rights Education. Accordingly, they recommend that each treaty body, in its examination of State Party reports, assiduously investigate compliance by States parties with the extensive obligations regarding education and the provision of public information on

human rights in general and concerning the human rights instruments and the proceedings of the treaty bodies in particular. Treaty bodies should, *inter alia*, inquire as to whether instruments have been translated and disseminated in local languages and whether States parties have put in place satisfactory human rights training programmes for all relevant categories of public officials. The chairpersons also recommend that treaty bodies both further elaborate relevant reporting guidelines or general comments and recommendations, and offer to individual States concrete suggestions and advice on the implementation of the obligations they have assumed regarding education and the provision of public information.

21. *Reporting.* The chairpersons note with regret that the problems of overdue reports and of severe backlogs in the consideration of reports persist in most of the treaty bodies. They welcome the initiatives taken by various treaty bodies to respond to these problems but warn against solutions resulting in excessively abbreviated or summary consideration of the situation in the respective countries.

22. *External relations of treaty bodies.* The chairpersons note the failure to involve the treaty bodies, in an appropriate manner, in either the preparations for or the formal negotiations of United Nations world conferences. A recent case in point was the non-involvement of the Committee on the Elimination of Discrimination against Women and the Committee on the Rights of the Child in the preparations for and the negotiations of the recent Fourth World Conference on Women, held in Beijing in September 1995. They request the Secretary-General to provide the seventh meeting of chairpersons with a study which proposes ways and means of establishing an appropriate *sui generis* status for the treaty bodies in the United Nations system. Such a status would clearly distinguish the treaty bodies from intergovernmental and non-governmental organizations and would enable them to play a full role, befitting their importance, within all future international conferences and *vis-à-vis* the organs of the United Nations system. They urge the General Assembly to ensure that the relevant treaty bodies will be invited to be fully involved in the ongoing preparations for the forthcoming Habitat II conference and other international conferences dealing with human rights.

23. The chairpersons reiterate the central role which non-governmental organizations play in providing reliable information necessary to the conduct of treaty body activities and recommend that the Secretariat facilitate the exchange of information between treaty bodies and such organizations. The Secretariat is requested to develop a database of national institutions for the promotion and protection of human rights and of nationally based non-governmental organizations which should be informed of the scheduled consideration of any reports of the country concerned by the treaty bodies. In addition, the Secretariat is requested to issue twice a year, taking account of the exigencies of the various committees, an integrated schedule of all reports expected to be considered by all of the treaty bodies during the relevant period. Such a list should include all appropriate caveats as to possible changes occurring in the schedule.

24. The chairpersons recommend that the human rights treaty bodies take increased cognizance of the related activities of regional human rights mechanisms. In particular, they recommend that modalities of cooperation and of

exchange of information be explored by the respective secretariats and that existing databases on the jurisprudence of regional human rights regimes interface with databases to be developed by the United Nations for the human rights treaty bodies. The chairpersons recommend that regional bodies continue to be invited to attend all future meetings of the chairpersons.
25. The chairpersons recommend that human rights treaty bodies increase their cooperation and exchange of information with United Nations non-conventional human rights bodies and mechanisms. The chairpersons suggest that they meet regularly with the chairperson and other officers of the Commission on Human Rights and the Sub-commission on Prevention of Discrimination and Protection of Minorities in order to discuss matters of mutual concern and to further develop strategies for cooperation. Modalities for participation by the chairpersons or their representatives in the annual meetings of the special rapporteurs should be explored.
26. Furthermore, the chairpersons expressed the view that it would be extremely valuable if their meetings with the Secretary-General were to be held on an annual basis.
27. The chairpersons welcome the increased participation of United Nations specialized agencies in the work of some of the human rights treaty bodies, though they observe that there remains considerable potential for an enhancement of such cooperation. The chairpersons recommend that at their seventh meeting they include this matter in their envisaged exchange of views with specialized agencies and United Nations bodies and that high-level officials of the bodies and agencies, including especially the United Nations Children's Fund, the United Nations Development Programme, the United Nations Population Fund, the Office of the United Nations High Commissioner for Refugees, the International Labour Organization, the United Nations Educational, Scientific and Cultural Organization, the World Health Organization and the World Bank, be invited to participate, on a specific date to be notified well in advance, in order to ensure that concrete proposals might be discussed and appropriate arrangements entered into. In advance of that meeting human rights treaty bodies are invited to reflect on and to indicate the optimal models for cooperation with United Nations bodies and specialized agencies.
28. *Secretariat support.* While welcoming the efforts made by the Centre for Human Rights to ensure adequate funding for the treaty bodies, the chairpersons recommend that the General Assembly consider providing each treaty body with a budget, to be dispensed from with the approval of the United Nations High Commissioner for Human Rights, for the contracting of special studies, the undertaking of essential missions and other matters associated with their mandates. They are of the view that this initiative would result in economic efficiencies and improve accountability of expenditure.
29. The chairpersons welcome the ongoing support provided to them by the Centre for Human Rights and they acknowledge the range of servicing initiatives which continue to be taken within existing resources. The chairpersons welcome the indication provided by the Secretariat that the country-specific and other information available to each of the treaty bodies will in the future be maintained in an integrated fashion. They emphasize the need to develop the fullest possible databases in this regard and to ensure the

ready accessibility of the collection to members of the treaty bodies. The chairpersons, however, express their deep concern at the continuing massive under-resourcing of the Centre for Human Rights which prevents the human rights treaty bodies from adequately carrying out their mandates. Among the persistent problems are under-staffing of the treaty body secretariats, lack of technical expertise and inadequate administrative support.

30. The chairpersons recommend that the General Assembly, the Secretary-General and the United Nations High Commissioner for Human Rights consider the adverse impact upon the reputation of the work and public image of the United Nations that results from the persistent failure to address adequately the problems referred to above. In this regard, during the fiftieth anniversary year of the United Nations, the chairpersons strenuously urge that the work of human rights be restored, in effective practical terms, to the central role in the United Nations which was envisaged for it in the Charter.

31. The chairpersons declare their conviction as to the importance of the integration of the Committee on the Elimination of Discrimination against Women into the mainstream of United Nations system-wide activity through its relocation to the Centre for Human Rights, as they have already stated at their fifth meeting. They accordingly welcome decision 14/II of January 1995 of the Committee on the Elimination of Discrimination against Women which requests the Secretary-General to locate it at Geneva with servicing provided by the Centre. The chairpersons also welcome the Secretary-General's agreement, in principle, to the transfer to the Centre of the responsibility for both the substantive and technical servicing of the Committee, while maintaining a close working relationship with the Division for the Advancement of Women. The chairpersons also note with satisfaction the proposed amendment to article 20 of the Convention on the Elimination of All Forms of Discrimination against Women adopted on 22 May 1995 by the States parties to the Convention, though they express concern regarding the present procedure for ratification which may lead to inordinate delays. The chairpersons recommend that the General Assembly approve this amendment at its fiftieth session.

32. The chairpersons note the slight progress which has been made with regard to the development of appropriate databases and on-line information services at the Centre for Human Rights. They recommend that work proceed speedily and with full regard for the importance of making provision for an efficient flow of information. They urge that arrangements currently under way be assured and that any necessary exemptions from possible expenditure freezes be authorized. They also recommend that future appeals to Governments for funds be rendered more persuasive through the inclusion of detailed information on the manner in which the funds would be deployed.

33. The chairpersons reiterate their long-standing request that office facilities at the Centre for Human Rights be set aside for use by the 97 members of the various treaty bodies when they are in Geneva.

Gender perspectives in the work of the treaty bodies

34. The chairpersons endorse the following recommendations proposed by an expert group on the integration of gender perspectives into United Nations human rights activities and programmes, which met at Geneva from 3 to 7

July 1995, in line with the recommendations of the Vienna Declaration and Programme of Action:
  (a) The treaty bodies shall fully integrate gender perspectives into their presessional and sessional working methods, including identification of issues and preparation of questions for country reviews, general comments, general recommendations, and concluding observations. In particular, the treaty bodies should consider the gender implications of each issue discussed under each of the articles of the respective instruments;
  (b) Guidelines for the preparation of reports by States parties should be amended to reflect the necessity of providing specific information on the human rights of women for consideration by the respective committees;
  (c) In undertaking investigative procedures, the treaty bodies should make special efforts to elicit information about the situation of women in the area of inquiry;
  (d) Treaty bodies should consistently request gender-disaggregated data from States parties and from United Nations specialized agencies and use the data in reviewing country reports;
  (e) The treaty bodies should make every effort to exchange information on progress, developments and situations concerning the human rights of women;
  (f) In preparing reports of the treaty body sessions, attention should be paid to the use of gender-inclusive language wherever possible.
35. The chairpersons recommend that each treaty body consider how it might most effectively incorporate these proposals into its work practices. The respective chairpersons undertake to report to the seventh meeting of chairpersons on progress made in this regard.

Prevention of human rights violations, including early warning and urgent procedures

36. The chairpersons reiterate that the promotion and protection of all human rights and fundamental freedoms is, as declared in the Vienna Declaration and Programme of Action, a priority objective of the United Nations. In this regard, the chairpersons encourage treaty bodies to continue their efforts to develop mechanisms for the prevention of gross human rights violations, including early warning and urgent procedures. They consider that coordinated action by human rights treaty bodies in this regard would increase their effectiveness. To this end, they suggest that any action undertaken by one of the treaty bodies be immediately brought to the attention of the other treaty bodies.
37. The chairpersons recommend that treaty bodies increasingly consult United Nations organs and bodies, including special rapporteurs of the Commission on Human Rights and the Sub-Commission on the Prevention of Discrimination and Protection of Minorities, exchanging information and utilizing existing expertise in order to detect and respond appropriately to situations of massive violations of human rights.

Assistance to States in implementing committee recommendations

38. The chairpersons reiterate the importance of appropriate action being taken by relevant United Nations bodies to assist States, through the provision of technical assistance, in implementing recommendations made by treaty

bodies. The commitment indicated in this regard by representatives of specialized agencies and organizations participating in the meeting of chairpersons is welcomed and the chairpersons recommend that they, together with the secretariats of the treaty bodies, give priority attention to the development of ongoing programmes in this regard.

39. The potentially important role of the United Nations High Commissioner for Human Rights and the Centre for Human Rights in the implementation of technical assistance recommendations by the treaty bodies is acknowledged. The chairpersons recommend that the High Commissioner and the Centre pay increased attention to such proposals in the advisory services and technical assistance programmes of the Centre.

40. With a view to improving coordination and effectiveness in the human rights activities of the United Nations, the chairpersons recommend that all programmes of human rights technical assistance be planned and implemented with the full cooperation and collaboration of all relevant parties, especially those which benefit from a presence in the country concerned. The chairpersons, for their part, will ensure that the treaty bodies will consult widely in considering recommendations for technical assistance to States parties.

A/51/482 — 11 October 1996
UNITED NATIONS GENERAL ASSEMBLY
Fifty-first session

EFFECTIVE IMPLEMENTATION OF INTERNATIONAL INSTRUMENTS ON HUMAN RIGHTS, INCLUDING REPORTING OBLIGATIONS UNDER INTERNATIONAL INSTRUMENTS ON HUMAN RIGHTS

Note by the Secretary-General

The Secretary-General has the honour to transmit to the General Assembly the report of the seventh meeting of persons chairing the human rights treaty bodies, convened pursuant to General Assembly resolution 50/170 of 22 December 1995.

ANNEX

Report of the seventh meeting of persons chairing the human rights treaty bodies

I. INTRODUCTION

1. Since the adoption of resolution 37/44 on 3 December 1982, the General Assembly has continuously kept under review the problems relating to the effective implementation of international instruments on human rights, including reporting obligations under international instruments on human rights. Those problems have also received careful attention during the various sessions of the treaty bodies, at some of the meetings of States parties and at meetings of other organs such as the Economic and Social Council and the Commission on Human Rights.

2. Pursuant to General Assembly resolution 38/117 of 16 December 1983, the Secretary-General convened the first meeting of the persons chairing the bodies entrusted with the consideration of State party reports in August 1984. The report of that meeting was presented to the General Assembly at its thirty-ninth session (A/39/484, annex). The second, third, fourth, fifth and sixth meetings were convened by the Secretary-General in October 1988, October 1990, October 1992, September 1994 and September 1995. The reports of those meetings were presented to the Assembly at its forty-fourth, forty-fifth, forty-seventh, forty-ninth and fiftieth sessions (in the annexes of documents A/44/98, A/45/636, A/47/628, A/49/537 and A/50/505 respectively). It may be recalled that, in accordance with General Assembly resolution

49/178 of 23 December 1994, the meetings of persons chairing the human rights treaty bodies have become annual since 1995.
3. In its resolution 50/170 of 22 December 1995, the General Assembly welcomed the report of the persons chairing the human rights treaty bodies on their sixth meeting, held at Geneva from 18 to 22 September 1995, and took note of the conclusions and recommendations in the report (A/50/505, annex); welcomed the continuing efforts by the treaty bodies and the Secretary-General aimed at streamlining, rationalizing and otherwise improving reporting procedures, and urged the treaty bodies and the meetings of persons chairing the human rights treaty bodies to continue to examine ways of reducing the duplication of reporting required under the different instruments, without impairing the quality of reporting, and of generally reducing the reporting burden on Member States. The Commission on Human Rights welcomed the report of the sixth meeting of the persons chairing the human rights treaty bodies and took note of its conclusions and recommendations in its resolution 1996/22 of 19 April 1996.
4. The seventh meeting of persons chairing the human rights treaty bodies was convened by the Secretary-General pursuant to General Assembly resolution 50/170.

II. ORGANIZATION OF THE MEETING

5. The meeting was held at the United Nations Office at Geneva from 16 to 20 September 1996. The following representatives of the human rights treaty bodies attended: Mr. Francisco José Aguilar Urbina (Chairperson, Human Rights Committee), Mr. Philip Alston (Chairperson, Committee on Economic, Social and Cultural Rights), Mr. Michael Banton (Chairperson, Committee on the Elimination of Racial Discrimination), Ms. Akila Belembaogo (Chairperson, Committee on the Rights of the Child), Ms. Ivanka Corti (Chairperson, Committee on the Elimination of Discrimination against Women) and Mr. Alexis Dipanda-Mouelle (Chairperson, Committee against Torture).
6. Representatives of the following United Nations bodies and specialized agencies attended the meeting: Division for the Advancement of Women of the United Nations Secretariat, the Joint United Nations Programme on HIV/AIDs (UNAIDS), the United Nations Children's Fund (UNICEF), the United Nations Population Fund (UNFPA), the Office of the United Nations High Commissioner for Refugees (UNHCR), the International Labour Organization (ILO), the United Nations Educational, Scientific and Cultural Organization (UNESCO) and the World Health Organization (WHO). A member of the Subcommission on Prevention of Discrimination and Protection of Minorities attended the meeting. The following regional intergovernmental organizations were represented at the meeting: Council of Europe (represented by the President of the European Commission on Human Rights), and the Organization for Security and Cooperation in Europe (OSCE). In addition, representatives of the following non-governmental organizations attended: Amnesty International, Anti-Racism Information Service (ARIS), Baha'i International Community, the Catholic Association

for Radio and Television, the Conference of European Justice and Peace Commissions, International Service for Human Rights, International Women's Rights Action Watch, the Women's International League for Peace and Freedom, the NGO Group for the Convention on the Rights of the Child and the World Organization against Torture.
7. In addition to his address to open the meeting (see para. 13 below), Mr. José Ayala-Lasso, the United Nations High Commissioner for Human Rights, participated in a closed meeting with the chairpersons, who appreciated the opportunity to have a frank dialogue with him. The chairpersons appreciated also that the High Commissioner had implemented the project of providing office space and facilities for experts and special rapporteurs.
8. Mr. Bacre W. N'diaye, chairperson of the third meeting of special rapporteurs, representatives, experts, and chairpersons of working groups of the special procedures of the Commission on Human Rights and the Advisory Services Programme addressed the chairpersons of the human rights treaty bodies on 19 September 1996.
9. The agenda for the meeting was as follows:
    1. Opening of the meeting.
    2. Election of the officers of the meeting.
    3. Adoption of the agenda.
    4. Organizational and other matters.
    5. Review of recent developments relating to the work of the treaty bodies.
    6. Improving the operation of the human rights treaty bodies.
    7. Cooperation of human rights treaty bodies with United Nations non-conventional human rights bodies and mechanisms and regional organizations.
    8. Gender perspectives in the work of the treaty bodies.
    9. Prevention of human rights violations, including early warning and urgent procedures.
    10. Assistance to States in implementing treaty body recommendations.
    11. Adoption of the report to the General Assembly.
10. Owing to lack of time, the chairpersons decided to postpone item 9 until the next meeting.
11. The following documentation was made available to the participants:
    (a) Provisional agenda and annotations (HRI/MC/1996/1);
    (b) Report of the Secretary-General on improving the operation of the human rights treaty bodies (HRI/MC/1996/2);
    (c) Report of the Secretary-General on the status of the international instruments and the general situation of overdue reports (HRI/MC/1996/3);
    (d) Reports of the fifth and sixth meetings of persons chairing the human rights treaty bodies (A/49/537, annex, and A/50/505, annex);
    (e) Report of the Fourth World Conference on Women (A/CONF.177/L.20);
    (f) Interim report on the updated study by the independent expert on enhancing the long-term effectiveness of the United Nations human rights treaty regime (A/CONF.157/PC/62/Add.11/Rev.1);
    (g) Vienna statement of the international human rights treaty bodies (A/CONF.157/TBB/4 and Add.1);
    (h) Vienna Declaration and Programme of Action adopted by the World

Conference on Human Rights on 25 June 1993 (A/CONF.157/24 (Part I), chap. III);
(i) Compilation of general comments and general recommendations adopted by human rights treaty bodies(HRI/GEN/1/Rev.2);
(j) Preparation of a plan of action for a United Nations decade for human rights education: report of the Secretary-General (A/49/261 and Add.1);
(k) Reports of the United Nations High Commissioner for Human Rights on the Implementation of the Plan of Action for the United Nations Decade for Human Rights Education: 1995–2004 (A/50/698 and E/CN.4/1996/51);
(l) General Assembly resolutions 50/170 and 50/177;
(m) Commission on Human Rights resolutions 1996/16, 1996/22, 1996/44, 1996/48 and 1996/78;
(n) Report of the Secretary-General on the Restructuring the Centre for Human Rights: Programme Budget for the Biennium 1996–1997 (A/C.5/50/71);
(o) Proposed medium-term plan for the period 1998–2001: Programme 19: Human rights (A/51/6 (Prog. 19)).

12. The following informal working documents were also made available to the participants:
(a) Recommendations for advisory services and technical assistance by treaty bodies: compilation prepared by the Secretariat;
(b) Actions being taken regarding recommendations made by treaty bodies for advisory services and technical assistance in the field of human rights: compilation prepared by the Secretariat;
(c) Status of the international human rights instruments: compilation prepared by the Secretariat;
(d) Status of State party reports to be submitted to the principal international human rights instruments: compilation prepared by the Secretariat;
(e) Plan of Action to strengthen the implementation of the Convention on the Rights of the Child, Centre for Human Rights;
(f) Document relating to the round table organized by UNFPA, Centre for Human Rights and the Division for the Advancement of Women on "Round Table on Approaches of Human Rights Treaty Bodies Towards Women's Health, with a Focus on Reproductive and Sexual Health Rights".

13. The meeting was opened by Mr. José Ayala-Lasso, the United Nations High Commissioner for Human Rights, who addressed the chairpersons.

14. Ms. Ivanka Corti was elected Chairperson-Rapporteur of the meeting unanimously. The chairpersons agreed that the principle of rotation among the treaty bodies should be taken into consideration in future meetings.

15. On 20 September 1996, the chairpersons considered the draft report of their seventh meeting. The report, as amended during the course of the meeting, was adopted unanimously by the chairpersons.

III. REVIEW OF DEVELOPMENTS RELATING TO THE WORK OF THE TREATY BODIES

16. Under this agenda item, the chairpersons provided information on recent activities of the treaty bodies they represented.
17. The chairperson of the Human Rights Committee referred to the increased active participation by specialized agencies and non-governmental organizations in the monitoring procedures under the International Covenant on Civil and Political Rights. He referred to the process to review the Committee's rules of procedures and its working methods. He also stated that the Committee had decided to prepare a series of new general comments and had appointed Committee members to prepare drafts. He pointed out that one of those general comments would concern article 3 of the Covenant regarding discrimination against women.
18. The chairperson of the Committee on Economic, Social and Cultural Rights stressed that the very existence of his Committee was legally tenuous because it had not been explicitly established by the Covenant of Economic, Social and Cultural Rights. Therefore, its legal existence could be called into question by the Economic and Social Council. Consideration should be given in the future to steps to be taken to remedy this situation.
19. The chairperson also regretted that his Committee had not been able to establish a constructive relationship with the World Bank and the United Nations Development Programme (UNDP), despite numerous requests. He noted the positive experience that the Committee on the Rights of the Child had had with UNICEF in terms of close cooperation, a relationship which had served not only to help promote knowledge of the Convention and its effective implementation, but which had also resulted in substantial additional financial and other resources being made available to that Committee. However, he questioned the wisdom of having one treaty body that was extremely well funded, while other treaty bodies had inadequate resources and administrative support with possibly no natural outside agencies to provide additional funding that could lead to increased effectiveness and more optimal functioning.
20. The chairperson of the Committee on the Rights of the Child indicated that the Committee had visited Bangladesh, Nepal, India, Sri Lanka and Pakistan, in cooperation with UNICEF, and subsequently participated in a seminar on the elimination of child labour.
21. The Committee had been asked to participate in a significant number of regional and international meetings. Most prominent among these had been the World Congress against Commercial Sexual Exploitation of Children in Stockholm. The chairperson pointed out that all these visits made the Convention and the work of the Committee better known but the virtual universal ratification of the Convention on the Rights of the Child, even if a positive achievement, posed the problem of the burden of work to the Committee in the present conditions.
22. The chairperson of the Committee against Torture commented that the major problems facing his Committee included ensuring that States parties to the Convention against Torture and Other Cruel, Inhuman or Degrading

Treatment and Punishment respect reporting deadlines and reservations by States to conducting investigations. He also stressed that the Committee continued to work closely with international and regional mechanisms established to fight against torture.

23. The chairperson of the Committee on the Elimination of Racial Discrimination referred to his Committee proposal of a new procedure for examining State parties initial reports when they are seriously overdue. He pointed out that the Committee's latest annual report to the General Assembly contains a new and detailed chapter on its methods of work, which explains how the Committee proceeds on a wide range of issues. The Committee had also decided to eliminate a summary of the discussions of initial and periodic reports in its annual report.

24. The chairperson of the Committee on the Elimination of Discrimination against Women referred to a seminar organized by a non-governmental organization on how to improve the content and quality of concluding observations. She drew particular attention to the development of the proposed optional protocol describing the progress made by the in-session Working Group of the Commission on the Status of Women at its fortieth session. She informed the meeting that the working group had accepted the participation of an expert from the Committee on the Elimination of Discrimination against Women as a resource person. The Committee had also decided to explore on the basis of experience of other treaty bodies how to regularly receive information from non-governmental organizations and to what extent their representatives could participate in its monitoring procedures. The Committee had also decided to adopt a new form of annual report to the General Assembly which would focus on its concluding observations. The Committee had appointed some members as focal points to follow the work of the other treaty bodies.

IV. CONCLUSIONS AND RECOMMENDATIONS

A. *Improving the operation of the human rights treaty bodies*

Promotion of international human rights treaties

25. The chairpersons recommend that any new human rights treaties should contain a provision that facilitates subsequent procedural amendments without going through the full constitutional ratification process in the State parties. It was suggested, for example, that any new human rights treaties should be drafted to provide that if two thirds of the States parties to such a treaty find that a decision to amend is procedural, then they can amend it in a meeting of States parties without referring it to their constitutional procedures for ratification.

26. The chairpersons further recommend that consideration be given to more creative approaches whereby several of the various procedural amendments to the human rights treaties could be packaged together in a single, comprehensive document to be transmitted to the States parties to allow them the option of invoking their constitutional amendment procedures only once for all the amendments.

27. The chairpersons also recommend that the view of the treaty body concerned

should be taken into account when the General Assembly considers proposals for optional protocols to human rights treaties.

States parties
28. The chairpersons note that a number of problems continue to exist between States parties and the treaty bodies, including the failure of some States to fulfil their reporting and financial obligations, and the increasing reporting burden upon States deriving from treaty bodies' requests for information. The chairpersons reiterate the recommendation of their fifth meeting (A/49/537, para. 17) that such problems be considered at regular meetings of States parties. These problems will demand extended attention when the independent expert has reported on possible long-term approaches to enhancing the effective operations of the treaty system.

Treaty-monitoring process
29. The chairpersons recommend that members of treaty bodies refrain from participating in any aspect of the consideration of the reports of the States of which they are nationals, or communications or inquiries concerning those States, in order to maintain the highest standards of impartiality, both in substance and in appearance. Human rights education
30. The chairpersons recommend that members of the various treaty bodies undertake substantial efforts in relation to all States parties, as well as their own national parliaments and human rights institutions, to publicize the six principal international instruments.
31. They further recommend that UNDP be invited to present at the next meeting of persons chairing the human rights treaty bodies a plan of action on how the principal human rights treaties and various reporting procedures could be promoted through its programmes. Similarly, when invited to the next meeting of persons chairing human rights treaty bodies, ILO, UNHCR, UNESCO, WHO, UNICEF should also be asked to indicate what contribution they could make to the dissemination of knowledge about the principal human rights treaties and the various reporting procedures. Also, the Inter-Parliamentary Union (IPU) should be asked to attend the next meeting for the same purpose. The United Nations information centres should be asked to prepare a report regarding what they have done to disseminate information about the various international human rights treaties and the work of the treaty bodies.
32. The chairpersons also recommend that national human rights institutions and non-governmental organizations take a more active role at the national level in monitoring and reporting upon the various steps States parties have taken or are in the process of taking to promote knowledge of the six principal human rights treaties, their translation into appropriate languages, as well as the dissemination to the public of States parties reports to the various treaty bodies and the concluding observations of the treaty bodies relating to such reports. International or regional non-governmental organizations that work in cooperation with national organizations, as well as national non-governmental organizations themselves, are encouraged to present such information to the next meeting of the chairpersons.

External relations of treaty bodies

33. The chairpersons recommend that the person elected to chair the meeting of chairpersons continue to represent all of the persons chairing human rights treaty bodies in between the annual meetings in order to follow-up on the implementation of the chairpersons' recommendations and have the opportunity to attend meetings that could affect the treaty bodies as a whole.
34. The chairpersons express the wish that the Economic and Social Council amend the rules of the Commission on Human Rights so that the treaty bodies are recognized as having a distinct status that would enable them to participate in all relevant meetings. They further request that the General Assembly indicate in a resolution that the treaty bodies should, as a matter of principle, be permitted to participate in international meetings of interest to them. The Secretariat should take the necessary steps to establish a special fund within available resources to facilitate travel by one or more treaty body members to United Nations meetings and conferences that are considered to be of direct importance to the work of the treaty body concerned. The chairpersons are of the view that the inability of the treaty bodies to participate in international meetings of vital importance constitutes a setback for the improvement of the knowledge of the work of the various treaty bodies and even the awareness of their importance.
35. The chairpersons affirm once again that non-governmental organizations play a vital role in supplying the treaty bodies with documentation and other information on human rights developments that is extremely useful for their monitoring activities and that each treaty body should consider how best to monitor and facilitate this role. The chairpersons agree that at their next meeting a specific opportunity would be provided to non-governmental organization representatives to present their views. This would not prejudice in any way their participation at appropriate points during the meeting as a whole.
36. The chairpersons encourage non-governmental organizations to continue to take an active role in critically examining the work of the treaty bodies. Their constructive criticism should stimulate more effective performance by the treaty bodies as a whole as well as the performance of their individual members.
37. The chairperson notes that there have been very extensive delays in efforts by the Centre for Human Rights to develop electronic information systems that were recommended by the Commission on Human Rights as long ago as 1989. They note that in the meantime there have been many major developments in human rights databases, especially on the World Wide Web, and that materials of direct relevance to the work of the treaty bodies are now available on databases such as those of the UNHCR, UNICEF, ILO and the University of Minnesota (http://www.unicc.org/unhcrcdr/; gopher://hqfaus01.unicef.org:70/1; http://www.unicc.org/ilo/index.html; http://www.umn.edu/humanrts/; http://heiww.unige.ch/humanrts/). They urge those involved in the development of these databases to seek to include treaty body materials as fully as possible on their sites and recommend that the Centre for Human Rights make a particular effort to cooperate in every possible way with the complementary development of such databases.
38. The chairpersons express the view that non-governmental organizations

should be invited by the chairperson of a treaty body to attend the press conference usually held at the end of each session without their participating in the dialogue between the journalists and the members of the treaty bodies. Individual treaty bodies may also wish to consider a separate non-governmental organization briefing at the end of their sessions in addition to the traditional press conference.

39. The chairpersons request each treaty body to make available to the public the addresses of their members so that communication, in particular between non-governmental organizations and treaty body members, can be facilitated. The request of treaty body members who object to their coordinates being made available to the public should be respected. Secretariat support

40. The chairpersons note with concern that the plans to restructure the Centre for Human Rights, which will have a major impact on existing long-standing arrangements in relation to the servicing of the five Geneva-based treaty bodies, have proceeded on the basis of no meaningful consultation with the chairpersons or with the treaty bodies. They note that, less than two weeks before very major changes are to be announced and implemented, they have not yet received any information that would enable them to understand how the new arrangements will look or how they will operate. In view of the need to ensure that an effective working partnership is developed between the treaty bodies and the Secretariat, the chairpersons call upon the United Nations High Commissioner for Human Rights to ensure that this lack of consultation and transparency be remedied in the following ways: (a) each chairperson should be notified of the details of the reorganization of the relevant part of the Centre for Human Rights as soon as they are announced; (b) each Committee should be briefed in detail as to the arrangements; and (c) genuine consultations should take place between representatives of the treaty bodies and the Secretariat to ensure the optimal use of available resources.

41. The chairpersons also consider it to be essential that the staff members servicing the treaty bodies be encouraged to discuss among themselves and with the treaty bodies the best ways in which to organize the work in which they are mutually engaged. This spirit of partnership and interaction has been notably absent in the past, despite the considerable contribution that it can make to improved working relations and more effective servicing.

42. On the basis of the extremely vague details provided thus far by the Secretariat in relation to the proposed restructuring of the Centre for Human Rights on the servicing to be provided to the treaty bodies, the chairpersons express their deep concern that the apparent elimination of individuals designated as Committee secretaries will be extremely inefficient, counter-productive and ultimately unworkable.

43. The annual meeting of chairpersons has the potential to perform very important functions in terms of ensuring a more effective as well as a more efficient functioning of the treaty supervisory system. If this potential is to be fully realized it is essential that a consistent flow of information be made available to the chairpersons so that they are in a position to discuss the relevant issues in an informed and focused manner. The chairpersons note, by way of example, that the key issue of a radical reduction of the resources concerning the documentation of the treaty bodies has not always been dealt

with in a satisfactory manner. If the chairpersons are to be in a position to discuss in a meaningful way an issue that has the potential to undermine the very foundation upon which the existing system of reports and supervision is based, it is essential that they be briefed in detail and provided with all of the relevant background documentation.

44. In order to ensure the availability of comprehensive documents submitted by some States parties to the treaty bodies, the chairpersons request the Secretary-General to exempt the treaty bodies from the rule established by the General Assembly in its resolution 36/117 B of 10 December 1981, according to which United Nations documents should be distributed only when they are available in all of the official working languages of the bodies concerned. For such documents, the chairpersons request discretion to designate in what working language or languages those documents should be made available to ensure the timely consideration by treaty bodies of all material submitted by the States parties concerned.

45. The chairpersons received during the meeting a copy of the "Plan of Action to strengthen the implementation of the Convention on the Rights of the Child" prepared in 1995 by the United Nations High Commissioner for Human Rights. Although the time remaining after the distribution of the document did not permit a discussion of its content, the chairpersons note with appreciation the efforts made to strengthen the support provided to the Committee on the Rights of the Child. They also note, however, that as a result of this programme and of the special support already received by the Committee from other sources, there is a risk of a radical imbalance emerging between the resources and support available to the Committee on the Rights of the Child and that available to the other five treaty bodies. While assurances have been given that there will be a significant flow-on effect and that the programme for the Committee on the Rights of the Child is a pilot programme that could subsequently be applied in relation to other treaty bodies, the chairpersons call for greater attention to be given to the measures necessary to ensure that such an imbalance does not occur.

46. The chairpersons reaffirm their support for the request of the Committee on the Elimination of Discrimination against Women to have its secretariat to be transferred to the Centre for Human Rights in Geneva, which is contained in Committee's resolution 14/II. The chairpersons regret that this resolution, as well as the numerous recommendations of the chairpersons of human rights treaty bodies on this matter, have not been respected. They share the Committee's view that the Committee cannot function properly if its secretariat is physically separated from the secretariat of all the other human rights treaty bodies.

47. The chairpersons recommend that the development and maintenance of the treaty body information database system be pursued and reinforced. They also recommend that, as soon as this information system is fully operational, each member of all treaty bodies be given the possibility to access the database; and that access to documents for general distribution be made available to the public by means of the Internet Web site to be established by the Centre for Human Rights.

48. The chairpersons request the Secretary-General to make the necessary arrangements so that all experts of the treaty bodies obtain the United Nations certificates to which they are entitled during their mandate.

B. *Cooperation of human rights treaty bodies with United Nations non-conventional human rights bodies and mechanisms and regional organizations*

49. The chairpersons note that one of the items on the agenda for the Ministerial Meeting of the World Trade Organization (WTO), to be held at Singapore in December 1996, concerns proposals to adopt a "social clause" which would link respect for certain human rights (notably freedom of association, non-discrimination in employment, and the elimination of exploitative child labour) to access to trade opportunities. They note that whatever the respective merits of such proposals, the system of treaty supervision in which the treaty bodies are engaged already provides an important avenue for monitoring compliance with States obligations in these and related areas and that a greater effort should be made to strengthen these existing opportunities.
50. The chairpersons note that some organizations such as ILO and UNHCR have established CD-ROM databases relating to their international instruments and fields of activity and recommend that such organizations make that material available to the Centre for Human Rights and to individual treaty body members, at a reduced price, to contribute to the improvement of their work.
51. The chairpersons recommend that in the future treaty bodies consider much more carefully what kind of assistance they would like from United Nations bodies and specialized agencies. They should do their upmost to describe as precisely as possible their requests to such bodies and specialized agencies.
52. The chairpersons recognize that cooperation is a reciprocal process and recommend that treaty bodies similarly work with United Nations bodies and specialized agencies to enhance the effectiveness of their work, by providing documentation and responding to specific requests.
53. The chairpersons recommend that, where appropriate, the treaty bodies take a more active role in supporting, suggesting topics for, and cooperating in the preparation of studies by the Subcommission on Prevention of Discrimination and Protection of Minorities, as well as by special rapporteurs and other experts appointed by the Commission on Human Rights. The chairpersons note the important contribution that special rapporteurs and other experts appointed by the Commission on Human Rights have made to the work of the treaty bodies and recommend that efforts continue to be made to increase existing cooperation. Special rapporteurs and other experts whose work is of direct relevance to the activities of a particular treaty body could schedule their visits to the United Nations in connection with the meeting of the treaty bodies concerned in order to have direct cooperation on issues of mutual concern.
54. The chairpersons recommend that written reports for general distribution be issued about the development of cooperation between the United Nations High Commissioner for Human Rights and the Bretton Woods institutions and UNDP, given the interest of various treaty bodies in developing a constructive relationship with these organizations.
55. The chairpersons are of the view that it would greatly assist the treaty bodies to have access to the country reports prepared by the World Bank and request that the Centre for Human Rights proceed expeditiously in its planned meeting with World Bank officials in November 1996 to put into place procedures for access to such documentation.

56. The chairpersons recommend that the Centre for Human Rights engage in an active dialogue with Bretton Woods institutions so that in the references to human rights standards by these institutions, the applicable United Nations human rights instruments will be given a preeminent role.
57. The chairpersons recommend that individual treaty bodies enhance cooperation with regional human rights mechanisms when appropriate. It notes with satisfaction that the Committee on the Elimination of Racial Discrimination and the Human Rights Committee are engaged in the process of establishing liaison relationships with a number of regional human rights organizations.

C. Gender perspectives in the work of the treaty bodies

58. The chairpersons wish to recall that at their sixth meeting they recommended the following:
    (a) The treaty bodies shall fully integrate gender perspectives into their presessional and sessional working methods, including identification of issues and preparation of questions for country reviews, general comments, general recommendations, and concluding observations. In particular, the treaty bodies should consider the gender implications of each issue discussed under each of the articles of the respective instruments;
    (b) Guidelines for the preparation of reports by States parties should be amended to reflect the necessity of providing specific information on the human rights of women for consideration by the respective committees;
    (c) In undertaking investigative procedures, the treaty bodies should make special efforts to elicit information about the situation of women in the area of inquiry;
    (d) Treaty bodies should consistently request gender-disaggregated data from States parties and from United Nations specialized agencies and use the data in reviewing country reports;
    (e) The treaty bodies should make every effort to exchange information on progress, developments and situations concerning the human rights of women;
    (f) In preparing reports of the treaty body sessions, attention should be paid to the use of gender-inclusive language wherever possible.
59. The chairpersons noted that the Committee on the Elimination of Racial Discrimination, having considered the recommendation to change its guidelines for the preparation of State party reports, decided that they did not need alteration.
60. In the light of the recommendations of the sixth meeting of chairpersons to incorporating gender perspectives in the work of the treaty bodies, the chairpersons recommend that each treaty body continue to consider how it might most effectively include this issue in its work practices.
61. The chairpersons recommend that the issue of gender perspective in the work of the treaty bodies be placed on the agenda of their next meeting to enable them to review the progress made in the meantime.

D. *Assistance to States in implementing committee recommendations*

62. The chairpersons recommend that treaty bodies be as specific as possible in elaborating concluding observations on State party reports involving recommendations for technical assistance to be made available by the Centre for Human Rights to the State concerned.

A/52/507 — 21 October 1997

UNITED NATIONS GENERAL ASSEMBLY
Fifty-second session

EFFECTIVE IMPLEMENTATION OF INTERNATIONAL INSTRUMENTS ON HUMAN RIGHTS, INCLUDING REPORTING OBLIGATIONS UNDER INTERNATIONAL INSTRUMENTS ON HUMAN RIGHTS

Note by the Secretary-General

The Secretary-General has the honour to transmit to the General Assembly the report of the eighth meeting of persons chairing the human rights treaty bodies, convened in Geneva from 15 to 19 September 1997, pursuant to General Assembly resolution 51/87 of 12 December 1996.

ANNEX

Report of the eighth meeting of persons chairing the human rights treaty bodies

I. INTRODUCTION

1. Since the adoption of resolution 37/44 on 3 December 1982, the General Assembly has continuously kept under review the issue of the effective implementation of international instruments on human rights, including reporting obligations under international instruments. Those matters have also received careful attention during the various sessions of the treaty bodies, at some of the meetings of States parties and at meetings of other organs such as the Economic and Social Council and the Commission on Human Rights.
2. Pursuant to General Assembly resolution 38/117 of 16 December 1983, the Secretary-General convened the first meeting of the persons chairing the bodies entrusted with the consideration of State party reports in August 1984. The report of that meeting was presented to the General Assembly at its thirty-ninth session (A/39/484, annex). The second, third, fourth, fifth, sixth and seventh meetings were convened by the Secretary-General in October 1988, October 1990, October 1992, September 1994, September 1995 and September 1996. The reports of those meetings were presented to the Assembly at its forty-fourth, forty-fifth, forty-seventh, forty-ninth, fiftieth and fifty-first sessions (in the annexes of documents A/44/98, A/45/636, A/47/628, A/49/537, A/50/505 and A/51/482 respectively). It may be recalled that, in accordance with General Assembly resolution 49/178 of 23 December 1994, the meetings

of persons chairing the human rights treaty bodies have become annual since 1995.
3. In its resolution 51/87 of 12 December 1996, the General Assembly welcomed the report of the persons chairing the human rights treaty bodies on their seventh meeting, held at Geneva from 16 to 20 September 1996, and took note of the conclusions and recommendations in the report (A/51/482, annex); welcomed the continuing efforts by the treaty bodies and the Secretary-General aimed at streamlining, rationalizing, rendering more transparent and otherwise improving reporting procedures, and urged the treaty bodies and the meetings of persons chairing the human rights treaty bodies to continue to examine ways of reducing the duplication of reporting under the different instruments, without impairing the quality of reporting, and of generally reducing the reporting burden on Member States. The Commission on Human Rights welcomed the report of the seventh meeting of the persons chairing the human rights treaty bodies and took note of its conclusions and recommendations in its decision 1997/105 of 3 April 1997.
4. At the fifty-third session of the Commission, the independent expert, Mr. Philip Alston, presented his final report on enhancing the long-term effectiveness of the United Nations human rights treaty system.
5. In its resolution 51/87, the General Assembly also requested the Secretary-General to prepare a detailed analytical study comparing the provisions of the International Covenant on Economic, Social and Cultural Rights, the International Covenant on Civil and Political Rights, the International Convention on the Elimination of All Forms of Racial Discrimination, the Convention on the Elimination of All Forms of Discrimination against Women, the Convention on the Rights of the Child and the Convention against Torture and Other Cruel, Inhuman or Degrading Treatment or Punishment, with a view to identifying duplication of reporting under those instruments. Pursuant thereto, the Secretariat prepared a working paper entitled "Preliminary analysis of the international human rights treaty system, with a view to offering guidance to the integration and cross-referencing of treaty provisions for the purpose of identifying duplication of reporting and reducing the reporting burden".[1] This preliminary analysis was made available to the chairpersons.
6. The eighth meeting of persons chairing the human rights treaty bodies was convened by the Secretary-General pursuant to General Assembly resolution 51/87.

II. ORGANIZATION OF THE MEETING

7. The meeting was held at the United Nations Office at Geneva from 15 to 19 September 1997. The following representatives of the human rights treaty bodies attended: Mr. Philip Alston (Chairperson, Committee on Economic, Social and Cultural Rights), Mr. Michael Banton (Chairman, Committee on the Elimination of Racial Discrimination), Ms. Christine Chanet (Chairperson,

---

[1] HRI/MC/1997/Misc.1.

Human Rights Committee), Mr. Alexis Dipanda-Mouelle (Chairperson, Committee against Torture), Ms. Salma Khan (Chairperson, Committee on the Elimination of Discrimination against Women) and Ms. Sandra P. Mason (Chairperson, Committee on the Rights of the Child). Ms. Ivanka Corti, former Chairperson of the Committee on the Elimination of Discrimination against Women, also participated in her capacity as Chairperson of the seventh meeting of chairpersons.
8. Mrs. Mary Robinson, the United Nations High Commissioner for Human Rights, addressed the chairpersons of the treaty bodies on 19 September 1997. She also participated in a closed meeting with the chairpersons, who appreciated the opportunity to have a frank dialogue with her.
9. Representatives of numerous States parties attended. The following United Nations bodies and specialized agencies participated in the meeting: Division for the Advancement of Women of the United Nations Secretariat; Joint United Nations Programme on HIV/AIDS (UNAIDS); United Nations Children's Fund (UNICEF); United Nations Population Fund (UNFPA); Office of the United Nations High Commissioner for Refugees (UNHCR); International Labour Organization (ILO); and World Health Organization (WHO).
10. Representatives of the following non-governmental organizations (NGOs) made oral interventions: Amnesty International; Association for World Education; Anti-Racism Information Service (ARIS); Defence of Children International; International Commission of Jurists; International Service for Human Rights; International Women's Rights Action Watch; Lawyers Committee for Human Rights; NGO Group for the Convention on the Rights of the Child; Women's International League for Peace and Freedom; and World Organization against Torture.
11. Mr. Paulo S. Pinheiro, Chairperson of the fourth meeting of special rapporteurs, representatives, experts and chairpersons of working groups on the special procedures of the Commission on Human Rights and the Advisory Services Programme, addressed the chairpersons of the human rights treaty bodies on 17 September 1997.
12. Mr. Miroslav Somol, Chairman of the fifty-third session of the Commission on Human Rights, and Ms. Halima Warzazi, member of the Bureau of the Subcommission on Prevention of Discrimination and Protection of Minorities, addressed the chairpersons. Ms. Therese Gastaut, Director of the United Nations Information Service at Geneva, also briefed the chairpersons.
13. The eighth meeting of chairpersons focused primarily on issues of reform. The agenda for the meeting included a review of recent developments relating to the work of the treaty bodies; methods of improving their operation; cooperation of human rights treaty bodies with United Nations non-conventional human rights bodies and mechanisms and regional organizations; gender perspectives; and assistance to States in implementing treaty body recommendations.[2]
14. Among the documents made available to the participants were the final report of the independent expert on enhancing the long-term effectiveness

---
[2] See HRI/MC/1997/1.

of the United Nations treaty system;[3] the report of the Secretary-General entitled "Renewing the United Nations: a programme for reform";[4] the report of the Secretary-General on improving the operation of the human rights treaty bodies;[5] the report of the Secretary-General on the status of the international instruments and the general situation of overdue reports;[6] the High Commissioner's plan of action to strengthen the implementation of the Convention on the Rights of the Child; the plan of action to strengthen the implementation of the International Covenant on Economic, Social and Cultural Rights; and an informal Secretariat paper containing a preliminary analysis of overlapping treaty provisions.[7]

15. Mr. Philip Alston was elected Chairperson-Rapporteur of the meeting. He will represent the persons chairing treaty bodies for a 12-month period and should be invited to attend any meetings which could affect the work of the treaty bodies as a whole.

16. On 19 September 1997, the chairpersons considered the draft report of their eighth meeting. The report, as amended during the course of the meeting, was adopted unanimously.

III. REVIEW OF DEVELOPMENTS RELATING TO THE WORK OF THE TREATY BODIES

17. Under this agenda item, the chairpersons provided information on recent activities of the treaty bodies they represented. Brief statements were made by each chairperson in relation to his or her committee's working methods, innovations over the past year and challenges to be addressed.

18. Several chairpersons made reference to three academic conferences on the future of the human rights treaty system, held respectively in November 1996 at the German Human Rights Centre in Potsdam; in March 1997 at the Research Centre for International Law at Cambridge University, United Kingdom of Great Britain and Northern Ireland; and in June 1997 at the York University of Toronto, Canada. Several members of the Committees attended those meetings, at which analytical papers were discussed and concrete recommendations for short- and long-term reform were formulated. The chairpersons welcomed the increasing attention being given by institutions outside the United Nations to the problems facing the treaty bodies.

19. The chairpersons welcomed the positive experience that the Committee on the Rights of the Child had with the United Nations Children's Fund (UNICEF) in terms of close cooperation, a relationship which not only had served to help promote knowledge of the Convention and its effective implementation, but had also resulted in substantial additional financial and other resources being made available to that Committee. However, it was noted with regret that a constructive relationship between the treaty bodies and

---

[3] E/CN.4/1997/74.
[4] A/51/950.
[5] HRI/MC/1997/2.
[6] HRI/MC/1997/Misc.2.
[7] HRI/MC/1997/Misc.1.

some key agencies, in particular the World Bank and the United Nations Development Programme (UNDP), had still not been established.
20. The chairpersons took note of the fact that the High Commissioner's plan of action for strengthening the implementation of the Convention on the Rights of the Child has succeeded in obtaining financing for its first year of operation and that a team of four staff members had been recruited and was already assisting the experts of the Committee on the Rights of the Child in carrying out their tasks, including issues of follow-up and technical assistance in the field. It is expected that a fifth member of the support team will soon be recruited so as to ensure representation from the five regions.
21. A plan of action on the strengthening of the implementation of the International Covenant on Economic, Social and Cultural Rights was adopted by the Committee on Economic, Social and Cultural Rights, envisaging the recruitment of two associate experts. It is hoped that sufficient voluntary funds will be received in 1997 in order to allow the plan to become operational at an early date.
22. The relationship between the treaty bodies and the media was discussed at length, with particular assistance from an informal discussion paper prepared by the United Nations Information Service (UNIS) at Geneva entitled "Raising awareness, appreciation and understanding of the role of the United Nations human rights treaty bodies". Comments on the paper were also submitted to the chairpersons by the United Nations Office of Communications and Public Information (formerly the Department of Public Information) in New York. In essence, the papers highlighted the need for a more proactive role on the part of the treaty bodies if they were to obtain the press coverage and broader media attention to which they aspired. End-of-session press briefings based on the full text of concluding observations were seen to be unlikely to attract significant coverage. Suggestions included making use of daily briefings given by UNIS, holding a press conference during the session and preferably not on Fridays or in the afternoon, an advocacy role for treaty body members in relation to the rights being dealt with by the relevant committee, and using stronger, clearer and more declarative language in both oral and written assessments.

IV. CONCLUSIONS AND RECOMMENDATIONS

Improving the operation of the human rights treaty bodies

Reform of the treaty system
23. The chairpersons acknowledged that there were considerable challenges confronting the treaty bodies in order to improve the effectiveness, efficiency and coordination of their activities. They noted that the overall process of United Nations reform and the restructuring of the Office of the High Commissioner for Human Rights also provided opportunities to promote continuing reform of the working methods of the different committees. They emphasized, however, that reform was only useful if its objective was to strengthen the capacity of the treaty bodies to perform their diverse functions aimed at promoting compliance by States parties with their human rights obligations.

24. The chairpersons believed that, meeting together, they could play a part in the process of reform. While ensuring that proper account was always taken of the features specific to each of the six treaty bodies, they could identify problems common to different treaty bodies and help them coordinate their responses.

Universal ratification

25. The chairpersons noted the call for universal ratification of the human rights treaties formulated in the Vienna Declaration and Programme of Action. They believed that universal participation in the core human rights treaties constituted an important means by which to respond to suggestions that human rights were more relevant in some cultures than in others and to ensure that the indivisibility of all human rights was reflected in practice. In this connection they noted the central role which must be played by the Office of the High Commissioner for Human Rights in encouraging and facilitating universal ratification.
26. The chairpersons called for the adoption of a constructive approach designed to assist States in relation to ratification in whatever ways might be most helpful. They recommended that a separate human rights treaty ratification fund be established to enable such assistance to be provided. The Office of the High Commissioner should designate a specialist coordinator for the purpose. Governments should be approached with a view to identifying the type of assistance that would be most useful to them in exploring the feasibility and modalities of ratification. The fund should be used in a flexible manner and enable the use of specialist consultants whenever appropriate.
27. The chairpersons considered that an important role in relation to the promotion of universal ratification could be played by international agencies and they requested the Office of the High Commissioner to engage in consultations with the World Bank, UNDP, the International Labour Organization (ILO), the United Nations Educational, Scientific and Cultural Organization (UNESCO) and UNICEF to explore the contributions those agencies might make to encouraging and assisting Governments to ratify the core international human rights treaties. The chairpersons warmly welcomed the initiative being taken by the Office of the High Commissioner and the Inter-Parliamentary Union to encourage national parliaments to play a stronger role in that regard. The chairpersons requested the Office of the High Commissioner to provide a written report in relation to progress made in those initiatives to the ninth meeting of chairpersons.
28. The chairpersons noted that regional ratification conferences had been held in 1996 at Addis Ababa, and in 1997 in Amman. While such initiatives were useful, they were far from being sufficient if universal ratification was to be actively promoted by the Office of the High Commissioner.

Denunciation of treaties

29. Serious concern was expressed by the chairpersons at the announcement on 25 August 1997 that the Government of the Democratic People's Republic of Korea intended to denounce the International Covenant on Civil and Political Rights. Such an action would be unprecedented and the chairpersons strongly questioned the conformity of the proposed course of action with existing international law. In particular, a careful review of all of the

relevant materials provided no basis upon which to conclude that the States parties to the Covenant intended to permit its unilateral denunciation by a State party. Moreover, the right to make such a denunciation would not seem to be compatible with the nature of the Covenant. The chairpersons therefore called upon all members of the international community to do everything possible to uphold the integrity of the human rights treaty system in general, and that of the International Covenant on Civil and Political Rights in particular.

Special situation of States with very small populations

30. The chairpersons noted that, as of January 1997, there were 29 countries with populations under 1 million which had ratified neither of the International Covenants and also had a relatively low rate of ratification of the other core treaties. They noted that the reporting requirements under the human rights treaties might appear particularly daunting to countries with very small populations, especially where there was a lack of available trained personnel to draft the reports due under the treaties. The chairpersons recommended that the Office of the High Commissioner for Human Rights should indicate its willingness to provide to all developing countries with a population of less than 1 million that ratified or acceded to any of the core treaties with the services of an expert who could advise on the preparation of the initial reports which would then be required. The chairpersons also suggested that the individual committees should give particular attention to the situation of those countries on a case-by-case basis, as appropriate.

31. The recommendation contained in paragraph 49 below would, if acted upon, also make it easier for such States, many of which do not have a permanent mission in Geneva, to report to the treaty bodies in the framework of a New York session.

The reporting system: reform proposals

32. The chairpersons took note of the report of the Secretary-General on the status of reporting,[8] which indicated that the treaty bodies as a whole were facing two major problems: (a) many States parties were failing to fulfil their obligations under the treaties to such an extent that some 1,000 State reports were overdue; and (b) even when reports had been submitted, they could frequently not be scheduled for examination until two or three years later, thus rendering much of the data obsolete.

33. Concern was expressed that, in the absence of appropriate reforms tailored to the needs of each committee, the examination of reports might become a ritual without much meaning for the States parties, the treaty bodies or the individuals whose human rights must be protected. The chairpersons thus gave careful consideration to various reform options designed to make the monitoring system more meaningful, avoid duplication and make the reporting burden on States more manageable.

34. No consensus was reached with regard to the frequently expressed proposal to consolidate reports into a single global report covering all six human rights treaties. Although such an approach would reduce the number of different reports requested of States parties and would serve to underline

---

[8] HRI/MC/1997/Misc.2.

the indivisibility of human rights by ensuring a comprehensive analysis of the situation, concerns were expressed in relation to problems resulting from the different periodicities of reporting under the treaties, and the risk that the specialist attention given to groups such as women and children would be lost in a single comprehensive report.
35. The chairpersons recognized, however, that in relation to periodic reports there might be significant advantages in seeking ways by which to focus the report of each State party on a limited range of issues, which might be identified by the committee in advance of the preparation of the report. Such an approach would greatly reduce the need for very lengthy reports, minimize duplication of reports, help to eliminate long delays between the submission and the examination of reports, enable problem areas to be dealt with in depth and facilitate the follow-up of concluding observations, both for the State party and for the committee concerned. Accordingly, the chairpersons requested their committees to examine the feasibility of adopting an approach along those lines, taking account of the particular needs of the treaty concerned and the preferred working methods of the committee.
36. Emphasis was also placed by the chairpersons upon the importance of strengthening the concluding observations adopted by each committee and of ensuring that they were clear, precise and sufficiently specific as to the measures that should be taken.
37. The chairpersons noted the anomalous situation whereby States that did not submit reports escaped scrutiny while those that were conscientious were held to account, and they noted that both the Committee on Economic, Social and Cultural Rights and the Committee on the Elimination of Racial Discrimination had moved to examine the situation in States whose reports were chronically overdue. It was noted that the General Assembly and the Commission on Human Rights had encouraged those initiatives and that a legal foundation for such an approach had been put forward. It was suggested that other committees might wish to keep that option under review in relation to their own working methods.

Consolidation of the treaty bodies
38. The general view of the chairpersons was that it was neither practicable nor desirable to envisage joining the six human rights treaty bodies into a single committee. The chairpersons believed, however, that the establishment of additional treaty bodies should be avoided to the greatest extent possible, in the interests of the existing system, of States and of the prospects for effective implementation of any new treaty. In that connection, they recommended that States consider the possibility of amending the International Convention on the Protection of the Rights of All Migrant Workers and Members of Their Families in order to provide that no new treaty body be established and that the monitoring tasks under the Convention be assured by other means based on the existing treaty body system. Bearing in mind that the Convention had not entered into force and that as of September 1997 eight States had ratified or acceded to it, it was felt that an amendment at the current stage should be feasible. The chairpersons emphasized that the proposal should not in any way be interpreted as diminishing the importance of the Convention itself. Rather, the intention was to ensure

effective monitoring of an important set of issues and to avoid a situation in which a new committee was established without the resources or personnel which would be required.

Amendment of treaties
39. The chairpersons requested that a report should be sought from the Legal Counsel which would explore the feasibility of devising more innovative approaches in dealing with existing and future amendments to the human rights treaties.
40. The chairpersons recommended that action be taken to write off the continuing backlog of contributions owed for the Committee on the Elimination of Racial Discrimination. As indicated in the report of the Independent Expert,[9] as of the end of 1996, 57 States parties owed a total of US$ 225,506 (see A/51/430). Given that those assessments are now anachronistic and that the cost incurred by the United Nations in calculating, updating and reporting on their non-payment would soon exceed the amount involved, agreement should be sought to cover the outstanding amount from the regular budget and close the file. For legal and policy reasons, it should be indicated that no precedent of broader application was thereby created.

Communications
41. The chairpersons noted that there were currently 147 registered communications pending under the Optional Protocol and awaiting a decision by the Human Rights Committee; 46 cases pending under the procedure governed by article 22 of the Convention Against Torture; and 5 cases pending under the procedure governed by article 14 of the Convention on the Elimination of All Forms of Racial Discrimination.
42. Incoming communications were not being expeditiously processed. Some 800 pieces of correspondence were currently awaiting reply, some dating back to 1996. The situation was particularly worrisome with regard to communications submitted in Russian, as no Russian-speaking lawyer had been assigned to individual complaints procedures.
43. The chairpersons recognized that, for the Human Rights Committee, the Committee Against Torture and the Committee on the Elimination of Racial Discrimination, individual communications procedures constituted an important part of their mandate, and the current situation called for urgent action.

Annual meeting with Secretary-General
44. The chairpersons recalled that, although a meeting had been held with the Secretary-General in 1995 and one had been scheduled for 1996, the latter had not eventuated. They believed that a meeting with the Secretary-General within the coming 12 months would be very useful, particularly in the light of his new reform plan for the United Nations and of the various challenges facing the treaty bodies. They emphasized the need for such a meeting to be carefully prepared and focused on issues of major concern.

---

[9] E/CN.4/1997/74, para. 101(e).

Staff and servicing
45. Note was taken of the stage reached in the process of restructuring the Office of the High Commissioner for Human Rights. The chairpersons considered, however, that there was still no clarity as to the result of that effort despite the disruption and confusion that had been generated. Nor could they yet conclude that the wholly inadequate staffing situation in Geneva had improved.
46. They welcomed the progress made with the plans of action for two committees (see paras. 20 and 21 above) and urged that every effort be made to ensure that the work performed for the committees concerned was also of benefit to as many of the treaty bodies as possible.
47. The chairpersons considered that it was essential for specialist training to be provided to the staff of the Office of the High Commissioner for Human Rights. In relation to the staff as a whole, a half-day training programme focused on the role of the treaty bodies, the relevance of their various outputs and their role within the human rights system as a whole would be very valuable. In relation to those staff responsible for the servicing of the treaty bodies, the chairpersons strongly recommended a training course focused on the specific challenges arising in that context, including information retrieval and analysis techniques, the drafting of reports and especially materials on the basis of which concluding observations were prepared, and the more effective dissemination of the results of the work of the treaty bodies.
48. The increasing complexity of the legal and institutional context in which the treaty bodies operated, and the fact that many members had limited exposure to the work of the relevant international organizations, also seemed to the chairpersons to warrant the organization of targeted technical briefings for treaty body members on an occasional basis. The chairpersons requested the Secretariat to present a proposal at their next meeting as to the possible content of such a briefing. Each committee should then consider setting aside half a day for that purpose perhaps every two or three years.

Role of the treaty bodies in relation to the overall United Nations human rights system
49. The chairpersons strongly believed that the existing system whereby one treaty body met only in New York and four of the other five met exclusively at Geneva was detrimental to the effectiveness of their work. They believed that occasional sessions in New York would enable the four committees concerned to establish better contact with States which did not have permanent missions at Geneva, to make their work much more widely known to a broader range of interested groups, to facilitate contact with those NGO and media representatives who were not active in Geneva and to provide an important opportunity for interaction with other international organizations which did not actively follow the work of the treaty bodies in Geneva. Similarly, an opportunity for the Committee on the Elimination of Discrimination against Women to meet occasionally at Geneva would greatly enhance its relationship with the other human rights mechanisms and give it access to a range of agencies, NGOs and other groups not present in New York. The chairpersons therefore called upon the Secretariat to propose a means by which any additional costs involved in such flexible arrangements

could be minimized and requested the Secretary-General to put a specific proposal before the relevant United Nations organs in order to facilitate such an approach.
50. The chairpersons recommended that one of their future meetings be timed in order to coincide with all or part of the meeting of the special rapporteurs, representatives, experts and chairpersons of working groups appointed under the special procedures of the Commission on Human Rights. Such synchronization would greatly facilitate formal and informal discussions designed to coordinate in a more effective manner the activities of the two groups.
51. The chairpersons noted the many advantages that would accrue if the treaty bodies were to be able to meet on an exceptional and occasional basis at the various United Nations regional offices. They requested that the High Commissioner approach the relevant offices to explore the conditions under which it might be possible to organize a treaty body session at the regional level without incurring costs significantly greater than those involved in meeting in New York or Geneva, as the case may be. The High Commissioner was requested to report back to the chairpersons on the matter at their next session.

New technologies
52. The rapid development over the past year of the Web site of the High Commissioner for Human Rights was very warmly welcomed by the chairpersons. They emphasized the indispensable role which the Web site can play in making treaty body materials accessible to a wide range of governmental, expert and scholarly audiences as well as to the public at large. They urged the High Commissioner to attach high priority to the further development of this resource and expressed the hope that the additional funding which that would require would be made available.
53. The chairpersons noted with regret that the important jurisprudence from the ILO supervisory bodies was available in electronic form only to that very limited audience which could afford to pay a fee of $200 per year for the CD-ROM and expressed the hope that that policy will be reviewed to ensure greater access by the human rights community in general, and the treaty bodies in particular.
54. In view of the rapid evolution of information technology systems, the chairpersons would welcome the preparation of a study of the types of measures that might be contemplated, either in the short or the medium term, to improve the efficiency of the information-processing techniques that could be used by treaty body members. In view of the important work already done in that direction by UNICEF, the chairpersons expressed the hope that UNICEF might be prepared to sponsor or undertake such a study and make it available to the meeting of chairpersons in September 1998.
55. In view of the costs and difficulties that some small developing States might face in relation to the presentation of reports before each committee, the chairpersons recommended that consideration be given to the possibility of examining State reports by means of a video conference link between the committee room and the national capital. The chairpersons requested that a report on such a possibility be sought from the appropriate Secretariat service for consideration by the chairpersons in September 1998.

Languages
56. The chairpersons recognized that it would not always be possible to work in working groups on the basis of a single language, thereby avoiding the need for interpretation. However, in view of the financial pressures within the United Nations, treaty bodies should seek to use that approach where possible and appropriate. In order not to delay the distribution of documents needed for the meetings of the treaty bodies, each committee should decide in a timely fashion the languages into which the documents should be translated for any given meeting. In that way the distribution of documents would not be delayed by the unavailability of a document in a language not absolutely necessary for the discussion of a given item. The Secretariat should draft guidelines in that regard for the consideration of the treaty bodies.

Time-saving practices in the consideration of States' reports
57. The chairpersons took note of time utilization statistics provided by the Secretariat which showed that most committees continued to delay the start of their meetings, thereby losing 15 minutes or more of conference services each day. They called for a greater effort to be made to make full use of all the time available.
58. The task of expressing appropriate courtesies towards the representatives of the reporting State should be entrusted solely to the chairperson of the relevant committee. Members should not feel the need to add their individual expressions of welcome and appreciation, in view of the time consumed by such formalities. Nor should members when asking questions and offering individual comments advance any appraisal of the State report.
59. The Secretariat, when notifying a State party that its report had been scheduled for consideration, should consult with it on the type of composition of the delegation. The Secretariat should ensure that each delegation was thoroughly briefed in advance on the procedures that would be followed during its participation in the Committee's session.

Honoraria
60. The chairpersons drew attention yet again to the fact that the members of three committees received honoraria, while those of the other three did not. In many instances, treaty body members worked for at least two months a year on committee business and received no compensation at all from the United Nations. While States had agreed that honoraria should be paid in the case of all of the treaty bodies, the Secretariat continued to resist placing an appropriate statement of financial implications before the relevant organs in order to obtain the final authorization required. The justification had never been provided in writing to the committees but apparently concerned the fact that the General Assembly had commenced a review of the appropriate levels of honoraria system-wide a number of years ago and it had not been completed. The chairpersons called upon the Secretary-General to take the necessary measures immediately, using the existing figures of $3,000 per annum, until such time as a higher amount might result from the review.

Role of non-governmental organizations
61. The chairpersons noted the vital role played by international and national non-governmental organizations in monitoring human rights implementation and supporting the work of the treaty bodies. They recommended that

treaty bodies continue to develop working methods that provided appropriately for NGO input and that the Secretariat facilitate communication between NGOs and the treaty bodies.

Gender perspectives

62. The chairpersons recalled that their 1995 and 1996 reports had contained a section emphasizing the importance of taking gender perspectives fully into account in relation to all of the activities of the treaty bodies. They noted that, while some progress had been achieved in that regard, considerably more could be done. In order to assess the current position, the chairpersons invited the Division for the Advancement of Women to prepare a background paper analysing what the various treaty bodies had done, and should do, in integrating gender perspectives into their work.
63. The chairpersons discussed the usefulness of convening a seminar on gender perspectives along similar lines to the 1995 meeting, which was considered to have been very helpful. A review of the progress achieved in that regard would be timely, and they invited the relevant United Nations agencies and secretariats to consider the organization of another such meeting.
64. The chairpersons welcomed the conclusions of the UNFPA round table on "Human Rights Approaches to Women's Health with a focus on Reproductive and Sexual Health and Rights", held at Glen Cove, New York, in December 1996. The chairpersons considered that the issues discussed at the round table were of relevance to all treaty bodies, and therefore recommended that the treaty bodies consider issuing general recommendations on health, including sexual and reproductive health and rights, and that a gender dimension be incorporated in the revision of general comments/recommendations and guidelines.

HIV/AIDS

65. The chairpersons took note of the report on the Second International Consultation on HIV/AIDS and Human Rights,[10] of Commission on Human Rights resolution 1997/33 and of the informative interventions made by six experts brought to the meeting by UNAIDS.
66. The chairpersons recommended that each treaty body give careful attention to the measures which it might take in relation to the relevant human rights aspects of HIV/AIDS, including, where appropriate, adopting or revising general comments and recommendations, amending reporting guidelines and addressing those issues in their dialogue with States parties and in their concluding observations.

Independence of experts

67. The chairpersons recommended that members of treaty bodies refrain from participating in any aspect of the consideration of the reports of the States of which they were nationals, or communications or inquiries concerning those States, in order to maintain the highest standards of impartiality, both in substance and in appearance.
68. States parties to human rights treaties should refrain from nominating or

---

[10] E/CN.4/1997/37.

electing to the treaty bodies persons performing political functions or occupying positions which were not readily reconcilable with the obligations of independent experts under the given treaty. The chairpersons also urged that consideration be given to the importance of expertise in areas related to the mandate of the treaty body, the need for balanced geographical composition, the desirability of an appropriate gender balance and the nominee's availability in terms of time to discharge the responsibilities of an expert member of a treaty body.

Public information
69. While recognizing that no single formula could apply in relation to all of the treaty bodies, the chairpersons believed that there was an important role to be played by the media in promoting news coverage and a better understanding of the work of the treaty bodies. The chairpersons noted it was highly unlikely that that objective could be achieved in the absence of a deliberate strategy on the part of each treaty body. They therefore urged each committee to give careful consideration to the type of measures that had been suggested by the United Nations Information Service at Geneva and the Office of Communications and Public Information of the Secretariat.
70. The chairpersons requested each of those services to compile some sample dossiers of the type of press coverage that different treaty bodies had achieved recently and to make them available to the treaty bodies so that they might gain a better appreciation of what was involved and what could be achieved.
71. A briefing on activities planned for the celebration of the fiftieth anniversary of the Universal Declaration of Human Rights was received by the chairpersons from Mr. Z. Kedzia, Special Adviser to the High Commissioner and coordinator of fiftieth anniversary activities. The chairpersons considered that greater emphasis should be placed upon the importance of the core treaties based on the Universal Declaration, as well as on the monitoring and other activities of the treaty bodies. They also noted the importance of seeking to reach out beyond a small circle of the initiated so as to reach the broadest possible public audience.

Preparation of ninth meeting of chairpersons
72. The annual meeting of chairpersons has the potential to perform very important functions in terms of ensuring a more effective as well as a more efficient functioning of the treaty supervisory system. If this potential is to be fully realized, it is essential that a consistent flow of information be made available to the chairpersons so that they are in a position to discuss the relevant issues in an informed and focused manner and so that they can provide the necessary leadership in relation to the system as a whole.
73. The Secretariat, in cooperation with the members of the treaty bodies, should prepare an "activities profile" for each committee, consisting of one page describing the salient activities of each committee and including relevant statistics. The chairpersons agreed to consider at their next ordinary meeting whether such profiles should usefully be included in their report.
74. The chairpersons requested the Secretariat to prepare, in advance of its next ordinary meeting, a chart showing the follow-up action that had been taken in response to each of the specific recommendations contained in the present

report. They also requested the Chairperson of the eighth session to prepare and circulate for comments a draft agenda for their ninth session.

Request for an extraordinary meeting

75. The treaty system is at a crossroads and the conjunction of the broader United Nations reform process and the arrival of a new United Nations High Commissioner for Human Rights provides a unique opportunity to promote sustained reforms designed to enhance its effectiveness and efficiency. Accordingly, the chairpersons request that the General Assembly authorize, on an exceptional basis, the holding of a three-day meeting of the chairpersons (on the tentatively suggested dates of 25 to 27 February 1998) to enable a review of the response to the present report by the treaty bodies and the General Assembly, to prepare recommendations, as may be appropriate, to the fifty-fourth session of the Commission on Human Rights, to be held from 16 March to 24 April 1998, and to ensure that momentum is maintained in relation to the reform process as it affects the work of the treaty bodies (for programme budget implications, see the appendix to the present report).

APPENDIX

Programme budget implications of an additional meeting of persons chairing human rights treaty bodies, to be held at Geneva from 25 to 27 February 1998

A. Conference services

Regular budget

	Estimated workload (workdays)	Workload expressed in calendar days, i.e. × (7/5) days[a]	1997 unit rate[b] (Swiss francs)	Estimated cost (Swiss francs)
1. *Meeting services*				
Number of meeting(s):				
6 Languages: E,F				
6 Interpreters	18	25	636	15,907
1 Meeting Room Attendant	3	4	157	627
Conference Officer	–	–	173	–
Total (1)				16,534
2. *Pre-session documentation*				
Languages: E,F				
Translation	–	–	452	–
Revision	–	–	543	–
Translation/self-revision	–	–	498	–
Typing	–	–	230	–
Reproduction[c] (originals)	–	..	0.05	–
Distribution[d]	–	..	0.264	–
Total (2)				–

Appendix 7: Meeting of Chairpersons of the Treaty Bodies   825

3	*In-session documentation*			
	2 documents (15 original pages/document)			
	Languages: A,E,F,R,S			
	Translation	7	10	452	4520
	Revision	2	3	543	1629
	Translation/self-revision	6	8	498	3984
	Typing	10	14	230	3220
	Reproduction[c] (originals)				
	(page impression)	11,250	..	0.05	630
	Distribution[d] (documents)	1500	..	0.264	396
	Total (3)				14379
4.	*Summary records*				
	Translation	–	–	452	–
	Revision	–	–	543	–
	Typing	–	–	286	–
	Reproduction[c]				
	(page impression)	–	..	0.05	–
	Distribution[d] (documents)	–	..	0.264	–
	Total (4)				–
5.	*Post-session documentation*				
	Languages: E,F				
	Translation	–	–	452	–
	Revision	–	–	543	–
	Translation/self-revision	–	–	498	–
	Typing	–	–	230	–
	Reproduction[c] (originals)				
	(page impression)	–	..	0.05	–
	Distribution[d] (documents)	–	..	0.264	–
	Total (5)				–
6.	*General Services*				
	2 Sound Technicians/Recording	6	8	219	1756
	Messenger	–	–	173	–
	Guards	–	–	157	–
	Overtime normal (hours)	–	..	30	–
	Total (6)				1756
7.	*Other requirements*				
	Secretary	–	–	270	–
	Overtime normal (hours)	–	..	41	–
	Editing	–	–	315	–
	Documents Control Officer	–	–	157	–
	Documents Distribution Officer	–	–	157	–
	Total (7)				–
	Total (1 to 7)				32,669
	Rental of conference room(s) (days)	–	..	3799	–
	Rental of office space (sq m) (days)	–	..	1.90	–

ESTIMATED GRAND TOTAL SwF 32,669
e or
US$ 21926

a Since short-term staff are normally hired for more than one week, these estimates take into account on a cost-sharing basis among various conferences the salary costs over the weekend.
b All salary rates are based on latest applicable circulars.
c Reproduction: in-session documentation: number of original pages × 4.49 + number of page impressions × SwF 0.05.
d Distribution: 264 SwF per 1,000 documents.
e Exchange rate for September 1997: $1.00 = SwF 1.49.

B. *Travel*

The estimated travel cost, including daily subsistence allowance (DSA), for three days, for the chairpersons of the five treaty bodies serviced by the Office of the High Commissioner for Human Rights amounts to US$ 14,698.00.

A/53/125 — 14 May 1998

UNITED NATIONS GENERAL ASSEMBLY
Fifty-third session

EFFECTIVE IMPLEMENTATION OF INTERNATIONAL INSTRUMENTS ON HUMAN RIGHTS, INCLUDING REPORTING OBLIGATIONS UNDER INTERNATIONAL INSTRUMENTS ON HUMAN RIGHTS

Note by the Secretary-General

The Secretary-General has the honour to transmit to the General Assembly the report of the ninth meeting of persons chairing the human rights treaty bodies, convened in Geneva from 25 to 27 February 1998, pursuant to General Assembly resolution 52/118 of 12 December 1997.

ANNEX

Report of the ninth meeting of persons chairing the human rights treaty bodies

I. INTRODUCTION

1. Since the adoption of its resolution 37/44 on 3 December 1982, the General Assembly has continuously kept under review the issue of the effective implementation of international instruments on human rights, including reporting obligations under international instruments. Those matters have also received careful attention during the various sessions of the treaty bodies, at some of the meetings of States Parties and at meetings of other organs such as the Economic and Social Council and the Commission on Human Rights.
2. Pursuant to General Assembly resolution 38/117 of 16 December 1983, the Secretary-General convened the first meeting of the persons chairing the bodies entrusted with the consideration of State Party reports in August 1984. The report of that meeting was presented to the General Assembly at its thirty-ninth session (A/39/484, annex). The second, third, fourth, fifth, sixth and seventh meetings were convened by the Secretary-General biannually from 1988 until 1994 and, in accordance with General Assembly resolution 49/178 of 23 December 1994, annually since 1995. The report of the eighth meeting (A/52/507, annex) was presented to the Assembly at its fifty-second session.
3. In its resolution 52/118 of 12 December 1997, the General Assembly welcomed the report of the persons chairing the human rights treaty bodies on their eighth meeting, held at Geneva from 15 to 19 September 1997, and took note

of their conclusions and recommendations; took note with appreciation of the efforts of the persons chairing the human rights treaty bodies, at their eighth meeting, to develop appropriate reforms of the reporting system, with a view to, *inter alia*, reducing the reporting burden on States Parties while maintaining the quality of reporting, and encouraged them to continue those efforts, including through the continued examination of the benefits of reports focused on a limited range of issues and of opportunities for harmonizing the general guidelines regarding the form and content of reports, and the timing of consideration of reports and the methods of work of the treaty bodies. The General Assembly welcomed the request of the persons chairing the human rights treaty bodies to hold an extraordinary three-day meeting early in 1998 to pursue the reform process aimed at improving the effective implementation of international instruments on human rights.
4. The ninth meeting of persons chairing the human rights treaty bodies was convened by the Secretary-General pursuant to General Assembly resolution 52/118.

II. ORGANIZATION OF THE MEETING

5. The meeting was held at the United Nations Office at Geneva from 25 to 27 February 1998. The following representatives of the human rights treaty bodies attended: Mr. Philip Alston (Chairperson, Committee on Economic, Social and Cultural Rights), Mr. Michael Banton (Chairman, Committee on the Elimination of Racial Discrimination), Ms. Christine Chanet (Chairperson, Human Rights Committee), Mr. Bent Sorensen (Vice-Chairperson, Committee against Torture), Ms. Salma Khan (Chairperson, Committee on the Elimination of Discrimination against Women) and Ms. Sandra P. Mason (Chairperson, Committee on the Rights of the Child). Mr. Alston, who had been elected Chairperson-Rapporteur of the eighth meeting of chairpersons, continued to serve in that capacity.
6. Mrs. Mary Robinson, the United Nations High Commissioner for Human Rights, participated in a closed meeting with the chairpersons, as she had during their eighth meeting.
7. Representatives of the following United Nations bodies and specialized agencies participated in the meeting: Division for the Advancement of Women of the United Nations Secretariat; International Labour Organization (ILO); Joint United Nations Programme on HIV/AIDS (UNAIDS); United Nations Development Programme (UNDP); United Nations Educational, Scientific and Cultural Organization (UNESCO); United Nations Children's Fund (UNICEF); Office of the United Nations High Commissioner for Refugees (UNHCR); and World Health Organization (WHO).
8. Mr. Paulo Sergio Pinheiro, Chairperson of the fourth meeting of special rapporteurs, representatives, experts and chairpersons of working groups on the special procedures of the Commission on Human Rights and the Advisory Services Programme, addressed the chairpersons of the human rights treaty bodies on 25 February 1998.
9. Among the documents made available to the participants were the report of the independent expert on enhancing the long-term effectiveness of the United

Nations human rights treaty monitoring system;[1] the report of the Secretary-General on effective implementation of international instruments on human rights, including reporting obligations under international instruments on human rights;[2] and the report of the Secretary-General on the status of the international instruments and the general situation of overdue reports.[3]

10. On 27 February 1998, the chairpersons considered the draft report of their ninth meeting. The report, as amended, was adopted during the course of the meeting.

11. The chairpersons wished to reaffirm the considerable importance they attach to the opportunity for discussion and coordination which is provided by the meetings of chairpersons. They considered the present meeting to have been especially productive in this regard.

12. On the afternoon of 27 February 1998, the chairpersons convened a meeting with the representatives of States Parties and any other interested individuals and groups. The Chairperson of the meeting outlined some of the results of the discussions and an opportunity was then provided for an exchange of ideas between the representatives and the chairpersons. The meeting was extremely well attended and provided a valuable opportunity for dialogue in relation to the role of the treaty bodies and their future evolution.

III. IMPROVING THE OPERATION OF THE HUMAN RIGHTS TREATY BODIES

Universal ratification

13. The chairpersons considered that universal ratification of the six core human rights treaties constituted an essential dimension of a global order committed to the full respect of human rights. The ratification of these treaties had benefits which went far beyond the strengthening of the treaty system itself. The work of the General Assembly and of the Commission on Human Rights in the human rights field was greatly facilitated by a strong level of ratification, as were efforts to promote virtually every other goal endorsed by the international community. For those reasons, and in order to give effect to the commitments undertaken by Governments in both the Vienna Declaration and Programme of Action, as well as the Beijing Declaration and Platform for Action, the chairpersons called upon the United Nations system as a whole to accord an even higher priority to efforts to encourage and facilitate ratification of each of the six treaties by every State.

14. The chairpersons welcomed the continuing emphasis on ratification by the Secretary-General and the High Commissioner for Human Rights in their high-level bilateral meetings with Governments. They considered, however, that additional measures were required and that these should be carefully designed to address the concerns of individual States in relation to specific treaties which they have not ratified. In some instances, reluctance to ratify seemed to be based on misconceptions which could easily be dispelled if the

---

[1] E/CN.4/1997/74.
[2] E/CN.4/1998/85 and Corr.1.
[3] HRI/MC/1998/2.

right type of assistance were available. Similarly, assistance should be available to States which request it to help them to review or modify legislation or other standards to ensure conformity with treaty standards, and to assist with the reporting process, especially where this was seen as an obstacle to ratification.

15. The chairpersons therefore recommended that a major priority of the technical cooperation programme of the Office of the High Commissioner for Human Rights should be to provide assistance to States, upon their request, with the process of ratifying the human rights treaties and, where needed, providing assistance in the preparation of reports. They noted that these activities had to date been accorded a relatively very minor place in the programme.

16. The chairpersons, while awaiting a report from the office of the High Commissioner for Human Rights in response to their request in the report on their eighth session[4] that consultations be held with key agencies in relation to the role of those agencies in encouraging ratifications, requested that a letter be sent by the High Commission for Human Rights, after consultation with the chairpersons, requesting UNDP to develop a comprehensive programme within the framework of its activities to facilitate ratification and reporting by States.

Reservations to treaties

17. The chairpersons considered the Preliminary Conclusions of the International Law Commission on reservations to normative multilateral treaties including human rights treaties which had been brought to their attention by the Chairman of the forty-ninth session of the International Law Commission and Special Rapporteur on the issue of reservations to treaties.[5] The chairpersons recalled the emphasis attached in the Vienna Declaration and Programme of Action to the importance of limiting the number and extent of reservations to human rights treaties[6] and welcomed the recognition contained in the draft that treaty monitoring bodies have an important competence in relation to reservations. They considered, however, that the draft was unduly restrictive in other respects and did not accord sufficient attention to the fact that human rights treaties, by virtue of their subject matter and the role they recognize to individuals, could not be placed on precisely the same footing as other treaties with different characteristics.

18. The chairpersons believed that the capacity of a monitoring body to perform its function of determining the scope of the provisions of the relevant convention could not be performed effectively if it was precluded from exercising a similar function in relation to reservations. They therefore recalled the two general recommendations adopted by the Committee on the Elimination of Discrimination against Women and noted the proposal by that Committee to adopt a further recommendation on the subject in conjunction with the fiftieth anniversary of the Universal Declaration of Human Rights, and

---

[4] A/52/507, para. 27.
[5] *Official Records of the General Assembly, Fifty-second Session Supplement No. 10* (A/52/10), paras. 125–127.
[6] A/CONF.157/24 (Part I), chap. III, sect. II, para. 5.

expressed their firm support for the approach reflected in General Comment No. 24, adopted by the Human Rights Committee.[7] They requested their Chairperson to address a letter to the International Law Commission on their behalf to reiterate their support for the approach reflected in General Comment No. 24, and to urge that the conclusions proposed by the International Law Commission be adjusted accordingly.

Periodicity of reporting

19. The chairpersons noted that the issue of determining the appropriate timing of a report which follows a long overdue report by a given State Party could be a difficult one for some treaty bodies. They believed that it was important to avoid the adoption of rules or approaches that would provide an incentive to States Parties to delay the submission of their reports, and that it was appropriate for a treaty body to adopt a flexible approach which enabled it to take full account of the circumstances of each case in determining when the subsequent report of a State Party which had been overdue in submitting its previous report should be submitted. The Committee on the Elimination of Racial Discrimination considered that it had no power to vary the date at which a report was due.

Staff and servicing

General concerns

20. The chairpersons regretted that the level of Secretariat assistance provided to the five Geneva-based committees had decreased radically in recent years. While overall numbers had not changed greatly, except for a major reduction in the staff available to process communications, there had been an exponential increase in the number of demands placed upon the treaty bodies as a result of, *inter alia*, rapidly expanding participation in the treaty regime, a correspondingly sharp increase in the number of reports to be processed and the number of communications received, an expansion in the range of activities undertaken by the treaty bodies, particularly in response to calls from States, and growing interest in the work of the treaty bodies by a wide range of actors, accompanied by many demands for information and assistance.

Future staffing needs

21. The chairpersons strongly believed that an increase in the number of staff available to service all aspects of their activities was indispensable. They considered existing arrangements to be clearly inadequate and noted that this constrained their ability to adopt and implement the type of procedural and other improvements in treaty body functioning which had consistently been endorsed by the General Assembly and the Commission on Human Rights.

Restructuring and Committee secretaries

22. The chairpersons noted with regret that the implications for their work of the new structure of the Office of the High Commissioner for Human Rights, which has been in effect since 1 February 1998, remained very unclear. They

---

[7] *Ibid., Fiftieth Session, Supplement No. 40* (A/50/40), vol. I, sect. VII and annex V, at 124–130.

unanimously considered that it was essential to have a designated committee secretary servicing each Committee on a full-time basis for reasons of continuity, efficiency and expertise. That person needed to serve as a focal point of communication for Governments, with and among committee members, and for interested persons, institutions and non-governmental organizations seeking information about each treaty body.

Specific problems relating to complaints procedures
23. In addition, the chairpersons strongly supported the view that servicing of the optional complaints procedure must be conducted by staff members with strong legal qualifications and detailed knowledge of the relevant jurisprudence and relevant experience. The significant decrease in the number of staff servicing the communications procedures over the past four years which had accompanied a steady increase in the number of communications, had led to a situation of crisis. The backlog of communications waiting to be processed was unconscionable and risked making a mockery of the commitment of States Parties to accept the relevant petitions procedures. The chairpersons requested that the Secretariat provide them at their next meeting with an estimate of the amount of professional staff time required on average to process each communication and a corresponding estimate of the number of staff required to eliminate the existing backlog and ensure the steady, timely and expert processing of anticipated levels of communications in the future.

A global plan of action
24. In order to give effect to the commitments clearly set out in the context of the Vienna Declaration and Programme of Action, and to be able to respond to specific concerns voiced by Governments, a concerted effort to strengthen the support available to the treaty bodies was now imperative. The chairpersons affirmed that the functions performed by the treaty bodies should be considered a core function of the United Nations and be adequately funded from the regular budget of the Organization. Nevertheless, taking account of the clear inadequacy of existing funding and the apparent certainty of continuing budgetary stringency within the Organization as a whole, they believed that it was now appropriate to build upon an approach which seemed capable of immediately increasing the support available, which was to seek voluntary funding for the work of the six treaty bodies. The chairpersons welcomed the success of the Plan of Action for the Convention on the Rights of the Child and the growing support for a more limited Plan of Action for the International Covenant on Economic, Social and Cultural Rights. Without in any way affecting the operation of these action plans, the chairpersons believed that the time was now ripe for an overall Plan of Action to be drawn up to help them meet the expectations of Governments and other interested parties. If this was to be done, the resources available to the treaty bodies must be increased. They therefore invited the High Commissioner for Human Rights, in consultation with their Chairperson, to draft a Plan of Action listing priorities and modalities and which would be considered by them at their next meeting in September 1998. They emphasized that additional resources generated in this way should not be

used as an excuse for failing to increase, or even for reducing, the level of servicing of treaty bodies provided by regular funds.

Examination of situations in the absence of reports

25. At their eighth meeting[8] the chairpersons noted the practice of the Committee on Economic, Social and Cultural Rights and of the Committee on the Elimination of Racial Discrimination to examine the human rights situation in States Parties whose reports are very long overdue, in the absence of a report by the State Party concerned and once all alternative approaches have been exhausted. That practice, which frequently stimulates a State to submit the requisite report, had been welcomed by the Commission on Human Rights and by the General Assembly and had now been operating successfully for a number of years. Nevertheless, in relation to the work of some of the committees, questions had been raised with regard to the legal basis for such an approach and it had even been suggested that such an approach might exceed the legal competence of a committee. The chairpersons considered that there was a very strong basis, in both law and policy, to support the consideration of a situation in the absence of a report, once repeated requests had failed to persuade a State party to honour its treaty obligation to report. By the same token, the chairpersons were aware of the disadvantages of that practice, bearing in mind the principle of equality of arms and practical considerations of efficacy.

26. The chairpersons noted that there was no express provision requiring such an approach contained in the relevant treaties, but that the relevant treaty provisions were, without exception, extremely brief and general in nature. They also recalled that many of the procedures which had become accepted as essential elements of the reporting procedure were not dealt with in the treaties. One such example was the universally accepted assumption that each State Party would send a delegation to present its reports. Although all committees had come to insist on that approach, it was not provided for in the text of the treaties, nor was it envisaged at the time of drafting of the earlier treaties.

27. The principle which should thus be applied in responding to a situation which threatened to undermine the entire system for supervising the obligations freely undertaken by States Parties by virtue of their ratification or accession to the relevant treaty was that of ensuring the effectiveness of the regime established by the treaty. In the absence of any provision to the contrary in a treaty, the question was whether or not a particular course of action contributed to the effectiveness of that regime. That approach was analogous to the principle of implied powers, according to which the acceptability of activities not explicitly provided for should be determined in the light of the object and purpose of the treaty in question.[9] The International Court of Justice had also noted that, even in the absence of specific enabling powers, an international body may act in ways not specifically forbidden, in order to achieve its purposes and objectives.[10]

---

[8] A/52/507, para. 37.
[9] See, generally, Reparations for Injuries Suffered in Service of the United Nations Case, Advisory Opinion of the International Court of Justice, I.C.J. Reports, 1949, at 174–188.
[10] Advisory Opinion in the Case of Certain Expenses, International Court of Justice Reports 1962, at 151.

28. Bearing in mind that all Parties to the human rights treaties have undertaken the obligation to submit reports on the measures they have adopted to give effect to the rights recognized in the conventions and accepted the competence of the respective committees to examine said reports, it would be an anomaly if delinquent States could avoid scrutiny simply by refusing to submit reports which they are under a treaty obligation to produce. In cases where a State Party had submitted an initial report but had failed to produce one or more subsequent reports, the Committee concerned clearly had the competence to revisit the prior report or reports. In cases where no report whatsoever had been submitted, a conclusion that the Committee was powerless to react would vest unilateral power in every State Party to undermine the purposes and objectives of the treaty. This was surely not a result that States Parties to a multilateral treaty in the human rights field could have intended. In the view of the chairpersons, committees faced with a situation of persistent non-reporting should explore every available alternative, including the offer of advisory services and technical assistance to the State in the preparation of the overdue report. As a final resort, however, committees should be willing to consider proceeding with a consideration of the situation, on the basis of information provided by the State Party to other international bodies and taking account of all other relevant information.

Problems of small States

29. The burden posed for low population States by reporting requirements under the treaties was again discussed. It was noted, for example, that some 29 States with a population of less than one million persons had not ratified either of the International Covenants. It was agreed that the principal challenge was to identify an approach which took account of the special needs of this group without prejudicing the integrity of the reporting system as a whole. The chairpersons requested the Secretariat to prepare an analysis for their September 1998 meeting which would: (a) explore the different approaches which might be used to defining "small States" for this purpose, such as using an arbitrary cut-off of one million or alternative approaches; (b) facilitate a differentiation between small but rich and well-resourced States and others; and (c) suggest ways in which the reporting burden for such States might be eased, such as the preparation of a consolidated report, the drawing up of special reporting guidelines, presentation of the report to only one committee with the others examining it *in absentia*, video-conferencing as a means of presentation, etc.

Focused reports
30. The chairpersons reiterated their view[11] that, in relation to periodic reports, there might be significant advantages in seeking ways by which to focus the report of each State Party on a limited range of issues, which might be identified by the Committee in advance of the preparation of the report. Such an approach would greatly reduce the need for very lengthy reports, minimize duplication of reports, help to eliminate long delays between the

---

[11] A/52/507, para. 35.

submission and the examination of reports, enable problem areas to be dealt with in depth and facilitate the follow-up of concluding observations, both for the State Party and for the committee concerned.
31. The chairpersons undertook to bring the issue to the attention of the members of their respective committees and to report back at the earliest opportunity on any measures that might have been taken in that regard. They believed that the principal criteria in determining the appropriate focus of more limited reports should include the recommendations contained in the previous concluding observations relating to the State in question, significant new measures of a legislative, judicial, administrative or policy nature adopted since the examination of the last report, and any issues identified by a pre-sessional working group as requiring a sustained focus. The chairpersons would return to this matter at their tenth meeting, to be held in September 1998.

Quality of concluding observations
32. The chairpersons reiterated the importance of high-quality concluding observations with particular emphasis on the identification of specific recommendations. They noted with approval that there was a strong trend towards a reduction in the length of those parts of the standard format dealing with "factors and difficulties" and "positive factors", and they supported the trend towards combining the sections on "concerns" and "suggestions and recommendations" into a single section, so that the recommendations and the underlying concerns that gave rise to them were presented in a coherent manner.
33. In addition, the chairpersons recommended that, in future, the Secretariat aim to provide each treaty body, as a minimum, with a structured analysis of the issues raised during the dialogue and the responses provided or not provided. This would ensure that the dialogue was used in a systematic and detailed way as a basis for the Committee's work. The analysis should be prepared in such a way as to provide a good foundation for the drafting of the concluding observations according to the approach adopted by each committee.

General comments and the possible use of joint statements
34. The chairpersons took note of the fact that some committees were beginning to make reference to the general comments or equivalent statements of other committees. They encouraged the development of that practice, insofar as the pronouncements of other committees appeared to be relevant and appropriate to the situation at hand.
35. Note was taken of a proposal by the Committee on the Elimination of Discrimination against Women that that Committee, along with the Human Rights Committee and the Committee on Economic, Social and Cultural Rights, consider issuing a joint statement on the indivisibility of rights and the centrality of gender awareness as part of the fiftieth anniversary celebration of the Universal Declaration of Human Rights. The chairpersons requested the Division for the Advancement of Women to prepare a draft to be considered by the three chairpersons concerned and then to be put to the respective committees.
36. It was agreed that a new genre of "joint statements" would be an appropriate

means by which to enable the committees to address issues of common concern without taking such matters to the level of general comments, in relation to which joint approaches would always be very difficult to achieve. Such joint statements would enable different treaty bodies to work together to address issues of current importance.

Human rights training
37. The chairpersons believed that the existing arrangements for training of national level officials in relation to reporting and the content of the treaties in general were entirely inadequate. They therefore proposed that the High Commissioner for Human Rights launch a major new programme to make available adequate training possibilities, provided by technically and pedagogically competent instructors, to a wide range of interested parties. Such training should be undertaken primarily at the national level, rather than on a regional basis, and should be made available to all government departments involved in implementation of the treaties, the judiciary, police, etc., and all interested parts of civil society. They recommended that an inventory of all training programmes in this area be undertaken, not only of those programmes organized by the Office of the High Commissioner, but also all relevant programmes of other international institutions. The chairpersons recommended that the Office of the High Commissioner make an effort to coordinate with those institutions, to maximize the effectiveness of the training provided and to explore the possibility of exploiting electronic means of providing target audiences with training materials and information.
38. They requested that a particular effort be made to expedite the translation and publication of the *Reporting Manual* in languages other than English, and recommended that the manual be made available on the Web site of the Office of the High Commissioner for Human Rights.
39. In addition, the chairpersons reiterated their view, expressed in previous reports, of the importance of providing human rights training to all United Nations personnel in the field, particularly those engaged in missions that may have an impact on the enjoyment of human rights in the areas where they are stationed, including peacekeepers. They encouraged the High Commissioner for Human Rights to continue to examine the matter and to implement, as soon as possible, a basic human rights training package for personnel throughout the United Nations system, including UNDP, the World Bank, the International Monetary Fund (IMF) and other relevant agencies.

Independence of experts
40. The chairpersons took note with appreciation of the guidelines for the exercise of their functions adopted by the Human Rights Committee in November 1997, and urged that careful consideration be given to the guidelines by each of the other committees. They also reaffirmed the vital importance of respect by States of the privileges and immunities of experts in relation to the exercise of their United Nations-related functions.

Honoraria
41. In the report of the eighth meeting of persons chairing the human rights treaty bodies,[12] the chairpersons drew attention to the fact that the members

---
[12] *Ibid.*, para. 60.

of three committees receive honoraria, while those of the other three do not. In resolution 52/118, the General Assembly requested the Secretary-General to include in his report prepared pursuant to the resolution a detailed explanation of the basis for the payment of honoraria to the members of the human rights treaty bodies and suggestions to improve coherence in this regard. The chairpersons called upon the Secretary-General to emphasize in his report the invidious nature of the existing disparities and the urgent need to remedy the situation. The chairpersons requested their Chairperson to address a letter to the Secretary-General further developing the need for appropriate action, and authorize the Chairperson to follow up on the matter, as appropriate, with the Advisory Committee on Administrative and Budgetary Questions.

Fiftieth anniversary of the Universal Declaration of Human Rights
42. Bearing in mind that the six human rights treaties constitute a codification and further elaboration of the rights enshrined in the Universal Declaration, the treaty bodies urged the High Commissioner for Human Rights to give greater emphasis to the importance of the treaties and to the monitoring and other activities of the treaty bodies in the context of activities designed to mark the anniversary. The chairpersons agreed to prepare a statement on the present and future role of the treaty bodies, to be widely circulated prior to the commencement of the fifty-fourth session of the Commission on Human Rights.

Reporting by the Committee on Economic, Social and Cultural Rights
43. The chairpersons endorsed the position adopted by the Committee on Economic, Social and Cultural Rights, in response to the proposal set out in the report of the Secretary-General entitled "Renewing the United Nations: A Programme for Reform",[13] that the Committee should in future report to the Economic and Social Council through the Commission on Human Rights, rather than directly to the Council. The chairpersons noted that this could greatly delay the Council's consideration of the Committee's report and would make that Committee the only one out of six human rights treaty bodies which must first submit its report to the Commission on Human Rights rather than to the Economic and Social Council or the General Assembly. The chairpersons believed that the same objective could be achieved by requesting the Secretary-General to ensure that the report of the Committee was made available to the Commission for its consideration, without altering the formal arrangements that exist.

Cooperation with the special rapporteurs
44. In order to give effect to the recommendation contained in the report of the previous meeting of chairpersons,[14] the chairpersons recommended that their eleventh meeting be organized to overlap with the meeting of special rapporteurs/representatives, experts and chairpersons of working groups of the special procedures of the Commission on Human Rights, to be held in

---

[13] See A/51/950, para. 135 (f).
[14] A/52/507, para. 50.

May 1999. They requested the Secretary-General to make the appropriate arrangements towards this end.

Tenth meeting of chairpersons

45. The chairpersons decided to make provision in the agenda envisaged for their tenth meeting for the holding of a private meeting with those members of the Secretariat who service the treaty bodies, in order to hold a mutual exchange of ideas in relation to working methods.

A/53/432 — 25 September 1998

UNITED NATIONS GENERAL ASSEMBLY
Fifty-third session

EFFECTIVE IMPLEMENTATION OF INTERNATIONAL INSTRUMENTS ON HUMAN RIGHTS, INCLUDING REPORTING OBLIGATIONS UNDER INTERNATIONAL INSTRUMENTS ON HUMAN RIGHTS

Note by the Secretary-General

The Secretary-General has the honour to transmit to the General Assembly the report of the persons chairing the human rights treaty bodies on their tenth meeting, held at Geneva from 14 to 18 September 1998, pursuant to General Assembly resolution 52/118 of 12 December 1997.

ANNEX

Report of the persons chairing the human rights treaty bodies on their tenth meeting

I. INTRODUCTION

1. Since the adoption of its resolution 37/44 on 3 December 1982, the General Assembly has continuously kept under review the issue of the effective implementation of international instruments on human rights, including reporting obligations under international instruments. Those matters have also received careful attention during the various sessions of the treaty bodies, at some of the meetings of States parties and at meetings of other organs such as the Economic and Social Council and the Commission on Human Rights.
2. Pursuant to General Assembly resolution 38/117 of 16 December 1983, the Secretary-General convened the first meeting of the persons chairing the bodies entrusted with the consideration of State party reports in August 1984. The report on that meeting was submitted to the General Assembly at its thirty-ninth session (A/39/484, annex). The second, third, fourth, fifth and sixth meetings were convened by the Secretary-General biannually from 1988 until 1994 and, in accordance with General Assembly resolution 49/178 of 23 December 1994, annually since 1995.
3. In its resolution 52/118 of 12 December 1997, the General Assembly welcomed the report of the persons chairing the human rights treaty bodies on their eighth meeting, held at Geneva from 15 to 19 September 1997 (A/52/507, annex), and took note of their conclusions and recommendations. The Assembly noted with appreciation the efforts of the persons chairing the treaty bodies, at their eighth meeting, to develop appropriate reforms of the

reporting system, with a view to, *inter alia*, reducing the reporting burden on States parties while maintaining the quality of reporting, and encouraged them to continue those efforts, including through the continued examination of the benefits of reports focused on a limited range of issues and of opportunities for harmonizing the general guidelines regarding the form and content of reports, and the timing of consideration of reports and the methods of work of the treaty bodies. The General Assembly endorsed the request of the persons chairing the treaty bodies to hold an extraordinary meeting from 25 to 27 February 1998 to pursue the reform process with the aim of improving the effective implementation of international instruments on human rights. The report on that meeting (ninth meeting) is before the General Assembly at its fifty-third session (A/53/125).
4. The tenth meeting of persons chairing the human rights treaty bodies was convened by the Secretary-General pursuant to General Assembly resolution 52/118.

II. ORGANIZATION OF THE MEETING

5. The meeting was held at the United Nations Office at Geneva from 14 to 18 September 1998. The following representatives of the human rights treaty bodies attended: Charlotte Abaka (Vice-Chairperson, Committee on the Elimination of Discrimination against Women), Mahmoud Aboul-Nasr (Chairperson, Committee on the Elimination of Racial Discrimination), Philip Alston (Chairperson, Committee on Economic, Social and Cultural Rights), Peter Thomas Burns (Chairperson, Committee against Torture), Omran El-Shafei (Vice-Chairperson, Human Rights Committee) and Sandra P. Mason (Chairperson, Committee on the Rights of the Child). Mr. Burns was elected Chairperson/Rapporteur of the meeting. At their first meeting the chairpersons adopted the agenda and the programme of work.
6. On behalf of the United Nations High Commissioner for Human Rights, the Deputy High Commissioner for Human Rights declared the meeting open and addressed the chairpersons of the human rights treaty bodies on 14 September 1998. Mary Robinson, the United Nations High Commissioner for Human Rights, participated in a closed meeting with the chairpersons on 18 September 1998, which was highly appreciated as it made it possible to continue the frank dialogue of previous meetings.
7. Representatives of the following United Nations bodies, specialized agencies and regional organizations participated in the meeting: Organization of American States (OAS); Organization of African Unity (OAU); Division for the Advancement of Women of the United Nations Secretariat; United Nations Population Fund (UNFPA); United Nations Development Programme (UNDP); United Nations Educational, Scientific and Cultural Organization (UNESCO); United Nations Children's Fund (UNICEF); Office of the United Nations High Commissioner for Refugees (UNHCR); and World Health Organization (WHO).
8. The Director of the Information Service of the United Nations Office of Geneva informed the meeting of chairpersons about the ongoing information activities covering the work of all treaty bodies. To ensure better coverage of

the meetings of treaty bodies, the Department of Public Information is planning (a) to continue working to make the activities of the committees better known, through radiocommunication with Geneva-based correspondents, making use of "points de presse"; (b) to prepare, for November 1998, an annual timetable for the six treaty bodies which would provide dates of meetings and list the State reports to be considered; this is to alert the press on the national level; and (c) to continue Department action to make television networks aware of the activities of the treaty bodies during public sessions.

9. Representatives of the following non-governmental organizations attended the meeting: Amnesty International; Anti-Racism Information Service (ARIS); Association for the Prevention of Torture (APT); Baha'i International Community; Defence for Children International; Friends World Committee for Consultation; International Service for Human Rights; International Women's Rights Action Watch; Lawyers Committee for Human Rights; and NGO Group for the Convention on the Rights of the Child.

10. Gallegos Chiriboga, Vice-Chairperson of the fifty-fourth session of the Commission on Human Rights, and Yimer Aboye, member of the Bureau of the Sub-Commission on Prevention of Discrimination and Protection of Minorities, addressed the meeting, as did Ms. Rishmawi, Chairperson of the fifth meeting of special rapporteurs and representatives, experts and chairpersons of working groups on the special procedures of the Commission on Human Rights and the Advisory Services Programme.

11. On 17 September 1998 the chairpersons convened a private meeting with the representatives of States parties to discuss ideas on how to improve the work of human rights treaty bodies and to promote implementation of their concluding observations. Fifty-five States parties were represented at the meeting, which provided a valuable opportunity for dialogue in relation to the role of the treaty bodies and their future evolution. The following issues were discussed: (a) the problem of human resources; the success in obtaining ratifications has not been accompanied by a growth in the human resources made available to meet the increased workload; (b) the serious backlog of communications in those committees having communications procedures; (c) two recent denunciations of the Optional Protocol to the International Covenant on Civil and Political Rights; (d) the backlog of State reports received and not yet examined; (e) the problem of overdue reports; and (f) the problem of giving effect to the recommendations of the expert committees. The chairpersons consider that informal consultations with States parties during their meetings are extremely useful and request the Secretariat to arrange for an informal consultation during their eleventh meeting.

12. The chairpersons further convened a private meeting with the internal Task Force of the Office of the High Commissioner for Human Rights, established with a mandate to facilitate and contribute to the parallel review of the United Nations mechanisms by the Commission on Human Rights and provide the Office of the High Commissioner with an input on measures to improve the effectiveness of the mechanisms. In this context, the chairpersons also had the opportunity to meet with Professor Anne Bayefsky of York University, Canada, who will conduct an academic study and review of the human rights treaty system for the Office of the High Commissioner.

13. Among the documents made available to the participants were the report of the Secretariat on universal ratification, improving the operation of the human rights treaty bodies, servicing of the treaty bodies and information technology;[1] the report of the Secretary-General on the status of the international human rights instruments and the general situation of overdue reports;[2] a background paper by the Division for the Advancement of Women on the integration of a gender perspective into the work of all treaty bodies;[3] and a proposal for a plan of action to strengthen the implementation of the Covenant on Civil and Political Rights, the Convention on the Elimination of Racial Discrimination and the Convention against Torture and Other Cruel, Inhuman or Degrading Treatment or Punishment.
14. On 18 September 1998, the chairpersons considered the draft report on their tenth meeting. The report, as amended during the course of the meeting, was adopted unanimously.
15. The chairpersons tentatively agreed to hold their eleventh meeting at the United Nations Office at Geneva from 31 May to 4 June 1998, to coincide with the meeting of special rapporteurs and representatives, experts and chairpersons of working groups.

III. COMPOSITION OF THE TREATY BODIES

16. The chairpersons expressed strong concern at the geographical and gender imbalances reflected in the composition of certain of the treaty bodies. In particular, they noted that the number of African experts within two of the committees was entirely unsatisfactory. They recognized that the election of members of the treaty bodies was entirely a matter for the States parties. Nevertheless they called upon States parties to make a concerted effort to remedy the imbalances.

IV. REVIEW OF RECENT DEVELOPMENTS RELATING TO THE WORK OF THE TREATY BODIES AND THEIR COOPERATION WTIH SPECIALIZED AGENCIES, UNITED NATIONS FUNDS AND PROGRAMMES AND REGIONAL AND NON-GOVERNMENTAL ORGANIZATIONS

17. The chairpersons provided information on recent activities of the treaty bodies they represented. Brief statements were made by each chairperson in relation to the working methods, innovations made and challenges to be addressed by the respective committees.
18. Appreciation was expressed at the increasing cooperation between the Sub-Commission on Prevention of Discrimination and Protection of Minorities and the Committee on the Elimination of Racial Discrimination, which has resulted in a joint paper on article 7 of the Convention on the Elimination

---

[1] HRI/MC/1998/4.
[2] HRI/MC/1998/5.
[3] HRI/MC/1998/6.

of All Forms of Racial Discrimination. The chairpersons recommended that the expertise of the treaty bodies in general, and the Committee on the Elimination of Racial Discrimination in particular, should be increasingly drawn upon by the Sub-Commission in its preparation of future studies on topics related to, *inter alia*, ethnic conflict, education and racial discrimination, globalization in the context of the increase in incidents of racism, racial discrimination and xenophobia, affirmative action, migrant workers and the rights of non-citizens.

19. The chairpersons emphasized the importance of the work of the special rapporteurs and representatives, experts and chairpersons of working groups and underlined the utility of and the need to have easy access to the reports of other existing United Nations mechanisms so as to improve the work of the human rights treaty bodies. It was recommended that ways to improve the communication and information flow between the various United Nations mechanisms be explored. The chairpersons further endorsed the conclusion reached at the fifth meeting of special rapporteurs that the current practice of special rapporteurs occasionally participating in meetings of treaty bodies should be institutionalized.

20. The chairpersons also noted with interest the wish expressed by the representative of UNESCO that the newly appointed Special Rapporteur on education should cooperate with UNESCO and be able to visit its headquarters to make use of its existing network and material.

21. The chairpersons further underlined the importance of the supportive work of and fruitful cooperation with a number of specialized agencies, United Nations bodies and non-governmental organizations. It was once again regretted that no such constructive relationship had yet been established between the treaty bodies and some key agencies, in particular the International Monetary Fund and the World Bank. The chairpersons welcomed the statement of UNDP that it intended to increase its cooperation with the Committee on Economic, Social and Cultural Rights, as a first step towards greater involvement in the work of the treaty bodies as a whole.

22. The representative of UNDP informed the chairpersons of the ongoing cooperation with the Office of the High Commissioner for Human Rights, in drafting a human rights programme, "Human rights strengthening – HURIST", with the aim of supporting the implementation of UNDP policy on human rights as presented in its policy document entitled "Integrating human rights with sustainable human development".

23. The chairpersons were briefed on the process under way, pursuant to the memorandum of understanding signed on 4 March 1998 by UNDP and the Office of the High Commissioner, to draft a training module on human rights for UNDP staff at headquarters and field levels as part of the UNDP training programme. Still within the framework of the memorandum of understanding, the possibilities of staff exchange and rotations of Junior Professional Officers between UNDP and the Office of the High Commissioner are being studied. The chairpersons very much hope that the strong commitment expressed in the memorandum of understanding will be translated into real action and support by UNDP at the national level.

24. The chairpersons noted with interest that, according to the memorandum of understanding, the recommendations of all special rapporteurs and the

concluding observations of all treaty bodies should be sent to UNDP resident representatives, a decision endorsed by the chairpersons.

V. UNIVERSAL RATIFICATION

25. Universal ratification has been a recurrent issue on the agenda of various treaty bodies and chairpersons' meetings. Commitments undertaken in the Vienna Declaration and Programme of Action and in the Beijing Declaration and Platform for Action towards universal ratification of the six principal human rights treaties must be given effect. In this framework, the chairpersons, at their ninth meeting, called upon the United Nations system as a whole to accord an even higher priority to efforts to encourage and facilitate ratification of each of the six treaties by every State.
26. The chairpersons reiterated their view that universal ratification of the six principal human rights treaties constituted an essential dimension of a global order committed to the full respect of human rights (see A/53/125, paras. 13–16).
27. The chairpersons noted that the memorandum of understanding referred to in paragraph 23 above includes in its annex, *inter alia*, a provision for cooperation with a view to promoting universal ratification of the international human rights instruments. In particular, it provides that UNDP shall, through its country offices, inform the Governments seeking assistance or advice on ratification of international human rights instruments about the availability of assistance under the technical cooperation programme of the Office of the High Commissioner for Human Rights.
28. In view of the above, the chairpersons recommended that the Office of the High Commissioner for Human Rights develop a concerted and comprehensive action programme to promote universal ratification in cooperation with specialized agencies and United Nations funds and programmes, in particular UNDP, and to report to the chairpersons at their eleventh meeting on the action taken in this regard.

VI. IMPROVING THE WORK OF HUMAN RIGHTS TREATY BODIES

A. *Focused and consolidated reports*

29. At their eighth and ninth meetings, the chairpersons expressed the view that, in relation to periodic reports, there might be significant advantages in seeking ways by which to focus the report of each State party on a limited range of issues, which might be identified by the committees in advance of the preparation of the report. Such an approach would greatly reduce the need for very lengthy reports, minimize duplication of reports, help to eliminate long delays between the submission and the examination of reports, allow problem areas to be dealt with in depth and facilitate the follow-up of concluding observations, both for the State party and for the committee concerned. The chairpersons undertook to bring the issue to the attention of the members of their respective committees and to report on any measures that might be taken in that regard.

30. Following the discussion of recent experiences of the respective committees, the chairpersons reiterated their view that it was desirable to strive towards focused periodic reports, adding that account must be taken of the limited scope of the issues covered by some of the treaties.
31. With regard to the frequently expressed idea of consolidating reports in a single global report covering all six human rights treaties, no consensus could be reached. As at the eighth meeting, although the chairpersons considered that such an approach would reduce the number of different reports requested of States parties and would serve to underline the indivisibility of human rights by ensuring a comprehensive analysis of the situation, concerns were expressed in relation to problems resulting from the different periodicities of reporting under the treaties and, in particular, the risk that the special attention given to groups such as women and children would be lost in a single comprehensive report.

B. *Venue of meetings*

32. At the tenth meeting of chairpersons, the issue of interchangeability of venues was once more discussed. The chairpersons strongly emphasized that it would be desirable for the treaty bodies to meet in both Geneva and New York, as that would enhance the effectiveness and visibility of their work. They also believed that occasional sessions in New York would enable the four committees concerned to establish better contacts with States parties which did not have permanent missions at Geneva, to make their work much more widely known to a broader range of interested groups, to facilitate contacts with those non-governmental organizations and media representatives that were not active at Geneva and to provide an important opportunity for interaction with other international organizations which did not actively follow the work of the treaty bodies at Geneva. Similarly, the chairpersons reiterated the view that an opportunity for the Committee on the Elimination of Discrimination against Women to meet at Geneva would greatly enhance its relationship with other human rights mechanisms and give it access to a range of agencies, non-governmental organizations and other groups not present in New York (A/52/507, para. 49).
33. Furthermore, the chairpersons noted the many advantages that would accrue if the treaty bodies were able to meet on an exceptional and occasional basis at the various United Nations regional offices. They requested the High Commissioner to approach the relevant offices to explore the conditions under which it might be possible to organize a treaty body session at the regional level without incurring costs significantly greater than those involved in meeting in New York or Geneva, as the case may be. The High Commissioner for Human Rights was requested to report to the chairpersons on the matter (A/52/507, para. 51).
34. Having been informed about the estimated financial implications of their proposal, the chairpersons reaffirmed their previous request. The chairpersons further underlined that the advantages and positive side-effects of holding meetings in both New York and Geneva, and occasionally in regional headquarters, by far outweighed the additional costs entailed.

C. Technical briefings for experts of human rights treaty bodies

35. At the eighth meeting of chairpersons, the Secretariat was requested to present a proposal as to the possible contents of technical briefings directed at treaty body members to expose them to the legal and institutional context in which the treaty bodies operate and to the work of the relevant international organizations.
36. Following the presentation of a proposal at their tenth meeting, the chairpersons welcomed the possibility of such technical briefings, especially as a means to familiarize new members with the workings of their committees. However, the chairpersons considered that the current proposal should be refined, bearing in mind, *inter alia*, that the briefings should be of a minimum of one day's duration, as well as procedures currently in place in the Committee on the Elimination of Discrimination against Women. The chairpersons recommended that the Secretariat amend its proposal accordingly.

D. Press coverage of the treaty bodies

37. At their tenth meeting, the chairpersons noted with interest the information received from the Information Service of the United Nations Office at Geneva on the ongoing information activities covering the work of all treaty bodies and measures planned to ensure better coverage of the meetings of treaty bodies, namely, (a) continuing work to make the activities of the committees better known, through radio communication with Geneva-based correspondents; (b) preparation, for November 1998, of an annual timetable for the six treaty bodies which would provide dates of meetings and list the State reports to be considered, so as to alert the press on the national level; and (c) continuing action to make television networks aware of the activities of the treaty bodies during public sessions.
38. It was noted that the United Nations press corps in New York and Geneva were heavily weighted in favour of Western countries. The chairpersons considered that this was particularly problematic insofar as it restricted the media coverage given to the examination of reports concerning other countries. They considered that the Department of Public Information and the United Nations Information Service offices at the country level should make a concerted effort to provide the local media with documentation and appropriate background briefings whenever a report from the State concerned or neighbouring States was being considered by any of the treaty bodies. They urged the Department to consider providing appropriate training to its field office representatives to enable them to perform this function effectively.

VII. SERVICING OF THE HUMAN RIGHTS TREATY BODIES

A. Staffing situation

39. The chairpersons have on several previous occasions expressed their concern at the level of Secretariat assistance provided to the five Geneva-based committees. The chairpersons note that the new structure of the Office of

the High Commissioner for Human Rights has not brought any improvement in the service for the human rights treaty bodies. The impact of the restructuring on their work has entailed a noticeable reduction of human resources assigned to the treaty bodies in terms of numbers of staff, as well as a loss of essential expertise and institutional memory.
40. The chairpersons expressed particular concern at the important turnover of staff servicing the human rights treaty bodies as a result of the restructuring, which has negatively affected the quality of the service received. In this context the chairpersons underlined the importance of appropriate training of staff members in drafting methods and document research.
41. Having considered the information contained in the report of the Secretariat on universal ratification, improving the operation of the human rights treaty bodies, servicing of the treaty bodies and information technology,[1] concerning the relevant tasks performed and the time required to perform those tasks, the chairpersons reiterated their appeals already contained in the reports on their eighth and ninth meetings that the specialized secretariat staff servicing the committees be significantly strengthened. In view of the current financial situation of the United Nations as a whole, the possibility of seeking voluntary funds must be further explored, although adequate provision to human rights treaty bodies should be developed within the regular budget allocated to the Office of the High Commissioner for Human Rights.
42. The chairpersons noted that while they had consistently called upon the High Commissioner to provide additional staff support, the High Commissioner had limited scope to respond as long as the States Members of the United Nations continued to reduce the already seriously inadequate resources available from the regular budget for human rights purposes. The failure of States to pay their longstanding arrears is particularly problematic in this respect and the honouring of financial obligations under the Charter of the United Nations could achieve a significant improvement of the situation. The chairpersons wished to highlight the fact that the reductions which had been made were inconsistent with the constant reaffirmations by States of the importance of the United Nations human rights mandate, and the dramatic expansion of tasks entrusted to the Office of the High Commissioner for Human Rights in general, particularly in relation to the treaty bodies.
43. Further, in view of the importance of finding concrete and innovative ways to improve the work of the human rights treaty bodies, the chairpersons emphasized the need for adequate resources to be made available to enable them to follow up and implement its various proposals.

B. *Backlog of work*

44. The chairpersons noted the growing backlog in the examination of reports of States parties and underlined the fact that it was detrimental to the proper functioning of the treaty bodies to press States parties to submit their reports in a timely fashion if those reports could not be examined before the data

---

[1] HRI/MC/1998/4.

submitted became obsolete. While the chairpersons insisted that the examination of reports must not be rushed, and that the quality of the dialogue and of the concluding observations could be further improved, they recognized that it would be desirable to complete the examination of reports in fewer meetings than is currently the case. In order to achieve such an improvement, the chairpersons believe that better preparation of documents by the Secretariat would significantly assist the committees in examining State party reports more expeditiously.
45. The chairpersons noted that while the Committee on the Elimination of Racial Discrimination does not at present have any backlog of pending communications, the Committee against Torture is experiencing a constant growth in the number of communications received and is concerned that appropriate measures be taken to ensure that a serious backlog does not develop in the near future. With respect to the Human Rights Committee, the chairpersons remained concerned about the excessive number of pending cases and growing backlog of unanswered correspondence, which seriously calls into question the effectiveness of the Human Rights Committee and consequently of the Optional Protocol procedure.
46. The chairpersons suggested that some possibilities be explored to respond adequately to the current backlog of communications in the Human Rights Committee and to similar situations for other committees in the future. The chairpersons considered it the responsibility of each committee to persevere in the ongoing examination of working methods and to find adequate solutions. The chairpersons noted, as an example of measures already taken, that the Human Rights Committee had reviewed its methods of work and amended its rules of procedure to allow the joint examination of admissibility and merits in appropriate cases. This change had already enabled the Committee to reduce substantially the time required to complete the examination of communications.
47. Furthermore, in view of the present situation, the chairpersons wished once again to emphasize the fact that the individual communications procedures constituted an important part of the human rights treaties monitoring system. It was imperative that individual communications be acknowledged promptly upon receipt and processed expeditiously, although that might require a substantial increase in the number of specialized lawyers assigned to the work.

C. *Plan of Action to strengthen the implementation of the international human rights treaties*

48. The chairpersons welcomed the information received concerning the success of the Plan of Action to strengthen the implementation of the Convention on the Rights of the Child, which has been in operation since 1997 and has significantly helped the Committee on the Rights of the Child in carrying out its mandate. They also welcomed the information concerning the funds already received for the Plan of Action for the Covenant on Economic, Social and Cultural Rights.
49. The chairpersons examined a proposed draft of a plan of action to strengthen the implementation of the Covenant on Civil and Political Rights, the

Convention on the Elimination of All Forms of Racial Discrimination and the Convention against Torture, prepared by the Secretariat pursuant to a recommendation contained in the report on the ninth meeting. The chairpersons confirmed the support expressed at their previous meetings for the adoption of such a plan of action, but requested the Secretariat to take due account of a number of concerns that needed to be addressed and to revise the proposal in close cooperation with the chairperson of the tenth meeting. They further requested the High Commissioner for Human Rights to ensure that the finalization and subsequent launching of a plan of action be given absolute priority so as to increase available resources.

VIII. RESERVATIONS TO THE HUMAN RIGHTS TREATIES

50. The chairpersons continued their discussion of the preliminary conclusions adopted by the International Law Commission at its forty-seventh session relating to reservations to normative multilateral treaties and noted the third report on reservations to treaties submitted by Mr. Alain Pellet, Special Rapporteur, to the Commission at its fiftieth session in 1998.
51. The chairpersons took note of the report of the Secretary-General reflecting the views of the six human rights treaty bodies on the preliminary conclusions of the International Law Commission,[4] paragraph 3 of which correctly reflects the position of the chairpersons: "At the ninth meeting of persons chairing the human rights treaty bodies, held at Geneva in February 1998, the chairpersons considered the Commission's Preliminary Conclusions and drew attention to the emphasis attached in the Vienna Declaration and Programme of Action to the importance of limiting the number and the extent of reservations to human rights treaties and welcomed the recognition contained in the text that treaty monitoring bodies have an important competence in relation to reservations. They considered, however, that the Preliminary Conclusions were unduly restrictive in other respects and did not accord sufficient attention to the fact that human rights treaties, by virtue of their subject matter and the role they recognize to individuals, cannot be placed on precisely the same footing as other treaties with different characteristics."
52. The chairpersons agreed to pursue the consideration of the preliminary conclusions in their respective committees with a view to formulating their comments and forwarding them to the International Law Commission as soon as possible.

IX. GENDER PERSPECTIVES IN THE WORK OF THE TREATY BODIES

53. At their eighth meeting, the chairpersons invited the Division for the Advancement of Women to prepare a background paper analysing what the various treaty bodies had done, and should do, in integrating a gender

---

[4] E/CN.4/Sub.2/1998/25.

perspective into their work. At their tenth meeting, the chairpersons were presented with a report reviewing the integration of a gender perspective into the work of the United Nations human rights treaty bodies. The chairpersons strongly endorsed the report and emphasized the usefulness of such a comprehensive study to the work of the treaty bodies, in particular in assessing current practices and in identifying and focusing on areas of improvements for the future. The chairpersons however expressed concern at the risk that this valuable analysis might not receive the attention deserved, and called upon each of the committees to take full account of the recommendations contained in the report within the framework of their respective mandates.

54. The chairpersons further noted with interest the proposed guidelines on gender perspective presented by the International Women's Rights Action Watch, which could prove to be an indispensable tool in integrating the gender perspective into the work of the treaty bodies in practice.

X. CONCLUSIONS AND RECOMMENDATIONS

55. The chairpersons expressed strong concern at the geographical and gender imbalances reflected in the composition of certain of the treaty bodies. In particular, they noted that the number of African experts within two of the committees was entirely unsatisfactory. They recognized that the election of members of the treaty bodies was entirely a matter for the States parties. Nevertheless they called upon States parties to make a concerted effort to remedy the imbalances.

56. In view of the recent successful outcome of cooperation between the Committee on the Elimination of Racial Discrimination and the Sub-Commission on Prevention of Discrimination and Protection of Minorities, the chairpersons recommended that the expertise of the treaty bodies in general, and the Committee on the Elimination of Racial Discrimination in particular, should be increasingly drawn upon by the Sub-Commission in its preparation of future studies on topics related to, *inter alia*, ethnic conflict, education and racial discrimination, globalization in the context of the increase in incidents of racism, racial discrimination and xenophobia, affirmative action, migrant workers and the rights of non-citizens.

57. Underlining the importance of the work of the special rapporteurs and representatives, experts and chairpersons of working groups, the chairpersons recommended that effective ways to improve the communication and information flow between the various United Nations mechanisms be explored. They further endorsed the conclusion reached at the fifth meeting of special rapporteurs that the current practice of special rapporteurs occasionally participating in meetings of treaty bodies should be institutionalized.

58. The chairpersons recommended that the Office of the High Commissioner for Human Rights develop a concerted and comprehensive action programme to promote universal ratification in cooperation with specialized agencies, and United Nations funds and programmes, in particular UNDP, and to report to the chairpersons at their eleventh meeting on the action taken in this regard.

59. The chairpersons also noted with interest the wish expressed by the representative of UNESCO that the newly appointed Special Rapporteur on education should cooperate with UNESCO and be able to visit its headquarters to make use of its existing network and material.
60. The chairpersons very much hope that the strong commitment expressed in the memorandum of understanding signed by the Office of the High Commissioner for Human Rights and UNDP will be translated into real action and support by UNDP at the national level. The chairpersons noted with interest that, according to the memorandum of understanding, the recommendations of all special rapporteurs and the concluding observations of all treaty bodies should be sent to UNDP resident representatives, a decision endorsed by the chairpersons.
61. For the reasons cited above (paras. 32–34), the chairpersons reiterated their request that necessary steps be taken to enable the four human rights treaty bodies meeting only at Geneva to hold occasional sessions in New York, and for the Committee on the Elimination of All Forms of Discrimination against Women to hold sessions at Geneva. They also reiterated their request to be enabled to meet, on occasion, at other United Nations regional offices.
62. The chairpersons recommended that a programme of technical briefings for committee experts be developed on the basis of the proposal presented by the Secretariat during the tenth meeting, incorporating elements suggested by the chairpersons.
63. The chairpersons recommended that the Secretariat, in conjunction with the Information Service of the United Nations Office at Geneva, explore ways to attract the interest of the media worldwide, through increased cooperation with national information offices. They also considered that the Department and the United Nations Information Service offices at the country level should make a concerted effort to provide the local media with documentation and appropriate background briefings whenever a report from the State concerned, or neighbouring States, was being considered by any of the treaty bodies. The chairpersons urged the Department to consider providing appropriate training to its field office representatives to enable them to perform this function effectively.
64. The chairpersons noted that while they had consistently called upon the High Commissioner to provide additional staff support, the High Commissioner had limited scope to respond as long as Member States continued to reduce the already seriously inadequate resources available from the regular budget for human rights purposes. The failure of States to pay their longstanding arrears is particularly problematic in this respect and the honouring of financial obligations under the Charter could achieve a significant improvement of the situation. The chairpersons wished to highlight the fact that the reductions which had been made were inconsistent with the constant reaffirmations by States of the importance of the United Nations human rights mandate, and the dramatic expansion of tasks entrusted to the Office of the High Commissioner for Human Rights in general, particularly in relation to the treaty bodies.
65. In view of the importance of finding concrete and innovative ways to improve the work of the human rights treaty bodies, the chairpersons wished to emphasize the need for adequate attention and resources to follow up and implement its various proposals.

66. So as to respond adequately to the current backlog of communications in the Human Rights Committee and to similar situations for other committees in the future, the chairpersons recommended all committees to persevere in their ongoing examination of working methods and to find adequate solutions to current difficulties and challenges ahead. The chairpersons suggested that the following possibilities might be explored: (a) an additional week to deal solely with individual communications; (b) an increase in the number of members of the committees, a suggestion which however should be seen as a long-term project as it would entail amendments of existing treaties and a subsequent ratification process; and (c) the creation of small working groups.
67. The chairpersons strongly endorsed the proposed plan of action to strengthen the implementation of the Covenant on Civil and Political Rights, the Convention on the Elimination of All Forms of Racial Discrimination and the Convention against Torture and Other Forms of Cruel, Inhuman or Degrading Treatment or Punishment, and requested the Secretariat to take account of a number of concerns that needed to be addressed and to revise the proposal presented in close cooperation with the chairperson of the tenth meeting. They further requested the High Commissioner for Human Rights to ensure that the finalization and subsequent launching of a plan of action be given absolute priority and that necessary resources be made available.
68. The chairpersons called upon each of the committees to take full account of the recommendations contained in the report of the Secretary-General on the question of integrating the human rights of women throughout the United Nations system,[5] within the framework of their respective mandates.
69. The chairpersons considered that informal consultations with States parties during the tenth meeting were extremely useful, and requested the Secretariat to arrange for the holding of an informal consultation during their eleventh meeting.

---

[5] E/CN.4/1998/49.

A/54/805 — 21 March 2000
UNITED NATIONS GENERAL ASSEMBLY
Fifty-fourth session

EFFECTIVE IMPLEMENTATION OF INTERNATIONAL INSTRUMENTS ON HUMAN RIGHTS, INCLUDING REPORTING OBLIGATIONS UNDER INTERNATIONAL INSTRUMENTS ON HUMAN RIGHTS

Note by the Secretary-General

The Secretary-General has the honour to transmit to the General Assembly the report of the persons chairing the human rights treaty bodies on their eleventh meeting, held at Geneva from 31 May to 4 June 1999, pursuant to General Assembly resolution 49/178 of 23 December 1994.

ANNEX

Report of the Chairpersons of human rights treaty bodies on their eleventh meeting

I. INTRODUCTION

1. Since the adoption of its resolution 37/44 on 3 December 1982, the General Assembly has continuously kept under review the issue of the effective implementation of international instruments on human rights, including reporting obligations under international instruments. Those matters have also received careful attention during the various sessions of human rights treaty bodies, at some of the meetings of States parties and at meetings of other organs such as the Economic and Social Council and the Commission on Human Rights.
2. Pursuant to General Assembly resolution 38/117 of 16 December 1983, the Secretary-General convened the first meeting of the chairpersons of bodies entrusted with the consideration of State party reports in August 1984. The report on that meeting was submitted to the General Assembly at its thirty-ninth session (A/39/484, annex). The meetings of the chairpersons were convened by the Secretary-General biennially from 1988 until 1994 and, in accordance with Assembly resolution 49/178 of 23 December 1994, annually since 1995. In its resolution 52/118 of 12 December 1997, the General Assembly endorsed a request of the persons chairing the treaty bodies to hold an extraordinary ninth meeting early in 1998 to pursue the reform process with the aim of improving the effective implementation of international instruments on human rights.

3. In its resolution 53/138 of 9 December 1998, the General Assembly welcomed the reports of the persons chairing the human rights treaty bodies on their ninth and tenth meetings, held at Geneva from 25 to 27 February 1998 and 14 to 18 September 1998, respectively (A/53/125, annex; and A/53/432, annex), and took note of their conclusions and recommendations. The General Assembly noted with appreciation the efforts of the persons chairing the human rights treaty bodies to propose appropriate reforms of the reporting system with a view to, *inter alia*, reducing the reporting burden on States parties while maintaining the quality of reporting, and encouraged them to continue those efforts, including through the continued examination of the benefits of reports focused on a limited range of issues and of opportunities for harmonizing the general guidelines regarding the form and content of reports, the timing of consideration of reports and the methods of work of the treaty bodies. It decided to continue to give priority consideration at its fifty-fifth session to the conclusions and recommendations of the meetings of persons chairing the human rights treaty bodies, in the light of the deliberations of the Commission on Human Rights, under the item entitled "Human rights questions".
4. The eleventh meeting of chairpersons of the human rights treaty bodies was convened by the Secretary-General from 31 May to 4 June 1999 pursuant to General Assembly resolution 49/178.

II. ORGANIZATION OF THE MEETING

5. The meeting was held at the United Nations Office at Geneva from 31 May to 4 June 1999. The following representatives of the human rights treaty bodies attended: Mr. Mahmoud Aboul-Nasr (Chairperson of the Committee on the Elimination of Racial Discrimination), Mrs. Virginia Bonoan-Dandan (Chairperson of the Committee on Economic, Social and Cultural Rights), Mr. Peter T. Burns (Chairperson of the Committee against Torture), Mrs. Aida González (Chairperson of the Committee on the Elimination of Discrimination against Women), Mrs. Nafsiah Mboi (Chairperson of the Committee on the Rights of the Child), and Mrs. Cecilia Medina Quiroga (Chairperson of the Human Rights Committee). Mrs. Medina Quiroga was elected Chairperson/Rapporteur of the meeting and Mrs. Bonoan-Dandan was elected Vice-Chairperson. At their first meeting the chairpersons adopted the agenda and the programme of work.
6. On behalf of the United Nations High Commissioner for Human Rights, Mr. Bertrand Ramcharan, Deputy High Commissioner for Human Rights, addressed persons chairing the human rights treaty bodies on 31 May 1999. Mrs. Mary Robinson, United Nations High Commissioner for Human Rights, addressed the chairpersons in a closed meeting on 4 June 1999, which was highly appreciated by the participants.
7. Representatives of the following United Nations bodies and specialized agencies participated in the meeting: the Division for the Advancement of Women of the United Nations Secretariat; the United Nations Development Programme (UNDP); the Joint United Nations Programme on HIV/AIDS (UNAIDS); the Office of the United Nations High Commissioner for Refugees

(UNHCR); the United Nations Children's Fund (UNICEF); the International Labour Organization (ILO); and the United Nations Educational, Scientific and Cultural Organization (UNESCO).
8. Representatives of Amnesty International and the Lawyers Committee for Human Rights also intervened during the meeting.
9. In addition to the above, the meeting was addressed by Mrs. Anne Anderson, Chairperson of the fifty-fifth session of the Commission on Human Rights; Mr. Yimer Aboye, member of the Bureau of the fiftieth session of the Subcommission on Prevention of Discrimination and Protection of Minorities; and Mrs. Thérèse Gastaut, Director of the Information Service of the United Nations Office at Geneva.
10. The chairpersons were also addressed by Ms. Anne Bayefsky of York University, Canada, entrusted by the High Commissioner for Human Rights to conduct a study on the effective functioning of the human rights treaties, including their impact at the national level.
11. On the afternoon of 2 June 1999, the chairpersons held a joint meeting with the participants of the sixth meeting of special rapporteurs and representatives, experts and chairpersons of working groups of the special procedures system of the Commission on Human Rights and of the advisory services programme.
12. On 3 June, the chairpersons convened a meeting with the representatives of States parties to discuss views on the functioning of the six human rights treaty bodies. Thirty-eight States parties were represented at the meeting. Appreciation was expressed by all participants for the opportunity to engage in a fruitful dialogue on the role of the treaty bodies and their future evolution.
13. On 4 June, the chairpersons considered the draft report on their eleventh meeting. The report, as amended during the course of the meeting, was adopted unanimously. The list of documents made available to the meeting is contained in appendix I.
14. The chairpersons tentatively agreed to hold their twelfth meeting at the United Nations Office at Geneva to coincide with the next annual meeting of special rapporteurs and representatives, experts and chairpersons of working groups, but not to interfere with any of the sessions of the treaty bodies.

III. REVIEW OF RECENT DEVELOPMENTS RELATING TO THE WORK OF THE TREATY BODY

15. The chairpersons briefed the meeting on recent developments in the work of their respective treaty bodies and the follow-up on recommendations of the tenth meeting of chairpersons. Positive results with respect to some treaty bodies were noted as a consequence of modifications in their methods of work. These included allowing additional time for States parties to respond to issues raised during the examination of reports, which has resulted in a higher quality of dialogue with the States parties concerned, as well as higher quality of the conclusions and recommendations adopted by the committees. The chairpersons expressed concern over continuing problems such as the large backlog of State reports to be examined and the growing backlog of

correspondence awaiting responses; the unbalanced geographical and gender representation in their committees; the inadequate meeting time allotted to them to deal with their workloads; and the lack of adequate interpretation services for all their work, including Bureau meetings.

16. The chairpersons were addressed by the Deputy High Commissioner for Human Rights, Mr. Bertrand Ramcharan, who, *inter alia*, informed them of the approach adopted by the High Commissioner with regard to fund-raising. While welcoming the success of the plans of action to strengthen the implementation of the Convention on the Rights of the Child and of the International Covenant on Economic, Social and Cultural Rights and noting the efforts of the chairpersons to develop a plan of action for the remaining three Geneva-based treaty bodies, the High Commissioner was seeking to ensure adequate resources for all treaty bodies through a consolidated approach. The High Commissioner would appeal to the international donor community, including Governments, businesses and institutions, to support the work of the treaty bodies.

17. The Deputy High Commissioner also highlighted the importance attached by the High Commissioner to the jurisprudence of the treaty bodies. In that regard, the High Commissioner was considering ways to reassemble within the Secretariat a core team to service their communications procedures, which should reinforce the work not only of the three treaty bodies that currently have such procedures in place but also of the other three bodies that are seeking to have such procedures developed in relation to the treaties whose implementation they monitor.

18. The chairpersons welcomed the proposal of the Deputy High Commissioner that a handbook for States parties be prepared which would present the core elements of treaty body "jurisprudence", in the broadest sense of the term. Such a handbook would bring together in a single volume significant decisions or views on communications, important general comments or recommendations, concluding observations, reporting guidelines of the six treaty bodies and other relevant material, and would be useful not only to States parties but to non-governmental organizations, other parts of the United Nations system and individuals interested in the work of the treaty bodies. They urged the Office of the High Commissioner to prepare such a handbook as soon as possible, in consultation with the chairpersons.

19. Mrs. Anne Anderson, Chairperson of the fifty-fifth session of the Commission on Human Rights, addressed the meeting and emphasized that the Commission and the treaty bodies shared a common interest, namely, the quality of interaction between them. She further made reference to the current review and reform of the mechanisms of the Commission, stating that once the process of reform within the Commission itself had been completed, it would be time to look closely at ways to improve the cooperation between the Commission's procedures and treaty bodies. For example, subsequent to the "special dialogues" organized by the Commission this year on a few priority issues, the Commission was already considering topics to be addressed during future "special dialogues". Mrs. Anderson suggested that consultation with human rights treaty bodies should be undertaken in that regard, a suggestion that was warmly welcomed by the chairpersons. She concurred with the view previously expressed by the chairpersons that

a representative of the committees should be granted formal status at the Commission on Human Rights to enable their participation on matters of relevance to them. She informed the chairpersons of her intention to raise that matter at her next meeting with the Economic and Social Council.

20. The chairpersons were also addressed by Mr. Yimer Aboye, member of the Bureau of the fiftieth session of the Subcommission on Prevention of Discrimination and Protection of Minorities. Among a number of interesting initiatives, the Subcommission was undertaking studies and working papers on topics including reservations to the human rights treaties and observance by States of the Universal Declaration of Human Rights. The chairpersons welcomed those important endeavours and expressed hope that the Subcommission would draw on the expertise of the treaty bodies when considering future studies. The representative of the Subcommission requested the Human Rights Committee and other treaty bodies to consider articles 8 and 24 of the International Covenant on Civil and Political Rights within the context of the work of the Working Group on Contemporary Forms of Slavery.

21. The representative of the Division for the Advancement of Women reviewed the recently concluded Workshop on Gender Integration into the Human Rights System, to which all chairpersons of treaty bodies and representatives from all special mechanisms had been invited. At the Workshop, the chairpersons were encouraged to review the working methods of the treaty bodies with a view to identifying areas where questions of gender could be raised, as well as the sources of information that they relied upon in order to have a more balanced view of country situations. The Workshop concluded, *inter alia*, that increased coordination among treaty bodies, in the form of joint meetings, coordinated general comments or recommendations and shared databases, could prove useful. The final report of the Workshop was distributed at the meeting.

22. The chairpersons were briefed by Ms. Anne Bayefsky on a global study which she had been commissioned to undertake by the High Commissioner for Human Rights on the effective functioning of the human rights treaties, including their impact at the national level. Part of the study would be devoted to the functioning of the treaty bodies. At the request of the High Commissioner, she presented to the meeting her discussion paper on secretariat servicing.

23. The chairpersons also took note of a decision adopted at a recent meeting of States parties to the Convention on the Rights of the Child in which States parties recommended that nominations of candidates be submitted in accordance with the two-month time period set out in the Convention.

24. Another development brought to the attention of the chairpersons was the issue of corporate responsibility for human rights. A representative of the Office of the High Commissioner for Human Rights (OHCHR) explained that the relationship between business and human rights was an area of special concern to the High Commissioner. Although the treaties are addressed to States parties, corporate entities were often directly responsible for the protection of certain human rights, particularly labour rights, and in some countries corporate entities exercised greater influence over society than did their Governments. The chairpersons welcomed the attention paid by the High Commissioner to that important area.

IV. COOPERATION OF HUMAN RIGHTS TREATY BODIES WITH SPECIALIZED AGENCIES, UNITED NATIONS DEPARTMENTS, FUNDS, PROGRAMMES AND MECHANISMS AND NON-GOVERNMENTAL ORGANIZATIONS

A. *Cooperation of human rights treaty bodies with specialized agencies, United Nations departments, funds and programmes*

25. The Director of the United Nations Information Service at Geneva, Mrs. Thérèse Gastaut, described the traditional and new strategic news coverage undertaken by the Department of Public Information of the Secretariat on the work of treaty bodies. The traditional news coverage undertaken was done through press releases, radio broadcasting, television coverage and press conferences. In view of their previous recommendation to the Information Service (A/53/432 para. 38) to explore ways to attract the interest of the media worldwide, the chairpersons noted with particular interest: (a) the efforts made to ensure that all information on reporting by a particular State was sent to the local UNDP field offices and that it was reflected in the national media; and (b) the foreseen launching, in June 1999, of the United Nations News Service through which important United Nations news would be sent by e-mail to subscribers of that service, with particular focus on developing countries. It was agreed that in order to keep the treaty bodies up to date as to the news coverage relating to their work in the international and local media, the Department of Public Information would send a dossier of each committee's press coverage to its respective committee secretary.

26. The chairpersons expressed appreciation for the information provided by Mrs. Gastaut. They acknowledged that there was a need for treaty bodies to make their work more appealing to members of the press and recognized the difficulties in ensuring the accuracy of press releases, since the speed with which they must be issued often precluded verification of facts. Nevertheless, a number of chairpersons expressed dissatisfaction with the quality of press releases for two reasons. First, inaccuracies were found to be contained in some press releases; and, secondly, press releases tended to highlight only problems encountered in treaty implementation by States parties. Both of those problems had on occasion placed some treaty bodies in awkward positions in relation to States parties. One Chairperson suggested, in order to make concluding observations more interesting to the press, that the responsible staff in the Department of Public Information who were drafting press releases should coordinate with the person with principal responsibility for the meeting in question with a view to identifying themes or issues that might attract interest.

27. Representatives of UNDP, UNAIDS, UNICEF, ILO and UNESCO informed the chairpersons of their work and of recently developed forms of cooperation with the treaty bodies. The representative from UNAIDS highlighted ways in which inadequate protection of human rights – civil and political rights, as well as economic, social and cultural rights – fuelled the HIV/AIDS epidemic, in particular among women and children. The representative of UNAIDS reported that an agreement had been reached on the

hiring of a full-time adviser to work directly with the treaty bodies in integrating HIV/AIDS concerns into their activities. The adviser would be funded by UNAIDS during the first year of service and was due to begin working in June 1999.

28. The representative of UNICEF reported on steps taken to update the Memorandum of Understanding with OHCHR. In connection with the cooperation with treaty bodies, she indicated that UNICEF also planned to embark on a compilation of "best practices" in the implementation of the Convention on the Rights of the Child, especially on general measures of implementation. In addition to its traditional cooperation with the Committee on the Rights of the Child, UNICEF had started to cooperate closely with other treaty bodies, in particular with the Committee on the Elimination of Discrimination against Women and the Human Rights Committee.

29. The representative of ILO informed the meeting that efforts were being made within that organization to improve the quality of information provided to the treaty bodies which at present was limited to copies of comments by the bodies supervising the ILO conventions. For example, information on the International Programme on the Elimination of Child Labour (IPEC) could be submitted to the Committee on the Rights of the Child and more targeted information could be submitted to the Committee on the Elimination of Discrimination against Women. To enhance the effectiveness and usefulness of the liaison system of those treaty bodies which had such a system in place, ILO would welcome visits by members designated to carry out liaison functions to speak with ILO staff working in areas of interest to them, to view ILO files that were too voluminous to submit to the treaty bodies and to consult the ILO resource centre. She further reported that information from the treaty bodies had been specifically designated as a source of information for follow-up reports to the Declaration on the Right and Responsibility of Individuals, Groups and Organs of Society to Promote and Protect Universally Recognized Human Rights and Fundamental Freedoms and that concluding observations were systematically brought to the attention of the ILO Committee of Experts.

30. The representative of UNDP informed the meeting of efforts under way in the organization to cooperate with the treaty bodies and other mechanisms. In particular, the Committee on Economic, Social and Cultural Rights and the Working Group on the Right to Development of the Commission on Human Rights were targeted as entry points for closer cooperation with human rights bodies. Information from UNDP field offices, particularly national development reports, where those existed and when relevant to the examination of a State report, was regularly submitted to the Committee. Making the reports available to other treaty bodies would soon be considered. UNDP encouraged, but as a decentralized organization did not obligate, Resident Representatives serving in countries under consideration to participate directly in relevant meetings of the Committee. Within the context of the Memorandum of Understanding concluded with the Office of the High Commissioner for Human Rights in March 1998, UNDP and the Office had launched in April a joint programme entitled "Human Rights Strengthening" (HURIST) to promote human rights at the regional and national levels.

B. *Cooperation of human rights treaty bodies with non-governmental organizations*

31. A joint written appeal from Amnesty International, the Association for the Prevention of Torture, the Carter Center, Fédération internationale des ligues des droits de l'homme, Human Rights Internet, Human Rights Watch, the International Commission of Jurists, the International League for Human Rights, the International Service for Human Rights, the Jacob Blaustein Institute for the Advancement of Human Rights, the Lawyers Committee for Human Rights, the Observatory for the Protection of Human Rights, and the World Organization against Torture was presented to the chairpersons related to the Declaration on the Right and Responsibility of Individuals, Groups and Organs of Society to Promote and Protect Universally Recognized Human Rights and Fundamental Freedoms, adopted by the General Assembly on 9 December 1998 (resolution 53/144, annex). The organizations urged the human rights treaty bodies to pay increased attention to the rights of human rights defenders, including their need to access the treaty bodies and the right to freedom of association.
32. In its intervention, Amnesty International expressed its concerns about the recent denunciation and subsequent re-accession with serious reservations to human rights treaties by some States parties. The organization proposed a number of possible measures to be taken by the human rights treaty bodies to discourage such a practice.

C. *Joint meeting with participants in the eleventh meeting of chairpersons of human rights treaty bodies and the sixth meeting of special rapporteurs and representatives, experts and chairpersons of working groups of the special procedures system of the Commission on Human Rights and of the advisory services programme*

33. On 2 June 1999, a joint meeting was held between the participants of the eleventh meeting of the persons chairing human rights treaty bodies and the sixth meeting of special rapporteurs and representatives, experts and chairpersons of working groups of the special procedures system of the Commission on Human Rights and of the advisory services programme.
34. The first joint meeting was welcomed.
35. The six chairpersons of the human rights treaty bodies and three representatives of the special procedures system[1] provided information on the activities of their respective mandates, as well as on present and future interaction between the two mechanisms. The presentations were followed by suggestions to enhance the cooperation between treaty bodies and the special procedures system, including the following:
    (a) The reports of the special rapporteurs and representatives, experts and chairpersons of working groups should contain a specific section on the situation of children;

---

[1] Mr. Roberto Garretón, Special Rapporteur on contemporary forms of racism, racial discrimination, xenophobia and related intolerance; Mr. Abid Hussain, Special Rapporteur on the promotion and protection of the right to freedom of opinion and expression; and Mr. Diego García-Sayán, member of the Working Group on Enforced or Involuntary Disappearances of the Commission on Human Rights.

(b) The reports of the special rapporteurs and representatives, experts and chairpersons of working groups should include a gender focus in their assessments of human rights situations;
(c) Greater use should be made by treaty bodies and the special procedures system of the findings of the other mechanism;
(d) Close cooperation should be sought in the preparations for the World Conference against Racism, Racial Discrimination, Xenophobia and Related Intolerance;
(e) More information should be shared on positive achievements and "best practices" in the implementation of human rights;
(f) Ways should be explored to enable the two mechanisms to jointly enhance the interpretation of human rights provisions in a consistent manner;
(g) Greater attention should be paid to the impact of armed conflict on the realization of human rights;
(h) There should be opportunities for the two mechanisms to discuss thematic issues of mutual interest such as environment and human rights, education, and human rights defenders;
(i) There is a need for an exchange of information and experience regarding "follow-up" procedures to ensure the implementation of conclusions and recommendations;
(j) Databases should be developed to facilitate the exchange of information;
(k) Consideration should be given to compiling an easily accessible chart on planned and recently completed missions in order to identify activities of mutual interest and opportunities for cooperation.

36. The joint meeting adopted recommendations relating to cooperation through better use of information technology, more direct consultation and improved coordination (see paras. 60–62 below).

V. UNIVERSAL RATIFICATION

37. The chairpersons were briefed by the Secretariat on the efforts of OHCHR to promote universal ratification of the principal international human rights treaties. In addition to the systematic encouragement the Secretary-General of the United Nations and the High Commissioner for Human Rights have given to promote ratification during their contacts with representatives of Governments, the Office continued to make use of its inter-agency contacts initiated within the framework of activities to commemorate the fiftieth anniversary of the Universal Declaration of Human Rights in 1998 to promote ratification. In addition, one of the activities provided for in the joint UNDP/OHCHR programme HURIST was entirely dedicated to the promotion of ratification. The activities foreseen under the programme would in part be based on the results of two regional meetings on this topic organized by the Office in the Africa and Asia/Pacific regions in 1996 and 1997, respectively.
38. The chairpersons discussed the possibility of treaty bodies encouraging States parties, during the examination of their reports, to ratify any of the human rights treaties as yet unratified by those States. They noted the concerns of

some States that a major obstacle to ratification was the onerous reporting obligations under the various treaties. In this connection, the chairpersons considered that it would be useful to have at their disposal a document presenting the reporting history of all States under all six treaties through which it could be readily ascertained which treaties each State was a party to. Such a document would be useful not only to treaty bodies but also to States and organizations and individuals interested in the reporting process.

VI. IMPROVING THE WORK OF THE TREATY BODIES

A. *Regional session*

39. The chairpersons considered the possibility that sessions of treaty bodies be held in locations other than their usual sites. They considered that varying session sites would bring the treaty bodies more visibility in regions where they might not be well known, make them more accessible to some States that might not have representation at their normal sites, or facilitate the participation of some small States that might not otherwise be in a position to attend sessions of the treaty bodies.
40. The chairpersons noted that the Committee on the Elimination of Racial Discrimination had made a formal request for one of its annual sessions to be held in New York, as it is stipulated in article 10.4 of the International Convention on the Elimination of All Forms of Racial Discrimination that the Committee shall normally meet at United Nations Headquarters. The Committee on Economic, Social and Cultural Rights had been requested by its parent body, the Economic and Social Council, to resubmit its request for a session to be held in New York, which it planned to do promptly. The Committee on the Elimination of Discrimination against Women, which was based in New York, planned to submit a formal request for a session to be organized in Geneva. However, the chairperson of the Committee against Torture reported that his Committee did not wish to use scarce resources to have its sessions held elsewhere but rather preferred to use any available additional resources for other priorities, such as missions.

B. *Technical briefings*

41. At their eighth meeting, held in September 1997, the chairpersons of the human rights treaty bodies requested the Secretariat to present a proposal as to the possible content of technical briefings for members of the treaty bodies that would help them better to face the increasing complexity of the legal and institutional context in which the treaty bodies operate (A/52/507, para. 48). At their eleventh meeting, the chairpersons considered a proposal by the Secretariat for a programme of technical briefings for committee experts, which had been prepared in accordance with suggestions made at their previous meeting (A/53/432, paras. 35 and 36). The chairpersons welcomed the proposal and recommended that OHCHR take appropriate steps to ensure that such technical briefings be made available, in particular, to newly elected committee experts, on the understanding that each briefing

would be adapted in accordance with the needs and methods of work of each treaty body.

C. *Measures to enhance cooperation among treaty bodies*

42. A suggestion was made to establish ad hoc joint working groups to draft common guidelines for State reports with regard to common provisions contained in several of the human rights treaties. Such working groups would consist of designated members of the treaty bodies concerned.
43. The chairpersons discussed various measures that could be taken to enhance cooperation among treaty bodies. They included the extension of reciprocal invitations by treaty bodies to attend each other's sessions when matters of mutual interest were scheduled for consideration. Such measures could also include the drafting of "coordinated general comments or recommendations", which was also a recommendation of the Workshop on Gender Integration into the Human Rights System.
44. The chairpersons discussed the suggestion that OHCHR publish a "human rights treaties series", each issue to be devoted to specific provisions of the treaties. Articles could be drafted by external experts in the field of human rights, with the proviso that the views contained in the articles were exclusively those of the author and were not endorsed by the treaty bodies or by OHCHR. Articles to be included in the publication could deal with such matters as interpretations of treaty provisions, issues relating to practical implementation and best practices.
45. The chairpersons discussed the possibility of their participation in meetings of their supervisory organs when their annual or biannual reports were being considered. For the Committee on Economic, Social and Cultural Rights, the supervisory organ is the Economic and Social Council, while for the other five it is the General Assembly. The chairpersons considered it would be useful to be able to highlight important findings of their Committees and see how their reports were received.

VII. DRAFT PLAN OF ACTION FOR STRENGTHENING THE IMPLEMENTATION OF THE INTERNATIONAL COVENANT ON CIVIL AND POLITICAL RIGHTS, THE INTERNATIONAL CONVENTION ON THE ELIMINATION OF ALL FORMS OF RACIAL DISCRIMINATION AND THE CONVENTION AGAINST TORTURE AND OTHER CRUEL, INHUMAN OR DEGRADING TREATMENT OR PUNISHMENT

46. The chairpersons welcomed the revised draft Plan of Action for strengthening the implementation of the International Covenant on Civil and Political Rights, the International Convention on the Elimination of All Forms of Racial Discrimination and the Convention against Torture and Other Cruel, Inhuman or Degrading Treatment or Punishment, which was submitted to them in accordance with a recommendation of their tenth meeting. Following a detailed discussion, they approved the draft Plan of Action, as modified during the meeting and subject to a final round of consultations with all

members of the three treaty bodies concerned. The meeting urged OHCHR to undertake such consultations with a view to finalizing and implementing the Plan of Action as soon as possible.

VIII. DEVELOPMENT OF INDICATORS AND BENCHMARKS TO ASSESS THE REALIZATION OF HUMAN RIGHTS

47. The chairpersons reviewed a proposal for a workshop to be organized for the purpose of developing indicators to measure the implementation of the right to education. Such a workshop was foreseen in Commission on Human Rights resolution 1999/25 of 26 April 1999; if the resolution was endorsed by the General Assembly, the chairpersons considered that the proposal would be most helpful for its implementation. They strongly supported the holding of a workshop and recommended that it be organized in close consultation with the Committee on Economic, Social and Cultural Rights along the lines presented therein.

48. The chairpersons were briefed by the Secretariat on efforts being made to develop human rights indicators within the United Nations system. It was pointed out that while a wealth of data was available on economic, social and cultural rights, which already formed a strong foundation for the development of indicators for the measurement of those rights, little was available in the area of civil and political rights. OHCHR sought to remedy that imbalance by developing indicators for the measurement of enjoyment of all human rights, as defined in the principal treaties. To this end, it is working with its partners in the United Nations system, particularly through the United Nations Development Group (UNDG).[2]

IX. INFORMAL CONSULTATIONS WITH GOVERNMENTS

49. On 3 June, the chairpersons met with representatives of States parties. The meeting provided an opportunity for the chairpersons to outline the difficulties faced by each treaty body and to hear the views of States parties on a wide range of topics relating to their interaction with treaty bodies. The chairpersons urged States parties to support their work, particularly by submitting instruments of acceptance of the proposed amendments to the various treaties and by allocating sufficient resources in the Fifth Committee. They also appealed to the States parties to consider gender and geographical balance in the treaty bodies when electing members.

50. Many representatives expressed appreciation for the improvements in methods of work that made possible better participation by States parties in the

---

[2] The United Nations Development Group is one of four executive committees established directly under the Secretary-General to advise him on matters relating to key areas of work undertaken by the United Nations system. The membership of UNDG is composed of the heads of the major development agencies and departments, including UNDP, UNICEF and the United Nations Population Fund (UNFPA). The High Commissioner for Human Rights is a member of all four executive committees, in accordance with the designation by the Secretary-General of human rights as a cross-cutting theme relevant to all the work of the Organization.

reporting process, particularly by allowing more time for delegations to respond to questions posed by treaty bodies and by requesting more focused information in periodic reports. They were pleased to learn that treaty bodies were beginning or continuing to invite States parties to comment on concluding observations adopted on their reports and that those comments would normally be included in the annual reports of treaty bodies. They considered that many of the matters raised in the report of the independent expert of the Commission on Human Rights on enhancing the long-term effectiveness of the United Nations human rights treaty monitoring system (E/CN.4/1997/74) were still valid, and suggested that treaty bodies should continue to consider ways to streamline and coordinate their work.

X. RECOMMENDATIONS

A. *Relationship with the General Assembly, the Economic and Social Council and the functional commissions of the Economic and Social Council*

51. The chairpersons recommend that treaty body chairpersons, or designated members of the treaty bodies, should be permitted to be present when their annual reports are considered by their supervisory organ, whether it be the General Assembly or the Economic and Social Council. They recommend that the Secretary-General consider ways to enable such a practice to be instituted.
52. The chairpersons further recommend that they be granted formal status within the Economic and Social Council, and hence with its functional commissions, to enable them to participate in discussions on matters of relevance to their respective committees.
53. The chairpersons welcome the suggestion by the chairperson of the Commission on Human Rights that treaty bodies should be consulted in relation to preparations for future "special dialogues" organized by the Commission.

B. *Public information*

54. The chairpersons welcome the offer by the Department of Public Information to transmit to each treaty body, through its respective secretariat, a dossier of media coverage of its work at both the national and international levels. They recommend that such dossiers be prepared on a regular basis.

C. *HIV/AIDS*

55. The chairpersons recommend that the treaty bodies pay closer attention to the situation of persons with HIV/AIDS, including women and children, during the examination of State reports.

D. *Cooperation with non-governmental organizations*

56. The chairpersons note the concerns and suggestions put forward by the non-governmental organizations and decide to bring them to the attention of their respective committees.

E. Documents and publications

57. The chairpersons warmly welcome the proposal of the Deputy High Commissioner for the preparation of a handbook for States parties which would present the core elements of treaty body "jurisprudence", in the broadest sense of the term. They urge the Office of the High Commissioner to prepare such a handbook, in consultation with the chairpersons.
58. In relation to efforts to promote compliance of States parties with their reporting obligations, as well as to promote universal ratification of the human rights treaties, the chairpersons recommend that OHCHR produce a document, on an annual basis, outlining the reporting history of States parties to the treaties.
59. The chairpersons fully endorse the proposal for OHCHR to publish a "human rights treaties series", each issue to be devoted to specific provisions of the treaties.

F. Recommendations of the joint meeting with the special procedures system

60. Subsequent to its general discussion, the joint meeting decided to adopt the following recommendations: the joint meeting emphasizes that the work of each group of mechanisms is equally important to the other. It also welcomes efforts made by OHCHR to make the documentation produced by both the treaty bodies and the special procedures of the Commission on Human Rights available to each mechanism and urges the intensification of such efforts. In particular, it urges OHCHR to institutionalize a system for drawing the attention of the different special procedures mandates to information of the treaty bodies relevant to their work, including observations on State party reports and views on individual cases.
61. It also encourages the treaty bodies to call, as they feel necessary, for the cooperation of the special procedures, including the possibility of a direct exchange of information during their sessions. It requests the Office of the High Commissioner to take steps to ensure the necessary funding for such cooperation.
62. In order to provide an opportunity to conduct more in-depth consultations and dialogue on areas of common concern, it is recommended that a full day of joint meetings be arranged for next year.

G. Regional meetings

63. The chairpersons reiterate their request made in previous reports that necessary steps be taken to enable the four human rights treaty bodies meeting only in Geneva to hold occasional sessions in New York, and for the Committee on the Elimination of Discrimination against Women to hold sessions in Geneva. They also reiterated their request to be enabled to meet, on occasion, at other United Nations regional offices.

H. Technical briefings

64. The chairpersons express appreciation for the revised proposal of the Secretariat on technical briefings that was requested at their tenth meeting. They agree in principle on the contents proposed, with the understanding

that the programme would be tailored in accordance with the specific requirements and methods of work of each treaty body.

I. *Coordination among treaty bodies*

65. The chairpersons agree that it would be useful to establish an ad hoc joint working group to explore the possibility of drafting possible common guidelines for State reports with regard to common provisions contained in several of the human rights treaties, consisting of designated members of the treaty bodies concerned. They call on OHCHR to take the necessary steps to organize meetings of such working group.

J. *Plan of Action for strengthening the implementation of the International Covenant on Civil and Political Rights, the International Convention on the Elimination of All Forms of Racial Discrimination and the Convention against Torture and Other Cruel, Inhuman or Degrading Treatment or Punishment*

66. The chairpersons welcome the revised draft Plan of Action, prepared by the Secretariat in consultation with the members of the three treaty bodies involved. They welcome the opportunity provided therein to develop and test new methods of work, to engage in closer cooperation among the six treaty bodies, as well as to strengthen the level of support provided to them. They therefore urge the High Commissioner for Human Rights to embark on consultations with members of all treaty bodies concerned, with a view to finalizing and launching the Plan of Action without delay.

K. *Human rights indicators*

67. The chairpersons note with interest the efforts being made by the Office of the High Commissioner for Human Rights to develop, in cooperation with its partners in the United Nations system, indicators that would make possible measurement of the level of enjoyment of all human rights. In this regard, they encourage the Office in these endeavours and express hope that they will lead to the development of useful tools for the human rights treaty bodies, among others.
68. In this regard, the chairpersons welcome the first such effort in the area of the right to education. They express full support for the proposal for OHCHR to organize a workshop of experts for the purpose of developing indicators to measure implementation of this right. They call upon the Office, in its preparations for this workshop, to cooperate closely with the Committee on Economic, Social and Cultural Rights.

L. *Corporate responsibility for human rights*

69. The chairpersons welcome the attention paid by the High Commissioner to the important issue of corporate responsibility for human rights and recommend that the treaty bodies consider what role, if any, they might play in this regard.

ANNEX I

Documents made available to the meeting

1. Provisional agenda and annotations (HRI/MC/1999/1)
2. Tentative programme of work
3. Activities profiles of treaty bodies
4. Reports of the ninth and tenth meetings of chairpersons (A/53/125 and A/53/432
5. Status of the international human rights instruments and the general situation of overdue reports: report of the Secretary-General (HRI/MC/1999/2 and Corr.1)
6. General Assembly resolution 53/138
7. Status of instruments: list of ratifications of the nine principal international human rights treaties
8. Report of the secretariat on follow-up to the recommendations of the tenth meeting of chairpersons (HRI/MC/1999/3)
9. Chart prepared by the secretariat on follow-up to the recommendations of the tenth meeting of chairpersons of the human rights treaty bodies
10. OHCHR/UNDP joint programme on "Human Rights Strengthening" (HURIST)
11. Annotated agenda and programme of work of the sixth meeting of special rapporteurs and representatives, experts and chairpersons of working groups of the special procedures system of the Commission on Human Rights and of the advisory services programme
12. Report of the fifth meeting of special rapporteurs and representatives, experts and chairpersons of working groups of the special procedures system of the Commission on Human Rights and of the advisory services programme, May 1998 (E/CN.4/1999/3 and addenda)
13. Preliminary conclusions of the International Law Commission on reservations to normative multilateral treaties including human rights treaties (A/52/10, chap. V.C)
14. Second report on reservations to treaties by the International Law Commission (A/CN.4/478/Rev.1)
15. Fourth report on reservations to treaties by the International Law Commission (A/CN.4/499)
16. Resolution 1997/41 of the Subcommission on Prevention of Discrimination and Protection of Minorities
17. Note by the secretariat on cost estimates associated with the possible organization of treaty body sessions in various regions requested by the eighth and tenth meetings of chairpersons (HRI/MC/1999/Misc.1)
18. Proposal of the secretariat for technical briefings for new members of treaty bodies (HRI/MC/1999/Misc.2)
19. Draft Plan of Action to strengthen the implementation of the International Covenant on Civil and Political Rights, the International Convention on the Elimination of All Forms of Racial Discrimination and the Convention against Torture and Other Forms of Cruel, Inhuman or Degrading Treatment or Punishment (HRI/MC/1999/Misc.3)
20. "Servicing the human rights treaty system", summary of a study by Ms. Anne Bayefsky (HRI/MC/1999/Misc.4)

21. Plan of Action to strengthen the implementation of the Convention on the Rights of the Child (CRC/SP/26)
22. Plan of Action to strengthen the implementation of the International Covenant on Economic, Social and Cultural Rights
23. Report of the secretariat on follow-up to the recommendations of the ninth meeting of chairpersons (HRI/MC/1998/4)
24. Proposal for the organization of a workshop on the development of indicators to assess the realization of the right to education, prepared by the Committee on Economic, Social and Cultural Rights
25. Background note prepared by the secretariat on the establishment of indicators/benchmarks to assess the realization of human rights (HRI/MC/1999/Misc.5)
26. Report on the expert seminar on "appropriate indicators to measure achievements in the progressive realization of economic, social and cultural rights" (A/CONF.157/PC.73)
27. Results of the twentieth session of the Committee on the Elimination of Discrimination against Women (E/CN.6/1999/CRP.1)
28. Draft resolution submitted by the Chairperson of the Open-ended Working Group on the Elaboration of a Draft Optional Protocol to the Convention on the Elimination of All Forms of Discrimination against Women (E/CN.6/1999/WG/L.3)

ANNEX II

Programme budget implications for the organization of technical briefings for members of human rights treaty bodies

1. The proposal for the organization of technical briefings for new members of treaty bodies assumes that the briefings would be held in association with a regularly scheduled session, normally on the Friday before the opening of the session. The only costs involved would therefore arise from the additional daily subsistence allowance (DSA) that members would be entitled to receive. In this scenario, that would amount to three additional days of DSA for each member participating in a briefing.
2. Assuming that half of the members of all treaty bodies are elected every two years, the maximum biennial costs involved would be as follows:

		(US dollars)
Committee on Economic, Social and Cultural Rights	9 members and chairperson (or designate)	8220
Human Rights Committee	9 members and chairperson (or designate)	8220
Committee against Torture	5 members and chairperson (or designate)	4932

Committee on the Elimination of Racial Discrimination	9 members and chairperson (or designate)	8220
Committee on the Rights of the Child	5 members and chairperson (or designate)	4932
Total maximum biennial costs		34 524

Appendix 8: Resolutions of the Commission on Human Rights relating to the Human Rights Treaties

Effective implementation of international instruments on human rights, including reporting obligations under international instruments on human rights

Commission on Human Rights Resolution 2000/75
adopted 26 April 2000

The Commission on Human Rights,

Taking note of General Assembly resolution 53/138 of 9 December 1998 and recalling its own resolution 1998/27 of 17 April 1998, as well as other relevant resolutions,

Reaffirming that the full and effective implementation of United Nations human rights instruments is of major importance to the efforts of the Organization, pursuant to the Charter of the United Nations and the Universal Declaration of Human Rights, to promote universal respect for and observance of human rights and fundamental freedoms,

Considering that the effective functioning of treaty bodies established pursuant to United Nations human rights instruments is indispensable for the full and effective implementation of such instruments,

Reiterating its concern about the large number of overdue reports under the United Nations human rights instruments, the increasing backlog of reports on the implementation by States parties and delays in consideration of reports by treaty bodies, as well as the lack of adequate resources, which impedes the effective functioning of the treaty bodies, including in regard to their ability to work in the applicable working languages,

Recalling that the effectiveness of the treaty bodies in encouraging the realization by States parties of their obligations under the United Nations human rights instruments requires constructive dialogue aimed at assisting States parties in identifying solutions to human rights problems and should be based on the reporting process supplemented by information from all relevant sources, which should be shared with all interested parties,

Conscious of the importance of coordination of the human rights promotion and protection activities of the United Nations system,

1. *Takes note with appreciation* of the report of the 10th meeting of the persons chairing the human rights treaty bodies (A/53/432), held at Geneva from 14 to 18 September 1998, and the holding of the 11th meeting at Geneva from 31 May to 4 June 1999, and takes note of the conclusions and recommendations of those meetings;

2. *Encourages* each treaty body to continue to give careful consideration to the relevant conclusions and recommendations contained in the reports of the meetings of the chairpersons of the human rights treaty bodies and, in this context, encourages enhanced cooperation and coordination between the human rights treaty bodies;
3. *Takes note with interest* of the report of the Secretary-General on implementation of international instruments on human rights, including reporting obligations under international instruments on human rights (E/CN.4/2000/106);
4. *Welcomes* the submission of comments by Governments, United Nations bodies and specialized agencies, non-governmental organizations and interested persons on the final report of the independent expert on enhancing the long-term effectiveness of the United Nations human rights treaty system (E/CN.4/1997/74) and the Secretary-General's report thereon (E/CN.4/2000/98);
5. *Notes with appreciation* the continuing attention given by the human rights treaty bodies, the chairpersons of those bodies, Governments, United Nations bodies and specialized agencies, the United Nations High Commissioner for Human Rights, non-governmental organizations and interested persons to the question of enhancing the long-term effectiveness of the United Nations human rights treaty system, including the final report of the independent expert and other contributions;
6. *Emphasizes* the need to ensure financing and adequate staff and information resources for the operations of the human rights treaty bodies and, with this in mind:
   (a) Reiterates its request that the Secretary-General provide adequate resources in respect of each treaty body, while making the most efficient use of existing resources, in order to give the human rights treaty bodies adequate administrative support and better access to technical expertise and relevant information;
   (b) Calls upon the Secretary-General to seek in the next biennium the resources within the United Nations regular budget necessary to give the human rights treaty bodies adequate administrative support and better access to technical expertise and relevant information;
   (c) Welcomes the plans of action prepared by the United Nations High Commissioner for Human Rights to enhance the resources available to all the human rights treaty bodies and thereby strengthen the implementation of these human rights treaties and encourages all Governments, United Nations bodies and specialized agencies, non-governmental organizations and interested persons to consider contributing to the appeal for extrabudgetary resources for the treaty bodies made by the United Nations High Commissioner for Human Rights until the regular budget funding meets their needs;
7. *Takes note* of the measures taken by each of the human rights treaty bodies to improve their functioning, as reflected in their respective annual reports, and encourages continuing efforts by the human rights treaty bodies and the Secretary-General to help improve the meeting of reporting obligations by States parties and to reduce the backlog in the consideration of reports by treaty bodies;
8. *Welcomes* the continuing efforts by the human rights treaty bodies and the

Secretary-General aimed at streamlining, rationalizing, rendering more transparent and otherwise improving reporting procedures, and encourages the Secretary-General, the treaty bodies and the next meeting of the chairpersons of the treaty bodies to continue to examine ways of reducing the duplication of reporting required under the different instruments, without impairing the quality of reporting, and of generally reducing the reporting burden on States parties, including through an ongoing examination of proposals for reports focused on a limited range of issues, the harmonization of the general guidelines regarding the form and content of reports, the possibility of consolidating overdue reports, the timing of consideration of reports and the methods of work of the treaty bodies;

9. *Urges* States parties to contribute, individually and collectively, such as through meetings of States parties, to identifying practical proposals and ideas for improving the functioning of the treaty bodies;

10. *Also urges* States parties to make every effort to meet their reporting obligations under United Nations human rights instruments;

11. *Reiterates* that a priority of the programme of advisory services and technical assistance of the Office of the United Nations High Commissioner for Human Rights should be to provide assistance to States parties, upon their request and, if possible, in coordination with other United Nations bodies, Governments and other interested parties in order to:
    (a) Assist those States in the process of ratifying United Nations human rights instruments;
    (b) Assist States with the implementation of their obligations under such instruments, including the preparation of their initial reports;

12. *Welcomes* the publication of the revised *Manual on Human Rights Reporting*, and requests the United Nations High Commissioner for Human Rights, in accordance with Economic and Social Council decision 1998/252 of 30 July 1998, to take the necessary measures to ensure the translation into all the official United Nations languages of the revised *Manual* as soon as possible;

13. *Also welcomes* the availability of documentation regarding the treaty bodies on the Website of the Office of the High Commissioner for Human Rights and urges the Secretary-General to ensure that United Nations practices concerning access to treaty information are consistent with Commission resolutions 1999/60 of 28 April 1998 on public information activities and 1999/64 of 28 April 1998 on human rights education;

14. *Invites* States parties that have not yet submitted their initial reports under United Nations human rights instruments to avail themselves, where necessary, of technical assistance for this purpose;

15. *Encourages* the human rights treaty bodies to continue to identify specific possibilities for technical assistance, to be provided at the request of the State concerned, in the regular course of their work of reviewing the periodic reports of States parties, and encourages States parties to consider carefully the concluding observations of the treaty bodies in identifying their needs for technical assistance;

16. *Urges* each State party whose report has been examined by a human rights treaty body to translate, publish and make available in its territory the full text of the concluding observations of the treaty body on its report and to provide adequate follow-up to those observations;

17. *Welcomes* the contribution to the work of the human rights treaty bodies made by the specialized agencies and other United Nations bodies and encourages the specialized agencies and other United Nations bodies, the Commission on Human Rights, including its special procedures, the Sub-Commission on the Promotion and Protection of Human Rights, the Office of the High Commissioner for Human Rights and the chairpersons of the human rights treaty bodies to continue to explore specific measures to intensify this cooperation among themselves and improve communication and information flow to improve further the quality of their work, including by avoiding unnecessary duplication;
18. *Recognizes* the important role played by non-governmental organizations in all parts of the world in the effective implementation of all human rights instruments, and encourages the exchange of information between the human rights treaty bodies and such organizations;
19. *Recalls*, with regard to the election of the members of the human rights treaty bodies, the importance of giving consideration to equitable geographical distribution and gender balance of membership and to the representation of the principal legal systems, and of bearing in mind that the members shall be elected and serve in their personal capacity and shall be of high moral character, acknowledged impartiality and recognized competence in the field of human rights, and encourages States parties, individually and through meetings of States parties, to consider how to give better effect to these principles;
20. *Welcomes* the continuing emphasis by the chairpersons of the human rights treaty bodies that the enjoyment of the human rights of women should be monitored closely by each treaty body within the purview of its mandate and, in this regard, takes note of the report of the Gender Integration Workshop (E/CN.4/2000/118) and the report of the Division for the Advancement of Women on trends regarding the integration of a gender perspective into the work of the United Nations human rights bodies (HRI/MC/1998/6);
21. *Also welcomes* the contribution of the human rights treaty bodies, within their mandates, to the prevention of violations of human rights, in the context of their consideration of reports submitted under their respective treaties;
22. *Encourages* the chairpersons of the human rights treaty bodies to pursue at their future meetings the reform process aimed at improving the effective implementation of international instruments on human rights;
23. *Requests* the Secretary-General to report to the Commission at its fifty-eighth session on measures taken to implement the present resolution and obstacles to its implementation, and on measures taken or planned to ensure financing and adequate staff and information resources for the effective operation of the human rights treaty bodies;
24. *Decides* to consider this question on a priority basis at its fifty-eighth session under the agenda item entitled "Effective functioning of bodies established pursuant to United Nations human rights instruments".

Status of International Covenants on Human Rights

Commission on Human Rights Resolution 2000/67
adopted 26 April 2000

The Commission on Human Rights,

Recalling General Assembly resolution 54/157 of 17 December 1999 and its own resolution 1998/9 of 3 April 1998,

Mindful that the International Covenants on Human Rights constitute the first all-embracing and legally binding international treaties in the field of human rights and, together with the Universal Declaration of Human Rights, form the core of the International Bill of Human Rights,

Having considered the reports of the Secretary-General on the status of the International Covenants on Human Rights (E/CN.4/2000/89) and on the status of withdrawals and reservations with respect to the International Covenants on Human Rights (E/CN.4/2000/96),

Recalling the International Covenant on Economic, Social and Cultural Rights and the International Covenant on Civil and Political Rights, and reaffirming that all human rights and fundamental freedoms are universal, indivisible, interdependent and interrelated and that the promotion and protection of one category of rights should never exempt or excuse States from the promotion and protection of the other rights,

Recognizing the important role of the Human Rights Committee and the Committee on Economic, Social and Cultural Rights in examining the progress made by States parties in implementing the obligations undertaken in the International Covenants on Human Rights and the Optional Protocols to the International Covenant on Civil and Political Rights and in providing recommendations to States parties on their implementation,

Recognizing also the importance of regional human rights instruments and their monitoring mechanisms for the promotion and protection of human rights which complement the universal system of human rights protection,

1. *Reaffirms* the importance of the International Covenants on Human Rights as major parts of international efforts to promote universal respect for and observance of human rights and fundamental freedoms;
2. *Appeals strongly* to all States that have not yet done so to become parties to the International Covenant on Economic, Social and Cultural Rights and the International Covenant on Civil and Political Rights, as well as to accede to the Optional Protocols to the International Covenant on Civil and Political Rights and to make the declaration provided for in article 41 of that Covenant;

3. *Invites* the United Nations High Commissioner for Human Rights to intensify systematic efforts to encourage States to become parties to the International Covenants on Human Rights and, through the programme of technical cooperation and advisory services in the field of human rights, to assist such States, at their request, in ratifying or acceding to the Covenants and to the Optional Protocols to the International Covenant on Civil and Political Rights;
4. *Emphasizes* the importance of the strictest compliance by States parties with their obligations under the International Covenant on Economic, Social and Cultural Rights and the International Covenant on Civil and Political Rights and, where applicable, the Optional Protocols to the International Covenant on Civil and Political Rights;
5. *Stresses* the importance of avoiding the erosion of human rights by derogation, and underlines the necessity of strict observance of the agreed conditions and procedures for derogation under article 4 of the International Covenant on Civil and Political Rights, bearing in mind the need for States parties to provide the fullest possible information during states of emergency so that the justification for the appropriateness of measures taken in those circumstances can be assessed;
6. *Also stresses* the importance of fully taking into account a gender perspective in the implementation of the International Covenants on Human Rights at the national level, including in the reports of States parties and in the work of the Human Rights Committee and the Committee on Economic, Social and Cultural Rights;
7. *Encourages* States parties to consider limiting the extent of any reservations they lodge to the International Covenants on Human Rights, to formulate any reservations as precisely and narrowly as possible and to ensure that no reservation is incompatible with the object and purpose of the relevant treaty or otherwise contrary to international law;
8. *Also encourages* States parties to review regularly any reservations made in respect of the provisions of the International Covenants on Human Rights and the Optional Protocols to the International Covenant on Civil and Political Rights with a view to withdrawing them;
9. *Takes note* of General Comments Nos. 27 and 28 adopted by the Human Rights Committee and General Comments Nos. 9, 10, 11, 12 and 13 adopted by the Committee on Economic, Social and Cultural Rights since the fifty-fourth session of the Commission;
10. *Urges States* parties to fulfil in good time such reporting obligations under the International Covenants on Human Rights as may be requested and to make use of gender-disaggregated data in their reports;
11. *Also urges* States parties to take duly into account, in implementing the provisions of the International Covenants on Human Rights, the observations made at the conclusion of the consideration of their reports by the Human Rights Committee and by the Committee on Economic, Social and Cultural Rights, as well as the views adopted by the Human Rights Committee under the Optional Protocol to the International Covenant on Civil and Political Rights;
12. *Invites* States parties to give particular attention to the dissemination at the national level of the reports they have submitted to the Human Rights Committee and the Committee on Economic, Social and Cultural Rights,

the summary records relating to the examination of those reports by the Committees and the observations made by the Committees at the conclusion of the consideration of the reports;

13. *Once again encourages* all Governments to publish the texts of the International Covenant on Economic, Social and Cultural Rights, the International Covenant on Civil and Political Rights and the Optional Protocols to the International Covenant on Civil and Political Rights in as many local languages as possible and to distribute them and make them known as widely as possible in their territories;

14. *Invites* the Human Rights Committee and the Committee on Economic, Social and Cultural Rights, when considering the reports of States parties, to continue to identify specific needs that might be addressed by United Nations departments, funds and programmes and the specialized agencies, including through the advisory services and technical assistance programme of the Office of the United Nations High Commissioner for Human Rights;

15. *Stresses* the need for improved coordination between relevant United Nations mechanisms and bodies in supporting States parties, upon their request, in implementing the International Covenants on Human Rights and the Optional Protocols to the International Covenant on Civil and Political Rights, and encourages continued efforts in this direction;

16. *Welcomes* Economic and Social Council decision 287 of 30 July 1999 approving the holding of two additional three-week extraordinary sessions of the Committee on Economic, Social and Cultural Rights, as well as respective pre-sessional working groups of one week's duration during the years 2000–2001 in order to reduce the backlog of reports;

17. *Welcomes* the efforts of the Human Rights Committee and the Committee on Economic, Social and Cultural Rights to improve the efficiency of their working methods and encourages them to continue to consider further ways and means to that end;

18. *Invites* States to continue to contribute, with practical proposals and ideas, to the dialogue on ways of improving the functioning of the Human Rights Committee and the Committee on Economic, Social and Cultural Rights;

19. *Welcomes* the continuing efforts of the Human Rights Committee and the Committee on Economic, Social and Cultural Rights to strive for uniform standards in the implementation of the provisions of the International Covenants on Human Rights, and appeals to other bodies dealing with similar human rights questions to respect those uniform standards, as expressed in the general comments of the Committees;

20. *Stresses* the need for further efforts towards developing indicators and benchmarks to measure progress in the realization of the rights set forth in the International Covenant on Economic, Social and Cultural Rights as well as the desirability of considering the issue of justiciability of economic, social and cultural rights in order to strengthen the enjoyment of these rights;

21. *Encourages* the Secretary-General to continue to assist States parties to the International Covenants on Human Rights in the preparation of their reports, including by convening seminars or workshops at the national level for the purpose of training government officials engaged in the preparation of such reports and by exploring other possibilities available under the regular programme of technical cooperation advisory services in the field of human rights;

22. *Requests* the Secretary-General to ensure that the Office of the United Nations High Commissioner for Human Rights effectively assists the Human Rights Committee and the Committee on Economic, Social and Cultural Rights in the implementation of their respective mandates, including by the provision of adequate Secretariat staff resources;
23. *Welcomes* the initiative by the Secretary-General, taking into account the suggestions of the Human Rights Committee, to take determined steps, in particular through the Department of Public Information of the Secretariat, to give more publicity to the work of that Committee and, similarly, to the work of the Committee on Economic, Social and Cultural Rights;
24. *Requests* the Secretary-General to submit to the Commission on Human Rights, at its fifty-seventh and fifty-eighth sessions, a report on the status of the International Covenant on Economic, Social and Cultural Rights, the International Covenant on Civil and Political Rights and the Optional Protocols to the International Covenant on Civil and Political Rights, including all reservations and declarations;
25. *Decides* to consider this question at its fifty-eighth session under the agenda item entitled "Status of the International Covenants on Human Rights".

Question of the realization in all countries of the economic, social and cultural rights contained in the Universal Declaration of Human Rights and in the International Covenant on Economic, Social and Cultural Rights, and study of special problems which the developing countries face in their efforts to achieve these human rights

Commission on Human Rights Resolution 2000/9
adopted 17 April 2000

The Commission on Human Rights,

Guided by the principles relating to economic, social and cultural rights enshrined in the Universal Declaration of Human Rights and the International Covenant on Economic, Social and Cultural Rights,

Recalling its previous resolutions on the realization of economic, social and cultural rights, including resolution 1998/33 of 17 April 1998, in which it decided, *inter alia* as part of its efforts to impart a higher visibility to economic, social and cultural rights, to appoint, for a period of three years, a special rapporteur whose mandate would focus on the right to education,

Taking note with interest of ongoing new approaches to the realization of economic, social and cultural rights, and considering that to ensure the fulfilment of economic, social and cultural rights, additional approaches should be examined,

I

1. *Notes with interest*:
    (a) The report of the Secretary-General on the implementation of resolution 1999/25 of 26 April 1999 (E/CN.4/2000/47), the report submitted to the Economic and Social Council by the High Commissioner for Human Rights pursuant to General Assembly resolution 48/141 of 20 December 1993 (E/1999/96), the report of the High Commissioner on the draft optional protocol to the International Covenant on Economic, Social and Cultural Rights (E/CN.4/2000/49), as well as all other relevant reports of the High Commissioner on economic, social and cultural rights and activities of intergovernmental and non-governmental organizations in that regard;
    (b) The unanimous adoption by the International Labour Conference, in July

1999, of Convention (No. 182) concerning the Prohibition and Immediate Action for the Elimination of the Worst Forms of Child Labour;
  (c) The work carried out by the Committee on Economic, Social and Cultural Rights, including the assistance given to States parties in the fulfilment of their obligations through its general comments No. 11 on plans of action for primary education, No. 12 on the right to adequate food, and No. 13 on the right to education;
  (d) The work of the Committee on the Rights of the Child in the promotion of economic, social and cultural rights of children;
  (e) The convening in March 1999 by the United Nations Centre for Human Settlements (Habitat)and the Office of the United Nations High Commissioner for Human Rights of an expert group meeting on practical aspects of the human right to adequate housing, which recommended, *inter alia*, the appointment of a special rapporteur on housing rights;
  (f) Efforts of the High Commissioner for Human Rights within the United Nations Development Group to promote economic, social and cultural rights;
  (g) The elaboration of training programmes in the Office of the High Commissioner for Human Rights to develop in-house expertise in incorporating economic, social and cultural rights in technical cooperation projects, and the inclusion of economic, social and cultural rights aspects in the Office's manuals and methodological materials for technical cooperation programmes and field activities;
2. *Welcomes* ongoing efforts by the Economic and Social Council and the General Assembly towards a coordinated follow-up to relevant United Nations world conferences and summits, notably the World Food Summit held in Rome in 1996, the second United Nations Conference on Human Settlements (Habitat II) held in Istanbul in 1996, the World Summit for Social Development, held in Copenhagen in 1995, the Fourth World Conference on Women, held in Beijing in 1995, the International Conference on Population and Development, held in Cairo in 1994 and the World Conference on Education for All, held in Jomtien, Thailand, in 1990, which should provide a rights-based framework for setting goals, outlining new approaches and developing supportive partnerships for the promotion and protection of all human rights, notably economic, social and cultural rights;
3. *Reaffirms*:
  (a) That, in accordance with the Universal Declaration of Human Rights, the ideal of free human beings enjoying freedom from fear and want can be achieved only if conditions are created whereby everyone may enjoy his or her economic, social and cultural rights, as well as his or her civil and political rights;
  (b) The inextricable link between full respect for the rights contained in the International Covenant on Economic, Social and Cultural Rights and the process of development, the central purpose of which is the realization of the potentialities of the human person with the effective participation of all members of society in relevant decision-making processes as agents and beneficiaries of development, as well as with a fair distribution of its benefits;
  (c) That all persons in all countries are entitled to the realization of their

economic, social and cultural rights, which are indispensable to their dignity and the free development of their personality;
  (d) The universality, indivisibility, interdependence and interrelatedness of all human rights and fundamental freedoms and that promoting and protecting one category of rights should therefore never exempt or excuse States from the promotion and protection of other rights;
  (e) The importance of international cooperation for the promotion and protection of all human rights, including economic, social and cultural rights;
  (f) That the realization of all human rights and fundamental freedoms, and particularly economic, social and cultural rights, is a dynamic process and that, as is evident in today's world, a great deal remains to be accomplished;
4. *Calls upon* all States:
  (a) To give full effect to economic, social and cultural rights;
  (b) To consider signing and ratifying, and the States parties to implement, the International Covenant on Economic, Social and Cultural Rights;
  (c) To consider ratifying, as soon as possible, and the States parties to fully implement the Convention (No. 182) concerning the Prohibition and Immediate Action for the Elimination of the Worst Forms of Child Labour of the International Labour Organization;
  (d) To guarantee that economic, social and cultural rights will be exercised without discrimination of any kind;
  (e) To secure progressively, through national development policies and with international assistance and cooperation, full realization of economic, social and cultural rights, giving particular attention to the individuals, most often women and children, especially girls, and communities living in extreme poverty and therefore most vulnerable and disadvantaged;
  (f) To consider in this context, as appropriate, the desirability of drawing up national action plans identifying steps to improve the situation of human rights in general with specific benchmarks designed to give effect to minimum essential levels of enjoyment of economic, social and cultural rights;
  (g) To help alleviate the unsustainable external debt burden of countries that meet the criteria of the highly indebted poor countries initiative, which should further strengthen the efforts of the Governments of these countries to realize economic, social and cultural rights, *inter alia* through the development and implementation of programmes such as the "Bolsa Escola" programme in Brazil, as well as the prevention of the spread of the HIV/AIDS pandemic in Africa and the reconstruction of countries affected by natural disasters;
  (h) To promote the effective and wide participation of representatives of civil society in decision-making processes related to the promotion and protection of economic, social and cultural rights;
5. *Calls upon* States parties to the International Covenant on Economic, Social and Cultural Rights:
  (a) To submit their reports to the Committee on Economic, Social and Cultural Rights in a regular and timely manner;
  (b) To promote a concerted national effort to ensure the participation of representatives of all sectors of civil society in the process of preparation of their periodic reports to the Committee on Economic, Social and

Cultural Rights and in the implementation of the recommendations of the Committee;
   (c) To withdraw reservations incompatible with the object and purpose of the Covenant and to consider reviewing other reservations with a view to withdrawing them;
6. *Recalls* that international cooperation in solving international problems of an economic, social and cultural character, and in promoting and encouraging respect for human rights and fundamental freedoms for all is one of the purposes of the United Nations and affirms that wider international cooperation would contribute to lasting progress in implementing economic, social and cultural rights;
7. *Decides*:
   (a) To encourage the Committee on Economic, Social and Cultural Rights to continue its efforts towards the promotion and protection of human rights at the national and international levels and the full realization of specific rights, notably through the drafting of further general comments, thus making the experience gained so far through the examination of States parties' reports available for the benefit of all States parties in order to assist and promote their further implementation of the Covenant;
   (b) To request the High Commissioner for Human Rights to invite all States, intergovernmental organizations and non-governmental organizations which have not yet done so to submit their comments on the report by the Committee on Economic, Social and Cultural Rights on a draft optional protocol for the consideration of communications in relation to the Covenant (E/CN.4/1997/105, annex), as well as to invite all States to submit their comments on the options relating to the proposal for a draft optional protocol, contained in her report on the draft optional protocol (E/CN.4/2000/49), or to propose any other option that would be conducive to a substantive dialogue, giving due regard to the respective roles of the Committee on Economic, Social and Cultural Rights and the Sub-Commission on the Promotion and Protection of Human Rights;
   (c) To appoint, for a period of three years, a special rapporteur whose mandate will focus on adequate housing as a component of the right to an adequate standard of living, as reflected in article 25, paragraph 1, of the Universal Declaration of Human Rights, article 11, paragraph 1, of the International Covenant on Economic, Social and Cultural Rights, and article 27, paragraph 3, of the Convention on the Rights of the Child, and on the right to non-discrimination as reflected in article 14 (h) of the Convention on the Elimination of All Forms of Discrimination against Women, and article 5 (e) of the International Convention on the Elimination of All Forms of Racial Discrimination;
   (d) To request the Special Rapporteur, in the fulfilment of her/his mandate:
      (i) To report on the status, throughout the world, of the realization of the rights that are relevant to the mandate, in accordance with the provisions of the relevant instrument, and on developments relating to these rights, including on laws, policies and good practices most beneficial to the enjoyment and difficulties and obstacles encountered domestically and internationally, taking into account information received from Governments, organizations and bodies of the United

Nations system, other relevant international organizations and non-governmental organizations;
 (ii) To promote, as appropriate, assistance to Governments in their efforts to progressively secure housing rights and to develop, wherever they do not exist, national strategies for the full realization of housing rights;
 (iii) To apply a gender perspective in her/his work and to propose particular measures in support of the housing rights of women;
 (iv) To develop a regular dialogue and discuss possible areas of collaboration with Governments, relevant United Nations bodies, specialized agencies, international organizations in the field of housing rights, *inter alia* the United Nations Centre for Human Settlements (Habitat), non-governmental organizations and international financial institutions, and to make recommendations on the realization of the rights relative to the mandate;
 (v) To identify possible types and sources of financing for advisory services and technical cooperation;
 (vi) To facilitate, where appropriate, the inclusion of issues relating to the mandate in relevant United Nations missions, field presences and national offices;
 (vii) To submit to the Commission on Human Rights an annual report covering the activities relating to the mandate;
(e) To request the High Commissioner for Human Rights to provide all the necessary resources for the effective fulfilment of the mandate of the Special Rapporteur;
(f) To encourage the High Commissioner for Human Rights to strengthen the research and analytical capacities of her Office in the field of economic, social and cultural rights, and to share her expertise *inter alia* through the holding of expert meetings;
(g) To encourage the High Commissioner for Human Rights to continue to ensure better support for the Committee on Economic, Social and Cultural Rights, in particular under the programme of action to strengthen the implementation of the International Covenant on Economic, Social and Cultural Rights (E/1997/22-E/C.12/1996/6, annex VII) adopted by the Committee at its fifteenth session;
(h) To encourage the High Commissioner for Human Rights to continue to provide or to facilitate practical support aimed at building capacities for the full realization of economic, social and cultural rights;
(i) To support the efforts carried out by the High Commissioner for Human Rights to implement the proposed programme of action designed to enhance the ability of the Committee on Economic, Social and Cultural Rights to assist interested Governments in their reporting obligations and its capacity to process and follow up the examination of States parties' reports and, accordingly, to request States parties to the International Covenant on Economic, Social and Cultural Rights to make voluntary financial contributions to ensure the adequate implementation of that programme of action;

II

8. *Notes with interest*:
   (a) The report of the Special Rapporteur on the right to education (E/CN.4/2000/6 and Add.1 and 2 and Corr.1);
   (b) The work of the Committee on the Rights of the Child in the promotion of the right to education;
   (c) The established cooperation between the Special Rapporteur and the Committee on Economic, Social and Cultural Rights and the Committee on the Rights of the Child;
   (d) The established dialogue with the World Bank to promote the right to education in its strategies;
9. *Welcomes*:
   (a) The focus given by the Special Rapporteur to the identification of obstacles to the realization of the right to education at the domestic and international levels, to the mainstreaming of gender and to the legal enforcement of the right to education;
   (b) The convening of the World Education Forum held in (Dakar from 26 to 28 April 2000 which constitutes the follow-up to the World Conference on Education for All), which should provide a rights-based framework for setting goals, outlining new approaches and developing supportive partnerships and reaffirm the need for primary education to be universal, compulsory and free of charge;
10. *Invites* the Special Rapporteur to continue to work in accordance with her mandate and notably to intensify her efforts to identify ways and means to overcome obstacles and difficulties in the realization of the right to education, notably through international cooperation;
11. *Calls upon* all States:
    (a) To give full effect to the right to education;
    (b) To guarantee that the right to education will be exercised without discrimination of any kind;
    (c) To cooperate with the Special Rapporteur;
12. *Decides*:
    (a) To request the Special Rapporteur on the right to education to submit a report to the Commission at its fifty-seventh session;
    (b) To reiterate its request to the High Commissioner for Human Rights to organize in 2001, the year of the twenty-fifth anniversary of the entry into force of the International Covenant on Economic, Social and Cultural Rights, a workshop to identify progressive developmental benchmarks and indicators related to the right to education, as set out in paragraph 6 (b) of resolution 1999/25 to 26 April 1999;
    (c) To reiterate its invitation to the United Nations Children's Fund and the United Nations Educational, Scientific and Cultural Organization to continue to develop a regular dialogue with the Special Rapporteur on the right to education and to submit to the Commission on Human Rights information pertaining to their activities in promoting primary education, with specific reference to women and children, particularly girls,
13. *Requests* the Secretary-General to provide the Special Rapporteur on the

right to education with all the assistance necessary for the execution of the mandate.

III

14. *Requests* the Secretary-General to submit to the Commission at its fifty-seventh session a report on the implementation of the present resolution.
15. *Recommends* the following draft decision to the Economic and Social Council for adoption:

"The Economic and Social Council, taking note of Commission on Human Rights resolution 2000/... of ... April 2000, endorses the Commission's decision to appoint, for a period of three years, a special rapporteur whose mandate will focus on aspects related to the right to adequate housing contained in the right to an adequate standard of living as reflected, *inter alia* in article 25, paragraph 1, of the Universal Declaration on Human Rights, article 11, paragraph 1, of the International Covenant on Economic, Social and Cultural Rights, article 14(h) of the Convention on the Elimination of All Forms of Discrimination against Women, article 27, paragraph 3, of the Convention on the Rights of the Child and article 5(e) of the International Convention on the Elimination of All Forms of Racial Discrimination, including the questions of secure tenure and forced evictions (housing rights). The Council also endorses the Commission's request to the United Nations High Commissioner for Human Rights to provide all the necessary resources for the effective fulfilment of the mandate of the Special Rapporteur."

Torture and other cruel, inhuman or degrading treatment or punishment

Commission on Human Rights Resolution 2000/43
adopted 20 April 2000

The Commission on Human Rights,

Reaffirming that no one should be subjected to torture or to cruel, inhuman or degrading treatment or punishment, that such actions constitute a criminal attempt to destroy a fellow human being physically and mentally, which can never be justified under any circumstances, by any ideology or by any overriding interest, and convinced that a society that tolerates torture can never claim to respect human rights,

Recalling that freedom from torture and cruel, inhuman or degrading treatment or punishment is a non-derogable right and that the prohibition of torture is explicitly affirmed in article 5 of the Universal Declaration of Human Rights, article 7 of the International Covenant on Civil and Political Rights, the Declaration on the Protection of All Persons from Being Subjected to Torture and Other Cruel, Inhuman or Degrading Treatment or Punishment and the Convention against Torture and Other Cruel, Inhuman or Degrading Treatment or Punishment, as well as in the relevant provisions of other international human rights instruments such as the Convention on the Rights of the Child, the Vienna Declaration and Programme of Action, the Declaration on the Elimination of All Forms of Violence against Women, the four Geneva Conventions of 1949 for the protection of war victims, and in the Rome Statute of the International Criminal Court,

Recalling also the definition of torture contained in article 1 of the Convention against Torture and Other Cruel, Inhuman or Degrading Treatment or Punishment,

Appalled at the widespread occurrence of torture and other cruel, inhuman or degrading treatment or punishment,

Recalling all relevant resolutions of the General Assembly, the Economic and Social Council and the Commission on Human Rights, in particular General Assembly resolution 51/86 of 12 December 1996 and Commission resolution 1999/32 of 26 April 1999 and General Assembly resolution 54/156 of 17 December 1999,

Mindful of the proclamation by the General Assembly, in its resolution 52/149 of 12 December 1997, of 26 June as United Nations International Day in Support of Victims of Torture,

Commending the persistent efforts by non-governmental organizations to combat torture and to alleviate the suffering of victims of torture,

1. *Calls upon* all Governments to implement fully the prohibition of torture and other cruel, inhuman or degrading treatment or punishment;
2. *Urges* all Governments to promote the speedy and full implementation of the Vienna Declaration and Programme of Action, in particular Part II, section B.5, relating to freedom from torture, in which it is stated that States should abrogate legislation leading to impunity for those responsible for grave violations of human rights such as torture and prosecute such violations, thereby providing a firm basis for the rule of law;
3. *Reminds* Governments that corporal punishment, including of children, can amount to cruel, inhuman or degrading punishment or even to torture;
4. *Condemns* all forms of torture, including through intimidation, as described in article 1 of the Convention against Torture and Other Cruel, Inhuman or Degrading Treatment or Punishment;
5. *Draws* the attention of Governments to the Principles on the effective investigation and documentation of torture and other cruel, inhuman or degrading treatment or punishment annexed to the present resolution, requests the Office of the High Commissioner for Human Rights to disseminate them widely, encourages Governments to reflect upon the Principles as a useful tool in efforts to combat torture and requests the Special Rapporteur, in the normal course of his work, to solicit views from Governments and non-governmental organizations thereon;
6. *Stresses in particular* that all allegations of torture or other cruel, inhuman or degrading treatment or punishment be promptly and impartially examined by the competent national authority, that those who encourage, order, tolerate or perpetrate acts of torture must be held responsible and severely punished, including the officials in charge of the place of detention where the prohibited act is found to have taken place, and that national legal systems should ensure that the victims of such acts obtain redress and are awarded fair and adequate compensation and receive appropriate socio-medical rehabilitation;
7. *Reminds* all States that prolonged incommunicado detention may facilitate the perpetration of torture and can in itself constitute a form of cruel, inhuman or degrading treatment, and urges all States to respect the safeguards concerning the liberty, security and dignity of the person;
8. *Calls upon* all Governments, the United Nations High Commissioner for Human Rights and United Nations bodies and agencies, as well as relevant intergovernmental and non-governmental organizations, to commemorate on 26 June the United Nations International Day in Support of Victims of Torture, this year with particular emphasis on reparation for torture victims;
9. *Takes note with appreciation* of the report of the Secretary-General on the status of the Convention against Torture and Other Cruel, Inhuman or Degrading Treatment or Punishment (E/CN.4/2000/59) and the ratifications and accessions to the Convention since the fifty-fifth session of the Commission;
10. *Urges* all States to become parties to the Convention against Torture as a matter of priority;
11. *Encourages* States parties to consider limiting the extent of any reservations

they lodge to the Convention against Torture, to formulate any reservations as precisely and narrowly as possible and to ensure that no reservation is incompatible with the object and purpose of the Convention;
12. *Also encourages* States parties to review regularly any reservations made in respect of the provisions of the Convention against Torture with a view to withdrawing them;
13. *Invites* all States ratifying or acceding to the Convention against Torture and those States parties that have not yet done so to make the declaration provided for in articles 21 and 22 of the Convention and to avoid making, or consider the possibility of withdrawing, reservations to article 20;
14. *Urges* States parties to notify the Secretary-General of their acceptance of the amendments to articles 17 and 18 of the Convention against Torture as soon as possible;
15. *Also urges* all States parties to comply strictly with their obligations in accordance with article 19 of the Convention against Torture, including their reporting obligations, and, in particular, those States parties whose reports are long overdue to submit their reports forthwith, and invites States parties to incorporate a gender perspective and information concerning children and juveniles when submitting reports to the Committee;
16. *Stresses* that under article 4 of the Convention against Torture acts of torture must be made an offence under domestic criminal law and that acts of torture during armed conflict are considered a grave breach of the Geneva Conventions of 1949, with the perpetrators liable to prosecution and punishment;
17. *Emphasizes* the obligation of States parties under article 10 of the Convention against Torture to ensure education and training for personnel who may be involved in the custody, interrogation or treatment of any individual subjected to any form of arrest, detention or imprisonment, and calls upon the United Nations High Commissioner for Human Rights, in conformity with her mandate established in General Assembly resolution 48/141 of 20 December 1993, to provide, at the request of Governments, advisory services in this regard, as well as technical assistance in the development, production and distribution of appropriate teaching material for this purpose;
18. *Stresses* in this context that States must not punish personnel referred to in the preceding paragraph for not obeying orders to commit acts amounting to torture or other cruel, inhuman or degrading treatment or punishment;
19. *Welcomes* the report of the Committee against Torture on its twenty-first and twenty-second sessions (A/54/44);
20. *Also welcomes* the work of the Committee against Torture and its practice of formulating concluding observations after the consideration of reports, as well as its practice of carrying out inquiries into cases where there are indications of the systematic practice of torture within the jurisdiction of States parties;
21. *Urges* States parties to take fully into account, in implementing the provisions of the Convention against Torture, the conclusions and recommendations made by the Committee against Torture at the end of its consideration of their reports;
22. *Requests* the Secretary-General to continue to submit to the Commission an annual report on the status of the Convention against Torture;

23. *Commends* the Special Rapporteur for his work as reflected in his report (E/CN.4/2000/9 and Add.1–5);
24. *Notes* the recommendations of the Special Rapporteur contained in his report, as well as the recommendations made in previous years, and encourages him to continue to include amongst his recommendations proposals on the prevention and investigation of torture, taking into account information received on training manuals and activities aimed at facilitating the practice of torture;
25. *Approves* the methods of work employed by the Special Rapporteur as set out in a previous report (E/CN.4/1997/4, annex), in particular with regard to urgent appeals, encourages him to continue to respond effectively to credible and reliable information that comes before him and invites him to continue to seek the views and comments of all concerned, including Governments, in the elaboration of his report;
26. *Invites* the Special Rapporteur to continue to consider questions concerning torture and other cruel, inhuman or degrading treatment or punishment directed against women and conditions conducive to such torture, to make appropriate recommendations concerning the prevention and redress of gender-specific forms of torture, including rape or any other form of sexual violence, and to exchange views with the Special Rapporteur on violence against women with a view to enhancing further their mutual cooperation;
27. *Also invites* the Special Rapporteur to continue to consider questions relating to the torture of children and conditions conducive to such torture and other cruel, inhuman or degrading treatment or punishment and to make appropriate recommendations concerning the prevention of such torture;
28. *Calls upon* all Governments to cooperate with and assist the Special Rapporteur on the question of torture in the performance of his task, to supply all necessary information requested by him and to react appropriately and expeditiously to his urgent appeals;
29. *Urges* those Governments that have not yet responded to communications transmitted to them by the Special Rapporteur to answer without further delay;
30. *Calls upon* all Governments to give serious consideration to the Special Rapporteur's requests to visit their countries and urges them to enter into a constructive dialogue with the Special Rapporteur with respect to the follow-up to his recommendations, so as to enable him to fulfil his mandate even more effectively;
31. *Requests* the Special Rapporteur to continue to consider inclusion of information in his report on the follow-up by Governments to his recommendations, visits and communications, including both improvements and problems encountered;
32. *Considers it desirable* that the Special Rapporteur continue to exchange views with the relevant human rights mechanisms and bodies, especially the Committee against Torture and the Office of the United Nations High Commissioner for Human Rights, in particular with a view to enhancing further their effectiveness and mutual cooperation, while avoiding unnecessary duplication with other special procedures, and that he should pursue cooperation with relevant United Nations programmes, notably that on crime prevention and criminal justice;

33. *Invites* the Special Rapporteur to present an interim report to the General Assembly at its fifty-fifth session on the overall trends and developments with regard to his mandate and a full report to the Commission at its fifty-seventh session, including all replies sent by Governments that are received in any of the official languages of the United Nations;
34. *Takes note* of the reports of the Secretary-General on the United Nations Voluntary Fund for Victims of Torture (A/54/177 and E/CN.4/2000/60 and Add.1);
35. *Expresses its appreciation* to the Board of Trustees of the United Nations Voluntary Fund for Victims of Torture for the work it has accomplished and to those Governments, organizations and individuals that have contributed to the Fund, and encourages them to continue to do so;
36. *Appeals* to all Governments, organizations and individuals to contribute annually to the Fund and preferably by 1 March before the annual meeting of the Board, if possible with a substantial increase in the contributions in order to take into consideration the ever-increasing requests for assistance;
37. *Stresses in particular* the increasing need for assistance to rehabilitation services for victims of torture and to small projects of humanitarian assistance to victims of torture;
38. *Requests* the Secretary-General to continue to include the Fund, on an annual basis, among the programmes for which funds are pledged at the United Nations Pledging Conference for Development Activities;
39. *Renews* its request to the Secretary-General to transmit to all Governments the appeals of the Commission for contributions to the Fund;
40. *Calls upon* the Board of Trustees of the Fund to report to the Commission at its fifty-seventh session and to present an updated assessment of the global need for international funding of rehabilitation services for victims of torture and of lessons learned from the activities of the Fund;
41. *Requests* the Secretary-General to continue to keep the Commission informed of the operations of the Fund on an annual basis;
42. *Urges* States parties whose arrears pre-date the provision made by the Secretary-General for funding the Committee against Torture from the regular budget to fulfil their obligations forthwith;
43. *Requests* the Secretary-General to ensure, within the overall budgetary framework of the United Nations, the provision of an adequate and stable level of staffing, as well as the necessary technical facilities for the United Nations bodies and mechanisms dealing with torture, in order to ensure their effective performance;
44. *Decides* to continue to consider these questions at its fifty-seventh session, as a matter of priority.

Annex

Principles on the effective investigation and documentation of torture and other cruel, inhuman or degrading treatment or punishment

1. The purposes of effective investigation and documentation of torture and other cruel, inhuman or degrading treatment (hereafter torture or other ill-treatment) include the following:

(i) Clarification of the facts and establishment and acknowledgement of individual and State responsibility for victims and their families;
(ii) Identification of measures needed to prevent recurrence;
(iii) Facilitating prosecution and/or, as appropriate, disciplinary sanctions for those indicated by the investigation as being responsible, and demonstrating the need for full reparation and redress from the State, including fair and adequate financial compensation and provision of the means for medical care and rehabilitation.

2. States shall ensure that complaints and reports of torture or ill-treatment shall be promptly and effectively investigated. Even in the absence of an express complaint, an investigation should be undertaken if there are other indications that torture or ill-treatment might have occurred. The investigators, who shall be independent of the suspected perpetrators and the agency they serve, shall be competent and impartial. They shall have access to, or be empowered to commission investigations by impartial medical or other experts. The methods used to carry out such investigations shall meet the highest professional standards, and the findings shall be made public.

3. (a) The investigative authority shall have the power and obligation to obtain all the information necessary to the inquiry.[1] The persons conducting the investigation shall have at their disposal all the necessary budgetary and technical resources for effective investigation. They shall also have the authority to oblige all those acting in an official capacity allegedly involved in torture or ill-treatment to appear and testify. The same shall apply to any witness. To this end, the investigative authority shall be entitled to issue summonses to witnesses, including any officials allegedly involved, and to demand the production of evidence.

(b) Alleged victims of torture or ill-treatment, witnesses, those conducting the investigation and their families shall be protected from violence, threats of violence or any other form of intimidation that may arise pursuant to the investigation. Those potentially implicated in torture or ill-treatment shall be removed from any position of control or power, whether direct or indirect, over complainants, witnesses and their families, as well as those conducting the investigation.

4. Alleged victims of torture or ill-treatment and their legal representatives shall be informed of, and have access to any hearing as well as to all information relevant to the investigation, and shall be entitled to present other evidence.

5. (a) In cases in which the established investigative procedures are inadequate because of insufficient expertise or suspected bias, or because of the apparent existence of a pattern of abuse, or for other substantial reasons, States shall ensure that investigations are undertaken through an independent commission of inquiry or similar procedure. Members of such a commission shall be chosen for their recognized impartiality, competence and independence as individuals. In particular, they shall be independent of any suspected perpetrators and the institutions or agencies they may serve. The commission shall have the authority to obtain all information

---

[1] Under certain circumstances, professional ethics may require information to be kept confidential. These requirements should be respected.

necessary to the inquiry and shall conduct the inquiry as provided for under these Principles.[1]
- (b) A written report, made within a reasonable time, shall include the scope of the inquiry, procedures and methods used to evaluate evidence as well as conclusions and recommendations based on findings of fact and on applicable law. On completion, this report shall be made public. It shall also describe in detail specific events that were found to have occurred, the evidence upon which such findings were based, and list the names of witnesses who testified with the exception of those whose identities have been withheld for their own protection. The State shall, within a reasonable period of time, reply to the report of the investigation and, as appropriate, indicate steps to be taken in response.

6. (a) Medical experts involved in the investigation of torture or ill-treatment should behave at all times in conformity with the highest ethical standards and in particular shall obtain informed consent before any examination is undertaken. The examination must conform to established standards of medical practice. In particular, examinations shall be conducted in private under the control of the medical expert and outside the presence of security agents and other government officials.
- (b) The medical expert should promptly prepare an accurate written report. This report should include at least the following:
   - (i) Circumstances of the interview: name of the subject and name affiliation of those present at the examination; the exact time and date; the location, nature and address of the institution (including, where appropriate, the room) where the examination is being conducted (e.g. detention centre, clinic, house, etc.); the circumstances of the subject at the time of the examination (e.g. nature of any restraints on arrival or during the examination, presence of security forces during the examination, demeanour of those accompanying the prisoner, threatening statements to the examiner, etc.); and any other relevant factor;
   - (ii) History: a detailed record of the subject's story as given during the interview, including alleged methods of torture or ill-treatment, the times when torture or ill-treatment is alleged to have occurred and all complaints of physical and psychological symptoms;
   - (iii) Physical and psychological examination: a record of all physical and psychological findings on clinical examination including appropriate diagnostic tests and, where possible, colour photographs of all injuries;
   - (iv) Opinion: an interpretation as to the probable relationship of the physical and psychological findings to possible torture or ill-treatment. A recommendation for any necessary medical and psychological treatment and/or further examination should be given;
   - (v) Authorship: the report should clearly identify those carrying out the examination and should be signed.
- (c) The report should be confidential and communicated to the subject or

---

[1] Under certain circumstances, professional ethics may require information to be kept confidential. These requirements should be respected.

his or her nominated representative. The views of the subject and his or her representative about the examination process should be solicited and recorded in the report. It should also be provided in writing, where appropriate, to the authority responsible for investigating the allegation of torture or ill-treatment. It is the responsibility of the State to ensure that it is delivered securely to these persons. The report should not be made available to any other person, except with the consent of the subject or on the authorization of a court empowered to enforce such transfer.

Draft optional protocol to the Convention against Torture and Other Cruel, Inhuman or Degrading Treatment or Punishment

Commission on Human Rights Resolution 2000/35
adopted 20 April 2000

The Commission on Human Rights,

Recalling its resolution 1992/43 of 3 March 1992, in which it established an open-ended working group to elaborate a draft optional protocol to the Convention against Torture and Other Cruel, Inhuman or Degrading Treatment or Punishment, using as a basis for its discussions the draft text proposed by the Government of Costa Rica at the forty-seventh session of the Commission (E/CN.4/1991/66), and decided to consider the question at its forty-ninth session,

Recalling also the subsequent resolutions on the subject and in particular decision 1999/237 of 27 July 1999 of the Economic and Social Council, in which the Council authorized the working group to meet in order to continue its work,

Recalling further that the World Conference on Human Rights firmly declared that efforts to eradicate torture should, first and foremost, be concentrated on prevention and called for the early adoption of an optional protocol to the Convention against Torture and Other Cruel, Inhuman or Degrading Treatment or Punishment, which is intended to establish a preventive system of regular visits to places of detention,

1. *Takes note* of the report of the working group on the draft optional protocol to the Convention against Torture and Other Cruel, Inhuman or Degrading Treatment or Punishment (E/CN.4/2000/58);
2. *Requests* the working group, in order to continue its work, to meet prior to the fifty-seventh session of the Commission for a period of two weeks, with a view to completing expeditiously a final and substantive text, and to report to the Commission at its fifty-seventh session;
3. *Requests* the Secretary-General to transmit the report of the working group to all Governments, the specialized agencies, the chairpersons of the human rights treaty bodies and intergovernmental and non-governmental organizations, and to invite them to submit their comments to the working group;
4. *Also requests* the Secretary-General to invite Governments, the specialized agencies and relevant intergovernmental and non-governmental organizations, as well as the Chairperson of the Committee against Torture and the Special Rapporteur on the question of torture, to participate if needed in the activities of the working group;
5. *Further requests* the Secretary-General to extend all necessary facilities to the

working group for its meeting prior to the fifty-seventh session of the Commission;

6. *Encourages* the Chairman-Rapporteur of the working group to conduct informal inter-sessional consultations with all interested parties in order to facilitate the completion of a consolidated text;
7. *Decides* to examine the report of the working group at its fifty-seventh session under the same sub-item;
8. *Recommends* the following draft decision to the Economic and Social Council for adoption:

"The Economic and Social Council, taking note of Commission on Human Rights resolution 2000/35 of April 2000:

(a) Authorizes the open-ended working group of the Commission on Human Rights to meet for a period of two weeks, prior to the fifty-seventh session of the Commission, in order to continue or conclude the elaboration of a draft optional protocol to the Convention against Torture and Other Cruel, Inhuman or Degrading Treatment or Punishment;
(b) Encourages the Chairman-Rapporteur of the working group to conduct informal inter-sessional consultations with all interested parties in order to facilitate the completion of a consolidated text."

Rights of the child

Commission on Human Rights Resolution 2000/85
adopted 27 April 2000

The Commission on Human Rights,

Bearing in mind the Convention on the Rights of the Child, emphasizing that the provisions of the Convention on the Rights of the Child and other relevant human rights instruments must constitute the standard in the promotion and protection of the rights of the child, and reaffirming that the best interest of the child shall be the primary consideration in all actions concerning children,

Reaffirming its resolution 1999/80 of 28 April 1999 and General Assembly resolutions 54/149 and 54/148 of 17 December 1999, as well as all previous resolutions on this subject,

Welcoming the tenth. anniversary of the entry into force of the Convention on the Rights of the Child, which constitutes an occasion for the renewal of commitment to the rights of the child,

Welcoming also the preparatory process for the special session of the General Assembly to be convened in 2001 in the follow-up to the World Summit for Children and encouraging States to participate actively therein in order to promote an effective review of progress made, as well as the identification of obstacles affecting the full implementation of the outcome of the World Summit for Children, as a reaffirmation of their commitment to children, and encouraging the establishment of forward-looking strategies,

Reaffirming the Declaration and Plan of Action adopted by the World Summit for Children in 1990 (A/45/625, annex) and the Vienna Declaration and Programme of Action adopted by the World Conference on Human Rights in June 1993 (A/CONF.157/23), which, *inter alia*, states that national and international mechanisms and programmes for the safeguard and protection of children, in particular those in especially difficult circumstances, should be strengthened, including through effective measures to combat exploitation and abuse of children, female infanticide, harmful child labour, sale of children and organs, child prostitution and child pornography, as well as other forms of sexual abuse, and which reaffirms that all human rights and fundamental freedoms are universal,

Profoundly concerned that the situation of children in many parts of the world remains critical as a result of poverty, inadequate social and economic conditions in an increasingly globalized world economy, pandemics, natural disasters, armed conflicts, displacement, exploitation, illiteracy, hunger, intolerance, disability and inadequate legal protection, and convinced that urgent and effective national and international action is called for,

Alarmed by the reality of daily violations of children's rights, including the right to life, to physical security and to freedom from arbitrary detention, torture and any form of exploitation, as laid out in relevant international instruments,

Reaffirming that the family is the fundamental group of society and the natural environment for the growth and well-being of the children and recognizing that the child should grow up in a family, environment and social atmosphere of happiness, love and understanding,

Concerned at the number of illegal adoptions, of children growing up without parents and of child victims of family and social violence, neglect and abuse,

Reaffirming the importance of access by children to the highest attainable standard of social services, which are an integral part of, and contribute positively to, social and economic development and recognizing that the primary responsibility for ensuring provision of and universal access to social services rests with Governments, and that international cooperation to enhance social development would facilitate the provision of basic services for all,

Calling for the further mainstreaming of a gender perspective in all policies and programmes relating to children,

Reaffirming the fundamental principle set forth in the Vienna Declaration and Programme of Action and in the Beijing Declaration and Platform for Action that the human rights of women and girls are an inalienable, integral and indivisible part of universal human rights,

Welcoming the adoption by the Commission on Human Rights in resolution 2000/59 of 26 April 2000, of a draft optional protocol to the Convention on the Rights of the Child on the sale of children, child prostitution and child pornography and of a draft optional protocol to the Convention on the Rights of the Child on the involvement of children in armed conflicts, which develop the principles and provisions of the Convention on the Rights of the Child and represent an important step towards improving the standards of protection accorded to children,

Welcoming also the unanimous adoption in June 1999 of the International Labour Organization Convention (No. 182) on the Prohibition and Immediate Action for the Elimination of the Worst Forms of Child Labour and reaffirming the right of the child to be protected from economic exploitation and from performing any work that is likely to be hazardous or to interfere with the child's education, or to be harmful to the child's health or physical, mental, spiritual, moral or social development, in accordance with obligations under the Convention on the Rights of the Child and the aim of effective abolition of child labour contrary to accepted international standards, giving priority to immediate and concrete action for the elimination of the worst forms of child labour and to the rehabilitation and social reintegration of the children concerned, as well as to the search for alternatives to child labour and for a better socio-economic environment to prevent child labour,

Reaffirming the need for States to ensure that every child alleged to have or recognized as having infringed the penal law is treated with dignity in accordance with their obligations under the Convention on the Rights of the Child and other relevant international human rights instruments, including the International Covenant on Civil and Political Rights, and expressing deep concern *inter alia* about cases of children prosecuted without account being taken of their special needs, kept in arbitrary detention, subjected to torture or cruel, inhuman or degrading treatment or punishment or subjected to punishment contrary to accepted international standards,

Reaffirming also the obligation of States to protect children from torture, other cruel, inhuman or degrading treatment or punishment, and other forms of abuse welcoming the decision of the Committee on the Rights of the Child to devote a theme day during its twenty-fifth session to "State violence against children",

Noting with appreciation the commemorative meeting on the tenth anniversary of the Convention on the Rights of the Child held jointly by the Committee on the Rights of the Child and the Office of the United Nations High Commissioner for Human Rights, and taking note of the decision of the Committee to adopt a general comment on child participation as envisaged in the Convention, bearing in mind that participation includes, but is not limited to, consultation and proactive initiatives by children and youth themselves,

Welcoming the proclamation by the General Assembly of the International Decade for a Culture of Peace and Non-Violence for the Children of the World (2001–2010) and the Declaration and Programme of Action of Culture of Peace, which serve as the basis for the International Decade,

Welcoming also the ongoing implementation by the United Nations Children's Fund of the human rights-based approach in fulfilling its mandate to promote the rights of the child, including through its medium-term plan and encouraging the organization to continue to derive lessons and identify best practices from this process,

Welcoming further the development of a global strategic framework on young people and HIV/AIDS, based on a rights approach, initiated by the Joint United Nations Programme on HIV/AIDS working in partnership with the UNAIDS co-sponsors and in consultation with relevant parts of the United Nations system,

Recognizing that partnership between Governments, international organizations and all sectors of civil society, in particular non-governmental organizations, as well as the private sector, is important to realizing the rights of the child,

Stressing the importance of integrating child-related issues into the work of the World Conference against Racism, Racial Discrimination, Xenophobia and Related Intolerance to be held in the year 2001,

I

Implementation of the Convention on the Rights of the Child

1. *Welcomes* the report of the Secretary-General on the status of the Convention on the Rights of the Child (E/CN.4/2000/70);
2. *Urges once again* those States that have not yet done so to positively consider signing and ratifying or acceding to the Convention as a matter of priority having in mind the tenth anniversary of the entry into force of the Convention on the Rights of the Child;
3. *Welcomes* the unprecedented number of 191 States that have ratified or

acceded to the Convention on the Rights of the Child, as an indication of the universal commitment to the rights of the child;

4. *Calls upon* States parties to implement the Convention fully and to ensure that the rights set forth in the Convention are respected without discrimination of any kind, that the best interests of the child are a primary consideration in all actions concerning children, and that children are able to express their opinions on matters affecting them and that these opinions are listened to and given due weight;

5. *Also calls upon* States parties to assure to the child who is capable of forming his or her own views the right to express those views freely in all matters affecting the child, the views being given due weight in accordance with the age and maturity of the child;

6. *Urges* States parties to withdraw reservations incompatible with the object and purpose of the Convention and to consider reviewing other reservations with a view to withdrawing them;

7. *Calls upon* States parties:
    (a) To accept, as a matter of priority, the amendment to paragraph 2, article 43, of the Convention;
    (b) To comply in a timely manner with their reporting obligations under the Convention, in accordance with the guidelines elaborated by the Committee on the Rights of the Child, as well as to take into account the recommendations made by the Committee in the implementation of the provisions of the Convention and to strengthen their cooperation with the Committee;

8. *Welcomes* the role of the Committee on the Rights of the Child in examining the progress made by States parties in implementing the obligations undertaken in the Convention, and in providing recommendations to States parties on its implementation and, in cooperation with the Office of the United Nations High Commissioner for Human Rights, in creating awareness of the principles and provisions of the Convention;

9. *Calls upon* States parties to ensure when electing the members of the Committee on the Rights of the Child in accordance with article 43 of the Convention, that the members are of high moral standing and recognized competence in the field covered by the Convention, serving in their personal capacity, consideration being given to equitable geographical distribution, as well as to the principal legal systems;

10. *Calls upon* States to strengthen efforts to improve national systems for the collection of comprehensive and disaggregated data, including gender-specific data, for all areas covered by the Convention on the Rights of the Child;

11. *Reaffirms* the importance of ensuring adequate and systematic training in the rights of the child for professional groups working with and for children, *inter alia*, specialized judges, law enforcement officials, lawyers, social workers, medical doctors and teachers, and coordination between various governmental bodies involved in children's rights;

12. *Urges* States to take all appropriate measures for the implementation of their obligations under the Convention on the Rights of the Child, bearing in mind article 4 of the Convention:

13. *Recommends* that, within their mandates, all relevant human rights mechanisms, in particular special rapporteurs and working groups, and all other

relevant organs and mechanisms of the United Nations system and the specialized agencies, regularly and systematically take a child's rights perspective into account in the implementation of their mandates, especially by paying attention to particular situations in which children are in danger and where their rights are violated, and that they take into account the work of the Committee on the Rights of the Child;
14. *Decides*, with regard to the Committee on the Rights of the Child, to request to the Secretary-General to ensure the provision of appropriate staff and facilities from the United Nations regular budget for the effective and expeditious performance of the functions of the Committee, while noting the temporary support given by the Plan of Action of the United Nations High Commissioner for Human Rights to strengthen the implementation of the Convention on the Rights of the Child and invites the Committee to continue to enhance its constructive dialogue with the States parties and its transparent and effective functioning;

II

Protection and promotion of rights of children

Identity, family relations and birth registration
15. *Calls upon* all States:
    (a) To intensify efforts to ensure the registration of all children immediately after birth, including by the consideration of simplified, expeditious and effective procedures;
    (b) To undertake to respect the right of the child to preserve his or her identity, including nationality, name and family relations as recognized by law without unlawful interference and, where a child is illegally deprived of some or all of the elements of his or her identity, to provide appropriate assistance and protection with a view to re-establishing speedily his or her identity;
    (c) To ensure, as far as possible, the right of the child to know and be cared for by his or her parents;
    (d) To ensure that a child shall not be separated from his or her parents against their will, except when the competent authorities, subject to judicial review, determine, in accordance with applicable law and procedures, that such separation is necessary for the best interest of the child; such determination may be necessary in a particular case, such as one involving abuse or neglect of the child by the parents, or one where the parents are living separately and a decision must be made as to the child's place of residence.

Health
16. *Calls upon* all States:
    (a) And relevant bodies and organizations of the United Nations system, in particular the World Health Organization, to pay particular attention to the development of sustainable health systems and social services to ensure the effective prevention of diseases, malnutrition, disabilities and

infant and child mortality, including through prenatal and postnatal health care, as well as the provision of necessary medical treatment and health care to all children, taking into consideration the special needs of young children, including prevention of common infectious diseases, the special needs of adolescents, including relating to reproductive and sexual health and threats from substance abuse and violence, and the particular needs of children living in poverty, children in situations of armed conflict and vulnerable groups;

(b) And relevant bodies and organizations of the United Nations system, in particular the World Health Organization, to continue to promote education and training of health professionals and other relevant health-related workers in human rights, in particular the rights of the child and the human rights of women and girls;

(c) To adopt all necessary measures to ensure the full and equal enjoyment of all human rights and fundamental freedoms by children affected by disease and malnutrition, including protection from all forms of discrimination, abuse or neglect, in particular in access to and the provision of health care;

17. *Encourages* the Committee on the Rights of the Child to continue to give attention to the realization of the highest attainable standard of health and access to health care, and takes note of the recommendations adopted on HIV/AIDS;

18. *Urges* Governments to take all necessary measures to protect children infected and/or affected by HIV/AIDS from all forms of discrimination, stigma, abuse and neglect, in particular in the access to and provision of health, education and social services;

19. *Calls upon* the international community, relevant United Nations agencies, funds and programmes and intergovernmental and non-governmental organizations;

(a) To give importance also to the treatment and rehabilitation of children infected with HIV/AIDS and invites them to consider further involving the private sector;

(b) To intensify their support of national efforts against HIV/AIDS aimed at providing assistance to children infected or affected by the epidemic, focusing particularly on the worst-hit regions of Africa and where the epidemic is severely setting back national development gains;

Education

20. *Calls upon* States:

(a) To recognize the right to education on the basis of equal opportunity by making primary education compulsory and ensuring that all children have access to free and relevant primary education, as well as making secondary education generally available and accessible to all, and in particular by the progressive introduction of free education;

(b) Which have not been able to secure compulsory primary education, free of charge, to work out and adopt a detailed plan of action for the progressive implementation of the principle of compulsory education free of charge for all;

(c) To ensure that emphasis is given to the qualitative aspects of education, that the education of the child is carried out and that States parties develop and implement programmes for the education of the child, in accordance with articles 28 and 29 of the Convention on the Rights of the Child, and that education is directed, *inter alia*, to the development of respect for human rights and fundamental freedoms and to the preparation of the child for a responsible life in a free society, in a spirit of understanding, peace, tolerance, gender equality and friendship among peoples, ethnic, national and religious groups, and persons of indigenous origin;

(d) To take all appropriate measures to prevent racist, discriminatory and xenophobic attitudes and behaviour, through education, keeping in mind the important role that children have to play in changing these practices;

(e) To remove educational disparities and make education accessible to children living in poverty, children living in remote areas, children with special educational needs and children requiring special protection, including refugee children, migrant children, street children, children deprived of their liberty, indigenous children and children belonging to minorities;

(f) And educational institutions and the United Nations system, in particular the United Nations Children's Fund, the United Nations Development Fund for Women and the United Nations Educational, Scientific and Cultural Organization, to develop and implement gender-sensitive strategies to address the particular needs of the girl child in education;

21. *Encourages* all relevant actors to strengthen action at the national, regional and international levels, particularly through education, to:
   (i) Ensure that children, from an early age, benefit from education on values, attitudes, modes of behaviour and ways of life to enable them to resolve any dispute peacefully and in a spirit of respect for human dignity and of tolerance and non-discrimination;
   (ii) Involve children in activities for instilling in them the values and goals of a culture of peace;

Freedom from violence

22. *Reaffirms* the obligation of States to protect children from torture and other cruel, inhuman or degrading treatment or punishment;

23. *Calls upon* States:
   (a) To take all appropriate national, bilateral and multilateral measures to prevent all forms of violence against children and to protect them from torture and other forms of violence, including physical, mental and sexual violence, abuse by the police, other law enforcement authorities or employees in juvenile detention centres or orphanages and domestic violence;
   (b) To investigate and submit cases of torture and other forms of violence against children to the competent authorities for the purpose of prosecution and to impose appropriate disciplinary or penal sanctions against those responsible for such practices;

24. *Requests* all relevant human rights mechanisms, in particular special rapporteurs and working groups, within their mandates, to pay attention to the special situations of violence against children, reflecting their experiences in the field;

III

Non-discrimination

25. *Reaffirms* the obligation of States to ensure the rights of the child without discrimination of any kind, irrespective of the child's or his or her parent's or legal guardian's race, colour, sex, language, religion, political or other opinion, national, ethnic or social origin, property, disability, birth or other status, and to take all appropriate measures to ensure that the child is protected against all forms of discrimination;

The girl child

26. *Reaffirms* General Assembly resolutions 54/148 on the girl child, and 54/133 on traditional practices affecting the health of women and the girl child of 17 December 1999, and takes note of resolution 1999/13 of 25 August 1999 on traditional practices affecting the health of women and the girl child, adopted by the Sub-Commission on the Promotion and Protection of Human Rights;
27. *Calls upon* all States:
    (a) To take all necessary measures and to institute legal reforms to ensure the full and equal enjoyment by girls of all human rights and fundamental freedoms, to take effective actions against violations of those rights and freedoms and to base programmes and policies for the girl child on the rights of the child and women;
    (b) And non-governmental organizations, individually and collectively, to set goals and to develop and effectively implement gender-sensitive strategies to address the rights and needs of children, in accordance with the Convention on the Rights of the Child, especially the rights and particular needs of girls in education, health and nutrition, and to eliminate harmful traditional or customary attitudes and practices against girls;
    (c) To eliminate all forms of discrimination against girls and the root causes of son preference, which result in harmful and unethical practices, *inter alia*, by enacting and enforcing legislation and where appropriate formulating comprehensive, multidisciplinary and coordinated national plans, programmes or strategies protecting girls from violence, including female infanticide and prenatal sex selection, genital mutilation, incest, rape, domestic violence, sexual abuse and exploitation, and by developing age-appropriate, safe and confidential programmes and medical, social and psychological support services to assist girls who are subjected to violence;
    (d) To eradicate traditional or customary practices, particularly female genital mutilation, that are harmful to or discriminatory against women and girls and that are violations of human rights and fundamental freedoms of women and girls through the development and implementation of legislation and policies prohibiting such practices, the prosecution of perpetrators of such practices, and awareness-raising programmes, education and training, involving, among others, leaders of public opinion, educators, religious leaders, medical practitioners, women's health and family planning organizations, the media, parents and young people, in

order to achieve the total elimination of these practices, and to support women's organizations at the national and local levels that are working for the elimination of female genital mutilation and other harmful traditional or customary practices violating the human rights of women and girls;

(e) To enact and enforce strictly laws to ensure that marriage is entered into only with the free and full consent of the intending spouses, to enact and to enforce strictly laws concerning the minimum legal age of consent and the minimum age for marriage and to raise the minimum age for marriage where necessary;

28. *Urges* the Office of the United Nations High Commissioner for Human Rights to provide administrative assistance to the Special Rapporteur on traditional practices affecting the health of women and the girl child of the Sub-Commission on the Promotion and Protection of Human Rights to enable her to proceed with her work;

Children with disabilities
29. *Calls upon* all States:
    (a) To adopt all necessary measures to ensure the full and equal enjoyment of all human rights and fundamental freedoms by children with disabilities and to develop policy measures and to develop and enforce legislation prohibiting discrimination against children with disabilities;
    (b) To adopt an integrated approach to providing adequate support and appropriate education for children with disabilities and their parents, in a manner which promotes the child's achievement of self-reliance and the fullest possible social integration, individual development and active participation in the community;

Migrant children
30. *Also calls upon* States:
    (a) To protect all the human rights of migrant children, in particular unaccompanied migrant children, and ensure that the best interests of the child shall accordingly be a primary consideration, and encourages the Committee on the Rights of the Child, the United Nations Children's Fund and other relevant United Nations bodies, within their respective mandates, to pay particular attention to the conditions of migrant children, and as appropriate, make recommendations to strengthen their protection;
    (b) To cooperate fully with and assist the Special Rapporteur on migrants, in order to address the particular vulnerable conditions of migrant children;

IV

Protection and promotion of the rights of children in particularly vulnerable situations

Children working and/or living on the street
31. *Further calls upon* all States:
    (a) To examine and devise comprehensive economic and social solutions, at

the national and international levels, to the problems causing children to work and/or to live on the street;
(b) To adopt, promote and implement appropriate programmes and policies for the protection and the rehabilitation and reintegration of these children, taking into account that such children are particularly vulnerable to all forms of violence, abuse, exploitation and neglect, especially the girl child;
(c) To ensure that services are provided for children to divert them from, and address the economic imperatives for, involvement in harmful, exploitative and abusive activity;
(d) To recognize the right to education by making primary education compulsory, to ensure that all children have access to free primary education as a key strategy to prevent children working on the street, recognizing in particular the important role of the United Nations Educational, Scientific and Cultural Organization and the United Nations Children's Fund in this regard, to recognize that primary education is one of the main instruments for reintegrating child workers and to implement and develop programmes designed to integrate working children into the formal education sector;
(e) To take the situation of children working and/or living on the street into account when preparing reports to the Committee on the Rights of the Child, and encourages the Committee and other relevant bodies and organizations of the United Nations system, within their existing mandates, to increase attention to the question of children working and/or living on the street;
(f) To guarantee respect for all human rights and fundamental freedoms, particularly the right to life, and to take urgent and effective measures to prevent the killing of children working and/or living on the street and to combat torture and violence against them, as well as their recruitment into armed forces or groups in breach of international standards and their sexual exploitation, to bring the perpetrators to justice and to ensure strict compliance with applicable international human rights instruments, including the Convention on the Rights of the Child, including the requirement that legal and juridical processes respect the rights of the child;

Refugee and internally displaced children
32. *Calls upon* all States:
(a) And other parties to armed conflicts to bear in mind that refugee and internally displaced children are particularly exposed to risks in connection with armed conflicts, such as being recruited in violation of international standards or subjected to sexual violence, abuse or exploitation, and stresses the special vulnerability of unaccompanied refugee and internally displaced children, and calls upon Governments and United Nations bodies and organizations to give those situations urgent attention, enhancing protection and assistance mechanisms;
(b) To increase protection of refugee and internally displaced children, including through policies for their care, well-being and development, in such areas as health, education and psychosocial rehabilitation, with the

necessary international cooperation, in particular with the Office of the United Nations High Commissioner for Refugees, the United Nations Children's Fund, the Representative of the Secretary-General on internally displaced persons and the International Committee of the Red Cross and the International Federation of Red Cross and Red Crescent Societies, in accordance with their obligations under the Convention on the Rights of the Child;
   (c) And United Nations bodies and agencies, in coordination with other international humanitarian organizations such as the International Committee of the Red Cross, to ensure the early identification and registration of unaccompanied refugee and internally displaced children, to give priority to programmes for family tracing and reunification, and to pay particular attention to the special protection of children with a view to developing programmes for voluntary repatriation, local integration and resettlement;
   (d) To cooperate with and assist the Representative of the Secretary-General on internally displaced persons in his ongoing efforts to pay specific attention to the special needs of children;

Progressive elimination of child labour
33. *Calls upon* all States:
   (a) To translate into concrete action their commitment to the progressive and effective elimination of child labour contrary to accepted international standards, and urges them, as a matter of priority, to eliminate the worst forms of child labour, such as forced labour, forced or compulsory recruitment of children for use in armed conflict, bonded labour and other forms of slavery;
   (b) That have not yet done so to consider ratifying the conventions of the International Labour Organization relating to child labour, in particular the Convention concerning the Prohibition and Immediate Action for the Elimination of the Worst Forms of Child Labour, 1999 (Convention No. 182), the Forced Labour Convention, 1930 (Convention No. 29) and the Minimum Age for Admission to Employment Convention, 1973 (Convention No. 138);
   (c) To examine and devise economic policies, where necessary, in cooperation with the international community, that address factors contributing to child labour contrary to accepted international standards;
   (d) To promote education as a key strategy to prevent child labour contrary to accepted international standards, including the creation of vocational training opportunities and apprenticeship programmes and integrating working children into the formal education system;
34. *Also calls upon* all States systematically to assess and examine the magnitude, nature and causes of child labour and to elaborate and implement strategies for the elimination of child labour contrary to accepted international standards, giving special attention to specific dangers faced by girls, as well as to the rehabilitation and social reintegration of the children concerned;

Children alleged to have or recognized as having infringed the penal law
35. *Reaffirms* the need for States to ensure that every child alleged to have or recognized as having infringed the penal law is treated with dignity in

accordance with their obligations under the Convention on the Rights of the Child and other relevant international human rights instruments, including the International Covenant on Civil and Political Rights, expressing deep concern, *inter alia*, about cases of children prosecuted without account being taken of their special needs, kept in arbitrary detention, subjected to torture or cruel, inhuman or degrading treatment or punishment or subjected to punishment contrary to accepted international standards and, in this regard, calls upon States to take all the necessary measures to protect children from these practices;

36. *Calls upon* States:
    (a) To ensure that all structures, procedures and programmes in the administration of justice with regard to children who infringe the penal law promote their re-education and rehabilitation, encouraging, whenever appropriate and desirable, measures for dealing with such children without resorting to judicial proceedings, and providing that human rights and legal safeguards are fully respected;
    (b) To take appropriate steps to ensure compliance with the principle that depriving children of their liberty should be used only as a measure of last resort and for the shortest appropriate period of time, in particular before trial, and to ensure that, if they are arrested, detained or imprisoned, children are separated from adults, to the greatest extent feasible, unless it is considered in their best interest not to do so;
    (c) Also to take appropriate steps to ensure that no child in detention is sentenced to forced labour or deprived of access to and provision of health-care services, hygiene and environmental sanitation, education and basic instruction, taking into consideration the special needs of children with disabilities in detention, in accordance with the Convention on the Rights of the Child;
    (d) Parties to comply with the Convention, in their national legislation and practice, and all States to bear in mind the Guidelines for Action on Children in the Criminal Justice System which appear in the annex to Economic and Social Council resolution 1997/30 of 21 July 1997, the United Nations Guidelines for the Prevention of Juvenile Delinquency (The Riyadh Guidelines) adopted by the General Assembly in resolution 45/112 of 14 December 1990, the United Nations Standard Minimum Rules for the Administration of Juvenile Justice (The Beijing Rules) adopted by the Assembly in resolution 40/33 of 29 November 1985 and the United Nations Rules for the Protection of Juveniles Deprived of their Liberty adopted by the Assembly in resolution 45/113 of 14 December 1990, taking into account the best interest of the child;

V

Prevention and eradication of the sale of children, child prostitution and child pornography

37. *Welcomes* the report of the Special Rapporteur on the sale of children, child prostitution and child pornography (E/CN.4/2000/73 and Add.1–3);
38. *Calls upon* States:

(a) To take:
   (i) All appropriate national, bilateral and multilateral measures to ensure the effective application of relevant international standards concerning the prevention and the combat of trafficking and sale of children, child prostitution and child pornography and encourages all actors of civil society and the media to cooperate in efforts to this end;
   (ii) Into account the particular problems posed by the use of the Internet in this regard and to protect children from the practices referred to in subparagraph (i) above, while ensuring that, in the treatment by the criminal justice system of children who are victims, the best interest of the child shall be a primary consideration, and taking into account the concrete measures outlined in the Vienna Declaration and Programme of Action and in the Programmes of Action adopted by the Commission in 1992, 1993 and 1996;
(b) And, in this regard, to enact, review and revise, where appropriate, relevant laws, policies, programmes and practices;
(c) And, in this context, to consider the positive input by other international initiatives outside the United Nations system and to encourage regional and interregional efforts with the objective of identifying best practices and issues requiring particularly urgent action, such as the Declaration and Agenda for Action of the World Congress against Commercial Sexual Exploitation of Children, held in Stockholm in August 1996 (A/51/385, annex) and the Declaration of the Vienna International Conference "Combating Child Pornography on the Internet", held in Vienna from 29 September to 1 October 1999;
(d) To criminalize and effectively penalize all forms of sexual exploitation and sexual abuse of children, including within the family or for commercial purposes, child pornography and child prostitution, including child sex tourism, while ensuring that, in the treatment by the criminal justice system of children who are victims, the best interest of the child shall be a primary consideration, and to take effective measures to ensure prosecution of offenders, whether local or foreign, by the competent national authorities, either in the offender's country of origin or in the country of destination, in accordance with due process of law;
(e) To enhance, in cases of child sex tourism, international cooperation among all relevant authorities, in particular law enforcement authorities, including sharing relevant data, in order to eradicate this practice;

39. *Requests* States to increase cooperation and concerted action, at the national, regional and international levels, including in the context of the United Nations, by all relevant authorities and institutions, in particular law enforcement authorities, in order to adopt and implement effective measures, including the sharing of relevant data, for the prevention and eradication of child sex tourism, the sale of children and of their sexual exploitation and abuse, and to prevent and dismantle networks trafficking in children;

40. *Stresses* the need to combat the existence of a market that encourages such criminal practices against children, including through preventive and enforcement measures targeting customers or individuals who sexually exploit or sexually abuse children;

41. *Encourages* Governments to facilitate the active participation of child victims of sexual exploitation or abuse in the development and implementation of strategies to protect children from sexual exploitation and abuse;
42. *Expresses* its support for the work of the Special Rapporteur on the sale of children, child prostitution and child pornography, calls upon States to cooperate closely with and assist her and to furnish all information requested, including by inviting her to visit their countries, invites further voluntary contributions through the Office of the United Nations High Commissioner for Human Rights and all the necessary human and financial assistance to be provided for her work for the effective fulfilment of her mandate and to enable her to submit an interim report to the General Assembly at its fifty-fifth session and a report to the Commission at its fifty-seventh session;

VI

Protection of children affected by armed conflict

43. *Welcomes* the report of the Special Representative of the Secretary-General on Children and Armed Conflict to the General Assembly at its fifty-fourth session (A/54/430, annex) and his report to the Commission on Human Rights at its fifty-sixth session (E/CN.4/2000/71);
44. *Calls upon* all States:
    (a) And other parties to armed conflict to respect fully international humanitarian law and, in this regard, calls upon States parties to respect fully the provisions of the Geneva Conventions of 12 August 1949 and the Additional Protocols thereto of 1977, while bearing in mind the Plan of Action adopted by the twenty-seventh International Conference of the Red Cross and Red Crescent of 1999, and to respect the provisions of the Convention on the Rights of the Child which accord children affected by armed conflict special protection and treatment;
    (b) And relevant United Nations bodies and agencies and regional organizations to integrate the rights of the child into all activities in conflict and post-conflict situations, including training programmes and emergency relief operations, country programmes and field operations aimed at promoting peace and preventing and resolving conflicts, as well as negotiating and implementing peace agreements and, given the long-term consequences for society, underlines the importance of including specific provisions for children, including resourcing, in peace agreements and in arrangements negotiated by parties;
45. *Calls upon* all States and other parties concerned to continue to cooperate with the Special Representative, to implement the commitments they have undertaken, to consider carefully all the recommendations of the Special Representative and to address the issues identified, and welcomes the continued support and voluntary contributions that are being provided to the work of the Special Representative;
46. *Recognizes*, in this regard, the contribution of the establishment of the International Criminal Court to ending impunity for perpetrators of certain crimes committed against children, as defined in the Rome Statute of the International Criminal Court (see A/CONF.183/9, art. 8), *inter alia* those involving sexual violence or child soldiers, and thus to the prevention of

such crimes, and calls upon States to consider signing and ratifying the Rome Statute;

47. *Condemns* the abduction of children in situations of armed conflict and into armed conflicts, urges States, international organizations and other concerned parties to take all appropriate measures to secure the unconditional release of all abducted children and urges States to bring the perpetrators to justice, in accordance with due process of law;

48. *Notes* the importance of the second debate held by the Security Council, on 25 August 1999, on children and armed conflict and the undertaking by the Council to give special attention to the protection, welfare and rights of children when taking action aimed at maintaining peace and security, and reaffirms the essential role of the General Assembly and the Economic and Social Council for the promotion and protection of the rights and welfare of children;

49. *Calls upon* all parties to armed conflicts to ensure the full, safe and unhindered access of humanitarian personnel and the delivery of humanitarian assistance to all children affected by armed conflict;

50. *Calls upon* States and relevant United Nations bodies to continue to support national and international mine action efforts, including by financial contributions, mine awareness programmes, victim assistance and child-centred rehabilitation, taking note of the Convention on the Prohibition of the Use, Stockpiling, Production and Transfer of Anti-Personnel Mines and on Their Destruction and its implementation by those States that become parties to it, and welcomes the positive effects on children of concrete legislative measures with respect to anti-personnel mines;

51. *Notes with concern* the impact of small arms and light weapons on children in situations of armed conflict, in particular as a result of their illicit production and traffic, and calls upon States to address this problem;

52. *Welcomes* the ongoing efforts by, *inter alia*, regional organizations, intergovernmental organizations and non-governmental organizations to ensure the effective application of international standards concerning the participation of children in armed conflict, and their demobilization, recovery and social reintegration;

53. *Urges* all parties to armed conflicts to ensure that the protection, welfare and rights of children are taken into account during peace negotiations and throughout the process of consolidating peace in the aftermath of conflict;

54. *Urges* States and United Nations agencies and bodies, in particular the United Nations Children's Fund, non-governmental organizations and the Special Representative of the Secretary-General on Children and Armed Conflict, to continue to put pressure on those who involve children as soldiers in armed conflicts in breach of international standards;

55. *Decides*, with regard to the Special Representative of the Secretary-General on Children and Armed Conflict, to recommend that the Special Representative and the relevant parts of the United Nations system continue to develop a concerted approach on the rights, protection and welfare of children affected by armed conflict, and to increase cooperation among their respective mandates and with national and international non-governmental organizations including, as appropriate, in the planning of field visits and follow-up to the recommendations of the Special Representative;

56. *Recommends* that, whenever sanctions are imposed in the context of armed conflict their impact on children be assessed and monitored and, to the extent that they are humanitarian exemptions, they be child-focused and formulated with clear guidelines for their application, and reaffirms the recommendations of the General Assembly and the International Conference of the Red Cross and Red Crescent;

VII

Recovery and social reintegration

57. *Urges* States and all other relevant actors:
    (a) To take all appropriate measures to promote, where necessary, the physical and psychological recovery and social reintegration of a child victim of any form of neglect; exploitation, or abuse; torture to any other form of cruel, inhuman or degrading treatment or punishment; or armed conflicts;
    (b) To allocate appropriate resources for comprehensive and gender-sensitive programmes for the recovery of children victims of the above-mentioned violations of the rights of the child;
58. *Encourages* States to cooperate, including through bilateral and multilateral technical cooperation and financial assistance, in the implementation of their obligations under the Convention on the Rights of the Child, including in the prevention of any activity contrary to the rights of the child and in the rehabilitation and social integration of the victims, such assistance and cooperation to be undertaken in consultation by concerned States and other relevant international organizations;

VIII

59. *Decides*:
    (a) To request the Secretary-General to submit to the Commission at its fifty-seventh session a report on the rights of the child, with information on the status of the Convention on the Rights of the Child and on the problems addressed in the present resolution;
    (b) To continue its consideration of this question at its fifty-seventh session under the same agenda item.

Racism, racial discrimination, xenophobia and related intolerance

Commission on Human Rights Resolution 2000/14
adopted 17 April 2000

The Commission on Human Rights,

Reaffirming the Universal Declaration of Human Rights, the Charter of the United Nations, the International Covenants on Human Rights and the International Convention on the Elimination of All Forms of Racial Discrimination,

Reaffirming also its firm determination and its commitment to eradicate totally and unconditionally racism in all its forms and racial discrimination, and its conviction that racism and racial discrimination constitute a total negation of the purposes and principles of the Charter of the United Nations and the Universal Declaration of Human Rights,

Taking note of resolution 54/154 of 17 December 1999, in which the General Assembly welcomed the offer by the Government of South Africa to host the World Conference against Racism, Racial discrimination, Xenophobia and Related intolerance,

Reaffirming its resolution 1998/26 of 17 April 1998, in which it recommended that the activities of the Programme of Action for the Third Decade to Combat Racism and Racial Discrimination should be focused on the preparatory process for the World Conference,

Recalling the recommendations of the two World Conferences to Combat Racism and Racial Discrimination, held in Geneva in 1978 and 1983,

Bearing in mind the Vienna Declaration and Programme of Action adopted by the World Conference on Human Rights in June 1993 (A/CONF.157/23), which call for the speedy and comprehensive elimination of all forms of racism, racial discrimination, xenophobia and related intolerance,

Deeply concerned that, despite continuing efforts, contemporary forms of racism, racial discrimination, any form of discrimination against, *inter alia*, Blacks, Arabs and Muslims, xenophobia, Negrophobia, anti-Semitism and related intolerance persist and are even growing in magnitude, incessantly adopting new forms, including tendencies to establish policies based on racial, religious, ethnic, cultural and national superiority or exclusivity,

Particularly alarmed at the rise of racist and xenophobic ideas in political circles, in the sphere of public opinion and in society at large,

Conscious of the fundamental difference between, on the one hand, racism and racial discrimination as an institutionalized governmental policy or resulting from official doctrines of racial superiority or exclusivity and, on the other hand, other manifestations of racism, racial discrimination, xenophobia and related intolerance taking place in segments of many societies and perpetrated by individuals or groups, some of which are directed against migrant workers and their families,

Reaffirming, in this regard, the responsibility of Governments for safeguarding and protecting the rights of individuals residing in their territory against crimes perpetrated by racist or xenophobic individuals or groups,

Noting with concern that racism, racial discrimination, xenophobia and related intolerance may be aggravated by, *inter alia*, inequitable distribution of wealth, marginalization and social exclusion,

Deeply concerned about the fact that the phenomenon of racism and racial discrimination against migrant workers continues to increase despite efforts undertaken by the international community to improve the protection of the human rights of migrant workers and members of their families,

Taking note of the report of the Special Rapporteur on the human rights of migrants (E/CN.4/2000/82),

Noting with grave concern that, despite the efforts of the international community, the principal objectives of the two Decades for Action to Combat Racism and Racial Discrimination have not been attained and that millions of human beings continue to this day to be victims of varied forms of racism and racial discrimination,

Noting also with grave concern that, despite the efforts undertaken by the international community at various levels, racism, racial discrimination, xenophobia and related forms of intolerance, ethnic antagonism and acts of violence are showing signs of increase,

Deeply concerned that those advocating racism and racial discrimination misuse new communication technologies, including the Internet, to disseminate their repugnant views,

Aware that racism, being one of the exclusionist phenomena plaguing many societies, requires resolute action and cooperation for its eradication,

Recalling General Assembly resolution 48/91 of 20 December 1993, in which the Assembly proclaimed the Third Decade to Combat Racism and Racial Discrimination, beginning in 1993, and adopted the Programme of Action proposed for the Decade,

Having examined the report of the Special Rapporteur on contemporary forms of racism, racial discrimination, xenophobia and related intolerance (E/CN.4/2000/16 and Add.1),

Observing that the manifestations of contemporary forms of racism, racial discrimination, xenophobia and related intolerance bode ill for the international community, that racist propaganda and incitement to racial hatred are spreading and that racism is taking increasingly violent forms,

Stressing the need to recognize that acts of violence motivated by racial discrimination and xenophobia are crimes punishable by law,

Also stressing the importance of urgently eliminating growing and violent trends of racism and racial discrimination, and conscious that any form of impunity for crimes motivated by racist and xenophobic attitudes plays a role in weakening the rule of law and democracy and tends to encourage the recurrence of such crimes, and requires resolute action and cooperation for its eradication,

Recognizing that failure to combat racial discrimination and xenophobia, especially by public authorities and politicians, is a factor encouraging their perpetuation in society,

I

General

1. *Expresses its profound concern at and unequivocal condemnation* of all forms of racism and racial discrimination, including related acts of racially motivated violence, xenophobia and related intolerance, as well as all propaganda activities and organizations which attempt to justify or promote racism, racial discrimination, xenophobia and related intolerance in any form;
2. *Declares* that racism and racial discrimination are among the most serious violations of human rights in the contemporary world and must be combated by all available means;
3. *Calls upon* all States resolutely to bring to justice the perpetrators of crimes motivated by racism and calls upon those who have not done so, to consider including racist motivation as an aggravating factor for the purposes of sentencing;
4. *Recognizes* the vulnerability of victims of acts of racial discrimination, which violate their human rights and fundamental freedoms, as well as the difficulties they often face in seeking legal remedies, and in this regard calls upon all States to provide, when needed, legal assistance, in order to facilitate access to justice, as well as to consider establishing appropriate policies and structures as a national level, *inter alia*, an ombudsman to deal with these kinds of acts;
5. *Calls* upon all States to intensify their efforts in taking appropriate measures to prevent political parties from promoting and inciting racial discrimination in violation of human rights;
6. *Underlines* the importance of effective action to create conditions that foster greater harmony and tolerance within societies;
7. *Expresses its deep concern and condemnation* of manifestations of racism, racial discrimination, xenophobia and related intolerance against migrant workers and members of their families and other vulnerable groups in many societies;
8. *Calls upon* all States to review and, where necessary, revise their immigration policies which are inconsistent with international human rights instruments, with a view to eliminating all discriminatory policies and practices against migrants;
9. *Condemns* all forms of racial discrimination and xenophobia as regards access to employment, vocational training, housing, schooling, health services and social services, as well as services intended for use by the public;
10. *Categorically condemns* any role played by some print, audio-visual or electronic media in inciting acts of violence motivated by racial hatred;

11. *Urges* Governments to take all necessary measures against incitement to racial hatred, including through print, audio-visual and electronic media;
12. *Urges* all States to intensify their efforts for the implementation of the obligations they have accepted under article 4 of the International Convention on the Elimination of All Forms of Racial Discrimination, with due regard to the principles of the Universal Declaration of Human Rights and to article 5 of the International Convention on the Elimination of all Forms of Racial Discrimination, with respect to:
    (a) Declaring an offence punishable by law all dissemination of ideas based on racial superiority or hatred, incitement to racial discrimination, as well as all acts of violence or incitement to such acts, against any race or group of persons of another colour or ethnic origin, and also the provision of any assistance to racist activities, including the financing thereof;
    (b) Declaring illegal and prohibit organizations, and also organized and all other propaganda activities, which promote and incite racial discrimination, and recognizing participation in such organizations or activities as an offence punishable by law;
    (c) Not permitting public authorities or public institutions, national or local, to promote or incite racial discrimination;
13. *Calls upon* all States, where appropriate, to strengthen their national legislation and institutions for the promotion of racial harmony and notes the conclusions and recommendations of the Special Rapporteur on contemporary forms of racism, racial discrimination, xenophobia and related intolerance in this regard, including those on the importance of integration of vulnerable groups in mainstream societies;
14. *Invites* all States, in their efforts aimed at promoting racial harmony, to involve, or, as necessary, to establish, national institutions and other appropriate organizations;
15. *Welcomes* the active role played by non-governmental organizations in combating racism and assisting individual victims of racist acts;
16. *Encourages* the mass media to promote ideas of tolerance and understanding among peoples and between different cultures and to refrain from disseminating racist and xenophobic ideas, through all appropriate means, such as codes of conduct;
17. *Takes note with interest* of general recommendation XV (42) of 17 March 1993 of the Committee on the Elimination of Racial Discrimination on article 4 of the International Convention on the Elimination of All Forms of Racial Discrimination, in which the Committee concluded that the prohibition of the dissemination of all ideas based on racial superiority or racial hatred is compatible with the right to freedom of opinion and expression as embodied in article 19 of the Universal Declaration of Human Rights and recalled in article 5 of the Convention;

II

Implementation of the Programme of Action for the Third Decade to Combat Racism and Racial Discrimination and coordination of activities

18. *Regrets* the continued lack of interest, support and financial resources for the Third Decade and the Programme of Action, and that very few of the

activities planned for the period 1994–1998 were carried out;
19. *Recognizes* the laudable and generous efforts by donors that have made contributions to the Trust Fund for the Programme for the Decade to Combat Racism and Racial Discrimination, but feels that these financial contributions have proved inadequate and that the General Assembly should consider all ways and means of financing the Programme of Action, including through the United Nations regular budget;
20. *Recommends* that the General Assembly, through the Economic and Social Council, should request the Secretary-General to assign high priority to the activities of the Programme of Action and to earmark adequate resources to finance the activities of the Programme;
21. *Warmly calls upon* all Governments, United Nations bodies, the specialized agencies and intergovernmental organizations, as well as interested non-governmental organizations, to contribute fully to the effective implementation of the Programme of Action for the Third Decade to Combat Racism and Racial Discrimination;
22. *Strongly appeals* to all Governments, intergovernmental and non-governmental organizations and individuals in a position to do so to contribute generously to the Trust Fund, and, to this end, requests the Secretary-General to continue to undertake appropriate contacts and initiatives to encourage contributions;
23. *Welcomes* the establishment of the racism project team in the Office of the United Nations High Commissioner for Human Rights with a view to coordinating all activities of the Third Decade;
24. *Affirms* its determination to combat violence stemming from intolerance on the basis of ethnicity, which it considers to be as particularly serious a problem as violence based on racism, racial discrimination, xenophobia and related intolerance;
25. *Requests* all States to encourage the reporting of all acts motivated by racism, racial discrimination, xenophobia or ethnic reasons in order to facilitate the necessary inquiries and bring the persons who commit such acts to trial;
26. *Recommends* that States give priority to education as a principal means of preventing and eradicating racism and racial discrimination and of creating awareness of the principles of human rights, particularly among young people, and to the training of law enforcement personnel, *inter alia* through the promotion of tolerance and respect for cultural diversity;
27. *Calls upon* all Member States to consider signing and ratifying or acceding to the International Convention on the Protection of the Rights of All Migrant Workers and Members of Their Families as a matter of priority;

III

Special Rapporteur on contemporary forms of racism, racial discrimination, xenophobia and related intolerance and follow-up to his visits

28. *Takes note with satisfaction* of the report of the Special Rapporteur (E/CN.4/2000/16 and Add.1);
29. *Expresses* its full support and appreciation for the work of the Special Rapporteur and for its continuation;

30. *Requests* the Special Rapporteur to continue his exchange of views with Member States and relevant mechanisms and treaty bodies within the United Nations system in order to enhance further their effectiveness and mutual cooperation;
31. *Also requests* the Special Rapporteur to examine the issue of political platforms which promote or incite racial discrimination in violation of human rights and to submit recommendations thereon to the Preparatory Committee for the World Conference at its second session;
32. *Calls upon* all Governments, intergovernmental organizations and other relevant organizations of the United Nations system, as well as non-governmental organizations, to supply information to the Special Rapporteur;
33. *Urges* all Governments to cooperate fully with the Special Rapporteur with a view to enabling him to fulfil his mandate to examine incidents of contemporary forms of racism, racial discrimination, any form of discrimination against, *inter alia*, Blacks, Arabs and Muslims, xenophobia, Negrophobia, anti-Semitism and related intolerance;
34. *Requests* the Special Rapporteur to make the fullest use of all appropriate sources of information, including country visits and evaluation of the mass media, and to elicit responses from Governments with regard to allegations;
35. *Commends* those States that have so far invited and received the Special Rapporteur;
36. *Invites* the Governments of the States so far visited to consider ways to implement the recommendations contained in the reports of the Special Rapporteur and requests the Special Rapporteur to include in his report to the Commission at its fifty-seventh session, under the same agenda item, information on the measures taken to implement those recommendations, and to undertake follow-up visits, if necessary;
37. *Notes with concern* the increase in the use of new communications technologies, in particular the Internet, to disseminate racist ideas and incite racial hatred;
38. *Notes* that the use of such technologies can contribute to combating racism, racial discrimination, xenophobia and related intolerance, for example through the creation of Internet sites to disseminate anti-racist and anti-xenophobic messages;
39. *Requests* the United Nations High Commissioner for Human Rights to undertake research and consultations on the use of the Internet for purposes of incitement to racial hatred, racist propaganda and xenophobia, to study ways of promoting international cooperation in this area, and to draw up a programme of human rights education and exchanges over the Internet on experience in the struggle against racism, xenophobia and anti-Semitism;
40. *Urges* the High Commissioner to provide those countries which were visited by the Special Rapporteur, at their request, with advisory services and technical assistance to enable them to implement fully the recommendations of the Special Rapporteur;

IV

International Convention on the Elimination of All Forms of Racial Discrimination

41. *Appeals* to those States that have not yet done so to consider ratifying or acceding to the relevant international instruments, particularly the

International Convention on the Elimination of All Forms of Racial Discrimination and the Convention against Discrimination in Education, and calls upon the States that have done so to implement them;

42. *Recommends* that the issue of universal ratification of the International Convention on the Elimination of All Forms of Racial Discrimination as well as the reservations thereto and the question of recognition of the competence of the Committee on the Elimination of Racial Discrimination to receive individual complaints be considered at the World Conference against Racism, Racial Discrimination, Xenophobia and Related Intolerance;

43. *Calls upon* States parties that have not submitted initial or periodic reports in accordance with article 9 of the Convention to do so;

44. *Urges States* to limit the extent of any reservations they lodge to the International Convention on the Elimination of All Forms of Racial Discrimination and to formulate any reservation as precisely and as narrowly as possible, while ensuring that no reservation is incompatible with the object and purpose of the Convention;

45. *Calls upon* States parties to the Convention, as appropriate, to adopt immediately positive measures aimed at the elimination of all forms of racial discrimination, xenophobia and related intolerance;

46. *Requests* the States parties to the Convention that have not yet done so to consider the possibility of making the declaration provided for in article 14 of the Convention;

47. *Invites* the States parties to ratify the amendment to article 8 of the Convention on the financing of the Committee on the Elimination of Racial Discrimination;

V

World Conference against Racism, Racial Discrimination, Xenophobia and Related Intolerance

48. *Takes note* of the report of the Secretary-General on racism, racial discrimination, xenophobia and all forms of racial discrimination concerning the implementation of Commission resolution 1999/78 of 28 April 1999 (E/CN.4/2000/15);

49. *Welcomes* the offer by the Government of South Africa to host in 2001 the World Conference against Racism, Racial Discrimination, Xenophobia and Related Intolerance and invites the international community to support the host country with financial resources;

50. *Recalls* its decision, in resolution 1999/78, and decides to appoint an 11-member Bureau for the two sessions of the Preparatory Committee, comprising two representatives per regional group and a representative of the host country as an ex-officio member, in order to ensure continuity and the adequate representation of all Member States:

51. *Requests* the High Commissioner, in her capacity as Secretary-General of the World Conference, to continue and intensify the activities already initiated within the framework of the world information campaign with a view to mobilization and support for the objectives of the World Conference by all sectors of political, economic, social and cultural life, as well as other interested sectors;

52. *Welcomes* the efforts by the High Commissioner to include, *inter alia*, in her strategy for informing international public opinion and raising awareness about the objectives of the World Conference, and encourages her to continue these efforts;
53. *Also welcomes* the efforts of the High Commissioner for Human Rights in initiating consultations with various international sporting and other organizations to enable them to contribute to the struggle against racism and racial discrimination in the framework of the World Conference;
54. *Urges* all States, United Nations bodies, international, regional and subregional governmental organizations, non-governmental organizations and any interested body to support the High Commissioner and the Department of Public Information of the Secretariat and give them full and complete cooperation for the coordination of information activities;
55. *Encourages* the participation of non-governmental organizations in the World Conference and in the sessions of the Preparatory Committee and calls upon the Secretary-General of the Conference to expedite arrangements for accreditation of non-governmental organizations, including those that are not in consultative status with the Economic and Social Council, in accordance with Council resolution 1996/31 of 25 July 1996;
56. *Requests* the High Commissioner to undertake appropriate consultations with non-governmental organizations on the possibility that they might hold a forum before and partly during the World Conference and, insofar as possible, to provide them with technical assistance for that purpose;
57. *Welcomes* the offers made by the Governments of Senegal, Islamic Republic of Iran and Brazil, and by the Council of Europe, to host regional preparatory meetings for the World Conference;
58. *Expresses* concern at the lack of financial support to hold regional meetings in preparation of the World Conference, and invites all States to contribute generously to the trust fund established by the High Commissioner in order to cover the activities foreseen within the framework of the World Conference and, in particular, to respond positively and in a timely manner to the appeal for the preparation of the Conference contained in the Annual Appeal of the Office of the High Commissioner for Human Rights and also invites the specialized agencies and regional commissions of the United Nations to contribute to the organization of regional conferences;
59. *Requests* the Secretary-General, the United Nations specialized agencies and the regional economic commissions to provide financial and technical assistance for the organization of the regional preparatory meetings planned in the context of the World Conference and stresses that such assistance should be supplemented by voluntary contributions;
60. *Recommends* that the regional preparatory processes should include the campaign for information and sensitization of public opinion to the objectives of the World Conference on their agenda;
61. *Requests* the regional preparatory processes to identify trends, priorities and obstacles at the national and regional levels, to formulate specific recommendations for the action to be carried out in future to combat racism, racial discrimination, xenophobia and related intolerance and to submit to the Preparatory Committee, by its 2001 session at the latest, the conclusions of these regional preparatory processes;

62. *Encourages* the regional preparatory processes to coordinate among themselves, with a view to facilitating and optimizing their contributions to the preparatory process of the World Conference;
63. *Calls upon* the regional preparatory meetings to submit to the Preparatory Committee, through the High Commissioner, reports on the results of their deliberations, with concrete and pragmatic recommendations aimed at combating racism, racial discrimination, xenophobia and related intolerance, which will be duly reflected in the texts of the draft final documents of the World Conference to be prepared by the Committee;
64. *Invites* Governments to promote the participation of national institutions and local non-governmental organizations in the preparations and in regional meetings and to organize debates in national parliaments on the objectives of the World Conference;
65. *Encourages* all parliaments to participate actively in the preparation of the World Conference and requests the High Commissioner to explore ways and means for the effective involvement of parliaments through the relevant international organizations;
66. *Invites* United Nations bodies and mechanisms dealing with the question of racism, racial discrimination, xenophobia and related intolerance, the Committee on the Elimination of Racial Discrimination, the Sub-Commission on the Promotion and Protection of Human Rights and the special rapporteurs concerned to participate actively in the preparatory process with a view to ensuring the success of the World Conference and to coordinate their activities in this regard with the assistance of the High Commissioner;
67. *Recommends* that the World Conference should adopt a declaration and programme of action containing concrete and practical recommendations to combat racism, racial discrimination, xenophobia and related intolerance;
68. *Stresses* the importance of systematically adopting a gender-based approach throughout the preparations for and in the outcome of the World Conference;
69. *Recommends* that the particular situation of children should receive special attention during the preparations for and during the World Conference itself, especially in its outcome;
70. *Welcomes* the decision of the General Assembly to declare 2001 the International Year of Mobilization against Racism, Racial Discrimination, Xenophobia and Related Intolerance;
71. *Calls upon* all States, United Nations bodies, specialized agencies, regional organizations and intergovernmental as well as non-governmental organizations to mobilize their efforts in realizing the objectives of the International Year;
72. *Emphasizes* that the activities which will be implemented within the framework of the International Year should be directed towards the preparation of the World Conference;
73. *Requests* the Secretary-General to submit to the Commission at its fifty-seventh session a report on the implementation of the present resolution under the agenda item entitled "Racism, racial discrimination, xenophobia and all forms of discrimination";
74. *Decides* to continue its consideration of this question at its fifty-seventh session under the same agenda item.

Appendix 9: Resolutions of the General Assembly relating to the Human Rights Treaties

A/RES/53/138

UNITED NATIONS GENERAL ASSEMBLY

Effective implementation of international instruments on human rights, including reporting obligations under international instruments on human rights

General Assembly Resolution 53/138
adopted 9 December 1998

The General Assembly,

Recalling its resolution 52/118 of 12 December 1997, as well as other relevant resolutions, and taking note of Commission on Human Rights resolution 1998/27 of 17 April 1998, See *Official Records of the Economic and Social Council, 1998, Supplement No. 3* (E/1998/23), chap. II, sect. A.

Recalling also the relevant paragraphs of the Vienna Declaration and Programme of Action, adopted by the World Conference on Human Rights on 25 June 1993, A/CONF.157/24 (Part I), chap. III.

Reaffirming that the full and effective implementation of United Nations human rights instruments is of major importance to the efforts of the Organization, pursuant to the Charter of the United Nations and the Universal Declaration of Human Rights, Resolution 217A(III), to promote universal respect for and observance of human rights and fundamental freedoms,

Considering that the effective functioning of the human rights treaty bodies established pursuant to United Nations human rights instruments is indispensable for the full and effective implementation of such instruments,

Conscious of the importance of coordination of the human rights promotion and protection activities of the United Nations bodies active in the field of human rights,

Recalling that the effectiveness of the human rights treaty bodies in encouraging the realization by States parties of their obligations under United Nations human rights instruments requires constructive dialogue, which should be based on the reporting process supplemented by information from all relevant sources and aimed at assisting States parties in identifying solutions to human rights problems,

Recalling also the initiatives taken by a number of human rights treaty bodies to elaborate early warning measures and urgent procedures, within their mandates, with a view to preventing the occurrence or recurrence of serious human rights violations,

Reaffirming its responsibility for the effective functioning of human rights treaty bodies, and reaffirming also the importance of:

(a) Promoting the effective functioning of the periodic reporting by States parties to those instruments,
(b) Securing sufficient financial, human and information resources to overcome the under-resourcing of the Office of the United Nations High Commissioner for Human Rights, which impedes the ability of the human rights treaty bodies to carry out their mandates effectively,
(c) Promoting greater efficiency and effectiveness through better coordination of the activities of the United Nations bodies active in the field of human rights, taking into account the need to avoid unnecessary duplication and overlapping of their mandates and tasks,
(d) Addressing questions of both reporting obligations and financial implications when elaborating any further instruments on human rights,

Concerned that the lack of adequate resources should not impede the effective functioning of the human rights treaty bodies, including in regard to their ability to work in the applicable working languages,

Taking note of the report of the Secretary-General on the effective implementation of international instruments on human rights, including reporting obligations under international instruments on human rights, A/53/469.

1. *Welcomes* the submission of the reports of the persons chairing the human rights treaty bodies on their ninth A/53/125, annex. and tenth A/53/432, annex. meetings, held at Geneva from 25 to 27 February and 14 to 18 September 1998, respectively, and takes note of their conclusions and recommendations;
2. *Encourages* each treaty body to give careful consideration to the relevant conclusions and recommendations contained in the report of the persons chairing the human rights treaty bodies;
3. *Welcomes* the submission to the Commission on Human Rights of the final report of the independent expert on enhancing the long-term effectiveness of the United Nations human rights treaty monitoring system E/CN.4/1997/74, annex. and of the report of the Secretary-General containing the comments and observations of Governments, United Nations bodies, the specialized agencies, non-governmental organizations and interested persons on the report of the independent expert, as well as his views on the legal, administrative and other implications of the recommendations made in the report, E/CN.4/1998/85 and Add.1 and Corr.1. taking into account further developments;
4. *Invites* the Secretary-General to continue to solicit the views of Governments, United Nations bodies, the specialized agencies, non-governmental organizations and interested persons on the final report of the independent expert and to submit a further report thereon, including his own views on the legal, administrative and other implications of the recommendations made in the report, taking into account further developments;
5. *Encourages* ongoing efforts to identify measures for more effective implementation of the United Nations human rights instruments;
6. *Emphasizes* the need to ensure financing and adequate staff and information

resources for the operations of the human rights treaty bodies, and, with this in mind:
   (a) *Reiterates* its request that the Secretary-General provide adequate resources in respect of each human rights treaty body;
   (b) *Calls upon* the Secretary-General to make the most efficient use of existing resources and to seek the resources necessary to give the human rights treaty bodies adequate administrative support and better access to technical expertise and relevant information;
   (c) *Also calls upon* the Secretary-General to seek, in the next biennium, the resources within the United Nations regular budget necessary to give the human rights treaty bodies adequate administrative support and better access to technical expertise and relevant information without diverting resources from the development programmes and activities of the United Nations;
7. *Takes note with appreciation* of the revised plan of action to strengthen the implementation of the Convention on the Rights of the Child, Resolution 44/25, annex. and the plan of action to strengthen the implementation of the International Covenant on Economic, Social and Cultural Rights, See resolution 2200 A (XXI), annex. recalls the importance of administering those plans in accordance with established United Nations procedures, welcomes the information provided by the Secretary-General on the implementation of those plans, and requests him to include in his report prepared pursuant to the present resolution further information in this regard;
8. *Notes with interest* the work being done by the United Nations High Commissioner for Human Rights on a plan of action to enhance the resources available to all human rights treaty bodies;
9. *Reaffirms* the need for human rights treaty bodies to better complement each other in their work, and emphasizes that the universal ratification of international human rights treaties containing reporting obligations adopted within the framework of the United Nations system is important for the realization of that complementarity;
10. *Welcomes* the continuing efforts by the human rights treaty bodies and the Secretary-General aimed at streamlining, rationalizing, rendering more transparent and otherwise improving reporting procedures, and urges the Secretary-General, the treaty bodies and the meetings of persons chairing the treaty bodies to continue to examine ways of reducing the duplication of reporting required under the different instruments, without impairing the quality of reporting, and of generally reducing the reporting burden on States parties;
11. *Takes note with appreciation*, in this regard, of the efforts of the persons chairing the human rights treaty bodies, at their ninth and tenth meetings, to propose appropriate reforms of the reporting system with a view to, *inter alia*, reducing the reporting burden on States parties while maintaining the quality of reporting, and encourages them to continue these efforts, including through the continued examination of the benefits of reports focused on a limited range of issues and of opportunities for harmonizing the general guidelines regarding the form and content of reports, the timing of consideration of reports and the methods of work of the treaty bodies;
12. *Invites* the Chairperson of the periodic meetings of the persons chairing the

human rights treaty bodies to submit the reports of the meetings to the General Assembly at its fifty-fifth session;
13. *Welcomes* the initiative undertaken by the persons chairing the human rights treaty bodies of inviting representatives of Member States to participate in a dialogue within the framework of their periodic meetings, and encourages them to continue this practice in the future;
14. *Calls upon* the Secretary-General to complete as soon as possible the detailed analytical study comparing the provisions of the International Covenant on Economic, Social and Cultural Rights, See resolution 2200 A (XXI), annex. the International Covenant on Civil and Political Rights, see resolution 2200 A (XXI), annex. the International Convention on the Elimination of All Forms of Racial Discrimination, Resolution 2106 A (XX), annex. the Convention on the Elimination of All Forms of Discrimination against Women, Resolution 34/180, annex. the Convention on the Rights of the Child, Resolution 2106 A (XX), annex. and the Convention against Torture and Other Cruel, Inhuman or Degrading Treatment or Punishment, Resolution 39/46, annex. which is being prepared with a view to identifying duplication of reporting required under those instruments;
15. *Urges* States parties to contribute, individually and through meetings of States parties, to identifying and implementing ways of further streamlining, rationalizing, avoiding duplication in and otherwise improving reporting procedures;
16. *Welcomes* the publication of the revised *Manual on Human Rights Reporting*; United Nations publication, Sales No. E.GV.97.0.16.
17. *Underlines* the importance of providing technical assistance to a State, upon its request, in the process of ratifying human rights instruments and in the preparation of its initial reports;
18. *Requests* the Secretary-General to compile in a single volume all the general guidelines regarding the form and content of reports to be submitted by States parties that have been issued by the Human Rights Committee, the Committee on Economic, Social and Cultural Rights, the Committee on the Elimination of Discrimination against Women, the Committee on the Elimination of Racial Discrimination, the Committee on the Rights of the Child and the Committee against Torture;
19. *Reiterates its concern* about the increasing backlog of reports on the implementation by States parties of certain United Nations instruments on human rights and about delays in consideration of reports by the treaty bodies;
20. *Also reiterates its concern* about the large number of overdue reports under the United Nations instruments on human rights, and again urges States parties to make every effort to meet their reporting obligations;
21. *Invites* States parties that have been unable to comply with the requirements to submit their initial report to avail themselves of technical assistance;
22. *Urges* all States parties whose reports have been examined by human rights treaty bodies to provide adequate follow-up to the observations and final comments of the treaty bodies on their reports;
23. *Encourages* the human rights treaty bodies to continue to identify specific possibilities for technical assistance, to be provided at the request of the State concerned, in the regular course of their work of reviewing the periodic reports of States parties;

24. *Recalls* the recommendation by the meeting of persons chairing the human rights treaty bodies that treaty bodies urge each State party to translate, publish and make widely available in its territory the full text of the concluding observations on its reports to the treaty bodies;
25. *Welcomes* the contribution to the work of the human rights treaty bodies made by the specialized agencies and other United Nations bodies, and invites the specialized agencies, other United Nations bodies and the treaty bodies to continue to pursue further cooperation between them;
26. *Notes* that efforts continue to be made at coordination and cooperation between the human rights treaty bodies and the special procedures, rapporteurs, representatives, experts and working groups of the Commission on Human Rights and the Subcommission on Prevention of Discrimination and Protection of Minorities of the Commission, all acting within their respective mandates;
27. *Recognizes* the important role played by non-governmental organizations in all parts of the world in the effective implementation of all human rights instruments, and encourages the exchange of information between the human rights treaty bodies and such organizations;
28. *Recalls*, with regard to the election of the members of the human rights treaty bodies, the importance of giving consideration to equitable geographical distribution of membership and to the representation of the principal legal systems and of bearing in mind that the members shall be elected and shall serve in their personal capacity and shall be of high moral character, acknowledged independence and recognized competence in the field of human rights, and encourages States parties, individually and through meetings of States parties, to consider how to give better effect to these principles;
29. *Takes note* of the discussion of the payment of honorariums to the members of the human rights treaty bodies included in the report of the Secretary-General on the effective implementation of international instruments on human rights, including reporting obligations under international instruments on human rights, A/53/469, and of other work being done by the Secretary-General on this subject;
30. *Encourages* the Economic and Social Council, as well as its functional commissions and their subsidiary bodies, other United Nations bodies and the specialized agencies to consider the feasibility of participation by representatives of the human rights treaty bodies in their meetings;
31. *Welcomes* the continuing emphasis by the persons chairing the human rights treaty bodies that the enjoyment of the human rights of women should be monitored closely by each treaty body within the purview of its mandate, and, in this context, takes note of the recommendation made at their tenth meeting A/53/432, annex, para. 53 that the treaty bodies take full account of the recommendations contained in the report prepared by the Division for the Advancement of Women of the Secretariat; HRI/MC/1998/6;
32. *Also welcomes* the contributions of the human rights treaty bodies, within their mandates, to the prevention of violations of human rights, in the context of their consideration of reports submitted under their respective treaties;
33. *Requests* the Secretary-General to report to the General Assembly at its fifty-fifth session on measures taken to implement the present resolution, on

obstacles to its implementation and on measures taken or planned to ensure financing and adequate staff and information resources for the effective operation of the human rights treaty bodies;
34. *Decides* to continue to give priority consideration at its fifty-fifth session to the conclusions and recommendations of the meetings of persons chairing human rights treaty bodies, in the light of the deliberations of the Commission on Human Rights, under the item entitled "Human rights questions".

A/RES/53/131

UNITED NATIONS GENERAL ASSEMBLY

International Convention on the Elimination of All Forms of Racial Discrimination

General Assembly Resolution 53/131
adopted 9 December 1998

The General Assembly,

Recalling its previous resolutions concerning the reports of the Committee on the Elimination of Racial Discrimination and its resolutions on the status of the International Convention on the Elimination of All Forms of Racial Discrimination, Resolution 2106 A (XX), annex. most recently resolutions 51/80 of 12 December 1996 and 52/110 of 12 December 1997,

Bearing in mind the Vienna Declaration and Programme of Action adopted by the World Conference on Human Rights on 25 June 1993, A/CONF.157/24 (Part I), chap. III. in particular section II.B of the Declaration, relating to equality, dignity and tolerance,

Reiterating the need to intensify the struggle to eliminate all forms of racial discrimination throughout the world, especially its most brutal forms,

Recalling its resolution 52/111 of 12 December 1997, in which it decided to convene a World Conference against Racism, Racial Discrimination, Xenophobia and Related Intolerance no later than the year 2001,

Taking note of Commission on Human Rights resolution 1998/26 of 17 April 1998 on racism, racial discrimination, xenophobia and related intolerance, See *Official Records of the Economic and Social Council, 1998, Supplement No. 3* (E/1998/23), chap. II, sect. A. and of agreed conclusions 1998/2 on the coordinated follow-up to and implementation of the Vienna Declaration and Programme of Action, See *Official Records of the General Assembly, Fifty-third Session, Supplement No. 3* and corrigendum (A/53/3 and Corr.1), chap. VI, para. 3. adopted by the Economic and Social Council on 28 July 1998,

Reiterating the importance of the Convention, which is one of the most widely accepted human rights instruments adopted under the auspices of the United Nations,

Mindful of the importance of the contributions of the Committee to the effective implementation of the Convention and to the efforts of the United Nations to combat racism and all other forms of discrimination based on race, colour, descent or national or ethnic origin,

Noting that the reports submitted by States parties under the Convention contain, *inter alia*, information about the causes of, as well as measures to combat, contemporary forms of racism, racial discrimination, xenophobia and related intolerance,

Calling upon States that have not yet become parties to the Convention to ratify it or accede thereto,

Emphasizing the obligation of all States parties to the Convention to take legislative, judicial and other measures in order to secure full implementation of the provisions of the Convention,

Recalling its resolution 47/111 of 16 December 1992, in which it welcomed the decision, taken on 15 January 1992 by the Fourteenth Meeting of States Parties to the International Convention on the Elimination of All Forms of Racial Discrimination, See CERD/SP/45, annex. to amend paragraph 6 of article 8 of the Convention and to add a new paragraph, as paragraph 7 of article 8, with a view to providing for the financing of the Committee from the regular budget of the United Nations, and reiterating its deep concern that the amendment to the Convention has not yet entered into force,

Stressing the importance of enabling the Committee to function smoothly and to have all necessary facilities for the effective performance of its functions under the Convention,

Recalling the provisions of paragraph 4 of article 10 of the Convention regarding the location of the meetings of the Committee and the provisions of paragraph 1 of article 8 regarding the composition of the Committee,

I

REPORT OF THE COMMITTEE ON THE ELIMINATION OF RACIAL DISCRIMINATION

1. *Takes note* of the report of the Committee on the Elimination of Racial Discrimination on its fifty-second and fifty-third sessions; *Official Records of the General Assembly, Fifty-third Session, Supplement No. 18* (A/53/18).
2. *Commends* the Committee for its work with regard to the implementation of the International Convention on the Elimination of All Forms of Racial Discrimination, Resolution 2106A (XX), Annex, especially the examination of reports under article 9 and action on communications under article 14 of the Convention;
3. *Calls upon* States parties to fulfil their obligation, under paragraph 1 of article 9 of the Convention, to submit their periodic reports on measures taken to implement the Convention in due time;
4. *Expresses its concern* at the fact that a great number of reports are overdue and continue to be overdue, in particular initial reports, which constitutes an obstacle to the full implementation of the Convention, and encourages the Secretariat to extend technical assistance to those States whose reports are seriously overdue, upon their request, in the preparation of the reports;
5. *Commends* the Committee on its continuing efforts to contribute to the effective implementation of the Convention, and notes its continuing efforts to improve its working methods;
6. *Also commends* the Committee for its continuing contribution to the prevention of racial discrimination, and welcomes its relevant action thereon;

7. *Encourages* the Committee to continue to contribute fully to the implementation of the Third Decade to Combat Racism and Racial Discrimination and its revised Programme of Action, Resolution 49/146, annex. including by continuing to collaborate with the Subcommission on Prevention of Discrimination and Protection of Minorities of the Commission on Human Rights, as well as by cooperating, as appropriate, with the Special Rapporteur of the Commission on contemporary forms of racism, racial discrimination, xenophobia and related intolerance;
8. *Welcomes and encourages* the cooperation and exchange of information between the Committee and relevant structures and mechanisms of the United Nations, including the Office of the United Nations High Commissioner for Human Rights, as well as with the General Assembly and the States parties to the Convention;
9. *Takes note* of the initial suggestions made by the Committee regarding the World Conference against Racism, Racial Discrimination, Xenophobia and Related Intolerance, and invites the Committee to give high priority to the preparatory process for the World Conference, to present to the Commission on Human Rights, which will act as the preparatory committee for the Conference, its contribution to the objectives of the Conference, including the undertaking of a series of studies, and to participate actively in the preparatory process and at the Conference itself;
10. *Also takes note* of Committee decisions 7 (53) and 8 (53) of 19 August 1998, See *Official Records of the General Assembly, Fifty-third Session, Supplement No. 18* (A/53/18), chap. I, sect. F, para. 14. regarding organizational matters, authorizes the Secretary-General to extend, on a temporary basis, the 1999 and 2000 summer sessions of the Committee by five working days, and decides to consider the two decisions further at its fifty-fifth session;

II

FINANCIAL SITUATION OF THE COMMITTEE ON THE ELIMINATION OF RACIAL DISCRIMINATION

11. *Takes note* of the report of the Secretary-General on the financial situation of the Committee on the Elimination of Racial Discrimination; A/53/255.
12. *Expresses its profound concern* about the fact that a number of States parties to the International Convention on the Elimination of All Forms of Racial Discrimination have still not fulfilled their financial obligations, as shown in the report of the Secretary-General, and strongly appeals to all States parties that are in arrears to fulfil their outstanding financial obligations under paragraph 6 of article 8 of the Convention;
13. *Strongly urges* States parties to the Convention to accelerate their domestic ratification procedures with regard to the amendment to the Convention concerning the financing of the Committee and to notify the Secretary-General expeditiously in writing of their agreement to the amendment, as decided upon at the Fourteenth Meeting of States Parties to the International Convention on the Elimination of All Forms of Racial Discrimination on 15 January 1992, See Official Records of the Economic and Social Council, 1998, Supplement No. 3 (E/1998/23), chap. II, sect. A. endorsed by the

General Assembly in its resolution 47/111 of 16 December 1992 and further reiterated at the Sixteenth Meeting of States Parties on 16 January 1996;

14. *Requests* the Secretary-General to continue to ensure adequate financial arrangements and appropriate means and to provide the necessary support, including an adequate level of Secretariat assistance, in order to ensure the functioning of the Committee and to enable it to cope with its increasing amount of work;

15. *Also requests* the Secretary-General to invite those States parties to the Convention that are in arrears to pay the amounts in arrears and to report thereon to the General Assembly at its fifty-fifth session;

III

STATUS OF THE INTERNATIONAL CONVENTION ON THE ELIMINATION OF ALL FORMS OF RACIAL DISCRIMINATION

16. *Takes note* of the report of the Secretary-General on the status of the International Convention on the Elimination of All Forms of Racial Discrimination; A/53/256.

17. *Expresses its satisfaction* at the number of States that have ratified the Convention or acceded thereto;

18. *Reaffirms once again its conviction* that ratification of or accession to the Convention on a universal basis and the implementation of its provisions are necessary for the realization of the objectives of the Third Decade to Combat Racism and Racial Discrimination and for action beyond the Decade;

19. *Urges* all States that have not yet become parties to the Convention to ratify it or accede thereto;

20. *Urges* States to limit the extent of any reservation they lodge to the Convention and to formulate any reservation as precisely and as narrowly as possible in order to ensure that no reservation is incompatible with the objective and purpose of the Convention or otherwise contrary to international treaty law, to review their reservations regularly with a view to withdrawing them and to withdraw reservations that are contrary to the objective and purpose of the Convention or that are otherwise incompatible with international treaty law;

21. *Requests* the States parties to the Convention that have not yet done so to consider the possibility of making the declaration provided for in article 14 of the Convention;

22. *Decides* to consider at its fifty-fifth session, under the item entitled "Elimination of racism and racial discrimination", the reports of the Committee on the Elimination of Racial Discrimination and the reports of the Secretary-General on the financial situation of the Committee and the status of the Convention.

A/RES/54/157

UNITED NATIONS GENERAL ASSEMBLY

International Covenants on Human Rights

General Assembly Resolution 54/157
adopted 17 December 1999

The General Assembly,

Recalling its resolution 52/116 of 12 December 1997 and Commission on Human Rights resolution 1998/9 of 3 April 1998, See *Official Records of the Economic and Social Council, 1998, Supplement No. 3* (E/1998/23), chap. II, sect. A.

Mindful that the International Covenants on Human Rights, Resolution 2200 A (XXI), annex. constitute the first all-embracing and legally binding international treaties in the field of human rights and, together with the Universal Declaration of Human Rights, Resolution 217 A (III) form the core of the International Bill of Human Rights,

Taking note of the report of the Secretary-General A/54/277 and Corr. 1, on the status of the International Covenants on Human Rights and the Optional Protocols to the International Covenant on Civil and Political Rights, See resolution 2200 A (XXI), annex, and resolution 44/128, annex.

Recalling the International Covenant on Economic, Social and Cultural Rights and the International Covenant on Civil and Political Rights, and reaffirming that all human rights and fundamental freedoms are universal, indivisible and interdependent and interrelated and that the promotion and protection of one category of rights should never exempt or excuse States from the promotion and protection of the other rights,

Recognizing the important role of the Human Rights Committee and the Committee on Economic, Social and Cultural Rights in examining the progress made by State parties in implementing the obligations undertaken in the two International Covenants on Human Rights and the Optional Protocols to the International Covenant on Civil and Political Rights and in providing recommendations to States parties on their implementation,

1. *Reaffirms* the importance of the International Covenants on Human Rights as major parts of international efforts to promote universal respect for and observance of human rights and fundamental freedoms;
2. *Appeals strongly* to all States that have not yet done so to become parties to the International Covenant on Economic, Social and Cultural Rights and the International Covenant on Civil and Political Rights, as well as to accede to the Optional Protocols to the International Covenant on Civil and Political Rights and to make the declaration provided for in article 41 of the Covenant;

3. *Invites* the United Nations High Commissioner for Human Rights to intensify systematic efforts to encourage States to become parties to the International Covenants on Human Rights and, through the programme of advisory services in the field of human rights, to assist such States, at their request, in ratifying or acceding to the Covenants and to the Optional Protocols to the International Covenant on Civil and Political Rights;
4. *Emphasizes* the importance of the strictest compliance by States parties with their obligations under the International Covenant on Economic, Social and Cultural Rights and the International Covenant on Civil and Political Rights and, where applicable, the Optional Protocols to the International Covenant on Civil and Political Rights;
5. *Stresses* the importance of avoiding the erosion of human rights by derogation, and underlines the necessity of strict observance of the agreed conditions and procedures for derogation under article 4 of the International Covenant on Civil and Political Rights, bearing in mind the need for States parties to provide the fullest possible information during states of emergency so that the justification for the appropriateness of measures taken in those circumstances can be assessed;
6. *Encourages* States parties to consider limiting the extent of any reservations they lodge to the International Covenants on Human Rights, to formulate any reservations as precisely and narrowly as possible and to ensure that no reservation is incompatible with the object and purpose of the relevant treaty or otherwise incompatible with international treaty law;
7. *Also encourages* States parties to review regularly any reservations made in respect of the provisions of the International Covenants on Human Rights and the Optional Protocols to the International Covenant on Civil and Political Rights, with a view to withdrawing them;
8. *Takes note with appreciation* of the annual report of the Human Rights Committee submitted to the General Assembly at its fifty-fourth session, *Official Records of the General Assembly, Fifty-fourth Session, Supplement No. 40* (A/54/40) and takes note of general comments Nos. 25 Ibid., *Fifty-first Session, Supplement No. 40* (A/51/40), vol. I, annex V and 26 Ibid., *Fifty-third Session, Supplement No. 40* (A/53/40), vol. I, annex VII adopted by the Committee;
9. *Also takes note with appreciation* of the reports of the Committee on Economic, Social and Cultural Rights on its sixteenth and seventeenth *Official Records of the Economic and Social Council, 1998, Supplement No. 2* (E/1998/22) and eighteenth and nineteenth Ibid., *1999, Supplement No. 2* (E/1999/22) sessions and takes note of general comments Nos. 8, Ibid., *1998, Supplement No. 2* (E/1998/22), annex V. 9, Ibid., *1999, Supplement No. 2* (E/1999/22), annex IV. 10, Ibid., *1999, Supplement No. 2* (E/1999/22), annex V. 11 E/C.12/1999/4 Adopted on 10 May 1999 during the twentieth session and 12 E/C.12/1999/5 Adopted on 12 May 1999 during the twentieth session adopted by the Committee;
10. *Urges* States parties to fulfil in good time such reporting obligations under the International Covenants on Human Rights as may be requested and in their reports to make use of gender-disaggregated data;
11. *Stresses* the importance of fully taking into account a gender perspective in the implementation of the International Covenants on Human Rights at the

national level, including in the national reports of States parties and in the work of the Human Rights Committee and the Committee on Economic, Social and Cultural Rights;
12. *Urges* States parties to take duly into account, in implementing the provisions of the International Covenants on Human Rights, the concluding observations made at the conclusion of the consideration of their reports by the Human Rights Committee and by the Committee on Economic, Social and Cultural Rights, as well as the views adopted by the Human Rights Committee under the first Optional Protocol to the International Covenant on Civil and Political Rights;
13. *Invites* States parties to give particular attention to the dissemination at the national level of the reports they have submitted to the Human Rights Committee and the Committee on Economic, Social and Cultural Rights, the summary records relating to the examination of those reports by the Committees and the observations made by the Committees at the conclusion of the consideration of the reports;
14. *Once again encourages* all Governments to publish the texts of the International Covenant on Economic, Social and Cultural Rights, the International Covenant on Civil and Political Rights and the Optional Protocols to the International Covenant on Civil and Political Rights in as many local languages as possible and to distribute them and make them known as widely as possible in their territories;
15. *Invites* the Human Rights Committee and the Committee on Economic, Social and Cultural Rights when considering the reports of States parties to continue to identify specific needs that might be addressed by United Nations departments, funds and programmes and the specialized agencies, including through the advisory services and technical assistance programme of the Office of the United Nations High Commissioner for Human Rights;
16. *Stresses* the need for improved coordination between relevant United Nations mechanisms and bodies in supporting States parties, upon their request, in implementing the International Covenants on Human Rights and the Optional Protocols to the International Covenant on Civil and Political Rights and encourages continued efforts in this direction;
17. *Invites* States parties to continue to contribute, with practical proposals and ideas, to the dialogue on ways of improving the functioning of the Human Rights Committee and the Committee on Economic, Social and Cultural Rights;
18. *Welcomes* the continuing efforts of the Human Rights Committee and the Committee on Economic, Social and Cultural Rights to strive for uniform standards in the implementation of the provisions of the International Covenants on Human Rights, and appeals to other bodies dealing with similar human rights questions to respect those uniform standards, as expressed in the general comments of the Committees;
19. *Encourages* the Secretary-General to continue to assist States parties to the International Covenants on Human Rights in the preparation of their reports, including by convening seminars or workshops at the national level for the purpose of training government officials engaged in the preparation of such reports, and by exploring other possibilities available under the regular programme of advisory services in the field of human rights;

20. *Requests* the Secretary-General to ensure that the Office of the United Nations High Commissioner for Human Rights effectively assists the Human Rights Committee and the Committee on Economic, Social and Cultural Rights in the implementation of their respective mandates, including by the provision of adequate Secretariat staff resources;
21. *Welcomes* the initiative by the Secretary-General, taking into account the suggestions of the Human Rights Committee, to take determined steps, in particular through the Office of Communications and Public Information of the Secretariat, to give more publicity to the work of that Committee and, similarly, to the work of the Committee on Economic, Social and Cultural Rights;
22. *Requests* the Secretary-General to submit to the General Assembly at its fifty-sixth session, under the item entitled "Human rights questions", a report on the status of the International Covenant on Economic, Social and Cultural Rights, the International Covenant on Civil and Political Rights and the Optional Protocols to the International Covenant on Civil and Political Rights, including all reservations and declarations.

A/RES/54/156

UNITED NATIONS GENERAL ASSEMBLY

Torture and other cruel, inhuman or degrading treatment or punishment

General Assembly Resolution 54/156
adopted 17 December 1999

The General Assembly,

Recalling article 5 of the Universal Declaration of Human Rights, Resolution 217 A (III). article 7 of the International Covenant on Civil and Political Rights, See resolution 2200 A (XXI), annex. the Declaration on the Protection of All Persons from Being Subjected to Torture and Other Cruel, Inhuman or Degrading Treatment or Punishment, Resolution 3452 (XXX), annex. and its resolution 39/46 of 10 December 1984, by which it adopted and opened for signature, ratification and accession the Convention against Torture and Other Cruel, Inhuman or Degrading Treatment or Punishment, and all its subsequent relevant resolutions,

Recalling that freedom from torture is a right that must be protected under all circumstances, including in times of internal or international disturbance or armed conflict,

Recalling also that the World Conference on Human Rights, held in Vienna from 14 to 25 June 1993, firmly declared that efforts to eradicate torture should, first and foremost, be concentrated on prevention and called for the early adoption of an optional protocol to the Convention against Torture and Other Cruel, Inhuman or Degrading Treatment or Punishment, which is intended to establish a preventive system of regular visits to places of detention, A/CONF.157/24 (Part I), chap. III, sect. II, para. 61.

Urging all Governments to promote the speedy and full implementation of the Vienna Declaration and Programme of Action, adopted by the World Conference on Human Rights on 25 June 1993, A/CONF.157/24 (Part I), chap. III. in particular the section relating to freedom from torture, in which it is stated that States should abrogate legislation leading to impunity for those responsible for grave violations of human rights, such as torture, and prosecute such violations, thereby providing a firm basis for the rule of law, Ibid., sect. II, paras. 54–61.

Recalling its resolution 36/151 of 16 December 1981, in which it noted with deep concern that acts of torture took place in various countries, recognized the need to provide assistance to the victims in a purely humanitarian spirit and established the United Nations Voluntary Fund for Victims of Torture,

Recalling also the recommendation in the Vienna Declaration and Programme of Action that high priority should be given to providing the necessary resources to assist victims of torture and effective remedies for their physical, psychological and social rehabilitation, *inter alia*, by additional contributions to the Fund, Ibid., para. 59.

Noting with satisfaction the existence of a considerable international network of centres for the rehabilitation of torture victims, which plays an important role in providing assistance to victims of torture, and the collaboration of the Fund with the centres,

Mindful of the proclamation by the General Assembly in its resolution 52/149 of 12 December 1997 of 26 June as United Nations International Day in Support of Victims of Torture,

1. *Welcomes* the work of the Committee against Torture, and takes note of the report of the Committee, *Official Records of the General Assembly, Fifty-fourth Session, Supplement No. 44* (A/54/44) submitted in accordance with article 24 of the Convention against Torture and Other Cruel, Inhuman or Degrading Treatment or Punishment;
2. *Notes with appreciation* that one hundred and eighteen States have become parties to the Convention;
3. *Urges* all States that have not yet done so to become parties to the Convention as a matter of priority;
4. *Invites* all States ratifying or acceding to the Convention and those States which are parties to the Convention and have not yet done so to consider joining the States parties that have already made the declarations provided for in articles 21 and 22 of the Convention and to consider the possibility of withdrawing their reservations to article 20;
5. *Urges* all States parties to the Convention to notify the Secretary-General of their acceptance of the amendments to articles 17 and 18 of the Convention as soon as possible;
6. *Urges* States parties to comply strictly with their obligations under the Convention, including their obligation to submit reports in accordance with article 19 of the Convention, in view of the high number of reports not submitted, and invites States parties to incorporate a gender perspective and to include information concerning children and juveniles when submitting reports to the Committee;
7. *Calls upon* the United Nations High Commissioner for Human Rights, in conformity with her mandate established in General Assembly resolution 48/141 of 20 December 1993, to continue to provide, at the request of Governments, advisory services for the preparation of national reports to the Committee and for the prevention of torture, as well as technical assistance in the development, production and distribution of teaching material for this purpose;
8. *Urges* States parties to take fully into account the conclusions and recommendations made by the Committee after its consideration of their reports;
9. *Emphasizes* the obligation of States parties under article 10 of the Convention to ensure education and training for personnel who may be involved in the custody, interrogation or treatment of any individual subjected to any form of arrest, detention or imprisonment;
10. *Stresses* in this context that States must not punish personnel referred to in

paragraph 9 above for not obeying orders to commit or conceal acts amounting to torture or other cruel, inhuman or degrading treatment or punishment;

11. *Welcomes* the progress made by the inter-sessional open-ended working group of the Commission on Human Rights on the development of a draft optional protocol to the Convention against Torture and other Cruel, Inhuman or Degrading Treatment or Punishment, and urges the inter-sessional open-ended working group to complete as soon as possible a final text for submission to the General Assembly, through the Economic and Social Council, for consideration and adoption;

12. *Takes note with appreciation* of the interim report by the Special Rapporteur of the Commission on Human Rights on the question of torture and other cruel, inhuman or degrading treatment or punishment, A/54/426, annex., describing the overall trends and developments with regard to his mandate, and encourages the Special Rapporteur to continue to include in his recommendations proposals on the prevention and investigation of torture;

13. *Invites* the Special Rapporteur to continue to examine questions of torture or other cruel, inhuman or degrading treatment or punishment directed against women and conditions conducive to such torture, and to make appropriate recommendations for the prevention and redress of gender-specific forms of torture, including rape or any other form of sexual violence, and to exchange views with the Special Rapporteur on violence against women, its causes and consequences, with a view to enhancing further their effectiveness and mutual cooperation;

14. *Also invites* the Special Rapporteur to continue to consider questions relating to the torture of children and conditions conducive to such torture and other cruel, inhuman or degrading treatment or punishment and to make appropriate recommendations for the prevention of such torture;

15. *Calls upon* all Governments to cooperate with and to assist the Special Rapporteur in the performance of his task, in particular by supplying all necessary information requested by him, to react appropriately and expeditiously to his urgent appeals, to give serious consideration to his requests to visit their countries, and urges them to enter into a constructive dialogue with the Special Rapporteur with respect to the follow-up to his recommendations;

16. *Approves* the methods of work employed by the Special Rapporteur, in particular as regards urgent appeals, reiterates his need to be able to respond effectively to credible and reliable information that comes before him, invites him to continue to seek the views and comments of all concerned, in particular Member States, and expresses its appreciation for the discreet and independent way in which he continues to carry out his work;

17. *Requests* the Special Rapporteur to continue to consider including in his report information on the follow-up by Governments to his recommendations, visits and communications, including progress made and problems encountered;

18. *Stresses* the need for the continued regular exchange of views between the Committee, the Special Rapporteur and other relevant United Nations mechanisms and bodies, as well as the pursuance of cooperation with relevant United Nations programmes, notably the United Nations Crime Prevention

and Criminal Justice Programme, with a view to enhancing further their effectiveness and cooperation on issues relating to torture, *inter alia*, by improving their coordination;

19. *Expresses its gratitude and appreciation* to the Governments, organizations and individuals who have already contributed to the United Nations Voluntary Fund for Victims of Torture;
20. *Appeals* to all Governments and organizations to contribute annually to the Fund, if possible with a substantial increase in the level of contributions, so that consideration may be given to the ever-increasing demand for assistance;
21. *Expresses its appreciation* to the Board of Trustees of the Fund for the work it has accomplished;
22. *Requests* the Secretary-General to transmit to all Governments the appeals of the General Assembly for contributions to the Fund;
23. *Also requests* the Secretary-General to continue to include the Fund on an annual basis among the programmes for which funds are pledged at the United Nations Pledging Conference for Development Activities;
24. *Further requests* the Secretary-General to assist the Board of Trustees of the Fund in its appeal for contributions and its efforts to make better known the existence of the Fund and the financial means currently available to it, as well as its assessment of the global need for international funding of rehabilitation services for torture victims, and in this effort, to make use of all existing possibilities, including the preparation, production and dissemination of information materials;
25. *Requests* the Secretary-General to ensure the provision of adequate staff and facilities for the bodies and mechanisms involved in combating torture and assisting victims of torture, commensurate with the strong support expressed by Member States for combating torture and assisting victims of torture;
26. *Invites* donor countries and recipient countries to consider including in their bilateral programmes and projects relating to the training of armed forces, security forces, prison and police personnel, as well as health-care personnel, matters relating to the protection of human rights and the prevention of torture and to keep in mind a gender perspective;
27. *Calls upon* all Governments, the United Nations High Commissioner for Human Rights and other United Nations bodies and agencies, as well as relevant intergovernmental and non-governmental organizations, to commemorate, on 26 June, the United Nations International Day in Support of Victims of Torture;
28. *Requests* the Secretary-General to submit to the Commission on Human Rights at its fifty-sixth session and to the General Assembly at its fifty-fifth session a report on the status of the Convention against Torture and Other Cruel, Inhuman or Degrading Treatment or Punishment and a report on the operations of the United Nations Voluntary Fund for the Victims of Torture;
29. *Decides* to consider the reports of the Secretary-General, including the report on the United Nations Voluntary Fund for Victims of Torture, the report of the Committee against Torture and the interim report of the Special Rapporteur of the Commission on Human Rights on the question of torture and other cruel, inhuman or degrading treatment or punishment at its fifty-fifth session.

A/RES/54/137

UNITED NATIONS GENERAL ASSEMBLY

Convention on the Elimination of All Forms of Discrimination against Women

General Assembly Resolution 54/137
adopted 17 December 1999

The General Assembly,

Recalling its resolution 53/118 of 9 December 1998,

Bearing in mind that one of the purposes of the United Nations, as stated in Articles 1 and 55 of the Charter, is to promote universal respect for human rights and fundamental freedoms for all without distinction of any kind, including distinction as to sex,

Affirming that women and men should participate equally in social, economic and political development, should contribute equally to such development and should share equally in improved conditions of life,

Recalling the Vienna Declaration and Programme of Action, adopted by the World Conference on Human Rights on 25 June 1993, A/CONF.157/24 (Part I), chap. III in which the Conference reaffirmed that the human rights of women and the girl child were an inalienable, integral and indivisible part of universal human rights,

Acknowledging the need for a comprehensive and integrated approach to the promotion and protection of the human rights of women, which includes the integration of the human rights of women into the mainstream of United Nations activities system-wide, and, in this context, calling for the implementation of agreed conclusions 1998/2 of the Economic and Social Council, See *Official Records of the General Assembly, Fifty-third Session, Supplement No. 3* and corrigendum (A/53/3 and Corr.1), chap. VI, para. 3.

Noting that 1999 is the twentieth anniversary of the adoption of the Convention on the Elimination of All Forms of Discrimination against Women, Resolution 34/180, annex. welcoming the progress made in its implementation, but concerned with the remaining challenges,

Bearing in mind its resolution 54/4 of 6 October 1999 in which it adopted and opened for signature, ratification and accession the Optional Protocol to the Convention on the Elimination of All Forms of Discrimination against Women,

Bearing in mind also the recommendation of the Committee on the Elimination of Discrimination against Women that national reports include information on the implementation of the Beijing Platform for Action of the Fourth World

Conference on Women, *Report of the Fourth World Conference on Women, Beijing, 4–15 September 1995 (United Nations publication, Sales No. E.96.IV.13), chap. I, resolution 1, annex II,*

Welcoming the growing number of States parties to the Convention on the Elimination of All Forms of Discrimination against Women, which now stands at one hundred and sixty-five,

Noting the elaboration and adoption by the Committee on the Elimination of Discrimination against Women, at its twentieth session, of general recommendation 24 on article 12 of the Convention, women and health, *Official Records of the General Assembly, Fifty-fourth Session, Supplement No. 38 (A/54/38/Rev.1), chap. I, sect. A.*

Having considered the reports of the Committee on the Elimination of Discrimination against Women on its twentieth and twenty-first sessions, *Ibid.*, parts one and two.

Expressing concern at the great number of reports overdue and which continue to be overdue, in particular initial reports, which constitute an obstacle to the full implementation of the Convention on the Elimination of All Forms of Discrimination against Women,

1. *Welcomes* the report of the Secretary-General on the status of the Convention on the Elimination of All Forms of Discrimination against Women; A/54/224 and Corr. 1.
2. *Urges* all States that have not yet ratified or acceded to the Convention to do so as soon as possible, so that universal ratification of the Convention can be achieved by the year 2000;
3. *Emphasizes* the importance of full compliance by States parties with their obligations under the Convention;
4. *Takes note with appreciation* of the adoption by the General Assembly, by resolution 54/4, of the Optional Protocol to the Convention on the Elimination of All Forms of Discrimination against Women;
5. *Notes* that some States parties have modified their reservations, expresses satisfaction that some reservations have been withdrawn, and urges States to limit the extent of any reservations they lodge to the Convention, to formulate any such reservations as precisely and as narrowly as possible, to ensure that no reservations are incompatible with the object and purpose of the Convention or otherwise incompatible with international treaty law, to review their reservations regularly with a view to withdrawing them and to withdraw reservations that are contrary to the object and purpose of the Convention or that are otherwise incompatible with international treaty law;
6. *Urges* States parties to the Convention to make all possible efforts to submit their reports on the implementation of the Convention in accordance with article 18 thereof and with the guidelines provided by the Committee on the Elimination of Discrimination against Women and to cooperate fully with the Committee in the presentation of their reports;
7. *Encourages* the Secretariat to extend further technical assistance to States parties, upon their request, in the preparation of reports, in particular initial reports, and invites Governments to contribute to these efforts;
8. *Commends* the Committee on its contributions to the effective implementation of the Convention;

9. *Urges* States parties to the Convention to take appropriate measures so that acceptance of the amendment to article 20, paragraph 1, of the Convention by a two-thirds majority of States parties can be reached as soon as possible in order for the amendment to enter into force;
10. *Expresses its appreciation* for the additional meeting time allowing the Committee to hold two sessions annually, each of three weeks' duration, preceded by a pre-session working group of the Committee;
11. *Emphasizes* the need to ensure adequate financing and staff support for the effective functioning of the Committee, including for the dissemination of information;
12. *Invites* Governments, agencies and organizations of the United Nations system and intergovernmental as well as non-governmental organizations to disseminate the Convention and its Optional Protocol;
13. *Encourages* all relevant entities of the United Nations system, within their mandates, to continue to assist, upon their request, States parties to implement the Convention and, in this regard, to pay attention to the concluding comments as well as the general recommendations of the Committee;
14. *Also encourages* all relevant entities of the United Nations system to continue building women's knowledge and understanding of and capacity to utilize human rights instruments, in particular of the Convention and its Optional Protocol;
15. *Welcomes* the submission of reports by the specialized agencies at the invitation of the Committee on the implementation of the Convention in areas falling within the scope of their activities and the contribution of non-governmental organizations to the work of the Committee, and encourages those agencies to continue the submission of their reports;
16. *Requests* the Secretary-General to submit to the General Assembly at its fifty-fifth session a report on the status of the Convention and the implementation of the present resolution under the appropriate agenda item.

A/RES/54/148

UNITED NATIONS GENERAL ASSEMBLY

The girl child

General Assembly Resolution 54/148
adopted 17 December 1999

The General Assembly,

Recalling its resolution 53/127 of 9 December 1998 and all previous relevant resolutions, including the agreed conclusions of the Commission on the Status of Women, *Official Records of the Economic and Social Council, 1999, Supplement No. 7* (E/1999/27), chap. I, sect. B.IV. in particular those relevant to the girl child,

Recalling also all relevant previous United Nations conferences and the Declaration and Agenda for Action of the World Congress against Commercial Sexual Exploitation of Children, held at Stockholm from 27 to 31 August 1996, A/51/385, annex. including the recent five-year review of the implementation of the Programme of Action of the International Conference on Population and Development, *Report of the International Conference on Population and Development, Cairo, 5–13 September 1994 (United Nations publication, Sales No. E.95.XIII.18), chap. I, resolution 1, annex.,*

Deeply concerned about discrimination against the girl child and the violation of the rights of the girl child, which often result in less access for girls to education, nutrition, physical and mental health care and in girls enjoying fewer of the rights, opportunities and benefits of childhood and adolescence than boys and often being subjected to various forms of cultural, social, sexual and economic exploitation and to violence and harmful practices such as female infanticide, incest, early marriage, prenatal sex selection and female genital mutilation,

Recognizing the need to achieve gender equality so as to ensure a just and equitable world for girls,

Deeply concerned that, in situations of poverty, war and armed conflict, girl children are among the victims most affected and that thus their potential for full development is limited,

Concerned that the girl child has furthermore become a victim of sexually transmitted diseases and the human immunodeficiency virus, which affects the quality of her life and leaves her open to further discrimination,

Noting that 1999 is the tenth anniversary of the Convention on the Rights of the Child Resolution 44/25, annex. and the twentieth anniversary of Convention on the Elimination of All Forms of Discrimination against Women, Resolution 34/180, annex.

Reaffirming the equal rights of women and men as enshrined, *inter alia*, in the

Preamble to the Charter of the United Nations, the Convention on the Elimination of All Forms of Discrimination against Women and the Convention on the Rights of the Child,

1. *Stresses* the need for full and urgent implementation of the rights of the girl child as guaranteed to her under all human rights instruments, including the Convention on the Rights of the Child, Resolution 44/25, annex. and the Convention on the Elimination of All Forms of Discrimination against Women, Resolution 34/180, annex. as well as the need for universal ratification of those instruments;
2. *Urges* all States to take all necessary measures and to institute legal reforms to ensure the full and equal enjoyment by the girl child of all human rights and fundamental freedoms, to take effective action against violations of those rights and freedoms and to base programmes and policies for the girl child on the rights of the child;
3. *Urges* States to enact and strictly enforce laws to ensure that marriage is entered into only with the free and full consent of the intending spouses, to enact and strictly enforce laws concerning the minimum legal age of consent and the minimum age for marriage and to raise the minimum age for marriage where necessary;
4. *Also urges* all States to fulfil obligations they have under the Convention on the Rights of the Child and the Convention on the Elimination of all Forms of Discrimination against Women as well as the commitment to implement the Platform of Action of the Fourth World Conference on Women; *Report of the Fourth World Conference on Women, Beijing, 4–15 September 1995* (United Nations publication, Sales No. E.96.IV.13), chap. I, resolution 1, annex II;
5. *Further urges* all States to enact and enforce legislation to protect girls from all forms of violence, including female infanticide and prenatal sex selection, female genital mutilation, rape, domestic violence, incest, sexual abuse, sexual exploitation, child prostitution and child pornography, and to develop age-appropriate safe and confidential programmes and medical, social and psychological support services to assist girls who are subjected to violence;
6. *Calls upon* all States and international and non-governmental organizations, individually and collectively to further implement the Platform for Action of the Fourth World Conference on Women, in particular the strategic objectives relating to the girl child;
7. *Urges* States to take special measures for the protection of children, in particular to protect girls from rape and other forms of sexual abuse and gender-based violence in situations of armed conflict, paying special attention to refugee and displaced girls and taking into account the special needs of the girl child in the delivery of humanitarian assistance;
8. *Also urges* States to formulate comprehensive, multidisciplinary and coordinated national plans, programmes or strategies to eliminate all forms of violence against women and girls, which should be widely disseminated and should provide targets and timetables for implementation, as well as effective domestic enforcement procedures through the establishment of monitoring mechanisms involving all parties concerned, including consultations with women's organizations, giving attention to the recommendations relating to

the girl child of the Special Rapporteur of the Commission on Human Rights on violence against women, its causes and consequences;
9. *Calls upon* Governments, civil society, including the media, and non-governmental organizations, to promote human rights education and the full respect for and enjoyment of the human rights of the girl child, *inter alia*, through the translation, production and dissemination of age-appropriate information materials on these rights to all sectors of society, in particular to children;
10. *Requests* the Secretary-General, as Chairman of the Administrative Committee on Coordination, to ensure that all organizations and bodies of the United Nations system, individually and collectively, in particular the United Nations Children's Fund, the United Nations Educational, Scientific and Cultural Organization, the World Food Programme, the United Nations Population Fund, the United Nations Development Fund for Women, the World Health Organization and the Office of the United Nations High Commissioner for Refugees, take into account the rights and the particular needs of the girl child in the country programme of cooperation in accordance with the national priorities, including through the United Nations Development Assistance Framework. See A/53/226, paras. 72–77, and A/53/226/ Add. 1, paras. 88–98;
11. *Requests* all human rights treaty bodies, special procedures and other human rights mechanisms of the Commission on Human Rights and the Subcommission on the Promotion and Protection of Human Rights. Formerly known as the Sub-commission on Prevention of Discrimination and Protection of Minorities; see E/1999/INF/2/ Add. 2. For the final text, see *Official Records of the Economic and Social Council, 1999, Supplement No. 1, (E/1999/99)*, decision 1999/256 to adopt regularly and systematically a gender perspective in the implementation of their mandates and to include in their reports information on the qualitative analysis of violations of human rights of women and girls, and encourages the strengthening of cooperation and coordination in that regard;
12. *Calls upon* States and international and non-governmental organizations to mobilize all necessary resources, support and efforts to realize the goals, strategic objectives and actions set out in the Platform for Action of the Fourth World Conference on Women;
13. *Stresses* the importance of a substantive assessment of the implementation of the Platform for Action with a life cycle perspective so as to identify gaps and obstacles in the implementation process and to develop further actions for the achievement of the goals of the Programme for Action;
14. *Calls upon* Governments, the United Nations system, in particular the Division for the Advancement of Women, non-governmental organizations and women's organizations to ensure that, in the preparation for the special session of the General Assembly entitled "Women 2000: gender, equality, development and peace for the twenty-first century", the needs and rights of the girl child are duly taken into account and integrated into all activities;
15. *Requests* the Secretary-General to ensure that the needs and the rights of the girl child are specifically assessed in the five-year review of the Programme of Action of the World Summit for Social Development, *Report of the World Summit for Social Development, Copenhagen, 6–12 March 1995*

(United Nations publication, Sales No. E.96.IV.8), chap. I, resolution 1, annex. II to be held in June 2000;

16. *Also requests* the Secretary-General, in consultation with the United Nations Development Programme, the United Nations Educational, Scientific and Cultural Organization, the United Nations Population Fund, the United Nations Children's Fund and the World Bank, to ensure that the needs and the rights of the girl child are given special attention in all preparatory processes at the national, regional and international levels, including the Education for All 2000 Assessment See A/54/128-E/1999/70 and the agenda of the World Education Forum, to be held in April 2000;

17. *Further requests* the Secretary-General to ensure that the needs and the rights of the girl child are integrated in the preparatory work of the special session of the General Assembly on the follow-up to the World Summit for Children in 2001, *inter alia*, by providing the General Assembly with a comprehensive report drawing on the experiences and outcomes of the five-year reviews of the International Conference on Population and Development, the Fourth World Conference on Women and the World Summit for Social Development, and the World Education Forum.

A/RES/54/149

UNITED NATIONS GENERAL ASSEMBLY

The rights of the child

General Assembly Resolution 54/149
adopted 17 December 1999

The General Assembly,

Recalling its resolutions 53/128 and 53/127 of 9 December 1998 and Commission on Human Rights resolution 1999/80 of 28 April 1999, See *Official Records of the Economic and Social Council 1999, Supplement No. 3 (E/1999/23), chap. II,* sect. A,

Bearing in mind the Convention on the Rights of the Child, Resolution 44/25, annex. emphasizing that the provisions of the Convention and other relevant human rights instruments must constitute the standard in the promotion and protection of the rights of the child, and reaffirming that the best interest of the child shall be the primary consideration in all actions concerning children,

Reaffirming the World Declaration on the Survival, Protection and Development of Children and the Plan of Action for Implementing the World Declaration on the Survival, Protection and Development of Children in the 1990s adopted by the World Summit for Children held in New York on 29 and 30 September 1990, A/45/625, annex. notably the solemn commitment to give high priority to the rights of children, to their survival and to their protection and development, and reaffirming also the Vienna Declaration and Programme of Action adopted by the World Conference on Human Rights, held at Vienna from 14 to 25 June 1993, A/CONF.157/24 (Part I), chap. III. which, *inter alia*, states that national and international mechanisms and programmes for the defence and protection of children, in particular those in especially difficult circumstances, should be strengthened, including through effective measures to combat exploitation and abuse of children, such as female infanticide, harmful child labour, sale of children and organs, child prostitution and child pornography, and which reaffirms that all human rights and fundamental freedoms are universal,

Profoundly concerned that the situation of girls and boys in many parts of the world remains critical as a result of poverty, inadequate social and economic conditions in an increasingly globalized world economy, pandemics, natural disasters, armed conflicts, displacement, exploitation, illiteracy, hunger, intolerance, discrimination and inadequate legal protection, and convinced that urgent and effective national and international action is called for,

Underlining the need for mainstreaming a gender perspective into all policies and programmes relating to children,

Recognizing the need for the realization of a standard of living adequate for the child's physical, mental, spiritual, moral and social development, as well as the provision of universal and equal access to primary education,

Recognizing also that partnership between Governments, international organizations and all sectors of civil society, in particular non-governmental organizations, is important to realizing the rights of the child,

Emphasizing the importance of the tenth anniversary of the Convention on the Rights of the Child for mobilizing and taking further action towards the full realization of the rights of the child,

Welcoming the preparations for the special session of the General Assembly on the follow-up to the World Summit for Children in 2001,

I

Implementation of the Convention on the Rights of the Child

1. *Once again urges* the States that have not yet done so to sign and ratify or accede to the Convention on the Rights of the Child[1] as a matter of priority, with a view to reaching the goal of universal adherence by the tenth anniversaries, in 2000, of both the World Summit for Children[2] and the entry into force of the Convention;
2. *Reiterates its concern* at the great number of reservations to the Convention, and urges States parties to withdraw reservations incompatible with the object and purpose of the Convention and to regularly review any reservations with a view to withdrawing them;
3. *Calls upon* States parties to implement fully the Convention, and stresses that the implementation of the Convention contributes to the achievement of the goals of the World Summit for Children;
4. *Urges* States to involve children and youth in their efforts to implement the goals of the World Summit for Children and the Convention on the Rights of the Child;
5. *Calls upon* States parties to cooperate closely with the Committee on the Rights of the Child and to comply in a timely manner with their reporting obligations under the Convention, in accordance with the guidelines elaborated by the Committee, and encourages States parties to take into account the recommendations made by the Committee in the implementation of the provisions of the Convention;
6. *Also calls upon* States parties to encourage training on the rights of the child for those involved in activities concerning children, for example through the programme of advisory services and technical cooperation in the field of human rights;
7. *Requests* the Secretary-General to ensure the provision of appropriate staff and facilities for the effective and expeditious performance of the functions of the Committee, and takes note of the temporary support given by the plan of action of the United Nations High Commissioner for Human Rights to strengthen the important role of the Committee in advancing the implementation of the Convention on the Rights of the Child, and to make available information on the follow-up to the plan of action;

8. *Calls upon* States parties to the Convention to urgently take appropriate measures so that acceptance of the amendment to paragraph 2 of article 43 of the Convention by a two-thirds majority of States parties can be reached as soon as possible, in order for the amendment to enter into force, increasing the membership of the Committee from ten to eighteen experts;
9. *Invites* the Committee on the Rights of the Child to continue to enhance its constructive dialogue with the States parties and its transparent and effective functioning;
10. *Welcomes* the attention given by the Committee to the realization of the highest attainable standards of health and access to health care, and to the rights of children affected by human immunodeficiency virus/acquired immunodeficiency syndrome (HIV/AIDS) and urges Governments, in cooperation with relevant United Nations bodies and organizations, to adopt all appropriate measures with a view to the realization of all their rights;
11. *Calls upon* States to protect all human rights of migrant children, in particular unaccompanied migrant children, and to ensure that the best interest of the child shall accordingly be a primary consideration, and encourages the Committee on the Rights of the Child, the United Nations Children's Fund as well as other relevant United Nations bodies, within their respective mandates, to pay particular attention to the conditions of migrant children in all States, and as appropriate, to make recommendations to strengthen their protection;
12. *Recommends* that, within their mandates, all relevant human rights mechanisms and all other relevant organs and mechanisms of the United Nations system and the supervisory bodies of the specialized agencies pay attention to particular situations in which children are in danger and where their rights are violated and that they take into account the work of the Committee on the Rights of the Child, and encourages the further development of the rights-based approach adopted by the United Nations Children's Fund and further steps to increase system-wide coordination and inter-agency cooperation for the promotion and protection of the rights of the child;
13. *Encourages* the Committee, in monitoring the implementation of the Convention, to continue to pay attention to the needs of children in especially difficult circumstances;
14. *Encourages* Governments, relevant United Nations bodies as well as relevant non-governmental organizations and child rights advocates to contribute to, as appropriate, to the web-based database launched by the United Nations Children's Fund, in order to continue to provide information on laws, structures, policies and processes adopted at the national level to translate the Convention on the Rights of the Child into practice;

II

Prevention and eradication of the sale of children and of their sexual exploitation and abuse, including child prostitution and child pornography

1. *Welcomes* the interim report of the Special Rapporteur of the Commission on Human Rights on the sale of children, child prostitution and child pornography, A/54/411. and expresses its support for her work;

2. *Requests* the Secretary-General to provide the Special Rapporteur with all necessary human and financial assistance to enable her to discharge her mandate fully;
3. *Invites* further voluntary contributions through the Office of the United Nations High Commissioner for Human Rights and support to be provided for the work of the Special Rapporteur for the effective fulfilment of her mandate;
4. *Strongly supports* the work of the open-ended inter-sessional working group of the Commission on Human Rights on the elaboration of a draft optional protocol to the Convention on the Rights of the Child, Resolution 44/25, annex. related to the sale of children, child prostitution and child pornography, and urges the working group to finalize its work before the tenth anniversary of the entry into force of the Convention on the Rights of the Child in 2000;
5. *Reaffirms* the obligation of States parties to prevent the abduction of, sale of or trafficking in children for any purpose or in any form and to protect the child from all forms of sexual exploitation or abuse, in accordance with articles 35 and 34 of the Convention on the Rights of the Child;
6. *Calls upon* States to criminalize and effectively penalize all forms of sexual exploitation and sexual abuse of children, including within the family or for commercial purposes, child pornography and child prostitution, including child sex tourism, while ensuring that the children victims of such practices are not penalized, and to take effective measures to ensure the prosecution of offenders, whether local or foreign, by the competent national authorities, either in the offender's country of origin or in the country of destination, in accordance with due process of law;
7. *Also calls upon* States, in cases of child sex tourism, to enhance international cooperation among all relevant authorities, in particular law enforcement authorities, including sharing relevant data, in order to eradicate this practice;
8. *Requests* States to increase cooperation and concerted action, at the national, regional and international levels, including in the context of the United Nations, by all relevant authorities and institutions, in order to adopt and implement effective measures for the prevention and eradication of the sale of children and of their sexual exploitation and abuse and to prevent and dismantle networks trafficking in children;
9. *Stresses* the need to combat the existence of a market that encourages such criminal practices against children, including through preventive and enforcement measures targeting customers or individuals who sexually exploit or sexually abuse children;
10. *Also calls upon* States to enact and enforce, review and revise, as appropriate, laws, and implement policies, programmes and practices to protect children from and to eliminate all forms of sexual exploitation and abuse, including commercial sexual exploitation, taking into account the particular problems posed by the use of the Internet in this regard;
11. *Encourages* Governments to facilitate the active participation of child victims of sexual exploitation or abuse in the development and implementation of strategies to protect children from sexual exploitation and abuse;
12. *Encourages* continued regional and interregional efforts, with the objective of identifying best practices and issues requiring particularly urgent action,

to follow up the implementation of the measures in line with those outlined in the Declaration and Agenda for Action of the World Congress against Commercial Sexual Exploitation of Children held at Stockholm, from 27 to 31 August 1996; A/51/385, annex.
13. *Invites* States and relevant United Nations bodies and agencies to allocate appropriate resources for rehabilitation of child victims of sexual exploitation and abuse and to take all appropriate measures to promote their full recovery and social reintegration;

III

Protection of children affected by armed conflict

1. *Welcomes* the report of the Special Representative of the Secretary-General on the impact of armed conflict on children; A/54/430.
2. *Expresses its support* for the work of the Special Representative of the Secretary-General, in particular in raising worldwide awareness and mobilizing official and public opinion for the protection of children affected by armed conflict, in order to promote respect for children's rights and needs in conflict and post-conflict situations, and recommends that the Secretary-General extend his mandate, as established in paragraphs 35, 36 and 37 of General Assembly resolution 51/77 of 12 December 1996, for a further period of three years;
3. *Urges* the Secretary-General and all relevant parts of the United Nations system, including the Special Representative and the United Nations Children's Fund, to intensify their efforts to develop a concerted approach to the rights, protection and welfare of children affected by armed conflict, including, as appropriate, in the preparations of the field visits of the Special Representative and in the follow-up to such visits;
4. *Calls upon* all States and other parties concerned to continue to cooperate with the Special Representative, to implement the commitments they have undertaken and to consider carefully all the recommendations of the Special Representative and address the issues identified;
5. *Welcomes* the continued support and voluntary contributions that are being provided to the work of the Special Representative;
6. *Urges* all States and other parties to armed conflict to respect international humanitarian law, to put an end to any form of targeting of children and to attacking sites that usually have a significant presence of children, calls upon States parties to respect fully the provisions of the Geneva Conventions of 12 August 1949, United Nations, *Treaty Series*, vol. 75, Nos. 970–973 and the additional protocols thereto of 1977, Ibid., vol. 1125, Nos. 17512 and 17513 and calls upon all parties to armed conflict to take all measures required to protect children from acts constituting violations of international humanitarian law, including prosecution by States, within their national legal framework, of those responsible for such violations;
7. *Recognizes*, in this regard, the contribution of the establishment of the International Criminal Court to ending impunity for perpetrators of certain crimes committed against children, as defined in the Rome Statute of the International Criminal Court, See A/CONF.183/9, art. 8 which include, *inter*

alia, those involving sexual violence or child soldiers, and thus to the prevention of such crimes;
8. *Condemns* the abduction of children in situations of armed conflict and into armed conflicts, and urges States, international organizations and other concerned parties to take all appropriate measures to secure the unconditional release of all abducted children, and urges States to bring the perpetrators to justice;
9. *Notes* the importance of the second open debate, held in the Security Council on 25 August 1999, on children and armed conflict, see S/PV.4037 and Corr. 1 and S/PV.4037 (Resumption 1). For the final text, see *Official Records of the Security Council, Fifty-fourth Year, Plenary Meetings, 4037th meeting,* and the undertaking by the Council to give special attention to the protection, welfare and rights of children when taking action aimed at maintaining peace and security: see Security Council resolution 1261 (1999), and reaffirms the essential role of the General Assembly and the Economic and Social Council for the promotion and protection of rights and welfare of children;
10. *Calls upon* all parties to armed conflicts to ensure the full, safe and unhindered access of humanitarian personnel and the delivery of humanitarian assistance to all children affected by armed conflict;
11. *Welcomes* the decision by the Economic and Social Council to call for systematic, concerted and comprehensive inter-agency efforts on behalf of children as well as adequate and sustainable resource allocation to provide both the immediate emergency assistance and long-term measures to children throughout all phases of an emergency, see A/54/3, chap. VI, para. 5, agreed conclusions 1999/1, para. 22. For the final text, see *Official Records of the General Assembly, Fifty-fourth Session, Supplement No. 3 (A/54/3/Rev.1);*
12. *Urges* States and all other parties to armed conflict to end the use of children as soldiers and to ensure their demobilization and effective disarmament, and to implement effective measures for the rehabilitation, physical and psychological recovery and reintegration into society of all child victims in cases of armed conflict, and invites the international community to assist in this endeavour and emphasizes that no support which enables or contributes to the use of child soldiers should be given to those who use child soldiers;
13. *Calls upon* States and relevant United Nations bodies to continue to support national and international mine action efforts, including by financial contributions, mine awareness programmes, victim assistance and child centred rehabilitation, and welcomes also the positive effects on children of concrete legislative measures with respect to anti-personnel mines;
14. *Notes with concern* the impact of small arms and light weapons on children in situations of armed conflict, in particular as a result of their illicit production and traffic, and calls upon States to address this problem;
15. *Recommends* that whenever sanctions are imposed their impact on children be assessed and monitored and that humanitarian exemptions be child-focused and formulated with clear guidelines for their application;
16. *Calls upon* States, relevant United Nations bodies and agencies and regional organizations to integrate the rights of the child into all activities in conflict and post-conflict situations, including training programmes and emergency relief operations, country programmes and field operations aimed at promoting peace, preventing and resolving conflicts as well as negotiating and

implementing peace agreements, and, given the long-term consequences for society, underlines the importance of including specific provisions for children, including resourcing, in peace agreements and in arrangements negotiated by parties;

17. *Welcomes* the ongoing efforts by, *inter alia*, regional organizations, intergovernmental organizations and non-governmental organizations, to bring to an end the use of children as soldiers in armed conflicts, and reaffirms the urgent need to raise the current minimum age-limit set by article 38 of the Convention on the Rights of the Child, Resolution 44/25, annex. on the recruitment and participation of any person in armed conflicts with the aim to end the use of child soldiers;

18. *Strongly supports* the work of the open-ended inter-sessional working group of the Commission on Human Rights on the elaboration of a draft optional protocol to the Convention on the Rights of the Child related to the involvement of children in armed conflict, and the consultations conducted by the chairperson of the working group in order to make further progress with the aim of finalizing its work before the tenth anniversary of the entry into force of the Convention on the Rights of the Child;

IV

Refugee and internally displaced children

1. *Urges* Governments to improve the implementation of policies and programmes for the protection, care and well-being of refugee and internally displaced children, with the necessary international cooperation, in particular with the Office of the United Nations High Commissioner for Refugees, the United Nations Children's Fund and the representative of the Secretary-General on internally displaced persons, in accordance with the obligations under the Convention on the Rights of the Child, Resolution 44/25, annex.;

2. *Calls upon* all States and other parties to armed conflicts, as well as United Nations bodies and organizations, to give urgent attention, in terms of protection and assistance, to the fact that refugee and internally displaced children are particularly exposed to risks in connection with armed conflicts, such as being forcibly recruited or subjected to sexual violence, abuse or exploitation;

3. *Expresses its deep concern* about the growing number of unaccompanied refugee and internally displaced children, and calls upon all States and United Nations bodies and agencies and other relevant organizations to give priority to programmes for family tracing and reunification and to continue to monitor the care arrangements for unaccompanied refugee and internally displaced children;

V

Progressive elimination of child labour

1. *Reaffirms* the right of the child to be protected from economic exploitation and from performing any work that is likely to be hazardous or to interfere with the child's education, or to be harmful to the child's health or physical, mental, spiritual, moral or social development;

2. *Welcomes* the adoption by the International Labour Organization, at the eighty-seventh session of the International Labour Conference, held at Geneva from 1 to 17 June 1999, of the Convention concerning the Prohibition and Immediate Action for the Elimination of the Worst Forms of Child Labour, Convention No. 182, and encourages all States to consider ratifying it as a matter of priority with a view to its entry into force as soon as possible;
3. *Calls upon* all States that have not yet done so to consider ratifying the conventions of the International Labour Organization relating to child labour, in particular the Convention concerning Forced or Compulsory Labour, 1930, Convention No. 29, and the Convention concerning Minimum Age for Admission to Employment, 1973, Convention No. 138, and to implement those Conventions;
4. *Calls upon* all States to translate into concrete action their commitment to the progressive and effective elimination of child labour contrary to accepted international standards, and urges them, *inter alia*, to immediately eliminate the worst forms of child labour as set out in the new International Labour Organization Convention No. 182;
5. *Also calls upon* all States to systematically assess and examine the magnitude, nature and causes of child labour and to elaborate and implement strategies for the elimination of child labour contrary to accepted international standards, giving special attention to specific dangers faced by girls, as well as to the rehabilitation and social reintegration of the children concerned;
6. *Recognizes* that primary education is one of the main instruments for reintegrating child workers, and calls upon all States to recognize the right to education by making primary education compulsory and to ensure that all children have access to free primary education as a key strategy to prevent child labour, and recognizes, in particular, the important role of the United Nations Educational, Scientific and Cultural Organization and the United Nations Children's Fund in this regard;
7. *Calls upon* all States and the United Nations system to strengthen international cooperation as a means of assisting Governments in preventing or combating violations of the rights of the child and in attaining the objective of the elimination of child labour contrary to accepted international standards;
8. *Calls upon* all States to strengthen cooperation and coordination at the national and the international level to address effectively the problem of child labour, also in close cooperation, *inter alia*, with the International Labour Organization and the United Nations Children's Fund;

VI

The plight of children working and/or living on the streets

1. *Calls upon* Governments to seek comprehensive solutions to the problems causing children to work and/or live on the streets, and to implement appropriate programmes and policies for the protection and the rehabilitation and reintegration of these children, taking into account that such children are particularly vulnerable to all forms of violence, abuse, exploitation and neglect;
2. *Calls upon* all States to ensure that services are provided for children to divert them from, and address the economic imperatives for, involvement in harmful, exploitative and abusive activity;

3. *Strongly urges* all Governments to guarantee the respect for all human rights and fundamental freedoms, in particular the right to life, to take urgent and effective measures to prevent the killing of children living and/or working on the streets, to combat torture and abusive treatment and violence against them and to bring the perpetrators to justice;
4. *Calls upon* the international community to support, through effective international cooperation, including technical advice and assistance, the efforts of States to improve the situation of children working and/or living on the streets;

VII

Children with disabilities

1. *Welcomes* the establishment of a working group, following the decision by the Committee on the Rights of the Child, with the aim of elaborating a plan of action on children with disabilities, in close cooperation with the Special Rapporteur on Disability of the Commission for Social Development and other relevant parts of the United Nations system, see CRC/C/69, paras. 310–339, CRC/C/80, paras. 244–247, and CRC/C/84, paras. 219–222;
2. *Calls upon* all States to take all necessary measures to ensure the full and equal enjoyment of all human rights and fundamental freedoms by children with disabilities and to develop and enforce legislation against their discrimination;
3. *Also calls upon* all States to promote for children with disabilities a full and decent life, in conditions which ensure dignity, promote self-reliance and facilitate the child's active participation in the community, including effective access to education and health services;

VIII

Decides:
(a) To request the Secretary-General to submit a report on the rights of the child to the General Assembly at its fifty-fifth session containing information on the status of the Convention on the Rights of the Child and the problems addressed in the present resolution;
(b) To request the Special Representative of the Secretary-General for Children and Armed Conflict to submit to the General Assembly and the Commission on Human Rights reports containing relevant information on the situation of children affected by armed conflict, bearing in mind existing mandates and reports of relevant bodies;
(c) To continue its consideration of this question at its fifty-fifth session under the item entitled "Promotion and protection of the rights of the child".

A/RES/54/153

UNITED NATIONS GENERAL ASSEMBLY

Measures to combat contemporary forms of racism, racial discrimination, xenophobia and related intolerance

General Assembly Resolution 54/153
adopted 17 December 1999

The General Assembly,

Recalling its resolution 53/133 of 9 December 1998, and Commission on Human Rights resolution 1999/78 of 28 April 1999, *Official Records of the Economic and Social Council, 1999, Supplement No. 3* (E/1999/23-E/CN.4/1999/167), chap. II, sect. A.

Stressing that the Vienna Declaration and Programme of Action A/CONF.157/24 (Part I), chap. III. adopted by the World Conference on Human Rights on 25 June 1993 attaches importance to the elimination of racism, racial discrimination, xenophobia and other forms of intolerance,

Convinced that racism, as one of the exclusionist phenomena plaguing many societies, requires resolute action and cooperation for its eradication,

Having examined the report of the Special Rapporteur of the Commission on Human Rights on contemporary forms of racism, racial discrimination, xenophobia and related intolerance, See A/54/347 including its conclusions and recommendations,

Deeply concerned that, despite continued efforts, racism, racial discrimination, xenophobia and related intolerance, as well as acts of violence, persist and even grow in magnitude, incessantly adopting new forms, including tendencies to establish policies based on racial, religious, ethnic, cultural and national superiority or exclusivity,

Deeply concerned also that those advocating racism and racial discrimination misuse new communication technologies, including the Internet, to disseminate their repugnant views,

Noting that the use of such technologies can also contribute to combating racism, racial discrimination, xenophobia and related intolerance,

Conscious of the fundamental difference between, on the one hand, racism and racial discrimination as governmental policy or resulting from official doctrines of racial superiority or exclusivity and, on the other hand, other manifestations of racism, racial discrimination, xenophobia and related intolerance that are increasingly visible in segments of many societies and are perpetrated by individuals or groups, some of which manifestations are directed against migrant workers and members of their families,

Reaffirming, in this regard, the responsibility of Governments for safeguarding and protecting the rights of individuals residing in their territory against crimes perpetrated by racist or xenophobic individuals or groups,

Noting with concern that racism, racial discrimination, xenophobia and related intolerance may be aggravated by, *inter alia*, inequitable distribution of wealth, marginalization and social exclusion,

Deeply concerned about the fact that racism and racial discrimination against migrant workers continues to increase despite the efforts undertaken by the international community to protect the human rights of migrant workers and members of their families,

Noting that the Committee on the Elimination of Racial Discrimination, in its general recommendation XV (42) of 17 March 1993 See *Official Records of the General Assembly, Forty-eighth Session, Supplement No. 18* (A/48/18), chap. VIII, sect. B. on article 4 of the International Convention on the Elimination of All Forms of Racial Discrimination, Resolution 2106 A (XX), annex. holds that the prohibition of the dissemination of ideas based on racial superiority or racial hatred is compatible with the right to freedom of opinion and expression as outlined in article 19 of the Universal Declaration of Human Rights Resolution 217 A (III) and in article 5 of the Convention,

Noting also that the reports that the States parties submit under the Convention contain, *inter alia*, information about the causes of, as well as measures to combat, contemporary forms of racism, racial discrimination, xenophobia and related intolerance,

Particularly alarmed at the rise of racist and xenophobic ideas in political circles, in the sphere of public opinion and in society at large,

Noting with appreciation that the Special Rapporteur will continue to pay attention to the rise of racist and xenophobic ideas in political circles, in the sphere of public opinion and in society at large,

Underlining the importance of urgently eliminating growing and violent trends of racism and racial discrimination, and conscious that any form of impunity for crimes motivated by racist and xenophobic attitudes plays a role in weakening the rule of law and democracy and tends to encourage the recurrence of such crimes, and requires resolute action and cooperation for its eradication,

Emphasizing the importance of creating conditions that foster greater harmony and tolerance within societies,

1. *Reaffirms* the proclamation of 2001 as the International Year of Mobilization against Racism, Racial Discrimination, Xenophobia and Related Intolerance; Resolution 53/132, sect. III.
2. *Calls upon* the relevant bodies of the United Nations, Member States, intergovernmental organizations and non-governmental organizations to carry out, promote and disseminate activities and actions in the framework of this commemorative year, in order to ensure its success, in particular the outcome of the World Conference against Racism, Racial Discrimination, Xenophobia and Related Intolerance;

3. *Expresses its full support and appreciation* for the work of the Special Rapporteur of the Commission on Human Rights on contemporary forms of racism, racial discrimination, xenophobia and related intolerance and for its continuation, and welcomes the report of the Special Rapporteur, See A/54/347;
4. *Requests* the Special Rapporteur to continue his exchange of views with Member States, related United Nations organs and the specialized agencies, and other relevant mechanisms in order to further their effectiveness and mutual cooperation;
5. *Recommends* that the Commission on Human Rights consider the implementation of the recommendation of the Special Rapporteur with regard to all forms of xenophobia and related intolerance; See A/53/269, para. 41(b).
6. *Commends* the Committee on the Elimination of Racial Discrimination for its contribution to the effective implementation of the International Convention on the Elimination of All Forms of Racial Discrimination, Resolution 2106A (XX), annex. which contributes to the fight against contemporary forms of racism, racial discrimination, xenophobia and related intolerance;
7. *Reaffirms* that acts of racist violence against others stemming from racism do not constitute expressions of opinion but rather offences;
8. *Declares* that racism and racial discrimination are amongst the most serious violations of human rights in the contemporary world and must be combated by all available means;
9. *Expresses its profound concern about and unequivocal condemnation* of all forms of racism and racial discrimination, in particular all racist violence, and related acts of random and indiscriminate violence;
10. *Also expresses its profound concern about and unequivocal condemnation* of all forms of racism and racial discrimination, including propaganda, activities and organizations based on doctrines of superiority of one race or group of persons that attempt to justify or promote racism and racial discrimination in any form;
11. *Expresses its profound concern about and condemnation* of manifestations of racism, racial discrimination, xenophobia and related intolerance against, as well as stereotyping of, migrant workers and members of their families, persons belonging to minorities and members of vulnerable groups in many societies;
12. *Expresses deep concern* about the increase in racial and xenophobic violence, in particular in Europe and North America, including the increasing number of associations established on the bases of racist and xenophobic platforms and constitutions;
13. *Encourages* all States to include in their educational curricula and social programmes at all levels, as appropriate, knowledge of and tolerance and respect for, foreign cultures, peoples and countries;
14. *Recognizes* that the increasing gravity of different manifestations of racism, racial discrimination and xenophobia in various parts of the world requires a more integrated and effective approach on the part of the relevant mechanisms of United Nations human rights machinery;
15. *Encourages* Governments to take appropriate measures to eradicate all forms of racism, racial discrimination, xenophobia and related intolerance;

16. *Calls upon* all States to review and, where necessary, revise their immigration policies with a view to eliminating all discriminatory policies and practices against migrants which are inconsistent with relevant international human rights instruments;
17. *Condemns* the misuse of print, audio-visual and electronic media and new communication technologies, including the Internet, to incite violence motivated by racial hatred;
18. *Recognizes* that Governments should implement and enforce appropriate and effective legislation to prevent acts of racism, racial discrimination, xenophobia and related intolerance;
19. *Calls upon* all Governments and intergovernmental organizations, with the assistance of non-governmental organizations, as appropriate, to continue to supply relevant information to the Special Rapporteur to enable him to fulfil his mandate;
20. *Commends* non-governmental organizations for the work that they have undertaken against racism and racial discrimination and for the continuous support and assistance that they have provided to the victims of racism and racial discrimination;
21. *Urges* all Governments to cooperate fully with the Special Rapporteur, with a view to enabling him to fulfil his mandate, including the examination of incidence of contemporary forms of racism and racial discrimination, *inter alia*, against blacks, Arabs and Muslims, xenophobia, Negrophobia, anti-Semitism and related intolerance;
22. *Requests* the Secretary-General to provide the Special Rapporteur with all the necessary human and financial assistance to carry out his mandate efficiently, effectively and expeditiously and to enable him to submit an interim report to the General Assembly at its fifty-fifth session.

Appendix 10: Regional Human Rights Instruments

COUNCIL OF EUROPE

European Treaties
ETS No. 5

CONVENTION FOR THE PROTECTION OF HUMAN RIGHTS AND FUNDAMENTAL FREEDOMS
(Rome, 4.XI.1950)

As Amended

"The text of the Convention had been amended according to the provisions of *Protocol No. 3* (ETS No. 45), which entered into force on 21 September 1970, of *Protocol No. 5* (ETS No. 55), which entered into force on 20 December 1971 and of *Protocol No. 8* (ETS No. 118), which entered into force on 1 January 1990, and comprised also the text of *Protocol No. 2* (ETS No. 44) which, in accordance with Article 5, paragraph 3 thereof, had been an integral part of the Convention since its entry into force on 21 September 1970. All provisions which had been amended or added by these Protocols are replaced by *Protocol No. 11* (ETS No. 155), as from the date of its entry into force on 1 November 1998. As from that date, *Protocol no. 9* (ETS No. 140), which entered into force on 1 October 1994, is repealed and *Protocol no. 10* (ETS No. 146), which has not entered into force, has lost its purpose."

The governments signatory hereto, being members of the Council of Europe,

Considering the Universal Declaration of Human Rights proclaimed by the General Assembly of the United Nations on 10th December 1948;

Considering that this Declaration aims at securing the universal and effective recognition and observance of the Rights therein declared;

Considering that the aim of the Council of Europe is the achievement of greater unity between its members and that one of the methods by which that aim is to be pursued is the maintenance and further realisation of human rights and fundamental freedoms;

Reaffirming their profound belief in those fundamental freedoms which are the foundation of justice and peace in the world and are best maintained on the one hand by an effective political democracy and on the other by a common understanding and observance of the human rights upon which they depend;

Being resolved, as the governments of European countries which are like-minded and have a common heritage of political traditions, ideals, freedom and the rule of law, to take the first steps for the collective enforcement of certain of the rights stated in the Universal Declaration,

Have agreed as follows:

Article 1[1] *– Obligation to respect human rights*
The High Contracting Parties shall secure to everyone within their jurisdiction the rights and freedoms defined in Section I of this Convention.

Section I – Rights and freedoms

Article 2[1] *– Right to life*
1. Everyone's right to life shall be protected by law. No one shall be deprived of his life intentionally save in the execution of a sentence of a court following his conviction of a crime for which this penalty is provided by law.
2. Deprivation of life shall not be regarded as inflicted in contravention of this article when it results from the use of force which is no more than absolutely necessary:
   (a) in defence of any person from unlawful violence;
   (b) in order to effect a lawful arrest or to prevent the escape of a person lawfully detained;
   (c) in action lawfully taken for the purpose of quelling a riot or insurrection.

Article 3[1] *– Prohibition of torture*
No one shall be subjected to torture or to inhuman or degrading treatment or punishment.

Article 4[1] *– Prohibition of slavery and forced labour*
1. No one shall be held in slavery or servitude.
2. No one shall be required to perform forced or compulsory labour.
3. For the purpose of this article the term "forced or compulsory labour" shall not include:
   (a) any work required to be done in the ordinary course of detention imposed according to the provisions of Article 5 of this Convention or during conditional release from such detention;
   (b) any service of a military character or, in case of conscientious objectors in countries where they are recognised, service exacted instead of compulsory military service;
   (c) any service exacted in case of an emergency or calamity threatening the life or well-being of the community;
   (d) any work or service which forms part of normal civic obligations.

Article 5[1] *– Right to liberty and security*
1. Everyone has the right to liberty and security of person. No one shall be deprived of his liberty save in the following cases and in accordance with a procedure prescribed by law:
   (a) the lawful detention of a person after conviction by a competent court;
   (b) the lawful arrest or detention of a person for non- compliance with the lawful order of a court or in order to secure the fulfilment of any obligation prescribed by law;
   (c) the lawful arrest or detention of a person effected for the purpose of bringing him before the competent legal authority on reasonable suspicion of having committed an offence or when it is reasonably considered

---

[1] Heading added according to the provisions of Protocol No. 11 (ETS No. 155).

necessary to prevent his committing an offence or fleeing after having done so;
(d) the detention of a minor by lawful order for the purpose of educational supervision or his lawful detention for the purpose of bringing him before the competent legal authority;
(e) the lawful detention of persons for the prevention of the spreading of infectious diseases, of persons of unsound mind, alcoholics or drug addicts or vagrants;
(f) the lawful arrest or detention of a person to prevent his effecting an unauthorised entry into the country or of a person against whom action is being taken with a view to deportation or extradition.
2. Everyone who is arrested shall be informed promptly, in a language which he understands, of the reasons for his arrest and of any charge against him.
3. Everyone arrested or detained in accordance with the provisions of paragraph 1.c of this article shall be brought promptly before a judge or other officer authorised by law to exercise judicial power and shall be entitled to trial within a reasonable time or to release pending trial. Release may be conditioned by guarantees to appear for trial.
4. Everyone who is deprived of his liberty by arrest or detention shall be entitled to take proceedings by which the lawfulness of his detention shall be decided speedily by a court and his release ordered if the detention is not lawful.
5. Everyone who has been the victim of arrest or detention in contravention of the provisions of this article shall have an enforceable right to compensation.

Article 6[1] *– Right to a fair trial*
1. In the determination of his civil rights and obligations or of any criminal charge against him, everyone is entitled to a fair and public hearing within a reasonable time by an independent and impartial tribunal established by law. Judgment shall be pronounced publicly but the press and public may be excluded from all or part of the trial in the interests of morals, public order or national security in a democratic society, where the interests of juveniles or the protection of the private life of the parties so require, or to the extent strictly necessary in the opinion of the court in special circumstances where publicity would prejudice the interests of justice.
2. Everyone charged with a criminal offence shall be presumed innocent until proved guilty according to law.
3. Everyone charged with a criminal offence has the following minimum rights:
   (a) to be informed promptly, in a language which he understands and in detail, of the nature and cause of the accusation against him;
   (b) to have adequate time and facilities for the preparation of his defence;
   (c) to defend himself in person or through legal assistance of his own choosing or, if he has not sufficient means to pay for legal assistance, to be given it free when the interests of justice so require;
   (d) to examine or have examined witnesses against him and to obtain the attendance and examination of witnesses on his behalf under the same conditions as witnesses against him;
   (e) to have the free assistance of an interpreter if he cannot understand or speak the language used in court.

---
[1] Heading added according to the provisions of Protocol No. 11 (ETS No. 155).

Article 7[1] *– No punishment without law*
1. No one shall be held guilty of any criminal offence on account of any act or omission which did not constitute a criminal offence under national or international law at the time when it was committed. Nor shall a heavier penalty be imposed than the one that was applicable at the time the criminal offence was committed.
2. This article shall not prejudice the trial and punishment of any person for any act or omission which, at the time when it was committed, was criminal according to the general principles of law recognised by civilised nations.

Article 8[1] *– Right to respect for private and family life*
1. Everyone has the right to respect for his private and family life, his home and his correspondence.
2. There shall be no interference by a public authority with the exercise of this right except such as is in accordance with the law and is necessary in a democratic society in the interests of national security, public safety or the economic well-being of the country, for the prevention of disorder or crime, for the protection of health or morals, or for the protection of the rights and freedoms of others.

Article 9[1] *– Freedom of thought, conscience and religion*
1. Everyone has the right to freedom of thought, conscience and religion; this right includes freedom to change his religion or belief and freedom, either alone or in community with others and in public or private, to manifest his religion or belief, in worship, teaching, practice and observance.
2. Freedom to manifest one's religion or beliefs shall be subject only to such limitations as are prescribed by law and are necessary in a democratic society in the interests of public safety, for the protection of public order, health or morals, or for the protection of the rights and freedoms of others.

Article 10[1] *– Freedom of expression*
1. Everyone has the right to freedom of expression. This right shall include freedom to hold opinions and to receive and impart information and ideas without interference by public authority and regardless of frontiers. This article shall not prevent States from requiring the licensing of broadcasting, television or cinema enterprises.
2. The exercise of these freedoms, since it carries with it duties and responsibilities, may be subject to such formalities, conditions, restrictions or penalties as are prescribed by law and are necessary in a democratic society, in the interests of national security, territorial integrity or public safety, for the prevention of disorder or crime, for the protection of health or morals, for the protection of the reputation or rights of others, for preventing the disclosure of information received in confidence, or for maintaining the authority and impartiality of the judiciary.

Article 11[1] *– Freedom of assembly and association*
1. Everyone has the right to freedom of peaceful assembly and to freedom of association with others, including the right to form and to join trade unions for the protection of his interests.

---
[1] Heading added according to the provisions of Protocol No. 11 (ETS No. 155).

2. No restrictions shall be placed on the exercise of these rights other than such as are prescribed by law and are necessary in a democratic society in the interests of national security or public safety, for the prevention of disorder or crime, for the protection of health or morals or for the protection of the rights and freedoms of others. This article shall not prevent the imposition of lawful restrictions on the exercise of these rights by members of the armed forces, of the police or of the administration of the State.

Article 12[1] – Right to marry
Men and women of marriageable age have the right to marry and to found a family, according to the national laws governing the exercise of this right.

Article 13[1] – Right to an effective remedy
Everyone whose rights and freedoms as set forth in this Convention are violated shall have an effective remedy before a national authority notwithstanding that the violation has been committed by persons acting in an official capacity.

Article 14[1] – Prohibition of discrimination
The enjoyment of the rights and freedoms set forth in this Convention shall be secured without discrimination on any ground such as sex, race, colour, language, religion, political or other opinion, national or social origin, association with a national minority, property, birth or other status.

Article 15[1] – Derogation in time of emergency
1. In time of war or other public emergency threatening the life of the nation any High Contracting Party may take measures derogating from its obligations under this Convention to the extent strictly required by the exigencies of the situation, provided that such measures are not inconsistent with its other obligations under international law.
2. No derogation from Article 2, except in respect of deaths resulting from lawful acts of war, or from Articles 3, 4 (paragraph 1) and 7 shall be made under this provision.
3. Any High Contracting Party availing itself of this right of derogation shall keep the Secretary General of the Council of Europe fully informed of the measures which it has taken and the reasons therefor. It shall also inform the Secretary General of the Council of Europe when such measures have ceased to operate and the provisions of the Convention are again being fully executed.

Article 16[1] – Restrictions on political activity of aliens
Nothing in Articles 10, 11 and 14 shall be regarded as preventing the High Contracting Parties from imposing restrictions on the political activity of aliens.

Article 17[1] – Prohibition of abuse of rights
Nothing in this Convention may be interpreted as implying for any State, group or person any right to engage in any activity or perform any act aimed at the destruction of any of the rights and freedoms set forth herein or at their limitation to a greater extent than is provided for in the Convention.

---

[1] Heading added according to the provisions of Protocol No. 11 (ETS No. 155).

Article 18[1] *– Limitation on use of restrictions on rights*
The restrictions permitted under this Convention to the said rights and freedoms shall not be applied for any purpose other than those for which they have been prescribed.

Section II – European Court of Human Rights[2]

Article 19 – Establishment of the Court
To ensure the observance of the engagements undertaken by the High Contracting Parties in the Convention and the Protocols thereto, there shall be set up a European Court of Human Rights, hereinafter referred to as "the Court". It shall function on a permanent basis.

Article 20 – Number of judges
The Court shall consist of a number of judges equal to that of the High Contracting Parties.

Article 21 – Criteria for office
1. The judges shall be of high moral character and must either possess the qualifications required for appointment to high judicial office or be jurisconsults of recognised competence.
2. The judges shall sit on the Court in their individual capacity.
3. During their term of office the judges shall not engage in any activity which is incompatible with their independence, impartiality or with the demands of a full-time office; all questions arising from the application of this paragraph shall be decided by the Court.

Article 22 – Election of judges
1. The judges shall be elected by the Parliamentary Assembly with respect to each High Contracting Party by a majority of votes cast from a list of three candidates nominated by the High Contracting Party.
2. The same procedure shall be followed to complete the Court in the event of the accession of new High Contracting Parties and in filling casual vacancies.

Article 23 – Terms of office
1. The judges shall be elected for a period of six years. They may be re-elected. However, the terms of office of one-half of the judges elected at the first election shall expire at the end of three years.
2. The judges whose terms of office are to expire at the end of the initial period of three years shall be chosen by lot by the Secretary General of the Council of Europe immediately after their election.
3. In order to ensure that, as far as possible, the terms of office of one-half of the judges are renewed every three years, the Parliamentary Assembly may decide, before proceeding to any subsequent election, that the term or terms of office of one or more judges to be elected shall be for a period other than six years but not more than nine and not less than three years.
4. In cases where more than one term of office is involved and where the

---
[1] Heading added according to the provisions of Protocol No. 11 (ETS No. 155).
[2] New Section II according to the provisions of Protocol No. 11 (ETS No. 155).

Parliamentary Assembly applies the preceding paragraph, the allocation of the terms of office shall be effected by a drawing of lots by the Secretary General of the Council of Europe immediately after the election.
5. A judge elected to replace a judge whose term of office has not expired shall hold office for the remainder of his predecessor's term.
6. The terms of office of judges shall expire when they reach the age of 70.
7. The judges shall hold office until replaced. They shall, however, continue to deal with such cases as they already have under consideration.

Article 24 – Dismissal
No judge may be dismissed from his office unless the other judges decide by a majority of two-thirds that he has ceased to fulfil the required conditions.

Article 25 – Registry and legal secretaries
The Court shall have a registry, the functions and organisation of which shall be laid down in the rules of the Court. The Court shall be assisted by legal secretaries.

Article 26 – Plenary Court
The plenary Court shall
(a) elect its President and one or two Vice-Presidents for a period of three years; they may be re-elected;
(b) set up Chambers, constituted for a fixed period of time;
(c) elect the Presidents of the Chambers of the Court; they may be re-elected;
(d) adopt the rules of the Court, and
(e) elect the Registrar and one or more Deputy Registrars.

Article 27 – Committees, Chambers and Grand Chamber
1. To consider cases brought before it, the Court shall sit in committees of three judges, in Chambers of seven judges and in a Grand Chamber of seventeen judges. The Court's Chambers shall set up committees for a fixed period of time.
2. There shall sit as an *ex officio* member of the Chamber and the Grand Chamber the judge elected in respect of the State Party concerned or, if there is none or if he is unable to sit, a person of its choice who shall sit in the capacity of judge.
3. The Grand Chamber shall also include the President of the Court, the Vice-Presidents, the Presidents of the Chambers and other judges chosen in accordance with the rules of the Court. When a case is referred to the Grand Chamber under Article 43, no judge from the Chamber which rendered the judgment shall sit in the Grand Chamber, with the exception of the President of the Chamber and the judge who sat in respect of the State Party concerned.

Article 28 – Declarations of inadmissibility by committees
A committee may, by a unanimous vote, declare inadmissible or strike out of its list of cases an application submitted under Article 34 where such a decision can be taken without further examination. The decision shall be final.

Article 29 – Decisions by Chambers on admissibility and merits
1. If no decision is taken under Article 28, a Chamber shall decide on the admissibility and merits of individual applications submitted under Article 34.
2. A Chamber shall decide on the admissibility and merits of inter-State applications submitted under Article 33.

3. The decision on admissibility shall be taken separately unless the Court, in exceptional cases, decides otherwise.

Article 30 – Relinquishment of jurisdiction to the Grand Chamber
Where a case pending before a Chamber raises a serious question affecting the interpretation of the Convention or the protocols thereto, or where the resolution of a question before the Chamber might have a result inconsistent with a judgment previously delivered by the Court, the Chamber may, at any time before it has rendered its judgment, relinquish jurisdiction in favour of the Grand Chamber, unless one of the parties to the case objects.

Article 31 – Powers of the Grand Chamber
The Grand Chamber shall
(a) determine applications submitted either under Article 33 or Article 34 when a Chamber has relinquished jurisdiction under Article 30 or when the case has been referred to it under Article 43; and
(b) consider requests for advisory opinions submitted under Article 47.

Article 32 – Jurisdiction of the Court
1. The jurisdiction of the Court shall extend to all matters concerning the interpretation and application of the Convention and the protocols thereto which are referred to it as provided in Articles 33, 34 and 47.
2. In the event of dispute as to whether the Court has jurisdiction, the Court shall decide.

Article 33 – Inter-State cases
Any High Contracting Party may refer to the Court any alleged breach of the provisions of the Convention and the protocols thereto by another High Contracting Party.

Article 34 – Individual applications
The Court may receive applications from any person, non-governmental organisation or group of individuals claiming to be the victim of a violation by one of the High Contracting Parties of the rights set forth in the Convention or the protocols thereto. The High Contracting Parties undertake not to hinder in any way the effective exercise of this right.

Article 35 – Admissibility criteria
1. The Court may only deal with the matter after all domestic remedies have been exhausted, according to the generally recognised rules of international law, and within a period of six months from the date on which the final decision was taken.
2. The Court shall not deal with any application submitted under Article 34 that
   (a) is anonymous; or
   (b) is substantially the same as a matter that has already been examined by the Court or has already been submitted to another procedure of international investigation or settlement and contains no relevant new information.
3. The Court shall declare inadmissible any individual application submitted under Article 34 which it considers incompatible with the provisions of the Convention or the protocols thereto, manifestly ill-founded, or an abuse of the right of application.

4. The Court shall reject any application which it considers inadmissible under this Article. It may do so at any stage of the proceedings.

Article 36 – Third party intervention
1. In all cases before a Chamber or the Grand Chamber, a High Contracting Party one of whose nationals is an applicant shall have the right to submit written comments and to take part in hearings.
2. The President of the Court may, in the interest of the proper administration of justice, invite any High Contracting Party which is not a party to the proceedings or any person concerned who is not the applicant to submit written comments or take part in hearings.

Article 37 – Striking out applications
1. The Court may at any stage of the proceedings decide to strike an application out of its list of cases where the circumstances lead to the conclusion that
    (a) the applicant does not intend to pursue his application; or
    (b) the matter has been resolved; or
    (c) for any other reason established by the Court, it is no longer justified to continue the examination of the application.
   However, the Court shall continue the examination of the application if respect for human rights as defined in the Convention and the protocols thereto so requires.
2. The Court may decide to restore an application to its list of cases if it considers that the circumstances justify such a course.

Article 38 – Examination of the case and friendly settlement proceedings
1. If the Court declares the application admissible, it shall
    (a) pursue the examination of the case, together with the representatives of the parties, and if need be, undertake an investigation, for the effective conduct of which the States concerned shall furnish all necessary facilities;
    (b) place itself at the disposal of the parties concerned with a view to securing a friendly settlement of the matter on the basis of respect for human rights as defined in the Convention and the protocols thereto.
2. Proceedings conducted under paragraph 1.b shall be confidential.

Article 39 – Finding of a friendly settlement
If a friendly settlement is effected, the Court shall strike the case out of its list by means of a decision which shall be confined to a brief statement of the facts and of the solution reached.

Article 40 – Public hearings and access to documents
1. Hearings shall be in public unless the Court in exceptional circumstances decides otherwise.
2. Documents deposited with the Registrar shall be accessible to the public unless the President of the Court decides otherwise.

Article 41 – Just satisfaction
If the Court finds that there has been a violation of the Convention or the protocols thereto, and if the internal law of the High Contracting Party concerned allows only partial reparation to be made, the Court shall, if necessary, afford just satisfaction to the injured party.

Article 42 – Judgments of Chambers
Judgments of Chambers shall become final in accordance with the provisions of Article 44, paragraph 2.

Article 43 – Referral to the Grand Chamber
1. Within a period of three months from the date of the judgment of the Chamber, any party to the case may, in exceptional cases, request that the case be referred to the Grand Chamber.
2. A panel of five judges of the Grand Chamber shall accept the request if the case raises a serious question affecting the interpretation or application of the Convention or the protocols thereto, or a serious issue of general importance.
3. If the panel accepts the request, the Grand Chamber shall decide the case by means of a judgment.

Article 44 – Final judgments
1. The judgment of the Grand Chamber shall be final.
2. The judgment of a Chamber shall become final
   (a) when the parties declare that they will not request that the case be referred to the Grand Chamber; or
   (b) three months after the date of the judgment, if reference of the case to the Grand Chamber has not been requested; or
   (c) when the panel of the Grand Chamber rejects the request to refer under Article 43.
3. The final judgment shall be published.

Article 45 – Reasons for judgments and decisions
1. Reasons shall be given for judgments as well as for decisions declaring applications admissible or inadmissible.
2. If a judgment does not represent, in whole or in part, the unanimous opinion of the judges, any judge shall be entitled to deliver a separate opinion.

Article 46 – Binding force and execution of judgments
1. The High Contracting Parties undertake to abide by the final judgment of the Court in any case to which they are parties.
2. The final judgment of the Court shall be transmitted to the Committee of Ministers, which shall supervise its execution.

Article 47 – Advisory opinions
1. The Court may, at the request of the Committee of Ministers, give advisory opinions on legal questions concerning the interpretation of the Convention and the protocols thereto.
2. Such opinions shall not deal with any question relating to the content or scope of the rights or freedoms defined in Section I of the Convention and the protocols thereto, or with any other question which the Court or the Committee of Ministers might have to consider in consequence of any such proceedings as could be instituted in accordance with the Convention.
3. Decisions of the Committee of Ministers to request an advisory opinion of the Court shall require a majority vote of the representatives entitled to sit on the Committee.

Article 48 – Advisory jurisdiction of the Court
The Court shall decide whether a request for an advisory opinion submitted by the Committee of Ministers is within its competence as defined in Article 47.

Article 49 – Reasons for advisory opinions
1. Reasons shall be given for advisory opinions of the Court.
2. If the advisory opinion does not represent, in whole or in part, the unanimous opinion of the judges, any judge shall be entitled to deliver a separate opinion.
3. Advisory opinions of the Court shall be communicated to the Committee of Ministers.

Article 50 – Expenditure on the Court
The expenditure on the Court shall be borne by the Council of Europe.

Article 51 – Privileges and immunities of judges
The judges shall be entitled, during the exercise of their functions, to the privileges and immunities provided for in Article 40 of the Statute of the Council of Europe and in the agreements made thereunder.

Section III – Miscellaneous provisions[3,1]

Article 52[1] – Inquiries by the Secretary General
On receipt of a request from the Secretary General of the Council of Europe any High Contracting Party shall furnish an explanation of the manner in which its internal law ensures the effective implementation of any of the provisions of the Convention.

Article 53[1] – Safeguard for existing human rights
Nothing in this Convention shall be construed as limiting or derogating from any of the human rights and fundamental freedoms which may be ensured under the laws of any High Contracting Party or under any other agreement to which it is a Party.

Article 54[1] – Powers of the Committee of Ministers
Nothing in this Convention shall prejudice the powers conferred on the Committee of Ministers by the Statute of the Council of Europe.

Article 55[1] – Exclusion of other means of dispute settlement
The High Contracting Parties agree that, except by special agreement, they will not avail themselves of treaties, conventions or declarations in force between them for the purpose of submitting, by way of petition, a dispute arising out of the interpretation or application of this Convention to a means of settlement other than those provided for in this Convention.

Article 56[1] – Territorial application
1. [4]Any State may at the time of its ratification or at any time thereafter declare by notification addressed to the Secretary General of the Council of Europe that the present Convention shall, subject to paragraph 4 of this Article,

---
[3] The articles of this Section are renumbered according to the provisions of Protocol No. 11 (ETS No. 155).
[1] Heading added according to the provisions of Protocol No. 11 (ETS No. 155).
[4] Text amended according to the provisions of Protocol No. 11 (ETS No. 155).

extend to all or any of the territories for whose international relations it is responsible.
2. The Convention shall extend to the territory or territories named in the notification as from the thirtieth day after the receipt of this notification by the Secretary General of the Council of Europe.
3. The provisions of this Convention shall be applied in such territories with due regard, however, to local requirements.
4. [4]Any State which has made a declaration in accordance with paragraph 1 of this article may at any time thereafter declare on behalf of one or more of the territories to which the declaration relates that it accepts the competence of the Court to receive applications from individuals, non-governmental organisations or groups of individuals as provided by Article 34 of the Convention.

Article 57[1] – Reservations
1. Any State may, when signing this Convention or when depositing its instrument of ratification, make a reservation in respect of any particular provision of the Convention to the extent that any law then in force in its territory is not in conformity with the provision. Reservations of a general character shall not be permitted under this article.
2. Any reservation made under this article shall contain a brief statement of the law concerned.

Article 58[1] – Denunciation
1. A High Contracting Party may denounce the present Convention only after the expiry of five years from the date on which it became a party to it and after six months' notice contained in a notification addressed to the Secretary General of the Council of Europe, who shall inform the other High Contracting Parties.
2. Such a denunciation shall not have the effect of releasing the High Contracting Party concerned from its obligations under this Convention in respect of any act which, being capable of constituting a violation of such obligations, may have been performed by it before the date at which the denunciation became effective.
3. Any High Contracting Party which shall cease to be a member of the Council of Europe shall cease to be a Party to this Convention under the same conditions.
4. [4]The Convention may be denounced in accordance with the provisions of the preceding paragraphs in respect of any territory to which it has been declared to extend under the terms of Article 56.

Article 59[1] – Signature and ratification
1. This Convention shall be open to the signature of the members of the Council of Europe. It shall be ratified. Ratifications shall be deposited with the Secretary General of the Council of Europe.
2. The present Convention shall come into force after the deposit of ten instruments of ratification.

---

[4] Text amended according to the provisions of Protocol No. 11 (ETS No. 155).
[1] Heading added according to the provisions of Protocol No. 11 (ETS No. 155).

3. As regards any signatory ratifying subsequently, the Convention shall come into force at the date of the deposit of its instrument of ratification.
4. The Secretary General of the Council of Europe shall notify all the members of the Council of Europe of the entry into force of the Convention, the names of the High Contracting Parties who have ratified it, and the deposit of all instruments of ratification which may be effected subsequently.

COUNCIL OF EUROPE

European Treaties
ETS No. 163

EUROPEAN SOCIAL CHARTER
(Revised)

Strasbourg, 3.V.1996

Preamble

The governments signatory hereto, being members of the Council of Europe,

Considering that the aim of the Council of Europe is the achievement of greater unity between its members for the purpose of safeguarding and realising the ideals and principles which are their common heritage and of facilitating their economic and social progress, in particular by the maintenance and further realisation of human rights and fundamental freedoms;

Considering that in the *European Convention for the Protection of Human Rights and Fundamental Freedoms* signed at Rome on 4 November 1950, and the Protocols thereto, the member States of the Council of Europe agreed to secure to their populations the civil and political rights and freedoms therein specified;

Considering that in the *European Social Charter* opened for signature in Turin on 18 October 1961 and the *Protocols* thereto, the member States of the Council of Europe agreed to secure to their populations the social rights specified therein in order to improve their standard of living and their social well-being;

Recalling that the Ministerial Conference on Human Rights held in Rome on 5 November 1990 stressed the need, on the one hand, to preserve the indivisible nature of all human rights, be they civil, political, economic, social or cultural and, on the other hand, to give the European Social Charter fresh impetus;

Resolved, as was decided during the Ministerial Conference held in Turin on 21 and 22 October 1991, to update and adapt the substantive contents of the Charter in order to take account in particular of the fundamental social changes which have occurred since the text was adopted;

Recognising the advantage of embodying in a Revised Charter, designed progressively to take the place of the European Social Charter, the rights guaranteed by the Charter as amended, the rights guaranteed by the *Additional Protocol* of 1988 and to add new rights,

Have agreed as follows:

Part I

The Parties accept as the aim of their policy, to be pursued by all appropriate means both national and international in character, the attainment of conditions in which the following rights and principles may be effectively realised:
1. Everyone shall have the opportunity to earn his living in an occupation freely entered upon.
2. All workers have the right to just conditions of work.
3. All workers have the right to safe and healthy working conditions.
4. All workers have the right to a fair remuneration sufficient for a decent standard of living for themselves and their families.
5. All workers and employers have the right to freedom of association in national or international organisations for the protection of their economic and social interests.
6. All workers and employers have the right to bargain collectively.
7. Children and young persons have the right to a special protection against the physical and moral hazards to which they are exposed.
8. Employed women, in case of maternity, have the right to a special protection.
9. Everyone has the right to appropriate facilities for vocational guidance with a view to helping him choose an occupation suited to his personal aptitude and interests.
10. Everyone has the right to appropriate facilities for vocational training.
11. Everyone has the right to benefit from any measures enabling him to enjoy the highest possible standard of health attainable.
12. All workers and their dependents have the right to social security.
13. Anyone without adequate resources has the right to social and medical assistance.
14. Everyone has the right to benefit from social welfare services.
15. Disabled persons have the right to independence, social integration and participation in the life of the community.
16. The family as a fundamental unit of society has the right to appropriate social, legal and economic protection to ensure its full development.
17. Children and young persons have the right to appropriate social, legal and economic protection.
18. The nationals of any one of the Parties have the right to engage in any gainful occupation in the territory of any one of the others on a footing of equality with the nationals of the latter, subject to restrictions based on cogent economic or social reasons.
19. Migrant workers who are nationals of a Party and their families have the right to protection and assistance in the territory of any other Party.
20. All workers have the right to equal opportunities and equal treatment in matters of employment and occupation without discrimination on the grounds of sex.
21. Workers have the right to be informed and to be consulted within the undertaking.

22. Workers have the right to take part in the determination and improvement of the working conditions and working environment in the undertaking.
23. Every elderly person has the right to social protection.
24. All workers have the right to protection in cases of termination of employment.
25. All workers have the right to protection of their claims in the event of the insolvency of their employer.
26. All workers have the right to dignity at work.
27. All persons with family responsibilities and who are engaged or wish to engage in employment have a right to do so without being subject to discrimination and as far as possible without conflict between their employment and family responsibilities.
28. Workers' representatives in undertakings have the right to protection against acts prejudicial to them and should be afforded appropriate facilities to carry out their functions.
29. All workers have the right to be informed and consulted in collective redundancy procedures.
30. Everyone has the right to protection against poverty and social exclusion.
31. Everyone has the right to housing.

Part II

The Parties undertake, as provided for in Part III, to consider themselves bound by the obligations laid down in the following articles and paragraphs.

Article 1 – The right to work
With a view to ensuring the effective exercise of the right to work, the Parties undertake:

1. to accept as one of their primary aims and responsibilities the achievement and maintenance of as high and stable a level of employment as possible, with a view to the attainment of full employment;
2. to protect effectively the right of the worker to earn his living in an occupation freely entered upon;
3. to establish or maintain free employment services for all workers;
4. to provide or promote appropriate vocational guidance, training and rehabilitation.

Article 2 – The right to just conditions of work
With a view to ensuring the effective exercise of the right to just conditions of work, the Parties undertake:

1. to provide for reasonable daily and weekly working hours, the working week to be progressively reduced to the extent that the increase of productivity and other relevant factors permit;
2. to provide for public holidays with pay;
3. to provide for a minimum of four weeks' annual holiday with pay;
4. to eliminate risks in inherently dangerous or unhealthy occupations, and

where it has not yet been possible to eliminate or reduce sufficiently these risks, to provide for either a reduction of working hours or additional paid holidays for workers engaged in such occupations;
5. to ensure a weekly rest period which shall, as far as possible, coincide with the day recognised by tradition or custom in the country or region concerned as a day of rest;
6. to ensure that workers are informed in written form, as soon as possible, and in any event not later than two months after the date of commencing their employment, of the essential aspects of the contract or employment relationship;
7. to ensure that workers performing night work benefit from measures which take account of the special nature of the work.

Article 3 – The right to safe and healthy working conditions
With a view to ensuring the effective exercise of the right to safe and healthy working conditions, the Parties undertake, in consultation with employers' and workers' organisations:

1. to formulate, implement and periodically review a coherent national policy on occupational safety, occupational health and the working environment. The primary aim of this policy shall be to improve occupational safety and health and to prevent accidents and injury to health arising out of, linked with or occurring in the course of work, particularly by minimising the causes of hazards inherent in the working environment;
2. to issue safety and health regulations;
3. to provide for the enforcement of such regulations by measures of supervision;
4. to promote the progressive development of occupational health services for all workers with essentially preventive and advisory functions.

Article 4 – The right to a fair remuneration
With a view to ensuring the effective exercise of the right to a fair remuneration, the Parties undertake:

1. to recognise the right of workers to a remuneration such as will give them and their families a decent standard of living;
2. to recognise the right of workers to an increased rate of remuneration for overtime work, subject to exceptions in particular cases;
3. to recognise the right of men and women workers to equal pay for work of equal value;
4. to recognise the right of all workers to a reasonable period of notice for termination of employment;
5. to permit deductions from wages only under conditions and to the extent prescribed by national laws or regulations or fixed by collective agreements or arbitration awards.

The exercise of these rights shall be achieved by freely concluded collective agreements, by statutory wage-fixing machinery, or by other means appropriate to national conditions.

Article 5 – The right to organise
With a view to ensuring or promoting the freedom of workers and employers to form local, national or international organisations for the protection of their economic and social interests and to join those organisations, the Parties undertake that national law shall not be such as to impair, nor shall it be so applied as to impair, this freedom. The extent to which the guarantees provided for in this article shall apply to the police shall be determined by national laws or regulations. The principle governing the application to the members of the armed forces of these guarantees and the extent to which they shall apply to persons in this category shall equally be determined by national laws or regulations.

Article 6 – The right to bargain collectively
With a view to ensuring the effective exercise of the right to bargain collectively, the Parties undertake:

1. to promote joint consultation between workers and employers;
2. to promote, where necessary and appropriate, machinery for voluntary negotiations between employers or employers' organisations and workers' organisations, with a view to the regulation of terms and conditions of employment by means of collective agreements;
3. to promote the establishment and use of appropriate machinery for conciliation and voluntary arbitration for the settlement of labour disputes;

   and recognise:
4. the right of workers and employers to collective action in cases of conflicts of interest, including the right to strike, subject to obligations that might arise out of collective agreements previously entered into.

Article 7 – The right of children and young persons to protection
With a view to ensuring the effective exercise of the right of children and young persons to protection, the Parties undertake:

1. to provide that the minimum age of admission to employment shall be 15 years, subject to exceptions for children employed in prescribed light work without harm to their health, morals or education;
2. to provide that the minimum age of admission to employment shall be 18 years with respect to prescribed occupations regarded as dangerous or unhealthy;
3. to provide that persons who are still subject to compulsory education shall not be employed in such work as would deprive them of the full benefit of their education;
4. to provide that the working hours of persons under 18 years of age shall be limited in accordance with the needs of their development, and particularly with their need for vocational training;
5. to recognise the right of young workers and apprentices to a fair wage or other appropriate allowances;
6. to provide that the time spent by young persons in vocational training during the normal working hours with the consent of the employer shall be treated as forming part of the working day;

7. to provide that employed persons of under 18 years of age shall be entitled to a minimum of four weeks' annual holiday with pay;
8. to provide that persons under 18 years of age shall not be employed in night work with the exception of certain occupations provided for by national laws or regulations;
9. to provide that persons under 18 years of age employed in occupations prescribed by national laws or regulations shall be subject to regular medical control;
10 to ensure special protection against physical and moral dangers to which children and young persons are exposed, and particularly against those resulting directly or indirectly from their work.

Article 8 – The right of employed women to protection of maternity
With a view to ensuring the effective exercise of the right of employed women to the protection of maternity, the Parties undertake:
1. to provide either by paid leave, by adequate social security benefits or by benefits from public funds for employed women to take leave before and after childbirth up to a total of at least fourteen weeks;
2. to consider it as unlawful for an employer to give a woman notice of dismissal during the period from the time she notifies her employer that she is pregnant until the end of her maternity leave, or to give her notice of dismissal at such a time that the notice would expire during such a period;
3. to provide that mothers who are nursing their infants shall be entitled to sufficient time off for this purpose;
4. to regulate the employment in night work of pregnant women, women who have recently given birth and women nursing their infants;
5. to prohibit the employment of pregnant women, women who have recently given birth or who are nursing their infants in underground mining and all other work which is unsuitable by reason of its dangerous, unhealthy or arduous nature and to take appropriate measures to protect the employment rights of these women.

Article 9 – The right to vocational guidance
With a view to ensuring the effective exercise of the right to vocational guidance, the Parties undertake to provide or promote, as necessary, a service which will assist all persons, including the handicapped, to solve problems related to occupational choice and progress, with due regard to the individual's characteristics and their relation to occupational opportunity: this assistance should be available free of charge, both to young persons, including schoolchildren, and to adults.

Article 10 – The right to vocational training
With a view to ensuring the effective exercise of the right to vocational training, the Parties undertake:
1. to provide or promote, as necessary, the technical and vocational training of all persons, including the handicapped, in consultation with employers' and workers' organisations, and to grant facilities for access to higher technical and university education, based solely on individual aptitude;

2. to provide or promote a system of apprenticeship and other systematic arrangements for training young boys and girls in their various employments;
3. to provide or promote, as necessary:
   (a) adequate and readily available training facilities for adult workers;
   (b) special facilities for the retraining of adult workers needed as a result of technological development or new trends in employment;
4. to provide or promote, as necessary, special measures for the retraining and reintegration of the long-term unemployed;
5. to encourage the full utilisation of the facilities provided by appropriate measures such as:
   (a) reducing or abolishing any fees or charges;
   (b) granting financial assistance in appropriate cases;
   (c) including in the normal working hours time spent on supplementary training taken by the worker, at the request of his employer, during employment;
   (d) ensuring, through adequate supervision, in consultation with the employers' and workers' organisations, the efficiency of apprenticeship and other training arrangements for young workers, and the adequate protection of young workers generally.

Article 11 – The right to protection of health
With a view to ensuring the effective exercise of the right to protection of health, the Parties undertake, either directly or in co-operation with public or private organisations, to take appropriate measures designed *inter alia*:

1. to remove as far as possible the causes of ill-health;
2. to provide advisory and educational facilities for the promotion of health and the encouragement of individual responsibility in matters of health;
3. to prevent as far as possible epidemic, endemic and other diseases, as well as accidents.

Article 12 – The right to social security
With a view to ensuring the effective exercise of the right to social security, the Parties undertake:

1. to establish or maintain a system of social security;
2. to maintain the social security system at a satisfactory level at least equal to that necessary for the ratification of the European Code of Social Security;
3. to endeavour to raise progressively the system of social security to a higher level;
4. to take steps, by the conclusion of appropriate bilateral and multilateral agreements or by other means, and subject to the conditions laid down in such agreements, in order to ensure:
   (a) equal treatment with their own nationals of the nationals of other Parties in respect of social security rights, including the retention of benefits arising out of social security legislation, whatever movements the persons protected may undertake between the territories of the Parties;
   (b) the granting, maintenance and resumption of social security rights by

such means as the accumulation of insurance or employment periods completed under the legislation of each of the Parties.

Article 13 – The right to social and medical assistance
With a view to ensuring the effective exercise of the right to social and medical assistance, the Parties undertake:

1. to ensure that any person who is without adequate resources and who is unable to secure such resources either by his own efforts or from other sources, in particular by benefits under a social security scheme, be granted adequate assistance, and, in case of sickness, the care necessitated by his condition;
2. to ensure that persons receiving such assistance shall not, for that reason, suffer from a diminution of their political or social rights;
3. to provide that everyone may receive by appropriate public or private services such advice and personal help as may be required to prevent, to remove, or to alleviate personal or family want;
4. to apply the provisions referred to in paragraphs 1, 2 and 3 of this article on an equal footing with their nationals to nationals of other Parties lawfully within their territories, in accordance with their obligations under the *European Convention on Social and Medical Assistance*, signed at Paris on 11 December 1953.

Article 14 – The right to benefit from social welfare services
With a view to ensuring the effective exercise of the right to benefit from social welfare services, the Parties undertake:

1. to promote or provide services which, by using methods of social work, would contribute to the welfare and development of both individuals and groups in the community, and to their adjustment to the social environment;
2. to encourage the participation of individuals and voluntary or other organisations in the establishment and maintenance of such services.

Article 15 – The right of persons with disabilities to independence, social integration and participation in the life of the community
With a view to ensuring to persons with disabilities, irrespective of age and the nature and origin of their disabilities, the effective exercise of the right to independence, social integration and participation in the life of the community, the Parties undertake, in particular:

1. to take the necessary measures to provide persons with disabilities with guidance, education and vocational training in the framework of general schemes wherever possible or, where this is not possible, through specialised bodies, public or private;
2. to promote their access to employment through all measures tending to encourage employers to hire and keep in employment persons with disabilities in the ordinary working environment and to adjust the working conditions to the needs of the disabled or, where this is not possible by reason of the disability, by arranging for or creating sheltered employment according to the level of disability. In certain cases, such measures may require recourse to specialised placement and support services;

3. to promote their full social integration and participation in the life of the community in particular through measures, including technical aids, aiming to overcome barriers to communication and mobility and enabling access to transport, housing, cultural activities and leisure.

Article 16 – The right of the family to social, legal and economic protection
With a view to ensuring the necessary conditions for the full development of the family, which is a fundamental unit of society, the Parties undertake to promote the economic, legal and social protection of family life by such means as social and family benefits, fiscal arrangements, provision of family housing, benefits for the newly married and other appropriate means.

Article 17 – The right of children and young persons to social, legal and economic protection
With a view to ensuring the effective exercise of the right of children and young persons to grow up in an environment which encourages the full development of their personality and of their physical and mental capacities, the Parties undertake, either directly or in co-operation with public and private organisations, to take all appropriate and necessary measures designed:
1. (a) to ensure that children and young persons, taking account of the rights and duties of their parents, have the care, the assistance, the education and the training they need, in particular by providing for the establishment or maintenance of institutions and services sufficient and adequate for this purpose;
   (b) to protect children and young persons against negligence, violence or exploitation;
   (c) to provide protection and special aid from the state for children and young persons temporarily or definitively deprived of their family's support;
2. to provide to children and young persons a free primary and secondary education as well as to encourage regular attendance at schools.

Article 18 – The right to engage in a gainful occupation in the territory of other Parties
With a view to ensuring the effective exercise of the right to engage in a gainful occupation in the territory of any other Party, the Parties undertake:
1. to apply existing regulations in a spirit of liberality;
2. to simplify existing formalities and to reduce or abolish chancery dues and other charges payable by foreign workers or their employers;
3. to liberalise, individually or collectively, regulations governing the employment of foreign workers;

and recognise:
4. the right of their nationals to leave the country to engage in a gainful occupation in the territories of the other Parties.

Article 19 – The right of migrant workers and their families to protection and assistance
With a view to ensuring the effective exercise of the right of migrant workers and their families to protection and assistance in the territory of any other Party, the Parties undertake:

1. to maintain or to satisfy themselves that there are maintained adequate and free services to assist such workers, particularly in obtaining accurate information, and to take all appropriate steps, so far as national laws and regulations permit, against misleading propaganda relating to emigration and immigration;
2. to adopt appropriate measures within their own jurisdiction to facilitate the departure, journey and reception of such workers and their families, and to provide, within their own jurisdiction, appropriate services for health, medical attention and good hygienic conditions during the journey;
3. to promote co-operation, as appropriate, between social services, public and private, in emigration and immigration countries;
4. to secure for such workers lawfully within their territories, insofar as such matters are regulated by law or regulations or are subject to the control of administrative authorities, treatment not less favourable than that of their own nationals in respect of the following matters:
   (a) remuneration and other employment and working conditions;
   (b) membership of trade unions and enjoyment of the benefits of collective bargaining;
   (c) accommodation;
5. to secure for such workers lawfully within their territories treatment not less favourable than that of their own nationals with regard to employment taxes, dues or contributions payable in respect of employed persons;
6. to facilitate as far as possible the reunion of the family of a foreign worker permitted to establish himself in the territory;
7. to secure for such workers lawfully within their territories treatment not less favourable than that of their own nationals in respect of legal proceedings relating to matters referred to in this article;
8. to secure that such workers lawfully residing within their territories are not expelled unless they endanger national security or offend against public interest or morality;
9. to permit, within legal limits, the transfer of such parts of the earnings and savings of such workers as they may desire;
10. to extend the protection and assistance provided for in this article to self-employed migrants insofar as such measures apply;
11. to promote and facilitate the teaching of the national language of the receiving state or, if there are several, one of these languages, to migrant workers and members of their families;
12. to promote and facilitate, as far as practicable, the teaching of the migrant worker's mother tongue to the children of the migrant worker.

Article 20 – The right to equal opportunities and equal treatment in matters of employment and occupation without discrimination on the grounds of sex
With a view to ensuring the effective exercise of the right to equal opportunities and equal treatment in matters of employment and occupation without discrimination on the grounds of sex, the Parties undertake to recognise that right and to take appropriate measures to ensure or promote its application in the following fields:

(a) access to employment, protection against dismissal and occupational reintegration;
(b) vocational guidance, training, retraining and rehabilitation;
(c) terms of employment and working conditions, including remuneration;
(d) career development, including promotion.

Article 21 – The right to information and consultation
With a view to ensuring the effective exercise of the right of workers to be informed and consulted within the undertaking, the Parties undertake to adopt or encourage measures enabling workers or their representatives, in accordance with national legislation and practice:

(a) to be informed regularly or at the appropriate time and in a comprehensible way about the economic and financial situation of the undertaking employing them, on the understanding that the disclosure of certain information which could be prejudicial to the undertaking may be refused or subject to confidentiality; and
(b) to be consulted in good time on proposed decisions which could substantially affect the interests of workers, particularly on those decisions which could have an important impact on the employment situation in the undertaking.

Article 22 – The right to take part in the determination and improvement of the working conditions and working environment
With a view to ensuring the effective exercise of the right of workers to take part in the determination and improvement of the working conditions and working environment in the undertaking, the Parties undertake to adopt or encourage measures enabling workers or their representatives, in accordance with national legislation and practice, to contribute:

(a) to the determination and the improvement of the working conditions, work organisation and working environment;
(b) to the protection of health and safety within the undertaking;
(c) to the organisation of social and socio-cultural services and facilities within the undertaking;
(d) to the supervision of the observance of regulations on these matters.

Article 23 – The right of elderly persons to social protection
With a view to ensuring the effective exercise of the right of elderly persons to social protection, the Parties undertake to adopt or encourage, either directly or in co-operation with public or private organisations, appropriate measures designed in particular:

1. to enable elderly persons to remain full members of society for as long as possible, by means of:

(a) adequate resources enabling them to lead a decent life and play an active part in public, social and cultural life;
(b) provision of information about services and facilities available for elderly persons and their opportunities to make use of them;

2. to enable elderly persons to choose their life-style freely and to lead independent lives in their familiar surroundings for as long as they wish and are able,

by means of:
(a) provision of housing suited to their needs and their state of health or of adequate support for adapting their housing;
(b) the health care and the services necessitated by their state;
3. to guarantee elderly persons living in institutions appropriate support, while respecting their privacy, and participation in decisions concerning living conditions in the institution.

Article 24 – The right to protection in cases of termination of employment
With a view to ensuring the effective exercise of the right of workers to protection in cases of termination of employment, the Parties undertake to recognise:
(a) the right of all workers not to have their employment terminated without valid reasons for such termination connected with their capacity or conduct or based on the operational requirements of the undertaking, establishment or service;
(b) the right of workers whose employment is terminated without a valid reason to adequate compensation or other appropriate relief.

To this end the Parties undertake to ensure that a worker who considers that his employment has been terminated without a valid reason shall have the right to appeal to an impartial body.

Article 25 – The right of workers to the protection of their claims in the event of the insolvency of their employer
With a view to ensuring the effective exercise of the right of workers to the protection of their claims in the event of the insolvency of their employer, the Parties undertake to provide that workers' claims arising from contracts of employment or employment relationships be guaranteed by a guarantee institution or by any other effective form of protection.

Article 26 – The right to dignity at work
With a view to ensuring the effective exercise of the right of all workers to protection of their dignity at work, the Parties undertake, in consultation with employers' and workers' organisations:
1. to promote awareness, information and prevention of sexual harassment in the workplace or in relation to work and to take all appropriate measures to protect workers from such conduct;
2. to promote awareness, information and prevention of recurrent reprehensible or distinctly negative and offensive actions directed against individual workers in the workplace or in relation to work and to take all appropriate measures to protect workers from such conduct.

Article 27 – The right of workers with family responsibilities to equal opportunities and equal treatment
With a view to ensuring the exercise of the right to equality of opportunity and treatment for men and women workers with family responsibilities and between such workers and other workers, the Parties undertake:
1. to take appropriate measures:
   (a) to enable workers with family responsibilities to enter and remain in

employment, as well as to re-enter employment after an absence due to those responsibilities, including measures in the field of vocational guidance and training;
(b) to take account of their needs in terms of conditions of employment and social security;
(c) to develop or promote services, public or private, in particular child daycare services and other childcare arrangements;

2. to provide a possibility for either parent to obtain, during a period after maternity leave, parental leave to take care of a child, the duration and conditions of which should be determined by national legislation, collective agreements or practice;

3. to ensure that family responsibilities shall not, as such, constitute a valid reason for termination of employment.

Article 28 – The right of workers' representatives to protection in the undertaking and facilities to be accorded to them
With a view to ensuring the effective exercise of the right of workers' representatives to carry out their functions, the Parties undertake to ensure that in the undertaking:

(a) they enjoy effective protection against acts prejudicial to them, including dismissal, based on their status or activities as workers' representatives within the undertaking;
(b) they are afforded such facilities as may be appropriate in order to enable them to carry out their functions promptly and efficiently, account being taken of the industrial relations system of the country and the needs, size and capabilities of the undertaking concerned.

Article 29 – The right to information and consultation in collective redundancy procedures
With a view to ensuring the effective exercise of the right of workers to be informed and consulted in situations of collective redundancies, the Parties undertake to ensure that employers shall inform and consult workers' representatives, in good time prior to such collective redundancies, on ways and means of avoiding collective redundancies or limiting their occurrence and mitigating their consequences, for example by recourse to accompanying social measures aimed, in particular, at aid for the redeployment or retraining of the workers concerned.

Article 30 – The right to protection against poverty and social exclusion
With a view to ensuring the effective exercise of the right to protection against poverty and social exclusion, the Parties undertake:

(a) to take measures within the framework of an overall and co-ordinated approach to promote the effective access of persons who live or risk living in a situation of social exclusion or poverty, as well as their families, to, in particular, employment, housing, training, education, culture and social and medical assistance;
(b) to review these measures with a view to their adaptation if necessary.

Article 31 – The right to housing
With a view to ensuring the effective exercise of the right to housing, the Parties undertake to take measures designed:

1. to promote access to housing of an adequate standard;
2. to prevent and reduce homelessness with a view to its gradual elimination;
3. to make the price of housing accessible to those without adequate resources.

Part III

Article A – Undertakings
1. Subject to the provisions of Article B below, each of the Parties undertakes:
   (a) to consider Part I of this Charter as a declaration of the aims which it will pursue by all appropriate means, as stated in the introductory paragraph of that part;
   (b) to consider itself bound by at least six of the following nine articles of Part II of this Charter: Articles 1, 5, 6, 7, 12, 13, 16, 19 and 20;
   (c) to consider itself bound by an additional number of articles or numbered paragraphs of Part II of the Charter which it may select, provided that the total number of articles or numbered paragraphs by which it is bound is not less than sixteen articles or sixty-three numbered paragraphs.
2. The articles or paragraphs selected in accordance with sub-paragraphs b and c of paragraph 1 of this article shall be notified to the Secretary General of the Council of Europe at the time when the instrument of ratification, acceptance or approval is deposited.
3. Any Party may, at a later date, declare by notification addressed to the Secretary General that it considers itself bound by any articles or any numbered paragraphs of Part II of the Charter which it has not already accepted under the terms of paragraph 1 of this article. Such undertakings subsequently given shall be deemed to be an integral part of the ratification, acceptance or approval and shall have the same effect as from the first day of the month following the expiration of a period of one month after the date of the notification.
4. Each Party shall maintain a system of labour inspection appropriate to national conditions. Article B – Links with the *European Social Charter* and the 1988 Additional Protocol. No Contracting Party to the European Social Charter or Party to the Additional Protocol of 5 May 1988 may ratify, accept or approve this Charter without considering itself bound by at least the provisions corresponding to the provisions of the European Social Charter and, where appropriate, of the Additional Protocol, to which it was bound.

Acceptance of the obligations of any provision of this Charter shall, from the date of entry into force of those obligations for the Party concerned, result in the corresponding provision of the European Social Charter and, where appropriate, of its Additional Protocol of 1988 ceasing to apply to the Party concerned in the event of that Party being bound by the first of those instruments or by both instruments.

Part IV

Article C – Supervision of the implementation of the undertakings contained in this Charter
The implementation of the legal obligations contained in this Charter shall be submitted to the same supervision as the European Social Charter.

Article D – Collective complaints
1. The provisions of the Additional Protocol to the European Social Charter providing for a system of collective complaints shall apply to the undertakings given in this Charter for the States which have ratified the said Protocol.
2. Any State which is not bound by the Additional Protocol to the European Social Charter providing for a system of collective complaints may when depositing its instrument of ratification, acceptance or approval of this Charter or at any time thereafter, declare by notification addressed to the Secretary General of the Council of Europe, that it accepts the supervision of its obligations under this Charter following the procedure provided for in the said Protocol.

Part V

Article E – Non-discrimination
The enjoyment of the rights set forth in this Charter shall be secured without discrimination on any ground such as race, colour, sex, language, religion, political or other opinion, national extraction or social origin, health, association with a national minority, birth or other status.

Article F – Derogations in time of war or public emergency
1. In time of war or other public emergency threatening the life of the nation any Party may take measures derogating from its obligations under this Charter to the extent strictly required by the exigencies of the situation, provided that such measures are not inconsistent with its other obligations under international law.
2. Any Party which has availed itself of this right of derogation shall, within a reasonable lapse of time, keep the Secretary General of the Council of Europe fully informed of the measures taken and of the reasons therefor. It shall likewise inform the Secretary General when such measures have ceased to operate and the provisions of the Charter which it has accepted are again being fully executed.

Article G – Restrictions
1. The rights and principles set forth in Part I when effectively realised, and their effective exercise as provided for in Part II, shall not be subject to any restrictions or limitations not specified in those parts, except such as are prescribed by law and are necessary in a democratic society for the protection of the rights and freedoms of others or for the protection of public interest, national security, public health, or morals.
2. The restrictions permitted under this Charter to the rights and obligations

set forth herein shall not be applied for any purpose other than that for which they have been prescribed.

Article H – Relations between the Charter and domestic law or international agreements
The provisions of this Charter shall not prejudice the provisions of domestic law or of any bilateral or multilateral treaties, conventions or agreements which are already in force, or may come into force, under which more favourable treatment would be accorded to the persons protected.

Article I – Implementation of the undertakings given
1. Without prejudice to the methods of implementation foreseen in these articles the relevant provisions of Articles 1 to 31 of Part II of this Charter shall be implemented by:
   (a) laws or regulations;
   (b) agreements between employers or employers' organisations and workers' organisations;
   (c) a combination of those two methods;
   (d) other appropriate means.
2. Compliance with the undertakings deriving from the provisions of paragraphs 1, 2, 3, 4, 5 and 7 of Article 2, paragraphs 4, 6 and 7 of Article 7, paragraphs 1, 2, 3 and 5 of Article 10 and Articles 21 and 22 of Part II of this Charter shall be regarded as effective if the provisions are applied, in accordance with paragraph 1 of this article, to the great majority of the workers concerned.

Article J – Amendments
1. Any amendment to Parts I and II of this Charter with the purpose of extending the rights guaranteed in this Charter as well as any amendment to Parts III to VI, proposed by a Party or by the Governmental Committee, shall be communicated to the Secretary General of the Council of Europe and forwarded by the Secretary General to the Parties to this Charter.
2. Any amendment proposed in accordance with the provisions of the preceding paragraph shall be examined by the Governmental Committee which shall submit the text adopted to the Committee of Ministers for approval after consultation with the Parliamentary Assembly. After its approval by the Committee of Ministers this text shall be forwarded to the Parties for acceptance.
3. Any amendment to Part I and to Part II of this Charter shall enter into force, in respect of those Parties which have accepted it, on the first day of the month following the expiration of a period of one month after the date on which three Parties have informed the Secretary General that they have accepted it.
   In respect of any Party which subsequently accepts it, the amendment shall enter into force on the first day of the month following the expiration of a period of one month after the date on which that Party has informed the Secretary General of its acceptance.
4. Any amendment to Parts III to VI of this Charter shall enter into force on the first day of the month following the expiration of a period of one month after the date on which all Parties have informed the Secretary General that they have accepted it.

Part VI

Article K – Signature, ratification and entry into force
1. This Charter shall be open for signature by the member States of the Council of Europe. It shall be subject to ratification, acceptance or approval. Instruments of ratification, acceptance or approval shall be deposited with the Secretary General of the Council of Europe.
2. This Charter shall enter into force on the first day of the month following the expiration of a period of one month after the date on which three member States of the Council of Europe have expressed their consent to be bound by this Charter in accordance with the preceding paragraph.
3. In respect of any member State which subsequently expresses its consent to be bound by this Charter, it shall enter into force on the first day of the month following the expiration of a period of one month after the date of the deposit of the instrument of ratification, acceptance or approval.

Article L – Territorial application
1. This Charter shall apply to the metropolitan territory of each Party. Each signatory may, at the time of signature or of the deposit of its instrument of ratification, acceptance or approval, specify, by declaration addressed to the Secretary General of the Council of Europe, the territory which shall be considered to be its metropolitan territory for this purpose.
2. Any signatory may, at the time of signature or of the deposit of its instrument of ratification, acceptance or approval, or at any time thereafter, declare by notification addressed to the Secretary General of the Council of Europe, that the Charter shall extend in whole or in part to a non-metropolitan territory or territories specified in the said declaration for whose international relations it is responsible or for which it assumes international responsibility. It shall specify in the declaration the articles or paragraphs of Part II of the Charter which it accepts as binding in respect of the territories named in the declaration.
3. The Charter shall extend its application to the territory or territories named in the aforesaid declaration as from the first day of the month following the expiration of a period of one month after the date of receipt of the notification of such declaration by the Secretary General.
4. Any Party may declare at a later date by notification addressed to the Secretary General of the Council of Europe that, in respect of one or more of the territories to which the Charter has been applied in accordance with paragraph 2 of this article, it accepts as binding any articles or any numbered paragraphs which it has not already accepted in respect of that territory or territories. Such undertakings subsequently given shall be deemed to be an integral part of the original declaration in respect of the territory concerned, and shall have the same effect as from the first day of the month following the expiration of a period of one month after the date of receipt of such notification by the Secretary General.

Article M – Denunciation
1. Any Party may denounce this Charter only at the end of a period of five years from the date on which the Charter entered into force for it, or at the end of any subsequent period of two years, and in either case after giving six

months' notice to the Secretary General of the Council of Europe who shall inform the other Parties accordingly.
2. Any Party may, in accordance with the provisions set out in the preceding paragraph, denounce any article or paragraph of Part II of the Charter accepted by it provided that the number of articles or paragraphs by which this Party is bound shall never be less than sixteen in the former case and sixty-three in the latter and that this number of articles or paragraphs shall continue to include the articles selected by the Party among those to which special reference is made in Article A, paragraph 1, sub-paragraph b.
3. Any Party may denounce the present Charter or any of the articles or paragraphs of Part II of the Charter under the conditions specified in paragraph 1 of this article in respect of any territory to which the said Charter is applicable, by virtue of a declaration made in accordance with paragraph 2 of Article L.

Article N – Appendix
The *appendix* to this Charter shall form an integral part of it.

Article O – Notifications
The Secretary General of the Council of Europe shall notify the member States of the Council and the Director General of the International Labour Office of:
(a) any signature;
(b) the deposit of any instrument of ratification, acceptance or approval;
(c) any date of entry into force of this Charter in accordance with Article K;
(d) any declaration made in application of Articles A, paragraphs 2 and 3, D, paragraphs 1 and 2, F, paragraph 2, L, paragraphs 1, 2, 3 and 4;
(e) any amendment in accordance with Article J;
(f) any denunciation in accordance with Article M;
(g) any other act, notification or communication relating to this Charter.

APPENDIX TO THE REVISED EUROPEAN SOCIAL CHARTER

Scope of the Revised European Social Charter in terms of persons protected

1. Without prejudice to Article 12, paragraph 4, and Article 13, paragraph 4, the persons covered by Articles 1 to 17 and 20 to 31 include foreigners only in so far as they are nationals of other Parties lawfully resident or working regularly within the territory of the Party concerned, subject to the understanding that these articles are to be interpreted in the light of the provisions of Articles 18 and 19. This interpretation would not prejudice the extension of similar facilities to other persons by any of the Parties.
2. Each Party will grant to refugees as defined in the Convention relating to the Status of Refugees, signed in Geneva on 28 July 1951 and in the Protocol of 31 January 1967, and lawfully staying in its territory, treatment as favourable as possible, and in any case not less favourable than under the obligations accepted by the Party under the said convention and under any other existing international instruments applicable to those refugees.
3. Each Party will grant to stateless persons as defined in the Convention on the Status of Stateless Persons done in New York on 28 September 1954 and

lawfully staying in its territory, treatment as favourable as possible and in any case not less favourable than under the obligations accepted by the Party under the said instrument and under any other existing international instruments applicable to those stateless persons.

Part I, paragraph 18, and Part II, Article 18, paragraph 1

It is understood that these provisions are not concerned with the question of entry into the territories of the Parties and do not prejudice the provisions of the European Convention on Establishment, signed in Paris on 13 December 1955.

Part II

Article 1, paragraph 2
This provision shall not be interpreted as prohibiting or authorising any union security clause or practice.

Article 2, paragraph 6
Parties may provide that this provision shall not apply:
(a) to workers having a contract or employment relationship with a total duration not exceeding one month and/or with a working week not exceeding eight hours;
(b) where the contract or employment relationship is of a casual and/or specific nature, provided, in these cases, that its non-application is justified by objective considerations.

Article 3, paragraph 4
It is understood that for the purposes of this provision the functions, organisation and conditions of operation of these services shall be determined by national laws or regulations, collective agreements or other means appropriate to national conditions.

Article 4, paragraph 4
This provision shall be so understood as not to prohibit immediate dismissal for any serious offence.

Article 4, paragraph 5
It is understood that a Party may give the undertaking required in this paragraph if the great majority of workers are not permitted to suffer deductions from wages either by law or through collective agreements or arbitration awards, the exceptions being those persons not so covered.

Article 6, paragraph 4
It is understood that each Party may, insofar as it is concerned, regulate the exercise of the right to strike by law, provided that any further restriction that this might place on the right can be justified under the terms of Article G.

Article 7, paragraph 2
This provision does not prevent Parties from providing in their legislation that young persons not having reached the minimum age laid down may perform work in so far as it is absolutely necessary for their vocational training where

such work is carried out in accordance with conditions prescribed by the competent authority and measures are taken to protect the health and safety of these young persons.

Article 7, paragraph 8
It is understood that a Party may give the undertaking required in this paragraph if it fulfils the spirit of the undertaking by providing by law that the great majority of persons under eighteen years of age shall not be employed in night work.

Article 8, paragraph 2
This provision shall not be interpreted as laying down an absolute prohibition. Exceptions could be made, for instance, in the following cases:
(a) if an employed woman has been guilty of misconduct which justifies breaking off the employment relationship;
(b) if the undertaking concerned ceases to operate;
(c) if the period prescribed in the employment contract has expired.

Article 12, paragraph 4
The words "and subject to the conditions laid down in such agreements" in the introduction to this paragraph are taken to imply *inter alia* that with regard to benefits which are available independently of any insurance contribution, a Party may require the completion of a prescribed period of residence before granting such benefits to nationals of other Parties.

Article 13, paragraph 4
Governments not Parties to the European Convention on Social and Medical Assistance may ratify the Charter in respect of this paragraph provided that they grant to nationals of other Parties a treatment which is in conformity with the provisions of the said convention.

Article 16
It is understood that the protection afforded in this provision covers single-parent families.

Article 17
It is understood that this provision covers all persons below the age of 18 years, unless under the law applicable to the child majority is attained earlier, without prejudice to the other specific provisions provided by the Charter, particularly Article 7.
This does not imply an obligation to provide compulsory education up to the above-mentioned age.

Article 19, paragraph 6
For the purpose of applying this provision, the term "family of a foreign worker" is understood to mean at least the worker's spouse and unmarried children, as long as the latter are considered to be minors by the receiving State and are dependent on the migrant worker.

Article 20
1. It is understood that social security matters, as well as other provisions relating to unemployment benefit, old age benefit and survivor's benefit, may be excluded from the scope of this article.

2. Provisions concerning the protection of women, particularly as regards pregnancy, confinement and the post-natal period, shall not be deemed to be discrimination as referred to in this article.
3. This article shall not prevent the adoption of specific measures aimed at removing *de facto* inequalities.
4. Occupational activities which, by reason of their nature or the context in which they are carried out, can be entrusted only to persons of a particular sex may be excluded from the scope of this article or some of its provisions. This provision is not to be interpreted as requiring the Parties to embody in laws or regulations a list of occupations which, by reason of their nature or the context in which they are carried out, may be reserved to persons of a particular sex.

Articles 21 and 22
1. For the purpose of the application of these articles, the term "workers' representatives" means persons who are recognised as such under national legislation or practice.
2. The terms "national legislation and practice" embrace as the case may be, in addition to laws and regulations, collective agreements, other agreements between employers and workers' representatives, customs as well as relevant case law.
3. For the purpose of the application of these articles, the term "undertaking" is understood as referring to a set of tangible and intangible components, with or without legal personality, formed to produce goods or provide services for financial gain and with power to determine its own market policy.
4. It is understood that religious communities and their institutions may be excluded from the application of these articles, even if these institutions are "undertakings" within the meaning of paragraph 3. Establishments pursuing activities which are inspired by certain ideals or guided by certain moral concepts, ideals and concepts which are protected by national legislation, may be excluded from the application of these articles to such an extent as is necessary to protect the orientation of the undertaking.
5. It is understood that where in a state the rights set out in these articles are exercised in the various establishments of the undertaking, the Party concerned is to be considered as fulfilling the obligations deriving from these provisions.
6. The Parties may exclude from the field of application of these articles, those undertakings employing less than a certain number of workers, to be determined by national legislation or practice.

Article 22
1. This provision affects neither the powers and obligations of states as regards the adoption of health and safety regulations for workplaces, nor the powers and responsibilities of the bodies in charge of monitoring their application.
2. The terms "social and socio-cultural services and facilities" are understood as referring to the social and/or cultural facilities for workers provided by some undertakings such as welfare assistance, sports fields, rooms for nursing mothers, libraries, children's holiday camps, etc.

Article 23, paragraph 1
For the purpose of the application of this paragraph, the term "for as long as possible" refers to the elderly person's physical, psychological and intellectual capacities.

Article 24
1. It is understood that for the purposes of this article the terms "termination of employment" and "terminated" mean termination of employment at the initiative of the employer.
2. It is understood that this article covers all workers but that a Party may exclude from some or all of its protection the following categories of employed persons:
   (a) workers engaged under a contract of employment for a specified period of time or a specified task;
   (b) workers undergoing a period of probation or a qualifying period of employment, provided that this is determined in advance and is of a reasonable duration;
   (c) workers engaged on a casual basis for a short period.
3. For the purpose of this article the following, in particular, shall not constitute valid reasons for termination of employment:
   (a) trade union membership or participation in union activities outside working hours, or, with the consent of the employer, within working hours;
   (b) seeking office as, acting or having acted in the capacity of a workers' representative;
   (c) the filing of a complaint or the participation in proceedings against an employer involving alleged violation of laws or regulations or recourse to competent administrative authorities;
   (d) race, colour, sex, marital status, family responsibilities, pregnancy, religion, political opinion, national extraction or social origin;
   (e) maternity or parental leave;
   (f) temporary absence from work due to illness or injury.
4. It is understood that compensation or other appropriate relief in case of termination of employment without valid reasons shall be determined by national laws or regulations, collective agreements or other means appropriate to national conditions.

Article 25
1. It is understood that the competent national authority may, by way of exemption and after consulting organisations of employers and workers, exclude certain categories of workers from the protection provided in this provision by reason of the special nature of their employment relationship.
2. It is understood that the definition of the term "insolvency" must be determined by national law and practice.
3. The workers' claims covered by this provision shall include at least:
   (a) the workers' claims for wages relating to a prescribed period, which shall not be less than three months under a privilege system and eight weeks under a guarantee system, prior to the insolvency or to the termination of employment;
   (b) the workers' claims for holiday pay due as a result of work performed during the year in which the insolvency or the termination of employment occurred;

(c) the workers' claims for amounts due in respect of other types of paid absence relating to a prescribed period, which shall not be less than three months under a privilege system and eight weeks under a guarantee system, prior to the insolvency or the termination of the employment.
4. National laws or regulations may limit the protection of workers' claims to a prescribed amount, which shall be of a socially acceptable level.

Article 26
It is understood that this article does not require that legislation be enacted by the Parties. It is understood that paragraph 2 does not cover sexual harassment.

Article 27
It is understood that this article applies to men and women workers with family responsibilities in relation to their dependent children as well as in relation to other members of their immediate family who clearly need their care or support where such responsibilities restrict their possibilities of preparing for, entering, participating in or advancing in economic activity. The terms "dependent children" and "other members of their immediate family who clearly need their care and support" mean persons defined as such by the national legislation of the Party concerned.

Articles 28 and 29
For the purpose of the application of this article, the term "workers' representatives" means persons who are recognised as such under national legislation or practice.

Part III

It is understood that the Charter contains legal obligations of an international character, the application of which is submitted solely to the supervision provided for in *Part IV* thereof.

Article A, paragraph 1
It is understood that the numbered paragraphs may include articles consisting of only one paragraph.

Article B, paragraph 2
For the purpose of paragraph 2 of Article B, the provisions of the revised Charter correspond to the provisions of the Charter with the same article or paragraph number with the exception of:

(a) Article 3, paragraph 2, of the revised Charter which corresponds to Article 3, paragraphs 1 and 3, of the Charter;
(b) Article 3, paragraph 3, of the revised Charter which corresponds to Article 3, paragraphs 2 and 3, of the Charter;
(c) Article 10, paragraph 5, of the revised Charter which corresponds to Article 10, paragraph 4, of the Charter;
(d) Article 17, paragraph 1, of the revised Charter which corresponds to Article 17 of the Charter.

Part V

Article E
A differential treatment based on an objective and reasonable justification shall not be deemed discriminatory.

Article F
The terms "**in time of war or other public emergency**" shall be so understood as to cover also the *threat* of war.

Article I
It is understood that workers excluded in accordance with the appendix to Articles 21 and 22 are not taken into account in establishing the number of workers concerned.

Article J
The term "**amendment**" shall be extended so as to cover also the addition of new articles to the Charter.

COUNCIL OF EUROPE

European Treaties
ETS No. 126

EUROPEAN CONVENTION FOR THE PREVENTION OF TORTURE AND INHUMAN OR DEGRADING TREATMENT OR PUNISHMENT

Strasbourg, 26.XI.1987

The member States of the Council of Europe, signatory hereto,

Having regard to the provisions of the Convention for the Protection of Human Rights and Fundamental Freedoms,

Recalling that, under Article 3 of the same Convention, "no one shall be subjected to torture or to inhuman or degrading treatment or punishment";

Noting that the machinery provided for in that Convention operates in relation to persons who allege that they are victims of violations of Article 3;

Convinced that the protection of persons deprived of their liberty against torture and inhuman or degrading treatment or punishment could be strengthened by non-judicial means of a preventive character based on visits,

Have agreed as follows:

Chapter I

Article 1
There shall be established a European Committee for the Prevention of Torture and Inhuman or Degrading Treatment or Punishment (hereinafter referred to as "the Committee"). The Committee shall, by means of visits, examine the treatment of persons deprived of their liberty with a view to strengthening, if necessary, the protection of such persons from torture and from inhuman or degrading treatment or punishment.

Article 2
Each Party shall permit visits, in accordance with this Convention, to any place within its jurisdiction where persons are deprived of their liberty by a public authority.

Article 3
In the application of this Convention, the Committee and the competent national authorities of the Party concerned shall co-operate with each other.

Chapter II

Article 4
1. The Committee shall consist of a number of members equal to that of the Parties.
2. The members of the Committee shall be chosen from among persons of high moral character, known for their competence in the field of human rights or having professional experience in the areas covered by this Convention.
3. No two members of the Committee may be nationals of the same State.
4. The members shall serve in their individual capacity, shall be independent and impartial, and shall be available to serve the Committee effectively.

Article 5
1. The members of the Committee shall be elected by the Committee of Ministers of the Council of Europe by an absolute majority of votes, from a list of names drawn up by the Bureau of the Consultative Assembly of the Council of Europe; each national delegation of the Parties in the Consultative Assembly shall put forward three candidates, of whom two at least shall be its nationals.
2. The same procedure shall be followed in filling casual vacancies.
3. The members of the Committee shall be elected for a period of four years. They may only be re-elected once. However, among the members elected at the first election, the terms of three members shall expire at the end of two years. The members whose terms are to expire at the end of the initial period of two years shall be chosen by lot by the Secretary General of the Council of Europe immediately after the first election has been completed.

Article 6
1. The Committee shall meet in camera. A quorum shall be equal to the majority of its members. The decisions of the Committee shall be taken by a majority of the members present, subject to the provisions of Article 10, paragraph 2.
2. The Committee shall draw up its own rules of procedure.
3. The Secretariat of the Committee shall be provided by the Secretary General of the Council of Europe.

Chapter III

Article 7
1. The Committee shall organise visits to places referred to in Article 2. Apart from periodic visits, the Committee may organise such other visits as appear to it to be required in the circumstances.
2. As a general rule, the visits shall be carried out by at least two members of the Committee. The Committee may, if it considers it necessary, be assisted by experts and interpreters.

Article 8
1. The Committee shall notify the Government of the Party concerned of its intention to carry out a visit. After such notification, it may at any time visit any place referred to in Article 2.
2. A Party shall provide the Committee with the following facilities to carry out its task:
   (a) access to its territory and the right to travel without restriction;
   (b) full information on the places where persons deprived of their liberty are being held;
   (c) unlimited access to any place where persons are deprived of their liberty, including the right to move inside such places without restriction;
   (d) other information available to the Party which is necessary for the Committee to carry out its task.
In seeking such information, the Committee shall have regard to applicable rules of national law and professional ethics.
3. The Committee may interview in private persons deprived of their liberty.
4. The Committee may communicate freely with any person whom it believes can supply relevant information.
5. If necessary, the Committee may immediately communicate observations to the competent authorities of the Party concerned.

Article 9
1. In exceptional circumstances, the competent authorities of the Party concerned may make representations to the Committee against a visit at the time or to the particular place proposed by the Committee. Such representations may only be made on grounds of national defence, public safety, serious disorder in places where persons are deprived of their liberty, the medical condition of a person or that an urgent interrogation relating to a serious crime is in progress.
2. Following such representations, the Committee and the Party shall immediately enter into consultations in order to clarify the situation and seek agreement on arrangements to enable the Committee to exercise its functions expeditiously. Such arrangements may include the transfer to another place of any person whom the Committee proposed to visit. Until the visit takes place, the Party shall provide information to the Committee about any person concerned.

Article 10
1. After each visit, the Committee shall draw up a report on the facts found during the visit, taking account of any observations which may have been submitted by the Party concerned. It shall transmit to the latter its report containing any recommendations it considers necessary. The Committee may consult with the Party with a view to suggesting, if necessary, improvements in the protection of persons deprived of their liberty.
2. If the Party fails to co-operate or refuses to improve the situation in the light of the Committee's recommendations, the Committee may decide, after the Party has had an opportunity to make known its views, by a majority of two-thirds of its members to make a public statement on the matter.

Article 11
1. The information gathered by the Committee in relation to a visit, its report and its consultations with the Party concerned shall be confidential.
2. The Committee shall publish its report, together with any comments of the Party concerned, whenever requested to do so by that Party.
3. However, no personal data shall be published without the express consent of the person concerned.

Article 12
Subject to the rules of confidentiality in Article 11, the Committee shall every year submit to the Committee of Ministers a general report on its activities which shall be transmitted to the Consultative Assembly and made public.

Article 13
The members of the Committee, experts and other persons assisting the Committee are required, during and after their terms of office, to maintain the confidentiality of the facts or information of which they have become aware during the discharge of their functions.

Article 14
1. The names of persons assisting the Committee shall be specified in the notification under Article 8, paragraph 1.
2. Experts shall act on the instructions and under the authority of the Committee. They shall have particular knowledge and experience in the areas covered by this Convention and shall be bound by the same duties of independence, impartiality and availability as the members of the Committee.
3. A Party may exceptionally declare that an expert or other person assisting the Committee may not be allowed to take part in a visit to a place within its jurisdiction.

Chapter IV

Article 15
Each Party shall inform the Committee of the name and address of the authority competent to receive notifications to its Government, and of any liaison officer it may appoint.

Article 16
The Committee, its members and experts referred to in Article 7, paragraph 2 shall enjoy the privileges and immunities set out in the Annex to this Convention.

Article 17
This Convention shall not prejudice the provisions of domestic law or any international agreement which provide greater protection for persons deprived of their liberty.
Nothing in this Convention shall be construed as limiting or derogating from the competence of the organs of the European Convention on Human Rights or from the obligations assumed by the Parties under that Convention.
The Committee shall not visit places which representatives or delegates of Protecting Powers or the International Committee of the Red Cross effectively

visit on a regular basis by virtue of the Geneva Conventions of 12 August 1949 and the Additional Protocols of 8 June 1977 thereto.

Chapter V

Article 18
This Convention shall be open for signature by the member States of the Council of Europe. It is subject to ratification, acceptance or approval. Instruments of ratification, acceptance or approval shall be deposited with the Secretary General of the Council of Europe.

Article 19
1. This Convention shall enter into force on the first day of the month following the expiration of a period of three months after the date on which seven member States of the Council of Europe have expressed their consent to be bound by the Convention in accordance with the provisions of Article 18.
2. In respect of any member State which subsequently expresses its consent to be bound by it, the Convention shall enter into force on the first day of the month following the expiration of a period of three months after the date of the deposit of the instrument of ratification, acceptance or approval.

Article 20
1. Any State may at the time of signature or when depositing its instrument of ratification, acceptance or approval, specify the territory or territories to which this Convention shall apply.
2. Any State may at any later date, by a declaration addressed to the Secretary General of the Council of Europe, extend the application of this Convention to any other territory specified in the declaration. In respect of such territory the Convention shall enter into force on the first day of the month following the expiration of a period of three months after the date of receipt of such declaration by the Secretary General.
3. Any declaration made under the two preceding paragraphs may, in respect of any territory specified in such declaration, be withdrawn by a notification addressed to the Secretary General. The withdrawal shall become effective on the first day of the month following the expiration of a period of three months after the date of receipt of such notification by the Secretary General.

Article 21
No reservation may be made in respect of the provisions of this Convention.

Article 22
1. Any Party may, at any time, denounce this Convention by means of a notification addressed to the Secretary General of the Council of Europe.
2. Such denunciation shall become effective on the first day of the month following the expiration of a period of twelve months after the date of receipt of the notification by the Secretary General.

Article 23
The Secretary General of the Council of Europe shall notify the member States of the Council of Europe of:

(a) any signature;
(b) the deposit of any instrument of ratification, acceptance or approval;
(c) any date of entry into force of this Convention in accordance with Articles 19 and 20;
(d) any other act, notification or communication relating to this Convention, except for action taken in pursuance of Articles 8 and 10.

ANNEX

Privileges and immunities

(Article 16)
1. For the purpose of this annex, references to members of the Committee shall be deemed to include references to experts mentioned in Article 7, paragraph 2.
2. The members of the Committee shall, while exercising their functions and during journeys made in the exercise of their functions, enjoy the following privileges and immunities:
   (a) immunity from personal arrest or detention and from seizure of their personal baggage and, in respect of words spoken or written and all acts done by them in their official capacity, immunity from legal process of every kind;
   (b) exemption from any restrictions on their freedom of movement on exit from and return to their country of residence, and entry into and exit from the country in which they exercise their functions, and from alien registration in the country which they are visiting or through which they are passing in the exercise of their functions.
3. In the course of journeys undertaken in the exercise of their functions, the members of the Committee shall, in the matter of customs and exchange control, be accorded:
   (a) by their own Government, the same facilities as those accorded to senior officials travelling abroad on temporary official duty;
   (b) by the Governments of other Parties, the same facilities as those accorded to representatives of foreign Governments on temporary official duty.
4. Documents and papers of the Committee, in so far as they relate to the business of the Committee, shall be inviolable. The official correspondence and other official communications of the Committee may not be held up or subjected to censorship.
5. In order to secure for the members of the Committee complete freedom of speech and complete independence in the discharge of their duties, the immunity from legal process in respect of words spoken or written and all acts done by them in discharging their duties shall continue to be accorded, notwithstanding that the persons concerned are no longer engaged in the discharge of such duties.
6. Privileges and immunities are accorded to the members of the Committee, not for the personal benefit of the individuals themselves but in order to safeguard the independent exercise of their functions. The Committee alone shall be competent to waive the immunity of its members; it has not only the

right, but is under a duty, to waive the immunity of one of its members in any case where, in its opinion, the immunity would impede the course of justice, and where it can be waived without prejudice to the purpose for which the immunity is accorded.

COUNCIL OF EUROPE

European Treaties
ETS No. 151

PROTOCOL No. 1 TO THE EUROPEAN CONVENTION FOR THE PREVENTION OF TORTURE AND INHUMAN OR DEGRADING TREATMENT OR PUNISHMENT

Strasbourg, 4.XI.1993

The member States of the Council of Europe, signatories to this Protocol to the European Convention for the Prevention of Torture and Inhuman or Degrading Treatment or Punishment, signed at Strasbourg on 26 November 1987 (hereinafter referred to as "the Convention"),

Considering that non-member States of the Council of Europe should be allowed to accede to the Convention at the invitation of the Committee of Ministers,

Have agreed as follows:

Article 1
A sub-paragraph shall be added to Article 5, paragraph 1, of the Convention as follows:

"Where a member is to be elected to the Committee in respect of a non-member State of the Council of Europe, the Bureau of the Consultative Assembly shall invite the Parliament of that State to put forward three candidates, of whom two at least shall be its nationals. The election by the Committee of Ministers shall take place after consultation with the Party concerned."

Article 2
Article 12 of the Convention shall read as follows:

"Subject to the rules of confidentiality in Article 11, the Committee shall every year submit to the Committee of Ministers a general report on its activities which shall be transmitted to the Consultative Assembly and to any non-member State of the Council of Europe which is a party to the Convention, and made public."

Article 3
The text of Article 18 of the Convention shall become paragraph 1 of that article and shall be supplemented by the following second paragraph:

"2. The Committee of Ministers of the Council of Europe may invite any non-member State of the Council of Europe to accede to the Convention."

Article 4
In paragraph 2 of Article 19 of the Convention, the word "member" shall be deleted and the words "or approval," shall be replaced by "approval or accession.".

Article 5
In paragraph 1 of Article 20 of the Convention, the words "or approval" shall be replaced by "approval or accession,".

Article 6
The introductory sentence of Article 23 of the Convention shall read as follows:

> "The Secretary General of the Council of Europe shall notify the member States and any non-member State of the Council of Europe party to the Convention of:"

In Article 23.b of the Convention, the words "or approval;" shall be replaced by "approval or accession;".

Article 7
1. This Protocol shall be open for signature by member States of the Council of Europe signatories to the Convention, which may express their consent to be bound by:
   (a) signature without reservation as to ratification, acceptance or approval; or
   (b) signature subject to ratification, acceptance or approval, followed by ratification, acceptance or approval.
2. Instruments of ratification, acceptance or approval shall be deposited with the Secretary General of the Council of Europe.

Article 8
This Protocol shall enter into force on the first day of the month following the expiration of a period of three months after the date on which all Parties to the Convention have expressed their consent to be bound by the Protocol, in accordance with the provisions of Article 7.

Article 9
The Secretary General of the Council of Europe shall notify the member States of the Council of Europe of:
(a) any signature;
(b) the deposit of any instrument of ratification, acceptance or approval;
(c) the date of entry into force of this Protocol, in accordance with Article 8;
(d) any other act, notification or communication relating to this Protocol.

COUNCIL OF EUROPE

European Treaties
ETS No. 152

PROTOCOL No. 2 TO THE EUROPEAN CONVENTION FOR THE PREVENTION OF TORTURE AND INHUMAN OR DEGRADING TREATMENT OR PUNISHMENT

Strasbourg, 4.XI.1993

The States, signatories to this Protocol to the European Convention for the Prevention of Torture and Inhuman or Degrading Treatment or Punishment, signed at Strasbourg on 26 November 1987 (hereinafter referred to as "the Convention"),

Convinced of the advisibility of enabling members of the European Committee for the Prevention of Torture and Inhuman and Degrading Treatment (hereinafter referred to as "the Committee") to be re-elected twice;

Also considering the need to guarantee an orderly renewal of the membership of the Committee,

Have agreed as follows:

Article 1
In Article 5, paragraph 3, the second sentence shall read as follows:

"They may be re-elected twice."

1. Article 5 of the Convention shall be supplemented by the following paragraphs 4 and 5:
    "4. In order to ensure that, as far as possible, one half of the membership of the Committee shall be renewed every two years, the Committee of Ministers may decide, before proceeding to any subsequent election, that the term or terms of office of one or more members to be elected shall be for a period other than four years but not more than six and not less than two years.
    5. In cases where more than one term of office is involved and the Committee of Ministers applies the preceding paragraph, the allocation of the terms of office shall be effected by the drawing of lots by the Secretary General, immediately after the election."

Article 2
1. This Protocol shall be open for signature by States signatories to the Convention or acceding thereto, which may express their consent to be bound by:

(a) signature without reservation as to ratification, acceptance or approval; or
(b) signature subject to ratification, acceptance or approval, followed by ratification, acceptance or approval.

2. Instruments of ratification, acceptance or approval shall be deposited with the Secretary General of the Council of Europe.

Article 3

This Protocol shall enter into force on the first day of the month following the expiration of a period of three months after the date on which all Parties to the Convention have expressed their consent to be bound by the Protocol, in accordance with the provisions of Article 2.

Article 4

The Secretary General of the Council of Europe shall notify the member States of the Council of Europe and non-member States Parties to the Convention of:
(a) any signature;
(b) the deposit of any instrument of ratification, acceptance or approval;
(c) the date of any entry into force of this Protocol, in accordance with Article 3;
(d) any other act, notification or communication relating to this Protocol.

ORGANIZATION OF AMERICAN STATES

AMERICAN DECLARATION OF THE RIGHTS AND DUTIES OF MAN

Adopted by the Ninth International Conference of American States, Bogotá, Colombia, 1948

Whereas,

The American peoples have acknowledged the dignity of the individual, and their national constitutions recognize that juridical and political institutions, which regulate life in human society, have as their principal aim the protection of the essential rights of man and the creation of circumstances that will permit him to achieve spiritual and material progress and attain happiness;

The American States have on repeated occasions recognized that the essential rights of man are not derived from the fact that he is a national of a certain state, but are based upon attributes of his human personality;

The international protection of the rights of man should be the principal guide of an evolving American law;

The affirmation of essential human rights by the American States together with the guarantees given by the internal regimes of the states establish the initial system of protection considered by the American States as being suited to the present social and juridical conditions, not without a recognition on their part that they should increasingly strengthen that system in the international field as conditions become more favorable,

The Ninth International Conference of American States
Agrees,
To adopt the following

AMERICAN DECLARATION OF THE RIGHTS AND DUTIES OF MAN

Preamble

All men are born free and equal, in dignity and in rights, and, being endowed by nature with reason and conscience, they should conduct themselves as brothers one to another.

The fulfillment of duty by each individual is a prerequisite to the rights of all. Rights and duties are interrelated in every social and political activity of man. While rights exalt individual liberty, duties express the dignity of that liberty.

Duties of a juridical nature presuppose others of a moral nature which support them in principle and constitute their basis.

Inasmuch as spiritual development is the supreme end of human existence and the highest expression thereof, it is the duty of man to serve that end with all his strength and resources.

Since culture is the highest social and historical expression of that spiritual development, it is the duty of man to preserve, practice and foster culture by every means within his power.

And, since moral conduct constitutes the noblest flowering of culture, it is the duty of every man always to hold it in high respect.

CHAPTER ONE

Rights

Article I. Every human being has the right to life, liberty and the security of his person.	Right to life liberty and personal security.
Article II. All persons are equal before the law and have the rights and duties established in this Declaration, without distinction as to race, sex, language, creed or any other factor.	Right to equality before the law.
Article III. Every person has the right freely to profess a religious faith, and to manifest and practice it both in public and in private.	Right to religious freedom and worship.
Article IV. Every person has the right to freedom of investigation, of opinion, and of the expression and dissemination of ideas, by any medium whatsoever.	Right to freedom of investigation, opinion, expression and dissemination.
Article V. Every person has the right to the protection of the law against abusive attacks upon his honor, his reputation, and his private and family life.	Right to protection of honor, personal reputation and private and family life.
Article VI. Every person has the right to establish a family, the basic element of society, and to receive protection therefor.	Right to a family and to protection thereof.
Article VII. All women, during pregnancy and the nursing period, and all children have the right to special protection, care and aid.	Right to protection for mothers and children.
Article VIII. Every person has the right to fix his residence within the territory of the state of which he is a national, to move about freely within such territory, and not to leave it except by his own will.	Right to residence and movement.
Article IX. Every person has the right to the inviolability of his home.	Right to inviolability of the home.
Article X. Every person has the right to the inviolability and transmission of his correspondence.	Right to the inviolability and transmission of correspondence.

Article XI. Every person has the right to the preservation of his health through sanitary and social measures relating to food, clothing, housing and medical care, to the extent permitted by public and community resources.

Article XII. Every person has the right to an education, which should be based on the principles of liberty, morality and human solidarity.

Likewise every person has the right to an education that will prepare him to attain a decent life, to raise his standard of living, and to be a useful member of society.

The right to an education includes the right to equality of opportunity in every case, in accordance with natural talents, merit and the desire to utilize the resources that the state or the community is in a position to provide.

Every person has the right to receive, free, at least a primary education.

Article XIII. Every person has the right to take part in the cultural life of the community, to enjoy the arts, and to participate in the benefits that result from intellectual progress, especially scientific discoveries.

He likewise has the right to the protection of his moral and material interests as regards his inventions or any literary, scientific or artistic works of which he is the author.

Article XIV. Every person has the right to work, under proper conditions, and to follow his vocation freely, insofar as existing conditions of employment permit.

Every person who works has the right to receive such remuneration as will, in proportion to his capacity and skill, assure him a standard of living suitable for himself and for his family.

Article XV. Every person has the right to leisure time, to wholesome recreation, and to the opportunity for advantageous use of his free time to his spiritual, cultural and physical benefit.

Article XVI. Every person has the right to social security which will protect him from the consequences of unemployment, old age, and any disabilities arising from causes beyond his control that make it physically or mentally impossible for him to earn a living.

Article XI	Right to the preservation of health and to well-being.
Article XII	Right to education.
Article XIII	Right to the benefits of culture.
Article XIV	Right to work and to fair remuneration.
Article XV	Right to leisure time and to the use thereof.
Article XVI	Right to social security.

Article XVII. Every person has the right to be recognized everywhere as a person having rights and obligations, and to enjoy the basic civil rights. — Right to recognition of juridical personality and civil rights.

Article XVIII. Every person may resort to the courts to ensure respect for his legal rights. There should likewise be available to him a simple, brief procedure whereby the courts will protect him from acts of authority that, to his prejudice, violate any fundamental constitutional rights. — Right to a fair trial.

Article XIX. Every person has the right to the nationality to which he is entitled by law and to change it, if he so wishes, for the nationality of any other country that is willing to grant it to him. — Right to nationality.

Article XX. Every person having legal capacity is entitled to participate in the government of his country, directly or through his representatives, and to take part in popular elections, which shall be by secret ballot, and shall be honest, periodic and free. — Right to vote and to participate in government.

Article XXI. Every person has the right to assemble peaceably with others in a formal public meeting or an informal gathering, in connection with matters of common interest of any nature. — Right of assembly.

Article XXII. Every person has the right to associate with others to promote, exercise and protect his legitimate interests of a political, economic, religious, social, cultural, professional, labor union or other nature. — Right of association.

Article XXIII. Every person has a right to own such private property as meets the essential needs of decent living and helps to maintain the dignity of the individual and of the home. — Right to property.

Article XXIV. Every person has the right to submit respectful petitions to any competent authority, for reasons of either general or private interest, and the right to obtain a prompt decision thereon. — Right of petition.

Article XXV. No person may be deprived of his liberty except in the cases and according to the procedures established by pre-existing law. — Right of protection from arbitrary arrest.

No person may be deprived of liberty for nonfulfillment of obligations of a purely civil character.

Every individual who has been deprived of his liberty has the right to have the legality of his detention ascertained without delay by a court, and the right to be tried without undue delay or, otherwise, to be released. He also has the right to humane treatment during the time he is in custody.

Article XXVI. Every accused person is presumed to be innocent until proved guilty. — Right to due process of law.

Every person accused of an offense has the right to be given an impartial and public hearing, and to be tried by courts previously established in accordance with pre-existing laws, and not to receive cruel, infamous or unusual punishment.

Article XXVII. Every person has the right, in case of pursuit not resulting from ordinary crimes, to seek and receive asylum in foreign territory, in accordance with the laws of each country and with international agreements. — Right of asylum.

Article XXVIII. The rights of man are limited by the rights of others, by the security of all, and by the just demands of the general welfare and the advancement of democracy. — Scope of the rights of man.

CHAPTER TWO

Duties

Article XXIX. It is the duty of the individual so to conduct himself in relation to others that each and every one may fully form and develop his personality. — Duties to society.

Article XXX. It is the duty of every person to aid, support, educate and protect his minor children, and it is the duty of children to honor their parents always and to aid, support and protect them when they need it. — Duties toward children and parents.

Article XXXI. It is the duty of every person to acquire at least an elementary education. — Duty to receive instruction.

Article XXXII. It is the duty of every person to vote in the popular elections of the country of which he is a national, when he is legally capable of doing so. — Duty to vote.

Article XXXIII. It is the duty of every person to obey the law and other legitimate commands of the authorities of his country and those of the country in which he may be. — Duty to obey the law.

Article XXXIV. It is the duty of every able-bodied person to render whatever civil and military service his country may require for its — Duty to serve the community and the nation.

defense and preservation, and, in case of public disaster, to render such services as may be in his power.

It is likewise his duty to hold any public office to which he may be elected by popular vote in the state of which he is a national.

Article XXXV. It is the duty of every person to cooperate with the state and the community with respect to social security and welfare, in accordance with his ability and with existing circumstances. — Duties with respect to social security and welfare.

Article XXXVI. It is the duty of every person to pay the taxes established by law for the support of public services. — Duty to pay taxes.

Article XXXVII. It is the duty of every person to work, as far as his capacity and possibilities permit, in order to obtain the means of livelihood or to benefit his community. — Duty to work.

Article XXXVIII. It is the duty of every person to refrain from taking part in political activities that, according to law, are reserved exclusively to the citizens of the state in which he is an alien. — Duty to refrain from political activities in a foreign country.

ORGANIZATION OF AMERICAN STATES

AMERICAN CONVENTION ON HUMAN RIGHTS

Signed at the Inter-American Specialized Conference on Human Rights, San José, Costa Rica, 22 November 1969

Preamble

The American states signatory to the present Convention,

Reaffirming their intention to consolidate in this hemisphere, within the framework of democratic institutions, a system of personal liberty and social justice based on respect for the essential rights of man;

Recognizing that the essential rights of man are not derived from one's being a national of a certain state, but are based upon attributes of the human personality, and that they therefore justify international protection in the form of a convention reinforcing or complementing the protection provided by the domestic law of the American states;

Considering that these principles have been set forth in the Charter of the Organization of American States, in the American Declaration of the Rights and Duties of Man, and in the Universal Declaration of Human Rights, and that they have been reaffirmed and refined in other international instruments, worldwide as well as regional in scope;

Reiterating that, in accordance with the Universal Declaration of Human Rights, the ideal of free men enjoying freedom from fear and want can be achieved only if conditions are created whereby everyone may enjoy his economic, social, and cultural rights, as well as his civil and political rights; and

Considering that the Third Special Inter-American Conference (Buenos Aires, 1967) approved the incorporation into the Charter of the Organization itself of broader standards with respect to economic, social, and educational rights and resolved that an inter-American convention on human rights should determine the structure, competence, and procedure of the organs responsible for these matters,

Have agreed upon the following:

Part I – State Obligations and Rights Protected

CHAPTER I – GENERAL OBLIGATIONS

Article 1 – Obligation to Respect Rights
1. The States Parties to this Convention undertake to respect the rights and freedoms recognized herein and to ensure to all persons subject to their

jurisdiction the free and full exercise of those rights and freedoms, without any discrimination for reasons of race, color, sex, language, religion, political or other opinion, national or social origin, economic status, birth, or any other social condition.
2. For the purposes of this Convention, "person" means every human being.

Article 2 – Domestic Legal Effects
Where the exercise of any of the rights or freedoms referred to in Article 1 is not already ensured by legislative or other provisions, the States Parties undertake to adopt, in accordance with their constitutional processes and the provisions of this Convention, such legislative or other measures as may be necessary to give effect to those rights or freedoms.

CHAPTER II – CIVIL AND POLITICAL RIGHTS

Article 3 – Right to Juridical Personality
Every person has the right to recognition as a person before the law.

Article 4 – Right to Life
1. Every person has the right to have his life respected. This right shall be protected by law and, in general, from the moment of conception. No one shall be arbitrarily deprived of his life.
2. In countries that have not abolished the death penalty, it may be imposed only for the most serious crimes and pursuant to a final judgment rendered by a competent court and in accordance with a law establishing such punishment, enacted prior to the commission of the crime. The application of such punishment shall not be extended to crimes to which it does not presently apply.
3. The death penalty shall not be reestablished in states that have abolished it.
4. In no case shall capital punishment be inflicted for political offenses or related common crimes.
5. Capital punishment shall not be imposed upon persons who, at the time the crime was committed, were under 18 years of age or over 70 years of age; nor shall it be applied to pregnant women.
6. Every person condemned to death shall have the right to apply for amnesty, pardon, or commutation of sentence, which may be granted in all cases. Capital punishment shall not be imposed while such a petition is pending decision by the competent authority.

Article 5 – Right to Humane Treatment
1. Every person has the right to have his physical, mental, and moral integrity respected.
2. No one shall be subjected to torture or to cruel, inhuman, or degrading punishment or treatment. All persons deprived of their liberty shall be treated with respect for the inherent dignity of the human person.
3. Punishment shall not be extended to any person other than the criminal.
4. Accused persons shall, save in exceptional circumstances, be segregated from convicted persons, and shall be subject to separate treatment appropriate to their status as unconvicted persons.

5. Minors while subject to criminal proceedings shall be separated from adults and brought before specialized tribunals, as speedily as possible, so that they may be treated in accordance with their status as minors.
6. Punishments consisting of deprivation of liberty shall have as an essential aim the reform and social readaptation of the prisoners.

Article 6 – Freedom from Slavery
1. No one shall be subject to slavery or to involuntary servitude, which are prohibited in all their forms, as are the slave trade and traffic in women.
2. No one shall be required to perform forced or compulsory labor. This provision shall not be interpreted to mean that, in those countries in which the penalty established for certain crimes is deprivation of liberty at forced labor, the carrying out of such a sentence imposed by a competent court is prohibited. Forced labor shall not adversely affect the dignity or the physical or intellectual capacity of the prisoner.
3. For the purposes of this article, the following do not constitute forced or compulsory labor:
   (a) work or service normally required of a person imprisoned in execution of a sentence or formal decision passed by the competent judicial authority. Such work or service shall be carried out under the supervision and control of public authorities, and any persons performing such work or service shall not be placed at the disposal of any private party, company, or juridical person;
   (b) military service and, in countries in which conscientious objectors are recognized, national service that the law may provide for in lieu of military service;
   (c) service exacted in time of danger or calamity that threatens the existence or the well-being of the community; or
   (d) work or service that forms part of normal civic obligations.

Article 7 – Right to Personal Liberty
1. Every person has the right to personal liberty and security.
2. No one shall be deprived of his physical liberty except for the reasons and under the conditions established beforehand by the constitution of the State Party concerned or by a law established pursuant thereto.
3. No one shall be subject to arbitrary arrest or imprisonment.
4. Anyone who is detained shall be informed of the reasons for his detention and shall be promptly notified of the charge or charges against him.
5. Any person detained shall be brought promptly before a judge or other officer authorized by law to exercise judicial power and shall be entitled to trial within a reasonable time or to be released without prejudice to the continuation of the proceedings. His release may be subject to guarantees to assure his appearance for trial.
6. Anyone who is deprived of his liberty shall be entitled to recourse to a competent court, in order that the court may decide without delay on the lawfulness of his arrest or detention and order his release if the arrest or detention is unlawful. In States Parties whose laws provide that anyone who believes himself to be threatened with deprivation of his liberty is entitled to recourse to a competent court in order that it may decide on the lawfulness

of such threat, this remedy may not be restricted or abolished. The interested party or another person in his behalf is entitled to seek these remedies.
7. No one shall be detained for debt. This principle shall not limit the orders of a competent judicial authority issued for nonfulfillment of duties of support.

Article 8 – Right to a Fair Trial
1. Every person has the right to a hearing, with due guarantees and within a reasonable time, by a competent, independent, and impartial tribunal, previously established by law, in the substantiation of any accusation of a criminal nature made against him or for the determination of his rights and obligations of a civil, labor, fiscal, or any other nature.
2. Every person accused of a criminal offense has the right to be presumed innocent so long as his guilt has not been proven according to law. During the proceedings, every person is entitled, with full equality, to the following minimum guarantees:
   (a) the right of the accused to be assisted without charge by a translator or interpreter, if he does not understand or does not speak the language of the tribunal or court;
   (b) prior notification in detail to the accused of the charges against him;
   (c) adequate time and means for the preparation of his defense;
   (d) the right of the accused to defend himself personally or to be assisted by legal counsel of his own choosing, and to communicate freely and privately with his counsel;
   (e) the inalienable right to be assisted by counsel provided by the state, paid or not as the domestic law provides, if the accused does not defend himself personally or engage his own counsel within the time period established by law;
   (f) the right of the defense to examine witnesses present in the court and to obtain the appearance, as witnesses, of experts or other persons who may throw light on the facts;
   (g) the right not to be compelled to be a witness against himself or to plead guilty; and
   (h) the right to appeal the judgment to a higher court.
3. A confession of guilt by the accused shall be valid only if it is made without coercion of any kind.
4. An accused person acquitted by a nonappealable judgment shall not be subjected to a new trial for the same cause.
5. Criminal proceedings shall be public, except insofar as may be necessary to protect the interests of justice.

Article 9 – Freedom from Ex Post Facto Laws
No one shall be convicted of any act or omission that did not constitute a criminal offense, under the applicable law, at the time it was committed. A heavier penalty shall not be imposed than the one that was applicable at the time the criminal offense was committed. If subsequent to the commission of the offense the law provides for the imposition of a lighter punishment, the guilty person shall benefit therefrom.

Article 10 – Right to Compensation
Every person has the right to be compensated in accordance with the law in the event he has been sentenced by a final judgment through a miscarriage of justice.

Article 11 – Right to Privacy
1. Everyone has the right to have his honor respected and his dignity recognized.
2. No one may be the object of arbitrary or abusive interference with his private life, his family, his home, or his correspondence, or of unlawful attacks on his honor or reputation.
3. Everyone has the right to the protection of the law against such interference or attacks.

Article 12 – Freedom of Conscience and Religion
1. Everyone has the right to freedom of conscience and of religion. This right includes freedom to maintain or to change one's religion or beliefs, and freedom to profess or disseminate one's religion or beliefs, either individually or together with others, in public or in private.
2. No one shall be subject to restrictions that might impair his freedom to maintain or to change his religion or beliefs.
3. Freedom to manifest one's religion and beliefs may be subject only to the limitations prescribed by law that are necessary to protect public safety, order, health, or morals, or the rights or freedoms of others.
4. Parents or guardians, as the case may be, have the right to provide for the religious and moral education of their children or wards that is in accord with their own convictions.

Article 13 – Freedom of Thought and Expression
1. Everyone has the right to freedom of thought and expression. This right includes freedom to seek, receive, and impart information and ideas of all kinds, regardless of frontiers, either orally, in writing, in print, in the form of art, or through any other medium of one's choice.
2. The exercise of the right provided for in the foregoing paragraph shall not be subject to prior censorship but shall be subject to subsequent imposition of liability, which shall be expressly established by law to the extent necessary to ensure:
   (a) respect for the rights or reputations of others; or
   (b) the protection of national security, public order, or public health or morals.
3. The right of expression may not be restricted by indirect methods or means, such as the abuse of government or private controls over newsprint, radio broadcasting frequencies, or equipment used in the dissemination of information, or by any other means tending to impede the communication and circulation of ideas and opinions.
4. Notwithstanding the provisions of paragraph 2 above, public entertainments may be subject by law to prior censorship for the sole purpose of regulating access to them for the moral protection of childhood and adolescence.
5. Any propaganda for war and any advocacy of national, racial, or religious hatred that constitute incitements to lawless violence or to any other similar action against any person or group of persons on any grounds including those of race, color, religion, language, or national origin shall be considered as offenses punishable by law.

Article 14 – Right of Reply
1. Anyone injured by inaccurate or offensive statements or ideas disseminated to the public in general by a legally regulated medium of communication has the right to reply or to make a correction using the same communications outlet, under such conditions as the law may establish.
2. The correction or reply shall not in any case remit other legal liabilities that may have been incurred.
3. For the effective protection of honor and reputation, every publisher, and every newspaper, motion picture, radio, and television company, shall have a person responsible who is not protected by immunities or special privileges.

Article 15 – Right of Assembly
The right to peaceful assembly, without arms, is recognized. No restrictions may be placed on the exercise of this right other than those imposed in conformity with the law and necessary in a democratic society in the interest of national security, public safety or public order, or to protect public health or morals or the rights or freedom of others.

Article 16 – Freedom of Association
1. Everyone has the right to associate freely for ideological, religious, political, economic, labor, social, cultural, sports, or other purposes.
2. The exercise of this right shall be subject only to such restrictions established by law as may be necessary in a democratic society, in the interest of national security, public safety or public order, or to protect public health or morals or the rights and freedoms of others.
3. The provisions of this article do not bar the imposition of legal restrictions, including even deprivation of the exercise of the right of association, on members of the armed forces and the police.

Article 17 – Rights of the Family
1. The family is the natural and fundamental group unit of society and is entitled to protection by society and the state.
2. The right of men and women of marriageable age to marry and to raise a family shall be recognized, if they meet the conditions required by domestic laws, insofar as such conditions do not affect the principle of nondiscrimination established in this Convention.
3. No marriage shall be entered into without the free and full consent of the intending spouses.
4. The States Parties shall take appropriate steps to ensure the equality of rights and the adequate balancing of responsibilities of the spouses as to marriage, during marriage, and in the event of its dissolution. In case of dissolution, provision shall be made for the necessary protection of any children solely on the basis of their own best interests.
5. The law shall recognize equal rights for children born out of wedlock and those born in wedlock.

Article 18 – Right to a Name
Every person has the right to a given name and to the surnames of his parents or that of one of them. The law shall regulate the manner in which this right shall be ensured for all, by the use of assumed names if necessary.

Article 19 – Rights of the Child
Every minor child has the right to the measures of protection required by his condition as a minor on the part of his family, society, and the state.

Article 20 – Right to Nationality
1. Every person has the right to a nationality.
2. Every person has the right to the nationality of the state in whose territory he was born if he does not have the right to any other nationality.
3. No one shall be arbitrarily deprived of his nationality or of the right to change it.

Article 21 – Right to Property
1. Everyone has the right to the use and enjoyment of his property. The law may subordinate such use and enjoyment to the interest of society.
2. No one shall be deprived of his property except upon payment of just compensation, for reasons of public utility or social interest, and in the cases and according to the forms established by law.
3. Usury and any other form of exploitation of man by man shall be prohibited by law.

Article 22 – Freedom of Movement and Residence
1. Every person lawfully in the territory of a State Party has the right to move about in it, and to reside in it subject to the provisions of the law.
2. Every person has the right lo leave any country freely, including his own.
3. The exercise of the foregoing rights may be restricted only pursuant to a law to the extent necessary in a democratic society to prevent crime or to protect national security, public safety, public order, public morals, public health, or the rights or freedoms of others.
4. The exercise of the rights recognized in paragraph 1 may also be restricted by law in designated zones for reasons of public interest.
5. No one can be expelled from the territory of the state of which he is a national or be deprived of the right to enter it.
6. An alien lawfully in the territory of a State Party to this Convention may be expelled from it only pursuant to a decision reached in accordance with law.
7. Every person has the right to seek and be granted asylum in a foreign territory, in accordance with the legislation of the state and international conventions, in the event he is being pursued for political offenses or related common crimes.
8. In no case may an alien be deported or returned to a country, regardless of whether or not it is his country of origin, if in that country his right to life or personal freedom is in danger of being violated because of his race, nationality, religion, social status, or political opinions.
9. The collective expulsion of aliens is prohibited.

Article 23 – Right to Participate in Government
1. Every citizen shall enjoy the following rights and opportunities:
    (a) to take part in the conduct of public affairs, directly or through freely chosen representatives;
    (b) to vote and to be elected in genuine periodic elections, which shall be by

universal and equal suffrage and by secret ballot that guarantees the free expression of the will of the voters; and
(c) to have access, under general conditions of equality, to the public service of his country.
2. The law may regulate the exercise of the rights and opportunities referred to in the preceding paragraph only on the basis of age, nationality, residence, language, education, civil and mental capacity, or sentencing by a competent court in criminal proceedings.

Article 24 – Right to Equal Protection
All persons are equal before the law. Consequently, they are entitled, without discrimination, to equal protection of the law.

Article 25 – Right to Judicial Protection
1. Everyone has the right to simple and prompt recourse, or any other effective recourse, to a competent court or tribunal for protection against acts that violate his fundamental rights recognized by the constitution or laws of the state concerned or by this Convention, even though such violation may have been committed by persons acting in the course of their official duties.
2. The States Parties undertake:
   (a) to ensure that any person claiming such remedy shall have his rights determined by the competent authority provided for by the legal system of the state;
   (b) to develop the possibilities of judicial remedy; and
   (c) to ensure that the competent authorities shall enforce such remedies when granted.

CHAPTER III – ECONOMIC, SOCIAL, AND CULTURAL RIGHTS

Article 26 – Progressive Development
The States Parties undertake to adopt measures, both internally and through international cooperation, especially those of an economic and technical nature, with a view to achieving progressively, by legislation or other appropriate means, the full realization of the rights implicit in the economic, social, educational, scientific, and cultural standards set forth in the Charter of the Organization of American States as amended by the Protocol of Buenos Aires.

CHAPTER IV – SUSPENSION OF GUARANTEES, INTERPRETATION, AND APPLICATION

Article 27 – Suspension of Guarantees
1. In time of war, public danger, or other emergency that threatens the independence or security of a State Party, it may take measures derogating from its obligations under the present Convention to the extent and for the period of time strictly required by the exigencies of the situation, provided that such measures are not inconsistent with its other obligations under international law and do not involve discrimination on the ground of race, color, sex, language, religion, or social origin.

2. The foregoing provision does not authorize any suspension of the following articles: Article 3 (Right to Juridical Personality), Article 4 (Right to Life), Article 5 (Right to Humane Treatment), Article 6 (Freedom from Slavery), Article 9 (Freedom from Ex Post Facto Laws), Article 12 (Freedom of Conscience and Religion), Article 17 (Rights of the Family), Article 18 (Right to a Name), Article 19 (Rights of the Child), Article 20 (Right to Nationality), and Article 23 (Right to Participate in Government), or of the judicial guarantees essential for the protection of such rights.
3. Any State Party availing itself of the right of suspension shall immediately inform the other States Parties, through the Secretary General of the Organization of American States, of the provisions the application of which it has suspended, the reasons that gave rise to the suspension, and the date set for the termination of such suspension.

Article 28 – Federal Clause
1. Where a State Party is constituted as a federal state, the national government of such State Party shall implement all the provisions of the Convention over whose subject matter it exercises legislative and judicial jurisdiction.
2. With respect to the provisions over whose subject matter the constituent units of the federal state have jurisdiction, the national government shall immediately take suitable measures, in accordance with its constitution and its laws, to the end that the competent authorities of the constituent units may adopt appropriate provisions for the fulfillment of this Convention.
3. Whenever two or more States Parties agree to form a federation or other type of association, they shall take care that the resulting federal or other compact contains the provisions necessary for continuing and rendering effective the standards of this Convention in the new state that is organized.

Article 29 – Restrictions Regarding Interpretation
No provision of this Convention shall be interpreted as:
(a) permitting any State Party, group, or person to suppress the enjoyment or exercise of the rights and freedoms recognized in this Convention or to restrict them to a greater extent than is provided for herein;
(b) restricting the enjoyment or exercise of any right or freedom recognized by virtue of the laws of any State Party or by virtue of another convention to which one of the said states is a party;
(c) precluding other rights or guarantees that are inherent in the human personality or derived from representative democracy as a form of government; or
(d) excluding or limiting the effect that the American Declaration of the Rights and Duties of Man and other international acts of the same nature may have.

Article 30 – Scope of Restrictions
The restrictions that, pursuant to this Convention, may be placed on the enjoyment or exercise of the rights or freedoms recognized herein may not be applied except in accordance with laws enacted for reasons of general interest and in accordance with the purpose for which such restrictions have been established.

Article 31 – Recognition of Other Rights
Other rights and freedoms recognized in accordance with the procedures established in Articles 76 and 77 may be included in the system of protection of this Convention.

CHAPTER V – PERSONAL RESPONSIBILITIES

Article 32 – Relationship between Duties and Rights
1. Every person has responsibilities to his family, his community, and mankind.
2. The rights of each person are limited by the rights of others, by the security of all, and by the just demands of the general welfare, in a democratic society.

Part II – Means of Protection

CHAPTER VI – COMPETENT ORGANS

Article 33
The following organs shall have competence with respect to matters relating to the fulfillment of the commitments made by the States Parties to this Convention:
(a) the Inter-American Commission on Human Rights, referred to as "The Commission;" and
(b) the Inter-American Court of Human Rights, referred to as "The Court."

CHAPTER VII – INTER-AMERICAN COMMISSION ON HUMAN RIGHTS

Section 1 – Organization

Article 34
The Inter-American Commission on Human Rights shall be composed of seven members, who shall be persons of high moral character and recognized competence in the field of human rights.

Article 35
The Commission shall represent all the member countries of the Organization of American States.

Article 36
1. The members of the Commission shall be elected in a personal capacity by the General Assembly of the Organization from a list of candidates proposed by the governments of the member states.
2. Each of those governments may propose up to three candidates, who may be nationals of the states proposing them or of any other member state of the Organization of American States. When a slate of three is proposed, at least one of the candidates shall be a national of a state other than the one proposing the slate.

Article 37
1. The members of the Commission shall be elected for a term of four years and may be reelected only once, but the terms of three of the members chosen in the first election shall expire at the end of two years. Immediately following that election the General Assembly shall determine the names of those three members by lot.
2. No two nationals of the same state may be members of the Commission.

Article 38
Vacancies that may occur on the Commission for reasons other than the normal expiration of a term shall be filled by the Permanent Council of the Organization in accordance with the provisions of the Statute of the Commission.

Article 39
The Commission shall prepare its Statute, which it shall submit to the General Assembly for approval. It shall establish its own Regulations.

Article 40
Secretariat services for the Commission shall be furnished by the appropriate specialized unit of the General Secretariat of the Organization. This unit shall be provided with the resources required to accomplish the tasks assigned to it by the Commission.

Section 2 – Functions

Article 41
The main function of the Commission shall be to promote respect for and defense of human rights. In the exercise of its mandate, it shall have the following functions and powers:
(a) to develop an awareness of human rights among the peoples of America;
(b) to make recommendations to the governments of the member states, when it considers such action advisable, for the adoption of progressive measures in favor of human rights within the framework of their domestic law and constitutional provisions as well as appropriate measures to further the observance of those rights;
(c) to prepare such studies or reports as it considers advisable in the performance of its duties;
(d) to request the governments of the member states to supply it with information on the measures adopted by them in matters of human rights;
(e) to respond, through the General Secretariat of the Organization of American States, to inquiries made by the member states on matters related to human rights and, within the limits of its possibilities, to provide those states with the advisory services they request;
(f) to take action on petitions and other communications pursuant to its authority under the provisions of Articles 44 through 51 of this Convention; and
(g) to submit an annual report to the General Assembly of the Organization of American States.

Article 42
The States Parties shall transmit to the Commission a copy of each of the reports and studies that they submit annually to the Executive Committees of the Inter-American Economic and Social Council and the Inter-American Council for Education, Science, and Culture, in their respective fields, so that the Commission may watch over the promotion of the rights implicit in the economic, social, educational, scientific, and cultural standards set forth in the Charter of the Organization of American States as amended by the Protocol of Buenos Aires.

Article 43
The States Parties undertake to provide the Commission with such information as it may request of them as to the manner in which their domestic law ensures the effective application of any provisions of this Convention.

Section 3 – Competence

Article 44
Any person or group of persons, or any nongovernmental entity legally recognized in one or more member states of the Organization, may lodge petitions with the Commission containing denunciations or complaints of violation of this Convention by a State Party.

Article 45
1. Any State Party may, when it deposits its instrument of ratification of or adherence to this Convention, or at any later time, declare that it recognizes the competence of the Commission to receive and examine communications in which a State Party alleges that another State Party has committed a violation of a human right set forth in this Convention.
2. Communications presented by virtue of this article may be admitted and examined only if they are presented by a State Party that has made a declaration recognizing the aforementioned competence of the Commission. The Commission shall not admit any communication against a State Party that has not made such a declaration.
3. A declaration concerning recognition of competence may be made to be valid for an indefinite time, for a specified period, or for a specific case.
4. Declarations shall be deposited with the General Secretariat of the Organization of American States, which shall transmit copies thereof to the member states of that Organization.

Article 46
1. Admission by the Commission of a petition or communication lodged in accordance with Articles 44 or 45 shall be subject to the following requirements:
   (a) that the remedies under domestic law have been pursued and exhausted in accordance with generally recognized principles of international law;
   (b) that the petition or communication is lodged within a period of six months from the date on which the party alleging violation of his rights was notified of the final judgment;
   (c) that the subject of the petition or communication is not pending in another international proceeding for settlement; and
   (d) that, in the case of Article 44, the petition contains the name, nationality, profession, domicile, and signature of the person or persons or of the legal representative of the entity lodging the petition.
2. The provisions of paragraphs 1.a and 1.b of this article shall not be applicable when:
   (a) the domestic legislation of the state concerned does not afford due process of law for the protection of the right or rights that have allegedly been violated;
   (b) the party alleging violation of his rights has been denied access to the

remedies under domestic law or has been prevented from exhausting them; or
(c) there has been unwarranted delay in rendering a final judgment under the aforementioned remedies.

Article 47
The Commission shall consider inadmissible any petition or communication submitted under Articles 44 or 45 if:
(a) any of the requirements indicated in Article 46 has not been met;
(b) the petition or communication does not state facts that tend to establish a violation of the rights guaranteed by this Convention;
(c) the statements of the petitioner or of the state indicate that the petition or communication is manifestly groundless or obviously out of order; or
(d) the petition or communication is substantially the same as one previously studied by the Commission or by another international organization.

Section 4 – Procedure

Article 48
1. When the Commission receives a petition or communication alleging violation of any of the rights protected by this Convention, it shall proceed as follows:
   (a) If it considers the petition or communication admissible, it shall request information from the government of the state indicated as being responsible for the alleged violations and shall furnish that government a transcript of the pertinent portions of the petition or communication. This information shall be submitted within a reasonable period to be determined by the Commission in accordance with the circumstances of each case.
   (b) After the information has been received, or after the period established has elapsed and the information has not been received, the Commission shall ascertain whether the grounds for the petition or communication still exist. If they do not, the Commission shall order the record to be closed.
   (c) The Commission may also declare the petition or communication inadmissible or out of order on the basis of information or evidence subsequently received.
   (d) If the record has not been closed, the Commission shall, with the knowledge of the parties, examine the matter set forth in the petition or communication in order to verify the facts. If necessary and advisable, the Commission shall carry out an investigation, for the effective conduct of which it shall request, and the states concerned shall furnish to it, all necessary facilities.
   (e) The Commission may request the states concerned to furnish any pertinent information and, if so requested, shall hear oral statements or receive written statements from the parties concerned.
   (f) The Commission shall place itself at the disposal of the parties concerned with a view to reaching a friendly settlement of the matter on the basis of respect for the human rights recognized in this Convention.
2. However, in serious and urgent cases, only the presentation of a petition or communication that fulfills all the formal requirements of admissibility shall

be necessary in order for the Commission to conduct an investigation with the prior consent of the state in whose territory a violation has allegedly been committed.

Article 49
If a friendly settlement has been reached in accordance with paragraph 1.f of Article 48, the Commission shall draw up a report, which shall be transmitted to the petitioner and to the States Parties to this Convention, and shall then be communicated to the Secretary General of the Organization of American States for publication. This report shall contain a brief statement of the facts and of the solution reached. If any party in the case so requests, the fullest possible information shall be provided to it.

Article 50
1. If a settlement is not reached, the Commission shall, within the time limit established by its Statute, draw up a report setting forth the facts and stating its conclusions. If the report, in whole or in part, does not represent the unanimous agreement of the members of the Commission, any member may attach to it a separate opinion. The written and oral statements made by the parties in accordance with paragraph 1.e of Article 48 shall also be attached to the report.
2. The report shall be transmitted to the states concerned, which shall not be at liberty to publish it.
3. In transmitting the report, the Commission may make such proposals and recommendations as it sees fit.

Article 51
1. If, within a period of three months from the date of the transmittal of the report of the Commission to the states concerned, the matter has not either been settled or submitted by the Commission or by the state concerned to the Court and its jurisdiction accepted, the Commission may, by the vote of an absolute majority of its members, set forth its opinion and conclusions concerning the question submitted for its consideration.
2. Where appropriate, the Commission shall make pertinent recommendations and shall prescribe a period within which the state is to take the measures that are incumbent upon it to remedy the situation examined.
3. When the prescribed period has expired, the Commission shall decide by the vote of an absolute majority of its members whether the state has taken adequate measures and whether to publish its report.

THE AFRICAN CHARTER ON HUMAN AND PEOPLES' RIGHTS AND THE RULES OF PROCEDURE

Adopted by the eighteenth Assembly of Heads of State and Government,
Nairobi, Kenya, 27 June 1981

Preamble

The African States members of the Organization of African Unity, parties to the present convention entitled "African Charter on Human and Peoples Rights"

Recalling Decision 115 (XVI) of the Assembly of Heads of State and Government at its Sixteenth Ordinary Session held in Monrovia, Liberia, from 17 to 20 July 1979 on the preparation of a "preliminary draft on an African Charter on Human and Peoples' Rights provided *inter alia* for the establishment of bodies to promote and protect human and peoples' rights";

Considering the Charter of the Organization of African Unity, which stipulates that "freedom, equality, justice and dignity are essential objectives for the achievement of the legitimate aspirations of the African peoples";

Reaffirming the pledge they solemnly made in Article 2 of the said Charter to eradicate all forms of colonialism from Africa, to co-ordinate and intensify their co-operation and efforts to achieve a better life for the peoples of Africa and to promote international co-operation, having due regard to the Charter of the United Nations and the Universal Declaration of Human Rights;

Taking into consideration the virtues of their historical tradition and the values of African civilization which should inspire and characterize their reflection on the concept of human and peoples' rights;

Recognizing on the one hand, that fundamental human rights stem from the attributes of human beings, which justifies their international protection and on the other hand, that the reality and respect of peoples' rights should necessarily guarantee human rights;

Considering that the enjoyment of rights and freedoms also implies the performance of duties on the part of everyone;

Convinced that it is henceforth essential to pay a particular attention to the right to development and that civil and political rights cannot be dissociated from economic, social and cultural rights in their conception as well as universality and that the satisfaction of economic, social and cultural rights is a guarantee for the enjoyment of civil and political rights;

Conscious of their duty to achieve the total liberation of Africa, the peoples of which are still struggling for their dignity and genuine independence, and undertaking to eliminate colonialism, neo-colonialism, apartheid, zionism and to dismantle aggressive foreign military bases and all forms of discrimination, particularly those based on race, ethnic group, colour, sex, language, religion or political opinions;

Reaffirming their adherence to the principles of human and peoples' rights and freedoms contained in the declarations, conventions and other instruments adopted by the Organization of African Unity, the Movement of Non-Aligned Countries and the United Nations;

Firmly convinced of their duty to promote and protect human and peoples' rights and freedoms taking into account the importance traditionally attached to these rights and freedoms in Africa;

Have agreed as follows:

Part I – Rights and Duties

CHAPTER I

Human and Peoples' Rights

Article 1
The Member States of the Organization of African Unity parties to the present Charter shall recognize the rights, duties and freedoms enshrined in this Charter and shall undertake to adopt legislative or other measures to give effect to them.

Article 2
Every individual shall be entitled to the enjoyment of the rights and freedoms recognized and guaranteed in the present Charter without distinction of any kind such as race, ethnic group, colour, sex, language, religion, political or any other opinion, national and social origin, fortune, birth or other status.

Article 3
1. Every individual shall be equal before the law.
2. Every individual shall be entitled to equal protection of the law.

Article 4
Human beings are inviolable. Every human being shall be entitled to respect for his life and the integrity of his person. No one may be arbitrarily deprived of this right.

Article 5
Every individual shall have the right to the respect of the dignity inherent in a human being and to the recognition of his legal status. All forms of exploitation and degradation of man particularly slavery, slave trade, torture, cruel, inhuman or degrading punishment and treatment shall be prohibited.

Article 6
Every individual shall have the right to liberty and to the security of his person. No one may be deprived of his freedom except for reasons and conditions previously laid down by law. In particular, no one may be arbitrarily arrested or detained.

Article 7
1. Every individual shall have the right to have his cause heard. This comprises:
    (a) The right to an appeal to competent national organs against acts of violating his fundamental rights as recognized and guaranteed by conventions, laws, regulations and customs in force;
    (b) The right to be presumed innocent until proved guilty by a competent court or tribunal;
    (c) The right to defence, including the right to be defended by counsel of his choice;
    (d) The right to be tried within a reasonable time by an impartial court or tribunal.
2. No one may be condemned for an act or omission which did not constitute a legally punishable offence at the time it was committed. No penalty may be inflicted for an offence for which no provision was made at the time it was committed. Punishment is personal and can be imposed only on the offender.

Article 8
Freedom of conscience, the profession and free practice of religion shall be guaranteed. No one may, subject to law and order, be submitted to measures restricting the exercise of these freedoms.

Article 9
1. Every individual shall have the right to receive information.
2. Every individual shall have the right to express and disseminate his opinions within the law.

Article 10
1. Every individual shall have the right to free association provided that he abides by the law.
2. Subject to the obligation of solidarity provided for in Article 29 no one may be compelled to join an association.

Article 11
Every individual shall have the right to assemble freely with others. The exercise of this right shall be subject only to necessary restrictions provided for by law in particular those enacted in the interest of national security, the safety, health, ethics and rights and freedoms of others.

Article 12
1. Every individual shall have the right to freedom of movement and residence within the borders of a State provided he abides by the law.
2. Every individual shall have the right to leave any country including his own, and to return to his country. This right may only be subject to restrictions, provided for by law for the protection of national security, law and order, public health or morality.

3. Every individual shall have the right, when persecuted, to seek and obtain asylum in other countries in accordance with the law of those countries and international conventions.
4. A non-national legally admitted in a territory of a State party to the present Charter, may only be expelled from it by virtue of a decision taken in accordance with the law.
5. The mass expulsion of non-nationals shall be prohibited. Mass expulsion shall be that which is aimed at national, racial, ethnic or religious groups.

Article 13
1. Every citizen shall have the right to participate freely in the government of his country, either directly or though freely chosen representatives in accordance with the provisions of the law.
2. Every citizen shall have the right of equal access to the public service of his country.
3. Every individual shall have the right of access to public property and services in strict equality of all persons before the law.

Article 14
The right to property shall be guaranteed. It may only be encroached upon in the interest of public need or in the general interest of the community and in accordance with the provisions of appropriate laws.

Article 15
Every individual shall have the right to work under equitable and satisfactory conditions, and shall receive equal pay for equal work.

Article 16
1. Every individual shall have the right to enjoy the best attainable state of physical and mental health.
2. States Parties to the present Charter shall take the necessary measures to protect the health of their people and to ensure that they receive medical attention when they are sick.

Article 17
1. Every individual shall have the right to education.
2. Every individual may freely take part in the cultural life of his community.
3. The promotion and protection of morals and traditional values recognized by the community shall be the duty of the State.

Article 18
1. The family shall be the natural unit and basis of society. It shall be protected by the State which shall take care of its physical and moral health.
2. The State shall have the duty to assist the family which is the custodian of morals and traditional values recognized by the community.
3. The State shall ensure the elimination of every discrimination against women and also ensure the protection of the rights of the women and the child as stipulated in international declarations and conventions.
4. The aged and the disabled shall also have the right to special measures of protection in keeping with their physical or moral needs.

Article 19
All peoples shall be equal; they shall enjoy the same respect and shall have the same rights. Nothing shall justify the domination of a people by another.

Article 20
1. All peoples shall have right to existence. They shall have the unquestionable and inalienable right to self-determination. They shall freely determine their political status and shall pursue their economic and social development according to the policy they have freely chosen.
2. Colonized or oppressed peoples shall have the right to free themselves from the bonds of domination by resorting to any means recognized by the international community.
3. All peoples shall have the right to the assistance of the States Parties to the present Charter in their liberation struggle against foreign domination, be it political, economic or cultural.

Article 21
1. All peoples shall freely dispose of their wealth and natural resources. This right shall be exercised in the exclusive interest of the people. In no case shall a people be deprived of it.
2. In case of spoliation the dispossessed people shall have the right to lawful recovery of its property as well as to an adequate compensation.
3. The free disposal of wealth and natural resources shall be exercised without prejudice to the obligation of promoting international economic cooperation based on mutual respect, equitable exchange and the principles of international law.
4. States Parties to the present Charter shall individually and collectively exercise the right to free disposal of their wealth and natural resources with a view to strengthening African unity and solidarity.
5. States Parties to the present Charter shall undertake to eliminate all forms of foreign exploitation particularly that practised by international monopolies so as to enable their peoples to fully benefit from the advantages derived from their natural resources.

Article 22
1. All peoples shall have the right to their economic, social and cultural development with due regard to their freedom and identify and in the equal enjoyment of the common heritage of mankind.
2. States shall have the duty, individually or collectively, to ensure the exercise of the right to development.

Article 23
1. All peoples shall have the right to national and international peace and security. The principles of solidarity and friendly relations implicitly affirmed by the Charter of the United Nations and reaffirmed by that of the Organization of African Unity shall govern relations between States.
2. For the purpose of strengthening peace, solidarity and friendly relations, States parties to the present Charter shall ensure that:
   (a) any individual enjoying the right of asylum under Article 12 of the present Charter shall not engage in subversive activities against his country of

origin or any other State party to the present Charter;
(b) their territories shall not be used as bases for subversive or terrorist activities against the people of any other State party to the present Charter.

Article 24
All peoples shall have the right to a general satisfactory environment favourable to their development.

Article 25
States parties to the present Charter shall have the duty to promote and ensure through teaching, education and publication, the respect of the rights and freedoms contained in the present Charter and to see to it that these freedoms and rights as well as corresponding obligations and duties are understood.

Article 26
States parties to the present Charter shall have the duty to guarantee the independence of the Courts and shall allow the establishment and improvement of appropriate institutions entrusted with the promotion and protection of the rights and freedoms guaranteed by the present Charter.

CHAPTER II

Duties

Article 27
1. Every individual shall have duties towards his family and society, the State and other legally recognized communities and the international community.
2. The rights and freedoms of each individual shall be exercised with due regard to the rights of others, collective security, morality and common interest.

Article 28
Every individual shall have the duty to respect and consider his fellow beings without discrimination, and to maintain relations aimed at promoting, safeguarding and reinforcing mutual respect and tolerance.

Article 29
The individual shall also have the duty:
1. To preserve the harmonious development of the family and to work for the cohesion and respect of the family; to respect his parents at all times, to maintain them in case of need;
2. To serve his national community by placing his physical and intellectual abilities at its service;
3. Not to compromise the security of the State whose national or resident he is;
4. To preserve and strengthen social and national solidarity, particularly when the latter is threatened;
5. To preserve and strengthen the national independence and the territorial integrity of his country and to contribute to his defence in accordance with the law;
6. To work to the best of his abilities and competence, and to pay taxes imposed by law in the interest of the society;

7. To preserve and strengthen positive African cultural values in his relations with other members of the society, in the spirit of tolerance, dialogue and consultations and, in general, to contribute to the promotion of the moral well being of society;
8. To contribute to the best of his abilities, at all times and at all levels, to the promotion and achievement of African unity.

Part II – Measures of Safeguard

CHAPTER I

Establishment and Organization of the African Commission on Human and People's Rights

Article 30
An African Commission on Human and People's Rights, hereinafter called "the Commission", shall be established within the Organization of African Unity to promote human and people's rights and ensure their protection in Africa.

Article 31
1. The Commission shall consist of eleven members chosen from amongst African personalities of the highest reputation, known for their high morality, integrity, impartiality and competence in matters of human and people's rights; particularly consideration being given to persons having legal experience.
2. The members of the Commission shall serve in their personal capacity.

Article 32
The Commission shall not include more than one national of the same State.

Article 33
The members of the Commission shall be elected by secret ballot by the Assembly of Heads of State and Government, from a list of persons nominated by the States parties to the present Charter.

Article 34
Each State party to the present Charter may not nominate more than two candidates. The candidates must have the nationality of one of the States Parties to the present Charter. When two candidates are nominated by a State, one of them may not be a national of that State.

Article 35
1. The Secretary-General of the Organization of African Unity shall invite State parties to the present Charter at least four months before the elections to nominate candidates.
2. The Secretary-General of the Organization of African Unity shall make an alphabetical list of the persons thus nominated and communicate it to the Heads of State and Government at least one month before the elections.

Article 36
The members of the Commission shall be elected for a six year period and shall be eligible for re-election. However, the term of office of four of the members elected at the first election shall terminate after two years and the term of office of three others, at the end of four years.

Article 37
Immediately after the first election, the Chairman of the Assembly of Heads of State and Government of the Organization of African Unity shall draw lots to decide the names of those referred to in Article 36.

Article 38
After their election, the members of the Commission shall make a solemn declaration to discharge their duties impartially and faithfully.

Article 39
1. In case of death or resignation of a member of the Commission, the Chairman of the Commission shall immediately inform the Secretary-General of the Organization of African Unity, who shall declare the seat vacant from the date of death or from the date on which the resignation takes effect.
2. If, in the unanimous opinion of other members of the Commission, a member has stopped discharging his duties for any reason other than a temporary absence, the Chairman of the Commission shall inform the Secretary-General of the Organization of African Unity, who shall then declare the seat vacant.
3. In each of the cases anticipated above, the Assembly of Heads of State and Government shall replace the member whose seat became vacant for the remaining period of his term unless the period is less than six months.

Article 40
Every member of the Commission shall be in office until the date his successor assumes office.

Article 41
The Secretary-General of the Organization of African Unity shall appoint the Secretary of the Commission. He shall provide the staff and services necessary for the effective discharge of the duties of the Commission. The Organization of African Unity shall bear the cost of the staff and services.

Article 42
1. The Commission shall elect its Chairman and Vice Chairman for a two-year period. They shall be eligible for re-election.
2. The Commission shall lay down its rules of procedure.
3. Seven members shall form the quorum.
4. In case of an equality of votes, the Chairman shall have a casting vote.
5. The Secretary-General may attend the meetings of the Commission. He shall neither participate in deliberations nor shall he be entitled to vote. The Chairman of the Commission may, however, invite him to speak.

Article 43
In discharging their duties, members of the Commission shall enjoy diplomatic privileges and immunities provided for in the General Convention on the Privileges and Immunities of the Organization of African Unity.

Article 44
Provision shall be made for the emoluments and allowances of the members of the Commission in the Regular Budget of the Organization of African Unity.

CHAPTER II

Mandate of the Commission

Article 45
The functions of the Commission shall be:
1. To promote Human and People's Rights and in particular:
   (a) to collect documents, undertake studies and researches on African problems in the field of human and people's rights, organise seminars, symposia and conferences, disseminate information, encourage national and local institutions concerned with human and people's rights and, should the case arise, give its views or make recommendations to Governments.
   (b) to formulate and lay down, principles and rules aimed at solving legal problems relating to human and people's rights and fundamental freedoms upon which African Governments may base their legislation.
   (c) co-operate with other African and international institutions concerned with the promotion and protection of human people's rights.
2. Ensure the protection of human and people's rights under conditions laid down by the present Charter.
3. Interpret all the provisions of the present Charter at the request of a State party, an institution of the Organization of African Unity or an African organization recognized by the Organization of African Unity.
4. Perform any other tasks which may be entrusted to it by the Assembly of Heads of State and Government.

CHAPTER III

Procedure of the Commission

Article 46
The Commission may resort to any appropriate method of investigation; it may hear from the Secretary-General of the Organization of African Unity or any other person capable of enlightening it.

Communication from States

Article 47
If a State Party to the present Charter has good reasons to believe that another State Party to this Charter has violated the provisions of the Charter, it may draw, by written communication, the attention of that State to the matter. This communication shall also be addressed to the Secretary-General of the Organization of African Unity and to the Chairman of the Commission. Within three months of the receipt of the communication the State to which the communication is addressed shall give the enquiring State, written explanation or

statement elucidating the matter. This should include as much as possible relevant information relating to the laws and rules of procedure applied and applicable and the redress already given or course of action available.

Article 48
If within three months from the date on which the original communications is received by the State to which it is addressed, the issue is not settled to the satisfaction of the two States involved through bilateral negotiations or by any other peaceful procedure, either State shall have the right to submit the matter to the Commission through the Chairman and shall notify the other State involved.

Article 49
Notwithstanding the provisions of Article 47, if a State party to the present Charter considers that another State Party has violated the provisions of the Charter, it may refer the matter directly to the Commission by addressing a communication to the Chairman, to the Secretary-General of the Organization of African Unity and the State concerned.

Article 50
The Commission can only deal with a matter submitted to it after making sure that all local remedies, if they exist, have been exhausted, unless it is obvious to the Commission that the procedure of achieving these remedies would be unduly prolonged.

Article 51
1. The Commission may ask the States concerned to provide it with all relevant information.
2. When the Commission is considering the matter, States concerned may be represented before it and submit written or oral representations.

Article 52
After having obtained from the States concerned and from the other sources all the information it deems necessary and after having tried all appropriate means to reach an amicable solution based on the respect of human and people's rights, the Commission shall prepare, within a reasonable period of time from the notification referred to in Article 48, a report stating the facts and its findings. This report shall be sent to the States concerned and communicated to the Assembly of Heads of State and Government.

Article 53
While transmitting its report, the Commission may make to the Assembly of Heads of State and Government such recommendations as it deems useful.

Article 54
The Commission shall submit to each Ordinary Session of the Assembly of Heads of State and Government a report on its activities.

Other Communications

Article 55
1. Before each Session, the Secretary of the Commission shall make a list of the communications other than those of States parties to the present Charter and

transmit them to the members of the Commission, who shall indicate which communications should be considered by the Commission.
2. A communication shall be considered by the Commission if a simple majority of its members so decide.

Article 56
Communication relating to human and people's rights referred to in Article 55 received by the Commission, shall be considered if they:

1. Indicate their authors even if the latter request anonymity;
2. Are compatible with the Charter of the Organization of African Unity or with the present Charter;
3. Are not written in disparaging or insulting language directed against the State concerned and its institutions or the Organization of African Unity;
4. Are not based exclusively on news disseminated through the mass media;
5. Are sent after exhausting local remedies, if any unless it is obvious that this procedure is unduly prolonged;
6. Are submitted within a reasonable period from the time local remedies are exhausted or from the date the Commission is seized of the matter; and
7. Do not deal with cases which have been settled by these States involved in accordance with the principles of the Charter of the United Nations, or the Charter of the Organization of African Unity or the provisions of the present Charter.

Article 57
Prior to any substantive consideration, all communications shall be brought to the knowledge of the State concerned by the Chairman of the Commission.

Article 58
1. When it appears after deliberations of the Commission that one or more communications apparently relate to special cases which reveal the existence of a series of serious or massive violations of human and people's rights, the Commission shall draw the attention of the Assembly of Heads of State and Government to these special cases.
2. The Assembly of Heads of State and Government may then request the Commission to undertake an in-depth study of these cases and make a factual report, accompanied by its finding and recommendations.
3. A case of emergency duly noticed by the Commission shall be submitted by the latter to the Chairman of the Assembly of Heads of State and Government who may request an in-depth study.

Article 59
1. All measures taken within the provisions of the present Chapter shall remain confidential until such a time as the Assembly of Heads of State and Government shall otherwise decide.
2. However, the report shall be published by the Chairman of the Commission upon the decision of the Assembly of Heads of State and Government.
3. The report on the activities of the Commission shall be published by its Chairman after it has been considered by the Assembly of Heads of State and Government.

CHAPTER IV

Applicable Principles

Article 60
The Commission shall draw inspiration from international law on human and people's rights, particularly from the provisions of various African instruments on human and people's rights, the Charter of the United Nations, the Charter of the Organization of African Unity, the Universal Declaration of Human Rights, other instruments adopted by the United Nations and by African countries in the field of human and people's rights as well as from the provisions of various instruments adopted within the Specialized Agencies of the United Nations of which the parties to the present Charter are members.

Article 61
The Commission shall also take into consideration, as subsidiary measures to determine the principles of law, other general or special international conventions, laying down rules expressly recognised by Member States of the Organization of African Unity, African practices consistent with international norms on human and people's rights, customs generally accepted as law, general principles of law recognised by the African states as well as legal precedents and doctrine.

Article 62
Each State Party shall undertake to submit every two years, from the date the present Charter comes into force, a report on the legislative or other measures taken with a view to giving effect to the rights and freedoms recognised and guaranteed by the present Charter.

Article 63
1. The present Charter shall be open to signature, ratification or adherence of the Member States of the Organization of African Unity.
2. The instruments of ratification or adherence to the present Charter shall be deposited with the Secretary-General of the Organization of African Unity.
3. The present Charter shall come into force three months after the reception by the Secretary-General of the instruments of ratification or adherence of a simple majority of the Member States of the Organization of African Unity.

Part III – General Provisions

Article 64
1. After the coming into force of the present Charter, members of the Commission shall be elected in accordance with the relevant Articles of the present Charter.
2. The Secretary-General of the Organization of African Unity shall convene the first meeting of the Commission at the Headquarters of the Organization within three months of the constitution of the Commission. Thereafter, the Commission shall be convened by its Chairman whenever necessary but at least once a year.

Article 65
For each of the States that will ratify or adhere to the present Charter after its coming into force, the Charter shall take effect three months after the date of the deposit by that State of its instrument of ratification or adherence.

Article 66
Special Protocols or agreements may, if necessary, supplement the provisions of the present Charter.

Article 67
The Secretary-General of the Organization of African Unity shall inform Member States of the Organization of the deposit of each instrument of ratification or adherence.

Article 68
The present Charter may be amended if a State party makes a written request to that effect to the Secretary-General of the Organization of African Unity. The Assembly of Heads of State and Government may only consider the draft amendment after all the States parties have been duly informed of it and the Commission has given its opinion on it at the request of the sponsoring State. The amendment shall be approved by a simple majority of the States parties. It shall come into force for each State which has accepted it in accordance with its constitutional procedure three months after the Secretary-General has received notice of the acceptance.

AMENDED RULES OF PROCEDURE OF THE AFRICAN COMMISSION ON HUMAN AND PEOPLE'S RIGHTS

Deliberated and Adopted by the Commission at its 18th Session held in Praia, Cape Verde, 6 October 1995

General Provisions – Organization of the Commission

CHAPTER I – SESSIONS

Rule 1 – Number of Sessions
The African Commission on Human and Peoples' Rights (hereinafter referred to as "the Commission") shall hold the sessions which may be necessary to enable it to carry out satisfactorily its functions in conformity with the African Charter on Human and People's Rights (hereinafter referred to as "The Charter").

Rule 2 – Opening Date
1. The Commission shall normally hold two ordinary sessions a year each lasting for about two weeks.
2. The ordinary sessions of the Commission shall be convened on a date fixed by the Commission on the proposal of its Chairman and in consultation with the Secretary-General of the Organization of African Unity (OAU) (hereinafter referred to as "The Secretary-General").
3. The Secretary-General may change, under exceptional circumstances, the opening date of a session, in consultation with the Chairman of the Commission.

Rule 3 – Extraordinary Session
1. The Commission may decide to hold extraordinary sessions. When the Commission is not in session, the Chairman may convene extraordinary sessions in consultation with the members of the Commission. The Chairman of the Commission shall also convene extraordinary sessions:
   (a) At the request of the majority of the members of the Commission or
   (b) At the request of the current Chairman of the Organization of African Unity.
2. Extraordinary sessions shall be convened as soon as possible on a date fixed by the Chairman, in consultation with the Secretary-General and the other members of the Commission.

Rule 4 – Place of Meetings
The sessions shall normally be held at the Headquarters of the Commission. The Commission, in consideration with the Secretary-General, may decide to hold a Session elsewhere.

Rule 5 – Notification of the Opening Date of the Sessions
The Secretary of the Commission (hereinafter referred to as the Secretary, shall inform members of the Commission of the date and venue of the first meeting of each session. This notification shall be sent, in the case of an Ordinary Session, at least eight (8) weeks and, in the case of an Extraordinary Session, at least three (3) weeks, if possible, before the Session.

CHAPTER II – AGENDA

Rule 6 – Drawing up the Provisional Agenda
1. The Provisional Agenda for each Ordinary Session shall be drawn up by the Secretary in consultation with the Chairman of the Commission in accordance with the provisions of the Charter and these Rules.
2. The Provisional Agenda shall include, if necessary, items on: "Communications from States", and "Other Communications" in conformity with the provisions of Article 55 of the Charter. It should not contain any information relating to such communications.
3. Except as specified above on the communications, the Provisional Agenda shall include all the items listed by the present Rules of Procedure as well as the items proposed by:
   (a) The Commission at a previous Session;
   (b) The Chairman of the Commission or another member of the Commission;
   (c) A State party to the Charter;
   (d) The Assembly of Heads of State and Government or the Council of Ministers of the Organization of African Unity;
   (e) The Secretary-General of the Organization of African Unity on any issue relating to the functions assigned to him by the Charter;
   (f) A national liberation movement recognized by the Organization of African Unity or by a non-governmental organization;
   (g) A specialized institution of which the State parties to the Charter are members.
4. The items to be included in the provisional agenda under sub paragraphs b, c, f and g of paragraph 3 must be communicated to the Secretary, accompanied by essential documents, not later than eight (8) weeks before the Opening of the Session.
5. (a) All national liberation movements, specialized institutions, intergovernmental or non-governmental organizations wishing to propose the inclusion of an item in the Provisional Agenda must inform the Secretary, at least ten (10) weeks before the opening of the meeting. Before formally proposing the inclusion of an item in the Provisional Agenda, the observations likely to be made by the Secretary must duly be taken into account;
   (b) All proposals made under the provisions of the present paragraph shall be included only in the Provisional Agenda of the Commission, if at least two thirds (2/3) of the members present and voting so decide.

6. The Provisional Agenda of the Extraordinary Session of the Commission shall include only the item proposed to be considered at that Extraordinary Session.

Rule 7 – Transmission and Distribution of the Provisional Agenda
1. The Provisional Agenda and the essential documents relating to each item shall be distributed to the members of the Commission by the Secretary who shall endeavour to transmit them to members at least six (6) weeks before the opening of the Session.
2. The Secretary shall communicate the Provisional Agenda of that session and have the essential documents relating to each Agenda item distributed at least six weeks before the opening of the Session of the Commission to the members of the Commission, member States parties to the Charter, to the current Chairman of the Organization of African Unity and observers.
3. The draft agenda shall also be sent to the specialized agencies, to non-governmental organizations and to the national liberation movements concerned with the agenda.
4. In exceptional cases the Secretary may, while giving his reasons in writing, have the essential documents relating to some items of the Provisional Agenda distributed at least four (4) weeks prior to the opening of the Session.

Rule 8 – Adoption of the Agenda
At the beginning of each session, the Commission shall if necessary, after the election of officers in conformity with rule 17, adopt the agenda of the Session on the basis of the Provisional Agenda referred to in Rule 6.

Rule 9 – Revision of the Agenda
The Commission may, during the Session, revise the Agenda if need be, adjourn, cancel or amend items. During the Session, only urgent and important issues may be added to the Agenda.

Rule 10 – Draft Provisional Agenda for Next Session
The Secretary shall, at each session of the Commission, submit a Draft Provisional Agenda for the next session of the Commission, indicating with respect to each item, the documents to be submitted on that item and the decisions of the deliberative organ which authorized their preparation so as to enable the Commission to consider these documents as regards the contribution they make to its proceedings, as well as their urgency and relevance to the prevailing situation.

CHAPTER III – MEMBERS OF THE COMMISSION

Rule 11 – Composition of the Commission
The Commission shall be composed of eleven (11) members elected by the Assembly of Heads of State and Government hereinafter referred to as "the Assembly", in conformity with the relevant provisions of the Charter.

Rule 12 – Status of the Members
1. The members of the Commission shall be the eleven (11) personalities appointed in conformity with the provisions of Article 31 of the Charter.
2. Each member of the Commission shall sit on the Commission in a personal capacity. No member may be represented by another person.

Rule 13 – Term of Office of the Members
1. The term of office of the members of the Commission elected on 29 July 1987 shall begin from that date. The term of office of the members of the Commission elected at subsequent elections shall take effect the day following the expiry date of the term of office of the members of the Commission they shall replace.
2. However, if a member is re-elected at the expiry of his or her term of office, or elected to replace a member whose term of office has expired or will expire, the term of office shall begin from that expiry date.
3. In conformity with Article 39(3) of the Charter, the member elected to replace a member whose term has not expired, shall complete the term of office of his or her predecessor, unless the remaining term of office is less than six (6) months. In the latter case, there shall be no replacement.

Rule 14 – Cessation of Functions
1. If in the unanimous opinion of the other members of the Commission, a member has stopped discharging his duties for any reason other than a temporary absence, the Chairman of the Commission shall inform the Secretary-General of the Organization of African Unity, who shall then declare the seat vacant.
2. In case of the death or resignation of a member of the Commission, the Chairman shall immediately inform the Secretary-General who shall declare the seat vacant from the date of the death or from that on which the resignation took effect. The member of the Commission who resigns shall address a written notification of his or her resignation directly to the chairman or to the Secretary-General and steps to declare his or her seat vacant shall only be taken after receiving the said notification. The resignation shall make the seat vacant.

Rule 15 – Vacant Seat
Every seat declared vacant in conformity with Rule 14 of the present Rules of Procedure shall be filled on the basis of Article 39 of the Charter.

Rule 16 – Oath
Before coming into office, every member of the Commission shall make the following solemn commitment at a public sitting: "I swear to carry out my duties well and faithfully in all impartiality".

CHAPTER IV – OFFICERS

Rule 17 – Election of Officers
1. The Commission shall elect among its members a Chairman and Vice Chairman.

2. The elections referred to in the present Rule shall be held by secret ballot. Only the members present shall vote, the member who shall obtain the two-thirds majority of the votes of the members present and voting shall be elected.
3. If no member obtains this two-thirds majority in a second, third and fourth ballot, the member having the highest number of votes at the fifth ballot shall be elected.
4. The officers of the Commission shall be elected for a period of two (2) years. They shall be eligible for re-election. None of them may, however, exercise his or her functions if he or she ceases to be a member of the Commission.

Rule 18 – Power of the Chairman
The Chairman shall carry out the functions assigned to him by the Charter, the Rules of Procedure and the decisions of the Commission. In the exercise of his functions the chairman shall be under the authority of the Commission.

Rule 19 – Absence of the Chairman
1. The Vice Chairman shall replace the Chairman during a session if the latter is unable to attend a whole or part of a sitting of a session.
2. In the absence of both the Chairman and Vice Chairman, members shall elect an acting Chairman.

Rule 20 – Functions of the Vice Chairman
The Vice Chairman and or ad hoc Chairman, acting in the capacity of the Chairman, shall have the same rights and the same duties as the Chairman.

Rule 21 – Cessation of the Functions of an Officer
If any of the officers ceases to carry out his or her functions or declares that he or she is no longer available to serve as an officer or exercise the functions of a member of the Commission, a new officer shall be elected for the remaining term of office of his or her predecessor.

CHAPTER V – SECRETARIAT

Rule 22 – Functions of the Secretary-General
1. The Secretary-General or his representative may attend the meeting of the Commission. He shall neither participate in the deliberations, nor in the voting. He may, however, be called upon by the Chairman of the Commission to make written or oral statements at the sittings of the Commission.
2. He shall appoint, in consultation with the Chairman of the Commission, a Secretary of the Commission.
3. He shall, in consultation with the Chairman, provide the Commission with the necessary staff, means and services for it to carry out effectively the functions and missions assigned to it under the Charter.
4. The Secretary-General shall take all the necessary steps for the meetings of the Commission.

Rule 23 – Functions of the Secretary to the Commission
The Secretary of the Commission shall be responsible for the activities of the Secretariat under the general supervision of the Chairman, and particularly:

(a) He/she shall assist the Commission and its members in the exercise of their functions;
(b) He/she shall serve as an intermediary for all the communications concerning the Commission;
(c) He/she shall be the custodian of the archives of the Commission;
(d) The Secretary shall bring immediately to the knowledge of the members of the Commission all the issues that will be submitted to him/her.

Rule 24 – Estimates
Before the Commission approves a proposal entailing expenses, the Secretary shall prepare and distribute, as soon as possible, to the members of the Commission, the financial implications to the proposal. It is incumbent on the Chairman to draw the attention of the members to those implications so that they discuss them when the proposal is considered by the Commission.

Rule 25 – Financial Rules
The Financial Rules adopted pursuant to the provisions of Articles 41 and 44 of the Charter, shall be appended to the present Rules of Procedure.

Rule 26 – Financial Responsibility
The Organization of African Unity shall bear the expenses of the staff and the facilities and services placed at the disposal of the Commission to carry out its functions.

Rule 27 – Records of Cases
A special record, with a reference number and initialled, in which shall be entered the date of registration of each petition and communication and that of the closure of the procedure relating to them before the Commission, shall be kept at the Secretariat.

CHAPTER VI – SUBSIDIARY BODIES

Rule 28 – Establishment of Committees and Working Groups
1. The Commission may during a session, taking into account the provisions of the Charter, establish, if it deems it necessary for the exercise of its functions, committees or working groups, composed of the members of the Commission and send them any agenda item for consideration and report.
2. These committees or working groups may, in consultation with the Secretary-General, be authorized to sit when the Commission is not in session.
3. The members of the committees or working groups shall be appointed by the Chairman subject to the approval of the absolute majority of the other members of the Commission.

Rule 29 – Establishment of Sub-Commissions
1. The Commission may establish Sub-Commissions of experts after the prior approval of the Assembly.
2. Unless the assembly decides otherwise, the Commission shall determine the functions and composition of each Sub-Commission.

Rule 30 – Officers of the Subsidiary Bodies
Unless the Commission decides otherwise, the subsidiary bodies of the Commission shall elect their own officers.

Rule 31 – Rules of Procedure
The Rules of Procedure of the Commission shall apply, as far as possible, to the proceedings of its subsidiary bodies.

CHAPTER VII – PUBLIC SESSIONS AND PRIVATE LESSONS

Rule 32 – General Principle
The sittings of the Commission and of its subsidiary bodies shall be held in public unless the Commission decides otherwise, or it appears from the relevant provisions of the charter that the meeting shall be held in private.

Rule 33 – Publication of Proceedings
At the end of each private or public sitting, the Commission or its subsidiary bodies may issue a communiqué.

CHAPTER VIII – LANGUAGES

Rule 34 – Working Languages
The working language of the Commission and of all its institutions shall be those of the Organization of African Unity.

Rule 35 – Interpretation
1. The address delivered in one of the working languages shall be interpreted in the other working languages.
2. Any person addressing the Commission in a language other than one of the working languages, shall, in principle, ensure the interpretation in one of the working languages. The interpreters of the Secretariat may take the interpretation of the original language as source language for their interpretation in the other working languages.

Rule 36 – Languages to be used for Minutes of Proceedings
The summary minutes of the sittings of the Commission shall be drafted in the working languages.

Rule 37 – Languages to be used for Resolutions and other Official Decisions
The Secretariat shall record and preserve the tapes of the sessions of the Commission. It may also record and conserve the tapes of the sessions of the committees, working groups and sub-commissions if the Commission so decides.

Rule 38 – Tape Recordings of the Sessions
The Secretariat shall record and preserve the tapes of the sessions of the Commission. It may also record and conserve the tapes of the sessions of the Committee, working groups and sub-commissions if the Commission so decides.

Rule 39 – Summary Minutes of the Sessions
1. The Secretariat shall draft the summary minutes of the private and public sessions of the Commission and of its subsidiary bodies. It shall distribute them as soon as possible in a draft form to the members of the Commission

and to all other participants in the session. All those participants may, in the 30 days following receipt of the draft minutes of the session, submit corrections to the Secretariat. The Chairman may, under special circumstances, in consultation with the Secretary, extend the time for the submission of the corrections.
2. In case the corrections are contested, the Chairman of the Commission or the Chairman of the subsidiary body whose minutes they are shall resolve the disagreement after having listened to, if necessary, the tape recording of the discussions. If the disagreement persists, the Commission or the subsidiary body shall decide. The corrections shall be published in a distinct volume after the closure of the session.

Rule 40 – Distribution of the Minutes of the Private Sessions and Public Sessions
1. The final summary minutes of the public and private sessions shall be the document intended for general distribution, unless the Commission decides otherwise.
2. The minutes of the private sessions of the Commission shall be distributed forthwith to all members of the Commission.

Rule 41 – Reports to be submitted after each Session
The Commission shall submit to the current Chairman of the Organization of African Unity, a report on the deliberations of each session. This report shall contain a brief summary of the recommendations and statements on issues to which the Commission would like to draw the attention of the current Chairman and member States of the Organization of African Unity.

Rule 42 – Submission of official decisions and reports
The text of the decisions and reports officially adopted by the Commission shall be distributed to all members of the Commission as soon as possible.

CHAPTER X – CONDUCT OF THE DEBATES

Rule 43 – Quorum
The quorum shall be constituted by seven (7) members of the Commission, as specified in Article 42(3) of the Charter.

Rule 44 – Additional Functions of the Chairman
1. In addition to the powers entrusted to him/her under other provisions of the present Rules of Procedure, the Chairman shall have the responsibility to open and close each session; he/she shall direct the debates, ensure the application of the present Rules of Procedure, grant the use of floor, submit to a vote matters under discussion and announce the result of the vote taken.
2. Subject to the provisions of the present Rules of Procedure, the Chairman shall direct the discussions of the Commission and ensure order during meetings. The Chairman may during the discussion of an agenda item, propose to the Commission to limit the time allotted to speakers, as well as the number of interventions of each speaker on the same issue and close the list of speakers.
3. He/she shall rule on the points of order. He/she shall also have the power to propose the adjournment and the closure of debates as well as the adjournment and suspension of a sitting. The debates shall deal solely with the issues

submitted to the Commission and the chairman may call a speaker, whose remarks are irrelevant to the matter under discussion, to order.

Rule 45 – Points of Order
1. During the debate of any matter a member may, at any time, raise a point of order and the point of order shall be immediately decided by the Chairman, in accordance with the Rules of Procedure. If a member appeals against the decision, the appeal shall immediately be put to the vote and if the Chairman's ruling is not overruled by the majority of the members present, it shall be maintained.
2. A member raising a point of order cannot, in his or her comments, deal with the substance of the matter under discussion.

Rule 46 – Adjournment of debates
During the discussion on any matter, a member may move the adjournment of the debate on the matter under discussion. In addition to the proposer of the motion one member may speak in favour of and one against the motion after which the motion shall be immediately put to the vote.

Rule 47 – Limit the time accorded to speakers
The Commission may limit the time accorded to each speaker on any matter, when the time allotted for debates is limited and a speaker spends more time than the time accorded, the Chairman shall immediately call him to order.

Rule 48 – Closing the list of speakers
The Chairman may, during a debate, read out the list of speakers and with the approval of the Commission, declare the list closed. Where there are no more speakers, the Chairman shall, with the approval of the Commission, declare the debate closed.

Rule 49 – Closure of Debate
A member may, at any time, move for the closure of the debate on the matter under discussion, even if the other members or representatives expressed the desire to take the floor. The authorization to take the floor on the closure of the debate shall be given only to two speakers before the closure, after which the motion shall immediately be put to the vote.

Rule 50 – Suspension or Adjournment of the Meeting
During the discussion of any matter, a member may move for the suspension or adjournment of the meeting. No discussion on any such motion shall be permitted and it shall be immediately put to the vote.

Rule 51 – Order of the Motions
Subject to the provision of Rule 45 of the present Rules of Procedure, the following motions shall have precedence in the following order over all the other proposals or motions before the meeting.
(a) To suspend the meeting
(b) To adjourn the meeting
(c) To adjourn the debate on the item under discussion
(d) For the closure of the debate of the item under discussion

Rule 52 – Submission of Proposals and Amendment of Substance
Unless the Commission decides otherwise the proposals, amendments or motions of substance made by members shall be submitted in writing to the Secretariat; they shall be considered at the first sitting following their submission.

Rule 53 – Decisions on Competence
Subject to the provisions of Rule 45 of the Procedure, any motion tabled by a member for a decision on the competence of the Commission to adopt a proposal submitted to it shall immediately be put to the vote.

Rule 54 – Withdrawal of a Proposal or a Motion
The sponsor of a motion or a proposal may still withdraw it before it is put to the vote, provided that it has not been amended. A motion or a proposal thus withdrawn may be submitted again by another member.

Rule 55 – New Consideration or a Motion
When a proposal is adopted or rejected, it shall not be considered again at the same session, unless the Commission decides otherwise. When a member moves for the new consideration of a proposal, only one member may speak in favour of and one against the motion, after which it shall immediately be put to the vote.

Rule 56 – Interventions
1. No member may take the floor at a meeting of the Commission without prior authorization of the Chairman. Subject to Rules 45, 48, 49 and 50 the Chairman shall grant the use of the floor to the speakers in the order in which it has been requested.
2. The debates shall deal solely with the matter submitted to the Commission and the Chairman may call to order a speaker whose remarks are irrelevant to the matter under discussion.
3. The Chairman may limit the time accorded to speakers and the number of the interventions which each member may make on the same issue, in accordance with Rule 44 of the present Rules.
4. Only two members in favour and two against the motion of fixing such time limits shall be granted the use of the floor after which the motion shall immediately be put to the vote. For questions of procedure the time allotted to each speaker shall not exceed five minutes, unless the Chairman decides otherwise. When the time allotted discussions is limited and a speaker exceeds the time accorded the Chairman shall immediately call him to order.

Rule 57 – Right to Reply
The right of reply shall be granted by the chairman to any member requesting it. The member must, while exercising this right, be as brief as possible and take the floor preferably at the end of the sitting at which this right has been requested.

Rule 58 – Congratulations
The congratulations addressed to the newly elected members of the Commission shall only be presented by the Chairman or a member designated by the latter. Those addressed to the newly elected officers shall only be presented by the outgoing Chairman or a member designated by him.

Rule 59 – Condolences
Condolences shall be exclusively presented by the Chairman on behalf of all the members. The Chairman may, with the consent of the Commission, send a message of condolence.

CHAPTER XI – VOTE AND ELECTIONS

Rule 60 – Right to Vote
Each member of the Commission shall have one vote. In the case of an equal number of votes the Chairman shall have a casting vote.

Rule 61 – Asking for a Vote
A proposal or a motion submitted for the decision of the Commission shall be put to the vote if a member so requests. If no member asks for a vote, the Commission may adopt a proposal or a motion without a vote.

Rule 62 – Required Majority
1. Except as otherwise provided by the Charter or other Rules of the present Rules of Procedure, decisions of the Commission shall be taken by a simple majority of the members present and voting.
2. For the purpose of the present Rules of Procedure, the expression "members present and voting" shall mean members voting for or against or blank. The members who shall abstain from voting shall be considered as non-voting members.
3. Decisions may be taken by consensus, failing which, Commission shall resort to voting.

Rule 63 – Method of Voting
1. Subject to the provisions of Rule 68, the Commission, unless it otherwise decides, shall normally vote by show of hands, but any member may request the roll-call vote, which shall be taken in the alphabetical order of the names of the members of the Commission beginning with the member whose name is drawn by lot by the Chairman. In all the votes by roll-call each member shall reply "yes", "no" or "abstention". The Commission may decide to hold a secret ballot.
2. In case of vote by roll-call, the vote of each member participating in the ballot shall be recorded in the minutes.

Rule 64 – Explanation of Vote
Members may make brief statements for the only purpose of explaining their vote, before the beginning of the vote or once the vote has been taken. The member who is the sponsor of a proposal or a motion cannot explain his vote on that proposal or motion except if it has been amended.

Rule 65 – Rules to be Observed while Voting
A ballot shall not be interrupted except if a member raises a point of order relating to the manner in which the ballot is held. The Chairman may allow members to intervene briefly, whether before the ballot beginning or when it is closed, but solely to explain their vote.

Rule 66 – Division of Proposals and Amendments
Proposals and amendments may be separated if requested. The parts of the proposals or of the amendments which have been adopted shall later be put to the vote as a whole; if all the operative parts of a proposal have been rejected, the proposal shall be considered to have been rejected as a whole.

Rule 67 – Amendment
An amendment to a proposal is an addition to, deletion from or revision of part of that proposal.

Rule 68 – Order of Vote on Amendments
When an amendment is moved to a proposal, the amendment shall be voted on first.
When two or more amendments are moved to a proposal, the Commission shall first vote on the amendment furthest removed in substance from the original proposal and then on the amendment next furthest removed therefrom and so on until all the amendments have been put to the vote. Nevertheless when the adoption of an amendment implies the rejection of another amendment, the latter shall not be put to the vote. If one or several amendments are adopted, the amended proposal shall then be put to the vote.

Rule 69 – Order of Vote on the Proposals
1. If two or more proposals are made on the same matter, the Commission, unless it decides otherwise, shall vote on these proposals in the order in which they were submitted.
2. After each vote the Commission may decide whether it shall put the next proposal to the vote.
3. However, the motions which are not on the substance of the proposals shall be voted upon before the said proposals.

Rule 70 – Elections
Elections shall be held by secret ballot unless the election is for a post for which only one candidate has been proposed and that candidate has been agreed upon by the members of the Commission.

CHAPTER XII – PARTICIPATION OF NON-MEMBERS OF THE COMMISSION

Rule 71 – Participation of States in the deliberations
1. The Commission or its subsidiary bodies may invite any State to participate in the discussion of any issue that shall be of particular interest to that State.
2. A State thus invited shall have no voting right, but may submit proposals which may be put to the vote at the request of any member of the Commission or of the subsidiary body concerned.

Rule 72 – Participation of other Persons or Organizations
The Commission may invite any organization or persons capable of enlightening it, to participate in its deliberations without voting rights.

Rule 73 – Participation of Specialized Institutions and Consultation with the latter
1. Pursuant to the agreements concluded between the Organization of African Unity and the Specialized Institutions, the latter shall have the right to:

(a) Be represented in the public sessions of the Commission and its subsidiary bodies;
(b) Participate, without voting rights, through their representatives in deliberations on issues which shall be of interest to them and to submit, on these issues, proposals which may be put to vote at the request of any member of the Commission or the interested subsidiary body.
2. Before placing on the provisional agenda an issue submitted by a Specialized Institution, the Secretary-General should initiate such preliminary consultations as may be necessary, with this institution.
3. When the issue proposed for inclusion on the provisional agenda of a session, or which has been added to the agenda of a session pursuant to Rule 5 of the present Rules of Procedure, contains a proposal requesting the Organization of African Unity to undertake additional activities relating to issues concerning directly one or more specialized institutions, the Secretary-General should enter into consultation with the institutions concerned and inform the Commission of the ways and means of ensuring co-ordinated utilization of the resources of the various institutions.
4. When at a meeting of the Commission, a proposal calling upon the Organization of African Unity to undertake additional activities relating to issues directly concerning one or several specialized institutions, the Secretary-General, after consulting as far as possible, the representatives of the interested institutions, should draw the attention of the Commission to the effects of that proposal.
5. Before taking a decision on the proposals mentioned above, the Commission shall make sure that the institutions concerned have been duly consulted.

Rule 74 – Participation of other Inter-Governmental Organizations
1. The Secretary shall inform, not later than 4 weeks before a session, non-governmental organizations with observer status of the days and agenda of a forthcoming session.
2. Representatives of Inter-Governmental Organizations to which the Organization of African Unity has granted permanent observer status and other Organizations recognized by the Commission, may participate, without voting rights, in the deliberations of the Commission on issues falling within the framework of the activities of these organizations.

CHAPTER XIII – RELATIONS WITH AND REPRESENTATION OF NON-GOVERNMENTAL ORGANIZATIONS

Rule 75 – Representation
Non-governmental organizations, granted observer status by the Commission, may appoint authorized observers to participate in the public sessions of the Commission and of its subsidiary bodies.

Rule 76 – Consultation
The Commission may consult the non-governmental organizations either directly or through one of several committees set up for this purpose. These consultations may be held at the invitation of the Commission or at the request of the organization.

CHAPTER XIV – PUBLICATION AND DISTRIBUTION OF THE REPORTS AND OTHER OFFICIAL DOCUMENTS OF THE COMMISSION

Rule 77 – Report of the Commission
Within the framework of the procedure of communication among States parties to the Charter, referred to in Articles 47 and 49 of the Charter, the Commission shall submit to the Assembly a report containing, where possible, recommendations it shall deem necessary. The report shall be confidential. However, it shall be published by the Chairman of the Commission after reporting unless the Assembly directs otherwise.

Rule 78 – Periodical Reports of Member States
Periodical Reports and other information submitted by States parties to the Charter as requested under Article 62 of the Charter, shall be documents for general distribution. The same thing shall apply to other information supplied by a State party to the Charter, unless the Commission decides otherwise.

Rule 79 – Reports on the Activities of the Commission
1. As stipulated in Article 54 of the Charter, the Commission shall each year submit to the Assembly, a report on its deliberations, in which it shall include a summary of the activities.
2. The report shall be published by the Chairman after the Assembly has considered it.

Rule 80 – Translation of reports and other documents
The Secretary shall endeavour to translate all reports and other documents of the Commission into the working languages.

Part Two – Provisions Relating to the Functions of the Commission

CHAPTER XV – PROMOTIONAL ACTIVITIES REPORT SUBMITTED BY STATES PARTIES TO THE CHARTER UNDER ARTICLE 62 OF THE CHARTER

Rule 81 – Contents of Reports
1. States parties to the Charter shall submit reports in the form required by the Commission on measures they have taken to give effect to the rights recognized by the Charter and on the progress made with regard to the enjoyment of these rights.
2. If a State party fails to comply with Article 62 of the Charter, the Commission shall fix the date for the submission of that State party's report.
3. The Commission may, through the Secretary-General, inform State parties to the Charter of its wishes regarding the form and contents of the reports to be submitted under Article 62 of the Charter.

Rule 82 – Transmission of the Reports
1. The Secretary may, after consultation with the Commission, communicate to the specialized institutions concerned, copies of all parts of the reports which may relate to their areas of competence, produced by member States of these institutions.

2. The Commission may invite the specialized institutions to which the Secretary has communicated parts of the report, to submit observations relating to these parts within a time limit that it may specify.

Rule 83 – Submission of Reports

The Commission shall inform, as early as possible, member States parties to the Charter, through the Secretary, of the opening date, duration and venue of the Session at which their respective reports shall be considered.

Representatives of the States parties to the Charter may participate in the sessions of the Commission at which their reports shall be considered. The Commission may also inform a State party to the Charter from which it wanted complementary information, that it may authorize its representative to participate in a specific session. This representative should be able to reply to questions put to him/her by the Commission and make statements on reports already submitted by this State. He may also furnish additional information from his State.

Rule 84 – Non-submission of Reports

1. The Secretary shall, at each session, inform the Commission of all cases of non-submission of reports or of additional information requested pursuant to Rule 81 and 85 of the Rules of Procedure. In such cases, the Commission may send, through the Secretary, to the State party to the Charter concerned, a report or reminder relating to the submission of the report or additional information.
2. If, after the reminder referred to in paragraph 1 of this Rule, a State party to the Charter does not submit the report or the additional information requested pursuant to Rules 81 and 85 of the Rules and Procedure, the Commission shall point it out in its yearly report to the Assembly.

Rule 85 – Examination of information contained in reports

1. When considering a report submitted by a State party to the Charter under Article 62 of the Charter, the Commission should first make sure that the report provides all the necessary information including relevant legislation pursuant to the provisions of Rule 81 of the Rules and Procedure.
2. If, in the opinion of the Commission, a report submitted by a Sate party to the Charter, does not contain adequate information, the Commission shall request this State to furnish the additional information required by indicating the data on which the information needed should be submitted.
3. If, following the consideration of the reports, and the information submitted by a State party to the Charter, the Commission decides that the State has not discharged some of its obligations under the Charter, it may address all general observations to the State concerned as it may deem necessary.

Rule 86 – Adjournment and Transmission of the Reports

1. The Commission shall, through the Secretary, communicate to States parties to the Charter for comments, its general observations made following the consideration of the reports and the information submitted by States parties to the Charter which shall be public documents. The Commission may, when necessary, fix a time limit for the submission of the comments by the States parties to the Charter.

2. The Commission may also transmit to the Assembly, the observations mentioned in paragraph 1 of this Rule, accompanied by copies of the reports it has received from the States parties to the Charter as well as the comments supplied by the latter if possible.

Rule 87 – Promotional Activities
1. The Commission shall adopt and carry out a programme of action which gives effect to its obligations under the Charter, particularly Article 45(1).
2. The Commission shall carry out other promotional activities in member states and elsewhere on a continuing basis.
3. Each member of the Commission shall file a written report on his/her activities at each session including countries visited and organizations contacted.

CHAPTER XVI – PROTECTION ACTIVITIES

COMMUNICATIONS FROM THE STATES PARTIES TO THE CHARTER

SECTION I – PROCEDURE FOR THE CONSIDERATION OF COMMUNICATIONS RECEIVED IN CONFORMITY WITH ARTICLE 47 OF THE CHARTER: PROCEDURE FOR COMMUNICATIONS – NEGOTIATIONS

Rule 88 – Procedure
1. A communication under Article 47 of the Charter should be submitted to the Secretary-General, the Chairman of the Commission and the State party concerned.
2. The communication referred to above should be in writing and contain a detailed and comprehensive statement on the actions denounced as well as the provisions of the Charter alleged to have been violated.
3. The notification of the communications to the State party to the Charter, the Secretary-General and the Chairman of the Commission shall be done through the most practicable and reliable means.

Rule 89 – Register of Communications
The Secretary shall keep a permanent register for all communications received under Article 47 of the Charter.

Rule 90 – Reply and time limit
1. The reply of the State party to the Charter to which a communication is addressed should reach the requesting State party to the Charter within 3 months following the receipt of the notification of the communication.
2. It shall be accompanied particularly by:
    (a) Written explanations, declarations or statements relating to the issues raised;
    (b) Possible indications and measures taken to end the situation denounced;
    (c) Indications on the law and rules of procedure applicable or applied;
    (d) Indications on the local procedures for appeal already used, in process or still open.

Rule 91 – Non-Settlement of the Issue
1. If within three (3) months from the date of notification of the original communication is received by the addressee State, the issue has not been settled to the satisfaction of the two interested parties, through the selected channel of negotiation or through any other peaceful procedure selected by common consent of the parties, the issue shall be referred to the Commission, in accordance with the provisions of Article 48 of the Charter.
2. The issue shall also be referred to the Commission if the addressee State party to the Charter fails to react to the request made under Article 47 of the Charter, within the same 3 months' period of time.

Rule 92 – Seisin of the Commission
At the expiration of the 3 months' time limit referred to in Article 47 of the Charter, and in the absence of a satisfactory reply or in case the addressee State fails to respond, the party may submit the communication to the Commission through a notification addressed to its Chairman, the other interested State party and the Secretary-General.

SECTION II – PROCEDURE FOR THE CONSIDERATION OF THE COMMUNICATIONS RECEIVED IN CONFORMITY WITH ARTICLE 48 AND 49 OF THE CHARTER: PROCEDURE FOR COMMUNICATION – COMPLAINT

Rule 93 – Seisin of the Commission
1. Any communication submitted under Article 48 and 49 of the Charter may be submitted to the Commission by any one of the interested States parties through notification addressed to the Chairman of the Commission, the Secretary and the State party concerned.
2. The notification referred to in paragraph 1 of the present Rule shall contain information on the following elements or accompanied particularly by:
   (a) Measures taken to try to resolve the issue pursuant to Article 47 of the Charter including the text of the initial communications and any further written explanation from the interested States parties to the Charter relating to the issue;
   (b) Measures taken to exhaust local procedure for appeal;
   (c) Any other procedure for the international investigation or international settlement to which the interested State parties have resorted.

Rule 94 – Permanent Register of Communications
The Secretary shall keep a permanent register for all communications received by the Commission under Articles 48 and 49 of the Charter.

Rule 95 – Seisin of the Members of the Commission
The Secretary shall immediately inform the members of the Commission of any notification received pursuant to Rule 91 of the Rules and Procedure and shall send them, as early as possible, a copy of the notification as well as the relevant information.

Rule 96 – Private Session and Press Release
1. The Commission shall consider the communications referred to in Articles 48 and 49 of the Charter in closed session.
2. After consulting the interested State parties to the Charter, the Commission may issue through the Secretary, releases on its private sessions for the attention of the media and the public.

Rule 97 – Consideration of the Communication
The Commission shall consider a communication only when:
(a) The procedure offered to the State parties by Article 47 of the Charter has been exhausted;
(b) The time limit in Article 48 of the Charter has expired;
(c) The Commission is certain that all the available local remedies have been utilized and exhausted, in accordance with the generally recognized principles of international law, or that the application of these remedies is unreasonably prolonged or that there are no effective remedies.

Rule 98 – Amicable Settlement
Except the provisions of Rule 97 of the present Rules of Procedure, the Commission shall place its good offices at the disposal of the interested States parties to the Charter so as to reach an amicable solution on the issue based on the respect of human rights and fundamental liberties, as recognized by the Charter.

Rule 99 – Additional Information
The Commission may through the Secretary, request the States parties or one of them to communicate additional information or observations orally or in writing. The Commission shall fix a time limit for the submission of the written information or observations.

Rule 100 – Right of Representation
1. The States parties to the Charter concerned shall have the right to be represented during the consideration of the issue by the Commission and to submit observations orally and in writing or in either form.
2. The Commission shall notify, as soon as possible, the States parties concerned, through the Secretary, of the opening date, the duration and the venue of the session at which the issue will be examined.
3. The procedure to be followed for the presentation of the oral or written observations shall be determined by the Commission.

Rule 101 – Report of the Commission
1. The Commission shall adopt a report pursuant to Article 52 of the Charter within 12 months, following the notification referred to in Article 48 of the Charter and Rule 90 of the present Rules of Procedure.
2. The provisions of paragraph 1 of Rule 99 of these Rules of Procedure shall not apply to the deliberations of the Commission, relating to the adoption of the report.
3. The report referred to above shall concern the decisions and conclusions that the Commission will reach.
4. The report of the Commission shall be communicated to the States parties concerned through the Secretary.

5. The report of the Commission shall be sent to the Assembly through the Secretary-General, together with the recommendations that it shall deem useful.

CHAPTER XVII – OTHER COMMUNICATIONS
PROCEDURE FOR THE CONSIDERATION OF THE COMMUNICATIONS RECEIVED IN CONFORMITY WITH ARTICLE 55 OF THE CHARTER

SECTION I – TRANSMISSION OF COMMUNICATIONS TO THE COMMISSION

Rule 102 – Seisin of the Commission
1. Pursuant to these Rules of Procedure, the Secretary shall transmit to the Commission the communications submitted to him for consideration by the Commission in accordance with the Charter.
2. No communications concerning a State which is not a party to the Charter shall be received by the Commission or placed on a list under Rule 103 of the present Rules.

Rule 103 – List of Communication
1. The Secretary of the Commission shall prepare lists of communications submitted to the Commission pursuant to Rule 101 above, to which he/she shall attach a brief summary to their contents and regularly cause the lists to be distributed to members of the Commission. Besides, the Secretary shall keep a permanent register of all these communications which shall be made public.
2. The full text of each communication referred to the Commission shall be communicated to each member of the Commission on request.

Rule 104 – Request for Clarifications
1. The Commission, through the Secretary, may request the author of a communication to furnish clarifications on the applicability of the Charter to his/her communication, and specify in particular:
   (a) His name, address, age and profession by justifying his very identity, if ever he/she is requesting the Commission to be kept anonymous;
   (b) Name of the State party referred to in the communication;
   (c) Purpose of the communication;
   (d) Provision(s) of the Charter allegedly violated;
   (e) The facts of the claim;
   (f) Measures taken by the author to exhaust local remedies; or explanation why local remedies will be futile;
   (g) The extent to which the same issue has been settled by another international investigating or settlement body.
2. When asking for clarification or information, the Commission shall fix an appropriate time limit for the author to submit the communication so as to avoid undue delay in the procedure provided for by the Charter.
3. The Commission may adopt a questionnaire for use by the author of the communication in providing the above-mentioned information.

4. The request for clarification referred to in paragraph 1 of this rule shall not prevent the inclusion of the communication on the lists mentioned in paragraph 1 of Rule 102 above.

Rule 105 – Distribution of Communications
For each communication recorded, the Secretary shall prepare as soon as possible, a summary of the relevant information received, which shall be distributed to the members of the Commission.

SECTION II – GENERAL PROVISIONS GOVERNING THE CONSIDERATION OF THE COMMUNICATIONS BY THE COMMISSION OR ITS SUBSIDIARY BODIES

Rule 106 – Private Sessions
The sessions of the Commission or of its subsidiary bodies during which the communications are examined as provided for in the Charter shall be private.

Rule 107 – Public Sessions
The sessions during which the Commission may consider general issues, such as the application procedure of the Charter, shall be public.

Rule 108 – Press Releases
The Commission may issue, through the Secretary and for the attention of the media and public, releases on the activities of the Commission in its private session.

Rule 109 – Incompatibilities
1. No member shall take part in the consideration of a communication by the Commission:
   (a) If he/she has any personal interests in the case, or
   (b) If he/she has participated, in any capacity, in the adoption of any decision relating to the case which is the subject of the communication.
2. The Rapporteur responsible for a communication shall not be a national of the State concerned. Any issue relating to the application of paragraph 1 above shall be resolved by the Commission.

Rule 110 – Provisional Measures
If, for any reason, a member considers that he/she should not take part or continue to take part in the consideration of a communication, he/she shall inform the Chairman of his/her decision to withdraw.

Rule 111 – Provisional Measures
1. Before making its final views known to the Assembly on the communication, the Commission may inform the State party concerned of its views on the appropriateness of taking provisional measures to avoid irreparable damage being caused to the victim of the alleged violation. In so doing, the Commission shall inform the State party that the expression of its views on the adoption of those provisional measures does not imply a decision on the substance of the communication.
2. The Commission, or when it is not in session, the Chairman, in consultation

with other members of the Commission, may indicate to the parties any interim measure the adoption of which seems desirable in the interest of the parties or the proper conduct of the proceedings before it.
3. In case of urgency when the Commission is not in session, the Chairman, in consultation with other members of the Commission, may take any necessary action on behalf of the Commission. As soon as the Commission is again in session, the Chairman shall report to it on any action taken.

Rule 112 – Information to the State party to the Charter
Prior to any substantive consideration, every communication should be made known to the State concerned through the Chairman of the Commission, pursuant to Article 57 of the Charter.

SECTION III – PROCEDURES TO DETERMINE ADMISSIBILITY

Rule 113 – Time limits for consideration of the admissibility
The Commission shall decide, as early as possible and pursuant to the following provisions, whether or not the communication shall be admissible under the Charter.

Rule 114 – Order of consideration of Communications
1. Unless otherwise decided, the Commission shall consider the communications in the order they have been received by the Secretariat.
2. The Commission may decide, if it deems it good, to consider jointly two or more communications.

Rule 115 – Working groups
The Commission may set up one or more working groups; each composed of three of its members at most, to submit recommendations on admissibility as stipulated in Article 56 of the Charter.

Rule 116 – Admissibility of the Communications
The Commission shall determine questions of admissibility pursuant to Article 56 of the Charter.

Rule 117 – Additional Information
1. The Commission or a working group set up under Rule 113, requests the State party concerned or the author of the communication to submit in writing additional information or observations relating to the issue of admissibility of the communication. The Commission or the working group shall fix a time for the submission of the information or observations to avoid the issue dragging on too long.
2. A communication may be declared admissible if the State party concerned has been give the opportunity to submit information and observations pursuant to paragraph 1 of this Rule.
3. A request made under paragraph 1 of this Rule should indicate clearly that the request does not mean that any decision whatsoever has been taken on the issue of the admissibility.
4. However, the Commission shall decide on the issue of admissibility if the

State party fails to send a written response within three (3) months from the date of notification of the text of the communication.

Rule 118 – Decision of the Commission on Admissibility
1. If the Commission decides that a communication is inadmissible under the Charter, it shall make its decision known as early as possible, through the Secretary to the author of the communication and, if the communication has been transmitted to a State party concerned, to that State.
2. If the Commission has declared a communication admissible under the Charter, it may reconsider this decision at a later date if it receives a request for reconsideration.

SECTION IV – PROCEDURES FOR THE CONSIDERATION OF COMMUNICATIONS

Rule 119 – Proceedings
1. If the Commission decides that a communication is admissible under the Charter, its decision and text of the relevant documents shall as soon as possible, be submitted to the State party concerned, through the Secretary. The author of the communication shall also be informed of the Commission's decision through the Secretary.
2. The State party to the Charter concerned shall, within the 3 ensuing months, submit in writing to the Commission, explanations or statements elucidating the issue under consideration and indicating, if possible measures it was able to take to remedy the situation.
3. All explanations or statements submitted by a State party pursuant to the present Rule shall be communicated, through the Secretary, to the author of the communication who may submit in writing additional information and observations within a time limit fixed by the Commission.
4. State parties from whom explanations or statements are sought within specified times shall be informed that if they fail to comply within those times the Commission will act on the evidence before it.

Rule 120 – Final Decision of the Commission
1. If the communication is admissible, the Commission shall consider it in the light of all the information that the individual and the State party concerned has submitted in writing; it shall make known its observations on this issue. To this end, the Commission may refer the communication to a working group, composed of 3 of its members at most, which shall submit recommendations to it.
2. The observations of the Commission shall be communicated to the Assembly through the Secretary-General and to the State party concerned.
3. The Assembly or its Chairman may request the Commission to conduct an in-depth study on these cases and to submit a factual report accompanied by its findings and recommendations, in accordance with the provisions of Article 58 sub-paragraph 2 of the Charter. The Commission may entrust this function to a Special Rapporteur or a working group.

FINAL CHAPTER – AMENDMENT AND SUSPENSION OF THE RULES OF PROCEDURE

Rule 121 – Method of Amendment
The Commission may suspend temporarily, the application of any Rule of the present Rules of Procedure, on condition that such a suspension shall not be incompatible with any applicable decision of the Commission or the Assembly or with any relevant provision of the Charter and that the proposal shall have been submitted 24 hours in advance. This condition may be set a side if no member opposes it. Such a suspension may take place only with a specific and precise object in view and should be limited to the duration necessary to achieve that aim.

PROTOCOL TO THE AFRICAN CHARTER ON THE ESTABLISHMENT OF THE AFRICAN COURT ON HUMAN AND PEOPLES' RIGHTS

The Member States of the Organization of African Unity, States Parties to the African Charter on Human and Peoples' Rights,

Considering that the Charter of the Organization of African Unity recognizes that freedom, equality, justice and dignity are essential objectives for the achievement of the legitimate aspirations of the African peoples,

Noting that the African Charter on Human and Peoples' Rights reaffirms adherence to the principles of human and peoples' rights and freedoms contained in the declarations, conventions and other instruments adopted by the Organization of African Unity, and other international organizations,

Recognizing that the two-fold objective of the African Charter on Human and Peoples' Rights is to ensure on the one hand promotion and on the other protection of Human and Peoples' Rights, freedoms and duties,

Recognizing further, the efforts of the African Commission on Human and Peoples' Rights in the protection and promotion of human and peoples' rights since its inception in 1987,

Recalling Resolution 230 (XXX) adopted by the Assembly of Heads of State and Government requesting the Secretary-General to convene as a government experts' meeting to ponder, in conjunction with the African Commission, over the means to enhance the efficiency of the African Commission in considering particularly the establishment of an African Court of Human and Peoples' Rights,

Firmly convinced that the attainment of the objectives of the African Charter on Human and Peoples' Rights requires the establishment of an African Court of Human and Peoples' Rights to complement and reinforce the mission of the African Commission on Human and Peoples' Rights,

Have agreed as follows:

Article 1 – Establishment of the Court
There shall be established an African Court of Human and Peoples' Rights ("Court") whose jurisdiction and functioning of which shall be governed by the present Protocol.

Article 2 – Relationship between the Commission and the Court
The Court shall complement the protective mandate of the African Commission on Human and Peoples' Rights ("Commission") conferred upon it by the African Charter on Human and Peoples' Rights ("Charter").

Article 3 – Jurisdiction
1. The jurisdiction of the Court shall extend to all cases and disputes submitted to it concerning the interpretation and application of the Charter, this Protocol and any other African human rights Convention.

2. In the event of a dispute as to whether the Court has jurisdiction, the matter shall be settled by decision of the Court.

Article 4 – Advisory opinions
1. At the request of a Member State of the OAU any of its organs, or an African organization recognised by the OAU, the Court may provide an opinion on any legal matter relating to the Charter or any African human rights instrument.
2. The court shall give reasons for its advisory opinions provided that every judge shall be titled to deliver a separate or dissenting opinion.

Article 5 – Seizure of the Court
1. The following are entitled to submit cases to the Court:
   (a) The Commission
   (b) The State party which has lodged a complaint to the Commission
   (c) The State party against which the complaint has been lodged at the Commission

Article 6 – Exceptional jurisdiction
1. Notwithstanding the provisions of Article 5, the Court may, on exceptional grounds, allow individuals, non-governmental organisations and groups of individuals to bring cases before the Court, without first proceeding under Article 55 of the Charter.
2. The Court will consider such a case, taking into account the conditions enunciated in Article 56 of the Charter.
3. The Court itself may consider the case or refer it to the Commission.

Article 7 – Sources of law
In its deliberations, the Court shall be guided by the provisions of the Charter and the applicable principles stipulated in Articles 60 and 61 of the Charter.

Article 8 – Conditions for considering communications
1. The Court shall not consider a matter before it originating under the provisions of Article 9 of the Charter until such time as the Commission has prepared a report in terms of Article 52 of the Charter.
2. The Court may not consider a case originating under the provisions of Article 55 of the Charter until the Commission has considered the matter and prepared a report or taken a decision.
3. The Court may deal with a case only if the matter is brought before it, within three months, after the submission of the report of the Commission to the Assembly of Heads of States and Government.
4. Having accepted a case as stipulated in the above provisions, the Court may, by a two-thirds majority of its members decide to reject it if, after due consideration, the Court establishes the existence of one of the grounds of inadmissibility in Article 56 of the Charter.

Article 9 – Hearings and presentations
1. The Court shall conduct its proceedings in public. The Court may however conduct proceedings in camera, in cases where it is satisfied it is in the interest of justice.
2. Any party to a case shall be entitled to be represented by a legal representative

of the party's choice. Free legal representation may be provided where the interests of justice so require.
3. Any person, witness, or representative of the parties, who appears before the Court, shall enjoy the immunities and privileges in accordance with international law necessary for the discharging of their functions, tasks and duties in relation to the Court.

Article 10 – Composition
1. The Court shall consist of eleven judges, nationals of the Member States of the OAU, elected in an individual capacity from among jurists of high moral character and of recognized practical, judicial or academic competence and experience in the field of human and peoples' rights.
2. No two judges shall be nationals of the same State.

Article 11 – Nominations
States parties to the Charter may each propose up to three candidates, at least two of whom shall be nationals of that State. States Due consideration shall be given to adequate gender representation in the nomination process.

Article 12 – List of candidates
1. Upon the entry into force of this Protocol, the Secretary-General of the OAU shall request each State party to the Charter to present, within 90 days of such a request, its nominees for membership of the Court.
2. The Secretary-General of the OAU shall prepare a list in alphabetical order of the candidates presented and transmitted to the Member States of the OAU at least thirty days prior to the next session of the Assembly of Heads of State and Government of the OAU ("Assembly").

Article 13 – Elections
1. The judges of the Court shall be elected by secret ballot by two-thirds majority of votes of the members present and voting in the Assembly from the list referred to in Article 12(2) of the present Protocol.
2. States parties shall ensure that in the Court as a whole there is representation of the main regions of Africa and of their principal legal traditions.
3. Due consideration shall be given to adequate gender representation during the election process.
4. The same procedure as set out in Articles 11, 12, and 13(1), (2) and (3) shall be followed for the filling of vacancies.

Article 14 – Term of office
1. The judges of the Court shall be elected for a period of six years and may be re-elected only once. The terms of four judges elected at the first election shall expire at the end of two years, and the terms of four more judges shall expire at the end of four years.
2. The judges whose terms are to expire at the end of the initial periods of two and four years shall be chosen by lot to be drawn by the Secretary-General of the OAU immediately after the first election has been completed.
3. A judge elected to replace a judge whose term of office has not expired shall hold office for the remainder of the predecessor's term.
4. The expiration of their term notwithstanding, judges shall continue to hear cases part heard by them.

Article 15 – Independence
1. The independence of the judges shall be ensured. The Court shall decide matters before it impartially, on the basis of fact and in accordance with the law, without any restrictions, undue influence, inducement, pressure, threat or interference, direct or indirect, from any quarter for any reason.
2. No judge may hear a case in which the same judge has previously taken part as agent, counsel or advocate for one of the parties or as a member of a national or international court or a commission of enquiry or in any other capacity. Any doubt on this point shall be settled by decision of the Court.
3. The judges of the Court shall enjoy, from the moment of their election and throughout their term of office, the immunities extended to diplomatic agents in accordance with international law.
4. At no time shall the judges of the Court be held liable for any decisions or opinions issued in the exercise of their functions.

Article 16 – Incompatibility
The position of judge of the Court is incompatible with any other activity that might interfere with the independence or impartiality of such a judge or the demands of the office, as determined in the Rules of Procedure of the Court. Any doubt on this point shall be settled by decision of the Court.

Article 17 – Cessation of office
1. A judge shall not be suspended or removed from office unless, by the unanimous decision of other members of the Court, the judge concerned has been found to be no longer fulfilling the required conditions to be a judge of the Court.
2. Such a judgement of the Court shall be final and take effect immediately.

Article 18 – Presidency of the Court
1. The Court shall elect its President and one Vice President for a period of two years. They may be re-elected only once.
2. The President shall perform judicial functions on a full-time basis and shall reside at the seat of the Court.

Article 19 – Right to hear cases
If a judge is a national of any of the State parties to a case submitted to the Court, that judge shall retain the right to hear the case.

Article 20 – Quorum
The Court will examine cases brought before it in principle by seven judges. However, the Court may establish, if the need arises, two chambers consisting of five judges each.

Article 21 – Registry of the Court
1. The Court shall appoint its own Registrar and other staff of the registry according to the Rules of Procedure.
2. The office and residence of the Registrar shall be at the place where the Court has its seat.

Article 22 – Seat of Court
1. The court shall have its seat at the place determined by the Assembly. However, it may convene in the territory of any Member State of the OAU when a majority of the Court consider it desirable, and with the prior consent of the State concerned.

2. The seat of the Court may be changed by the Assembly after due consultation with the Court.

Article 23 – Evidence
1. As far as possible, after due consideration, the Court will hear submissions by all parties and if deemed necessary, hold an enquiry. The States concerned shall assist by providing relevant facilities for the efficient handling of the case.
2. The Court may receive written and oral evidence and other representations including expert testimony and it shall make a decision on the basis of such evidence and representations.

Article 24 – Findings
1. If the Court finds that there has been a violation of a human or peoples' right, it shall, order an appropriate measure to remedy the violation.
2. The Court may also order, that the consequences of the measure or situation that constituted the breach of such right be remedied and that fair compensation or reparation be paid or made to the injured party.
3. In cases of extreme gravity and urgency, and when necessary to avoid irreparable damage to persons, the Court shall adopt such provisional measures as it deems necessary.

Article 25 – Judgement
1. The judgement of the Court taken by majority shall be final and not subject to appeal.
2. The judgement of the Court shall be read in open court, due notice having been given to the parties.
3. Reasons shall be given for the judgement of the Court.
4. If the judgement of the Court does not represent, in whole or in part, the unanimous opinion of the judges, any judge shall be entitled to deliver a separate or dissenting opinion.

Article 26 – Execution of judgement
The States parties to the present Protocol undertake to comply with the judgement in any case to which they are parties to and to guarantee its execution.

Article 27 – Notification of judgement
1. The parties to the case shall be notified of the judgement of the Court and shall be transmitted to the Member States of the OAU.
2. The Council of Ministers shall also be notified of the judgement and shall monitor its execution on behalf of the Assembly.

Article 28 – Report
The Court shall submit to each regular session of the Assembly, a report on its work during the previous year. The report shall specify, in particular, the cases in which the State has not complied with the Court's judgement.

Article 29 – Budget
Expenses of the Court emoluments and allowances for judges and the budget of its registry, shall be determined and borne by the OAU in accordance with criteria laid down by the OAU in consultation with the Court bearing in mind the Independence of the Court.

Article 30 – Rules of procedure
The Court shall draw up its Rules and determine its own procedures.

Article 31 – Ratification
1. The Protocol shall be open for signature and ratification or adherence by any State party to the Charter.
2. The instrument of ratification or adherence to the present Protocol shall be deposited with the Secretary-General of the OAU.
3. The Protocol shall come into effect one month after eleven instruments of ratification or adherence have been deposited.
4. For any State party ratifying subsequently, the present Protocol shall come into force in respect of that State on the date of the deposit of its instrument of ratification or adherence.
5. The Secretary-General shall inform all Member States of the OAU of the entry into force of the present Protocol.

Article 32 – Amendments
1. The present Protocol may be amended if a State party to the Protocol makes a written request to that effect to the Secretary-General of the OAU. The Assembly may adopt by two-thirds majority, the draft amendment after all the States parties to the present Protocol have been duly informed of it and the Court has given its opinion on the amendment.
2. The Court shall also be entitled to propose such amendments to the present Protocol as it may deem necessary, through the Secretary-General of the OAU.
3. The amendment shall come into force for each State party which has accepted it, one month after the Secretary-General of the OAU has received notice of the acceptance.

Index

abuse of children 419, 424, 425, 947, 950
  refugees 956
  street children 957, 958
  UN Commission resolutions 898, 899, 904, 913
  see also sexual exploitation of children
ad hoc international criminal tribunals 74–5, 95
  Former Yugoslavia 67, 74[n37], 113, 217[n30]
  Rwanda 67, 74[n37], 83, 111
adoption 419, 420, 439
advisory opinions
  African Court of Human and Peoples' Rights 1070
  European Court of Human Rights 974–5
advisory services
  Centre for Human Rights 280, 563, 615, 779, 796
  CERD Committee 709, 712, 723
  chairpersons' meetings
  (1984) 710, 712–14; (1989) 730–1, 736, 737; (1990) 746; (1992) 763, 771; (1994) 779
  CRC Committee 43
  children's rights 951
  Conference recommendations 338
  cross-referencing 563
  independent expert's report 519, 527, 543, 546, 614–15
  comments regarding 640–3, 660, 670; state reporting 553–4, 605, 606, 626, 627
  International Covenants 879, 937
  ratification 603
  Special Rapporteur on racism recommendations 919
  torture reports 890, 940

training workshops 677
  UN Commission resolution 875
  see also training programmes
Africa 281
African Charter on Human and Peoples' Rights 1033–68
  individual complaints procedures 140
  NGOs 188
  Protocol 1069–74
African Charter on the Rights and Welfare of the Child 536
African Commission on Human and Peoples' Rights 536, 591, 772, 1039–45, 1046–68, 1069–70
African Court of Human and Peoples' Rights 1069–74
Agenda 21 564, 582
AIDS see HIV/AIDS
Akdivar and Others v. Turkey (1996) 121[n19], 124[n37], 270[n69]
Akeyesu case (1998) 74[n37]
Aksoy v. Turkey (1996) 123, 124[n37], 174, 270[n69]
Albert and Le Compte v. Belgium (1983) 260[n28]
Algeria
  CAT draft optional protocol 499, 501
  CEDAW Optional Protocol 156[n61]
  dialogue with Committee on Economic, Social and Political Rights 685
amendments
  African Charter on Human and Peoples' Rights 1045, 1057, 1068
  Protocol 1074
  CAT 412–13, 445, 446, 490–512, 622, 940
  draft optional protocol 509
  CCPR 163, 370
  First Optional Protocol 374

1075

1076 Index

CEDAW   794, 945
   Optional Protocol   401–2
CERD   354, 445, 446, 622–3, 649, 932, 933
CESCR   385–6, 471–89
   draft optional protocol   489
   chairpersons' meeting (1997)   818
   comments regarding   631, 649–50, 662
   CRC   429–30, 448, 650, 952
      Optional Protocols   436, 443
   European Social Charter   993, 1001
   independent expert's report   524, 622–3, 628, 649, 671
   International Law Association report   699
   new human rights treaties   802
American Association for the Advancement of Science (AAAS)   197[n5], 229, 785
American Bar Association   299[n1]
American Convention on Human Rights   72, 80, 105, 106, 107, 1019–32
   Additional Protocol   473–4, 475
   individual complaints procedures   140
   NGOs   188
   see also Inter-American Commission on Human Rights
American Declaration of the Rights and Duties of Man   140[n9], 1013–18, 1019, 1027
Amnesty International   7, 16[n66], 79, 186–7, 209, 219
   attendance at state reporting   687
   CAT draft optional protocol   492
   individual complaints   188
   Iraq   98
   Peru   220–1
   Rwanda   83
   Torture Convention   189
   treaty denunciations   860
   use of the press   222
   women's rights   201
Angola
   CCPR Optional Protocol   688
   UN peace operations   99
anti-personnel mines   912, 955
Anti-Racism Information Service (ARIS)   16[n66], 49
apartheid   529, 551, 595–6, 714, 726
Arevalo et al. v. Colombia (1984)   236[n16]
Argentina
   Marzioni v. Argentina (1996)   71[n21]
   Siderman de Blake v. Republic of Argentina (1992)   76
   truth commission   86
   women's rights   202[n15]

ARIS *see* Anti-Racism Information Service
armed conflict
   CEDAW reports   27–8, 29
   children   425, 431–6, 899, 907, 911–13, 954–6
Artico v. Italy (1980)   173[n16], 259
Ashby v. Jamaica (1994)   147[n29]
Assenov and Others v. Bulgaria (1998)   70[n16]
Association for the Prevention of Torture   492, 493, 502
asylum seeking   213, 214, 224, 1017
   adjudication   75
   African Charter on Human and Peoples' Rights   1036, 1037
   American Convention on Human Rights   1025
   individual complaints   144[n19]
Australia
   CAT draft optional protocol   499–500, 501, 502, 503
   CCPR Optional Protocol   145–6
   comments regarding the independent expert's report   630–1, 637, 644–5, 650, 652, 655
   CRC   211[n5]
   follow-up activities   240–1
   Human Rights Committee   148[n31]
   Toonen v. Australia (1992)   150[n38], 241
Austria
   Chorherr v. Austria (1993)   69[n12], 257[n6]
   European Convention review   272[n76]
   European Court judgements   252
   Kremzow v. Austria (1993)   259[n22]
   Pauger v. Austria (1990)   237[n18]
   Ringeisen v. Austria (1972)   259[n23]
   Simon-Herold v. Austria (1971)   126
Aydin v. Turkey (1997)   68[n9]

B. v. The United Kingdom (1988)   260[n28]
Bangladesh
   CRC Committee visit   801
   non-ratification of treaties   51[n17]
Beijing Declaration and Platform for Action   24, 196, 599, 829, 844, 899, 943–4
Belgium
   Albert and Le Compte v. Belgium (1983)   260[n28]
   De Weer v. Belgium (1980)   259
   European Convention review   272[n77]
   implementation of judgements   233[n5]
   law changes   261–2

Marckx v. Belgium (1979) 233[n5], 260, 261, 262, 270
Pauwels v. Belgium (1985) 260[n28]
Piersack v. Belgium (1984) 259[n21]
Vermeire v. Belgium (1991) 262
Belgrade Rules 67[n4], 74, 82, 110[n18], 113[n27]
Benin, CRC Committee follow-up activities 245[n52]
Berrehab v. The Netherlands (1988) 259
bias, fact-finding 65, 86–91, 103
Bolivia
 follow-up consultations 236[n15], 239
 NGO reporting 212[n9]
Bosnia
 Dayton Agreement 633
 Human Rights Chamber 251
 independence of treaty body members 253
 UN field presence 99, 100
Bosnia-Herzegovina, fact-finding 80
Bozano v. France (1986) 261
Brannigan and McBride v. The United Kingdom (1993) 265[n53]
Brazil
 "Bolsa Escola" programme 883
 fact-finding 87[n90]
 World Conference against Racism 921
Bretton Woods institutions 18, 807, 808
Brogan and Others v. The United Kingdom (1988) 264–5, 270
budget analysis 824–6, 869–70
Bulgaria
 Assenov and Others v. Bulgaria (1998) 70[n16]
 Loukanov v. Bulgaria (1997) 270
burden of proof 74, 125–7, 166
Burma
 European Union sanctions 85–6
 ILO Commission of Inquiry 66[n3]
 UN field operations 101
 see also Myanmar
Burundi, report to CEDAW Committee 28

Çagirga v. Turkey (1995) 124[n37]
Cambodia
 advisory services 614
 UN mission 82, 97, 101
Cameroon, follow-up consultations 239
Canada
 CAT 167, 499, 503
 comments regarding the independent expert's report 630–1, 634, 637, 639, 643, 645–6, 650, 656
 Cox v. Canada (1993) 150[n38]
 draft optional protocol to CAT 499, 503
 follow-up activities 240–1
 individual complaints 144[n19], 145, 147[n29, n30]
 Kindler v. Canada (1991) 150[n38]
 legal protection of human rights 305, 307–12
 Lubicon Lake Band v. Canada (1984) 147[n29]
 Ng v. Canada (1991) 147[n30], 150[n38]
 Singh v. Canada (1998) 147[n29]
 Stewart v. Canada (1993) 150[n38], 165
 Supreme Court 309–12
  R. (B.) v. Children's Aid Society of Metropolitan Toronto (1995) 310; *R. v. Brydges* (1990) 309; *R. v. Keegstra* (1990) 311; *R. v. L. (D.O.)* (1993) 310; *R. v. Milne* (1987) 310; *Slaight Communications Inc. v. Davidson* (1989) 311[n23]; *United States of America v. Cotroni* (1989) 310
Canadian Charter of Rights and Freedoms (1982) 305, 309–10, 311–12
Caribbean 145
Castells v. Spain (1992) 261[n34]
CAT *see* Committee Against Torture; Convention Against Torture
CCPOQ *see* Consultative Committee on Program and Operational Questions
CCPR *see* International Covenant on Civil and Political Rights
CEDAW *see* Committee on the Elimination of All Forms of Discrimination Against Women; Convention on the Elimination of All Forms of Discrimination Against Women
Central African Republic, follow-up consultations 239
Central Europe
 Council of Europe membership 265–6, 270–1
 European Convention on Human Rights 70, 118, 176
Centre for Human Rights
 advisory services 280, 563, 615, 779, 796
 committee resource room 732, 747–8, 760, 767, 783
 computerization 745
 coordination of UN organs 709, 721
 core documents 727
 database 576, 592, 611–12, 626–7, 804–5, 806

expert missions 713
field operations 98
gender integration 203
independence of treaty body
   members 691
independent expert's report 518, 521
information available to treaty
   bodies 692
length of reports 609
NGOs 586, 692
public information 747, 748, 762, 768
ratifications 715
regional advisors 279
resources 742–3, 760, 766, 783, 784–5, 793–4
restructuring 805
secretariat servicing 576, 577, 734, 743, 793–4
CEDAW Committee 521, 577, 760, 773, 784, 794, 806
studies and surveys 558
technical assistance 809
training programmes 714, 728, 730, 746, 752
website 611–12, 626–7, 806
working conditions 575
World Bank meeting (1996) 808
see also Office of the High Commissioner for Human Rights
CERD *see* Committee on the Elimination of All Forms of Racial Discrimination; Convention on the Elimination of All Forms of Racial Discrimination
CESCR *see* International Covenant on Economic, Social and Cultural Rights
Chad, CCPR Optional Protocol 688
Chahal v. The United Kingdom (1996) 69[n10], 69[n14], 174–5
Charter of the United Nations *see* United Nations Charter
CRC Committee *see* Committee on the Rights of the Child
child labour 801, 859, 882, 883, 899, 908, 956–7
children
   American Convention on Human Rights 1024, 1025
   CCPR 363
   CEDAW 388, 389, 393
   CESCR 381
   European Social Charter 979, 982–3, 986, 997
   pornography/prostitution 424, 431, 437–43

UN resolutions 898, 909–11, 947, 952–4; Vienna Declaration 950
torture 424, 425, 891, 900, 913, 941
World Conference on Racism 922
see also Committee on the Rights of the Child; Convention on the Rights of the Child; young people
Chile
   on-site visits 81
   truth commission 86, 114
China
   avoidance of UN scrutiny 184
   CAT draft optional protocol 499, 501, 502
   CEDAW Optional Protocol 156[n61]
   CERD reports 90
   reports to CAT 222
Chorherr v. Austria (1993) 69[n12], 257[n6]
civil rights
   African Charter on Human and Peoples' Rights 1033
   American Convention on Human Rights 1020–6
   American Declaration of the Rights and Duties of Man 1016
   CERD 348
   European Convention on Human Rights 967
   justiciability 160
   women 205
   see also International Covenant on Civil and Political Rights
coalitions of NGOs 52–3, 324, 337
Coeriel and Aurick v. The Netherlands (1991) 237
Cold War xvii, 89, 315, 579, 682
   end of 89, 299, 526, 582, 602
collaboration *see* cooperation
collective bargaining 979, 982
collective complaints 129–30, 132, 992
Colombia
   appearances before Human Rights Committee 211–12
   Arevalo et al. v. Colombia (1984) 236[n16]
   enabling law 242
   follow-up consultations 236, 239
   media coverage of reporting 687
   Páez v. Colombia (1985) 236[n16]
   response to concluding observations 293[n11]
   UN missions 82

Commission on Human Rights *see* United Nations Commission on Human Rights
Committee Against Torture (CAT) 407–12, 530
  asylum-seekers 224
  briefing on regional counterpart 589[n80]
  communications workload 533, 655
  concluding observations 693
  coordination with other bodies 538
  draft optional protocol 493, 503, 506, 621
  examination of state without report 606
  fact-finding 81, 84–5, 87, 92, 95
  financing arrangements 445, 446, 526, 571, 622
  chairpersons' meetings 724, 726–7, 733, 741, 750, 759
  General Assembly resolution 940, 941, 942
  general comments 531
  Global Plan of Action 18
  individual complaints 94, 146[n28], 166–7, 465–6, 818
  interim measures 147; International Law Association report 688, 697–8
  jurisprudential issues 214
  membership 295[n17], 407–8, 411, 618
  Morocco 221–2
  national courts' decision-making 327
  NGOs 49, 93, 191
  participation 15, 15[n62]; publicity 187; role 189; submissions 584
  non-payment of members 618
  resources 862
  state reporting 571, 726–7, 801–2
    backlog 848; country rapporteur 13[n50]; guidelines 928; length of reports 609; overdue reports 604
  technical briefing costs 869
  Turkey investigation 225
  UN Commission resolution 890, 891, 892
  US refugee practice 212[n8]
  see also Convention Against Torture
Committee on Economic, Social and Cultural Rights 530, 837, 863
  Algeria dialogue with 685
  concluding observations 6[n14], 625
  cooperation with other agencies 538, 653, 747
  draft optional protocol 160–2, 471–3, 475–89
  examination of state without report 89, 554, 606, 817, 833
  General Assembly resolution 935, 936, 937, 938
  general comments 531
  implementation 790–1, 814, 864
  individual complaints 79, 160–2, 689[n28]
  International Convention on the Protection of the Rights of Migrant Workers and Members of Their Families 621
  joint statements 835
  lack of interagency cooperation 580–1
  legal existence 801
  lists of issues 291[n8]
  meeting arrangements 572, 790, 862
  new functions 541
  NGOs 48–9, 50, 93, 190, 191–2, 227–30
    cooperation with 653; state reporting 15, 52, 317; thematic discussions 61
  non-payment of members 618
  overlapping competences 560, 562, 563, 761, 773
  specific proposals 539, 566
  state reporting 6–7, 9, 19, 291[n9], 292[n10], 721–2, 728
    delay between submission and examination 608; guidelines 928; NGOs 15, 52, 317; objectives 547–8; overdue reports 89, 770, 817; Plan of Action 18; pre-sessional working group 13–14; specifically-focused reports 569–70
  technical briefing costs 869
  thematic sessions 91–2
  UN Commission resolutions 877–9, 880, 882, 883–4, 885, 886
  UNDP relationship 677, 843, 859
  see also International Covenant on Economic, Social and Cultural Rights
Committee on the Elimination of All Forms of Discrimination Against Women (CEDAW) 393–5, 530, 535
  Committee on Economic, Social and Political Rights relationship 229
  computerization 745, 751
  concluding observations 693, 802
  conflicts of interest 90
  draft optional protocol 473
  examination of state without report 606

fact-finding 92
gender integration 565
General Assembly resolution 943–5
general comments 531
individual complaints 94, 155[n54], 159
influence of 538
IWRAW relationship 747
joint statements 835
lack of interagency cooperation 580–1
lists of issues 291[n8]
meeting arrangements 12[n45], 24–5, 572, 607, 695
  chairpersons' meetings 725–6, 784, 790, 819, 845, 851, 862, 866; International Law Association report 683–4, 687
membership 12, 13[n46], 31, 216, 328, 393–4, 618, 735
NGOs 15, 16[n66], 49, 93, 183[n1], 684
  international action 200–2; limited role 190–1
non-involvement in Beijing Conference 792
Optional Protocol 156–60, 398–401
overlapping competences 562–3, 761, 773
payment of members 574, 618
pre-sessional working group 14, 54
recommended move to Geneva 329
reservations 763, 830
resources 17, 736, 784
secretariat servicing
  by Centre for Human Rights 521, 577, 734, 760, 773, 784, 794, 806; problems 742–3
separation from other treaty bodies 294
slavery 566
state reporting 19, 23–34, 291[n9]
  chairpersons' meetings 714, 725–6; concluding observations 6[n14], 15[n59]; country rapporteur 13[n50]; delay between submission and examination 608; delegations 11; guidelines 928; overdue reports 605, 607; pre-sessional working group 14; reports on an exceptional basis 27–9; resources 17; Yearbooks 610
technical assistance 746
technical briefings 846
treaty amendments 622
UNDP 602
UNICEF relationship 859
UNIFEM 18
Yugoslavia 540

see also Convention on the Elimination of All Forms of Discrimination Against Women
Committee on the Elimination of All Forms of Racial Discrimination (CERD) 349–53, 530
backlog of contributions 818
communications workload 533, 655
concluding observations 625, 693
conflicts of interest 90
coordination with other bodies 538
examination of state without report 89, 554, 606, 817, 833
exchange of information 710–11
fact-finding 67, 78, 92
financing arrangements 445, 446, 526, 571, 622
chairpersons' meetings 724, 733, 741, 759, 766; General Assembly resolution 932, 933–4
first report 528–9
General Assembly resolutions 931, 932–4, 960, 961
general comments 531
Global Plan of Action 18
individual complaints 94, 147, 688, 698, 818
lack of interagency cooperation 580–1
meeting arrangements 572, 683–4, 862
membership 349–50, 618
Mexico dialogue with 685
national courts' decision-making 327
NGOs 15, 16[n66], 49, 50, 93
Nigeria dialogue with 685
non-payment of members 618
on-site visits 95
regional human rights organizations 808
special reports 615–16
state reporting 6[n13], 9, 19, 291[n9]
  chairpersons' meetings 707–9, 711–12, 714, 722–4, 790, 802, 831, 848; concluding observations 6[n14]; country rapporteur 13[n50]; guidelines 928; length of reports 609; overdue reports 89, 723, 770, 802, 817; time between submission and examination 668
Sub-Commission on Minorities cooperation 538, 842–3, 850, 933
technical briefing costs 870
Third Decade to Combat Racism and Racial Discrimination 540
UN Commission resolution 917, 920, 922
urgent action procedure 51

Yugoslavia 540
see also Convention on the Elimination of All Forms of Racial Discrimination; racial discrimination
Committee on the Rights of the Child (CRC) 427–9, 448, 530
  concluding observations 321–2
  conscientiousness of 600–1
  cooperation with other agencies 538, 579, 580, 625
  CRC Plan of Action 848
  economic, social and cultural rights 882, 886
  examination of state without report 606
  follow-up activities 244–5, 686[n17]
  General Assembly resolutions 448, 951–2
  general human rights 59
  HIV/AIDS discussion 674–5
  informal visits 294[n14]
  Jamaica dialogue with 685
  lists of issues 291[n8]
  Manual on Human Rights Reporting 785
  meeting arrangements 12[n45], 572, 607–8, 683, 695, 790
  membership 427, 618, 622, 650
  NGOs 93, 183[n1], 191–2, 212, 684
    comments regarding 653, 654, 655; state reporting 15–16, 47–8, 50, 51–6; thematic discussions 61
  non-involvement in Beijing Conference 792
  notebook computer provision 612
  on-site fact-finding 83–4, 95
  Optional Protocol on the Involvement of Children in Armed Conflict 435
  Optional Protocol on the Sale of Children, Child Prostitution and Child Pornography 442
  overlapping competences 561–2, 761, 773
  Pakistan dialogue with 685
  payment of members 618
  Plan of Action 18, 814
  regional meetings 762
  resources 806
  Senegal dialogue with 685
  slavery 566
  specialist secretariat unit 577–8
  specific proposals 539
  state reporting 9, 19, 20, 35–44, 292[n10]
    common themes 662; concluding observations 6[n14]; delay between submission and examination 608; experts 12, 38[n5]; guidelines 35[n1], 38–9, 51, 928; length of reports 609; NGOs 15–16, 47–8, 50, 51–6; number of meetings 607–8; Plan of Action 18; pre-sessional working group 13–14; schedule 59–60; United Kingdom report 7, 11[n41]; yearbooks 610
  submission of information 325
  technical briefing costs 870
  thematic sessions 91
  UN Commission resolution 900, 901, 902, 903, 907
  UNICEF relationship 41–2, 92, 635, 641, 651, 677
    best practice 859; cooperation 625; fact-finding missions 83–4; financial rewards 801, 813; success 18; technical assistance 43[n29]; urgent action 20
  urgent action procedure 20, 50–1
  see also Convention on the Rights of the Child
Commonwealth 632
compensation 259, 999, 1022
computerization 731–2, 736, 744–5, 750–1, 760, 767, 784–5
  Centre for Human Rights database 576
  General Assembly Resolution 445
  Office of UN High Commissioner for Human Rights 296
  state reporting schedules 559
  UNICEF notebook provision 612
concluding observations xix, 6, 14–15, 45, 89, 290, 291–2
  benefits of state reports 316–17
  CEDAW Committee 29–30, 32, 33, 802
  CRC 43
  Committee on Economic, Social and Political Rights 228, 606
  Conference recommendations 334, 335, 337, 338
  follow-up activities 244–9, 325, 326
  independent expert's report 531, 652
  International Covenants 937
  International Law Association report 686, 687, 693–4
  NGOs 61, 224, 226
  publicity 783
  quality of 625–6, 628, 652–3, 662, 673–4, 817, 835
  specificity 809
  state response to 293
  usefulness of 321–2

Conference for Security and Cooperation in
    Europe (CSCE)   536
confidentiality
    CAT draft optional protocol   493–4
    CERD Committee procedure   352
    European Committee of Ministers
        monitoring procedure   268
    individual complaints procedures   149
    new international instruments   745
    torture investigations   894–5
    truth commission witnesses   109–11
Congo, Democratic Republic of
    follow-up consultations   239
    report to CEDAW Committee   27, 28–9
    see also Zaire
consolidation of reports   223–4, 295, 300,
    301, 329, 340
    chairpersons' meetings   727–9, 816–17,
        845
    comments regarding   644–9, 661, 666, 667
    Conference discussion   318
    independent expert's report   549, 567–9,
        616, 619, 627, 644, 671
    NGOs   61–2, 193–4
consolidation of treaty bodies   21, 94, 295,
    299–302, 567, 817–18
    comments regarding   645, 646, 648–9, 662
    Conference conclusions   329–30, 340, 341
    core reports   93
    critique of   224
    independent expert's report   193, 616, 620,
        627, 644, 671
    NGO viewpoint   194
constructive dialogue   6, 9, 13, 37–8, 45, 925
    CEDAW reporting   26, 27, 29, 33
    critique of   683, 684–6
    NGOs   192, 193, 585
Consultative Committee on Program and
    Operational Questions (CCPOQ)   248
Convention Against Torture (CAT)   xvii
    amendments   412–13, 445, 446, 490–512,
        622, 940
    analytical study on duplication   928
    Canadian Supreme Court references
        to   309
    draft optional protocol   490–512, 532,
        621, 627, 896–7, 941
    enforcement of decisions   233
    financing arrangements
    chairpersons' meetings   733, 741–2, 750,
        759, 766, 783–4; independent expert's
        report   595
    General Assembly resolution   939–42

individual complaints   140, 167, 465–6,
    633, 688, 818
    asylum-seekers   144[n19]; Conference
        conclusions   327, 339; inquiry
        procedure   157, 158–9
    inter-state complaints procedure   476
    International Criminal Court
        jurisdiction   656–7
    jurisprudential issues   214, 590
    NGOs   49
    non-ratification of   595, 598–9
    overlap with other treaties   300
    Plan of Action   849, 852, 863, 867
    ratification   412, 451–8, 542, 682[n2],
        889–90, 940
        implementation   306, 315; independent
            expert's report   542
    reservations   413, 889–90, 940
    state reporting   5[n12], 12[n42], 408,
        726–7, 801–2, 890
        number of meetings   552, 607; overdue
            reports   550, 551, 604
    treaty text   403–13
    UN Commission resolution   888, 889–90
    see also Committee Against Torture
Convention on the Elimination of All Forms
    of Discrimination Against Women
    (CEDAW)   xvii, 195, 565
    amendments   794, 945
    analytical study on duplication   928
    Canadian Supreme Court references
        to   309
    complaints procedure changes   596
    economic, social and cultural rights   884,
        887
    General Assembly resolution   943–5
    girl child   947
    inter-state complaints procedure   476
    International Law Association
        report   689, 695, 698
    new communications procedures   590
    NGOs   191, 198
    Optional Protocol   398–402, 473, 476,
        533
    General Assembly resolutions   943, 944,
        945; individual complaints   xviii, 4,
        140–1, 155–60, 188[n14], 655, 698;
        state reporting   252[n4]
    ratification   3, 295[n16], 306, 396, 944
        chart of states   451–8; independent
            expert's report   595, 598, 599, 602,
            603–4
    reservations   200, 396, 763, 944

state reporting   5, 9, 23–34, 394–5, 714, 725–6
  Denmark   10[n35]; guidelines   295; Morocco   10[n38]; number of meetings   552, 607; Optional Protocol   252[n4]; overdue reports   9, 551, 604, 944; rules of procedure   26[n9]
treaty text   387–97
UNICEF programmes   641
violence against women   206
World Summit for Social Development   779
see also Committee on the Elimination of All Forms of Discrimination Against Women
Convention on the Elimination of All Forms of Racial Discrimination (CERD)   xvii, 529
  amendments   354, 445, 446, 622–3, 649, 932, 933
  analytical study on duplication   928
  Canadian Supreme Court references to   309, 311
  economic, social and cultural rights   884, 887
  enforcement of decisions   233, 234
  financing arrangements
    chairpersons' meetings   733, 741–2, 750, 759, 766, 783–4; independent expert's report   595
  General Assembly resolutions   931–4, 960, 961
  individual complaints   140, 157, 327, 467, 633, 688, 818
  inter-state complaints procedure   476
  jurisprudential issues   590
  Plan of Action   849, 852, 863, 867
  ratification   306, 354, 451–8, 603, 919–20, 934
  reservations   354, 920, 934
  state reporting   5[n12], 9, 88, 89, 350
    chairpersons' meetings   708–9, 711, 714, 722–4, 729; guidelines   295; number of meetings   552, 607; overdue reports   551, 604, 668, 932; periodic reports   646
  Sub-Commission on Minorities cooperation   842–3
  treaty text   345–55
  UN Commission resolution   917, 919–20
  victim identity   484
  women's rights   565
  see also Committee on the Elimination of All Forms of Racial Discrimination; racial discrimination
Convention on the Prevention and Punishment of the Crime of Genocide   80, 358
Convention on the Prohibition of the Use, Stockpiling, Production and Transfer of Anti-Personnel Mines and on Their Destruction   912
Convention on the Protection of the Rights of Migrant Workers and Members of Their Families see International Convention on the Protection of the Rights of Migrant Workers and Members of Their Families
Convention on the Reduction of Statelessness (1961)   213
Convention Relating to the Status of Refugees (1951)   75, 213–14, 995
Convention on the Rights of the Child (CRC)   xvii
  amendments   429–30, 448, 650, 952
  analytical study on duplication   928
  Australia   211[n5]
  Canadian Supreme Court references to   309, 310
  Conference of States Parties   448
  cooperation with other agencies   579
  cross-referencing   743
  database system   638
  dissemination of information   637
  draft optional protocol   899, 953, 956
  economic, social and cultural rights   884, 887
  follow-up procedure   244–5
  General Assembly resolution   950–8
  girl child   947
  honoraria payments   574
  individual petition   698
  International Law Association report   695, 698
  length of committee sessions   572
  Manual on Human Rights Reporting   785
  NGO–CRC Group   16[n66], 42, 43[n28], 48, 52–5, 653–4
    comments regarding   630, 637; consolidation of reports   647; information-finding   93; language issues   650–1
  NGOs   15–16, 46–8, 49, 50, 52–5, 183[n1]
  nomination of candidates   857
  Optional Protocol on the Involvement of Children in Armed Conflict   431–6

Optional Protocol on the Sale of Children, Child Prostitution and Child Pornography 431–2, 437–43
overlapping competences 561–2
Plan of Action for implementation 18, 806, 814, 832, 848, 856, 927
ratification 3, 59, 295[n16], 429, 451–8, 801
  comments regarding 632, 665; independent expert's report 545, 595, 598, 599–600, 603; number of states 306, 448; UN Commission resolution 900–1
refugees 214
regional meetings 762
reservations 430, 690[n29], 763–4, 901, 951
state reporting 5[n12], 7, 35–44, 428, 635
  guidelines 10[n32], 295; number of meetings 607; overdue reports 551, 604
torture 598, 888
training programmes 677
treaty text 414–30
UN Commission resolution 898–913
UNICEF 100, 641, 651, 791, 859
  CRC/UNICEF link 84, 92
women's rights 565
see also Committee on the Rights of the Child
Convention on the Status of Stateless Persons 995–6
Convention on the Suppression and Punishment of the Crime of Apartheid 529, 551, 595–6, 714, 726
cooperation
  between treaty bodies 294–5, 527, 538–9, 677
    analysis of standards 292; chairpersons' meetings 302, 786, 863; Conference conclusions 328–9, 334, 336
  CAT Committee and other bodies 941–2
  CAT draft optional protocol 494–5, 496–9
  chairpersons' meetings
    2nd (1989) 732; 3rd (1990) 741, 747; 5th (1994) 780, 782; 6th (1995) 793; 7th (1996) 807; 10th (1998) 843; 11th (1999) 858–9
  CRC and NGOs 40, 41–3, 51, 52
  child protection 428–9, 435, 442, 953, 957
  fact-finding 91–4

holistic approach 36
ILO assistance 276
intergovernmental agencies 579–81
NGOs 40, 41–3, 51, 52, 860, 865
sexual exploitation of children prevention 910
special procedures system 860–1, 866, 929
specialized agencies 32, 624–5, 651–2, 672–3, 876
Coordinadora Nacional de Derechos Humanos 186–7, 220–1
core documents/reports 93, 559–60, 727
Corigliano v. Italy (1982) 261
corporate responsibility 857
Costa Rica, CAT draft optional protocol 502
Cote d'Ivoire, UNICEF programmes 641
Council of Europe 116–17, 255, 535
  Additional Protocol to the European Social Charter Providing for a System of Collective Complaints 474, 475
  advisory opinions 974, 975
  aim of 965, 978
  Central/Eastern Europe membership 265–6, 270–1
  Committee of Ministers 172, 176, 271–2, 975
  Additional Protocol to the European Social Charter 474; *Brogan* case 265; Committee for the Prevention of Torture elections 1003, 1009, 1011; European Social Charter 128–9, 131, 132, 993; follow-up activities 154–5; judgements 117–18, 259, 260, 262–3; legal enforcement 251, 253; monitoring procedure 266–8; sanctions 264; state commitments 115–16
  cultural traditions 542
  European Convention on Human Rights 257, 969, 975, 976
  European Convention for the Prevention of Torture 1006–7, 1009, 1010, 1011, 1012
  European Social Charter 978, 993, 994
  exchange of information 731
  fact-finding methodology 69–70, 95
  follow-up activities 154, 155
  implementation 68, 233[n5]
  legal aid 145

member states 170
overlapping competences 559
political will 169
public emergencies 969
public information 640
reservations to European Convention on
    Human Rights 257
treaty body membership 216[n24]
World Conference against Racism 921
Covenant on Civil and Political Rights *see*
    International Covenant on Civil and
    Political Rights
Covenant on Economic, Social and Cultural
    Rights *see* International Covenant on
    Economic, Social and Cultural Rights
Cox v. Canada (1993) 150[n38]
CPT *see* European Committee for the
    Prevention of Torture and Inhuman or
    Degrading Treatment or Punishment
CRC *see* Committee on the Rights of the
    Child; Convention on the Rights of the
    Child
credibility 333, 552–3, 758
    European Court 172
    fact-finding 111–12
    normative inconsistency 587–8
criminal proceedings
    African Charter on Human and Peoples'
        Rights 1035
    American Convention on Human
        Rights 1020–1, 1022
    American Declaration of the Rights and
        Duties of Man 1016–17
    CCPR 359, 360–1
    children 425–6, 440–1, 899–900, 908–9
    European Convention on Human
        Rights 966–8
    torture offenders 405–6
    see also International Criminal Court
Croatia
    CERD mission 78[n53]
    reports to CEDAW Committee 27
cross-referencing 520, 560–4, 662, 728–9,
    743
Cruz Varas and Others v. Sweden
    (1991) 68[n7], 123, 125[n38], 171
CSCE *see* Conference for Security and
    Cooperation in Europe
CSW *see* United Nations Commission on the
    Status of Women
Cuba
    CAT draft optional protocol 499, 501,
        502, 503

CEDAW Optional Protocol 156[n61]
comments regarding the independent
    expert's report 664, 665, 666–7,
    672–3, 674
cultural rights
    African Charter on Human and Peoples'
        Rights 1033
    American Convention on Human
        Rights 1026
    American Declaration of the Rights and
        Duties of Man 1015
    CEDAW 392
    CERD 348
    CESCR 378–86
    CRC 416, 423–4
    justiciability 160
    lack of awareness 230
    UN Commission resolution 881–7
    women 205
    see also European Social Charter;
        International Covenant on
        Economic, Social and Cultural
        Rights
culture of human rights 37–8, 283, 307,
    308–9, 312
Cyprus
    comments regarding independent expert's
        report 630, 631, 643, 646
    European Convention review 272[n77]
    European Social Charter 131
Cyprus v. Turkey cases 124, 128[n53]
Czech Republic, follow-up consultations 239

D. v. United Kingdom (1997) 128[n52]
databases 611, 612, 636, 638–9, 669
    centralized 94
    Centre for Human Rights 576, 592,
        611–12, 626–7, 804–5, 806
    chairpersons' meeting
        recommendations 750–1, 767, 785,
        793, 794
    committee yearbooks 610
    Human Rights Committee 464
    NGOs 334, 336, 807
    treaty body 56
    UNICEF 952
DCI *see* Defence of Children International
De Weer v. Belgium (1980) 259
death penalty 72[n24], 145, 146[n27], 178,
    358, 375–7, 1020
Declaration and Agenda of the World
    Congress against Commercial Sexual
    Exploitation of Children 910, 946, 954

1086 *Index*

Declaration of the Committee of Ministers on the Compliance with Commitments Accepted by Member States of the Council of Europe (1994) 266, 267, 271–2
Declaration on the Elimination of All Forms of Racial Discrimination 345
Declaration on the Elimination of All Forms of Violence against Women 206, 388, 888
Declaration on the Granting of Independence to Colonial Countries and Peoples 345, 353, 373
Declaration and Programme of Action of Culture of Peace 900
Declaration on the Protection of All Persons from Being Subjected to Torture and Other Forms of Cruel, Inhuman or Degrading Treatment or Punishment 888
Declaration on the Protection of All Persons from Enforced Disappearance 77
Declaration on the Protection of Women and Children in Emergency and Armed Conflict 415
Declaration on the Right and Responsibility of Individuals, Groups and Organs of Society to Promote and Protect Universally Recognized Human Rights and Fundamental Freedoms 860
Declaration on the Rights of the Child 415
Declaration on Social and Legal Principles relating to the Protection and Welfare of Children, with Special Reference to Foster Placement and Adoption Nationally and Internationally 415
Declaration of the Vienna International Conference "Combating Child Pornography on the Internet" 910
Defence of Children International (DCI) 296[n18]
Denmark
  CAT 167, 502, 503
  CEDAW reports 10[n35]
  European Convention review 272[n77]
detention *see* imprisonment
developing countries
  advisory services 603
  assistance to 661, 670, 763
  CRC 421, 422, 423
  disabled children 421
  economic, social and cultural rights 379, 883
  expert advice 816
  resources 672

development, right to 1033, 1037
dialogue
  analytical studies 291
  Conference recommendations 334, 335
  quality of 320, 691
  usefulness of 321
  see also constructive dialogue
disabilities
  African Charter on Human and Peoples' Rights 1036
  children 420–1, 906, 958
  European Social Charter 979, 985–6
  independent expert's report 566
disappearance cases 74, 77
discrimination
  American Convention on Human Rights 1026
  CCPR 363
  CESCR 379
  children 415, 905
  European Convention on Human Rights 969
  European Social Charter 992, 1001
  not addressed by committees 566
  see also Convention on the Elimination of All Forms of Discrimination against Women; Convention on the Elimination of All Forms of Racial Discrimination; equal opportunities; racial discrimination
Dombo Beheer B.V. v. The Netherlands (1993) 259[n22]
Dominican Republic
  follow-up consultations 239
  state reporting 11[n39]
DPI *see* United Nations Department of Public Information; United Nations Office of Communications and Public Information
Draft Program of Action in the Field of Juvenile Justice 43[n30]
drug use 424
due process 143, 148–9
duties
  African Charter on Human and Peoples' Rights 1038–9
  American Convention on Human Rights 1028
  American Declaration of the Rights and Duties of Man 1017–18

East Timor, fact-finding 82
Eastern Europe
  Council of Europe membership 265–6, 270–1

European Convention on Human
    Rights 70, 118, 176
  truth commissions 86
Eastern Slavonia, UN field operations 99,
    101
economic rights
  African Charter on Human and Peoples'
    Rights 1033
  American Convention on Human
    Rights 1026
  CEDAW 392
  CERD 348
  CESCR 378–86
  CRC 416
  justiciability 160
  lack of awareness 230
  permeability 587
  UN Commission resolution 881–7
  women 205
  see also International Covenant on
    Economic, Social and Cultural
    Rights
Economic and Social Council
    (ECOSOC) 227, 228, 253, 477, 865
  Beijing Rules 557
  CAT draft optional protocol 491, 897
  CCPR 366, 369
  CEDAW Committee 395
  CESCR 383, 475, 477
  CRC Committee submissions 428, 429
  children's rights 955
  Committee on Economic, Social and
    Cultural Rights 572, 837, 863
  Conference recommendations 338
  consultative status 583–4
  draft optional protocol to CESCR 475,
    477
  fact-finding 81
  follow-up to world conferences 882
  housing special rapporteur 887
  Human Rights Committee 537
  independent expert's report 522
  NGO consultation 49
  normative consistency 586–7
  periodicity of reporting 721
  status of treaty bodies 804
  treaty body participation 929
  UN Charter 384
ECOSOC see Economic and Social Council
Ecuador, follow-up activities 238[n27], 239
education 780, 886–7, 1015, 1036
  African Charter on Human and Peoples'
    Rights 1037
  anti-racism 918, 961

CEDAW 390–1, 392
CERD 348, 349
CESCR 382–3
CRC Committee reporting
    guidelines 36[n1], 39
child labour 908, 957
CRC 422–3, 441
European Social Charter 986, 997
Optional Protocol on the Sale of Children,
    Child Prostitution and Child
    Pornography 441
street children 907
UN Commission resolution 903–4
UNESCO Convention against
    Discrimination 346
United Nations Decade for Human Rights
    Education 791–2
Egypt
  Amnesty International submissions 189
  CAT draft optional protocol 499, 501
  CAT examination 84–5, 87, 95, 225
  CEDAW Optional Protocol 156[n61]
  discriminatory nationality laws 20[n83]
  state party meetings 225
El Salvador
  fact-finding 85, 86
  field operations 78–9, 82, 97, 98, 101
  truth commission 110–11, 112, 113–14
elderly persons 566, 980, 988–9, 999, 1036
electoral rights 363, 390, 1016, 1025–6
employment see work
enforcement 251–4, 305–12
  CCPR Optional Protocol 164
  European Convention on Human
    Rights 255–72
  see also follow-up activities;
    implementation
Engel and Others v. The Netherlands
    (1976) 258[n13]
Ensslin, Baader and Raspe v. Federal Republic
    of Germany (1978) 68[n7], 126[n43]
equal opportunities 979, 987–8, 989, 1015
  see also discrimination
Equatorial Guinea, follow-up
    consultations 239
Errol Johnson v. Jamaica (1994) 165
European Commission Against Racism and
    Intolerance 116
European Commission on Human
    Rights 117, 170, 255, 772
  Akdivar and Others v. Turkey
    (1996) 121[n19], 124[n37]
  Aksoy v. Turkey (1996) 123, 124[n37]
  Aydin v. Turkey (1997) 68[n9]

Çagirga v. Turkey (1995)   124[n37]
conflicts of interest   90
Cruz Varas and Others v. Sweden
    (1991)   68[n7], 123, 171
Cyprus v. Turkey cases   124, 128[n53]
Ensslin, Baader and Raspe v. Federal
    Republic of Germany
    (1978)   68[n7], 126[n43]
fact-finding   68, 69, 70, 79–80, 121–8
Farrel v. The United Kingdom
    (1982)   126[n44]
France, Norway, Denmark, Sweden and The
    Netherlands v. Turkey (1985)   124
Greece v. The United Kingdom
    (1958)   124
The Greek Case (1969)   80, 124
H.L.R. v. France (1997)   70[n14],
    127[n50]
individual complaints   257
interim measures   171
Ireland v. The United Kingdom (1978)   79,
    124, 125[n38, n40]
jurisprudence   536
Kapan v. Turkey (1997)   122[n19]
Klaas v. Germany (1993)   123–4
McCann and Others v. United Kingdom
    (1995)   123
Marcella and Robert Sands v. United
    Kingdom (1981)   68[n7]
margin of appreciation   256
membership rules   216
Mentes v. Turkey (1997)   68[n9],
    70[n15]
Protocol No.11   258[n10, n11]
remuneration of members   574
Sands v. The United Kingdom   126[n42]
Sargin and Yagci v. Turkey
    (1989)   124[n37]
secretariat servicing   576
serious allegations   179
Simon-Herold v. Austria (1971)   126
Stocké v. Germany (1991)   123
Tomasi v. France (1992)   123
workload   176, 177
European Committee for the Prevention of
    Torture and Inhuman or Degrading
    Treatment or Punishment
    (CPT)   132–6, 493, 1002–5, 1007–8
independent expert's report   536,
    559[n45]
membership   216–17, 1003, 1005, 1007–8,
    1009, 1011
European Convention for the Prevention of
    Torture and Inhuman or Degrading

Treatment or Punishment   132–6,
    179–80, 589[n80], 1002–8
CAT Optional Protocol comparison   495,
    496, 497, 500
ratification   1006, 1010, 1012
European Convention for the Protection of
    Human Rights and Fundamental
    Freedoms   115–16, 117–28, 169–80,
    633, 965–77
Eastern/Central European states   70
effectiveness   175–6, 255–72
fact-finding   68, 69, 79–80, 121–8, 135
follow-up activities   154–5, 251, 253
individual complaints   140, 141, 233
judicial developments   173–5
membership rules   216
NGOs   188
petition system   171–3
Protocol No.1   1009–10
Protocol No.2   1011–12
Protocol No.11   116, 117–18, 121–3, 169
    effectiveness   170, 173, 176–7, 179;
    reservations   271; transitional
    arrangements   258[n10, n11]
refugees   213
reservations   179, 256–7, 976
success of   177–9
torture   1002
weaknesses   179–80, 257, 271–2
European Convention on Social and Medical
    Assistance   985, 997
European Court of Human Rights   117–18,
    135, 772, 970–5
Akdivar and Others v. Turkey
    (1996)   121[n19], 124[n37],
    270[n69]
Aksoy v. Turkey (1996)   123, 124[n37],
    174, 270[n69]
Albert and Le Compte v. Belgium
    (1983)   260[n28]
Artico v. Italy (1980)   173[n16], 259
Assenov and Others v. Bulgaria
    (1998)   70[n16]
Aydin v. Turkey (1997)   68[n9]
B. v. The United Kingdom
    (1988)   260[n28]
Berrehab v. The Netherlands (1988)   259
Bozano v. France (1986)   261
Brannigan and McBride v. The United
    Kingdom (1993)   265[n53]
Brogan and Others v. The United Kingdom
    (1988)   264–5, 270
Castells v. Spain (1992)   261[n34]

Chahal v. The United Kingdom
  (1996)   69[n10], 69[n14], 174–5
Chorherr v. Austria (1993)   69[n12],
  257[n6]
conflicts of interest   90
Corigliano v. Italy (1982)   261
Cruz Varas and Others v. Sweden
  (1991)   68[n7], 123, 125[n38], 171
D. v. United Kingdom (1997)   128[n52]
damages   73
De Weer v. Belgium (1980)   259
Dombo Beheer B.V. v. The Netherlands
  (1993)   259[n22]
effectiveness   175–6, 255
Engel and Others v. The Netherlands
  (1976)   258[n13]
fact-finding   67, 68, 69, 70, 79, 122–8
follow-up procedure   154–5
Georgiadis v. Greece (1997)   172[n12]
Golder v. The United Kingdom (1975)   258
The Greek Case (1969)   264
Guillot v. France (1996)   69[n13]
Guincho v. Portugal (1980)   258[n14]
H.L.R. v. France (1997)   70[n14]
increasing challenges to   180
individual complaints   233, 258–9
Ireland v. The United Kingdom
  (1978)   260–1
judgements   258–9, 260–3, 264–5, 270
judicial developments   173–5
jurisprudence   536
Karakaya v. France (1995)   259
Klaas and Others v. Germany
  (1978)   173[n17], 256[n3]
Klaas v. Germany (1993)   123–4
Kremzow v. Austria (1993)   259[n22]
legal enforcement   251–2
Loizidou v. Turkey (1995)   173[n19, n20],
  256[n4], 270[n69]
Loukanov v. Bulgaria (1997)   270
McCann and Others v. United Kingdom
  (1995)   123
McElduff and Others v. United Kingdom
  (1998)   70[n14]
McGoff v. Sweden (1984)   260[n28]
Manifattura and Others v. Italy
  (1992)   261[n34]
Marckx v. Belgium (1979)   233[n5], 260,
  261, 262, 270
margin of appreciation   256
membership rules   216
Mentes v. Turkey (1997)   68[n9],
  70[n15]
monitoring system   264–5

Moreira De Azevedo v. Portugal
  (1991)   259[n22]
NGOs   173
Olsson v. Sweden (No.1) (1988)   262
Olsson v. Sweden (No.2) (1992)   262
Pakelli v. Federal Republic of Germany
  (1983)   260[n28]
Pauwels v. Belgium (1985)   260[n28]
Piersack v. Belgium (1984)   259[n21]
Pine Valley Development Ltd and Others v.
  Ireland (1993)   172[n11]
Protocol No.11   170, 176–7
reform   169
Ringeisen v. Austria (1972)   259[n23]
Schönenberger and Durmaz v. Switzerland
  (1988)   259
secretariat servicing   576
settlements   171–2
Soering v. The United Kingdom
  (1989)   173[n18], 260
Stocké v. Germany (1991)   123
Stran Greek Refineries and Stratis
  Andreadis v. Greece (1994)   172
success of   177–9
Sunday Times v. The United Kingdom
  (1980)   258[n14]
Tinnelly & Sons Ltd. v. United Kingdom
  (1998)   70[n14]
Tomasi v. France (1992)   123, 172[n12]
Tsirlis and Kouloumpas v. Greece
  (1997)   172[n12]
Vermeire v. Belgium (1991)   262
X v. Federal Republic of Germany
  (1965)   256[n4]
Yagci and Saragin v. Turkey
  (1995)   270[n69]
European Social Charter   128–32, 481,
  559[n45], 978–1001
  additional protocol   474, 478
  individual complaints   479
European Union   85–6, 632
evidentiary standards   68–9, 73, 108–9, 112,
  114, 126, 405
expertise   12–15, 193–4, 223–4, 226, 571,
  765–6
  advisory services   615
  allocation by subject area   588–9
  CAT Subcommittee   507
  CEDAW Committee   31
  CRC Committee   38[n5]
  European Committee for the Prevention of
    Torture   136, 1005
  independence   253
  ratification procedure   546

secretariat 577–8
extradition 173, 404, 405, 407, 439–40

fact-finding 65–95, 294, 322–5
  Belgrade Rules 110[n18]
  bias 65, 86–91, 103
  credibility 111–12
  European Convention on Human Rights 116, 121–8
  European Convention for the Prevention of Torture 133–6
  European Social Charter 130–2
  Inter-American human rights system 106–9
  International Law Association report 693
  Jamaica 240
  on-site visits 79–80, 81–5, 92, 95, 97–104, 324
  situations/patterns 66–7, 79–86
  judicial methods 79–81; non-judicial methods 81–6
  specific incidents 66, 67–79
  judicial methods 67–77; non-judicial methods 77–9
  torture investigations 893–5
  see also field operations; follow-up activities
family
  African Charter on Human and Peoples' Rights 1036, 1038
  American Convention on Human Rights 1024
  American Declaration of the Rights and Duties of Man 1014
  CCPR 363
  CEDAW 388, 389, 393
  CESCR 381
  CRC 414, 417, 420, 902
  European Social Charter 979, 980, 986, 989–90, 997, 1000
  privacy rights 968
  see also children; parents
FAO see Food and Agriculture Organization of the United Nations
Farrel v. The United Kingdom (1982) 126[n44]
Faurisson v. France (1993) 150[n38], 165–6
FIAN see Food First Information and Action Network
field operations 82–3, 97–104, 248, 316, 323
  see also on-site visits
financial issues
  African Commission on Human and Peoples' Rights procedural rules 1051
  budget analysis 824–6, 869–70
  CAT 445, 446, 526, 571, 595, 622
  chairpersons' meetings
    2nd (1989) 724, 726–7, 733; 3rd (1990) 741–2, 750; 4th (1992) 759, 766; 5th (1994) 783–4; draft optional protocol 507–8
  CERD 445, 446, 526, 571, 595, 622
  chairpersons' meetings
    2nd (1989) 724, 733; 3rd (1990) 741–2, 750; 4th (1992) 759, 766; 5th (1994) 783–4; General Assembly resolution 932, 933–4
  funding of chairpersons' meetings 788
  General Assembly Resolution 445
  independent expert's report 520–1, 571
  reforms 617, 619
  state arrears 847, 851
  Third Decade to Combat Racism and Racial Discrimination 918
  UN Commission resolution 874
  World Conference against Racism 921
Finland
  CAT draft optional protocol 503
  comments regarding the independent expert's report 630, 631–2, 634, 636, 637, 646, 650
  European Convention review 272[n77]
  individual complaints 150–1
  Kivenmaa v. Finland (1990) 150–1
  law changes 251
follow-up activities 233–49, 251–4, 277–83, 290, 325–6
  CCPR violations 72[n23]
  CESCR draft optional protocol 486, 487
  concluding observations 652
  Conference recommendations 337–8, 339–40
  exchange of information 861
  independent expert's report 550
  individual complaints 144, 151–5, 339–40
  International Labour Organization 273–6, 277
  International Law Association report 686, 694, 698
  NGOs 316
  state reporting 293–4, 319
  time required for 730
  see also enforcement; fact-finding; implementation; monitoring

Food and Agriculture Organization of the United Nations (FAO) 580[n67], 602, 603, 728
Food First Information and Action Network (FIAN) 229
Fourth World Conference on Women (Beijing 1995) 11, 24, 30, 32, 196, 943–4
　follow up to 882
　girl child rights 947, 948, 949
　impact on ratifications 599
　NGOs 198[n6]
　non-involvement of CEDAW Committee 792
　see also Beijing Declaration and Platform for Action
France
　Bozano v. France (1986) 261
　European Convention review 272[n77]
　follow-up activities 238[n27], 239
　Guillot v. France (1996) 69[n13]
　H.L.R. v. France (1997) 70[n14], 127[n50]
　Karakaya v. France (1995) 259
　Tomasi v. France (1992) 123, 172[n12]
France, Norway, Denmark, Sweden and The Netherlands v. Turkey (1985) 124
freedom of assembly
　African Charter on Human and Peoples' Rights 1035
　American Convention on Human Rights 1024
　American Declaration on the Rights and Duties of Man 1016
　CCPR 362
　CRC 418
　European Convention on Human Rights 968–9
　Finland case 150–1
　Hong Kong 151[n41]
freedom of association
　African Charter on Human and Peoples' Rights 1035
　American Convention on Human Rights 1024
　American Declaration on the Rights and Duties of Man 1016
　CCPR 362–3
　CERD 348
　CESCR 380
　CRC 418
　European Convention on Human Rights 968–9
　European Social Charter 979
　NGOs 582
freedom of expression
　African Charter on Human and Peoples' Rights 1035
　American Convention on Human Rights 1023
　American Declaration of the Rights and Duties of Man 1014
　CCPR 362
　CERD 348
　CRC 417, 418
　European Convention on Human Rights 968
　racial hatred ban 917, 960
freedom of movement 348, 360, 1014, 1025, 1035
freedom of thought, conscience and religion
　African Charter on Human and Peoples' Rights 1035
　American Convention on Human Rights 1023
　CCPR 361–2
　CERD 348
　CRC 418
　European Convention on Human Rights 968
friendly settlement 171, 172, 484–5, 973, 1031, 1032, 1063

GAATW *see* Global Alliance Against Traffic in Women
Gailius v. I.N.S. (1998) 75[n41]
Gambia, CERD review 89[n94]
gender 565, 794–5, 808–9, 822, 849–50, 857
　CAT 940
　children 950
　General Assembly resolutions 936–7, 940, 943, 948, 950
　International Covenants 878, 936–7
　NGOs 195, 196–7, 203–5
　UN Commission resolution 876
　World Conference on Racism 922
　see also CEDAW; women
general comments 190, 224, 226, 328, 835–6
　consultation 750
　ILA recommendations 696–7
　independent expert's report 529–31, 590–1
Geneva Conventions (1949) 506, 888, 890, 911, 954, 1005
Geneva Declaration on the Rights of the Child 414–15
genital mutilation 905–6, 946, 947

genocide
  Convention on the Prevention and
    Punishment of the Crime of
    Genocide 80, 358
  Rwanda 83, 98–9, 103
Georgia
  CAT draft optional protocol 503
  European Convention on Human
    Rights 170
  European Convention on the Prevention
    of Torture 133[n74]
  response to concluding
    observations 293[n11]
  UN field presence 99
Georgiadis v. Greece (1997) 172[n12]
Germany
  avoidance of UN scrutiny 184
  *Ensslin, Baader and Raspe v. Federal
    Republic of Germany*
    (1978) 68[n7], 126[n43]
  Klaas and Others v. Germany
    (1978) 173[n17], 256[n3]
  Klaas v. Germany (1993) 123–4
  Pakelli v. Federal Republic of Germany
    (1983) 260[n28]
  Stocké v. Germany (1991) 123
  X v. Federal Republic of Germany
    (1965) 256[n4]
girl child 903, 904, 905–6, 946–9
Global Alliance Against Traffic in Women
  (GAATW) 199
Golder v. The United Kingdom (1975) 258
governance 280–1, 283
Grand Council of the Crees (of
  Quebec) 630, 654–5
Greece
  CESCR ratification 544[n30]
  European Convention review 272[n77]
  Georgiadis v. Greece (1997) 172[n12]
  Greece v. The United Kingdom
    (1958) 124
  The Greek Case (1969) 80, 124, 264
  *Stran Greek Refineries and Stratis
    Andreadis v. Greece* (1994) 172
  Tsirlis and Kouloumpas v. Greece
    (1997) 172[n12]
Greece v. The United Kingdom (1958) 124
The Greek Case (1969) 80, 124, 264
Group of Three 529, 726
Guatemala
  CAT draft optional protocol 503
  field operations 97–8, 101, 103
  witness confidentiality 111
Guillot v. France (1996) 69[n13]

Guincho v. Portugal (1980) 258[n14]
Guinea Bissau, CESCR
  ratification 544[n30]
Guyana
  CCPR Optional Protocol
    denunciation 153[n46]
  death penalty 72[n24]

Habitat International Coalition (HIC) 229
Hague Convention on the Civil Aspects of
  Child Abduction 437–8
Hague Convention on Jurisdiction,
  Applicable Law, Recognition,
  Enforcement and Co-operation in
  Respect of Parental Responsibility and
  Measures for the Protection of
  Children 438
Hague Convention on the Protection of
  Children and Co-operation with
  Respect to Intercountry Adoption 437
Hague Convention on the Protection of
  Cultural Property in the Event of
  Armed Conflict 494
Haiti
  advisory services 614
  CCPR ratification 544[n30]
  CRC Committee follow-up
    activities 245[n52]
  field operations 83, 97, 98, 101, 102, 103
  reporting mechanism 60
  truth commission 113
  UN Security Council enforcement 253
  witness confidentiality 111
Hamilton v. Jamaica (1988) 241[n38]
health issues
  African Charter on Human and Peoples'
    Rights 1036
  American Declaration of the Rights and
    Duties of Man 1015
  CEDAW 392
  CESCR 381–2
  children 421–2, 902–3, 952
  European Social Charter 979, 981, 984
Herzegovina
  Dayton Agreement 633
  Human Rights Chamber 251
  UN field presence 99, 100
  see also Bosnia-Herzegovina
HIC *see* Habitat International Coalition
HIV/AIDS 674, 822, 858–9, 865, 883
  independent expert's report 539, 566
  Joint United Nations Programme on
    (UNAIDS)
    chairpersons' meeting 822, 858–9;

comments on independent expert's
  report 664, 665, 668, 670, 673,
  674–5; young people 900
 young people 900, 903, 952
H.L.R. v. France (1997) 70[n14], 127[n50]
holistic implementation 36–7, 44
Honduras, CESCR ratification 544[n30]
Honduras Disappearance Cases 107–8
Hong Kong
 Human Rights Committee 212[n8],
  294[n14]
 right to assembly 151[n41]
 state reporting 7
honoraria 12, 521, 574, 821, 836–7, 929
housing rights 348, 885, 887, 980, 991
HRFOR *see* Human Rights Field Operation
  in Rwanda
Hugo van Alphen v. The Netherlands
  (1988) 237
Human Rights Act (1998) 269[n65]
Human Rights Commission *see* United
  Nations Commission on Human Rights
Human Rights Committee 363–9, 633, 801
 advisory services 280
 African members 215
 Arevalo et al. v. Colombia
  (1984) 236[n16]
 Ashby v. Jamaica (1994) 147[n29]
 backlog 300
 CAT Committee membership 407
 CCPR First Optional Protocol 70–1,
  372–3, 461–4, 484, 485, 529
 CCPR Second Optional Protocol 376
 Coeriel and Aurick v. The Netherlands
  (1991) 237
 collaboration with other treaty bodies 92
 Colombia appearances before 211–12
 communications workload 531–2, 533,
  655
 concluding observations 625
 Cox v. Canada (1993) 150[n38]
 critiques of state records 222–3
 cross-referencing 728–9
 enforcement 251, 254
 Errol Johnson v. Jamaica (1994) 165
 examination of state without report 606
 exchange of information 710–11
 fact-finding 66[n2], 67, 70–2
 Faurisson v. France (1993) 150[n38],
  165–6
 follow-up activities 234–43, 246, 278, 486,
  487, 652
 gender equality 206

General Assembly resolution 935, 936,
  937, 938
general comments 530, 531
Global Plan of Action 18
group complaints 479
Guidelines for the Exercise of their
  Functions by Members 215–16,
  836
Hamilton v. Jamaica (1988) 241[n38]
harmonization of reports 563[n52]
Hugo van Alphen v. The Netherlands
  (1988) 237
individual complaints xix, 94–5, 145–55,
  162, 163–6, 818
 CESCR draft optional protocol 479;
  First Optional Protocol 372–3,
  461–4; International Law
  Association report 688–9, 697, 698;
  number of cases 327
influence of 537–8
interim measures 484
International Convention on the
  Protection of the Rights of Migrant
  Workers and Members of Their
  Families 621
Ireland 7
joint statements 835
jurisprudential issues 210, 212, 214, 590
Kandu-Bo et al. v. Sierra Leone
  (1998) 147[n29]
Kennedy v. Trinidad & Tobago
  (1999) 153[n46]
Kindler v. Canada (1991) 150[n38]
Kivenmaa v. Finland (1990) 150–1
K.N. v. Switzerland (1997) 147[n29]
Kulomin v. Hungary (1992) 71[n20]
Laureano v. Peru (1993) 71[n19]
limited periodic reports 619
Lubicon Lake Band v. Canada
  (1984) 147[n29]
meeting arrangements 572–3, 683, 684,
  695
membership 364–5, 369, 574, 618
national courts' decision-making 326–7
new functions 541
Ng v. Canada (1991) 147[n30], 150[n38]
NGOs 49, 93, 184–5, 191, 209
normative consistency 587
overlapping competences 561, 562, 761,
  773
Páez v. Colombia (1985) 236[n16]
Pauger v. Austria (1990) 237[n18]
payment of members 574, 618
Peru 186, 187, 220–1, 245

Piandiong v. Philippines (1999) 147[n29]
Pratt v. Attorney-General for Jamaica (1993) 146[n27]
pre-sessional working group 14, 54
problems 524–5
public information 296, 612–13
regional human rights organizations 808
reporting period 318
reservations 791, 831
secretariat servicing 575, 576–7
self-determination 480–1
Singh v. Canada (1998) 147[n29]
special reports 615–16
specific issues 566
state reporting 8–9, 19, 290–1, 292[n10], 571, 635
   backlog 848, 852; chairpersons' meetings 706, 709, 711, 714, 719–21; concluding observations 6[n14]; criticism of 685–6; delay between submission and examination 608; experts 12; guidelines 928; NGO participation 15; overdue reports 604, 605; pre-sessional working group 14; technical assistance 712, 713–14; yearbooks 610
Stewart v. Canada (1993) 150[n38], 165
technical briefing costs 869
terminology 477
Toonen v. Australia (1992) 150[n38], 241
Tunisia dialogue with 684–5
UN Commission resolution 877, 878–9, 880
UNICEF relationship 859
urgent action procedure 51
visits to Hong Kong 294[n14]
Yearbooks 626, 636, 669
see also International Covenant on Civil and Political Rights
Human Rights Field Operation in Rwanda (HRFOR) 83, 99, 101[n9]
Human Rights Watch 201, 492
Hungary
   European Convention review 272[n77]
   Kulomin v. Hungary (1992) 71[n20]
HURIST (Human Rights Strengthening) programme 843, 859, 861

ICJ *see* International Court of Justice
ILA *see* International Law Association
ILO *see* International Labour Organization
IMF *see* International Monetary Fund
immigration *see* migrant workers
implementation xviii, xix, 233–4, 758, 795–6
   advisory services 714
   CAT draft optional protocol 507
   CCPR 369
   CEDAW 944, 945
   CESCR 722, 790–1
   Conference recommendations 338
   CRC 428–9, 806, 951–2
      Optional Protocols 433, 435
   crisis in 306–7, 596, 600, 689–90
   draft Plan of Action 848–9, 863–4
   European Social Charter 993
   fact-finding 65–95
   follow-up activities 235, 237, 240
   General Assembly resolutions 925–30
   indicators 864, 867
   International Covenants 369, 722, 790–1, 935, 937
   International Law Association report 682–3, 686, 687–8, 689–90
   national 210–13
   NGO role 209–17, 220, 225–6
   problems 333
   state reporting 3–21, 547
      CEDAW 23–34; CRC Committee 35–44; NGOs 45–56, 57–62
   state responsibility 277
   treaty body advice to states 294
   UN Commission resolution 873–6
   UN General Assembly resolution 444–7
   see also enforcement; follow-up activities
implied powers doctrine 234–5, 240, 252, 833
imprisonment
   American Convention on Human Rights 1020, 1021
   American Declaration of the Rights and Duties of Man 1016–17
   CCPR 359–60
   children 424–5, 909
   European Convention on Human Rights 966–7
   torture offenders 405, 406
incident facts 66, 67–79
independence of treaty body members 12–15, 214–17, 253, 340, 691, 822–3, 836
independent expert's report xix, 4–5, 193, 445, 865, 926
   comments regarding 629–77
   final report 593–629

interim report   515–92
India
   avoidance of UN scrutiny   184
   CEDAW Optional Protocol   156[n61]
   CERD reports   90
   CRC Committee visit   801
   gendered violations of CCPR   199
   implementation issues   687–8
   NGO critiques of   222–3
indigenous peoples   423, 558, 654, 685
individual complaints   xviii, xix, 139–62, 818, 848, 852
   accessibility/awareness of   143, 144–5
   African Commission on Human and Peoples' Rights   1042–3, 1064–7
   CAT   410–11, 465–6
   CAT Committee   166–7
   CCPR
      First Optional Protocol   372–3, 461–4; Second Optional Protocol   376
   CEDAW Optional Protocol   398–400
   CERD   352, 467
   CESCR draft optional protocol   478, 479–80, 482, 483
   comments regarding   633, 655
   Conference conclusions   326–8, 338–40, 341
   consolidated committee proposal   299, 300–1, 329–30, 341
   decision-making   143, 149–51, 164, 165, 166, 328
   enforcement of decisions   233, 251
   European Convention on Human Rights   257–9
   European Court of Human Rights   972
   fact-finding   78, 79, 94
   follow-up activities   235, 249
   Human Rights Committee   71–2, 94, 95, 163–6, 372–3, 531–2
   implementation   3–4
   International Law Association report   688–9, 697–9
   NGO role   187–90
   speed of procedures   143, 146–7
   staffing requirements   832
Indonesia, reservations to CRC   690[n29]
information and communication technologies   526–7, 820, 919
INSTRAW see International Research and Training Institute for the Advancement of Women
Inter-American Commission on Human Rights   105–10, 140[n9], 637, 772, 1028–32

exchange of information   731
fact-finding   70, 71, 72–3, 81, 323
Honduras Disappearance Cases   107–8
jurisprudence   536, 590
Marzioni v. Argentina (1996)   71[n21]
NGO participation   654
see also American Convention on Human Rights
Inter-American Convention on the Prevention, Punishment and Eradication of Violence against Women   140[n9]
Inter-American Court of Human Rights   105, 107–9, 648, 772
   fact-finding   73–4, 80
   jurisprudence   536, 590
   Protocol of San Salvador   474
   see also American Convention on Human Rights
Inter-American human rights system   105–14, 216
Inter-Church Committee for Refugees   630, 647–8, 654
inter-country adoption   420
Inter-Parliamentary Union (IPU)   803, 815
intergovernmental organizations (IGOs)
   African Commission on Human and Peoples' Rights   1047, 1058
   anti-racism   918, 919, 922, 960, 962
   bias   90, 91
   CEDAW   945
   CRC Committee   47
   child refugees   420
   children in armed conflict   912, 956
   enforcement measures   252
   fact-finding   76, 78, 79, 81–3, 85–7, 97
   independent expert's report   521, 579–81
   ratification of treaties   602
Interights   188, 211
interim measures
   CEDAW Optional Protocol   159, 399
   CESCR draft optional protocol   484
   European Convention on Human Rights   171
   individual complaints   143, 147
International Bill of Human Rights   282, 877, 935
   see also International Covenant on Civil and Political Rights; International Covenant on Economic, Social and Cultural Rights; Universal Declaration of Human Rights
International Committee of the Red Cross   136, 491, 506, 908, 1005

International Conference on Combating
  Child Pornography on the Internet
  (Vienna 1999) 437, 910
International Conference on Population and
  Development (Cairo 1994) 32, 540,
  882, 946, 949
International Conference of the Red
  Cross 433, 911, 913
International Convention on the Protection
  of the Rights of Migrant Workers and
  Members of Their Families 560, 617,
  621, 918
  amendments 623, 649, 817–18
  ratification 3[n4]
International Court of Justice (ICJ)
  advisory opinion on reservations 769
  CAT arbitration 413
  CERD 354
  fact-finding 80
  implied powers principle 833
  judge selection 639
  membership rules 216, 217
  UN Court for Human Rights
    proposal 301
International Covenant on Civil and Political
  Rights (CCPR) xvii
  amendments 163, 370
  analytical study on duplication 928
  Canadian Supreme Court references
    to 309–10, 311
  CESCR comparison 230
  children 414, 415, 900, 909
  core document submissions 560[n46]
  denunciation by Democratic People's
    Republic of Korea 815–16
  enforcement of decisions 233, 234
  European Convention comparison 251,
    272
  fact finding 66[n2]
  family equality 200
  First Optional Protocol (OPT) xviii, 135,
    372–4
    amendments 374; CESCR draft
      optional protocol comparison 476,
      477–8, 479, 480–1, 483–8; constraints
      to 163–4, 165–6; European
      Convention comparison 251;
      follow-up activities 234–6, 237, 240,
      242, 243, 246, 278; individual
      complaints 71–2, 140, 143–6, 152,
      157, 461–4, 633, 688–9; NGO
      activity 188; number of
      communications 818;
    permeability 587;
    ratifications 451, 452–8
  freedom of assembly 150–1
  gender issues 199, 206
  General Assembly resolution 935–8
  governance 281
  honoraria payments 574
  independent expert's report 524
  individual complaints xix, 688
  Iran 682–3
  lack of expertise in the state 709
  membership 691
  monitoring procedures 801
  NGO role 209, 282
  non-ratification of 518, 595, 598–601,
    759, 773, 816, 834
  Optional Protocols
    General Assembly resolution 935, 936,
      937, 938; UN Commission
      resolution 877, 878, 879, 880
  overlapping competences 300, 559, 561–2
  Plan of Action 848–9, 852, 863, 867
  ratification 306, 370, 451–8, 542, 544–5,
    602, 714–15
  resourcing 288[n3]
  Second Optional Protocol
    (OPT2) 375–7, 451, 452–8
  self-determination 480–1
  sexual equality 387, 398
  slavery 857
  state reporting 5[n12], 295, 366, 524, 720
    number of meetings 552, 607; overdue
      reports 551, 604
  torture 403, 598–9, 888
  treaty text 356–71
  UN Commission resolution 877–80
  withdrawals from 633
  women's rights 565
  see also Human Rights Committee
International Covenant on Economic, Social
  and Cultural Rights (CESCR) xvii,
  227–30
  amendments 385–6, 471–89
  analytical study on duplication 928
  Canadian Supreme Court references
    to 309
  children's rights 414, 415
  complaints procedure changes 596
  draft optional protocol 160–2, 471–89,
    533, 884
  General Assembly resolution 935–8
  governance 281
  Human Rights Commission
    relationship 539

implementation 790–1, 814
individual complaints 4, 141, 155, 160–2, 590, 655, 698
International Law Association
 report 689, 695, 698
legal existence of Committee on Economic, Social and Political Rights 801
NGOs 49
non-ratification 518, 595, 598–601, 759, 773, 816, 834
non-reporting 676
overlapping competences 559, 561, 562, 563
permeability 587
Plan of Action 814, 832, 848, 856, 927
ratification 306, 385, 451–8, 542, 544–5, 602, 714–15, 883
reservations 884
Sessional Working Group 529, 707, 710, 711, 712, 714
sexual equality 387, 398
state reporting 5[n12], 383, 547–8
 chairpersons' meetings
  1st (1984) 707, 710, 711, 712, 714;
  2nd (1989) 722, 729;
 guidelines 295; number of meetings 552, 607; overdue reports 550[n39], 551, 604
treaty text 378–86
UN Commission resolutions 877–80, 881–7
women's rights 565
World Summit for Social Development 779
see also Committee on Economic, Social and Cultural Rights
International Criminal Court
 CAT draft optional protocol 494
 children in armed conflict 432
 crimes against children 911–12, 954–5
 Rome Statute 888
 treaty-based crimes 656–7
 UN Court for Human Rights proposal 301
International Criminal Tribunals 74–5, 95
 Akeyesu case (1998) 74[n37]
 Former Yugoslavia 67, 74[n37], 113, 217[n30]
 Prosecutor v. Delacic et al. (1997) 74[n37]
 Rwanda 67, 74[n37], 83, 111
International Decade for a Culture of Peace and Non-Violence 900
International Federation of ACAT (Action of

Christians for the Abolition of Torture) 492
International Human Rights Court proposal 301, 330, 341
International Human Rights Law Group 196
International Labour Organization (ILO)
 CESCR draft optional protocol 472, 475, 478, 484
 chairperson meetings 732, 737
 CRC Committee relationship 625
 comments regarding independent expert's report 630, 632
 Convention concerning Discrimination in respect of Employment and Occupation 273, 346
 Convention concerning Equal Remuneration for Men and Women Workers for Work of Equal Value 562–3
 Convention concerning Freedom of Association and Protection of the Right to Organize 273, 362–3, 380, 560, 632
 Convention Concerning the Prohibition and Immediate Action for the Elimination of the Worst Forms of Child Labour 433, 438, 881–2, 883, 899, 908, 957
 Convention on the Right to Organize and Collective Bargaining 273, 560
 cooperation 732, 747
  with CRC Committee 625; with other agencies 580, 652; with treaty bodies 625, 793
 database 612, 627, 638, 669, 807
 European Social Charter 128, 130, 132
 expert group 592
 fact-finding 66
 follow-up activities 234, 273–6, 277
 independent expert's report 520, 535
 individual complaints 140
 inter-state complaints procedure 476
 jurisprudence CD-ROM 820
 quality of information 859
 ratification of treaties 602, 632, 815
 regional advisors 279, 615, 642
 secretariat servicing 576
 standards 279–80, 543, 564
 state reporting 294[n15], 319, 556, 803
 statistical reports 728
 training programmes 224, 746
 World Conference on Human Rights 772

International Law Association (ILA)
  Belgrade Rules   67[n4], 74, 82, 110[n18], 113[n27]
  Helsinki Conference (1996)   681–99
  implementation crisis   596
International Law Commission   574, 830, 831, 849
International Monetary Fund (IMF)   18, 42[n25], 580, 728, 736
International Programme on the Elimination of Child Labour (IPEC)   859
International Research and Training Institute for the Advancement of Women (INSTRAW)   611
International Service for Human Rights   219, 221, 224–5
International Women's Rights Watch (IWRAW)   7, 16[n66], 31, 49, 93, 747
  Committee on Economic, Social and Political Rights   229
  gender integration   850
  national women's groups   191
  shadow reports   296[n18]
  state reporting guidelines   24
Internet
  Centre for Human Rights website   611–12, 626–7, 806
  chairpersons' meetings   785
  child pornography   437, 910
  European Court website   176
  Office of the High Commissioner for Human Rights website   10[n36], 58, 60, 248, 292[n10], 296, 637–9, 669, 820
  racism   919, 959, 962
  training/educational materials   640
  United Nations Division for the Advancement of Women website   10[n36], 17
  United Nations High Commissioner for Refugees website   612, 638–9, 669
  United Nations Human Rights website   676–7
IPEC see International Programme on the Elimination of Child Labour
Iran, Islamic Republic of
  CCPR   682–3
  ILO criticism   273–4, 275
  World Conference against Racism   921
Iraq, human rights field presence   98, 101
Ireland
  Pine Valley Development Ltd and Others v. Ireland (1993)   172[n11]
  state reporting   7

Ireland v. The United Kingdom (1978)   79, 124, 125[n38, n40], 260–1
Islamic law   690
Israel, comments regarding the independent expert's report   630, 634, 637, 643, 646, 656
Italy
  Artico v. Italy (1980)   173[n16], 259
  Bozano case   261
  Corigliano v. Italy (1982)   261
  Manifattura and Others v. Italy (1992)   261[n34]
Ivory Coast see Cote d'Ivoire
IWRAW Asia-Pacific   7, 200–1

Jamaica
  Ashby v. Jamaica (1994)   147[n29]
  CCPR Optional Protocol denunciation   153[n46], 633
  dialogue with CRC Committee   685
  Errol Johnson v. Jamaica (1994)   165
  fact-finding mission   240
  follow-up activities   236, 239, 240, 241[n38]
  Hamilton v. Jamaica (1988)   241[n38]
  Human Rights Committee visit   72[n24]
  individual complaints   147[n29], 464
  Pratt v. Attorney-General for Jamaica (1993)   146[n27]
Japan
  CAT draft optional protocol   499
  media coverage of reporting   687
just satisfaction   258, 259, 260, 261, 263, 973
justiciability   158, 160–1, 698–9, 879

Kandu-Bo et al. v. Sierra Leone (1998)   147[n29]
Kapan v. Turkey (1997)   122[n19]
Karakaya v. France (1995)   259
Kennedy v. Trinidad & Tobago (1999)   153[n46]
Kenya, marital rape   206
Kindler v. Canada (1991)   150[n38]
Kivenmaa v. Finland (1990)   150–1
Klaas and Others v. Germany (1978)   173[n17], 256[n3]
Klaas v. Germany (1993)   123–4
K.N. v. Switzerland (1997)   147[n29]
Korea, Republic of
  comments regarding the independent expert's report   630, 633, 636, 647, 650
  denunciation of CCPR   633, 815–16
  follow-up consultations   239

NGOs 224
Kosovo 81
Kremzow v. Austria (1993) 259[n22]
Kulomin v. Hungary (1992) 71[n20]

language issues 548, 610, 650–1, 671–2
   African Commission on Human and Peoples' Rights procedural rules 1052
   CAT 167
   chairpersons' meetings 771, 806, 821
   migrant workers 987
   NGO documents 53
   translation 623–4
Laureano v. Peru (1993) 71[n19]
Lawyers Committee for Human Rights 16[n66], 210, 212
Lebanon, failure to answer treaty body questions 245[n53]
legal aid 145, 152[n44], 171, 309
legal rights
   African Charter on Human and Peoples' Rights 1035
   American Convention on Human Rights 1022, 1026
   American Declaration of the Rights and Duties of Man 1016
   CAT 406
   CCPR 360–1, 363
   CEDAW 392–3
   CRC 425–6, 440–1
   European Convention on Human Rights 967–8
   Optional Protocol on the Sale of Children, Child Prostitution and Child Pornography 440–1
leisure 380, 423–4, 1015
liberty, right to 359, 966–7, 1014, 1021–2, 1035
Libya, criticism of state report by Human Rights Committee 686
life, right to 358, 416, 907, 966, 1014, 1020
Loizidou v. Turkey (1995) 173[n19, n20], 256[n4], 270[n69]
Loukanov v. Bulgaria (1997) 270
Lubicon Lake Band v. Canada (1984) 147[n29]
Luxembourg, European Convention review 272[n76]

McCann and Others v. United Kingdom (1995) 123
McElduff and Others v. United Kingdom (1998) 70[n14]

McGoff v. Sweden (1984) 260[n28]
Madagascar, follow-up consultations 239
Malaysia, reservations to CRC 690[n29]
Malta
   European Convention review 272[n76]
   right to organize 131
Manifattura and Others v. Italy (1992) 261[n34]
Manual on Human Rights Reporting 640, 641, 762, 768, 785, 836, 875, 928
Marcella and Robert Sands v. United Kingdom (1981) 68[n7]
Marckx v. Belgium (1979) 233[n5], 260, 261, 262, 270
Marcu v. I.N.S. (1998) 75[n40]
marriage
   American Convention on Human Rights 1024
   CCPR 363
   CEDAW 381, 390, 393
   CERD 348
   European Convention on Human Rights 969
   minimum age 906, 947
Marzioni v. Argentina (1996) 71[n21]
"massive" violations of human rights 616, 764, 765, 780
maternity 388, 389, 391–2, 979, 983, 1014
Mauritius 215
media 11, 17, 222, 734, 748, 814
   accessibility of treaty body process 322
   African Commission on Human and Peoples' Rights 1063, 1065
   CRC 418–19
   human rights programmes 780
   International Law Association report 687, 694
   NGO role 337
   public information 658
   racism 917
   treaty body activities 841, 846, 851, 858
   see also publicity
membership of treaty bodies 12, 16–17, 297, 328, 340, 341
   bias 90
   CAT Committee 295[n17], 407–8, 411, 618
   CAT Subcommittee 504–6, 509
   CEDAW Committee 12, 13[n46], 31, 216, 328, 393–4
   CERD Committee 349–50
   CRC Committee 427, 622, 650
   conditions of service 574–5
   CRC 901

gender balance 735, 737
General Assembly resolution 929
geographical imbalance 842, 850
government officials 185
Human Rights Committee 364–5, 369
independence 822–3, 836
International Law Association
  recommendations 691
Meetings of Chairpersons 302
NGO input 214–17, 224–5, 226
payment of members 574, 618, 821,
  836–7, 929
technical briefings 746, 751, 819, 846,
  851, 862–3, 866–7, 869–70
UN Commission resolution 876
unequal 674
see also expertise
Mentes v. Turkey (1997) 68[n9], 70[n15]
Mexico
  dialogue with CERD Committee 685
  Inter-American Commission scrutiny 73
MICIVIH see Mission Civil Internationale en Haiti
migrant workers
  children 906, 952
  European Social Charter 979, 986–7, 997
  racism against 915, 960, 961, 962
  see also International Convention on the
    Protection of the Rights of Migrant
    Workers and Members of Their
    Families
*Minister for Immigration and Ethnic Affairs v.
  Teoh* (1996) 211[n5]
minorities see United Nations Sub-
  Commission on Prevention of
  Discrimination and Protection of
  Minorities
MINUGUA (United Nations Mission for the
  Verification of Human Rights in
  Guatemala) 97–8, 101[n9]
Mission Civil Internationale en Haiti
  (MICIVIH) 97, 101[n9], 102, 103
Mission d'observation des Nations Unies en
  El Salvador see ONUSAL
monitoring 315, 316, 322, 803
  CEDAW Committee 33
  CRC Committee 36, 37, 39
  European Convention 264–8
  field operations 82–3, 97–104, 248, 323
  following up reports 319
  independent expert's report 525, 578
  new international instruments 745
  NGOs 56, 204, 653, 803, 804

state reporting 35, 45–6, 547, 548, 553, 567
  see also follow-up activities
Montenegro, ICJ fact-finding 80
Moreira De Azevedo v. Portugal
  (1991) 259[n22]
Morocco
  CAT examination 221–2
  CRC Committee visits 84[n78]
  ILO sanctions 275
  state party meetings 225
  state reporting 10[n38]
  women's rights 203
movement, freedom of 348, 360, 1014, 1025, 1035
Mozambique, UN field operations 100
Myanmar (Burma)
  European Union sanctions 85–6
  ILO Commission of Inquiry 66[n3]
  ILO sanctions 275
  non-ratification of treaties 51[n17]
  UN field operations 101

name, right to a 416, 1024
national courts
  Australia, *Minister for Immigration and
    Ethnic Affairs v. Teoh*
    (1996) 211[n5]
  Canada
    *R. (B.) v. Children's Aid Society of
      Metropolitan Toronto* (1995) 310;
    R. v. Brydges (1990) 309; *R. v.
      Keegstra* (1990) 311; *R. v. L. (D.O.)*
      (1993) 310; *R. v. Milne*
      (1987) 310; *Slaight Communications
      Inc. v. Davidson* (1989) 311[n23];
    United States of America v. Cotroni
      (1989) 310
  fact-finding 76
  New Zealand
    *Tangiora v. Wellington District Legal
      Services Corporation*
      (2000) 145[n22]; *Wellington
      District Legal Services Corporation v.
      Tangiora* (1997) 145[n22]
  United States
    Gailius v. I.N.S. (1998) 75[n41];
    Marcu v. I.N.S. (1998) 75[n40];
    *Siderman de Blake v. Republic of
      Argentina* (1992) 76
national implementation 210–13
nationality 20[n83], 216[n29], 390, 416, 1016, 1025

Nepal
  CCPR Optional Protocol   145
  CRC Committee visit   801
Netherlands
  Berrehab v. The Netherlands (1988)   259
  CAT   167
  Coeriel and Aurick v. The Netherlands (1991)   237
  comments regarding the independent expert's report   630, 632, 646–7
  custody of infants   269–70
  Dombo Beheer B.V. v. The Netherlands (1993)   259[n22]
  Engel and Others v. The Netherlands (1976)   258[n13]
  follow-up replies   236[n15], 237
  Hugo van Alphen v. The Netherlands (1988)   237
  law changes   251
New Zealand
  comments regarding the independent expert's report   660–2, 664, 667–8, 670, 673
  legal aid   145[n22], 152[n44]
  occupational diseases   275
Ng v. Canada (1991)   147[n30], 150[n38]
NGOs *see* non-governmental organizations
Nicaragua, follow-up consultations   239
Nigeria
  dialogue with CERD Committee   685
  ILO sanctions   275
non-governmental organizations (NGOs)   xviii
  Additional Protocol to the European Social Charter Providing for a System of Collective Complaints   474
  African Commission on Human and Peoples' Rights procedural rules   1047, 1048, 1058
  anti-racism   917, 918, 919, 921, 922, 960, 962
  attendance at press conferences   222, 805
  CAT draft optional protocol   491–2
  CEDAW   24, 29, 31, 33, 945
  CESCR draft optional protocol   472
  chairpersons' meetings   773, 782–3, 791, 792, 821–2
  CRC Committee   36, 37, 40, 41–3
  see also non-governmental organizations, NGO-CRC Group
  children
    in armed conflict   912, 956;
    refugees   420; rights   951

comments regarding the independent expert's report
groups present   630; public information   639; state reporting   635, 637, 652, 653–5; universal ratification   633
Committee on Economic, Social and Political Rights   227–30, 722
concluding observations   322, 653
Conference recommendations   336–7, 338, 339
consolidation of reports   647–8
cooperation   860, 865
CRC recognition   46–8
critique of treaty system   288
enforcement measures   252
European Court recognition   173
European Social Charter   129, 130
European Torture Convention   136
fact-finding   66[n3], 76, 79, 81, 86–7, 95
  bias   90; collaboration   91, 93–4; Conference discussion   323–5; field operations   97, 101, 103
flexible meeting arrangements   819, 845
follow-up activities   238, 278, 282–3, 316, 326, 652
gender-sensitive strategies   905
General Assembly resolution   929
girl child objectives   947, 948
growing burden on treaty bodies   617
impartiality   675
implementation of treaty systems   209–17, 220, 225–6
independent expert's report   521, 581–6
individual complaints   145, 327, 339, 479
informal reports   614
information   637, 684, 746–7, 751, 768, 802
Inter-American human rights system   105, 106
international   211, 212, 226, 324–5, 337
  CRC Committee   53; individual complaints   339; monitoring   803; state reporting   317; women's rights   197–8, 200–3
language issues   650–1
members of treaty bodies   340
monitoring   322, 803, 804
national NGOs   186, 210–12, 219, 226, 324–5, 337
  CRC Committee   47–8, 50, 53; individual complaints   339; monitoring   803; state

reporting 57, 60, 317; women's
rights 197–200, 207
NGO-CRC Group 16[n66], 42,
43[n28], 48, 52–5, 653–4
 comments regarding the independent
 expert's report 630, 637;
 consolidation of reports 647;
 information-finding 93; language
 issues 650–1
publicity 734
role 183–94, 219–26, 333, 653–5, 821–2,
876
state reporting 7, 8, 13, 15–17, 20, 45–62
 attendance 687; CEDAW 24, 29, 31,
 33; CRC Committee 36, 37, 40,
 41–3; comments regarding 635,
 637, 652, 653–5; Committee on
 Economic, Social and Political
 Rights 722; committee
 recommendations 290; concluding
 observations 694; Conference
 conclusions 317, 334–5; follow-up
 activities 282, 652; independent
 expert's report 549, 635, 637;
 information-sharing 88;
 International Law Association
 report 683, 684, 687, 690, 692–3;
 publicity 293; role of 183, 184–5,
 186, 211; technical assistance 292
treaty system changes 296
women's rights 195–207, 390
normative consistency 521, 586–9, 648, 742,
744
North–South XXI 630, 633, 635, 639, 651,
652
Northern Ireland
 CAT draft optional protocol 503
 NGO publicity 187
Norway
 comments regarding the independent
 expert's report 630
 European Convention review 272[n76]
 legal aid 171

OAS *see* Organization of American States
OAU *see* Organization of African Unity
Office of the High Commissioner for Human
 Rights (OHCHR) [formerly Centre for
 Human Rights]
 absence of support 210
 advisory services 641, 875, 879
 Annual Appeal 18, 921
 assistance programmes 43, 247, 660–1,
 816, 830, 844

 best practices 248
 CERD Committee collaboration 933
 CRC Committee 901
 Colombian field office 211–12
 computerization 296
 concluding observations 61
 Conference recommendations 336, 337–8,
 339
 cooperation with other agencies 651, 672,
 673, 807, 876, 901
 coordination of treaty bodies 867
 corporate responsibility 857
 economic, social and cultural rights 882
 enforcement 253–4
 establishment of 279, 777
 expertise 226
 fact-finding 82, 323
 field operations 104
 follow-up activities 242, 243, 325–6,
 337–8
 human rights treaty series 863, 866
 implementation indicators 864, 867
 increase in legal staff proposal 662
 individual complaints 327, 339
 internal Task Force 841
 International Covenants 879, 880, 938
 jurisprudence handbook 856, 866
 memorandum of understanding with
 UNDP 843, 851, 859
 NGOs 50, 93
 public information 640
 racism project team 918
 referrals to 59, 62
 reform 814
 resources 166, 668, 793, 794, 847, 926
 restructuring 819, 831–2, 846–7
 secretariat servicing 846–7
 Special Rapporteur on child
 exploitation 911
 staffing 819, 847
 state reporting 17, 18, 24
 torture 889, 891
 training programmes 224, 641, 642, 819,
 836
 universal ratification 631, 675, 815, 850,
 861
 website 10[n36], 58, 60, 248, 292[n10],
 296, 637–9
 women's rights 32, 906
 see also Centre for Human Rights; United
 Nations High Commissioner for
 Human Rights
Olsson v. Sweden (No.1) (1988) 262
Olsson v. Sweden (No.2) (1992) 262

on-site visits
    CAT Committee   409
    CAT draft optional protocol   495, 496–7, 499–502, 506–7, 509, 510–12
    CEDAW Committee   400
    CERD Committee   78
    CESCR draft optional protocol   485
    CRC Committee   40–1
    European Committee for the Prevention of Torture   134, 135–6, 1002, 1003–4
    fact-finding   79–80, 81–5, 92, 95, 97–104, 324
    follow-up activities   239–40
    individual complaints   161
    Inter-American Commission on Human Rights   72, 106–7
    Working Group on Enforced or Involuntary Disappearances   77
    see also field operations
ONUSAL (La Mission d'observation des Nations Unies en El Salvador)   78–9, 82, 97, 101[n9]
oral hearings
    African Commission on Human and Peoples' Rights   1063
    CAT   167
    Committee on Economic, Social and Political Rights   228
    Conference conclusions   320, 328, 339
    Human Rights Committee   164–5
    individual complaints   148–9, 339
    Inter-American Commission   106
    International Law Association report   692–3
    see also individual complaints
Organization of African Unity (OAU)   535, 632, 1034, 1037
    African Court of Human and Peoples' Rights   1070, 1071, 1072, 1073
    Charter of   1033, 1043, 1044, 1069
    Commission on Human and Peoples' Rights   1039–41, 1044, 1046, 1047, 1053
    ratification of African Charter Protocol   1074
    Specialized Institutions   1057–8
Organization of American States (OAS)   72, 73, 473, 535
    Charter of   1019, 1026, 1029
    Haiti mission   83, 97
    Inter-American Commission on Human Rights   1028, 1029, 1030
    Inter-American human rights system   105, 106, 108

Organization of the Islamic Conference   632
Organization for Security and Cooperation in Europe (OSCE)   81, 99, 190, 266, 272, 603

Páez v. Colombia (1985)   236[n16]
Pakelli v. Federal Republic of Germany (1983)   260[n28]
Pakistan, CRC Committee   685, 801
Panama, follow-up consultations   236[n14], 239
parents   382, 416–17, 418, 419, 421, 902
Pauger v. Austria (1990)   237[n18]
Pauwels v. Belgium (1985)   260[n28]
peace   1037–8
permeability   587
Peru
    American Convention of Human Rights withdrawal   105[n2]
    Amnesty International role   186–7
    enabling law   241
    failure to respond to recommendations   245
    follow-up consultations   239
    Laureano v. Peru (1993)   71[n19]
    NGO role   220–1
    OAS General Assembly   106
    severe violations   73
Philippines
    executions   147[n29]
    Piandiong v. Philippines (1999)   147[n29]
Piandiong v. Philippines (1999)   147[n29]
Piersack v. Belgium (1984)   259[n21]
Pine Valley Development Ltd and Others v. Ireland (1993)   172[n11]
Poland
    CAT draft optional protocol   502
    European Social Charter   129
political rights
    African Charter on Human and Peoples' Rights   1033, 1036, 1037
    American Convention on Human Rights   1025–6
    American Declaration of the Rights and Duties of Man   1016
    CEDAW   390
    CERD   348
    justiciability   160
    women   205
    see also International Covenant on Civil and Political Rights
pornography
    children   424, 431, 437–43

UN resolutions 898, 909–11, 947, 952–4;
    Vienna Declaration 950
Portugal
  Guincho v. Portugal (1980) 258[n14]
  Moreira De Azevedo v. Portugal
    (1991) 259[n22]
poverty
  children 898, 950
  economic, social and cultural rights 883
  European Social Charter 980, 990
  girl child 946
Pratt v. Attorney-General for Jamaica
    (1993) 146[n27]
pre-sessional working groups
  CEDAW Committee 14, 25, 26–7, 54
  CRC Committee 13–14, 47, 54
  Committee on Economic, Social and
      Political Rights 13–14, 227–8, 229
  Human Rights Committee 14, 54
  scheduling of 335
prisoners *see* imprisonment
privacy 361, 418, 441, 968, 1023
Programme of Action for the Prevention of
    the Sale of Children, Child Prostitution
    and Child Pornography 438
propaganda, racist 347–8, 916, 917, 961,
    1023
property rights
  African Charter on Human and Peoples'
      Rights 1036
  American Convention on Human
      Rights 1025
  American Declaration of the Rights and
      Duties of Man 1016
  CERD 348
Prosecutor v. Delacic et al. (1997) 74[n37]
prostitution
  children 424, 431, 437–43
  UN resolutions 898, 909–11, 947, 952–4;
      Vienna Declaration 950
public emergencies
  American Convention on Human
      Rights 1026
  CCPR 357
  European Convention on Human
      Rights 969
  European Social Charter 992, 1001
public information
  chairpersons' meetings
    (1990) 747, 748, 753; (1992) 761–2,
      768–9; (1994) 783; (1995) 791–2;
      (1997) 823; (1999) 858, 865
  Human Rights Committee 296

independent expert's report 523, 527, 550,
    612–14, 627, 639–40, 669–70
UN News Service 858
United Nations Information
    Centres 658–9
publicity
  CAT draft optional protocol 498
  chairpersons' meetings
    (1984) 708; (1989) 734, 737;
    (1990) 752, 753; (1992) 757, 768;
    (1994) 783
  follow-up activities 237–8, 242
  ILO procedures 275, 276
  individual complaints procedure 149,
      152, 153
  International Covenants 938
  NGOs 187, 200, 222
  state reporting 293, 753
  see also media

*R. (B.) v. Children's Aid Society of
    Metropolitan Toronto* (1995) 310
R. v. Brydges (1990) 309
R. v. Keegstra (1990) 311
R. v. L. (D.O.) (1993) 310
R. v. Milne (1987) 310
racial discrimination 388, 914–22, 931–4,
    959–62
  see also Committee on the Elimination of
      All Forms of Racial Discrimination;
      Convention on the Elimination of
      All Forms of Racial Discrimination
racism
  American Convention on Human
      Rights 1023
  children 904
  General Assembly resolutions 931–4,
      959–62
  racial hatred 346, 347, 362
  UN Commission resolution 914–22
ratification xvii-xviii, 3, 20, 51, 220, 306, 315
  African Charter on Human and Peoples'
      Rights 1044, 1045
  Protocol 1074
  CAT 412, 542, 889, 890, 940
    draft optional protocol 496, 508
  CCPR 370, 542, 544, 545
    First Optional Protocol 373–4, 529;
    Second Optional Protocol 375,
      376–7
  CEDAW 295[n16], 396, 598, 599, 944
    Optional Protocol 401
  CERD 354, 919–20, 934
  CESCR 385, 542, 544, 545, 883

draft optional protocol 488
chairpersons' meetings
  (1984) 714–15; (1990) 749;
  (1994) 778; (1995) 791;
  (1997) 815; (1999) 861–2;
  (Feb 1998) 829–30;
  (Sep 1998) 844, 850
comments on independent expert's
  report 631–4, 660, 665, 675–6
Conference recommendations 333
CRC 295[n16], 429, 448, 545, 598–600,
  900–1
Optional Protocols 431–2, 434, 435–6,
  442–3
European Convention on Human
  Rights 271[n71], 976–7
European Convention on the Prevention
  of Torture 1006, 1010, 1012
European Social Charter 991, 994
independent expert's report 518, 541–6,
  595, 598–604, 626, 631
International Covenants 935–6
International Law Association
  report 682, 689–90
Migrant Workers Convention 918
status of 451–8
Red Crescent 433, 908, 911, 913
Red Cross
  International Committee of 136, 491,
    506, 908, 1005
  International Conference of 433, 911, 913
refugees
  CAT 167
  children 420, 907–8, 956
  Convention Relating to the Status of
    Refugees (1951) 75
  European Social Charter 995
  treaty protection 213–14
  UNHCR role 100
  Zaire 28
  see also United Nations High
    Commissioner for Refugees
regional advisors 279, 281, 615, 642–3, 676,
  713
regional human rights bodies 527–8, 535–6,
  589–92, 603, 731, 792–3, 963–1074
religion 361–2, 418, 968, 998, 1014, 1023
reservations
  CAT 413, 889–90, 940
  draft optional protocol 494
  CCPR Second Optional Protocol 375
  CEDAW 200, 396, 763, 944
  CERD 354, 920, 934
  CESCR 884

draft optional protocol 488
chairpersons' meetings
  (1992) 755, 756, 763–4, 769; (1994) 781;
  (1995) 791; (Feb 1998) 830–1;
  (Sep 1998) 849
Conference recommendations 334
CRC 430, 690[n29], 763–4, 901, 951
European Convention on Human
  Rights 179, 256–7, 976
independent expert's report 523
International Covenants 878, 936
International Law Association
  report 690, 696
objection to 316
residence, freedom of 348, 360, 1014, 1025,
  1035
Resident Coordinators 247
resources xx, 166, 288, 289, 296–7
  advisory services 614
  CEDAW Committee 736, 742–3, 784
  chairpersons' meetings
    (1990) 740, 741–3; (1992) 755, 757–8,
    759–60, 766–7; (1994) 783, 784;
    (1999) 856; (Feb 1998) 832–3;
    (Sep 1998) 847, 851
  comments regarding 655, 668
  Conference recommendations 334
  conference servicing 617
  developing countries 672
  enforcement measures 254
  fact-finding 95, 324
  follow-up activities 243, 248–9
  General Assembly resolution 926–7
  imbalances between treaty bodies 801,
    806
  independent expert's report 518, 523, 527,
    575–8, 596, 597
  individual complaints procedures 162
  overlapping competences 562
  ratification of treaties 546, 599, 601, 631
  reduction of 164, 596, 597
  state reporting 17–18, 20, 619, 627
  training programmes 642
  travel to international meetings 804
  truth commissions 112–13
  UN Commission resolution 874
  see also financial issues; secretariat
    servicing
right of reply 1024, 1055
right to life 358, 416, 907, 966, 1014, 1020
right to organize 979, 982
Ringeisen v. Austria (1972) 259[n23]
rural areas 392

Russia
  European Torture Convention 134[n74]
  individual complaints 818
  NGO use of the press 222
Russian Federation
  Amnesty International role 187
  avoidance of UN scrutria 184
  critique of treaty bodies 225
  European Convention on Human Rights 170
  see also Soviet Union, former
Rwanda
  International Criminal Tribunal 67, 74[n37], 83, 111
  reports to CEDAW Committee 27, 28
  UN field operations 82, 83, 98–9, 101, 102, 103
  UN Security Council enforcement 253
  witness confidentiality 111

sale of children 424, 431–2, 437–43, 898, 909–11, 950, 952–4
Sands v. The United Kingdom 126[n42]
Sargin and Yagci v. Turkey (1989) 124[n37]
Saudi Arabia, CAT draft optional protocol 499, 501
Schönenberger and Durmaz v. Switzerland (1988) 259
scientific rights 383
secretariat servicing
  CESCR draft optional protocol 487–8
  chairpersons' meetings
    (1989) 733–4; (1990) 742–3, 750; (1992) 757, 759–60, 766–7, 773; (1994) 784; (1995) 793–4; (1996) 806; (Feb 1998) 831; (Sep 1998) 846–7
  follow-up activities 242–3
  independent expert's report 521, 523, 575–8, 617
self-determination 356–7, 378–9, 480–1, 1037
Senegal
  dialogue with CRC Committee 685
  World Conference against Racism 921
Serbia, fact-finding 80
sexual exploitation of children 424, 431, 437–43, 801
  General Assembly resolutions 946, 947, 952–4
  refugees 956
  UN Commission resolutions 898, 904, 905, 907, 909–11

Siderman de Blake v. Republic of Argentina (1992) 76
Sierra Leone
  executions 147[n29]
  Kandu-Bo et al. v. Sierra Leone (1998) 147[n29]
Simon-Herold v. Austria (1971) 126
Singh v. Canada (1998) 147[n29]
situation fact-finding 66–7, 79–86
Slaight Communications Inc. v. Davidson (1989) 311[n23]
slavery 358–9, 566, 966, 1021, 1034
social exclusion 960, 980, 990
social rights
  African Charter on Human and Peoples' Rights 1033
  American Convention on Human Rights 1026
  CEDAW 392
  CERD 348
  CESCR 378–86
  CRC 416
  justiciability 160
  lack of awareness 230
  UN Commission resolution 881–7
  women 205
  see also European Social Charter; International Covenant on Economic, Social and Cultural Rights
social security
  American Declaration of the Rights and Duties of Man 1015
  CEDAW 391, 392
  CESCR 381
  CRC 422
  European Social Charter 979, 983, 984–5, 990, 997
Soering v. The United Kingdom (1989) 173[n18], 260
Solomon Islands, CESCR ratification 544[n30]
Somalia
  state reporting 60
  UN Security Council enforcement 253
South Africa
  NGO pressure 220
  Truth and Reconciliation Commission 86, 109, 113[n27]
  UNICEF programmes 641
  World Conference against Racism 920
sovereignty xvii, 209, 497, 501
Soviet Union, former
  CCPR Optional Protocol 164

sovereignty xvii
see also Russian Federation
Spain, *Castells v. Spain* (1992) 261[n34]
Special Rapporteur for Follow-Up on Concluding Observations 246–7
Special Rapporteur for Follow-Up on Views 235–7, 238–9, 240, 242, 243, 247, 252
Special Rapporteur on Violence Against Women 92, 205[n27]
Sri Lanka
 CRC Committee visit 801
 response to concluding observations 293[n11]
standard of living 381, 422, 979, 981
state reporting xviii, 3–21
 access by victims 333
 advisory services 641–2
 African Charter on Human and Peoples' Rights 1059–61
 bias in fact-finding 88–90, 95
 CAT 5[n12], 408, 726–7, 801–2, 890
  experts 12[n42]; number of meetings 552, 607; overdue reports 550, 551, 604
 CCPR 5[n12], 295, 366, 524, 720
  number of meetings 552, 607; overdue reports 551, 604
 CEDAW 5, 9, 23–34, 394–5, 714, 725–6
  Denmark 10[n35]; guidelines 295; Morocco 10[n38]; number of meetings 552, 607; Optional Protocol 252[n4]; overdue reports 9, 551, 604, 944; rules of procedure 26[n9]
 CERD 5[n12], 9, 88, 89, 350
  chairpersons' meetings 708–9, 711, 714, 722–4, 729; guidelines 295; number of meetings 552, 607; overdue reports 551, 604, 668, 723, 770, 802, 817, 932; periodic reports 646
 CESCR 5[n12], 383, 547–8
  chairpersons' meetings 707, 710, 711–12, 714, 722, 729; guidelines 295; number of meetings 552, 607; overdue reports 550[n39], 551, 604
 chairpersons' meetings
  (1984) 706–10, 711, 712–14, 715; (1989) 719–31, 735–7; (1990) 740, 741, 743–4, 746, 748–9, 751–2; (1992) 755, 758, 760–1, 763, 768, 770–1; (1994) 775, 778–9, 781–2;

  (1995) 790, 791–2; (1996) 803, 809; (1997) 816–17, 821, 828; (1999) 855–6, 862; (Feb 1998) 831, 833–5; (Sep 1998) 844–5, 847–8, 854
 Committee on Economic, Social and Political Rights monitoring 227–8
 Conference conclusions 316–20, 334–7, 340
 consolidated committee proposal 299–300, 301, 329, 340
 consolidated guidelines 748, 752–3
 CRC 5[n12], 7, 35–44, 428, 635
  guidelines 10[n32], 295; number of meetings 607; Optional Protocol on Involvement of Children in Armed Conflict 435; Optional Protocol on the Sale of Children, Child Prostitution and Child Pornography 442; overdue reports 551, 604
 critiques of 193, 288, 683–8
 cross-referencing 520, 560–4, 662, 728–9, 743
 dependencies 8–18
 description 5–8
 documentation problems 636–8, 661–2, 669
 effectiveness 289–96
 expertise 223–4
 failure to report 319–20
 follow-up activities 244–9, 325, 652
 General Assembly resolution 927, 928
 implementation 444, 446
 inadequacy of supervisory system 635–6, 666–8
 independent expert's report 193, 518–20, 523, 532, 546–71
  advisory services 605, 606, 614–15, 626, 627; documentation problems 608–10, 626, 636–8, 669; inadequacy of supervisory system 607–8, 626, 635–6, 666; overdue reports 519, 550–2, 555, 596, 604–6, 626, 634, 665–6; reforms 616–21, 627, 644–9, 666, 671
 indigenous peoples 654–5
 International Covenants 878–9, 936–7
 International Law Association
  critique of 683–8;
  recommendations 690–6
 length of committee sessions 573, 574
 limitations of system 18–20

limited periodic reports   619–20, 834–5, 844
NGOs   7, 8, 13, 15–17, 20, 45–62
   attendance   687; CEDAW   24, 29, 31, 33; CRC Committee   36, 37, 40, 41–3; comments regarding   652, 653–5; Committee on Economic, Social and Political Rights   722; committee recommendations   290; concluding observations   694; Conference conclusions   317, 334–5; follow-up activities   282, 652; independent expert's report   549, 635, 637; information-sharing   88; International Law Association report   683, 684, 687, 690, 692–3; publicity   293; role of   183, 184–5, 186, 211; technical assistance   292
normative consistency   521, 586–9, 648, 742, 744
overdue reports   xviii, 9, 89, 676, 683, 690–1
   chairpersons' meetings
      2nd (1989)   722, 723, 729, 735–6; 3rd (1990)   741, 749; 4th (1992)   758, 770–1; 5th (1994)   778–9; 6th (1995)   792; 8th (1997)   816, 817; CAT   550, 551, 604; CCPR   551, 604; CEDAW   9, 551, 604, 944; CERD   551, 604, 668, 723, 770, 802, 817, 932; CESCR   550[n39], 551, 604; comments regarding   634–5, 660–1, 665–6, 667; CRC   551, 604; General Assembly resolution   928; independent expert's report   519, 550–2, 555, 596, 604–6, 626, 634, 665–6; UN Commission resolution   873
reforms   644–9, 666, 667, 671
reporting period   318–19
special/exceptional reports   615–16, 627, 634, 643–4, 670–1
   Conference conclusions   319, 335
   International Law Association recommendations   696
specifically-focused reports   569–71
state failures   525, 683–6
thematic reporting   39–40, 317–18, 340
UN Commission resolutions   873, 875
unreliability of   323
see also consolidation of reports
state responsibility   277–8, 333–4
statelessness   213, 214, 995–6

Stewart v. Canada (1993)   150[n38], 165
Stocké v. Germany (1991)   123
Stran Greek Refineries and Stratis Andreadis v. Greece (1994)   172
street children   906–7, 957–8
subsidiarity principle   178
successions   769–70, 781
Sudan
   CAT draft optional protocol   499, 501
   ILO case against   274, 275
Sunday Times v. The United Kingdom (1980)   258[n14]
Suriname, follow-up consultations   236[n14], 239
Swaziland
   ILO sanctions   275
   UNICEF programmes   641
Sweden
   CAT   167
   comments regarding the independent expert's report   660, 661, 662
   Cruz Varas and Others v. Sweden (1991)   68[n7], 123, 125[n38], 171
   draft optional protocol to CAT   503
   individual complaints   144[n19]
   McGoff v. Sweden (1984)   260[n28]
   Olsson v. Sweden (No.1) (1988)   262
   Olsson v. Sweden (No.2) (1992)   262
Switzerland
   CAT   167
   draft optional protocol to CAT   502, 503
   European Convention review   272[n76]
   individual complaints   144[n19]
   K.N. v. Switzerland (1997)   147[n29]
   Schönenberger and Durmaz v. Switzerland (1988)   259
Syrian Arab Republic, CAT draft optional protocol   499, 501

Tajikistan   100
Tangiora v. Wellington District Legal Services Corporation (2000)   145[n22]
thematic reporting   39–40, 317–18, 340
Third Decade to Combat Racism and Racial Discrimination   540, 914, 915, 917–18, 933, 934
Tinnelly & Sons Ltd. v. United Kingdom (1998)   70[n14]
Togo, criticism of state report by Human Rights Committee   686
Tomasi v. France (1992)   123, 172[n12]
Toonen v. Australia (1992)   150[n38], 241

Index 1109

torture
  American Convention on Human
    Rights 1020
  CCPR 358
  children 424, 425, 891, 900, 913, 941
  European Convention on Human
    Rights 966
  fact-finding 79–80, 84–5, 87
  General Assembly resolution 939–42
  NGO role in publicising 189–90
  UN Commission resolutions 888–95,
    900, 904, 913
  women 205, 891, 941
  see also Committee against Torture;
    Convention Against Torture;
    European Committee for the
    Prevention of Torture and Inhuman
    or Degrading Treatment or
    Punishment; European Convention
    for the Prevention of Torture and
    Inhuman or Degrading Treatment or
    Punishment
trade unions 362, 380, 968, 999
training programmes 614–15, 627, 635,
    641–2, 670, 677
  annual courses 223–4
  chairpersons' meetings
    (1984) 713; (1989) 721, 736;
    (1990) 746, 752; (1992) 763, 771;
    (1998) 836
  children's rights 951
  custody/security personnel 507, 940, 942
  economic, social and cultural rights 882
  law enforcers 406
  UN staff 819, 836, 843
  UNIFEM/IWRAW Asia Pacific 201–2
  see also advisory services; vocational
    training
Trinidad & Tobago, *Kennedy v. Trinidad &
  Tobago* (1999) 153[n46]
Trinidad and Tobago
  American Convention of Human Rights
    withdrawal 105[n2]
  CCPR Optional Protocol
    denunciation 153[n46]
  death penalty 72[n24]
  follow-up consultations 239
  individual complaints 464
truth commissions
  Inter-American human rights
    system 109–14
  South Africa 86
Truth and Reconciliation Commission, South
  Africa 86

Tsirlis and Kouloumpas v. Greece
  (1997) 172[n12]
Tunis Declaration 548
Tunisia
  dialogue with Human Rights
    Committee 684–5
  Human Rights Committee members 215
Turkey
  Akdivar and Others v. Turkey
    (1996) 121[n19], 124[n37],
    270[n69]
  Aksoy v. Turkey (1996) 123, 124[n37],
    174, 270[n69]
  Amnesty International submissions
    on 189–90
  Aydin v. Turkey (1997) 68[n9]
  CAT draft optional protocol 503
  CAT examination 84, 95, 225
  Cyprus v. Turkey cases 124, 128[n53]
  European Commission fact-finding 179
  European Committee for the Prevention of
    Torture report 134, 135
  European Convention violations 252,
    270, 272[n77]
  European Court applications
    against 124, 127
  European Social Charter 131
  Kapan v. Turkey (1997) 122[n19]
  lack of political will against 223
  Loizidou v. Turkey (1995) 173[n19, n20],
    256[n4], 270[n69]
  Mentes v. Turkey (1997) 68[n9],
    70[n15]
  on-site testimony 70
  Sargin and Yagci v. Turkey
    (1989) 124[n37]
  state party meetings 225
  UNICEF programmes 641
  Yagci and Saragin v. Turkey
    (1995) 270[n69]
  Çagirga v. Turkey (1995) 124[n37]

Uganda
  CESCR ratification 544[n30]
  CRC Committee follow-up
    activities 245[n52]
Ukraine
  Canadian judicial assistance
    program 308
  European Convention on Human
    Rights 170
  European Convention for the Prevention
    of Torture 134[n74]

UNAIDS *see* HIV/AIDS, Joint United
    Nations Programme on
UNDG *see* United Nations Development
    Group
UNDP *see* United Nations Development
    Program
UNESCO *see* United Nations Educational,
    Scientific and Cultural Organization
UNFPA *see* United Nations Population
    Fund
UNIFEM *see* United Nations Development
    Fund for Women
UNIS *see* United Nations Information
    Service
UNITAR *see* United Nations Institute for
    Training and Research
United Kingdom
    avoidance of UN scrutiny   184
    B. v. The United Kingdom
        (1988)   260[n28]
    *Brannigan and McBride v. The United
        Kingdom* (1993)   265[n53]
    Brogan and Others v. The United Kingdom
        (1988)   264–5, 270
    CAT draft optional protocol   503
    Chahal v. The United Kingdom
        (1996)   69[n10], 69[n14], 174–5
    D. v. United Kingdom (1997)   128[n52]
    European Convention on Human
        Rights   269
    Farrel v. The United Kingdom
        (1982)   126[n44]
    Golder v. The United Kingdom (1975)   258
    Greece v. The United Kingdom
        (1958)   124
    Ireland v. The United Kingdom (1978)   79,
        124, 125[n38, n40], 260–1
    McCann and Others v. United Kingdom
        (1995)   123
    McElduff and Others v. United Kingdom
        (1998)   70[n14]
    *Marcella and Robert Sands v. United
        Kingdom* (1981)   68[n7]
    media coverage of reporting   687
    NGO use of the press   222
    reservations   690
    Sands v. The United Kingdom   126[n42]
    Soering v. The United Kingdom
        (1989)   173[n18], 260
    state reporting   7
    Sunday Times v. The United Kingdom
        (1980)   258[n14]
    Tinnelly & Sons Ltd. v. United Kingdom
        (1998)   70[n14]

United Nations Charter   xvii, 287, 288, 305,
    522, 943
CAT   403
    draft optional protocol   512
CCPR   356
CEDAW   387
    Optional Protocol   398
CERD   345, 349
CESCR   378, 384–5
colonial peoples   373
CRC   414, 423
    Optional Protocols   433
Economic and Social Council
    (ECOSOC)   384
equal rights   947
financial obligations   847
racism and racial discrimination   914
requests for information   556[n44]
solidarity and friendly relations   1037
state reporting   546
treaty financing arrangements   733
treaty implementation   925
United Nations Children's Fund (UNICEF)
    armed conflict   954
    CRC Committee relationship   41–2, 92,
        635, 641, 651, 677
    best practice   859; cooperation   625; fact-
        finding missions   83–4; financial
        rewards   801, 813; success   18;
        technical assistance   43[n29];
        urgent action   20
    children in armed conflict   912
    comments regarding the independent
        expert's report   630
    databases   638; dissemination of
        information   637; state
        reporting   635; universal
        ratification   632
    concluding observations   652
    consolidation of reports   647
    cooperation with treaty bodies   625, 793
    CRC   50, 428–9, 602
        amendments   650; publication of
            compliance with   791;
            ratification   599, 791;
            recognition   47[n3], 53; regional
            meeting   762
    field visits   40[n15], 41
    gender-sensitive education   904
    girl child rights   948, 949
    human rights approach   100
    information technology   820
    migrant children   906, 952
    refugees   908, 956

reporting procedures 803
right to education 886, 907, 957
state reporting 16
statistical reports 728, 736
UN Commission resolution 900
universal ratification 665, 815
United Nations Commission on Crime Prevention and Criminal Justice 535
United Nations Commission on Human Rights xix, 184
  access to complaints procedure 482
  amendments to treaties 622–3, 649
  CAT draft optional protocol 491, 503, 897, 941
  CESCR draft optional protocol 161–2, 471–2, 488
  chairpersons' meetings
    (1992) 755, 756–7, 769; (1994) 775; (1995) 798; (1996) 811; (1999) 865
  child rights 898–913
  Committee for Economic, Social and Cultural Rights 837
  committee resource room 760
  Conference recommendations 338
  cooperation with treaty bodies 793, 795, 929
  CRC
    draft optional protocol 953, 956;
    length of committee sessions 572;
    Optional Protocols 431
  critique of resolution language 288
  Economic and Social Council (ECOSOC) submissions 384
  examination of state without report 833
  exchange of information 710–11, 731, 737
  expert seminar 625
  fact-finding procedure 67[n4], 74, 81, 82
  field operations 98
  financial issues
    chairpersons' meetings 788; treaty bodies 733, 741
  follow-up activities xix, 326
  gender integration 948
  independent expert's report 515–16, 522–3, 525, 527–8, 534, 539–40, 926
    comments on 630, 664; General Assembly resolution 445
  intergovernmental agencies 579, 580[n67]
  International Law Association recommendations 694, 695

  interpretation of international standards 537
  NGOs 47[n4], 219, 223, 583
  ratification 542, 543, 829
  reform 856–7
  reservations 769
  resolutions 873–922
    CAT draft optional protocol 896–7;
    economic, social and cultural rights 881–7;
    implementation 873–6;
    International Covenants 877–80;
    racism and racial discrimination 914–22;
    torture 888–95
  rules 804
  special procedures 860, 866
  special rapporteurs 61, 807, 860–1, 961
  special reports 643, 644
  specific concerns 566
  state reporting 546, 555–6, 687, 710, 712–13, 714
    overdue reports 817; special procedures 557; technical assistance 712–13, 730
  substantive protocols 699
  technical assistance 446, 746
  torture allegations 190
  treaty amendments 622–3
  treaty body decisions 253
  women's rights 196
  Working Group on Enforced or Involuntary Disappearances 77
  Working Group on the Right to Development 859
  World Conference on Racism 933
United Nations Commission on Social Development 534–5
United Nations Commission on the Status of Women (CSW) xix, 156–7, 191, 196, 446
  CEDAW reports 395
  Conference recommendations 338
  girl child 946
  independent expert's report 534–5, 538, 565
  individual petition 689[n28]
  International Law Association recommendations 694, 695
  optional protocol 156–60, 473
  secretariat 743
  state reporting 687
  Working Group 802

1112   Index

United Nations Conference on Environment and Development (1992)   582
United Nations Conference on Human Settlements (Habitat II) 1996   882
United Nations Crime Prevention and Criminal Justice Division   43, 630
United Nations Crime Prevention and Criminal Justice Programme   941–2
United Nations Decade for Human Rights Education   791–2
United Nations Declarations *see* Declaration on...
United Nations Department of Public Information (DPI)   613, 658, 747, 783, 841, 846
  critique of   17
  International Covenants   880
  media dossiers   865
  news coverage   858
  see also United Nations Office of Communications and Public Information
United Nations Development Fund for Women (UNIFEM)   7, 18, 200–3, 611, 904, 948
United Nations Development Group (UNDG)   864, 882
United Nations Development Program (UNDP)   18, 248, 276, 280–1, 791
  Committee on Economic, Social and Political Rights relationship   677, 801, 843, 859
  Conference recommendations   338
  cooperation with treaty bodies   580, 793
  girl child rights   949
  HURIST (Human Rights Strengthening) programme   843, 859, 861
  memorandum of understanding   843–4, 851, 859
  ratification of treaties   602, 603
  reporting procedures   803
  training programmes   642
  UNHCHR relationship   807
  universal ratification   675, 815, 830, 844, 850
United Nations Division for the Advancement of Women   32, 794, 876, 929
  CESCR draft optional protocol   472
  Conference recommendations   336, 337–8, 339
  gender integration   822, 849–50, 857
  girl children   948
  joint statements   835
  secretariat servicing   577, 734
  website   10[n36], 17
  'Women Watch' project   611
United Nations Educational, Scientific and Cultural Organization (UNESCO)
  comments regarding independent expert's report   664, 673
  Convention against Discrimination in Education   346
  cooperation with other bodies   580, 625, 732, 747, 793
  gender-sensitive education   904
  girl child rights   948, 949
  independent expert's report   535
  individual complaints   139–40, 475
  ratification of treaties   602, 603, 815
  reporting procedures   803
  right to education   886, 907, 957
  special rapporteur on education   843, 851
  state reporting   556
  statistical reports   728
  World Conference on Human Rights   772
United Nations General Assembly
  adoption of treaties   529
  amendments   622, 623, 649
  CAT Committee decisions   697
  CEDAW meeting time   25
  chairpersons' meetings
    (1984)   704, 706, 707–8, 717;
    (1989)   717–18, 724, 733, 735, 736, 738; (1990)   738–9, 741, 742, 743, 746; (1991)   755; (1992)   759, 764–5, 767, 769; (1993)   775, 787–8; (1995)   794, 798; (1996)   803, 804, 811; (1997)   824, 827–8
  CRC Committee   428, 448
  children in armed conflict   192, 912
  Conference recommendations   338
  consolidated reports   619, 692
  coordinated global resolution   695
  critique of resolution language   288
  documentation language   806
  examination of states without report   817
  follow-up activities   xix, 246, 278, 326, 694
  honoraria payments   574, 821, 837
  implementation   444–7
  independent expert's report   515, 522, 523, 525, 526, 664
  individual complaints   698
  linguistic diversity   624, 651
  massive human rights violations   616
  membership of treaty bodies   215[n19]
  Programme of Action for Decade to Combat Racism   918

racism/racial discrimination 915, 918, 922, 959–62
ratification of treaties 542
regional human rights initiatives 535, 589
reports 530
resolutions 925–62
  CEDAW 943–5; CERD 931–4; CRC 950–8; girl child 946–9; implementation 925–30; International Covenants 935–8; racism/racial discrimination 959–62; torture 939–42
resources 17, 693
state reporting 546–7, 606, 676, 687–8, 691
substantive protocols 699
torture 403, 888
treaty body decisions 253
treaty body meeting times 572, 573
UN Declaration on the Granting of Independence to Colonial Countries and Peoples 373
Vienna Declaration 601
World Conference on Human Rights 749, 762, 763, 772
United Nations High Commissioner for Human Rights (UNHCHR)
  advisory services 615, 796, 890, 919, 940
  CESCR Optional Protocol 162
  consultation 805
  cooperation with other agencies 625, 628, 672, 807
  coordination mandate 602, 779, 780
  corporate responsibility 867
  CRC implementation 806, 814
  economic, social and cultural rights 881, 882, 885, 887
  enforcement 253
  establishment of 777
  field operations 98–9, 102
  International Covenants 878, 936
  Internet racism 919
  jurisprudence 856
  mandate 656
  Manual on Human Rights Reporting 875
  overdue reports 691
  Plan of Action 832, 849, 852, 867, 902, 927, 951
  ratification 603, 632–4, 665, 675, 778, 791, 829–30
  referrals to 62
  regional advisors 676
  regional meetings 820, 845
  resources 793, 794, 856, 874
  selection of 217[n33]
  staff support 847, 851
  technical cooperation 633
  training programmes 836
  United Nations Development Group 864[n2]
  Universal Declaration of Human Rights anniversary 837
  website 626–7, 820
  World Conference against Racism 920–1, 922
  see also Office of the High Commissioner for Human Rights
United Nations High Commissioner for Refugees (UNHCR)
  children 908, 956
  comments regarding independent expert's report 630
  cooperation with treaty bodies 580, 625, 793
  databases 807
  fact-finding 323
  field operations 100
  girl child rights 948
  Handbook 75
  PARINAC project 654
  Refugee Convention (1951) 213–14
  reporting procedures 803
  website 612, 638–9, 669
United Nations Human Rights Website 676–7
United Nations Information Centres (UNICs) 58–9, 640, 658–9
  chairpersons' meeting recommendations 734, 747, 803
  independent expert's report 586, 614
United Nations Information Service (UNIS) 814, 823, 846, 851
United Nations Institute for Training and Research (UNITAR) 713, 728, 736, 749, 751, 763
United Nations Mission for the Verification of Human Rights in Guatemala (MINUGUA) 97–8, 101[n9]
United Nations Office of Communications and Public Information (DPI) [formerly Department of Public Information] 814, 823, 938
United Nations Population Fund (UNFPA)
  cooperation with treaty bodies 580, 793
  girl child rights 948, 949
  reporting system 18
  reproductive and sexual health 32, 822

United Nations Security Council
  ad hoc criminal tribunals 67, 74
  children in armed conflict 912, 955
  emergencies/massive violations 540, 764, 765–6, 780–1
  enforcement measures 253
  field operations 102
United Nations Standard Minimum Rules for the Administration of Juvenile Justice (Beijing Rules) 415, 909
United Nations Standard Minimum Rules for the Treatment of Prisoners 557
United Nations Sub-Commission on Prevention of Discrimination and Protection of Minorities 707, 732, 807
  CEDAW Committee relationship 742
  CERD Committee relationship 538, 842–3, 850, 933
  CESCR draft optional protocol 486
  cooperation with treaty bodies 538, 793, 795, 842–3, 850, 929, 933
  exchange of information 711, 731, 737
  independent expert's report 522, 534, 538, 543
  requests for information 556
  reservations 756, 764, 769
  Slavery Conventions 557
  studies 857
  substantive protocols 699
United Nations Sub-Commission on the Promotion and Protection of Human Rights (formerly Sub-Commission on the Prevention of Discrimination and Protection of Minorities) 905–6, 922, 948
United Nations Transitional Authority in Cambodia (UNTAC) 82, 97
United Republic of Tanzania, UNICEF programmes 641
United States
  American Declaration of the Rights and Duties of Man 140[n9], 1013–18, 1019, 1027
  asylum adjudication 75[n40], 75[n42]
  avoidance of UN scrutiny 184
  CAT draft optional protocol 502
  CCPR ratification 544[n30]
  fact-finding 85
  ILO case against 274–5
  media coverage of reporting 687
  NGOs 220, 222
  refugee practice 212[n8]
  reservations 690
  tort suits 76

United States of America v. Cotroni (1989) 310
  see also American Convention on Human Rights; Inter-American Commission on Human Rights; Inter-American Court of Human Rights
United States of America v. Cotroni (1989) 310
Universal Declaration of Human Rights 305, 632, 877, 935, 1019
  50th anniversary 632, 633, 823, 835, 837, 861
  CCPR 356
  CEDAW 387, 398
  CERD 345, 347, 349
  CESCR 378
  childhood 414
  death penalty abolition 375
  economic, social and cultural rights 881, 882, 884, 887
  freedom of expression 960
  racism/racial discrimination 914, 917
  state reporting 546
  torture 403, 888
  treaty implementation 925
UNTAC *see* United Nations Transitional Authority in Cambodia
Uruguay, follow-up consultations 239, 241[n39]

Vermeire v. Belgium (1991) 262
Vienna Declaration and Programme for Action xvii[n2], 3[n3], 98, 471–2, 477
  children 898, 910, 950
  equality 931
  objectives 778, 795
  racism 914, 959
  ratification 598, 601, 815, 829, 844
  reservations 830, 849
  torture 888, 889, 939–40
  training for civil servants 779
  withdrawals from CCPR 633
  women's rights 899, 943
Vienna Summit (1994) 266
violence
  against women 92, 140[n9], 205, 205[n27], 206, 947–8
  racist 347, 915–16, 917–18, 959, 961, 962
vocational training 391, 979, 982, 983–4, 996–7
Voluntary Fund for the Victims of Torture 892, 939, 942

websites *see* databases; Internet
Wellington District Legal Services Corporation v. Tangiora (1997) 145[n22]
WHO *see* World Health Organization
witness confidentiality 109–11
women
   African Charter on Human and Peoples' Rights 1036
   American Declaration of the Rights and Duties of Man 1014
   chairpersons' meetings 779, 781, 786, 808–9
   European Social Charter 998
   General Assembly resolution 929
   housing rights 885
   independent expert's report 564–6
   marginalization 58
   maternity 388, 389, 391–2, 979, 983, 1014
   NGOs 195–207
   torture 205, 891, 941
   UN Commission resolution 876
   see also Committee on the Elimination of All Forms of Discrimination Against Women; Convention on the Elimination of All Forms of Discrimination Against Women; gender integration; girl children
Women's Rights Advocacy Program (WRAP) 196, 199, 201[n12]
work
   African Charter on Human and Peoples' Rights 1036
   American Declaration of the Rights and Duties of Man 1015
   CEDAW 391, 392
   CERD 348
   CESCR 379–80
   CRC 424, 437
   European Social Charter 979–90, 996–1000
   ILO conventions 273
   see also child labour
Working Group on Arbitrary Detention 77
Working Group on Enforced or Involuntary Disappearances 77, 78[n51, n52]
World Bank 18, 728, 736
   Committee on Economic, Social and Political Rights relationship 801
   cooperation with treaty bodies 793
   country reports 808
   girl child rights 949
   independent expert's report 580, 602, 603, 625
   right to education 886

universal ratification 815
World Conference against Racism, Racial Discrimination, Xenophobia and Related Intolerance 861, 900, 914, 920–2, 931, 933, 960
World Conference on Education for All (Jomtien 1990) 882
World Conference on Housing 41[n17]
World Conference on Human Rights (Vienna 1993) 3, 41[n17], 98, 287, 515–16, 594
   CESCR draft optional protocol 471, 473, 475, 476
   children 950
   dialogue 603
   independent expert's report 522
   objectives 778
   original proposals for 749, 751, 762–3, 771–2
   ratification 598, 660, 675–6
   resources 17, 783
   torture 896, 939
   women 196, 781
   see also Vienna Declaration and Platform for Action
World Congress against Commercial Sexual Exploitation of Children (Stockholm 1996) 41[n17], 438, 801, 910, 946, 954
World Education Forum 886, 949
World Food Programme 948
World Food Summit (Rome 1996) 882
World Health Organization (WHO) 580[n67], 602, 603, 803
   children's health 902, 903
   cooperation with treaty bodies 747, 793
   girl child rights 948
   statistical reports 728
World Summit for Children (New York 1990) 431, 898, 950, 951
World Summit for Social Development (Copenhagen 1995) 779, 882, 948, 949
World Trade Organization (WTO) 807
WRAP *see* Women's Rights Advocacy Program

X v. Federal Republic of Germany (1965) 256[n4]
xenophobia 914–22, 959–62
   see also racial discrimination

Yagci and Saragin v. Turkey (1995) 270[n69]

Yemen, state party meetings 225
young people
    European Social Charter 979, 982–3, 986, 996–7
    HIV/AIDS 900, 903, 952
Yugoslavia, Federal Republic of, reports to CEDAW Committee 27
Yugoslavia, former
    breaches of international law 766
    country rapporteur 19[n77]
    International Criminal Tribunal 67, 74[n37], 113, 217[n30]

    treaty body concerns 540
    UN field operations 98
    UN Security Council enforcement 253
    witness protection 113

Zaire
    follow-up consultations 236[n14]
    political refugees 224
    women's rights 27, 28–9, 202[n15]
    see also Congo, Democratic Republic of
Zambia, follow-up consultations 239